Marketing

Real People, Real Choices

Ninth Edition

Global Edition

Marketing

Real People, Real Choices

Ninth Edition

Global Edition

Michael R. **SOLOMON**
SAINT JOSEPH'S UNIVERSITY

Greg W. **MARSHALL**
ROLLINS COLLEGE

Elnora W. **STUART**
UNIVERSITY OF SOUTH CAROLINA UPSTATE

Pearson

Harlow, England • London • New York • Boston • San Francisco • Toronto • Sydney • Dubai • Singapore • Hong Kong
Tokyo • Seoul • Taipei • New Delhi • Cape Town • Sao Paulo • Mexico City • Madrid • Amsterdam • Munich • Paris • Milan

Vice President, Business Publishing: Donna Battista
Director of Portfolio Management: Stephanie Wall
Portfolio Manager: Emily Tamburri
Editorial Assistant: Eric Santucci
Senior Project Manager, Global Edition: Vamanan Namboodhiri
Acquisitions Editor, Global Edition: Tahnee Wager
Senior Project Editor, Global Edition: Daniel Luiz
Managing Editor, Global Edition: Steven Jackson
Manager, Media Production, Global Edition: M. Vikram Kumar
Senior Manufacturing Controller, Production, Global Edition: Trudy Kimber
Vice President, Product Marketing: Roxanne McCarley
Director of Strategic Marketing: Brad Parkins
Strategic Marketing Manager: Deborah Strickland
Product Marketer: Becky Brown
Field Marketing Manager: Lenny Ann Kucenski
Product Marketing Assistant: Jessica Quazza
Vice President, Production and Digital Studio, Arts and Business: Etain O'Dea

Director of Production, Business: Jeff Holcomb
Managing Producer, Business: Ashley Santora
Content Producer: Claudia Fernandes
Operations Specialist: Carol Melville
Creative Director: Blair Brown
Manager, Learning Tools: Brian Surette
Content Developer, Learning Tools: Sarah Peterson
Managing Producer, Digital Studio, Arts and Business: Diane Lombardo
Digital Studio Producer: Monique Lawrence
Digital Studio Producer: Alana Coles
Full-Service Project Management and Composition: Integra Software Services Pvt. Ltd.
Interior Designer: Integra Software Services Pvt. Ltd.
Cover Designer: Lumina Datamatics, Inc.
Cover Art: zentilia/ShutterStock
Printer/Binder: RR Donnelley/Crawfordsville
Cover Printer: Phoenix Color/Hagerstown

Pearson Education Limited
KAO Two
KAO Park
Harlow
CM17 9NA
United Kingdom

And Associated Companies throughout the world

Visit us on the World Wide Web at:
www.pearsonglobaleditions.com

© Pearson Education Limited 2018

ISBN 10:   1-292-22108-9
ISBN 13: 978-1-292-22108-3

British Library Cataloguing-in-Publication Data
A catalogue record for this book is available from the British Library.

10 9 8 7 6 5 4 3 2 1
21 20 19 18 17

Typeset by Integra Software Services Pvt. Ltd.

Printed and bound by Vivar, Malaysia.

To Gail, Amanda, Zachary, Alex, Orly, Rose, Evey,
and Arya—my favorite market segment

—M.S.

To Patti and Justin

—G.M.

To Sonny, Patrick, Gabriela, Allyson, and Marge

—E.S.

▶Brief Contents

▶Contents

PART 2 Determine the Value Propositions Different Customers Want   116

CHAPTER 4: Market Research.......116

Real **People**, Real **Choices:** Here's my problem...   117

KNOWLEDGE IS POWER   118

CHAPTER 5: Marketing Analytics: Welcome to the Era of Big Data!.............148

Real **People**, Real **Choices:** Here's my problem...   149

CUSTOMER RELATIONSHIP MANAGEMENT (CRM): A KEY DECISION TOOL FOR MARKETERS   150

CHAPTER 6: Understand Consumer and Business Markets.............................182

Real **People**, Real **Choices:** Here's my problem...   183

THE CONSUMER DECISION-MAKING PROCESS   184

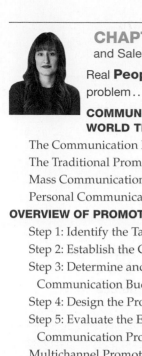

▶Preface

WHAT'S **NEW** IN THE NINTH EDITION?

What's new in the ninth edition is what's new in marketing. To put it simply, we feel a newcomer to marketing today needs to grapple with three core issues: Value, analytics and metrics, and ethical and sustainable marketing.

Here's just a sample of what we changed in this edition:

- Today's marketer needs to be "a numbers person." Increasingly, the field is data driven, and sophisticated analytics are revolutionizing the options organizations have at their fingertips to create, deliver, and measure value. We're proud to say that with each edition we continue to lead the field of marketing principles books in coverage of analytics and metrics, and in this edition we've continued to expand that coverage significantly to show how marketers use the exciting new tools they have available to understand and harness "Big Data" as they strive to identify and meet customer needs. To reinforce this focus throughout the book, each chapter provides a *Metrics Moment* box that describes some important ways to measure key marketing concepts and each chapter also includes an *Apply Marketing Metrics* exercise at the end.

- In the eighth edition, we were proud to be the first marketing principles textbook to devote an entire chapter (Chapter 5) to the emerging and vital topic of Big Data and marketing analytics. Now in the ninth edition we've greatly expanded that chapter's coverage to include numerous new key terms, many more application examples to connect concepts to practice, and several new tables and figures to further illustrate this fascinating chapter material.

- The ninth edition shines an even larger spotlight on the importance of ethical and sustainable marketing. The topic is so important to today's students that our coverage of ethical issues begins right up front in Chapter 2. As soon as the student basically understands what marketing *is*, he or she begins to learn how it *should be*. And each chapter provides a boxed feature called Ripped from the Headlines: Ethical/Sustainable Decisions in the Real World. Here we describe a questionable marketing practice and then ask students for their opinion on the subject. All 14 of these boxes are new for the ninth edition, including attention to such firms as Coca-Cola, Chipotle, Volkswagen, Kimberly Clark, and Allstar (the "Snuggie").

- Each chapter continues to feature a Marketing in Action mini-case at the end, and 13 of these are brand new for the ninth edition. Among the exciting firms with interesting problems and opportunities featured in these cases are GetFeedback, Airbus, Sprig, Facebook, Disney, Target, and Alibaba.

- The decision-focused Real People vignettes that frame each chapter are one of the signature features of our book. We continue this tradition in the ninth edition with seven new vignettes (50 percent of the total). These new vignettes include executives from Twitter, Campbell Soup, Weight Watchers, Levi Strauss, Quaker, BDP International, and Pitch (the advertising agency for Burger King).

- We emphasize active learning and decision making because we know that is what employers seek in today's graduates. We further sharpen our focus on employability in the ninth edition with the debut of a new supplemental feature, found in MyLab Marketing, called "Rising Stars in Marketing." Here we present video clips contributed by recent successful graduates of marketing programs around the country. Each person shares advice about job-seeking and offers "do's and don'ts" to current readers. These clips are indexed by job type, so students have the option of exploring career wisdom from those who have followed the same path they hope to take.

- Last but certainly not least, as always we pride ourselves on the currency of our content. Today's student deserves to know what is going on in the marketing world *today*—and also tomorrow to the extent we can predict it. Here is a sampling of new Key Terms we introduce in the ninth edition:

Chapter 1
accountability
return on marketing
    investment (ROMI)
mobile marketing
user-generated content
corporate citizenship
screen addicts
growth hackers
haul videos
competitive advantage
consumer addiction
Web 1.0
Web 3.0
Web 4.0
screen addicts
Cloud
positioning

Chapter 2
Arab Spring
Greenhouse Effect
global warming
World Bank
International Monetary Fund (IMF)
foreign exchange rate (forex rate)
balance of payments
BRICS countries
drones
unmanned aerial vehicles (UAVs)

Chapter 3
market planning
activity metrics
outcome metrics
leading indicators

Chapter 4
market research online
    community (MROC)
mechanical observation
eye tracking technology

internal validity
external validity

Chapter 5
mar-tech
marketing automation
channel partner model
emotion analysis
digital marketing channels
A/B test
landing page
churn rate
margin on sales

Chapter 6
evoked set
consideration set
determinant attributes
compensatory decision rules
multitasking
rich media
sadvertising
conscientious consumerism

Chapter 7
generational marketing
digital natives
buying power
organizational demographics
positioning statement
brand anthropomorphism

Chapter 8
technical success
commercial success
beta test
bleeding edge technology

Chapter 9
brand dilution
sustainable packaging
copycat packaging

Chapter 10
vertical integration
shopping for control
keystoning
high/low pricing
promo pricing
price segmentation
peak load pricing
surge pricing
bottom of the pyramid pricing
decoy pricing
prestige or premium pricing

Chapter 11
direct channel
product diversion
diverter
grey market
level loading
subscription boxes

Chapter 12
experiential merchandising
destination retailer
omnichannel marketing
organized retail crime (ORC)
beacon marketing
digital wallets
fair trade goods
bifurcated retailing
services

Chapter 13
comparative advertising
brand storytelling
slice of life advertising
lifestyle advertising
ad fraud
ad blocking
mobile hijacking
search engines
search marketing
search engine marketing (SEM)
sponsored search ads
text message advertising
monetize
in-app advertising
QR code advertising

Chapter 14
partner relationship
    management (PRM)
telecommute
virtual office
key account
cross-functional team
multilevel selling
direct selling
video news release (VNR)
sock puppeting
paid influencer programs

Features of the Ninth Edition of *Real People, Real Choices*

Meet Real Marketers

Many of the Real People, Real Choices vignettes are new to this edition, featuring a variety of decision makers, from CEOs to brand managers. Here is just a sample of the marketers we feature:

- Michael Baumwoll, Twitter
- Keith Sutter, Johnson & Johnson
- Dondeena Bradley, Weight Watchers
- Becky Frankiewicz, Quaker Foods
- Neal Goldman, Under Armour
- Jennifer Sey, Levi Strauss
- Stephanie Nashawaty, Oracle
- Stan Clark, Eskimo Joe's

Ethics and Sustainability in Marketing

Because the role of ethics and sustainability in business and in marketing is so important, we focus on these topics not just in a single chapter but in *every chapter* of the book. These *Ripped from the Headlines* boxes feature real-life examples of ethical and sustainable decisions marketers are faced with on a day-to-day basis.

Easy-to-Follow Marketing Plan Template

Marketing: Real People, Real Choices, ninth edition, includes a handy supplement at the end of Chapter 3 that is a template of a marketing plan you can use as a road map as you make your way through the book. The template provides a framework that is keyed to the major topics in the book, which will enable you to organize marketing concepts by chapter and create a solid marketing plan of your own.

Marketing Plan Appendix

Appendix A, Marketing Plan: The S&S Smoothie Company, provides a basic marketing plan for this interesting, if fictitious, firm. The extended example gives students the foundation they need to craft a complete marketing plan for a class project. In addition, the plan includes helpful "how to" guidelines that answer many of the questions that students ask while developing their own plans.

Career Appendix

Appendix B, Your Future in a Marketing Career, provides guidance for students on how to plan for a successful and rewarding career in the field. Success is framed as developing a unique brand for yourself that meets the needs of the job market. Career guidance recommendations follow the steps in a marketing plan with suggestions at each step for critical thinking and specific actions.

End-of-Chapter Study Map

Each chapter has an integrative study map for students that includes an Objective Summary, Key Terms, and student assessment opportunities of several types: Concepts: Test Your Knowledge; Activities: Apply What You've Learned; Apply Marketing Metrics (more on this one follows); Choices: What Do You Think?, and Miniproject: Learn by Doing. By completing these assessments, students and instructors achieve maximum assurance of learning.

Measuring the Value of Marketing through Marketing Metrics

Just how do marketers add value to a company, and how can they quantify that value? More and more, businesses demand accountability, and marketers respond as they develop a variety of "scorecards" that show how specific marketing activities directly affect their company's return on investment (ROI). And on the job, the decisions that marketers make increasingly are informed by a mix of data-based facts coupled with good old marketing instinct. Each chapter provides a *Metrics Moment* box that describes some important ways to measure key marketing concepts, including a short *Apply the Metric* exercise that asks the student to actually work with some of these measures. And every end-of-chapter includes an *Apply Marketing Metrics* exercise that provides additional opportunities for students to practice measures that marketers use to help them make good decisions. Pricing exercises included at the end of the Marketing Math Supplement following Chapter 10 provide the opportunity for students to work real-life pricing problems.

New and Updated End-of-Chapter Cases in This Edition

Each chapter concludes with an exciting Marketing in Action mini-case about a real firm facing real marketing challenges. Questions at the end let you make the call to get the company on the right track.

Instructor Resources

At the Pearson's Higher Ed catalog, https://www.pearsonglobaleditions.com, instructors can easily register to gain access to a variety of instructor resources available with the book in downloadable format. If assistance, is needed, Pearson's dedicated technical support team is ready to help with the media supplements that accompany the book. Visit https://support.pearson.com/getsupport for answers to frequently asked questions and toll-free user support phone numbers.

The following supplements are available with the ninth edition:

- Instructor's Resource Manual
- Test Bank
- TestGen® Computerized Test Bank
- PowerPoint Presentation

This title is available as an eBook and can be purchased at most eBook retailers.

About the Authors

Michael R. Solomon, Elnora W. Stuart, Greg W. Marshall

Michael R. Solomon

MICHAEL R. SOLOMON, Ph.D., joined the Haub School of Business at Saint Joseph's University in Philadelphia as Professor of Marketing in 2006. From 2007 to 2013, he also held an appointment as Professor of Consumer Behaviour at the University of Manchester in the United Kingdom. From 1995 to 2006, he was the Human Sciences Professor of Consumer Behavior at Auburn University. Before joining Auburn in 1995, he was chairman of the Department of Marketing in the School of Business at Rutgers University, New Brunswick, New Jersey. Professor Solomon's primary research interests include consumer behavior and lifestyle issues; branding strategy; the symbolic aspects of products; the psychology of fashion, decoration, and image; services marketing; and the development of visually oriented online research methodologies. He currently sits on the editorial boards of the *Journal of Consumer Behaviour*, the *Journal for the Advancement of Marketing Education*, the *Journal of Marketing Theory and Practice*, and *Critical Studies in Fashion and Beauty*. In addition to other books, he is also the author of Prentice Hall's text *Consumer Behavior: Buying, Having, and Being*, which is widely used in universities throughout the world. Professor Solomon frequently appears on television and radio shows, such as *The Today Show, Good Morning America*, Channel One, the *Wall Street Journal* Radio Network, and National Public Radio to comment on consumer behavior and marketing issues.

Greg W. Marshall

GREG W. MARSHALL, Ph.D., is the Charles Harwood Professor of Marketing and Strategy in the Crummer Graduate School of Business at Rollins College in Winter Park, Florida. For three years, he also served as vice president for strategic marketing for Rollins. Before joining Rollins, he was on the faculty of Oklahoma State University, the University of South Florida, and Texas Christian University. He also holds a visiting professorship in the Marketing Group at Aston Business School, Birmingham, United Kingdom. Professor Marshall earned a BSBA in marketing and an MBA from the University of Tulsa and a Ph.D. in marketing from Oklahoma State University. His research interests include sales management, marketing management decision making, and intraorganizational relationships. He is editor-in-chief of the *Journal of Marketing Theory and Practice* and former editor of the *Journal of Personal Selling & Sales Management* and currently serves on the editorial boards of the *Journal of the Academy of Marketing Science*, the *Journal of Business Research*, and *Industrial Marketing Management*. Professor Marshall is a member of the board of directors of the American Marketing Association, past president of the American Marketing Association Academic Division, a distinguished fellow and past president of the Academy of Marketing Science, and a distinguished fellow and past president of the Society for Marketing Advances. His industry experience before entering academe includes product management, field sales management, and retail management positions with firms such as Warner-Lambert, the Mennen Company, and Target Corporation.

Elnora W. Stuart

ELNORA W. STUART, Ph.D., is professor of marketing and associate dean of the George Dean Johnson, Jr. College of Business and Economics at the University of South Carolina Upstate. Prior to joining USC Upstate in 2008, she was professor of marketing and the BP Egypt Oil Professor of Management Studies at the American University in Cairo and professor of marketing at Winthrop University in Rock Hill, South Carolina, and on the faculty of the University of South Carolina. She has also been a regular visiting professor at Instituto de Empresa in Madrid, Spain. She earned a B.A. in theater and speech from the University of North Carolina at Greensboro and both an M.A. in journalism and mass communication and a Ph.D. in marketing from the University of South Carolina. Professor Stuart's research has been published in major academic journals, including the *Journal of Consumer Research*, the *Journal of Advertising*, the *Journal of Business Research*, and the *Journal of Public Policy and Marketing*. For over 25 years, she has served as a consultant for numerous businesses and not-for-profit organizations in the United States and in Egypt.

▶ Acknowledgments

We feature many talented marketers and successful companies in this book. In developing it, we also were fortunate to work with a team of exceptionally talented and creative people at Pearson. Emily Tamburri, Portfolio Manager, was instrumental in helping us solidify the vision for the ninth edition, and her assistance with decisions about content, organization, features, and supplements was invaluable. Kudos to Claudia Fernandes for managing the project with great efficiency and patience. Becky Brown deserves thanks for marketing the book successfully. And we'd like to add our special thanks to Stephanie Wall, Director of Portfolio Management, for working with the author team over the long term to ensure that our book continues its tradition as a creative and innovative leader in the principles of marketing space.

A special note of appreciation goes to Phillip Wiseman of the Crummer Graduate School of Business at Rollins College for his substantial contributions to Chapter 5—Marketing Analytics: Welcome to the Era of Big Data!—as well as his able assistance in bringing in fresh new ideas and a "millennial's perspective" to other aspects of the ninth edition. Phillip's hard work and commitment to excellence are most appreciated and he was a valued member of the ninth edition team. And thank you to Leroy Robinson of the University of Houston–Clear Lake, who so ably developed the Marketing in Action cases for this edition.

No book is complete without a solid supplements package. We extend our thanks to our dedicated supplement authors who devoted their time and shared their teaching ideas.

Finally, our utmost thanks and appreciation go to our families for their continued support and encouragement. Without them, this project would not be possible.

Many people worked to make this ninth edition a reality. Guidance and recommendations by the following professors and focus group participants helped us update and improve the chapters and the supplements:

REVIEWERS/FOCUS GROUP PARTICIPANTS

Pia A. Albinsson, Appalachian State University
Norma Anderson, Ivy Tech Community College
Eileen Archibald, Phoenix College
Michele Arpin, Chattanooga State Community College
Kelly Atkins, East Tennessee State University
Jacqueline Babb, Oakton Community College
Dana Bailey, East Tennessee State University
Koren Borges, University of North Florida
Susan Callender, Hudson Valley Community College
Ricky Caraballo, Miami Dade College
Jerome Christia, Coastal Carolina University
Christy Cole, Gulf Coast State College
Debbie Coleman, Miami University
Amy Danley, Wilmington University
Abid Din, Ivy Tech Community College
Jeff Fanter, Ivy Tech Community College
Monica Fine, Coastal Carolina University
Thomas F. Frizzell, Sr., Massasoit Community College
Gerald Yong Gao, University of Missouri–St. Louis
Roland Gau, University of Texas–El Paso
Tulay Girard, Penn State Altoona
Charles S. Gulas, Wright State University
Bonnie Guy, Appalachian State University
Mary Haines, Ohio University
Jennifer S. Hampton, Ivy Tech Community College
Eric Harvey, Ball State University
Karen Hawkins, Miami Dade College
Carol Heeter, Ivy Tech Community College
Donald Hoffer, Miami University
Eva Hyatt, Appalachian State University
Fernando R. Jimenez, University of Texas–El Paso
Sungwoo Jung, Columbus State University
Alex Kim, Long Island University–Post

Helen Koons, Miami University
Trina Lynch-Jackson, Ivy Tech Community College
Mark Mitchell, Coastal Carolina University
Lakshmi Nagarajan-Iyer, Middlesex County College
Denisse Olivas, University of Texas–El Paso
Timucin Ozcan, Southern Illinois University–Edwardsville
Courtney Pham, Missouri State University
Lisa Pucurs, University of North Carolina–Wilmington
Mohammed Rawwas, University of Northern Iowa
Julie Rigrish, Ivy Tech Community College
Kathryn Schifferle, California State University–Chico
Sarah M. Shepler, Ivy Tech Community College
Brent Smith, Saint Joseph's University
Randy Stuart, Kennesaw State University
Ronda Taylor, Ivy Tech Community College
Russell G. Wahlers, Ball State University
Jefrey R. Woodall, York College of Pennsylvania
Doula Zaharopoulos, Phoenix College

EXECUTIVES

In addition to our reviewers and focus group participants, we want to extend our gratitude to the busy executives who gave generously of their time for the Real People, Real Choices features.

Executives Featured in Real People, Real Choices Vignettes

Chapter 1: Michael Baumwoll, Twitter
Chapter 2: Keith Sutter, Johnson & Johnson
Chapter 3: Stephanie Nashawaty, Oracle
Chapter 4: Cindy Bean, Campbell Soup Company
Chapter 5: Lisa Arthur, Teradata Corporation
Chapter 6: Dondeena Bradley, Weight Watchers

Chapter 7: Jennifer Sey, Levi Strauss
Chapter 8: Neal Goldman, Under Armour
Chapter 9: Becky Frankiewicz, Quaker Foods
Chapter 10: Betsy Fleming, Converse College
Chapter 11: Michael Ford, BDP International
Chapter 12: Stan Clark, Eskimo Joe's
Chapter 13: Sara Bamossy, Pitch
Chapter 14: Rohan Deuskar, Stylitics, Inc.

REVIEWERS OF PREVIOUS EDITIONS

The following individuals were of immense help in reviewing all or part of previous editions of this book and the supplement package:

Camille Abbruscato, Stony Brook University
Roy Adler, Pepperdine University
Lydia Anderson, Fresno City College
Christopher Anicich, California State University–Fullerton
Carole S. Arnone, Frostburg State University
Gerald Athaide, Loyola College
Nathan Austin, Morgan State University
Xenia Balabkins, Middlesex County College
Fred Beasley, Northern Kentucky University
Gary Benson, Southeast Community College
Jas Bhangal, Chabot College
Gregory Spencer Black, Metropolitan State College of Denver
Greta Blake, York College of Pennsylvania
Silvia Borges, Miami Dade CC–Wolfson Campus
Norm Borin, California State Polytechnic University
Deborah Boyce, State University of New York Institute of Technology, Utica, New York
Tom Boyd, California State University–Fullerton
Henry C. Boyd III, University of Maryland–College Park
Rich Brown, Harding University
Val Calvert, San Antonio College
Charles R. Canedy, University of Hartford
Richard Celsi, California State University–Long Beach
Swee-Lim Chia, LaSalle University
Ruth Clottey, Barry University
Paul Cohen, Florida Atlantic University
Brian Connett, California State University–Northridge
Robert M. Cosenza, University of Mississippi
C. Brad Cox, Midlands Technical College
Brent Cunningham, Jacksonville State University
Mayukh Dass, Texas Tech University
Mark Davis, Harding University
Mark DeFanti, Providence College
George D. Deitz, University of Memphis
Patricia Doney, Florida Atlantic University
Michael Dotson, Appalachian State University
Laura Dwyer, Rochester Institute of Technology
Rita Dynan, LaSalle University
Jill S. Dybus, Oakton Community College
Joyce Fairchild, Northern Virginia Community College
Elizabeth Ferrell, Southwestern Oklahoma State University
Angel M. Fonseca, MSCTE, Jackson College
Jie G. Fowler, Valdosta State University
Joanne Frazier, Montgomery College
Jon Freiden, Florida State University
Marlene Frisbee, AB-Tech College
Patricia Galitz, Southeast Community College
Debbie Gaspard, Southeast Community College

Mike Gates, South Hills School of Business and Technology
Kenneth C. Gehrt, San Jose State University
Michael Goldberg, Berkeley College
Karen Welte Gore, Ivy Tech Community College
Kimberly Goudy, Central Ohio Technical College
Kimberly D. Grantham, University of Georgia
Arlene Green, Indian River State College
David Hansen, Texas Southern University
John Hardjimarcou, University of Texas–El Paso
Jeffrey S. Harper, Texas Tech University
Dana L. E. Harrison, East Tennessee State University
Manoj Hastak, American University
Kelli S. Hatin, SUNY Adirondack
John Heinemann, Keller Graduate School of Management
Dorothy Hetmer-Hinds, Trinity Valley Community College
Tarique Hossain, California State Polytechnic University, Pomona
Mark B. Houston, Texas Christian University
Gary Hunter, Case Western Reserve University
Annette Jajko, Triton College
Jacqueline J. Kacen, University of Houston
Jack E. Kant, San Juan College
Janice M. Karlen, LaGuardia Community College/City University of New York
Laura Lynn Kerner, Athens State University
Cheryl Keymer, North Arkansas College
Gail Kirby, Santa Clara University
David Knuff, Oregon State University–Cascades
Kathleen Krentler, San Diego State University
Nancy P. LaGuardia, Capital Community College
Sandra J. Lakin, Hesser College
Linda N. LaMarca, Tarleton State University
Debra A. Laverie, Texas Tech University
Freddy Lee, California State University–Sacramento
David Lehman, Kansas State University
Ron Lennon, Barry University
Marilyn Liebrenz-Himes, George Washington University
Anne Weidemanis Magi, University of South Florida
Cesar Maloles, California State University–East Bay
Norton Marks, California State University–San Bernardino
Doug Martin, Forsyth Technical Community College
Kelly Duggan Martin, Washington State University
Carolyn Massiah, University of Central Florida
Jane McKay-Nesbitt, Bryant University
Juan (Gloria) Meng, Minnesota State University, Mankato
Mohan K. Menon, University of South Alabama
Laura M. Milner, University of Alaska
Timothy R Mittan, Southeast Community College
Jakki Mohr, University of Montana
Rex T. Moody, Angelo State University
Linda Morable, Richland College
Michael Munro, Florida International University
Jeff B. Murray, University of Arkansas
Lynn M. Murray, Pittsburg State University
Jun Myers, California State Polytechnic University–Pomona
Mark A. Neckes, Johnson & Wales University
Linda Newell, Saddleback College
Eric Newman, California State University–San Bernardino
Hieu P. Nguyen, California State University–Long Beach
David A. Norton, University of Connecticut
Elaine M. Notarantonio, Bryant University

David Oliver, Edison College
Beng Ong, California State University–Fresno
A. J. Otjen, Montana State University–Billings
Jason Keith Phillips, West Chester University
Lucille Pointer, University of Houston–Downtown
Abe Qastin, Lakeland College
Kevin Raiford, College of Southern Nevada
Rosemary P. Ramsey, Wright State University
John E. Robbins, Winthrop University
Matthew Roberts, California Polytechnic State University–San Luis Obispo
Bruce Robertson, San Francisco State University
Leroy Robinson, University of Houston–Clear Lake
Carlos M. Rodriguez, Delaware State University
L. Renee J. Rogers, Forsyth Technical College
Ann Renee Root, Florida Atlantic University
Barbara Rosenthal, Miami Dade Community College–Kendall Campus
Behrooz Saghafi, Chicago State University
Ritesh Saini, George Mason University
Charles Jay Schafer, Johnson & Wales University
Mary Schramm, Quinnipiac University
Joseph A. Schubert, Delaware Technical Community College, Wilmington Campus
Marcianne Schusler, Prairie State College
Susan Silverstone, National University
Lisa R. Simon, California Polytechnic State University
Samuel A. Spralls III, Central Michigan University
Melissa St. James, California State University–Dominguez Hills

Frank Svestka, Loyola University of Chicago
James Swartz, California State Polytechnic University–Pomona
Kim Taylor, Florida International University–Park Campus
Steven Taylor, Illinois State University
Susan L. Taylor, Belmont University
Nancy J. Thannert, Robert Morris University Illinois
John Thanopoulos, University of Piraeus, Greece
Jane Boyd Thomas, Winthrop University
Scott Thorne, Southeast Missouri State University
Mary Jean Thornton, Capital Community College
Judee A. Timm, Monterey Peninsula College
Sue Umashankar, University of Arizona
Sal Veas, Santa Monica College
Mary K. Wachter, Pittsburg State University
Beth Ghiloni Wage, University of Hartford
D. Roger Waller, San Joaquin Delta College
James R. Walton, Arkansas Tech University
Leatha Ware, Waubonsee Community College
Steve Wedwick, Heartland Community College
Casey Wilhelm, North Idaho University
Kathleen Williamson, University of Houston–Clear Lake
Mary Wolfinbarger, California State University–Long Beach
Kim Wong, Albuquerque TVI Community College
Steve Wong, Rock Valley College
Richard Wozniak, Northern Illinois University
Brent M. Wren, University of Alabama in Hunstville
Merv Yeagle, University of Maryland at College Park
Mark Young, Winona State University
Srdan Zdravkovic, Bryant University
Marybeth Zipperer, Montgomery College

Global Edition Acknowledgments

Pearson would like to thank Geoff Fripp, University of Sydney, for his contributions to the Global Edition, and David Ahlstrom, The Chinese University of Hong Kong; Jie Liu, Manchester Metropolitan University; Stephen Tustain, Glion Institute of Higher Education; and Jimmy Wong Shiang Yang, Singapore University of Social Sciences, for their reviews of the new content.

Marketing

Real People, Real Choices

Ninth Edition

Global Edition

Welcome to the World of Marketing
Create and Deliver Value

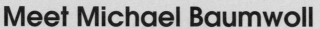

Meet Michael Baumwoll
▼ A Decision Maker at Twitter

Courtesy of Michael Baumwoll

I am currently an Account Manager at Twitter. After I graduated from Lafayette College in 2009, my career focused on digital media and advertising with brief stints in entrepreneurship. For the first five years of my professional life, I worked for an advertising technology company with the goal of revolutionizing the digital media landscape. Similar to exchanges like Nasdaq and eBay, this company built a platform that allowed websites (publishers) to auction off their advertising space to the highest advertising bidder. I joined this young, growth startup and quickly learned the robust, technical, and (highly) relationship-driven industry of digital advertising. Working in a fun, supportive, Google-esque culture, I was able to grow personally and ultimately manage relationships with major advertising agencies and their digital media-buying arms, called "trading desks." I was also lucky enough to manage a small group of coworkers and help them develop their understanding of the advertising landscape, technical skills and—most importantly, to me—themselves, professionally.

Simultaneously, I co-founded an iPhone application called BarSocial with the goal of creating a social media platform for nightlife. On the app, users connected with their friends and other bar-hoppers to determine the best places to go out. It was, essentially, Twitter for bars. BarSocial was live in the App Store for more than a year and was briefly featured on Wired.com. I quickly learned the facets of maintaining and building a technology business. Building BarSocial was one of the most exhilarating and challenging experiences I've ever had; I'd highly recommend building something of your own if the opportunity presents itself.

With a passion for social media, I now have the pleasure of working at one of the world's most recognized technology companies, Twitter. Twitter is a social media platform that democratizes the world by providing a forum for users to share their experiences and views. Similar to my previous professional experience, Twitter has successfully built a culture designed to help their employees thrive professionally. My role at Twitter is to manage and develop relationships with advertisers and their creative and media agencies. To simplify, I am a Twitter consultant helping to demystify the ever-growing world of Twitter and showcase the power of its advertising solutions to my clients.

Michael's Info

What I do when I'm not working:
Watching movies, spending time with my family, and breaking it down on the dance floor.

A job-related mistake I wish I hadn't made:
I avoided speaking up in meetings where I could have contributed value.

Business book I'm reading now:
Contagious: Why Things Catch On by Jonah Berger

My motto to live by:
Always focus on developing relationships—new and old. They will be the driving force in your professional and personal growth.

What drives me:
The opportunity to impact the world in my own personal way.

Don't do this when interviewing with me:
Be inauthentic

My pet peeve:
Talking during movies

Here's my problem...

Real **People**, Real **Choices**

Twitter is a public microphone that gives those with a handheld device or access to the Internet the ability to step up and speak. It gives each of us the opportunity to share our experiences and thoughts 24 hours a day, 7 days a week. As a result, Twitter has become a democratized platform for human expression and thought.

Just like the product externally, Twitter's management team creates an environment that encourages team members to speak up and share ideas. Employees are constantly reminded of their value and given channels to be creative and productive. It's an internal cultural choice that was made in the early days of Twitter to reflect the founders' beliefs in transparency and cooperation.

Internally at Twitter, there are multiple ways to share ideas and feedback. There are e-mail chains, discussion boards, water cooler conversations, feedback forms, and many other methods that allow you to express yourself. Although there are a number of options, it's (a) difficult to navigate and select the right method to share your idea and (b) hard to determine who the ideal person is with whom to share it.

As a member of the sales team, my focus is to understand the needs and concerns of my clients and relay that information to the Twitter team. It addition, and just as important, as an involved member of the Twitter community, it's my responsibility to contribute to building an even stronger product and experience for users. The question then becomes: how do we harness the innovation within Twitter's walls and leverage it to solve challenges the team faces with employees, consumers, and marketers? And subsequently, how can we track it?

Michael considered his **Options** 1·2·3

1 **Option**
Make a case for the management team to hold weekly meetings to discuss ideas and innovations within Twitter. This change would provide a dedicated time for team members to share their opinions, views, and ideas in an hour-long weekly meeting. Employees feel they are part of the process when they help to make decisions for the company. And different teams could interact with one another to come up with productive ideas because of this cross-pollination that only comes from face-to-face encounters. However, some employees are hesitant to voice their concerns and suggestions in such a public forum. Also getting a bunch of busy people to give up an hour of their time each week might not go over well with some people.

2 **Option**
Build an internal online tool to allow employees to share, build, and measure ideas (i.e., a Twitter within Twitter). Like Twitter, the forum would allow any team member to carefully think and craft ideas he or she could then share with coworkers or with entire teams. Employees could vote on ideas to showcase demand for an idea or product. And we could measure the success of the platform by tracking posts, votes, comments, etc. On the other hand, some employees might be reluctant to post ideas to the group if everyone votes on the ones they like and don't like. It's also not clear that there would be enough demand for merit the time and other resources to build this app that could be devoted to building business for Twitter instead.

3 **Option**
Share ideas on Twitter to galvanize support and subsequently share findings with the Twitter team. This approach would include the external Twitter community to help shape Twitter's product vision. We could get real-time feedback from potential customers about the ideas we're considering and engage them as partners rather than just as customers. On the other hand, we wouldn't be able to share some sensitive issues with non-Twitter employees. And we couldn't always be confident about the perspectives we get—not everyone necessarily has the experience and perspective to weigh in on how to run a complex business like ours.

Now, put yourself in Michael's shoes. Which option would you choose, and why?

You Choose

Which **Option** would you choose, and **why**?

☐ **Option 1** ☐ **Option 2** ☐ **Option 3**

See what **option** Michael chose in **MyLab Marketing**™

MyLab Marketing™

⭐ **Improve Your Grade!**

Over 10 million students improved their results using the Pearson MyLabs. Visit **mymktlab.com** for simulations, tutorials, and end-of-chapter problems.

1.1 Marketing: What Is It?

OBJECTIVE

Explain what marketing is, the marketing mix, what can be marketed, and the value of marketing.

(pp. 28–35)

Marketing. People either love it or hate it. The crazy part of this is that whether they love it or hate it, most folks really do not understand what marketing really is! How about when a Chris Cornell concert in Australia entices fans from Peoria, Illinois, to travel around the globe just to scream in ecstasy alongside the Aussies. Is that marketing? When Donald Trump and Hillary Clinton spend millions to get your vote—is that marketing? And then, of course, there are those e-mails that fill your inbox from Amazon.com, suggesting products that might entice you to let go of some hard-earned cash. Yes, these are all examples of marketing. And that's just scratching the surface.

Of course you already know a lot about marketing; it's been a part of your life from day one. As one of millions of **consumers**, you are the ultimate user of a good or service. Every time you purchase or use your car, your clothes, your lunch at the cafeteria (whether an old-school burger or a vegan version), a movie, or a haircut, you are part of the marketing process. In this book, we'll tell you why—and why you should care.

Indeed, consumers like you (and your humble authors!) are at the center of all marketing activities. By the way, when we refer to consumers, we don't just mean individuals. Organizations, whether a company, government, sorority, or charity, are made up of consumers.

Here's the key: *Marketing is first and foremost about satisfying consumer needs.* We like to say that the consumer is king (or queen), but it's important not to lose sight of the fact that the seller also has needs—to make a profit, to remain in business, and even to take pride in selling the highest-quality products possible. Products are sold to satisfy both consumers' and marketers' needs; it's a two-way street.

When you ask people to define **marketing**, you get many answers. Some people say, "That's what happens when a pushy salesman tries to sell me something I don't want." Many people say, "Oh, that's simple—TV commercials." Students might answer, "That's a course I have to take before I can get my business degree." Each of these responses has a grain of truth to it, but the official definition of marketing the American Marketing Association adopted in 2013 is as follows:

> Marketing is the activity, set of institutions, and processes for creating, communicating, delivering, and exchanging offerings that have value for customers, clients, partners, and society at large.[2]

The basic idea behind this somewhat complicated definition is that marketing is all about delivering value to everyone whom a transaction affects. That's a long-winded explanation. Let's take it apart to understand exactly what marketing is all about.

"Marketing Is the Activity, Institutions, and Processes..."

As we will discuss throughout this book, marketing includes a great number of activities—from top-level market planning by the chief marketing officer (CMO) of a big company to the creation of a Facebook page by your university. The importance organizations assign to marketing activities varies a lot. Top management in some firms is marketing oriented (especially when the chief executive officer, or CEO, comes from the marketing ranks), whereas in other companies marketing is an afterthought. Ten percent of the *Fortune 100* U.S. CEOs, more than one out of five (21%) of the Financial Times Stock Exchange (FTCE) 100 CEOs in the United Kingdom, and 40 percent of those with consumer and healthcare firms come from a marketing background—so stick with us![3]

---

consumer
The ultimate user of a good or service.

marketing
Marketing is the activity, set of institutions, and processes for creating, communicating, delivering, and exchanging offerings that have value for customers, clients, partners, and society at large.[1]

In the text we discuss many of the activities of marketing that include:

- Better understanding of customer needs through marketing research
- Selecting the people or organizations in the market that are your best bets for success
- Developing the product
- Pricing the product
- Getting the product to the consumer

We'll also learn about a variety of institutions that help firms create a better marketing program:

- Advertising agencies that firms work with to create and deliver a variety of marketing communication activities including traditional advertising as well as newer digital communications, sales promotion, and research activities
- Marketing research firms such as Nielsen that provide data vital to the planning and implementation of successful marketing programs
- The traditional media
- The Internet and social media
- Governments that enforce laws and regulations to make sure marketing occurs in a fair and ethical manner
- Logistics firms that get the product to the consumer most efficiently
- Retailers that interact directly with the final customer

We also talk about some of the processes marketers use in combination with these institutions to satisfy customer needs—the end-all for all marketing activities.

Whether it is a giant global producer of consumer products such as Proctor & Gamble or a smaller organization such as Eskimo Joe's of Stillwater, Oklahoma (we'll talk more about Eskimo Joe's in Chapter 12), a marketer's decisions affect—and are affected by—the firm's other activities. Marketing managers must work with financial and accounting officers to figure out whether products are profitable, to set marketing budgets, and to determine prices. They must work with people in manufacturing to be sure that the new iPhone is produced on time and in the right quantities for those avid iPhone fans that camp out in front of Apple stores to get their hands on the new model. Marketers also must work with research-and-development specialists to create products that meet consumers' needs.

"… for Creating, Communicating, Delivering, and Exchanging: The Marketing Mix…"

As we said, marketing is about satisfying needs. To do this, marketers need many tools. The **marketing mix** is the marketer's strategic toolbox. It consists of the tools the organization uses to create a desired response among a set of predefined consumers. These tools include the product itself, the price of the product, the promotional activities (such as advertising) that introduce it to consumers, and the places where it is available. We commonly refer to the elements of the marketing mix as the **Four Ps**: *product, price, promotion*, and *place*.

Although we talk about the Four Ps as separate parts of a firm's marketing strategy, in reality, product, price, promotion, and place decisions are interdependent. Decisions about any single one of the four are affected by, and affect every other marketing mix decision. For example, what if Superdry (a rapidly growing Japanese apparel company) decides to introduce a leather biker jacket that is higher end than the ones it makes now? If the company uses more expensive materials to make this item, it has to boost the selling price to cover these higher costs; this also signals to consumers that the garment is more upscale. In addition, Superdry would have to create advertising and other promotional strategies to convey a top-quality image. Furthermore, the firm must include high-end retailers like Neiman Marcus,

marketing mix
A combination of the product itself, the price of the product, the promotional activities that introduce it, and the place where it is made available, that together create a desired response among a set of predefined consumers.

Four Ps
Product, price, promotion, and place.

Figure 1.1 📷 *Snapshot* | The Marketing Mix

The marketing mix is the marketer's strategic toolbox.

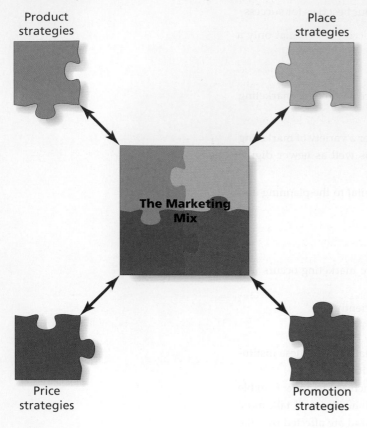

Product strategies

Place strategies

The Marketing Mix

Price strategies

Promotion strategies

product
A tangible good, service, idea, or some combination of these that satisfies consumer or business customer needs through the exchange process; a bundle of attributes including features, functions, benefits, and uses.

promotion
The coordination of a marketer's communication efforts to influence attitudes or behavior.

place
The availability of the product to the customer at the desired time and location.

channel of distribution
The series of firms or individuals that facilitates the movement of a product from the producer to the final customer.

price
The assignment of value, or the amount the consumer must exchange to receive the offering.

Bergdorf Goodman, and Bloomingdale's in its distribution strategy to ensure that shoppers who seek out high-end items will come across the jacket. Thus, all the pieces in the puzzle we call the marketing mix work together. As 📷 Figure 1.1 shows, each P is interconnected with each of the other three Ps. This shows us that the activities of each of the Four Ps must be coordinated with each of the other three Ps.

We'll examine these components of the marketing mix in detail later in this book. For now, let's briefly look at each of the Four Ps to gain some more insight into their role in the marketing mix.

Product

What have you spent your money and time to get recently? A pizza on Friday night, a concert on the weekend, a new tennis racket so you can beat all your buddies on the court, maybe even a "wonderful" Marketing textbook? These are all products. A **product** can be a good, a service, an idea, a place, a person—whatever a person or organization offers for sale in the exchange. Creating new products is vital to the success and even the life of an organization. The product, one aspect of the marketing mix, includes the design and packaging of a good as well as its physical features and any associated services, such as free delivery.

The product is a combination of many different elements, all of which are important to the product's success. Think about your college education—an expensive product. You are buying more than the boring lecture in that chemistry class (or the awesome lecture in your marketing class). You are also paying for the health center with a weight room, pool and a rock-climbing wall, for the classroom building, and maybe for the bragging rights of graduating from a "Big Ten" school.

Promotion

Although we all are familiar with advertising, **promotion**, also referred to as *marketing communication*, includes many different activities marketers undertake to inform consumers about their products and to encourage potential customers to buy these products. Marketing communication takes the form of personal selling, TV advertising, store coupons, billboards, magazine ads, publicity releases, web pages, social media sites, and a lot more. Today marketers are quickly moving much of their energy and money to devising and implementing digital marketing communications including mobile marketing, location-based marketing, behavioral digital marketing, and, of course, social media marketing.

Place

Place refers to the availability of the product to the customer at the desired time and location. This P relates to a **channel of distribution**, which is the series of firms or individuals that facilitates the movement of a product from the producer to the final customer. For clothing or electronics, this channel includes local retailers as well as other outlets, such as retail sites on the web that strive to offer the right quantity of products in the right styles at the right time.

Price

Price—we all know what price is—it's the amount you have to pay for the pizza, the concert tickets, the tennis racket, and, yes, this book. Price is the assignment of value, or the amount the consumer must exchange to receive the offering. Marketers often turn to price to increase consumers' interest in a product. This happens when they put an item on sale, but in other cases marketers actually try to sell a product with a higher price than people are used to if they want to communicate that it's high quality or cutting edge. For example, designer clothes and accessories are priced so high that only a few consumers can afford them. Not many of us can afford a Prada Python/Crocodile Arcade-Stripe Frame Satchel Bag priced at $9,600 or a pair of Valentino Rockstud Metallic Leather Mid-Heel Pumps at $1,045. If you can, you probably don't need to take this course!

At the heart of every marketing act—big or small—is something we refer to as an "exchange relationship." An **exchange** occurs when a person gives something and gets something else in return. The buyer receives an object, service, or idea that satisfies a need and the seller receives something he or she feels is of equivalent value. Today, most exchanges occur as monetary transactions in which one party surrenders currency (in the form of cash, check, credit card, or even Bitcoin) in return for a good or a service. But there are also other kinds of exchanges. A politician, for example, can agree to work toward certain goals in exchange for your vote, city officials may offer you a cleaner environment if you recycle, and health officials tell you that you can save lives (perhaps your own) if you wash your hands properly.

For an exchange to occur, at least two people or organizations must be willing to make a trade, and each must have something the other wants. Both parties must agree on the value of the exchange and how it will be carried out. Each party also must be free to accept or reject the other's terms for the exchange. Under these conditions, a knife-wielding robber's offer to "exchange" your money for your life does *not* constitute a valid exchange. In contrast, although someone may complain that a store's prices are "highway robbery," an exchange occurs if he or she still forks over the money to buy something there—even if he or she still grumbles about it weeks later.

To complicate things a bit more, everyone does not always agree on the terms of the exchange. Think, for example, about movie piracy. That's what happens when a new Leonardo DiCaprio blockbuster is available on street corners for a few dollars—or free on *Bit Torrent*— before it even opens in theaters.

"… Offerings …": What Can We Market?

Is there any limit to what marketers can and will market? Marketing applies to more than just the new iPhone and the Microwavable S'Mores Maker your mother bought you before you came to college.

Some of the best marketers come from the ranks of services companies such as American Express or not-for-profit organizations like Greenpeace. Politicians, athletes, and performers use marketing to their advantage (the Kardashians have figured it out). Ideas such as political systems (democracy, totalitarianism), religion (Christianity, Islam), and art (realism, abstract) also compete for acceptance in a "marketplace." In this book, we'll refer to any good, service, person, place, or idea that we can market as a product, even though what you buy may not take a physical form.

Consumer Goods and Services

Consumer goods are the tangible products that individual consumers purchase for personal or family use. **Services** are intangible products that we pay for and use but don't own. Service transactions contribute more than 75 percent

exchange
The process by which some transfer of value occurs between a buyer and a seller.

consumer goods
The goods individual consumers purchase for personal or family use.

services
Intangible products that are exchanged directly between the producer and the customer.

A robbery is NOT a valid exchange.

bennymarty/Fotolia

This British fence company offers to exchange money for the guarantee of privacy.

business-to-business marketing
The marketing of goods and services from one organization to another.

industrial goods
Goods that individuals or organizations buy for further processing or for their own use when they do business.

e-commerce
The buying or selling of goods and services electronically, usually over the Internet.

of the gross domestic product (GDP) in the U.S. and other developed countries.[4] Marketers need to understand the special challenges that arise when they market an intangible service rather than a tangible good.[5] Because both goods and services are products, it's more accurate to say "goods and services" rather than "products and services."

Business-to-Business Goods and Services

Business-to-business marketing is about the exchange of goods and services from one organization to another. Although we usually think of marketing in terms of the piles of consumer goods that beg for our dollars every day, the reality is that businesses and other organizations buy a lot more stuff than consumers do. They purchase these **industrial goods** for further processing or to use in their own business operations. For example, automakers buy tons of steel to use in the manufacturing process, and they buy computer systems to track manufacturing costs and other information essential to operations.

Similarly, the growth of **e-commerce** isn't just about things people buy for themselves—books, CDs, cars, and so forth—on the Internet. Just like in the offline world, much of the real online action is in the area of business-to-business marketing.

Not-for-Profit Marketing

As we noted previously, you don't have to be a businessperson to use marketing principles. Many **not-for-profit organizations** (also known as **nongovernmental organizations [NGOs]**), including museums, zoos, and even churches, practice the marketing concept to survive. Local governments adopt marketing techniques to attract new businesses and industries to their counties and cities. Even states are getting into the act: We've known for a long time that I♥NY, but recently Kentucky and Oregon hired advertising agencies to develop statewide branding campaigns (the official state motto of Oregon is now "Oregon. We love dreamers.").[6]

Idea, Place, and People Marketing

Marketing principles also encourage people to endorse ideas or to change their behaviors in positive ways. Many organizations work hard to "sell" everything from fatherhood involvement to shelter-pet adoption to stopping teen bullying. We are all familiar with tourism marketing that promotes wonderful places with slogans such as, "Smile! You are in Spain! or "Live your myth in Greece."

You may have heard the expression "Stars are made, not born." There's a lot of truth to that. Adele may have a killer voice and Chris Davis may have a red-hot baseball bat, but talent alone doesn't make thousands or even millions of people buy CDs or stadium seats. Some of the same principles that go into "creating" a celebrity apply to you. An entertainer—whether Miranda Lambert, Selena Gomez, or Drake—must "package" his or her talents, identify a market that is likely to be interested, and work hard to gain exposure to these potential customers by appearing in the right musical venues.

In the same way, everyday people like you "package" themselves when they create a great social media profile. And this person-marketing perspective is more valid than ever—now that almost everyone can find "15 minutes of fame" on a website, a blog, or a YouTube video. We even have a new word—*microcelebrity*—to describe those who are famous, not necessarily to millions of people but certainly to hundreds or even thousands who follow their comings and goings on

Today, almost anyone can have their "15 minutes of fame" online.

Facebook, Flickr, or Twitter. Whether it's the guy who sang the "Bed Intruder Song," Boxxy, Gary the Goat, "Alex from Target," or even Grumpy Cat, the Internet churns out hundreds of temporarily famous people who probably won't be remembered for long.

"... Value for Customers ..."

Most successful firms today practice the **marketing concept**—that is, marketers first identify consumer needs and then provide products that satisfy those needs to ensure the firm's long-term profitability. Practicing the marketing concept is, of course, more complex and requires that marketers understand the most basic elements of successful marketing.

These elements—needs, wants, benefits, demand, a market, and a marketplace—are listed and explained in Table 1.1.

This Italian ketchup brand illustrates how the condiment satisfies a simple need.

Table 1.1	Value for Customers	
Term	**Definition**	**In Practice**
Need	The difference between a consumer's actual state and some ideal or desired state	If the difference is big enough, the consumer is motivated to take action to satisfy the need. When you're hungry, you buy a snack. If you're not happy with your hair, you get a new hairstyle.
Want	A desire for a particular product we use to satisfy a need in specific ways that are culturally and socially influenced	If two students are hungry, the first student may be a health nut who fantasizes about gulping down a big handful of trail mix, whereas the second person may lust for a greasy cheeseburger and fries. The first student's want is trail mix, whereas the second student's want is fast food (and some antacid for dessert).
Benefit	A product delivers a benefit when it satisfies a need or want.	After several years when sales were down, McDonald's responded to the number-one request of its customers, breakfast all day. The new program attracted lapsed customers back and increased lunch business.[7]
Demand	Consumers' want for a product coupled with the means to obtain it.	Demand for a snappy red BMW convertible includes the people who want the car minus those who can't afford to buy or lease one.
Market	All the consumers who share a common need that can be satisfied by a specific product and who have the resources, willingness, and authority to make the purchase.	The availability of scholarships, government aid, and loans has increased the market for college education as more students can afford an education.
Marketplace	Location where buying and selling occurs	Today the exchange may be face-to-face, or through a mail-order catalog, a TV shopping network, an eBay auction, or a phone app.

not-for-profit organizations (also known as nongovernmental organizations [NGOs])
Organizations with charitable, educational, community, and other public service goals that buy goods and services to support their functions and to attract and serve their members.

marketing concept
A management orientation that focuses on identifying and satisfying consumer needs to ensure the organization's long-term profitability.

need
The recognition of any difference between a consumer's actual state and some ideal or desired state.

want
The desire to satisfy needs in specific ways that are culturally and socially influenced.

benefit
The outcome sought by a customer that motivates buying behavior that satisfies a need or want.

demand
Customers' desires for products coupled with the resources needed to obtain them.

market
All the customers and potential customers who share a common need that can be satisfied by a specific product, who have the resources to exchange for it, who are willing to make the exchange, and who have the authority to make the exchange.

marketplace
Any location or medium used to conduct an exchange.

Uber and other ride-sharing services are disrupting the transportation marketplace.

rentrepreneurs
Enterprising consumers who make money by renting out their possessions when they aren't using them.

collaborative consumption
A term used to refer to the activities practiced by rentrepreneurs.

utility
The usefulness or benefit that consumers receive from a product.

Rent the Runway is a service started by two recent business school grads. It rents high-end dresses from designers like Diane Von Furstenberg, for about one-tenth of the cost of buying the same garment in a store. A woman can rent a dress for four nights; it's shipped directly to her doorstep much like a Netflix video. The customer returns the dress in a prepaid envelope and the rental price includes the cost of dry cleaning. Place utility at work!

For example, you may *need* transportation but *want* a new Mazda MX-5 Miata convertible. The Miata will not only get you from Point A to Point B; it also will provide the *benefit* of a cool image. Unfortunately, it's possible that Mazda can't count you in their estimates of *demand* or the size of the *market* for the MX-5 because you can't afford such an expensive car. In that case you need to check out a different *marketplace*, a used car lot.

Of course, marketplaces continue to evolve. Increasingly consumers, especially younger ones, would rather rent than purchase the products they use. One of the biggest changes is in the domain of car sales, which are plummeting among newer drivers. Innovative start-ups like Zipcar figured out that many people, especially those who live in urban areas, would rather rent a ride by the hour instead of dealing with the hassles of car loans and hunting for parking spots when they weren't using their cars. Now the big guys are testing the waters. Volkswagen's Quicar project rents cars in Hanover, Germany, whereas BMW continues its international expansion of the DriveNow electric vehicle car-sharing program from Europe to the U.S.

A second change in the transportation marketplace is ride-sharing. Uber has become a global phenomenon based on this concept. Uber drivers use their own cars and work when they want to. Customers prefer Uber to traditional taxis; many say that Uber drivers treat you better than taxi drivers and because they use their own cars you aren't as likely to find a "science project" in the back seat.[8]

Millions of enterprising consumers in turn are becoming **rentrepreneurs** as they make money by renting out their stuff when they aren't using it; they're offering everything from barbecue grills and power tools to Halloween costumes and who knows what else on sites like Zilok in France and Craigslist in the United States. Some analysts refer to this mushrooming trend as **collaborative consumption**.

Marketing Creates Utility

Marketing transactions create **utility**, which refers to the usefulness or benefit we receive when we use a good or service. When it ensures that people have the type of product they want, where and when they want it, the marketing system makes our lives easier. Utility is what creates value.

Marketing processes create several different kinds of utility to provide value to consumers:

- *Form utility* is the benefit marketing provides by transforming raw materials into finished products, as when a dress manufacturer combines silk, thread, and zippers to create a bridesmaid's gown.

- *Place utility* is the benefit marketing provides by making products available where customers want them. The most sophisticated evening gown sewn in New York's garment district is of little use to a bridesmaid in Kansas City if it isn't shipped to her in time.

- *Time utility* is the benefit marketing provides by storing products until they are needed. Some women rent their wedding gowns instead of buying them and wearing them only once (they hope!).

- *Possession utility* is the benefit marketing provides by allowing the consumer to own, use, and enjoy the product. The bridal store provides access to a range of styles and colors that would not be available to a woman outfitting a bridal party on her own.

As we've seen, marketers provide utility in many ways. Now, let's see how customers and others "take delivery" of this added value.

Value for Clients and Partners

Marketing doesn't just meet the needs of consumers—it meets the needs of diverse stakeholders. The term **stakeholders** refers to buyers, sellers, or investors in a company, community residents, and even citizens of the nations where goods and services are made or sold—in other words, any person or organization that has a "stake" in the outcome. Thus, marketing is about satisfying everyone involved in the marketing process.

Value for Society at Large

Is it possible to contribute in a positive way to society and the earth and still contribute to your paycheck? Target, one of the nation's largest retailers, seems to think so. The company announced in its 2012 corporate responsibility report that two of its top five priorities are environmental sustainability and responsible sourcing. For example, one goal Target set is to ensure that the seafood sold in its stores is 100 percent sustainable (caught without negatively impacting ecosystems) and traceable (fish can be traced through the supply chain from point of harvest to final product). Also, the retailer gives back to its customers and helps them save money. Through its reusable-bag program, Target has returned more than $7 million to customers (those who bring their reusable bags save five cents per bag off their bill). And more than half of the chain's apparel line is labeled "machine wash cold," meaning customers reduce energy when they wash their clothes (thereby lowering customers' electricity bills).[9]

Green marketing in action.

stakeholders

Buyers, sellers, or investors in a company; community residents; and even citizens of the nations where goods and services are made or sold; in other words, any person or organization that has a "stake" in the outcome.

1.2

OBJECTIVE

Explain the evolution of the marketing concept.

(pp. 35–39)

When Did Marketing Begin? The Evolution of a Concept

Now that we have an idea of how the marketing process works, let's take a step back and see how this process worked (or didn't work) in "the old days." Although it just sounds like common sense to us, believe it or not, the notion that businesses and other organizations succeed when they satisfy customers' needs actually is a pretty recent idea. Before the 1950s, organizations only needed to make products faster and cheaper to be successful. Let's take a quick look at how the marketing discipline has developed since then. Table 1.2 tells us about a few of the more recent events in this marketing history.

Table 1.2 | Marketing's "Greatest Hits"

Year	Marketing Event
1961	Procter & Gamble launches Pampers.
1964	Blue Ribbon Sports (now known as Nike) ships its first shoes.
1971	Cigarette advertising is banned on radio and TV.
1980	Ted Turner creates CNN.
1981	MTV begins.
1985	New Coke is launched; old Coke rebranded as Coca-Cola Classic is brought back 79 days later.
2004	Online sales in the U.S. top $100 billion.
2010	Apple launches the iPad; sells 300,000 of the tablets on the first day and 1 million iPads in 28 days—less than half of the 74 days it took to sell 1 million iPhones. Consumers watch more than 30 billion videos online per month.
2014	Facebook spends $2 billion to buy Oculus Rift, a manufacturer of virtual reality headsets, as it signals the next frontier for social networks.
2016	Microsoft buys LinkedIn for $26.1 billion.

Sources: Patricia Sellers, "To Avoid Trampling, Get Ahead of the Mass," *Fortune*, 1994, 201–2, except as noted. Keith Regan, "Report: Online Sales Top $100 Billion," June 1, 2004, http://www.ecommercetimes.com/story/34148.html.

The Production Era

We think about the history of marketing as moving through four distinct eras, summarized in Table 1.3 and briefly described here. Many people say that Henry Ford's Model T changed America forever. From the start in 1908, when the "Tin Lizzie," or "flivver" as the T was known, sold for $825, Ford continued to make improvements in production

Ford's focus illustrates a **production orientation**, which works best in a seller's market when demand is greater than supply because it focuses on the most efficient ways to produce and distribute products.

production orientation
A management philosophy that emphasizes the most efficient ways to produce and distribute products.

The Sales Era

When product availability exceeds demand in a buyer's market, businesses may engage in the "hard sell," in which salespeople aggressively push their wares. This **selling orientation** means that management views marketing as a sales function, or a way to move products out of warehouses so that inventories don't pile up. The selling orientation gained in popularity after World War II and prevailed well into the 1950s. But consumers as a rule don't like to be pushed, and the hard sell gave marketing a bad image.

selling orientation
A managerial view of marketing as a sales function, or a way to move products out of warehouses to reduce inventory.

Companies that still follow a selling orientation tend to be more successful at making one-time sales rather than at building repeat business. We are most likely to find this focus among companies that sell *unsought goods*—products that people don't tend to buy without some prodding. For example, most of us aren't exactly "dying" to shop for cemetery plots, so some encouragement may be necessary to splurge on a final resting place. Even in these categories, however, we still may find that competitors try to stay on top of consumers' evolving needs. That's why we see the rise in popularity of *eco burials* that avoid embalming and encourage cremation and also online funerals that stream images of the loved one on the Internet.

The Relationship Era

At Plaza Fiesta outside Atlanta, Georgia, Hispanic customers are in for a treat: Instead of shopping at a mall, it's more like they're visiting a traditional Mexican village. With a bus station for ease of access, services like hairdressers or a doctor's office, and live music on Sundays, customers come for the experience, not just the shopping.[10] Plaza Fiesta found that it pays to have a **customer orientation**.

customer orientation
A business approach that prioritizes the satisfaction of customers' needs and wants.

As the world's most successful firms began to adopt a customer orientation, marketers had a way to outdo the competition, and firms began to develop more of an appreciation

Table 1.3 | The Evolution of Marketing

Icon	Era	Description	Example
Vira Honcharenko/Shutterstock	Production Era	Consumers have to take whatever is available marketing plays a relatively insignificant role.	Henry Ford's Model T sold for less than $575 and owned 60% of the market.
HitToon/Shutterstock	Sales Era	When product availability exceeds demand in a buyer's market. Management views marketing as a sales function, or a way to move products out of warehouses so that inventories don't pile up. Businesses engage in the "hard sell," in which salespeople aggressively push their wares.	The selling orientation gained in popularity after World War II when post-war demand had been satisfied and companies needed to sell more.
marcojavier/DigitalVision Vectors/Getty Image	Relationship Era	Firms have a customer orientation that satisfies customers' needs and wants.	Organizations research customer needs and develop products to meet the needs of various groups.
Kakigori Studio/Fotolia; wannasak saetia/Shutterstock; Dawn Hudson/Shutterstock	Triple-Bottom Line Era	Business emphasizes the need to maximize three components: 1. *The financial bottom line* 2. *The social bottom line* 3. *The environmental bottom line*	Companies try to create financial profits for stakeholders, contribute to the communities in which the company operates, and engage in sustainable business practices that minimize damage to the environment or that even improve it.

for the ways they could contribute to profits. Companies increasingly concentrated on improving the quality of their products. By the early 1990s, many in the marketing community followed a **total quality management (TQM)** approach, which is a management philosophy that involves all employees from the assembly line onward in continuous product quality improvement. We'll learn more about TQM in Chapter 9.

The Triple-Bottom-Line Orientation

More recently, organizations began to wake up to the idea that making monetary profit is important, but there's more to think about than just the financial bottom line. Instead, they began to focus on a **triple-bottom-line orientation**.[11] This new way of looking at business emphasizes the need to maximize not just one, but three components:

1. *The financial bottom line:* Financial profits to stakeholders
2. *The social bottom line:* Contributing to the communities in which the company operates
3. *The environmental bottom line:* Creating sustainable business practices that minimize damage to the environment or that even improve it

One result of this new way of long-term thinking is the **societal marketing concept**. It states that marketers must satisfy customers' needs in ways that also benefit society while

total quality management (TQM)
A management philosophy that focuses on satisfying customers through empowering employees to be an active part of continuous quality improvement.

triple-bottom-line orientation
A business orientation that looks at financial profits, the community in which the organization operates, and creating sustainable business practices.

societal marketing concept
A management philosophy that marketers must satisfy customers' needs in ways that also benefit society and deliver profit to the firm.

Habitat for Humanity does well by doing good.

sustainability
A product design focus that seeks to create products that meet present consumer needs without compromising the ability of future generations to meet their needs.

green marketing
A marketing strategy that supports environmental stewardship, thus creating a differential benefit in the minds of consumers.

accountability
A process of determining just how much value an organization's marketing activities create and their impact on the bottom line.

return on investment (ROI)
The direct financial impact of a firm's expenditure of a resource, such as time or money.

they still deliver a profit to the firm. A similar important trend now is for companies to think of ways to design and manufacture products with a focus on **sustainability**, which we define as "meeting present needs without compromising the ability of future generations to meet their needs."[12] One way to think about this philosophy is "doing well by doing good." Many big and small firms alike practice sustainability through their efforts that include satisfying society's environmental and social needs for a cleaner, safer environment.

Adidas is one of the world's most admired companies when it comes to sustainability. In 2015, Adidas was ranked No. 3 of the *Global 100 Most Sustainable Corporations*. Adidas's sustainability initiatives come from its "open source" program comprised of searching for ideas from various stakeholders. One Adidas open source partner, Parley for the Oceans, has a primary goal of getting plastic out of the ocean. Beginning in 2016, Adidas integrated materials made from ocean plastic waste into its products.[13]

Sustainability applies to many aspects of doing business, including social and economic practices (e.g., humane working conditions and diplomacy to prevent wars that deplete food supplies, atmospheric quality, and of course, lives). One other crucial pillar of sustainability is the environmental impact of the product. **Green marketing** means developing marketing strategies that support environmental stewardship by creating an environmentally founded differential benefit in the minds of consumers. Green marketing is one aspect of a firm's overall commitment to sustainability.

In addition to building long-term relationships and focusing on social responsibility, triple-bottom-line firms place a much greater focus on **accountability**—measuring just how much value an organization's marketing activities create. This means that marketers at these organizations ask hard questions about the true value of their efforts and their impact on the bottom line. These questions all boil down to the simple acronym of **ROI (return on investment)** or, specifically for marketing, *ROMI (return on marketing investment)*. Marketers now realize that if they want to assess just how much value they create for the firm, they need to know exactly what they are spending and what the concrete results of their actions are. You will learn more about ROMI in Chapter 3.

However, it's not always so easy to assess the value of marketing activities. Many times, managers state their marketing objectives using vague phrases like "increase awareness of our product" or "encourage people to eat healthier snacks." These goals are important, but their lack of specificity makes it pretty much impossible for senior management to determine marketing's true impact. Because management may view these efforts as costs rather than investments, marketing activities often are among the first to be cut out of a firm's budget. To win continued support for what they do (and sometimes to keep their jobs), marketers in triple-bottom-line firms do their best to prove to management that they generate measurable value by aligning marketing activities with the firm's overall business objectives.[14]

MillerCoors believes that a critical part of implementing accountability is that finance people respect marketing people for their knowledge and vice versa. The company has made this possible by developing a closer bond between the two groups. The CFO and CMO have adjacent offices and finance people have been dispersed among their marketing counterparts.[15]

What's Next in the Evolution of Marketing?

Although no one can really predict the future, most agree that in the years ahead we will see an acceleration of the most important factors that marketers think about today. These predictions include: Good content, big data, mobile marketing, marketing metrics, customer interaction, and the demand for companies to do good even as they do well.[16] Let's briefly dive in and see what these terms mean.

Mobile marketing, interacting with consumers via mobile phones, tablets, and wearable screens such as smart watches, will be one of the prime factors in marketing's future. Not only will these small screens allow for more personalized relationships with customers but the growth of mobile screens in developing countries will exponentially increase the number of potential customers.

Customers' demand for good content will continue to dominate online marketing. **User-generated content** (also known as consumer-generated content), in which consumers engage in marketing activities such as creating advertisements, will grow and overtake the importance of **branded content**. Branded content has been an important communication strategy for a number of years. It is produced by a brand and may even indicate the brand is the sponsor but still presents itself as something other than an attempt to sell a product. *The Lego Movie* was a great example of branded content. Despite the claims that the movie was not created to sell Legos, the company did have a major say-so in decisions about details of the movie.

Consumers' use of online reviews, blogs, and social media will require more than ever that brands create a positive image with every customer and in any place that the company touches him or her whether online or offline. All of this means that branding will increasingly become a two-way conversation allowing consumers to have a greater voice. Because this increases the ability of marketers to track consumer behavior, they will be able to provide a more personalized brand communication experience.

Firms that do well by doing good will become more important than ever. Customers will continue the current trend of rewarding brands that do good and punishing those that do not. **Corporate citizenship**, also called corporate social responsibility, refers to a firm's responsibility to the community in which it operates and to society in general. In the future, good corporate citizenship will become a major marketing function.

The ability to effectively interpret the increasing volume of consumer data will actually improve consumer lives. Although the primary purpose of consumer big data is to increase the ability of marketers to create better products to improve customer service, the use of that same data can provide better health care and even improved traffic. Ever wonder why there are two or three Starbucks' locations only a block away from each other? Starbucks' uses big data that includes street traffic analysis and demographic information to find new store locations that will be successful.[17] We'll do a deeper dive into big data in Chapter 5.

mobile marketing
Interacting with consumers via mobile devices (i.e., phones, tablets, and wearable screens such as smart watches).

user-generated content (also referred to as consumer-generated content)
Marketing content and activities created by consumers and users of a brand such as advertisements, online reviews, blogs, social media, input to new product development or serving as wholesalers or retailers. online reviews, blogs, and social media.

branded content
Marketing communication developed by a brand to provide educational or entertainment value rather than to sell the brand in order to develop a relationship with consumers; may indicate the brand is the sponsor.

corporate citizenship
Also referred to a corporate social responsibility, refers to a firm's responsibility to the community in which they operate and to society in general.

screen addicts
Consumers who spend so much time on smartphones, tablets, and computers that it interferes with more normal activities and productivity.

growth hacker
Experts who work on apps and sites to better hook consumers and keep them coming back and staying longer.

Ripped from the Headlines

Ethical/Sustainable Decisions in the Real World

How much time do you spend using your smartphone and your tablet each day? Are you one of the millions of college students who pulls out your smartphone to read your email, check your Facebook page, or play a game before class begins? What about during class (never!)? If so, you may be one of the millions of college students who are addicted to their small screens. Nearly three-quarters of Americans (71%) sleep with their smartphones, and 3 percent actually hold them all night long while they're in Dreamland. And, get this: More than 1/3 of respondents to a recent survey said their phones are the first thing on their minds when they wake up (only 10 percent said their significant other was).[18]

Of course, it isn't just college students who are addicted to their phones and tablets. Children have traded in their Barbie dolls, Hot Wheels, and Ninja Turtles for small screens as well. The problem is that young children, teens, and adults can rapidly become **screen addicts**.

Some experts suggest when children become addicted, this can damage their physical and mental health, just as addiction to alcohol or drugs. A British Heart Foundation study found that only 1 in 10 toddlers in the iPad generation is active enough to be healthy.[19]

And the tech companies continue to work to increase the amount of time consumers, young and old, spend on smartphones and tablets. The industry term for experts who work on apps and sites to better hook consumers, keep them coming back and staying longer is **growth hackers**.[20]

There are some company leaders and designers who would like to do things differently, but there are greater incentives to continue growth hacking. Is this unethical? Should industry leaders, as good corporate citizens, work to inhibit Internet addiction? Should they develop apps to send an alert to users when they stay too long or provide some other means to stop addiction?

ETHICS CHECK:

Should companies try to increase the amount of time consumers spend with their small screens?

☐ YES   ☐ NO

1.3 The Value of Marketing and the Marketing of Value

OBJECTIVE
Understand value from the perspectives of customers, producers, and society.
(pp. 40–47)

We said that marketing is all about delivering value to everyone who is affected by a transaction. That includes the customer, the seller, and society at large.

How do customers decide how much value they will get from a purchase? One way to look at value is to think of it simply as a ratio of benefits to costs—that is, customers "invest" their precious time and money to do business with a firm, and they expect a certain bundle of benefits in return.

Let's look at value from the different perspectives of the parties that are involved in an exchange: the customers, the sellers, and society.

Value from the Customer's Perspective

Think about something you would like to buy, say, a new pair of shoes. You have narrowed the choice down to several options. Your purchase decision no doubt will be affected by the ratio of costs versus benefits for each type of shoe. When you buy a pair of shoes, you consider the price (and other costs) along with all the other benefits (utilities) that each competing pair of shoes provides you.

value proposition
A marketplace offering that fairly and accurately sums up the value that will be realized if the good or service is purchased.

Marketers communicate these benefits to the customer in the form of a **value proposition**, which is a marketplace offering that fairly and accurately sums up the value that the customer will realize if he or she purchases the product. The value proposition includes the whole bundle of benefits the firm promises to deliver, not just the benefits of the product itself. For example, although most people probably won't get to their destination sooner if they drive a BMW versus a Mercedes-Benz or Audi, many die-hard loyalists swear by their favorite brand.

These archrival brands are largely marketed in terms of their images—meaning the images their respective marketing communication firms have carefully crafted for them with the help of slickly produced commercials, YouTube videos, and millions of dollars. When you buy a BMW, you do more than choose a car to get you around town, you may also make a statement about the type of person you are or wish you were. In addition to providing a luxury ride or superior maintenance services, that statement also is part of the value the product delivers to you. The challenge to the marketer is to create a killer value proposition. A big part of this challenge is to convince customers that this value proposition is superior to others they might choose from competitors.

Value from the Seller's Perspective

We've seen that marketing transactions produce value for buyers, but how do sellers experience value, and how do they decide whether a transaction is valuable? One answer is obvious: They determine whether the exchange is profitable to them. Has it made money for the company's management, its workers, and its shareholders?

That's an important factor, but not the only one. Just as we can't measure the value of an automobile from the consumer's perspective only in terms of basic transportation, value from the seller's perspective can take many forms. For example, in addition to making a buck or two, many firms measure value along other dimensions, such as prestige among rivals or pride in doing what they do well. The online shoe retailer Zappos's top-core value is to "Deliver WOW through service." Some organizations by definition don't even care about making money, or they may not even be allowed to make money. Nonprofits like

Greenpeace, the Smithsonian Institution, or National Public Radio regard value in terms of their ability to motivate, educate, or delight the public.

In recent years, many firms have transformed the way they do business. They now regard consumers as *partners* in the transaction rather than as passive "victims." That explains why it's becoming more common for companies to host events (sometimes called **brandfests**) to thank customers for their loyalty. For example, Jeep builds strong bonds with its Jeep 4 × 4 owners when it holds several off-road adventure weekends every year. These Jeep Jamborees are where other Jeep owners get to challenge the limits of their 4 × 4s on off-road trails and commune with fellow brand loyalists.[21]

Jeep's cultivation of its 4 × 4 enthusiasts reflects an important lesson the company understands very well: *It is more expensive to attract new customers than it is to retain current ones.* This notion has transformed the way many companies do business, and we'll repeat it several times in this book. However, there is an important exception to the rule: In recent years, companies have been working harder to calculate the true value of their relationships with customers by asking, "How much is this customer *really* worth to us?" Firms recognize that it can be costly in terms of both money and human effort to do whatever it takes to keep some customers loyal to the company. Often these actions pay off, but there are cases in which keeping a customer is a losing proposition.

Companies that calculate the **lifetime value of a customer** look at how much profit they expect to make from a particular buyer, including each and every purchase he or she will make from them now and in the future. To calculate lifetime value, companies estimate the amount the person will spend and then subtract what it will cost to maintain this relationship. The Metrics Moment box illustrates one approach to how marketers measure customer value.

Provide Value through Competitive Advantage

Firms of all types seek to gain a **competitive advantage**—an edge over its competitors that allows it to have higher sales, higher profits, more customers—in short to enjoy greater success year after year. In general, a competitive advantage comes from either a *cost advantage* or a *differential advantage*. A firm has a cost advantage when the firm can produce a good or service at a lower cost than competitors and thus charge customers a lower price. A differential advantage means that the firm produces a product that differs significantly from competitors' products and customers see the product as superior.

How does a firm go about creating a competitive advantage? The first step is to identify what it does really well. A **distinctive competency** is a firm's capability that is superior to that of its competition. For example, Coca-Cola's success in global markets—Coke commands 50 percent of the world's soft-drink business—is related to its distinctive competencies in distribution and marketing communications. Coke's distribution system got a jump on the competition during World War II, when Coke partnered with the military to make sure every soldier had access to its soft drink. The military actually paid for the transportation of Coca-Cola and helped the company to build bottling plants to keep the troops happy.[22] Coke's skillful marketing communications program, a second distinctive competency, has contributed to its global success. Coke doesn't market its product; it sells "happiness. "

The second step to develop a competitive advantage is to turn a distinctive competency into a **differential benefit**—value that competitors don't offer. Differential benefits set products apart from competitors' products by providing something unique that customers want, that is the competitive advantage. Differential benefits provide reasons for customers to pay a premium for a firm's products and exhibit a strong brand preference. For many years, loyal Apple computer users benefited from superior graphics capability compared to their PC-using counterparts. Later, when PC manufacturers caught up with this competitive advantage, Apple relied on its inventive product designers to create another differential benefit—futuristic-looking computers in a multitude of colors.

brandfests
Events that companies host to thank customers for their loyalty.

lifetime value of a customer
The potential profit a single customer's purchase of a firm's products generates over the customer's lifetime.

competitive advantage
A firm's edge over its competitors that allows it to have higher sales, higher profits, and more customers and enjoy greater success year after year.

distinctive competency
A superior capability of a firm in comparison to its direct competitors.

differential benefit
Properties of products that set them apart from competitors' products by providing unique customer benefits.

Metrics Moment

This section highlights the concepts of value and the value proposition that firms and their offerings bring to customers. But how do marketers actually measure value? Increasingly, they develop a **marketing scorecard** that reports (often in the form of numerical values) how the company or brand is actually doing in achieving various goals. We can think of a scorecard as a marketing department's report card. Scorecards tend to be short and to the point, and they often include charts and graphs to summarize information in an easy-to-read format. They might report "grades" on factors such as actual cost per sale, a comparison of web hits (the number of people who visit an e-commerce site) versus web conversions (the number who actually buy something at the site), a measure of customers' satisfaction with a company's repair facilities, or perhaps even a percentage of consumers who respond to a mail piece

that asks them to make a donation to a charity that the firm sponsors. You can see an example of a simple scorecard in Table 1.4. Throughout this book, we'll give you the opportunity to "get your hands dirty" as you calculate various kinds of scores, or **metrics**.

Apply the Metrics

1. Using Table 1.4 as a template, develop a scorecard for student satisfaction with your marketing class. You will need to develop your own relevant items for satisfaction measurement.
2. Then have the students in your class complete the scorecard now and again in the middle of the semester.
3. Summarize, interpret, and present the results.

marketing scorecards
Feedback vehicles that report (often in quantified terms) how the company or brand is actually doing in achieving various goals.

metrics
Measurements or "scorecards" that marketers use to identify the effectiveness of different strategies or tactics.

Table 1.4	An Example of a Customer Service Scorecard		
	Quarterly Scores		
Item	1st Qtr.	2nd Qtr.	3rd Qtr.
Satisfaction with			
C1 Employee responsiveness	60%	65%	68%
C2 Product selection	60%	62%	63%
C3 Service quality	60%	62%	55%
C4 Cleanliness of facility	75%	80%	85%
C5 Knowledge of employees	62%	62%	58%
C6 Appearance of employees	60%	62%	63%
C7 Convenience of location	60%	65%	68%

Source: Adapted from C. F. Lunbdy and C. Rasinowich, "The Missing Link: Cause and Effect Linkages Make Marketing Scorecards More Valuable," *Marketing Research*, Winter 2003, 14–19, p. 18. Copyright © 2003 American Marketing Association.

This competitive advantage even tempted many loyal PC users to take a bite of the Apple (see Table 1.5).

Add Value through the Value Chain

Many different players—both within and outside a firm—need to work together to create and deliver value to customers. The **value chain** is a useful way to appreciate all the players that work together to create value. This term refers to a series of activities involved in designing, producing, marketing, delivering, and supporting any product. In addition to marketing activities, the value chain includes business functions such as human resource management and technology development.[23]

value chain
A series of activities involved in designing, producing, marketing, delivering, and supporting any product. Each link in the chain has the potential to either add or remove value from the product the customer eventually buys.

The value chain concept reminds us that every product starts with raw materials such as iron ore or crude oil that are of relatively limited value to the end customer. Each link in the chain has the potential to either add or remove value from the product the customer eventually buys. The successful firm is the one that can perform one or more of these activities better than other firms; this is its distinctive competency and thus provides an opportunity to gain a competitive advantage. The main activities of value chain members include the following:

- *Inbound logistics:* Bringing in materials or component parts necessary to make the product
- *Operations:* Converting the materials into another form or the final product

Table 1.5 | How Firms Achieve a Competitive Advantage with a Distinctive Competency[24]

Company	Distinctive Competency	Differential Benefit	Competitive Advantage
Coca-Cola	Distribution and marketing communications	Convenience and brand awareness for customers all over the world	Other soft drinks are unable to take loyal customers away from Coke. Coca-Cola has more than 50% of the world soft-drink market.
Apple	Product quality and design	Easy access to cutting-edge technology	Apple's sales of its Mac computer increased 28.5% as the overall market for PCs decreased.
Southwest Airlines	Price point	Appeals to budget-conscious consumers	Southwest is the number one domestic carrier in the U.S.
Amazon.com	Fulfillment and distribution	Availability, convenience, and ease of access of product	Amazon holds about a 50% market share for books sold via the Internet.
Starbucks	Product quality	Customer satisfaction	Starbucks has just under 33% of the market share in its industry.

- *Outbound logistics:* Shipping out the final product
- *Marketing:* Promoting and selling the final product
- *Service:* Meeting the customer's needs by providing any additional support required

To better understand the value chain, consider a new iPad you buy at your local Apple store. Do you think about all the people and steps involved in designing, producing, and delivering that product to the store? And there are other people who create brand advertising, conduct consumer research to figure out what people like or dislike about their small tablet, or even make the box it comes in or the packaging that keeps the unit from being damaged in shipment? Without these people, there simply would be no iPad, only a box of raw materials and parts.

As 📷 Figure 1.2 shows, all these activities and companies belong to Apple's value chain. This means that Apple must make a lot of decisions. What electronic components will go into its music players? What accessories will it include in the package? What trucking companies, wholesalers, and retailers will deliver the iPods to stores? What service will it

Figure 1.2 📷 *Snapshot* | Apple's Value Chain

Apple's value chain includes inbound logistics, operations, outbound logistics, marketing and sales, and service.

Inbound Logistics	Operations	Outbound Logistics	Marketing and Sales	Service
• Planar lithium battery (Sony) • Hard drive (Toshiba) • MP3 decoder and controller chip (PortalPlayer) • Flash memory chip (Sharp Electronics Corp.) • Stereo digital-to-analog converter (Wolfson Microelectronics Ltd.) • Firewire interface controller (Texas Instruments)	• Consumer research • New product development team • Engineering and production	• Trucking companies • Wholesalers • Retailers	• Advertising • Sales force	• Computer technicians

Source: Based on information from Erik Sherman, "Inside the Apple iPod Design Triumph," May 27, 2006, http://www.designchain.com/coverstory.asp?issue=summer02.

Figure 1.3 ⨮ *Process* | Create and Deliver Value

This book is organized around the sequence of steps necessary to ensure that the appropriate value exchange occurs and that both parties to the transaction are satisfied. Each step corresponds to one of the book's five parts.

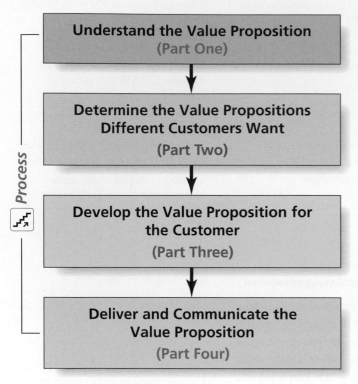

Understand the Value Proposition
(Part One)

Determine the Value Propositions Different Customers Want
(Part Two)

Develop the Value Proposition for the Customer
(Part Three)

Deliver and Communicate the Value Proposition
(Part Four)

haul videos
Videos consumers post on YouTube that detail the latest stuff they bought.

provide to customers after the sale? And what marketing strategies will it use? In some cases, members of a value chain will work together to coordinate their activities to be more efficient and thus create a competitive advantage.

We've organized this book around the series of steps in the marketing process. Each of these steps is essential to ensuring that the appropriate value exchange occurs and that both parties to the transaction are satisfied—making it more likely they'll continue to do business in the future. ⨮ Figure 1.3 shows these steps. Basically, we're going to learn about what marketers do as a product makes its way through the firm's value chain from obtaining the raw materials and component parts to produce the product to delivery into the customer's hands.

We'll start in Part 1 with a focus on how companies plan for success with global and ethical marketing strategies. In Part 2, we'll see how research and Big Data help marketers understand and meet the different needs of different customers. Then Part 3 takes a look at how firms decide to "position" the product in the marketplace, including choices about what it should look like, how its value should be communicated to customers, and how much to charge for it. As we reach the end of our marketing journey in Part 4, we'll talk about how the product gets delivered and promoted to consumers.

Consumer-Generated Value: From Audience to Community

As we discussed earlier, one of the most exciting changes in the world of marketing is that everyday people actually *generate* value instead of just buying it; consumers are turning into advertising directors, retailers, and new-product-development consultants. They create their own ads (some flattering, some not) for products and post them on sites like YouTube. They buy and sell merchandise ranging from Beatles memorabilia to washing machines (to body parts, but that's another story) on eBay. They share ideas for new styles with fashion designers, design new advertising, and customize their own unique versions of products on websites. Some even proudly announce the latest stuff they've bought in "**haul videos**" they shoot and post on YouTube (if you don't believe us, just search for "haul videos" and see how many people take the time to do this).

These profound changes mean that marketers must adjust their thinking about customers: They need to stop thinking of buyers as a passive audience and start thinking of them as a community that is motivated to participate in both the production and the consumption of what companies sell. They also are part of the brand communication process as they create their own videos, provide product reviews, and participate in blogs. Some examples of this **consumer-generated content** include:

- Ghirardelli Chocolate broadcast consumer-generated comments in New York's Times Square about when and where they most enjoyed eating its chocolate squares.[25]
- At iReport, budding citizen journalists can upload photos and videos to CNN in response to breaking news. The most timely and compelling of these stories have the potential to be vetted (cleared) and aired on the CNN TV network.[26]
- Rite-Solutions, a software company that builds advanced command-and-control systems for the U.S. Navy, sets up an internal "prediction market" in which any employee can propose that the company acquire a new technology, enter a new business, or make an efficiency improvement. These proposals become stocks, complete with ticker

symbols, discussion lists, and e-mail alerts. Employees buy or sell the stocks, and prices change to reflect the sentiments of the company's engineers, computer scientists, and project managers—as well as its marketers, accountants, and even the receptionist. One "stock" resulted in the development of a new product that now accounts for 30% of the company's sales.[27]

- For almost a decade, Doritos cashed in on its "Crash the Super Bowl" contest, where fans submitted their best 30-second commercials. The winning commercial (as voted on by fans) was aired during the Super Bowl game, and the winner received not only bragging rights but also took home a cool $1 million.[28]

Consumer-Generated Value: Social Networking

In the 1990s, the Internet (**Web 1.0**) was typified by static content provided by a site's creator. Businesses and institutions permitted little consumer involvement on websites.[29] These commercially and technically based organizations created sites that were crude, simple, and designed to accomplish one specific function. Later, **Web 2.0** offered marketers two-way communication through social networking sites such as Facebook. People wrote blogs and E-commerce expanded.

Web 3.0, where we are now, offers consumers real-time instant communications through live chats and instant messaging. When a marketing blunder is announced on the news such as Chipotle Grill's tainted food crisis, consumers blanket Twitter and Facebook with comments and complaints. Marketers are able to track customers' browser behavior so that if a customer searched for a sleeping bag, sleeping bags would be advertised/promoted on the main page and often on a totally different web page later. Maybe you've noticed that the things you search for tend to "follow" you around even as you visit other sites.

Marketers are now beginning to enjoy the benefits provided by **Web 4.0**, which offers customer engagement, cloud operations, and web participation as necessities. This means that marketers can now do much more than sell products to customers and the customers post their experiences and opinions of the products. To be successful in our fast-changing Internet-connected lives, companies must engage customers with the brand through social media, blogs and other online channels. Although we may imagine the **Cloud** as a physical place, in reality it's a network of servers, all having different functions. Because the Cloud provides an almost infinite amount of storage space, your school may have moved your e-mail to the Cloud. Some software companies have moved their programs to the Cloud. For example, small business owners now have the option of buying or paying a monthly subscription to QuickBooks.[30]

With the web, consumers create value through *social media*, which are Internet-based platforms that allow users to create their own content and share it with others who access their sites. Social media include, among others, social networks such as Facebook and Twitter and product review sites such as TripAdvisor. On **social networking platforms**, a user posts a profile on a website and he or she provides and receives links to other members of the network to share input about common interests. The odds are that you and most of your classmates checked your Facebook page before (or during?) class today.

Social media platforms like this are very hot today; more and more advertisers realize that these sites are a great way to reach an audience that tunes in regularly and enthusiastically to catch up with friends, check out photos of what they did at that outrageous party Saturday night (ouch!), proclaim opinions about political or social issues, or share discoveries of new musical artists.[31] They share several important characteristics:

- They improve as the number of users increases. For example, Amazon's ability to recommend books to you based on what other people with similar interests have bought gets better as it tracks more and more people who enter search queries.
- Their currency is eyeballs. Google makes its money by charging advertisers according to the number of people who see their ads after they type in a search term.

Web 1.0
The beginning phase of the Internet that offered static content provided by the owner of the site.

Web 2.0
The second generation of the World Wide Web that incorporated social networking and user interactivity via two-way communication.

Web 3.0
The current generation of the web that offers consumers real-time instant communications through live chats and instant messaging and marketers the ability to track customers' online behavior.

Web 4.0
The web gives consumers access to thousands of apps and makes the ability to use their smartphones and tablets to access brands anywhere and anytime a necessity.

Cloud
A network of servers that provide an almost infinite amount of storage space.

social networking platforms
Online platforms that allow a user to represent himself or herself via a profile on a website and provide and receive links to other members of the network to share input about common interests.

folksonomy
A classification system that relies on users rather than preestablished systems to sort contents.

wisdom of crowds
Under the right circumstances, groups are smarter than the smartest people in them, meaning that large numbers of consumers can predict successful products.

crowdsourcing
A practice where firms outsource marketing activities (such as selecting an ad) to a community of users.

- They are version free and in perpetual beta. Unlike static websites or books, content is always a work in progress. Enthusiastic users who serve as volunteer editors constantly update Wikipedia, the online encyclopedia and "correct" others' errors.

- They categorize entries according to **folksonomy** rather than "taxonomy." In other words, sites rely on users rather than preestablished systems to sort contents. Listeners at Pandora create their own "radio stations" that play songs by artists they choose as well as other similar artists.[32]

This last point highlights a key change in the way some new media companies approach their businesses: Think of it as marketing strategy by committee. The **wisdom of crowds** perspective (from a book by that name) argues that under the right circumstances, groups are smarter than the smartest people in them. If this is true, it implies that large numbers of (nonexpert) consumers can predict successful products.[33] Marketers rely on **crowdsourcing** when they outsource marketing activities to a large group of people, often through a social networking community. For example, Lego offers up its Lego CUUSOO crowdsourcing platform to solicit product and concept ideas from fans. The company periodically reviews the ideas that garner 10,000 supporters to see which ones might merit the chance to become a real Lego product, such as the *Ghostbusters* 30th Anniversary set, and "winners" earn 1 percent of the profits on net sales.[34] We'll talk more about crowdsourcing in Chapter 13.

Value from Society's Perspective

Every company's activities influence the world around it in ways both good and bad. Therefore, we must also consider how marketing transactions add or subtract value from society. In many ways, we as consumers are at the mercy of marketers, because we trust them to sell us products that are safe and perform as promised. We also trust them to price and distribute these products fairly. Conflicts often arise in business when the pressure to succeed in the marketplace provokes dishonest business practices; the huge failure of major financial services organizations like AIG and Goldman Sachs is a painful case in point.

Companies usually find that stressing ethics and social responsibility also is good business. The Internet and social media mean that consumers communicate about unsafe or faulty products, bad service, or scams. Some find this out the hard way:

The U.S. Environmental Protection Agency accused Volkswagen AG of using software to make 482,000 Volkswagen diesel-powered cars appear cleaner than they were. After first denying the accusation, Volkswagen later admitted to the charge. VW stock lost a third of its value in one day and the company faced the possibility of billions of dollars in fines.[35] In contrast, Procter & Gamble voluntarily withdrew its Rely tampons from the market following reports of women who had suffered toxic shock syndrome (TSS). Although scientists did not claim a causal link between Rely and TSS, the company agreed with the Food and Drug Administration that they would undertake extensive advertising notifying women of the symptoms of TSS and asking them to return their boxes of Rely for a refund. The company took a $75 million loss and sacrificed an unusually successful new product that had already captured about one-quarter of the billion-dollar sanitary product market.[36]

The Dark Side of Marketing and Consumer Behavior

For some—hopefully not many and hopefully not *you* after you read this book—marketing is a four-letter word. Whether intentionally or not, some marketers *do* violate their bond of trust with consumers, and unfortunately the "dark side" of marketing often is the subject of harsh criticism.[37] In some cases, these violations are illegal, such as when a retailer adopts a "bait-and-switch" selling strategy, luring consumers into the store with promises of inexpensive products with the sole intent of getting them to switch to higher-priced goods.

In other cases, marketing practices have detrimental effects on society even though they are not actually illegal. Some alcohol and tobacco companies advertise in low-income neighborhoods where abuse of these products is a big problem. Others sponsor commercials that depict groups of people in an unfavorable light or sell products that encourage antisocial behavior. An online game based on the Columbine High School massacre drew criticism from some who say it trivializes the actions of the two teen killers. We'll talk more about marketing ethics in Chapter 2.

Despite the best efforts of researchers, government regulators, and concerned industry people, sometimes consumers' worst enemies are themselves. We tend to think of ourselves as rational decision makers, calmly doing our best to obtain products and services that will maximize our health and well-being and that of our families and society. In reality, however, our desires, choices, and actions often result in negative consequences to ourselves and the society in which we live. Some of these actions are relatively harmless, but others have more onerous consequences. Some harmful consumer behaviors, such as excessive drinking or cigarette smoking, stem from social pressures, and the cultural value that people place on money encourages activities such as shoplifting or insurance fraud. Exposure to unattainable ideals of beauty and success can create dissatisfaction with the self. Let's briefly review some dimensions of the "dark side" of consumer behavior:

Addictive consumption: **Consumer addiction** is a physiological or psychological dependency on goods or services. These problems, of course, include alcoholism, drug addiction, and cigarettes, and many companies profit from addictive products or by selling solutions. More recently, as we've already seen many have become concerned about small screen addiction. Although most people equate addiction with drugs, consumers can use virtually anything to relieve (at least temporarily) some problem or satisfy some need to the point that reliance on it becomes extreme. "Shopaholics" turn to shopping much the way addicted people turn to drugs or alcohol.[38] Numerous treatment centers in China, South Korea, and Taiwan (and now a few in the U.S. also) deal with cases of Internet or small screen addiction—some hardcore gamers have become so hooked that they literally forget to eat or drink and die of dehydration. There is even a Chap Stick Addicts support group with approximately 250 active members![39]

consumer addiction
A physiological or psychological dependency on goods or services including alcoholism, drug addiction, cigarettes, shopping, and use of the Internet.

Illegal activities: The cost of crimes that consumers commit against businesses has been estimated at more than $40 billion per year. A survey the McCann-Erickson advertising agency conducted revealed the following tidbits:[40]

- Ninety-one percent of people say they lie regularly. One in three fibs about their weight, one in four fudges their income, and 21 percent lie about their age. Nine percent even lie about their natural hair color.

- Four out of 10 Americans have tried to pad an insurance bill to cover the deductible.

- Nineteen percent say they've snuck into a theater to avoid paying admission.

- More than three out of five people say they've taken credit for making something from scratch when they have done no such thing. According to Pillsbury's CEO, this "behavior is so prevalent that we've named a category after it—speed scratch."

Shrinkage: In 2014, shrinkage cost retailers an average of 1.38 percent of their total sales or $44 million. **Shrinkage** is the industry term for inventory and cash losses from shoplifting, employee theft, and damage to merchandise. As we'll see in Chapter 12, this is a massive problem for businesses, one that they in turn pass on to consumers in the form of higher prices. Analysts attribute about 40 percent of the losses to employees rather than shoppers.

shrinkage
Losses experienced by retailers as a result of shoplifting, employee theft, and damage to merchandise.

Anticonsumption: Some types of destructive consumer behavior are **anticonsumption**, when people deliberately deface or otherwise damage products. This practice ranges from relatively mild acts like spray-painting graffiti on buildings and subways, to serious incidences of product tampering or even the release of computer viruses that can bring large corporations to their knees.

anticonsumption
The deliberate defacement of products.

1.4 Marketing as a Process

OBJECTIVE

Explain the basics of market planning.

(p. 48)

Our definition of marketing also refers to *processes*. This means that marketing is not a one-shot operation. When it's done right, marketing is a decision process in which marketing managers determine the strategies that will help the firm meet its objectives and then execute those strategies using the tools they have at their disposal. In this section, we'll look at how marketers make business decisions and plan actions and the tools they use to execute their plans. We'll build on this brief overview in Chapter 3.

A big part of the marketing process is *market planning*, where we think carefully and strategically about the "big picture" and where our firm and its products fit within it. The first phase of market planning is to analyze the marketing environment. This means understanding the firm's current strengths and weaknesses by assessing factors that might help or hinder the development and marketing of products. The analysis must also take into account the opportunities and threats the firm will encounter in the marketplace, such as the actions of competitors, cultural and technological changes, and the economy.

Firms (or individuals) that engage in market planning ask questions like these:

- What product benefits will our customers look for in three to five years?
- What capabilities does our firm have that set it apart from the competition?
- What additional customer groups might provide important market segments for us in the future?
- How will changes in technology affect our production process, our communication strategy, and our distribution strategy?
- What changes in social and cultural values are occurring now that will impact our market in the next few years?
- How will customers' awareness of environmental issues affect their attitudes toward our manufacturing facilities?
- What legal and regulatory issues may affect our business in both domestic and global markets?

Answers to these and other questions provide the foundation for developing an organization's *marketing plan*. This is a document that describes the marketing environment, outlines the marketing objectives and strategy, and identifies who will be responsible for carrying out each part of the marketing strategy. Marketing plans will be discussed in full detail in Chapter 3—in fact, in that chapter you will learn about the basic layout and content of a marketing plan. A major marketing decision for most organizations is which products to market to which consumers without simultaneously turning off other consumers. Some firms choose to reach as many customers as possible, so they offer their goods or services to a **mass market** that consists of all possible customers in a market regardless of the differences in their specific needs and wants. Market planning then becomes a matter of developing a basic product and a single strategy to reach everyone.

Although this approach can be cost effective, the firm risks losing potential customers to competitors whose marketing plans instead try to meet the needs of specific groups within the market. A **market segment** is a distinct group of customers within a larger market who are similar to one another in some way and whose needs differ from other customers in the larger market. For example, automakers such as Ford, General Motors, and BMW offer different automobiles for different market segments. Depending on its goals and resources, a firm may choose to focus on one or on many segments. A **target market** is the segment(s) on which an organization focuses its marketing plan and toward which it directs its marketing efforts. Marketers develop *positioning* strategies to create a desired perception of the product in consumers' minds in comparison to competitors' brands. We'll learn more about these ideas in Chapter 7.

mass market
All possible customers in a market, regardless of the differences in their specific needs and wants.

market segment
A distinct group of customers within a larger market who are similar to one another in some way and whose needs differ from other customers in the larger market.

target market
The market segments on which an organization focuses its marketing plan and toward which it directs its marketing efforts.

Objective Summary ➥ Key Terms ➥ Apply

CHAPTER 1
Study Map

1.1 Objective Summary (pp. 28–35)

Explain what marketing is, the marketing mix, what can be marketed, and the value of marketing.

Marketing is the activity, set of institutions, and processes for creating, communicating, delivering, and exchanging offerings that have value for customers, clients, partners, and society at large. Therefore, marketing is all about delivering value to stakeholders, that is, to everyone who is affected by a transaction. Organizations that seek to ensure their long-term profitability by identifying and satisfying customers' needs and wants adopt the marketing concept.

The marketing mix includes product, price, place, and promotion. The product is what satisfies customer needs. The price is the assigned value or amount to be exchanged for the product. The place or channel of distribution gets the product to the customer. Promotion is the organization's efforts to persuade customers to buy the product.

Any good, service, or idea that can be marketed is a product, even though what is being sold may not take a physical form. Consumer goods are the tangible products that consumers purchase for personal or family use. Services are intangible products that we pay for and use but never own. Business-to-business goods and services are sold to businesses and other organizations for further processing or for use in their business operations. Not-for-profit organizations, ideas, places, and people can also be marketed.

Marketing provides value for customers when they practice the marketing concept and focus on identifying and satisfying customer needs. Marketing provides form, place, time, and possession utility. In addition, marketing provides value through satisfying the needs of diverse stakeholders, society, and the earth.

Key Terms

consumer, p. 28

marketing, p. 28

marketing mix, p. 29

Four Ps, p. 29

product, p. 30

promotion, p. 30

place, p. 30

channel of distribution, p. 30

price, p. 30

exchange, p. 31

consumer goods, p. 31

services, p. 31

business-to-business marketing, p. 32

industrial goods, p. 32

e-commerce, p. 32

not-for-profit organizations (also known as nongovernmental organizations [NGOs], p. 32

marketing concept, p. 33

need, p. 33

want, p. 33

benefit, p. 33

demand, p. 33

market, p. 33

marketplace, p. 33

rentrepreneurs, p. 34

collaborative consumption, p. 34

utility, p. 34

stakeholders, p. 35

1.2 Objective Summary (pp. 35–39)

Explain the evolution of the marketing concept.

Early in the twentieth century, firms followed a production orientation in which they focused on the most efficient ways to produce and distribute products. Beginning in the 1930s, some firms adopted a selling orientation that encouraged salespeople to aggressively sell products to customers. In the 1950s, organizations adopted a customer orientation that focused on customer satisfaction. This led to the development of the marketing concept. Today, many firms are moving toward a triple-bottom-line orientation that includes a commitment to quality and value, a concern for both economic and social profit while protecting the environment. The societal marketing concept maintains that marketers must satisfy customers' needs in ways that also benefit society while still delivering a profit to the firm. Similarly, companies think of ways to design and manufacture products with a focus on *sustainability*, or "doing well by doing good." Experts believe marketing will continue to change with greater use of good content, big data, mobile marketing, metrics and accountability, customer interaction and corporate citizenship.

Key Terms

production orientation, p. 36

selling orientation, p. 36

customer orientation, p. 36

total quality management (TQM), p. 37

triple-bottom-line orientation, p. 37

societal marketing concept, p. 37

sustainability, p. 38

green marketing, p. 38

accountability, p. 38

return on investment (ROI), p. 38

mobile marketing, p. 39

user-generated content (also known as consumer-generated content), p. 39

branded content, p. 39

corporate citizenship, p. 39

screen addicts, p. 39

growth hackers, p. 39

1.3 Objective Summary (pp. 40–47)

Understand value from the perspectives of customers, producers, and society.

Value is the benefits a customer receives from buying a good or service. Marketing communicates these benefits as the value proposition to the customer. For customers, the value proposition includes the whole bundle of benefits the product promises to deliver, not just the benefits of the product itself. Sellers determine value by assessing whether their transactions are profitable, whether they are providing value to stakeholders by creating a competitive advantage, and whether they are providing value through the value chain. Customers generate value when they turn into advertising directors, retailers, and new-product-development

consultants, often through social networking using social media. Society receives value from marketing activities when producers stress ethics and social responsibility. Criticisms of both marketing and consumer activities may be valid in a few instances, but most are unfounded.

Key Terms

value proposition, p. 40

brandfests, p. 41

lifetime value of a customer, p. 41

competitive advantage, p. 41

distinctive competency, p. 41

differential benefit, p. 41

marketing scorecards, p. 42

metrics, p. 42

value chain, p. 42

haul videos, p. 44

Web 1.0, p. 45

Web 2.0, p. 45

Web 3.0, p. 45

Web 4.0, p. 45

Cloud, p. 45

social networking platforms, p. 45

folksonomy, p. 46

wisdom of crowds, p. 46

crowdsourcing, p. 46

consumer addiction, p. 47

shrinkage, p. 47

anticonsumption, p. 47

1.4 Objective Summary (p. 48)

Explain the basics of market planning.

The strategic process of market planning begins with an assessment of factors within the organization and in the external environment that could help or hinder the development and marketing of products. On the basis of this analysis, marketers set objectives and develop strategies. Many firms use a target marketing strategy in which they divide the overall market into segments and then target the most attractive one. Then they design the marketing mix to gain a competitive position in the target market.

Key Terms

mass market, p. 48

market segment, p. 48

target market, p. 48

Chapter **Questions** and **Activities**

MyLab Marketing™
Go to **mymktlab.com** to watch this chapter's Rising Star video(s) for career advice and to respond to questions.

Concepts: Test Your Knowledge

1-1. Briefly explain what marketing is.

1-2. List and describe the elements of the marketing mix.

1-3. Define the terms *consumer goods, services*, and *industrial goods*.

1-4. Explain needs, wants, and demands. What is the role of marketing in each of these?

1-5. What is utility? How does marketing create different forms of utility?

1-6. Trace the evolution of the marketing concept.

1-7. Explain how marketers practice the societal marketing concept and sustainability.

1-8. Describe the Internet and how Web 3.0 and 4.0 provide greater opportunities for marketers to interact with their customers.

1-9. To what does the *lifetime value of the customer* refer, and how is it calculated?

1-10. What does it mean for a firm to have a competitive advantage? What gives a firm a competitive advantage?

1-11. What is involved in marketing planning?

Activities: Apply What You've Learned

⭐ **1-12.** *In Class, 10–25 Minutes for Teams* Assume that you are a marketing consultant employed by a large retail chain that offers consumers products in a number of brick-and-mortar stores and online. The retail organization wishes to increase its loyal customer base by engaging customers through interaction opportunities on social networks. Develop a list of at least 10 specific social network activities that will work together to increase customer engagement.

1-13. *In Class, 15–25 Minutes for Teams* Table 1.5 lists five well-known companies and highlights their distinctive competencies, differential benefits, and competitive advantages. First, review this table in your group and discuss how these three factors are interrelated. Then choose three other well-known companies (note: choose firms so that most of your team members have a reasonable knowledge of their marketing strategies) and construct a similar table for these companies. Finally, for each of these new firms, do you think that their competitive advantage is sustainable, or will they need to work to further improve their competitive position in the future?

1-14. *In Class, 10–25 Minutes for Teams* As college students, you and your friends sometimes discuss the various courses you are taking. One of your friends says to you, "Marketing's not important. It's just dumb advertising." Another friend says, "Marketing doesn't really affect people's lives in any way." As a role-playing exercise, present your arguments against these statements to your class.

1-15. *For Further Research (Individual)* Over time, marketing has moved through different eras, and some organizations are have adopted a triple-bottom-line orientation; they are looking beyond just the financial bottom-line to also consider social and environmental outcomes. Review the websites of three to five well-known companies. To what extent do they highlight the importance of social and environmental activities in their overall operations? Make a list of some of the activities (or contributions that they make) in this area.

1-16. *For Further Research (Groups)* Today's marketers recognize that the Internet and Big Data have changed marketing and will continue to change it in the years to come. Your team assignment is to first find examples of how the Internet and Big Data have improved marketing for some for-profit and not-for-profit organizations. Then develop your ideas on how the Internet and Big Data could make contributions to society as a whole in the future. Develop a short presentation for your class.

Concepts: Apply Marketing Metrics

The chapter discusses the growing importance of sustainability, and it notes that companies and consumers increasingly consider other costs in addition to financial kinds when they decide what to sell or buy. One of these cost categories is damage to the environment. How can marketers make it easier for shoppers to compute these costs? The answer is more apparent in some product categories than in others. For example, American consumers often are able to compare the power consumption and annual costs of appliances by looking at their EnergyStar™ rating. In other situations, we can assess the *carbon footprint* implications of a product or service; this tells us how much CO_2 our purchase will emit into the atmosphere (e.g., if a person flies from New York to London). The average American is responsible for 9.44 tons of CO_2 per year![41] A carbon footprint comes from the sum of two parts, the direct, or primary, footprint and the indirect, or secondary, footprint:

- The *primary footprint* is a measure of our direct emissions of CO_2 from the burning of fossil fuels, including domestic energy consumption and transportation (e.g., cars and planes).
- The *secondary footprint* is a measure of the indirect CO_2 emissions from the whole life cycle of products we use, from their manufacture to their eventual breakdown.[42]

Although many of us are more aware today that our consumption choices carry unseen costs, there is still a lot of confusion about the best way to communicate the environmental costs of our actions, and in many cases, consumers aren't motivated to take these issues into account unless the costs impact them directly and in the short term.

⭐ **1-17.** As a consumer, what other metrics would you suggest that might reflect benefits of sustainability initiatives that would motivate you to purchase from one provider or the other?

⭐ **1-18.** Would you buy from a demonstrably more expensive provider just because they exhibited a higher level of commitment to sustainability?

Choices: What Do You Think?

1-19. *Critical Thinking* Journalists, government officials, and consumers have been highly critical of companies for gathering and storing large amounts of data on consumers (i.e., Big Data). Others argue that such practices are essential for firms to provide high-quality, affordable products that satisfy consumers' varied needs. What do you think? Should the government regulate such practices? How can such practices hurt consumers? How can these practices help consumers?

⭐ **1-20.** *Ethics* Despite best efforts to ensure product safety, products that pose a danger to consumers sometimes reach the marketplace. At what point should marketers release information about a product's safety to the public? How should marketers be held accountable if their product harms a consumer?

1-21. *Critical Thinking* The marketing mix consists of four interdependent sets of tools that brands use in combination to obtain a desired response from targeted consumers. Think about two or three key competitors within the same industry (such as fast-food outlets, fashion retailers, food/snack brands, and so on)—do these firms (or brands) structure their marketing in a similar or different ways? That is, for each of their four Ps, outline what you see as similar in their approaches and also highlight where you see clear areas of difference in their marketing mix elements.

1-22. *Critical Thinking* Many consumers are concerned about the environment. They demand green marketing activities and more green products. Still, most do not buy green products because they are a few cents more expensive. How do you explain this? What are marketers doing wrong? Should government intervene? What are your suggestions for successful green marketing?

⭐ **1-23.** *Critical Thinking* Consumer-generated commercials seem to be part of a broader trend toward consumer-generated content of all sorts. Examples include MySpace, Flickr (where users post photos and comment on others' pictures), blogging, and video-sharing sites like YouTube. Do you think this is a passing fad or an important trend? How (if at all) should marketers be dealing with these activities?

1-24. *Ethics* The American Psychological Association formally recognizes Internet addiction as a psychological disorder. Should it? Why or why not?

1-25. *Ethics* Crowdsourcing has a lot of up side—for the company initiating the crowdsourcing anyway. The company gets to generate buzz among its fans as well as generate new product ideas and inventive advertising campaigns for little to no investment. Is there an up side to crowdsourcing for the customer, or are companies exploiting their users?

Miniproject: Learn by Doing

The purpose of this miniproject is to develop an understanding of the practice of marketing and the importance of societal marketing and sustainability to different organizations.

1-26. This task needs to be undertaken by a student team (with up to five students) and at least one student in the group should know a contact person in a business (the firm may be large or small). Step one in this task is to schedule an appointment with your contact and arrange for your entire group to both visit the business's premises and discuss how the firm undertakes its marketing activities (please refer to the next step in this project below for a list of possible questions).

1-27. Divide the following list of topics among your team and ask each person to be responsible for developing a set of questions to ask during the interview to learn about the company's program:
- What customer segments the company targets.
- How it determines customer needs and wants.
- What products it offers, including features, benefits, and goals for customer satisfaction.
- What its pricing strategies are.
- How it uses interactive content to engage customers.
- How it distributes products and whether it has encountered any problems.
- How it determines whether the needs and wants of customers are being met.
- Explain what marketers mean by the "societal marketing concept" and "sustainability" and ask if these are areas of concern to the organization. If so, how do they address them in their organization's activities? If not, ask if they have any plans to move in this direction in the future and, if so, how.

1-28. Develop a team report of your findings. In each section of the report, share what you learned that is new or surprising to you compared to what you expected.

1-29. Develop a team presentation for your class that summarizes your findings. Conclude your presentation with comments on what your team believes the company was doing that was particularly good and what was not quite so good.

Marketing in **Action** Case Real Choices at Coca-Cola

What do you do when your customer starts to shrink, both literally and figuratively? The sale of soft drinks in the U.S. is not what it used to be. The $98 billion soft-drink industry is being challenged by changes in consumers' attitudes toward both sugar-sweetened and diet drinks. Historically, soft drinks have

been a significant portion of the American diet and sales have grown year after year.

In the U.S. the rates of obesity, diabetes, and other weight-related health issues are on the rise. In 2014, the Centers for Disease Control and Prevention found that 35 percent of U.S.

adults were obese. And the problem is not limited to adults; with distressing regularity children are being diagnosed as obese. Although obesity and its related issues are complicated and have many different causes, soft drink manufacturers, like Coca-Cola, have been forced to bear a large share of the blame. This combined with the current consumer trend toward a healthier lifestyle has dealt a blow to the beverage industry. Since the 1990s, the sales of soft drinks have fallen by more than 25 percent.

J. Alexander M. Douglas Jr., president of Coca-Cola North America, stated that the public's change toward better health and wellness is transforming the long-term competitive environment. As many consumers have changed their attitudes toward sweetened soft drinks, they have also begun to question the safety of artificial sweeteners used in diet soft drinks. According to Barry M. Popkin, a professor of nutrition at the University of North Carolina, this has led to consumers changing from regular to diet soft drinks and finally to other beverages. The decision for many consumers has ultimately been to choose water.

Ironically, health and wellness were a key component of the beginning of the Coca-Cola story. In 1886, Dr. John S. Pemberton, a pharmacist, created a flavored syrup that was mixed with carbonated water and sold to customers. The motivation was to create a non-alcoholic alternative to the French Wine Coca, a concoction Dr. Pemberton used to cure his addiction to morphine. Dr. Pemberton promoted his new product as having a variety of health benefits, claiming that it was a cure for headaches, it relieved exhaustion, and it calmed nerves.

This mixture, which would eventually evolve into Coca-Cola, was primarily sold in pharmacies. However, instead of promoting it as a medicine, Dr. Pemberton decided to sell it as a fountain drink.

The association of obesity and soft drinks has become so much of a problem that in some cities, politician are proposing "soda taxes" to reduce the amount of sugar consumed. For now the soft-drink manufacturers are winning the political battles but are in jeopardy of losing overall. One of the consequences of these policy fights is that consumers are being reminded that soft drinks may not be the healthiest choice.

Coca-Cola has documented in a recent annual report that "Obesity concerns may reduce demand for some of our products." It has also stated that obesity and its corresponding health concerns are important risk considerations for Coca-Cola's business growth and sustained profitability.

How will this ongoing concern by public health officials effect how Americans feel about soft drinks in the long run? Will soft drinks ever attain the negative status of tobacco products, which many consumers have abandoned? Will Coca-Cola be able to reclaim its former position as market leader or must Coke change its focus to something else?

You Make the Call

1-30. What is the decision facing Coca-Cola?

1-31. What factors are important in understanding this decision situation?

1-32. What are the alternatives?

1-33. What decision(s) do you recommend?

1-34. What are some ways to implement your recommendation?

Based on: Margot Sanger-Katz, "The Decline of 'Big Soda'—The Drop in Soda Consumption Represents the Single Largest Change in the American Diet in the Last Decade," *New York Times* (October 2, 2015), http://www.nytimes.com/2015/10/04/upshot/soda-industry-struggles-as-consumer-tastes-change.html?_r=0 (accessed April 2, 2016); Claire Suddath, "Coke Confronts Its Big Fat Problem: Inside the Relaunch of America's No. 1 Soft Drink," *Bloomberg BusinessWeek* (July 31, 2014), http://www.bloomberg.com/news/articles/2014-07-31/coca-cola-sales-decline-health-concerns-spur-relaunch (accessed April 2, 2016); "Is This the Real Thing? Coca-Cola's Secret Formula 'Discovered'," *Time*, Inc. (February 15, 2011), http://newsfeed.time.com/2011/02/15/is-this-the-real-thing-coca-colas-secret-formula-discovered/ (accessed April 3, 2016).

MyLab Marketing™

Go to **mymktlab.com** for the following Assisted-graded writing questions:

1-35. *Creative Homework/Short Project.* An old friend of yours has been making and selling vitamin-fortified smoothies to acquaintances and friends of friends for some time. He is now thinking about opening a shop in a small college town, but he is worried about whether just having a great smoothie is enough to be successful. Knowing that you are a marketing student, he's asked you for some advice. What can you tell him about product, price, promotion, and place (distribution) strategies that will help him get his business off the ground?

1-36. *Creative Homework/Short Project.* As a marketing professional, you have been asked to write a short piece for a local business newsletter about the state of marketing today. You think the best way to address this topic is to review how the marketing concept has evolved and to discuss the triple-bottom-line orientation. Write the short article you will submit to the editor of the newsletter.

Global, Ethical, and Sustainable Marketing

Courtesy of Keith Sutter/Johnson & Johnson

Keith Sutter

▼ **A Decision Maker at Johnson & Johnson**

Keith Sutter is the senior product director for sustainable brand marketing at Johnson & Johnson. In that role, Keith leads Johnson & Johnson's 250 operating companies in developing sustainable products, business, and marketing strategies. He translates the value of Johnson & Johnson's extensive product stewardship and environmental successes to the company's trade customers and consumers, including championing the Earthwards® process.

Keith began his career at Johnson & Johnson in 2001 as a marketing associate. He subsequently held positions of increasing responsibility as a brand marketer on brands such as Band-Aid®, Neutrogena®, Lactaid®, and Ludens®.

Keith has a BS in economics from the Wharton School at the University of Pennsylvania and an MBA from the S.C. Johnson Graduate School of Management at Cornell University. He lives in Center City, Philadelphia, with his wife, Amy, and two sons, Leo and Charlie.

Keith's Info

What I do when I'm not working?
Triathlons and other outdoor sports.

First job out of school?
Marketing associate at Johnson & Johnson on the Decorated Band-Aid® Brand bandages, which was a great job working with licensees and cartoon characters like SpongeBob SquarePants and Elmo.

Business book I'm reading now?
David & Goliath by Malcom Gladwell.

What drives me?
New business opportunities and innovative new products and business models.

My management style?
Pacesetting. I like to set a good example for my team while allowing them the freedom to develop innovative solutions to our business problems that drive results.

Don't do this when interviewing with me.
Neglect to provide detailed examples of results you drove when asked for specific experiences.

Here's my problem...

Real **People**, Real **Choices**

Johnson & Johnson is one of the world's leading manufacturers of healthcare products. It sells many familiar consumer brands such as Band-Aid®, Neutrogena®, Listerine®, Splenda®, and Tylenol®, as well as medical devices and prescription drugs. Within this global company, the Earthwards® approach motivates employees to improve the sustainability of products. It defines how Johnson & Johnson thinks about and addresses its environmental and social impacts and challenges its people to design innovative and more sustainable solutions across a product's life cycle—from formulation and manufacturing to product use and safe disposal.

When Johnson & Johnson launched the Earthwards® process in 2009, Keith and his team used it to encourage J&J's product teams to make significant improvements to 60 products. Today, Johnson & Johnson has integrated and expanded the original process across the company. It uses the Earthwards® approach to drive continuous innovation by requiring every new product to:

- *Meet product stewardship requirements.* Every new product must achieve regulatory compliance and deliver on Johnson & Johnson's high standards.
- *Understand life cycle impact areas.* The life cycle impacts of products are reviewed at the category level, and opportunities to drive improvements are considered at the design, procurement, manufacturing, and marketing stages of a product's development.

Inviting every product team to:
- *Implement and validate improvements.* Product teams collaborate with sustainability experts to implement recommended improvements, and environmental marketing claims are reviewed and approved in accordance with applicable guidelines.

Encouraging the most sustainable product teams to:
- *Achieve Earthwards® recognition, an honor celebrating our most innovative and improved products.* If a product achieves at least three significant improvements across seven impact areas (materials used, packaging, energy reduction, waste reduction, water reduction, positive social impact or benefit, and product innovation), a board of internal and external experts determines if the product warrants Earthwards® recognition and provides suggestions for additional improvements. Teams who receive Earthwards® recognition are publicly congratulated on Earthwards.com and rewarded for their innovations by Johnson & Johnson leadership.

As he considered the best strategy to promote Earthwards®, Keith knew that one of his biggest challenges was to convince J&J's 127,000 employees around the globe to buy in to the idea. He needed a way to drive awareness and interest in the Earthwards® approach to sustainable product development across Johnson & Johnson. Generating awareness, understanding, and adoption of the process across J&J's business units was a key performance metric against which his team would be measured.

Keith had only limited resources to accomplish this objective.

Keith considered his **Options** 1·2·3

1 Option
Continue a successful tactic from the early roll-out of Earthwards®: Host regional green marketing conferences to bring together key stakeholders once per year. These meetings would showcase key tools and resources available that would then be distributed as requested by e-mail to other employees. This is high touch and engaging but hard to scale effectively across such a large company.

2 Option
Develop a customer intranet site, including an on-line scorecard to take Earthwards® submissions from an Excel spreadsheet to an online database accessible by all employees. The site would also house all the tools and materials Keith and his team had developed to date to explain Earthwards® and drive its adoption across J&J's varied businesses. This solution is low-touch and not engaging, but it is efficient because everyone in the company can access it easily. This database would free up resources that Keith and his team could use to further develop the Earthwards® program both internally and in the marketplace.

3 Option
Develop a high-touch strategy of identifying 20 to 30 influential leaders within Johnson & Johnson. Then set up multiple in-person meetings and training sessions with the goal of making the case for adoption of Earthwards® into each leader's business process and then encouraging each of these leaders to drive adoption of the program within J&J. This option would really engage people, but its impact would be hard to measure.

Now, put yourself in Keith's shoes. Which option would you choose, and why?

You Choose

Which **Option** would you choose, and **why**?
☐ **Option 1**   ☐ **Option 2**   ☐ **Option 3**

See what **option** Keith chose in **MyLab Marketing™**

Chapter 2

2.1 Take a Bow: Marketing on the Global Stage

OBJECTIVE

Understand the big picture of international marketing and the decisions firms must make when they consider globalization.

(pp. 56–59)

Here's an important question: Do you primarily see yourself only as a resident of Smalltown, USA, or as a member of a global community? The reality is that you and all your classmates are citizens of the world and participants in a global marketplace. It is likely that you eat bananas from Ecuador, drink beer from Mexico, and sip wine from Australia, South Africa, or Chile. When you come home, you may take off your shoes that were made in Thailand, put your feet up on the cocktail table imported from Indonesia, and watch the World Cup football (soccer) match being played in Brazil or Canada on your Smart TV while checking your Facebook page on your smartphone, both made in China. Hopefully, you also have some knowledge and concern for important world events such as the recent Ebola epidemic in Africa, terrorist attacks in Europe, and recent developments in North Korea and Syria. And you may even be looking for an exciting career with a firm that does business around the globe.

Firms doing business in this global economy face uncertainty in the future of the global marketplace. For a number of years, consumers and world leaders have argued that the development of free trade and a single global marketplace will benefit us all because it allows people who live in developing countries to enjoy the same economic benefits as citizens of more developed countries.

There are other reasons that many leaders want a single marketplace. One important reason comes from fears that the **Greenhouse Effect** may threaten the future of the planet. What is the Greenhouse Effect? In simple terms, our factories and automobiles continue to pump more and more carbon dioxide (the most important of the greenhouse gasses) into our atmosphere while at the same time we cut down the rain forests and reduce the amount of oxygen the trees add to the atmosphere. This increase in greenhouse gasses causes the earth to get warmer, just like a greenhouse provides a warm place for tender plants. The result, many believe, is **global warming**, a warming of the earth which will have disastrous effects on the planet. These fears have caused many to demand international agreements that would force industries and governments to develop and adhere to the same environmental standards to protect the future of the planet.

Of course, there is another side to the issue of a single marketplace. The **Arab Spring**, a series of anti-government protests and uprisings in a number of Arab countries that were largely aided by new social media tools available to people in the region, gave hope to many that dictatorships in countries in the Middle East would become democracies and bring a better life to peoples of the countries. Instead, new violent radical groups such as ISIS took over large portions of these countries. This was accompanied by a growing number of terrorist attacks in other parts of the world, causing citizens and country leaders to propose greater restrictions on immigration and on trade with countries that aid or harbor terrorists. At the same time, the decrease in the price of oil has increased concerns about a downturn in the global economy where each individual country will want to protect its own industries.

You may be asking, "What do these current events have to do with a marketing course?" Whether we like it or not, we are a global community. Everything that happens in any part of the world has a potential to influence what marketers need to do to be successful at home and around the globe. We'll be talking about these influences in this chapter and throughout the book.

The global marketing game is exciting, the stakes are high, and it's easy to lose your shirt. Competition comes from both local and foreign firms, and differences in national laws, customs, and consumer preferences can make your head spin. In this section, we will first discuss the status of world trade today. Then, we'll look at the decisions firms must make as they consider their global opportunities.

Greenhouse Effect

The turning of our atmosphere into a kind of greenhouse as a result of the addition of carbon dioxide and other greenhouse gasses.

global warming

A warming of the planet earth that will have disastrous effects on the planet.

Arab Spring

A series of anti-government protests and uprisings in a number of Arab countries facilitated by new social media tools available to people in the region.

World Trade

World trade refers to the flow of goods and services among different countries—the total value of all the exports and imports of the world's nations. In 2009, the world suffered a global economic crisis that resulted in dramatic decreases in worldwide exports. Today, we see increasing growth in world trade with world exports of merchandise increasing from $12 trillion in 2009 to nearly $19 trillion in 2014. Just how much is $19 trillion? Think about it this way: A recent lottery prize grew to a whopping $1 billion. If a lottery awarded a $1 billion prize every day, it would take more than 50 years to equal $19 trillion. Of course, not all countries participate equally in the trade flows among nations. Understanding the "big picture" of who does business with whom is important to marketers when they devise global trade strategies. 📷 Figure 2.1 shows the value of merchandise North American countries traded with major partners around the world in 2014.

It's often a good thing to have customers in remote markets but to serve their needs well requires flexibility and the ability to adapt to local social and economic conditions. For example, you may have to adapt to the needs of foreign trading partners when those firms can't pay cash for the products they want to purchase. Believe it or not, the currencies of as many as 100 countries—from the Albanian "lek" to the Uzbekistan "sum"—are not *convertible*; you can't spend or exchange them outside the country's borders. In other countries, because sufficient cash or credit simply is not available, trading firms work out elaborate deals in which they trade (or *barter*) their products with each other or even supply goods in return for tax breaks from the local government. This **countertrade** accounts for as much as 25 percent of all world trade.[1]

Our ever-increasing access to products from around the world does have a dark side: The growth in world trade in recent years has been accompanied by a glut of unsafe products—toys with lead paint, toothpaste containing poisonous diethylene glycol, and more recently, crayons laced with cancer-causing asbestos—many of which have come from China.[2] In 2014, the European Commission's early warning system for dangerous products (RAPEX) reported a notable increase in alerts of unsafe products; of the more than 2,000 alert issues the commission received, almost two-thirds of the unsafe products came from China.[3] Although most Chinese manufacturers make quality products, some unscrupulous producers have damaged the reputation of Chinese manufacturers and prompted U.S. and European officials to increase their inspections of Chinese imports.

world trade
The flow of goods and services among different countries—the value of all the exports and imports of the world's nations.

countertrade
A type of trade in which goods are paid for with other items instead of with cash.

Figure 2.1 📷 *Snapshot* | North American Merchandise Trade Flows (in Billions $)

Knowing who does business with whom is essential to develop an overseas marketing strategy. As this figure shows, North America trades most heavily with Asia, Europe, and Latin America.

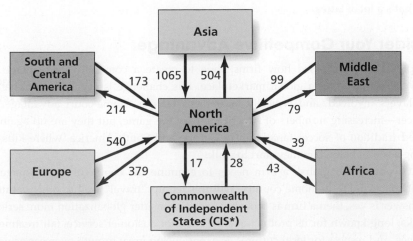

* Armenia, Azerbaijan, Belarus, Kazakhstan, Kyrgyzstan, Republic of Moldova, Russian Federation, and Ukraine

Figure 2.2  *Process* | Steps in the Decision Process to Enter Global Markets

Entering global markets involves a sequence of decisions.

Step 1: Whether to Go Global

Step 2: Which Market(s) to Enter

Step 3: Level of Commitment

Step 4: How to Adapt Marketing Mix Strategies
- **Localize**
- **Standardize**

Should We Go Global?

Figure 2.2 shows that when firms consider going global they must think about this in four steps:

- *Step 1.* "Go" or "no go"—is it in our best interest to focus exclusively on our home market or should we cast our net elsewhere as well?
- *Step 2.* If the decision is "go," which global markets are most attractive? Which country or countries offer the greatest opportunity for us?
- *Step 3.* What market-entry strategy, or rather, what level of commitment is best? As we'll see, it's pretty low risk to simply export products to overseas markets. On the other hand, although the commitment and the risk is substantial if the firm decides to build and run manufacturing facilities in other countries, the potentially greater payoff may be worth the extra risk.
- *Step 4.* How do we develop successful marketing mix strategies in these foreign markets—should we standardize what we do across all the countries where we operate or develop a unique localized marketing strategy for each country?

We'll look at the first of these decisions now—whether or not to go global.

The Globalization Decision

Although the prospect of millions—or even billions—of consumers salivating for your goods in other countries is tempting, not all firms can or should go global. When they make these decisions, marketers need to consider a number of factors that may enhance or detract from their success abroad. Let's review two that are critical to the decision: domestic demand and the competitive advantage the firm enjoys at home.

Look at Domestic and Global Market Conditions and Opportunities

Many times, a firm decides it's time to go global because the opportunity for growing the business and greater profit within its domestic market has already peaked and may even be declining while foreign markets offer opportunities for large growth. Of course, if there is still room to grow business and profits at home, it may not be a good idea to invest in the larger global market for now.

Starbucks has served coffee to just about every American who drinks coffee. The company opened its first store in 1971 in Seattle. After conquering its home city, the company spread across the U.S. The company's global expansion began in 1996 when it opened its first store outside of North America in Tokyo. Starbucks has opened stores in additional countries every year since. Today, Starbucks operates more than 24,000 stores in 70 countries.[4] That's a lot of lattes.

Consider Your Competitive Advantage

In Chapter 1, we discussed how firms hope to create a competitive advantage over rivals. When firms enter a global marketplace, this challenge is even greater. There are more players involved, and typically local firms have a "home-court advantage." It's like soccer—increasing numbers of Americans play the game, but they are up against an ingrained tradition of soccer fanaticism in Europe and South America, where kids start dribbling a soccer ball when they start to walk.

If it wants to go global, a firm needs to examine the competitive advantage that makes it successful in its home country. Will this leg up "travel" well to other countries? If the answer is yes, then a firm is probably wise to consider globalization more seriously. Starbucks, long known for its product quality, superior customer service, fair treatment of employees, and respect for local cultures, is experiencing great growth overseas as well as strong sales in the U.S.[5]

Now that we've discussed this first step in the global decision process, we'll look at important factors that help marketers make decisions about what markets to enter, including global trade controls that governments have in place and the various elements of the external environment that influence marketing decisions both at home and abroad. Finally, we'll examine marketers' decisions on the level of commitment and if and how to adapt marketing strategies used in the domestic market for success in other countries.

2.2 Understand International, Regional, and Country Global Trade Controls

OBJECTIVE

Explain how international organizations such as the World Trade Organization (WTO), economic communities, and individual country regulations facilitate and limit a firm's opportunities for globalization.

(pp. 59–61)

Even the most formidable competitive advantage does not guarantee success in foreign markets. Many governments participate in activities that support the idea that the world should be one big open marketplace where companies from every country are free to compete for business. The actions of others frequently say the reverse. In many countries, the local government may "stack the deck" in favor of domestic competitors. Often, they erect roadblocks (or at least those pesky speed bumps) designed to favor local businesses over outsiders, making it even more difficult to expand into foreign markets. Indeed, here in the U.S. the issue of whether to regulate trade to give American companies an advantage—or to lessen the advantage that companies based in other countries have from their own governments—is one of the most divisive issues in political and business circles.

Initiatives in International Cooperation and Regulation

In recent years, a number of international initiatives have diminished barriers to unfettered world trade. Most notably, after World War II, the United Nations established the **General Agreement on Tariffs and Trade (GATT)**, which did a lot to establish free trade among nations. During a meeting in 1984 known as the Uruguay Round, GATT created the **World Trade Organization (WTO)**. With 161 members, the WTO member nations account for 98 percent of world trade. The WTO has made giant strides to create a single, open world market. It is the only international organization that deals with the global rules of trade between nations. Its main function is "to ensure that trade flows as smoothly, predictably and freely as possible."[6]

The WTO also tackles other issues that stand in the way of an open and fair world market. If you spend any time in Asia, you immediately notice the huge numbers of luxury watches, leather bags, and current music CDs that sell for ridiculously low prices. Who can resist a Rolex watch for $20? Of course, there is a catch: They're fake or pirated illegally. Protection of copyright and patent rights is a huge headache for many companies, and it's a priority the WTO tries to tackle. *Pirating* is a serious problem for U.S. companies because illegal sales significantly erode their profits. All too often, we see news headlines from New York, Rome, or Dubai about police confiscating millions of dollars' worth of goods—from counterfeit luxury handbags to fake Viagra.[7]

Two additional organizations have a strong influence on the advancement of global trade.: the **World Bank** and the **International Monetary Fund (IMF)**. The World Bank, founded in 1944 and owned by its 181 member countries, is an international lending institution. The goal of the World Bank is to reduce poverty and improve the lives of people by

General Agreement on Tariffs and Trade (GATT)
International treaty to reduce import tax levels and trade restrictions.

World Trade Organization (WTO)
An organization that replaced GATT; the WTO sets trade rules for its member nations and mediates disputes between nations.

World Bank
An international lending institution that seeks to reduce poverty and improve the lives of people by improving economies and promoting sustainable development.

International Monetary Fund (IMF)
An international organization that seeks to ensure the stability of the international monetary exchange by controlling fluctuations in exchange rates.

improving economies and promoting sustainable development. In pursuit of this goal, the World Bank lends about $20 billion a year to development projects. The poorest countries may have up to 50 years to repay the loans without interest.[8]

The primary purpose of the IMF, also founded in 1944, is to ensure the stability of the international monetary exchange by controlling fluctuations in **foreign exchange rates,** also referred to as **forex rates**. Exchange rates are simply the price of one currency in terms of another currency. Stabilizing exchange rates can help to prevent severe **balance of payments** problems and thereby make it possible for countries to trade with each other. A country's balance of payments is a statement of how much trade a country has going out compared to how much it has coming in. If a country is buying more than it is selling, it will have a negative balance of payments (which is not necessarily a bad thing).[9] When we look in Figure 2.1 at the amount of merchandise various regions of the world import and export, we can get a good picture of the inequality of the balance of payments around the globe.

Protected Trade: Quotas, Embargoes, and Tariffs

Whereas the WTO works for free trade, some governments adopt policies of **protectionism** when they enforce rules on foreign firms to give home companies an advantage. Many governments set **import quotas** on foreign goods to reduce competition for their domestic industries. Quotas can make goods more expensive to a country's citizens because the absence of cheaper foreign goods reduces pressure on domestic firms to lower their prices.

While we normally think of import quotas that protect manufacturing and agricultural producers within a country, China also has strict import quotas on foreign films. A Hollywood-China co-production is exempt from the quota. Matt Damon created buzz in China when he began production as the star of a film in March 2016. The story of the co-production is about an army of elite warriors who must transform the Great Wall into a weapon "in order to combat wave after wave of otherworldly creatures hellbent on devouring humanity."[10]

An **embargo** is an extreme quota that prohibits commerce and trade with a specified country altogether. For over 50 years, hardcore cigar smokers in the U.S, have had to do without as the U.S. government prohibited the import of Cuban cigars as well as rum and other products because of political differences with its island neighbor. Now that the U.S. government has moved toward the normalization of relations between the two countries, Americans may again enjoy these uniquely Cuban products.

Governments also use **tariffs**, or taxes on imported goods, to give domestic competitors an advantage in the marketplace by making foreign competitors' goods more expensive than their own products. New Balance makes the only sneakers produced exclusively in the U.S. To protect this domestic industry, there is a 48 percent tariff on foreign shoes imports. No wonder those "Nike's Air Jordan III Retro Infrared 23" shoes are so expensive![11]

Economic Communities

Groups of countries may also band together to promote trade among themselves and make it easier for member nations to compete elsewhere. These **economic communities** coordinate trade policies and ease restrictions on the flow of products and capital across their borders. Economic communities are important to marketers because they set policies in areas such as product content, package labeling, and advertising regulations. The U.S., for example, is a member of the *North American Free Trade Agreement (NAFTA)*, which includes the U.S, Canada, and Mexico. *The European Union (EU)* represents 490 million consumers, more than 300 million of whom use the euro as their currency. In June 2016, voters in the U.K. approved the U.K.'s withdrawal from the European Union, causing alarm and concern around the globe. The long-term effects of this move will only be known after the passage of time. Table 2.1 lists the world's major economic communities.

foreign exchange rate (forex rate)
The price of a nation's currency in terms of another currency.

balance of payments
A statement of how much trade a country has going out compared to how much it has coming in. If a country is buying more than it is selling, it will have a negative balance of payments.

protectionism
A policy adopted by a government to give domestic companies an advantage.

import quotas
Limitations set by a government on the amount of a product allowed to enter a country.

embargo
A quota completely prohibiting specified goods from entering or leaving a country.

tariffs
Taxes on imported goods.

economic communities
Groups of countries that band together to promote trade among themselves and to make it easier for member nations to compete elsewhere.

Table 2.1 | Some Major Economic Communities around the World

Community	Member Countries
Andean Community (www.comunidadandina.org)	Bolivia, Colombia, Ecuador, Peru
Association of Southeast Asian Nations (ASEAN) (www.aseansec.org)	Brunei, Cambodia, Indonesia, Lao PDR, Malaysia, Myanmar, Philippines, Singapore, Thailand, Vietnam
Central American Common Market (CACM)	Costa Rica, El Salvador, Guatemala, Honduras, Nicaragua, Panama
Common Market for Eastern and Southern Africa (COMESA) (www.comesa.int)	Burundi, Comoros, Democratic Republic of Congo, Djibouti, Egypt, Eritrea, Ethiopia, Kenya, Libya, Madagascar, Malawi, Mauritius, Rwanda, Seychelles, Sudan, Swaziland, Uganda, Zambia, Zimbabwe
European Union (EU) (www.Europa.eu.int)	Austria, Belgium, Bulgaria, Croatia, Cyprus, Czech Republic, Denmark, Estonia, Finland, France, Germany, Greece, Hungary, Ireland, Italy, Latvia, Lithuania, Luxembourg, Malta, Netherlands, Poland, Portugal, Romania, Slovakia, Slovenia, Spain, Sweden (The United Kingdom was a member until it withdrew from the EU in 2016.)
MERCOSUR (www.mercosur.org)	Brazil, Paraguay, Uruguay, Argentina
NAFTA North American Free Trade Agreement (NAFTA) (www.nafta-sec-alena.org)	Canada, Mexico, United States
SAPTA South Asian Preferential Trade Arrangement (SAPTA) (www.saarc-sec.org)	Afghanistan, Bangladesh, Bhutan, India, Maldives, Nepal, Pakistan, Sri Lanka

2.3 Analyze the External Marketing Environment

OBJECTIVE

Understand how factors in a firm's external business environment influence marketing strategies and outcomes in both domestic and global markets.

(pp. 61–73)

Whether or not you decide to venture out of your own country (at least for now), to succeed you can't simply bury your head in the sand and ignore what's going on in the rest of the world. You can be sure your competitors aren't! Marketing planning demands that marketers understand the firm's internal and external environments. We'll talk about the internal environment of a firm in Chapter 3. In this chapter we'll look at how an understanding of a firm's external environment is even more important if your firm has decided to go global.

Things can happen very quickly, and new developments can trip up even the most sophisticated marketers. Just ask Tata Motors, which is a major player in the Indian auto industry. In 2016, Tata prepared to launch a new hatchback with the name Zica. Oops, too close to the Zika virus that's spreading headaches around the world so the company has to rename the car quickly.[12]

And, if you have decided to go global, understanding local conditions in a potential new country or in regional markets helps you to figure out where to go. 📷 Figure 2.3 provides a snapshot of these different external environments we'll dive into now.

The Economic Environment

After several rocky years of economic stumbling caused by the Great Recession of 2008–2009, the global economy is finally starting to make a comeback. It's a slow process—the global economy grew by only 2.6 percent in 2014 and 3.0 percent and 3.3 percent in 2015 and 2016, respectively. Countries with the highest incomes have experienced lower growth rates (2.4 percent in 2016) compared to much higher growth rates in lower income countries (5.3 percent) and 5.9 percent in countries with the lowest level of development, the **least developed countries (LDCs).**

least developed country (LDC)
A country at the lowest stage of economic development.

Figure 2.3 📷 *Snapshot* | Elements of the External Environment

It's essential to understand elements of the firm's external environment to succeed in both domestic and global markets.
Source: "World Trade Report," World Trade Organization, https://www.wto.org/english/res_e/publications_e/wtr15_e.htm

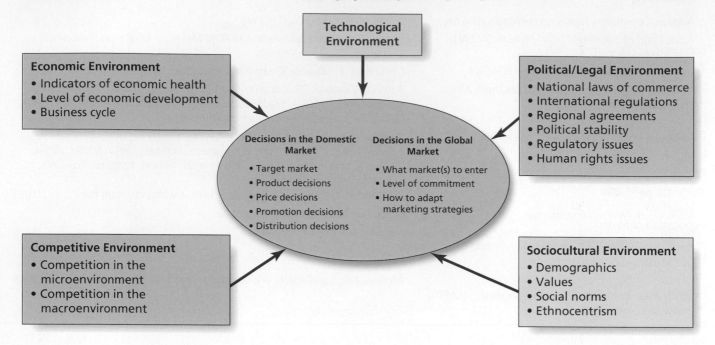

When we look at the future of the world economy, two areas of concern may impact future growth: the decline in oil prices because of a decrease in demand coupled with an increase in supply and the disruptive effects on trade due to geopolitical tensions in some regions of the world.[13] Marketers need to understand the state of the economy from two different perspectives: (1) the overall economic health and level of development of a country and (2) the current stage of its business cycle. Let's take a look at each now.

Indicators of Economic Health

Just as a doctor takes your temperature during a medical checkup, companies need to know about the overall "health" of a country's *economic environment* before they conduct a more detailed exam. You can easily find information about most countries in the *World Factbook* of the Central Intelligence Agency (CIA) (no, you don't need high-level security clearance to access this information online).

The most commonly used measure of economic health is a country's **gross domestic product (GDP)**: the total dollar value of goods and services it produces within its borders in a year. Table 2.2 shows the GDP and other economic and demographic characteristics of a sampling of countries. In addition to total GDP, marketers may also compare countries on the basis of *per capita GDP*: the total GDP divided by the number of people in a country. The *per capita* GDP is the better indicator of economic health because it is adjusted for the population size of each country.

Still, these comparisons may not tell the whole story. *Per capita* GDP can be deceiving, because of the income equality where the wealth of a country may be concentrated in the hands of a few, whereas most of its citizens don't have the means to obtain basic necessities. Furthermore, the costs of the same goods and services are much lower in some global markets. This is why it's important for companies that want to enter a foreign market to consider exchange rates as well.

The foreign exchange rate that we mentioned earlier is simply the price of a nation's currency in terms of what a bank will exchange it for with another currency. For example, if we want to know how much a U.S. dollar is worth in countries that are members of the

gross domestic product (GDP)
The total dollar value of goods and services produced by a nation within its borders in a year.

Table 2.2 | Selected Comparisons of Economic and Demographic Characteristics

	Democratic Republic of Congo	India	China	Brazil	Russia	United States	Qatar
Ranking*	2	61	103	107	135	177	185
Total GDP	$63.27 Billion	$8.027 Trillion	$11.38 Trillion	$3,166 Trillion	$3,471 Trillion	$17.97 Trillion	$324 Billion
Per capita GDP	$800	$6,300	$14,300	$15,800	$23,700	$56,300	$145,000
Population below poverty level	63%	29.8%	6.1%	21.4%	11.2%	15.1%	NA
Inflation rate	1.1%	5.6%	1.5%	10.6%	15.4%	0.2%	1.6%
Unemployment rate	NA	7.1%	4.2%	6.4%	5.4%	5.2%	0.45
Population	79 Million	1,251 Million	1,367 Million	204 Million	142 Million	321 Million	2.2 Million
Birthrate per 1,000 population	34.88	19.55	12.49	14.46	11.6	12.49	9.84
Population growth rate	2.45%	1.22%	0.45%	0.77%	−0.04%	.78%	3.07%
Population aged 0–14	42.65%	28.09%	17.08%	23.27%	16.68%	19.0%	12.52%
Population aged 15–24	21.41%	18.06%	13.82%	16.47%	10.15%	13.64%	12.96%
Population aged 25–54	29.75%	40.745	47.95%	43.80%	45.54%	37.76%	70.23%
Population aged 55–64	3.56%	7.16%	11.14%	8.66%	14.01%	12.73%	3.39%
Population aged 65 and older	2.63%	5.95%	10.01%	7.8%	13.61%	14.88%	0.89%
Life expectancy	56.93 yrs	68.13 yrs	75.41 yrs	73.53 yrs	70.47 yrs	79.68 yrs	78.59 yrs
Literacy rate	63.8%	71.2%	96.4%	92%	99.7%	NA	97.3%
School life expectancy	10 yrs	12 yrs	13 yrs	14 yrs	15 yrs	16 yrs	14 yrs
Mobile phones per 100 population	48	76	94	139	155	94	156
Internet users	<1%	19.2%	46.0%	53.4%	59.3%	86.8%	96.7%

*Based on values expressed in current international dollars, reflecting a single year's (the current year) currency exchange rates and purchasing-power-parity (PPP) adjustments. The ranking goes from the poorest (#1) to the wealthiest (#185).

Source for ranking: Valentina Pasquali, "The Poorest Countries in the World," *Global Finance Magazine,* April 2, 2016, https://www.gfmag.com/global-data/economic-data /the-poorest-countries-in-the-world?page=12 (accessed April 2, 2016); data based on, https://www.cia.gov/library/publications/the-world-factbook/geos/rs.html (accessed April 2, 2016). *The World Factbook* is updated biweekly.

European Union, we might find that it is only worth 87.8 cents in Europe ($1 = €0.878). If our neighbors in Europe look at the same exchange rate with the euro as the base currency, they would find that a euro is worth about 15 percent more in the U.S. (i.e., the forex rate would be €1 = $1.14). Why does the exchange rate matter? The rate determines the price of a product in a different country and thus a firm's ability to sell outside its borders. If the dollar becomes stronger so that for example it takes fewer dollars to equal one Euro, a dollar can buy more French wine or escargot, and customers in the U.S will buy more of it. If the dollar drops in value compared to the euro, then the dollar will buy less when you hike through Italy, whereas European tourists will flock to the U.S for a "cheap" vacation.

Of course, GDP and exchange rates alone do not provide the information marketers need to decide if a country's economic environment makes for an attractive market. They also need to consider whether they can conduct "business as usual" in another country.

economic infrastructure
The quality of a country's distribution, financial, and communications systems.

A country's **economic infrastructure** refers to the availability of the resources that make doing business in a country possible. These resources include transportation, distribution networks, financial institutions, communications networks, and energy resources. For example, countries with less-developed financial institutions may operate as a cash economy in which consumers and business customers must pay for goods and services with cash rather than with credit cards or checks. In poorer countries without good road systems, sellers may use donkey carts, hand trucks, or bicycles to deliver goods to the many small retailers who are their customers.

Level of Economic Development

level of economic development
The broader economic picture of a country.

standard of living
An indicator of the average quality and quantity of goods and services consumed in a country.

When marketers scout the world for opportunities, it helps to consider a country's **level of economic development**. Economists look past simple facts such as growth in GDP to decide this; they also look at what steps the country is taking to reduce poverty, inequality, and unemployment. Analysts also take into account a country's **standard of living**, an indicator of the average quality and quantity of goods and services a country consumes. They describe the following three basic levels of development:

1. As we said earlier, a country at the lowest stage of economic development is a least developed country (LDC). In most cases, its economic base is agricultural. Analysts consider many nations in Africa and South Asia to be LDCs. In LDCs, the standard of living is low, as are literacy levels. Opportunities to sell many products, especially luxury items such as diamonds and caviar, are minimal because most people don't have enough spending money. They grow what they need and barter for the rest. These countries are attractive markets for staples such as rice and inexpensive goods such as shoes and fabrics from which people can make clothing. In addition, they present opportunities for new products that these consumers need, such as solar-operated mobile phones and computers that will survive without air conditioning.

2. When an economy shifts its emphasis from agriculture to industry, standards of living, education, and the use of technology rise. These countries are **developing countries**. In such locales, there may be a viable middle class, often composed largely of entrepreneurs working hard to run successful small businesses. Because more than 8 out of 10 consumers now live in developing countries, the number of potential customers and the presence of a skilled labor force attract many firms to these areas. Marketers see these developing countries as the future market for consumer goods like skin care products and laundry detergents.

developing countries
Countries in which the economy is shifting its emphasis from agriculture to industry.

Within these LDCs and developing countries is a group of consumers known as the **bottom of the pyramid (BOP)**, which is the collective name for the group of more than 4 billion consumers throughout the world who live on less than $2 a day.[14] These BOP consumers represent a potentially huge marketing opportunity with purchasing power parity of $5 billion. They also present a big challenge for marketers, as unlike other consumer groups, they generally are unable to afford to purchase "inventory," such as a bottle of shampoo. Procter & Gamble, Unilever, and other companies meet these needs when they offer cleaning products, fabric softeners, and shampoo that can be used in cold water in affordable one-use **sachet** packaging.

bottom of the pyramid (BOP)
The collective name for the group of consumers throughout the world who live on less than $2 a day.

sachet
Affordable one-use packages of cleaning products, fabric softeners, shampoo, etc., for sale to consumers in least developed and developing countries.

The largest of the developing or newly industrialized countries—Brazil, Russia, India, China and South Africa—are referred to as the **BRICS countries**, or simply as the BRICS. Originally known as "BRIC," they became BRICS when South Africa joined in 2010. These five countries are the fastest growing of the developing countries; with more than 3 billion people, they represent over 42 percent of the world's population. Their total GDP of $16.039 trillion is equivalent to about 20 percent of the gross world product (GWP). Marketers are attracted to these countries because of the masses of consumers who are not wealthy but who are beginning their move toward economic prosperity.[15] The BRICS present exciting opportunities to marketers, but we must approach with

BRICS countries
Also referred to as the brics, Brazil, Russia, India, China, and South Africa are the fastest growing of the developing countries. With more than 3 billion people, they represent over 42% of the world's population and about 20% of the gross world product.

caution because of the many ups-and-downs that make these economies unstable. As examples, the political crisis in Brazil discourages foreign investment, Russia's "oil rush" has been reduced to a trickle because of the drop in oil prices, and China's exploding economy is starting to sputter.

A **developed country** boasts sophisticated marketing systems, strong private enterprise, and bountiful market potential for many goods and services. Such countries are economically advanced, and they offer a wide range of opportunities for international marketers.

In 1976, the most economically developed countries in the world—France, West Germany, Italy, Japan, the U.K, and the U.S.—formed what became known as the Group of Six, or G6. Later with the addition of Canada in 1976 and Russia in 1998, the G6 became the Group of Eight (G8). In 2014, Russia's membership was revoked because of its involvement in the Crimean crisis, so we are down to the **Group of Seven (G7)**.[16] The purpose of the G7 is to provide a way for these countries, democracies with highly developed economies, to deal with major economic and political issues that other countries and the international community face. In addition to topics of the world economy and international trade, G7 summits have more recently included discussions of other issues, such as energy, terrorism, unemployment, the information highway, crime and drugs, arms control, and the environment.[17]

The Business Cycle

The **business cycle** describes the overall pattern of changes or fluctuations of an economy. All economies go through cycles of *prosperity* (high levels of demand, employment, and income), *recession* (falling demand, employment, and income), and *recovery* (gradual improvement in production, lowering unemployment, and increasing income). A severe recession is a *depression*, a period during which prices fall but there is little demand because few people have money to spend and many are out of work.

Inflation occurs when prices and the cost of living rise while money loses its purchasing power because the cost of goods escalates. During inflationary periods, dollar incomes may increase, but real income—what the dollar will buy—decreases because goods and services cost more.

The business cycle is especially important to marketers because of its effect on customer purchasing behavior. During times of prosperity, consumers buy more goods and services. Marketers try to grow their businesses, maintain inventory levels and develop new products that meet customers' willingness to spend. During periods of recession, such as that experienced by countries all over the globe beginning in 2008, consumers simply buy less. They may also "trade down" as they substitute less expensive or lower-quality brands to stretch a dollar (or euro, etc.).

The Competitive Environment

A second important element of a firm's external environment is the *competitive environment*. For products ranging from toothpaste to sport utility vehicles, firms must keep abreast of what the competition is doing so they can develop new product features, new pricing schedules, or new advertising to maintain or gain market share. As we will see, marketers need to understand their competitive position among product alternatives in their microenvironment and in the structure of their industries, that is, their macroenvironment.

Like players in a global chess game, marketing managers size up their competitors according to their strengths and weaknesses, monitor their marketing strategies, and try to predict their next moves. To do this, an increasing number of firms around the globe engage in **competitive intelligence (CI)** activities where they gather and analyze publicly available information about rivals from such sources as the Internet, the news media, and publicly available government documents, such as building permits and patents. Successful CI

developed countries
A country that boasts sophisticated marketing systems, strong private enterprise, and bountiful market potential for many goods and services.

Group of 7 (G7)
An informal forum of the seven most economically developed countries that meets annually to discuss major economic and political issues facing the international community. Formerly the G8, Russia was excluded from the group as a result of its invasion of Crimea in 2014.

business cycle
The overall patterns of change in the economy—including periods of prosperity, recession, depression, and recovery—that affect consumer and business purchasing power.

competitive intelligence (CI)
The process of gathering and analyzing publicly available information about rivals.

means that a firm learns about a competitor's new products, its manufacturing processes, or the management styles of its executives. Then the firm uses this information to develop superior marketing strategies (we'll learn more about collecting marketing intelligence in Chapter 4).

Competition in the Microenvironment

Competition in the *microenvironment* means the product alternatives from which members of a target market may choose. We think of these choices at three different levels:

discretionary income
The portion of income people have left over after paying for necessities such as housing, utilities, food, and clothing.

1. Competition for consumers' **discretionary income** or the amount of money people have left after they pay for necessities such as housing, utilities, food, and clothing. Do we plow "leftover" money into a new computer tablet, donate it to charity, or turn over a new leaf and lose those extra pounds by investing in a healthy lifestyle? These choices vary by country. For Russians, the bulk of monthly income goes to food, alcohol, and tobacco. In the United States, health care is the biggest expenditure. In Japan, housing costs take just over a quarter of the average income, while in Saudi Arabia almost 10 percent is spent on furniture.[18]

product competition
When firms offering different products compete to satisfy the same consumer needs and wants.

2. **Product competition**: Other organizations offer different ways to satisfy the same consumers' needs and wants. So, for example, if a couch potato decides to use some discretionary income to get buff, he or she may consider either joining a health club or buying a used Soloflex machine on eBay to pump iron at home might be a good idea.

brand competition
When firms offering similar goods or services compete on the basis of their brand's reputation or perceived benefits.

3. **Brand competition**, where competitors offer similar goods or services, vying for consumer dollars. So, our flabby friend who decides to join a gym still must choose among competitors within this industry, such as Gold's Gym, Soul Cycle, or the humble YMCA, or he or she may forgo the exercise thing altogether and just buy bigger pants.

Competition in the Macroenvironment

When we talk about examining competition in the *macroenvironment*, we mean that marketers need to understand the big picture—the overall structure of their industry. This structure can range from one firm having total control to numerous firms that compete on an even playing field.

monopoly
A market situation in which one firm, the only supplier of a particular product, is able to control the price, quality, and supply of that product.

1. No, it's not just a board game: A **monopoly** exists when one seller controls a market. Because the seller is "the only game in town," it feels little pressure to keep prices low or to produce quality goods or services. In most U.S. industries today, the government attempts to ensure consumers' welfare by limiting monopolies through the prosecution of firms that engage in activities that would limit competition and thus violate antitrust regulations.

oligopoly
A market structure in which a relatively small number of sellers, each holding a substantial share of the market, compete in a market with many buyers.

2. In an **oligopoly**, there are a relatively small number of sellers, each holding substantial market share, in a market with many buyers. Because there are few sellers, the actions of each directly affect the others. Oligopolies most often exist in industries that require substantial investments in equipment or technology to produce a product. The airline industry is an oligopoly.

monopolistic competition
A market structure in which many firms, each having slightly different products, offer unique consumer benefits.

3. In a state of **monopolistic competition**, many sellers compete for buyers in a market. Each firm, however, offers a slightly different product, and each has only a small share of the market. For example, many athletic shoe manufacturers, including Nike, New Balance, and Under Armour, vigorously compete with one another to offer consumers some unique benefit—even though only Adidas (at least for now) offers you a $250 computerized running shoe that senses how hard the ground is where you are running and adapts to it.

4. Finally, **perfect competition** exists when there are many small sellers, each offering basically the same good or service. In such industries, no single firm has a significant impact on quality, price, or supply. Although true conditions of perfect competition are rare, agricultural markets (in which there are many individual farmers, each producing the same corn or jalapeño peppers) come the closest.

The Technological Environment

The *technological environment* profoundly affects marketing activities. Of course, the Internet is the biggest technological change in marketing within recent times—even bigger than hoverboards! Online sales offer consumers virtually anything they want (and even some things they don't want) without ever leaving home.

Some people believe the next innovation to be a game changer in marketing is already here. In 2013, Amazon CEO Jeff Bezos surprised CBS journalist Charlie Rose with the announcement that Amazon had been secretly working on "Prime Air," a project to use "octocopters" or **drones** to deliver packages to homes all over the country within 30 minutes.[19] A drone is an unmanned aircraft or flying robot controlled remotely using GPS. Drones, also known as **unmanned aerial vehicles or UAVs**, are already in demand by hobbyists and businesses. Drones have been equally successful at filming the Golden Globes and monitoring Iowa cornfields. They have been on the sets of *Game of Thrones* and the newest *Star Wars* films. While originally placing a ban on commercial use of small drones, more recently the FAA has dropped the ban and established rules for their use, opening the way for companies like Amazon to use drones for delivery.[20]

Successful marketers continuously scan the external business environment in search of ideas and trends to spark their own research efforts. When inventors feel they have come across something exciting, they usually want to protect their exclusive right to produce and sell the invention by applying for a **patent**. This is a legal document that grants inventors exclusive rights to produce and sell a particular invention in that country.

The Political and Legal Environment

The *political and legal environment* refers to the local, state, national, and global laws and regulations that affect businesses. Legal and regulatory controls can be prime motivators for many business decisions. Although firms that choose to remain at home have to worry about local regulations only, global marketers must understand more complex political issues that can affect how they are allowed to do business around the world.

American Laws

U.S. laws governing business generally have one or both of two purposes. Some, such as the Sherman Antitrust Act and the Wheeler-Lea Act, make sure that businesses compete fairly with each other. Others, such as the Food and Drug Act and the Consumer Products Safety Commission Act, make sure that businesses don't take advantage of consumers. Although some businesspeople argue that excessive legislation only limits competition, others say that laws ultimately help firms because they maintain a level playing field for businesses and support troubled industries.

Table 2.3 lists a few of the major federal laws that protect and preserve the rights of U.S. consumers and businesses. Federal and state governments have created a host of regulatory agencies—government bodies that monitor business activities and enforce laws. Table 2.4 lists some of the agencies whose actions affect marketing activities.

perfect competition
A market structure in which many small sellers, all of whom offer similar products, are unable to have an impact on the quality, price, or supply of a product.

drones
Unmanned aerial vehicles or flying robots controlled remotely using GPS technology.

unmanned aerial vehicles (UAVs)
Another name for drones.

patent
A legal mechanism to prevent competitors from producing or selling an invention, aimed at reducing or eliminating competition in a market for a period of time.

Table 2.3 | Significant American Legislation Relevant to Marketers

Law	Purpose
Sherman Antitrust Act (1890)	Developed to eliminate monopolies and to guarantee free competition. Prohibits exclusive territories (if they restrict competition), price fixing, and predatory pricing.
Food and Drug Act (1906)	Prohibits harmful practices in the production of food and drugs.
Federal Trade Commission Act (FTC) (1914)	Created the Federal Trade Commission to monitor unfair practices.
Robinson-Patman Act (1936)	Prohibits price discrimination (offering different prices to competing wholesalers or retailers) unless cost justified.
Wheeler-Lea Amendment to the FTC Act (1938)	Revised the FTC Act. Makes deceptive and misleading advertising illegal.
Lanham Trademark Act (1946)	Protects and regulates brand names and trademarks.
Child Protection and Toy Safety Act (1969)	Sets standards for child-resistant packaging.
Consumer Credit Protection Act (1968)	Protects consumers by requiring full disclosure of credit and loan terms and rates.
National Do Not Call Registry (2003)	Established by the Federal Trade Commission to allow consumers to limit number of telemarketing calls they receive.
Credit Card Accountability, Responsibility, and Disclosure Act of 2009	Bans unfair rate increases, prevents unfair fee traps, requires disclosures be in plain language, and protects students and young people.
The Affordable Care Act of 2013	Mandates health care coverage for Americans who do not receive benefits through an employer. Revises insurance regulations by eliminating denial of coverage for preexisting conditions, ending lifetime limits on coverage, and so on.[21]
Data Broker and Accountability Act of 2014 (DATA Act)	Gives consumers access to files of personal information a data broker compiles, the ability to correct inaccuracies, and the chance to opt out of the sale of that data to other companies.
USA Freedom Act of 2015	A result of Edward Snowden's revelations about the National Security Agency's (NSA) practices regarding collecting and monitoring of phone conversations. Requires that phone metadata be stored by phone companies, not the U.S. government.

Table 2.4 | U.S. Regulatory Agencies and Responsibilities

Regulatory Agency	Responsibilities
Consumer Product Safety Commission (CPSC)	Protects the public from potentially hazardous products. Through regulation and testing programs, the CPSC helps firms make sure their products won't harm customers.
Environmental Protection Agency (EPA)	Develops and enforces regulations aimed at protecting the environment. Such regulations have a major impact on the materials and processes that manufacturers use in their products and thus on the ability of companies to develop products.
Federal Communications Commission (FCC)	Regulates telephone, radio, TV and more recently the use of the Internet. FCC regulations directly affect the marketing activities of companies in the communications industries, and have indirect effects on all firms that use these media.
Federal Trade Commission (FTC)	Enforces laws, primarily through fines, against deceptive advertising and product labeling regulations.
Food and Drug Administration (FDA)	Enforces laws and regulations on foods, drugs, cosmetics, and veterinary products. FDA approval is required before marketers can introduce many products to the market.
Interstate Commerce Commission (ICC)	Regulates interstate bus, truck, rail, and water operations and therefore affects the ability of a firm to efficiently move products to its customers.

Political Constraints on Trade

Global firms know that the political actions a government takes can drastically affect their business operations. At the extreme, of course, when two countries go to war, the business environment changes dramatically.

Short of war, a country may impose *economic sanctions* that prohibit trade with another country as the U.S. has done with several countries, including Cuba, North Korea, and, more recently, Russia. After Russia invaded eastern Ukraine in 2014, the U.S. and European countries increased economic sanctions against the country. In retaliation, Russia banned the import of certain foods from the European Union and other countries.[22]

In some situations, internal pressures may prompt the government to take over the operations of foreign companies that do business within its borders. **Nationalization** occurs when the domestic government reimburses a foreign owned company (often not for the full value) for its assets after taking it over. One of the more famous examples of nationalization occurred when Egyptian president Gamal Abdel Nasser nationalized the Suez Canal Company in 1956. Similarly, following World War II, Germany and other European countries nationalized privately owned businesses. **Expropriation** is when a government seizes a foreign company's assets without any reimbursement (and that firm is just out of luck). In 1959, following the Cuban Revolution, the Cuban government expropriated all foreign-owned private companies, most of which were owned by U.S. firms or individuals. Now that the U.S. has normalized relations with Cuba, will these firms seek reimbursement for their lost property?

nationalization
When a domestic government reimburses a foreign company (often not for the full value) for its assets after taking it over.

expropriation
When a domestic government seizes a foreign company's assets without any reimbursement.

Regulatory Constraints on Trade

Governments and economic communities regulate what products are allowed in the country, what products should be made of, and what claims marketers can make about them. Other regulations ensure that the host country gets a piece of the action. **Local content rules** are a form of protectionism that stipulates that a certain proportion of a product must consist of components supplied by industries in the host country or economic community. For example, Brazil has recently tightened its local content rules regarding the manufacture and assembly of wind turbines. Under these rules, a minimum of 70 percent of the steel plates and 100 percent of the cement used to build the towers must be of Brazilian origin. In addition, the tower's nacelles (the assemblies that house the machinery) must be assembled locally.[23] Such rules ensure that Brazil is able to create more domestic manufacturing jobs for its citizens.

local content rules
A form of protectionism stipulating that a certain proportion of a product must consist of components supplied by industries in the host country or economic community.

Human Rights Issues

Some governments and companies are vigilant about denying business opportunities to countries that mistreat their citizens. They are concerned about conducting trade with local firms that exploit their workers or that keep costs down by employing children or prisoners for slave wages or by subjecting workers to unsafe working conditions, like locked factory doors. Nike, once the poster child for unsafe labor practices, has spent almost two decades admitting to and correcting its formerly abusive practices with increased wages and factory audits, and is now a company others can learn from and look up to.[24]

The U.S. Generalized System of Preferences

The **U.S. Generalized System of Preferences (GSP)** is a program Congress established to promote economic growth in the developing world. GSP regulations allow developing

U.S. Generalized System of Preferences (GSP)
A program to promote economic growth in developing countries by allowing duty-free entry of goods into the U.S.

Jodi Cobb/National Geographic Creative/Alamy Stock Photo

A culture's history often influences the way people respond to products. What does Spam mean to you?

countries to export goods duty free to the U.S. The catch is that each country must constantly demonstrate that it is making progress toward improving the rights of its workers. On the other side of the coin, the low wages that U.S. firms can pay to local workers often entices them to expand or entirely move their operations overseas. Although they provide needed jobs, some companies have been criticized for exploiting workers when they pay wages that fall below local poverty levels, for damaging the environment, or for selling poorly made or unsafe items to consumers.

The Sociocultural Environment

The *sociocultural environment* refers to the characteristics of the society, the people who live in that society, and the culture that reflects the values and beliefs of the society. Whether at home or in global markets, marketers need to understand and adapt to the customs, characteristics, and practices of its citizens. Basic beliefs about cultural priorities, such as the role of family or proper relations between the sexes, affect people's responses to products and promotional messages in any market.

To understand some of these values requires a knowledge of a culture's history. For example, someone who appreciates that South Korea has long had a significant U.S. military presence might not be as surprised to learn that SPAM—that American mystery meat—sells $235 million of the pork shoulder product there every year. During the Korean War, food was scarce and only a select few Koreans could gain access to PX stores on U.S. military bases. As a result the humble product became a status symbol; and it remains so today though many young Koreans who love to order "military stew" have no idea of its origins.[25]

Demographics

The first step toward understanding the characteristics of a society is to look at its **demographics**. These are statistics that measure observable aspects of a population, such as population size, age, gender, ethnic group, income, education, occupation, and family structure. The information demographic studies reveal is of great value to marketers when they want to predict the size of markets for many products, from home mortgages to brooms and can openers. We'll talk more about how demographic factors impact marketing strategies in Chapter 7.

Tupperware's explosive growth in overseas markets illustrates the importance of demographics. Faced with a static market (for one thing, many American women work so having Tupperware parties isn't as easy as it used to be), the company is prospering by planting its flag in other countries where there are more favorable conditions. One such sweet spot is Indonesia. It turns out there is an Indonesian tradition called an *arisan* ("gathering") where women meet with a group of friends to socialize, share recipes and even pool their money to buy gifts for one another. Tupperware, which relies on social networks like these, sends sellers to arisans to promote their products and to recruit new agents. For the container company, it's a natural fit.[26]

Values

Every society has a set of **cultural values**, or deeply held beliefs about right and wrong ways to live, that it imparts to its members.[27] Those beliefs influence virtually every aspect of our lives, even the way we mark the time we live them. For example, for most

demographics
Statistics that measure observable aspects of a population, including size, age, gender, ethnic group, income, education, occupation, and family structure.

cultural values
A society's deeply held beliefs about right and wrong ways to live.

Americans, *punctuality* is a core value; indeed, business leaders often proclaim that "time is money." For countries in Latin America and other parts of the world, this is not at all true. If you schedule a business meeting at 10:00, you can be assured most people will not arrive until around 10:30—or later.

These differences in values often explain why marketing efforts that are a big hit in one country can flop in another. In 2009, Mattel sought to invade China with a 36,000 square foot store in the most fashionable area of Shanghai. Barbie could get all her needs met in the store from a fashion consultation to getting lots of Barbie dolls and clothes.

Two years later the House of Barbie closed. What went wrong? Mattel failed to understand differences in values of Chinese and American families. The doll was too frivolous for parents who only have one child and who emphasize education over style. Two years after the House of Barbie closed, Mattel reintroduced Barbie as "Violin Soloist" Barbie, targeting Chinese parents who want their daughters to be "geniuses."[28]

Amnesty International campaigns for human rights around the world. This Swiss ad aims to combat domestic abuse.

One important dimension on which cultures differ is their emphasis on collectivism versus individualism. In **collectivist cultures**, such as those we find in Venezuela, Pakistan, Taiwan, Thailand, Turkey, Greece, and Portugal, people tend to subordinate their personal goals to those of a stable community. In contrast, consumers in **individualist cultures**, such as the U.S., Australia, Great Britain, Canada, and the Netherlands, tend to attach more importance to personal goals, and people are more likely to change memberships when the demands of the group become too costly.[29]

collectivist cultures
Cultures in which people subordinate their personal goals to those of a stable community.

individualist cultures
Cultures in which people tend to attach more importance to personal goals than to those of the larger community.

You may not do the Downward Facing Dog, but if like many other consumers you love to shop at Lululemon, you probably look like you do. The *yoga* craze is sweeping America, but not surprisingly it's (for now at least) even bigger in India, where it originates. *Yoga* is closely tied to other long-standing spiritual practices in that country that link to food, medicinal treatments (*Ayurveda*), and even home furnishings. Indian consumers crave modern versions of these products, and a new wave of businesspeople known as the "Baba Cool Movement" are giving them what they want as they market healthy items based upon ancient beliefs. For example, Baba Ramdev is a *swami* (holy man), but he's also an effective marketer who translates traditional values into modern versions. He and other entrepreneurs have been so successful that sales of large multinationals have suffered. They in turn have to adapt or die—that is why Colgate recently introduced toothpastes containing the extract of neem, an Indian tree, and charcoal that Indian villagers use to clean their teeth.[30]

social norms
Specific rules dictating what is right or wrong, acceptable or unacceptable.

Social Norms

Values are general ideas about good and bad behaviors. From these values flow **social norms**, or specific rules that dictate what is right or wrong, acceptable or unacceptable, within a society. Social norms indicate what ways to dress, how to speak, what to eat (and how to eat), and how to behave. For example, local customs dictate the appropriate hour at which the meal should be served—many Europeans, Middle Easterners, and Latin Americans do not begin dinner until around 9:00

It's common for store employees in Japan to wear uniforms, which help to symbolize the collective culture in that country.

AMERICANO, MAS COM UM TOQUE DE MÉXICO.

Mustang Sally

Marketers often "borrow" imagery from other cultures to communicate with local customers. This ad is for a Mexican restaurant in Brazil.

p.m. or later, and they are amused by American visitors whose stomachs growl by 7:00 p.m. Customs tell us how to eat the meal, including such details as the utensils, table etiquette, and even the appropriate apparel for dinnertime (no thongs at the dinner table!).

Conflicting customs can be a problem when U.S. marketers try to conduct business in other countries where executives have different ideas about what is proper or expected. These difficulties even include body language; people in Latin countries tend to stand much closer to each other than do Americans, and they will be insulted if their counterpart tries to stand farther away.

In many countries, even casual friends greet each other with a kiss (or two) on the cheek. In the U.S., one should kiss only a person of the opposite sex—and one kiss only, please. In Spain and other parts of Europe, kissing includes a kiss on each cheek for both people of the same and the opposite sex, whereas in the Middle East, unless a special friend, it is unacceptable for a man to kiss a woman or a woman to kiss a man. Instead, it is the norm to see two men or two women holding hands or walking down the street with their arms entwined.

Language

The language barrier is one obvious problem that confronts marketers who wish to break into foreign markets. A notice at a hotel in Acapulco proclaimed, "The manager has personally passed all the water served here." These translation snafus are not just embarrassing. They can affect product labeling and usage instructions, advertising, and personal selling as well. It's vital for marketers to work with local people who understand the subtleties of language to avoid confusion. Tell that to Audi, which may encounter a bit of trouble when it sells its new e-tron line of electric cars in France. In the French language, the word *Étron* doesn't conjure up images of speed, sustainability, or sophistication—it means another four-letter word that starts with s.[31]

Consumer Ethnocentrism

consumer ethnocentrism
Consumers' feeling that products from their own country are superior or that it is wrong to buy products produced in another country.

Ethnocentrism refers to the belief that one's own national or ethnic group is superior to others. Similarly, **consumer ethnocentrism** refers to consumers' beliefs about products produced in their country versus those from another. Consumers may feel that products from their own country are superior, or they may feel it is wrong, immoral, or unpatriotic to buy products produced in another country. Consumer ethnocentrism can cause consumers to be unwilling to try products made elsewhere.

2.4 How "Global" Should a Global Marketing Strategy Be?

OBJECTIVE
Explain some of the strategies and tactics that a firm can use to enter global markets.
(pp. 72–77)

Going global is not a simple task. Even a company known for its keen marketing prowess can make blunders when it reaches beyond its familiar borders. Disney, for example, learned several lessons from mistakes it made when it opened Hong Kong Disneyland:[32]

- Bigger is better. Unlike giant American parks, which Chinese visitors to the U.S. are accustomed to, Hong Kong Disneyland is Disney's smallest park, easily seen in a single day.

- Cinderella who? Chinese visitors know characters from recent movies like *Toy Story*, but they didn't grow up hearing about Cinderella, so that emotional connection to Disney's traditional characters is lacking, even though they're seen throughout the park.

When Disney opened its first mainland China Disney theme park in June, 2016, in Shanghai, it was clear that the company learned its lesson. Unlike the Hong Kong Disneyland, the new park includes the Enchanted Storybook Castle—the largest Disney castle on the planet, and six unique and unforgettable lands that relate to Disney characters Chinese families are familiar with: Mickey Avenue, Gardens of Imagination, Fantasyland, Adventure Isle, Treasure Cove, and Tomorrowland. There is also a Toy Story hotel.[33]

Company-Level Decisions: The Market Entry Strategy

If a firm decides to expand beyond its home country, it must make important decisions about how to structure its business and whether to adapt its product marketing strategy to accommodate local needs. Just like a romantic relationship, a firm must determine the level of commitment it is willing to make to operate in another country. This commitment ranges from casual involvement to a full-scale "marriage." At one extreme the firm simply exports its products, whereas at the other extreme it directly invests in another country by buying a foreign subsidiary or opening its own stores or manufacturing facility. This decision about the extent of commitment entails a trade-off between *control* and *risk*. Direct involvement gives the firm more control over what happens in the country, but its risk also increases if the operation is not successful.

Let's review four globalization strategies representing increased levels of involvement: exporting, contractual arrangements, strategic alliances, and direct investment. Table 2.5 summarizes these options.

Exporting

If a firm chooses to export, it must decide whether it will attempt to sell its products on its own or rely on intermediaries to represent it in the target country. These specialists, or **export merchants**, understand the local market and can find buyers and negotiate terms. An exporting strategy allows a firm to sell its products in global markets and cushions it against downturns in its domestic market. Because the firm actually makes the products at home, it is able to maintain control over design and production decisions.

Contractual Agreements

The next level of commitment a firm can make to a foreign market is a contractual agreement with a company in that country. Two of the most common forms of contractual agreements are licensing and franchising:

1. In a **licensing agreement**, a firm (the *licensor*) gives another firm (the *licensee*) the right to produce and market its product in a specific country or region in return for royalties on goods sold. The licensee is able to avoid many of the barriers to entry that the licensor would have but the licensor also loses control over how the product is produced and marketed.

2. **Franchising** is a form of licensing that gives the franchisee the right to adopt an entire way of doing

export merchants
Intermediaries a firm uses to represent it in other countries.

licensing agreement
An agreement in which one firm gives another firm the right to produce and market its product in a specific country or region in return for royalties.

franchising
A form of licensing involving the right to adapt an entire system of doing business.

Many consumers today hunger for new variations of familiar products from around the world. This German ad for crisps (i.e., potato chips) reads, "Discover Africa's spiciest secret."

| Table 2.5 | Market-Entry Strategies |

Strategy	Exporting Strategy	Contractual Agreements		Strategic Alliances	Direct Investment
Level of risk	Low	Medium		Medium	High
Level of control	Low	Medium		Medium	High
Options	Sell on its own Rely on export merchants	Licensing License a local firm to produce the product	Franchising A local firm adopts your entire business model	Joint venture, where firm and local partner pool their resources	Complete ownership often buying a local company
Advantages	Low investment, so presents the lowest risk of financial loss Can control quality of product Avoid difficulties of producing some products in other countries	Avoid barriers to entry Limit financial investment and thus risk	Local franchisee avoids barriers to entry Limit financial investment and risk	Easy access to new markets Preferential treatment by governments and other entities	Maximum freedom and control Avoid import restrictions
Disadvantages	May limit growth opportunities Perceived as a "foreign" product	Lose control over how product is produced and marketed, which could tarnish company and brand image Potential unauthorized use of formulas, designs, or other intellectual property	Franchisee may not use the same-quality ingredients or procedures, thus damaging brand image	High level of financial risk	Highest level of commitment and financial risk Potential for nationalization or expropriation if government is unstable

business in the host country. Firms need to monitor these operations carefully to ensure the partner maintains their brand image.

Strategic Alliances

strategic alliance
Relationship developed between a firm seeking a deeper commitment to a foreign market and a domestic firm in the target country.

Firms that choose to develop an even deeper commitment to a foreign market enter a **strategic alliance** with one or more domestic firms in the form of a **joint venture**, in which two or more firms create a new entity. Strategic alliances also allow companies easy access to new markets and preferential treatment in the partner's home country.

Direct Investment

joint venture
A strategic alliance in which a new entity owned by two or more firms allows the partners to pool their resources for common goals.

An even deeper level of commitment occurs when a firm expands internationally through ownership. When a firm buys all or part of a domestic firm, it can take advantage of a domestic company's political savvy and market position in the host country.

Marketing Mix Strategies

In addition to "big-picture" decisions about how a company will operate in other countries, managers must decide on how to market their product in each country. Do they need to modify or create new Four Ps—product, price, promotion, and place—to suit local conditions?

Standardization versus Localization

When they go global, marketers ask such questions as these:

1. To what extent will the company need to adapt its marketing communications to the specific styles and tastes of each local market?

2. Will the same product appeal to people there?

3. Will it have to be priced differently?

4. And, of course, how does the company get the product into people's hands?

Marketers must decide which is better—*standardization* or *localization*? Advocates of standardization argue that basic needs and wants are the same everywhere. A focus on the similarities among cultures means a firm doesn't have to make any changes to its marketing strategy to compete in foreign countries and can realize large economies of scale because it can spread the costs of product development and promotional materials over many markets. Widespread, consistent exposure also helps create a global brand like Coca Cola because it forges a strong, unified image all over the world.

In contrast, those in favor of localization feel that the world is not *that* small; you need to tailor products and promotional messages to local environments. These marketers argue that each culture is unique, with a distinctive set of behavioral and personality characteristics. If you visit the World of Coke in Atlanta, you can sample the products Coke sells around the globe.

To P or Not to P: Tweak the Marketing Mix

Once a firm decides whether it will adopt standardization or a localization strategy, it is time to plan for the Four Ps.

Product Decisions

A firm has three localization/standardization choices when it decides on a product strategy: to offer the same, a modified, or a new product:

1. A **straight extension strategy** (standardization) retains the same product for domestic and foreign markets. The Apple iPad is a good example of a straight extension strategy. No matter where you go in the world, every iPad is basically the same.

   straight extension strategy
   Product strategy in which a firm offers the same product in both domestic and foreign markets.

2. A **product adaptation strategy** (modified localization) recognizes that in many cases people in different cultures do have strong and different product preferences. Sometimes these differences can be subtle yet important. In South Korea, for example, the familiar pink and orange neon Dunkin' Donuts sign beckons customers inside to sample its gourmet coffee and traditional glazed donuts, but also on the menu is more Korean fare, such as black rice donuts, jalapeño sausage pie donuts, and rice sticks.[34]

   product adaptation strategy
   Product strategy in which a firm offers a similar but modified product in foreign markets.

   A product adaptation strategy also means a company adapts the same basic product to sync with local sensibilities. You may fondly recall Thomas the Tank Engine and his locomotive pals from your youth. Thomas is, in fact, one of the world's largest toy and TV franchises that delivers more than $1 billion per year to Mattel, which bought the company in 2012. Mattel started to catch some heat about the lack of diversity of Thomas's friends, who are primarily male and white. Mattel's answer: The company is introducing 14 new friends (four are female) who represent different countries. You can decide whether these new characters are valuable additions to the team, or if they just reflect cultural stereotypes. Here's a sample of them:[35]

   Raul of Brazil: "feisty"; "strong and agile."

   Yong Bao of China: "driven to achieve and make progress."

This Turkish ad for CNN implies that everyone has at least some things in common.

Ashima of India (female): "shows no fear"; "happy to help out."
Carlos of Mexico: "proud"; "always wearing a smile."

product invention strategy
Product strategy in which a firm develops a new product for foreign markets.

backward invention
Product strategy in which a firm develops a less advanced product to serve the needs of people living in countries without electricity or other elements of a developed infrastructure.

3. A **product invention strategy** (localization) means a company develops a new product as it expands to foreign markets. In some cases, a product invention strategy takes the form of **backward invention**. For example, there are still nearly one and a half billion people or more than 20 percent of the world's population who have no access to reliable electricity, primarily in Africa, Asia, and the Middle East. This provides a challenge for firms to develop products such as refrigerators, smartphones, and computers that can operate without electric power.[36]

Many of these people use kerosene lamps for light that are hazardous to both themselves and the environment. Here are just a few startling statistics:

- Fumes from kerosene lamps kill approximately 1.5 million African women and children annually.
- More than 1.5 million people in India suffer burns from kerosene lamps each year.
- Kerosene lamps burn fossil fuels and emit carbon dioxide (more than two pounds annually when used daily for four hours), contributing to greenhouse gas emissions.[37]

To combat these and other serious problems co-creators Jim Reeves and Martin Riddiford developed the $5 GravityLight, a small, batteryless LED that is powered by gravity. The light, which is attached to a bag filled with up to 28 pounds of sand, dirt, or rock (or whatever you have handy), works when the bag is hoisted into the air. As gravity pulls the weight of the bag downward, a notched belt spins a series of gears that drives the motor for the light. After you've used up approximately 25 minutes of light, you simply raise up the weight for another go.[38] As long as you've got a little muscle, you've got sustainable light.

Promotion Decisions

Marketers must also decide whether it's necessary to modify how they speak to consumers in a foreign market. Some firms endorse the idea that the same message will appeal to everyone around the world, whereas others feel the need to customize it. Unilever, maker of Lipton tea, is doing a bit of both in its first-ever global ad campaign to encourage its current and would-be tea drinkers to "Be More Tea"—that is, to "get off autopilot." The ads, which star Kermit the Frog from *The Muppets*, target both hot-tea and iced-tea drinkers. Although all of the global ads will include the same "Be More Tea" slogan (or translations thereof), only those global markets where *The Muppets* are well known will feature ads starring Kermit.[39]

Price Decisions

free trade zones
Designated areas where foreign companies can warehouse goods without paying taxes or customs duties until they move the goods into the marketplace.

gray market goods
Items manufactured outside a country and then imported without the consent of the trademark holder.

It's often more expensive to manufacture a product in a foreign market than at home. This may occur when there are higher costs stemming from transportation, tariffs, differences in currency exchange rates, and the need to source local materials. To ease the financial burden of tariffs on companies that import goods, some countries have established **free trade zones**. These are designated areas where foreign companies can warehouse goods without paying taxes or customs duties until they move the goods into the marketplace.

One danger of pricing too high is that competitors will find ways to offer their product at a lower price, even if they do so illegally. **Gray market goods** are items that are imported without the consent of the trademark holder. Although gray market goods are not counterfeit, they may be different from authorized products in warranty coverage and compliance with local regulatory requirements. Products such as toothpaste and pharmaceuticals may have the same formula but consist of inferior ingredients. The Internet offers exceptional opportunities for marketers of gray market goods ranging from toothpaste to textbooks. But, as the saying goes, "If it seems too good to be true, it probably is."

Another unethical and often illegal practice is **dumping**, through which a company prices its products lower than it offers them at home. This removes excess supply from home markets and keeps prices up there. And dumping isn't relegated to just retail products—agricultural products can be dumped, too.

dumping
A company tries to get a toehold in a foreign market by pricing its products lower than it offers them at home.

Place/Distribution Decisions

Getting your product to consumers in a remote location can be quite a challenge. It's essential for a firm to establish a reliable distribution system if it's going to succeed in a foreign market. Marketers used to dealing with a handful of large wholesalers or retailers in their domestic market may have to rely instead on thousands of small "mom-and-pop" stores or distributors, some of whom transport goods to remote rural areas on oxcarts, wheelbarrows, or bicycles. In LDCs, marketers may run into problems when they want to package, refrigerate, or store goods for long periods.

So far we've talked about marketers' need to understand the external environment and make good marketing mix decisions to be successful both at home and globally. In the next section, we'll discuss an even more important part of long-term marketing success: ethical marketing practices.

2.5 Ethics Is Job One in Marketing Planning

OBJECTIVE
Understand the importance of ethical marketing practices.
(pp. 77–81)

It's hard to overemphasize the importance of ethical marketing decisions. Businesses touch many stakeholders, and they need to do what's best for all of them where possible. On a more selfish level, unethical decisions usually come back to bite you later. The consequences of low ethical standards become visible when you consider the number of highly publicized corporate scandals that have made news headlines since the turn of the century. The fallout from unethical practices often means people lose their jobs and even their pensions. Stockholders lose their investments and consumers pay for worthless merchandise or services.

In 2015, the U.S. Environmental Protection Agency (EPA) accused Volkswagen AG of dodging air-pollution requirements by fitting about 482,000 U.S. diesel-powered vehicles with a "defeat device" in the form of computer software that would make the cars appear to be running cleaner than they were. Later Volkswagen admitted that they had fitted 8 million vehicles with the software. The result: Volkswagen's stock value plunged, sales dropped, car owners and investors filed lawsuits, and Volkswagen was last in *Fortune* magazine's 2016 ranking of the 100 largest companies by business reputation.[40]

Ethical Philosophies

Of course, what constitutes ethical behavior is often different for different people. We can point to various ethical philosophies and look at how each guides people to make their decisions. Table 2.6 presents a few of these different philosophies and how they reflect on ethical decision making.

Table 2.6 | Some Common Ethical Philosophies

Ethical Philosophy	Description of the Ethical Decision	Questions for Decision Making
Utilitarian approach	The decision that provides the most good or the least harm (i.e., the best balance of good and harm).	Which option will produce the most good and do the least harm?
Rights approach	The decision that does the best job of protecting the moral rights of all affected. These include the following: • The rights to decide what kind of life to lead • The right to be told the truth • The right not to be injured • The right to privacy	Which option best respects the rights of all who have a stake?
Fairness or justice approach	The decision that treat all human beings equally—or, if unequally, then fairly based on some standard that is defensible.	Which option treats people equally?
Common good approach	The decision that contributes to the good of all in the community.	Which option best serves the community as a whole, not just some members?
Virtue approach	The decision is in agreement with certain ideal virtues. Honesty, courage, compassion, generosity, tolerance, love, fidelity, integrity, fairness, self-control, and prudence are all examples of virtues.	Which option leads me to act as the sort of person I want to be?

utilitarian approach
Ethical philosophy that advocates a decision that provides the most good or the least harm.

rights approach
Ethical philosophy that advocates the decision that does the best job of protecting the moral rights of all.

fairness or justice approach
Ethical philosophy that advocates the decision that treats all human beings equally.

common good approach
Ethical philosophy that advocates the decision that contributes to the good of all in the community.

virtue approach
Ethical philosophy that advocates the decision that is in agreement with certain ideal values.

ethical relativism
Suggests that what is ethical in one culture is not necessarily the same as in another culture.

business ethics
Basic values that guide a firm's behavior.

For example, if one uses the *utilitarian approach* to make a decision on different safety features to include in a new product, the ethical choice is the one that provides the most good and the least harm. The *fairness or justice approach* suggests that the ethical decision about employee compensation is to pay everyone the same or to be able to justify why one salary is higher than another.

Of course, there are other factors that influence behavior. **Ethical relativism** suggests that what is ethical in one culture is not necessarily the same as in another culture. In other words, what is right or wrong is relative to the moral norms within the culture. Business leaders who have experienced a sheltered life in American companies are often shocked to find that they cannot expect the same ethical standards of others in the global community. Westerners, for example, are often painfully honest. If an American business contact cannot meet a deadline or attend a meeting or provide the needed services, he or she will normally say so. In other cultures, the answer, even if untrue, will always be "yes." Westerners see such dishonest answers as unethical, but in some areas of the world, people believe saying "no" to any request is extremely rude—even if there's no way they intend to honor the request.

Codes of Business Ethics

Ethics are rules of conduct—how most people in a culture judge what is right and what is wrong. **Business ethics** are basic values that guide the behavior of individuals within a business organization. Ethical values govern all sorts of marketing planning decisions that managers make, including what goes into their products, where they source raw materials, how they advertise, and what type of pricing they establish. Developing sound business ethics is a major step toward creating a strong relationship with customers and others in the marketplace.

To let employees and other stakeholders know definitively what is expected of them, many firms develop their own **code of ethics**—written standards of behavior to which everyone in the organization must subscribe—as part of the planning process. For example, AT&T's *Code of Business Conduct*, an 11-page document available via its website at www.att .com, details its commitments to honesty and to each other (to act with integrity and create a safe workplace), to the business and its shareholders (to work lawfully and to protect physical assets and intellectual property), to its customers (to follow ethical sales practices and guard customer communications), to its communities (to be responsible for the environment), to others (to maintain integrity in recording and reporting and to comply with antitrust laws), and to the code itself.[41]

To help marketers adhere to ethical behavior in their endeavors, the American Marketing Association (AMA) developed a code of ethics for marketers. We present the highlights of that code in Table 2.7.

code of ethics
Written standards of behavior to which everyone in the organization must subscribe.

Is Marketing Unethical?

Most marketers want to be ethical. Some follow the Rights Approach Philosophy and behave ethically because it's the right thing to do, whereas others are motivated by a desire not to get into trouble with consumers or government regulators. Still there are

Table 2.7	Highlights of the American Marketing Association Statement of Ethics

Ethical Norms and Values for Marketers

PREAMBLE

The American Marketing Association commits itself to promoting the highest standard of professional ethical norms and values for its members (practitioners, academics, and students). Norms are established standards of conduct that are expected and maintained by society and/or professional organizations. Values represent the collective conception of what communities find desirable, important and morally proper. Values also serve as the criteria for evaluating our own personal actions and the actions of others. As marketers, we recognize that we not only serve our organizations but also act as stewards of society in creating, facilitating, and executing the transactions that are part of the greater economy. In this role, marketers are expected to embrace the highest professional ethical norms and the ethical values implied by our responsibility toward multiple stakeholders (e.g., customers, employees, investors, peers, channel members, regulators, and the host community).

ETHICAL NORMS

As Marketers, we must:

1. **Do no harm.**
2. **Foster trust in the marketing system.**
3. **Embrace ethical values**

ETHICAL VALUES

Honesty—to be forthright in dealings with customers and stakeholders.
Responsibility—to accept the consequences of our marketing decisions and strategies.
Respect—to acknowledge the basic human dignity of all stakeholders.
Transparency—to create a spirit of openness in marketing operations.
Citizenship—to fulfill the economic, legal, philanthropic, and societal responsibilities that serve stakeholders.

IMPLEMENTATION

We expect AMA members to be courageous and proactive in leading and/or aiding their organizations in the fulfillment of the explicit and implicit promises made to those stakeholders.

The American Marketing Association helps its members adhere to ethical standards of business through its Code of Ethics.

Source: Copyright © American Marketing Association.

examples of questionable or unethical marketing. We'll discuss some of these criticisms here:

1. *Marketing serves the rich and exploits the poor:* Many marketers are concerned about their bottom line, but they also want to provide a better quality of life for all consumers, that is, the societal marketing concept that we discussed in Chapter 1. But there are exceptions. For example, because of decreasing sales of cigarettes in developed countries, tobacco companies target smokers in LDCs and developing countries and thus contribute to the health problems of those populations.[42]

2. *Products are not safe:* Whether marketers are truly dedicated to providing their customers with the safest products possible or because of the fear of government regulation and liability issues, most firms do make safe products and, if they find a problem, quickly notify customers and recall the defective product.

3. *Poor-quality products:* Many people bemoan the loss of U.S. manufacturing, feeling that imported products such as textiles and furniture are of poor quality. Product quality, however, is determined by what consumers want in a product. Do you want a refrigerator that lasts 50 years? Home appliance manufacturers could design and sell that, but would consumers be willing to pay what it would cost? Until consumers are willing to pay for higher quality, marketers have to provide products at the prices consumers want.

4. *Planned obsolescence:* To remain profitable, marketers must offer new products after an existing product has been on the market a period of time. The iPhone is an example. Have you noticed that about the time your cellular provider contract runs out, there is a newer and better iPhone that you just must have? For many people this is a good thing because new phones have better features. There are others who still like their old flip phone and will use it until if falls apart in their hands.

5. *Easy consumer credit makes people buy things they don't need and can't afford:* Many are concerned about businesses such as payday loan and car title loan companies that charge interest rates that can exceed 400 percent annually. Their customers typically are people with limited financial resources and even less knowledge about how to manage their money. One firm leases tires to consumers who can't afford to buy them. Of course, by the time the tires are paid off, the customer has spent enough to buy several sets of tires.

When Is a Bribe Not a Bribe? Ethical Issues for Global Business

In many LDCs and developing countries, salaries for midlevel people are, sadly, very low; the economy runs on a system we would call *blatant bribery or extortion*. Some of these "payments" are only petty corruption, and the "favors" are inconsequential, whereas others may involve high-level government or business officials and can have devastating consequences. If you need to park your car or your delivery truck illegally where there is no parking space, you give a little money to the policeman. If the shopkeeper wants the policeman to watch out for his store, he gives the policeman a shirt from his stock once in a while. If an importer wants to get her merchandise out of customs before it spoils, she pays off the government worker who can hold up her shipment for weeks. And if someone wants the contract to build a new building or wants an unsafe building to pass inspection—well, you get the idea.

Bribery occurs when someone voluntarily offers payment to get an illegal advantage. **Extortion** occurs when someone in authority extracts payment under duress. The Foreign Corrupt Practices Act of 1977 (FCPA), however, puts U.S. businesses at a disadvantage

bribery
When someone voluntarily offers payment to get an illegal advantage.

extortion
When someone in authority extracts payment under duress.

because it bars them from paying bribes to sell overseas. The FCPA does, however, allow payments for "routine governmental action … such as obtaining permits, licenses, or other official documents; processing governmental papers, such as visas and work orders; [and] providing police protection."[43]

2.6 Sustainability: Marketers Do Well by Doing Good

OBJECTIVE

Explain the role of sustainability in marketing planning.

(pp. 81–83)

In Chapter 1, we saw that many firms today have adopted a *triple-bottom-line orientation*. These firms don't just look at their financial successes but also focus on how they contribute to their communities (their social bottom line) and create sustainable business practices (the environmental bottom line). Today, many believe that sustainability is no longer an option. It's necessary, it's happening, and it will continue to be a part of strategic planning into the future.

Why are sustainable business practices so important? It's really simple. All of the things we need today or in the future to maintain life as we know it depend on the natural resources of our planet—air, water, our mineral resources in the earth, and ore reserves that we mine. Today, our earth's population continues to grow at staggering rates. Economic growth, especially the growth in developing countries, means we consume our natural resources at higher rates. The massive growth of developing countries like China and India doesn't just provide expanding marketing opportunities; the growing middle classes in these countries look at the lives of consumers in developed countries and want that same life, thus creating even greater levels of unsustainable consumption.

green customers
Those consumers who are most likely to actively look for and buy products that are eco-friendly.

Sustainability Is a Sensible Business Decision

To understand sustainable marketing better, we might go back to the marketing concept: identifying and satisfying consumer needs to ensure the organization's long-term profitability. Sustainability adds to this the need of the firm to sustain itself and the long-term future of society.

Today we see an increasing number of firms moving toward greater sustainability by increasing operational efficiencies, decreasing their use of raw materials, conserving energy, increasing the use of recycled materials, and preventing the discharge of wastes into the natural and social environment.[44]

Developing a Sustainable Marketing Mix

We can examine how some companies already implement sustainable marketing practices to gather some clues about the best ways to do that as we tweak our target marketing and Four Ps to do well by doing good:

- *Target marketing strategies:* Marketers need to understand the attitudes of their customers toward sustainability. They must know which consumers are willing to pay a few cents more for an environmentally friendly product? This allows marketers to successfully target **green customers**—those consumers who are most likely to actively look for and buy products that are eco-friendly.

- *Product strategies:* Sustainable product strategies include the use of environmentally friendly and recycled materials in products and in packaging. Marketers need to develop and put into production more environmentally

A campaign for fair trade bananas from New Zealand.

Ripped from the Headlines

Ethical/Sustainable Decisions in the Real World

Are you a *smombie*? That's smartphone plus zombie—a term the Germans have crafted for people who text and walk at the same time. For a while, it was a joke when we saw YouTube videos of people running into walls or falling over fences and into holes, all because of walking while texting (WWT). But when garages hire guards just to save pedestrians from walking in front of a car and governments pass laws against texting while walking, it's no longer a joke.

As smartphone makers develop new phone features and there are more and more apps, the problem is increasing. Emergency room visits and even deaths of distracted pedestrians using cell phones are up. And it's not just a lack of attention. Studies show that using a smartphone changes the way we walk: we walk slower and we can veer way off course.

The big question is what should be done about it? Some cities have put signs in stairwells and at intersections. New York has reduced speeds for cars and San Francisco has made some corridors pedestrian only. Hawaiian lawmakers have proposed a $250 fine for anyone who crosses a street with an electronic device.

More important, however, is whether the smartphone makers have an obligation to address the problem, just as auto manufacturers have designed cars with air bags, automatic braking systems, rear view cameras, drift warning signals and warning lights if another car is close by. After all, the product engineers have developed the phones to get and keep your attention. Could phones not be designed to prevent injuries? If an activity band can detect a wearer's walking and count the steps, why can't a smartphone do the same and tell you to watch out for traffic?

Should phone companies voluntarily do this? If not, should there be government intervention?

ETHICS CHECK: ↖

Do you think phone makers have an ethical obligation to cut down injuries and deaths from walking while texting?

☐ YES ☐ NO

SOME THINGS NEED ARTIFICIAL COLORS.

WE DON'T.

Oscar Mayer

NATURAL
SLOW ROASTED
TURKEY BREAST

"NO ARTIFICIAL INGREDIENTS
NO ARTIFICIAL PRESERVATIVES
NO ADDED HORMONES
NO ARTIFICIAL FLAVORS
NO ARTIFICIAL COLORS
NO GLUTEN
NO BY-PRODUCTS

American consumers' values are changing as many more of us are prioritizing "natural" food products that don't contain extra additives.

The Kraft Heinz Company

friendly products, such as electric automobiles. Some firms also strive to choose **fair trade suppliers**. This term refers to companies that outsource production only to firms that pay workers in developing countries a fair/living wage.

- *Price strategies:* Many consumers would like to buy green products, but they don't because the price is higher than comparable traditional products. Sustainable marketing practices aim to establish prices for green products that are the same or close to the prices of other products. A truly sustainable strategy actually reduces prices in the long term because it encourages more efficiency and less waste.

- *Place/distribution strategies:* Sustainable distribution strategies can include retailers who focus on a reduction in the use of energy to benefit from both monetary savings and the loyalty of green consumers. Both producers and retailers can choose to buy from nearby suppliers to reduce dependence on long-haul trucking, a major source of air pollution. Within the food industry in particular, the growing trend of **locavorism** means that many shoppers actively look for products that come from farms within 50 to 100 miles of where they live.[45]

- *Promotion strategies:* The most obvious sustainable promotion strategies are those that inform customers of the firm's commitment to the planet and future generations through advertising and other messages. But there are other opportunities. The cost of creating a TV commercial is enormous and may take two or three days of shooting to complete. Some firms have begun to "reuse" old commercials while letting customers know that this is their way of practicing sustainability.

Metrics Moment

Most organizations today measure business success using the traditional bottom line—profitability—as profits are essential for the survival of both nonprofit and for-profit organizations. However, sustainable businesses take two other bottom lines into consideration: natural capital and social capital. As we said in Chapter 1, this concept is called the triple-bottom-line orientation. Every decision made by a sustainable business must not harm (or may even improve) environmental quality and must have a social/community building component. Companies should treat their employees as valuable resources and give back to their community. Luckily, the same business practices that improve environmental and social capital have been shown to also improve long-term firm profitability. When implemented, sustainable business practices provide an avenue to achieve mutual benefits in the natural world, the community, and the economy.

Sustainability metrics are tools that measure the benefits an organization achieves through the implementation of sustainability. Unfortunately, unlike many widely used financial metrics, today there is no standardized method of measuring the other two elements of the triple-bottom-line. Hence, it is extremely hard to compare one company working toward sustainability with another. The social capital metrics are possibly the hardest set of metrics to develop; there are simply too many variables to measure societal progress, and as a result, it is extremely difficult to develop standardized metrics. Nonetheless, here are five examples of fairly common sustainability metrics:

- *Material intensity:* Pounds of material wasted per unit of organizational output
- *Energy intensity:* Net fuel energy in BTUs consumed to provide organizational heat and power requirements
- *Water consumption:* Gallons of fresh water consumed per unit of organizational output
- *Toxic emissions:* Pounds of toxic materials emitted in the process of creating organizational output
- *Pollutant (greenhouse gas) emissions:* Pounds of pollutants emitted in the process of creating organizational output

Complementary metrics within each of these categories can be developed by a firm to customize a dashboard of metrics to meet its needs.[46]

Apply the Metrics

1. Today, most large firms have a section on their website that points to their sustainability initiative. Select any large company that manufactures products (i.e., not a purely service firm like a bank or retail store). Review their website and find their section on sustainability (if the first firm you select doesn't have one, pick another firm to investigate).
2. What are several of the key specific activities the firm points to as evidence that they are engaged in sustainability-related activities?
3. What specific evidence do they report (i.e., what metrics do you find reported) that quantify their level of success in sustainability?

Sustainable Customer Behavior

A sustainability approach doesn't end with an improvement in manufacturing processes. Marketers also need to motivate customers to seek out, pay for, and use sustainable options. Many do buy products that minimize the use of natural resources; encourage the use of recycled, reused, and repurposed products; purchase fair trade and organic food; use environmentally friendly cleaning products and toiletries not tested on animals; and share cars, even at the expense of higher prices, less convenience, and lower product performance. Consumers can be an important part of sustainable marketing practices when they become knowledgeable about environmental concerns and environmentally friendly products.

fair trade suppliers
Companies that pledge to pay a fair price to producers in developing countries, to ensure that the workers who produce the goods receive a fair wage, and to ensure that these manufacturers rely where possible on environmentally sustainable production practices.

locavorism
The trend for shoppers to actively look for products that come from farms within 50 to 100 miles of where they live.

sustainability metrics
Tools that measure the benefits an organization achieves through the implementation of sustainability.

MyLab Marketing™
Go to **mymktlab.com** to complete the problems marked with this icon ⭐ as well as additional Marketing Metrics questions only available in MyLab Marketing.

Objective Summary ➡ Key Terms ➡ Apply

2.1 Objective Summary (pp. 56–59)

Understand the big picture of international marketing and the decisions firms must make when they consider globalization.

The increasing amount of world trade—the flow of goods and services among countries—may take place through cash, credit payments, or countertrade. A decision to go global often comes when further domestic growth opportunities dwindle and the firm perceives likelihood for success in foreign markets as a result of a competitive advantage. After a firm has decided to go global, they must consider which markets are most attractive, what market-entry strategy is best, and how to best develop the marketing mix.

Key Terms

Greenhouse Effect, p. 56

global warming, p. 56

Arab Spring, p. 56

world trade, p. 57

countertrade, p. 57

2.2 Objective Summary (pp. 59–61)

Explain how international organizations such as the World Trade Organization (WTO), economic communities, and individual country regulations facilitate and limit a firm's opportunities for globalization.

Established by the General Agreement on Tariffs and Trade (GATT) in 1984, the World Trade Organization with its 161 members seeks to create a single open world market where trade flows "smoothly, predictably and freely as possible." Some governments, however, adopt policies of protectionism with rules designed to give home companies an advantage. Such policies may include trade quotas, embargoes, or tariffs that increase the costs of foreign goods. Many countries have banded together to form economic communities to promote free trade.

Key Terms

General Agreement on Tariffs and Trade (GATT), p. 59

World Trade Organization (WTO), p. 59

World Bank, p. 59

International Monetary Fund (IMF), p. 59

foreign exchange rate (forex rate), p. 60

balance of payments, p. 60

protectionism, p. 60

import quotas, p. 60

embargo, p. 60

tariffs, p. 60

economic communities, p. 60

2.3 Objective Summary (pp. 61–72)

Understand how factors in a firm's external business environment influence marketing strategies and outcomes in both domestic and global markets.

The economic environment refers to the economic health of a country that may be gauged by its gross domestic product (GDP), its economic infrastructure, level of economic development, and stage in the business cycle. Marketers use competitive intelligence to examine brand, product, and discretionary income competition in the microenvironment. They also consider the structure of the industry in the macroenvironment. A country's political and legal environment includes laws and regulations that affect business. Marketers must understand any local political constraints, that is, the prospects for nationalization or expropriation of foreign holdings, regulations such as local content rules, and labor and human rights regulations. Because technology can affect every aspect of marketing, marketers must be knowledgeable about technological changes, often monitoring government and private research findings. Marketers also examine a country's sociocultural environment, including demographics, values, social norms and customs, language, and ethnocentricity. The ethical environment in some countries can cause problems for marketers if they do not understand the differences in the ethical perspective on such things such as honesty. In many least developed and developing countries, corruption is a major stumbling block for Western businesses. Bribery and extortion present ethical dilemmas for U.S. companies who must abide by the Foreign Corrupt Practices Act of 1977 (FCPA).

Key Terms

least developed country (LDC), p. 61

gross domestic product (GDP), p. 62

economic infrastructure, p. 64

level of economic development, p. 64

standard of living, p. 64

developing countries, p. 64

bottom of the pyramid (BOP), p. 64

sachet, p. 64

BRICS countries, p. 64

developed countries, p. 65

Group of 7 (G7), p. 65

business cycle, p. 65

competitive intelligence (CI), p. 65

discretionary income, p. 66

product competition, p. 66

brand competition, p. 66

monopoly, p. 66

oligopoly, p. 66

monopolistic competition, p. 66

perfect competition, p. 67

drones, p. 67

unmanned aerial vehicles (UAVs), p. 67

patent, p. 67

nationalization, p. 69

expropriation, p. 69

local content rules, p. 69

U.S. Generalized System of Preferences (GSP), p. 69

demographics, p. 70

cultural values, p. 70

collectivist cultures, p. 71

individualist cultures, p. 71

social norms, p. 71

consumer ethnocentrism, p. 72

2.4 Objective Summary (pp. 72–77)

Explain some of the strategies and tactics that a firm can use to enter global markets.

Different foreign-market-entry strategies represent varying levels of commitment for a firm. Exporting of goods entails little commitment but allows little control over how products are sold. Contractual agreements such as licensing or franchising allow greater control. With strategic alliances through joint ventures, commitment increases. Finally, the firm can choose to invest directly by buying an existing company or starting a foreign subsidiary in the host country. Firms that operate in two or more countries can choose to standardize their marketing strategies by using the same approach in all countries or to localize by adopting different strategies for each market. The firm needs to decide whether to sell an existing product, change an existing product, or develop a new product. In many cases, the promotional strategy, the pricing strategy, the place/distribution strategy, and the product itself must be tailored to fit the needs of consumers in another country.

Key Terms

export merchants, p. 73

licensing agreement, p. 73

franchising, p. 73

strategic alliance, p. 74

joint venture, p. 74

straight extension strategy, p. 75

product adaptation strategy, p. 75

product invention strategy, p. 76

backward invention, p. 76

free trade zones, p. 76

gray market goods, p. 76

dumping, p. 77

2.5 Objective Summary (pp. 77–81)

Understand the importance of ethical marketing practices.

Ethical business practices are important in order for the firm to do the best for all stakeholders and to avoid the consequences of low ethical standards for the firm and to society. Differing philosophies of ethics provide different results in ethical decision making. Business ethics, values that guide the firm, are often used to develop a business code of ethics. Although most marketers do make ethical decisions, there are examples of actions that justify some of the criticisms of marketing. In many countries, bribery and extortion are an accepted way of doing business.

Key Terms

utilitarian approach, p. 78

rights approach, p. 78

fairness or justice approach, p. 78

common good approach, p. 78

virtue approach, p. 78

ethical relativism, p. 78

business ethics, p. 78

code of ethics, p. 79

bribery, p. 80

extortion, p. 80

2.6 Objective Summary (pp. 81–83)

Explain the role of sustainability in marketing planning.

With growing world populations and increasing demand for products, sustainable business practices are necessary for life in the future. Many firms practice sustainability when then develop target marketing, product, price, place/distribution, and promotion strategies designed to protect the environment and the future of our communities.

Key Terms

green customers, p. 81

fair trade suppliers, p. 83

locavorism, p. 83

sustainability metrics, p. 83

Chapter **Questions** and **Activities**

MyLab Marketing™
Go to **mymktlab.com** to watch this chapter's Rising Star video(s) for career advice and to respond to questions.

Concepts: Test Your Knowledge

2-1. Describe the market conditions that influence a firm's decision to enter foreign markets.

2-2. Explain what *world trade* means. What is the role of the WTO and economic communities in encouraging free trade? What is the role of the World Bank and the International Monetary Fund in global trade? What is protectionism? Explain import quotas, embargoes, and tariffs.

2-3. Explain how GDP, the categories of economic development, and the business cycle influence marketers' decisions in entering global markets. What are the BRICS countries? What is the Group of Seven (G7)?

2-4. Explain the types of competition marketers face: discretionary income competition, product competition, and brand competition.

2-5. What are a monopoly, an oligopoly, monopolistic competition, and pure competition?

2-6. What aspects of the political and legal environment influence a firm's decision to enter a foreign market? Why are human rights issues important to firms in their decisions to enter global markets?

2-7. What do marketers mean when they refer to technological and sociocultural environments? Why do they need to understand these environments in a global marketplace?

2-8. What is ethnocentrism?

2-9. Describe the four globalization strategies representing different levels of involvement for a firm: exporting, contractual agreements, strategic alliances, and direct investment.

2-10. What are the arguments for standardization of marketing strategies in the global marketplace? What are the arguments for localization? What are some ways a firm can standardize or localize its marketing mix?

2-11. Describe the utilitarianism, rights, fairness or justice, common good, and virtue approaches to ethical decision making. What is ethical relativism?

2-12. Why is it increasingly important that firms engage in sustainability? What are some ways that strategies for the Four Ps can include sustainability?

Activities: Apply What You've Learned

2-13. *In Class, 10–25 Minutes for Teams* Using the data in Table 2.2, select two countries that are substantively dissimilar. Then select one of the products below. Use the data for the two countries to develop arguments why each of the two countries would and would not be a good opportunity for expansion of the market for your product.
1. New and more environmentally friendly method for heating and cooling houses.
2. A small automobile that runs on electricity.

3. Barbie and Ken dolls and accessories
4. A low-priced, easy to use, sewing machine that does not require electricity.

2-14. *Creative Homework/Short Project* With several members of your class, assume you are in the marketing department for a low end retail store chain; you might think of a chain similar to Dollar General. Your firm has decided to begin an expansion into the global market. Currently you are considering building stores in France, Ecuador, Brazil and Australia. Gather information about these countries using the CIA Factbook available online and other sources. Using the data you have about each country, develop ideas on the pros and cons of entering each country. Which country do you feel is best? Present your findings to your class.

2-15. *For Further Research (Individual)* Consider the six different ethical philosophies described in the chapter. Apply these six philosophies to one of the following ethical dilemmas. What would be the most ethical decision for each? Explain why you think so. Which would you be most likely to follow?
Decisions:
1. You see a fellow student cheating. Should you ignore what you saw, report it, or do something else?
2. You are the president of a school club, which gives you access to the club's money. You need to buy a new tire for your car but you won't have enough money for a week. You are considering borrowing the money from the club and paying it back in a week.
3. You have been assigned to a class project team. In a different class, you have been on a team with one of the members of your current team, and you know he or she refuses to do any work but expects others on the team to help him or her out. What are your options, and what should you do?

2-16. *In Class, 15–20 Minutes for Teams* One of the key questions for global marketers is whether to standardize (globally) or localize their product and related marketing mix offerings. For this activity, let's consider three different firms:
- a well-known women's fashion brand that is both a manufacturer and a retailer,
- an established fast food restaurant chain, and
- a manufacturer of household furniture.
If each of these firms plans to expand into China, would you recommend that they standardize or localize their offerings? (Remember to consider both product and non-product marketing mix elements.) Why do you take this view?

2-17. *Creative Homework/Short Project* Consumer ethnocentrism is the tendency for individuals to prefer products from one's own culture. Sometimes people think products made at home are better than imported goods. Develop a small study to find out what students at your university think about products made at home and abroad. Develop a survey that asks other students to evaluate 10 or more products (not brands) that are imported versus made at home. You might wish to ask if they feel the domestic or imported products are superior in quality and which they would purchase. Prepare a report on your study for your class.

2-18. *In Class, 10–25 Minutes for Teams* Some people argue that our environment is not in jeopardy and that sustainability efforts will only make products more expensive. Plan a debate in your class with two teams, one arguing for sustainability efforts and one against.

2-19. *For Further Research (Individual)* You are planning a trip to another country for your summer vacation. You are considering traveling to Greece, to Peru, to England and to Egypt. Determine the current forex rate for all four countries as well as the average forex over the past five years for each. Based solely on the information you collect about forex rates, explain where you would go and why.

2-20. *For Further Research (Groups)* Search the Internet for a recent ethical marketing dilemma involving a large brand or firm. Marketing ethics issues are becoming more commonly reported in business media, and you should be able to identify a practical and current challenge to investigate.

Your initial task is to outline the issues faced by the brand and to outline why you believe this to be an ethical challenge. Then you need to identify the two sides of the argument; that is, outline an approach that is highly ethical and an approach that is highly centered on the needs of the firm. Do you think there is a suitable solution to this particular issue? What would you recommend? Do you think there are circumstances where firms will appear to be behaving unethically regardless of their actions?

Concepts: Apply Marketing Metrics

Many Western firms see their futures in the growing populations of developing countries, where 8 out of 10 consumers now live. Consumers from the BRICS countries—Brazil, Russia, India, China, and South Africa—offer new opportunities for firms because growing numbers are accumulating significant amounts of disposable income. Firms such as worldwide cosmetics giant Beirsdorf, the producer of Nivea products, are adapting their products and their marketing activities to meet the needs of these populations. Often this means selling miniature or even single-use sachet packages of shampoo, dishwashing detergent, or fabric softener for only a few cents. The huge Swiss company Nestlé sells shrimp-flavored instant soup cubes for two cents each in Ghana; similarly the financial company Allianz, in a joint program with CARE, sells microinsurance for five cents a month to the very poor in India.

How do these firms measure their success in these new markets? Firms in developed countries normally use standard marketing metrics such as customer awareness, customer satisfaction, increases in market share or profits, or return on customer investment or return on marketing investment. But these metrics are based on standard market-entry strategies with full-size products and correspondingly typical pricing and promotional strategies—very different from the approach just described. Hence, these metrics are likely not too useful for the new markets in the developing world, where many millions of people buy streamlined versions of a firm's products at a fraction of their usual price.

⭐ **2-21.** Do you think the approach described is effective for entering BRICS markets to appeal to consumers with small but growing disposable income?

⭐ **2-22.** How would the success of this approach be better measured—that is, what metrics would be more useful than the typical metrics used in developed countries? Be creative and develop a list of several possible metrics that firms might use to measure their success in these new developing markets. *Hint:* Keep closely in mind what firms hope to accomplish by increasing their presence and sales in those markets.

Choices: What Do You Think?

⭐ **2-23.** *Critical thinking* International expansion is one pathway for growth for established firms, particularly when their domestic markets reach maturity or have become quite competitive. However, as highlighted in the chapter, when brands expand internationally, they will compete against established brands in the host country that have a "home-court advantage."

Outline the array of advantages that an established brand in its own domestic market would have over potential new entrants from international markets. Given these advantages, how can a new entrant to an international market succeed against the local, established players?

2-24. *Critical Thinking* What role has technology played in the globalization of businesses? Has technology leveled the economic playing field, or has it merely increased the distance between the "haves" and the "have-nots"? Give at least one example of each and explain your position.

2-25. *Critical Thinking* LDCs are not required by the WTO to meet the same environment standards as developed countries. Do you think LDCs should be excluded from WTO standards for pollution and other environmental protection issues? Why or why not?

2-26. *Critical Thinking* Economic communities are groups of countries that reach agreements to help facilitate trade. While most countries will actively pursue trade agreements for the long-term benefit of their economies, in recent years the United Kingdom has voted to withdraw from the European Union, and the United States is also reconsidering some of its existing trade agreements.

When choosing international markets to enter, how important do you think economic and political stability factors are in the firm's overall selection criteria? How do you think the change toward trade agreements and economic communities by the United States and the United Kingdom will affect international trade overall?

2-27. *Critical Thinking* Some of the U.S. population supports free trade, whereas others are unhapppy, even angry, that the government has reduced regulations on imports of such products as textiles and furniture, causing factories to shut down and employees to lose their jobs. They feel that the U.S. government should legislate greater regulation of imported goods to give American companies an advantage or at least to lessen the advantage that companies in other countries receive from their government. What do you think? How do you justify your answer?

2-28. *Critical Thinking* In 1999, several single European nations banded together to form the European Union and converted their individual monetary systems over to the euro. Do you believe there will ever be other economic communities that would follow this path? Explain your reasoning and, if necessary, provide some possible examples. What about the possibility of a single world currency? Could this happen? Why or why not?

2-29. *Ethics* Ethical relativism suggests that what is ethical in one culture may not be considered ethical in another. What should the attitude of businesses be when differences occur? Should businesses follow the ethical values and practices of their own country or those of the host country? What should governments do about this if anything? What is the role of the WTO?

2-30. *Ethics* Review the *AMA Code of Ethical Norms and Values for Marketers*, available on the AMA website, https://www.ama.org/AboutAMA/Pages/Statement -of-Ethics.aspx. Which of the areas represented within the document do you anticipate are the most challenging for marketers to consistently follow? What makes these issues particularly troublesome? Do you think marketing in general does a good job adhering to the AMA Code? Provide specific evidence from your knowledge and experience to support your position.

Miniproject: Learn by Doing

The purpose of this miniproject is to gain experience in understanding what it takes to move a product that is successful in its home market into a global market in which it will continue to be successful. Assume that you are the director of marketing for a firm that produces its own high-end brands of makeup, skin care, and hair care products for both men and women. The products have been endorsed by a number of male and female musicians who are highly popular with young people. The products are sold only in the company's own retail outlets.

2-31. Describe your local competitive advantage and why you believe this competitive advantage will serve you globally.

2-32. Determine which global market(s) is or are most attractive for your products. Will you target a single country or an economic community? Describe your reasoning.

2-33. Decide which market-entry strategy you will pursue. Again, explain your reasoning.

2-34. Describe your marketing mix strategy:
- How might you need to adapt your product?
- What other product decisions do you need to make?
- How will you promote your products?
- How will you price your products?
- What place/distribution decisions must you consider?

Prepare a short presentation to share with your class.

Marketing in **Action** Case Real Choices at Ford

Ford Motor Company has committed to investing $1.6 billion to construct a small car plant in the San Luis Potosi State in Mexico. This will result in the creation of more than 2,800 jobs in the country. The Center for Automotive Research states that U.S. automotive labor costs average around $30 per hour and are substantially higher than those in Mexico which average around $5 per hour. This means that moving production to Mexico will allow Ford to lower its cost for small cars and make Ford more competitive in the global auto marketplace. The move will, in turn, allow Ford to reallocate its U.S. facilities toward larger vehicles with higher profit margins, like SUVs and F-Series trucks. Furthermore, Mexico has the necessary transportation infrastructure to efficiently export the cars back to the U.S. and other markets.

Mexico has been a part of Ford's manufacturing history since 1925 when the company became the first automobile manufacturer in the country. According to Gabriel Lopez, president and CEO of Ford of Mexico, "Ford of Mexico is the fourth largest producer of vehicles, the fourth largest producer of engines and the second country in the global auto parts supply company facilities." Over the past 90 years Ford has provided more than $8 billion to build and develop its production capabilities in the country. Currently, Ford has two assembly plants, two stamping plants, and an engine plant in Mexico. Increasing production output in the country is consistent with Ford's long-term manufacturing plans.

The additional investment in Mexico is not without its critics. The issue of jobs leaving the country has always been a part of political debate in Washington, D.C. The announcement of Ford's plans was made during the most recent presidential campaign and created dissent among the candidates. One candidate called for increased tariffs and penalties for U.S. firms, like Ford, that choose to relocate manufacturing to foreign markets to lower costs. Ford has reacted with a vigorous defense of its business practices. As per CEO Mark Fields, "more than 80 percent of our North American investment annually is in the U.S., and 97 percent of our North American engineering is conducted in the U.S."

Dennis Williams, President of the United Auto Workers (UAW) union, is another voice of dissent to the move. He states that as production moves outside of the U.S. to low-wage countries, American workers suffer at home. This is a serious issue for the company, but it is projected that UAW members will see their wages grow domestically. This will make Ford's move to Mexico even more advantageous for the company. Moreover, top management at the company explained that over the next few years, Ford will spend more than $9 billion in the U.S., which is expected to create or maintain 8,500 jobs.

Increasing its presence in Mexico is not the only initiative Ford is implementing. As a part of its strategic "One Ford" plan the company has allocated billions of dollars to expand its global production capabilities in places like Spain, Germany, China, the Middle East, and Africa. While Ford's improves its financial outlook, how will it deal with the negative attention generated by moving jobs outside the United States? Is it possible for the company to increase its profitability and reduce its dependence on foreign production? In the current political climate should the company rethink its plans?

You Make the Call

2-35. What is the decision facing Ford?

2-36. What factors are important in understanding this decision situation?

2-37. What are the alternatives?

2-38. What decision(s) do you recommend?

2-39. What are some ways to implement your recommendation?

Based on: Daniel Miller, "Ford Motor Company's Move to Mexico Isn't a New Development," *The Motley Fool* (April 8, 2016), http://www.fool.com/investing/general/2016/04/08/ford-motor-companys-move-to-mexico-isnt-a-new-deve.aspx (accessed April 11, 2016); Brent Snavely, "6 Reasons Ford Picked Mexico for a New Plant," *Detroit Free Press* (April 7, 2016), http://www.freep.com/story/money/cars/ford/2016/04/06/6-reasons-ford-mexico-new-plant/82693218/ (accessed April 11, 2016); Ana Laura Alvarado Olivares, "Celebrating 90 Years of Great Stories in Mexico," *Ford.com* (July 20, 2015), http://www.at.ford.com/news/cn/Pages/Celebrating%2090%20Years%20of%20Great%20Stories%20in%20Mexico.aspx (accessed April 13, 2016).

MyLab Marketing™

Go to **mymktlab.com** for the following Assisted-graded writing questions:

2-40. *Creative Homework/Short Project.* As a marketing manager, you must consider whether to delay the production and introduction of a new automobile because of a small problem with the door locks; they could become nonfunctional when temperatures drop very low. Using (1) the utilitarian approach, (2) the rights approach, and (3) the common good approach, what would the different decisions be?

2-41. *Ethics.* Some companies have been criticized for moving their manufacturing to other countries where laws protecting the environment are more lenient and goods can be produced more cheaply because the firms do not have to invest in ways to protect the environment. What do you think of this practice? What can governments and/or consumers do to prevent such actions?

Strategic Market Planning

Stephanie Nashawaty

Stephanie Nashawaty

▼ **A Decision Maker at Oracle**

Stephanie Stewart Nashawaty is group vice president of customer experience (CX) transformation sales at Oracle. She has more than 15 years of software sales experience and extensive expertise in enterprise marketing solutions for Global 2000 leading companies.

Stephanie is currently responsible for CX sales at Oracle (this includes Oracle's application solutions for customer-facing functions, such as sales, services, and marketing). She leads an elite sales team of enterprise sales executives who are tasked with creating and delivering $1 million to $30 million Cloud deals with Oracle's most strategic customers. In this capacity, Stephanie also works on joint business development opportunities with selected systems integrators, such as Accenture and Deloitte, as well as digital agencies.

Prior to joining Oracle, Stephanie was a vice president with Unica Corporation, which was acquired by IBM in 2010. She helped to build and launch IBM's Enterprise Marketing Management (EMM) business unit. The unit's focus on "Smarter Marketing" is a key foundational pillar of IBM's current "Smarter Planet" campaign and go-to-market strategy. Stephanie led the EMM global sales team ($400 million in annual revenues), which focused on selling to the office of the chief marketing officer (CMO). She was recognized for her achievements and team contribution by her selection for IBM's Acquisition Talent Acceleration Program. During this time, she was also the executive sales leader for the acquisition and integration of three companies in the marketing domain (DemandTec, Tealeaf, and Xtify). Stephanie has significant international experience working with CMOs in retail, travel, telecommunications, and other industries focused on optimizing the customer experience with a brand across all channels.

Stephanie holds a BA in political science from the University of Vermont and was a candidate in the master's degree program at Stanford University. She and her family reside in Needham, Massachusetts.

Stephanie's Info

What I do when I'm not working?
Spend time with my two teenage daughters, ideally doing something outside like hiking, swimming, skiing, and tennis.

First job out of school?
Management trainee, Enterprise Rent-A-Car.

Career high?
Selected for IBM's Acquisition Talent Acceleration Program. Less than 1 percent of IBM employees were selected for this program.

Business book I'm reading now?
Converge: Transforming Business at the Intersection of Marketing and Technology by Bob Lord and Ray Velez.

My motto to live by?
"Don't let the perfect be the enemy of the good," that is, execute and iterate rather than be stuck in overanalyzing decisions.

What drives me?
Fear of failure.

My management style?
Collaborative and decisive.

Here's my problem...

Oracle is a huge player in a booming industry that helps businesses manage the vast amount of information they need to operate. Its initial business focus was on relational databases. For example, the global communications company British Telecom (BT) uses Oracle's database solution to increase control and improve customer service with a streamlined global information technology (IT) infrastructure and standardized database administration. With Oracle's help, BT can now deploy a database in 20 minutes as compared to the several weeks this task required before the company used Oracle's solution.

Companies now have the ability to access an incredible amount of information about customers and prospects. These data points come from all of our interactions with a brand, including online web-surfing behavior, interactions in stores and kiosks, our calls into service call centers, and even when we tweet about an airline losing our baggage. Marketing departments need automation technology to help them make sense of all of the data and to interact with their loyal customers on an almost constant basis. Today, U.S. companies spend more than $1.5 trillion per year on marketing technologies. The research firm Gartner predicts that by 2017, a typical firm's CMO will spend more on technology than will its chief information officer (CIO).

As business operations become more complex, the demand for change in IT increases, along with the associated risks a company has to address. Today's IT professionals are asked to manage a flood of information and to deliver it to their users in a timely manner with ever-increasing quality of service. And in today's economic climate, IT must also reduce budgets and derive greater value out of existing investments.

Over the years, Oracle has moved into offering software applications that help all of the various lines of business, such as human resources and sales, to do their jobs better. Oracle acquired its customer relationship management (CRM) application when it bought Siebel Systems in 2005. Siebel CRM is an on-premise application that allows salespeople to manage their prospects and accounts and forecast their business. It is the key to maintaining contact with the client's customers. For example, a company that maintains a loyalty program where it tracks consumers' transactions and awards points and other goodies in return has to monitor thousands and sometimes even millions of interactions every month.

It's a huge understatement to say that the technological environment is changing rapidly. In particular, the industry is moving toward a new model called software as a service (SaaS). Instead of purchasing and installing software on its own computers, this "software-on-demand" approach allows a company to take advantage of new "distributed computing" technology. This approach stores these programs remotely so that a user can access the software from any location. Users can customize the software, obtain faster answers, and analyze larger volumes of data, making it easier for clients with global operations to coordinate data management across locations. Many people refer to this revolution in information storage as "cloud computing" because data live "in the cloud" rather than being physically stored in a machine in the building.

This sea change in the technological environment creates both a huge opportunity and a big headache for Oracle. The opportunity is that Oracle traditionally sold its products exclusively to the CIO. Now that the CMO and his team is so attuned to data-driven decision making, Oracle suddenly finds itself with an entirely new set of potential customers. Companies will be increasing their "spend" on sophisticated technology to keep up with a wired world, and the relative amount of this money they spend across functions will shift toward fatter marketing budgets for data-related products and services.

The downside: Oracle ironically faces a challenge because it is so successful in the on-premise product space, with hundreds of major corporate clients that equate the company with this traditional solution to data management. The company has faced challenges for the past few years as it struggles with concerns about its ability to compete in a new cloud-based business environment.

If Oracle tries to change with the times and move its vast number of clients "to the cloud," these companies may now think twice about sticking with the company. A CIO who wants to totally revamp the way his or her company manages information probably will explore what competing SaaS solutions companies have to offer. In that case, it would be open season on Oracle's clients.

Oracle needs to make important adjustments in its strategic planning to move to where the market is going. It needs to figure out how to structure its sales force to go after this new source of revenue and at the same time Oracle has to rebrand itself as a leader in cloud computing technology. The company needs to increase its focus on developing new cloud-computing capabilities or perhaps acquiring other companies that already have SaaS-based solutions and a sales team that understands this new marketing space.

Oracle needs to win in the emerging cloud-based market but at the same time retain the loyalty of its existing client base. The company needs to convince CMOs that it still has the ability to solve their most pressing database marketing challenges and that Oracle's solutions will help them acquire, upsell, and retain customers as the business world continues to move to the cloud.

Stephanie considered her Options 1·2·3

1 **Option**

Stay the course with marketing clients. Oracle is extremely successful as a premise-based solutions provider. The company still boasts a huge roster of corporate clients that are satisfied with what it does for them. A shift to cloud-based solutions will confuse these clients and open the door to a host of competitors.

Of course, the long-term writing is on the wall: CMOs will continue to move their operations to the cloud and over time Oracle may be stuck with obsolete technologies and lose its reputation as an industry innovator.

You Choose

Which **Option** would you choose, and **why**?
☐ Option 1   ☐ Option 2   ☐ Option 3

See what **option** Stephanie chose in **MyLab Marketing™**

MyLab Marketing™

⭐ **Improve Your Grade!**

Over 10 million students improved their results using the Pearson MyLabs.
Visit **mymktlab.com** for simulations, tutorials, and end-of-chapter problems.

Chapter 3

2 **Option**

Acquire companies that already offer new SaaS marketing technologies. Go to market with a dedicated sales team that focuses only on selling cloud solutions to current and new clients. If Oracles buys up companies with this expertise, it will quickly acquire a customer base, products, and organization that were designed exclusively for this technology. These new products also will cross-pollinate across Oracle so that its own software engineers will come up to speed quickly on state-of-the-art applications. This choice would also create an immediate revenue stream from SaaS clients, and Oracle will be able to rebrand itself as an organization that truly is on the cutting edge of database management. On the other hand, it will be expensive to acquire these companies. Oracle's biggest rivals, including IBM, Salesforce.com, Adobe, and SAP, also are on the lookout for them, so the company might find itself in bidding wars that could up the ante quite a bit. An acquisition strategy might also create market confusion about what Oracle sells, and in addition the company's strategic partners are not as familiar with these new offerings as they are with legacy applications like Siebel. In fact, Oracle might lose clients who use the Seibel system now if they decide the company is not committed to the platform for the long haul. Finally, it was unclear if the salespeople at these smaller companies would stick with Oracle after it acquired their employers. Some of them might prefer to work for a young start-up rather than a huge corporation.

3 **Option**

Stick to your knitting. Continue to promote the Siebel system for basic data management function. "De-invest" in the marketing solutions category, where it will be expensive to compete against the numerous other companies that were gearing up to swoop into this market. This would be a much less costly decision because Oracle would not have to spend the billions of dollars it would probably take to acquire new companies as in option 2. As is the case with option 1, Oracle already is well known as a market leader in database solutions. The messages it would send to the market would be much simpler and more straightforward, and it would benefit from a sales force that already knows the product and is familiar to clients.

However, Oracle would have to counter the perception that the company is trying to "ride an old horse" in a technology industry that richly rewards innovative solutions. In a few years, it may find itself the market leader in an obsolete category as all kinds of businesses eventually migrate to the cloud. Oracle might well find itself "penny wise and pound foolish" if it focuses on what it does well right now but fails to invest in the marketing category. By all indications, marketing functions will account for a steadily increasing share of the money that organizations spend on technology. If Oracle decides to enter this lucrative but competitive category down the road, it may discover that the ship has already sailed.

Now, put yourself in the team's shoes. Which option would you choose, and why?

3.1 Business Planning: Compose the Big Picture

OBJECTIVE

Explain business planning and its three levels.

(pp. 92–94)

There's an old saying in business that "planning is everything"—well, almost. Planning allows a firm like Oracle to define its distinctive identity and purpose. Careful planning enables a firm to speak in a clear voice in the marketplace so that customers understand what the firm is and what it has to offer that competitors don't—especially as it decides how to create value for customers, clients, partners, and society at large. In this chapter, you will experience the power of effective business planning—and especially market planning—and lay the groundwork for your own capability to do successful planning.

We think this process is really important. That's why we're starting with a discussion about what planners do and the questions they need to ask to be sure they keep their companies and products on course. In many ways, developing great business planning is like taking an awesome digital photo with your smartphone (maybe a "selfie"?)—hence the title of this section. The metaphor works because success in photography is built around capturing the right information in the lens of your camera, positioning the image correctly, and snapping the picture you'll need to set things in motion. A business plan is a lot like that.

The knowledge you gain from going through a formal planning process is worth its weight in gold. Without market planning as an ongoing activity in a business, there's no real way to know where you want the firm to go, how it will get there, or even if it is on the right or wrong track right now. There's nothing like a clear road map when you're lost in the wilderness. And speaking of road maps, we even include a handy guide as a supplement at the end of this chapter that shows you step-by-step how to build a marketing plan and where to find the information throughout the book to be able to do it. This road map will be highly useful as you make your way through the book, keeping the "big-picture" viewpoint of marketing in mind no matter which chapter you're reading.

What exactly is **business planning**? Put simply, it's an ongoing process of decision making that guides the firm in both the short term and the long term. Planning identifies and builds on a firm's strengths, and it helps managers at all levels make informed decisions in a changing business environment. *Planning* means that an organization develops objectives before it takes action. In large firms like IBM and Ford, which operate in many markets, planning is a complex process involving many people from different areas of the company's operations. At a small business like Mac's Diner in your hometown, however, planning is quite different in scope. Yet regardless of firm size or industry, great planning can only increase the chances of success.

In the sections that follow, we'll look at the different steps in an organization's planning. First, we'll see how managers develop a **business plan** to specify the decisions that guide the entire organization or its business units. Then we'll examine the entire strategic planning process and the stages in that process that lead to the development and implementation of a **marketing plan**—a process and resulting document that describes the marketing environment, outlines the marketing objectives and strategies, and identifies how the company will implement and control the strategies embedded in the plan.

business planning
An ongoing process of making decisions that guides the firm both in the short term and in the long term.

business plan
A plan that includes the decisions that guide the entire organization.

marketing plan
A document that describes the marketing environment, outlines the marketing objectives and strategy, and identifies how the company will implement and control the strategies embedded in the plan.

The Three Levels of Business Planning

We all know in general what planning is—we plan a vacation or a great Saturday night party. Some of us even plan how we're going to study and get our assignments completed without stressing out at the last minute. When businesses plan, the process is more complex. As Figure 3.1 shows, planning occurs at three levels: strategic, functional, and operational. The top level is big-picture stuff, whereas the bottom level specifies the "nuts-and-bolts" actions the firm will need to take to achieve these lofty goals.

Figure 3.1 *Snapshot* | Levels of Business Planning

During planning, an organization determines its objectives and then develops courses of action to accomplish them. In larger firms, planning takes place at the strategic, functional, and operational levels.

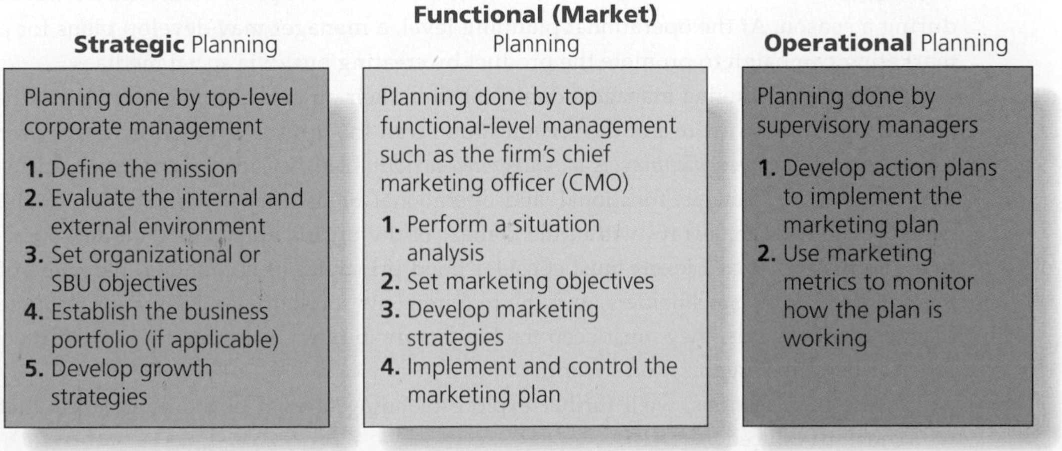

Strategic Planning	**Functional (Market)** Planning	**Operational** Planning
Planning done by top-level corporate management	Planning done by top functional-level management such as the firm's chief marketing officer (CMO)	Planning done by supervisory managers
1. Define the mission 2. Evaluate the internal and external environment 3. Set organizational or SBU objectives 4. Establish the business portfolio (if applicable) 5. Develop growth strategies	1. Perform a situation analysis 2. Set marketing objectives 3. Develop marketing strategies 4. Implement and control the marketing plan	1. Develop action plans to implement the marketing plan 2. Use marketing metrics to monitor how the plan is working

Source: Copyright © American Marketing Association.

strategic planning
A managerial decision process that matches an organization's resources and capabilities to its market opportunities for long-term growth.

strategic business units (SBUs)
Individual units within the firm that operate like separate businesses, with each having its own mission, business objectives, resources, managers, and competitors.

functional planning
A decision process that concentrates on developing detailed plans for strategies and tactics for the short term, supporting an organization's long-term strategic plan.

market planning
The functional planning marketers do. Market planning typically includes both a broad three- to five-year marketing plan to support the firm's strategic plan and a detailed annual plan for the coming year.

operational planning
A decision process that focuses on developing detailed plans for day-to-day activities that carry out an organization's functional plans.

First-Level Planning

Strategic planning is the managerial decision process that matches the firm's resources (such as its financial assets and workforce) and capabilities (the things it is able to do well because of its expertise and experience) to its market opportunities for long-term growth. In a strategic plan, top management—usually the chief executive officer (CEO), president, and other top executives—define the firm's purpose and specify what the firm hopes to achieve over the next five years or so. For example, Oracle's strategic plan may set an objective to increase total revenues by 20 percent in the next five years.

Large firms, such as the Walt Disney Company, have a number of self-contained divisions called **strategic business units (SBUs)**—individual units that represent different areas of business within a firm that are unique enough to each have their own mission, business objectives, resources, managers, and competitors. Disney's SBUs include parks and resorts, media networks, consumer products and interactive media, and studios. Hence, strategic planning occurs both at the overall corporate level (Disney headquarters in Burbank, California, plans for the whole corporation globally) and at the SBU level. We'll discuss these two levels later in the chapter.

Second-Level Planning

The next level of planning is **functional planning**. This level gets its name because it involves the various functional areas of the firm, such as marketing, finance, and human resources. Vice presidents or functional directors usually do this. We refer to the functional planning that marketers do as **market planning**. The person in charge of such planning may have the title of director of marketing, vice president of marketing, chief marketing officer, or something similar. Such marketers might set an objective to gain 40 percent of a particular market by successfully introducing three new products during the coming year. This objective would be part of a marketing plan. Market planning typically includes both a broad three- to five-year marketing plan to support the firm's strategic plan and a detailed annual plan for the coming year.

Third-Level Planning

Still farther down the planning ladder are the managers who are responsible for planning at a third level called **operational planning**. In marketing, these include people such as sales managers, marketing communication managers, brand managers, and market research managers. This level of planning focuses on the day-to-day execution of the functional plans and includes detailed annual, semiannual, or quarterly plans. Operational plans might show exactly how many units of a product a salesperson needs to sell per month or how many TV commercials the firm will place on certain networks during a season. At the operational planning level, a manager may develop plans for a marketing campaign to promote the product by creating buzz via social media.

Of course, marketing managers don't just sit in their offices dreaming up plans without any concern for the rest of the organization. Even though we've described each layer separately, *all business planning is an integrated activity*. This means that at an organization like Oracle, strategic, functional, and operational plans must work together for the benefit of the whole, always within the context of the organization's mission and objectives. So planners at all levels must consider good principles of accounting, the value of the company to its stockholders, and the requirements for staffing and human resource management—that is, they must keep the big picture in mind even as they plan for their little corner of the organization's world.

In the next sections, we'll further explore planning at each of the three levels that we've just introduced.

3.2 Strategic Planning: Frame the Picture

OBJECTIVE

Describe the steps in strategic planning.

(pp. 95–101)

Many large firms realize it's risky to put all their eggs in one basket and rely on only one product, so they have become multiproduct companies with self-contained divisions organized around product lines or brands.

In firms with multiple SBUs (as illustrated previously by Disney), the first step in strategic planning is for top management to establish a mission for the entire corporation. Top managers then evaluate the internal and external environments of the business and set corporate-level objectives that guide decision making within each individual SBU. In small firms that are not large enough to have separate SBUs, strategic planning simply takes place at the overall firm level. Whether or not a firm has SBUs, the process of strategic planning is basically the same. Let's look at the planning steps in a bit more detail, guided by 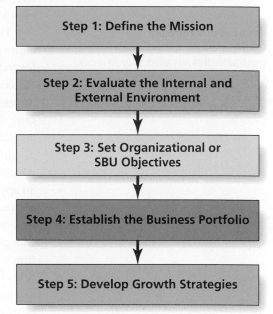 Figure 3.2.

Figure 3.2 〽 *Process* | Steps in Strategic Planning

The strategic planning process includes a series of steps that results in the development of growth strategies.

Step 1: Define the Mission

Step 2: Evaluate the Internal and External Environment

Step 3: Set Organizational or SBU Objectives

Step 4: Establish the Business Portfolio

Step 5: Develop Growth Strategies

Step 1: Define the Mission

Ideally, top management's first step in the strategic planning stage is to answer questions such as the following:

- What business are we in?
- What customers should we serve?
- How should we develop the firm's capabilities and focus its efforts?

In many firms, the answers to questions such as these become the lead items in the organization's strategic plan. The answers become part of a **mission statement**—a formal document that describes the organization's overall purpose and what it intends to achieve in terms of its customers, products, and resources. For example, Twitter's mission statement is "To give everyone the power to create and share ideas and information instantly, without barriers."[1] The ideal mission statement is not too broad, too narrow, or too shortsighted. A mission that is too broad will not provide adequate focus for the organization. It doesn't do much good to claim, "We are in the business of making high-quality products" or "Our business is keeping customers happy," because it is hard to find a firm that doesn't make these claims. It's also important to remember that the need for a clear mission statement applies to virtually any type of organization.

mission statement

A formal statement in an organization's strategic plan that describes the overall purpose of the organization and what it intends to achieve in terms of its customers, products, and resources.

Step 2: Evaluate the Internal and External Environment

The second step in strategic planning is to assess the firm's internal and external environments. We refer to this process as a **situation analysis**, *environmental analysis*, or sometimes a *business review*. The analysis includes a discussion of the firm's internal environment, which can identify a firm's strengths and weaknesses, as well as the external environment in which the firm does business so the firm can identify opportunities and threats.

By **internal environment** we mean all the controllable elements inside a firm that influence how well the firm operates. Internal strengths may lie in the firm's technologies. What is the firm able to do well that other firms would find difficult to duplicate? What patents does it hold? A firm's physical facilities can be an important strength or weakness, as can its level of financial stability, its relationships with suppliers, its corporate reputation, its ability to produce consistently high-quality products, and its ownership of strong brands

situation analysis

An assessment of a firm's internal and external environments.

internal environment

The controllable elements inside an organization, including its people, its facilities, and how it does things that influence the operations of the organization.

in the marketplace. Internal elements include a firm's structure, organizational culture, and all sorts of assets—financial and otherwise.

Internal strengths and weaknesses often reside in the firm's employees—the firm's *human and intellectual capital*. What skills do the employees have? What kind of training have they had? Are they loyal to the firm? Do they feel a sense of ownership? Has the firm been able to attract top researchers and good decision makers?

external environment

The uncontrollable elements outside an organization that may affect its performance either positively or negatively.

The **external environment** consists of elements outside the firm that may affect it either positively or negatively. For Oracle and many other firms, the external environment for today's businesses is global, so managers/marketers must consider elements such as the economy, competition, technology, law, ethics, and sociocultural trends. Unlike elements of the internal environment that management can control to a large degree, the firm can't directly control these external factors, so management must respond to them through its planning process.

In Chapter 2, you read about the various elements of the external environment in which marketing takes place, within the context of today's global enterprise. You gained an appreciation of why it is important for you to be aware that opportunities and threats can come from any part of the external environment. On the one hand, trends or currently unserved customer needs may provide opportunities for growth. On the other hand, if changing customer needs or buying patterns mean customers are turning away from a firm's products, it's a signal of possible danger or threats down the road. Even successful firms have to change to keep up with external environmental pressures. Oracle's business, like that of most marketing-related suppliers, is greatly impacted by the marketing budgets of its clients, which in turn are driven by economic conditions and ultimately consumer demand.

SWOT analysis

An analysis of an organization's strengths and weaknesses and the opportunities and threats in its external environment.

What is the outcome of an analysis of a firm's internal and external environments? Managers often synthesize their findings from a situation analysis into a format called a **SWOT analysis**. This document summarizes the ideas from the situation analysis. It allows managers to focus clearly on the meaningful strengths (S) and weaknesses (W) in the firm's internal environment and opportunities (O) and threats (T) coming from outside the firm (the external environment). A SWOT analysis enables a firm to develop strategies that make use of what the firm does best in seizing opportunities for growth while at the same time avoiding external threats that might hurt the firm's sales and profits.

Step 3: Set Organizational or SBU Objectives

After they construct a mission statement, top management translates it into *organizational* or *SBU objectives*. These goals are a direct outgrowth of the mission statement and broadly identify what the firm hopes to accomplish within the general time frame of the firm's long-range business plan. If the firm is big enough to have separate SBUs, each unit will have its own objectives relevant to its operations.

To be effective, objectives need to be *specific, measurable* (so firms can tell whether they've met them), *attainable*, and *sustainable over time*. Attainability is especially important—firms that establish "pie-in-the-sky" objectives they can't realistically obtain can create frustration for their employees (who work hard but get no satisfaction of accomplishment) and other stakeholders in the firm, such

Southwest Airlines has always been very focused on hiring and developing employees who reflect the "Southwest Spirit" to customers. Anyone who has flown on Southwest can attest to the fact that the atmosphere is lively and fun, and flight attendants are likely to do most any crazy stunt—bowling in the aisle or serenading the captain and first officer (and passengers) with a favorite tune. One of our favorites is a guy who does galloping horse hooves and neighing sounds during takeoff and landing. For Southwest, a real strength—one that's hard for the competition to crack—lies in this employee spirit.

B Christopher/Alamy Stock Photo

as vendors and shareholders who are affected when the firm doesn't meet its objectives. That a firm's objectives are sustainable over time is also critical—usually there's little advantage to investing in attaining an objective for only a very short term? This often happens when a firm underestimates the likelihood that a competitor will come to market with a better offering. Without some assurance that an objective is sustainable over time, the financial return on an investment likely will not be positive.

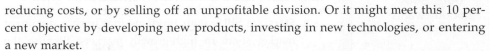

Samsung has hefty growth objectives for the remainder of the decade.

Objectives may relate to revenue and sales, profitability, the firm's standing in the market, return on investment, productivity, product development, customer satisfaction, social responsibility, and many other attributes. To ensure measurability, marketers increasingly try to state objectives in numerical terms. For example, a firm might have as an objective a 10 percent increase in profitability. It could reach this objective by increasing productivity, by reducing costs, or by selling off an unprofitable division. Or it might meet this 10 percent objective by developing new products, investing in new technologies, or entering a new market.

Samsung Electronics recently identified as part of its vision for 2020 two ambitious goals that include reaching $400 billion in annual revenue and achieving a position as one of the top five brands in the world. Samsung's plan to more than double its annual revenue by 2020 may seem ambitious, but the firm has identified an aggressive roadmap for enhancing its position within its current industries and markets as well as entering into new opportunities.[2]

Step 4: Establish the Business Portfolio

For companies with several different SBUs, strategic planning includes making decisions about how to best allocate resources across these businesses to ensure growth for the total organization. Each SBU has its own focus within the firm's overall strategic plan, and each has its own target market and strategies to reach its objectives. Just like an independent business, each SBU is a separate *profit center* within the larger corporation—that is, each SBU within the firm is responsible for its own costs, revenues, and profits. These items can be accounted for separately for each SBU.

Just as we call the collection of different stocks an investor owns a portfolio, the range of different businesses that a large firm operates is its **business portfolio**. These different businesses usually represent different product lines, each of which operates with its own budget and management. Having a diversified business portfolio reduces the firm's dependence on one product line or one group of customers. For example, if the economy sours and consumers don't travel as much in a bad year for Disney theme park attendance and cruises, its managers hope that the sales will be made up by stay-at-homers who watch Disney's TV networks and who purchase Mickey Mouse collectibles from the Disney website.

Portfolio analysis is a tool management uses to assess the potential of a firm's business portfolio. It helps management decide which of its current SBUs should receive more—or less—of the firm's resources and which of its SBUs are most consistent with the firm's overall mission. There are a host of portfolio models available. To illustrate how one works, let's examine the especially popular model the Boston Consulting Group (BCG) developed: the **BCG growth–market share matrix**.

The BCG model focuses on determining the potential of a firm's existing successful SBUs to generate cash that the firm can then use to invest in other businesses. The BCG

business portfolio
The group of different products or brands owned by an organization and characterized by different income-generating and growth capabilities.

portfolio analysis
A management tool for evaluating a firm's business mix and assessing the potential of an organization's strategic business units.

BCG growth–market share matrix
A portfolio analysis model developed by the Boston Consulting Group that assesses the potential of successful products to generate cash that a firm can then use to invest in new products.

Figure 3.3 📷 *Snapshot* | BCG Matrix

The Boston Consulting Group's (BCG) growth–market share matrix is one way a firm can examine its portfolio of different SBUs and their related products. By categorizing SBUs as stars, cash cows, question marks, or dogs, the matrix helps managers make good decisions about how the firm should grow.

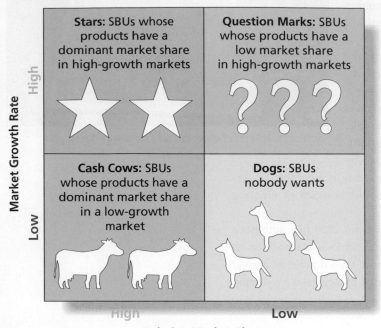

Stars: SBUs whose products have a dominant market share in high-growth markets

Question Marks: SBUs whose products have a low market share in high-growth markets

Cash Cows: SBUs whose products have a dominant market share in a low-growth market

Dogs: SBUs nobody wants

Market Growth Rate — High / Low

Relative Market Share — High / Low

Relative Market Share

Source: Product Portfolio Matrix, © 1970, The Boston Consulting Group.

stars
SBUs with products that have a dominant market share in high-growth markets.

cash cows
SBUs with a dominant market share in a low-growth-potential market.

question marks
SBUs with low market shares in fast-growth markets.

Disney's retail stores are question marks for the diversified company.

matrix in 📷 Figure 3.3 shows that the vertical axis represents the attractiveness of the market: the *market growth rate*. Even though the figure shows "high" and "low" as measurements, marketers might ask whether the total market for the SBU's products is growing at a rate of 10, 50, 100, or 200 percent annually.

The horizontal axis in Figure 3.3 shows the SBU's current strength in the market through its relative market share. Here, marketers might ask whether the SBU's share is 5, 25, or perhaps 75 percent of the current market. Combining the two axes creates four quadrants representing four different types of SBUs. Each quadrant of the BCG grid uses a symbol to designate business units that fall within a certain range for market growth rate and market share. Let's take a closer look at each cell in the grid:

- **Stars** are SBUs with products that have a dominant market share in high-growth markets. Because the SBU has a dominant share of the market, stars generate large revenues, but they also require large amounts of funding to keep up with production and promotion demands. Hence, stars need investment capital from other parts of the business because they don't generate it themselves. Of course, any profits generated directly by stars presumably would be reinvested right back in the star. For example, in recent years, Disney has viewed its studios as a star and has been able to generate significant revenues from its acquisition of Lucasfilm and the intellectual property within the *Star Wars* universe. *Star Wars Episode VII: The Force Awakens* broke the domestic box office record, ousting *Avatar* and generating well more than $2 billion in revenue worldwide.[3]

- **Cash cows** have a dominant market share in a low-growth potential market. Because there's not much opportunity for new companies, competitors don't often enter the market. At the same time, the SBU is well established and enjoys a high market share that the firm can sustain with minimal funding. Firms usually milk cash cows of their profits to fund the growth of other SBUs. Of course, if the firm's objective is to increase revenues, having too many cash cows with little or no growth potential can become a liability. For Disney, its theme parks unit fits into the cash cow category in that sales have been basically steady for an extended period of time. Walt Disney World in Orlando's Hollywood Studios closed a number of attractions to make way for the construction of a 14-acre section of the part dedicated to the *Star Wars* Universe so the park will remain fresh and appealing for its visitors.[4]

- **Question marks**—sometimes called "problem children"—are SBUs with low market shares in fast-growth markets. When a business unit is a question mark, they key issue is whether through investment and new strategy it can be transformed into a star. For example, the firm could pump more money into marketing the product and hope that relative market share will improve. But the problem with question marks is that despite investment many times they make a beeline straight into the annals of market failures. Hence, the firm must carefully evaluate the likelihood that investment in a question mark will pay off else it may find itself "throwing good money after bad" if it gains nothing but a negative cash flow and disappointment. For Disney, its brick-and-mortar retail operation falls into the question-mark category because its performance compared to the overall specialty retail market has somewhat lagged. Like most retail operators today, the online version of the Disney Store provides a better growth trajectory than the four walls version.

The recent acquisition of Marvel Comics by Disney most likely will add to the entertainment company's stable of stars.

- **Dogs** command a small share of a slow-growth market. They are businesses that offer specialized products in limited markets that are not likely to grow quickly. When possible, large firms may sell off their dogs to smaller firms that may be able to nurture them—or they may take the SBU's products off the market. Disney, being a savvy strategic planner, apparently identified its Miramax film studio as a long-term dog (to Pluto and Goofy: no pun intended) because they sold it off in 2010 ending a 17-year involvement with that studio.[5] In addition, in 2011, Disney Vacation Club (its time-share unit) scrapped plans to launch a major new facility at National Harbor near Washington, D.C.[6] This move was no doubt reflective of the general malaise in the time-share market (also called "vacation ownership") since the Great Recession.

dogs
SBUs with a small share of a slow-growth market. They are businesses that offer specialized products in limited markets that are not likely to grow quickly.

Like Disney, Oracle could use the BCG matrix to evaluate its product lines to make important decisions about where to invest for future growth. It would look across Oracle's various offerings to assess the market growth rate and relative market share, determine the degree to which each is a cash generator or a cash user, and decide whether to invest further in these or other business opportunities.

Step 5: Develop Growth Strategies

Although the BCG matrix can help managers decide which SBUs they should invest in for growth, it doesn't tell them much about *how* to make that growth happen. Should the growth of an SBU come from finding new customers, from developing new variations of the product, or from some other growth strategy? Part of strategic planning at the SBU level entails evaluating growth strategies.

market penetration strategies
Growth strategies designed to increase sales of existing products to current customers, nonusers, and users of competitive brands in served markets.

Marketers use the product–market growth matrix, shown in Figure 3.4, to analyze different growth strategies. The vertical axis in the matrix represents opportunities for growth either in existing markets or in new markets. The horizontal axis considers whether the firm would be better off putting its resources into existing products or whether it should acquire new products. The matrix provides four fundamental marketing strategies: market penetration, market development, product development, and diversification:

Figure 3.4 📷 *Snapshot* | Product–Market Growth Matrix

Marketers use the product–market growth matrix to analyze different growth strategies.

- **Market penetration strategies** seek to increase sales of existing products to existing markets, such as current users, nonusers, and users of competing brands within a market. The voice assistant market is relatively crowded with the likes of Apple's Siri, Microsoft's Cortana, and Google Now, but Amazon has found a way in recent years to introduce a standalone product that has been able to gain increasing adoption. Amazon's Echo (and the software it runs on called Alexa) is a

Product Emphasis

	Existing Products	New Products
Existing Markets	**Market penetration strategy** • Seek to increase sales of existing products to existing markets	**Product development strategy** • Create growth by selling new products in existing markets
New Markets	**Market development strategy** • Introduce existing products to new markets	**Diversification strategy** • Emphasize both new products and new markets to achieve growth

Market Emphasis

Cuba is a promising market for American companies now that government restrictions have been lifted.

market development strategies
Growth strategies that introduce existing products to new markets.

product development strategies
Growth strategies that focus on selling new products in existing markets.

diversification strategies
Growth strategies that emphasize both new products and new markets.

voice assistant speaker that enables users to communicate verbally with the device to make requests to play a specific song on Spotify or hail an Uber. Through Echo, Amazon has been able to gain greater market by developing and highlighting the growing list of integrations available for the device aimed at adding greater levels of convenience to different tasks. For Super Bowl 50, Amazon spent big money on a primetime television spot to feature the Echo and the Alexa software that it utilizes.[7] In the not too distant future, a user may be able to treat the product as, among other things, a "virtual teller" capable of performing different banking activities.[8]

- **Market development strategies** introduce existing products to new markets. This strategy can mean expanding into a new geographic area, or it may mean reaching new customer segments within an existing geographic market. For example, Boeing sells its airplanes in many countries throughout the world, but it just recently entered the African market for the first time. In recent years as the U.S. relationship with Cuba has improved, many American companies have begun to look at this nearby island as a new opportunity for growth close to home. Early in 2016 Starwood Hotels and Resorts edged out Marriott to become the first U.S. company in about 60 years to take over the operation of a hotel in Cuba. For global hotelier Starwood, Cuba represents an attractive market that for decades has been artificially constrained due to governmental policies.[9]

- **Product development strategies** create growth by selling new products in existing markets. *Product development* may mean extending the firm's product line by developing new variations of the item, or it may mean altering or improving the product to provide enhanced performance. In Southern California, McDonald's started a test of healthier breakfast bowls that feature kale, egg whites, and other nontraditional Mickey D ingredients.[10] Riding on the success of their all-day breakfast menu, such product development tests have the opportunity to generate considerable additional revenue in this case from more health-conscious consumers.

- **Diversification strategies** emphasize both new products and new markets to achieve growth. Coke offers a wide range of brands and products beyond the high fructose corn syrup goodness of its namesake Coca-Cola, largely in response to a global backlash on poor nutrition and obesity. With declining sales of the core brand, recently Coke stepped up efforts to acquire companies such as China's Culiangwang Beverages Holding Ltd. that is well known for its multigrain beverages branded as health drinks.[11] In addition, Coca-Cola developed products in recent years such as Coca-Cola Life that shifts to a sweetener called Stevia, a purportedly healthier plant extract. As the demand for healthier products accelerates, count on Coke to turn to more diversification strategies including opportunities in emerging economies to replace growth that is waning in its portfolio of traditional high-calorie products.[12]

To review what we've learned so far, strategic planning includes developing the mission statement, assessing the internal and external environment (resulting in a SWOT analysis), setting objectives, establishing the business portfolio, and developing growth strategies. In the next section, we'll look at marketers' functional plans as we examine the process of market planning.

Ripped from the Headlines

Ethical/Sustainable Decisions in the Real World

Previously in this chapter, you learned about portfolio management and the different ways that stars, cash cows, question marks, and dogs are identified and managed by firms. Within the pharmaceutical industry a cash cow can take the form of a drug that has been around for a while and is considered a staple for treating a specific medical condition. This particular drug might not have a substantially large market, but for those who suffer from a specific condition it may be the only option. In this regard we could argue that this drug enjoys a monopolistic position and that the sensitivity to price for this product is most likely extremely low. This may especially be true if the drug is prescribed by doctors who view it as the only suitable option for the condition it treats.

Pharmaceutical firms are under increasing public and governmental scrutiny to balance societal needs with the profit motive. Traditionally, the pharma industry argues back that product development costs in bringing innovative new drugs to market are sky high and approval timelines are very long. A study by the Tufts Center for the Study of Drug Development pegged total cost of bringing an approved drug to market at $2.6 billion with a typical developmental timespan more than 10 years.[13]

Pharma is a high-risk business model, but when a firm does hit on the "next big drug," the payoff is astronomical. One way to help fund innovation in this environment is to substantially raise the prices of existing drugs that serve small specialized markets with low or no growth potential, but because of the overwhelming need of those patients for the medicine no drop in revenue would be anticipated (in Chapter 10 we'll talk about price changes that do not cause much change in demand as *price inelasticity*). Recently, in a scenario played out heavily in the media, Turing Pharmaceuticals argued that an increase in the price of a dose of its product Daraprim from $13.50 to a whopping $750 would help the company invest in the development of new drugs that would benefit far more consumers. At the time Daraprim served fewer than ten thousand individuals, but for them it was indeed a potential lifesaver in fighting a parasitic infection encountered by folks whose immune systems were compromised. Public outcry against Turing was extreme. The CEO (who ultimately resigned and was later indicated on unrelated charges) was reviled as the "bad boy of biotech" and many other names unfit to print in a family textbook.[14]

Although they may be wildly unpopular, such huge price increases are not illegal. Pharma firms assume high financial risks, and not every new medication is a blockbuster. Most failing along the long road to product development, forcing those that do succeed to pay for themselves and also the products that didn't make it to the finish line.[15]

ETHICS CHECK:

Is it appropriate for pharma companies to set prices of prescription drugs at any level they want based on the needs of their business?

☐ YES   ☐ NO

3.3

OBJECTIVE

Describe the steps in market planning.

(pp. 101–108)

Market Planning: Develop and Execute Marketing Strategy

Until now, we have focused on fairly broad strategic plans. This big-picture perspective, however, does not provide details about how to reach the objectives we set. Strategic plans "talk the talk" but put the pressure on lower-level functional-area managers, such as the marketing manager, production manager, and finance manager, to "walk the walk" by developing the functional plans—the nuts and bolts—to achieve organizational and SBU objectives. Because you're taking a marketing course and this is a marketing book, our focus at the functional planning level is naturally on developing marketing plans, which is the next step in planning as we showed back in Figure 3.1.

The Four Ps of the marketing mix we discussed in Chapter 1 remind us that successful firms must have viable *products* at *prices* consumers are willing to pay, a way to *promote* the products to the right consumers, and the ability to get the products to the *place* where consumers want to buy them.

Making this happen requires a tremendous amount of planning by the marketer. The steps in this market planning process are quite similar to the steps at the strategic planning level. An important distinction between strategic planning and market planning, however, is that marketing professionals focus much of their planning efforts on issues related to the

Figure 3.5  *Process* Steps in Market Planning

marketing mix—the firm's product, its price, promotional approach, and distribution (place) methods. In the end, as you learned in Chapter 1, marketing focuses on creating, communicating, delivering, and exchanging offerings that have value, and market planning plays a central role in making these critical components of marketing successful. Let's use Figure 3.5 as a guide to look at the steps involved in the market planning process in a bit more detail.

Step 1: Perform a Situation Analysis

The first step to develop a marketing plan is to conduct an analysis of the *marketing* environment. In Chapter 2, you learned about four key external elements that impact marketers: the economic, technological, political and legal, and sociocultural environments. To do this, managers build on the company's SWOT analysis and search out information about the environment that specifically affects the marketing plan. For example, for Oracle to develop an effective marketing communication program for any one of its products, it's not enough to have just a general understanding of the target market. Oracle needs to know *specifically* what media potential customers like to connect with, what messages about the product are most likely to make them buy, and how they prefer to communicate with the firm about new services and customer care issues. Oracle also must know how competitors market to customers so that the company can plan effectively.

Step 2: Set Marketing Objectives

Once marketing managers have a thorough understanding of the marketing environment, the next step is to develop specific marketing objectives. How do marketing objectives differ from corporate objectives? Generally, marketing objectives are more specific to the firm's marketing mix–related elements. Think of the connection between business objectives and marketing objectives this way: Business objectives guide the entire firm's operations, whereas marketing objectives state what the marketing function must accomplish if the firm is ultimately to achieve these overall business objectives. So for Oracle, setting marketing objectives means deciding what the firm wants to accomplish in terms of a product line's marketing mix–related elements: product development, pricing strategies, or specific marketing communication approaches.

Step 3: Develop Marketing Strategies: Target Markets and the Marketing Mix

In the next stage of the market planning process, marketing managers develop their actual marketing strategies—that is, they make decisions about what activities they must accomplish to achieve the marketing objectives. Usually this means they decide which markets to target and actually develop the marketing mix strategies (product, price, promotion, and place [supply chain]) to support how they want to position the product in the market. At this stage, marketers must figure out how they want consumers to think of their product compared to competing products.

As we mentioned in Chapter 1, the target market is the market segment(s) a firm selects because it believes its offerings are most likely to win those customers. The firm assesses the potential demand—the number of consumers it believes are willing and able to pay for its products—and decides if it is able to create a sustainable competitive advantage in the marketplace among target consumers.

Lee jeans offers a very diverse product portfolio.

Marketing mix decisions identify how marketing will accomplish its objectives in the firm's target markets by using product, price, promotion, and place. To make the point, we'll compare several different airlines' approaches:

- Because the product is the most fundamental part of the marketing mix—firms simply can't make a profit without something to sell—carefully developed *product strategies* are essential to achieve marketing objectives. Product strategies include decisions such as product design, packaging, branding, support services (e.g., maintenance); if there will be variations of the product; and what product features will provide the unique benefits targeted customers want. For example, Alaska Airlines became the first carrier to fly a version of the Boeing 737 aircraft that offers a type of overhead bin that can hold 48 percent more luggage than a standard pivot bin.[16] If you've ever packed a carry-on bag with the express purpose of not having to deal with the cost and hassle of checking a bag, only to find when you get to the gate that the bins are full and you end up checking the bag anyway, you might be tempted by Alaska's bigger bins and book them over other carriers.[17]

Many airline passengers today crave a bigger luggage bin as a product feature.

- A *pricing strategy* determines how much a firm charges for a product. Of course, that price has to be one that customers are willing to pay. If not, all the other marketing efforts are futile. In addition to setting prices for the final consumer, pricing strategies usually establish prices the company will charge to wholesalers and retailers. A firm may base its pricing strategies on costs, demand, or the prices of competing products. In recent years, most airlines have been charging extra fees (checked baggage anyone?) for services and perks they used to include in the ticket price, a practice known as *debundling*, in an effort to increase their revenues. Consumer backlash on such "nickel-and-diming" for everything led Delta Air Lines began offering a new option for travelers called Comfort+™ that includes many benefits built back into its price; these include Sky Priority boarding, premium content on the entertainment console, Wi-Fi access, alcoholic beverages and premium snacks, and seating with greater leg room. Travelers can easily add up the individual costs of these "rebundled" services to determine if Comfort+™ is a good deal for them.[18]

- A *promotional strategy* is how marketers communicate a product's value proposition to the target market. Marketers use promotion strategies to develop the product's message and the mix of advertising, sales promotion, public relations and publicity, direct marketing, and personal selling that will deliver the message. Many firms use all these elements to communicate their message to consumers. Emirates, an international airline company that operates flights to destinations all around the world, has cultivated a strong association with luxury and comfort through a focus on features and experiences within its airplanes that are clearly uncommon in today's commoditized world of air travel. To heighten public awareness that Emirates is different, the airline launched a major advertising campaign featuring its new brand ambassador Jennifer Aniston. In the ad Aniston (on an Emirates plane) emerges from a nightmare in which she was flying a U.S. carrier that had no walk-up bar, no private bedrooms in the first class cabin, and no in-flight showers (oh, the horror!). The ad closes with her kibitzing with the bartender about her horrible dream, asking him if the pilots can fly around for another hour or so to allow her to take advantage of Emirates' luxury product amenities.[19]

- *Distribution strategies* outline how, when, and where the firm will make the product available to targeted customers (the *place* component). When they develop a distribution strategy, marketers must decide whether to sell the product directly to the final customer or to sell through retailers and wholesalers. And the choice of which retailers should be involved depends on the product, pricing, and promotion decisions. Back in the day,

California's almond growers have a marketing strategy to increase consumption by promoting the nut's health benefits.

control

A process that entails measuring actual performance, comparing this performance to the established marketing objectives, and then making adjustments to the strategies or objectives on the basis of this analysis.

activity metrics

Metrics focused on measuring and tracking specific activities taken within a firm that are part of different marketing processes.

outcome metrics

Metrics focused on measuring and tracking specific events identified as key business outcomes that result from marketing processes.

airlines used to sell tickets in person or by phone directly to customers or through independent travel agents, but customers now largely purchase tickets online, often through third-party vendors such as Travelocity. And there are benefits to this strategy, especially for consumers. For example, travelers can see at a glance the best airlines fares and flight schedules; they can get discounts for booking multiple travel services, such as flights, hotels, and car rentals; and they can get access to top deals such as when Expedia offered 29 percent off on select hotel reservations made using the Expedia app on February 29, 2016, in celebration of the extra leap year day.[20]

Step 4: Implement and Control the Marketing Plan

Once the marketing plan is developed, it's time to get to work and make it succeed. In practice, marketers spend much of their time managing the various elements involved in implementing the marketing plan. Once Oracle understands the marketing environment, determines the most appropriate objectives and strategies, and gets its ideas organized and on paper in the formal plan, the rubber really hits the road. Like all firms, how Oracle actually implements its plan is what will make or break it in the marketplace.

During the implementation phase, marketers must have some means to determine to what degree they actually meet their stated marketing objectives. Often called **control**, this formal process of monitoring progress entails three steps:

1. Measure actual performance.

2. Compare this performance to the established marketing objectives or strategies.

3. Make adjustments to the objectives or strategies on the basis of this analysis. This issue of making adjustments brings up one of the most important aspects of successful market planning: Marketing plans aren't written in stone, and marketers must be flexible enough to make such changes when changes are warranted.

For effective control, Oracle has to establish appropriate *metrics* related to each of its marketing objectives and then track those metrics to know how successful the marketing strategy is and determine whether it needs to change the strategy along the way. For example, what happens if Oracle sets an objective for the first quarter of a year to increase its market share for a particular product line by 20 percent but after the first-quarter sales are only even with those of last year? The *control process* means that market planners would have to look carefully at *why* the company isn't meeting its objectives. Is it due to internal factors, external factors, or a combination of both? Depending on the cause, Oracle would then have to adjust the marketing plan's strategies (such as to implement product alterations, modify the price, change distribution channels, or increase or alter promotion). Alternatively, Oracle could decide to adjust the marketing objective so that it is more realistic and attainable. This scenario illustrates the important point we made earlier in our discussion of strategic planning: Objectives must be specific and measurable but also *attainable* (and *sustainable over time*) in the sense that if an objective is not realistic, it can become demotivating for everyone involved in the marketing plan.

For Oracle and all firms, effective control requires appropriate *marketing metrics*, which, as we discussed in Chapter 1, are measurements that marketers use to identify the effectiveness of different strategies or tactics. Two common ways that metrics can be categorized include: (1) **activity metrics**, which are focused on measuring and tracking specific activities taken within a firm that are part of different marketing processes; and (2) **outcome metrics**, which are focused on measuring and tracking specific events identified as key business outcomes that result from marketing processes. An example of an activity metric is the number of calls that a salesperson makes to customers over a month, whereas a related outcome metric is the number of orders gained from sales calls made during that month.

Metrics are so important in marketing today that you will find extensive treatment of the topic (along with marketing analytics and "Big Data") in Chapter 5. For now, it is important to understand that marketers must balance attention to marketing control and the measurement of marketing performance against sustainability and corporate social responsibility (CSR) objectives, which you read about in Chapter 2. Recall that sustainability has to do with firms doing well by doing good—that is, paying attention to important issues such as ethics, the environment, and social responsibility as well as the bottom line. In market planning, we certainly don't want to drive firms toward strategies that compromise sustainability by focusing only on controlling relatively short-term aspects of performance.

Today's CEOs are keen to quantify just how an investment in marketing has an impact on the firm's success, financially and otherwise, over the long haul. You've heard of the financial term *return on investment (ROI)*—in a marketing context we refer to **return on marketing investment (ROMI)**. *In fact, it's critical to consider marketing as an investment rather than an expense*; this distinction drives firms to use marketing more strategically to enhance the business. For many firms today, ROMI is the metric du jour to analyze how the marketing function contributes to the bottom line.

So, what exactly is ROMI? It is the revenue or profit margin (both are widely used) generated by investment in a specific marketing campaign or program divided by the cost of that program (expenditure) at a given risk level (the risk level is determined by management's analysis of the particular program). Again, the key word is *investment*—that is, in the planning process, thinking of marketing as an investment rather than an expense keeps managers focused on using marketing dollars to achieve specific objectives.[21]

Here's a quick and simple example of the ROMI concept. Let's say that a relatively routine marketing campaign costs $30,000 and generates $150,000 in new revenue. Thus, the ROMI for the program is 5.0 (the ROI is five times the investment). If the firm has a total marketing budget of $250,000 and an objective for new revenue of $1,000,000, then the ROMI hurdle rate could be considered 4.0 ($1,000,000/$250,000), meaning that each program should strive to meet or exceed that ROMI benchmark of $4.00 in revenue for every $1.00 in marketing expenditure. Because the marketing campaign exceeds the ROMI hurdle rate, it would be deemed acceptable to proceed with that investment.[22]

For an organization to use ROMI properly it must (1) identify the most appropriate and consistent measure to apply, (2) combine review of ROMI with other critical marketing metrics (one example is marketing payback—how quickly marketing costs are recovered), and (3) fully consider the potential long-term impact of the actions ROMI drives (i.e., is the impact sustainable for the organization over the long term).[23] Fortunately for the marketer, there are many other potential marketing metrics beyond ROMI that measure specific aspects of marketing performance. In Chapter 5 you will encounter other useful metrics that marketers can use to gauge the level of success of their plans, strategies, and tactics.

Action Plans

How does the implementation and control step actually manifest itself within a marketing plan? One convenient way is through the inclusion of a series of **action plans** that support the various marketing objectives and strategies within the plan. The best way to use action plans (which also are sometimes called "marketing programs") is to include a separate action plan for each important element involved in implementing the marketing plan. Table 3.1 provides a template for an action plan.

For example, let's consider the use of action plans in the context of supporting the objective we came up with for Oracle earlier to increase market share of a particular product line by 20 percent in the first quarter of the year. To accomplish this, the marketing plan

return on marketing investment (ROMI)
Quantifying just how an investment in marketing has an impact on the firm's success, financially and otherwise.

action plans
Individual support plans included in a marketing plan that provide guidance for implementation and control of the various marketing strategies within the plan. Action plans are sometimes referred to as "marketing programs."

Metrics Moment

Is ROMI always appropriate or sufficient to judge marketing's effectiveness and efficiency? Here are six common objections to relying *exclusively* on ROMI to measure marketing success:

1. In a company's accounting statements, marketing expenditures tend to appear as a cost, not an investment. This practice perpetuates the "marketing-is-an-expense" mentality in the firm.
2. ROMI requires the profit to be divided by expenditure, yet all other bottom-line performance measures (like the ones you learned in your finance course) consider profit or cash flow after deducting expenditures.
3. Calculating ROMI requires knowing what would have happened if the marketing expenditure in question had never taken place. Few marketers have those figures.
4. ROMI has become a fashionable term for marketing productivity in general, yet much evidence exists that firms interpret how to calculate ROMI quite differently. When executives discuss ROMI with different calculations of it in mind, only confusion can result.

5. ROMI, by nature, ignores the effect of marketing assets of the firm (e.g., its brands) and tends to lead managers toward a more short-term decision perspective. That is, it typically considers only short-term incremental profits and expenditures without looking at longer-term effects or any change in brand equity.
6. And speaking of short-term versus long-term decisions, ROMI (like a number of other metrics focused on snapshot information—in this case, a particular marketing campaign) often can lead to actions by management to shore up short-term performance to the detriment of a firm's sustainability commitment. Ethics in marketing should not be an oxymoron—but often unethical behavior is driven by the demand for quick, short-term marketing results.[24]

Apply the Metrics

1. Review the six objections to ROMI above and discuss them with your classmates.
2. Select any two of the objections and develop a specific example of how they might lead to a bad decision in market planning.

would likely include a variety of strategies related to how Oracle will use the marketing mix elements to reach this objective. Important questions will include the following:

- What are the important needs and wants of this target market?
- How will the product be positioned in relation to this market?
- What will be the product and branding strategies?
- What will be the pricing strategy for this group?
- How will the product be promoted to them?
- What is the best distribution strategy to access the market?

Any one of these important strategic issues may require several action plans to implement.

Action plans also help managers when they need to assign responsibilities, time lines, budgets, and measurement and control processes for market planning. In Table 3.1, notice

Table 3.1	Action Plan Template
Title of action plan	Give the action plan a relevant name.
Purpose of action plan	What do you hope to accomplish by the action plan—that is, what specific marketing objective and strategy within the marketing plan does it support?
Description of action plan	Be succinct—but still thorough—when you explain the action plan. What are the steps involved? This is the core of the action plan. It describes what must be done in order to accomplish the intended purpose of the action plan.
Responsibility for the action plan	What person(s) or organizational unit(s) are responsible for carrying out the action plan? What external parties are needed to make it happen? Most importantly, who specifically has final "ownership" of the action plan—that is, who within the organization is accountable for it?
Timeline for the action plan	Provide a specific timetable of events leading to the completion of the plan. If different people are responsible for different elements of the time line, provide that information.
Budget for the action plan	How much will implementation of the action plan cost? This may be direct costs only or may also include indirect costs, depending on the situation. The sum of all the individual action plan budget items will ultimately be aggregated by category to create the overall budget for the marketing plan.
Measurement and control of the action plan	Indicate the appropriate metrics, how and when they will be measured, and who will measure them.

that these four elements are the final items that an action plan documents. Sometimes when we view a marketing plan in total, it can seem daunting and nearly impossible to actually implement. Like most big projects, implementation of a marketing plan is best done one step at a time, paying attention to maximizing the quality of executing that step. In practice, what happens is that marketers combine the input from these last four elements of each action plan to form the overall implementation and control portion of the marketing plan. Let's examine each element a bit further.

Assign Responsibility

A marketing plan can't be implemented without people. And not everybody who will be involved in implementing a marketing plan is a marketer. The truth is, marketing plans touch most areas of an organization. Upper management and the human resources department will need to deploy the necessary employees to accomplish the plan's objectives. You learned in Chapter 1 that marketing isn't the responsibility only of a marketing department. Nowhere is that idea more apparent than in marketing plan implementation. Sales, production, quality control, shipping, customer service, finance, information technology—the list goes on—all will likely have a part in making the plan successful.

Create a Timeline

Notice that each action plan requires a timeline to accomplish the various tasks it requires. This is essential to include in the overall marketing plan. Most marketing plans portray the timing of tasks in flowchart form so that it is easy to visualize when the pieces of the plan will come together. Marketers often use *Gantt charts* or *PERT charts*, popular in operations management, to portray a plan's timeline. These are the same types of tools that a general contractor might use to map out the different elements of building a house from the ground up. Ultimately, managers develop budgets and the financial management of the marketing plan around the timeline so they know when cash outlays are required.

Set a Budget

Each element of the action plan links to a *budget item*, assuming there are costs involved in carrying out the plan. Forecasting the needed expenditures related to a marketing plan is difficult, but one way to improve accuracy in the budgeting process overall is to ensure estimates for expenditures for the individual action plans that are as accurate as possible. At the overall marketing plan level, managers create a master budget and track it throughout the market planning process. They report variances from the budget to the parties responsible for each budget item. For example, a firm's vice president of sales might receive a weekly or monthly report that shows each sales area's performance against its budget allocation. The vice president would note patterns of budget overage and contact affected sales managers to determine what, if any, action they need to take to get the budget back on track. The same approach would be repeated across all the different functional areas of the firm on which the budget has an impact. In such a manner, the budget itself becomes a critical element of control.

Decide on Measurements and Controls

Previously, we described the concept of control as a formal process of monitoring progress to measure actual performance, compare the performance to the established marketing objectives or strategies, and make adjustments to the objectives or strategies on the basis of this analysis. The metric(s) a marketer uses to monitor and control individual action plans ultimately forms the overall control process for the marketing plan. Metrics can serve as **leading indicators** or **lagging indicators** of marketing outcomes. Leading indicators provide insight into the performance of *current efforts* in a way that allows a marketer to adjust relevant marketing activities (hopefully) resulting in performance improvements against the current action plan. Lagging indicators reflect the performance of an action plan based on outcomes realized. Lagging indicators provide a basis for review and analysis of the

leading indicators
Performance indicators that provide insight into the performance of *current efforts* in a way that allows a marketer to adjust relevant marketing activities (hopefully) resulting in performance improvements against the current action plan.

lagging indicators
Performance indicators that provide insight into the performance of an action plan based on outcomes realized.

action plan with implications for improvement that are focused beyond the scope of the current action plan itself. That is, they provide post hoc insights for next actions.

It is an unfortunate fact that many marketers do not consistently do a good job of measurement and control, which, of course, compromises their market planning. And remember that selection of good metrics needs to take into account short-term objectives balanced against the firm's focus on long-term sustainability.

Operational Planning: Day-to-Day Execution of Marketing Plans

operational plans
Plans that focus on the day-to-day execution of the marketing plan. Operational plans include detailed directions for the specific activities to be carried out, who will be responsible for them, and time lines to accomplish the tasks.

Recall that planning happens at three levels: strategic, functional (such as market planning), and operational. In the previous section, we discussed market planning—the process by which marketers perform a situation analysis, set marketing objectives, and develop, implement, and control marketing strategies. But talk is cheap: The best plan ever written is useless if it's not properly carried out. That's what **operational plans** are for. They put the pedal to the metal by focusing on the day-to-day execution of the marketing plan.

The task of operational planning falls to first-line managers such as sales managers, marketing communications managers, brand managers, and market research managers. Operational plans generally cover a shorter period of time than either strategic plans or marketing plans—perhaps only one or two months—and they include detailed directions for the specific activities to be carried out, who will be responsible for them, and timelines for accomplishing the tasks. In reality, the action plan template we provide in Table 3.1 is most likely applied at the operational level.

Significantly, many of the important marketing metrics managers use to gauge the success of plans actually get used at the operational planning level. For example, sales managers in many firms are charged with the responsibility of tracking a wide range of metrics related to the firm–customer relationship, such as number of new customers, sales calls per month, customer turnover, and customer loyalty. The data are collected at the operational level and then sent to upper management for use in planning at the functional level and above.

Make Your Life Easier! Use the Market Planning Template

Ultimately, the planning process we've described in this section is documented in a formal, written marketing plan. You'll find a template for building a marketing plan in the Supplement at the end of this chapter. The template will come in handy as you make your way through the book, as each chapter will give you information you can use to "fill in the blanks" of a marketing plan. You will note that the template is cross-referenced with the questions you must answer in each section of the plan. It also provides you with a general road map of the topics covered in each chapter that need to flow into building the marketing plan. By the time you're done, we hope that all these pieces will come together and you'll understand how real marketers make real choices.

As we noted previously, a marketing plan should provide the best possible guide for the firm to successfully market its products. In large firms, top management often requires such a written plan because putting the ideas on paper encourages marketing managers to formulate concrete objectives and strategies. In small entrepreneurial firms, a well-thought-out marketing plan is often the key to attracting investors who will help turn the firm's dreams into reality.

MyLab Marketing™

Go to **mymktlab.com** to complete the problems marked with this icon ⊗ as well as additional Marketing Metrics questions only available in MyLab Marketing.

Objective Summary → Key → Terms Apply

3.1 Objective Summary (pp. 92–94)

Explain business planning and its three levels.

Business planning is the ongoing process of decision making that guides the firm in both the short term and the long term. A business plan, which includes the decisions that guide the entire organization or its business units, is different from a marketing plan, which is a process and resulting document that describes the marketing environment, outlines the marketing objectives and strategies, and identifies how the company will implement and control the strategies embedded in the plan.

Planning takes place at three key levels. Strategic planning is the managerial decision process that matches the firm's resources and capabilities to its market opportunities for long-term growth. Large firms may have a number of self-contained divisions called *strategic business units (SBUs)*. In such cases, strategic planning takes place at both the overall corporate level and within the SBU. Functional planning gets its name because the various functional areas of the firm, such as marketing, finance, and human resources, get involved. And operational planning focuses on the day-to-day execution of the functional plans and includes detailed annual, semiannual, or quarterly plans.

Key Terms

business planning, p. 93

business plan, p. 93

marketing plan, p. 93

strategic planning, p. 94

strategic business units (SBUs), p. 94

functional planning, p. 94

market planning, p. 94

operational planning, p. 94

3.2 Objective Summary (pp. 95–101)

Describe the steps in strategic planning.

For large firms that have a number of self-contained business units, the first step in strategic planning is for top management to establish a mission for the entire corporation. Top managers then evaluate the internal and external environment of the business and set corporate-level objectives that guide decision making within each individual SBU. In small firms that are not large enough to have separate SBUs, strategic planning simply takes place at the overall firm level.

The first step in strategic planning is defining the mission—a formal document that describes the organization's overall purpose and what it hopes to achieve in terms of its customers, products, and resources. Step 2 is to evaluate the internal and external environment through a process known as situational analysis, which is later formatted as a SWOT analysis that identifies the organization's strengths, weaknesses, opportunities, and threats. Step 3 is to set organizational or SBU objectives that are specific, measurable, attainable, and sustainable. Step 4 is to establish the business portfolio, which is the range of different businesses that a large firm operates. To determine how best to allocate resources to the various businesses, or units, managers use the Boston Consulting Group (BCG) growth–market share matrix to classify SBUs as stars, cash cows, question marks, or dogs. The final step, Step 5, in strategic planning is to develop growth strategies. Marketers use the product–market growth matrix to analyze four fundamental marketing strategies: market penetration, market development, product development, and diversification.

Key Terms

mission statement, p. 95

situation analysis, p. 95

internal environment, p. 95

external environment, p. 96

SWOT analysis, p. 96

business portfolio, p. 97

portfolio analysis, p. 97

BCG growth–market share matrix, p. 97

stars, p. 98

cash cows, p. 98

question marks, p. 98

dogs, p. 99

market penetration strategies, p. 99

market development strategies, p. 100

product development strategies, p. 100

diversification strategies, p. 100

3.3 Objective Summary (pp. 101–108)

Describe the steps in market planning.

Once big-picture issues are considered, it's up to the lower-level functional-area managers, such as the marketing manager, production manager, and finance manager, to develop the unctional marketing plans—the nuts and bolts—to achieve organizational and SBU objectives. The steps in this market planning process are quite similar to the steps at the strategic planning level. An important distinction between strategic planning and market planning, however, is that marketing professionals focus much of their planning efforts on issues related to the Four Ps of the marketing mix. Managers start off by performing a situational analysis of the marketing environment. Next, they develop marketing objectives specific to the firm's brand, sizes, and product features. Then marketing managers select the target market(s) for the organization and decide what marketing mix strategies they will use. Product strategies include decisions about products and product characteristics that will appeal to the target market. Pricing strategies state the specific prices to be charged to channel members and final consumers. Promotion strategies include plans for advertising, sales promotion, public relations, publicity, personal selling, and direct marketing used to reach the target market. Distribution (place) strategies outline how the product will be made available to targeted customers when and where they want it. Once the marketing strategies are developed, they must be implemented, which is the last step in developing the marketing plan. Control is the measurement of actual performance and comparison with planned performance. Maintaining control implies the need for concrete measures of marketing performance called "marketing metrics."

Operational planning is done by first-line supervisors such as sales managers, marketing communication managers, and market research managers and focuses on the day-to-day execution of the marketing plan. Operational plans generally cover a shorter period of time and include detailed directions for the specific activities to be carried out, who will be responsible for them, and time lines for accomplishing the tasks. To ensure effective implementation, a marketing plan must include individual action plans, or programs, that support the plan at the operational level. Each action plan necessitates providing a budget estimate, schedule, or time line for its implementation and appropriate metrics so that the marketer can monitor progress and control for discrepancies or variation from the plan. Sometimes, variance from a plan requires shifting or increasing resources to make the plan work; other times, it requires changing the objectives of the plan to recognize changing conditions.

Key Terms

control, p. 104

activity metric, p. 104

outcome metric, p. 104

return on marketing investment (ROMI), p. 105

action plans, p. 105

leading indicator, p. 107

lagging indicator, p. 107

operational plans, p. 108

Chapter **Questions** and **Activities**

> **MyLab Marketing™**
> Go to **mymktlab.com** to watch this chapter's Rising Star video(s) for career advice and to respond to questions.

Concepts: Test Your Knowledge

3-1. What is a marketing plan, and how does it differ from a business plan?

3-2. Describe the three levels of business planning: strategic, functional, and operational planning.

3-3. What is a mission statement? What is a SWOT analysis? What role do these play in the planning process?

3-4. What is a strategic business unit (SBU)? How does strategic planning differ at the corporate and the SBU levels?

3-5. Describe the five steps in the strategic planning process.

3-6. How do firms use the BCG model for portfolio analysis in planning for their SBUs?

3-7. Describe the four business growth strategies: market penetration, product development, market development, and diversification.

3-8. Explain the four steps in the market planning process.

3-9. What is return on marketing investment (ROMI)? How does considering marketing as an investment instead of an expense affect a firm?

3-10. Give several examples of marketing metrics. How might a marketer use each metric to track progress of some important element of a marketing plan?

3-11. What is an action plan? Why are action plans such an important part of market planning? Why is it so important for marketers to break the implementation of a marketing plan down into individual elements through action plans?

3-12. How does operational planning support the marketing plan?

Activities: Apply What You've Learned

★ **3-13.** *Creative Homework/Short Project* As a marketing student, you know that large firms often organize their operations into a number of strategic business units (SBUs). A university might develop a similar structure in which different academic schools or departments are seen as separate businesses. Consider how your university or college might divide its total academic units into separate SBUs. What would be the problems with implementing such a plan? What would be the advantages and disadvantages for students and for faculty? Be prepared to share your analysis of university SBUs to your class.

3-14. *Creative Homework/Short Project* Search the Internet for the mission statements of three well-known firms (for publicly listed companies, you should look under investor information on their corporate websites). Review each of the mission statements and answer these questions:
- What do the mission statements have in common?
- Do they specify products that the firm should deliver?

- Do they specify any target markets?
- Do they suggest an overall strategic approach?
- Do they talk about corporate values?
- Do they refer to their staff?
- In what ways are these mission statements different from each other?

Once you have completed the review, identify how these mission statements, as they are currently framed, will influence or drive the firm's marketing strategy and overall decision-making.

3-15. *Creative Homework/Short Project* Accor Hotels is a French-based corporation that operates a multi-brand hotel strategy in almost 100 countries. They operate a number of well-known hotel chains that range from budget to very exclusive. Via their website, review Accor's current business portfolio (that is, the hotel chains that they own in the countries they operate within). If possible, identify any hotel brands that they have recently acquired or divested.

Why do you think they operate multiple hotel brands rather than offering one overall hotel chain throughout the world? What are the advantages and disadvantages of this multi-brand approach?

3-16. *In Class, 10–25 Minutes for Teams* As an employee of a business consulting firm that specializes in helping people who want to start small businesses, you have been assigned a client who is interested in introducing a new concept in health clubs—one that offers its customers both the usual exercise and weight-training opportunities and certain related types of medical assistance, such as physical therapy, a weight-loss physician, and basic diagnostic testing. As you begin thinking about the potential for success for this client, you realize that developing a marketing plan is going to be essential. Take a role-playing approach to present your argument to the client as to why he or she needs to spend the money on your services to create a formal marketing plan.

3-17. *For Further Research (Individual)* All businesses—big and small—need to plan if they want to be profitable and sustainable. Contact one of your favorite local businesses and make an appointment with someone who has a hand in developing the firm's business plan. Find out how much time the planning process takes, how often the business plan is updated, and what types of information the business plan contains. Summarize your findings in a short report.

3-18. *For Further Research (Groups)* Identify a large company, like Disney, that has several SBUs. Using the BCG model, assign at least one SBU to each category in the model: star, cash cow, question mark, and dog. Include at least two pieces of data for each to justify your categorization. Prepare a short presentation to share with your class.

Concepts: Apply Marketing Metrics

You learned in the chapter that most marketers today feel pressure to measure (quantify) their level of success in market planning. They do this by setting and then measuring marketing objectives. One popular metric is market share, which in essence represents the percentage of total product category sales your products represent versus category competitors. For example,

recent statistics indicate that Lenovo holds the number-one market share in global PC sales with about 21 percent, topping HP with about 19 percent. Ranked third through fifth are Dell, Apple, and Acer, respectively.[25] But, despite its common appearance in marketing objectives, market share has been heavily criticized as a metric. Often it can become more of a "bragging right" for a firm than a profit enhancer. This is because—especially in situations like the global PC market that is seeing heavy annual declines in sales as tablets and other devices replace PCs—investing in being number one in market share may deflect focus away from more lucrative new and growing product lines.

★ 3-19. Under what conditions do you believe market share as a metric is important to a firm? What are the potential pitfalls of relying too much on market share as a key metric? What self-defeating behaviors might this over-reliance lead a firm to undertake?

★ 3-20. Come up with some other product categories besides PCs that are declining and identify the firms within those categories that have the highest market share. What does their profit picture look like?

Choices: What Do You Think?

★ 3-21. *Critical Thinking* In today's dynamic world, the marketing environment appears to be changing faster than ever, particularly with regard to technology and related customer lifestyles. Do you think that a structured approach to developing marketing plans is beneficial for the success of an organization, or do you think that planning would be overly restrictive to its operations and entrepreneurial spirit, with the result that it would miss out on opportunities?

3-22. The Boston Consulting Group (BCG) growth–market share matrix identifies SBUs and their related products as stars, cash cows, question marks, and dogs. Do you think this is a useful way for organizations to examine their businesses? What are some examples of product lines that fit in each category?

3-23. Within the BCG matrix, products that earn the dog label have limited market potential for the firm and also only hold a small relative market share. Products identified as dogs within this framework are typically obvious candidates for divestment, but are there any cases where doing so would not be wise for an organization? That is, why would a firm want to hold onto a dog?

3-24. In this chapter, we talked about how firms do strategic, functional, and operational planning. Yet some firms seem to be successful without formal planning. Do you think planning is essential to a firm's success? How might planning hurt an organization? Under what circumstances do you believe that formal planning is and is not important to an organization?

3-25. Most planning involves strategies for growth. But is growth always the right direction to pursue? Can you think of some organizations that should have contraction rather than expansion as their objective? Do you know of any organizations that have actually planned to get smaller rather than larger to increase their success?

3-26. When most people think of successful marketing, internal firm culture doesn't immediately come to mind as a contributing factor. You may have learned about corporate culture in a management course. What is a corporate culture? What are some reasons a firm's culture is important to the capability of doing good marketing? Give some examples of aspects that you consider indicate a good corporate culture for marketing.

3-27. Many companies operate on the mentality that "marketing is an expense." Do you agree that marketing is an expense, or should marketing be treated as an investment? Should there be a business standard as to whether marketing is treated as an expense/investment, or should individual organizations be given the freedom to choose which line item to assign it to? Explain your reasoning.

3-28. A common saying among managers is "if we can't measure it, we can't manage it." Is there such a thing as an overreliance on marketing metrics? Are there cases or specific aspects of marketing where a single-minded focus on metrics is inappropriate or detrimental to the firm?

Miniproject: Learn by Doing

The purpose of this miniproject is to gain an understanding of market planning through actual experience.

3-29. The product-market matrix provides four quadrants where firms may pursue growth opportunities. For this activity, you need to consider the range of growth opportunities that are potentially available to a book retailer that is struggling against online providers, such as Amazon, in the current environment.

Let's assume you are a consultant for an independent book store located in a busy city. This bookstore has been established for over 50 years but has seen a fall in sales and regular customers over the last five years as more consumers purchase books through online channels.

Initially, you should conduct research regarding book retailing throughout the world, looking for innovation in operations in particular and trying to find some success stories in this competitive marketplace.

Once you have conducted your research, your next task is to utilize the four quadrants of the product-market matrix to recommend a series of growth strategies for the book retailer. Keep in mind that their budget is probably going to be somewhat restrictive, so your ideas need to be reflective of that limitation. Otherwise, feel free to be as creative as possible and adapt any ideas that you identify through your research.

Marketing in **Action** Case   Real Choices at Amazon

In marketing, yesterday's success quickly becomes old news. How should one of the world's largest retailers plan to build on its' previous achievements? In the retail marketplace, it is becoming harder for companies to differentiate themselves from the competition beyond simply price. Amazon is now faced with this challenge and must develop offerings to protect and grow its customer base. One of its primary offerings to meet this task has been the creation of Amazon Prime. The service was created in 2005 offering free two-day shipping within the U.S. on qualified purchases. The initial annual membership fee was $79 and also allowed discounted one-day shipping rates on those same purchases. In 2014, the fee was increase to $99 and more services were added to increase customer value.

Prime Instant Video allows customers to stream movies and TV shows to their web browsers or multiple Amazon video-compatible devices. The current library of tens of thousands of titles provides a wide array of choice to lure potential customers. Subscribers can also purchase online video subscriptions from premium content providers like Showtime, Starz, and other streaming entertainment channels. The objective of the add-on services is to attract new customers to Amazon Prime in a crowded competitive environment. As of 2016, Netflix is the world's largest provider of streaming video content with more than 75 million subscribers. In addition, Hulu is a joint venture of Walt Disney, 21st Century Fox, and Comcast's NBCUniversal that similarly provides streaming services.

One of Amazon's latest additions to its Prime service is the Prime Store Card. The card rewards subscribers with 5 percent cash back on all Amazon purchases. Or, in lieu of the 5 percent cash back, members can choose a tiered financing option for purchases more than $149. In this plan, when customers reach cost thresholds they can avoid paying interest

if the outstanding balance is paid within 6, 12, or 24 months, as applicable. In addition, periodically on select items sold by Amazon offers 0 percent APR financing with 12 equal monthly payments. One of the key benefits to Amazon is that compared to the use of traditional cards like Visa, MasterCard, or AmEx, transaction processing costs for its Prime Store Card are lower.

One of the best benefits that brick-and-mortar retail stores have maintained over online retailers is the ability to provide customers with instant gratification. Amazon aims to decrease that advantage through its services. Recently introduced in select cities is Prime Now. a service that allows customers to receive their order within one hour for a fee of $7.99, or within two hours for no additional fee. Currently, the products available for Prime Now delivery are limited to 15,000 to 40,000 available items, which may seem like a lot but Prime members currently have access to millions of items to select from for two-day shipping. Prime Now is definitely an innovative service, but in some markets it is faced with other competitors for on-demand delivery offerings, like Google Express and UberRush.

Amazon continues to establish more services under the Prime umbrella. Prime Pantry is an option by which members can fill a virtual box with groceries and household products and have them delivered for $5.99 per box. Prime Music offers ad-free access to playlists and a catalog of more than1 million songs and albums. Prime Photo provides unlimited photo storage on the Amazon Cloud. This wide variety of associated services draws the attention of numerous varied competitors, and the key question as Amazon move forward is: How will the company successfully manage such a large portfolio of offerings? For success to be sustained over time, Amazon must carefully consider what long-term strategies are necessary to continue to make Amazon Prime a profitable winner in a competitive marketplace.

You Make the Call

3-30. What is the decision facing Amazon?

3-31. What factors are important in understanding this decision situation?

3-32. What are the alternatives?

3-33. What decision(s) do you recommend?

3-34. What are some ways to implement your recommendation?

Based on: Tricia Duryee, "Future-Proofing Prime: Amazon's Plans Go Way Beyond Free Shipping," *GeekWire.com*, (April 26, 2014), http://www.geekwire.com/2014/future-proofing-prime-amazons-ambitious-plans-go-way-beyond-shipping/ (accessed April 5, 2016); Amazon.com, "About Amazon Prime," https://www.amazon.com/gp/help/customer/display.html?ref=hp_468520_norush?nodeId=20044 4160 (accessed April 5, 2016); Taylor Tepper, "Should You Get the Amazon Prime Store Card?" *Time.com*, July 24, 2015, http://time.com/money/3970639/amazon-prime-store-credit-card/ (accessed April 5, 2016); Jason Del Rey, "Prime Now Has Become Amazon's Biggest Retail Bet," *Re/code.net*, December 14, 2015, http://recode.net/2015/12/14/prime-now-has-become-amazons-biggest-retail-bet/ (accessed April 5, 2016).

MyLab Marketing™

Go to **mymktlab.com** for the following Assisted-graded writing questions:

3-35. *Creative Homework/Short Project.* Assume that you are the marketing director for Mattel Toys. Your boss, the company vice president for marketing, has decided that it's time to develop some new objectives for some of their product lines as the company begins market planning. Your VP has asked you to help out by writing several initial objectives. Select any product line at Mattel and develop several objectives that fulfill the criteria for objectives discussed in the chapter.

3-36. *Creative Homework/Short Project.* An important part of planning is a SWOT analysis, understanding an organization's strengths, weaknesses, opportunities, and threats. Prepare a SWOT analysis for Panera Bread that includes three or four items in each of the four SWOT categories.

OUTLINE

C. DEVELOP MARKETING STRATEGIES
> **3. Pricing Strategies**

QUESTION

• How will we price our product to the consumer and through the channel?

CHAPTER

Chapter 10: Price: What is the Value Proposition Worth?

build a
Marketing
Plan

HOW TO USE This Template

Here's a handy template that serves as a road map both to develop a marketing plan and to guide you through the course.

1. The first column provides the basic marketing plan **OUTLINE**.

2. The second column gives you **QUESTIONS** you must answer in each of the sections of the marketing plan.

3. The third column shows you where to go to find the answers as you work your way through the **CHAPTERS** of the book.

By the time you're done, all these pieces will come together and you'll understand how real marketers make real choices.

The Marketing Plan OUTLINE

A. PERFORM A SITUATION ANALYSIS

1. Internal Environment

2. External Environment

3. SWOT Analysis

B. SET MARKETING OBJECTIVES

C. DEVELOP MARKETING STRATEGIES

1. Select Target Markets and Positioning

2. Product Strategies

3. Pricing Strategies

4. Distribution Strategies

5. Promotional Strategies

D. IMPLEMENT AND CONTROL THE MARKETING PLAN

1. Action Plans (for all marketing mix elements)

2. Responsibility

3. Timeline

4. Budget

5. Measurement and Control

QUESTIONS the Plan Addresses	CHAPTERS Where You'll Find These Questions
• How does marketing support my company's mission, objectives, and growth strategies? • What is the corporate culture and how does it influence marketing activities? • What has my company done in the past with its: Target markets? Products? Pricing? Promotion? Supply chain? • What resources including management expertise does my company have that make us unique? How has the company added value through its offerings in the past?	**Chapter 1:** Welcome to the World of Marketing: Create and Deliver Value **Chapter 2:** Global, Ethical, and Sustainable Marketing **Chapter 3:** Strategic Market Planning **Chapter 4:** Market Research **Chapter 5:** Marketing Analytics: Welcome to the Era of Big Data
• What is the nature of the overall domestic and global market for our product? How big is the market? Who buys our product? • Who are our competitors? What are their marketing strategies? • What are the key trends in the economic environment? The technological environment? The regulatory environment? The social and cultural environment?	
• Based on this analysis of the internal and external environments, what are the key Strengths, Weaknesses, Opportunities, and Threats (SWOT)?	
• What does marketing need to accomplish to support the objectives of my firm?	**Chapter 2:** Global, Ethical, and Sustainable Marketing **Chapter 3:** Strategic Market Planning
• How do consumers and organizations go about buying, using, and disposing of our products? • Which segments should we select to target? If a consumer market: What are the relevant demographic, psychographic, and behavioral segmentation approaches and the media habits of the targeted segments? If a business market: What are the relevant organizational demographics? • How will we position our product for our market(s)?	**Chapter 4:** Market Research **Chapter 5:** Marketing Analytics: Welcome to the Era of Big Data! **Chapter 6:** Understand Consumer and Business Markets **Chapter 7:** Segmentation, Target Marketing, and Positioning
• What is our core product? Actual product? Augmented product? • What product line/product mix strategies should we use? • How should we package, brand, and label our product? • How can attention to service quality enhance our success?	**Chapter 8:** Product I: Innovation and New Product Development **Chapter 9:** Product II: Product Strategy, Branding, and Product Management
• How will we price our product to the consumer and through the channel? How much must we sell to break even at this price? What pricing tactics should we use?	**Chapter 10:** Price: What Is the Value Proposition Worth?
• How do we get our product to consumers in the best and most efficient manner? • How do we integrate supply chain elements to maximize the value we offer to our customers and other stakeholders? • What types of retailers, if any, should we work with to sell our product?	**Chapter 11:** Deliver the Goods: Determine the Distribution Strategy **Chapter 12:** Deliver the Customer Experience: Goods and Services via Bricks and Clicks
• How do we develop a consistent message about our product? How do we best generate buzz? • What approaches to Advertising, Sales Promotion, Social Media, Direct/Database Marketing, Personal Selling, and Public Relations should we use? • What role should a sales force play in the marketing communications plan? How should direct marketing be used?	**Chapter 13:** Promotion I: Advertising and Sales Promotion **Chapter 14:** Promotion II: Social Media Marketing, Direct/Database Marketing, Personal Selling, and Public Relations
• How do we make our marketing plan happen?	**Chapter 3:** Strategic Market Planning
• Who is responsible for accomplishing each aspect of implementing the marketing plan?	**Chapter 4:** Market Research
• What is the timing for the elements of our marketing plan?	**Chapter 5:** Marketing Analytics: Welcome to the Era of Big Data!
• What budget do we need to accomplish our marketing objectives?	
• How do we measure the actual performance of our marketing plan and compare it to our planned performance and progress toward reaching our marketing objectives?	

Market Research

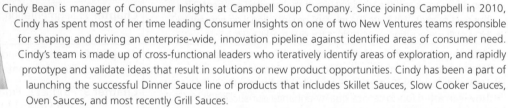

Meet Cindy Bean
▼ A Decision Maker at Campbell Soup Company

Cindy Bean is manager of Consumer Insights at Campbell Soup Company. Since joining Campbell in 2010, Cindy has spent most of her time leading Consumer Insights on one of two New Ventures teams responsible for shaping and driving an enterprise-wide, innovation pipeline against identified areas of consumer need. Cindy's team is made up of cross-functional leaders who iteratively identify areas of exploration, and rapidly prototype and validate ideas that result in solutions or new product opportunities. Cindy has been a part of launching the successful Dinner Sauce line of products that includes Skillet Sauces, Slow Cooker Sauces, Oven Sauces, and most recently Grill Sauces.

Prior to Campbell, Cindy worked in a variety of industries, managing a variety of businesses. Cindy worked as a Qualitative Research Consultant, achieving her moderating certification. She synthesized and interpreted sales and market share data, competitive intelligence, syndicated research, current industry conditions, and other relevant information to deliver the monthly state of the vision care business to Johnson & Johnson's Vistakon executives (J&J's Vision Care Division). She improved marketing effectiveness for Wyeth Pharmaceutical's (now Pfizer) Women's Health Care products by planning, designing, and managing a portfolio-wide consumer segmentation study and led the insights for the anti-depressant drug, Pristiq. She led research activities for McNeil Consumer Healthcare's Tylenol pediatrics, upper respiratory, and the Sleep franchise (Tylenol PM and Simply Sleep). And, she managed research functions within The Vanguard Group's Institutional business, including company 401(k) and 403(b) plans.

Cindy holds a bachelor's degree from Drexel University and an MBA from Pennsylvania State University.

Cindy's Info

What I do when I'm not working:
When I'm not spending time with my husband and two kids, I'm practicing yoga, reading a book, or trying out a new recipe.

First job out of school:
Financial Analyst at The Vanguard Group

A job-related mistake I wish I hadn't made:
Taking too long to launch a new product. Perfection does not exist, but it's easier to get closer to what the consumer wants by seeing them interact with it in real time and tweaking as we go.

Business book I'm reading now:
Thinking, Fast and Slow by Daniel Kahneman

My motto to live by:
Worry only about what you can control

What drives me:
Besides being a positive role model for my kids, I have a constant need to understand people to the point of knowing how to make their lives better.

My management style:
Highly collaborative and action-oriented

Don't do this when interviewing with me:
Tell vague stories about your past when I'm looking for clear examples of your actions

My pet peeve:
People not being accountable for their actions

Here's my problem...

A few years ago, Campbell set out on a mission to grow an otherwise stagnant soup business. Canned soup still is popular among Baby Boomers. However, younger consumers just aren't as interested. They turn to alternatives like microwaveable and mini meals (such as pizza and tacos). Campbell realized its core business is at risk if the company can't come up with products to entice the emerging group of millennial consumers who are between the ages of 18 and 34. These customers are 25 percent of the U.S. population, or approximately 80 million people. They spend a lot of money on food, but very little of it on soup.

To understand what makes millennials tick, Campbell went through a deep immersion. We scrutinized millennials' culture and habits to learn what kind of soups appeal to them. I lead a cross-functional innovation team that conducted dozens of extensive face-to-face in-depth interactions with young consumers, both one-on-one and in groups. We ate meals with young people in their homes, checked out their pantries, and tagged along with them on shopping trips to the supermarket.

After that immersion, the team listed all the pain points millennials associated with canned soup. For example, they told us they think these products are too "processed" and they taste bland, homogeneous, and unexciting. Another common complaint was the lack of healthy ingredients these consumers look for, such as quinoa and on-trend veggies like kale. We found this group includes "flexitarians," that is, they eat vegetarian for a few days and then eat meat on the weekends, special occasions, to satisfy a craving, etc. They tend to care about sustainability, local sourcing, and company practices.

As a result of these insights, we then created concepts and prototypes to test our potential solutions for the pain points we identified. We continued to put these ideas in front of a series of focus groups as we fine-tuned our solutions based on the feedback we got from actual millennials.

This process gave us some great insights about what we could do to boost our appeal to millennials. One no-brainer was to change the packaging from a can to a pouch; our respondents told us that a pouch communicates a "fresher ingredients" message. And, we knew the flavor profile of the soup had to be bolder than the varieties that Baby Boomers are used to. We ultimately aligned on the following as our guardrails to create this new product platform:

- Young adults looking for satisfying, easy meals for one
- Satisfies demanding tastes for a more flavorful life
- Always delivers of-the-moment flavors and packaging from a trusted brand

However, given Campbell's current portfolio of soups, we needed to position this millennial-focused platform differently from existing products we already sold under the Campbell's name. Specifically, most of the ideas we tested overlapped with Campbell's Slow Kettle brand. The Slow Kettle brand was created to bring Campbell's into the packaged premium soup category. Because consumers were becoming more interested in the rich, complex flavors they enjoy from restaurant soups, we saw an opportunity to bring that experience home. Our culinary team created Slow Kettle to bring a "prepared with care" feeling even though it still comes from the supermarket soup aisle. The flavors are familiar, they are hearty and filling, the quality is better than other canned soups, and the package is meant to convey homemade (it comes in a tub, like

Campbell's Slow Kettle and Go brands.

Tupperware). The brand skews toward higher-income millennials. Because the price point is at a premium for the category, $3.25, it represents a small but interesting opportunity for Campbell.

Clearly we would need to do more work to figure out the best way to create a new offering that would grab millennials' attention, make it clear that this is "not your father's soup," but at the same time avoid confusion with the Slow Kettle brand.

You Choose

Which **Option** would you choose, and **why**?
☐ Option 1   ☐ Option 2   ☐ Option 3

See what **option** Cindy chose in **MyLab Marketing™**

Cindy considered her Options 1·2·3

1

Option

Carve out a new space within the soup portfolio for this millennial-driven soup offering. We would have to demonstrate that the new offering serves a unique need for prepared soup that is not already available in Campbell's other brands. This strategy would give us an opportunity to build a new brand from scratch entirely based on millennials' needs. The brand could include soups but also possibly other food products such as mini-meals and hearty on-the-go snacks, positioned to meet the needs of the millennial. This new product line would be so distinct that we wouldn't have to worry about cannibalizing sales from other parts of our portfolio, especially Slow Kettle. However, it's expensive and risky to build a brand. We would have to commit to at least a three-year investment to build awareness and encourage trial. Because we do offer somewhat similar products like Slow Kettle, if we fail to create a really tight message to set apart the new brand we might shoot ourselves in the foot by injecting some confusion into the marketplace.

2

Option

Reposition an existing brand to be the face of the millennial portfolio. Our Slow Kettle Brand already has many elements that could meet the needs of these young consumers. With a few tweaks, we could probably transform it into the kind of product that would resonate with this target market. This approach would involve less investment than building an entirely new brand, and we already have the internal manufacturing capability to turn out these soups. On the other hand, we could commit the cardinal sin when marketing to millennials: offer a product they perceive as inauthentic. Because the Slow Kettle brand has already been on the market, these savvy young consumers might decide that a few tweaks to an existing offering doesn't really speak to them. Millennials run from products they view as "fake" faster than soup boils on a hot stove.

3

Option

Don't take the risk, and stick with our existing solutions. Investing in a unique millennial product might be just too costly and time-consuming, and it's possible that a new solution wouldn't deliver enough return on investment to justify our efforts. This conservative solution would allow us to focus our resources on maintaining our solid (though stagnant) base business. We could ramp up our advertising to appeal to the nostalgia of the familiar Campbell brand, because millennials sometimes do respond well to this kind of appeal. On the other hand, if this stay-the-course strategy backfires we risk becoming irrelevant to an entire generation of new consumers. In that event we would continue to experience a decline in our bottom line as an aging group of loyal consumers eventually died off. And, if competitors eventually enter the millennial space we might be forced to sit on the sidelines as they capture this valuable target. We know that most consumer packaged goods (CPG) companies are taking similar steps to satisfy this new generation. Many traditional brands are transitioning to natural colors, removing artificial sweeteners and high fructose corn syrup, and in some cases moving toward a non-GMO label to address consumers' concerns about genetically modified food. There's no doubt that changes are coming.

Now, put yourself in Cindy's shoes. Which option would you choose, and why?

4.1 Knowledge Is Power

OBJECTIVE

Explain the role of a marketing information system and a marketing decision support system in marketing decision making.

(pp. 118–123)

By now we know that successful market planning means that managers make informed decisions to guide the organization. But how do marketers actually make these choices? Specifically, how do they find out what they need to know to develop marketing objectives, select a target market, position (or reposition) their product, and develop product, price, promotion, and place strategies?

The answer is (drumroll ...): information. Information is the fuel that runs the marketing engine. There's a famous acronym in the marketing information systems field: GIGO, which stands for *Garbage In, Garbage Out*. To make good decisions, marketers must have information that is not "garbage"—rather, it must be accurate, up to date, and relevant. To understand these needs, marketers first must engage in various forms of research and data collection to identify them.

In this chapter, we will discuss some of the tools that marketers use to get that information. Then in Chapter 5, we'll drill down further on applying market research for decision making via marketing analytics. In the chapters that follow, we will look closely at how and why both consumers and organizations buy, and then how marketers sharpen their focus via target marketing.

Before we jump into the topic of market research, here's a question for you. A marketer who conducts research to learn more about his customers shouldn't encounter any ethical challenges, right? Well, maybe in a perfect world. In reality though, several aspects of market research are fraught with the *potential* for ethics breaches. **Market research ethics** refers to taking an ethical and aboveboard approach to conducting market research that does no harm to the participant in the process of conducting the research.

When the organization collects data, important issues of privacy and confidentiality come into play. Marketers must be clear when they work with research respondents about how they will use the data and give respondents full disclosure on their options for confidentiality and anonymity. For example, it is unethical to collect data under the guise of market research when your real intent is to develop a **database** of potential customers for direct marketing. A database is an organized collection (often electronic) of data that can be searched and queried to provide information about contacts, products, customers, inventory, and more. Firms that abuse the trust of respondents run a serious risk of damaging their reputation when word gets out that they are engaged in unethical research practices. This makes it difficult to attract participants in future research projects—and it "poisons the well" for other companies when consumers believe that they can't trust them.

market research ethics
Taking an ethical and aboveboard approach to conducting market research that does no harm to the participant in the process of conducting the research.

database
An organized collection (often electronic) of data that can be searched and queried to provide information about contacts, products, customers, inventory, and more.

The Marketing Information System

Many firms use a **marketing information system (MIS)** to collect information. The MIS is a process that first determines what information marketing managers need. Then it gathers, sorts, analyzes, stores, and distributes relevant and timely marketing information to users. As shown in 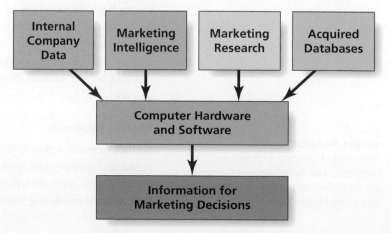 Figure 4.1, the MIS system includes three important components:

marketing information system (MIS)
A process that first determines what information marketing managers need and then gathers, sorts, analyzes, stores, and distributes relevant and timely marketing information to system users.

1. Four types of data (internal company data, market intelligence, market research, and acquired databases)
2. Computer hardware and software to analyze the data and to create reports
3. Output for marketing decision makers

Various sources "feed" the MIS with data, and then the system's software "digests" it. MIS analysts use the output to generate a series of regular reports for various decision makers.

Let's take a closer look at each of the four different data sources for the MIS.

Internal Company Data

The *internal company data system* uses information from within the organization to produce reports on the results of sales and marketing activities. Internal company data include a firm's sales records—information such as which customers buy which products in what quantities and at what intervals, which items are in stock and which are back-ordered because they are out of stock, when items were shipped to the customer, and which items have been returned because they are defective.

Figure 4.1 🔀 *Process* | The Marketing Information System

A firm's marketing information system (MIS) stores and analyzes data from a variety of sources and turns the data into information for useful marketing decision making.

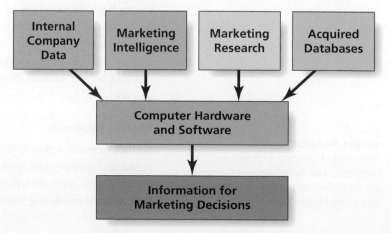

intranet
An internal corporate communication network that uses Internet technology to link company departments, employees, and databases.

Often, an MIS allows salespeople and sales managers in the field to access internal records through a company **intranet**. This is an internal corporate communications network that uses Internet technology to link company departments, employees, and databases. Intranets are secured so that only authorized employees have access. When salespeople and sales managers in the field can use an intranet to access their company's MIS, they can better serve their customers because they have immediate access to information on pricing, inventory levels, production schedules, shipping dates, and the customer's sales history. Related to the company intranet concept is the concept of *customer relationship management (CRM)*, which we'll develop more fully in Chapter 5.

Marketing managers at company headquarters also can see daily or weekly sales data by brand or product line from the internal company data system. They can view monthly sales reports to measure progress toward sales goals and market share objectives. For example, buyers and managers at Walmart's headquarters in Arkansas use up-to-the-minute sales information they obtain from store cash registers around the country so they can quickly detect problems with products, promotions, price competitiveness, and even the firm's distribution system.

Market Intelligence

market intelligence system
A method by which marketers get information about what's going on in the world that is relevant to their business.

As we saw in Chapter 2, to make good decisions, marketers need to have information about the marketing environment. Thus, a second important element of the MIS is the **market intelligence system**, a method by which marketers get information about what's going on in the world that is relevant to their business. Although the name *intelligence* may suggest cloak-and-dagger spy activities, in reality nearly all the information that companies need about their environment—including the competitive environment—is available by monitoring everyday sources: company websites, industry trade publications, or direct field observations of the competitive marketplace.

And because salespeople are the ones "in the trenches" every day, talking with customers, distributors, and prospective customers, they are a key to sourcing this valuable information. Retailers often hire "mystery shoppers" to visit their stores and those of their competitors posing as customers to see how people are treated. (Imagine being paid to shop!) Other information may come from speaking with organizational buyers about competing products, attending trade shows, or simply purchasing, using, and even **reverse engineering** competitors' products, which means physically deconstructing the product to determine how it's put together.

reverse engineering
The process of physically deconstructing a competitor's product to determine how it's put together.

Marketing managers may use market intelligence data to predict fluctuations in sales as a result of a variety of external environmental factors you read about in Chapter 2, including economic conditions, political issues, and events that heighten consumer awareness, or to forecast the future so that they will be on top of developing trends. Television networks have observed how consumers increasingly "binge-watch" shows through platforms such as Netflix, and as a result have begun to offer their shows in ways that appeal to the changing preferences and expectations of consumers when they watch. For instance, TBS premiered all of the episodes for its comedic series *Angie Tribeca* in a single 25-hour event that they labeled a "binge-a-thon." The strategy worked to attract tons of young viewers; one-third of the audience was totally new to TBS![1]

Market Research

market research
The process of collecting, analyzing, and interpreting data about customers, competitors, and the business environment in order to improve marketing effectiveness.

Market research refers to the process of collecting, analyzing, and interpreting data about customers, competitors, and the business environment to improve marketing effectiveness. (Note that the term *marketing research* is often used interchangeably with *market research*, but to be precise marketing research is broader in scope and often refers to the type of research that academics in marketing conduct about the field, whereas market research refers to the type of research that marketing professionals conduct about markets and consumers.) Although companies collect market intelligence data continuously to keep managers abreast of happenings in the marketplace, market research also is called for when managers need unique information to help them make specific decisions. Whether their business is selling cool fashion accessories to teens or industrial coolant to factories, firms succeed when they know what customers want, when they want it, where they want it—and what competing firms are doing about it. In other words, the better a firm is at obtaining valid market information, the more successful it will be. Therefore, virtually all companies rely on some form of market research, though the amount and type of research they conduct varies dramatically. In general, market research data available in an MIS come in two flavors: syndicated research reports and custom research reports.

Syndicated research is general information specialized firms collect on a regular basis and then sell to other firms. INC/The QScores Company, for instance, reports on consumers' perceptions of more than 1,800 celebrity performers for companies that want to feature a well-known person in their advertising. The company also rates consumer appeal of cartoon characters, sports stars, and even deceased celebrities.[2] Comedian Bill Cosby holds the record for the highest QScore ever recorded. Unfortunately, in light of recent criminal allegations and the related onslaught of negative media attention, the previously beloved comedian's QScore dropped into oblivion, possibly the greatest QScore change in history.[3] Other examples of syndicated research reports include Nielsen's TV ratings and Nielsen Audio's (formerly Arbitron's) radio ratings. Experian Simmons Market Research Bureau and GfK Mediamark Research & Intelligence are two syndicated research firms that combine information about consumers' buying behavior and their media usage with geographic and demographic characteristics.

> **syndicated research**
> Research by firms that collect data on a regular basis and sell the reports to multiple firms.

As valuable as it may be, syndicated research doesn't provide all the answers to marketing questions because the information it collects typically is broad but shallow. For example, it gives good insights about general trends, such as who is watching what TV shows or what brand of perfume is hot this year. In contrast, a firm conducts **custom research** to provide answers to specific questions. This kind of research is especially helpful for firms when they need to know more about *why* certain trends have surfaced.

> **custom research**
> Research conducted for a single firm to provide specific information its managers need.

Some firms maintain an in-house research department that conducts studies on its behalf. Many firms, however, hire outside research companies that specialize in designing and conducting projects based on the needs of the client. Hint: This is a great career path if you love solving puzzles and getting into the weeds about what makes consumers tick! These custom research reports are another kind of information an MIS includes. Marketers may use market research to identify opportunities for new products, to promote existing ones, or to provide data about the quality of their products, who uses them, and how.

Acquired Databases

A large amount of information that can be useful in marketing decision making is available in the form of external databases. Firms may acquire these databases from any number of sources. For example, some companies are willing to sell their customer database to noncompeting firms. Government databases, including the massive amounts of economic and demographic information the U.S. Census Bureau, Bureau of Labor Statistics, and other agencies collect, are available at little or no cost. State and local governments may make information such as automobile license data available for a fee.

In recent years, the use of databases for marketing purposes has come under increased government scrutiny because some consumer advocates are quite concerned

Sophisticated companies like Harrah's closely track what people do in venues like Las Vegas. If the data show that some of the company's clientele favor one property over another, one form of gaming over another, or even one type of show over another, those customers will receive promotional materials tailored to their specific preferences. Slot players are notified of slot tournaments, while fans of magic shows get a heads up when Lance Burton is scheduled to appear.

marketing decision support system (MDSS)
The data, analysis software, and interactive software that allow managers to conduct analyses and find the information they need.

about the potential invasion of privacy these may cause. Using the data to analyze overall consumer trends is one thing—using it for outbound direct mailings and unsolicited phone calls and e-mails has evoked a backlash resulting in a tidal wave of "do-not-call" lists and anti-spam laws. Maybe you have noticed that when you sign up for most anything online that requires your contact information, you receive an invitation to "opt out" of receiving promotional mailings from the company or from others who may acquire your contact information from the organization later. By law, if you decide to opt out, companies cannot use your information for marketing purposes.

We'll further develop the overall issue of database usage by marketers in the context of the popular phrase "Big Data" in Chapter 5. For now, just know that it's a good bet that every website or mobile link you search—and maybe even every tweet or Facebook message you post today—will wind up in a marketer's database.

Marketing Decision Support System

As we have seen, a firm's MIS generates regular reports for decision makers on what is going on in the internal and external environment. But sometimes these reports alone are inadequate. Different managers may want different information, and in some cases the problem they must address is too vague or unusual for the MIS process to easily answer. As a result, many firms beef up their MIS with a **marketing decision support system (MDSS).** Figure 4.2 shows the elements of an MDSS. An MDSS includes analysis and interactive software that allows marketing managers, even those who are not computer experts, to access MIS data and conduct their own analyses, often within the context of the company intranet.

A few years ago MasterCard developed an application of an MDSS it called the "Conversation Suite." This product offered marketers

Figure 4.2 *Process* | The MDSS

Although an MIS provides many reports managers need for decision making, it doesn't answer all their information needs. The marketing decision support system (MDSS) is an enhancement to the MIS that makes it easy for marketing managers to access the MIS system and find answers to their questions.

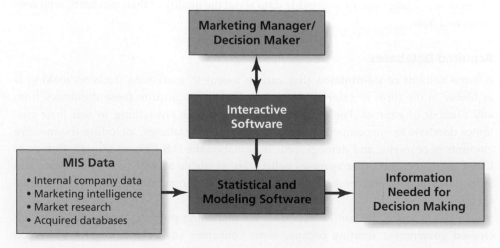

a single, intensive source of data and insights to further inform decisions about allocating a firm's massive global advertising budget. The Conversation Suite includes features such as a 40-foot display showcasing various marketing metrics and data visualizations grouped by market, as well as a number of touchscreen computers programmed to make digging into the various sources of information shown on the massive platform easy to perform.[4]

Typically, an MDSS includes sophisticated statistical and modeling software tools. Statistical software allows managers to examine complex relationships among factors in the marketplace. For example, a marketing manager who wants to know how consumers perceive his or her company's brand in relation to the competition's brand might use a sophisticated statistical technique called *multidimensional scaling* to create a "perceptual map," or a graphic presentation of the various brands in relationship to each other. You'll see an example of a perceptual map in Chapter 7.

Modeling software allows decision makers to examine possible or preconceived ideas about relationships in the data—to ask "what-if" questions. For example, media modeling software allows marketers to see what would happen if they made certain decisions about where to place their advertising. A manager may be able to use sales data and a model to find out how many consumers stay with his brand and how many switch, thus developing projections of market share over time. Table 4.1 gives some examples of the different marketing questions an MIS and an MDSS might answer.

For MasterCard, the Conversation Suite provides a readily accessible way for marketing managers to see and interact with high-value data and insights without requiring the technical skills that are typically necessary to perform these activities.

Digital Communications

Table 4.1 | Examples of Questions an MIS and an MDSS Might Answer

Questions an MIS Answers	Questions an MDSS Answers
What were our company sales of each product during the past month and the past year?	Has our decline in sales simply reflected changes in overall industry sales, or is there some portion of the decline that industry changes cannot explain?
What changes are happening in sales in our industry, and what are the demographic characteristics of consumers whose purchase patterns are changing the most?	Do we see the same trends in our different product categories? Are the changes in consumer trends similar among all our products? What are the demographic characteristics of consumers who seem to be the most and the least loyal?
What are the best media to reach a large proportion of heavy, medium, or light users of our product?	If we change our media schedule by adding or deleting certain media buys, will we reach fewer users of our product?

data
Raw, unorganized facts that need to be processed.

information
Interpreted data.

customer insights
The collection, deployment, and interpretation of information that allows a business to acquire, develop, and retain their customers.

4.2 Customer Insights and Marketing

OBJECTIVE
Understand the concept of customer insights and the role it plays in making good marketing decisions.

(p. 124)

It's getting easier all the time for organizations to collect huge amounts of data. **Data** are raw, unorganized facts that need to be processed. Analysts then process, organize, structure and present the data so that it is useful for decision making. This transformation creates **information**, which is interpreted data. But, there is a downside to knowing too much! All of these data can be overwhelming—and not very useful—if no one has any idea what they all mean. As some describe the ocean, "water, water everywhere and not a drop to drink!" can be repurposed "data, data everywhere and nothing insightful to find!"

Enter the customer insight specialists to save the day. At its essence, the idea of **customer insights** refers to the collection, deployment, and interpretation of information that allows a business to acquire, develop, and retain its customers. Like Cindy Bean at Campbell's, most companies today maintain a dedicated team of experts whose jobs are to sift through all the information available to support market planning decisions. This group does its best to understand how customers interact with the organization (including the nasty encounters they may have) and to guide planners when they think about future initiatives.

The job is more complicated than it sounds. Traditionally, most companies have operated in "silos," so that, for example, the people in new product development would have zero contact with anyone in customer service who actually had to deal with complaints about the items they designed. The insights manager is like an artist who has to work with a lot of different colors on a palette—the job is to integrate feedback from syndicated studies, marketing research, customer service, loyalty programs, and other sources to paint a more complete picture the organization can use. As such, this function in the organization usually plays a supporting role across the firm's strategic business units (SBUs).

For example, to gain greater insight into the preferences and characteristics of those consumers who made purchases within a specific product line of soups, a product line manager at Campbell's could reach out to Cindy Bean's consumer insights team for help. The team would then gather a wide array of data about the specific types of consumers who enjoy soup from that product line as well as other data such as frequency of purchases by consumer segment and what key factors influence consumption of specific types of soup by consumer segment. Cindy's team no doubt would deliver this information in an easy-to-understand format to highlight the most actionable insights. This analysis would enable the manager of the product line to determine how to better allocate resources to drive market performance of the products. Like Campbell's, many organizations are "catching the wave" by adding customer (consumer) insights departments—this growing trend in turn offers a lot of promising job opportunities for graduates who know how to fish for usable knowledge in the huge information ocean. More on using data to gain customer insights in Chapter 5.

4.3 Steps in the Market Research Process

OBJECTIVE
List and explain the steps and key elements of the market research process.

(pp. 124–142)

The collection and interpretation of information is hardly a one-shot deal that managers engage in "just out of curiosity." Ideally, market research is an ongoing process; a series of steps marketers take repeatedly to learn about the marketplace. Whether a company conducts the research itself or hires another firm to do it, the goal is the same: to help managers make informed marketing decisions.

Figure 4.3 provides a great road map of the steps in the research process. You can use it to track our discussion of each step.

Step 1: Define the Research Problem

The first step in the market research process is to clearly understand what information managers need. This step is called defining the research problem. You should note that the word *problem* here does not necessarily refer to "something that is wrong" but instead refers to the overall questions for which the firm needs answers. Defining the problem has three components:

1. *Specify the research objectives:* What questions will the research attempt to answer?

2. *Identify the consumer population of interest:* What are the characteristics of the consumer group(s) of interest?

3. *Place the problem in an environmental context:* What factors in the firm's internal and external business environment might influence the situation?

It's not as simple as it may seem to provide the right kind of information for each of these pieces of the problem. Suppose a luxury car manufacturer wants to find out why its sales fell off dramatically over the past year. The research objective could center on any number of possible questions: Is the firm's advertising failing to reach the right consumers? Is the right message being sent? Do the firm's cars have a particular feature and related benefit (or lack of one) that turns customers away? Does a competitor offer some features and benefits that have better captured customer imaginations? Is there a problem with the firm's reputation for providing quality service? Do consumers believe the price is right for the value they get? The particular objective researchers choose depends on a variety of factors, such as the feedback the firm gets from its customers, the information it receives from the marketplace, and sometimes even the intuition of the people who design the research.

Often the focus of a research question comes from marketplace feedback that identifies a possible problem. Volvo, long known for the safety records of its cars, had a tough time competing with luxury brands like Mercedes-Benz, BMW, Lexus, and Audi. How could Volvo improve its market share among luxury car buyers?

The *research objective* determines the consumer population the company will study. In the case of Volvo, the research could have focused on current owners to find out what they especially like about the car. Or it could have been directed at non-owners to understand their lifestyles, what they look for in a luxury automobile, or their beliefs about the Volvo brand that discourage them from buying the cars. Instead, the company chose to focus on why consumers didn't buy the competing brands. Managers figured it would be a good idea to identify the "pain points" shoppers experienced when they looked at rivals so that they could try to address these objections with their own marketing activities.

So what did Volvo find out? Its research showed that many car shoppers were too intimidated by the "ostentatious" image of Mercedes and BMW to consider actually buying one. Others felt that too many of their neighbors were driving a Lexus, and they wanted to make more of an individual statement. Volvo's vice president of marketing explained that Volvo owners' "interpretation of luxury is different but very real. They're more into life's experiences, and more into a Scandinavian simple design [of vehicles] versus a lot of clutter. They are very much luxury customers and love luxury products, but they don't feel a need to impress others." Based on the research findings, Volvo developed a

Figure 4.3 *Process* | Steps in the Market Research Process

The market research process includes a series of steps that begins with defining the problem or the information needed and ends with the finished research report for managers.

Define the Research Problem
- Specify the research objectives
- Identify the consumer population of interest
- Place the problem in an environmental context

Determine the Research Design
- Determine whether secondary data are available
- Determine whether primary data are required
  —Exploratory research
  —Descriptive research
  —Causal research

Choose the Method to Collect Primary Data
- Determine which survey methods are most appropriate
  —Mail questionnaires
  —Telephone interviews
  —Face-to-face interviews
  —Online questionnaires
- Determine which observational methods are most appropriate
  —Personal observation
  —Unobtrusive measures
  —Mechanical observation

Design the Sample
- Choose between probability sampling and nonprobability sampling

Collect the Data
- Translate questionnaires and responses if necessary
- Combine data from multiple sources (if available)

Analyze and Interpret the Data
- Tabulate and cross-tabulate the data
- Interpret or draw conclusions from the results

Prepare the Research Report
- In general, the research report includes the following:
  —An executive summary
  —A description of the research methods
  —A discussion of the results of the study
  —Limitations of the study
  —Conclusions and recommendations

new ad campaign, showing consumers that it was OK—and even desirable—to be different. The company even pokes fun at rival luxury brands. In one TV commercial, a sophisticated woman sits at a stoplight in her Mercedes-Benz SUV and checks out her makeup in the rear-view mirror. Another woman pulls up next to her in a Volvo XC60—but she's more down to earth. The Volvo driver looks into her own rear-view mirror. The difference is she makes a funny face to make her kids in the backseat crack up. The voice-over says, "Volvos aren't for everyone, and we kinda like it that way."[5]

Step 2: Determine the Research Design

research design
A plan that specifies what information marketers will collect and what type of study they will do.

Once we isolate specific problems, the second step of the research process is to decide on a "plan of attack." This plan is the **research design**, which specifies exactly what information marketers will collect and what type of study they will do. Research designs fall into two broad categories based on whether the analysts will use primary or secondary data (see Figure 4.4). All marketing problems do not call for the same research techniques, and marketers solve many problems most effectively with a combination of approaches.

Research with Secondary Data

The first question marketers must ask when they determine their research design is whether the information they require to make a decision already exists. For example, a coffee producer who needs to know the differences in coffee consumption among different demographic and geographic segments of the market may find that the information it needs is available from one or more studies already conducted by the National Coffee Association, the leading trade association of U.S. coffee companies and a major generator of industry research. Information that has been collected for some purpose other than the problem at hand is **secondary data**.

secondary data
Data that have been collected for some purpose other than the problem at hand.

Many marketers thrive on going out and collecting new, "fresh" data from consumers. In fact, getting new data seems to be part of the marketing DNA. However, if secondary data are available, it saves the firm time and money because it has already incurred the expense to design a study and collect the data. Sometimes the information that marketers need may be "hiding" right under the organization's nose in the form of company reports; previous company research studies; feedback received from customers, salespeople, or stores; or even in the memories of longtime employees (it's amazing how many times a manager commissions a study without knowing that someone else who was working on a different problem already submitted a similar report!).

Figure 4.4 🎯 *Process* | Market Research Designs

For some research problems, secondary data may provide the information needed. At other times, one of the primary data collection methods may be needed.

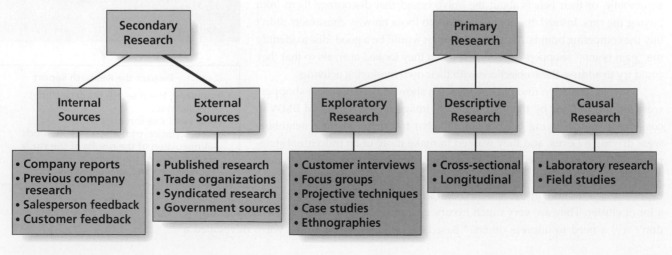

More typically, though, researchers need to look elsewhere for secondary data. They may obtain reports published in the popular and business press, studies that private research organizations or government agencies conduct, and published research on the state of the industry from trade organizations. For example, many companies subscribe to reports such as the *National Consumer Study*, a survey conducted by syndicated research firm Experian Simmons. The company publishes results that it then sells to marketers, advertising agencies, and publishers. Access to its data is even available in some college libraries. This database contains more than 60,000 data variables with usage behavior on all major media, over 500 product categories, and over 8,000 brands. Data from Experian Simmons can give a brand manager a profile of who uses a product, identify heavy users, or even provide data on what information sources a target market is likely to consult prior to purchase.[6] As examples, popular online sources of useful data for marketers include Opinion Research Corporation (ORC), the U.S. Census Bureau and Bureau of Labor Statistics, the American Marketing Association, and LexisNexus.

Research with Primary Data

Of course, secondary data are not always the answer. When a company needs to make a specific decision, marketers often collect **primary data**: information they gather directly from respondents to specifically address the question at hand. Primary data include demographic and psychological information about customers and prospective customers, customers' attitudes and opinions about products and competing products, as well as their awareness or knowledge about a product and their beliefs about the people who use those products. In the next few sections, we'll talk briefly about the various designs options to collect primary data.

primary data
Data from research conducted to help make a specific decision.

Exploratory Research

Marketers use **exploratory research** to come up with ideas for new strategies and opportunities or perhaps just to get a better handle on a problem they are currently experiencing with a product. Because the studies are usually small scale and less costly than other techniques, marketers may do this to test their hunches about what's going on without too much risk or expense.

exploratory research
A technique that marketers use to generate insights for future, more rigorous studies.

Exploratory studies often involve in-depth probing of a few consumers who fit the profile of the "typical" customer. Researchers may interview consumers, salespeople, or other employees about products, services, ads, or stores. They may simply "hang out" and watch what people do when they choose among competing brands in a store aisle. Or they may locate places where the consumers of interest tend to be and ask questions in these settings. For example, some researchers find that younger people often are too suspicious or skeptical in traditional research settings, so they may interview them while they wait in line to buy concert tickets or in clubs.[7]

We refer to most exploratory research as *qualitative*; that is, the results of the research project tend to be nonnumeric and instead might be detailed verbal or visual information about consumers' attitudes, feelings, and buying behaviors in the form of words rather than in numbers. For example, consumer packaged goods (CPG) company Reckitt Benckiser came to believe that for their Finish® dishwashing detergent the best way to compete for market share was to focus on the functional performance of the product. Through their ads, they typically would demonstrate how effective it was at cleaning dishware and glassware, in some cases comparing results to those of direct competitors' products such as P&G (who as a competitor in soap is no slouch). But then, Reckitt Benckiser brought in a market research firm to conduct a series of ethnographic studies (we will cover ethnography later in this section) focused on the observation of families in their homes actually using the product. The result of this research was the realization that a functionally oriented focus on the cleanness of dishware and glassware products resulting from the use of Finish® was masking a more compelling advertising message. This related to the dishwasher's role (and in turn the dishwashing detergent's role) as a central part of the home, one that spanned a wide range of social and family events. As a result of this insight, a whole new advertising campaign was launched that showcased all of the small and big life events in which dirty dishes are produced, closing with the message: "Everything in life creates dirty dishes. Love your dishwasher. Give it Finish®." The campaign met with positive responses from consumers, and even earned industry acclaim in the form of a silver trophy at the Cannes Lions Festival of Creativity.[8]

focus group
A product-oriented discussion among a small group of consumers led by a trained moderator.

A **focus group** is the technique that market researchers employ most often for exploratory research. Focus groups typically consist of five to nine consumers who have been recruited because they share certain characteristics (they all play golf at least twice a month, are women in their twenties, etc.). These people sit together to discuss a product, ad, or some other marketing topic a discussion leader introduces. Typically, the leader records (by videotape or audiotape) these group discussions, which may be held at special interviewing facilities that allow for observation by the client who watches from behind a one-way mirror. As a result of insights gathered from focus groups, MillerCoors decided to revise the packaging design for one of its brands to brighten it up and better appeal to consumers. The company heard from millennials in focus group sessions that the packaging on its Blue Moon Belgian White Ale was perceived as "dark," "lonely," and "mystical," which prompted the change in packaging to a more "perky" motif.[9]

market research online community (MROC)
A privately assembled group of people, usually by a market research firm or department, utilized to gain insight into customer sentiments and tendencies.

Today it's common to find focus groups in cyberspace as well as in person. Firms such as IKEA and Volvo use online focus group sites that resemble other social networking sites. IKEA used consumer consulting boards, also known as a **market research online community (MROC)** in five different countries to solicit feedback for an update of its catalog.[10] An MROC is a privately assembled group of people, usually by a market research firm or department, used to gain insight into customer sentiments and tendencies. The MROC-based research is generally thought of as exploratory in nature and as a qualitative method. MROC's are useful for many market research questions including product ideas, branding strategies, and packaging decisions.[11] In a different approach from Ikea's, Volvo launched a focus group via Twitter Chat to gather feedback about advertisements that the firm had developed. Volvo marketers said that the instant feedback they got from consumers helped strike the right balance in the ads. The rapid back-and-forth between the company and the online community allows for real-time data collection.[12]

case study
A comprehensive examination of a particular firm or organization.

The **case study** is a comprehensive examination of a particular firm or organization. In business-to-business market research in which the customers are other firms, for example, researchers may try to learn how one particular company makes its purchases. The goal is to identify the key decision makers, to learn what criteria they emphasize when they choose among suppliers, and perhaps to learn something about any conflicts and rivalries among these decision makers that may influence their choices.

ethnography
An approach to research based on observations of people in their own homes or communities.

Another qualitative approach is **ethnography**, which uses a technique that marketers borrow from anthropologists who go to "live with the natives" for months or even years. Some market researchers visit people's homes or participate in real-life consumer activities to get a handle on how they really use products. Imagine having a researcher follow you around while you shop and then, while you use the products you bought, see what kind of consumer you are. This is basically marketing's version of a reality show—though, we hope, the people they study are a bit more "realistic" than the ones on TV!

Descriptive Research

We've seen that marketers have many qualitative tools in their arsenal, including focus groups and observational techniques, to help them better define a problem or opportunity. These are usually modest studies of a small number of people, enough to get some indication of what is going on but not enough for the marketer to feel confident about generalizing what she observes to the rest of the population.

descriptive research
A tool that probes more systematically into the problem and bases its conclusions on large numbers of observations.

The next step in market research, then, often is to conduct **descriptive research**. This kind of research probes systematically into the marketing problem and bases its conclusions on a

Ripped from the Headlines

Ethical/Sustainable Decisions in the Real World

Should companies that offer products or services that may pose health risks be allowed to fund research that could suggest that those products share little or no responsibility for those health risks? Are there any potential conflicts of interest that could manifest in the form of unethical practices on the part of the funding company or the company conducting the research?

In the soft-drink industry, Coca-Cola disclosed early in 2016 that it spent more than $132 million on scientific research on soft drinks from 2010 to 2015.[13] Coke, like its industry competitors, has had to adapt to increasing societal concerns over the health effects of consuming large amounts of sugar and high fructose corn syrup, which are found in many of the firm's best-selling products. For many soft beverage companies this has meant diversifying into offerings that are lower in sugar and perceived to be healthier. Coke CEO Muhtar Kens says their disclosure of all research funding contributions was a step taken to help avoid any public feelings of "confusion and mistrust." The timing of the disclosure came soon after it was documented that a group called the Global Energy Balance Network had failed to initially disclose that its work was funded by Coca-Cola. The organization maintained as one of its positions that Americans held an illegitimate fixation on calorie consumption and were losing sight of the importance of exercise.[14]

Some have suggested that Coke's funding of anti-obesity research is an attempt to place greater focus on the role that a lack of exercise has on obesity to shift focus away from the role that sweetened soda beverages have on obesity. Absent solid proof of such accusations, it is worth considering the ethics of exerting influence on research groups funded by an organization with a conflict of interest that explicitly or implicitly makes it clear that the desired results would support a friendlier position for a potentially harmful product.

ETHICS CHECK:

As a marketing executive, is it OK to commission and fund research that supports the position that the product posed no health risk when you are aware that other independent research studies contradict that view?

☐ YES ☐ NO

---

large sample of participants. Results typically are expressed in quantitative terms—averages, percentages, or other statistics that result from a large set of measurements. In such *quantitative approaches* to research, the project can be as simple as counting the number of Listerine bottles sold in a month in different regions of the country or as complex as statistical analyses of responses to a survey mailed to thousands of consumers about their flavor preferences in mouthwash. In each case, marketers conduct the descriptive research to answer a specific question, in contrast to the "fishing expedition" they may undertake in exploratory research. However, don't downplay the usefulness of qualitative approaches—initial qualitative market research serves to greatly inform and shape subsequent quantitative approaches.

Market researchers who employ descriptive techniques most often use a **cross-sectional design**. This approach usually involves the systematic collection of responses to a consumer survey instrument, such as a *questionnaire*, from one or more samples of respondents at one point in time. They may collect the data on more than one occasion but usually not from the same pool of respondents.

In contrast to these one-shot studies, a **longitudinal design** tracks the responses of the same sample of respondents over time. Market researchers sometimes create consumer panels to get information; in this case, a sample of respondents that are representative of a larger market agrees to provide information about purchases on a weekly or monthly basis. Major consumer package goods firms like P&G, Unilever, Colgate Palmolive, and Johnson & Johnson, for example, recruit consumer advisory panels on a market-by-market basis to keep their fingers on the pulse of local shoppers. P&G maintains two key advisory panels: one for teens (Tremor) and one for moms (Vocalpoint). With more than 750,000 members weighing in on everything from package design to promotional material, P&G estimates that the loyalty and advocacy of these members have boosted P&G's sales by 10 to 30 percent.[15]

cross-sectional design
A type of descriptive technique that involves the systematic collection of quantitative information.

longitudinal design
A technique that tracks the responses of the same sample of respondents over time.

Causal Research

It's a fact that purchases of both diapers and beer peak between 5:00 P.M. and 7:00 P.M. Can we say that purchasing one of these products caused shoppers to purchase the other as well—and, if so, which caused which? Does taking care of a baby drive a parent to drink? Or is the answer simply that this happens to be the time when young fathers stop at the

Sales of diapers and beer are correlated, but does one cause the other?

store on their way home from work to pick up some brew and Pampers?[16]

And what about hemlines? Since the 1920s, George Taylor's "hemline theory" has posited that the length of women's hemlines reflects overall economic health. The theory originated at a time when women wore silk stockings—when the economy was strong, they shortened their hemlines to show off the stockings; when the economy took a dive, so did the hemlines, to cover up the fact that women couldn't afford the fancy stockings. Don't believe it? The same was true in 2009—when runway designs were "shockingly short"—the stock market rallied 15 percent for the year.[17]

The descriptive techniques we've mentioned do a good job of providing valuable information about what is happening in the marketplace, but by its nature, descriptive research can only *describe* a marketplace phenomenon—it cannot tell us *why* it occurs. Sometimes marketers need to know if something they've done has brought about some change in behavior. For example, does placing one product next to another in a store mean that people will buy more of each? We can't answer this question through simple observation or description.

causal research
A technique that attempts to understand cause-and-effect relationships.

Causal research attempts to identify cause-and-effect relationships. Marketers use causal research techniques when they want to know if a change in something (e.g., placing cases of beer next to a diaper display) is responsible for a change in something else (e.g., a big increase in diaper sales). They call the factors that might cause such a change *independent variables* and the outcomes *dependent variables.* The independent variable(s) cause some change in the dependent variable(s). In our example, then, the beer display is an independent variable, and sales data for the diapers are a dependent variable—that is, the study would investigate whether an increase in diaper sales "depends" on the proximity of beer. Researchers can gather data and test the causal relationship statistically.

experiments
A technique that tests predicted relationships among variables in a controlled environment.

This form of causal research often involves using experimental designs. **Experiments** attempt to establish causality by ruling out alternative explanations, and to maintain a high level of control, experiments may entail bringing subjects (participants) into a lab so that researchers can control precisely what they experience. For the diaper example, a group of men might be paid to come into a testing facility and enter a "virtual store" on a computer screen. Researchers would then ask the men to fill a grocery cart as they click through the virtual aisles. The experiment might vary the placement of the diapers—next to shelves of beer in one scenario and near paper goods in another scenario. The objective of the experiment is to find out which placement gets more of the guys to put diapers into their carts.

Step 3: Choose the Method to Collect Primary Data

When the researcher decides to work with primary data, the next step in the market research process is to figure out just how to collect it. We broadly describe primary data collection methods as either *survey* or *observation*. There are many ways to collect data, and marketers try new ones all the time. In fact, today, more and more marketers are turning to sophisticated brain scans to directly measure a consumers' brain for reactions to various advertisements or products. This **neuromarketing** approach uses technologies such

neuromarketing
A type of brain research that uses technologies such as functional magnetic resonance imaging (fMRI) to measure brain activity to better understand why consumers make the decisions they do.

as functional magnetic resonance imaging (fMRI) to measure brain activity to better understand why consumers make the decisions they do, and some firms have even invested in their own labs and in-house scientists to establish an ongoing neuromarketing research program.

Neuromarketing has gained increasing popularity among companies such as Facebook, Twitter, and Time Warner as a tool to understand consumer reactions to elements of various forms of marketing communication. Facebook, for example, learned in recent years that people take more away from ad information provided on a mobile phone compared to ad information provided on a TV. This insight came as a result of research the company commissioned from a firm called SalesBrain. SalesBrain's analysts attached a number of sensors to volunteers' bodies to measure such factors as perspiration, heart rate, eye movement, and brain activity as they watched ads on phones and televisions.[18] Because most of us don't have access to fMRI machines to conduct market research, in this section we'll focus more on explaining other methods to collect primary data.

In contrast to neuromarketing as a primary data collection approach, surveys provide a more "traditional" approach. Survey methods involve some kind of interview or other direct contact with respondents who answer questions. Questionnaires can be administered on the phone, in person, through the mail, or over the Internet. Table 4.2 summarizes the advantages and disadvantages of different survey methods to collect data.

Table 4.2 | Advantages and Disadvantages of Survey Data Collection Methods

Data Collection Method	Advantages	Disadvantages
Mail questionnaires	• Respondents feel anonymous • Low cost • Good for ongoing research	• It may take a long time for questionnaires to be returned • Low rate of response; many consumers may not return questionnaires • Inflexible questionnaire format • Length of questionnaire is limited by respondents' interest in the topic • Unclear whether respondents understand the questions • Unclear who is responding • No assurance that respondents are being honest
Telephone interviews	• Fast • High flexibility in questioning • Low cost • Limited interviewer follow-up • Limited questionnaire length	• Decreasing levels of respondent cooperation • High likelihood of respondent misunderstanding • Respondents cannot view materials • Cannot survey households without phones • Consumers screen calls with answering machines and caller ID • Do-not-call lists allow many research subjects to opt out of participation
Face-to-face interviews	• Flexibility of questioning • Can use long questionnaires • Can determine whether respondents have trouble understanding questions • Take a lot of time • Can use visuals or other materials	• High cost • Interviewer bias a problem
Online questionnaires	• Instantaneous data collection and analysis • Questioning very flexible • Low cost • No interviewer bias • No geographic restrictions • Can use visuals or other materials	• Unclear who is responding • No assurance that respondents are being honest • Limited questionnaire length • Unable to determine whether respondent understands the question • Self-selected samples

Sophisticated new technologies like virtual stores allow marketers to re-create shopping experiences on a respondent's computer screen or mobile device.

telemarketing
The use of the telephone to sell directly to consumers and business customers.

mall intercept
A study in which researchers recruit shoppers in malls or other public areas.

Questionnaires

Questionnaires differ in their degree of structure. With a totally *unstructured questionnaire*, the researcher loosely determines the items in advance. Questions may evolve from the respondent's answers to previous questions. At the other extreme, the researcher uses a *completely structured questionnaire*, asking every respondent the exact same questions, and each participant responds to the same set of fixed choices. You have probably experienced this kind of questionnaire, where you might have had to respond to a statement by saying if you "strongly agree," "somewhat agree," and so on. *Moderately structured questionnaires* ask each respondent the same questions, but the respondent is allowed to answer the questions in his or her own words.

Mail questionnaires are easy to administer and offer a high degree of anonymity to respondents. On the downside, because the questionnaire is printed and mailed, researchers have little flexibility in the types of questions they can ask and little control over the circumstances under which the respondent answers them. Mail questionnaires also take a long time to get back to the company and are likely to have a much lower response rate than other types of data collection methods because people tend to ignore them.

Telephone interviews usually consist of a brief phone conversation in which an interviewer reads a short list of questions to the respondent. There are several problems with using telephone interviews as a data collection method. The respondent also may not feel comfortable speaking directly to an interviewer, especially if the survey is about a sensitive subject.

Another problem with this method is that the growth of **telemarketing**, in which businesses sell directly to consumers over the phone, has eroded consumers' willingness to participate in phone surveys. In addition to aggravating people by barraging them with telephone sales messages (usually during dinnertime!), some unscrupulous telemarketers disguise their pitches as research. They contact consumers under the pretense of doing a study when, in fact, their real intent is to sell the respondent something or to solicit funds for some cause. This in turn prompts increasing numbers of people to use voice mail and caller ID to screen calls, further reducing the response rate. And, as we noted previously, state and federal *do-not-call lists* allow many would-be research subjects to opt out of participation in both legitimate market research and unscrupulous telemarketing.[19]

Using *face-to-face interviews*, a live interviewer asks questions of one respondent at a time. Although in "the old days" researchers often went door-to-door to ask questions, that's much less common today because of fears about security and because the large numbers of two-income families make it less likely to find people at home during the day. Typically, today's face-to-face interviews occur in a **mall intercept** study in which researchers recruit shoppers in malls or other public areas. You've probably seen this going on in your local mall, where a smiling person holding a clipboard stops shoppers to see if they are willing to answer a few questions. For example, have you seen pictures of super-hot models that show off cars at auto shows? Although you might think this strategy of using what the industry refers to as "booth babes" to get buyers' attention is pretty "old school" and probably obsolete, in fact car companies have doubled their use of what they euphemistically call "product specialists." Aspiring models or actors earn as much as $1000 per day to answer questions about new vehicles. The difference is that today they're as likely to be *asking* the questions; many companies now want the models to extract as much information as they can from visitors about their preferences. Do they like the car's color options? What about the style? Are they still worried about the economy? Many product specialists record each show goer's responses the minute he or she leaves the booth. Others write daily briefs or file a comprehensive report at the end of a show. These researchers offer more than just a pretty face.[20]

Mall intercepts offer good opportunities to get feedback about new package designs, styles, or even reactions to new foods or fragrances. However, because only certain groups of the population frequently shop at malls, a mall intercept study does not provide the researcher with a representative sample of the population (unless the population of interest is mall shoppers). In addition to being more expensive than mail or phone surveys, respondents may be reluctant to answer questions of a personal nature in a face-to-face context.

Auto show models today double as "product specialists."

Online questionnaires are growing in popularity, but the use of such questionnaires is not without concerns. Many researchers question the quality of responses they will receive—particularly because (as with mail and phone interviews) no one can be really sure who is typing in the responses on the computer. In addition, it's uncertain whether savvy online consumers are truly representative of the general population.[21] However, these concerns are rapidly evaporating as research firms devise new ways to verify identities; present surveys in novel formats, including the use of images, sound, and animation; and recruit more diverse respondents.[22]

Observational Methods

A second major primary data collection method is *observation*. This term refers to situations where the researcher simply records the consumer's behaviors.

When researchers use *personal observation*, they simply watch consumers in action to understand how they react to marketing activities. Although a laboratory allows researchers to exert control over what test subjects see and do, marketers don't always have the luxury of conducting this kind of "pure" research. But it is possible to conduct field studies in the real world, as long as the researchers still can control the independent variables. For example, a diaper company might choose two grocery stores that have similar customer bases in terms of age, income, and so on. With the cooperation of the grocery store's management, the company might place its diaper display next to the beer in one store and next to the paper goods in the other and then record diaper purchases men make over a two-week period. If a lot more guys buy diapers in the first store than in the second (and the company was sure that nothing else was different between the two stores, such as a dollar-off coupon for diapers being distributed in one store and not the other), the diaper manufacturer might conclude that the presence of beer in the background does indeed result in increased diaper sales.

When they suspect that subjects will probably alter their behavior if they know someone is watching them, researchers may use **unobtrusive measures** to record traces of physical evidence that remain after people have consumed something. For example, instead of asking a person to report on the alcohol products currently in her home, the researcher might go to the house and perform a "pantry check" by actually counting the bottles in her liquor cabinet. Another option is to sift through garbage to search for clues about each family's consumption habits. The "garbologists" can tell, for example, which soft drink is accompanied

unobtrusive measures
Measuring traces of physical evidence that remain after some action has been taken.

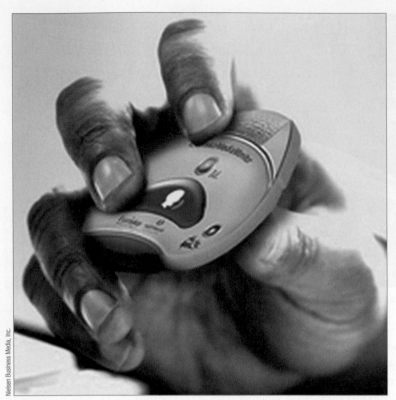

Nielsen's "People Meter" monitors what a large sample of American consumers watch.

mechanical observation
A method of primary data collection that relies on machines to capture human behavior in a form that allows for future analysis and interpretation.

eye tracking technology
A type of mechanical observation technology that uses sensors and sophisticated software to track the position and movement of an individual's eyes to gain context-specific insights into how individuals interact with and respond to different visual elements and stimuli.

by what kind of food. Because people in these studies don't know that researchers are looking through products they've discarded, the information is totally objective—although a bit smelly!

Mechanical observation is a method of primary data collection that relies on nonhuman devices to record behavior. For example, one of the classic applications of mechanical observation is the Nielsen Company's famous use of "people meters"—boxes the company attaches to the TV sets of selected viewers to record patterns of TV watching. The data that Nielsen obtains from these devices indicate who is watching which shows. These "television ratings" help network clients determine how much to charge advertisers for commercials and which shows to cancel or renew. Nielsen also measures user activity on digital media. The research company's U.S. panel alone is comprised of more than 200,000 Internet users across 30,000 sites covering all the potential devices that a consumer would use to access digital media.[23] This allows Nielsen to give clients a more updated understanding of how viewers interact with their favorite TV shows. For example, it tracks the number of TV-related tweets people post and provides demographic information including age and gender of individuals who post TV-related tweets.[24]

Similarly, Nielsen Audio (formerly Arbitron) deploys thousands of "portable people meters" (PPMs).[25] PPMs resemble pagers and automatically record the wearer's exposure to any media that has inserted an inaudible code into its promotion such as TV ads or shelf displays. Thus, when the consumer is exposed to a broadcast commercial, cinema ad, or other form of commercial, the PPM registers, records, and time-stamps the signal. Portability ensures that all exposures register; this eliminates obtrusive people meters and written diaries that participants often forget to fill out.[26]

Another form of mechanical observation that some firms use is **eye tracking technology**. This method relies on portable or stationary equipment to track the movement of a participant's eyes and can provide greater insight into what people look and for how long they look at it. For marketers this provides the opportunity to better understand how consumers engage with various forms of marketing of a visual nature. Examples of its use include tracking the viewing of print, television, and mobile ads, and product placement in televised sporting events. Improvements in the portable or wearable version of eye tracking technology offer greater opportunities for data to be gathered outside of lab settings—in the "real world" —thus offering potential for more applicable insights for marketers.[27]

Some retailers use sophisticated technology to observe where shoppers travel in their stores so they can identify places that attract a lot of traffic and those that are dead spots. In some cases these "heat maps" use the signals from shoppers' mobile phones to record their movements through the aisles.

Online Research

Many companies find that an online approach is a superior way to collect data—it's fast, it's relatively cheap, and it lends itself well to forms of

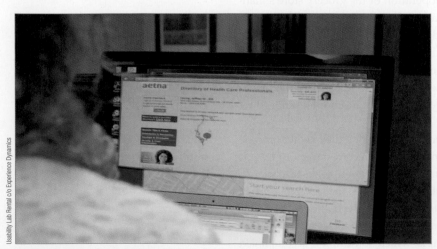

Sophisticated eye tracking technology gives marketers a close-up perspective on what people look at.

research from simple questionnaires to online focus groups. In fact, some large companies like P&G now collect a large portion of their consumer intelligence online. Developments in online research are happening quickly, so let's take some time now to see where things are headed.

There are two major types of online research. One type is information that organizations gather when they track consumers while they surf the web. The second type is information they gather more selectively through questionnaires on websites, including of course social media sites, through e-mail, or from focus groups that virtual moderators conduct in chat rooms. Most social media platforms, such as Twitter or Facebook, offer numerous ways to analyze trends and conduct market research. By simply searching the latest posts and popular terms—or, as marketers refer to it, "scraping the web"—you can gain insight into emerging trends and see what customers are talking about in real time. One example of this approach is conducting hashtag searches on Twitter. By setting up a few searches with hashtags related to your brand, industry, or product, you can receive instant notifications when customers, clients, or competitors use key terms.[28]

For marketers who want to collect data via surveys on the web, a platform such as Amazon Mechanical Turk (MTurk) is an effective medium. MTurk provides a place on the web where market researchers can post requests for one-off tasks that are typically not time intensive, but do require human intelligence to be completed effectively.[29] Using MTurk or a similar platform for collecting market research data could be potentially quicker and less costly than other methods used to gather large amount of responses because of the audience of workers available to the firm and the relatively lower prices for the performance of required tasks (in some cases, participants engage in quick tasks in return for what amounts to pocket change for completing each assignment). For market research that requires the inclusion of a specific group of respondents, such a platform may not be well suited and instead seeking out focused panel data may be more appropriate.

You may like to share selfies with friends, but it's possible companies are diving into Instagram and Pinterest to take a close look at your latest gems as well. Some firms use special software to scan photos to identify logos, facial expressions, and contexts so that they can learn more about how consumers use a client's brands in daily life. There are huge numbers of photos to look at; Instagram alone has about 20 billion photos to share with another 60 million being added every day. The practice is so new that privacy concerns are just starting to bubble up. For now, think twice about what you post.[30]

Across all of its platforms and forms, the Internet offers unprecedented ability to track consumers as they search for information on Google, Bing, Ask, and other search engines. We've become so accustomed to just looking up stuff online that *google* has become a verb (as has *friend*). As consumers enter search terms like "lowest prices on J Brand jeans" or "home theaters," these queries become small drops in the ocean of data available to marketers that engage in online behavioral tracking. How do they know what we're looking at online? Beware the Cookie Monster! **Cookies** are text files that a website sponsor inserts into a user's hard drive when the user connects with the site. Cookies remember details of a visit to a website and track which pages the user visits. Some sites request or require that visitors "register" on the site by answering questions about themselves and their likes and dislikes. In such cases, cookies also allow the site to access these details about the customer.

cookies
Text files inserted by a website sponsor into a web surfer's hard drive that allows the site to track the surfer's moves.

The technology associated with cookies allows websites to customize services, such as when Amazon recommends new books to users on the basis of what books they have ordered in the past. Consider this one: It is late evening, and you should be studying, but you just can't make yourself do it. So you grab your tablet and sign in to Netflix. And like every other time you sign in, Netflix offers up a bunch of movies and TV shows to tempt you away from the textbooks. But how does Netflix know what you want to see—sometimes they seem to anticipate your tastes better than your friends can!

predictive technology
Analysis techniques that use shopping patterns of large numbers of people to determine which products are likely to be purchased if others are.

No, there isn't someone sitting at their office whose only job is to follow you around online to guess what you'll want to see next. These surprising connections are the results of **predictive technology**, which uses shopping patterns of large numbers of people to determine which products are likely to be purchased if others are—except in this case what you're "shopping" for is movies to watch. To figure out what movies or TV shows you are likely to enjoy, Netflix trained teams of people to watch thousands of movies and tag them according to attributes such as "goriness" or "plot conclusiveness." Netflix then combines those attributes with the viewing habits of millions of users.[31] And voilà—Netflix knows just what to serve up to satisfy your viewing fix.

You can block cookies or curb them by changing settings on your computer, although this makes life difficult if you are trying to log on to many sites, such as online newspapers or travel agencies that require this information to admit you. The information generated from tracking consumers' online journeys has become big business, and in massive quantities it has become popularly known as "Big Data," a topic we will discuss in more detail in Chapter 5. To date, the Federal Trade Commission has relied primarily on firms and industries to develop and maintain its own standards instead of developing its own extensive privacy regulations, but many would like to see that situation changed, and much discussion is afoot at all levels of government regarding online privacy rights. Proponents advocate the following guiding principles:

- Information about a consumer belongs to the consumer.
- Consumers should be made aware of information collection.
- Consumers should know how information about them will be used.
- Consumers should be able to refuse to allow information collection.
- Information about a consumer should never be sold or given to another party without the permission of the consumer.

No data collection method is perfect, and online research is no exception—though many of the criticisms of online techniques also apply to offline techniques. One potential problem is the representativeness of the respondents. Many segments of the consumer population, mainly the economically disadvantaged and elderly, do not have the same level of access to the Internet as other groups.

In addition, in many studies (just as with mail surveys or mall intercepts), there is a *self-selection bias* in the sample. That is, because respondents have agreed to receive invitations to take part in online studies, by definition they tend to be the people who like to participate in surveys. As with other kinds of research, such as live focus groups or panel members, it's not unusual to encounter "professional respondents"—people who just enjoy taking part in studies (and getting paid for it). Quality online research specialists such as Harris Interactive, SSI—Survey Sampling International—and Toluna address this problem by monitoring their participants and regulating how often they are allowed to participate in different studies over a period of time. However, unfortunately, with the proliferation of online data collection, many new and unproven data providers continue to come into the industry—therefore, in terms of online research, the venerable phrase *caveat emptor* (let the buyer beware) rules.

There are other disadvantages of online research. Hackers can actually try to influence research results. Competitors can learn about a firm's marketing plans, products, advertising, and other proprietary elements when they intercept information from these studies (though this can occur in offline studies just as easily). Because cheating has become so rampant, some companies today use fraud-busting software that creates a digital fingerprint of each computer involved in a survey to identify respondents who fake responses or professionals who game the industry by doing as many surveys as possible.[32]

Metrics Moment

More and more, marketing is responsible for the e-commerce aspect of firms' web strategies. **Bounce rate** is a marketing metric for analyzing website traffic. It represents the percentage of visitors who enter the site (typically at the home page) and "bounce" (leave the site) rather than continuing to view other pages on the site. It is a straightforward metric to understand and is based on the following formula:

$$\text{Bounce rate} = \frac{\text{Total number of visitors viewing one page only}}{\text{Total entries to the web page}}$$

A site's bounce rate is easy to track with tools like Google Analytics. They can show the bounce rates on different pages of a website, how the user came to the site (organic search, paid search, banner ad, etc.), how the bounce rate has changed over time, and other data so that the marketer can really dig into where the leak is occurring.

Marketers use bounce rates to determine whether an entry page effectively generates visitors' interest. A bounce rate, simply put, is the measure of how many visitors come to a page on a website and leave without viewing any other pages. An entry page with a low bounce rate means that this first page encourages visitors to view still more pages and continue deeper into the website. High bounce rates, on the other hand, typically indicate that whatever visitors encounter on that first "hit" isn't interesting enough to make them want to check out more.[33]

Apply the Metrics

1. A rule of thumb for website effectiveness is that great websites should fulfill three basic criteria: (1) the site should be attractive, (2) the site should be easy to navigate and get where you want to go, and (3) the site should have up-to-date information (no old stuff). When you bounce off of a website, does it tend to be for one or more of these reasons? Are any of them more important than others to you?

2. Consider the bounce rate metric we describe. Like any marketing metric, decisions should not be made based on the bounce rate alone. What other considerations should the marketer use to evaluate the effectiveness of a website?

Data Quality: Garbage In, Garbage Out

We've seen that a firm can collect data in many ways, including focus groups, ethnographic approaches, observational studies, and controlled experiments. But how much faith should marketers place in what they find out from the research?

All too often, marketers who commission a study assume that because the researchers give them a massive report full of impressive-looking numbers and tables, they must be looking at the "truth." Unfortunately, there are times when this "truth" is really just one person's interpretation of the facts. At other times, the data researchers use to generate recommendations are flawed. Previously in the chapter we brought up GIGO: "garbage in, garbage out."[34] That is, your conclusions can be only as good as the *quality* of the information you use to make them. Typically, three factors influence the quality of research results—validity, reliability, and representativeness.

Validity is the extent to which the research actually measures what it was intended to measure. Validity can be further broken down into internal validity and external validity. **Internal validity** relates to the extent that the research design was set up in such a manner that what was intended to be measured was accurately measured and not obscured (for instance, by the accidental inclusion of any factors not intended to be included in the study). This is typically accomplished in a highly controlled setting (such as a laboratory) where it is easier to avoid the introduction of extraneous factors that could muddy the results obtained. **External validity** relates to the extent that research results are practically applicable to the relevant target market (and not just the specific study participants who were intended to represent that target market). Another way of thinking about this is whether the research findings would hold up when leveraged out in the real world.

Validity was part of the problem underlying the famous New Coke fiasco in the 1980s, in which Coca-Cola underestimated people's loyalty to its flagship soft drink after it replaced "Old Coke" with a new, sweeter formula. This blunder was so huge that we still talk about it today even though it happened before your humble authors were even born (well, not quite …)! In a blind taste test, the company assumed testers' preferences for one

bounce rate
A marketing metric for analyzing website traffic. It represents the percentage of visitors who enter the site (typically at the home page) and "bounce" (leave the site) rather than continuing to view additional pages on the site.

validity
The extent to which research actually measures what it was intended to measure.

internal validity
The extent to which the results of a research study accurately measure what the study intended to measure by ensuring proper research design, including efforts to ensure that any potentially confounding factors were not included or introduced at any point during the execution of the research study.

external validity
The extent to which the results of a research study can be generalized to the population its sample was intended to represent, providing a higher level of confidence that the findings can be applied outside of the setting where the research was conducted.

anonymous cola over another was a valid measure of consumers' preferences for a cola brand. Arguably, we can also say that the use of a sip test is flawed (and lacking degrees of external validity) in that it is set up so that consumers try the colas in small quantities, as opposed to the larger quantities more typically experienced by consumers when enjoying a can, a bottle, or a glass of cola in a more leisurely setting.[35] Coca-Cola found out the hard way that measuring taste only is not the same as measuring people's deep allegiances to their favorite soft drinks. After all, Coke is a brand that elicits strong consumer loyalty and is nothing short of a cultural icon. Tampering with the flavors was like assaulting mom and apple pie. Sales eventually recovered after the company brought back the old version as "Coca-Cola Classic."[36]

reliability
The extent to which research measurement techniques are free of errors.

Reliability is the extent to which the research measurement techniques are free of errors. Sometimes, for example, the way in which a researcher asks a question creates error by biasing people's responses. Imagine that an attractive female interviewer who works for Trojans condoms stops male college students on campus and asks them if they use contraceptive products. Do you think their answers might change if they were asked the same questions on an anonymous survey they received in the mail? Most likely, their answers would be different because people are reluctant to disclose what they actually do when their responses are not anonymous. Researchers try to maximize reliability by thinking of several different ways to ask the same questions, by asking these questions on several occasions, or by using several analysts to interpret the responses. Thus, they can compare responses and look for consistency and stability.

Reliability is a problem when the researchers can't be sure that the consumer population they're studying even understands the questions. For example, kids are difficult subjects for market researchers because they tend to be undependable reporters of their own behavior, they have poor recall, and they often do not understand abstract questions. In many cases, the children cannot explain why they prefer one item over another (or they're not willing to share these secrets with grown-ups).[37] For these reasons, researchers have to be especially creative when they design studies involving younger consumers. 📷 Figure 4.5 shows part of a completion test that a set of researchers used to measure children's preferences for TV programming in Japan.

representativeness
The extent to which consumers in a study are similar to a larger group in which the organization has an interest.

sampling
The process of selecting respondents for a study.

Representativeness is the extent to which consumers in the study are similar to a larger group in which the organization has an interest. This criterion underscores the importance of **sampling**: the process of selecting respondents for a study. The issue then becomes how large the sample should be and how to choose these people. We'll talk more about sampling in the next section.

Figure 4.5 📷 *Snapshot* | Completion Test

It can be especially difficult to get accurate information from children. Researchers often use visuals, such as this Japanese completion test, to encourage children to express their feelings. The test asked boys to write in the empty balloon what they think the boy in the drawing will answer when the girl asks, "What program do you want to watch next?"

Step 4: Design the Sample

Once the researcher defines the problem, decides on a research design, and determines how to collect the data, the next step is to decide from whom to obtain the needed information. Of course, he or she *could* collect data from every single customer or prospective customer, but this would be extremely expensive and time consuming if possible at all (this is what the U.S. Census spends millions of dollars to do every 10 years). Not everyone has the resources of the U.S. government to poll *everyone* in their market. So they typically collect most of their data from a small proportion, or *sample*, of the population of interest. Based on the answers from this sample, researchers generalize to the larger population. Whether such inferences are accurate or inaccurate depends on the type and quality of the study sample. There are two main types of samples: probability and nonprobability samples.

Probability Sampling

In a **probability sample**, each member of the population has some known chance of being included. Using a probability sample ensures that the sample represents the population and that inferences we make about the population from what members of the sample say or do are justified. For example, if a larger percentage of males than females in a probability sample say they prefer action movies to "chick flicks," one can infer with confidence that a larger percentage of males than females in the general population also would rather see a character get sliced and diced than kissed and dissed (okay, we wouldn't really use these descriptions in a study, but you get the idea).

The most basic type of probability sample is a *simple random sample*, in which every member of a population has a known and equal chance of being included in the study. For example, if we simply take the names of all 40 students in a class, put them in a hat, and draw one out, each member of the class has a 1 in 40 chance of being included in the sample. In most studies, the population from which the sample will be drawn is too large for a hat, so marketers use a computer program to generate a random sample from a list of members.

Sometimes researchers use a *systematic sampling procedure* to select members of a population; they select the *n*th member of a population after a random start. For example, if we want a sample of 10 members of your class, we might begin with the second person on the roll and select every fourth name after that—the second, sixth, tenth, fourteenth, and so on. Researchers know that studies that use systematic samples are just as accurate as those that use simple random samples. But unless a list of members of the population of interest is already in a computer data file, it's a lot simpler just to create a simple random sample.

Yet another type of probability sample is a *stratified sample*, in which a researcher divides the population into segments that relate to the study's topic. For example, imagine you want to study what movies most theatergoers like. You have learned from previous studies that men and women in the population differ in their attitudes toward different types of movies—men like action flicks, and women like romantic comedies. To create a stratified sample, you would first divide the population into male and female segments. Then you would randomly select respondents from each of the two segments in proportion to their percentage of the population. In this way, you have created a sample that is proportionate to the population on a characteristic that you know will make a difference in the study results.

Nonprobability Sampling

Sometimes researchers do not believe that the time and effort required to develop a probability sample is justified, perhaps because they need an answer quickly or just want to get a general sense of how people feel about a topic. They may choose a **nonprobability sample**, which entails the use of personal judgment to select respondents—in some cases, they just ask anyone they can find. With a nonprobability sample, some members of the population have no chance at all of being included. Thus, there is no way to ensure that the sample is representative of the population. Results from nonprobability studies can be generally suggestive of what is going on in the real world but are not necessarily definitive.

A **convenience sample** is a nonprobability sample composed of individuals who just happen to be available when and where the data are being collected. For example, if you were to simply stand in front of the student union and ask students who walk by to complete your questionnaire, the "guinea pigs" you get to agree to do it would be a convenience sample.

Finally, researchers may also use a *quota sample*, which includes the same proportion of individuals with certain characteristics as in the population. For example, if you are

---

probability sample
A sample in which each member of the population has some known chance of being included.

nonprobability sample
A sample in which personal judgment is used to select respondents.

convenience sample
A nonprobability sample composed of individuals who just happen to be available when and where the data are being collected.

studying attitudes of students in your university, you might just go on campus and find freshmen, sophomores, juniors, and seniors in proportion to the number of members of each class in the university. The quota sample is much like the stratified sample except that, with a quota sample, the researcher uses his or her individual judgment to select respondents.

Step 5: Collect the Data

At this point, the researcher has determined the nature of the problem to address. She chose a research design that will specify how to investigate the problem and what kinds of information (data) she will need. The researcher has also selected the data collection and sampling methods. Once she's made these decisions, the next task is to collect the data.

We noted previously that the quality of your conclusions is only as good as the data you use. The same logic applies to the people who collect the data: *The quality of research results is only as good as the poorest interviewer in the study*. Careless interviewers may not read questions exactly as written, or they may not record respondent answers correctly. So marketers must train and supervise interviewers to make sure they follow the research procedures exactly as outlined. In the next section, we'll talk about some of the problems in gathering data and some solutions.

Challenges to Gathering Data in Foreign Countries

Conducting market research around the world is big business for U.S. firms— for the top 50 companies (as measured by revenue), more than half of their income comes from work done outside the U.S.[38] However, as we saw in Chapter 2 market conditions and consumer preferences vary worldwide, and there are major differences in the sophistication of market research operations and the amount of data available to global marketers. In Mexico, for instance, because there are still large areas where native tribes speak languages other than Spanish, researchers may end up bypassing these groups in surveys. In Egypt, where the government must sign off on any survey, the approval process can take months or years. And in many developing countries, infrastructure is an impediment to executing phone or mail surveys, and lack of online connectivity blocks web-based research.

For these and other reasons, choosing an appropriate data collection method is difficult. In some countries, many people may not have phones, or low literacy rates may interfere with mail surveys. Understanding *local customs* can be a challenge, and *cultural differences* also affect responses to survey items. Both Danish and British consumers, for example, agree that it is important to eat breakfast. However, the Danish sample may be thinking of fruit and yogurt, whereas the British sample has toast and tea in mind. Sometimes marketers can overcome these problems by involving local researchers in decisions about the research design.

Another problem with conducting market research in global markets is *language*. Sometimes translations just don't come out right. In some cases, entire subcultures within a country might be excluded from the research sample. In fact, this issue is becoming more and more prevalent inside the U.S. as non-English speakers increase as a percentage of the population.

back-translation
The process of translating material to a foreign language and then back to the original language.

To overcome language difficulties, researchers use a process of **back-translation**, which requires two steps. First, a native speaker translates the questionnaire into the language of the targeted respondents. Then someone fluent in the second language translates this new version back into the original language to ensure that the correct meanings survive the process. Even with precautions such as these, researchers must interpret the data they obtain from other cultures with care.

Step 6: Analyze and Interpret the Data

Once market researchers collect the data, what's next? It's like a spin on the old "if a tree falls in the woods" question: "If results exist, but there's no one to interpret them, do they have a meaning?" Let's leave the philosophers out of it and just say that marketers would answer "no." Data need interpretation if the results are going to be useful.

To understand the important role of data analysis, let's take a look at a hypothetical research example. Say a company that markets frozen foods wishes to better understand consumers' preferences for varying levels of fat content in their diets. They conducted a descriptive research study where they collected primary data via telephone interviews. Because they know that dietary preferences relate to gender (among other aspects), they used a stratified sample that includes 175 males and 175 females.

Typically, marketers first tabulate the data as Table 4.3 shows—that is, they arrange the data in a table or other summary form so they can get a broad picture of the overall responses. The data in Table 4.3 indicate that 43 percent of the sample prefers a low-fat meal. In addition, there may be a desire to cross classify or cross tabulate the answers to questions by other variables. *Cross tabulation* means that we examine the data that we break down into *subgroups*, in this case males and females separately, to see how results vary between categories. The cross-tabulation in Table 4.3 reveals that 59 percent of females versus only 27 percent of males prefer a meal with low-fat content. Researchers may wish to apply additional statistical tests that you may learn about in subsequent courses (now there's something to look forward to!).

Based on the tabulation and cross tabulations, the researcher interprets the results and makes recommendations. For example, the study results in Table 4.3 may lead to the conclusion that females are more likely than males to be concerned about a low-fat diet. Based on these data, the researcher might then recommend that the firm target females when it introduces a new line of low-fat foods.

Step 7: Prepare the Research Report

The final step in the market research process is to prepare a report of the research results. In general, a research report must clearly and concisely tell the readers—top management, clients, creative departments, and many others—what they need to know in a way that they

Table 4.3 | Examples of Data Tabulation and Cross-Tabulation Tables

Fat Content Preference (number and percentages of responses)

Do you prefer a meal with high-fat content, medium-fat content, or low-fat content?

Questionnaire Response	Number of Responses	Percentage of Responses
High fat	21	6
Medium fat	179	51
Low fat	150	43
Total	350	100

Fat Content Preference by Gender (number and percentages of responses)

Do you prefer a meal with high-fat content, medium-fat content, or low-fat content?

Questionnaire Response	Number of Females	Percentage of Females	Number of Males	Percentage of Males	Total Number	Total Percentage
High fat	4	2	17	10	21	6
Medium fat	68	39	111	64	179	51
Low fat	103	59	47	27	150	43
Total	175	100	175	100	350	100

can easily understand and that won't bore you to tears (just like a good textbook should keep you engaged). A typical research report includes the following sections:

- An executive summary of the report that covers the high points of the total report
- An understandable description of the research methods
- A complete discussion of the results of the study, including the tabulations, cross tabulations, and additional statistical analyses
- Limitations of the study (no study is perfect)
- Conclusions drawn from the results and the recommendations for managerial action based on the results

---

MyLab Marketing™

Go to **mymktlab.com** to complete the problems marked with this icon as well as additional Marketing Metrics questions only available in MyLab Marketing.

Objective Summary ➡ Key Terms ➡ Apply

CHAPTER 4
Study Map

4.1 Objective Summary (pp. 118–123)

Explain the role of a marketing information system and a marketing decision support system in marketing decision making.

A marketing information system (MIS) is composed of internal data, market intelligence, market research data, acquired databases, and computer hardware and software. Firms use an MIS to gather, sort, analyze, store, and distribute information needed by managers for marketing decision making. The marketing decision support system (MDSS) allows managers to use analysis software and interactive software to access MIS data and to conduct analyses and find the information they need about their products and services.

Key Terms

market research ethics, p. 119

database, p. 119

marketing information system (MIS), p. 119

intranet, p. 120

market intelligence system, p. 120

reverse engineering, p. 120

market research, p. 120

syndicated research, p. 121

custom research, p. 121

marketing decision support system (MDSS), p. 122

4.2 Objective Summary (p. 124)

Understand the concept of customer insights and the role it plays in making good marketing decisions.

Organizations today are collecting massive amounts of data, but they need customer insight specialists to sift through that data in order to make it useful. The concept of customer insights refers to the collection, deployment, and interpretation of information that allows a business to acquire, develop, and retain its customers. This information supports market planning decisions and guides planners about future business initiatives.

Key Terms

data, p. 124

information, p. 124

customer insights, p. 124

4.3 Objective Summary (pp. 124–142)

List and explain the steps and key elements of the market research process.

The research process begins by defining the problem and determining the research design or type of study. Next, researchers choose the data collection method—that is, whether there are secondary data available or whether primary research with a communication study or through observation is necessary. Then researchers determine what type of sample is to be used for the study and then collect the data. The final steps in the research are to analyze and interpret the data and prepare a research report.

Exploratory research typically uses qualitative data collected by individual interviews, focus groups, or observational methods, such as ethnography. Descriptive research includes cross-sectional and longitudinal studies. Causal research goes a step further by designing controlled experiments to understand cause-and-effect relationships between independent marketing variables, such as price changes, and dependent variables, such as sales.

Researchers may choose to collect data via survey methods and observation approaches. Survey approaches include mail questionnaires, telephone interviews, face-to-face interviews, and online questionnaires. A study may use a probability sample, such as a simple random or stratified sample, in which inferences can be made to a population on the basis of sample results. Nonprobability sampling methods include a convenience sample and a quota sample. The researcher tries to ensure that the data are valid, reliable, and representative.

Internet-based research, including via various social media platforms, accounts for a rapidly growing proportion of all market research. Online tracking uses cookies to record where consumers go on a website. Consumers have become increasingly concerned about privacy and how this information is used and made available to others. Online approaches also provide an attractive alternative to traditional communication data collection methods because of its speed and low cost. Many firms use the Internet to conduct online focus groups.

Key Terms

research design, p. 126
secondary data, p. 126
primary data, p. 127
exploratory research, p. 127
focus group, p. 128
market research online community (MROC), p. 128
case study, p. 128
ethnography, p. 128
descriptive research, p. 128
cross-sectional design, p. 129
longitudinal design, p. 129
causal research, p. 130
experiments, p. 130
neuromarketing, p. 130
telemarketing, p. 132
mall intercept, p. 132
unobtrusive measures, p. 133
mechanical observation, p. 134
eye tracking technology, p. 134
cookies, p. 135
predictive technology, p. 136
bounce rate, p. 137
validity, p. 137
internal validity, p. 137
external validity, p. 137
reliability, p. 138
representativeness, p. 138
sampling, p. 138
probability sample, p. 139
nonprobability sample, p. 139
convenience sample, p. 139
back-translation, p. 140

Chapter Questions and Activities

MyLab Marketing™
Go to **mymktlab.com** to watch this chapter's Rising Star video(s) for career advice and to respond to questions.

Concepts: Test Your Knowledge

4-1. What is a marketing information system (MIS)? What types of information does it include?
4-2. How does a marketing decision support system (MDSS) allow marketers to easily get the information they need?
4-3. Define the concept of customer insights and the role it plays in market planning decisions.
4-4. Why is defining the problem to be researched so important to ultimate success with the research project?
4-5. Explain the difference between primary data and secondary data.
4-6. What techniques can marketers use to gather data in exploratory research? How is this type of data collection useful?
4-7. Explain what descriptive research is.

4-8. Describe the purpose of casual research. How does it differ from descriptive research?

4-9. What are the main methods to collect primary data?

4-10. GIGO—garbage in, garbage out—is mentioned in the chapter. What is the significance of this concept to market research?

4-11. What is a (computer) cookie? What ethical and privacy issues relate to cookies?

4-12. What important issues must researchers consider when they plan to collect data online?

4-13. When we consider data quality, what are the differences among validity, reliability, and representativeness? How can you know the data have high levels of these characteristics?

4-14. How do probability and nonprobability samples differ? What are some types of probability samples? What are some types of nonprobability samples?

4-15. What is a cross tabulation? How are cross tabulations useful to analyze and interpret data?

Activities: Apply What You've Learned

4-16. *In Class, 10–20 Minutes for Teams* Figure 4.1 outlines the four types of data that make up a marketing information system (MIS). Thinking about a large retail bank (that has an extensive customer database) as well as a large snack food manufacturer (which sells its products via wholesalers and retailers), which of the four types of data would each of these firms mainly utilize (that is, they would have lots of available and reliable data) and which ones would they use less (as they would limited data)? How would the difference in the availability of data impact their marketing decision making?

⭐ 4-17. *Creative Homework/Short Project* Select a multinational company that sells products to consumers.
  a. Identify a particular product and a research question related to that product that is most appropriately studied using a cross-sectional design. Justify your reasoning for selecting this design.
  b. Identify a particular product and research question related to that product that is most appropriately studied using a longitudinal design. Justify your reasoning for selecting this design.

4-18. *Creative Homework/Short Project* As an account executive with a market research firm, you are responsible for deciding on the type of research to be used in various studies conducted for your clients. For each of the following client questions, list your choices of research approaches.
  a. Will TV or mobile device advertising be more effective for a local bank to use in its marketing communication plan?
  b. Should a California winemaker operating on a national scale switch from bottling its mid-tier wine ($9 to $15 per bottle) with corks to bottling it with screwcaps?
  c. Are consumers more likely to buy brands from firms that support strong sustainability initiatives?
  d. What existing features of an e-commerce site selling clothing to women are most important for making a purchase decision?

4-19. *Creative Homework/Short Project* For each of the topics you selected in item 4-17, how might you use a more passive (observation) approach to support the communication methods you employ?

4-20. *Creative Homework/Short Project* To what degree could secondary data sources be used to address the topics you selected in item 4-17? What specific secondary sources (if any) might be most useful to help address your selected issues?

4-21. *In Class, 10–25 Minutes for Teams* Your market research firm is planning to conduct surveys to gather information for a number of clients. Your boss has asked you and a few other new employees to do some preliminary work. She has asked each of you to choose three of the topics (from among the following six listed) that will be included in the project and to prepare an analysis of the advantages and disadvantages of each these communication methods of collecting primary data: mail questionnaires, telephone interviews, face-to-face interviews, and online questionnaires.
  a. The amount of sports nutrition drinks consumed in a city
  b. Why a local bank has been losing customers
  c. How heavily the company should invest in manufacturing and marketing home fax machines
  d. The amount of money being spent "over the state line" for lottery tickets
  e. What local doctors would like to see changed in the city's hospitals
  f. Consumers' attitudes toward several sports celebrities

4-22. *For Further Research (Individual)* Some companies use neuromarketing to gain an edge over their competitors. Research at least two companies that employ this technique. Explain how they use neuromarketing to gain a competitive advantage and assess whether the value of the information these marketers gained was worth the investment. (Hint: Just start by googling the term *neuromarketing*.)

4-23. *For Further Research (Individual)* For each of the types of mechanical observation listed within the chapter (people meters, portable people meters, eye tracking technology), conduct research online to identify (and document) the benefits and limitations of using each method.

Concepts: Apply Marketing Metrics

Marketers historically have tended to rely too much on click-through rates as a metric for success of web advertising. *Click-through rate* means the proportion of visitors who initiated action with respect to an advertisement that redirected them to another page where they might purchase an item or learn more about a product or service. Technically, click-through rate is the number of times a click is made on the advertisement divided by the total impressions (the times an advertisement was served up to the consumer during the visit to the website). Thus,

$$\text{Click-through rate (\%)} = \frac{\text{Number of click-throughs}}{\text{Number of impressions}}$$

Although providing useful information, click-through rates merely measure quantity, not quality, of consumer response. Consider what you learned in this chapter about various approaches to market research.

4-24. What other two or three data collection approaches to measuring the success of a web advertising campaign might be fruitful in providing more meaningful data than just clicks? Hint: Just because the metric relates to the web doesn't mean non-web-based research approaches are inappropriate.[39]

Choices: What Do You Think?

4-25. *Critical Thinking* A recent consumer insight from KFC is that young adults tend to buy snacks and play on their smartphone (or other device) in the mid-afternoon, not because they are hungry, but because they just want a mental break from work or study. Given this consumer insight, is it possible to create a marketing tactic (that is, product, offer, communication) that can leverage it for KFC to sell more afternoon snack items to the young adult market segment?

4-26. *Ethics* Some marketers attempt to disguise themselves as market researchers who want to ask you questions when their real intent is to sell something to the consumer. What is the impact of this practice on legitimate researchers? What do you think might be done about this practice?

⭐ **4-27.** *Critical Thinking* Do you believe that there could be a relationship between the amount of compensation received for actively participating in a research study and the level of effort put forth by a participant in that study? Are there forms of research that are more or less susceptible to such a relationship?

4-28. *Critical Thinking* It is likely that many of you have been directly involved in a market research study (either via a survey or a focus group) as a respondent. Reflect upon the research study that you were involved in. Try to determine which firm most likely conducted the study and what information that they were trying to obtain. How do you think they incorporated this information into their marketing decision making?

4-29. *Critical Thinking* More and more companies are starting to employ customer insight specialists to make sense of the data collected about their customers. Do you think this position is really needed within companies, or is it just a fad? Explain your reasoning.

4-30. *Ethics* Marketers in numerous industries can benefit from conducting market research on children. What do you think is the youngest age that would be appropriate to conduct research on a child? Why did you select this age?

4-31. *Critical Thinking* Are you willing to divulge personal information to market researchers? How much are you willing to tell, or where would you draw the line?

4-32. *Critical Thinking* Would you be willing to participate in an ethnographic research study within your own home? Why or why not?

4-33. *Critical Thinking* Would you alter the settings on your computer to disallow cookies? Why or why not?

⭐ **4-34.** *Critical Thinking* During the 2014 legislative session, the Data Broker and Accountability Act of 2014 was introduced in the hopes of giving consumers more control over the types of information data brokers collect about them as well as letting consumers opt out of the sale of such information to other companies. Would you support such legislation? Why or why not?

4-35. *Ethics* One unobtrusive measure mentioned in this chapter involved going through consumers' or competitors' garbage. Do you think marketers should have the right to do this? Is it ethical?

4-36. *Critical Thinking* Consider the approach to tracking consumers' exposure to promotions via portable people meters (PPMs). Would you be willing to participate in a study that required you to use a PPM? Why or why not?

4-37. *Ethics* One of the potential opportunities offered by neuromarketing is the capability to look at patterns in brain activity and identify (a) how the presence of different product attributes and variations of those attributes can help to predict what choices a consumer prior to their actually making those choices, (b) and how those attributes can be manipulated to influence other choices without the consumer realizing the impact that those changes are having on their choices. Do you believe that marketers should be able to use this type of knowledge to their advantage? Would you have any personal qualms with doing so?

Miniproject: Learn by Doing

Research a recent successful advertising/promotional campaign. Review the material provided by the advertising or digital agency in terms of how they structured and prepared the campaign or, if possible, find a case study for the campaign (which is often submitted for an advertising award by the advertising/digital agency) that provides deeper insight into what it was trying to achieve and how successful it was in achieving these objectives.

For this mini project, we are primarily focused on the customer insight that was the foundation of the communications plan. Typically, you would not be able to guess this insight accurately as an outsider, which is why you will need to do some Internet research to find relevant case study material.

4-38. At the end of your research, you should provide:
- A summary of the overall campaign
- What the communication goals were
- Who the target market was
- How the campaign was executed
- What were some of the key results achieved
- The foundational customer insight used to help structure the central creative communication message

Once you have this summary of the campaign as outlined above, highlight the role of customer insight in developing the central idea of the overall campaign. Do you think that customer insights can be identified through creative methods or do insights need to be derived from extensive analysis of data and market information?

Marketing in **Action** Case   Real Choices at GetFeedback

We all know that the world has gone mobile! But how does this change impact the way market research is done? According to the Pew Research Center, 30 percent of cell phone owners use their phones as their primary Internet access point. Consumers are changing how they interact with companies, products, and services and recent research indicates that about 38 percent of all market research surveys began on mobile devices. In particular, when considering traditional market research data collection methods (mail, phone), millennials have the lowest reported response rates of any group. However, they are more willing to respond to studies offered on mobile devices. Amazingly though, Forrester Research estimates that as little as 17 percent of market researchers have taken their survey processes mobile, indicating that most market research companies still use outdated technology and techniques.

In 2013, Kraig Swensrud and Sean Whiteley recognized the information collection gap in the marketplace and decided to close the gap with mobile-first customer surveys. The two former Salesforce.com employees created a startup called GetFeedback with a goal to be on the frontlines of the changeover to mobile computing. GetFeedback is a service that creates surveys for smartphones, tablets, and mobile web browsers. Campaign Monitor, an online e-mail marketing application and software firm, acquired GetFeedback about a year later. Currently, GetFeedback has more than 1,000 enterprise users that includes high profile organizations like United Way, ESPN, Facebook, LinkedIn, and Nike. Available data collection services include package sizes from Personal ($25/month) for up to 100 responses/month to Enterprise ($150/month) for up to 10,000 responses/month. Additionally, service plans may include web, e-mail, and telephone technical support.

Swensrud knew that mobile surveys present many challenges including how to optimize them for smaller screen sizes to allow for quick scrolling and processing. GetFeedback offers templates to integrate video clips, photographs, or other images to reinforce a company's marketing. Clients can create surveys and then add style through colors, fonts, logos, and images. To attain deeper participant engagement and higher completion rates of online surveys, imagery and video are essential. The objective is to have the survey reflect the personality of the brand. Other key features of GetFeedback include push notifications that provide alerts and a set of analytical tools that allows customers to more fully use the collected information. All of this can happen in real-time, which gives GetFeedback's customers a speed advantage over their competitors. Collected information is owned by the customer and is readily available to share within their company. The information can easily be downloaded and exported into Microsoft Excel or any analytical software that can handle comma separated values (CSV).

In its 2015 Global Market Research Report, ESOMAR estimates total annual global expenditures of $43 billion on telephone polls, online surveys, questionnaires, and other market research—$19 billion in the U.S. alone. The market for consumer research is immense and steadily growing especially in the online and mobile devise space. SurveyMonkey is the current market leader with more than 25 million customers including Kraft Foods, Samsung, and Facebook. The CEO of SurveyMonkey, Zander Lurie, stresses "Now it's about execution. We have all the opportunity to thrive and succeed but if we're not super-focused and crisp about how we do it, then competition will take it."

To continue to be successful, GetFeedback has to challenge the market leader, make surveys as efficient to answer as possible for respondents, maintain information quality, and deliver great value to its customers. At the same time, the company must help its parent Campaign Monitor generate attractive shareholder gains. In a competitive, changeable growth environment as dynamic as this one, it's often difficult to decide what the next strategic move should be. GetFeedback needs to step back, consider the competitive environment, weigh opportunities and risks, and formulate its growth plans for the future.

You Make the Call

4-39. What is the decision facing GetFeedback?

4-40. What factors are important in understanding this decision situation?

4-41. What are the alternatives?

4-42. What decision(s) do you recommend?

4-43. What are some ways to implement your recommendation?

Based on: Heather Clancy, "With Mobile Surveys, Market Research Gets a Makeover," *Fortune* (March 25, 2014), http://tech.fortune.cnn.com/2014/03/25/with-mobile-surveys-market-research-gets-a-makeover (accessed April 13, 2016); Ted Saunders, "Improving the Survey Experience for Mobile Respondents," *Marketing Research Association* (August 13, 2015), http://www.marketingresearch.org/article/improving-survey-experience-mobile-respondents (accessed April 13, 2016); Sarah Kimmorley, "Zander Lurie explains How It felt to Be SurveyMonkey's CEO After His Best Mate Dave Goldberg Died," *Business Insider* (Apr 7, 2016), http://www.businessinsider.com.au/zander-lurie-on-taking-over-the-role-of-surveymonkeys-ceo-after-his-best-mate-dave-goldberg-died-2016-4 (accessed April 13, 2016).

MyLab Marketing™

Go to **mymktlab.com** for the following Assisted-graded writing questions:

4-44. *Creative Homework/Short Project.* Your company recently launched a new "dry" shampoo. Although initial sales were strong, they have steadily declined over the last year and a half. You have decided to conduct further market research, but first you have to define the research problem. What are your research objectives? What is the population of interest? How does the problem fit within the environmental context? Prepare a short report that clearly and fully defines the research problem for your product.

4-45. *Creative Homework/Short Project.* You work for a small company that designs and sells women's trendy rubber rain boots throughout the U.S. Sales have been strong, but you think they could be stronger. You have begun the market research process and are now ready to design the sample. Will you design a probability sample or a nonprobability sample? What type of probability or nonprobability sample will you use? What are the advantages of the method that you chose? What are the limitations of the method you chose?

Marketing Analytics: Welcome to the Era of Big Data!

Lisa Arthur

▼ **A Decision Maker at Teradata Corporation**

As Teradata's chief marketing officer (CMO), Lisa Arthur drives global market and demand strategy, product and solutions marketing, and customer-centric initiatives and serves as global industry thought leader around data-driven marketing and Teradata's Integrated Marketing Cloud solutions. A 30-year marketing veteran, she has also served as CMO for Internet leader Akamai Technologies, B2B2C application provider Mindjet, and most recently, Aprimo (now Teradata). She is the author of *Big Data Marketing; Engage Your Customers More Effectively to Drive Value* (2013).

Lisa spent nearly seven years at Oracle, where as a vice president of marketing she managed the market entry and growth for Oracle CRM and E-Business Suite On-Demand. Also, as the founder of Cinterim, she applied her market-centric processes and insight to provide strategic counsel for Silicon Valley start-ups and *Fortune 50* technology companies.

A seasoned keynote speaker, Lisa has addressed diverse topics at Web 2.0, Office 2.0, the Direct Marketing Association, the Australian Direct Marketing Association, the American Marketing Association (AMA) Strategy Conference, Stanford University, and the MIT Sloan CMO Summit and various CMO Executive Forums. She is frequently quoted in industry media, has a syndicated blog in *B2C Community*, and has appeared on Asia's *Wall Street Journal* broadcast and published numerous papers with the AMA. Her industry thought-leadership blogs have appeared on the Forbes.com CMO Network, and she is a contributor to *Lean back,* a marketing blog of The Economist Group. Lisa's recent honors include the *Direct Marketing News* 2013 "Marketing Hall of Femme," honoring today's top women marketers, and the American Business Association's 2012 Gold "Stevie Award" for Marketing Executive of the Year. And, in 2014, 2012, and 2011, she was named a "Woman to Watch" by the Sales and Lead Management Association. She is also a trustee with the Marketing Sciences Institute. She earned a BA degree from Ohio State University.

Lisa's Info

What I do when I'm not working?
Writing, cooking, and photography.

First job out of school?
I had school loans, and it was a tough job market, so I began my professional career as a temporary employment recruiter and placement professional. Needless to say, I'm thrilled I switched to marketing.

Career high?
Publishing my first book, *Big Data Marketing*, in October 2013.

A job-related mistake I wish I hadn't made?
Not listening to my intuition. I've made this mistake a couple of times, and while data is essential for decision making, so is gut instinct.

Business book I'm reading now?
The Singularity Is Near by Ray Kurtzweil.

My hero?
My husband. Every day, he is the "superman" in my life, and I couldn't do what I do without his love and support.

My motto to live by?
It's never too late.

What drives me?
I'm on a quest along with my company, Teradata, to make marketing a more valued function through the use of data to innovate and transform customer engagement and experiences.

My management style?
Collaborative coach.

My pet peeve?
The word *can't.*

Here's my problem...

Real **People**, Real **Choices**

When Lisa joined Aprimo in 2009 (now part of Teradata Corporation, a public company listed on the New York Stock Exchange) as its CMO, the company had been in business for 11 years and had enjoyed strong success in the marketing resource management (MRM), the multichannel campaign management, and in the enterprise marketing management space. It boasted a blue-chip client list of more than 200 companies that used its marketing software and services to improve their marketing results and effectiveness. Acquired in 2011 by Teradata, the applications have expanded to also include Big Data discovery and marketing attribution through its TeradataAster solutions. Marketers are both the consumers and the generators of Big Data and can gain insight and then take action with consumers and buyers to engage in real time to provide next-best offer or next-best message. Because Teradata is the leader in data and analytic platforms as well as its own leading multichannel campaign management solution, the combination of marketing applications along with Big Data and advanced analytics adds value to the company's already robust marketing solution.

Before the Teradata acquisition, Lisa was recruited to be a change agent—to reposition Aprimo, the company, and its brand as *the* platform for marketers. There had been branding and positioning work that had created a great logo, but the company still was missing a clear connection between what it could offer to marketing executives and their teams.

The company was growing quickly and needed to broaden its appeal to a wider market. At the same time, it was launching a next-generation cloud offering comprised of marketing operations, campaign management, and digital messaging solutions, along with associated analytics to help make real-time sense of customer data. The cloud analytics category was an emerging market with all the hallmarks of a sector ready to explode. But the Aprimo brand was not well known, and most people in the marketing analytics industry perceived that the firm was only an MRM technology solutions provider. In reality, the company offered a lot more—a marketing software platform to enable global companies to manage the entire business of marketing, immediately and for the long term. Beyond managing marketing operations, Aprimo offered clients advanced campaign management capabilities to communicate online or offline with their consumers and prospects as well as integrated digital messaging for its online platform to simplify and accelerate the delivery of e-mails and Short Message Service.

The company was gearing up for the launch of Aprimo Marketing Studio On Demand, a cloud-based platform. The launch of its cloud product was strategically important to the company to provide more flexible implementation and usage of its marketing solutions. The launch was scheduled to happen within the quarter during which Lisa joined the company, and the annual global user conference was just six months away. Resources in the marketing department were extremely limited because the leadership team of the company had awaited the arrival of the incoming CMO to staff up. In Lisa's strategic view, the Aprimo brand needed to be refreshed, evolved, and invigorated. Clearly, this market was ready for a true thought leader. The challenge was limited human and capital resources and not much time to "relaunch the company."

Lisa considered her **Options** 1·2·3

1 Option
Continue on the current course and pace and focus only on the launch of the product for the short term to provide more time and resources to relaunch the brand. Wait 9 to 12 months to do the more extensive brand work that would do a better job of communicating the company's abilities. This choice would allow Lisa and her team to focus on a "big-bang" product launch that would generate a lot of interest among potential clients in the short term. Because the marketing department was understaffed, this choice would allow the team to focus on getting the product launch right. On the other hand, the new cloud product was going to spearhead a major repositioning for Aprimo, and Lisa feared that the impact of the launch would get lost without a more full-scale, integrated approach.

2 Option
Launch the product and the brand in a "two-prong" release. Aprimo could use the revenue it would earn from the new cloud product to fund aggressive growth plans it had for the following year. This choice would allow the company to meet its revenue goals and also provide two (rather than one) anchor points for the relaunch of the company; there would be some buzz generated by the new cloud product, and then the brand relaunch a few months later could build on that. This decision would also give the company time to tweak its cloud product among early adopter clients so it could be confident that it was rolling on all cylinders when the entire Aprimo brand relaunched. Still, it wasn't clear if the team's minimal staff could pull off two separate launches within a fairly short period of time. And, this was a fairly unusual strategy, so it was a high-risk move for a brand-new CMO.

3 Option
Delay the cloud product launch, accelerate efforts to rebrand Aprimo, and then launch both the cloud product and the new brand together. This option was a big-bang approach that would energize the company. The relaunch would be even more impactful because it would be accompanied by the release of an innovative product to signal the company's arrival in the cloud. All of the company's event planning resources could focus on one truly integrated plan. On the other hand, this delay would probably result in a loss of revenue for Aprimo. The time lag might give competitors an opportunity to bring out similar products beforehand and steal Aprimo's thunder. Also, the delay would force Teradata to miss the industry's big autumn trade show, DreamForce, where people in the industry traditionally expected to see big new launches announced.

Now, put yourself in Lisa's shoes. Which option would you choose, and why?

You Choose

Which **Option** would you choose, and **why**?
☐ **Option 1**   ☐ **Option 2**   ☐ **Option 3**

See what **Option** Lisa chose in **MyLab Marketing**™

Chapter 5

5.1 Customer Relationship Management (CRM): A Key Decision Tool for Marketers

OBJECTIVE

Explain how marketers increase long-term success and profits by practicing customer relationship management.

(pp. 150–155)

A good place to kick off our discussion of how marketers use large quantities of data and advanced analytic tools is by introducing the concept of **customer relationship management (CRM)**. CRM systems serve as a central hub of customer data for most successful firms, integrating various data sources that can be used to develop powerful analytical capabilities oriented toward enhancing an organization's relationship with its customers. Vast amounts of data have enabled marketers to understand and interact with customers in ways that would never have been possible in the past. Did you know that chief marketing officers (CMOs) now spend more on technology than do chief information officers (CIOs)? There are roughly 3000 vendors that sell technology specifically for *marketing analytics* (we'll formally define this term later in the chapter) and this numbers grows by 300 to 500 each year! This explosion has created a new category of technology called **mar-tech**.[1]

In Chapter 1, you learned that a *consumer orientation* is a business approach that prioritizes the satisfaction of customers' needs and wants. Now it's time to drill down a bit more on how firms actually accomplish this prioritization. Toward this end, most highly successful firms embrace CRM programs that involve systematically tracking consumers' preferences and behaviors over time to tailor the value proposition as closely as possible to each individual's unique wants and needs. CRM allows firms to talk to individual customers and to adjust elements of their marketing programs in light of how each customer reacts.[2] The CRM trend facilitates **one-to-one marketing**, which includes several steps:[3]

1. Identify customers and get to know them in as much detail as possible.
2. Differentiate among these customers in terms of both their needs and their value to the company.
3. Interact with customers and find ways to improve cost efficiency and the effectiveness of the interaction.
4. Customize some aspect of the goods or services that you offer to each customer. This means treating each customer differently based on what the organization has learned about him or her through prior interactions.[4]

Remember, successful one-to-one marketing depends on CRM, which allows a company to identify its best customers, stay on top of their needs, and increase their satisfaction.[5]

At its core, CRM is about communicating with customers and about customers being able to communicate with a company "up close and personal." CRM systems are applications that use computers, specialized computer software, databases, and often the Internet to capture information at each **touchpoint**, which is any point of direct interface between customers and a company (online, by phone, or in person).

These systems include everything from websites that let you check on the status of a bill or package to call centers that solicit your business. When you log on to the FedEx website to track a lost package, that's part of a CRM system. When you get a phone message from the dentist reminding you about your appointment tomorrow to get a root canal, that's CRM (sorry about that). And when you get a call from the car dealer asking how you like your new vehicle, that's also CRM. Remember how we said in Chapter 4 that information is the fuel that runs the marketing engine? It is through CRM that companies act on and manage the information they gather from their customers.

---

customer relationship management (CRM)
A systematic tracking of consumers' preferences and behaviors over time to tailor the value proposition as closely as possible to each individual's unique wants and needs.

mar-tech
Short for "marketing technology," this term is commonly used to denote the fusion of marketing and technology. A particular focus is placed on the application of marketing through digital technologies.

one-to-one marketing
Facilitated by CRM, one-to-one marketing allows for customization of some aspect of the goods or services that are offered to each customer.

touchpoint
Any point of direct interface between customers and a company (online, by phone, or in person).

It quickly can become overwhelming to think about how to both maintain and utilize all of the data that can be collected from customers through all potential touch-points. To help reduce the cognitive load (and clerical effort) required to fully take advantage of all this data, firms deploy **marketing automation**. Marketing automation is a set of systems and technologies that the organization can use to put in place a set of rules for handling different processes in an automated fashion. These rules can relate to the collection and processing of data, as well as the execution of different customer-oriented actions.

Consider for example a potential customer who has subscribed to receive an e-mail notification whenever a new post is made on your company's blog. A few weeks later he or she reads and comments on a blog post that discusses the value that a client obtained from one of your company's products. Then in a few more days he or she downloads a document from your website that outlines the technical features of that same product. At this point if you're on your toes it should be increasingly clear that the potential customer has a fair amount of interest in one of your company's products, but with everything else that's going on it's often easy for managers to miss these activity patterns. In this example an organization could use a marketing automation system from the onset to watch for sequenced events like this, and based on an understanding of their contextual significance and relationship with each other, managers could instruct the system to send out an e-mail to the potential customer inviting her to speak to a sales representative, attend a webinar, or other follow-up options. Such customized responses greatly increase the likelihood of customer follow through.

On the e-commerce front, direct shopping company JD Williams deployed Oracle's marketing automation technology to advance the targeting and person-alization capabilities for its e-mail marketing campaigns. The organization went from a basic level of personalization in communications that involved using very simple data such as the customer's name, to being able to thoroughly cus-tomize communications based on lifecycle stage of the customer, the channel(s) customers were using to explore and shop, and other customer behavior data. The result of this investment in marketing automation has been incredible—JD Williams saw a 268 percent increase in e-mail click-through rates and a 92 per-cent increase in purchases attributed to customers who clicked on one of these e-mails. For a company like JD Williams that sends more than 42 million e-mails per month and wishes to take a personalized approach, there's no doubt that greater automation of analytical and operational marketing processes is not just desirable in today's competitive marketplace; it's a necessity.[6]

As we noted previously, CRM doesn't just drive automated methods, it also plays a key role in enabling employees to maximize high-touch and personal relationships with customers. For example, consider the experience of USAA, which began as an insurance company catering to the military market and today is a leading global financial services powerhouse. In 1922, when 25 army officers met in San Antonio and decided to insure each other's vehicles, they could not have imagined that their tiny organization would one day serve 6 million members and become the only fully integrated financial services company in America. Unlike State Farm, Allstate, and other traditional insurance providers, USAA does not provide field agents with an office you can go to, sit down, and shoot the breeze about your latest fishing trip. In fact, USAA's employees conduct business almost entirely over the phone. But just ask any USAA member how they feel about the service, and you'll get a glowing report.

The secret sauce in USAA's success is largely its state-of-the-art CRM system. No matter where on the globe you are, no matter what time of day or night, a USAA repre-sentative will pull up your profile, and you'll feel that he or she knows you. Of course, it takes a good dose of employee training to enable those folks to use the system to its

marketing automation
A group of systems and technologies that can be used to establish a set of rules for handling different marketing related processes in an automated fashion.

potential. But USAA does a great job of building and maintaining long-term customer relationships and, more important, getting customers to move many or all of their business over to USAA, including banking, credit cards, money management, investments, and financial planning. To further build loyalty, USAA even runs an online company store that sells all sorts of popular product lines and brands for which members get purchase discounts.[7]

USAA's success helps illustrate and explain why CRM has become a driving philosophy in many successful firms. Gartner, a leading information technology (IT) research firm, notes that the CRM market grew from \$20.4 billion to \$23.2 billion from 2013 to 2014.[8] Clearly, CRM has increasingly become an important part of how businesses operate, and there does not seem to be any signs of that trend slowing down. Gartner predicts that more organizations will adopt or migrate towards cloud-based CRM systems, which will make them even more powerful.[9] Here are some great examples of CRM at work:

- Amazon.com is the world champion master of the happy customer approach to CRM. For loyal users, Amazon tracks visits so that it can customize product recommendations on the website as well as enable the delivery of relevant product recommendations and promotions via e-mail.[10] On Amazon's homepage, a user can find product recommendations organized into sections that relate to such factors as past browsing and shopping behavior and observed relationships between a product that the user recently purchased and one or more products that the user has not yet purchased. These sections include: "Related to Items You've Viewed," "Inspired by Your Shopping Trends," and "Inspired by Your Wish List."[11] This focus on personalizing the customer experience helps keep customers engaged during each of their visits and helps ensure that they continue to come back for more.

- Tommy Bahama's focus on customer service is facilitated by CRM-related technologies that enable the brand to collect a wide array of data around customers and to respond more agilely and precisely to customer feedback. If a customer rates his or her new martini glass camp shirt unfavorably or posts negative comments about it on social media, the company automatically contacts him or her to determine how it can fix the problem. Tommy Bahama also uses technology integrated with its CRM system that can capture customer feedback in retail locations, outlets, and in-store kiosks and provide it to employees in real-time. This capability offers instant opportunities for employees to become heroes to customers by addressing problems and providing superior service immediately after the feedback has come in, ideally while the originating customer is still in the store.[12]

- Disney launched MyMagic+, a system that allows Disney World visitors to more efficiently plan out their vacation experience and reduce the need to carry around tickets and other items previously necessary to tour the park. Visitors can book events in advance, reserve times on rides, and review the park activities that they have experienced in the past, to name a few of the main features. MyMagic+ is designed to be partnered with a wearable computer called the Disney Magic Band, which enables users to verify all of the actions they have taken through the MyMagic+ system without carrying around receipts or other forms of proof. In addition, they can use the wearable Magic Band to make transactions while in the park. The benefits and convenience for visitors is obvious, but for Disney another big advantage is

Disney's Magic Band is a wearable computer that allows visitors to interact with the theme park.

the amount of data it can collect on visitors' behavior and actions. These data better enable the firm to understand how to communicate with each customer and manage each relationship more effectively.[13] Yep—one-to-one marketing even within a massive theme park!

Customer-Related Metrics

In addition to having a different mind-set, companies that successfully practice CRM have different goals, use different measures of success, and look at customers in some different ways from firms that do not. CRM facilitates the capability for users to look at three critical customer-related metrics (see 📷 Figure 5.1): share of customer, customer lifetime value (CLV), and customer prioritization. Let's have a look at each of these ideas now.

Share of Customer

Because it is always easier and less expensive to keep an existing customer than to get a new one, CRM firms try to increase their **share of customer**, not share of market; this is the percentage of an individual customer's purchase of a product over time that is the same brand. Let's say that a consumer buys six pairs of shoes a year—two pairs from each of three different manufacturers. Assume that one shoemaker has a CRM system that allows it to send letters to its current customers inviting them to receive a special price discount or a gift if they buy more of the firm's shoes during the year. If the firm can get the consumer to buy three or four or perhaps all six pairs from it, it has increased its *share of customer*. And that may not be too difficult because the customer already likes the firm's shoes. Without the CRM system, the shoe company would probably use traditional advertising to increase sales, which would be far costlier than the customer-only direct mail campaign. So the company can increase sales and profits at a much lower cost than it would spend to get one, two, or three new customers.

Customer Lifetime Value (CLV)

As you'll recall from Chapter 1, *customer lifetime value (CLV)* represents how much profit a firm expects to make from a particular customer, including each and every purchase he or she will make from them now and in the future. Thus, this metric describes the potential profit that a single customer's purchase of a firm's products generates over the customer's lifetime. It just makes sense that a firm's profitability and long-term success will be far greater if it develops long-term relationships with its customers so that those customers buy from it again and again. Costs will be far higher and profits lower if each customer's purchase is a first-time sale. That's why we keep repeating this mantra: *It's much more profitable to retain an existing customer than to acquire a new one.*

How do marketers calculate the lifetime value of a customer? Here's an example using an auto dealer we'll call Millennial Motors, so buckle your seatbelt because it's time to put the pedal to the metal on this critical concept in marketing. Using data from the CRM system, a Millennial Motors marketing manager would first estimate a customer's future purchases across all products from the firm over the next 20 or 30 years. The goal is to try to figure out what profit the company could make from the customer in the future (obviously this will just be an estimate).

For example, Millennial might calculate the lifetime value of a single customer by first calculating the total profit the customer will generate for the company during his or her life. This figure includes the number of automobiles he or she will probably buy

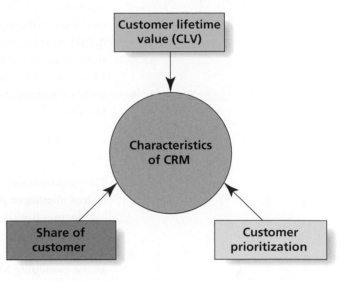

Figure 5.1 📷 *Snapshot* | CRM-Enabled Customer Metrics

Followers of CRM look at share of customer, lifetime value of a customer, and customer prioritization.

share of customer
The percentage of an individual customer's purchase of a product that is a single brand.

times their average gross margin (the price of the related automobiles less what the dealer paid for them and the costs associated with selling them to the customer). We add to this figure an estimate of any service and repairs that Millennial would provide for the cars over the years and even possibly the income from auto loan financing. We would subtract the cost of initially acquiring the customer in terms of sales and marketing efforts. The resulting figure would also need to take into account the *likelihood* that Millennial will retain the customer for the calculated period (this can be estimated based on historical data of all customers), as well as any other unique potential risks or uncertainties associated with the expected value of the customer through the life of the relationship. The lifetime value of the customer would be the total profit the revenue stream generates. Here's what the process of calculating CLV looks like as a formula:

$$\text{CLV (\$)} = \text{Margin (\$)}/[1 + \text{Discount Rate (\%)} - \text{Retention Rate (\%)}] - \text{Acquisition Cost (\$)}^{14}$$

The "discount rate" calculation is the one that takes into account the risk or uncertainty factors mentioned previously.

In practice CLV calculations companies use may be more complex because they factor in changes that occur in the relationship with a customer from one period of time to the next that do not assume constant values over the whole relationship (such as the preceding Millennial Motors example). The loyalty program that might be used by an airline company and the tiers contained within that program provide us with a suitable framework for exploring one type of approach to calculating customer lifetime value that can more accurately capture how a customer's relationship with a company may change from one point in time to the next. A customer within a loyalty program may move over time from one tier in a given loyalty program into another tier (with the American Airlines AAdvantage program, for example, from Gold to Platinum to Executive Platinum in status) based on specific purchase behaviors. Progression through the status ranks is clearly associated with increasing levels of a customer's value to the airline.

A more complex version of a CLV calculation might combine the defined tiers within its customer loyalty program, the likelihood that in a given period of time a customer will move from one tier to another, and the value associated with a customer being in a given tier during a given period of time to extrapolate what that customer's value will be over the lifetime of his or her relationship with the airline. This type of approach is tricky to represent as a simple formula; instead, marketers rely on more complex statistical approaches such as Markhov chain modeling to estimate CLV. Nevertheless, the example should provide you with a general idea of how a company can engage in a more nuanced approach to calculating customer lifetime value that is not limited to the assumption of constant values over the course of the company's relationship with a customer.

With all that in mind, the calculation of CLV that was initially provided does offer a suitable starting place to understand the basics of how companies work to determine the value of customers and the implications for marketing management. A key to the importance of CLV is that nobody sets out to acquire a customer that will cost them more money than they bring in! But without an effective estimate such as CLV, one might invest a lot of marketing dollars in the wrong customers over time.

Customer Prioritization

Using a CRM approach, the organization prioritizes its customers and customizes its communications to them accordingly. For example, any banker will

Redsnapper/Alamy Stock Photo

A bank's customers are not equal when it comes to profitability. Some use it primarily as a place to pick up cash for the weekend.

tell you that not all customers are equal when it comes to profitability. Some generate a lot of revenue because they pay interest on loans or credit cards, whereas others simply use the bank as a convenient place to store a small amount of money and take out a little bit each week to buy beer. Banks use CRM systems to generate a profile of each customer based on factors such as value, risk, attrition, and interest in buying new financial products. This automated system helps the bank decide which current or potential customers it will target with certain communications or how much effort it will expend to retain an account—all the while cutting its costs by as much as a third. It just makes sense to use different types of communication contacts based on the value of each individual customer. For example, personal selling (the most expensive form of marketing communication per contact) may constitute 75 percent of all contacts with high-volume customers, whereas direct mail or telemarketing is more often the best way to talk to low-volume customers.

5.2 Big Data: Terabytes Rule

OBJECTIVE

Understand Big Data, data mining, and how marketers can put these techniques to good use.

(pp. 155–164)

CRM systems provide a great internal organizational data repository. But as more consumer experiences shift into the digital space and new means of connecting and interacting with both individuals and corporations becomes possible and widely accepted, it is no surprise that *Big Data* is becoming an increasingly important concept. You were briefly introduced to **Big Data** in Chapter 1, where you learned that it is the popular term to describe the exponential growth of data—both structured and unstructured—in massive amounts that are hard or impossible to process using traditional database techniques.

Big Data
A popular term to describe the exponential growth of data—both structured and unstructured—in massive amounts that are hard or impossible to process using traditional database techniques.

According to SAS, a leading provider of data analytics software, "Big Data refers to the ever-increasing volume, velocity, variety, variability and complexity of information."[15] Think about the amount of time that you spend online looking up information through search engines such as Google, connecting with friends through social media sites such as Facebook and Twitter, listening to music on sites such as Spotify and YouTube, or myriad other activities on the web or through a mobile app that all of us engage in, and you'll begin to comprehend the sheer volume of data that we (perhaps unwittingly) create each and every day. Each action you take online leaves a digital footprint, and all of your footprints—especially when analysts combine them with the footprints of thousands or even millions of others—have the potential to yield valuable insights for a wide range of stakeholders within society. Table 5.1 provides some examples of common user actions that create these valuable footprints for marketers to follow.

The hugely successful Netflix show *House of Cards* became one of Netflix's first original programs thanks in part to the use of Big Data. This is because Netflix is able to use a treasure trove of consumer data pulled from its site to help inform content acquisitions, including consumer viewing habits (e.g., when, where, and with what devices do they watch) and content preferences (recall Chapter 4's coverage of *predictive technology* and how Netflix trained teams of people to watch thousands of movies and tag them according to attributes such as "goriness" or "plot conclusiveness" to figure out what movies or TV shows you are likely to enjoy—and thus be able to make better recommendations). All of this data helped Netflix to more accurately predict whether buying the rights to *House of Cards* was a sound decision based on a higher degree of confidence that the company could find a suitable group of current (and perhaps potential) customers who would enjoy the show, and promptly start binge-watching it. Netflix leverages large quantities of data to

Table 5.1 | Examples of Data Created on Digital Platforms

	Examples of User Actions	**Potential Use of the Related Data for a Marketer**
Facebook	"Like" an Internet celebrity's Facebook page	Data representing each "like" are recorded and associated with the individual user who committed the action. For example, if a marketer believes that the related Internet celebrity is well suited to endorse a product for female millennials, the Internet celebrity could show the marketer the related "like" data that would show that the majority of her followers fall within the correct age range and gender for which the marketer's product is designed to appeal.
YouTube	Watch a video	Data are recorded representing the view of the video and based on the characteristics of the video (e.g., its topic) related videos will be recommended to the user in the future that have the potential to increase the user's engagement on the platform (e.g., views of videos and time spent). A marketer could see that a large enough group of users view videos within the given topic and choose to use YouTube to distribute a video ad to users within this group (based on the assumption that the related video topic attracts a group of consumers with interests relevant to the product being advertised).
	Skip an ad displayed before a video	Data are recorded representing the action of pressing the "Skip Video" button for the user. If the marketer saw that a particular video ad was being skipped often enough through a review of this data in aggregate (across all users who were exposed to the ad), this could provide a good basis to dig deeper and determine if there are specific issues with the content of the video ad or the audience(s) to which it is delivered.

drive a wide array of choices on what shows and movies to license, as well as which ones to buy the rights to and produce.[16]

For marketers, Big Data has potential to provide competitive advantages in three main areas:

1. Identifying new opportunities through analytics that yield greater return on investment (ROI) on marketing efforts

2. Turning insights they gain into products and services that are better aligned with the desires of consumers

3. Delivering communications on products and services to the marketplace more efficiently and effectively

Internet of Things
Describes a system in which everyday objects are connected to the Internet and in turn are able to communicate information throughout an interconnected system.

The amount of data that all of us produce does not appear to be slowing down either, as new technologies continue to enhance the ways we connect to people, machines, and organizations. The **Internet of Things** is a term that increasingly appears in articles and stories on technology trends. It describes a system in which everyday objects are connected to the Internet and in turn are able to communicate information throughout an interconnected system.[17] Areas that would become part of this network include medical devices, cars, toys, video games, and even a six-pack of beer in your refrigerator—the list goes on and on. Within the context of Big Data, this means that an even larger amount of data will be accessible, offering insight into the extent and ways in which consumers use everyday objects. Like the marketing automation technologies we mentioned previously, this knowledge will allow companies to automate processes that were previously done manually. We're already seeing these changes in small

"Smart refrigerators" that can scan product codes are part of the "Internet of Things." It may not be long before your fridge will compile a shopping list for you as you run out of staples and even e-mail the grocery store to arrange for a delivery.

ways; just ask anyone who uses a Google Nest system to automatically regulate the thermostats in their home so that the A/C kicks in 10 minutes before the owner walks through the door!

For marketers, this interconnection of objects and collection of data could mean gaining insights into how we use products via data captured through sensors embedded in products that track a user's interaction with the product. This information would then be transmitted via an Internet connection at or near real time. Not only would this enable us to gain greater knowledge about how people use products, but this also could be done on a scale that traditional market research can achieve only through astronomical financial investments—essentially tracking the actions of each and every product user!

So it's easy to begin to see how much data we would produce in a world where the Internet of Things has fully taken hold. Consider the following quote from Jan Wassen, Director of Business Analytics at automobile manufacturer Volvo, about the possibilities stemming from the Internet of Things: "We can learn from it how customers are driving their car; at what speed it's being driven, which types of behavior that the customers have and learn it for developing future models. We can learn whether they're utilizing the center screen for getting at their different entertainment functions or if they use the turn button of the steering wheel or the voice control. We can also utilize the particular data for this particular customer to tell them, 'You actually have a function in your vehicle. It doesn't seem like you're utilizing this and it works like this,' and we could provide them with a video showing that 'This is something you should know.'"[18]

Big Data Creation, Sources, and Usage

The millions of pieces of information that make up Big Data originate from a number of different sources. Some of the most important sources of Big Data for marketers are listed here and illustrated in 📷 Figure 5.2:

1. *Social media sources:* With an increasing array of social media sites that boast a large number of consumers interacting with each other, with brands, and with other entities, a wealth of information is being produced about how individuals feel about products and just about everything else in their lives. It is not uncommon today for consumers to either praise or condemn a product online. That information can be very valuable to marketers not only in terms of what they're saying but also in terms of factors that triggered them to say it. Today, several companies engage in **web scraping** (using computer software to extract large amounts of data from websites), **sentiment analysis** (a process of identifying a follower's attitude (e.g., "positive," "negative," or "neutral") toward a product or brand by assessing the context or emotion of comments they post), and other advanced techniques that involve analyzing and mapping millions of posts on Facebook, Twitter, and other social media platforms to track what people say about their experiences with products and services. They depict the themes in these posts visually so that managers can easily see the kinds of words customers use in their posts. (Hint: If your brand's name appears a lot of time with terms like "awful" or "sucks," you probably have a problem.)

2. *Corporate IT sources:* These are the sources of data that live within the organization and might include: CRM databases, web analytic databases (e.g., Google Analytics), enterprise

web scraping
The process of using computer software to extract large amounts of data from websites.

sentiment analysis
The process of identifying a follower's attitude (e.g., "positive," "negative," or "neutral") toward a product or brand by assessing the context or emotion of his or her comments.

Figure 5.2 📷 *Snapshot* | Sources of Big Data for Marketers

Big Data can come from many sources. These sources can be both within and outside of the organization and created and compiled from different groups.

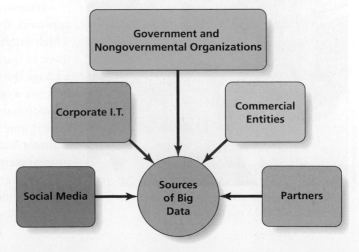

resource planning databases, and even accounting-related databases. Each of these sources can contain a treasure trove of information on an organization's consumers. Unfortunately, too often these systems live in departmental "silos"; one group in the company may not share this information with others in the firm, so each group gets only an incomplete picture of its customers. Hence, marketing needs to be the function within the organization that cuts across these groups to mine these databases and connect the dots.

3. *Government and nongovernmental organization sources:* Provided by the government, these types of data could be most anything from extracted U.S. Census results (quickly check out www.census.gov to begin to be overwhelmed with census data) to data on the economic conditions in developing countries that allow marketers to better understand the demographics of consumers at home and the opportunities for global expansion. Ever-increasing types and amounts of government-generated data that are accessible and machine readable will continue to provide new opportunities for enterprising marketers.[19]

4. *Commercial entity sources:* Many companies today collect data in large quantities to sell to organizations that can derive value from them. For some provider firms, this activity is their primary source of revenue; for others, it is a nice additional source of revenue over and above their principal business activities. For example (and this may or may not come as a surprise to you), many credit card companies, such as American Express and MasterCard, sell your purchase data to advertisers so that they can better target their ads. And supermarkets like Safeway for years have sold **scanner data**—data derived from all those items you scan at the cash register when you check out with your loyalty card (which just happens to have your demographic profile information in its record!). Supermarkets sell the data in aggregated form so that it's not possible to identify the actions of a specific customer, but scanner data still provide extremely useful information to both manufacturers and retailers about how much shoppers buy in different categories and which brands they choose.[20]

5. *Partner database sources:* In Chapter 11, you will read about different members of a channel of distribution. Many firms today have adopted a **channel partner model** in which there is a two-way exchange of information between purchasing organizations and their vendors through shared or integrated IT systems (more on channel relationships in Chapter 11). If you're the producer of a product that is sold by a large retailer such as Walmart, think about the information and insights you could gain from access to the consumer information that Walmart gathers from its interactions with shoppers in its stores.

Indeed, Walmart in particular is already well known for employing this approach through its vendor management system known as Retail Link, which provides real-time purchase data to suppliers, making it possible for them to track purchase data for their products in real time. Vendors are able manage the process of replenishment so that they can ensure that their products are available for consumers exactly when and where they need them. In addition, for marketers, this provides a valuable source of purchase data in real time that they can use to analyze purchase patterns within different Walmart locations. It also saves Walmart the costs of having to manage this process themselves.[21]

For organizations, being able to leverage large amounts of data to yield new insights and provide a clearer understanding of both consumers and internal business operations is an attractive proposition and a potential source

scanner data
Data derived from items that are scanned at the cash register when you check out with your loyalty card.

channel partner model
A relationship between channel partners in which a two-way exchange of information between purchasing organizations and their respective vendors is facilitated through shared or integrated IT systems.

Mangostock/Shutterstock

The loyalty card you use at the supermarket provides the store with valuable data about your purchase history.

of competitive advantage. As we noted in the previous section, increased integration within supply chains allows organizations to more efficiently track the movement of goods at every point. This helps them to create a more efficient balance between supply and demand and can create greater confidence among supply chain members when it comes to supplying either raw materials or products at exactly the point when they are needed (more on this when we discuss distribution, and in particular *just in time (JIT)* delivery and inventory techniques in Chapter 11). Ultimately, this means cost savings that retailers can pass down to the consumer in the form of lower prices.

A little known—and also quite important—source of Big Data for marketers is an aspect of daily life you may not have considered from a marketing perspective. Specifically, weather data collected in real time can be a great asset to marketers thanks to advances in technology (i.e., marketing automation) that makes its use in micro-local contexts more cost effective and valuable. You may be surprised to learn that venerable tech firm IBM, who is best known for its Big Data and business analytics capabilities, recently purchased the digital assets of the Weather Company (aka, The Weather Channel). It's a brilliant move! Among other things it enables Big Blue (that's IBM's historical nickname) to integrate a vast amount of weather-related data into a number

Brand Association Map

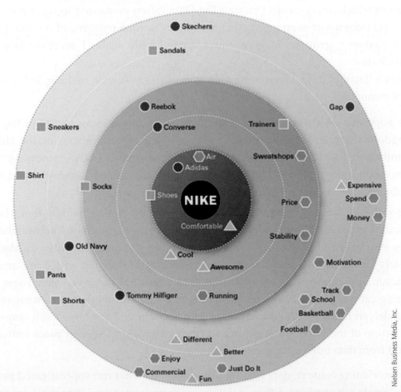

Nielsen's BAM (Brand Association Map) analyzes consumer conversations online and plots the words and phrases that most closely relate to a client's brand. The closer a word appears to the map's center, the stronger the association. And the proximity of words to each other also indicates the strength of their relationship in online posts.

of its current products and services, as well as develop new offerings that make use of the data.[22]

To fully appreciate the value of this acquisition to IBM, think about how consumer behavior may shift as a result of the weather. For example, a national spa company might decide to use location-specific weather data to trigger the delivery of a rainy day promotion to potential customers when the weather in the related area has taken a turn for the worse. Imagine if you had plans to go hiking (or some other outdoor activity) on a Saturday. Upon rolling out of bed you look out the window to see that the sun is nowhere to be found. New plan: a spa day! Oh, and thanks to the e-mail promotion you just received it is a top-of-mind alternative to salvage the day as a result of the inclement weather. This approach also comes in handy in more extreme situations. For example, when part of the country lies in the path of a hurricane, Walmart knows from experience what products to quickly load on its trucks that service stores in that region—two top-sellers are strawberry Pop Tarts and beer.[23]

Data Mining

Who says you can't have too much of a good thing? For organizations today, the challenge with data is not about having enough of it. To the contrary, many have far too much information than they can handle! Big Data can easily exacerbate the problem of **information overload**, in which the marketer is buried in so much data that it becomes nearly paralyzing to decide which of it provides useful information and which does not.

Most *marketing information systems* include internal customer transaction databases, and many include acquired databases. Often, these databases are extremely large. To take advantage of the massive amount of data now available, a sophisticated analysis technique called **data mining** is now a priority for many firms. This refers to a process in which analysts sift through Big Data (often measured in terabytes—much larger than kilobytes or even gigabytes) to identify unique patterns of behavior among different customer groups. To give you a sense of the scale, 1 terabyte is equal to 1,024 gigabytes!

To get a flavor of how data mining aids in marketing decision making, let's consider a couple of examples

- The supermarket chain Safeway learned from its data mining efforts in the United Kingdom that the upper 25 percent of most valuable customers for the chain frequently purchased a cheese that ranked only 209th in sales. Without knowing that this item was heavily preferred by the most profitable customers, Safeway would have no doubt dropped it from inventory for poor overall performance.[24]

- The web-based travel company Orbitz discovered by mining its data that Mac users spend as much as 30 percent more than PC users on nightly hotel accommodations. This insight led Orbitz to offer higher-end options more frequently to Mac users. Clearly Orbitz made a sound business decision, but it was met with a fair amount of criticism at the time of its implementation as a result of perceived unfairness.[25] Data mining can yield valuable insights, but it is important for marketers to remember that data-driven decisions should not occur in a vacuum and they must still consider the full scope of the impact that can result from putting strategies in place that a single result from data mining suggests.

In a marketing context, data mining uses computers that run sophisticated programs so that analysts can combine different databases to understand relationships among buying decisions, exposure to marketing messages, and in-store promotions. These operations are so complex that often companies need to build a **data warehouse** (which can cost more than $10 million) simply to store and process the data.[26] As you've no doubt

information overload
A state in which the marketer is buried in so much data that it becomes nearly paralyzing to decide which of the data provide useful information and which do not.

data mining
Sophisticated analysis techniques to take advantage of the massive amount of transaction information now available.

data warehouse
A system to store and process the data that result from data mining.

read in the news because it can be controversial, marketers at powerful consumer data generators Google, Netflix, Amazon, Facebook, and Twitter are into data mining big time. For example, Facebook has access to vast sums of data created as a result of the various posts, comments, and reactions by the one billion plus users that use the social media platform on a daily basis.[27]

Primary Data Types for Data Mining

As data mining techniques improve and software becomes more adept at understanding and analyzing information in its various formats, the ability to gain deeper insights about consumers from data is increasing. Data in electronic format can be considered either structured or unstructured. **Structured data** are what you might find in an Excel spreadsheet or in a statistics table on a sports website such as ESPN.com. These datasets typically are either numeric or categorical; they usually are organized and formatted in a way that is easy for computers to read, organize, and understand; they can be inserted into a database in a seamless fashion; and typically they can be easily placed within rows and columns.

Massive data warehouses (or server farms) store the huge amounts of information that marketers need to data mine and examine purchasing patterns to yield insights about their customers' preferences.

Scanrail/Fotolia

structured data

Data that (1) are typically numeric or categorical; (2) can be organized and formatted in a way that is easy for computers to read, organize, and understand; and (3) can be inserted into a database in a seamless fashion.

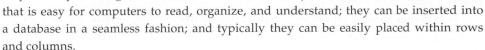

Ripped from the Headlines

Ethical/Sustainable Decisions in the Real World

Software algorithms have become a significant part of our daily lives and a major source of advancements in personal and organizational productivity. Algorithms comb through vast amounts of data to find hidden patterns and determine how to use those patterns. The formula may prompt the system to offer a highly personalized experience to a user when shopping or to provide new content on the user's website or phone based on what has already been viewed.

T-shirt company Solid Gold Bomb learned this the hard way when it used an algorithm to automate the design of thousands of variations of a T-shirt, all around the concept of modifying the well-known saying "keep calm and carry on." The British used this phrase during World War II to keep up civilians' morale during German bombing runs. The algorithm generated all kinds of variations including "keep calm and play football" and "keep calm and dance." These and thousands of other alternatives lived on the web—including at least one version that featured a distasteful saying (we can't publish it here!). The shirt went viral, and needless to say many people weren't happy. The company received a lot of criticism from those who strongly felt the firm should not be let off the hook just because the offending variation was the accidental result of an algorithm. In the end, the negativity this incident generated was too much for the small company to handle, and a few months later Solid Gold Bomb closed down shop.[28]

Algorithms also placed Facebook in the middle of some controversy. A source publicly claimed that some contractors within Facebook known as "news curators" may have selectively excluded news stories from the platform's "Trending Topics" module based on the view that those stories would be of interest to individuals with conservative political leanings.[29] Even if the claims were true that Facebook's workers were selectively excluding stories from the "Trending Topics" module based on their own personal biases or the company's biases, such activity would not have been illegal. Regardless, the situation does point out a potentially gray ethical area that can arise when algorithms require human intervention in order to effectively serve their purpose.

It is also worth considering that an algorithm may contain systemic biases as a result of the personal preferences of the designers, developers, and testers involved in its creation. This leads to other potential ethical quandaries about the algorithm's use and performance.[30] As such, it's possible that even without human intervention in Facebook's process of selecting "Trending Topics," the algorithms used could have exhibited a bias toward one or more particular views because the formula was programmed to highlight some terms or phrases over others.

ETHICS CHECK: ✎

Should social media companies who use algorithms to select news stories for display and distribution on their platforms be required to provide transparency into the inner workings of the related algorithms?

☐ YES ☐ NO

Figure 5.3 📈 *Process* | Structured and Unstructured Data Examples

Far more unstructured data than structured data are created on a daily basis through different business processes, but both have the potential to offer marketers greater insights into their customers and markets.

Structured Data	Unstructured Data
• **Date** • **Time** • **Census Data** • **Facebook "Likes"**	• **Body of Emails** • **Tweets** • **Facebook Status Update Messages** • **Video Transcripts**

unstructured data
Nonnumeric information that is typically formatted in a way that is meant for human eyes and not easily understood by computers.

emotion analysis
A sophisticated process for identifying and categorizing the emotions a follower possesses in relation to a product or brand by assessing the content of that communication.

In contrast, **unstructured data** contain nonnumeric information that is typically formatted in a way that is meant for human eyes and not easily understood by computers.[31] A good example of unstructured data is the body of an e-mail message. The e-mail carries a lot of meaning to a human, but poses a greater challenge for a machine to understand or organize. 📈 Figure 5.3 lists other examples of different types of structured and unstructured data.

In the past, data mining and data analysis were focused on structured data because computers could easily analyze a large number of data points at one time. For instance, a baseball statistician can put into a computer all of the "at bats" that a player has had throughout the course of a season along with their outcomes and easily tell the computer to predict his batting average for the year (as well as a number of other useful measures). This output yields a better understanding of each player's performance on the field.

It becomes more challenging—but also potentially more interesting—to derive meaning from large quantities of *unstructured* data. For instance, imagine that you are the social media manager for a company that sells candy bars and you spend a lot of time engaging with customers through Facebook and Twitter. You are lucky to have a lot of likes and followers and a high level of interaction as well, but you're not satisfied with these data and believe that this is only the tip of the iceberg. In addition, you know that all of these comments from your customers could be a source of a lot of great information—the only problem is that there are thousands of them flooding in, and you're only one person. How could you possibly find the time to effectively analyze their contents and discern valuable patterns from all of this information? Even a huge team would have significant challenges trying to cull through the vast amount of unstructured data customers create every day when they talk about different companies online.

Technology to the rescue! Significant advances in data-analytic technologies make the process of unstructured data analysis easier through the development of computer logic that can search through and extract patterns from large amounts of textual data. It also makes it more cost effective through the use of automated processes as opposed to manual intervention (imagine having to sift through every message by hand to pull out and record the information that you believed was meaningful).[32] The other advantage is that these types of technologies give unstructured data a "structure," enabling it to be shared and leveraged when combining it with data sources held elsewhere in an organization.

Previously in the chapter we introduced *sentiment analysis* which is commonly used with social media data to determine the attitudes held by consumers in relation to a brand. As technology becomes even more advanced, marketers are moving beyond sentiment (which might simply be recorded as either "positive," "negative," or "neutral") into a wide range of more complex feelings and emotions. This method, known as **emotion analysis**, can analyze the content of social media communications within the context of a specific brand or product and determine what emotional category or categories the communication fits within. The media conglomerate Viacom (which includes MTV, Nickelodeon, and BET to name a few) recently chose to use a technology startup called Canvs for emotion analysis to offer its advertising partners greater insight into how viewers are reacting to the advertisements they place through Viacom's programming and other content offerings. Canvs is able to categorize comments into 56 categories (in other words provide and translate *unstructured data* into *structured data*) that include such categories as "trippy," "awkward," "guilty pleasure," and "mind blown." The company is able to do this by allowing its algorithm to look at social media comments within the context of the company's own database of more than 4 million words and phrases, which includes short-hand expressions popular on social media as well as generation specific vernacular (e.g., "bae" and "on fleek").[33] Being able to leverage both structured and unstructured data in data mining efforts offers marketers the opportunity to gain a deeper understanding of their customers.

Data Mining: Applications for Marketers

A key theme of this chapter and the previous chapter is that better understanding of both current and potential customers should be a central goal for all marketers. Every interaction the firm has with a consumer—every touchpoint, regardless of which department might facilitate the interaction—can provide valuable information for marketers to leverage. Data mining techniques that enhance the value of Big Data provide opportunities for marketers to increase organizational performance. To help identify the data needed for these efforts and bring them together, organizations often assemble teams of individuals from different functions, such as marketing, sales, in-store operations, and IT to help identify and gather the needed data sources for analysis.[34]

As illustrated in 📷 Figure 5.4, data mining has four important applications for marketers:[35]

1. *Customer acquisition:* Many firms include demographic and other information about customers in their database. For example, a number of supermarkets offer weekly special price discounts for store "members." These stores' membership application forms require that customers indicate their age, family size, address, and so on. With this information, the supermarket determines which of its current customers respond best to specific offers and then sends the same offers to noncustomers who share the same demographic characteristics. You read previously that Safeway's U.K. division learned through mining supermarket scanner data that many of their most valuable customers prefer a particular type of cheese. This insight is quite handy to create special promotional offers on that cheese to attract more noncustomers that match the characteristics of the current cheese fans.

2. *Customer retention and loyalty:* The firm identifies big-spending customers, who may or may not be at risk of defecting, and then targets them with special offers and inducements other customers won't receive to reward them for their loyalty and increase

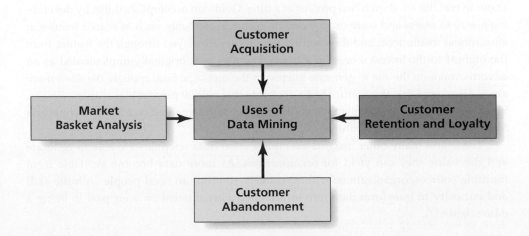

Figure 5.4 📷 *Snapshot* | Uses of Data Mining

Data mining has four primary applications for marketers.

their likelihood of retention.[36] Keeping the most profitable customers coming back is a great way to build business success because—here we go again!—keeping good customers is less expensive than constantly finding new ones.

3. *Customer abandonment:* Strange as it may sound, sometimes a firm wants customers to take their business elsewhere because servicing them actually costs the firm too much. Today, this is popularly called "firing a customer." For example, a department store may use data mining to identify unprofitable customers—those who don't spend enough or who return most of what they buy. Data mining has allowed Sprint to famously identify its customers as "the good, the bad, and the ugly" (we're not sure who the ugly are ...).[37]

4. *Market basket analysis:* Develops focused promotional strategies based on the records of which customers have bought certain products. Hewlett-Packard, for example, carefully analyzes which of its customers recently bought new printers and targets them to receive e-mails about specials on ink cartridges and tips to get the most out of their machines. Another example is when a user purchases one item on Amazon and then is recommended a set of items that other users who purchased the first item also purchased (such as recommending a Rachel Ray Cooking Pan after a customer purchases a Rachel Ray Cooking Pot).

Data Scientists: Transforming Big Data into Winning Information

In Chapter 4, we talked about the important role of customer insights for marketing decision making. Being able to transform data into insights and leveraging data to enhance the way that organizations interact with consumers is a really challenging proposition. It is one that analysts execute with the help of powerful databases and complex software. These analysts (also known as *business intelligence developers)* are employed by the biggest names in technology. A **data scientist** is someone who searches through multiple, disparate data sources to discover hidden insights that will provide a competitive advantage.[38] These individuals frequently have Ph.D.s, often command six-figure starting salaries (according to Glassdoor.com, the median salary as of 2016 was $113,436[39]), and are becoming an increasingly important source of competitive advantage for organizations that want to leverage Big Data. Traditional data analysts often looked at one data source, whereas data scientists typically look at multiple sources of data across the organization.

If you have ever used LinkedIn, you'll be interested to learn that one of the most frequently used features on the site was developed through experimentation by one of the organization's data scientists named Jonathan Goldman. Specifically, Goldman developed the "People You May Know" feature on the site, where LinkedIn users whom you may know in real life are shown two profiles at a time. Goldman accomplished this by developing a way to assess and score users based on common elements, such as shared tenures at educational institutions, and then sorting the profiles displayed through the feature from the highest to the lowest scores (to a limit). The idea was originally implemented as an advertisement on the site to generate interest in the message. Sure enough, the site's managers discovered that this feature had a click rate that was 30 percent higher than average. Soon after that, top management within the organization signed off on adding "People You May Know" as a standard feature.[40]

These and many other insights exemplify what data scientists are able to generate and the value they can yield for organizations. As more data become available from multiple sources, organizations will most likely continue to need people with the skill and curiosity to transform data into information (any interest on your part in being a data scientist?).

data scientist
An individual who searches through multiple, disparate data sources to discover hidden insights that will provide a competitive advantage.

5.3 Marketing Analytics

OBJECTIVE
Describe what marketing analytics include and how organizations can leverage both marketing analytics and predictive analytics to improve marketing performance.

(pp. 165–174)

Marketing analytics have become an increasingly important part of a marketer's toolbox as technological advances enable consumers to engage in an increasing number of activities online that were previously possible only within the physical space. In a general sense we can think of analytics as the identification, interpretation, and articulation of patterns within data that one or more groups view as meaningful.[41]

At its core, **marketing analytics** comprises a group of technologies and processes that enable marketers to collect, measure, analyze, and assess the effectiveness of marketing efforts. Marketing analytic solutions provide marketers with a holistic means to look at the performance of different marketing initiatives.[42] They are capable of providing a level of analysis and a degree of accuracy and speed that is crucial in our data-driven world. Put simply, then, marketing analytics takes the Big Data and makes sense out of it for use in marketing decision making! That is, the breadth and depth of information that today's marketers have at their disposal requires the ability to leverage technology that can move through massive and often disparate data sets to provide useful information that can power decisions and help marketers better understand the value of their investments.

The need to be able to tie specific actions in advertising to measurable results (such as sales) has been a long-standing challenge for marketers. Especially for those who have spent money on TV advertising, billboards, and other forms of traditional advertising, there is a real challenge to quantify the value of those efforts. You may have seen a TV advertisement for McDonald's featuring a Big Mac and chosen the next day to purchase one because of the advertisement, but how would anyone else know that it was <u>that</u> commercial that pushed you over the fast-food edge, as opposed to any of the other marketing investments that McDonald's has made? Digital marketing offers an attractive solution due to the easy application of marketing analytics it brings. It enables marketers to get a better sense of the specific ROI they receive when they use a specific channel as opposed to the guesswork of earlier days.

marketing analytics
A group of technologies and processes that enable marketers to collect, measure, analyze, and assess the effectiveness of marketing efforts.

digital marketing channels
The paths of distribution through which a company's digital marketing communications can be delivered to reach their respective audiences.

Connect Digital Marketing Channels to Marketing Analytics

One of the perennial challenges marketers face is being able to determine the effectiveness of different marketing campaigns and channels. This is because it is not always clear where a lead came from, or what led to a purchase by a consumer, without being able to track it from its origin. For instance, did a consumer learn about and ultimately purchase a product because of the commercial he or she saw on TV, because of the ad he or she viewed in a magazine, or perhaps both? For traditional media such as TV and magazines, it is still not always clear what actions yield the greatest impact for the marketer.

However, with the proliferation of digital media and digital marketing channels, it has become more straightforward to understand what actions on the part of marketers drive consumers to ultimately make a decision that aligns with the interests of the organization. **Digital marketing channels** are those specific means of distribution through

Retailers increasingly send promotional codes to customers' mobile phones to entice them to buy online.

NicoElNino/Shutterstock

which digital marketing communications can be delivered to current and potential customers. The distribution of communications through digital marketing channels often requires the use of one or more technology platforms that serve as intermediaries.

Let's consider as an example a fictional clothing company that has decided to send out a promotional e-mail to let you know about its new fall collection (and hopefully induce a purchase). The e-mail includes images of a few models who wear some of the clothing items, a link to a specific part of the website that displays the Fall collection, as well as a special promotional code to input at checkout (e.g., FALL20) that will take 20 percent off of any fall collection items that the recipient chooses to purchase.

Now, let's see how marketing analytics kick in to help this retailer. Hint: In the next paragraph, we are going to note some of the key parts of the process in which data is recorded (watch for the phrase "*data recorded*") based on your hypothetical actions in the scenario we describe. Figure 5.5 illustrates this process in terms of the relationship

Figure 5.5 *Process* | Digital Marketing Channel Example

This figure illustrates examples of several aspects of a digital marketing channel initiative for a fictional clothing company.

To: customer123@email.com
From: donotreply@genericclothingco.com
Subject: Check Out The New Fall Collection

Generic Clothing Company

Check Out The New Fall Collection!

The New Fall Collection has Arrived

Fall's latest styles are in from Generic Clothing Company and you won't want to miss out. From sweaters to jackets we have the looks that you'll love.

For a limited time enter Promo Code FALL20 when checking out to get 20% off of any purchases that you make from the fall collection. Offer Expires 11/24.

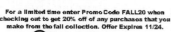

Get Started Shopping Now!

To remove your name from our mailing list, please click here.

Questions or comments? E-mail us at someone@example.com or call 555-555-5555

User Action	a. Open the email and review its contents (Image Displayed).
	b. Click the "Get Started Shopping Now!" button to go to the company's website.
Example of Data Recorded (Considered in Aggregate for all Recipients of the Email)	a. Opening of email.
	b. Specific button selected.
Marketing Analytics Application	a. The percentage of recipients who opened the email).
	b. The percentage of email recipients who opened the email who then clicked on the link to the website.
Example Consideration for Marketers related to Analytics Application	a. Was the subject line of the email effective at capturing the attention and interest of the email's recipients?
	b. How effective was the content of the email at conveying the purpose of the email and its relevance to its recipients?

Generic Clothing Company

Checkout 🛒

The Fall Collection

Fall Sweater (for Her)
List Price: $19.99

Fall Jacket (for Her)
List Price: $49.99

Fall Scarf (for Her)
List Price: $14.99

Fall Sweater (for Him)
List Price: $19.99

Fall Jacket (for Him)
List Price: $49.99

Fall Scarf (for Him)
List Price: $14.99

User Action	c. Review the "Fall Collection" page and click on the "Fall Sweater (for Her)" image/link to go to its individual page.
Example of Data Recorded (Considered in Aggregate for all Recipients of the Email)	c. Specific Image/link clicked on and the page that the link is on.
Marketing Analytics Application	c. The percentage that each page (clothing item) accounted for of the total pages that users visited from this page (for all users directed to the site by the promotional email).
Example Consideration for Marketers related to Analytics Application	c. Which pages (clothing items) are consumers visiting after being directed to the "Fall Collection" page from the promotional email? If some are more frequently being visited to a significant degree, what might that suggest about the content of the promotional email or the audience being targeted?

The Fall Collection > Fall Sweater (For Her)

Fall Sweater (for Her)

List Price: $19.99

Quantity: 1

(d) **Add to Shopping Cart**

User Action	d. Select the "Add to Shopping Cart" button to add the clothing item to the shopping cart.
	e. Select the "Checkout" link to go to the checkout page.
Example of Data Recorded (Considered in Aggregate for all Recipients of the Email)	d. Specific clothing item added to shopping cart.
	e. Specific link clicked on and the page that the link is on.
Marketing Analytics Application	d. The percentage that each individual clothing item accounted for of the total clothing items added to each user's shopping cart (for all users directed to the site by the promotional email).
	e. The percentage of clicks that each page accounted for out of the total count of clicks that directed users to the "Checkout page" (for all users directed to the site by the promotional email).
Example Consideration for Marketers related to Analytics Application	d. Which clothing items appear to be the most popular among consumers and why?
	e. Which pages do consumers tend to visit last before making the decision to proceed to the "Checkout" page to finalize a purchase and why?

Generic Clothing Company

Checkout 🛒

Checkout

Item Summary

Quantity	Description	Amount
1	Fall Sweater (for Her)	$19.99

Subtotal: $19.99

Shipping Cost: $4.99

Tax: $2.50

Total: $27.48

Input Promo Code (if Applicable) (f) FALL20

(g) **Continue to Payment**

User Action	f. Enters Promotional Code (FALL20).
	g. Select the "Continue to Payment" link to go to the page where the payment is made and finalized.
Example of Data Recorded (Considered in Aggregate for all Recipients of the Email)	f. N/A (the recording of the promotional code used is dependent on the user selecting the "Continue to Payment" link).
	g. The promotional code input; the specific link clicked on and the page that the link is on.
Marketing Analytics Application	f. N/A.
	g. The percentage of users that input the valid promotional code out of those users who selected the "Continue to Payment" link (for all users directed to the site by the promotional email).
Example Consideration for Marketers related to Analytics Application	f. N/A.
	g. How effective is the promotional code at motivating consumers to make a purchase? Do consumers seem to purchase more items or spend more when using the promotional code (compared to those who did not use it)?

between some of your actions in this scenario, the specific data created as a result of those actions, and the data's potential analytics-related applications.

OK, here goes. You receive the e-mail in your inbox, read the subject line and decide to open the e-mail (*data recorded*). After reviewing the e-mail's contents you decide that you are interested in checking out the new fall collection so you click on the link to that part of the website (*data recorded*). You take a look at a few of the specific details related to the items by clicking on links corresponding to their individual product pages (*data recorded*) and ultimately choose to add a sweater to your shopping cart (*data recorded*). You go to the checkout page (*data recorded*), input the promotional code and select a button to process it (*data recorded*), and then pay for the item (*data recorded*).

All of the data the preceding paragraph identified as "recorded" now can be transformed using marketing analytics to gain a greater understanding of whether the related e-mail campaign is achieving a satisfactory ROI for this retailer. Presumably you were not the only one who received the promotional e-mail and it is likely that other variations of it were distributed (perhaps with higher and lower discounts, as well as different images of models in different clothing items). Each of these variations would be identifiable within the data and the marketer could analyze at a more detailed level how each variation performed in terms of the ultimate goal of driving sales as well as along each step in the process leading to a sale. Perhaps best of all, the marketer can now measure the investment associated with each variation of the e-mail promotion (and the effort as a whole) relative to its cost and identify how the company might make further improvements. In its simplest form, the retailer might conduct an **A/B test**, which is a method to test the effectiveness of altering one characteristic of a marketing asset (e.g., a web page, a banner advertisement, or an e-mail). Essentially, this involves sending out two variations of the same message to determine if one version "pulls higher" than the other. The test is conducted by randomly exposing some users to the original version and other users to an altered version. The behavior of users within each group is recorded and the results are used to determine if the altered version performs better on some measure of interest (e.g., click-through rates). When you compare the power of this test to the old-fashioned, "let's run an ad in the Sunday paper and see what store traffic looks like on Monday," you can easily appreciate the benefit of this approach.

A/B test
A method to test the effectiveness of altering one characteristic of a marketing asset (e.g., a web page, a banner advertisement, or an e-mail).

Omni-channel Connectivity

To help understand the increasing value that marketing analytics offers to organizations, it is important to recognize how much the way that we ingest information has changed over time. As we'll see in later chapters, today's consumer has evolved into an omni-channel media user. This means that most of us get our information about the world from multiple sources including computers, tablets, and phones, and we freely move from one to another in the course of a day. With more individuals having access to and spending time on the Internet, digital marketing has become an increasingly important element of the marketer's toolbox. According to one survey conducted in 2013 by the Pew Research Center, 87 percent of Americans use the Internet (up from 14 percent in 1995), and 74 percent of Americans use at least one social networking site, with 42 percent using multiple social networking sites.[43]

Across the globe, more people use the Internet for an increasingly wider array of purposes. Who knows how many more functions will be made faster, easier, or more intuitive as developers continually introduce new apps? A survey of marketing executives for organizations in North America and the U.K. (with annual revenue greater than $500 million) conducted by Gartner, a leading IT research and consulting firm, noted that 98 percent of respondents view online and offline marketing as merging. In addition, the survey indicates that overall marketing budgets grew by 10 percent in 2015. Gartner's group vice president notes within the context of the survey's results that "marketers no longer make a clear distinction between offline and online marketing disciplines. As customers opt for digitally led experiences, digital marketing stops being a discrete discipline and instead becomes the context for all marketing. Digital marketing is now marketing in a digital world." That change helps to explain why digital commerce (or the purchase and sale of products and services using digital technologies) has seen an increase in investment with it accounting for 11 percent of the digital marketing budget, up from 8 percent in the prior year.[44] As marketers continue to feel pressure to demonstrate the ROI of their efforts, the emphasis on digital marketing and specifically digital commerce will most likely continue into the future.

The options for investment in digital marketing channels are diverse with consumers spending large amounts across a variety of options. 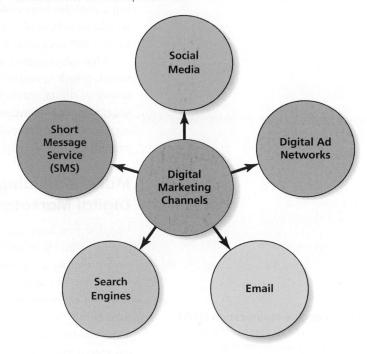 Figure 5.6 illustrates five major groupings of different digital marketing channels: social media, digital ad networks, e-mail, search engines, and short message service (SMS), which are digital messages delivered to mobile phones as text messages. Note that we will discuss digital advertising options that are available to marketers in detail in Chapter 13. For all of these entities, there is a lot of money to be made by selling advertising space to organizations. Facebook, which more than a billion people use, offers users the ability to create a profile for free, but its business model relies heavily on being able to generate revenue by selling advertisements on the site. Increasingly, social networking sites are looking for creative ways to provide advertisements on their sites in a way that does not turn off users. The objective is to create a source of value for organizations that does not compromise the website's user experience and relevance.

In addition, most if not all social networking sites invest a lot of effort to offer their advertisers access to analytic tools and capabilities that will help them to assess and further optimize the performance of their marketing efforts. For instance, the popular Internet meme generator and image sharing platform Imgur added advanced analytic capabilities to help its users and advertisers better understand how their images were spreading. The added capabilities allowed users to go beyond just knowing how many views an image has to understanding things such as how many of those views are being captured in a given day and in a given hour, which websites are linking back to the original version of the image, and where within those websites the image is shared. Bottom line, advertisers can use Imgur's analytics to track the performance of their images and better understand the specific stages on the path to going viral (or not viral) and also where the image was best received.[45]

Business Models for Digital Marketing

For marketers, investments in digital marketing are especially attractive because their cost is often directly tied to specific actions users take. For instance, Google's paid search ads can be purchased or bid upon on a **cost-per-click** basis. This means the cost of the advertisement is charged only each time an individual clicks on the advertisement and is directed to the web page that the marketer placed within the advertisement. This method of charging for advertisements is common for online vendors of advertisement space. Other methods of purchasing advertisements digitally include **cost-per-impression**, in which the cost of the advertisement is charged each time the advertisement shows up on a page that the user views.

Companies that sell online advertising space commonly use both of these methods to charge for advertisements. Cost-per-click purchases of advertisements are typically more expensive, as they demand a higher level of interaction from the user (i.e., the users have actually visited the page on which the ad appears and hence are one step closer to becoming a customer). In contrast, cost-per-impression purchases of advertisements can provide a good value but they typically require a greater leap of faith because it's not so easy

Figure 5.6 📷 *Snapshot* | Major Digital Marketing Channels

Digital marketing channels are typically broken up into five main categories. Within these, there are multiple types of marketing efforts and campaigns that marketers can develop and track.

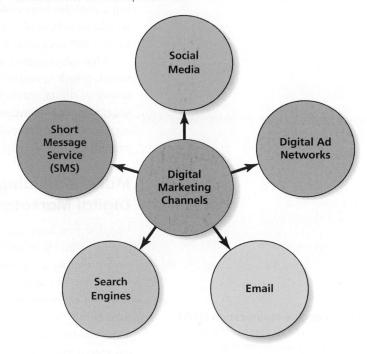

cost-per-click
An online ad purchase in which the cost of the advertisement is charged only each time an individual clicks on the advertisement and is directed to the web page that the marketer placed within the advertisement.

cost-per-impression
An online ad purchase in which the cost of the advertisement is charged each time the advertisement shows up on a page that the user views.

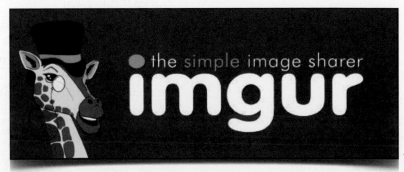

Imgur is a popular image-sharing platform that provides powerful analytics to marketers.

to measure the value of an impression (or view of an advertisement). For instance, if a marketer knew (or had a good idea) that a certain number of impressions from an advertisement translated into a specific number of clicks, then he or she would be able to more accurately estimate the cost of the ad in terms of clicks even while using a cost-per-impression structure to price advertisements. In this way, the marketer would be able to obtain a better value through cost-per-impression pricing as opposed to cost-per-click pricing.

One advantage of digital marketing is that data come in at the speed at which data travel, which is almost instantaneous. This means that marketers can track the performance of digital marketing initiatives and determine their performance both in the very short term and over the long term. Marketing analytics enable them to capture these data across all of the channels in which they have invested and present the data in a way that provides valuable insights into the performance of each channel.

Make Marketing Accountable: Determine the Value of Digital Marketing Investments across Channels

Imagine you have an e-commerce website to sell specialty headphones and you have begun to invest in attracting new customers to your website. You've purchased some online banner advertisements that are being strategically shown to individuals who visit different music websites, and you've also purchased some ads on Facebook that are showing up as sponsored posts in people's feeds who frequently "like" different indie rock bands' pages. You've even looked into **search engine optimization (SEO)**, which is a systematic process to ensure that your firm comes up at or near the top of lists of typical search phrases related to your business. As a result, you've hired a SEO specialist to help ensure that your website ranks highly on search engines such as Google and Bing when people type in search phrases such as "high-quality headphones" and "best way to listen to music."

Now that you have invested in your different marketing channels, you start to see that sales are increasing. It seems as though your investment in all of these different digital marketing channels is paying off, but what if some are paying off more than others because they are engaging more effectively with your target audience and in turn helping to create more sales? How would you determine which channels to invest in even more, and which to drop like a hot potato?

Answer: Marketing analytics would enable you to analyze the performance of all of these channels to help you make the best investment of your marketing dollars moving forward. To understand what's really working on your e-commerce site, you might look to see whether more sales come from your customers who arrive at your site because they typed a search term into Google or whether those who come there because they clicked on a Facebook ad spend more. Or you might find that the banner advertisements bring in relatively few customers and that the transactions they make are relatively small.

If you compare the average cost per customer transaction from each of these channels against the average value of the customer transaction from each channel, it would become clear which channel provides your e-commerce site with the most value. You might even discover that one of these channels costs more than it wins in sales! Table 5.2 provides sample data for the above example as an illustration of how you could perform the relevant calculations for each digital marketing channel. In the example you will see that SEO provides the highest sales, but Facebook ads actually provide the greatest amount of value per customer transaction (or profitability per transaction). This insight might encourage our specialty headphone company to invest more heavily in Facebook advertising in the future.

search engine optimization (SEO)
A systematic process to ensure that your firm comes up at or near the top of lists of typical search phrases related to your business.

Table 5.2 | Sample Marketing Performance Calculation and Comparison

Digital Marketing Channel	Average Customer Transaction (Total Sales Attributed to Channel/Total Number of Customers Acquired Through Channel)	Average Cost per Customer Transaction (Total Spend Attributed to Channel/ Total Number of Customers Acquired Through Channel)	Average Value of Digital Marketing Channel Investment (Average Customer Transaction – Average Cost Per Customer)
Banner Ads	$450,000 (Sales)/10,000 (Customer Transactions) = **$45 (Average Customer Transaction)**	$100,000 (Spent)/10,000 (Customer Transactions) = **$10 (Average Cost per Customer Transaction)**	$45 (Avg. Customer Transaction) – $10 (Avg. Cost per Customer Transaction) = **$35 (Average Value of Digital Marketing Channel Investment)**
Facebook Ads	$1,200,000 (Sales)/15,000 (Customer Transactions) = **$80 (Average Customer Transaction)**	$240,000 (Spent)/15,000 (Customer Transactions) = **$16 (Average Cost per Customer Transaction)**	$80 (Avg. Customer Transaction) – $16 (Avg. Cost per Customer Transaction) = **$64 (Average Value of Digital Marketing Channel Investment)**
Search Engine Optimization	$2,100,000 (Sales)/40,000 (Customer Transactions) = **$55 (Average Customer Transaction)**	$200,000 (Spent)/40,000 (Customer Transactions) = **$5 (Average Cost per Customer Transaction)**	$55 (Avg. Customer Transaction) – $5 (Avg. Cost per Customer Transaction) = **$50 (Average Value of Digital Marketing Channel Investment)**
Total across Channels (Sum of Total Values in Each Channel Input into the Formulas)	$3,75,000 (Sales)/65,000 (Customer Transactions) = **$57.69 (Average Customer Transaction)**	$440,000 (Spent)/65,000 (Customer Transactions) = **$6.77 (Average Cost per Customer Transaction)**	$57.69 (Avg. Customer Transaction) – $6.77 (Avg. Cost per Customer Transaction) = **$50.92 (Average Value of Digital Marketing Channel Investment)**

Without marketing analytics and the data digital marketing initiatives produce, this result would have been more challenging to determine, and as a result there would have been more waste within your e-commerce site's marketing mix. These are the types of challenging questions that companies such as Zappos.com and Overstock.com deal with every day as they look to ensure that their marketing investments provide a healthy ROI. Marketing analytics help them to better understand how their different marketing channels perform.

It is worth noting that some caution can be beneficial when relying on marketing analytics data to attribute a specific effort to a related outcome. For example, suppose an individual sees a TV advertisement for a product and decides to go online to learn more about it. At that point, he or she comes across a banner advertisement online that includes a coupon for the product. Then he or she clicks on the banner advertisement to redeem the coupon and buy the product. On the surface, to a marketer it might look as though all of the credit for the sale should go to the banner advertisement because the marketer has no awareness of the influence that the TV advertisement has had on the consumer, but, as we can see, that is not entirely accurate. The risk illustrated here is the misappropriation of the value that one particular effort has had in delivering a specific result.

Being able to determine the effectiveness of digital marketing depends on having clear goals that can be tracked and measured. In the case of an e-commerce site, one defined goal would most likely be the completion of a transaction with a consumer. However, for a business consulting company's website, it might be getting a prospective client to submit a request for information about what the consulting company can do to help with their particular problem. And being able to tie these data into a CRM system that tracks the individual from the point of filling out a request for information to when he or she ultimately becomes a customer enables the company to look back at the specific digital marketing initiative (or initiatives) that motivated that customer to come to the website in the first place, providing greater insight into what particular channels and factors help create new business.

This example serves to illustrate how different pieces of Big Data—in the form of the comprehensive information about a customer that resides in different parts of the organization (in this case, in the CRM system along with what is currently captured in the marketing analytics system for web-based interactions)—can be brought together. Through the use of marketing analytics, these data can be transformed into a more complete picture of each customer as well as each marketing channel to better understand where future investments should be made or how current marketing campaigns should be adjusted. Understanding each customer's full story enables marketers to better understand how to weave their own actions and communications into the fabric of that story in a way that is meaningful and compelling.

Marketing Accountability within Nondigital Marketing Channels

Although we have paid a lot of attention to marketing analytics within the context of digital marketing channels and efforts, we would be remiss not to take a little time to discuss how we can also use marketing analytics generate insights related to nondigital marketing channels. In particular, direct mail—which we will discuss as a promotion tool in Chapter 14—is one type of nondigital marketing channel that can be set up so that its value can be more effectively measured using marketing analytics. You might be asking yourself at this stage, how can you know that a direct mail marketing campaign led to a sale (or some other desired action)? The key is to put in place a mechanism to identify those current or potential customers who were targeted by a specific direct mail campaign and tie them to the specific desired goal (e.g., making a purchase).

A great example of how this works relates to an example we gave previously in the chapter of a clothing company that sent out a promotional e-mail to alert consumers of its new fall collection. As you may recall, one of its components was a promotional code that a customer could enter to redeem a discount. A direct mail campaign intended to generate sales of a product or service can use similar tactics by creating a unique promotional code to measure the effectiveness of the campaign. When that code is used by a customer (either in an online store or a physical store) the company can effectively attribute that transaction to the related direct mail campaign using marketing analytics. Knowing how many direct mail items were sent out with the related promotional code (and the cost of doing so) along with how many times the code was used (and the total dollar amount of the related transactions) gives the company strong evidence of how effective the campaign was.

Another example would be to use a specific URL within a direct mail campaign that is not used or displayed elsewhere. The URL could lead to a **landing page**, which is a single page on a website that is built for a particular direct marketing opportunity. Landing pages are usually designed to include specific information that is logically connected to the content of the marketing communication that led the user to the page, and typically feature one or more interactive elements that provide the user with a means of engaging in one or more actions desired by the marketer (e.g., filling out a contact form). Through marketing analytics, each visitor to the landing page can then be associated with the related direct mail campaign. Then the company can determine how effective the specific campaign was at encouraging people to (a) RSVP for the event and (b) actually show up for the event).

We can apply similar tactics to other types of nondigital marketing channels to get a better picture of how effective they are at reaching the marketer's particular goals for a campaign. Essential to such an approach is being able to isolate the relationship between a specific marketing effort and its desired outcome. Hence, using identifiers such as unique

landing page
A single page on a website that is built for a particular direct marketing opportunity.

campaign-specific promotional codes, campaign-specific URLs, or campaign-specific phone numbers for customer follow up allows the direct marketer to tie a specific effort to a specific response. This link provides maximum opportunity to apply marketing analytic capabilities to understand the performance of the campaign.[46]

Predictive Analytics

Can we predict the future? Up to this point, we've looked at how organizations can leverage marketing analytics to better understand how *current* marketing channels and initiatives are performing—in other words, to understand how to validate the value of decisions we have already made and potentially to create fact-based triggers that will enable us to better determine how to make future investments. Another intriguing area for any marketer is the ability to actually *predict* the future and thus better understand the value of their marketing campaigns even *before* they implement them.

One interesting application of predictive analytics that may be implemented in the future comes in the form of a highly publicized patent application by Amazon for a process it calls "anticipatory package shipping." The idea is to develop a data driven system that will allow for starting delivery of packages even before customers click "buy." Essentially, Amazon will be able to box and ship products it expects customers in a specific area will want but for which a specific customer order has not actually yet been placed. Getting the right goods moving like this could cut delivery time and thus dissuade customers from visiting brick-and-mortar retailers instead of shopping online.[47]

This crystal-ball scenario is where **predictive analytics** can increasingly provide significant value to marketers. These techniques use large quantities of data and variables that the analysts know relate to one another to more accurately predict specific *future* outcomes (the key with "predictive" analytics is this focus on the future, not just the present).[48] Certainly, organizations have used these techniques for decades to help forecast sales and other important measures of business performance and outcomes, but don't fool yourself into thinking there's nothing new or exciting within this area. Thanks to Big Data and the new-age data mining capabilities we've discussed, the types of future outcomes that we can predict, and the level of accuracy possible with those predictions now enable marketers to obtain more accuracy than ever before when they forecast successful future marketing investments.

Vodafone Netherlands is the second-largest mobile carrier in the Netherlands, and predictive analytics solutions seemed to be a strong choice to better understand the behavior of its customers and better predict future behaviors. As the organization's senior information architect for business intelligence noted, "We have a reasonably large number of customers, a limited marketing budget, and the need to understand how to apply the money effectively and get the best results." Vodafone had a wealth of information and wanted to have the capabilities to identify opportunities to more effectively predict consumer behavior and better tailor service offerings to consumers based on the information. One way that Vodafone was able to create value through predictive analytics was to better understand winter roaming patterns and, in particular, which of their customers were most likely to go skiing during that time. Through the firm's analysis, Vodafone was better able to identify and predict which customers would fall within the category of going skiing in the winter and target them exclusively with a campaign that was tailored to offer great value for winter roamers.[49] What if the company had reached out with this offering to customers within their base who had no plans to hit the slopes? Most likely, the campaign would have been a disaster because of wasted money and the risk of potentially aggravating couch potato customers who didn't want to be bombarded with images of happy skiers while they sat at home (Marketing Rule #1: Never upset your current profitable customers).

Another potential application of predictive analytics involves using Big Data to predict the likelihood that a customer will defect. This invaluable "heads up" allows

predictive analytics
Uses large quantities of data within variables that have identified relationships to more accurately predict specific future outcomes.

a company to identify those customers most at risk and take steps to proactively bring them back into good standing before they actually bail out. XO Communications, a $1.5 billion per year enterprise-level provider of voice, data, and IP services leveraged predictive analytics to do just this. The company knew that the signals of defection were embedded within the data, but it needed a more advanced method to identify these signs and transform them into usable insights that the company's account representatives could then act on to reduce customer defection rates. Some of the predictors included "support call patterns" and "delinquent payment patterns." The key to effectively apply predictive analytics for XO Communications was to give its account representatives the insights in a timely manner so they could get ahead of the curve. A controlled rollout of the effort saw a 47 percent decrease in the company's **churn rate**, which is the percentage of a company's customers (within given a span of time) who by the end of that time span have defected (note that in the next section we will provide a formula for churn rate and elaborate on the concept further). For XO Communications the loss of a customer would have most likely counted as the cancellation of a customer's service contract with the company. The reduction in customer churn from the controlled rollout translated into XO holding onto $15 million in revenue that would otherwise have been lost had churn rates remained where they were before.[50]

For companies such as Vodafone and XO Communications, as well as most all marketers, finding that sweet spot of providing valuable services and support to customers when those particular customers need them is mission critical in today's global competitive marketplace. Predictive analytics and marketing analytics in general enable great execution of marketing strategies.

churn rate
The percentage of a company's customers (for a given span of time) who by the end of that time span can no longer be considered customers of the company (e.g. because they have cancelled their contract for a service or they have stopped shopping at the related retail location).

5.4   Metrics for Marketing Control

OBJECTIVE
Identify how organizations can use marketing metrics to measure performance and achieve marketing control.
(pp. 174–176)

Throughout this chapter and also at different points throughout the text, we touch on different types of metrics and the benefit they provide to marketers (e.g., the "Metrics Moment" features in each chapter and the "Apply the Metrics" exercises at the end of each chapter). In a data-rich and data-driven world, organizations have the ability to gain a more detailed understanding than ever before of what's going on both inside and outside their operations. For marketers, this means having the ability to show more clearly a return on their various investments and to use this knowledge to develop and execute marketing plans and strategies.

In Chapter 3, you learned that marketing control is a process that entails measuring actual performance, comparing this performance to the established marketing objectives, and then making adjustments to the strategies or objectives based on this analysis. **Marketing metrics** are specific measures that help marketers keep an eye on the performance of their marketing campaigns, initiatives, and channels and, when appropriate, serve as a control mechanism for when corrective action is necessary.

Hence, *marketing control* is the ability to calculate and track relevant marketing metrics to identify deviations in expected performance, both positive and negative, as soon as they occur. This important process enables marketers to adjust their actions before greater losses or inefficiencies occur. Another reason digital marketing is seeing increased growth in investment from marketers is the speed at which they can modify their investments in different media channels. For example, a charitable organization that detects an unusually high flow of donations from a Facebook campaign can almost instantly shift more resources to that channel to capitalize on the sudden interest.

marketing metrics
Specific measures that help marketers watch the performance of their marketing campaigns, initiatives, and channels and, when appropriate, serve as a control mechanism.

Metrics Moment

Three Examples of Metrics

Here are three great examples of metrics that are relevant to a chapter on Big Data and marketing analytics. In them, the following symbols are used: $ = a monetary figure, % = a percentage figure, and # = a figure in units.

Click-Through Rate

Within digital marketing, the **click-through** rate is a metric that indicates the percentage of users (viewers of the advertisement or the page that the link is on) who have decided to click on the advertisement in order to visit the website or web page associated with the advertisement:[51]

Click-through rate (%) = (Click-throughs (#)/Impressions (#)) × 100

Most digital marketing campaigns or initiatives use click-through rates as a means of determining marketing effectiveness. Specifically, they indicate what percentage of users who viewed the ad found it relevant and interesting enough to click on it in order to be redirected to another web page. However, from that point of landing on the web page or website, the visitor could have chosen to immediately leave the web page because of a lack of interest in the content on the page or for some other reason. Other metrics taken in tandem with click-through rates can provide a more complete picture.

Conversion Rate

A popular metric used to look at the effectiveness of digital marketing is the conversion rate, which is expressed as a percentage. A **conversion** based on a consumer's interaction with a web page might be the purchase of a product or a service (or multiple purchases in one sitting), the choice to sign up for a mailing list, or the decision to become a follower of the company via social media.[52] The conversion rate is calculated by taking the number of visitors to a website who complete the identified desired activity and dividing that by the total number of visitors to the website and then multiplying the result by 100 to arrive at a percentage value:

Conversion rate (%) = (Number of goal achievements/ Number of website visitors) × 100

Conversion rate can be tracked on a day-to-day basis or provided as a cumulative value and tied back to different marketing campaigns or channels to measure the impact of those activities and to answer questions, such as what is bringing customers to your site. It can also alert marketers to opportunities to take corrective action in order to improve the performance of their marketing efforts.

Cost-per-Order

Cost-per-order indicates the cost of gaining an order in terms of the marketing investment made to turn a visitor to a website into a customer who has chosen to make a transaction.[53] Within digital marketing, this metric can be broken down by specific campaigns or marketing channels to help marketers to get a more precise idea of how effective their marketing investments are:

Cost-per-order ($) = Advertising costs ($)/Orders (#)

For marketers, it provides a clearer idea of what the average cost in advertising dollars is to generate an order. For instance, one might learn that Facebook ads have a lower cost per order than YouTube video ads, and as a result more resources are directed toward Facebook.

Apply the Metrics

Consider the information generated by calculating click-through rate, conversion rate, and cost per order.

1. How does knowledge of the results of calculating these three aid marketers in making better investment decisions in web strategies?
2. Do you think one of these metrics is more useful than the others? If so, what leads you to this opinion?

Before we dive into more marketing metrics, one point worth making is that it is typically not practical to use too many metrics at once to measure marketing effectiveness. Identifying the right metrics that align with the desired outcomes of your marketing strategies ensures that the right controls are in place and that the organization focuses on synchronizing the most important outcomes with the correct marketing decisions.

For instance, imagine you're the CMO for a laundry detergent producer. To bring in more business, you have decided to give your team full latitude to use the department's resources to ramp up sales. You tell them that they are going to be judged by their ability to increase the number of detergent bottles they sell. In the following few weeks, you're pleased to see that the detergent seems to be flying off of supermarket shelves. But on further inspection, you also learn that despite the surge in sales, profits have not increased. As it turns out, your marketing team has been saturating the market with coupons for half-off detergent bottles, and this price promotion is what drove the influx of business. You console yourself that, although profits may not have been positively impacted due to the reduced prices people are paying for the brand, surely this effort will bring in more business over the *long run* as new customers try the brand because they received a coupon.

click-through
A metric that indicates the percentage of website users who have decided to click on an advertisement to visit the website or web page associated with it.

conversion
Signifies an event that occurs on a web page that indicates the meeting of a predefined goal associated with the consumer's interaction with that page.

cost-per-order
The cost of gaining an order in terms of the marketing investment made to turn a website visitor into a customer who has chosen to make a transaction.

Unfortunately, the marketing team did not do an effective job of targeting new customers. It turns out that the shoppers who redeemed the coupons were primarily regulars (existing users) of the product who just bought as they normally would but at a reduced price. As a result, sales actually decline over the next month. The reason: Customers who stocked up on laundry detergent in the past month continue to use their reserves of the product they purchased at a promotional price! Had the goals of the effort been more clearly defined and the right metrics selected related to both gaining market share and increasing sales, then perhaps a more targeted approach with better controls could have been implemented.

Now, let's consider a couple of additional metrics. For each, the following symbols are used: \$ = a monetary figure, % = a percentage figure, and # = a figure in units.

Margin on Sales

margin on sales
The difference between the price at which a product is sold and the cost of the product.

Margin on sales represents the difference between the price at which a product is sold and its cost. This metric can be represented as either a dollar amount or as a percentage of the price that the product is sold for.

$$\text{Margin on Sales (\#)} = \text{Selling Price per Unit (\$)} - \text{Cost per Unit (\$)}$$
$$\text{Margin on Sales (\%)} = (\text{Unit Margin on Sales}/\text{Selling Price per Unit}) \times 100^{54}$$

It is crucial for marketers to have a strong understanding of the margin on sales associated with a product or service for a number of decisions. Examples of relevant decisions may include pricing a product within the different distribution channels and regions it is sold in, determining the ROMI of a particular marketing investment, and evaluating the profitability of a customer or segment of customers. We'll discuss margins in greater detail in Chapter 10.

Churn Rate

Churn rate, introduced previously in the chapter, is an important metric for many companies given the expense associated with acquiring new customers compared to the cost of retaining current customers. Reducing the churn rate can be an important financial goal for an organization and a sign that customer retention efforts are working (as was seen in the XO Communications example). An increase in a company's churn rate can also serve as an indicator that there has been a shift in the competitive environment, such as when a competitor offers large incentives to customers to switch to their product or service. A good example of this is when Sprint launched a marketing campaign around the claim that it would halve the bills of any customers who switched from using AT&T and Verizon to using Sprint for their wireless phone services.[55]

$$\text{Churn Rate (\%)} = (\text{Number of Customers Lost at the end of the Prior Period}/$$
$$\text{Total Number of Customers at the Beginning of the Prior Period}) \times 100^{56}$$

In the preceding formula we can define a period as any given span of time, but it is commonly defined as the period of time in which we can accurately observe customer churn. Depending on the specific product or service this may be a quarter or a year. Examples of customer behaviors (or lack thereof) we can use to identify that a customer has been lost at the end of a period may include unsubscribing from a service, not renewing a service contract, or the passing of a set number of days without a purchase (where the normal expectation would be that the customer would make another purchase at least once within a given span of time since the last purchase).

Objective Summary ➡ Key Terms ➡ Apply

5.1 Objective Summary (pp. 150–155)

Explain how marketers increase long-term success and profits by practicing customer relationship management.

Companies using CRM programs establish relationships and differentiate their behavior toward individual customers on a one-to-one basis through dialogue and feedback. The ability to effectively manage all of the available data has been greatly aided by marketing automation capabilities, which facilitate the capability of sales and marketing professionals to gain critical insights from customer data. Success of CRM is often measured one customer at a time using the metrics of share of customer, customer lifetime value (CLV), and customer prioritization. CRM also provides marketers with the means to better tailor their communications to customers based on the wealth of data that is being effectively captured and organized within the system.

Key Terms

customer relationship management (CRM), p. 150

mar-tech, p. 150

one-to-one marketing, p. 150

touchpoint, p. 150

marketing automation, p. 151

share of customer, p. 153

5.2 Objective Summary (pp. 155–164)

Understand Big Data, data mining, and how marketers can put these techniques to good use.

Big Data refers to data that are growing in terms of both volume and velocity. It comes from a wider range of sources within different functions within organizations as well as society at large. Big Data offers marketers the ability to gain a deeper understanding of their customers when properly leveraged through methods such as data mining. When marketers use data mining, they methodically sift through large data sets using computers that run sophisticated programs to understand relationships among things like consumer buying decisions, exposure to marketing messages, and in-store promotions. Data mining leads to the ability to make important decisions about which customers to invest in further, which to abandon, and where the greatest opportunities for new investments lie.

Key Terms

Big Data, p. 155

Internet of Things, p. 156

web scraping, p. 157

sentiment analysis, p. 157

scanner data, p. 158

channel partner model, p. 158

information overload, p. 160

data mining, p. 160

data warehouse, p. 160

structured data, p. 161

unstructured data, p. 162

emotion analysis, p. 162

data scientist, p. 164

5.3 Objective Summary (pp. 165–174)

Describe what marketing analytics include and how organizations can leverage both marketing analytics and predictive analytics to improve marketing performance.

Marketing analytics offer marketers the means of better understanding and analyzing the wealth of data that are now at their disposal. With the proliferation of digital marketing and the speed at which data can be captured and analyzed, marketers are able to gain insights at or near real time in regard to the performance of their marketing investments. This capability to analyze across channels (both physical and digital) the performance of their different marketing initiatives provides a means through which to more precisely identify *where value is being created*. Predictive analytics have the potential to help marketers identify outcomes before they occur and in turn make smarter decisions as they plan marketing campaigns and investments.

Key Terms

marketing analytics, p. 165

digital marketing channels, p. 165

A/B test, p. 168

cost-per-click, p. 169

cost-per-impression, p. 169

search engine optimization (SEO), p. 170

landing page, p. 172

predictive analytics, p. 173

churn rate, p. 174

5.4 Objective Summary (pp. 174-176)

Identify how organizations can use marketing metrics to measure performance and achieve marketing control.

Marketing metrics provide marketers with the means to further understand the performance of their marketing campaigns and channels and a means of identifying potential red flags or opportunities as they arise. Increases in the popularity of digital marketing as well as tools that are able to easily capture data online have enabled marketers to track marketing performance at a level of detail that was either not possible or not cost effective in the past. The marketing metrics provided in this section were just a small sampling, but they do provide some examples of what kinds of metrics can be used to help

ensure that marketing control is achieved. Through the selection of the right metrics, marketers are better able to understand the performance of their marketing activities, identify opportunities for improvement, and take corrective actions at a point where greater benefits can be realized.

Key Terms

marketing metrics, p. 174

click-through, p. 175

conversion, p. 175

cost-per-order, p. 175

margin on sales, p. 176

Chapter **Questions** and **Activities**

> **MyLab Marketing™**
> Go to **mymktlab.com** to watch this chapter's Rising Star video(s) for career advice and to respond to questions.

Concepts: Test Your Knowledge

5-1. What is CRM? How do firms practice CRM?

5-2. Explain the concepts of share of customer, customer lifetime value (CLV), and customer prioritization.

5-3. How would you describe Big Data? What are some of the most significant sources of competitive advantage that Big Data offers?

5-4. Describe the various sources of Big Data for marketers.

5-5. What is data mining? For marketers, what are some of the most important applications?

5-6. What is the difference between structured and unstructured data? What are some examples of each?

5-7. What are marketing analytics, and what kinds of insights are enabled by today's marketing analytics solutions? What are predictive analytics?

5-8. What is the difference between purchasing digital advertisements with a cost-per-impression structure versus a cost-per-click structure? Is one better than the other?

5-9. Define marketing metrics. How can marketing metrics help marketers understand the performance of different marketing initiatives and provide greater control?

5-10. What is a click-through rate, and how is it calculated?

5-11. What is a conversion? What are some examples of conversions on an e-commerce website?

5-12. What is a cost-per-order? What kind of information do marketers gain from this metric?

Activities: Apply What You've Learned

5-13. *For Further Research (Individual)* Sentiment analysis is an approach to evaluating the degree of positive or negative commentary for a brand by analyzing comments posted by consumers on social media, online forums, and other discussion websites. This is done through an

automated computer process, but for this activity you will need to review one social media platform for your brand (that is, Facebook, Twitter, or even YouTube) and assess the degree of positive or negative commentary (using some form of market research scale) for the brand by looking at around 50 recent comments.

Given your manual summary of sentiment analysis, how helpful do you think this form of analysis would be to a firm? How easy is it to assess comments on a scale of positive to negative, or are some comments too ambiguous? Would it be worthwhile to combine this analysis with a review of the current marketing activities of the firm or its competitors?

5-14. *Creative Homework/Short Project* Imagine that you are building your own e-commerce site. Having a keen understanding of the importance of defining and putting in place a set of conversions and metrics in advance of launching the site, you have incorporated the definitions and development of specific conversions for tracking into the planning of the website. List which actions on the site would indicate a conversion for tracking purposes and how they would align with the goals of your business. Because this is your website, feel free to assume the inclusion of any sorts of features or elements (conventional or unconventional) that you believe would be valuable in terms of the website's look and feel that would enable better tracking and analysis of marketing performance.

5-15. *Creative Homework/Short Project* Consider that you are in charge of all paid search advertising through Google for your company. One of your colleagues is in charge of Instagram advertising. Your boss is in the process of putting together the marketing budget and has asked you to weigh in on how much should be allotted for Instagram advertising. He tells you that he feels that the organization's funds would be better put toward increasing spending on Instagram as opposed to Google paid search advertisements. He says, "Pictures on Instagram are just more compelling than little blocks of text in a search engine's results." You couldn't agree less with that sentiment, and you have the data to back it up.

a. How would you go about making the argument that Google paid search advertisements should receive more of the marketing budget compared to Instagram advertisements? What factors in your boss's statement are potentially not taking this into consideration?

b. What metrics would you use to help make your case, and how would you explain their relevance and importance?

5-16. *In Class, 10–25 Minutes for Teams* As an admissions manager for a college or university, you are interested in exploring the use of predictive analytics within the admissions process to bring in students with a higher likelihood of graduating from the school and achieving greater levels of success both during and after their studies. With another student who is acting as your boss the admissions director, discuss the specific reasons that predictive analytics might be of value to making admissions decisions on students. Be sure to discuss any areas where you might need to proceed with caution.

Concepts: Apply Marketing Metrics

In the chapter discussion about CRM, you read about four key characteristics of CRM: share of customer, lifetime value of a customer, customer equity, and customer prioritization. Each of these elements is discussed in the context of monitoring and assessing the effectiveness of a CRM initiative.

Consider J.C. Penney's loyalty program, JCP Rewards. Go to their website (www.jcprewards.com) and review the information about their reward program.

5-17. In what ways could J.C. Penney expect to measure the four elements of CRM within the context of a reward program such as this?

5-18. How would data be collected for each element, and how might management at J.C. Penney use that data to provide loyal customers with a very strong relationship with the firm?

Choices: What Do You Think?

5-19. *Critical Thinking* Established brands often shift their marketing focus to "share of customer" over time as they become more successful in the marketplace. What is the difference between share of customer and customer loyalty? Do you think it is necessary to focus on share of customer or should firms primarily focus their marketing efforts on acquiring new customers and improving the degree of customer loyalty?

5-20. *Critical Thinking* Are there any potential challenges that could arise related to the use of customer lifetime value (CLV) as a means of determining the allocation of resources to current or potential customer groups? If so, what might these challenges be?

5-21. *Critical Thinking* Google's advertising model uses a pay-per-click (PPC) payment system where advertisers only pay for ads or paid search listings that are clicked on by interested consumers. This is significantly different to the traditional approach to advertising, where advertisers usually pay for the placement of the ad based upon audience numbers. The PPC approach helps brands have a clearer measurement of the effectiveness of the ad.

How would you assess the other advantages and disadvantages of using a pay-per-click advertising approach as opposed to the traditional audience-based payment approach to advertising? (Note: In your answer, you will need to consider the different communication goals of the brand as well as how the different media may impact the message.)

5-22. *Critical Thinking* Predictive analysis relies on a significant understanding of consumer behavior and the likelihood of future purchases based on previous purchases and information searches. The goal of analysis is to predict an upcoming purchase by a consumer in order to deliver suitable marketing communication messages and offers at the right time.

With regard to different types of products, in which product categories do you think predictive analysis would be the most effective? As we need to rely on extensive consumer purchasing behavior, a good degree of analysis, and some form of automated marketing communications system, do you think that the use of predictive analysis is only suitable for more expensive products that have the ability to generate a better return on marketing investment?

5-23. *Critical Thinking* Spending on digital marketing has trended upward in recent years, and with so many individuals using the Internet for extended periods of time, it is easy to understand why. In some cases, some organizations spend more than half of their budget on digital marketing. How do you think they justify committing more than half of their marketing budget to digital efforts? Do you believe that more companies should invest primarily in digital marketing? What groups or factors would indicate to you that digital marketing does not make sense as an investment?

5-24. *Critical Thinking* A study conducted by Adobe found that 77 percent of marketers surveyed believe that data on customer purchase histories can improve marketing performance, yet only 21 percent actually use it. Similarly, 88 percent believe that behavioral data can have a similar impact, but only 20 percent use it.[57] These statistics highlight a contradiction between the perception of marketing analytics' value and the actual frequency of execution of marketing analytics. Why do you think this is? If you were in charge of implementing marketing analytics into an organization, what hurdles would you expect to encounter and from whom, and how would you overcome them?

5-25. *Critical Thinking* If a company of which you are a customer suffered a data breach (in which some of the data customers created or shared by customers with the company were compromised), would your perceptions of that company change and if so, why? Would it matter what type of data was compromised? Are there other factors that would lessen or heighten your view of the severity of the event? If so, what might they include?

5-26. *Ethics* Do you believe it is right for companies to target a higher (or lower) cost service to a consumer based on a data driven observation that the consumer possesses characteristics typically associated with a willingness to spend more (or less) money on the related service? Does this constitute a form of discrimination that would make you uncomfortable as a marketer who is exploring the possibility of employing this strategy? What about if you were the consumer on the receiving end of it?

Miniproject: Learn by Doing

Different types of businesses use different approaches to engaging with both current and potential consumers online. A company's website is usually a key source of information for potential and current customers. The purpose of this project is to gain a deeper understanding of how marketing analytics can be implemented in order to gain greater insights into and enable more effective control of marketing efforts.

a. Select three company website. These should include one ecommerce site (e.g., Amazon), one consulting company (e.g., IBM), and one consumer packaged goods company (e.g., Tide).

b. For each company's website, list what you believe the objectives of the organization are as communicated through the website and identify specific conversion actions on the website that would most closely align with these goals. For example, customer acquisition might be supported and ultimately achieved by getting users to sign up for an e-mail newsletter, which would be defined as a conversion action.

5-27. Rank the conversion actions in order of importance and include an explanation of why you have ordered them as such. Identify whether they are short-term oriented as they relate to the organization's objectives or long term-oriented (or, in some cases, both) and why.

5-28. If you could choose only two marketing metrics (remember metrics, not conversions) to track for each of these websites, identify which two you would select for each website and explain why.

5-29. Some of the websites visited should have a request-for-information form on them. Often, this is one of the ways that marketers begin to collect information on a customer to place within their CRM system. Locate this form and identify what information it is asking for. Write down the different potential uses of this information for the organization and in what ways it might be used by marketers to further engage with the customer. What are some creative ways that you would recommend leveraging these data for each website analyzed in terms of future communications?

Marketing in **Action** Case Real Choices at Novartis

How would you like it if every time you used your medication somebody knew about it? Novartis wants to collect information in the cloud whenever someone uses its Breezhaler inhaler. The company has entered into an agreement with Qualcomm Life, Inc. to create an inhaler with Internet connectivity that will transmit information when patients use the Breezhaler. The device delivers chronic obstructive pulmonary disease (COPD) treatments of Onbrez, Seebri, and Ultibro. The companies will be able to accumulate data concerning the user's medical condition, the efficacy of the drug, and the device itself from a huge number of patients. The collaboration may lead to broad healthcare benefits, but patient confidentiality will be an important issue.

The roots of Novartis go back over 250 years. The modern day enterprise is the union of three Swiss companies: Ciba, Geigy, and Sandoz. Headquartered today in Basel, Switzerland, Novartis is a global leader in innovative medicines, eye care, and cost-saving generic pharmaceuticals. The company's global research operations include publicly funded collaborative research projects involving other corporate and academic partners. Novartis owned companies employ approximately 120,000 full-time associates and provide pharmaceutical products in more than 180 countries.

With this new Breezehaler initiative, when patients use the product it will send tracking information on their smartphones or tablets. Patient statistics transmit wirelessly to a Novartis COPD mobile application, which then transmits the data to the cloud. David Epstein, a Division Head and CEO of Novartis Pharmaceuticals, stated, "By enabling near real-time data capture from the patient and the connected Breezhaler device, patients can monitor their adherence to the medication they take which is vital to their health outcomes." Novartis wants to be the first pharmaceutical company to provide a connected delivery device to give patients an easy-to-use and simple experience. In addition, physicians and other healthcare providers may have access to the data and use it to directly monitor the patient's condition and medicine usage.

Despite the potential benefits, the collection of large amounts of patient data comes with significant risk. The information gathered by the Breezhaler will reside on the patient's device, the healthcare provider's systems, and the cloud. This data creates an attractive opportunity for criminals to steal information like names, birth dates, insurance policy numbers, billing data, and medical diagnostic codes. Stolen medical data is handy to create fake IDs, buy medical equipment, or acquire drugs. Erik Vollebregt, a medical device cybersecurity and privacy attorney, remarked, "The more information, the easier identity theft is and the more valuable the profiles that the hacker can sell to third parties." In addition, he believes that the possibility increases for criminals who hack the information systems to use the data to threaten the lives of patients and blackmail the manufacturer.

Novartis can use the cloud-based medical information to acquire a better understanding of the impact of medications on the treatment of COPD. However, it has to develop methods to ensure that the data sharing is confidential yet will still be of practical use to their researchers. How should

Novartis use the information to create medical benefits to both patients and healthcare professionals and at the same time protect the sensitive data?

You Make the Call

5-30. What is the decision facing Novartis?

5-31. What factors are important in understanding this decision?

5-32. What are the alternatives?

5-33. What decision(s) do you recommend?

5-34. What are some ways to implement your recommendation?

Sources: John Miller, "Big Pharma's Bet on Big Data Creates Opportunities and Risks," *Reuters* (January 26, 2016), http://www.reuters.com/article/us-pharmaceuticals-data-idUSKCN0V41LY (accessed May 10, 2016); "Company History," *Novartis*, https://www.novartis.com/about-us/who-we-are/company-history (accessed May 10, 2016); "Novartis Pharmaceuticals Collaborates with Qualcomm in Digital Innovation with the Breezhaler Inhaler Device to Treat COPD," *Novartis*, https://www.novartis.com/news/media-releases/novartis-pharmaceuticals-collaborates-qualcomm-digital-innovation-breezhalertm (accessed May 10, 2016).

MyLab Marketing™

Go to **mymktlab.com** for the following Assisted-graded writing questions:

5-35. *Creative Homework/Short Project.* Assume that a firm hires you as marketing manager for a chain of retail bookstores. You believe that the firm should develop a CRM strategy. Outline the steps you would take in developing that strategy.

5-36. *Creative Homework/Short Project.* Your boss has been hearing about the importance of Big Data and data mining to marketers. Write a memo to your boss that describes the various applications that data mining has for marketers in order to convince him that the company should explore this topic.

Understand Consumer and Business Markets

Dondeena Bradley

Meet Dondeena Bradley
▼ A Decision Maker at Weight Watchers

Dondeena Bradley is an innovation strategist, health and well-being expert, and a visionary in the area of health innovation. She currently leads global innovation at Weight Watchers International. Prior to Weight Watchers she was at PepsiCo, serving as Vice President, Nutrition Ventures, and Vice President of Nutrition R&D. Her previous food and nutrition experience includes Johnson & Johnson, Campbell's Soup and M&M/Mars. Her education includes a Doctor of Philosophy, Food Science, from Ohio State University, a Master of Science from Purdue University, and a Bachelor of Science from Anderson University.

Dondeena's Info

What I do when I'm not working:
Reading, sketching, and live music

First job out of school:
Research Scientist, M&M Mars

Business book I'm reading now:
Super Better by Jane McGonigal

My management style:
Collaborative, co-creative, and emergent

My pet peeve:
People talking over each other

Here's my problem...

In the early 1960s, Weight Watchers founder Jean Nidetch began inviting friends into her Queens, New York, living room once a week to talk about their lives and how stay on their diets. Today, that group of friends has grown to millions of women and men around the world who have joined Weight Watchers to lose weight and lead healthier lives.

More than 50 years after Weight Watchers was founded, the need for this kind of support has never been greater. Two out of three American adults are overweight, and one-third are obese. We spend more than $60 billion per year on weight-loss solutions, ranging from diet drinks and gym memberships to programs like Weight Watchers and competitors like Jenny Craig and Nutrisystem.[1] Healthcare providers and employers are grappling with the best way to address this costly epidemic. And losing weight continues to be a top priority for many consumers.

Yet there has been a shift in how people think about weight loss. Today's consumers don't want dieting, deprivation and restriction; they want a more holistic and personalized solution that integrates healthier eating, fitness, and emotional well-being. They are also looking for success to be measured by more than just the number on the scale.

In an age of infinite options and choices, it is getting harder to get people to "join" or commit to a single program. Many people opt for a "do it yourself" approach using smartphones, apps, and trackers—and customized diets and exercise regimens that fit their preferences and needs. Many consumers say they don't want a one-size-fits-all approach like Weight Watchers, and that they aren't all that interested in carving out time for weekly meetings that don't seem current.

In January 2016, in response to this changing landscape, Weight Watchers launched a new "Beyond the Scale" program that takes a more personalized approach based on each member's unique lifestyle, goals, and challenges. After an initial assessment, each member receives a custom program that includes daily and weekly SmartPoints targets (to encourage them to eat better), a personalized activity goal (to nudge them to move more), and education and inspiration tailored to their unique situation.

Members can choose to participate in the program online, in person, or both. A typical member's experience consists of attending weekly meetings, each lasting about 45 minutes, at a Weight Watchers location where an inspiring leader who has been successful using the program supports the member group in achieving their stated weight-loss goals.

Whether a member engages with online or in person, the challenge is to find relevant ways to help them stay motivated, inspired, and positive week after week—because the weight-loss journey is typically a long haul, and clinical evidence shows that happier people tend to make healthier choices.

As leader of the global innovation team, my job was to focus on transforming the Weight Watchers face-to-face business. My challenge was to modernize the experience for today's busy, "always on" consumer and to appeal to more people than the segment of age 50+ women that make up Weight Watcher's core customer base.

My team also was asked to address the seasonal/cyclical nature of a business that starts strong at the beginning of the year and typically goes downhill from there. The fact is, after a big marketing and membership "burst" in January when new year/new me resolutions are at a peak, engagement and attendance at Weight Watchers begins to decline significantly throughout the year—as people lose motivation, their commitment wanes, and it gets harder to stay on track.

There's no doubt that people still want the benefits that Weight Watchers delivers, but I had to think hard about new ways for the company to show up and deliver our services given the realities of consumer behavior today.

Dondeena considered her Options 1·2·3

1 Option

Make the weekly meetings more productive and entertaining. Mix them up with lectures by lifestyle experts and offer classes in yoga, Pilates, and other forms of exercise to provide a "one-stop shopping" experience for attendees. These offerings would be attractive to busy people who want to maximize their "bang for the buck" when they allocate time to weight loss. They also sync nicely with the broader consumer trend of a heightened interest in wellness that continues to spread through the mainstream U.S. population. On the other hand, these activities would dilute the core Weight Watchers experience, which is unique because it emphasizes group support and provides a forum for people to share their anxieties and frustrations when they try to lose weight. In addition, Weight Watchers has no expertise in these areas, so becoming a broader lifestyle-oriented company is a departure from the company's strategic mission. Plus, it would require a massive amount of training for our field of 10,000+ meeting leaders and service providers.

2 Option

Design an immersive well-being event that would debunk and shift current assumptions about Weight Watchers (dated, diet-focused, boring) and give participants a contemporary, compelling, life-changing experience. Make it unique and unexpected enough to energize current members, re-engage those who have left, and entice individuals who have never considered Weight Watchers before. Capitalize on trends of people increasingly paying for "experiences" that range from 45-minute group cycling classes at Soul Cycle to a four-day Wanderlust retreat at a Hawaii resort featuring yoga and meditation instructors, chefs, and performers. The event would generate a lot of word of mouth (a critical driver to the Weight Watchers business), and my team could use feedback on the first one to modify subsequent events and determine whether this plan is feasible. On the other hand, a large dramatic event would be a far stretch from the traditional Weight Watchers model. It might alienate core members who expect Weight Watchers to be focused on food, not holistic practices and approaches. It would also require a lot of resources to plan and execute a novel experience like this from scratch.

You Choose

Which **Option** would you choose, and **why**?

☐ **Option 1**   ☐ **Option 2**   ☐ **Option 3**

See what **Option** Dondeena chose in **MyLab Marketing**™

MyLab Marketing™

⭐ **Improve Your Grade!**

Over 10 million students improved their results using the Pearson MyLabs.
Visit **mymktlab.com** for simulations, tutorials, and end-of-chapter problems.

3 Option

Organize a transformative event, but partner with an existing organization like Wanderlust to leverage their experience and infrastructure. Instead of trying to reinvent the wheel, Weight Watchers could move quickly to market with a proven business model and a competent co-sponsor that knows how to stage a complicated event for hundreds/thousands of people. On the other hand, a partner wouldn't be as familiar with the needs of the weight loss community so the experience might not be as "authentic" for our customers. In addition, even if the event is successful, Weight Watchers would not "own" it so the value to our ongoing program might be hard to assess.

Now, put yourself in Dondeena's shoes.

Chapter 6

6.1   The Consumer Decision-Making Process

OBJECTIVE

Define *consumer behavior*, and explain the purchase decision-making process.

(pp. 184–190)

Compelling new products, clever packaging, and creative advertising surround us, clamoring for our attention—and our money. And that's not all—the Internet offers us 24/7 shopping on our "small screens" for these products from any location, information on a gazillion different products from just about as many sellers, plus product and seller reviews by other consumers.

But consumers don't all respond in the same way. Each of us is unique, with our own reasons to choose one product over another. Remember: The focus of the marketing concept is to satisfy consumers' wants and needs. To accomplish that crucial goal, first we need to appreciate what those wants and needs are. What causes one consumer to step into an International House of Pancakes for an order of IHOP Rooty Tooty Fresh 'N Fruity® Pancakes, whereas another opts for a quick Starbucks latte and Danish, and a third person will only eat a healthy serving of "natural" Kashi cereal and fruit? And what, other than income, will cause one consumer to buy that box of Kashi cereal only when it's "on deal" while her neighbor never even looks at the price?

Consumer behavior is the process individuals or groups go through to select, purchase, use, and dispose of goods, services, ideas, or experiences to satisfy their needs and desires. Marketers recognize that consumer decision making is an ongoing process; it's much more than what happens at the moment a consumer forks over the cash and in turn receives a good or service.

Let's go back to the shoppers who want to buy a box of dry cereal. Although this may seem like a simple purchase, in reality there are quite a few steps in the process that cereal marketers need to understand. The first decision in the process is where to buy your cereal. If you eat a lot of it, you may choose to make a special trip to a warehouse-type retailer that sells super-duper-sized boxes rather than just picking up a box while you're at the local supermarket. If you want to choose from healthier organic alternatives, you may browse for cereal at Whole Foods or a local food co-op. Of course, if you get a craving for cereal in the middle of the night, you may dash to the local convenience store. Then, what type of cereal do you buy? Do you eat only low-fat, high-fiber bran cereals, or do you go for the sugar-coated varieties with marshmallows? Of course, you may also like to have a variety of cereals available so you can mix and match.

Marketers also need to know how and when you consume their products. Do you eat cereal only for breakfast, or do you snack on it while you sit in front of the TV at night? Do you eat certain kinds of cereal only at certain times (like sugary kids' cereals that serve as comfort food when you pull an all-nighter)? What about storing the product (if it lasts that long)? Do you have a kitchen pantry where you can store the supersized box, or is space an issue?

And there's more. Marketers also need to understand the many factors that influence each of these steps in the consumer behavior process—internal factors unique to

consumer behavior

The process involved when individuals or groups select, purchase, use, and dispose of goods, services, ideas, or experiences to satisfy their needs and desires.

each of us, situational factors at the time of purchase, and the social influences of people around us. In this chapter, we'll talk about how all these factors influence how and why consumers do what they do. But first we'll look at the types of decisions consumers make and the steps in the decision-making process.

Not All Decisions Are the Same

Old school researchers assumed that consumers carefully collect information about competing products, determine which products possess the characteristics or product attributes important to their needs, weigh the pluses and minuses of each alternative, and arrive at a satisfactory decision. But how accurate is this picture of the decision-making process? Is this the way *you* buy cereal?

Although it does seem that people take these steps when they make an important purchase such as a new car, is it realistic to assume that they do this for *everything* they buy, like that box of cereal? Today, we realize that decision makers actually employ a set of approaches that range from painstaking analysis to pure whim, depending on the importance of what they are buying and how much effort they choose to put into the decision.[2] Researchers find it convenient to think in terms of an "effort" continuum that is anchored on one end by *habitual decision making*, such as deciding to purchase a box of cereal, and at the other end by *extended problem solving*, such as deciding to purchase a new car.

When consumers engage in extended problem solving, they do indeed carefully go through the steps ⬛ Figure 6.1 outlines: problem recognition, information search, evaluation of alternatives, product choice, and postpurchase evaluation.

When we make habitual decisions, however, we make little or no conscious effort. Rather, the search for information and the comparison of alternatives may occur almost instantaneously, as we recall what we have done in the past and the satisfaction we received. You may, for example, simply throw the same brand of cereal in your shopping cart week after week without thinking about it too much. ⬛ Figure 6.2 provides a summary of the differences between extended problem solving and habitual decision making.

Many decisions fall somewhere in the middle and are characterized by *limited problem solving*, which means that we do *some* work to make a decision but not a great deal. This is probably how you decide on a new pair of running shoes or a cool new case for your smartphone. Just how much effort do we put into our buying decisions? The answer depends on our level of **involvement**—how important we perceive the consequences of the purchase to be.

As a rule, we are more involved in the decision-making process for products that we think are risky in some way. **Perceived risk** may be present if the product is expensive or complex and hard to understand, such as a new computer or a sports car. Perceived risk also can play a role when we think that making a bad choice will result in embarrassment or social rejection. For example, a young woman might decide against purchasing a nice-looking and functional Nine West purse from Kohl's for fear that she might be teased or ridiculed by her sorority sisters who all sport trendy Coach handbags.

Figure 6.1 🔀 *Process* | The Consumer Decision-Making Process

The consumer decision-making process involves a series of steps.

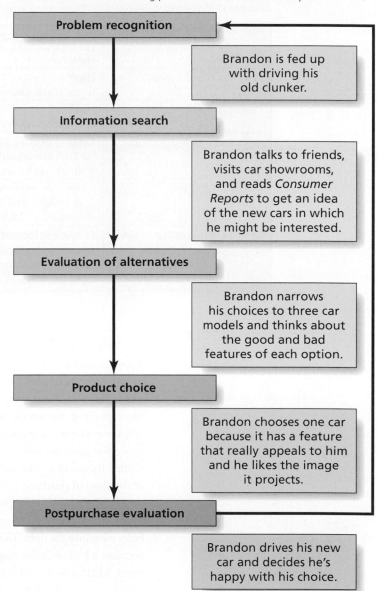

involvement
The relative importance of perceived consequences of the purchase to a consumer.

perceived risk
The belief that choice of a product has potentially negative consequences, whether financial, physical, or social.

Figure 6.2 ⚹ *Process* | Extended Problem Solving versus Habitual Decision Making

Decisions characterized as extended problem solving versus habitual decision making differ in a number of ways.

	Extended Problem Solving	*Habitual Decision Making*
Product	New car	Box of cereal
Level of involvement	High (important decision)	Low (unimportant decision)
Perceived risk	High (expensive, complex product)	Low (simple, low-cost product)
Information processing	Careful processing of information (search advertising, magazines, car dealers, websites)	Respond to environmental cues (store signage or displays)
Learning model	Cognitive learning (use insight and creativity to use information found in environment)	Behavioral learning (ad shows product in beautiful setting, creating positive attitude)
Needed marketing actions	Provide information via advertising, salespeople, brochures, websites. Educate consumers to product benefits, risks of wrong decisions, etc.	Provide environmental cues at point-of-purchase, such as product display

When perceived risk is low—such as when we buy a box of cereal—we experience a low amount of involvement in the decision-making process. In these cases, we're not overly concerned about which option we choose because it is not especially important or risky. The worst-case scenario is that you don't like the taste and pawn off the box on your unsuspecting roommate! In *low-involvement* situations, the consumer's decision is often a response to environmental cues, such as when you decide to try a new type of cereal because the grocery store prominently displays it at the end of the aisle, known as an *end cap*. Under these circumstances, managers must concentrate on how a store displays products at the time of purchase to influence the decision maker.

For *high-involvement* purchases, such as when we buy a house or a car, we are more likely to carefully process all the available information and to have thought about the decision well before we buy the item. The consequences of the purchase are important and risky, especially because a bad decision may result in significant financial losses, aggravation, or embarrassment. Most of us would not just saunter into an auto dealer's office at lunchtime and casually plunk down a deposit on a new Tesla Roadster. For high-involvement products, managers must start to reduce perceived risk by educating the consumer about why their product is the best choice well in advance of the time that the person is ready to make a decision.

To understand each of the steps in the decision-making process, we'll follow the fortunes of a consumer named Brandon, who, as Figure 6.1 shows, is in the market for a new ride—a highly involving purchase decision, to say the least.

Step 1: Problem Recognition

problem recognition
The process that occurs whenever the consumer sees a significant difference between his or her current state of affairs and some desired or ideal state; this recognition initiates the decision-making process.

Problem recognition occurs whenever a consumer sees a significant difference between his or her current state of affairs and some desired or ideal state. A woman whose 10-year-old Hyundai lives at the mechanic's shop has a problem, as does the man who thinks he'd look so much "cooler" if he traded his Toyota for a new sports car. You may fall into the latter category if your old clunker runs okay, but you want to sport some wheels that will get you admiring stares instead of laughs.

Do marketing decisions have a role in consumers' problem recognition? Although most problem recognition occurs spontaneously or when a true need arises, marketers often develop creative advertising messages that stimulate consumers to recognize that their

Stage in the Decision Process	Marketing Strategy	Example
Problem recognition	Encourage consumers to see that existing state does not equal desired state	• Create TV commercials showing the excitement of owning a new car
Information search	Provide information when and where consumers are likely to search	• Target advertising on TV programs with high target-market viewership • Provide sales training that ensures knowledgeable salespeople • Make new-car brochures available in dealer showrooms • Design exciting, easy-to-navigate, and informative websites • Provide information on blogs and social networks to encourage word-of-mouth strategies • Use search marketing to ensure that your website has preferential search engine positioning • Participate in consumer review/advisory websites such as tripadvisor.com
Evaluation of alternatives	Understand the criteria consumers use in comparing brands and communicate own brand superiority	• Conduct research to identify most important evaluative criteria • Create advertising that includes reliable data on superiority of a brand (e.g., miles per gallon, safety, comfort)
Product choice	Understand choice heuristics used by consumers and provide communication that encourages brand decision	• Advertise "Made in America" (country of origin) • Stress long history of the brand (brand loyalty)
Postpurchase evaluation	Encourage accurate consumer expectations	• Provide honest advertising and sales presentations

Figure 6.3 *Process* | Responses to Decision Process Stages

Understanding the consumer decision process means marketers can develop strategies to help move the consumer from recognizing a need to being a satisfied customer.

current state (that old car) just doesn't equal their desired state (a shiny, new convertible). Figure 6.3 provides examples of marketers' responses to consumers' problem recognition and the other steps in the consumer decision-making process.

Step 2: Information Search

Once Brandon recognizes his problem—he wants a newer car—he needs adequate information to resolve it. **Information search** is the step of the decision-making process in which the consumer checks his or her memory and surveys the environment to identify

information search
The process whereby a consumer searches for appropriate information to make a reasonable decision.

what options might solve his or her problem. Advertisements in on TV information we google on the Internet, or a video on YouTube often provide valuable guidance during this step. Brandon might rely on recommendations from his friends, Facebook drivers' clubs, information he finds at www.caranddriver.com, brochures from car dealerships, or the manufacturers' websites. We'll talk more about opportunities for consumers to gather information in the digital world in Chapter 14.

The search for information step includes finding out what alternatives are available and which meet our personal needs. We call the alternatives a consumer knows about the **evoked set** and the ones he or she seriously considers the **consideration set**. If a brand isn't in the consumer's evoked set, there's pretty much a zero chance of purchase. That's why marketers know it's important for consumers to be exposed to messages about their brand frequently, thus ensuring a place in the consumers' evoked set.

Increasingly, consumers use the Internet to search for information about products. Search engines, sites such as Google (www.google.com) and Bing (www.bing.com), help us locate useful information as they search millions of web pages for key words and return a list of sites that contain those key words. We'll talk more about marketing and search engines in Chapter 13.

Comparison-shopping agents (shopbots) such as Bizrate.com or Pricegrabber.com, are web applications that can help online shoppers find what they are looking for at the lowest price. In addition to listing where a product is available and the price, these sites often provide customer reviews and ratings of the product and the sellers. They enable consumers to view both positive and negative feedback about the product and the online retailer from other consumers. Increasingly, consumers also search out other consumers' opinions and experiences through networking websites such as YouTube and Facebook. We'll talk more about these sites and others similar to them later in the chapter.

Step 3: Evaluation of Alternatives

Once Brandon identifies his options, it's time to decide on a few true contenders. There are two components to this stage of the decision-making process. First, a consumer armed with information identifies a small number of products in which he or she is interested. Then he or she focuses on **determinant attributes**, the features most important to differentiate and compare among the product choices. Brandon has always wanted a red Ferrari. But after he allows himself to daydream for a few minutes, he returns to reality and reluctantly admits that an Italian sports car is probably not in the cards for him right now. He decides that the cars he likes—and can actually afford—are the Nissan Versa, the Kia Rio, the Chevrolet Spark, and the Honda Fit. He narrows down his options as he considers only affordable cars that come to mind or his Facebook friends suggest.

Now it's decision time. Brandon has to look more systematically at each of the three possibilities and identify the important product characteristics, what marketers refer to as **evaluative criteria**, he will use to decide among them. The characteristics may be power, comfort, price, the style of the car, and yes, even safety. Keep in mind that marketers often play a role in educating consumers about which product characteristics they should use as evaluative criteria—usually they will "conveniently" emphasize the dimensions on which their product excels. To make sure customers like Brandon come to the "right" conclusions in their evaluation of the alternatives, marketers must understand which criteria consumers use and which they believe are more and less important. With this information, sales and advertising professionals can point out a brand's superiority on the most important criteria as *they* have defined them.

Step 4: Product Choice

When Brandon examines his alternatives and takes a few test drives, it's time to "put the pedal to the metal." Deciding on one product and acting on this choice is the next step in the decision-making process. After agonizing over his choice for a few weeks, Brandon

---

evoked set

All of the alternative brands a consumer is aware of when making a decision.

consideration set

The alternative brands a consumer seriously considers in making a decision.

comparison shopping agents or shopbots

Web applications that help online shoppers find what they are looking for at the lowest price and provide customer reviews and ratings of products and sellers.

determinant attributes

The features most important to differentiate and compare among the product choices.

evaluative criteria

The dimensions consumers use to compare competing product alternatives.

decides that even though the Versa and the Fit have attractive qualities, the Honda Fit offers the affordability he needs, and its carefree image is the way he wants others to think about him. All this thinking about cars is "driving" him crazy, and he's relieved to make a decision to buy the Fit and get on with his life.

So just how do consumers like Brandon choose among the alternatives they consider? These decisions often are complicated because it's hard to juggle all the product characteristics in your head. One car may offer better gas mileage, another is $2,000 cheaper, whereas another boasts a better safety record. How do we make sense of all these qualities and arrive at a decision?

For extended problem solving decisions, we often consider all of the characteristics and the relative importance to us of each one. This type of decision uses **compensatory decision rules** that allow information about attributes of competing products to be averaged in some way. The poor standing on one attribute can potentially be offset by good standing on another.

Other times we rely on simple "rules of thumb," or heuristics, instead of painstakingly learning all the ins and outs of every product alternative. These **heuristics** provide consumers with shortcuts that simplify the decision-making process. One such heuristic is "price = quality"; many people willingly buy the more expensive brand because they assume that if it costs more, it must be better (even though this isn't always true).

Perhaps the most common heuristic is **brand loyalty**; this occurs when we buy the same brand over and over, and, as you might guess, it's the Holy Grail for marketers. People form preferences for a favorite brand and then may never change their minds in the course of a lifetime, making it extremely difficult for rivals to persuade them to switch.

Still another heuristic is based on *country of origin*. We assume that a product has certain characteristics if it comes from a certain country. In the car category, many people associate German cars with fine engineering and Swedish cars with safety. Brandon assumed that the Japanese Honda Fit would be more dependable than the Kia or the Chevrolet, so he factored that into his decision.

Step 5: Postpurchase Evaluation

In the last step of the decision-making process, the consumer evaluates just how good a choice he or she made. Everyone has experienced regret after making a purchase ("What was I *thinking*?"), and (it is hoped) we have all been pleased with something we've bought. The evaluation of the product results in a level of **consumer satisfaction/dissatisfaction**. This refers to the overall feelings, or attitude, a person has about a product after he or she purchases it.

Just how do we decide if we're satisfied with what we bought? When we buy a product, we have some *expectations* of product quality. How well a product or service meets or exceeds these expectations determines customer satisfaction. In other words, we tend to assess product quality by comparing what we have bought to a preexisting performance standard. Think about the customer who finds his new car gets 25 mpg fuel usage. If his expectation is the same 25 mpg, he will be satisfied; if his expectation is 20 mpg, he will be extremely satisfied; but if, based on the information he received before he purchases the auto, he expects the car to get 30 mpg, he will be dissatisfied.

We form our product expectations via a mixture of information from marketing communications, informal information sources such as friends and family, and our own prior experience with the product category. That's why it's important that marketers create accurate expectations of their product in advertising and other communications.

Even when a product performs to expectations, consumers may experience regret, or **cognitive dissonance**, after they make a purchase. When we reject product alternatives with attractive features, we may second-guess our decision. Brandon, for example, might begin to think, "Maybe I should have chosen the Kia Rio—Kia makes great cars and the price is right." To generate satisfied customers and remove dissonance,

compensatory decision rules
The methods for making decisions that allow information about attributes of competing products to be averaged in some way.

heuristics
A mental rule of thumb that leads to a speedy decision by simplifying the process.

brand loyalty
A pattern of repeat product purchases, accompanied by an underlying positive attitude toward the brand, based on the belief that the brand makes products superior to those of its competition.

consumer satisfaction/dissatisfaction
The overall feelings or attitude a person has about a product after purchasing it.

cognitive dissonance
The anxiety or regret a consumer may feel after choosing from among several similar attractive choices.

Figure 6.4 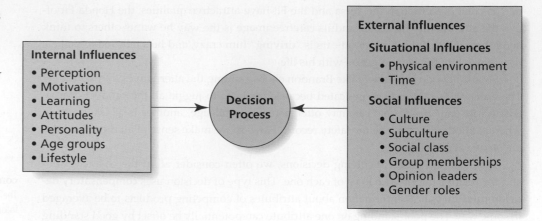 *Process* | Influences on Consumer Decision Making

A number of different factors in consumers' lives influence the consumer decision-making process. Marketers need to understand these influences and which ones are important in the purchase process.

marketers often seek to reinforce purchases through follow-up communications with the customer after the sale.

In a study, business students wrote complaint letters to companies. The companies responded with a free sample, a letter of apology, or no response at all. When the company sent a free sample, attitudes toward the company improved significantly; when the company sent a letter of apology, there was no change in attitude; and when the company did not respond, the attitude was more negative than before.[3]

In addition to understanding the mechanics of the consumer decision-making process, marketers need to understand what influences in consumers' lives affect this process. As we see in Figure 6.4, there are three main influences in the decision-making process: internal, situational, and social influences. All of these factors work together to affect the ultimate choice each person makes.

6.2 Internal Influences on Consumers' Decisions

OBJECTIVE

Explain how internal factors influence consumers' decision-making processes.

(pp. 190–198)

What is your dream car? It may be a sporty Ferrari. However, your roommate dreams of a tricked-out Mustang, and your dad is set on owning a big Mercedes. As the saying goes, "That's why they make chocolate and vanilla." We can attribute much of these differences to internal influences on consumer behavior—those things that cause each of us to interpret information about the outside world, including which car is the best, differently from one another.

Perception

perception

The process by which people select, organize, and interpret information from the outside world.

Perception is the process by which people select, organize, and interpret information from the outside world. We receive information in the form of sensations, the immediate response of our sensory receptors—eyes, ears, nose, mouth, and skin—to basic stimuli such as light, color, odors, touch, and sound. We try to make sense of the sensations we receive by interpreting them in light of our past experiences.

We are bombarded with information about products—thousands of ads both on and off-line, in-store displays, special offers, our friends' opinions we read on their Facebook page, and on and on. The perception process has important implications for marketers: As we absorb and make sense of the vast quantities of information that compete for our attention, the odds are that any single message will get lost in the clutter. And, if we do notice the message, there's no guarantee that the meaning we give it will be the same one the marketer intended. Marketers need to understand the three steps that occur during this process: *exposure, attention*, and *interpretation*.

Exposure

The stimulus must be within range of people's sensory receptors to be noticed; in other words, people must be physically able to see, hear, taste, smell, or feel the stimulus. For example, the lettering on a highway billboard must be big enough for a passing motorist to read easily, or the message will be lost. **Exposure** is the extent to which a person's sensory receptors are capable of registering a stimulus.

Marketers work hard to achieve exposure for their products, but sometimes it's just a matter of making sure that cool people use your product—and that others observe them doing so. One way marketers get their products into the hands of A-listers is to insert them into both official and unofficial gift bags that celebrities receive when they attend the Academy Awards—and then hope those celebrities like the swag so much they show it off for the cameras. One year, for example, actor Kevin James received as a gift a George Foreman grill that was such a hit that he wrote it into episodes of his hit show *The King of Queens*—where millions of viewers around the world saw it.[4]

Many people believe that even messages they can't see will persuade them to buy advertised products. Claims about **subliminal advertising** of messages hidden in ice cubes or baked into the tops of crackers have been surfacing since the 1950s. A survey of American consumers found that almost two-thirds believe in the existence of subliminal advertising, and more than one-half are convinced that this technique can get them to buy things they don't really want.[5]

There is not much evidence to support the argument that this technique actually has any effect at all on our perceptions of products and even less that marketers are or ever have used subliminal advertising methods. But still, concerns persist. ABC once rejected a commercial for KFC that invites viewers to slowly replay the ad to find a secret message, citing the network's long-standing policy against subliminal advertising. The ad (which other networks aired) is a seemingly ordinary pitch for KFC's $.99 Buffalo Snacker chicken sandwich. But if you replay it slowly on a digital video recorder, it tells you that viewers can visit KFC's website to receive a coupon for a free sandwich. Ironically, this technique is really the *opposite* of subliminal advertising because instead of secretly placing words or images in the ad, KFC blatantly publicized its campaign by informing viewers that it contains a message and how to find it.[6] The short story: Hidden messages are intriguing and fun to think about (if a little scary), but they don't really work. Sorry for the letdown—and don't bother trying to read this paragraph backward.

Attention

As you drive down the highway, you pass hundreds, maybe thousands, of other cars. But to how many do you pay attention? Probably only one or two—the bright pink and purple VW Bug and the Honda with the broken taillight that cut you off at the exit ramp. **Attention** is the extent to which we devote mental-processing activity to a particular stimulus.

New *augmented reality (AR)* applications add an exciting dimension to perception for marketers. AR combines a physical layer of information with a digital layer of information to create a dynamic image. This concept will be discussed further in Chapter 14.

dpa picture alliance archive/Alamy Stock Photo

exposure
The extent to which a stimulus is capable of being registered by a person's sensory receptors.

subliminal advertising
Supposedly hidden messages in marketers' communications.

attention
The extent to which a person devotes mental processing to a particular stimulus.

Novelty and contrast in a message are useful to capture consumers' attention.

Factors That Influence Attention

Because attention is critical to advertising effectiveness, marketers continue to look for ways to ensure that consumers will attend to their messages. Some factors that influence consumers' likelihood of devoting processing activity to a stimulus include the following:

Personal needs and goals: Consumers are more likely to pay attention to messages that speak to their current needs. A car that almost causes you to be in an accident will speak to your current need to get where you are going safely. That's the same reason you're far more likely to notice an ad for a fast-food restaurant when you're hungry.

Size: A larger magazine or newspaper ad or a longer TV commercial is more likely to command attention.

Novelty: Stimuli that present something unexpected tend to grab our attention. That includes the red-and-white polka-dot VW bug driving in front of us, ads that are in black and white in an all-color world, or ads in unconventional places such as painted on a sidewalk, on the backs of shopping carts or on bathroom walls. Novelty can also make product packaging stand out. When Pepsi came out with Pepsi One and Coke introduced Coca Cola Zero in black cans, these new versions stood out on store shelves.

Another problem marketers face when it comes to attention is **multitasking**; flitting back and forth among our e-mails, TV, instant messages, and so on. Getting the attention of young people in particular is a challenge—as your professor probably knows! More than half of teens report that they engage in multitasking, where they process information from more than one medium at a time as they alternate among their cell phones, TVs, and laptops.[7]

Online advertisers keep innovating to get visitors to watch their messages. Some have turned to **rich media**, a digital advertising term for an ad that includes advanced features like video and audio that encourage viewers to interact and engage with the content. The web page for the Chevrolet 2016 Spark allows viewers to see the car with different colors, trims, wheels and interiors.[8] Online rich media for the Metropolitan Museum of Art allows web visitors to view a moving panorama of an exhibit or to examine details of a painting by clicking on the image.

Interpretation

Interpretation is the process of assigning meaning to a stimulus based on prior associations we have with it and assumptions we make about it. Two people can see or hear the same event, but their interpretation of it can be as different as night and day, depending on what they had expected the stimulus to be. In one study, kids ages 3 to 5 who ate McDonald's French fries served in a McDonald's bag overwhelmingly thought they tasted better than those who ate the same fries out of a plain white bag. Even carrots tasted better when they came out of a McDonald's bag—more than half the kids preferred them to the same carrots served in a plain package! Ronald would be proud.[9]

Motivation

Motivation is an internal state that drives us to satisfy needs. Once we activate a need, a state of tension exists that drives the consumer toward some goal that will reduce this tension by eliminating the need. Have you ever been on an Interstate highway and seen a billboard with a giant picture of a hamburger available at the next exit, realized how good a big fat juicy hamburger would taste at that moment, and you decided to go for it? That's motivation at work.

multitasking
Moving back and forth between various activities such as e-mails TV, instant messages, and so on.

rich media
A digital advertising term for an ad that includes advanced features other elements like video and audio that encourage viewers to interact and engage with the content.

interpretation
The process of assigning meaning to a stimulus based on prior associations a person has with it and assumptions he or she makes about it.

motivation
An internal state that drives us to satisfy needs by activating goal-oriented behavior.

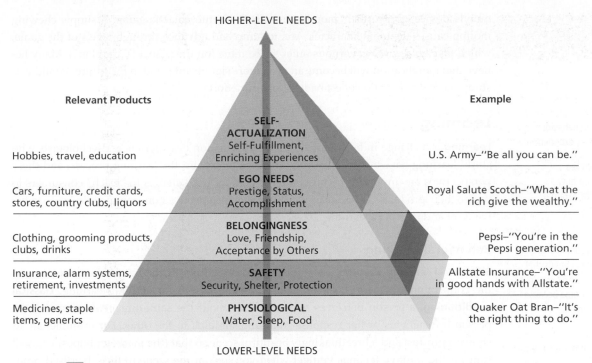

HIGHER-LEVEL NEEDS

Relevant Products

Example

SELF-ACTUALIZATION
Self-Fulfillment, Enriching Experiences

Hobbies, travel, education

U.S. Army–"Be all you can be."

EGO NEEDS
Prestige, Status, Accomplishment

Cars, furniture, credit cards, stores, country clubs, liquors

Royal Salute Scotch–"What the rich give the wealthy."

BELONGINGNESS
Love, Friendship, Acceptance by Others

Clothing, grooming products, clubs, drinks

Pepsi–"You're in the Pepsi generation."

SAFETY
Security, Shelter, Protection

Insurance, alarm systems, retirement, investments

Allstate Insurance–"You're in good hands with Allstate."

PHYSIOLOGICAL
Water, Sleep, Food

Medicines, staple items, generics

Quaker Oat Bran–"It's the right thing to do."

LOWER-LEVEL NEEDS

Figure 6.5 📷 *Snapshot* | Maslow's Hierarchy of Needs and Related Products

Abraham Maslow proposed a hierarchy of needs that categorizes motives. Savvy marketers know they need to understand the level of needs that motivates a consumer to buy a particular product or brand.
Source: Adapted from Maslow, Abraham H.; Frager, Robert D.; Fadiman, James, *Motivation and Personality*, 3rd Ed., ©1987. Reprinted and Electronically reproduced by permission of Pearson Education, Inc., Upper Saddle River, New Jersey.

Psychologist Abraham Maslow developed an influential approach to motivation.[10] He formulated a **hierarchy of needs** that categorizes motives according to five levels of importance, the more basic needs being on the bottom of the hierarchy and the higher needs at the top. The hierarchy suggests that before a person can meet needs at a given level, he or she must first meet the lower level's needs—somehow those hot new 7 For All Mankind jeans don't seem as enticing when you don't have enough money to buy food.

As you can see from 📷 Figure 6.5, people start at the lowest level with basic physiological needs for food and sleep. Then they progress to higher levels to satisfy more complex needs, such as the need to be accepted by others or to feel a sense of accomplishment. Ultimately, they can reach the highest-level needs, where they will be motivated to attain such goals as self-fulfillment. As the figure shows, if marketers understand the level of needs relevant to consumers in their target market, they can tailor their products and messages to them.

Marketers use their understanding of consumer needs for prestige, status, and accomplishment when they use gamification. **Gamification** is a strategy in which marketers apply game design techniques to non-gaming contexts like shopping. They often do this by awarding points or badges to motivate consumers. Nike+, for example, allows consumers to earn points and set goals to push themselves to exercise more. Foursquare and Zynga apps use gamification to encourage app usage. Stride gum introduced "Gumulon," the world's first chewing-based mobile game. Players position the camera on their

hierarchy of needs
An approach that categorizes motives according to five levels of importance, the more basic needs being on the bottom of the hierarchy and the higher needs at the top.

gamification
A strategy in which marketers apply game design techniques, often by awarding of points, badges, or levels, to non-game experiences to engage consumers.

Consumers purchase many products such as bathtubs for both functional and aesthetic reasons.

mobile devices to use their mouths to control the intergalactic game. A simple chewing motion causes the main character, Ace, to jump and advance through levels of the game, which takes place in a cavernous outer space mine (on the planet "Gumulon"). Many believe that gamification will become an even more significant trend in the future. Would you study more if you could collect badges for your efforts?

Learning

learning
A relatively permanent change in behavior caused by acquired information or experience.

Learning is a change in behavior caused by information or experience. Psychologists who study learning have advanced several theories to explain the learning process, and these perspectives are important because a major goal for marketers is to "teach" consumers to prefer their products. We refer to the two major perspectives on how people learn as behavioral and cognitive learning.

Behavioral Learning

behavioral learning theories
Theories of learning that focus on how consumer behavior is changed by external events or stimuli.

Behavioral learning theories assume that learning occurs as the result of experience and the connections we form between events. In one type of behavioral learning, **classical conditioning**, a person perceives two stimuli at about the same time. After a while, the person transfers his or her response from one stimulus to the other. For example, an ad shows a product and a breathtakingly beautiful scene so that (the marketer hopes) you will transfer the positive feelings you get when you look at the scene to the advertised product. Hint: Did you ever notice that car ads often show a new auto on a beautiful beach at sunset or speeding down a mountain road with brightly colored leaves blowing across the pavement?

classical conditioning
The learning that occurs when a stimulus eliciting a response is paired with another stimulus that initially does not elicit a response on its own but will cause a similar response over time because of its association with the first stimulus.

Another common form of behavioral learning is **operant conditioning**, which occurs when people learn that their actions result in rewards or punishments. This feedback

operant conditioning
Learning that occurs as the result of rewards or punishments.

data brokers
Companies that collect information on consumers, use it to create detailed profiles of individuals, and sell or share the information with others.

Ripped from the Headlines

Ethical/Sustainable Decisions in the Real World

Information about you, a typical consumer, is big business because it has huge financial value. Most of us know that companies place cookies on our computers to track our online activities. That's how Amazon offers you great books you'll like and why that ad for a Bosch refrigerator conveniently pops up when you're reading the *New York Times* online—and you happen to be in the market for a refrigerator. But exactly what data companies collect about consumers and what happens to it after they have it is a complex and very troubling question to many.

Data brokers are companies that collect information on consumers and use it to create detailed profiles of individuals. These companies then sell or share the personal information with others. It's not only your searches on Google that data brokers track. Data brokers are also monitoring what you post on Facebook, looking over your shoulder as you handle financial transactions online, even storing the information on the medications you take. Using a treasure box of analytical tools, the brokers are able to create a picture of you, with your name, your address, your likes and dislikes, your closest friends, your bad habits, even your daily movements, both online and offline. And then they sell that "picture" of you to advertisers, financial institutions, insurance companies, the hospitality industry, cable and telecommunications companies, political campaigns, retail stores, and even government entities and law enforcement agencies.

Many believe that consumers are in a kind of wild, wild West where the precious commodity that is being mined and sold is the innocent and unprotected consumer rather than gold. True, you benefit because you're much more likely to get useful information about the products and services you really want and not be bothered by ads for stuff you wouldn't buy in a million years. However, many critics are concerned because at the present time, there are no laws that require data brokers to maintain the privacy of consumer data *unless* they use that data for credit, employment, insurance, housing, or other similar purposes. There are no laws that give consumers the right to know the information the brokers have about them so that they can correct inaccuracies, and no laws that give consumers the right to "opt out" and prevent data brokers from selling their personal information. And, although platforms like Facebook do offer some forms of privacy protection, many users aren't aware of these options and in some cases they don't read "the fine print" closely enough to understand what happens to their data. Do you think that this business is unethical?

ETHICS CHECK:

Should there be more government regulations on data brokers to protect consumers' privacy?

☐ **YES** ☐ **NO**

If data on consumers has financial value, should consumers be financially compensated for their information?

☐ **YES** ☐ **NO**

influences how they will respond in similar situations in the future. Just as a rat in a maze learns the route to a piece of cheese, consumers who receive a "reward," like the toy that you used to get in your Happy Meal at McDonald's, will be more likely to buy that brand again. We don't like to think that marketers can train us like lab mice, but like it or not that kind of feedback does reward us for the behavior and make it more likely that we'll repeat it in the future.

Consumers learn to like or dislike products in part based on how others in their environment react. Marmite is an "acquired taste;" it's a yeast extract that is extremely salty and a local delicacy in the U.K. Australians favor a similar product called vegemite. Americans aren't wild about either.

Cognitive Learning

In contrast to behavioral theories of learning that emphasize simple stimulus-response connections, **cognitive learning theory** views people as problem solvers who learn as they proactively absorb new information. Supporters of this viewpoint stress the role of creativity and insight during the learning process. *Cognitive learning* occurs when consumers make a connection between ideas or by observing things in their environment.

Observational learning occurs when people watch the actions of others and note what happens to them as a result. They store these observations in memory and at some later point use the information to guide their own behavior. Marketers often use this process to create advertising and other messages that allow consumers to observe the benefits of using their products. Health clubs and manufacturers of exercise equipment feature ripped men and women pounding away on treadmills, whereas mouthwash makers imply that fresh breath is the key to romance.

Now we've discussed how the three internal processes of perception, motivation, and learning influence consumer behavior. But the results of these processes—the interpretation the consumer gives to a marketing message or action—differ depending on unique consumer characteristics. Let's talk next about some of these characteristics: existing consumer attitudes, the personality of the consumer, and consumer age groups.

cognitive learning theory
Theory of learning that stresses the importance of internal mental processes and that views people as problem solvers who actively use information from the world around them to master their environment.

observational learning
Learning that occurs when people watch the actions of others and note what happens to them as a result.

Attitudes

An **attitude** is a lasting evaluation of a person, object, or issue.[11] Consumers have attitudes toward brands, such as whether McDonald's or Wendy's has the best hamburgers. They also evaluate more general consumption-related behaviors, such as whether high-fat foods, including hamburgers, are a no-no in a healthy diet. Marketers often measure consumer attitudes because they believe attitudes predict behavior—people like Brandon who think Honda Fit is a "cool" car are more likely to buy one than consumers who cherish the plush comfort of a big Buick. To make attitude measurement meaningful, marketers understand that a person's attitude has three components: affect, cognition, and behavior.

Affect is the *feeling* component of attitudes. This term refers to the overall emotional response a person has to a product. Affect is usually dominant for expressive products, such as perfume, where we choose a fragrance if it makes us feel happy. In other cases, advertisers try to arouse more negative emotions to get our attention and create a bond with their products. This new trend even has a name, **sadvertising**. Ads that provoke a good cry are all around us; think about all the adorable puppies and ponies you see in modern Super Bowl spots.[12] These emotional reactions actually cause physiological changes, such as an increase in pulse and sweating when a well-done commercial really gets to us. Some advertising researchers measure heart rate and skin conductivity and track the eye gaze of consumers while they view ads over the Internet, mobile devices, and their TVs.[13]

Cognition, the *knowing* component, refers to the beliefs or knowledge a person has about a product and its important characteristics. Cognition is important for complex

attitude
A learned predisposition to respond favorably or unfavorably to stimuli on the basis of relatively enduring evaluations of people, objects, and issues.

affect
The feeling component of attitudes; refers to the overall emotional response a person has to a product.

sadvertising
Advertising designed to arouse more negative emotions to get our attention and create a bond with their products.

cognition
The knowing component of attitudes; refers to the beliefs or knowledge a person has about a product and its important characteristics.

behavior
The doing component of attitudes; involves a consumer's intention to do something, such as the intention to purchase or use a certain product.

personality
The set of unique psychological characteristics that consistently influences the way a person responds to situations in the environment.

self-concept
An individual's self-image that is composed of a mixture of beliefs, observations, and feelings about personal attributes.

products such as computers, for which we may develop beliefs on the basis of technical information.

Behavior, the *doing* component, involves a consumer's intention to do something, as the intention to purchase or use a certain product. For products such as cereal, consumers act (purchase and try the product) on the basis of limited information and then form an evaluation of the product simply on the basis of how the product tastes or performs.

Personality and the Self: Are You What You Buy?

Personality is the set of unique psychological characteristics that consistently influences the way a person responds to situations in the environment. One adventure-seeking consumer may always be on the lookout for new experiences and cutting-edge products, whereas another is happiest in familiar surroundings where he or she can use the same brands over and over. Today, popular online matchmaking services like Match.com, Matchmaker.com, and eHarmony.com offer to create your "personality profile" and then hook you up with other members whose profiles are a good match.

A person's **self-concept** is his or her attitude toward himself or herself. The self-concept is composed of a mixture of beliefs about one's abilities and observations of one's own behavior and feelings (both positive and negative) about one's personal attributes, such as body type or facial features. The extent to which a person's self-concept is positive or negative can influence the products he or she buys and even the extent to which he or she fantasizes about changing his or her life.

Self-esteem refers to how positive a person's self-concept is. Our society is obsessed with the self. Consumers track their health and diet on apps like Fitbit, they post updates on their relationships on Facebook, and they spend billions on apparel and beauty products to "edit" the person that others see. The "selfie" epidemic is another symptom of this infatuation, as people go to great lengths to record their presence at parties, museums, and many other locations. A recent survey of young consumers reported that they spend an average of 54 hours per year taking selfies. About half of the respondents were OK with the idea of snapping selfies during childbirth, and one in five think it's OK to take them during a funeral![14]

As Dondeena at Weight Watchers knows, the appeal of many products relates directly to their promise to improve self-image. A lot of these appeals focus on a person's body parts and how he or she feels about their physical condition. Of course in our society "thin is in," and women are constantly bombarded with images of anorexic-looking models. That focus may be starting to change as the movement toward more realistic body ideals gains steam. Recently a plus-size blogger with a huge following threatened to mobilize a boycott against Target because the chain didn't carry larger versions of the designer fashions she craved. Target's social media team picked up on this threat and the retailer nipped the problem in the bud: It now sells a line of plus-sized fashions called AVA & VIV and guess who is one of the models for the clothes? Sometimes the squeaky wheel does get the grease.[15]

Age

A person's age is another internal influence on purchasing behavior. Many of us feel we have more in common with those of our own age because we share a common set of experiences and memories about cultural events, whether these involve Woodstock, Woodstock II, or even Woodstock III. Goods and services often appeal to a specific age group. Although there are exceptions, it is safe to assume that most buyers of Rihanna's CDs are younger than those who buy Barbra Streisand discs.

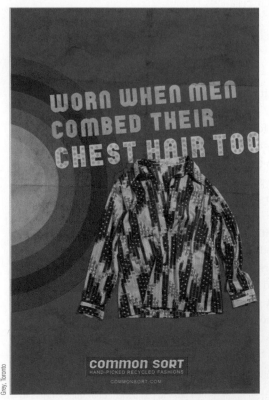

Grey, Toronto

Goods and services often appeal to a specific age-group.

Age is important, but regardless of how old we are, what we buy often depends more on our current position in the **family life cycle**—the stages through which family members pass as they grow older. Singles (of any age) are more likely to spend money on expensive cars, entertainment, and recreation. Couples with small children purchase baby furniture, insurance, and a larger house, whereas older couples whose children have "left the nest" are more likely to buy a retirement home in Florida.

Lifestyle

Demographic characteristics, such as age, income, and family life cycle, tell marketers *what* products people buy, but they don't reveal *why*. Two consumers can share the same demographic characteristics yet be totally different people—all 20-year-old male college students are hardly identical to one another. That's why marketers often further profile consumers in terms of their lifestyles. A **lifestyle** is a pattern of living that determines how people choose to spend their time, money, and energy and that reflects their values, tastes, and preferences.

Each stage in the family life cycle presents new challenges.

family life cycle
A means of characterizing consumers within a family structure on the basis of different stages through which people pass as they grow older.

lifestyle
The pattern of living that determines how people choose to spend their time, money, and energy and that reflects their values, tastes, and preferences.

Metrics Moment

There are many potential metrics available to assess aspects of consumer behavior. Here are some popular ones and an example of each.

- *Overall awareness:* The percentage of all consumers who recognize or know the name of a brand. This can be "aided" or "unaided." A marketer can measure unaided awareness for Sensodyne toothpaste simply by asking consumers to name all the brands of toothpaste that come to mind. Aided recognition is measured by asking consumers questions such as "Have you heard of Tom's of Maine toothpaste?" Then follow-up questions can be asked to ascertain additional pertinent information.
- *Top-of-mind awareness (TOMA):* The first brand that comes to a consumer's mind when he or she thinks of a product category. Marketers measure TOMA with questions such as "What school comes to mind when you think of Ivy League universities?"
- *Consumer knowledge:* Measured by asking consumers if they have some specific knowledge about a brand. To measure brand knowledge, marketers may ask consumers if they believe the brand possesses certain attributes or characteristics, such as "Does the Kia Soul come with Bluetooth wireless technology as a base feature?"
- *Attitude toward a brand:* Often measured with survey questions about beliefs that the brand possesses certain characteristics, the relative importance of those characteristics to the product category, and the overall measure of how much the consumer likes the brand. A resulting question might be "What is your overall feeling toward Chick-fil-A?" (measured on a scale from very unfavorable to highly favorable).
- *Purchase intentions:* A consumer's stated willingness to buy or expressed likelihood of certain behavior. A consumer survey may ask, "If you are in the market for a new pair of running shoes, what

is the likelihood that you would purchase a pair of Brooks running shoes?" (measured on a scale from highly unlikely to highly likely). Caution: Stated intent to purchase does not perfectly translate into actual purchase behavior!
- *Purchase habits:* Another measure of a consumer's self-reported behavior. Marketers ask questions such as "On average, how many times a month does your family eat out?"; "Which restaurant did you go to the last time you ate out?"; and "How much do you normally spend on a dinner out with your family?"
- *Customer loyalty:* A measure of a consumer's commitment to a specific brand. Once the marketer has determined which brand the consumer typically uses, they follow up with questions such as "If on your next trip to the store you plan to purchase hand soap and your favorite brand of hand soap is not available, would you buy another brand or wait until you find your favorite brand to make the purchase?"
- *Customer satisfaction:* A consumer survey may ask questions such as "How satisfied are you with the level of cabin service by JetBlue Airlines?" (measured on a scale from very dissatisfied to very satisfied).

Apply the Metrics

Consider the consumer behavior metrics mentioned. Pick out several metrics that you think would be most useful to gain a better understanding of each item that follows. How might you use each metric you choose to do the following?

1. Better understand a firm's existing customers
2. Identify potential new customers for a firm
3. Gauge the market potential for a new product

Savvy marketers often try to identify how consumers' lifestyle preferences create opportunities for products and services that relate to their values. Consider for example the growing cannabis revolution. Almost overnight, legal pot has become big business, with revenues in the United States of close to $3 billion per year already. As more states decide to legalize marijuana, businesses large and small are rushing in to satisfy customers' needs for the weed but also related items (Oreos, anyone?). The magazine *High Times*, founded by a former drug smuggler way back in 1974, is a "trade paper" for this lifestyle. Today it's at the forefront of the revolution. It hosts the High Times Cannabis Cups, weekend festivals that feature more than 500 vendors, seminars, and celebrity appearances such as Ice Cube and David Arquette. Now it's moving into other ventures, including nightclubs that offer cannabis menus and merchandise such as socks emblazoned with pot leaves.[16]

psychographics
The use of psychological, sociological, and anthropological factors to construct market segments.

activities, interests, and opinions (AIOs)
Measures of consumer activities, interests, and opinions used to place consumers into dimensions.

To determine the lifestyles of consumers, marketers turn to **psychographics**, which groups consumers according to psychological and behavioral similarities. One way to do this is to describe people in terms of their **activities, interests, and opinions (AIOs)**. These dimensions are based on preferences for vacation destinations, club memberships, hobbies, political and social attitudes, tastes in food and fashion, and so on. Using data from large samples, marketers create profiles of customers who resemble one another in terms of their activities and patterns of product use.[17]

6.3 Situational and Social Influences on Consumers' Decisions

OBJECTIVE
Show how situational factors and consumers' relationships with other people influence consumer behavior.

(pp. 198–203)

We've seen that internal factors, such as how people perceive marketing messages, their motivation to acquire products, and their unique personalities, age groups, family life cycle, and lifestyle, influence the decisions we make. In addition, situational and social influences—factors external to the consumer—have a big impact on the choices consumers make and how we make them.

Situational Influences

When, where, and how consumers shop—what we call *situational influences*—shape our purchase choices. Some important situational cues are our physical surroundings and time pressures.

Marketers know that dimensions of the physical environment, including factors such as decor, smells, lighting, music, and even temperature, can significantly influence consumption. When casino operators replaced old school "one-armed bandits" with electronic slot machines that no longer made the familiar whirring noises when players pulled the handle, earnings fell by 24 percent.[18] And the Hard Rock Hotel in Orlando, Florida, boosted ice cream sales by 50 percent simply by spraying a waffle cone scent into the air outside its shop.[19]

sensory marketing
Marketing techniques that link distinct sensory experiences such as a unique fragrance with a product or service.

Sensory marketing is becoming big business. Specialized companies sell scents to hotels, car manufacturers, and even banks (like customers don't know what money smells like). Some offer individual scents, like vanilla, whereas others sell combinations of popular scents. But for some retailers, like Victoria's Secret and Bloomingdale's, it's not enough to have just any scent; these retailers have actually purchased custom scents that not only appeal to their customers but also enhance their brand. And, coming soon: Books, movies, and even clothing that will deliver specific scents via pellets that you insert into your iPhone![20] Marketers term this strategy **sensory branding**.[21] Let's see how some other situational factors influence the consumer decision-making process.

sensory branding
The use of distinct sensory experiences not only to appeal to customers but also to enhance their brand.

The Physical Environment

It's no secret that physical surroundings strongly influence people's moods and behaviors. Despite all their efforts to presell consumers through advertising, marketers know that the store environment influences many purchases. For example, one study of purchasing habits showed that consumers decide on about three out of every four of their supermarket product purchases in the aisles (so always eat before you go to the supermarket). The study also showed that in-store marketing and branding had a strong influence on shoppers' purchasing decisions.[22]

Two dimensions, *arousal* and *pleasure*, determine whether a shopper will react positively or negatively to a store environment. In other words, the person's surroundings can be either dull or exciting (arousing) and either pleasant or unpleasant. Just because the environment is arousing doesn't necessarily mean it will be pleasant—we've all been in crowded, loud, hot stores that are anything but. The importance of these surroundings explains why many retailers focus on packing as much entertainment as possible into their stores. For example, Bass Pro Shops, a growing chain of outdoor sports equipment stores built in the style of an enormous hunting lodge, features giant aquariums, waterfalls, trout ponds, archery and rifle ranges, putting greens, fish and wildlife mounts at every turn, and free classes (for adults and kids) in everything from ice fishing to conservation to meat processing. And if all that sensory overload leaves you famished, many of the Bass Pro Shops stores even offer on-site restaurants at their more than 60 current locations.

Time

Time is one of consumers' most limited resources. We talk about "making time" or "spending time," and we remind one another that "time is money." Marketers know that the time of day, the season of the year, and how much time a person has to make a purchase affects decision making.

Indeed, many consumers believe that they are more pressed for time than ever before. This sense of **time poverty** makes consumers responsive to marketing innovations that allow them to save time, including services such as drive-through lanes at pharmacies, to-your-door grocery delivery, and mobile pet grooming. In fact, a funeral home in Farmville, Virginia, even offers drive-through viewing for mourners who don't want to get out of their cars to see the deceased.[23]

time poverty
Consumers' belief that they are more pressed for time than ever before.

Then of course there is the "always open" convenience of "stores" on the web, ready to serve you whenever, wherever, and however you want. In fact, online shopping is growing at about seven times the rate of overall retail spending in the United States But even though 70 percent of people said that they preferred to shop their favorite retailer online, that doesn't mean your favorite bricks-and-mortar store is going away anytime soon.[24] Instead, these stores are adapting their services to meet your needs. For example, many retailers now let you ship your online purchase to the store nearest you free of charge, and you can return items you purchased online at this location as well. And while you're in the store picking up that new summer tank top you ordered online, chances are you'll pick up a few extra items you didn't know you needed, like those matching earrings and to-die-for flip-flops.

Social Influences on Consumers' Decisions

Although we are all individuals, we are also members of many groups that influence our buying decisions. Families, friends, and classmates often sway us, as do larger groups with which we identify, such as ethnic groups and political parties. Now let's consider how social influences, such as culture, social class, influential friends and acquaintances, and trends within the larger society, affect the consumer decision-making process.

culture
The values, beliefs, customs, and tastes a group of people values.

Culture

We can think of **culture** as a society's personality. It is the values, beliefs, customs, and tastes a group of people produce or practice. Although we often assume that what people in one culture (especially our own) think is desirable or appropriate will be appreciated in other cultures as well, that's far from the truth. For example, simply translating American marketing messages into Spanish doesn't mean those messages will be accepted—especially among those Hispanic consumers living in the United States who have a strong desire to maintain their Hispanic identity. Instead, marketers must "recognize that Hispanics buy brands that empower their cultural relevancy."[25] That means developing relationships with customers and considering their family and religious values.

Values (Again)

As we also saw in Chapter 2, cultural values are deeply held beliefs about right and wrong ways to live.[26] Marketers who understand a culture's values can tailor their product offerings accordingly. But over time, cultural values do change. Consider, for example, that the values for collectivist countries differ greatly from those of individualistic cultures, where immediate gratification of one's own needs come before all other loyalties. In collectivist cultures, loyalty to a family or a tribe overrides personal goals. Today, we see the economic growth of some collectivist countries such as India, Japan, and China, making many consumers more affluent—and individualistic. For marketers, this means growth opportunities for products such as travel, luxury goods, sports activities like tennis and golf, and entertainment.

Subcultures

subculture
A group within a society whose members share a distinctive set of beliefs, characteristics, or common experiences.

microcultures
Groups of consumers who identify with a specific activity or art form.

A **subculture** is a group that coexists with other groups in a larger culture but whose members share a distinctive set of beliefs or characteristics, such as members of a religious organization or an ethnic group. **Microcultures** are groups of consumers who identify with a specific activity or art form. These form around TV shows like *The Voice* or *Grey's Anatomy*, online games like Candy Crush Saga, or leisure activities such as extreme sports. Social media have been a real boon to subcultures and microcultures; they provide an opportunity for like-minded consumers to share their thoughts, photographs, videos, and so on. More on these important new sharing platforms later in the book.

For marketers, some of the most important subcultures are racial and ethnic groups because many consumers identify strongly with their heritage, and products that appeal to this aspect of their identities appeal to them. To grow its business, Clorox got down and dirty with its Hispanic consumers. After studying how Hispanics traditionally clean their homes, Clorox introduced its Clorox Fraganzia line of cleaning products to meet all of their cleaning needs—a thorough process of cleaning, disinfecting, and aromatizing. Even their toilet-bowl cleaners, in the shape of little baskets, or *canastillas*, look like those used in Latin America.[27]

Conscientious Consumerism: An Emerging Lifestyle Trend

consumerism
A social movement that attempts to protect consumers from harmful business practices.

Powerful new social movements within a society also contribute to how consumers make decisions about what we want and what we don't. One such influence is **consumerism**, the social movement directed toward protecting consumers from harmful business practices. Much of the current focus of consumerism is about business activities that harm the environment and the potential damage to our planet. Worries about climate change, entire species going extinct, widespread exposure to carcinogens and harmful bacteria and many other issues are front and center.

As more and more emphasis has been placed on this by consumers and the media, many of us are much more mindful of environmental issues when we shop and when we make decisions about the foods we eat, the clothes we wear, the buildings in which we live and work, and the cars we drive. Even marketers are following the consumerism call to action. Unilever launched a campaign on Facebook and YouTube tied to its Axe brand to encourage reduced usage of hot water. The "Showerpooling" campaign asks fans to take a pledge to share a shower with a like-minded acquaintance or attractive stranger.[28] Some analysts call this new value **conscientious consumerism**.[29] We see evidence of its impact everywhere, in the form of vegan restaurants, electric cars, and solar heating panels on homes.

Social Class

Social class is the overall rank of people in a society. People who are within the same class tend to exhibit similarities in occupation, education, and income level, and they often have similar tastes in clothing, decorating styles, and leisure activities. Class members also share many political and religious beliefs as well as preferences for AIOs.

Many marketers design their products and stores to appeal to people in a specific social class. Working-class consumers tend to evaluate products in more utilitarian terms, such as sturdiness or comfort, instead of trendiness or aesthetics. They are less likely to experiment with new products or styles, such as modern furniture or colored appliances, because they tend to prefer predictability to novelty.[30] Marketers need to understand these differences and develop product and communication strategies that appeal to different social classes.

Luxury goods often serve as **status symbols**, visible markers that provide a way for people to flaunt their membership in higher social classes (or at least to make others believe they are members). The bumper sticker "He who dies with the most toys wins" illustrates the desire to accumulate these badges of achievement. However, it's important to note that over time, the importance of different status symbols rises and falls. For example, when James Dean starred in the 1956 movie *Giant*, the Cadillac convertible was the ultimate status symbol car in the United States. Today, wealthy consumers who want to let the world know of their success are far more likely to choose a Mercedes, a Tesla, or even a humbler Prius.

In addition, traditional status symbols today are available to a much wider range of consumers around the world with rising incomes. This change fuels demand for mass-consumed products that still offer some degree of *panache* or style. Think about the success of companies like Nokia, H&M, Zara, ING, Dell Computers, Gap, Nike, EasyJet, or L'Oréal. They cater to a consumer segment that analysts label **mass class**. This term refers to the hundreds of millions of global consumers who now enjoy a level of purchasing power that's sufficient to let them afford high-quality products offered by well-known multinational companies.

Group Membership

Anyone who's ever "gone along with the crowd" knows that people act differently in groups than they do on their own. When there are more people in a group, it becomes less likely that any one member will be singled out for attention, and normal restraints on behavior may evaporate (think about the last wild party you attended). In many cases, group members show a greater willingness to consider riskier alternatives than they would if each member made the decision alone.[31]

A **reference group** is a set of people that a consumer wants to please or imitate. Consumers "refer to" these groups when they decide what to wear, where they hang out, and what brands they buy. This influence can take the form of family and friends, a sorority or fraternity, a respected statesman like Martin Luther King Jr., celebrities like Angelina Jolie, or even (dare we say it) your professors. Marketers often try to cultivate a loyal community of fans who will spread the word about their clothing, cars, music, sports teams, or movies. Nobody does this better than Lucasfilm for its *Star Wars* franchise. The studio even employs a full-time head of fan relations.[32]

conscientious consumerism
A continuation of the consumerism movement in which consumers are much more mindful of environmental issues in their daily purchases and marketers support consumerism issues in their advertising.

social class
The overall rank or social standing of groups of people within a society according to the value assigned to factors such as family background, education, occupation, and income.

status symbols
Visible markers that provide a way for people to flaunt their membership in higher social classes (or at least to make others believe they are members).

mass class
The hundreds of millions of global consumers who now enjoy a level of purchasing power that's sufficient to let them afford high-quality products—except for big-ticket items like college educations, housing, or luxury cars.

reference group
An actual or imaginary individual or group that has a significant effect on an individual's evaluations, aspirations, or behavior.

Lucasfilm hosts a huge gathering every other year called *Star Wars Celebration*, which attracts almost 50,000 Jedis, Wookiees, and Stormtroopers.

Opinion Leaders

opinion leader
A person who is frequently able to influence others' attitudes or behaviors by virtue of his or her active interest and expertise in one or more product categories.

If, like Brandon, you are in the market for a new car, is there a certain person to whom you'd turn for advice? An **opinion leader** is a person who influences others' attitudes or behaviors because they believe that he or she possesses expertise about the product.[33] Opinion leaders usually exhibit high levels of interest in the product category. They continuously update their knowledge as they read blogs, talk to salespeople, or subscribe to podcasts about the topic. Because of this involvement, opinion leaders are valuable information sources.

Unlike commercial endorsers, who are paid to represent the interests of just one company, opinion leaders have no ax to grind and can impart both positive and negative information about the product (unless they're being compensated to blog on behalf of a brand, which is not unheard of these days!). In addition, these knowledgeable consumers often are among the first to buy new products, so they absorb much of the risk and reduce uncertainty for others who are not as courageous.

Gender Roles

gender roles
Society's expectations regarding the appropriate attitudes, behaviors, and appearance for men and women.

Some of the strongest pressures to conform come from our **gender roles**, society's expectations regarding the appropriate attitudes, behaviors, and appearance for men and women.[34] Of course, marketers play a part in teaching us how society expects us to act as men and women. Marketing communications and products often portray women and men differently. These influences teach us what the "proper" gender roles of women or men should be and which products are appropriate for each gender.

Gender roles vary across cultures, and they can change rapidly over time (as the recent debate over transgender people using bathrooms shows). In other cultures, however, old expectations can be hard to change: A husband in Italy (which has fairly traditional gender role expectations compared to some other countries) had the police formally charge his 40-year-old wife with "mistreatment of the family." He accused her of 2 years of neglect, including an unwillingness to cook and clean. She faces up to 6 years in prison if she is convicted for these offenses.[35]

Many products are sex-typed, which means they are intended specifically to appeal to one gender or the other. For years, consumers and feminists for example have claimed that the Barbie doll reinforces unrealistic ideas about what women's bodies should look like. In 2015, Mattel reintroduced its traditional blonde Barbie in a variety of skin tones, hairstyles, and outfits to attract a more diverse market. Even newer versions in three new body shapes: Tall, curvy and petite, followed in 2016.[36]

Sex roles constantly evolve; in a complex society like ours, we often encounter contradictory messages about "appropriate" behavior. We can clearly see this in the messages girls have been getting from the media for the last several years: It's cool to be overly provocative. Role models like Paris Hilton, Lindsay Lohan, Britney Spears, and Miley Cyrus convey standards about how far preteens and teens should go to broadcast their sexuality. Of course not everyone, especially parents, agree with this trend.

Every culture communicates expectations about the proper roles for men and women, as this ad from Chile for a line of power tools illustrates.

Men's sex roles are changing too. For one, men are concerned as never before with their appearance. In fact, appearance ranks as their second-biggest worry (topped only by money worries and weighing on them more than worries about their family and their health).[37] To prove this point, guys spend $17.5 billion on toiletries globally each year—and that doesn't include the cost of razors, razor blades, or shaving cream.[38] How does this obsession with hair gels and moisturizers coexist with the traditional "macho" guy who can hardly be bothered to comb his hair? Clearly, our cultural definition of masculinity is evolving as men try to redefine sex roles while they stay in a "safety zone" of acceptable behaviors bounded by danger zones of sloppiness at one extreme and effeminate behavior at the other. And, some cultural observers report the emergence of "retrosexuals"—men who want to emphasize their old-school masculinity as they get plastic surgery to create a more rugged look that includes hairier chests and beards, squarer chins, and more angular jawlines.[39]

6.4 Business Markets: Buying and Selling When the Customer Is Another Organization

OBJECTIVE

Understand the characteristics of business-to-business markets and business-to-business market demand and how marketers classify business-to-business customers.

(pp. 203–209)

You might think most marketers spend their days dreaming up the best way to promote cutting-edge products for consumers like new apps for your iPhone, a new power drink to keep you fit, or some funky shoes to add to your collection. But this is not the whole picture. Many marketers know that the "real action" also lies in products that companies sell to businesses and organizations rather than to end-user consumers like you—software applications to make a business more efficient, safety goggles for industrial plants, the carts shoppers push in supermarkets, or the sensors that keep track of your luggage at the airport. In fact, some of the most interesting and lucrative jobs for young marketers are in businesses you've never heard of because these companies don't deal directly with consumers.

Like an end consumer, a business buyer makes decisions—but with an important difference: The purchase may be worth millions of dollars, and both the buyer and the seller have a lot at stake (maybe even their jobs). A consumer may decide to buy two or three T-shirts at one time, each emblazoned with a different design. *Fortune* 500 companies such as ExxonMobil, PepsiCo Inc., and FedEx buy thousands of employee uniforms embroidered with their corporate logos in a single order.

Consider these transactions: P&G contracts with several advertising agencies to promote its brands at home and around the globe. The Metropolitan Opera buys costumes, sets, and programs. Mac's Diner buys a case of canned peas from BJ's Wholesale Club. The U.S. government places an order for 3,000 new HP laser printers. The country of Qatar purchases five new Boeing 787 Dreamliners to add to its fleet—at a price that can exceed $200 million each.[40]

All the these exchanges have one thing in common: they're part of *business-to-business (B2B) marketing*. As we saw in Chapter 1, this is the marketing of goods and services that businesses and other organizations buy for purposes other than personal consumption. Some firms resell these goods and services, so they are part of a *channel of distribution*, a concept we'll revisit in Chapters 11 and 12. Other firms use the goods and services they buy to produce still other goods and services that meet the needs of their customers or to support their own operations. These **business-to-business (B2B) markets**, also called **organizational markets**, include manufacturers and other product producers, wholesalers, retailers, and a variety of other organizations, such as hospitals, universities, and governmental agencies.

To put the size and complexity of business markets into perspective, let's consider a single product—a pair of jeans. A consumer may browse through several racks of jeans and ultimately purchase a single pair, but the buyer who works for the store at which the consumer shops had to purchase many pairs of jeans in different sizes, styles, and brands from different manufacturers. Each of these manufacturers purchases fabrics, zippers, buttons, and thread from other manufacturers, which in turn purchase the raw materials to make these components. In addition, all the firms in this chain need to purchase equipment, electricity, labor, computer systems, legal and accounting services, insurance, office supplies, packing materials, and countless other goods and services. So, even a single purchase of a pair of 7 For All Mankind jeans is the culmination of a series of buying and selling activities among many organizations; many people have been keeping busy while you're out shopping! In this section we'll first talk about the different types of business customers that buy goods and services, different types of B2B purchases and the steps in the B2B decision process. Finally, we'll look at B2B e-commerce and digital marketing.

Types of Business-to-Business Customers

As we noted before, many firms buy products in business markets so they can produce other goods. Other B2B customers resell, rent, or lease goods and services. Still other customers, including governments and not-for-profit institutions such as the Red Cross or a local church, serve the public in some way. In this section, we'll look at the three major classes of B2B customers we show in 📷 Figure 6.6 (producers, resellers, and organizations). Then we'll look at how marketers classify specific industries.

Producers

Producers purchase products for the production of other goods and services that they, in turn, sell to make a profit. For this reason, they are customers for a vast number of products from raw materials to goods that still other producers manufacture. For example, Dell buys microprocessor chips from Intel and AMD that go into its line of computers, and Marriott hotels buys linens, furniture, and food to produce the accommodations and meals their

---

business-to-business (B2B) markets
The group of customers that include manufacturers, wholesalers, retailers, and other organizations.

organizational markets
Another name for business-to-business markets.

producers
The individuals or organizations that purchase products for use in the production of other goods and services.

Figure 6.6 📷 *Snapshot* | The Business Marketplace

The business marketplace consists of three major categories of customers: producers, resellers, and organizations. B2B marketers must understand the different needs of these customers if they want to build successful relationships with them.

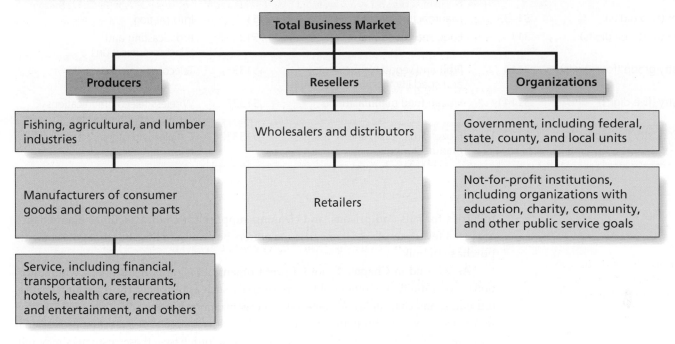

guests expect. In addition to manufacturers of goods, the fishing, agricultural and lumber industries are considered producers.

Resellers

Resellers buy finished goods for the purpose of reselling, renting, or leasing to consumers and other businesses. Although resellers do not actually produce goods, they do provide their customers with the time, place, and possession utility we talked about in Chapter 1 because they make the goods available to consumers when and where they want them. For example, Walmart buys toothpaste, peanuts, kids' shoes, and about a gazillion other products to sell in its more than 10,000 stores worldwide.[41]

Increasingly, large retail businesses such as Walmart, Walgreen's, and Kroger Supermarkets have taken over the functions that were previously the job of wholesalers and distributors. This means that there are fewer of these resellers today. More on that in Chapter 12.

Government and Not-for-Profit Organizations

Governments and not-for-profit institutions are two other types of organizations in the business marketplace. **Government markets** make up the largest single business and organizational market in the United States. The U.S. government market includes more than 3,000 county governments, 35,000 municipalities and townships, 37,000 special district governments, 50 states and the District of Columbia, plus the federal government. State and local government markets alone account for 15 percent of the U.S. gross national product.[42]

And of course, there are thousands more government customers around the globe, and many of those governments are just about the only customers for certain products, such as jet bombers and nuclear power plants. But many government expenditures are for more familiar items. Pens, pencils, and paper for offices; cots, bedding, and

resellers
The individuals or organizations that buy finished goods for the purpose of reselling, renting, or leasing to others to make a profit and to maintain their business operations.

government markets
The federal, state, county, and local governments that buy goods and services to carry out public objectives and to support their operations.

Table 6.1 | The North American Industry Classification System: A Sample

	Frozen Fruit Example		Cellular Telecommunications Example	
• Sector (two digits)	31–33	Manufacturing	51	Information
• Subsector (three digits)	311	Food manufacturing	513	Broadcasting and telecommunications
• Industry group (four digits)	3114	Fruit and vegetable preserving and specialty food manufacturing	5133	Telecommunications
• Industry (five digits)	31141	Frozen food manufacturing	51332	Wireless telecommunications carriers (except satellite)
• U.S. industry (six digits)	311311	Frozen fruit, juice, and vegetable manufacturing	513322	Cellular and other wireless telecommunications

toiletries for jails and prisons; and cleaning supplies for routine facilities maintenance are just a few examples of items that consumers buy one at a time but that governments purchase in bulk.

As we said in Chapter 1, not-for-profit organizations are organizations with educational, community, and other public service goals, such as hospitals, churches, universities, museums, and charitable and cause-related organizations like the Salvation Army and the Red Cross. These institutions tend to operate on low budgets. Because nonprofessional part-time buyers who have other duties often make purchases, these customers may rely on marketers to provide more advice and assistance before and after the sale.

The North American Industry Classification System

North American Industry Classification System (NAICS)
The numerical coding system that the United States, Canada, and Mexico use to classify firms into detailed categories according to their business activities.

In addition to looking at B2B markets within these three general categories, marketers rely on the **North American Industry Classification System (NAICS)** to identify their customers. This is a numerical coding of industries the United States, Canada, and Mexico developed. Table 6.1 illustrates how the NAICS coding system works. NAICS replaced the U.S. Standard Industrial Classification system in 1997 so that the North American Free Trade Agreement (NAFTA) countries could compare economic and financial statistics.[43] The NAICS reports the number of firms, the total dollar amount of sales, the number of employees, and the growth rate for industries, all broken down by geographic region. Many firms use the NAICS to assess potential markets and to determine how well they are doing compared to others in their industry group.

Firms may also use the NAICS to find new customers. A marketer might first determine the NAICS industry classifications of his or her current customers and then evaluate the sales potential of other firms occupying these categories.

Factors That Make a Difference in Business Markets

In theory, the same basic marketing principles should hold true in both consumer and business markets—firms identify customer needs and develop a marketing mix to satisfy those needs. For example, take the company that made the desks and chairs in your classroom. Just like a firm that markets consumer goods, the classroom furniture company first must create an important competitive advantage for its target market of universities. Next, the firm develops a marketing mix strategy that begins with a product—classroom furniture that will withstand years of use by thousands of students—while it provides a level of comfort that a good learning environment requires (and you thought those hardback chairs were intended just to keep you awake during class). The firm must offer the furniture at prices that universities will pay and that will allow the firm to make a reasonable profit. Then the firm must develop a sales force or other marketing

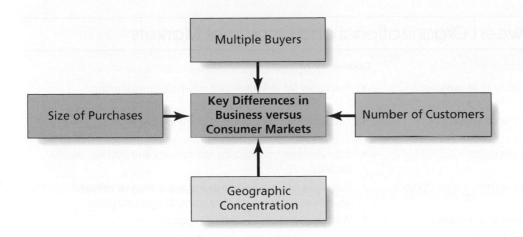

Figure 6.7 📷 *Snapshot* | Key Differences in Business versus Consumer Markets

There are a number of differences between business and consumer markets. To be successful, marketers must understand these differences and develop strategies specific to organizational customers.

communication strategy to make sure your university (and hundreds of others) considers—and hopefully chooses—its products when it furnishes classrooms.

Although marketing to business customers does have a lot in common with consumer marketing, there are differences that make this basic process more complex.[44] 📷 Figure 6.7 summarizes the key areas of difference, and Table 6.2 provides a more extensive set of comparisons between the two types of markets.

Multiple Buyers

In business markets, products often have to do more than satisfy an individual's needs. They must meet the requirements of everyone involved in the company's purchase decision. If you decide to buy a new chair for your room or apartment, you're the only one who has to be satisfied. For your classroom, the furniture must satisfy not only students but also faculty, administrators, campus planners, and the people at your school who actually do the purchasing. If your school is a state or other governmental institution, the furniture may also have to meet certain government-mandated engineering standards. If you have a formal green initiative, the purchase must satisfy environment-friendly criteria.

Number of Customers

Organizational customers are few and far between compared to end-user consumers. In the United States, there are about 100 million consumer households but less than half a million businesses and other organizations.

Size of Purchases

B2B products dwarf consumer purchases both in the quantity of items ordered and in how much a single item may cost. A company that rents uniforms to other businesses, for example, buys hundreds of large drums of laundry detergent each year to launder its uniforms. In contrast, even a hard-core soccer mom who deals with piles of dirty socks and shorts goes through a box of detergent only every few weeks.

Organizations purchase many products, such as a highly sophisticated piece of manufacturing equipment or computer-based marketing information systems that can cost a million dollars or more. Recognizing such differences in the size of purchases allows marketers to develop effective marketing strategies.

Geographic Concentration

Another difference between business markets and consumer markets is *geographic concentration*, meaning that many business customers may be located in a single region of

Table 6.2 | Differences between Organizational and Consumer Markets

Organizational Markets	Consumer Markets
• Purchases made for some purpose other than personal consumption	• Purchases for individual or household consumption
• Purchases made by someone other than the user of the product	• The ultimate user often makes the purchase
• Several people frequently make the decisions	• Individuals or small groups like couples and families usually decide
• Purchases made according to precise technical specifications based on product expertise	• Purchases often based on brand reputation or personal recommendations with little or no product expertise
• Purchases made after careful weighing of alternatives	• Purchases frequently made on impulse
• Purchases based on rational criteria*	• Purchases based on emotional responses to products or promotions
• Purchasers often engage in lengthy decision processes	• Individual purchasers often make quick decisions
• Interdependencies between buyers and sellers; long-term relationships	• Buyers engage in limited-term or one-time-only relationships with many different sellers
• Purchases may involve competitive bidding, price negotiations, and complex financial arrangements	• Most purchases made at "list price" with cash or credit cards
• Products frequently purchased directly from producer	• Products usually purchased from someone other than producer of the product
• Purchases frequently involve high risk and high cost	• Most purchases are relatively low risk and low cost
• Limited number of large buyers	• Many individuals or household customers
• Buyers often geographically concentrated in certain areas	• Buyers generally dispersed throughout total population
• Products often complex; classified based on how organizational customers use them	• Products: consumer goods and services for individual use
• Demand derived from demand for other goods and services, generally inelastic in the short run, subject to fluctuations, and may be joined to their demand for other goods and services	• Demand based on consumer needs and preferences, is generally price elastic, steady over time and independent of demand for other products
• Promotion emphasizes personal selling	• Promotion emphasizes advertising

the country. Whether they live in the heart of New York City or in a small fishing village in Oregon, consumers buy and use toothpaste and TVs. For years, Silicon Valley, a 50-mile-long corridor close to the California coast, has been home to thousands of electronics and software companies because of its high concentration of skilled engineers and scientists. For B2B marketers who wish to sell to these markets, this means that they can concentrate their sales efforts and perhaps even locate distribution centers in a single geographic area.

B2B Demand

Demand in business markets differs from consumer demand. Most demand for B2B products is derived, inelastic, fluctuating, and joint. Understanding how these factors influence B2B demand is important for marketers when they forecast sales and plan effective marketing strategies. Let's look at each of these concepts in a bit more detail.

Derived Demand

derived demand
Demand for business or organizational products caused by demand for consumer goods or services.

Consumer demand is based on a direct connection between a need and the satisfaction of that need. But business customers don't purchase goods and services to satisfy their own needs. Businesses instead operate on **derived demand** because a business's demand for goods and services comes either directly or indirectly from consumers' demand for what it produces.

To better understand derived demand, take a look at 🔀 Figure 6.8 (beginning at the bottom). Demand for forestry products comes from the demand for pulp, which in turn is derived from the demand for paper that publishers buy to make the textbooks you use in your classes. The demand for textbooks comes from the demand for education (yes, education is the "product" you're buying—with the occasional party or football game thrown in as a bonus). As a result of derived demand, the success of one company may depend on another company in a different industry. The derived nature of business demand means that marketers must constantly be alert to changes in consumer trends that ultimately will have an effect on B2B sales. So, if fewer students attend college and those who do increasingly choose to purchase digital textbooks, the forestry industry has to find other sources of demand for its products.

Inelastic Demand

Inelastic demand means that it usually doesn't matter if the price of a B2B product goes up or down—business customers still buy the same quantity. Demand in B2B markets is mostly inelastic because what an individual firm sells often is just one of the many parts or materials that go into producing the consumer product. It is not unusual for a large increase in a business product's price to have little effect on the final consumer product's price.

For example, you can buy a Limited Edition Porsche Boxster S "loaded" with options for about $64,000.[45] To produce the car, Porsche purchases thousands of different parts. If the price of tires, batteries, or stereos goes up or down, Porsche will still buy enough to meet consumer demand for its cars. As you might imagine, increasing the price by $30 or $40 or even $100 won't change consumer demand for Boxsters—so demand for parts remains the same. (If you have to ask how much it costs, you can't afford it!)

Fluctuating Demand

Business demand also is subject to greater fluctuations than is consumer demand. There are two reasons for this. First, even modest changes in consumer demand can create large increases or decreases in business demand. Take, for example, air travel. A rise in jet fuel prices, causing higher ticket prices and a shift by some consumers from flying to driving vacations, can cause airlines to postpone or cancel orders for new equipment. This change in turn creates a dramatic decrease in demand for planes from manufacturers such as Boeing and Airbus.

A product's life expectancy is another reason for fluctuating demand. Business customers tend to purchase certain products infrequently. They may need to replace some types of large machinery only every 10 or 20 years. Thus, demand for such products fluctuates—it may be high one year when a lot of customers' machinery wears out but low the following year because everyone's old machinery works fine.

Joint Demand

Joint demand occurs when two or more goods are necessary to create a product. For example, Porsche needs tires, batteries, and spark plugs to make that Limited Edition Boxster S that piqued your interest earlier. If the supply of one of these parts decreases, Porsche will be unable to manufacture as many automobiles, so it will not buy as many of the other items either.

Figure 6.8 🔀 *Process* | Derived Demand

B2B demand is derived demand. That is, the demand is derived directly or indirectly from consumer demand for another good or service. Some of the demand for forestry products is derived indirectly from the demand for education. At least until the day when all texts are available only online, publishers will need to buy paper.

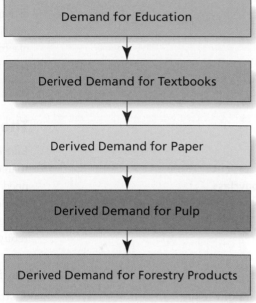

inelastic demand
Demand in which changes in price have little or no effect on the amount demanded.

joint demand
Demand for two or more goods that are used together to create a product.

6.5 Business Buying Situations and the Business Buying Decision Process

OBJECTIVE

Identify and describe the different business buying situations and the business buying decision process including the use of e-commerce and social media.

(pp. 210–218)

So far we've talked about how B2B markets are different from consumer markets and about the different types of customers that make up business markets. In this section, we'll discuss some of the important characteristics of business buying situations. This is important because just like companies that sell to end-user consumers, a successful B2B marketer needs to understand how his or her customers make decisions. Armed with this knowledge, the company is able to participate in the buyer's decision process from the start.

The Buyclass Framework

Like end-user consumers, business buyers spend more time and effort on some purchases than on others. This usually depends on the complexity of the product and how often they need to make the decision. A **buyclass** framework, as 📷 Figure 6.9 illustrates, identifies the degree of effort required of the firm's personnel to collect information and make a purchase decision. These classes, which apply to three different buying situations, are straight rebuys, modified rebuys, and new-task buys.

Straight Rebuy

A **straight rebuy** refers to the routine purchase of items that a B2B customer regularly needs. The buyer has purchased the same items many times before and routinely reorders them when supplies are low, often from the same suppliers. Reordering the items takes little time. Buyers typically maintain a list of approved vendors that have demonstrated their ability to meet the firm's criteria for pricing, quality, service, and delivery. GE Healthcare's customers routinely purchase its line of basic surgical scrubs (the clothing and caps doctors and nurses wear in the operating room) without much evaluation on each occasion.

Because straight rebuys often contribute the "bread-and-butter" revenue a firm needs to maintain a steady stream of income, many business marketers go to great lengths to cultivate and maintain relationships with customers who submit reorders on a regular basis. Salespeople may regularly call on these customers to personally handle orders and to see if there are additional products the customer needs—and to take the purchasing agent to lunch. The goal is to be sure that the customer doesn't even think twice about just buying the same product every time he or she runs low. Rebuys keep a supplier's sales volume up and help cover selling costs.

Modified Rebuy

Life is sweet for companies whose customers automatically do straight rebuys. Unfortunately, these situations don't last forever. A **modified rebuy** occurs when a firm decides to shop around for suppliers with better prices, quality, or delivery times. This situation also can occur when the organization confronts new needs for products it already buys. A buyer who purchased many BlackBerry smartphones, for example, may have to reevaluate several other options if the firm upgrades its cellular telecommunications system.

buyclass
One of three classifications of business buying situations that characterizes the degree of time and effort required to make a decision.

straight rebuy
A buying situation in which business buyers make routine purchases that require minimal decision making.

modified rebuy
A buying situation classification used by business buyers to categorize a previously made purchase that involves some change and that requires limited decision making.

Figure 6.9 📷 *Snapshot* | Elements of the Buyclass Framework

The classes of the buyclass framework relate to three different organizational buying situations: straight rebuy, modified rebuy, and new-task buy.

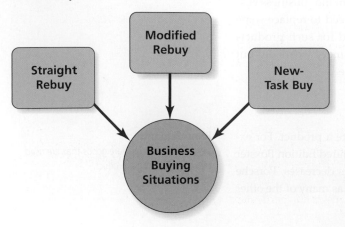

Modified rebuys require more time and effort than straight rebuys. The buyer generally knows the purchase requirements and has a few potential suppliers in mind. Marketers know that modified rebuys can mean that some vendors get added to a buyer's approved supplier list, whereas others may be dropped. So even if in the past a company purchased its smartphones from Blackberry, this doesn't necessarily mean it will do so in the future as this company's operating system steadily loses ground to newer rivals. Now, other platforms, like Apple and Google's Android, may gain approved supplier status going forward, and the race is on. Astute marketers routinely call on buyers to detect and define problems that can lead to winning or losing in such situations.

New-Task Buy

A first-time purchase is a **new-task buy**. Uncertainty and risk characterize buying decisions in this classification, and they require the most effort because the buyer has no previous experience on which to base a decision.

new-task buy
A new business-to-business purchase that is complex or risky and that requires extensive decision making.

Your university, for example, may decide (if it hasn't done so already) to develop "active-learning" classrooms. Furnishing the classrooms for a different form of learning that will meet the needs of classes in different disciplines is a complex new-task buy for a school. In new-task buying situations, not only do buyers lack experience with the product, but they also are often unfamiliar with firms that supply the product. Supplier choice is critical, and buyers gather much information about quality, pricing, delivery, and service from several potential suppliers.

Marketers know that to get the order in a new-buy situation, they must develop a close working relationship with the business buyer. There are many situations in which marketers focus on selling their product by wooing people who recommend their products—over and above the end consumers who actually buy them. To use an example close to home, think about all of the goods and services that make up the higher-education industry. For instance, even though you are the one who shelled out the money for this extremely awesome text, your professor was the one who made the exceptionally wise decision to assign it. He or she made this choice (did we mention it was a really wise choice?) only after carefully considering numerous texts and talking to several publishers' sales representatives.

Professional Buyers and Buying Centers

Just as it is important for marketers of consumer goods and services to understand their customers, it's essential that B2B marketers understand who handles the buying for their business customers. Trained professional buyers typically carry out buying in B2B markets. These people have titles such as *purchasing agents, procurement officers*, or *directors of materials management.*

Although some consumers like to shop 'til they drop almost every day, most of us spend far less time roaming the aisles. However, professional purchasers do it all day, every day—it's their job and their business to buy. These individuals focus on economic factors beyond the initial price of the product, including transportation and delivery charges, accessory products or supplies, maintenance, and other ongoing costs. They are responsible for selecting quality products and ensuring their timely delivery. They shop as if their jobs depend on it—because they do.

Many times in business buying situations, several people—ranging from a production worker to the CFO—work together to reach a decision. The **buying center** is the group of people in the organization who participate in the decision-making process. Although this term may conjure up an image of "command central" buzzing with purchasing activity, a buying center is not a place at all. Instead, it is a cross-functional team of decision makers. Generally, the members of a buying center have some expertise or interest in the particular decision, and as a group they are able to make the best decision.

buying center
The group of people in an organization who participate in a purchasing decision.

Table 6.3	Roles in the Buying Center		

Role	Potential Player		Responsibility
• Initiator	• Production employees, sales manager, almost anyone		• Recognizes that a purchase needs to be made
• User	• Production employees, secretaries, almost anyone		• Individual(s) who will ultimately use the product
• Gatekeeper	• Buyer/purchasing agent		• Controls flow of information to others in the organization
• Influencer	• Engineers, quality control experts, technical specialists, outside consultants		• Affects decision by giving advice and sharing expertise
• Decider	• Purchasing agent, managers, CEO		• Makes the final purchase decision
• Buyer	• Purchasing agent		• Executes the purchase decision

Depending on the complexity of the purchase and the size of the buying center, a participant may assume one, several, or all of the six roles that Table 6.3 shows. Let's review them now.

- The *initiator* begins the buying process by first recognizing that the firm needs to make a purchase. A production employee, for example, may notice that a piece of equipment is not working properly and notify a supervisor that it is slowing up the production line. Depending on the initiator's position in the organization and the type of purchase, the initiator may or may not influence the actual purchase decision. For marketers, it's important to make sure that individuals who might initiate a purchase are aware of improved products they offer.

- The *user* is the member of the buying center who actually needs the product. The user's role in the buying center varies. For example, an administrative assistant may give her input on the features a new copier should have because she will be chained to it for several hours a day. Marketers need to inform users of their products' benefits, especially if the benefits outweigh those that competitors offer.

- The *gatekeeper* is the person who controls the flow of information to other members. Typically, the gatekeeper is the purchasing agent, who gathers information and materials from salespeople, schedules sales presentations, and controls suppliers' access to other participants in the buying process. For salespeople, developing and maintaining strong personal relationships with gatekeepers is critical to being able to offer their products to the buying center.

- An *influencer* affects the buying decision when he or she dispenses advice or shares expertise. Highly trained employees, like engineers, quality control specialists, and other technical experts in the firm, generally have a great deal of influence in purchasing equipment, materials, and component parts the company uses in production. The influencers may or may not wind up using the product. Marketers need to identify key influencers in the buying center and persuade them of their product's superiority.

- The *decider* is the member of the buying center who makes the final decision. This person usually has the greatest power within the buying center; he or she often has power within the organization to authorize spending the company's money. For a routine purchase, the decider may be the purchasing agent. If the purchase is complex, a manager or even the CEO may be the decider. The decider is critical to a marketer's success and deserves a lot of attention in the selling process.

- The *buyer* is the person who has responsibility to execute the purchase. The buyer obtains competing bids, negotiates contracts, and arranges delivery dates and payment plans. Once a firm makes the purchase decision, marketers turn their attention to negotiating the details of the purchase with the buyer. Successful marketers are well aware that providing exemplary service in this stage of the purchase can be a critical factor in achieving future sales from this client.

The Business Buying Decision Process

We've seen that there are a number of players in the business buying process, beginning with an initiator and ending with a buyer. To make matters even more challenging to marketers, members of the buying team go through several stages in the decision-making process before the marketer gets an order. The *business buying decision process*, as Figure 6.10 shows, is a series of steps similar to those in the consumer decision process we discussed previously in this chapter. To help understand these steps, let's say you've just started working at the Way Radical Skateboard Company and your boss just assigned you to the buying center for the purchase of new software for web page design—a new-task buy for your firm.

Step 1: Recognize the Problem

As in consumer buying, the first step in the business buying decision process occurs when someone sees that a purchase can solve a problem. For straight rebuy purchases, this may occur because the firm has run out of paper, pens, or garbage bags. In these cases, the buyer places the order, and the decision-making process ends. Recognition of the need for modified rebuy purchases often comes when the organization wants to replace outdated existing equipment, from changes in technology, or from an ad, brochure, or some other marketing communication that offers the customer a better product or one at a lower price. Two events may occur in the problem-recognition step. First, a firm makes a request or requisition, usually in writing. Then, depending on the complexity of the purchase, the firm may form a buying center. The need for new-task purchases often occurs because the firm wants to enhance its operations in some way or when a smart salesperson tells the business customer about a new product that will increase the efficiency of the firm's operations or improve the firm's end products.

Step 2: Search for Information

In the second step of the decision process (for purchases other than straight rebuys), the buying center searches for information about products and suppliers. Members of the buying center may individually or collectively refer to reports in trade magazines and journals, seek advice from outside consultants, and pay close attention to marketing communications from different manufacturers and suppliers. As in consumer marketing, it's the job of marketers to make sure that information is available when and where business customers want it—by placing ads in trade magazines, by mailing brochures and other printed material to prospects, by having a well-trained sales force regularly calling on customers to build long-term relationships and by skillful use of the Internet. We'll talk more about how B2B firms can use the Internet and social media to increase their sales later in this chapter.

There are thousands of specialized publications out there that cater to just about any industry you can think of. Usually sponsored by leading industry trade associations, each is bursting with information from competing companies that cater to a specific niche. Who needs that fluffy romance novel at the beach? Try leafing through the latest issue of *Chemical Processing* or *Meat and Poultry Magazine* instead.

Of course, sometimes B2B marketers try to get the information about their product into the hands of buyers via less specialized media. For example, in recent years

Figure 6.10 *Process* | Steps in the Business Buying Decision Process

The steps in the business buying decision process are the same as those in the consumer decision process. But for business purchases, each step may be far more complex and require more attention from marketers.

Step 1: Recognize the problem
- Make purchase requisition or request
- Form buying center, if needed

Step 2: Search for Information
- Develop product specifications
- Identify potential suppliers
- Obtain proposals and quotations

Step 3: Evaluate the Alternatives
- Evaluate proposals
- Obtain and evaluate samples

Step 4: Select the Product and Supplier
- Issue purchase order

Step 5: Evaluate Postpurchase
- Survey users
- Document performance

AFLAC—the American Family Life Assurance Company of Columbus (the firm behind the famous duck)—has heavily advertised on TV even though most of its customers are in the B2B space. In fact, many end-user consumers don't have the foggiest notion what AFLAC sells—but they sure love to "quack up" over the duck's antics. The truth is, AFLAC's primary business is working with businesses (more than 400,000 of them, in fact) to enhance their employee benefits packages with various types of insurance and other benefits in order to improve recruiting and retention of the firms' people. But their strategy of advertising directly on mass media was brilliant; now when an organizational buyer or human resources manager searches for these services, AFLAC's name will surely be at the top of the list. Now there's a duck that's not out of water![46]

product specifications
A written description of the quality, size, weight, and other details required of a product purchase.

Business buyers often develop **product specifications**, that is, a written description of the quality, size, weight, color, features, quantity, training, warranty, service terms, and delivery requirements for the purchase. When the product needs are complex or technical, engineers and other experts are the key players who identify specific product characteristics they require and determine whether the organizations can get by with standardized, off-the-shelf items or if they need to acquire customized, made-to-order goods and services. Once the product specifications are in hand, the next step is to identify potential suppliers and obtain written or verbal proposals, or *bids*, from one or more of them. For standardized or branded products in which there are few if any differences in the products of different suppliers, this may be as simple as an informal request for pricing information, including discounts, shipping charges, and confirmation of delivery dates. At other times, the potential suppliers receive a formal written *request for proposal* or *request for quotation* that requires detailed information from vendors.

Step 3: Evaluate the Alternatives

In this stage of the business buying decision process, the buying center assesses the proposals it receives. Total spending for goods and services can have a major impact on the firm's profitability, so, all other things being equal, price can be a primary consideration. Pricing evaluations must take into account discount policies for certain quantities, returned-goods policies, the cost of repair and maintenance services, terms of payment, and the cost of financing large purchases. For capital equipment, cost criteria also include the life expectancy of the purchase, the expected resale value, and disposal costs for the old equipment. In some cases, the buying center may negotiate with the preferred supplier to match the lowest bidder.

Although a firm often selects a bidder because it offers the lowest price, there are times when it bases the buying decision on other factors. For example, in its lucrative B2B market, American Express wins bids for its travel agency business because it offers extra services other agencies don't or can't, such as a corporate credit card, monthly reports that detail the company's total travel expenses, and perks tied to the company's customer loyalty program.

customer reference program
A formalized process by which customers formally share success stories and actively recommend products to other potential clients, usually facilitated through an online community.

The more complex and costly the purchase, the more time buyers spend searching for the best supplier—and the more marketers must do to win the order. In some cases, a company may even ask one or more of its current customers to participate in a **customer reference program**. In these situations, customers formally share success stories and actively recommend products to other potential clients, often as part of an online community composed of people with similar needs.

Marketers often make formal presentations and product demonstrations to the buying center group. In the case of installations and large equipment, they may arrange for buyers to speak with or even visit other customers to examine how the product performs. For less complex products, the buying firm may ask potential suppliers for samples of the products so that its people can evaluate them personally. The buying center may ask salespeople from various companies to demonstrate their software for your Way Radical group so that you can all compare the capabilities of different products.

Step 4: Select the Product and Supplier

Once buyers have assessed all proposals, it's time for the rubber to hit the road. The next step in the buying process is the purchase decision when the group selects the best product and supplier to meet the organization's needs. Reliability and durability rank especially high for equipment and systems that keep the firm's operations running smoothly without interruption. For some purchases, warranties, repair service, and regular maintenance after the sale are important.

One of the most important decisions a buyer makes is how many suppliers can best serve the firm's needs. Sometimes having one supplier is more beneficial to the organization than having multiple suppliers. **Single sourcing**, in which a buyer and seller work quite closely, is particularly important when a firm needs frequent deliveries or specialized products. Single sourcing also helps assure consistency of quality of materials input into the production process. But reliance on a single source means that the firm is at the mercy of the chosen supplier to deliver the needed goods or services without interruption. If the single source doesn't come through, the firm's relationship with its own end users will likely be affected.

However, using one or a few suppliers rather than many has its advantages. A firm that buys from a single supplier becomes a large customer with a lot of clout when it comes to negotiating prices and contract terms. Having one or a few suppliers also lowers the firm's administrative costs because it has fewer invoices to pay, fewer contracts to negotiate, and fewer salespeople to see than if it uses many sources.

In contrast, **multiple sourcing** means buying a product from several different suppliers. Under this system, suppliers are more likely to remain price competitive. And if one supplier has problems with delivery, the firm has others to fall back on. The automotive industry practices this philosophy: A vehicle manufacturer often won't buy a new product from a supplier unless the vendor's rivals also are capable of making the same item. This policy tends to stifle innovation, but it does ensure a steady supply of parts to feed to the assembly line.

Sometimes supplier selection is based on **reciprocity**, which means that a buyer and seller agree to be each other's customers by saying, essentially, "I'll buy from you, and you buy from me." For example, a firm that supplies parts to a company that manufactures trucks would agree to buy trucks from only that firm.

The U.S. government frowns on reciprocal agreements and often determines that such agreements between large firms are illegal because they limit free competition; new suppliers simply don't have a chance against the preferred suppliers. Reciprocity between smaller firms, that is, firms that are not so large as to control a significant proportion of the business in their industry, is legal in the United States if both parties voluntarily agree to it. In other countries, reciprocity is a practice that is common and even expected in B2B marketing.

Outsourcing occurs when firms obtain outside vendors to provide goods or services that might otherwise be supplied in-house. For example, Sodexo is the world's largest outsourcer for food and facilities management services with more than 6,000 U.S. client sites. Colleges and universities are a major category of clientele for Sodexo (are they your school's vendor?) because these educational institutions want to focus on educating students rather than preparing and serving food. (Fortunately, your professors don't have to cook as well as teach!)

Outsourcing is an increasingly popular strategy, but in some cases it can be controversial. Many critics object when U.S. companies contract with companies or individuals in remote places like China or India to perform work they used to do at home, a process

single sourcing
The business practice of buying a particular product from only one supplier.

multiple sourcing
The business practice of buying a particular product from several different suppliers.

reciprocity
A trading partnership in which two firms agree to buy from one another.

outsourcing
The business buying process of obtaining outside vendors to provide goods or services that otherwise might be supplied in house.

offshoring
A process by which companies contract with companies or individuals in remote places like China or India to perform work they used to do at home.

reverse marketing
A business practice in which a buyer firm attempts to identify suppliers who will produce products according to the buyer firm's specifications.

known as **offshoring**. These tasks range from complicated jobs like writing computer code to fairly simple ones like manning reservations desks, staffing call centers for telephone sales, and even taking drive-through orders at U.S. fast-food restaurants. (Yes, in some cases, it's actually more efficient for an operator in India to relay an order from a customer for a #3 Burger Combo to the restaurant's cooks than for an on-site person to take the order.)

Yet another type of buyer–seller partnership is **reverse marketing**. Instead of sellers trying to identify potential customers and then "pitching" their products, buyers try to find suppliers that can produce specifically needed products and then attempt to "sell" the idea to the suppliers. Often large poultry producers practice reverse marketing. Purdue supplies baby chickens, chicken food, financing for chicken houses, medications, and everything else necessary for farmers to lay "golden eggs" for the company. This assures the farmer that he or she will have a buyer while at the same time Purdue knows it can rely on a steady supply of chickens.

Step 5: Evaluate Postpurchase

Just as consumers evaluate purchases, an organizational buyer assesses whether the performance of the product and the supplier lives up to expectations. The buyer surveys the users to determine their satisfaction with the product as well as with the installation, delivery, and service that the supplier provides. For producers of goods, this may relate to the level of satisfaction of the final consumer of the buying firm's product. Has demand for the producer's product increased, decreased, or stayed the same? By documenting and reviewing supplier performance, a firm decides whether to keep or drop the supplier.

An important element in postpurchase evaluation is measurement. When you think about measuring elements of a customer's experience with a company and its products and brands, we'll bet you automatically think about end-user consumers—like travelers' views of their Marriott hotel stay or the taste of that new Starbucks coffee flavor. Similarly, in the B2B world, managers pay a lot of attention to the feedback they get from their customers about the purchases they've made.

B2B E-Commerce and Social Media

We know that the Internet transformed marketing—from the creation of new products to providing more effective and efficient marketing communications to the actual distribution of some products. This is certainly true in business markets as well. **Business-to-business (B2B) e-commerce** refers to Internet exchanges of information, goods, services, and payments between two or more businesses or organizations. It's not as glitzy as consumer e-commerce, but it sure has changed the way businesses operate. Using the Internet for e-commerce allows business marketers to link directly to suppliers, factories, distributors, and their customers, radically reducing the time necessary for order and delivery of goods, tracking sales, and getting feedback from customers.

business-to-business (B2B) e-commerce
Online exchanges between companies and individual consumers.

In the simplest form of B2B e-commerce, the Internet provides an online catalog of goods and services that businesses need. Companies find that their Internet site is important to deliver online technical support, product information, order status information, and customer service to corporate customers. Many companies, for example, save millions of dollars a year when they replace hard-copy manuals with electronic downloads. And, of course, B2B e-commerce creates some exciting opportunities for a variety of B2B service industries.

Intranets and Extranets

Although the Internet is the primary means of B2B e-commerce, many companies maintain an *intranet*, which provides a more secure means of conducting business. As we said in

Chapter 4, this term refers to an internal corporate computer network that uses Internet technology to link a company's departments, employees, and databases. **Intranets** give access only to authorized employees. They allow companies to process internal transactions with greater control and consistency because of stricter security measures than those they can use on the entire web. Businesses also use intranets to videoconference, distribute internal documents, communicate with geographically dispersed branches, and train employees.

In contrast to an intranet, an **extranet** allows certain suppliers, customers, and others outside the organization to access a company's internal system. A business customer that a company authorizes to use its extranet can place orders online. Extranets can be especially useful for companies that need to have secure communications between the company and its dealers, distributors, or franchisees. As you can imagine, intranets and extranets are cost efficient and save money for organizations.

In addition to saving companies money, extranets allow business partners to collaborate on projects (such as product design) and build relationships. GE's extranet, the Trading Process Network, began as a set of online purchasing procedures and has morphed into an extensive online extranet community that connects GE with large buyers, such as Con Edison.

The Dark Side of B2B E-Commerce

Doing business the web-enabled way sounds great—perhaps too great. There are also security risks because so much information gets passed around in cyberspace. You've no doubt heard stories about hackers obtaining vast lists of consumers' credit card numbers from a number of retailers including Target and Neiman-Marcus. But companies have even greater worries. When hackers break into company sites, they can destroy company records and steal trade secrets. Both B2C and B2B e-commerce companies worry about *authentication* and ensuring that transactions are secure. This means making sure that only authorized individuals are allowed to access a site and place an order. Maintaining security also requires firms to keep the information transferred as part of a transaction, such as a credit card number, from criminals' hard drives.

Well-meaning employees also can create security problems. They can give out unauthorized access to company computer systems by being careless about keeping their passwords into the system a secret. For example, hackers can guess at obvious passwords— nicknames, birth dates, hobbies, or a spouse's name.

Some employees (and even nonemployees) are not so well-meaning; they deliberately create security breaches by leaking confidential documents or hacking into an organization's computer system for sensitive information. Edward Snowden became famous (or, rather, infamous) for his role in leaking thousands of classified documents to the media while working as a consultant for the National Security Agency. And Target's computer system was breached when hackers installed **malware** (software designed specifically to damage or disrupt computer systems) that captured more than 40 million credit card numbers and other customer data despite safeguards the retailer had in place.[47]

To increase security of their Internet sites and transactions, most companies now have safeguards in place—firewalls and encryption devices, to name the two most common methods, though, as we saw with Target, even these safeguards aren't always 100 percent hacker-proof.

A **firewall** is a combination of hardware and software that ensures that only authorized individuals gain entry into a computer system. The firewall monitors and controls all traffic between the Internet and the intranet to restrict access. Companies may even place additional firewalls within their intranet when they wish only designated employees to have access to certain parts of the system. Although firewalls can be fairly effective (even though none is totally foolproof), they require costly, constant monitoring.

intranet
An internal corporate communication network that uses Internet technology to link company departments, employees, and databases.

extranet
A private, corporate computer network that links company departments, employees, and databases to suppliers, customers, and others outside the organization.

malware
Software designed specifically to damage or disrupt computer systems.

firewall
A combination of hardware and software that ensures that only authorized individuals gain entry into a computer system.

encryption

The process of scrambling a message so that only another individual (or computer) with the right "key" can unscramble it.

Encryption means scrambling a message so that only another individual (or computer) with the right "key" can unscramble it. Otherwise, it looks like gobbledygook. The message is inaccessible without the appropriate encryption software—kind of like a decoder ring your favorite superhero might wear. Without encryption, it would be easy for unethical people to get a credit card number by creating a "sniffer" program that intercepts and reads messages. A sniffer finds messages with four blocks of four numbers, copies the data, and voilà!—someone else has your credit card number.

Despite firewalls, encryption, and other security measures, web security for B2B marketers remains a serious problem. The threat to intranet and extranet usage goes beyond competitive espionage. The increasing sophistication of hackers and Internet criminals who create viruses and worms and other approaches to disrupting individual computers and entire company systems mean that all organizations—and consumers—are vulnerable to attacks and must remain vigilant.

B2B and Social Media

Although most of us associate business use of social media such as Facebook, LinkedIn, and Twitter with consumer marketing, B2B organizations are increasing their use of and their budgets for social media:[48]

- A recent study found three social media sites that B2B marketers are most likely to use: LinkedIn (91 percent), Twitter (85 percent), and Facebook (81 percent). Effectiveness ratings for the three sites were lower: LinkedIn (62 percent), Twitter (50 percent), and Facebook (30 percent).

- Forty-five percent of B2B marketers have gained a customer through LinkedIn.

- Job postings on LinkedIn for social media marketers have increased by 1,300 percent since 2010.

- Seventy-six percent of B2B marketers say they maintain company blogs, and 52 percent say it is an important to their company for communicating content.

- How do B2B marketers use social media? Eighty-three percent say they use sites to increase brand exposure, 69 percent to increase web traffic, and 65 percent to gain marketing insights.

- Why are B2B and marketers turning to social media? Many say they are tired of the normal impersonal communication of advertising and that social media allow them to relate to one another.

- In 2013, global Internet ad spending including that by B2B firms grew to second place (20.6 percent) behind TV (40.2 percent), while newspaper advertising dropped to only 17.0 percent of total ad spending.

As with consumer marketing, a number of strategies can be successful in using social media marketing for B2B firms.[49] First, social media sites are good sources of information to identify target audiences. It's helpful to know which potential customers your competitors interact with on social media. And, one of the most important uses of social media for both consumer marketers and business marketers is to monitor what your customers and others say about your product, your firm, and your competitors. A number of tools, such as Google Analytics, Radian6, and Social Mention, have been developed for this purpose. Social media provide platforms for marketers or consumers to join in conversations, get answers to their questions, and share experiences. Marketers who understand social media contribute to conversations on Twitter, Facebook, and blogs. They give good answers to questions and establish their credibility and a leadership position in the industry.

MyLab Marketing™
Go to **mymktlab.com** to complete the problems marked with this icon ⭐ as well as additional Marketing Metrics questions only available in MyLab Marketing.

Objective Summary ➥ Key Terms ➥ Apply

CHAPTER 6
Study Map

6.1 Objective Summary (pp. 184–190)

Define *consumer behavior*, and explain the purchase decision-making process.

Consumer behavior is the process individuals or groups go through to select, purchase, use, and dispose of goods, services, ideas, or experiences to satisfy their needs and desires. Consumer decisions differ greatly, ranging from habitual, repeat (low-involvement) purchases to complex, extended problem-solving activities for important, risky (high-involvement) purchases. When consumers make important purchases, they go through a series of five steps. First, they recognize there is a problem to be solved. Then they search for information to make the best decision. Next, they evaluate a set of alternatives and judge them on the basis of various evaluative criteria. At this point, they are ready to make their purchasing decision. Following the purchase, consumers decide whether the product matched their expectations and may develop anxiety or regret or cognitive dissonance.

Key Terms

consumer behavior, p. 184

involvement, p. 185

perceived risk, p. 185

problem recognition, p. 186

information search, p. 187

evoked set, p. 188

consideration set, p. 188

comparison shopping agents or shopbots, p. 188

determinant attributes, p. 188

evaluative criteria, p. 188

compensatory decision rules, p. 189

heuristics, p. 189

brand loyalty, p. 189

consumer satisfaction/dissatisfaction, p. 189

cognitive dissonance, p. 189

6.2 Objective Summary (pp. 190–198)

Explain how internal factors influence consumers' decision-making processes.

Several internal factors influence consumer decisions. Perception is how consumers select, organize, and interpret stimuli. Motivation is an internal state that drives consumers to satisfy needs. Learning is a change in behavior that results from information or experience. Behavioral learning results from external events, whereas cognitive learning refers to internal mental activity. An attitude is a lasting evaluation of a person, object, or issue and includes three components: affect, cognition, and behavior. Personality influences how consumers respond to situations in the environment. Marketers seek to understand a consumer's self-concept to develop product attributes that match some aspect of the consumer's self-concept.

The age of consumers, family life cycle, and their lifestyle also are strongly related to consumption preferences. Marketers may use psychographics to group people according to activities, interests, and opinions that may explain reasons for purchasing products.

Key Terms

perception, p. 190

exposure, p. 191

subliminal advertising, p. 191

attention, p. 191

multitasking, p. 192

rich media, p. 192

interpretation, p. 192

motivation, p. 192

hierarchy of needs, p. 193

gamification, p. 193

learning, p. 194

behavioral learning theories, p. 194

classical conditioning, p. 194

operant conditioning, p. 194

data brokers, p. 194

cognitive learning theory, p. 195

observational learning, p. 195

attitude, p. 195

affect, p. 195

sadvertising, p. 195

cognition, p. 195

behavior, p. 196

personality, p. 196

self-concept, p. 196

family life cycle, p. 197

lifestyle, p. 197

psychographics, p. 198

activities, interests, and opinions (AIOs), p. 198

subculture, p. 200

microcultures, p. 200

consumerism, p. 200

conscientious consumerism, p. 201

social class, p. 201

status symbols, p. 201

mass class, p. 201

reference group, p. 201

opinion leader, p. 202

gender roles, p. 202

6.3 Objective Summary (pp. 198–203)

Show how situational factors and consumers' relationships with other people influence consumer behavior.

Situational influences include our physical surroundings and time pressures. Dimensions of the physical environment create arousal and pleasure and can determine how consumers react to the environment. The time of day, the season of the year, and how much time one has to make a purchase also affect decision making.

Consumers' overall preferences for products are determined by their membership in cultures and subcultures and by cultural values such as collectivism and individualism. Consumerism is a social movement directed toward protecting consumers from harmful business practices. Social class, group memberships, and opinion leaders are other types of social influences that affect consumer choices. A reference group is a set of people a consumer wants to please or imitate, and this affects the consumer's purchasing decisions. Purchases also result from conformity to real or imagined group pressures. Another way social influence is felt is in the expectations of society regarding the proper roles for men and women. Such expectations have led to many gender-typed products.

Key Terms

sensory marketing, p. 198

sensory branding, p. 199

time poverty, p. 199

culture, p. 200

6.4 Objective Summary (pp. 203–209)

Understand the characteristics of business-to-business markets and business-to-business market demand and how marketers classify business-to-business customers.

B2B markets include business or organizational customers that buy goods and services for purposes other than personal consumption. Business customers include producers, resellers, governments, and not-for-profit organizations. Producers purchase materials, parts, and various goods and services needed to produce other goods and services to be sold at a profit. Resellers purchase finished goods to resell at a profit as well as other goods and services to maintain their operations. Governments and other not-for-profit organizations purchase the goods and services necessary to fulfill their objectives. The NAICS, a numerical coding system developed by NAFTA countries, is a widely used classification system for business and organizational markets.

There are a number of major and minor differences between organizational and consumer markets. To be successful, marketers must understand these differences and develop strategies that can be effective with organizational customers. For example, business customers are usually few in number, they may be geographically concentrated, and they often purchase higher-priced products in larger quantities. Business demand derives from the demand for another good or service, is generally not affected by price increases or decreases, is subject to great fluctuations, and may be tied to the demand and availability of some other good.

Key Terms

business-to-business (B2B) markets, p. 204

organizational markets, p. 204

producers, p. 204

resellers, p. 205

government markets, p. 205

North American Industry Classification System (NAICS), p. 206

derived demand, p. 208

inelastic demand, p. 209

joint demand, p. 209

6.5 Objective Summary (pp. 210–218)

Identify and describe the different business buying situations and the business buying decision process including the use of e-commerce and social media.

The buyclass framework identifies the degree and effort required to make a business buying decision. Purchase situations can be straight rebuy, modified rebuy, and new-task buying. A buying center is a group of people who work together to make a buying decision. The roles in the buying center are (1) the initiator, who recognizes the need for a purchase; (2) the user, who will ultimately use the product; (3) the gatekeeper, who controls the flow of information to others; (4) the influencer, who shares advice and expertise; (5) the decider, who makes the final decision; and (6) the buyer, who executes the purchase. The steps in the business buying process are similar to those in the consumer decision process but are often somewhat more complex. For example, in the search for information, B2B firms often develop written product specifications, identify potential suppliers, and obtain proposals and quotations.

B2B e-commerce refers to Internet exchanges of information, goods and services, and payments between two or more businesses or organizations. B2B firms often maintain intranets that give access only to employees or extranets that allow access to certain suppliers and other outsiders. Firms often install firewalls and use encryption to prevent problems from hackers and other threats to the security of the firm's intranets and extranets. B2B firms are increasingly using social media to gather information on target audiences, increase brand exposure and web traffic, monitor what customers and others are saying, and provide a platform for conversations with customers.

Key Terms

buyclass, p. 210

straight rebuy, p. 210

modified rebuy, p. 210

new-task buy, p. 211

buying center, p. 211

product specifications, p. 214

customer reference program, p. 214

single sourcing, p. 215

multiple sourcing, p. 215

reciprocity, p. 215

outsourcing, p. 215

offshoring, p. 216

reverse marketing, p. 216

business-to-business (B2B) e-commerce, p. 216

intranet, p. 217

extranet, p. 217

malware, p. 217

firewall, p. 217

encryption, p. 218

Chapter Questions and Activities

> **MyLab Marketing™**
>
> Go to **mymktlab.com** to watch this chapter's Rising Star video(s) for career advice and to respond to questions.

Concepts: Test Your Knowledge

6-1. What is consumer behavior? Why is it important for marketers to understand consumer behavior?

6-2. Explain habitual decision making, limited problem solving, and extended problem solving. What is the role of perceived risk in the decision process?

6-3. Explain the steps in the consumer decision-making process.

6-4. What is perception? Explain the three parts of the perception process: exposure, attention, and interpretation.

6-5. Describe Maslow's hierarchy of needs as it relates to motivation.

6-6. How does gamification influence consumers' motivation to interact with brands?

6-7. What is behavioral learning? What is cognitive learning?

6-8. What are the three components of attitudes?

6-9. What is personality?

6-10. What is family life cycle?

6-11. Explain what lifestyle means.

6-12. How do situational influences, such as the physical environment and time, shape consumer purchase decisions?

6-13. What are cultures, subcultures, and microcultures?

6-14. What is the significance of social class to marketers?

6-15. What are reference groups, and how do they influence consumers?

6-16. What are opinion leaders?

6-17. What are gender roles? Define this term and give an example.

6-18. How do B2B markets differ from consumer markets?

6-19. Explain what we mean by derived demand, inelastic demand, fluctuating demand, and joint demand.

6-20. How do we generally classify B2B markets?

6-21. Describe the buyclass framework. What are new-task buys, modified rebuys, and straight rebuys?

6-22. What is a buying center? What are the roles of the members of in a buying center?

6-23. Explain the steps in the business buying decision process.

6-24. What is single sourcing? Multiple sourcing? Outsourcing?

6-25. Explain the role of intranets and extranets in B2B e-commerce. Describe the security issues firms face in B2B e-commerce and some safeguards firms use to reduce their security risks.

Activities: Apply What You've Learned

⭐ **6-26.** *Creative Homework/Short Project* This chapter indicated that consumers go through a series of steps (from problem recognition to postpurchase evaluation) as they make purchases. Write a detailed report describing what you as a consumer would do in each of these steps when deciding to purchase one of the following products:
   a. A suit for an upcoming job interview
   b. A piece of jewelry to be given to a special friend for his or her birthday
   c. A fast-food lunch
   d. A Christmas tree
   Then make suggestions for what marketers might do to make sure that consumers like you who are going through each step in the consumer decision process move toward the purchase of their brand. (*Hint:* Think about product, place, price, and promotion strategies.)

6-27. *In Class, 15–20 Minutes for Teams* Think about a TV show that you watched recently, or perhaps a magazine that you have flipped through, or the last time you were looking at various websites. Try to remember the advertisements from those experiences.

   Why did you notice certain ads, whereas others which you were also exposed to were essentially screened out? In other words, what made you pay attention to these ads? Try to think beyond just the ad design itself, and consider your personal situation at the time as well as your product interests.

   What was the key message of each of the advertisements that you can recall? And finally, given your responses, how important is it for marketers to understand the process of perception when designing ads and other marketing communications?

6-28. *In Class, 10-15 Minutes for Individuals* Sometimes brands have their own personalities and consumers will make purchases of these brands in line with their own self-concept. Do you have any family or friends who have a particularly strong attachment to a brand, so much so that it almost becomes part of their self-identity? What are some of the characteristics of brands that can communicate their own "personality"?

6-29. *Creative Thinking* B2B marketers have usually focused on building relationships and personal selling, whereas social media tends to be mainly used for personal relationships, entertainment, and light information. To what extent do you think B2B marketers can effectively use social media networks in their overall marketing efforts? Do you think that the way marketers use social media will differ between B2B and B2C marketing?

6-30. *In Class, 15–20 Minutes for Teams* A straight rebuy purchase for a business is similar to a habit purchase for a consumer. Given that this is virtually an automatic repurchase, how could a competitive firm structure their marketing activities to win market share from customers who have established business relationships with other firms?

6-31. *For Further Research (Individual)* In this chapter, we learned that firms may use rich media in their messages online to create interaction and engagement with consumers. "Surf" the web and find at least three examples of rich media. Develop a report that describes the three rich media examples you found, what you believe the advertiser was seeking to gain in terms of interaction and engagement, and your opinion about the rich media suggestions for use in this ad and how it might be improved.

6-32. *For Further Research (Groups)* We learned in this chapter that when considering a product need, consumers have an evoked set of brands and a consideration set of brands. With some of your classmates, conduct a simple research study and explain your results using the following steps.
   a. Select a product that students in college would might purchase.
   b. Develop a questionnaire that you will ask student participants to complete. The questionnaire should ask students to list all of the brands of the product you have selected that they are aware of. Give them at least five minutes to complete this question.
   c. Then ask them to tell you which ones would they seriously consider buying if they were going to make a purchase today.
   d. Develop a report using the results of the survey. What conclusions can you draw from the research?

Concepts: Apply Marketing Metrics

B2B customers (clients) are busy professionals and thus are notoriously reluctant to take time to provide data to marketers. To measure important issues described in the chapter, such as overall client satisfaction, service quality by the vendor firm, level of customer engagement, repurchase intentions, and speed and effectiveness of problem resolution, marketers must employ the most user-friendly and efficient data collection methods available when dealing with these professional business clients. Otherwise, it is highly unlikely that they will take time to provide any useful data for market planning and decision making.

⭐ **6-33.** Take a few minutes to go back and briefly review what you learned in Chapter 4 about the different approaches to collecting data. Propose an approach to collecting the types of information from a busy B2B customer in a way that is most likely to result in his or her cooperation. Be as specific as you can in describing your chosen approach and explain why you selected it.

Choices: What Do You Think?

⭐ **6-34.** *Critical Thinking* Changing demographics and cultural values are important to marketers. List at least three current trends that may affect the successful marketing of the following products:
   a. Housing
   b. Food
   c. Education
   d. Clothing
   e. Travel and tourism
   f. Automobiles

6-35. *Critical Thinking* Consumers often buy products because they feel pressure from reference groups to conform. Does conformity exert a positive or a negative influence on consumers? With what types of products is conformity more likely to occur?

⭐ **6-36.** *Ethics* Marketers have been shelling out the bucks on sensory marketing techniques for years to appeal to your subconscious mind. And studies show that it works. But is sensory marketing fair? Some say it's a way to enhance the purchasing process, while others say marketers are unethically manipulating consumers. What are some of the pros and cons associated with sensory marketing? What is your position?

6-37. *Critical Thinking* E-commerce is dramatically changing the way B2B transactions take place. What are the advantages of B2B e-commerce to companies? To society? Are there any disadvantages of B2B e-commerce?

6-38. *Critical Thinking* Mobile commerce (m-commerce) is a rapidly growing category of e-commerce that takes place via a smart phone or tablet instead of a desktop or laptop computer. How has m-commerce changed the way consumers shop? What do marketers need to do now and in the future to better support their m-commerce customers? What do you think the future of m-commerce will be?

6-39. *Critical Thinking* The practice of buying business products based on sealed competitive bids is popular among all types of business buyers. What are the advantages and disadvantages of this practice to buyers? What are the advantages and disadvantages to sellers? Should companies always give the business to the lowest bidder? Why or why not?

6-40. *Ethics* When firms implement a single sourcing policy in their buying, other possible suppliers do not have an opportunity to compete for the business. Is this ethical? What are the advantages to the company? What are the disadvantages?

6-41. *Critical Thinking* In the buying center, the gatekeeper controls information flow to others in the center. Thus, the gatekeeper determines which possible sellers are heard and which are not. Does the gatekeeper have too much power? What policies might be implemented to make sure that all possible sellers are treated fairly?

6-42. *Critical Thinking* Outsourcing and offshoring are practices often surrounded by controversy. What are the benefits of outsourcing for businesses? For consumers? What are the disadvantages of outsourcing for businesses? For consumers? Should outsourcing be regulated to protect U.S. interests both at home and abroad? Why or why not?

Miniproject: Learn by Doing

The purpose of this miniproject is to increase your understanding of the process that consumers go through when making a purchase decision. First, select one of the following products (or some other product of your choice) that now, or in the future, you might be in the market for.

• New or used car
• Spring break vacation
• Apartment
• Computer or smart phone

6-43. *Problem Recognition* Describe the problem that might lead you to purchase this product.

6-44. *Information Search* Use the Internet to gather some initial information about the product you chose. Visit at least two stores or locations where the product may be purchased to gather further information.

6-45. *Evaluation of Alternatives* Identify at least five alternative product options that you are interested in. Narrow down your selection to two or three choices. Which are the most feasible? What are the pros and cons of each?

6-46. *Product Choice* Make a final decision about which product you will purchase. Describe the heuristics that aided in your decision making.

6-47. *Postpurchase Evaluation* If this is a product you have actually purchased, explain the reasoning behind your current satisfaction or dissatisfaction with the product. If not, develop several reasons you might be satisfied or dissatisfied with the product.

6-48. Prepare a report that explains in detail the decision-making process for the product in your purchase scenario.

Marketing in **Action** Case Real Choices at Airbus

There is always room for more. At least that's what Airbus thinks. It has improved on its A320 product family (the world's best-selling aircraft) and introduced the A320neo (new engine option). The A320neo is available with two different engine configurations and will be a more fuel-efficient, single-aisle aircraft, for purchasing by the world's airlines. According to Airbus's estimates, the A320neo family of aircraft will lower per-seat fuel burn by 20 percent while providing additional range, reduced engine noise, and lower pollution emissions.

To create this level of efficiency, the new engine options are accompanied by Sharklets wingtips, which not only provide for better fuel efficiency but also add more passenger comfort. Sharklets cut down aerodynamic drag and offer airlines up to four percent fuel burn reduction on longer-range flights. The Sharklets derive their name from their resemblance to a shark's fin, are made from light-weight composites and are 2.4 meters tall. With other aerodynamic refinements and significant weight savings, the A320neo has an increased range of approximately 500 nautical miles. The interior enhancements incorporate a re-designed cabin that offers larger carry-on luggage space and an upgraded air purification system. The cabin upgrades will allow for 20 additional revenue-generating passengers.

Airbus also offers its customers other NEO type of aircraft including the A319neo and A321neo versions. These new planes share 95 percent of the spare parts used by their currently available versions. More compatibility will allow current A320 customers to make use of parts and equipment that they already own, thereby lowering implementation costs. In addition, the new aircraft include a variety of other improvements over current aircraft.

Airbus's greatest competition for the A320neo is from Boeing's most recent entry into the short-haul airliner market, the 737 MAX. Boeing's Senior Vice President of Program Management, Scott Fancher, calls this medium-size airplane "the heart of the market." The 737 MAX boasts increased fuel efficiency as the result of a redesigned wing, improved interface of the wing and engine, and the use of winglets. Boeing, however, is behind Airbus. The 787 MAX program is operating approximately 18 months behind Airbus. Boeing did not have its first flight of the 737 MAX until after the initial delivery of the Airbus A320neo. As of December 2015, Boeing had 3,072 firm orders for the new aircraft and the first 737 MAX is scheduled for delivery in 2017.

Since early 2015, there have been more than 4,500 worldwide orders for aircraft in the A320neo product line. In January 2016, German carrier Lufthansa became the first airline to receive and put into use the A320neo's improved airplanes. Airbus was thus first to the market with significant pre-orders and ready to take a commanding lead in the single-aisle market.

It is not uncommon in the aircraft business for manufacturers to experience small production issues during the introduction phase. The A320neo's problems are more significant than usual and are causing a delay in delivery schedules.

Although Lufthansa was the first to receive delivery of the A320neo, it was not the initial intention of Airbus. Qatar Airways had been scheduled to receive the first delivery in late 2015. However, after testing the aircraft, the airline complained of engine problems and refused to take possession. Airbus began dealing with these issues, but they still persist. They had to compensate Lufthansa because the airline was restricted to using the A320neo only at the airports where it had additional technical staff. Someone once said, "Good things take time."

The introduction of the A320neo has been plagued with problems. However, the delays in delivery are expected to end. With more than 4,000 awaiting orders from a multitude of customers, Airbus has the potential to turn something bad into something good. There are a lot of customer relationships that need soothing. How does the company get customers not to cancel orders and choose Boeing's aircraft? Airbus's challenges are far from over.

You Make the Call

6-49. What is the decision facing Airbus?

6-50. What factors are important in understanding this decision situation?

6-51. What are the alternatives?

6-52. What decision(s) do you recommend?

6-53. What are some ways to implement your recommendation?

Sources: Based on Dhierin Bechai, "Did The Airbus A320neo Lose Its Momentum?" *Seeking Alpha* (March 21, 2016), http://seekingalpha.com/article/3959986-airbus-a320neo-lose-momentum (accessed April 21, 2016); "Spotlight on … The neo: a Born Leader," *Airbus*, http://www.airbus.com/aircraftfamilies/passengeraircraft/a320family/spotlight-on-a320neo/ (accessed April 21, 2016); Dominic Gates, "Boeing's 737 MAX Takes Wing with New Engines, High Hopes," *Seattle Times* (January 29, 2016), http://www.seattletimes.com/business/boeing-aerospace/boeings-737-max-takes-off-on-first-flight/ (accessed April 21, 2016).

MyLab Marketing™

Go to mymktlab.com for the following Assisted-graded writing questions:

6-54. *Creative Homework/Short Project.* Sometimes advertising or other marketing activities cause problem recognition by showing consumers how much better off they would be with a new product or by pointing out problems with products they already own. Discuss problem recognition for the following product categories. Make a list of some ways marketers might try to stimulate problem recognition for each product. Present your ideas to your class.
   a. Toothpaste
   b. A home security system
   c. A new automobile
   d. An online dating service
   e. A health club membership

6-55. *Creative Homework/Short Project.* As a director of purchasing for a firm that manufactures motorcycles, you have been notified that the price of an important part used in the manufacture of the bikes has nearly doubled from $100 to nearly $200. You see your company having three choices: buying the part and passing the cost on to the customer by increasing your price; buying the part and absorbing the increase in cost, keeping the price of your bikes the same; or buying a lower-priced part that will be of lower quality. Prepare a list of pros and cons for each alternative. Then explain your recommendation and justification for it.

Segmentation, Target Marketing, and Positioning

Objective Outline

Meet Jen Sey

▼ **A Decision Maker at Levi Strauss**

Jen Sey is Chief Marketing Officer for the Levi's® Brand within Levi Strauss & Co. She has been with LS&Co. for more than 16 years, holding a variety of leadership positions within the Marketing, Strategy, and E-commerce teams. In 2013, Sey became the Global Chief Marketing Officer for the Levi's® Brand.

Twenty years ago, she began her career at an advertising agency, Foote Cone and Belding, where she worked on a variety of brands including Levi's®. She went on to become the advertising manager at Banana Republic before landing at Levi Strauss & Co in 1999.

At LS&Co she has held a broad range of assignments across both Levi's® and Dockers brands including Director of Marketing for U.S. Levi's®, Senior Director of Global Strategy for Levi's®, Vice President of Global Marketing for Levi Strauss & Co., and Senior Vice President for Dockers Global Marketing. In 2012, she stepped into the role of Senior Vice President of Global E-commerce, driving the business and replatforming efforts for both levi.com and dockers.com across the regions.

In 2013, Jen returned to the Levi's® Brand as CMO and quickly launched the Live in Levi's® campaign, notable for reconnecting the brand with its optimistic spirit that fans around the world have loved about Levi's® for decades. The campaign is a celebration of Levi's® products and brand, showcasing how people all over the world live in Levi's®. The Live in Levi's "Beautiful Morning" television spot was honored as a 2015 Taste Award's Special Achievement Spotlight winner, recognizing Jen's immediate impact.

Sey has received numerous awards, including the distinction of *AdAge's* Top 40 Marketers Under 40 in 2006; being named one of the Top Women in Retail by *Total Retail* in 2014 and one of *Brand Innovators'* Top 50 Women in Marketing in 2015. Most recently, she was named one of *Hot Topic's* Top 100 Retail Marketers in 2016.

As a child, Sey led an intense life of dedication, challenge, and competition. She won the U.S. National Gymnastics Championship title in 1986, less than one year after having suffered a devastating injury at the 1985 World Championships. As a result, the U.S. Olympic Committee named her Gymnastics' Athlete of the Year. She retired after eight years on the national team and went on to study at Stanford University where she double majored in Communications and Political Science. In 2008, Sey released her first book, *Chalked Up*, a memoir detailing her triumphs and struggles within the world of competitive gymnastics. She has been featured on a variety of talk shows including *Good Morning America* and the *CBS Morning Show* discussing the pros and cons of elite competitive childhood athletics.

Sey now lives in San Francisco, California, with partner Daniel and her three sons Virgil, Wyatt, and Oscar. She lends her voice to online outlets Salon.com, Mommytrackd.com and BasilandSpice.com, and she continues her work started with *Chalked Up* as an athlete advocate. In 2016, Sweaty Betty (leading British activewear brand) appointed Sey to the Company's Board of Directors.

Levi Strauss

What I do when I'm not working:
Spend time with my family (3 kids, 1 partner, 1 dog), read, cook, write, exercise

First job out of school:
Production assistant on a movie and gymnastics coach

Career high:
Levi's CMO—launch of Live in Levi's and Levi's Stadium

A job-related mistake I wish I hadn't made:
Got too attached to a single path forward in my career. Wish I'd been open to unexpected next steps sooner rather than later.

My motto to live by:
Get 'er done

My management style:
Be open and honest, practice humility always, roll up your sleeves and do the work, be direct in your communication style, and always remember—you don't know everything!

My pet peeve:
Leaders that think leadership is just telling people what to do. And mean people. No patience for meanness. Unnecessary.

Here's my problem...

Real **People**, Real **Choices**

The Levi's brand was losing relevance and market share. Although technically we were the leader in denim in terms of market share, it didn't necessarily feel like we were leading; our market share was being eaten up by premium brands and then most recently fast fashion. We needed to reposition for success—in terms of both financial and equity performance and the overall future health of the brand. We needed to create a clear brand value proposition that was relevant and differentiated, broadly appealing and globally viable. My job was to lead this process and create a long-standing marketing campaign off of this positioning, while inspiring the organization more broadly with this brand direction.

Jen considered her **Options** 1·2·3

1 Option
First and foremost we looked at the obvious: **Levi's is THE original blue jean.** Our founder Levi Strauss and tailor Jacob Davis obtained a U.S. patent on the process of putting rivets in men's work pants in 1873, and the company has a rich history that spans almost 150 years. This positioning asserts the brand's innovator status; it's the oldest but also the first. No other company can make this claim. No one else created the blue jean—or the product category. Although this is a powerful statement it's not that relevant to modern consumers. It doesn't give them a reason to choose the brand TODAY. We know that millennials value authenticity, but we need to either promote this attribute more forcefully or give them additional reasons to choose our brand.

2 Option
We also looked at a different definition of Originality. Our idea is that "originality" means not only "first." This concept also refers to the quality of being new, fresh, creative, and independent. We looked at creating an association between the brand and the wearer with a position built around the idea that **Levi's is as original as you are.** This statement is relevant and aspirational. Everyone wants to see themselves as original, unique, and individualistic. And it is certainly believable for Levi's to be associated with this position. The brand has long told a story about individuality, most notably through its strong association with the cultural

icon James Dean. The actor's appearance in the 1950s movie *Rebel Without a Cause* wearing a white shirt, leather jacket, and a pair of Levi's 501s is one of the most legendary images in pop culture. On the other hand, this link with originality no longer makes the statement it used to. Many jeans and apparel brands make this claim (justified or not). We couldn't be sure that this position would differentiate us in the market and give people a reason to choose Levi's versus another brand. However, there is no question that our brand has a legitimate claim to this space if we choose to remind consumers of our long heritage.

3 Option
As we embarked on research with consumers around the world, we heard a lot of people telling us about all the amazing life experiences they have had in their Levi's. They related stories about road trips, first loves, concerts, and all-night dance parties. They talked about the bond they have with their Levi's because of these experiences. And they said that they did not have this kind of relationship with their other jeans or clothing items. The relationship with their Levi's jeans was special. This inspired this idea of: **You wear other jeans but you live your life in Levi's.** This claim is highly differentiated and more importantly it makes an emotional connection with our customers. The down side is that today blue jeans are more of a fashion-oriented product than they used to be. We need to be able to drive a style message in addition to an emotional message. And this connection isn't as strong in all of our global markets. For example, in China, where people haven't been wearing Levi's for very long, people haven't had time to forge these connections yet.

Now, put yourself in Jen's shoes. Which option would you choose, and why?

You Choose

Which **Option** would you choose, and **why**?

☐ Option 1   ☐ Option 2   ☐ Option 3

See what **Option** Jen chose in **MyLab Marketing**™

MyLab Marketing™

⭐ **Improve Your Grade!**

Over 10 million students improved their results using the Pearson MyLabs.
Visit **mymktlab.com** for simulations, tutorials, and end-of-chapter problems.

7.1 Target Marketing:
Select and Enter a Market

OBJECTIVE

Identify the steps in the target marketing process.

(p. 228)

Way back in Chapter 1, we defined a market as all the customers and potential customers who share a common need that can be satisfied by a specific product, who have the resources to exchange for it, who are willing to make the exchange, and who have the authority to make the exchange. And at this point in your study of marketing, you know that key goals of the marketer are to create value, build customer relationships, and satisfy needs. But in our modern, complex society, it's naive to assume that everyone's needs are the same—even for a pair of blue jeans.

Today, it's a complex task to understand people's differing needs because technological and cultural advances create a condition of **market fragmentation**. This means that people's diverse interests and backgrounds naturally divide them into numerous groups with distinct needs and wants. Because of this diversity, the same good or service will not appeal to everyone.

Consider, for example, the effects of fragmentation in higher education. Before you faced the big decision of which classes to register for, including this one, you had the even bigger task of deciding on which one of the numerous types of colleges or universities you would attend. Not only did you have the more traditional schools to choose from—community or technical colleges and public or private four-year schools—but you also had newer schools, such as the for-profit University of Phoenix or Kaplan University, and several online-only schools, such as Western Governors University. Each of these institutions of higher learning serves a different market need, and what may meet your needs currently might not meet your needs in the future. Fortunately, there are plenty of options to choose from, depending on your abilities, background, and of course the old checkbook!

Marketers must balance the efficiency of mass marketing where they serve the same items to everyone, with the effectiveness that comes when they offer each individual exactly what he or she wants. Mass marketing certainly costs much less—when we offer one product to everyone, we eliminate the need for separate advertising campaigns and distinctive packages for each item. However, consumers see things differently. From their perspective the best strategy would be to offer the perfect product just for them. Unfortunately, that's often not realistic.

For 40 years, Burger King's motto was "Have It Your Way," but in 2014 the fast food company scrapped that iconic theme for an updated version of the slogan: "Be Your Way." Burger King says that the new motto is intended to remind people that "they can and should live how they want anytime. It's ok to not be perfect ... Self-expression is most important and it's our differences that make us individuals instead of robots."[1] This change is convenient for Burger King, because the huge chain could deliver on the old promise only to a point: "Having" it your way is fine as long as you stay within the confines of familiar condiments, such as mustard or ketchup. Don't dream of topping your burger with blue cheese, mango sauce, or some other "exotic" ingredient.

So, instead of trying to sell the same thing to everyone, marketers select a **target marketing strategy** in which they divide the total market into different segments based on customer characteristics, select one or more segments, and develop products to meet the needs of those specific segments. Figure 7.1 illustrates the three-step process of segmentation, targeting, and positioning, and it's what we're going to check out in this chapter. Let's start with the first step—segmentation.

market fragmentation
The creation of many consumer groups due to a diversity of distinct needs and wants in modern society.

target marketing strategy
Dividing the total market into different segments on the basis of customer characteristics, selecting one or more segments, and developing products to meet the needs of those specific segments.

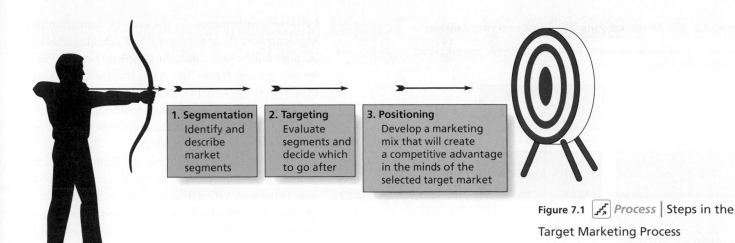

| 1. Segmentation Identify and describe market segments | 2. Targeting Evaluate segments and decide which to go after | 3. Positioning Develop a marketing mix that will create a competitive advantage in the minds of the selected target market |

Figure 7.1 ⬈ *Process* | Steps in the Target Marketing Process

Target marketing strategy consists of three separate steps. Marketers first divide the market into segments based on customer characteristics, then select one or more segments, and finally develop products to meet the needs of those specific segments.

7.2

OBJECTIVE

Understand the need for market segmentation and the approaches available to do it.

(pp. 229–241)

Step 1: Segmentation

Segmentation is the process of dividing a larger market into smaller pieces based on one or more meaningful, shared characteristics. This process is a way of life for almost all marketers in both consumer and business-to-business markets. The truth is that you can't please all the people all the time, so you need to take your best shot. Marriott, for example, segments its market by offering 16 separate brands that range from the value-oriented Courtyard to the deluxe Ritz-Carlton. Newer brands include the Moxy chain in partnership with IKEA and the uber-hip Edition hotels it is opening in partnership with Ian Schrager who created the boutique hotel concept in the 1980s and is most famous for his Studio 54 disco.[2] Just how do marketers segment a population? How do they divide the whole pie into smaller slices they can "digest"? The marketer must decide on one or more useful **segmentation variables**—that is, dimensions that divide the total market into fairly homogeneous groups, each with different needs and preferences. In this section, we'll take a look at this process, beginning with the types of segmentation variables that marketers use to divide up end-user consumers. Then we'll move on to business-to-business segmentation.

segmentation

The process of dividing a larger market into smaller pieces based on one or more meaningfully shared characteristics.

segmentation variables

Dimensions that divide the total market into fairly homogeneous groups, each with different needs and preferences.

Segment Consumer Markets

At one time, it was sufficient to divide the sports shoe market into athletes and non-athletes. But take a walk through any sporting goods store today and you'll quickly see that the athlete market has fragmented in many directions. Shoes designed for jogging, basketball, tennis, cycling, cross training, and even skateboarding beckon us from the aisles. We need several segmentation variables if we want to slice up the market for all the shoe variations available today. First, not everyone is willing or able to drop several hundred bucks on the latest sneakers, so marketers consider income (Note: A pair of Air Jordan Friends and Family edition kicks will run you a cool $6,000).[3] Second, men may be more interested in basketball shoes for shooting hoops with the guys, whereas women snap up the latest Pilates styles, so marketers also consider gender. Because not all age groups are equally interested in buying specialized athletic shoes, we slice the larger consumer "pie" into smaller pieces in a number of ways, including demographic, psychographic, and

Figure 7.2 📷 *Snapshot* | Segmenting Consumer Markets

Consumer markets can be segmented by demographic, psychographic, or behavioral criteria.

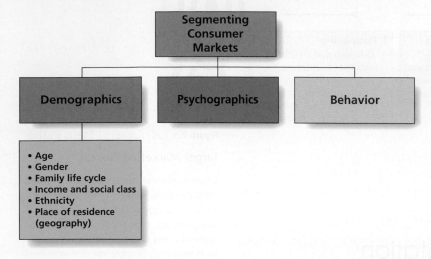

behavioral differences. In the case of demographic segmentation, there are several key subcategories of demographics: age (including generational differences), gender, family life cycle, income and social class, ethnicity, and place of residence, sometimes referred to separately as geographic segmentation. 📷 Figure 7.2 summarizes the dominant approaches to segmenting consumer markets.

In the sections that follow, we'll consider each of these segmentation approaches in turn, but first a note of caution. When it comes to marketing to some groups—in particular, lower-income individuals, the poorly educated, nonnative-language speakers, and children—it is incumbent on marketers to exercise the utmost care not to take undue advantage of their circumstances. In Chapter 2, we introduced a global segment called the *bottom of the pyramid (BOP)*, which is the collective name for the group of more than 4 billion consumers throughout the world who live on less than $2 a day. Ethical marketers must be sensitive to the different conditions in which people find themselves, and proactively work to uphold a high level of honesty and trust with all segments of the public. Doing so is nothing short of marketing's social responsibility.

One other caveat is needed before we jump into our discussion of different market segments. Identifying segments is not, repeat *not*, intended by marketers as a form of stereotyping. The idea of segmenting markets is to identify groups of consumers with similar needs so that marketing to them can be done more efficiently and effectively versus a mass-market approach. That doesn't necessarily mean that we want to pigeonhole a group of people because they happen to share an important characteristic such as gender or place of residence.

Segment by Demographics: Age

demographics

Statistics that measure observable aspects of a population, including size, age, gender, ethnic group, income, education, occupation, and family structure.

As we stated in Chapter 2, **demographics** are statistics that measure observable aspects of a population, including size, age, gender, ethnic group, income, education, occupation, and family structure. These descriptors are vital to identify the best potential customers for a good or service. Because they represent objective characteristics, they usually are easy to identify, and then it's just a matter of tailoring messages and products to relevant age groups. Consumers of different age groups have different needs and wants. Members of a generation tend to share the same outlook, values, and priorities. When these characteristics are combined for purposes of market segmentation and targeting, such an approach is called **generational marketing**.

generational marketing

Marketing to members of a generation, who tend to share the same outlook, values, and priorities.

For example, *children* are an attractive age segment for many marketers. Although kids obviously have a lot to say about purchases of toys and games, they influence other family purchases as well (just watch them at work in the grocery store!). According to a recent YouGov Omnibus survey, 42 percent of parents said that they gave in to a child's request to buy a product when the child put substantial effort into arguing for the purchase. Savvy children are famous for negotiation tactics such as promising to do more chores or to work harder in school to get better grades.[4] It's not hard to see how these persuasive little guys could quickly wear down a parent's resistance—buying the item is easier than fighting the fight. For Netflix, developing content to win over children to the platform has become a key strategy. The company developed 20 out of 70 "Netflix Original" programs specifically for children. Netflix recognizes the importance of this segment in cementing its position as the main source of entertainment for families and as a key source of growth in delivering long-term customer value.[5] **Generation Z** is a relatively new term coined to denote individuals who were born after 1994. This is the first generation of the 21st century and it's the most diverse we've ever experienced: 55 percent are Caucasian, 24 percent are Hispanic, 14 percent are African American, and 4 percent are Asian. They are accustomed to blurred gender roles, where household responsibilities don't split along traditional lines. And, of course they are **digital natives** who spend a big chunk of their time online, so they expect brands to engage them in two-way digital conversations.

Marketers are just starting to figure out what this new group of youngsters will be like as consumers. Having grown up during the "Great Recession," they are not as likely to believe in an idealized, carefree world. They tend to be independent and gravitate to stores like Free People rather than Abercrombie & Fitch.[6] They learn about new styles from around the globe via social media, so they are equally at home watching *The Hunger Games* or listening to Korean K-pop. Their idols are "self-made" Internet stars like the Swedish video producer PewDiePie, who has the world's most subscribed YouTube channel, and the teenage video sensation Evan who has 25 million followers.[7]

The 13- to 18-year-old age group is reported to spend more than $200 billion (both through purchases made by them and purchases made for them) on different products.[8] Much of this money goes toward "feel-good" products: music, video games, cosmetics, and fast food—with the occasional tattoo or hookah pen thrown in as well. Because they are so interested in many different products and have the resources to obtain them, many marketers avidly court the teen market.[9] Snapchat has designed a platform that contains cool features (such as the ability to manipulate selfies to incorporate some of the features of a unicorn into your face) that appeal heavily to a younger crowd, including teenagers. The platform is designed to make it hard for one user (say for instance a parent) to eavesdrop on the activity of another user (say for instance the child of that parent) without knowing their username. One of the platform's investors, social media guru Gary Vaynerchuk, states that, after Instagram, for "everyone from 14 to 24 in America, (Snapchat) is either the No. 1 or No. 2 app in their lives."[10]

Generation Y, often also called **millennials** or "Echo Boomers," consists of people born between the years 1979 and 1994. This age segment is the first generation to grow up online. Generation Y is an attractive market for a host of consumer products because of its size (approximately 27 percent of the population) and free-spending nature—as a group, it spends about $1.3 trillion annually.[11]

But Generation Y consumers can be hard to reach through traditional media because they resist reading and increasingly turn off the TV to opt instead for streaming video and digital video recordings. As a result, many marketers have had to develop other ways to reach this generation "where they live," which is in large measure through their smartphones and tablets, using social media and related technology. We'll talk more about the shift to new-age marketing communications techniques later in this book.

We already know that Gen Yers are tech savvy, but what else defines them as a generation compared to past generations? A Pew Research study shows that compared to past generations (when they were in the same age range) GenYers are more racially diverse and more highly educated. In addition, a greater proportion of them have never been married when compared to other generations (68 percent compared to 56 percent for Generation X, which is the next closest generation).[12]

The group of consumers born between 1965 and 1978 consists of 46 million Americans known as **Generation X**, who unfortunately and undeservedly came to be called slackers, or busters (for the "baby bust" that followed the "baby boom"). Many of these people have a cynical attitude toward marketing—a chapter in a famous book called *Generation X* is titled "I Am Not a Target Market!"[13]

Generation Z
The group of consumers born after 1994.

digital natives
Individuals who spend a big chunk of their time online, so they expect brands to engage them in two-way digital conversations.

Generation Y (millennials)
The group of consumers born between 1979 and 1994.

Generation X
The group of consumers born between 1965 and 1978.

baby boomers
The segment of people born between 1946 and 1964.

Despite this tough reputation, members of Generation X, the oldest of whom are now in their early fifties, have mellowed with age. In retrospect, they also have developed an identity for being an entrepreneurial group. One study revealed that Gen Xers led much of the modern technology revolution, and now firms seek them out for their entrepreneurial talents. Many people in this segment were determined to have stable families after being brought up as latch-key children themselves as both their parents put in long days at work. Gen Xers tend to view the home as an expression of individuality rather than material success. More than half are involved in home improvement and repair projects.[14] So much for Gen Xers as slackers!

Baby boomers, consumers born between 1946 and 1964 and who are now in their fifties and sixties, are an important segment to many marketers—if for no other reason than that there are so many of them who have a lot of money. The baby boom occurred when soldiers came flooding home after World War II and there was a rush to get married and start families. Back in the 1950s and 1960s, couples started having children younger and had more of them than the previous generation. The resulting glut of kids really changed the infrastructure of the country: more single-family houses, more schools, migration to the suburbs, and freeways to commute from home to work.

More recently some research has suggested that it may be beneficial for marketers to treat this generational segment as two different groups for purposes of considering their discretionary and non-discretionary spending capabilities. A survey by Gallup indicates that there are significant differences between baby boomer spending for those born in the first half of the generation's age range ("leading-edge Boomers") compared to those born in the second half of the generation's age range ("trailing-edge Boomers"). In general, the trailing-edge boomers find themselves spending significantly more on non-discretionary items (e.g., house maintenance, groceries, etc.) than their leading-edge boomer counterparts. One explanation for this difference in spending capabilities between these two groups may relate to differences in financial obligations. The older group of Baby Boomers (aged 59 to 68) may have reached a point where they are no longer paying off mortgages or higher education debts. For marketers that sell non-discretionary products, this knowledge provides important guidance to develop marketing strategies.[15]

Currently, the U.S. Census Bureau estimates that there are slightly more than 46 million Americans aged 65 or older, an increase from prior years. Florida and Maine ranked first and second in the highest percentage of individuals aged 65 and older with about 19 percent and 18 percent, respectively.[16] To better accommodate the senior market, companies are changing their stores and their products. CVS, for example, introduced carpeting in its stores to reduce slipping, and Walgreens added magnifying glasses in aisles that featured products with fine print. Kimberly-Clark not only redesigned its Depends line to look more like regular underwear but also will now shelve the product among other general hygiene products and not in an "old person's" section of the store.[17]

Many *mature consumers* enjoy leisure time and continued good health. Indeed, a key question today is, "Just what is a senior citizen, when people live longer and 80 is the new 60?" As we will see later in the chapter, perhaps it isn't age but rather lifestyle factors, including mobility, that best define this group. More and more marketers offer products that appeal to active-lifestyle seniors. And they often combine the product appeal with a nostalgia theme that includes music popular during the seniors' era of youth. People tend to prefer music that was released when they were teenagers or young adults, with interest peaking between ages 24 and 25. For years, Sandals Resorts, whose advertising imagery tends to favor Boomers, has used the song "(I've Had) The Time of My Life" in commercials for its romantic vacation destinations in the Caribbean. The song, recorded by Bill Medley and Jennifer Warnes, was made famous in the classic 1987 movie *Dirty Dancing*. As nostalgia, it does double duty because the movie itself was set in 1963, so it conjures up memories of both the 1980s and the 1960s for this key boomer demographic segment for Sandals.[18] And more recently history repeated itself, as ABC presented a three-hour remake of the show starring Abigail Breslin of *Scream Queens* fame.[19]

Segment by Demographics: Gender

Many products, from fragrances to fashion apparel and accessories, specifically appeal to men or women. Segmenting by gender starts at an early age—even diapers come in pink for girls and blue for boys.

In some cases, manufacturers develop parallel products to appeal to each sex. For example, male grooming products have traditionally been Gillette's priority since the company's founder King Gillette (yes, his first name was actually King) introduced the safety razor in 1903. But today, the Venus line by Gillette is a top-selling razor for women of all ages.

A small microbrewer in California called She Beverage Co. applied to register with the U.S. Patent and Trademark Office the phrase "Queen of Beer," which it has been using on its website as well as in its social media communications. "The King of Beers" Budweiser contested the application and general use of the phrase on the grounds that it might cause confusion for consumers, resulting in drawing the incorrect conclusion that the beer is affiliated with the Anheuser-Busch company (and all of the brand benefits that come along with that association). She Beverage Co. recently has begun to sell its beers in restaurants and stores with a focus on the female consumer and the claim that its beers are made to better fit to female taste and style preferences that are underserved within the male-dominated beer market. She Beverage continues to pursue its trademark, vowing to keep up the fight so the company can communicate to female beer drinkers that this is beer formulated specifically with their preferences in mind.[20]

Metrosexual as a marketing buzzword gained steam beginning in the late 2000s. The term describes a straight, urban man who is keenly interested in fashion, home design, gourmet cooking, and personal care. Metrosexuals are usually well-educated urban dwellers who are in touch with their feminine side. Although many men are reluctant to overtly identify with the metrosexual, there's no denying that a renewed interest in personal care products, fashion accessories, and other "formerly feminine" product categories creates many marketing opportunities. Mainstream newspapers such as the *New York Times* offer regular segments dedicated to male fashion and grooming.

Recently, there's been broad acceptance and assimilation of the values and behaviors ascribed to metrosexuals within the mainstream market. Retailers have been making an extra effort to provide a more pleasurable experience to men who are spending more time on extensive in-store browsing and purchasing across product lines, in stark contrast to the quick in-and-out style of shopping primarily associated with men before. For instance, the high-end retailer Club Monaco now offers bars, cafes, bookstores, and even barbershops in some of its retail locations.[21]

You've no doubt heard of the "Great Recession" that began in late 2007, which was a shock to marketers who had to quickly scramble to understand its impact on purchasing habits. An interesting trend related to gender segmentation fueled by the recession and its aftermath is that men now are increasingly likely to marry wives with more education and income than they have, and the reverse is true for women. In recent decades, with the rise of well-paid working wives, the economic gains of marriage have been a greater benefit for men. The education and income gap has grown even more in the latest recession, when men held about three in four of the jobs that were lost. In 1960, 13.5 percent of wives had husbands who were better educated, and 6.9 percent were married to men with less education. By 2012, the comparable figures were 19.9 percent and 20.7 percent—for the first time in history, more women "married down," educationally speaking, than men.[22] In 1960, 6.2 percent of husbands had wives who made more money; in 2007, 24 percent did.[23]

metrosexual
A straight, urban male who is keenly interested in fashion, home design, gourmet cooking, and personal care.

SHE Beer specifically targets female brew drinkers.

Segment by Demographics: Family Life Cycle

Because family needs and expenditures change over time, one way to segment consumers is to consider the stage of the family life cycle they occupy. (You learned about the family life cycle in Chapter 6.) Not surprisingly, consumers in different life cycle segments are unlikely to need the same products, or at least they may not need these things in the same quantities. Single-person households have grown over the years, influenced by such factors as changing views toward marriage and other shifting lifestyle choices. This trend is expected to continue to grow over time and is projected to have an impact on marketing in many industries including housing and health care.[24] A report from the research firm the NPD Group noted that recent growth in snack food consumption could be attributed largely to the growth in single-person households.[25,26]

But not all attempts at marketing to the family life cycle succeed. Gerber once tried to market single-serving food jars to single seniors—a quick meal for one person who lives alone. The manufacturer called these containers "Singles." However, Gerber's strong identification with baby food worked against it: The product flopped because their target market was embarrassed to be seen buying baby food.[27]

As families age and move into new life stages, different product categories ascend and descend in importance. Young bachelors and newlyweds are the most likely to exercise, go to bars and movies, and consume alcohol (in other words, party while you can). Older couples and bachelors are more likely to use maintenance services. Seniors are a prime market for resort condominiums and golf products. Marketers need to identify the family life cycle segment of their target consumers by examining purchase data by family life cycle group.

Cultural changes continually create new opportunities as people's roles change. For example, boomer women in their sixties are a hot new market for what the auto industry calls "reward cars": sexy and extravagant vehicles. Says president of Women-Drivers.com Anne Fleming, "As they graduate from baseball and ballerina mom, they are seizing their new-found freedom and buying sexy, indulgent 'me-mobiles.'"[28]

Segment by Demographics: Income and Social Class

buying power
A concept in segmentation that can help marketers to determine how to better match different products and versions of products to different consumer groups based on an understanding of what discretionary and nondiscretionary allocations of funds they are able to make.

The distribution of wealth is of great interest to marketers because it determines which groups have the greatest **buying power**. Buying power can help marketers to determine how to better match different products and versions of products to different consumer groups based on an understanding of what discretionary and nondiscretionary allocations of funds they are able to make. After a more than 50-year run during which the truly wealthy just kept getting richer, the Great Recession took some of the wind out of their sails because of heavy investment losses. While at this writing the losses have been moderated by a rebound in the stock market, that history of risk and volatility in investments has likely impacted the consumer behavior of the rich just as it has other income segments. Of course, households making $100,000 or more certainly do not in most cases come close to being part of that "truly wealthy" crowd, but marketers mightily depend on their discretionary spending. Although they represent only 20 percent of U.S. households, they control more than half of all income and are far less likely than everyone else to be restrained by tight credit markets. On average, historically the affluent are 2.6 times more likely to make purchases in general, and when they do, they spend 3.7 times more.[29]

In the past, it was popular for marketers to consider *social class segments*, such as upper class, middle class, and lower class. However, many consumers buy not according to where they actually fall in that framework but rather according to the image they wish to portray. In recent years, luxury car manufacturers such as Mercedes, BMW, and Audi have developed versions of cars that are priced at less than half the price they charge for one of their traditional models. Seeking to attract consumers who view the brands as aspirational purchases, the approach has been so successful at increasing sales and market share that *avant-garde* electric car manufacturer Tesla unveiled a "low-end" Model III for less than half the price of its roadster to compete for these consumers, and the company can't keep up with the demand after getting blanketed with preorders.[30]

Segment by Demographics: Ethnicity

A consumer's national origin is often a strong indicator of his or her preferences for specific magazines or TV shows, foods, apparel, and leisure activities. Marketers need to be aware of these differences and sensitivities—especially when they invoke outmoded stereotypes to appeal to consumers of diverse races and ethnic groups.

African Americans, Asian Americans, and Hispanic Americans are the largest ethnic groups in the U.S. The Census Bureau projects that by the year 2050, non-Hispanic whites will make up just less than 50 percent of the population (compared to 74 percent in 1995) as these other groups grow. Let's take a closer look at each of these important ethnic segments.

African Americans make up more than 13 percent of the U.S. population.[31] Many marketers recognize the huge impact of this racial subculture and work hard to identify products and services that will appeal to these consumers. The toy market is no exception—children tend to gravitate toward toys and characters that look like them. The Disney TV show *Doc McStuffins* that stars an African American character who fixes toys in her backyard clinic illustrates this appeal. The blockbuster show sold about $500 million in merchandise last year. Its success reflects demographic changes in the United States that create opportunities for a diversity of ethnic characters.[32]

Although their numbers are still relatively small, Asian Americans are the fastest-growing minority group in the U.S. Between 2002 and 2014, the Asian American population grew by 46 percent to reach 19.4 million individuals with an expected growth of 150 percent between 2015 and 2050. For marketers this segment is especially attractive given its' substantial buying power that is estimated to be close to $800 billion. An amazing fact is that this figure is almost quadruple the buying power estimated for *all* millennials ($200 billion)![33] BuzzFeed makes an effort to court Asian-Americans by publishing content on topics and experiences highly relatable to this group, such as posts tailored to specific Asian subsegments like "22 Signs You Grew up with Immigrant Chinese Parents" and "21 Annoying Comments Filipinos Are Tired of Hearing." This approach to delivering fresh and specifically relatable content to different segments enables BuzzFeed to connect with distinct cultural groups of Asian Americans as well as other types of consumer segments.[34] It also makes BuzzFeed attractive to marketers who want to develop **content marketing** that will resonate with specific customer groups. This term refers to the strategy of establishing thought leadership in the form of bylines, blogs, commenting opportunities, videos, sharable social images, and infographics. A key departure is that these messages look like the kind of content that "ordinary" people post rather than the traditional advertising messages consumers are used to seeing.

content marketing
The strategy of establishing thought leadership in the form of bylines, blogs, commenting opportunities, videos, sharable social images, and infographics.

The Hispanic American population is a real emerging superstar segment for this decade, a segment that mainstream marketers today actively cultivate. Hispanics have overtaken African Americans as the nation's largest minority group.[35] In the U.S., Hispanic buying power is estimated to exceed $1.5 trillion—a greater than 50 percent increase from where the segment's buying power was in 2010.[36] In addition to its rapid growth, five other factors make the Hispanic segment attractive to marketers:

- Hispanics tend to be brand loyal, especially to products made in their country of origin.
- They tend to be highly concentrated by national origin, which makes it easy to fine-tune the marketing mix to appeal to those who come from the same country.

- This segment is young (the median age of Hispanic Americans is 23.6, compared with the U.S. average of 32), which is attractive to marketers because it is a great potential market for youth-oriented products, such as cosmetics and music.

- The average Hispanic household contains 3.5 people, compared to only 2.7 people for the rest of the U.S. For this reason, Hispanic households spend 15 to 20 percent more of their disposable income than the national average on groceries and other household products.

- In general, Hispanic consumers are receptive to relationship-building approaches to marketing and selling. For this reason, there are many opportunities to build loyalty to brands and companies by emphasizing relationship aspects of the customer encounter.[37]

As with any ethnic group, appeals to Hispanic consumers need to take into account cultural differences. For example, Hispanics didn't appreciate the successful mainstream "Got Milk?" campaign because biting, sarcastic humor is not part of their culture. In addition, the notion of milk deprivation is not funny to a Hispanic mother—if she runs out of milk, this means she has failed her family. To make matters worse, "Got Milk?" translates as "Are You Lactating?" in Spanish. Thus, new Spanish-language versions were changed to "And you, have you given them enough milk today?" with tender scenes centered on cooking *flan* (a popular pudding) in the family kitchen. And Taco Bell's "Yo quiero Taco Bell" uttering Chihuahua dog was put out to pasture years ago.

It is not an overstatement to say that Latino youth are changing mainstream culture. Many of these consumers are "young biculturals" who bounce back and forth between hip-hop and rock en Español, blend Mexican rice with spaghetti sauce, and spread peanut butter and jelly on tortillas. In fact, we find many bicultural Hispanics in both younger and older age groups—one study reported that fully 44 percent of the Hispanic-American population identifies as bicultural. Within that group there are those who place a greater emphasis on preserving their heritage and those who are more open to experimenting with it in the context of new cultural influences.[38] One caution about the Hispanic market is that the term *Hispanic* itself actually is a misnomer. For example, Cuban Americans, Mexican Americans, and Puerto Ricans may share a common language, but their history, politics, and culture have many differences. Marketing to them as though they are a homogeneous segment can be a big mistake. However, the term is still widely used as a demographic descriptive. By 2020, the U.S. Census Bureau estimates, the number of Hispanic teens will grow by 62 percent, compared with 10 percent growth in teens overall. They seek spirituality, stronger family ties, and more color in their lives—three hallmarks of Latino culture. Music crossovers from the Latin charts to mainstream lead the trend, including pop idols Shakira, Enrique Iglesias, Marc Anthony, Jennifer Lopez, and Reggaeton sensation Daddy Yankee.

An important outcome of the increase in multiethnicity is the opportunity for increased cultural diversity in the workplace and elsewhere. **Cultural diversity**, a management practice that actively seeks to include people of different sexes, races, ethnic groups, and religions in an organization's employees, customers, suppliers, and distribution channel partners, is today business as usual rather than an exception. Marketing organizations benefit from employing people of all kinds because they bring different backgrounds, experiences, and points of view that help the firm develop strategies for its brands that will appeal to diverse customer groups.

cultural diversity
A management practice that actively seeks to include people of different sexes, races, ethnic groups, and religions in an organization's employees, customers, suppliers, and distribution channel partners.

Aristidis Vafeiadakis/Alamy Stock Photo

The crossover sensation Marc Anthony is helping to make Latino music mainstream.

Segment by Demographics: Place of Residence

Recognizing that people's preferences often vary depending on where they live, many marketers tailor their offerings to specific geographic areas, an approach called **geographic segmentation**. Google Earth and other similar applications of a **geographic information system (GIS)** have ramped up geographic approaches to segmentation. A GIS system can elegantly combine a geographic map with digitally stored data about the consumers in a geographic area. Thus, market information by geographic location is much more convenient for use in market planning and decision making than ever before.

When marketers want to segment regional markets even more precisely, they sometimes combine geography with demographics using the technique of **geodemography**. A basic assumption of geodemography is that "birds of a feather flock together"—people who live near one another share similar characteristics. Sophisticated statistical techniques identify geographic areas that share the same preferences for household items, magazines, and other products. This lets marketers construct segments of households with a common pattern of preferences. This way, they can hone in on those customers most likely to be interested in its specific offerings, in some cases so precisely that families living on one block will belong to a segment, whereas those on the next block will not.

One widely used geodemographic system is PRIZM, which is a large database developed by Nielsen Claritas. This system classifies the U.S. population into 66 segments based on various socioeconomic data, such as income, age, race, occupation, education, and household composition as well as lifestyle attributes that are critical to marketing strategies, shopping patterns such as where they vacation, what they drive and their favorite brands, and media preferences. The 66 segments range from the highly affluent "Upper Crust" and "Blue Blood Estates" to the lower-income "Big City Blues or "Low-Rise Living" neighborhoods.

Here are a few thumbnail sketches of different segments of relatively younger consumers a marketer might want to reach depending on the specific product or service he or she sells:

- *Young Digerati* are tech-savvy and live in fashionable neighborhoods on the urban fringe. Affluent, highly educated, and ethnically mixed, Young Digerati communities are typically filled with trendy apartments and condos, fitness clubs and clothing boutiques, casual restaurants, and all types of bars—from juice to coffee to microbrew. The Young Digerati are much more likely than the average American consumer to shop at Bloomingdale's, travel to Asia, read *Dwell*, watch the Independent Film Channel, and buy an Audi A3.

- *Kids & Cul-de-Sacs* are upper-middle-class, suburban, married couples with children—that's the skinny on Kids & Cul-de-Sacs, an enviable lifestyle of large families in recently built subdivisions. This segment has a high rate of Hispanics and Asian Americans. It is also a refuge for college-educated, white-collar professionals with administrative jobs and upper-middle-class incomes. Their nexus of education, affluence, and children translates into large outlays for child-centered products and services. They are much more likely than the average American consumer to order from target.com, play fantasy sports, read *Parents* magazine, watch X Games, and buy a Honda Odyssey.

- *Shotguns & Pickups* came by its moniker honestly: it scores near the top of all lifestyles for owning hunting rifles and pickup trucks. These Americans tend to be young, working-class couples with large families, living in small homes and manufactured housing. Nearly a third of residents live in mobile homes, more than anywhere else in the nation. They are much more likely than the average American consumer to order from Mary Kay, own a horse, read *Four Wheeler*, watch *Maury*, and drive a Ram diesel pickup.

---

geographic segmentation
An approach in which marketers tailor their offerings to specific geographic areas because people's preferences often vary depending on where they live.

geographic information system (GIS)
A system that combines a geographic map with digitally stored data about the consumers in a particular geographic area.

geodemography
A segmentation technique that combines geography with demographics.

Metrics Moment

It should be clear from your reading that geodemographic and related approaches to segmentation can be powerful and allow for a high level of precision in identifying potentially fruitful segments to target. When it comes to metrics, good data about the characteristics of the various consumer segments that you may wish to ultimately target is critical because target marketing is ultimately a strategic investment of resources in the segments that appear to have the best return on investment.

To make the power of the geodemographic technique and resulting information for decision making come alive, let's try a demonstration of the PRIZM database that gets close to home.

Apply the Metrics

1. Go to the Nielsen My Best Segments website (search for the phrase "Nielsen My Best Segments" website on any search engine).

2. Click on Zip Code Lookup, and then type in your own ZIP code along with the provided security code, then click SUBMIT.

3. Several segments should then come up that comprise your ZIP code. Click on each for more detail.

4. You will also see some quick facts in a box that further describe some basic demographics of your ZIP code (population, median age, median income, and consumer spend total and per household).

5. What is your reaction to the segment profiles and other information about your ZIP code? Are you surprised with the results, or was it what you expected?

6. Given the profile provided, what sort of products and services do you think are most likely to be particularly attractive to the segments represented?

---

geotargeting
Determining the geographic location of a website visitor and delivering different content to that visitor based on his or her location.

micromarketing
The ability to identify and target very small geographic segments that sometimes amount to individuals.

psychographics
The use of psychological, sociological, and anthropological factors to construct market segments.

One interesting specific approach to location-based targeting is **geotargeting**, which in Internet marketing refers to determining the geographic location of a website visitor and delivering different content to that visitor based on his or her location, such as country, region/state, city, metro code/ZIP code, organization, IP address, Internet service provider (ISP), or other criteria.[39] Campari America, for instance, targeted consumers who were between the ages of 21 and 34 while they were in neighborhoods with a high proportion of bars and restaurants during times when consumers are known to have a few drinks, using a promotion for $5 off of a future ride using the ride-sharing app Lyft. The deal was offered through specific mobile apps that this targeted segment is known to use while out unwinding at restaurants and bars. The overall intention of the campaign was to both promote responsible behavior while out drinking and to increase awareness and favorable attitudes toward Campari and some of its staple brands of alcohol. More than 20 percent of those who received the offer chose to accept it, a high rate of acceptance by digital advertising standards.[40,41]

Ultimately, highly precise geodemographic segmentation enables marketers to practice **micromarketing**, which is the ability to identify and target small geographic segments that sometimes amount to just one or a few individuals—a capability you read about in Chapter 5 that we referred to as one-to-one marketing.

Segment by Psychographics

Demographic information is useful, but it does not always provide enough information to divide consumers into meaningful segments. Although we can use demographic variables to discover, for example, that the female college student segment uses perfume, we won't be able to tell whether certain college women prefer perfumes that express an image of, say, sexiness rather than athleticism.

As we said in Chapter 6, **psychographics** segment consumers in terms of psychological and

Mediacolor's/Alamy Stock Photo

A Harley rider's profile includes both thrill-seeking and affinity for a countercultural image (at least on weekends).

behavioral similarities, such as shared activities, interests, and opinions, or AIOs.[42] Marketers often develop profiles of the typical customers for whom they desire to paint a more vivid picture. Although some marketers and their creative agencies develop their own psychographic techniques to classify customers, others subscribe to services that divide the entire U.S. population into segments and then provide this information to clients for use in proprietary marketing project applications such as strategy planning. The best known of these systems is **VALS™**, which is a product of Strategic Business Insights (SBI). VALS™ divides U.S. adults into eight groups according to what drives them psychologically as well as by their economic resources.

One segment that combines a psychographic/lifestyle component with a heavy dose of generational marketing is the **gamer segment**, sometimes referred to as the gamer generation—"gamer" as in "video games," of course. This group grew up playing video games as second nature for primary recreation, and as they have entered college and the workforce, they continue to carry many gaming sensibilities with them. Video gaming is clearly a lifestyle, and much as the company Google turned into the generic verb "to google" in the 2000s, in this decade the buzz term du jour is *gamification*, which, as we saw in Chapter 6, is a strategy in which marketers apply game design techniques, often by awarding points or badges to nongame experiences, to drive consumer behavior (e.g., the gamification of practice exams where you might earn badges for getting right answers and moving to the next level of difficulty in your homework). And, by the way, just in case you didn't know, a **badge** is some type of milestone or reward a player earns when he or she progresses through a gamified application. If you've ever checked into Foursquare and earned a badge for a (dubious) achievement like "Gym Rat," "Overshare," or even "Crunked," you know how this works. Marketers would be wise to think about what sorts of badges might appeal to the gamer segment as they become more and more engaged as consumers who are highly likely to do much of their shopping online.

Segment by Behavior

People may use the same product for different reasons, on different occasions, and in different amounts. So, in addition to demographics and psychographics, it is useful to study what consumers actually do with a product. **Behavioral segmentation** slices consumer segments on the basis of how they act toward, feel about, or use a product. One way to segment on the basis of behavior is to divide the market into users and nonusers of a product. Then marketers may attempt to reward current users or try to win over new ones. In addition to distinguishing between users and non-users, marketers can describe current customers as heavy, moderate, and light users. They often do this according to a rule of thumb we call the **80/20 Rule**: 20 percent of purchasers account for 80 percent of the product's sales (the ratio is an approximation, not gospel). This rule means that it often makes more sense to focus on the smaller number of people who are really into a product rather than on the larger number who are just casual users.

Starbucks recently chose to redefine its loyalty program to better reward consumers who spend more with the company, in contrast to the old structure that rewarded consumers for the number of transactions they made. Consider, for instance, that before the change a customer who bought a tall coffee received the same number of stars as a customer who purchased a venti white chocolate mocha and a breakfast sandwich—clearly a big difference in revenue generation for the firm. Although the change to Starbucks' loyalty program received a fair amount of initial negative feedback (presumably from those customers who will not benefit as greatly under the new terms of the program), industry analysts view the move as smart in the long term because it will ultimately enable Starbucks to offer greater rewards to its *most valuable customers* (those who spend more through larger purchases while also purchasing more frequently).[43]

VALS™
A psychographic segmentation system that divides U.S. adults into eight groups according to what drives them psychologically as well as by their economic resources.

gamer segment
A consumer segment that combines a psychographic/lifestyle component with a heavy dose of generational marketing.

badge
A milestone or reward earned for progressing through a video game.

behavioral segmentation
A technique that divides consumers into segments on the basis of how they act toward, feel about, or use a good or service.

80/20 Rule
A marketing rule of thumb that 20 percent of purchasers account for 80 percent of a product's sales.

The Biltmore Estate in Asheville, North Carolina, increased attendance during its annual Christmas celebration as part of a strategy to segment by usage occasion. The estate's marketers developed four separate strategies to target different types of visitors, including heavy users who have made a Christmas pilgrimage an annual family tradition.

usage rate
A measurement that reflects the quantity purchased or frequency of use among consumers of a particular product or service.

long tail
A new approach to segmentation based on the idea that companies can make money by selling small amounts of items that only a few people want, provided they sell enough different items.

usage occasions
An indicator used in behavioral market segmentation based on when consumers use a product most.

A related concept to the 80/20 Rule in behavioral segmentation is **usage rate**, which reflects the quantity purchased or frequency of use among consumers of a particular product or service. The entire travel and hospitality industry cultivates high users through their loyalty programs, such as American Airlines AAdvantage or Marriott Rewards. The high-use segment is often incredibly profitable over the long run.

Although the 80/20 Rule still holds true in the majority of situations, the Internet's ability to offer an unlimited choice of goods to billions of people has changed how marketers think about segmentation. An approach called the **long tail** turns traditional thinking about the virtues of selling in high volume on its head. The basic idea is that we need no longer rely solely on big hits (like blockbuster movies or best-selling books) to find profits. Companies can also make money when they sell small amounts of items that only a few people want—if they sell enough different items.

For many companies the selling of digital products that can be transferred to purchasers through an Internet connection helps to support a long tail approach because it reduces the cost of storage of products and allows for the fulfillment of consumer demand on an as-needed basis. Amazon, the Apple iTunes Store, and the Google Play Store are prime examples of sites that are set up to be able to benefit from the large and small sales of a wider array of goods, which should also benefit both the big and small sellers that offer products through their platforms.

Another way to segment a market on the basis of behavior is to look at **usage occasions**, or when consumers use the product most. We associate many products with specific occasions, whether time of day, holidays, business functions, or casual get-togethers. Businesses often divide up their markets according to when and how their offerings are in demand. Ruth's Chris Steakhouse is by far the market leader in the high-end steak restaurant category featuring USDA Prime Beef as its' signature dish. Ruth's is well aware that it is a special-occasion location—graduations, birthdays, promotions, you name it—and folks want to celebrate at Ruth's. And they are all too happy to accommodate, often surprising guests with special table decorations for the occasion and a nice dessert treat, compliments of the chef.

And in the online space, Google enables its advertising clients to target certain ads to certain segments of search engine users based on data such as Google domain, query entered, IP address, and language preference. This way, companies can have Google automatically sort and send the intended ad to certain market segments. Thus, it is possible for advertisers on Google to tailor their automatically targeted ads based on seasonality—you will see more TurboTax ads on Google pages during tax season, even if people aren't querying tax software.[44]

Segment B2B Markets

We've reviewed the segmentation variables marketers use to divide up the consumer pie, but how about all those B2B marketers out there? Adding to what we learned about business markets in Chapter 6, it's important to know that segmentation also helps them better understand their customers. Although the specific variables may differ, the underlying logic of classifying the larger market into manageable pieces that share relevant characteristics is the same whether the product you sell is pesto or pesticides.

Organizational demographics are organization-specific dimensions that marketers use to describe, classify, and organize different organizations for the purpose of segmenting business-to-business markets. Organizational demographics also help a B2B marketer understand the needs and characteristics of its potential customers. These classification dimensions include the size of the firms (either in total sales or in number of employees), the number of facilities, whether they are a domestic or a multinational company, their purchasing policies, and the type of business they are in. B2B markets may also be segmented on the basis of the production technology they use and whether the customer is a user or a nonuser of the product.

Many industries use the North American Industry Classification System (NAICS) we discussed in Chapter 6 to obtain information about the size and number of companies operating in a particular industry. B2B marketers often consult general informational business and industry databases on the web, such as Hoover's or Yahoo! Finance for insight and up-to-date information on private and public companies worldwide.

organizational demographics
Organization-specific dimensions that can be used to describe, classify, and organize different organizations for the purpose of segmenting business-to-business markets.

7.3
OBJECTIVE
Explain how marketers evaluate segments and choose a targeting strategy.
(pp. 241–244)

Step 2: Targeting

We've seen that the first step in a target marketing strategy is segmentation, in which the firm divides the market into smaller groups that share certain characteristics. The next step is **targeting**, in which marketers evaluate the attractiveness of each potential segment and decide in which of these groups they will invest resources to try to turn them into customers. The customer group or groups they select are the firm's **target market**, which, as you learned in Chapter 1, is the segment(s) on which an organization focuses its marketing plan and toward which it directs its marketing efforts.

In this section, we'll review the three phases of targeting: evaluate market segments, develop segment profiles, and choose a targeting strategy. Figure 7.3 illustrates these three phases.

targeting
A strategy in which marketers evaluate the attractiveness of each potential segment and decide in which of these groups they will invest resources to try to turn them into customers.

target market
The market segments on which an organization focuses its marketing plan and toward which it directs its marketing efforts.

Phases of Targeting

Phase 1: Evaluate Market Segments

Just because a marketer identifies a segment does not necessarily mean that it's a useful target. A viable target segment should satisfy the following requirements:

- *Are members of the segment similar to each other in their product needs and wants and, at the same time, different from consumers in other segments?* Without real differences in consumer needs, firms might as well use a mass-marketing strategy. It's a waste of time to develop two separate lines of skin care products for working women and nonworking women if both segments have the same complaints about dry skin.
- *Can marketers measure the segment?* Marketers must know something about the size and purchasing power of a potential *segment* before they decide if it's worth their efforts.
- *Is the segment large enough to be profitable now and in the future?* For example, a graphic designer who hopes to design web pages for Barbie-doll

Figure 7.3 *Process* | Phases of Targeting

Targeting involves three distinct phases of activities.

collectors must decide whether there are enough hard-core aficionados to make this business worthwhile and whether the trend will continue.

- *Can marketing communications reach the segment?* It is easy to select TV programs or magazines that will efficiently reach older consumers, consumers with certain levels of education, or residents of major cities because the media *they* prefer are easy to identify. However, it is unlikely that marketing communications can reach only left-handed blondes with multiple piercings who listen to Taylor Swift overdubbed in Mandarin Chinese.

- *Can the marketer adequately serve the needs of the segment?* Does the firm have the expertise and resources to satisfy the segment better than the competition? Some years ago, consumer-products manufacturer Warner-Lambert (now a part of Pfizer) made the mistake of trying to enter the pastry business by purchasing Entenmann's Bakery. Entenmann's sells high-end boxed cakes, cookies, pastries, and pies in super-markets. Unfortunately, Warner-Lambert's expertise at selling Listerine mouthwash and Trident gum did not transfer to baked goods, and it soon lost a lot of "dough" on the deal.

Phase 2: Develop Segment Profiles

segment profile
A description of the "typical" customer in a segment.

Once a marketer identifies a set of usable segments, it is helpful to generate a profile of each to really understand segment members' needs and to look for business op-portunities. This segment profile is a description of the "typical" customer in that segment. A **segment profile** might, for example, include customer demographics, location, lifestyle information, and a description of how frequently the customer buys the product. When the marketers of General Mills' product Hamburger Helper de-cided to target cash-strapped millennials, they had to adjust the image they presented on social media. On one April Fools' Day, the packaged food company announced through social media the release of a mixtape titled "Watch the Stove" containing five light-hearted Hamburger Helper–themed rap songs created by a group of college stu-dents at McNally Smith's College of Music. The mixtape was well received, and was played more than 270,000 times on SoundCloud by 5 P.M. on the day of release. One of the company's marketing communications planners describes the target segment of consumers as "a young, urban, millennial guy making Hamburger Helper in his dorm room."[45]

undifferentiated targeting strategy
Appealing to a broad spectrum of people.

Phase 3: Choose a Targeting Strategy

A basic targeting decision centers on how finely tuned the target should be: Should the company go after one large segment or focus on meeting the needs of one or more smaller segments? Let's look at four targeting strategies, which Figure 7.4 summarizes.

A company like Walmart that selects an **undifferentiated targeting strategy** appeals to a broad spectrum of people. If successful, this type of operation can be efficient because production, research, and promotion costs benefit from *economies of scale*—it's cheaper to develop one product or one advertising campaign than to choose several targets and create separate products or messages for each.

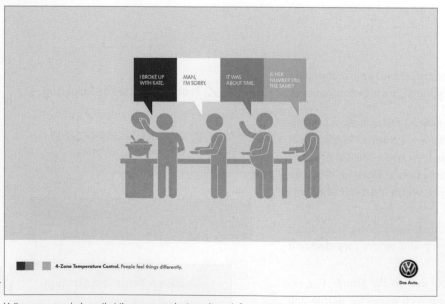

Volkswagen reminds us that the same product won't work for everyone.

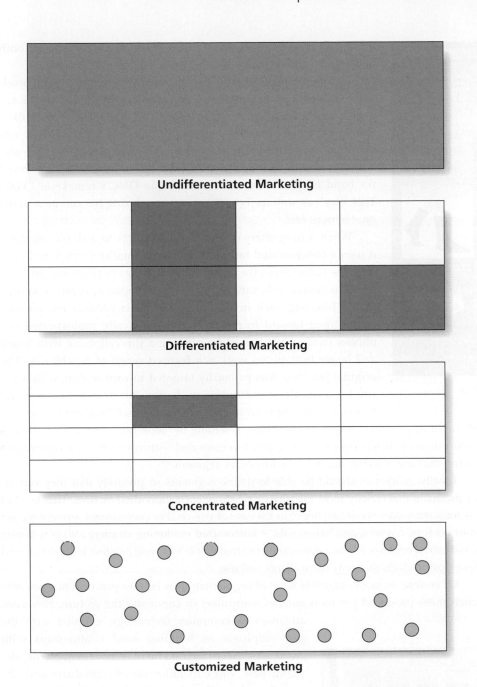

Undifferentiated Marketing

Differentiated Marketing

Concentrated Marketing

Customized Marketing

Figure 7.4 📷 *Snapshot* | Choose a Targeting Strategy

Marketers must decide on a targeting strategy. Should the company go after one total market, one or several market segments, or even target customers individually?

But the company must be willing to bet that people have similar needs so that the same product and message will appeal to many customers.

A company that chooses a **differentiated targeting strategy** develops one or more products for each of several customer groups with different product needs. A differentiated strategy is called for when consumers choose among well-known brands that have distinctive images, and the company can identify one or more segments that have distinct needs for different types of products.

Despite its highly publicized product safety issues in 2014, GM historically has been a leader in differentiated strategy with distinct product lines that satisfy the needs of multiple customer groups. Its Cadillac and Buick product lines cater to consumers who want luxury. The Chevrolet Volt hybrid provides value to drivers who want to save gas money and the environment. And finally, the GMC product line appeals to

differentiated targeting strategy
Developing one or more products for each of several distinct customer groups and making sure these offerings are kept separate in the marketplace.

Blacksocks US

Blacksocks practices a highly concentrated targeting strategy.

concentrated targeting strategy
Focusing a firm's efforts on offering one or more products to a single segment.

customized marketing strategy
An approach that tailors specific products and the messages about them to individual customers.

mass customization
An approach that modifies a basic good or service to meet the needs of an individual.

drivers who need an everyday truck, crossover, or SUV that is both dependable and stylish.

Differentiated marketing can also involve connecting one product with multiple segments by communicating differently to appeal to those segments. Again using the venerable "Got Milk?" campaign as an example, one of the campaign's most classic ads featured Aerosmith's Steven Tyler to appeal to both aging boomers who got into the band in the 1970s and Gen Yers who discovered the band in the 1990s as a result of Run-DMC's remake of "Walk This Way" as well as Tyler's resurgence during his run as a judge on *American Idol*.

When a firm offers one or more products to a single segment, it uses a **concentrated targeting strategy**. Smaller firms that do not have the resources or the desire to be all things to all people often do this. The company GreatCall Wireless developed a cellphone known as the Jitterbug back in the mid-2000s. This product ran counter to the trend toward increasingly technologically sophisticated cell phones (and smartphones) by offering a flip cellphone with fewer and larger buttons, as well as a focused range of capabilities. The original Jitterbug was primarily targeted toward seniors with a desire for a simpler communication device. But over the years it has evolved to offer options including a model that "resembles" a smartphone in appearance (important for today's seniors to "look hip") but with a streamlined range of choices on its touch screen interface and features such as an urgent care button that are of particular value to this older segment.[46]

Ideally, marketers should be able to define segments so precisely that they can offer products that exactly meet the unique needs of each individual or firm. This level of concentration does occur (we hope) in the case of personal or professional services we get from doctors, lawyers, and hairstylists. A **customized marketing strategy** also is common in industrial contexts where a manufacturer often works with one or a few large clients and develops products that only these clients will use.

Of course, in most cases this level of segmentation is neither practical nor possible when mass-produced products such as computers or cars enter the picture. However, advances in computer technology, coupled with the new emphasis on building solid relationships with customers, have focused managers' attention on devising new ways to tailor specific products and the messages about them to individual customers. In fact, some entrepreneurs are working on the possibility of using new 3-D printing technology to let you print your own car.[47] This is an extreme example of the growing trend of **mass customization**, where a manufacturer modifies a basic good or service to meet an individual's specific needs.[48] Levi Strauss was a pioneer in this area. Company researchers found that 80 percent of women around the world fall into three distinct body shapes, so it's physically impossible to offer a one-size-fits-all product. The Levi's CURVE ID program employs an interactive custom fit experience to tell a customer whether she should buy a Slight Curve, Demi Curve, or Bold Curve version of the jeans.[49]

Local Motors

New 3-D printing technology allows consumers to literally print their own car.

7.4

OBJECTIVE

Recognize how marketers develop and implement a positioning strategy.

(pp. 245–249)

Step 3: Positioning

The final stage of developing a target marketing strategy is to provide consumers who belong to a targeted market segment with a good or service that meets their unique needs and expectations. **Positioning** means developing a marketing strategy to influence how a particular market segment perceives a good or service in comparison to the competition. A key word in this definition is *perceives*—that is, positioning is in the eye of the beholder.

A firm may truly believe that its customers think about its offering in a certain way, but unless market research bears this out, what the marketer "thinks" doesn't matter as it is trumped by what the consumer perceives. To position a brand, marketers must clearly understand the criteria target consumers use to evaluate competing products and then convince them that their product, service, or organization will meet those needs. In addition, the organization has to come up with a plan to communicate this position to its target market.

Positioning happens in many ways. Sometimes it's just a matter of making sure that cool people use your product—and that others observe them doing this. After finding out that a close friend was flying to Los Angeles to audition for the film *Any Given Sunday*, the president of the high-performance sportswear company Under Armour sent along with him a bunch of free samples of its athletic wear to give to the film's casting director as a gift. The director liked the quality of the clothes so much that he gave them to the wardrobe company the filmmakers hired, and they also really liked the clothes. The next thing you know, the movie (starring Al Pacino and Jamie Foxx) featured both the actors wearing Under Armour clothes on screen—and there was even a scene in the film when Jamie Foxx undressed in the locker room with a clear shot of the Under

positioning

Developing a marketing strategy to influence how a particular market segment perceives a good or service in comparison to the competition.

Ripped from the Headlines

Ethical/Sustainable Decisions in the Real World

Candy companies have received scrutiny in the past for advertising directly to children, given the widely held belief that children are more impressionable and more susceptible to advertising than older groups. Recent massive publicity about childhood obesity, diabetes, and dental impacts because of too much sugar haven't helped matters any for candy marketers.

In 2007 the Children's Food and Beverage Advertising Initiative (CFBAI) was launched to help move the food and beverage industries toward creating advertising messages for children (defined as individuals under the age of 12) that promote healthier products and generally healthier nutritional habits.[50] Despite the launch of this initiative and some candy companies pledging to reduce or altogether eliminate their marketing efforts directed toward children, a research study found that between 2008 and 2011 children's exposure to ads for candy actually went up 74 percent along with evidence that candy ads children were exposed to peripherally (that is, not specifically directed to a child) also increased.[51]

Determining whether an advertisement is directed to a particular segment is a somewhat subjective exercise, which creates word games between advertisers and regulators as to whether a particular advertisement is "directed" to (in this case) children. The vagueness of this situation also potentially provides room for unscrupulous marketers to make a pledge to do one thing when in reality they plan on doing another without technically failing to honor their pledge (whether this is true in the candy company example is for them to say).

In 2016, soon after Easter passed, a large number of major candy companies announced that they would no longer advertise directly to children. These companies include the Ferrara Candy Company, Ghirardelli Chocolate Company, Jelly Belly Candy Company, Just Born Quality Confections, Promotion in Motion Inc., and the R.M. Palmer Company. This announcement was quickly praised by candy industry oversight groups.[52] But the extent to which this announced decision actually reduces the amount of candy-related marketing directed at children (as well as peripheral exposure of candy advertising) remains to be seen.

ETHICS CHECK:

Should candy companies be allowed to advertise directly to children?

☐ YES   ☐ NO

Figure 7.5 [⚡] *Process* | Steps in Positioning

Four key steps comprise the decision-making process in positioning.

Armour logo on his jock strap. After the movie's release, hits on Under Armour's website spiked, and, as they say, the rest is history.[53] More recently Under Armour was able to sign NBA phenom Stephen Curry to an endorsement deal that has benefitted the brand enormously as a result of Curry's popularity and meteoric success on the court. The company's CEO in a recent earnings call spoke about (among other things) how the footwear division saw a 95 percent increase in sales from the same period in the prior year. The reason he gave for the significant increase in sales within footwear: Stephen Curry's popularity. One analyst on Wall Street believes Curry adds $14 billion to the value of Under Armour's outstanding shares of stock.[54]

Steps in Positioning

[⚡] Figure 7.5 shows the steps marketers go through to decide just how to position their product or service: analyze competitors' positions, offer a good or service with a competitive advantage finalize the marketing mix, and evaluate responses and modify as needed. Let's take a closer look at each of these positioning steps.

Step 1: Analyze Competitors' Positions

The first stage is to analyze competitors' positions in the marketplace. To develop an effective positioning strategy, marketers must understand the current lay of the land. What competitors are out there, and how does the target market perceive them? Aside from direct competitors in the product category, are there other goods or services that provide similar benefits?

Sometimes the indirect competition can be more important than the direct, especially if it represents an emerging consumer trend. For years, McDonald's developed positioning strategies based only on its direct competition, which it defined as other large fast-food hamburger chains (translation: Burger King and Wendy's). McDonald's failed to realize that in fact many indirect competitors fulfilled consumers' needs for a quick, tasty, convenient meal—from supermarket delis to frozen microwavable single-serving meals to call-ahead takeout from full-service restaurants like Applebee's, T.G.I. Friday's, Outback, and Chili's—all of whom have convenient curbside service instead of backed-up drive-through lines. Ultimately, McDonald's began to understand that it must react to this indirect competition by serving up a wider variety of adult-friendly food and shoring up lagging service. These days the company also offers its McCafé concept, with coffee products aimed squarely at taking business away from morning mainstays Starbucks and Dunkin' Donuts, along with a tasty breakfast menu all day long to compete in a brand-new space.

Step 2: Define Your Competitive Advantage

positioning statement
An expression of a product's positioning that is internally developed and maintained in order to support the development of marketing communication that articulates the specific *value* offered by a product.

The second stage is to offer a good or service with a competitive advantage to provide a reason why consumers will perceive the product as better than the competition. Toward this end, a **positioning statement** can help the company frame internally how a product is positioned so that any associated marketing communication remains focused on articulating to consumers the specific *value* offered by a product. Positioning statements typically include the segment(s) to which the product is targeted, the most important claim (differentiator) to be attributed to the product for the targeted segment(s), and the most important piece of evidence that supports the claim made about the product. If the company offers only a "me-too product," it can induce people to buy for a lower price. Other forms of competitive advantage include offering a superior image (Giorgio Armani), a unique product feature (Levi's 501 button-fly jeans), better service (Cadillac's roadside assistance program), or even better-qualified people (the legendary salespeople at Nordstrom's department stores).

Step 3: Finalize the Marketing Mix

Once they settle on a positioning strategy, the third stage for marketers is to finalize the marketing mix as they put all the pieces into place. The elements of the marketing mix must match the selected segment. This means that the good or service must deliver benefits that the segment values, such as convenience or status. Put another way, it must add value and satisfy consumer needs (sound familiar?). Furthermore, marketers must price this offering at a level these consumers will pay, make the offering available at places they are likely to go, and correctly communicate the offering's benefits in locations where these targets are likely to take notice. In other words, the positioning strategy translates into the organization's marketing mix that we discussed in Chapter 1.

Beginning with Chapter 8, all the remaining chapters in the book provide you with the details of developing strategies for each element of the marketing mix: product, price, physical distribution, and promotion. The sum of these individual marketing mix strategies results in the overall positioning strategy for your offering.

Step 4: Evaluate Responses and Modify as Needed

In the fourth and final stage, marketers evaluate the target market's responses so they can modify strategies if necessary. Over time, the firm may find that it needs to change which segments it targets or even alter a product's position to respond to marketplace changes. Consider this classic example: Both TGI Fridays and Jack Daniel's are venerable brands in separate market spaces. But like peanut butter and chocolate in the case of a Reese's peanut butter cup, Fridays and Jack Daniel's partnered to create a set of new menu items like the Jack Daniel's® Burger which repositioned TGIF from "your father's restaurant" to a hipper place for the younger urban crowd.

A change in positioning strategy is **repositioning**, and it's fairly common to see a company try to modify its brand image to keep up with changing times. Take as an example Charles Schwab, which used to be pegged primarily as a self-service stock brokerage. Competition in the budget broker business, especially from online brokers, prompted Schwab's repositioning to a full-line, full-service financial services firm that still pays attention to frugal prices for its services. Think of it this way: There's not much value Schwab can add as one of a dozen or more online providers of stock trades. In that environment, customers simply will view the firm as a commodity (i.e., just a way to buy stocks) with no real differentiation. Schwab still has its no-frills products, but the real growth in sales and profits comes from its expanded product lines and provision of more information—both online and through personal selling—that warrant higher fees and build deeper customer relationships. Repositioning also occurs when a marketer revises a brand thought to be inextricably past its prime. Sometimes these products rise like a phoenix from the ashes to ride a wave of nostalgia and return to the marketplace as **retro brands**— venerable brands like Oxydol laundry detergent, Breck Shampoo, Ovaltine cereal, Frontier airlines, and Tab cola all are examples of brands that were nearly forgotten but got a new lease on life.[55]

Three guys built a powerful community through Facebook called the SURGE Movement to bring back the carbonated beverage that had some

repositioning
Redoing a product's position to respond to marketplace changes.

retro brands
A once-popular brand that has been revived to experience a popularity comeback, often by riding a wave of nostalgia.

The SoBe Beverage Company started in Miami's South Beach (hence the name "So-Be") in 1996 when the founders saw a lizard on the art deco façade of the Abbey Hotel, and the rest is history. SoBe has masterfully executed the process of segmentation, target marketing, and positioning you've read about in this chapter and today boasts an amazing brand and product line that appeals to a definitive set of demographic/psychographic targets.

ZUMA Press, Inc./Alamy Stock Photo

popularity in the 1990s but had been out of production for over a decade. The group amassed a large following of active supporters (more than 300,000 people support the Facebook Cause page) and worked fervently to let the Coca-Cola Company, the creators of SURGE, know about their love for the product. The SURGE Movement's efforts ultimately were successful and now the three founders of the movement are working hard to make sure the effort doesn't lose any steam and that SURGE remains a viable product into the future.[56]

Bring a Product to Life: Brand Personality

brand personality
A distinctive image that captures a good's or service's character and benefits.

In a way, brands are like people: We often describe them in terms of personality traits. We may use adjectives such as *cheap, elegant, sexy*, or *cool* when we talk about a store, a perfume, or a car. That's why a positioning strategy often tries to create a **brand personality** for a good or service—a distinctive image that captures its character and benefits. An advertisement for *Elle*, an amazingly chic fashion magazine for women, proclaimed, "She is not a reply card. She is not a category. She is not shrink-wrapped. *Elle* is not a magazine. She is a woman."

brand anthropomorphism
The assignment of human characteristics and qualities to a brand.

One of the more effective ways to give a brand a personality in the minds of consumers is to engage in deliberate marketing actions that make the brand seem more human. The phenomenon of attributing to a brand human characteristics is known as **brand anthropomorphism** and it can be seen in action when, for instance, a brand's Twitter account makes a quirky comment in reply to someone's tweet (that is, "humanizing the brand through a response") or through the interactions of a brand's mascot in a commercial. The Pillsbury Doughboy, who has been active in advertising for more than 50 years, is a prime example of the latter with his friendly demeanor and the trademark giggle he lets out when poked in the belly that help shape consumer perceptions of the brand.[57] We'll talk a lot more about brands in Chapter 9.

Products as people? It seems funny to say, yet marketing researchers find that most consumers have no trouble describing what a product would be like "if it came to life." People often give clear, detailed descriptions, including what color hair the product would have, the type of house it would live in, and even whether it would be thin, overweight, or somewhere in between.[58] If you don't believe us, try doing this yourself.

perceptual map
A technique to visually describe where brands are "located" in consumers' minds relative to competing brands.

Part of creating a brand personality is to develop an identity for the product that the target market will prefer over competing brands. How do marketers determine where their product actually stands in the minds of consumers? One solution is to ask consumers what characteristics are important and how competing alternatives would rate on these attributes, too. Marketers use this information to construct a **perceptual map**—a vivid way to construct a picture of where products or brands are "located" in consumers' minds.

For example, suppose you want to develop an idea for a new publication that will appeal to American women in their twenties. You might construct a perceptual map of how these target customers perceive the magazines out there now to help you develop an idea for a new publication they would like. After you interview a sample of female readers, you might identify two key questions women ask when they select a magazine: (1) Is it "traditional," that is, oriented toward family, home, or personal issues, or is it "fashion-forward," oriented toward personal appearance and fashion? (2) Is it for "upscale" women who are older and established in their careers or for relatively "downscale" women who are younger and just starting out in their careers?

The perceptual map in Figure 7.6 illustrates how these ratings might look for a set of major women's magazines. The map provides some guidance as to where you might position your new magazine. You might decide to compete directly with either the cluster of "service magazines" in the lower left or the traditional fashion magazines

Figure 7.6 📷 *Snapshot* | Perceptual Map

Perceptual mapping allows marketers to identify consumers' perceptions of their brand in relation to the competition.

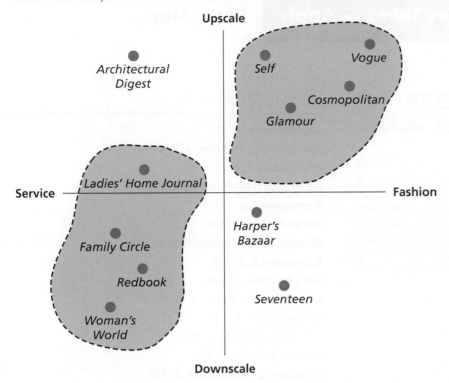

in the upper right. In this case, you would have to determine what benefits your new magazine might offer that these existing magazines do not. Media firm Condé Nast, for example, positions *Allure* to compete against other fashion magazines by going into more depth than they do on beauty issues, such as the mental, physical, and emotional dangers of cosmetic surgery.

You might try to locate an unserved or underserved area in this perceptual map. There may be room for a magazine that targets "cutting-edge" fashion for college-age women. A neglected segment is the "Holy Grail" for marketers: With luck, they can move quickly to capture a segment and define the standards of comparison for the category. This tactic paid off for Chrysler, which first identified the minivan market for soccer moms; JetBlue, which found a spot for low fares and high tech without the poor-boy service attitude and cattle-call boarding procedure of other budget airlines; and Liz Claiborne, which pioneered the concept of comfortable, "user-friendly" clothing for working women. In the magazine category, perhaps *Marie Claire* comes closest to this position.

Objective Summary ➡ Key Terms ➡ Apply

Chapter 7
Study Map

7.1 Objective Summary (p. 228)

Identify the steps in the target marketing process.

Marketers must balance the efficiency of mass marketing, serving the same items to everyone, with the effectiveness of offering each individual exactly what he or she wants. To accomplish this, instead of trying to sell something to everyone, marketers follow these steps: (1) select a target marketing strategy, in which they divide the total market into different segments based on customer characteristics; (2) select one or more segments; and (3) develop products to meet the needs of those specific segments.

Key Terms

market fragmentation, p. 228
target marketing strategy, p. 228

7.2 Objective Summary (pp. 229–241)

Understand the need for market segmentation and the approaches available to do it.

Market segmentation is often necessary in today's marketplace because of market fragmentation—that is, the splintering of a mass society into diverse groups due to technological and cultural differences. Most marketers can't realistically do a good job of meeting the needs of everyone, so it is more efficient to divide the larger pie into slices in which members of a segment share some important characteristics and tend to exhibit the same needs and preferences. Marketers frequently find it useful to segment consumer markets on the basis of demographic characteristics, including age, gender, family life cycle, social class, race or ethnic identity, and place of residence. A second dimension, psychographics, uses measures of psychological and social characteristics to identify people with shared preferences or traits. Consumer markets may also be segmented on the basis of how consumers behave toward the product, for example, their brand loyalty, usage rates (heavy, moderate, or light), and usage occasions. B2B markets are often segmented on the basis of industrial demographics, type of business based on the North American Industry Classification codes, and geographic location.

Key Terms

segmentation, p. 229
segmentation variables, p. 229
demographics, p. 230
generational marketing, p. 230
Generation Z, p. 231
digital natives, p. 231
Generation Y (millennials), p. 231
Generation X, p. 231
baby boomers, p. 232
metrosexual, p. 233
buying power, p. 234
content marketing, p. 235
cultural diversity, p. 236
geographic segmentation, p. 237
geographic information system (GIS), p. 237
geodemography, p. 237
geotargeting, p. 238
micromarketing, p. 238
psychographics, p. 238
VALS™, p. 239
gamer segment, p. 239
badge, p. 239
behavioral segmentation, p. 239
80/20 Rule, p. 239
usage rate, p. 240
long tail, p. 240
usage occasions, p. 240
organizational demographics, p. 241

7.3 Objective Summary (pp. 241–244)

Explain how marketers evaluate segments and choose a targeting strategy.

To choose one or more segments to target, marketers examine each segment and evaluate its potential for success as a target market. Meaningful segments have wants that are different from those in other segments, can be identified, can be reached with a unique marketing mix, will respond to unique marketing communications, are large enough to be profitable, have future growth potential, and possess needs that the organization can satisfy better than the competition.

After marketers identify the different segments, they estimate the market potential of each. The relative attractiveness of segments also influences the firm's selection of an overall marketing strategy. The firm may choose an undifferentiated, differentiated, concentrated, or custom strategy based on the company's characteristics and the nature of the market.

Key Terms

targeting, p. 241

target market, p. 241

segment profile, p. 242

undifferentiated targeting strategy, p. 242

differentiated targeting strategy, p. 243

concentrated targeting strategy, p. 244

customized marketing strategy, p. 244

mass customization, p. 244

7.4 Objective Summary (pp. 245–249)

Recognize how marketers develop and implement a positioning strategy.

After marketers select the target market(s) and the overall strategy, they must determine how they wish customers to perceive the brand relative to the competition—that is, should the brand be positioned like, against, or away from the competition? Through positioning, a brand personality is developed. Marketers can compare brand positions by using such research techniques as perceptual mapping. In developing and implementing the positioning strategy, firms analyze the competitors' positions, determine the competitive advantage offered by their product, tailor the marketing mix in accordance with the positioning strategy, and evaluate responses to the marketing mix selected. Marketers must continually monitor changes in the market that might indicate a need to reposition the product.

Key Terms

positioning, p. 245

positioning statement, p. 246

repositioning, p. 247

retro brands, p. 247

brand personality, p. 248

brand anthropomorphism, p. 248

perceptual map, p. 248

Chapter **Questions** and **Activities**

MyLab Marketing™
Go to **mymktlab.com** to watch this chapter's Rising Star video(s) for career advice and to respond to questions.

Concepts: Test Your Knowledge

7-1. What is market fragmentation, and what are its consequences for marketers?

7-2. What is a target marketing strategy?

7-3. What is market segmentation, and why is it an important strategy in today's marketplace?

7-4. List and explain the major demographic characteristics frequently used in segmenting consumer markets.

7-5. Explain the process of consumer psychographic segmentation.

7-6. What is behavioral segmentation?

7-7. What are some of the ways marketers segment B2B markets?

7-8. List the criteria marketers use to determine whether a segment may be a good candidate for targeting.

7-9. Explain the differences between undifferentiated, differentiated, concentrated, and customized marketing strategies. What is mass customization?

7-10. What is product positioning?

7-11. What do marketers mean by creating a brand personality? What examples can you come up with of uses of brand anthropomorphism?

7-12. How do marketers use perceptual maps to help them develop effective positioning strategies?

Activities: Apply What You've Learned

⭐ **7-13.** *In Class, 15-20 Minutes for Teams* A segment profile is a detailed description of the target consumer, their needs and preferences, lifestyle and demographics, media usage, family relationships, and so on. It is used to get a deeper sense of the consumers in that target market.

For this activity, identify two different target markets that would exist in the holiday/travel industry. Try to identify two segments that have distinct motivations and interests for travel, and prepare a detailed segment profile for each of these market segments (based on your general knowledge).

⭐ 7-14. *Creative Homework/Short Project* As the marketing director for a company that is planning to enter the B2B market for photocopy machines, you are attempting to develop an overall marketing strategy. You have considered the possibility of using mass-marketing, concentrated marketing, differentiated marketing, and custom marketing strategies.

a. Prepare a summary explaining what each type of strategy would mean for your marketing plan in terms of product, price, promotion, and distribution channel.

b. Evaluate the desirability of each type of strategy.

c. Describe your final recommendations for the best type of strategy.

7-15. *In Class, 10–25 Minutes for Teams* To better market the university to potential students, you and your classmates have been asked to create a segment profile of the typical college student at your school. Write up a descriptive segment profile, or "persona," of the targeted consumer. Share your description with the class.

7-16. *Creative Homework/Short Project* A positioning statement is used internally by the firm as a clear index of how the brand will be differentiated in the marketplace. We sometimes see a version of the positioning statement in the tagline used by the brand, although the internal statement is slightly more detailed.

Pick three well-known and defined brands and write one or two sentences which would be suitable as an internal statement to describe the desired positioning and differentiation of the brand. Do you think that all brands need an internal positioning statement? Why or why not?

7-17. *For Further Research (Individual):* A geographic information system (GIS) combines a geographic map with digitally stored data about the consumers in a particular geographic area. Using the web, find an example or case study of a business or nonprofit that is using a GIS such as Google Earth to generate market information by location. Write a short summary of this example or case study and present this summary to your class.

7-18. *For Further Research (Individual)* Select any consumer packaged goods company's product that has been around for at least two decades and find at least five print advertisements from throughout that time frame. From the marketing communication content, how has the product's target customers and positioning changed over time and why do you believe these changes have occurred? If the product's target customers or positioning have not changed, what might explain the product's ability to remain the same in its targeting and positioning?

7-19. *Creative Homework/Short Project* Imagine you are the marketing director for a new soft drink brand called

Verve and that you have been charged with determining what kind of brand personality the product should have in order for it to have broad appeal with members of Generation Z. Describe the desired brand personality and identify specific elements of the marketing mix (product, place, price, promotion) that should be implemented to assist in establishing the desired brand personality.

Concepts: Apply Marketing Metrics

When it comes to metrics, good data about the characteristics of the various consumer segments that you may wish to ultimately target is critical because target marketing is ultimately a strategic investment of resources in the segments that appear to have the best return on investment. In this chapter, we mentioned that VALS™ is a well-known approach to psychographic segmentation.

⭐ 7-20. To make the power of the psychographic technique and resulting information for decision making come alive, let's find out your own VALS™ category.

a. Go to the VALS™ website (either Google it or go directly to www.strategicbusinessinsights.com).

b. Click on "Take the VALS™ Survey." Complete all the questions and click SUBMIT to view your results.

c. What is your VALS™ type? Review the information on the website that describes it (found under the tabs About VALS™/VALS™ Types) along with the other VALS™ types.

d. What is your reaction to learning your own VALS™ type? Are you surprised with the result or was it consistent with what you would have expected? Why or why not?

e. What insights does the knowledge of your VALS™ type provide relative to your own consumer behavior?

Choices: What Do You Think?

7-21. *Ethics* Some critics of marketing have suggested that market segmentation and target marketing lead to an unnecessary proliferation of product choices that wastes valuable resources. These critics suggest that if marketers didn't create so many different product choices, there would be more resources to feed the hungry and house the homeless and provide for the needs of people around the globe. Are the results of segmentation and target marketing harmful or beneficial to society as a whole? Should firms be concerned about these criticisms? Why or why not?

⭐ 7-22. *Critical Thinking* One of the criteria for a usable market segment is its size. This chapter suggested that to be usable, a segment must be large enough to be profitable now and in the future and that some small segments get ignored because they can never be profitable. So how large should a segment be? How do you think a firm should go about determining if a segment is profitable? Have technological advances made it possible for smaller segments to be profitable? Do firms ever have a moral or ethical obligation to develop products for small, unprofitable segments? When?

7-23. *Ethics* Marketers are in business to make a profit, but they also have an ethical obligation not to take advantage of consumers, especially disadvantaged consumers like those at the bottom of the pyramid. Would you consider it ethical to sell mosquito nets in Africa to prevent the spread of malaria? Would you consider it ethical to sell Coca-Cola or Pepsi to consumers in rural India? Why or why not? Is there a line between what is ethical to sell and what is not? How would you describe that line?

7-24. *Critical Thinking* Sometimes marketers will develop strategies to target multiple social class segments with the same product by offering it at different prices. What are some examples of products or brands that use this strategy and how do they accomplish it? Are there any potential risks to taking this approach with specific products or brands and what might make some products or brands more susceptible to these kinds of risks?

7-25. *Critical Thinking* Age segmentation is a generally common approach for small businesses in particular, as it is a simple and easy method of segmentation. Considering your own peer group (which is likely to be about the same age), which product categories do you think age segmentation would be suited to and which product categories would it be unsuitable for?

7-26. *Critical Thinking* A few years ago, Anheuser-Busch Inc. created a new division dedicated to marketing to Hispanics and announced it would boost its ad spending in Hispanic media by two-thirds to more than $60 million, while Miller Brewing Co. signed a $100 million, three-year ad package with Spanish-language broadcaster Univision. But Hispanic activists immediately raised public health concerns about the beer ad blitz on the grounds that it targets a population that skews young and is disproportionately likely to abuse alcohol. Surveys of Hispanic youth show that they are much more likely to drink alcohol, get drunk, and engage in binge drinking than their white or black peers. A senior executive at Anheuser-Busch responded, "We would disagree with anyone who suggests beer billboards increase abuse among Latino or other minority communities. It would be poor business for us in today's world to ignore what is the fastest-growing segment of our population."

　　a. Manufacturers of alcohol and tobacco products have been criticized for targeting unwholesome products to certain segments of the market—the aged, ethnic minorities, the disabled, and others. Do you view this as a problem? Should a firm use different criteria in targeting such groups? Should the government oversee and control such marketing activities?

7-27. *Ethics* Gamification was discussed in Chapter 6. For specific segments of a market, a gamification approach might help elicit a desired behavior from consumers, and of course in many cases the desired behavior is an increase in consumption of the related product. When a product is generally associated with potential health problems if consumed in large quantities (e.g., alcohol, sugar) should a marketer be allowed to engage the consumer in gamification activities or similar "fun" approaches that encourage or induce excessive consumption of the product?

7-28. *Critical Thinking* Marketers commonly ask celebrities to endorse products, but tying a brand to a celebrity can come with risks if that celebrity falls out of favor with the public as the result of a something they do or say that is perceived negatively. How would you determine if the signing of a celebrity to an endorsement deal is worth the risk? What would you want to know to make that determination and reduce the risk potential?

Miniproject: Learn by Doing

7-29. Perceptual mapping is often an effective tool when there is a limited array of differences between competing brands. We often find this in products sold by supermarkets, for example. Your task for this mini project is to construct a perceptual map for a choice of brands for one product category within a supermarket setting.

　　You may choose from the following product categories or another product category of your instructor's choosing:

a. paper towels
b. milk
c. laundry detergent
d. canned vegetables

In many ways, these products are relatively "generic," which means that very precise positioning is required to generate and hold market share. To get the information to construct a perceptual map, you will need to visit a supermarket or review a supermarket's offerings online to identify how the products are differentiated from each other within their product category.

　　When you construct your perceptual map, you may need to think about different attributes that consumers use to make their purchase decision. You may need to construct multiple perceptual maps before you find one that is most effective in demonstrating the marketplace.

　　Once you have settled on your final perceptual map, identify any potential gaps for new entrants, and highlight which brands are well positioned and which brands potentially need to be repositioned.

Marketing in **Action** Case   Real Choices at Sprig

What's for dinner? Sprig would like to play a part in a health-conscious customer's answer to that question. Sprig is an on-demand delivery restaurant that offers balanced meals which are fully prepared and delivered in 15 to 20 minutes. The company focuses on using the freshest ingredients to create innovatively delicious food that supports a healthy lifestyle. Its target market includes those who have busy schedules and desire meals that include servings of fruits, vegetables, proteins, and other nutrients. Sprig's website claims, "We use the best ingredients to create dishes that are high on flavor and low on butter, oils, and sugar." Customers have a choice of ordering meals via the Internet or by an app.

CEO Gagan Biyani realized as he worked at ride-sharing company Lyft that when he ordered on-demand meal delivery he was relying way too much on unhealthy options like pizza. So in 2013 he created a company that gives the health-conscious consumer better choices without compromising speed or convenience. Jessica Entzel, executive R&D chef and Biyani's first employee, manages Sprig's menu development. She teams with Nate Keller, a former executive chef for Google, who develops relationships with local farmers and manages the company's sustainability efforts. Keller has a great deal of freedom and a large budget to experiment with recipes and then test them with a host of eager tasters. Sample menu selections include grilled jerk chicken with habanero slaw, beef keema with roasted red potatoes and cabbage, and truffled mac and cheese with cauliflower béchamel.

Sprig uses data continuously collected from customers to refine the menu and ensure consistent delivery of desirable, innovative meals that offer high value. Entzel studies customer feedback on each item to see if it meets and exceeds customer expectations. When the ratings are not as expected, she digs deeper into the responses to discover ways to fix the problem before including that item on the menu again. She also makes sure the presentation of the meal is first-rate, a difficult task to accomplish consistently in on-demand delivery. Hence, the meal development process takes into account how to transport the food without it arriving to the customer as an unattractive mess.

The on-demand delivery segment of the restaurant industry is developing and attracting attention from many new players. Munchery delivers fresh-food entrees, sides, desserts, drinks, and kids' meals in San Francisco, New York, Los Angeles, and Seattle. It offers ready-to-cook meals that are delivered with directions on how to successfully complete the dish. Postmates operates a network of local couriers to deliver meals through a service called Pop that promises food delivery in 15 minutes or less. Pop is fast because it eliminates the pickup leg. Rather than spending time traveling to a specific merchant location or waiting for the food to be prepared, Postmates drivers who participate in Pop carry an inventory of freshly made items ready to drop off immediately. Even Uber is in the market with UberEats, its own on-demand meal delivery service that uses existing Uber technology and customer relationships for competitive advantage.

So what's next for Sprig? Are they on the right track targeting only the smaller health-conscious segment of on-demand delivery? Biyani expects the on-demand delivery market to experience shake-out among competitors similar to what was experienced by the search engine, social media, and other tech markets—that is, a shake-out of initial providers with only a few remaining competitors today. How does Sprig become one of those few that survives?

You Make the Call

7-30. What is the decision facing Sprig?

7-31. What factors are important in understanding this decision situation?

7-32. What are the alternatives?

7-33. What decision(s) do you recommend?

7-34. What are some ways to implement your recommendation?

Sources: Based on Harry McCracken, "The R&D behind Meal Delivery Startup Sprig's New Recipes," *Fast Company* (January 27, 2016), http://www.fastcompany.com/3055772/the-rd-behind-meal-delivery-startup-sprigs-new-recipes (accessed April 21, 2016); "Homepage," *Sprig*, https://www.sprig.com/#/ (accessed April 21, 2016); Melia Robinson, "This Idealistic Food Startup Could Change the Way We Eat—If It Survives," *Business Insider* (April 21, 2016), http://www.techinsider.io/sprig-food-delivery-on-demand-startup-2016-4 (accessed April 21, 2016); http://blog.postmates.com/post/130627727422/poprocks (accessed April 29, 2016).

MyLab Marketing™

Go to **mymktlab.com** for the following Assisted-graded writing questions:

7-35. *Creative Homework/Short Project.* Assume that a small regional microbrewery has hired you to help them with their target marketing. They are pretty unsophisticated about marketing—you will need to explain some things to them and provide ideas for their future. In the past, the microbrewery has simply produced and sold a single beer brand to the entire market—a mass-marketing strategy. As you begin your work, you come to believe that the firm could be more successful if it developed a target marketing strategy. Write a memo to the owner outlining the following:
  a. The basic reasons for doing target marketing in the first place
  b. The specific advantages of a target marketing strategy for the micro-brewery
  c. An initial "short list" of possible target segment profiles

7-36. *Creative Homework/Short Project.* You have been a contributing author to several marketing newsletters, and you have been asked to submit a one-page article on market segmentation. First, describe the need for market segmentation and then, in turn, discuss the various approaches marketers can take, including the advantages of each approach.

Product I: Innovation and New Product Development

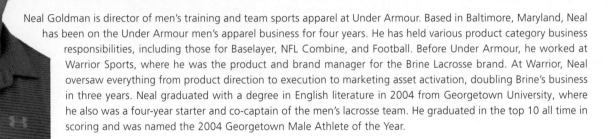

Neal Goldman
▼ A Decision Maker at Under Armour

Neal Goldman, Under Armour

Neal Goldman is director of men's training and team sports apparel at Under Armour. Based in Baltimore, Maryland, Neal has been on the Under Armour men's apparel business for four years. He has held various product category business responsibilities, including those for Baselayer, NFL Combine, and Football. Before Under Armour, he worked at Warrior Sports, where he was the product and brand manager for the Brine Lacrosse brand. At Warrior, Neal oversaw everything from product direction to execution to marketing asset activation, doubling Brine's business in three years. Neal graduated with a degree in English literature in 2004 from Georgetown University, where he also was a four-year starter and co-captain of the men's lacrosse team. He graduated in the top 10 all time in scoring and was named the 2004 Georgetown Male Athlete of the Year.

Neal's Info

What I do when I'm not working?
Playing with my wild two-year-old son and still pretending I'm as good of a lacrosse player as I was 10 years ago.

First job out of school?
Wrigley Gum sales rep.

Career high?
I feel like it's an evolving ranking, but currently it's the acknowledgment of being made director.

My motto to live by?
I have two: (1) If it was easy, anybody could do it. (2) Be the thermostat, not the thermometer.

What drives me?
Personally, making my family proud. Professionally, curiosity of the unknown.

My management style?
Lead by actions, not words. I want my team to see what empowerment to make decisions looks like.

My pet peeve?
Meetings where lots of words are said but no decisions are made.

Here's my problem...

Real **People**, Real **Choices**

In 1996, Kevin Plank, a football player at the University of Maryland, had the thought that there must be a better solution to the 100 percent cotton T-shirt he and his fellow teammates were wearing under their pads. Their shirts were quickly soaked with sweat within minutes of practice, and once they were saturated, it seemed like it took an eternity for them to dry. Not only did the wet, uncomfortable feeling of a heavy shirt bother him, but they also fit poorly; the shirts were constantly poking out of the jersey and becoming a distraction. He knew there had to be a better solution, so he scoured the garment district, found a synthetic blend that met his liking, and took that material along with a small underwear shirt to a tailor. With that, the first run of Under Armour compression shirts was created.

What started as Kevin's idea in 1996 has exploded into a $2 billion-plus empire 18 years later that now encompasses world-class footwear, outerwear, and women's and youth products. But no matter how much Under Armour grows and expands into new markets and categories around the world, the heritage product category, compression HeatGear, remains a vital part of the company. This Baselayer apparel line links directly to Under Armour's core message: "Protect This House."

In the spring of 2011, Under Armour started to see a gradual decline in HeatGear Baselayer sales during a time when historically business would begin ramping up. The brand's biggest sporting goods wholesale partners were telling us that for the first time since the company created this category, they were seeing severe competition from other brands. One major threat was Nike, which had just launched a new product campaign called Pro Combat. If Under Armour had created the story of compression apparel, Nike's Pro Combat was aiming to write the next chapter. The company clearly planned to target the next wave of athletes, who might not have ever been exposed to the Under Armour brand, for their new performance gear line.

The challenge we faced was twofold: product and marketing. At least from the consumer's perspective, the HeatGear Baselayer product line had not evolved in more than a decade. The core franchise business had been treated like "milk and eggs" in the sense that as long as these basic items were in stock, customers wouldn't forget to pick up key essentials. That mind-set contributed to a lack of new product initiatives within this range because we had been focusing on creating new category opportunities, such as women's apparel and athletic shoes. Marketing also played a critical role in this challenge, as Nike launched a full-on assault in all touch points with a heavy focus on retail in-store creative and social media. Our bigger rival was forging a new emotional connection with customers and leveraging its roster of professional athletes and creative resources to explode into the Baselayer category—and threaten our house.

To make matters worse, the product development calendar is an 18-month process from line architecture briefing to market delivery. When business began to dip, the reality of the situation was that any product line overhaul might be too little too late. The HeatGear compression line sells millions of units each year. Any product adjustment can send ripple effects through the supply chain, which in turn can affect delivery times, sales, and profit. On the other hand, the longer Under Armour waited to enact a new plan, the more we would see a dip in sales. A delay in responding to the threat had the potential to threaten long-term revenue and decrease Under Armour's overall market share in the athletic apparel category.

As the leader of the business unit, my role was to assess our options and deliver a strategy that took into account all cross-functional groups with the end goal of recouping short-term revenue as well as setting the brand up for long-term success.

Neal considered his **Options** 1·2·3

1 Option
Approach the decision as a product problem. Build new product offerings to get into retail ASAP. Try to reverse the sales trend with new, exciting styles. This emphasis on immediate new product development to produce a new collection of Baselayer apparel could capture *open-to-buy* dollars from retailers (i.e., the budget they have to purchase retail merchandise), who clearly were going to begin allocating more of their funds to Nike. It could also help Under Armour to look more enticing and competitive compared to other products in the market, which would draw shoppers back to our core brand. But because Under Armour's product development team would have to make this happen on an accelerated time line with no opportunity for delays, production expenses would go up. We would need to position materials, trims, and manufacturing with our current supplier so that once designs and fits were completed, production could start immediately. Combine speed to market with the substantial aesthetic and material direction this product line would demand, and the costs of producing these styles could climb anywhere from 25 to 50 percent. Under Armour wouldn't be able to pass these costs on to consumers in such a competitive market, so short-term gains at retail could come at the expense of bottom-line revenue. In addition, we had to assume that we wouldn't acquire more floor space in stores, so some of our current product offerings would have to come off the displays to make room for the new. The company might need to take back the current product and absorb those costs against sales as well as add more inventory to the books.

2 Option
Approach the decision as a marketing problem. Stay the course with the current product line and invest time, money, and resources immediately into ramping up the messaging that Under Armour sent to its target market of active athletes. This would allow us to continue investing in other new business categories and allow one of the brand's strengths—storytelling—to be on display. An overhaul of this presentation of our Baselayer products in stores would create new energy for the brand and encourage shoppers to take a closer look. Styles that had been treated like milk and eggs would now take center stage, and launching a social and digital campaign for Baselayer could reach millions of consumers instantly. However, although a marketing blitz could put Baselayer into the product spotlight, this might provide only a temporary shot in the arm to sales. The short-term

---

You Choose

Which **Option** would you choose, and **why**?

☐ Option 1   ☐ Option 2   ☐ Option 3

See what **option** Neal chose in **MyLab Marketing**™.

---

gain from a marketing blitz could even provide us with a false sense of security about our Baselayer business. The same issues with product inertia and attractive options from competitors could pop up again six to nine months later, and if so, we would find ourselves in an even deeper hole in terms of our ability to bring new products to market. In addition, other initiatives the marketing teams are working on would need to be put on hold. Finally, cost could be a real issue: Nike's marketing budget dwarfs Under Armour's, so going toe-to-toe with the larger company in a marketing showdown would be tough for us.

3
Option

Start over with a new business plan. Rebuild the Baselayer product from the ground up. Analyze every detail in terms of new fabric selections, design aesthetics, features and benefits, pricing, and consumer positioning. Instead of rushing through the process like option 1 proposes, play the long game: Develop a go-to-market product strategy to ensure that all business needs are addressed without compromising the supply chain and bottom-line revenue. Marketing would have more time, money, and resources to build out the consumer-facing message of what this relaunch means to athletes all over the world. Because this more drawn-out approach would not interrupt their project flow from the previous season, Under Armour's marketing team would have the bandwidth to fully focus on the new deliverables. However, it's nice to have the luxury to step back and reset the game. We didn't necessarily have that; this approach would cause us to lose out in sales and market share in the short term. We don't know how low the floor is yet: Will Under Armour still have the confidence of its retail partners when we come back to the table with new ideas after a tough year of stagnant or declining sales? Another major concern was that to overhaul the product line, we would have to move the category into a different direction from when the company was founded. Think about that for a second: Aside from questioning why we need a new course of action after 17 years of doing something the same way, imagine telling the CEO and COO that to be successful, we would need to go forward with a different product plan than what these two had built from the ground up! And from the marketing end, conventional branding wasn't going to make enough waves to let consumers know about the new line, so there is much more cost and risk associated with taking a bigger swing. If the product and marketing reset isn't successful, how deep is the hole Under Armour would have to dig itself out of?

Now, put yourself in Neal's shoes. Which option would you choose, and why?

Chapter 8

8.1 Build a Better Mousetrap— and Add Value

OBJECTIVE

Explain how value is derived through different product layers.

(pp. 258–261)

"Build a better mousetrap and the world will beat a path to your door." Although we've all heard that adage, the truth is that just because a product is better there is no guarantee it will succeed. For decades, the Woodstream Corp. built Victor brand wooden mousetraps. Then the company decided to build a better one. Woodstream's product-development people researched the eating, crawling, and nesting habits of mice (hey, it's a living). They built prototypes of different mousetraps to come up with the best possible design and tested them in homes. Then the company unveiled the sleek-looking "Little Champ," a black plastic miniature inverted bathtub with a hole. When the mouse went in and ate the bait, a spring snapped upward—and the mouse was history.

Sounds like a great new product (unless you're a mouse), but the Little Champ failed. Woodstream studied mouse habits, *not* consumer preferences. The company later discovered that husbands set the trap at night, but in the morning it was the wives who disposed of the "present" they found waiting for them. Unfortunately, many of them thought the Little Champ looked too expensive to throw away, so they felt they should empty the trap for reuse. This was a task most women weren't willing to do; they wanted a trap they could happily toss into the garbage.[1]

Woodstream's failure in the "rat race" underscores the importance of creating products that provide the benefits people want rather than just new gizmos that sound like a good idea. It also tells us that any number of products, from low-tech cheese to high-tech traps, potentially deliver these benefits. Despite Victor's claim to be the "World's Leader in Rodent Control Solutions," in this case cheese and a shoe box could snuff out a mouse as well as a high-tech trap.

We need to take a close look at how products successfully trap consumers' dollars when they provide value. In Chapter 1, we saw that the *value proposition* is the consumer's perception of the benefits he or she will receive if he or she buys a good or service. So the marketer's task is twofold: first, to create a better value than what's out there already and, second, to convince customers that this is true.

As we defined it in Chapter 1, a *product* is a tangible good, service, idea, or some combination of these that satisfies consumer or business customer needs through the exchange process; it is a bundle of **attributes**, including features, functions, benefits, and uses as well as its brand and packaging.

Products can be physical goods, services, ideas, people, or places. A **good** is a *tangible* product, something that we can see, touch, smell, hear, taste, or possess. It may take the form of a pack of yummy cookies, a shiny new iPad, a house, a part used in production of that Tesla electric sports car you'd like to buy, or a chic but pricey Coach handbag. In contrast, *intangible* products—services, ideas, people, and places—are products that we can't always see, touch, taste, smell, or possess. We'll talk more about intangible products in Chapter 12.

Welcome to Part 3 of this book, "Develop the Value Proposition for the Customer." The key word here is *develop*, and a large part of the marketer's role in developing the value proposition is to create and market products innovatively. In this chapter, we'll first examine what a product is and see how marketers classify consumer and business-to-business (B2B) products. Then we'll go on to look at new products, how marketers develop new products, and how markets accept them (or not).

More broadly speaking, Parts 3 and 4 of the book take you systematically through all of the elements of the marketing mix's four Ps: product and price in Part 3 and distribution ("place") and promotion in Part 4. As you learned in Chapter 7, developing and executing a great marketing mix is the heart and soul of positioning strategy. And the place to start is with your product—as an old saying in marketing goes, "If the product ain't right, the rest don't matter."

Layers of the Product Concept

No doubt you've heard someone say, "It's the thought, not the gift, that counts." Sometimes that's just an excuse for a lame present, but more broadly it means that the gift is a sign or symbol that the gift giver has remembered you. When we evaluate a gift, we may consider the following: Was it presented with a flourish? Was it wrapped in special paper? Was it obviously a "regift"—something the gift giver had received as a gift for himself or herself but wanted to pass on to you (like last year's fruitcake)? These dimensions are a part of the total gift you receive in addition to the actual goodie in the box.

Like a gift, a product is everything that a customer receives in an exchange. As 📷 Figure 8.1 shows, we distinguish among three distinct layers of the product—the core product, the actual product, and the augmented product. When they develop product strategies, marketers need to consider how to satisfy customers' wants and needs at each of these three layers—that is, how they can create value. Let's consider each layer in turn.

The Core Product

The **core product** consists of all the benefits the product will provide for consumers or business customers. As we noted in Chapter 1, a *benefit* is an outcome that the customer receives from owning or using a product. Wise old marketers (and some young ones, too) will tell you, "A marketer may make and sell a half-inch drill bit, but a customer buys a half-inch hole." This tried-and-true saying reminds us that people buy the core product, in this case, the ability to make a hole. If a new product, such as a laser, comes along that provides that outcome in a better way or more cheaply, the drill-bit maker has a problem. The moral of this story? *Marketing is about supplying benefits*, not *attributes*. And benefits are the foundation of any value proposition.

attributes
Include features, functions, benefits, and uses of a product. Marketers view products as a bundle of attributes that includes the packaging, brand name, benefits, and supporting features in addition to a physical good.

good
A tangible product that we can see, touch, smell, hear, or taste.

core product
All the benefits the product will provide for consumers or business customers.

Figure 8.1 📷 *Snapshot* | Layers of the Product

A product is everything a customer receives—the basic benefits, the physical product and its packaging, and the "extras" that come with the product.

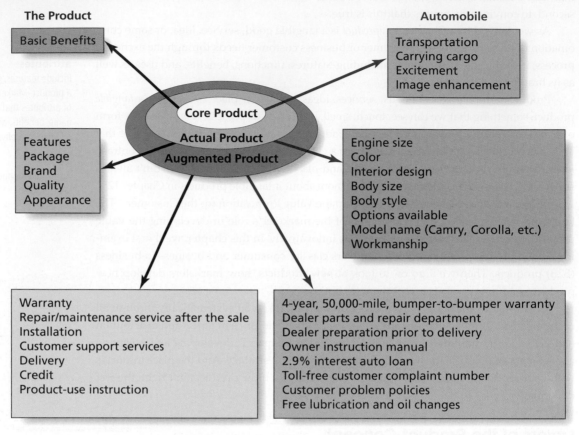

Many products actually provide multiple benefits. For example, the primary benefit of a car is transportation—all cars (in good repair) offer the ability to travel from point A to point B. But products also provide customized benefits—benefits customers receive because manufacturers add "bells and whistles" to win them over. Some drivers simply want economical transportation, others appreciate an environmentally friendly hybrid car, and still others want a top-of-the-line, all-terrain vehicle or perhaps a hot sports car that will be the envy of their friends. And some just like the expandable cup holder's ability to accommodate everything from your Red Bull to a Big Gulp!

The Actual Product

actual product
The physical good or the delivered service that supplies the desired benefit.

The second layer—the **actual product**—is the physical good or the delivered service that supplies the desired benefit. For example, when you buy a washing machine, the core product is the ability to get clothes clean, but the actual product is a large, square metal apparatus. When you get a medical exam, the core service is maintaining your health, but the actual one is a lot of annoying poking and prodding. The actual product also includes the unique features of the product, such as its appearance or styling, the package, and the brand name. Samsung makes a wide range of flat-screen TVs in dozens of sizes from low-end low-price to other models that might cause you to mortgage your house. But in the end, all offer the same core benefit of enabling you to catch Sheldon Cooper's antics on the latest episode of *The Big Bang Theory*.

The Augmented Product

Finally, marketers offer customers an **augmented product**—the actual product plus other supporting features, such as a warranty, credit, delivery, installation, and repair service after the sale. Marketers know that adding these supporting features to a product is an effective way for a company to stand out from the crowd.

For example, Apple truly revolutionized the music industry when it created its iTunes Store, which enabled consumers to download titles directly to their digital music and video libraries. It also conveniently saves you the trouble of correctly inserting, labeling, and sorting the new music. This innovation no doubt dealt a blow to firms that manufactured stands designed to hold hundreds of CDs. Apple's augmented product (convenience, extensive selection, and ease of use) pays off handsomely for the company in sales and profits, and customers adore the fact that you can do it all on your device of choice. As streaming services for music such as Spotify and Tidal have gained in popularity, Apple adapted to the change in consumer preferences by creating Apple Music. Apple Music offers users the ability to access an extensive collection of songs for a monthly fee as opposed to purchasing songs or albums individually.[2] One high profile benefit to attract users is the release of *exclusive content* from artists such as first-to-market singles by popular rapper Drake.[3]

augmented product
The actual product plus other supporting features such as a warranty, credit, delivery, installation, and repair service after the sale.

This diet dessert offers the value proposition of good taste without the extra calories.

8.2 How Marketers Classify Products

OBJECTIVE
Describe how marketers classify products.

(pp. 261–265)

So far, we've learned that a product may be a tangible good or an intangible service or idea and that there are different layers to the product through which a consumer can derive value. Now we'll build on these ideas as we look at how products differ from one another.

Marketers classify products into categories because they represent differences in how consumers and business customers feel about products and how they purchase different products. Such an understanding helps marketers develop new products and a marketing mix that satisfies customer needs.

Let's first consider differences in consumer products based on how long the product will last and on how the consumer shops for the product. Then we will discuss the general types of B2B products.

How Long Do Products Last?

Marketers classify consumer goods as durable or nondurable depending on how long the product lasts. You expect a refrigerator to last many years, but a gallon of milk will last only a week or so until it turns into a science project. **Durable goods** are consumer products that provide benefits over a period of months, years, or even decades, such as cars, furniture, and appliances. In contrast, we consume **nondurable goods**, such as *People* magazine and fresh sushi, in the short term.

We are more likely to purchase durable goods under conditions of *high involvement* (as we saw in Chapter 6), whereas nondurable goods are more likely to be *low-involvement* decisions. When consumers buy a new car or a house, most will spend a lot of time and energy on the decision process. When they offer high-involvement products, marketers

durable goods
Consumer products that provide benefits over a long period of time, such as cars, furniture, and appliances.

nondurable goods
Consumer products that provide benefits for a short time because they are consumed (such as food) or are no longer useful (such as newspapers).

need to understand consumers' desires for different product benefits and the importance of warranties, service, and customer support. So they must be sure that consumers can find the information they need. One way is to provide a "Frequently Asked Questions" (FAQ) section on a company website. Another is to host a Facebook page, Twitter feed, message board, or blog to build a community around the product. When a company itself sponsors such forums, the firm can keep track of what people say about its products and provide a place for users to share information with each other as well as ask questions of the company related to specific products. For high-tech products, this is especially valuable to support the consumer's experience and ensure they are able to gain maximum value from what they buy. Our friends at Apple maintain a popular online forum for iPad users to ask new questions, look up answers to prior questions, and answer active questions from others. The forum is divided into two communities based on how the iPad is used: one for general use and one for business and education use, providing maximum utility for each user group.[4]

In contrast to the higher involvement mode for durable goods, consumers usually don't "sweat the details" so much when they choose among nondurable goods. There is little if any search for information or deliberation. Sometimes this means that consumers buy whatever brand is available and is reasonably priced. In other instances, they base their decisions largely on past experience. Because a certain brand has performed satisfactorily before, customers often see no reason to consider other brands, and they choose the same one out of habit.

How Do Consumers Buy Products?

Marketers also classify products based on where and how consumers buy the product. Figure 8.2 portrays product classifications in the consumer and business marketplaces. We'll consider the consumer market first in which we think of both goods and services as convenience products, shopping products, specialty products, or unsought products. Recall that in Chapter 6 we talked about how consumer decisions differ in terms of effort they put into habitual decision making versus limited problem solving versus extended problem solving—a useful idea on which to base our understanding of why it's important to classify products.

A **convenience product** typically is a nondurable good or service that consumers purchase frequently with a minimum of comparison and effort. As the name implies, consumers expect these products to be handy, and they will buy whatever brands are easy to obtain. In general, convenience products are low priced and widely available. You can buy a gallon of milk or a loaf of bread at most any grocery store, drugstore, or convenience store. Consumers generally already know all they need or want to know about a convenience product, devote little effort to purchases, and willingly accept alternative brands if their preferred brand is not available in a convenient location.

What's the most important thing for marketers of convenience products? You guessed it—make sure the product is easily obtainable in all the places where consumers are likely to look for it. It's a good guess that shoppers don't put a lot of thought into buying convenience products, so a company that sells products like white bread might focus its strategy on promoting awareness of a

convenience product
A consumer good or service that is usually low priced, widely available, and purchased frequently with a minimum of comparison and effort.

Figure 8.2 📷 *Snapshot* | Classification of Products

Products are classified differently depending on whether they are in the consumer or business market.

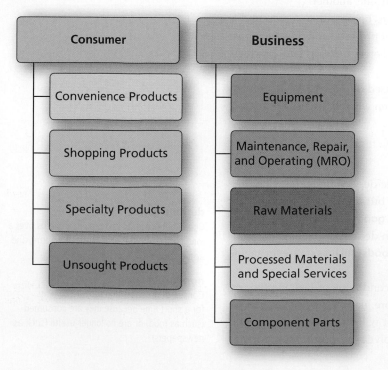

brand name (ever try Bunny Bread? It's white bread at its finest!) as opposed to providing a detailed "spec sheet" we might expect to find for a smartphone or other durable product.

There are several types of convenience products:

- **Staple products**, such as milk, bread, and gasoline, are basic or necessary items that are available almost everywhere. Most consumers don't perceive big differences among brands. A particular category of staple products is called consumer packaged goods. A **consumer packaged good (CPG)** or **fast-moving consumer good (FMCG)** is a low-cost good that we consume quickly and replace frequently.

  Like staple products in general, CPGs (or FMCGs) are also frequently purchased but are less basic, with more variations than general staples. Importantly, they are also more brand-centric, and consumers tend to perceive more differences in product quality, features, and benefits, so the brands are heavily advertised. And in terms of distribution, giant retailers use CPGs and FMCGs to bring shoppers into the store, thus building foot traffic and increasing the chances that other types of products will also end up in shopping baskets (see discussion on impulse and shopping products that follows). A few years back, the venerable treat Twinkies disappeared from distribution for a while because of a closing and sale of the manufacturer. Then, to celebrate the victorious re-debut of the fluffy delights, Walmart heavily promoted the arrival of Twinkies at its stores the weekend before the shipments arrived, resulting in a rush to their stores on arrival (and no doubt a sugar rush among consumers immediately thereafter). And if your Twinkie crave was on, who can go into Walmart and purchase just one item? Their sales for that week were up across the board.

- While a staple is something we usually decide to buy in advance (or at least before the fuel needle sits on "E" for too long), we buy **impulse products** on the spur of the moment. When you throw a copy of *People* magazine into your shopping cart because it has a cool photo of Christina Aguilera and her baby with a screaming headline "NEW BABY, NEW LIFE" on the cover, you're acting on impulse. When they want to promote impulse products, marketers have two challenges: (1) to create a product or package design that "reaches out and grabs the customer" and (2) to make sure their product is highly visible, for example, by securing prime end-aisle or checkout-lane space. That's why you'll often find brightly colored packages of yellow creme Oreos on end caps in the spring or cheery packages of gum and candy in the checkout lines. Package design and placement is becoming ever more important as customers come through the lines with "mobile blinders" on—that is, customers with mobile phones in hand are more likely to send texts or check Facebook while they stand in line, so they don't even notice the impulse products beckoning for their attention.[5] It's getting harder and harder for a package of Juicy Fruit gum to compete with a juicy Facebook post. And advances in technology (such as physical devices that can transmit information based on location called beacons—more on this in Chapter 12) have made it possible for marketers to provide highly targeted promotions to consumers' smartphones as they navigate through the store, driving impulse purchases that in the past would have been missed for retailers.[6]

- As the name suggests, we purchase **emergency products** when we're in dire need; examples include bandages, umbrellas, and something to unclog the nasty bathroom sink. Because we need the product badly and immediately, price and sometimes product quality may be irrelevant to our decision to purchase.

In contrast to convenience products, **shopping products** are goods or services for which consumers will spend time and effort to gather information on price, product attributes, and product quality. For these products, consumers are likely to compare alternatives before they buy.

Tablet computers are a good example of a shopping product. They offer an ever-expanding array of features and functions, and new versions constantly enter the market.

staple products
Basic or necessary items that are available almost everywhere.

consumer packaged good (CPG) or **fast-moving consumer good (FMCG)**
A low-cost good that is consumed quickly and replaced frequently.

impulse products
A product people often buy on the spur of the moment.

emergency products
Products we purchase when we're in dire need.

shopping products
Goods or services for which consumers spend considerable time and effort gathering information and comparing alternatives before making a purchase.

The shopper has many trade-offs and decisions to make about a variety of features that can be bundled, including speed, screen size, functionality, weight, and battery life. And tablet manufacturers understand your decision dilemma: They take great pains to communicate comparisons to you in their advertising—and, as you might expect, they usually find a way to make their version seem superior.

specialty products
Goods or services that have unique characteristics and are important to the buyer and for which he or she will devote significant effort to acquire.

Specialty products have unique characteristics that are important to buyers at almost any price. When gas prices are down, hybrid vehicles are less cost-effective versus standard cars yet many consumers still opt to shell out the premium prices to purchase them because of the importance they place on being environmentally friendly. Specialty products often have luxury connotations for which consumers are willing to pay a higher price to achieve a desired image—Rolex versus Timex for example. Both keep time quite accurately, but the Rolex mystique commands considerable attention. Rolex justifies its high price when the company points out that because of its high standards for quality and design it takes about a year to make one of its watches.[7]

Consumers usually know a good deal about specialty products, and they tend to be loyal to specific brands. Generally, a specialty product is an extended problem-solving purchase that requires a lot of effort to choose, meaning that firms that sell these kinds of products need to create marketing strategies that make their products stand apart from the rest.

unsought products
Goods or services for which a consumer has little awareness or interest until the product or a need for the product is brought to his or her attention.

Unsought products are goods or services (other than convenience products) for which a consumer has little awareness or interest until a need arises. When a college graduate lands his or her first "real" job, typically retirement plans and disability insurance are unsought products. It requires a good deal of advertising or personal selling to interest young people in these kinds of products—just ask any life insurance salesperson. One solution may be to make pricing more attractive; for example, reluctant consumers may be more willing to buy an unsought product for "only pennies a day" than if they have to think about their yearly or lifetime cash outlay.

How Do Businesses Buy Products?

Although consumers purchase products for their own use, as we saw in Chapter 6 organizational customers purchase items to enable them to produce still other goods or services. Marketers classify B2B products based on how organizational customers *use* them. As with consumer products, when marketers know how their business customers use a product, they are better able to design products and craft an appropriate marketing mix. Let's briefly review the five different types of B2B products that Figure 8.2 depicts.

equipment
Expensive goods that an organization uses in its daily operations that last for a long time.

- **Equipment** refers to the products an organization uses in its daily operations. *Heavy equipment*, sometimes called *installations* or *capital equipment*, includes items such as the sophisticated robotics Ford uses to assemble automobiles. Installations are big-ticket items and last for a number of years. Computers, photocopy machines, and water fountains are examples of *light* or *accessory equipment*; they are portable, cost less, and have a shorter life span than capital equipment.

maintenance, repair, and operating (MRO) products
Goods that a business customer consumes in a relatively short time.

- **Maintenance, repair, and operating (MRO) products** are goods that a business customer consumes in a relatively short time. *Maintenance products* include light bulbs, mops, cleaning supplies, and the like. Repair products are items such as nuts, bolts, washers, and small tools. *Operating supplies* include computer paper and oil to keep machinery running smoothly. Although some firms use a sales force to promote MRO products, others rely on catalog sales, the Internet, and telemarketing to keep prices as low as possible.

raw materials
Products of the fishing, lumber, agricultural, and mining industries that organizational customers purchase to use in their finished products.

- **Raw materials** are products of the fishing, lumber, agricultural, and mining industries that organizational customers purchase to use in their finished products. For example, a food company transforms soybeans into tofu, and a steel manufacturer changes iron ore into large sheets of steel that other firms use to build automobiles, washing machines, and lawn mowers.

- Firms produce **processed materials** when they transform raw materials from their original state. A builder uses treated lumber to add a deck onto a house. A company that creates aluminum cans for Red Bull buys aluminum ingots to make them.

- In addition to tangible processed materials, some business customers purchase **specialized services** from outside suppliers. These may be equipment based, such as repairing a copy machine or fixing an assembly line malfunction, or non–equipment-based, such as market research and legal services. These services are essential to the operation of an organization but are not part of the production of a product.

- **Component parts** are manufactured goods or subassemblies of finished items that organizations need to complete their own products. For example, a computer manufacturer needs silicon chips to make a computer, and an automobile manufacturer needs batteries, tires, and fuel injectors.

processed materials
Products created when firms transform raw materials from their original state.

specialized services
Services that are essential to the operation of an organization but are not part of the production of a product.

component parts
Manufactured goods or subassemblies of finished items that organizations need to complete their own products.

8.3 "New and Improved!" The Process of Innovation

OBJECTIVE

Understand the importance and types of product innovations.

(pp. 265–267)

"New and improved!" What exactly do we mean when we use the term *new product*? The Federal Trade Commission says that (1) a product must be entirely new or changed significantly to be called new and that (2) a product may be called new for only six months.

That definition is fine from a legal perspective. From a marketing standpoint, though, a new product or an **innovation** is *anything* that customers perceive as new and different. Innovation has its roots in an even more elemental concept that is a hot topic in boardrooms of most organizations today: creativity. **Creativity** describes a process that results in something new. Creative outcomes can take on many forms, but most often we experience them as something we can see, hear, smell, touch, or taste.[8] The outcome can be most anything—an idea, a joke, an artistic or literary work, a painting or musical composition, a novel solution to a problem, an invention, and of course, a new product. Scientific research into creativity provides strong evidence of the importance of creative processes in the production of novel, useful products.[9]

An innovation may be relatively minor, such as the thousands of new versions of current products, such as Chocolate Cheerios, we see on the market each year. Or it can be something game changing like wearable technology to monitor personal health and fitness worn on the wrist (e.g., the Fitbit Flex and the Jawbone Up) or headsets used to explore virtual reality (e.g., the Oculus Rift). It may come in the form of a new way to transmit information, such as when Skype VoIP telephony became available as a free service over the Internet, or as a new way to power a vehicle, such as the hydrogen fuel cells in the Honda FCX Clarity. In some cases, an innovation may be a completely new product that provides benefits never available before, like the original HP scientific calculator that nearly overnight made the slide rule obsolete (if the term *slide rule* is foreign to you, we suggest Googling it—a slide rule is how engineers used to make complex calculations before HP's innovation). In this section and the next, we focus heavily on the concept and process of product innovation, which, if done well, contributes mightily to organizational success.

innovation
A product that consumers perceive to be new and different from existing products.

creativity
A phenomenon whereby something new and valuable is created.

Figure 8.3 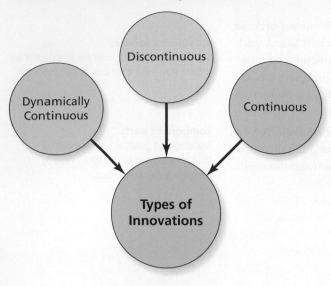 *Snapshot* | Types of Innovations

Three types of innovations are continuous, dynamically continuous, and discontinuous, based on their degree of newness.

Types of Innovations

Innovations differ in their *degree* of newness, and this helps determine how quickly the target market will adopt them. Because innovations that are more novel require us to exert greater effort to figure out how to use them, they are slower to spread throughout a population than new products that are similar to what is already available.

As Figure 8.3 shows, marketers classify innovations into three categories based on their degree of newness: continuous innovations, dynamically continuous innovations, and discontinuous innovations. However, it is better to think of these three types as ranges along a continuum that goes from a very small change in an existing product to a totally new product. We can then describe the three types of innovations in terms of the amount of change they bring to people's lives. For example, the first automobiles caused tremendous changes in the lives of people who were used to getting places by "horse power." Then airplanes came along and opened the entire world to us. And now, with innovations like the TripLingo app, you can communicate easily while traveling abroad. TripLingo comes with a real-time translator—just speak into your phone, and it speaks back to you, at whatever speed you choose. It even has a Slangslider so that you can set the level of formality.[10]

On the idea side, Airbnb changed how travelers book a place to stay at their destinations (by allowing virtually anyone to rent out space in their own homes), and Uber's app provides a new way to get to this destination (by allowing virtually anyone to become a taxi driver and pick up fares when people summon a ride on their phones). With a whole new world of travel opened up through these apps and all of the data those travel plans generate, an app such as TripIt is a nice innovation to have handy. The app allows a user to forward any confirmation e-mails received associated with a trip so that the important details can be automatically organized into an easy to use digital itinerary. Very convenient![11]

Continuous Innovations

A **continuous innovation** is a modification to an existing product, such as when Samsung and others reinvigorated the TV market by offering thinner sets that featured high-definition viewing. This type of modification can set one brand apart from its competitors. For example, people associate Volvo cars with safety—in fact, their taglines include "Safety first, always" and "You're not just driving a car, you're driving a promise." Those are strong words, and Volvo backs them up with a steady stream of safety-related innovations.

The consumer doesn't have to learn anything new to use a continuous innovation. From a marketing perspective, this means that it's usually relatively easy to convince consumers to adopt this kind of new product. For example, the current generation of high-definition plasma flat-screen monitors didn't require computer users to change their behaviors. We all know what a computer monitor is and how it works. The system's continuous innovation simply gives users the added benefits of taking up less space and being easier on the eyes than old-style monitors.

A **knockoff** is a new product that copies, with slight modification, the design of an original product. Firms deliberately create knockoffs of

continuous innovation
A modification of an existing product that sets one brand apart from its competitors.

knockoff
A new product that copies, with slight modification, the design of an original product.

Courtesy of Osborne Macharia/ProKraft Africa

Relatively new products like this African mascara brand need to work hard to create a distinctive image and stand out in a crowded marketplace.

clothing and jewelry, often with the intent to sell to a larger or different market. For example, companies may copy the *haute couture* clothing styles of top designers and sell them at lower prices to the mass market. It's likely that a cheaper version of the gown Jennifer Lawrence wears to the Academy Awards ceremony will be available at numerous websites within a few days after the event. It is difficult to legally protect a design (as opposed to a technological invention) because an imitator can argue that even a slight change—different buttons or a slightly wider collar on a dress or shirt—means the knockoff is not an exact copy.

Dynamically Continuous Innovations

A **dynamically continuous innovation** is a pronounced modification to an existing product that requires a modest amount of learning or change in behavior to use it. The history of audio equipment is a series of dynamically continuous innovations. For many years, consumers enjoyed listening to their favorite Frank Sinatra songs on record players (actually, when first introduced, they were called Gramophones). In the 1960s, teeny boppers screamed and swooned as they listened to the Beatles on a continuous-play eight-track tape (requiring the purchase of an eight-track tape player, of course). Then came cassette tapes to listen to the Eagles (oops, now a cassette player is needed). In the 1980s, consumers could hear Metallica songs digitally mastered on compact discs (that, of course, required the purchase of a new CD player).

But of course, in the 1990s, recording technology moved one big step forward with MP3 technology; it allowed Madonna fans to download music from the Internet or to exchange electronic copies of the music with others, and when mobile MP3 players hit the scene in 1998, fans could download the tunes directly into a portable player. Then, in November 2001, Apple Computer introduced its first iPod (can you believe it's been that long!). With the original iPod, music fans could take 1,000 songs with them wherever they went. By 2010, iPods could hold 40,000 songs, 25,000 photos, and 200 hours of video.[12] Music fans go to the Apple iTunes Store or elsewhere to download songs and to get suggestions for new music they might enjoy. Of course, today you can do all this on your smartphone. With improving data plans and coverage as well as Wi-Fi being available almost everywhere outside the home, it's easier than ever to stream music on your smartphone or tablet as opposed to downloading it on a device. Although Apple still sells iPods, sales plummeted from a peak of nearly 55 million in 2008 to less than 15 million in 2014 because many of us have moved on to using our iPhones instead. But in marketing, the story never ends: Now even mighty Apple sees sales dropping dramatically as the market for iPhones gets saturated and consumers wait to buy "the next big thing."[13] Maybe a virtual reality Gramophone?

Discontinuous Innovations

To qualify as a **discontinuous innovation**, the product must create *major changes* in the way we live. Consumers have to learn a great deal to be able to effectively use a discontinuous innovation because no similar product has ever been on the market. Major inventions, such as the airplane, the car, and the TV, are the sort of innovations that radically changed modern lifestyles. Another discontinuous innovation, the personal computer—developed in fairly close parallel to the rise of the Internet—changed the way we shop and allowed more people to work from home or anywhere else. Since the advent of PCs, the move toward processing the same information on tablets and on handheld devices became a follow-up journey in dynamically continuous innovation. One particular type of discontinuous innovation is **convergence**, which means the coming together of two or more technologies to create new systems that provide greater benefit than the original technologies alone.

What's the next discontinuous innovation? Is there a product out there already that will gain that distinction? Usually, marketers know for sure only through 20/20 hindsight; in other words, it's tough to plan for the next really big one (what the computer industry calls the "killer app").

dynamically continuous innovation
A change in an existing product that requires a moderate amount of learning or behavior change.

discontinuous innovation
A totally new product that creates major changes in the way we live.

convergence
The coming together of two or more technologies to create a new system with greater benefits than its separate parts.

research and development (R&D)
A well-defined and systematic approach to how innovation is done within the firm.

new product development (NPD)
The phases by which firms develop new products, including idea generation, product concept development and screening, marketing strategy development, business analysis, technical development, test marketing, and commercialization.

idea generation (ideation)
A phase of product development in which marketers use a variety of sources to come up with great new product ideas that provide customer benefits and that are compatible with the company mission.

value co-creation
The process by which benefits-based value is created through collaborative participation by customers and other stakeholders in the new product development process.

8.4 New Product Development

OBJECTIVE
Show how firms develop new products.

(pp. 268–273)

Building on our knowledge of the concept of creativity and the different types of innovations, we'll now turn our attention to how firms actually develop new products. This process is based on expenditures in **research and development (R&D)**, which in most organizations is a well-defined and systematic approach to how it innovates. Investors and financial markets closely scrutinize R&D investments because these expenditures tend to predict how robust the firm's oncoming new product stream will be. In fact, R&D investment in and of itself is often a central metric for organizational commitment to innovation. Higher levels of R&D activity are inherently more competitively important in some industries versus others (high tech and pharmaceuticals are examples on the high side), but as we saw in the case of Under Armour at the beginning of the chapter, in any firm new product development is fueled by investment in R&D.

There are seven phases in the process of **new product development (NPD)**, as Figure 8.4 shows: idea generation, product concept development and screening, marketing strategy development, business analysis, technical development, market test, and commercialization. Let's take a quick look at what goes on during each of these phases.

Phase 1: Idea Generation (Ideation)

In the initial **idea generation (or ideation)** phase of product development, marketers use a variety of sources to come up with great new product ideas that provide customer benefits and that are compatible with the company mission. Sometimes ideas come from customers. Ideas also come from salespeople, service providers, and others who have direct customer contact. **Value co-creation** refers to the process by which an organization creates worth through collaborative participation by customers and other stakeholders in the new product development process.

Metrics Moment

How do marketers measure innovation? Short answer: It's pretty complex. This is because it involves not only marketing but also the firm's overall culture, leadership, and processes in place that foster innovation. Here's a short list of measures that when taken as a whole can provide a firm's "Innovation Score Card."

Firm Strategy

- How aware are organization members of a firm's goals for innovation?
- How committed is the firm and its leadership to those goals?
- How actively does the firm support innovation among its organization members? Are there rewards and other incentives in place to innovate? Is innovation part of the performance evaluation process?
- To what degree do organization members perceive that resources are available for innovation (money and otherwise)?

Firm Culture

- Does the organization have an appetite for learning and trying new things?
- Do organization members have the freedom and security to try things, fail, and then go forward to try different things?

Outcomes of Innovation

- How many innovations have been launched in the past three years?
- What is the percentage of revenue attributable to launches of innovations during the past three years?[14]

Apply the Metrics

1. Select a firm that you are particularly interested in and that you believe is pretty innovative.
2. Do a little research on its website and elsewhere to get a sense for the evidence about how it performs on the Score Card's criteria for innovativeness.
3. Summarize your findings; how does the firm score on the Innovation Score Card. Consider each item that requires a rating (e.g., the "Firm Strategy" section of the scorecard) on a scale of 1 to 5 where 5 is the highest or most favorable rating and 1 is the lowest or least favorable rating?
4. In general, do you find that the firm is more or less innovative than you expected?

Lego developed an online platform called Lego Ideas where users can suggest new Lego sets and seek to have them turned into physical products by the company. Lego Ideas enables users to provide a description, a visual representation (build a representation of the product physically or digitally using Legos), and to specify the characteristics of their proposed Lego set. Then, any new ideas that attract more than 10,000 supporters in a two-year period on the platform move into a review phase, at which point Lego determines whether or not it's feasible to turn the idea into a mass-produced Lego set. As part of the vetting process, folks who throw their support behind a particular proposed product answer a series of questions to determine market potential (questions related to perceived price, segments of the market the set would appeal to, complexity of building the set, etc.).This approach to value co-creation has yielded some massive successes for Lego including the first Minecraft set that paved the way for future sets to be made that leverage the Minecraft intellectual property.[15] It's important to note that such a value co-creation approach is in stark contrast to "traditional" approaches in which firms develop products behind a curtain and send them to market, hoping that customers connect with the intended value proposition of the new offering.

Often firms use marketing research activities, such as the *focus groups* we discussed in Chapter 4, in their search for new product ideas. For example, a company like ESPN that wants to develop new channels or change the focus of its existing channels might hold focus group discussions across different groups of sports-minded viewers to get ideas for new types of programs.

Phase 2: Product Concept Development and Screening

The second phase in developing new products is **product concept development and screening**. Although ideas for products initially come from a variety of sources and, it is hoped, through co-creation with customers and others, ultimately the responsibility usually falls to marketers to manage the process and expand these ideas into more complete product concepts. Product concepts describe what features the product should have and the benefits those features will provide for consumers. Of course, just because an idea is unique doesn't mean it will sell. How about the Japanese company that invented an app to allow your smartphone to control your toilet? It lets you flush and lift the seat without touching the commode. But wait, there's more: You can play music through the toilet's speakers, and store your "usage history" in a "toilet diary" to track your progress. Now this idea is flush with possibilities![16]

In new product development, failures often come as frequently (or more so) than successes, and it is critical to screen ideas for *both* their technical and commercial value. When screening, marketers examine the chances that a new product concept might be successful while they weed out concepts that have little chance to make it in the market. They estimate **technical success** when they decide whether the new product is technologically feasible—is it possible to actually build this product? Then they estimate **commercial success** when they decide whether anyone is likely to buy the product. Lego uses its Lego Ideas process to estimate the potential commercial success of a new product in terms of the number of supporters the idea attracts. Its potential technical success comes into play only if the product gains enough support to make it to Lego's internal review. If the product concept reaches this benchmark, the company will then conduct an analysis of whether it can actually produce it.

Phase 3: Marketing Strategy Development

The third phase in new product development is to develop a marketing strategy to introduce the product to the marketplace, a process we began to talk about back in Chapter 3. This means that marketers must identify the target market, estimate its size, and determine how they can effectively position the product to address the target

Figure 8.4 ⚡ *Process* | Phases in New Product Development

New product development generally occurs in seven phases.

Phase 1: Idea Generation

Phase 2: Product Concept Development and Screening

Phase 3: Marketing Strategy Development

Phase 4: Business Analysis

Phase 5: Technical Development

Phase 6: Test Marketing

Phase 7: Commercialization

product concept development and screening
The second step of product development in which marketers test product ideas for technical and commercial success.

technical success
Indicates that a product concept is feasible purely from the standpoint of whether or not it is possible to physically develop it, regardless of whether it is perceived to be commercially viable.

commercial success
Indicates that a product concept is feasible from the standpoint of whether the firm developing the product believes there is or will be sufficient consumer demand to warrant its development and entry into the market.

The director of culinary innovation at McDonald's recently came up with a simple idea: He took the breaded chicken the chain uses in its Chicken Selects strips, topped it with shredded cheddar jack cheese and lettuce, added a few squirts of ranch sauce, and wrapped it in a flour tortilla. McDonald's dubbed it the "Snack Wrap" and put it on the menu at a starter price of $1.29. A hit was born—the Snack Wrap is one of the most successful new product launches in company history with sales exceeding projections by 20 percent.

business analysis
The step in the product development process in which marketers assess a product's commercial viability.

technical development
The step in the product development process in which company engineers refine and perfect a new product.

market's needs. And, of course, marketing strategy development includes planning for pricing, distribution, and promotion expenditures both for the introduction of the new product and for the long run.

Phase 4: Business Analysis

Once a product concept passes the screening stage, the next phase is a **business analysis**. Even though marketers have evidence that there is a market for the product, they still must find out if the product can make a profitable contribution to the organization's product mix. How much potential demand is there for the product? Does the firm have the resources it will need to successfully develop and introduce the product?

The business analysis for a new product begins with assessing how the new product will fit into the firm's total product mix. Will the new product increase sales, or will it simply take away sales of existing products (a concept called *cannibalization* that we'll discuss further in Chapter 9)? Are there possible synergies between the new product and the company's existing offerings that may improve visibility and the image of both? And what are the marketing costs likely to be?

Phase 5: Technical Development

If a new product concept survives the scrutiny of a business analysis, it then undergoes **technical development**, in which a firm's engineers work with marketers to refine the design and production process. A great example of the technical development phase involves

Ripped from the Headlines

Ethical/Sustainable Decisions in the Real World

Over the years, automobile companies have come under increasing pressure to produce cars that are more fuel efficient and better for the environment. Fuel efficiency is commonly measured in miles per gallon of gasoline. Measures of environmental benefit can include greenhouse gas and other air polluting emissions.[17] Driven in part by consumer sentiment—especially among millennials—and governmental regulations, car companies have worked hard to innovate to offer vehicles that provide more value for their money and a lesser impact on the environment.

Volkswagen (VW) found itself in a lot of trouble with government agencies and the public when it came to light that 11 million VW cars were manufactured with so-called "cheating software" that enabled each of those vehicles to essentially sense when an emissions test was being conducted and then direct the engine to operate in a manner that would significantly reduce both power and performance and in turn lower the level of pollutants the tests measured. When the vehicle's software sensed that a test was no longer being performed it reverted the vehicle back into normal operations, which meant a significant increase in the amount of environmental pollutants being emitted

including nitrogen oxide at 40 times greater than what is permitted in the U.S.[18] The discovery of this cheating software in many of VW's vehicles led to profound consumer backlash and shunning of the brand that will likely continue to impact VW for some time.

Diesel cars offer strong fuel economy on a par with hybrids. Unfortunately, the VW scandal has shaken consumer confidence. VW played a significant role in bringing diesel cars into the mainstream in the U.S., and it is quite possible that VW's admission that it cheated on tests will make buyers skeptical about the environmental performance of diesel cars in general.[19] When all is said and done, fines from governmental agencies against VW will be in the billions of dollars and the costs of physically correcting the issues on a car-to-car basis will be at a comparable level. The impact of this event on brand equity and consumer confidence over the long term also will be measurable and significant and the future of the VW brand is uncertain especially with environmentally conscious millennials.

ETHICS CHECK:

Should managers who are both knowingly and actively involved in the development of automobiles that are designed to cheat government mandated environmental tests be held criminally accountable?

☐ YES   ☐ NO

the company goTenna, which recently launched a product to enable people to be able to communicate with each other using their smartphones while in an area without cell phone coverage. The product (also named goTenna) uses radio signals to create a network between multiple goTenna devices that, along with the company's smartphone app, provides a means of communication between multiple users of the product within a given area. One valuable application of goTenna is during wilderness excursions, where potentially intense weather conditions make it even more difficult to receive cell phone signals. The goTenna's design is lightweight, it's easy to attach to the outside of a backpack or one of the belt loops on a pair of pants, and it's water-resistant. Although many of these characteristics were most likely identified to some degree during an earlier stage of the product development process, the company's marketers needed to work with the engineering team during the technical development phase to more fully flesh them out into a tangible form that fits with both consumer needs and the internal capabilities of the company.[20]

New flavors need to undergo rigorous technical development so companies can be sure they will satisfy consumers' expectations.

The better a firm understands how customers will react to a new product, the better its chances of commercial success. For this reason, typically a company allocates resources to develop one or more physical versions or **prototypes** of the product. Prospective customers may evaluate these mock-ups in focus groups or in field trials at home.

Prototypes also are useful for people within the firm. Those involved in the technical development process must determine which parts of a finished good the company will make and which ones it will buy from other suppliers. In the case of manufacturing goods, the company may have to buy new production equipment or modify existing machinery. Someone has to develop work instructions for employees and train them to make the product. When it's a matter of a new service process, technical development includes decisions such as which activities will occur within sight of customers versus in the "backroom" and whether the company can automate parts of the service to make delivery more efficient.

prototypes
Test versions of a proposed product.

Technical development sometimes requires the company to apply for a **patent**. Because patents legally prevent competitors from producing or selling the invention, this legal mechanism may reduce or eliminate competition in a market for many years so that a firm gains some time to recoup its investments in technical development.

patent
A legal mechanism to prevent competitors from producing or selling an invention, aimed at reducing or eliminating competition in a market for a period of time.

Phase 6: Market Test

The next phase of new product development is running a **market test** (also known as a **test market**). This usually means the firm tries out the complete marketing plan—the distribution, advertising, and sales promotion—in a small slice of the market that is similar to the larger market it ultimately hopes to enter with full force.

market test or **test market**
Testing the complete marketing plan in a small geographic area that is similar to the larger market the firm hopes to enter.

There are both pluses and minuses to market tests. On the negative side, market tests are extremely expensive. It can cost more than a million dollars to conduct a market test even in a single city. A market test also gives the competition a free look at the new product, its introductory price, and the intended promotional strategy—and an opportunity to get to the market first with a competing product. On the positive side, when they offer a new product in a limited area, marketers can evaluate and improve the marketing program. Sometimes, market tests uncover a need to improve the product itself. At other times, market tests indicate product failure, providing an advanced warning that allows the firm to save millions of dollars by "pulling the plug."

For years, the manufacturer of venerable Listerine wanted to introduce a mint-flavored version of its classic gold formulation to compete more directly with P&G's pleasant-tasting Scope (it originally introduced this alternative under the brand Listermint). Unfortunately,

Pepsi is moving into the restaurant business as it opens Kola House in a hip area of lower Manhattan. The restaurant–bar–event space will build buzz for Pepsi, but also serve as a testing ground for new products.

every time they tried to run a market test, P&G found out, and the rival poured substantial extra advertising and coupons for its Scope brand into the test market cities. This counterattack reduced the usefulness of the test market results for Listerine when its market planners tried to decide whether to introduce Listermint nationwide. Because P&G's aggressive response to Listermint's market tests actually *increased* Scope's market share in the test cities, there was no way to determine how well Listermint would actually do under normal competitive conditions. The company went ahead and introduced Listermint nationally anyway, but the new brand achieved only marginal success, and the company ultimately pulled it from the market. Today, thanks to better product development, the Listerine brand itself is available in mint flavor as well as several other choices and is the top-selling mouthwash.[21]

simulated market test
Application of special computer software to imitate the introduction of a product into the marketplace allowing the company to see the likely impact of price cuts and new packaging— or even to determine where in the store it should try to place the product.

Because of the potential problems and expense of market tests, marketers instead may use special computer software to conduct a **simulated market test** that imitates the introduction of a product into the marketplace. These simulations allow the company to see the likely impact of price cuts and new packaging—or even to determine where in the store it should try to place the product. The process entails gathering basic research data on consumers' perceptions of the product concept, the physical product, the advertising, and other promotional activity. The test market simulation model uses that information to predict the product's success much less expensively (and more discreetly) than a traditional test market. As this technology improves, traditional test markets may become a thing of the past.

Phase 7: Commercialization

commercialization
The final step in the product development process in which a new product is launched into the market.

The last phase in new product development is **commercialization**. This means the launching of a new product, and it requires full-scale production, distribution, advertising, sales promotion—the works. For this reason, commercialization of a new product cannot happen overnight. A launch requires planning and careful preparation.

Commercialization is expensive, but the Internet makes it much easier for start-ups to obtain the funding they need to get their new products into the market. Today, we witness the explosive growth of **crowdfunding**, where innovative websites such as Kickstarter.com, Indiegogo.com, and Crowdfunder.com have raised more than $5 billion for entrepreneurs and small companies (not to mention the popular TV show *Shark Tank*, which also provides funding for contestants who convince one or more Sharks to join them). On these sites, individuals can choose to either donate money (often in exchange for a product sample) or invest in the company.[22] Under this model, even small contributions add up when hundreds or thousands of people like an idea and pitch in.

crowdfunding
Online platforms that allow thousands of individuals to each contribute small amounts of money to fund a new product from a startup company.

As launch time nears, preparations gain a sense of urgency. First, the social media campaigns are likely to crank up and hopefully insiders will then start to buzz about the new product on Twitter and in the blogosphere. Then sales managers will have to explain special incentive programs to salespeople, who in turn will educate all of their customers in the channel of distribution. Soon the media announce to prospective customers why they should buy and where they can find the new product. And all of this has to be orchestrated with the precision of a symphony, with every player on top of his or her part, else the introduction into the market can easily disappoint customers when they first try to buy.

The late Apple innovation genius Steve Jobs was never one to squelch precommercialization hype about his new product introductions. It has been estimated that Apple achieved prelaunch publicity worth more than $500 million on the original iPhone before it spent a single penny on any actual paid advertising. And the introduction of the original iPad back in 2010 was no exception to the Apple hype-creation machine. Jobs claimed that the iPad would offer an experience superior to that of netbooks (a popular term at the time for notebook computers). He argued that the 751 million people who at that time owned iPhones and iPod Touches already knew how to use the iPad because it uses the same operating system and touch-screen interface. Well, as they say, the rest is history. Since 2010, the iPad and its bevy of competitors have had a major impact on how we work and entertain ourselves.[23] The reflection on the iPad introduction provides a perfect segue to the next section on adoption and diffusion of innovation.

8.5 Adoption and Diffusion of New Products

OBJECTIVE

Explain the process of product adoption and the diffusion of innovations.

(pp. 273–279)

In the previous section, we talked about the steps marketers take to develop new products from generating ideas to launch. Now we'll look at what happens *after* that new product hits the market—how an innovation spreads throughout a population.

A painting is not a work of art until someone views it. A song is not music until someone sings it. In the same way, new products do not satisfy customer wants and needs until the customer actually uses (consumes) them—hence the word *consumer*. **Product adoption** is the process by which a consumer or business customer begins to buy and use a new good, service, or idea.

The term **diffusion** describes how the use of a product spreads throughout a population. One way to understand how this process works is to think about a new product as if it were a computer virus that spreads from a few computers to infect many machines. A brand might just slog around—sometimes for years and years. At first, only a small number of people buy it, but change happens in a hurry when the process reaches the moment of critical mass. This moment of truth is called the **tipping point**.[24] After they spend months or even years to develop a new product, the real challenge for firms is to get consumers to buy and use the product and to do so quickly and in sufficient quantities so they can recover the costs of product development and launch. To accomplish this, marketers must understand the product adoption process.

Next we'll discuss the stages in this process. We'll also see how consumers and businesses differ in their eagerness to adopt new products and how the characteristics of a product affect its adoption (or "infection") rate.

product adoption
The process by which a consumer or business customer begins to buy and use a new good, service, or idea.

diffusion
The process by which the use of a product spreads throughout a population.

tipping point
In the context of product diffusion, the point when a product's sales spike from a slow climb to an unprecedented new level.

Stages in Consumers' Adoption of a New Product

Whether the innovation is the next breakthrough in smartphones or a better mousetrap, individuals and organizations pass through six stages in the adoption process. Figure 8.5 shows the **adoption pyramid**, which reflects how a person goes from being unaware of an innovation through stages from the bottom up of awareness, interest, evaluation, trial, adoption, and confirmation. At every stage in building the pyramid, people drop out of the process, so the proportion of consumers who wind up actually using the innovation on a consistent basis is a mere fraction of those who are exposed to it.

adoption pyramid
Reflects how a person goes from being unaware of an innovation through stages from the bottom up of awareness, interest, evaluation, trial, adoption, and confirmation.

Awareness

Awareness that the innovation exists at all is the first step in the adoption process. To educate consumers about a new product, marketers may conduct a massive advertising

Figure 8.5 *Process* | Adoption Pyramid

Consumers pass through six stages in the adoption of a new product—from being unaware of an innovation to becoming loyal adopters. The right marketing strategies at each stage help ensure a successful adoption.

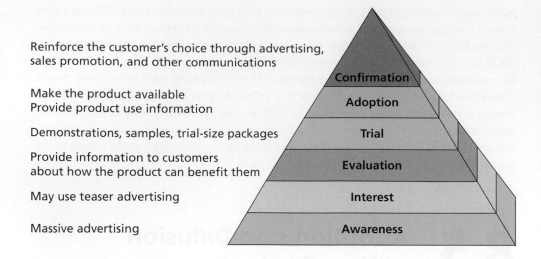

Reinforce the customer's choice through advertising, sales promotion, and other communications — **Confirmation**

Make the product available
Provide product use information — **Adoption**

Demonstrations, samples, trial-size packages — **Trial**

Provide information to customers about how the product can benefit them — **Evaluation**

May use teaser advertising — **Interest**

Massive advertising — **Awareness**

media blitz

A massive advertising campaign that occurs over a relatively short time frame.

campaign: a **media blitz**. For the launch of its Samsung Galaxy S7 smartphone, Samsung chose to place a significant emphasis on developing content that could be shared through social media. Before the product launched Samsung devoted significant resources to the development of a campaign called the "Seven Days of Unboxing," which included a special website and a series of short videos disseminated online. Each video featured a different character going into a sealed room for 30 seconds to unbox the product and then coming out and illustrating what they saw. The videos included (among others) a child, a llama that likes to paint, and a pastry chef. The campaign generated incredible buzz for the product leading up to its official unboxing.[25,26]

At this stage, though, some consumers will say, "So there's a new smartphone out there. So what?" Many of these consumers—a good portion of whom are probably not current Samsung smartphone owners—of course will fall by the wayside and thus drop out of the adoption process. But this strategy works for new products when at least some consumers see a new product as something they want and need and just can't live without.

Slyde Handboards faces a particularly daunting challenge: how to create a market for a product most people have never heard of, and for a sport they know nothing about. Handboards help bodyboarders move faster and have more control in the water, but a very small number of surfers know about them—so far.

Interest

For some of the people who become aware of a new product, a second stage in the adoption process is *interest*. In this stage, a prospective adopter begins to see how a new product might satisfy an existing or newly realized need. Interest also means that consumers look for and are open to information about the innovation. In the months after the launch of the Samsung Galaxy S7, the company continued to build interest in the product with a series of videos featuring the Grammy-winning rapper Lil' Wayne. One of the videos showcased the product's water-resistant capabilities through a comical scene in which Lil' Wayne is shown in a store dousing the device in expensive champagne and then using it to make a mobile payment for another bottle of champagne. The commercials featuring the rapper were viewed well over 10 million times on YouTube and videos and gifs created from them were viewed more than 30 million times on Facebook and Twitter.[27] Other ads featured the Galaxy S7's wireless charging capabilities and its role in enabling the use of the Samsung Gear VR headset for virtual reality experiences. Samsung's efforts to encourage consumers to consider an iPhone alternative paid off big time. The Galaxy S7 had a tremendous product introduction despite Apple's perennially tough competition.

However, this approach doesn't work with all products, so marketers often design teaser advertisements that give prospective customers just enough information about the new product to make them curious and to stimulate their interest. Despite marketers' best efforts, however, some more consumers drop out of the process at this point.

Evaluation

In the *evaluation* stage, we weigh the costs and benefits of the new product. On the one hand, for complex, risky, or expensive products, people think about the innovation a great deal before they will try it. For example, a firm will carefully evaluate spending hundreds of thousands of dollars on manufacturing robotics prior to purchase. Marketers for such products help prospective customers see how such products can benefit them.

In recent years, Callaway (the golf club manufacturer) has partnered with Boeing to deploy some of the aerodynamic know-how and design elements that Boeing has developed for use in airplanes into the development of a new set of drivers. Although some consumers might be initially skeptical of the end product of this partnership, Callaway has worked hard to educate consumers on why this odd coupling of two companies has resulted in better performing golf clubs. To hammer home the point, Callaway convinced several of its sponsored pro golf players to use the new clubs in the Masters tournament. If this product is good enough for arguably the most prestigious tournament in golf, it stands to reason they would make a great addition to most casual golfers' arsenals.[28]

As we've seen in the case of impulse products, sometimes little evaluation may occur before someone decides to buy a good or service. A person may do very little thinking before he or she makes an **impulse purchase**, like the virtual *Tamagotchi* (Japanese for "cute little egg") pets. For these goods, marketers design the product to be eye-catching and appealing to get consumers to notice the product quickly. Tamagotchis certainly did grab the attention of consumers, who bought more than 79 million of them since the first generation came out.[29]

Some potential adopters will evaluate an innovation positively enough to move on to the next stage. Those who do not think the new product will provide adequate benefits drop out at this point.

impulse purchase
A purchase made without any planning or search effort.

Trial

Trial is the stage in the adoption process when potential buyers will actually experience or use the product for the first time. Often marketers stimulate trial when they provide opportunities for consumers to sample the product. Mountain Dew's Kickstart product is positioned primarily as a carbonated energy drink for consumption at the start and end of the day. It is clearly targeted to a younger audience and has been successful since its initial

Mountain Dew's Kickstart truck offers samples to consumers to encourage trial of a new product.

launch in 2013. In 2015, Mountain Dew added two new flavors to the lineup. To stimulate trial of these new products, the company sent out five specially equipped Mountain Dew Kickstart trucks on an eight-month tour to college campuses and sports stadiums to offer samples to consumers. This sort of trial of a product like Kickstart can result in high rates of adoption by the target market, provided its members enjoy the product.[30] Those who do not are unlikely to adopt the new product and fall out at this point.

Adoption

In the *adoption* stage, a prospect actually buys the product (hooray, a sale!). Does this mean that all individuals or organizations that first choose an innovation are permanent customers? No, and that's a mistake many firms make. Marketers need to provide follow-up contacts and communications with adopters to ensure they are satisfied and remain loyal to the new product over time.

Confirmation

After he or she adopts an innovation, a customer weighs expected versus actual benefits and costs. Favorable experiences make it more likely that the customer will become a loyal adopter as initially positive opinions result in *confirmation*. Of course, nothing lasts forever; even a loyal customer may decide that a new product no longer meets his or her expectations and reject it. Hence, marketers understand that reselling the customer in the confirmation stage is often quite important. They provide advertisements, sales presentations, and other communications to reinforce a customer's choice.

Adopter Categories

As we saw previously, *diffusion* describes how the use of a product spreads throughout a population. Of course, marketers prefer their entire target market to immediately adopt a new product, but this is not the case. Both consumers and business customers differ in their willingness to try something new, lengthening the diffusion process by months or even years. Based on adopters' roles in the diffusion process, experts classify them into five categories, as shown in 📷 Figure 8.6: innovators, early adopters, early majority, late majority, and laggards.[31]

Some people like to try new products. Others are so reluctant that you'd think they're afraid of anything new (know anyone like that?). Many innovative technology products are released as a **beta test** to allow usage and feedback from a small number of users who are willing to test the product under normal, everyday conditions of use. The types of innovative technologies commonly beta tested are often called a **bleeding edge technology**—one that is not yet ready for release to the market as a whole, potentially because of issues related to reliability and stability, but is in a suitable state for beta testing and user feedback.[32] To understand how the adopter categories differ, we'll focus

beta test

Limited release of a product, especially an innovative technology, to allow usage and feedback from a small number of customers who are willing to test the product under normal, everyday conditions of use.

bleeding edge technology

An innovative technology that is not yet ready for release to the market as a whole, potentially because of issues related to reliability and stability, but is in a suitable state to be offered for beta testing to evaluate consumer perceptions of its performance and identify any potential issues in its usage.

Figure 8.6 📷 *Snapshot* | Categories of Adopters

Because consumers differ in how willing they are to buy and try a new product, it often takes months or years for most of the population to adopt an innovation.

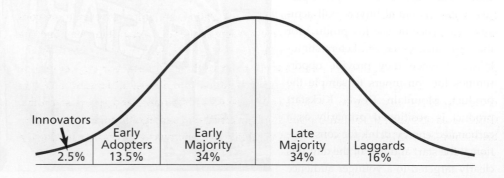

| Innovators 2.5% | Early Adopters 13.5% | Early Majority 34% | Late Majority 34% | Laggards 16% |

below on a threaded example of the adoption of one specific technology from the past that has had a big impact on all of us today—Wi-Fi (wireless fidelity). What would we do without it?

Innovators

Innovators make up roughly the first 2.5 percent of adopters. This segment is extremely adventurous and willing to take risks with new products. Innovators are typically well educated, younger, better off financially than others in the population, and worldly. Innovators who were into new technology knew all about Wi-Fi well before other people had even heard of it. Because innovators pride themselves on trying new products, they purchased laptops with Wi-Fi cards way back in ancient history (1999) when Apple first introduced them in its Mac laptops.

innovators
The first segment (roughly 2.5 percent) of a population to adopt a new product.

Early Adopters

Early adopters, approximately 13.5 percent of adopters, buy product innovations early in the diffusion process but not as early as innovators. Unlike innovators, early adopters are concerned about social acceptance, so they tend to gravitate toward products they believe will make others think they are cutting-edge or fashionable. Typically, they are heavy media users and often are heavy users of the product category. Others in the population often look to early adopters for their opinions on various topics, making early adopters critical to a new product's success. For this reason, marketers often heavily target them in their advertising and other communications efforts. Remember that the innovators pretty much already have the new product in hand before most early adopters purchase.

early adopters
Those who adopt an innovation early in the diffusion process but after the innovators.

Columnists who write about personal technology for most popular magazines and tech websites were testing Wi-Fi in mid-2000. They experienced some problems (like PCs crashing when they set up a wireless network at home), but still they touted the benefits of wireless connectivity. Road warriors adopted the technology as Wi-Fi access spread into airports, hotels, city parks, and other public spaces. Intel, maker of the Centrino mobile platform, launched a major campaign with field-leading Condé Nast's *Traveler* magazine and offered a location guide to T-Mobile hot spots nationwide.

Early Majority

The **early majority**, roughly 34 percent of adopters, avoid being either first or last to try an innovation. They are typically middle-class consumers and are deliberate and cautious. Early majority consumers have slightly above-average education and income levels. When the early majority adopts a product, we no longer consider it new or different—that is, when it gets into their hands, it is, in essence, "established." By 2002, Wi-Fi access was available in more than 500 Starbucks cafés, and monthly subscription prices were dropping rapidly (from $30 to $9.95 per month).

early majority
Those whose adoption of a new product signals a general acceptance of the innovation.

Late Majority

Late majority adopters, about 34 percent of the population, are older, are even more conservative, and typically have lower-than-average levels of education and income. The late majority adopters avoid trying a new product until it is no longer risky. By that time, the product has become an economic necessity for them, or there is pressure from peer groups to adopt. By 2004, Wi-Fi capability was being bundled into almost all laptops, and you could connect in mainstream venues like McDonald's restaurants and sports stadiums. Cities across the country began considering blanket Wi-Fi coverage throughout the entire town through WiMax (Worldwide Interoperability for Microwave Access) technology, a wireless communication standard.

late majority
The adopters who are willing to try new products when there is little or no risk associated with the purchase, when the purchase becomes an economic necessity, or when there is social pressure to purchase.

laggards
The last consumers to adopt an innovation.

Laggards

Laggards, about 16 percent of adopters, are the last in a population to adopt a new product. Laggards are typically lower in income level and education than other adopter categories and are bound by tradition. By the time laggards adopt a product, it may already be superseded by other innovations. By 2006, it would have seemed strange if Wi-Fi or a similar capability was not part of the standard package in even the lowest-priced laptop computer, and people began to become annoyed if Wi-Fi access wasn't available just about everywhere they might go.[33]

Understanding these adopter categories allows marketers to develop strategies that will speed the diffusion or widespread use of their products. For example, early in the diffusion process marketers may put greater emphasis on gaining buzz through targeted social media and advertising in special-interest magazines and websites to attract innovators and early adopters. Later, they may lower the product's price or come out with lower-priced models with fewer "bells and whistles" to attract the late majority. We will talk more about more strategies for new and existing products in the next chapter.

Product Factors That Affect the Rate of Adoption

Not all products are successful, to say the least. Let's see if you've ever heard of these classic boo-boos in new product introduction:

- *Clairol Look of Buttermilk shampoo:* Consumers pondered what exactly *was* the "Look of Buttermilk" and why they would want it.
- *Betamax video player:* Sony refused to allow anyone else to make the players, and the rest of the industry went to VHS format.
- *Snif-T-Panties:* Yes, women's underwear that smelled like bananas, popcorn, whiskey, or pizza. What were they thinking![34]
- *Heinz multicolored ketchup:* What's better than red ketchup? Blue, green, or purple, of course! Consumers, however, didn't equate the look with the flavor.
- *Wow! Chips:* Frito-Lay thought fat-free chips would be a smash hit among the health conscious. Too bad the main ingredient, Olestra, caused stomach cramping and other abdominal issues.[35]
- *Coors Rocky Mountain Sparkling Water:* Despite Coors' efforts to equate their beer's quality with the pureness of the Rocky Mountain water used to produce it, the Coors brand and its famous water source did not translate into successful sales of a sparkling water line. Perhaps this was because consumers were confused as to why a company known for brew was selling sparkling water with a label similar to the one on its more familiar beer cans and bottles.[36]

The reason for most product failures is really pretty simple; consumers did not perceive that the products satisfied a need better than competitive products already on the market. If you *could* predict which new products will succeed and which will fail, you'd quickly be in high demand as a marketing guru by companies worldwide. That's because companies make large investments in new products, but failures are all too frequent. Experts suggest that between one-third and one-half of all new products fail. As you might expect, a lot of people try to develop research techniques that enable them to predict whether a new product will be hot or not.

Researchers identify five characteristics of innovations that affect the rate of adoption: relative advantage, compatibility, complexity, trialability, and observability.[37]

The degree to which a new product has each of these characteristics affects the speed of diffusion. It may take years for a market to widely adopt a new product. Let's take a closer look at the humble microwave oven—a product that was highly innovative in its early days but now is generally a low-priced staple of every kitchen (and every college apartment and dorm)—as an example to better understand why each of these five factors is important:

- **Relative advantage** describes the degree to which a consumer perceives that a new product provides superior benefits. In the case of the microwave oven, consumers in the 1960s did not believe that the product provided important benefits that would improve their lives. But by the late 1970s, that perception had changed because more women had entered the workforce. In the 1960s, a woman had all day to prepare the evening meal, so she didn't need the microwave (yes, at that time there were very few males in the "househusband" role—that's really changed today!). In the 1970s, however, when many women left home for work at 8:00 A.M. and returned home at 6:00 P.M., an appliance that would "magically" defrost a frozen chicken and cook it in 30 minutes provided a genuine advantage.

- **Compatibility** is the extent to which a new product is consistent with existing cultural values, customs, and practices. Did consumers see the microwave oven as being compatible with existing ways of doing things? Hardly. Cooking on paper plates? If you put a paper plate in a conventional oven, you'll likely get a visit from the fire department. By anticipating compatibility issues early in the new-product-development stage, marketing strategies can address such problems in planning communications and consumer education programs, or there may be opportunities to alter product designs to overcome some consumer objections.

- **Complexity** is the degree to which consumers find a new product or its use difficult to understand. Many microwave users today haven't a clue about how a microwave oven cooks food. When appliance manufacturers introduced the first microwaves, they explained that this new technology causes molecules to move and rub together, which creates friction that produces heat. Voilà! Cooked pot roast. But that explanation was too complex and confusing for the homemaker of the Beaver Cleaver days back in the 1960s.

- **Trialability** is the ease of sampling a new product and its benefits. Marketers took an important step in the 1970s to speed up adoption of the microwave oven product trial. Just about every store that sold microwaves invited shoppers to visit the store and sample an entire meal a microwave cooked. Finally, consumers began to understand what the product even was and what it could do!

- **Observability** refers to how visible a new product and its benefits are to others who might adopt it. The ideal innovation is easy to see. For example, for a generation of kids, scooters like the Razor became the hippest way to get around as soon as one preteen saw his or her friends flying by. That same generation observed its friends trading Pokémon cards and wanted to join in (were you part of this craze when you were younger?). In the case of the microwave, it wasn't quite so readily observable for its potential adopters—only close friends and acquaintances who visited someone's home would likely see an early adopter using it. But the fruits of the microwave's labors—tasty food dishes—created lots of buzz at office watercoolers and social events, and its use spread quickly. Too bad they didn't have social media back then—if they had, it's a sure bet that the rate of adoption of microwaves would have been a whole lot faster.

relative advantage
The degree to which a consumer perceives that a new product provides superior benefits.

compatibility
The extent to which a new product is consistent with existing cultural values, customs, and practices.

complexity
The degree to which consumers find a new product or its use difficult to understand.

trialability
The ease of sampling a new product and its benefits.

observability
How visible a new product and its benefits are to others who might adopt it.

MyLab Marketing™

Go to **mymktlab.com** to complete the problems marked with this icon
as well as additional Marketing Metrics questions only available in
MyLab Marketing.

Objective Summary ➡ Key Terms ➡ Apply

CHAPTER 8
Study Map

8.1 Objective Summary (pp. 258–261)

Explain how value is derived through different product layers.

Products can be physical goods, services, ideas, people, or places. A good is a *tangible* product, something that we can see, touch, smell, hear, taste, or possess. In contrast, *intangible* products—services, ideas, people, and places—are products that we can't always see, touch, taste, smell, or possess. Marketers think of the product as more than just a thing that comes in a package. They view it as a bundle of attributes that includes the packaging, brand name, benefits, and supporting features in addition to a physical good. The key issue is the marketer's role in creating the value proposition to develop and market products appropriately.

The core product is the basic product category benefits and customized benefit(s) the product provides. The actual product is the physical good or delivered service, including the packaging and brand name. The augmented product includes both the actual product and any supplementary services, such as warranty, credit, delivery, installation, and so on.

Key Terms

attributes, p. 259

good, p. 259

core product, p. 259

actual product, p. 260

augmented product, p. 261

8.2 Objective Summary (pp. 261–265)

Describe how marketers classify products.

Marketers generally classify goods and services as either consumer or B2B products. They further classify consumer products according to how long they last and by how they

are purchased. Durable goods provide benefits for months or years, whereas nondurable goods are used up quickly or are useful for only a short time. Consumers purchase convenience products frequently with little effort. Customers carefully gather information and compare different brands on their attributes and prices before buying shopping products. Specialty products have unique characteristics that are important to the buyer. Customers have little interest in unsought products until a need arises. Business products are for commercial uses by organizations. Marketers classify business products according to how they are used, for example, equipment: maintenance, repair, and operating (MRO) products; raw materials; processed materials; specialized services; and component parts.

Key Terms

durable goods, p. 261

nondurable goods, p. 261

convenience product, p. 262

staple products, p. 263

**consumer packaged good (CPG) or
    fast-moving consumer good (FMCG), p. 263**

impulse products, p. 263

emergency products, p. 263

shopping products, p. 263

specialty products, p. 264

unsought products, p. 264

equipment, p. 264

maintenance, repair, and operating (MRO) products, p. 264

raw materials, p. 264

processed materials, p. 265

specialized services, p. 265

component parts, p. 265

8.3 Objective Summary (pp. 265–267)

Understand the importance and types of product innovations.

Innovations are anything consumers perceive to be new. Understanding new products is important to companies because of the fast pace of technological advancement, the high cost to companies of developing new products, and the contributions to society that new products can make. Marketers classify innovations by their degree of newness. A continuous innovation is a modification of an existing product, a dynamically continuous innovation provides a greater change in a product, and a discontinuous innovation is a new product that creates major changes in people's lives.

Key Terms

innovation, p. 265

creativity, p. 265

continuous innovation, p. 266

knockoff, p. 266

dynamically continuous innovation, p. 267

discontinuous innovation, p. 267

convergence, p. 267

8.4 Objective Summary (pp. 268–273)

Show how firms develop new products.

In new product development, marketers generate product ideas from which product concepts are first developed and then screened. Next, they develop a marketing strategy and conduct a business analysis to estimate the profitability of the new product. Technical development includes planning how the product will be manufactured and may mean obtaining a patent. Next, an actual or a simulated test market may be conducted to assess the effectiveness of the new product in the market. Finally, in the commercialization phase the product is launched, and the entire marketing plan is implemented.

Key Terms

research and development (R&D), p. 268

new product development (NPD), p. 268

idea generation (ideation), p. 268

value co-creation, p. 268

product concept development and screening, p. 269

technical success, p. 269

commercial success, p. 269

business analysis, p. 270

technical development, p. 270

prototypes, p. 271

patent, p. 271

market test (or test market), p. 271

simulated market test, p. 272

commercialization, p. 272

crowdfunding, p. 272

8.5 Objective Summary (pp. 273–279)

Explain the process of product adoption and the diffusion of innovations.

Product adoption is the process by which an individual begins to buy and use a new product, whereas the diffusion of innovations is how a new product spreads throughout a population. The stages in the adoption process are awareness, interest, trial, adoption, and confirmation. To better understand the diffusion process, marketers classify consumers—according to their readiness to adopt new products—as innovators, early adopters, early majority, late majority, and laggards.

Five product characteristics that have an important effect on how quickly (or if) a new product will be adopted by consumers are relative advantage, compatibility, product complexity, trialability, and observability. Similar to individual consumers, organizations differ in their readiness to adopt new products based on characteristics of the organization, its management, and characteristics of the innovation.

Key Terms

product adoption, p. 273

diffusion, p. 273

tipping point, p. 273

adoption pyramid, p. 273

media blitz, p. 274

impulse purchase, p. 275

beta test, p. 276

bleeding edge technology, p. 276

innovators, p. 277

early adopters, p. 277

early majority, p. 277

late majority, p. 277

laggards, p. 278

relative advantage, p. 279

compatibility, p. 279

complexity, p. 279

trialability, p. 279

observability, p. 279

Chapter **Questions** and **Activities**

Concepts: Test Your Knowledge

8-1. What is a good? What are the differences between tangible and intangible products?

8-2. What is the difference between the core product, the actual product, and the augmented product?

8-3. What is the difference between a durable good and a nondurable good? What are the main differences among convenience, shopping, and specialty products?

8-4. What is an unsought product? How do marketers make such products attractive to consumers?

8-5. What types of products are bought and sold in B2B markets?

8-6. What is a new product? Why is understanding new products so important to marketers? What are the types of innovations?

8-7. What is R&D, and what is its importance to marketers and the product development process?

8-8. List and explain the steps marketers undergo to develop new products.

8-9. What is a test market? What are some pros and cons of test markets?

8-10. Explain the stages a consumer goes through in the adoption of a new product.

8-11. List and explain the categories of adopters.

8-12. What product factors affect the rate of adoption of innovations?

Activities: Apply What You've Learned

⭐ **8-13.** *Creative Homework/Short Project* Assume that you are employed in the marketing department of a firm that is producing an electric scooter. In developing this product, you realize that it is important to provide a core product, an actual product, and an augmented product that meets the needs of customers. Develop an outline of how your firm might provide these three product layers in the electric scooter.

8-14. *In Class, 15–20 Minutes for Teams* Phase 4 of the new product development process is business analysis. This is when the organization decides on whether or not to bring their product concept to market. Read the following potential ideas for an airline: how would you go about evaluating each of them? That is, how should you structure your assessment criteria?

    1. The ability to order customized meals from the on-screen menu, as and when required

    2. Being able to book a seat in a section that does not have the ability to recline, ensuring that you always have space in your own seat

    3. Budget seating options where there is very restricted legroom but at very low prices

    4. Premium economy (midway between business-class and economy/coach), which is an adults-only section of the plane

    5. The premium economy section of the plane, which has a small circular walking track that passengers can access for 10 minutes at a time on long flights.

Then, with your class, screen one or more of the ideas for possible further product development.

8-15. *In Class, 10–25 Minutes for Teams* As an entrepreneur, you know that innovation will play a huge role in your new business. With your team, brainstorm briefly to define what your new business will be—let the sky be your limit. Then create a short outline that defines the various types of innovations—continuous, dynamically continuous, and discontinuous—and give examples of each. Which innovation type would be the easiest when starting out? Which innovation type brings the greatest reward? Which innovation type ultimately makes the most sense for your new business?

⭐ **8-16.** *Creative Homework/Short Project* As a member of a new product team with your company, you are working to develop an electric car jack that would make changing car tires easier. You are considering conducting a test market for this new product. Outline the pros and cons for test marketing this product. What are your recommendations?

8-17. *For Further Research (Individual)* Every year, marketers come out with many new or new and improved products. Using the web, research a new or new and improved product and summarize either how marketers developed and tested that product before taking it to market or how they created awareness about that new product once they developed it.

8-18. *Creative Homework/Short Project* Select a company and identify an existing product sold by that company that could potentially be further developed to meet new consumer needs. Using the selected product, develop an approach to engage consumers in the process of value co-creation with the objective of developing a new version of the selected product.

8-19. *For Further Research (Individual)* Select a recently successful product that you believe is innovative and do some research on how the product was introduced. Using the adopter categories in the chapter, identify adopters of the product that you consider to be innovators and provide evidence of specific behaviors and characteristics that support the placement of these consumers within that adopter category.

8-20. *For Further Research (Individual)* Identify an innovative product that was just recently introduced into the market and using the five characteristics that affect the rate of adoption (relative advantage, compatibility, complexity, trialability, and observability) evaluate the product on each respective characteristic. Based on your evaluation state whether you believe the innovation will be quickly adopted, slowly adopted, or adopted at a rate somewhere in between. Use your best judgment in making this determination.

8-21. *For Further Research (Individual)* Sometimes products are massively successful because consumers find a use for them separate from what the developing company initially envisioned. Find two products online that fit this description and identify their initial intended use(s), then what other use(s) consumers found for them, and finally whether companies adjusted their marketing efforts around the products after becoming aware of how consumers were actually using the products.

Concepts: Apply Marketing Metrics

In the chapter, we define creativity and discuss how it relates to innovation. Innovation can be measured in terms of number of successful new products as well as a variety of secondary measures related to those products (e.g., new product launches per year, per employee, and success rate versus failure rate—cast on the basis of how the firm defines product success and failure). Innovation is fueled by R&D expenditures, as the chapter notes.

But what about measuring creativity itself? Some experts have argued that an overfocus on metrics can kill creativity.[38] They might argue that the phrase "creativity metric" is an oxymoron. There's always been a right-brain/left-brain argument that marketing, to be optimally successful, has to nurture both the creative and the analytical. Has the obsession with marketing metrics over the past decade squelched essential creativity emanating from the right brain?

8-22. What is your viewpoint about measuring creativity? Do you believe it is more constructive or damaging to organizational innovation? Support your opinions.

8-23. Point out a few well-known organizations that you believe are quite creative. How do you know that they are creative—that is, what specific evidence can you cite that indicates that a high level of creativity is practiced?

Choices: What Do You Think?

8-24. *Critical Thinking* A market test (or some form of test marketing) is an optional step close to the full-scale launch of a new product. However, a market test is also likely to be quite expensive, reveal the firm's actions to its key competitors, and potentially send confusing signals to consumers in the tested marketplace. In what circumstances do you think that a market test would be warranted? (In your answer, think about competitive situations, degree of innovation of the product, potential product cannibalization, impact on service and logistics, and so on.)

8-25. *Critical Thinking* The chapter outlines five product factors that influence the rate of adoption for a new product. In this section, the textbook outlines the adoption of the microwave oven and some of the challenges it faced in becoming a mainstream kitchen product. In recent years, wearable fitness technology (e.g., Fit Bits) has become more common. Using the microwave oven discussion as a guide, evaluate the likely adoption of wearable fitness technology using the same five product factors. From your analysis, do you think that wearable technology will become as widely adopted as the microwave oven?

⭐ 8-26. *Critical Thinking* Discontinuous innovations are totally new products—something seldom seen in the marketplace. What are some examples of discontinuous innovations introduced in the past 50 years? Why are there so few discontinuous innovations? What products

have companies recently introduced that you believe will end up being regarded as discontinuous innovations?

⭐ 8-27. *Ethics* For several decades, consumer products—everything from vaccines to cosmetics—have been tested on animals. Do you think product testing on animals should be legal or illegal? Does your position change depending on what kind of animal the product is tested on (e.g., a mouse versus a dog)? What are some instances of when it would be acceptable or unacceptable to test products on animals (e.g., medical necessity versus enhancing one's looks)?

8-28. *Ethics* Should a company opt to manufacture a product with a cheaper component if it knows that its inclusion will moderately increase the physical safety risk of the product for consumers? What if it is known that the increase in cost of using the more expensive and safer component will lead to about a 50 percent lower adoption rate for the product by consumers, does it become more justifiable to do so then?

8-29. *Critical Thinking* Consider the differences in marketing to consumer markets versus business markets. Which aspects of the processes of product adoption and diffusion apply to both markets? Which aspects are unique to one or the other? Provide evidence of your findings.

8-30. *Ethics* In this chapter, we explained that knockoffs are slightly modified copies of original product designs. Should knockoffs be illegal? Who is hurt by knockoffs? Is the marketing of knockoffs good or bad for consumers in the short run? In the long run?

8-31. *Critical Thinking* It is not necessarily true that all new products benefit consumers or society. What are some new products that have made our lives better? What are some new products that have actually been harmful to consumers or to society? Should there be a way to monitor or "police" new products that are introduced to the marketplace?

8-32. *Critical Thinking* Patent trolling is the practice of acquiring patents with the sole purpose of making money off of them either by suing those who infringe on the patent or by licensing the patent. What do you think of the practice of patent trolling? What effect does patent trolling have on product innovation?

8-33. *Critical Thinking* Are there potential risks to involving consumers in the development of new products through processes associated with value co-creation as discussed in the chapter? What factors might make a value co-creation approach more or less suitable for the development of a new product?

8-34. *Critical Thinking* Products such as video games produced for traditional gaming consoles used to be sold only as physical items, but of course now they can also be downloaded onto a gaming console (such as Xbox One or PlayStation 4). For a video game that is *exclusively* sold as a download, how do you think the new product development process might vary compared to the process involved in producing a video game sold exclusively as a physical product?

Miniproject: Learn by Doing

One of the most successful consumer products of all time is the Apple iPhone. Launched in 2007 after 2½ years of development, it now generates more than half of Apple's revenue.

However, Apple's new product development path was not smooth, and they had multiple challenges along the way. The phone design changed several times, they had difficulties organizing suppliers, patents for certain technologies had to be acquired, and so on.

Your task in this mini project is to research the new product development process undertaken by Apple for the development of the iPhone.

8-35. How similar is the new product process undertaken by Apple with the development of the iPhone as compared to the new product process outlined in the textbook? Why do you think there may be some differences between the textbook process and the real-life process used by Apple?

Marketing in **Action** Case | Real Choices at Facebook

Can virtual reality go mainstream? Facebook would like to believe the answer to that question is a resounding "yes!" The company has big plans for its virtual reality offering, the Oculus Rift, which is designed to transform how people play games, view videos, and share the experiences of their social lives. The Rift is one of three premium virtual reality headsets new to the market, and it's no small market with estimated value at more than $16 billion. Facebook CEO Mark Zuckerberg believes that virtual reality has come a long way in a short time and that we are "entering the golden age of video and animation."

Inspired by the gaming market, Palmer Luckey, founder of Oculus, created a prototype for a virtual reality headset that would later become the Oculus Rift. In 2012, he began a Kickstarter crowdfunding campaign to finance the development of the product, eventually generating more than $2.4 million in funds. Over the next few years, the product went through five working prototypes released to developers and the public for feedback. In 2014, Zuckerberg raised the question of what will be the next best thing in tech, and the answer was that it would be the viewing of movies, television, and other content in an immersive 3-D environment. Soon after, Facebook purchased Oculus for $2 billion.

In 2016, the Rift went on sale for $599, supported by dozens of games. Other uses include viewing conventional movies and videos, 360° 3D videos, and "virtual reality movies." But alas, problems plagued the early stages of the product's introduction. The first shipments were delayed by a component shortage in the production process. Jason Rubin, Head of Studio, expressed the company's embarrassment, apologized for the delays, and offered free shipping to everyone who had placed orders. In addition, some people complained of motion sickness when using the Rift. Oculus has since issued developers a software fix that reduces the likelihood that anyone will suffer any nausea.

Other companies are rushing to join the virtual reality marketplace as well. Two of the major players are HTC and Sony. HTC, working with Valve Corp., introduced the Vive, a $799 headset designed to use while the user is standing up and walking around. Sony introduced the $399 PlayStation VR headset to compete as a lower priced option for the market. In conjunction with its launch, Sony created a new PlayStation 4 with better performance to effectively run the virtual reality options.

Facebook understands that the Rift represents a really new technology and thus will initially appeal to a limited market, although the growth potential is very high. Zuckerberg recognizes that video is presently the most popular mode of sharing but that virtual reality will soon be in second place. The outlook is favorable, and some professional reviewers have suggested that this may be the biggest tech product since the introduction of the iPhone (although using the Oculus Rift is significantly more complicated than using a smartphone). Yet despite the potential, success for the product and the technology overall is not guaranteed. Now that Facebook has taken the steps to develop its new product, it has to find ways to convince customers to adopt it.

You Make the Call

8-36. What is the decision facing Facebook?

8-37. What factors are important in understanding this decision situation?

8-38. What are the alternatives?

8-39. What decision(s) do you recommend?

8-40. What are some ways to implement your recommendation?

Sources: Based on Joshua Brustein, "Oculus Kicks Off Virtual Reality's Slow-Motion Revolution," *Bloomberg Businessweek* (March 28, 2016), http://www.bloomberg.com/news/articles/2016-03-28/oculus-kicks-off-virtual-reality-s-slow-motion-revolution (accessed April 28, 2016); Max Chafkin, "Why Facebook's $2 Billion Bet on Oculus Rift Might One Day Connect Everyone on Earth," *Vanity Fair* (September 8, 2015), http://www.vanityfair.com/news/2015/09/oculus-rift-mark-zuckerberg-cover-story-palmer-luckey (accessed April 28, 2016); Deepa Seetharaman and Sarah E. Needleman, "Some Oculus Rift Shipments Delayed by Parts Shortage," *The Wall Street Journal* (April 4, 2016), http://www.wsj.com/articles/some-oculus-rift-shipments-delayed-by-parts-shortage-1459705051 (accessed April 28, 2016).

MyLab Marketing™

Go to **mymktlab.com** for the following Assisted-graded writing questions:

8-41. *Creative Homework/Short Project.* Assume that you are the director of marketing for the company that has developed a smartphone to outdo the iPhone. How would you go about convincing the late majority to go ahead and adopt it—especially because they still haven't quite caught onto the iPhone yet?

8-42. *Creative Homework/Short Project.* You work for a large retailer and have been asked by a professor at the local university to give a presentation on how your business classifies products. Prepare a slide show that defines the various product categories, including any subcategories, and give at least three examples of each. Include photos of the products where possible.

Product II: Product Strategy, Branding, and Product Management

Courtesy of Becky Frankiewicz, PepsiCo, Inc.

Becky Frankiewicz
▼ **A Decision Maker at the Quaker Oats Company**

Becky Frankiewicz is the Senior Vice President and General Manager of Quaker Foods North America, a subsidiary of PepsiCo, Inc., an important better-for-you brand within the company's global growth strategy.

Becky began her PepsiCo career in finance working in the strategy/mergers and acquisitions practice for Frito Lay. Since then she's held a variety of roles across marketing and innovation for Quaker Foods North America and the Global Nutrition Group.

Most recently Becky spent two years operating in a sales capacity, leading and developing PepsiCo's Costco business globally across nine countries. As part of this role, she was responsible for setting the long-term strategic plan, delivering the annual operating plan, and managing the overall relationship with the customer.

In October 2014, Becky rejoined the Quaker Foods North America team as general manager, a role that allows her to serve as the keeper of a loved and trusted health and wellness brand, steeped in nearly 140 years of heritage.

Before PepsiCo, Becky worked in strategic consulting with Deloitte and Andersen Consulting and held a series of management and leadership roles at Procter & Gamble. She holds a BBA in Marketing from the University of Texas and an MBA in Finance from the University of Texas San Antonio.

Passionate about the development of female leaders in business, Becky is the executive sponsor of PepsiCo's Women's Inclusion Network and sits on the Board of Directors for Girls in the Game, a nonprofit committed to developing leadership in at-risk teen girls.

Becky resides in the suburbs of Chicago with her husband and three daughters.

Becky's Info

What I do when I'm not working:
I have three beautiful daughters—Parker (15), Payton (13), and Piper (11)—who keep me quite busy. They are all very strong students in school and all three dance competitively outside of school. They are my "why" to borrow Simon Sinek's term. I want to empower them to be and do whatever they choose in life and show them that you can have a family and achieve your career goals. My husband, Marek, and

I were college sweethearts and have been married for 20 years! He's a keeper.

First job out of school:
I worked in retail sales for Procter & Gamble going door to door to grocery stores. It was a critical experience as it taught me what retail managers' value and gave a bit of insight into how consumers make decisions. I say a bit of insight—as it's the reason I've stayed in this business.

With all of the tools we have today in marketing, there is not a reliable tool to predict consumer behavior. It's the beauty of humanity; we are all different in certain ways and we continue to change making us ultimately unpredictable!

Business book I'm reading now:
The Road to Character by David Brooks

My hero:
My mom. She worked outside the home at a time very few women did and although I intellectually know she worked long hours, I never felt her absence at home. She taught me very early that I could do whatever I wanted in life—and I believed her. She is truly remarkable!

My motto to live by:
Listen for what you do not want to hear. As you grow as a leader—it becomes harder for you to get the "real" story so you have to listen very well. A wise person once shared this motto with me, and I've adopted it.

What drives me:
My family, helping consumers live more balanced lives, feeling like I'm on the path for my purpose.

Here's my problem...

Real **People**, Real **Choices**

Quaker is one of the oldest registered trademarks in the United States. The original trademark was filed in 1877, so the brand has a rich history. We know (and love) that for many people, Quaker is synonymous with oatmeal. It's what they grew up eating, continue to eat in their adulthood, and in many cases feed their own children.

Through a commitment to innovation, over the last several decades the Quaker brand has been able to expand its offerings beyond traditional oatmeal to cross into many different types of products and sub-brands. This includes things like granola bars (e.g., the Quaker Chewy sub-brand) as well as ready-to-eat cereals (e.g., the Quaker Oatmeal Squares or Quaker Life Cereal sub-brands). Although oatmeal continues to—and will always—be our heart and soul, we actually make many different types of wholesome and delicious products for people to enjoy.

Further, although Quaker has always thought of our core consumer as moms (who act as the primary grocery shopper for their families), the brand has at times had to evolve how we position ourselves given that consumers and their preferences are constantly changing, especially when it comes to food.

When I joined the Quaker business in October 2014, one of the first things I did was examine our marketing approach. For the last several years, Quaker had been operating under what is called a "master brand strategy," in that it applied a singular brand position, message, and look and feel across all Quaker products and sub-brands. It also targeted the same, universal audience (in our case, women ages 25–44, with 2 + school-aged kids). This strategy came to life as a campaign called "Quaker Up," and carried the message that Quaker could help fuel families by delivering good energy through the power of whole grain oats.

Although our initial intent was to continue operating under this type of master brand strategy, we had to pause given that we were not seeing the halo we hoped for across our full portfolio. The hypothesis was that communicating a singular benefit was potentially a lowest common denominator across our full business, but it was clear that some products were benefiting from the singular message more than others.

The key question became clear: would using the Quaker Up/energy message across all products and sub-brands drive return on investment (ROI) as effectively and efficiently as having a separate message for each product?

Becky considered her **Options** 1·2

Option 1

Continue on the current path with the same brand positioning and target through the master brand approach. This would be the safest route to maintain the equity of the brand, and we could confidently estimate ROI based on the brand's performance in prior years. In addition, sticking with the master brand approach would be the most economical from a media buy perspective because it required a lower spend on each portion of the portfolio, and we hoped the singular Quaker message would have a halo effect that equally benefitted all of our products.

Option 2

Explore a new positioning and target through a consumer deep dive that could halo across all products yet be customized with different reasons to believe (meaning proof that the brand delivers the benefits that it promises) for each. At a minimum, this option would benefit the business because the brand management team would gain a deeper understanding of the benefits consumers are looking for in the current marketplace. Additionally, these insights would help improve our brand positioning with credible reasons to believe, which should accelerate growth. On the other hand, developing a new positioning strategy would be less efficient compared to the master brand approach because we would have to invest additional marketing funds for each category or sub-brand across the portfolio. Therefore, we would likely have to prioritize how we spent our dollars across products. Plus, there is the risk that the change in positioning may not resonate with consumers of a well-established, mature brand like Quaker.

Now put yourself in Becky's shoes: Which option would you choose, and why?

You Choose

Which **Option** would you choose, and **why**?
□ Option 1   □ Option 2

See what **option** Becky chose in **MyLab Marketing**™.

MyLab Marketing™

⭐ **Improve Your Grade!**

Over 10 million students improved their results using the Pearson MyLabs.
Visit **mymktlab.com** for simulations, tutorials, and end-of-chapter problems.

9.1 Product Planning: Develop Product Objectives and Product Strategy

OBJECTIVE
Discuss the different product objectives and strategies a firm may choose.

(pp. 288–294)

What makes one product fail and another succeed? It's worth reemphasizing what you learned in Chapter 3: *Firms that plan well succeed.* Product planning plays a big role in the firm's *market planning.* And among the famous four Ps of the marketing mix, each P is not created equal—that is, the best pricing, promotion, and physical distribution strategies cannot overcome fundamental problems with the product over the long run! Hence, product planning takes on special significance in marketing.

Strategies outlined within the product specify how the firm expects to develop a value proposition that will meet marketing objectives. Product planning is guided by the continual process of **product management**, which is the systematic and usually team-based approach to coordinating all aspects of a product's strategy development and execution. In some companies, product management is sometimes also called *brand management*, and the terms refer to essentially the same thing. The organization members that coordinate these processes are called *product managers* or *brand managers*. We discuss the role of these individuals in more detail later in the chapter.

As more and more competitors enter the global marketplace and as technology moves forward at an ever-increasing pace, firms create products that grow, mature, and then decline at faster and faster speeds. This acceleration underscores that smart product management strategies are more critical than ever. Marketers just don't have the luxury of trying one thing, finding out it doesn't work, and then trying the next thing; they have to multitask when it comes to product management!

In Chapter 8, we talked about how marketers think about products—both core and augmented—and about how companies develop and introduce new products. In this chapter, we finish the product part of the story as we see how companies manage products, and then we examine the steps in product planning, shown in 🏃 Figure 9.1. These steps include developing product objectives and the related strategies required to successfully market products as they evolve from "newbies" to tried-and-true favorites—and in some cases finding new markets for these favorites. Next, we discuss branding and packaging, two of the more important tactical decisions product planners make. Finally, we examine how firms organize for effective product management. Let's start with an overview of how firms develop product-related objectives.

Getting Product Objectives Right

When marketers develop product strategies, they make decisions about product benefits, features, styling, branding, labeling, and packaging. But what do they want to accomplish? Clearly stated product objectives provide focus and direction. They should support the broader marketing objectives of the business unit in addition to being consistent with the firm's overall mission. For example, the objectives of the firm may focus on return on investment (ROI). Marketing objectives then may concentrate on building market share or the unit or dollar sales volume necessary to attain that ROI. Product objectives need to specify how product decisions will contribute to reaching a desired market share or level of sales.

To be effective, product-related objectives must be measurable, clear, and unambiguous—and feasible. Also, they must indicate a specific time frame. Consider, for

product management
The systematic and usually team-based approach to coordinating all aspects of a product's strategy development and execution.

Figure 9.1 🏃 *Process* | Steps to Manage Products

Effective product strategies come from a series of orderly steps.

example, how Amy's, a popular organic and health-conscious frozen ethnic entrée manufacturer, might state its product objectives:

- "In the upcoming fiscal year, reduce the fat and calorie content of our products by 15 percent to satisfy consumers' health concerns."
- "Introduce three new products this quarter to the product line to take advantage of increased consumer interest in Mexican foods."
- "During the coming fiscal year, improve the chicken entrées to the extent that consumers will rate them better tasting than the competition."

Planners must keep in touch with their customers so that their objectives accurately respond to their needs. In Chapter 2, we introduced you to the idea of *competitive intelligence*, and an up-to-date knowledge of competitive product innovations is important to develop product objectives. Above all, these objectives should consider the *long-term implications* of product decisions. Planners who sacrifice the long-term health of the firm to reach short-term sales or financial goals choose a risky course. Product planners may focus on one or more individual products at a time, or they may look at a group of product offerings as a whole. Next, we briefly examine both of these approaches. We also look at one important product objective: product quality.

Objectives and Strategies for Individual Products

Everybody loves the MINI Cooper. But it wasn't just luck or happenstance that turned this product into a global sensation. Just how do you launch a new car that's only 142 inches long and makes people laugh when they see it? Its parent company BMW succeeded by deliberately but gently poking fun at the MINI Cooper's small size. The original launch of the MINI Cooper included bolting the MINI onto the top of a Ford Excursion with a sign reading, "What are you doing for fun this weekend?" BMW also mocked up full-size MINIs to look like coin-operated kiddie rides you find outside grocery stores with a sign proclaiming, "Rides $16,850. Quarters only." The advertising generated buzz in the 20- to 34-year-old target market, and today the MINI is no joke.

As a smaller brand, the MINI never had a huge advertising budget—in fact it was the first launch of a new car in modern times that didn't include TV advertising. Instead, the MINI launched with print, outdoor billboards, and online ads. It has an active and ongoing social media presence. The objective wasn't a traditional heavy car launch; rather, BMW envisioned a "discovery process" by which target consumers would find out about the brand on their own and fall in love with it. Ads promoted "motoring" instead of driving, and magazine inserts included MINI-shaped air fresheners and pullout games. *Wired* magazine even ran a cardboard foldout of the MINI suggesting that readers assemble and drive it around their desks making "putt-putt" noises. *Playboy* came up with the idea of a six-page MINI "centerfold" complete with the car's vital statistics and hobbies. By the end of its first year on the market, the MINI was rated the second-most memorable new product of the year!

Like the MINI, product strategies often focus on a single new product. (As an interesting sidebar, enough customers have complained about the cramped quarters in the MINI's backseat—it is, after all, a "mini"—that BMW acquiesced and introduced a "larger MINI." Now that's an oxymoron—something like a "jumbo shrimp"!)[1] Strategies for individual products may be quite different, depending on the situation: new products, regional products, mature products, or other differences. For new products, not surprisingly, the objectives relate heavily to producing a very successful introduction.

After a firm experiences success with a product in a local or regional market, it may decide to introduce it nationally. Trader Joe's, for example, opened its doors in Pasadena, California, in 1967 (and it's still there today). But it wasn't until 1993 that the brand moved outside of California, heading east to Phoenix, Arizona. Today, you can find Trader Joe's throughout most of the country, though you won't yet find it in all 50 states.[2]

For mature products like 80-year-old Lay's potato chips, product objectives may be focused on how to leverage the brand to develop new varieties of the product that appeal to changing consumer tastes. Today there are four different main categories of Lay's potato chips (Traditional Lay's, Wavy, Kettle Cooked, and Stax). Each of these categories has a variety of different flavors that range from the more traditional "Barbeque" to the more adventurous "Kettle Cooked Wasabi Ginger."[3] Lay's involves its consumers in the process of developing new flavors through its "Do Us A Flavor" contest in which anyone is allowed to submit a flavor idea and the public is able to vote on their favorite flavors, with the ultimate winner taking home a cool $1 million or 1 percent of net sales through a set time frame, whichever is higher). The winner also gets the satisfaction of knowing that this winning flavor actually will be taken to market as the newest Lay's potato chip flavor. In 2015 the winning submission was (drumroll please): Biscuits and Gravy, proving that creativity and fun have a place in keeping even an 80-plus-year-old brand alive.[4]

Objectives and Strategies for Multiple Products

Although a small firm might get away with a focus on one product, larger firms often sell a set of related products. This means that strategic decisions affect two or more products simultaneously. The firm must think in terms of its entire portfolio of products. As Figure 9.2 shows, product planning means developing *product line* and *product mix* strategies to encompass multiple offerings.

A **product line** is a firm's total product offering to satisfy a group of target customers. For example, as we saw in Chapter 4 Campbell's Soup offers several different brands to satisfy different consumer tastes and needs. One is Campbell's Slow Kettle® soup, which is positioned as a more luxurious experience for more discerning consumers. Slow Kettle® is preservative free, features creative combinations of ingredients, and employs a slow simmer method of cooking to draw out each soup's unique flavor. On the other hand,

product line
A firm's total product offering designed to satisfy a single need or desire of target customers.

Figure 9.2 *Process* | Objectives for Single and Multiple Products

Product objectives provide focus and direction for product strategies. Objectives can focus on a single product or a group of products.

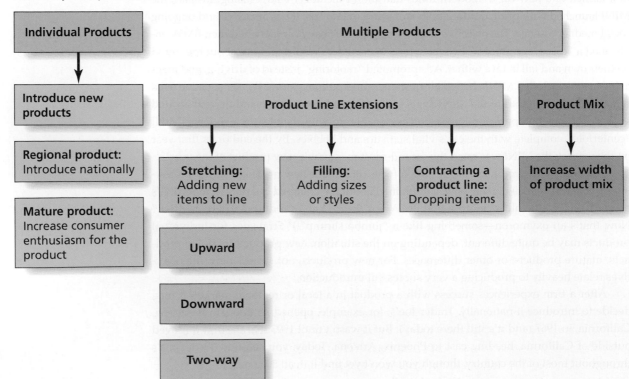

Campbell's Soup on the Go is positioned as a quick snack for those with limited time to eat. Soup on the Go features simple soups packaged in a cup that is microwavable for heating, easy to grip with one hand, and consumed by tilting the container in the same way one would do for a can of soda.

The **product line length** is determined by the number of separate items within the same category, in Campbell's case a total of nine brands each with multiple **stock-keeping units (SKUs)**. An SKU is a unique identifier for each distinct product. Hence, for Campbell's Soup on the Go, each SKU would represent a unique item within the brand, which in this case would be each of the different soup recipes sold under that brand.[5]

A full line strategy targets many customer segments to boost sales potential. In contrast, a *limited-line strategy*, with fewer product variations, can improve the firm's image if consumers perceive it as a specialist with a clear, specific position in the market. A great example is Rolls-Royce Motor Cars, which BMW also owns (how about that—from MINI Coopers to Rolls—quite a stable of brands!). Rolls-Royce makes expensive, handcrafted cars built to each customer's exact specifications and for decades maintained a unique position in the automobile industry. Every Rolls Phantom that rolls out the factory door is truly a unique work of art.[6]

Organizations may decide to extend their product line by adding more brands or models. In recent years the fragrance company Estee Lauder has acquired several high-end, niche fragrance brands such as "By Kilian" and "Le Labo" to take advantage of a consumer trend toward fragrances that more closely express each wearer's individuality.[7]

When a firm stretches its product line, it must decide on the best direction to go. If a firm's current product line includes middle- and lower-end items, an *upward line stretch* adds new items—higher-priced entrants that claim better quality or offer more bells and whistles. Kia has been working to stretch its low-priced product line upward with new brand-building activities and a new luxury car. To achieve that objective, in 2013 Kia launched its $66,000 luxury K900, positioning it between the BMW 5-Series (at about $50,000) and the BMW 7-Series (at about $75,000).[8] It is often challenging for a brand to make the move from offering products in the mid-to-low priced category to offering a high-end product, and the K900 has experienced this first hand in the few years since it was launched. Lower-than-expected sales motivated Kia to cut the price of the Premium trim version of the car (one tier below the luxury trim version initially launched and discussed) by $5,000 down to $55,400.[9]

Conversely, a *downward line stretch* augments a line when it adds items at the lower end. Here, the firm must take care not to blur the images of its higher-priced, upper-end offerings. Rolex, for example, may not want to run the risk of cheapening its image with a new watch line to compete with Timex or Swatch. In some cases, a firm may come to the realization that its current target market is too small. In this case, the product strategy may call for a *two-way stretch* that adds products at both the upper and lower ends.

A *filling-out strategy* adds sizes or styles not previously available in a product category. Mars Candy did this when it introduced Reese's Minis as a knockoff of its already crazy-popular full-sized product. In other cases, the best strategy may be to *contract*—meaning reduce the size of a product line, particularly when some of the items are not profitable and the complexity of managing them becomes detrimental to the company. For example, P&G agreed in 2015 to sell a number of its beauty brands and associated products to the company Coty. Included in the deal were such well-known brands as Cover Girl and Clairol. This strategic move was designed to free up company resources at P&G to focus on higher potential brands and reduce the costs and complexities associated with managing a large number of underperforming brands within the company's brand portfolio.[10]

We've seen that there are many ways a firm can modify its product line to meet the competition or take advantage of new opportunities. To further explore these product strategy decisions, let's stick with the P&G theme and return to the "glamorous" world of dish detergents. By the way, P&G basically invented the product management system

product line length
Determined by the number of separate items within the same category.

stock-keeping unit (SKU)
A unique identifier for each distinct product.

that is widely used in firms around the world, so it's certainly fitting to focus on this giant consumer products company. What does P&G do if the objective is to increase market share? One possibility would be to expand its line of liquid dish detergents—as the company did with its move to expand Gain's popularity from laundry soap to dishwashing liquid. If the line extension meets a perceived consumer need the company doesn't currently address, this would be a good strategic objective. Gain brought a bevy of laundry loyalists into its new category in dishes, making for a great base of business on which to build.

cannibalization
The loss of sales of an existing brand when a new item in a product line or product family is introduced.

But whenever a manufacturer extends a product line or a product family, there is risk of **cannibalization**. This occurs when the new item eats up sales of an existing brand as the firm's current customers simply switch to the new product. That may explain why P&G's Gain dishwashing positioning is all about the unique Gain scent. For Gain Flings (basically the Gain equivalent of Tide Pods), the message to consumers is "get 50 percent more of that original Gain scent you love—it's music to your nose!"

Product Mix Strategies

product mix
The total set of all products a firm offers for sale.

product mix width
The number of different product lines the firm produces.

A firm's **product mix** describes its entire range of products. When they develop a product mix strategy, marketers usually consider the **product mix width**, which is the number of different product lines the firm produces. If it develops several different product lines, a firm reduces the risk of putting all its eggs in one basket. Normally, firms develop a mix of product lines that have some things in common.

Constellation Brands, an international producer and marketer of wine, beer, and spirits, recently acquired craft beer producer Ballast Point Brewing & Spirits for $1 billion to add a line of craft beers to its current portfolio of beer brands. Constellation was originally more focused on wine and spirits but has been expanding its offering of beers since it acquired permission to sell Corona and Modelo beers in 2013. For Constellation the addition of Ballast Point makes sense as it increases the types of brands and products that it offers to meet the growing consumer demand for craft beers, a market that is expected to continue to grow for the foreseeable future. Some of Ballast Point's products bring with them a loyal following, and Constellation hopes these loyalists will ask local watering holes to sell the product. It stands to reason that Constellation also may be able to increase sales of some of their other beer brands to establishments that currently carry Ballast Point beers through cross selling opportunities. Strategically, the acquisition of Ballast Points has potential to increase Constellation's product mix width in a way that adds synergies and opportunities for further growth.[11]

product quality
The overall ability of the product to satisfy customer expectations.

Quality as a Product Objective: TQM and Beyond

Product objectives often focus on **product quality**, which is the overall ability of the product to satisfy customer expectations. Quality is tied to how customers *think* a product will perform, not necessarily to some technological level of perfection. That is, for all intents and purposes, perception is reality. Product quality objectives coincide with marketing objectives for higher sales and market share and to the firm's objectives for increased profits.

Courtesy of Ballast Point Brewing & Spirits

Constellation Brands acquired the Ballast Point craft beer brand to diversify its product mix.

In 1980, just when the economies of Germany and Japan were finally rebuilt from World War II and were threatening American markets with a flood of new products, an NBC documentary on quality titled *If Japan Can Do It, Why Can't We?* fired a first salvo to the American public—and to American CEOs—to warn that American product quality was becoming inferior to

Ripped from the Headlines

Ethical/Sustainable Decisions in the Real World

How precise must marketing messaging be about environmentally friendly or all natural products? Can we call a product "all natural" if it is made with 99 percent all natural ingredients and 1 percent artificial components? What if the ratio is 90 percent all natural ingredients and 10 percent artificial components. Would your opinion shift then?

Toward the end of 2015, a class-action lawsuit was filed against the consumer packaged goods company Kimberly Clark by two plaintiffs. They claimed that they had been deceived by the labeling of Huggies "Pure and Natural" diapers and Huggies "Natural Care" wipes. Huggies marketed its "Pure and Natural" diapers as a "super-premium diaper that includes natural, organic materials and ingredients to provide gentle protection for new babies, as well as initial steps toward environmental improvements, without sacrificing performance."[12] This rather vague statement was viewed as perpetrating misperceptions about the product's actual level of natural, organic content. The plaintiffs stated in their lawsuit that they would not have purchased either product had they known that they contained ingredients that were not naturally occurring and potentially harmful.[13]

So just what does a company have to deliver in the form of a product to label it as "pure," "natural," "green," or "sustainable" on its packaging and emphasize these attributes in its marketing communication? And what should consumers expect of the product in terms of its ingredients and attributes based on such labels and identifications? Although the company might argue that nothing about the Huggies labeling and messaging was technically false, it's not hard to see how consumers might have made certain assumptions about the product as a result of the specific information that it emphasized in its marketing communication about these products.

ETHICS CHECK:

Should marketers be allowed to promote a product to consumers as "green," or "natural" if they know that such claims are only partially accurate?

☐ YES   ☐ NO

---

other global players.[14] So began the **total quality management (TQM)** revolution in American industry. TQM is a business philosophy that calls for company-wide dedication to the development, maintenance, and continuous improvement of all aspects of the company's operations. Indeed, some of the world's most admired, successful companies—top-of-industry firms such as Nordstrom, 3M, Boeing, and Coca-Cola, to name a few—endorse a total quality focus.

Product quality is one way that marketing adds value to customers. However, TQM as an approach to doing business is far more sophisticated and impactful than simply paying attention to products that roll off the assembly line. TQM firms promote a culture among employees that *everybody* working there serves its customers—even employees who never interact with people outside the firm. In such cases, coworkers are **internal customers**—other employees with whom they interact, and these employees harbor an attitude and belief that providing a high quality of service internally will ultimately have an impact on external customers' experiences with the firm and its offerings. This **internal customer mind-set** comprises the following four beliefs: (1) employees who receive my work are my customers, (2) meeting the needs of employees who receive my work is critical to doing a good job, (3) it is important to receive feedback from employees who receive my work, and (4) I focus on the requirements of the person who receives my work.

The bottom line is that TQM maximizes external customer satisfaction by involving all employees, regardless of their function, in efforts to continually improve quality. This results in products that perform better and more fully meet customer needs. For example, TQM firms encourage all employees, even the lowest-paid factory workers, to suggest ways to improve products—and then reward them when they come up with good ideas.

TQM fired the first shot on product quality, and since then many companies around the world look to the uniform standards of the International Organization for Standardization (ISO) for quality guidelines. This Geneva-based organization developed a set of criteria to improve and standardize product quality in Europe. The **ISO 9000** is a broad set of guidelines that establish voluntary standards for quality management. These guidelines ensure that an organization's products conform to the customer's requirements.

ISO subsequently has developed a variety of other standards, including ISO 14000, which concentrates on environmental management, and ISO 22000 on food safety management and ISO 27001 on information security. Because members of the European Union and

total quality management (TQM)
A management philosophy that focuses on satisfying customers through empowering employees to be an active part of continuous quality improvement.

internal customers
Coworkers that interact who harbor the attitude and belief that all activities ultimately impact external customers.

internal customer mind-set
An organizational culture in which all organization members treat each other as valued customers.

ISO 9000
Criteria developed by the International Organization for Standardization to regulate product quality in Europe.

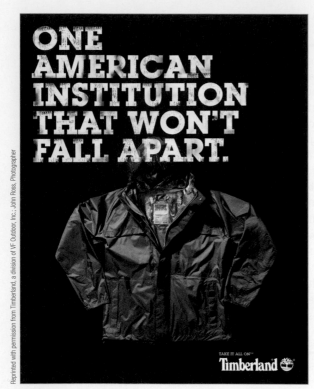

Timberland uses a patriotic message to underscore an emphasis on quality.

Six Sigma

A process whereby firms work to limit product defects to 3.4 per million or fewer.

other European countries prefer suppliers with ISO 9000 and ISO 14000 certification, U.S. companies must comply with these standards to be competitive there.[15]

One way that companies can improve quality is to use the **Six Sigma** method. The term *Six Sigma* comes from the statistical term *sigma*, which is a standard deviation from the mean. Six Sigma refers to six standard deviations from a normal distribution curve. In practical terms, that translates to no more than 3.4 defects per million—getting it right 99.9997 percent of the time. As you can imagine, achieving that level of quality requires a rigorous approach (try it on your term papers—even when you use spell-check!), and that's what Six Sigma offers. The method involves a five-step process called *DMAIC* (define, measure, analyze, improve, and control). The company trains its employees in the method, and as in karate they progress toward "black belt" status when they successfully complete all the levels of training. Employees can use Six Sigma processes to remove defects from services, not just products. In these cases, a "defect" means failing to meet customer expectations. For example, hospitals use Six Sigma processes to reduce medical errors, and airlines use the system to improve flight scheduling.

It's fine to talk about product quality, but exactly what is it? 📷 Figure 9.3 summarizes the many aspects of product quality. In some cases, product quality means durability. For example, athletic shoes shouldn't develop holes after their owner shoots hoops for a few weeks. Reliability also is an important aspect of product quality—customers want to know that a McDonald's hamburger is going to taste the same at any location. For many customers, a product's versatility and its ability to satisfy their needs are central to product quality.

For other products, quality means a high degree of precision. For example, purists compare HDTVs in terms of the number of pixels and their refresh rate. Quality, especially in business-to-business (B2B) products, also relates to ease of use, maintenance, and repair. Yet another crucial dimension of quality is product safety. Finally, the quality of products, such as a painting, a movie, or even a wedding gown, relates to the degree of aesthetic pleasure they provide. Of course, evaluations of aesthetic quality differ dramatically among people: To one person, the quality of a mobile device may mean simplicity, ease of use, and a focus on reliability in voice signal, whereas to another it's the cornucopia of apps and multiple communication modes available on the device.

Figure 9.3 📷 *Snapshot* | Product Quality

Some product objectives focus on quality, which is the ability of a product to satisfy customer expectations—no matter what those expectations are.

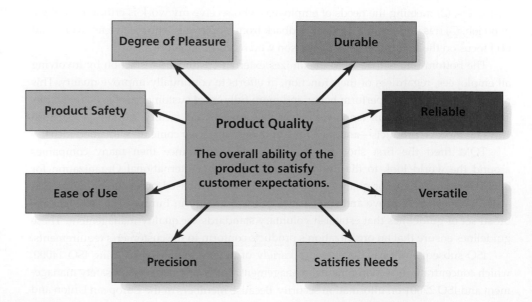

9.2 Marketing throughout the Product Life Cycle

OBJECTIVE

Understand how firms manage products throughout the product life cycle.

(pp. 295–298)

Many products have long lives. Others are "here today, gone tomorrow." The **product life cycle (PLC)** is a useful way to explain how the market's response to a product and marketing activities change over the life of a product. In Chapter 8, we talked about how marketers introduce new products, but the launch is only the beginning. Product marketing strategies must evolve and change as they continue through the product life cycle.

product life cycle (PLC)
A concept that explains how products go through four distinct stages from birth to death: introduction, growth, maturity, and decline.

Alas, some brands don't have long to live. Who remembers the Rambler car or Evening in Paris perfume? In contrast, other brands seem almost immortal. For example, Coca-Cola has been the number-one cola brand for more than 120 years, General Electric has been the number-one light bulb brand for over a century, and Kleenex has been the number-one tissue brand for more than 80 years.[16] Let's take a look at the stages of the PLC, which are portrayed in 📷 Figure 9.4. In addition, 📷 Figure 9.5 provides insights on marketing mix strategies throughout each phase of the PLC.

Introduction Stage

Like people, products are born, they "grow up," and eventually they die. We divide the life of a product into four stages. The first stage we see in Figure 9.4 is the **introduction stage**. Here, customers get the first chance to purchase the good or service. During this early stage, a single company usually produces the product. If it clicks and is profitable, competitors usually follow with their own versions.

introduction stage
The first stage of the product life cycle, in which slow growth follows the introduction of a new product in the marketplace.

During the introduction stage, the goal is to get first-time buyers to try the product. Sales (hopefully) increase at a steady but slow pace. As is also evident in Figure 9.4, the company usually does not make a profit during this stage. Why? Research-and-development (R&D) costs and heavy spending for advertising and promotional efforts cut into revenue.

As Figure 9.5 illustrates, during the introduction stage, pricing may be high to recover the R&D costs (demand permitting) or low to attract a large numbers of consumers. For example, when Microsoft's Xbox One and Sony's PlayStation 4 (PS4) were initially released, the PS4 had

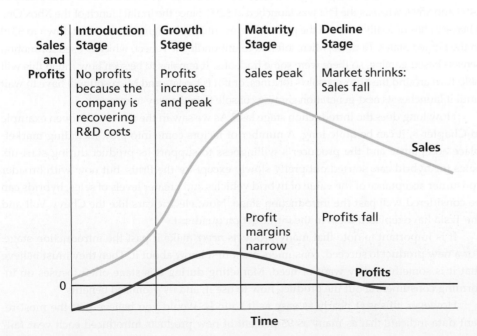

Figure 9.4 📷 *Snapshot* | The Product Life Cycle

The PLC helps marketers understand how a product changes over its lifetime and suggests how to modify their strategies accordingly.

Figure 9.5 📷 *Snapshot* | Marketing Mix Strategies and Other Characteristics through the Product Life Cycle

Marketing mix strategies (the Four Ps) and other characteristics change as a product moves through the life cycle.

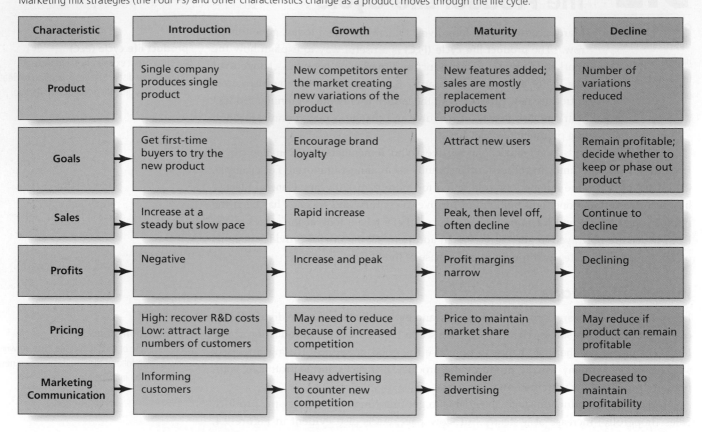

Characteristic	Introduction	Growth	Maturity	Decline
Product	Single company produces single product	New competitors enter the market creating new variations of the product	New features added; sales are mostly replacement products	Number of variations reduced
Goals	Get first-time buyers to try the new product	Encourage brand loyalty	Attract new users	Remain profitable; decide whether to keep or phase out product
Sales	Increase at a steady but slow pace	Rapid increase	Peak, then level off, often decline	Continue to decline
Profits	Negative	Increase and peak	Profit margins narrow	Declining
Pricing	High: recover R&D costs Low: attract large numbers of customers	May need to reduce because of increased competition	Price to maintain market share	May reduce if product can remain profitable
Marketing Communication	Informing customers	Heavy advertising to counter new competition	Reminder advertising	Decreased to maintain profitability

a substantial edge in pricing at $399 compared to the Xbox One's initial price of $499. To be fair, these two next-generation systems were bundled differently, but that initial difference in price had a big impact on initial sales, with the PS4 taking a strong lead. It's interesting to note that Sony had marketed the prior generation, the PS3, in two versions that were both pricey at $499 and $599, whereas the PS2 was launched at $299. Since the initial launch of the Xbox One Microsoft has officially lowered the price twice, eventually bringing the product down to $349 in the United States. To do so, Microsoft had to unbundle the Kinect, which is used for motion sensor–based gaming, so there were some tradeoffs. It remains to be seen how much this will help turn around the Xbox console's fortunes, or if it is too late and Microsoft will have to wait until it launches its next-generation gaming console to find a way to recoup.[17]

How long does the introduction stage last? As we saw in the microwave oven example in Chapter 8, it can be quite long. A number of factors come into play, including marketplace acceptance and the producer's willingness to support its product during start-up. Sales for hybrid cars started out pretty slowly except for the Prius, but now with broader consumer acceptance of the value of hybrid vehicles and greater levels of sales, hybrids can be considered well past the introduction stage. Now, electric cars like the Chevy Volt and the Tesla have replaced them in the introduction quadrant.

It is important to note that many products *never* make it past the introduction stage. For a new product to succeed, consumers must first know about it. Then they must believe that it is something they want or need. Marketing during this stage often focuses on informing consumers about the product, how to use it, and its promised benefits.

However, this isn't nearly as easy as it sounds: Would you believe that the most recent data indicate that as many as 95 percent of new products introduced each year fail?

Shocking as that number is, it's true. Ever heard of Parfum Bic, Pierre Cardin frying pans, or Jack Daniels mustard? These product blunders—which must have seemed good to some product manager at the time but sound crazy now—certainly didn't last on shelves very long. Ever heard of the Microsoft "Kin" mobile phone, positioned as a product for teens and tweens? It was both introduced and subsequently quickly withdrawn from the market because sales were abysmal (if you have one, keep it—it could be worth a fortune as a collector's item on eBay). It's noteworthy that these (as are many) product failures were backed by big companies and attached to already well-known brands. Just think of the product introduction risks for start-ups and unknown brands![18]

The "Snuggie" blanket was a new product success story, largely due to exceptionally well-executed product planning and management.

Growth Stage

In the **growth stage**, sales increase rapidly while profits increase and peak. Marketing's goal here is to encourage brand loyalty by convincing the market that this brand is superior to others. In this stage, marketing strategies may include the introduction of product variations to attract market segments and increase market share. Tablets and smartphones are examples of products that are still in the growth stage, as worldwide sales continue to increase. Continual new product innovations fuel what seems for now to be an endless growth opportunity. The iPhone 6s sold 13 million units within three days after it became available for purchase, beating out its predecessor (the iPhone 6) during that time period by 3 million units. This represented a new sales record for Apple and a sign of the continued growth opportunities within the smartphone market. Of course, the question over the longer term is whether Apple can keep up this momentum given the tough competition from Samsung in the smartphone market.[19]

When competitors appear on the scene, marketers must heavily rely on advertising and other forms of promotion. Price competition may develop, driving profits down. Some firms may seek to capture a particular segment of the market by positioning their product to appeal to a certain group. And, if it initially set the price high, the firm may now reduce it to meet increasing competition.

growth stage
The second stage in the product life cycle, during which consumers accept the product and sales rapidly increase.

Maturity Stage

The **maturity stage** of the PLC is usually the longest. Sales peak and then begin to level off and even decline while profit margins narrow. Competition gets intense when remaining competitors fight for their share of a shrinking pie. Firms may resort to price reductions and reminder advertising ("Did you brush your teeth today?") to maintain market share.

Because most customers have already accepted the product, they tend to buy to replace a worn-out item or to take advantage of product improvements. For example, almost everyone in the U.S. owns a TV (there are still more homes without indoor toilets than without a TV set), meaning that most people who buy a new set replace an older one—especially when TV stations nationwide stopped using analog signals and began to broadcast exclusively in a digital format. TV manufacturers hope that a lot of the replacements will be sets with the latest-and-greatest new technology—Samsung would love to sell you a Smart TV to replace that worn-out basic model. During the maturity stage, firms try to sell their product through as many outlets as possible because availability is crucial in a competitive market. Consumers will not go far to find one particular brand if satisfactory alternatives are close at hand.

To remain competitive and maintain market share during the maturity stage, firms may tinker with the marketing mix to extend this profitable phase for their product. Food

maturity stage
The third and longest stage in the product life cycle, during which sales peak and profit margins narrow.

manufacturers constantly monitor consumer trends, which of late have been heavily skewed toward healthier eating. This has resulted in all sorts of products that trumpet their low-carb, organic, or no-trans-fat credentials.

Decline Stage

decline stage
The final stage in the product life cycle, during which sales decrease as customer needs change.

The **decline stage** of the PLC is characterized by a decrease in overall product category sales. The reason may be obsolescence forced by new technology—where (other than in a museum) do you see a typewriter today? See many people using flip phones recently? Although a single firm may still be profitable, the market as a whole begins to shrink, profits decline, there are fewer variations of the product, and suppliers pull out. In this stage, there are usually many competitors, but none has a distinct advantage.

A firm's major product decision in the decline stage is whether to keep the product at all. An unprofitable product drains resources that the firm could use to develop newer products. If the firm decides to keep the product, it may decrease advertising and other marketing communication to cut costs and reduce prices if the product can still remain profitable. If the firm decides to drop the product, it can eliminate it in two ways: (1) phase it out by cutting production in stages and letting existing stocks run out or (2) simply dump the product immediately. If the established market leader anticipates that there will be some residual demand for the product for a long time, it may make sense to keep the product on the market. The idea is to sell a limited quantity of the product with little or no support from sales, merchandising, advertising, and distribution and just let it "wither on the vine."

9.3 Branding and Packaging:
Create Product Identity

OBJECTIVE
Explain how branding and packaging strategies contribute to product identity.

(pp. 298–307)

Successful marketers keep close tabs on their products' life cycle status, and they plan accordingly. Equally important, though, is to give that product an *identity* and a *personality*. For example, the mere word *Disney* evokes positive emotions around fun, playfulness, family, and casting day-to-day cares out the window. Folks pay a whole lot of money at Disney's theme parks in Florida and California (as well as in France, China, and Japan) to act on those emotions. Disney achieved its strong identity through decades of great branding. Branding along with packaging are extremely important (and expensive) elements of product strategies.

What's in a Name (or a Symbol)?

brand
A name, a term, a symbol, or any other unique element of a product that identifies one firm's product(s) and sets it apart from the competition.

How do you identify your favorite brand? By its name? By the logo (how the name appears)? By the package? By some graphic image or symbol, such as Nike's swoosh? A **brand** is a name, a term, a symbol, or any other unique element of a product that identifies one firm's product(s) and sets it apart from the competition. Consumers easily recognize the Coca-Cola logo, the Jolly Green Giant (a *trade character*), and the triangular red Nabisco logo (a *brand mark*) in the corner of the box. Branding provides the recognition factor products need to succeed in regional, national, and international markets.

A brand name is probably the most used and most recognized form of branding. Smart marketers use brand names to maintain relationships with consumers "from the cradle to the grave." McDonald's would like nothing better than to bring in kids for their Happy Meal and then convert them over time to its more adult Premium Grilled Chicken Ranch BLT (accompanied, they hope, by a Side Salad and a McCafé Frappé Chocolate Chip). A good brand name may position a product because it conveys a certain image (Ford Mustang, which is now more than 50 years old) or describes how it works (Drano).

Brand names such as Caress and Shield help position these different brands of bath soap by saying different things about the benefits they promise. Irish Spring soap provides an unerring image of freshness (can't you just smell it now?). The recently revived Coca-Cola Company brand Surge is a carbonated beverage meant to give consumers exactly what the brand name suggests through the beverage's caffeine and sugar content. Apple's use of "i-everything" is a brilliant branding strategy because it conveys individuality and personalization—characteristics that Gen Y buyers prize.

How does a firm select a good brand name? Good brand designers say there are four "easy" tests: *easy to say, easy to spell, easy to read*, and *easy to remember*—like P&G's Tide, Pampers, Bold, Gain, Downy, Bounty, and Crest (P&G is probably the undisputed branding king of all time). And the name should also pass the "fit test" on four dimensions:

1. Fit the target market
2. Fit the product's benefits
3. Fit the customer's culture
4. Fit legal requirements

When it comes to graphics for a brand symbol, name, or logo, the rule is that it must be recognizable and memorable. No matter how small or large, the triangular Nabisco logo in the corner of the box is a familiar sight. And it should have visual impact. That means that from across a store or when you quickly flip the pages in a magazine, the brand will catch your attention. Apple's apple with the one bite missing never fails to attract.

A **trademark** is the legal term for a brand name, brand mark, or trade character. The symbol for legal registration in the U.S. is a capital "R" in a circle: ®. Marketers register trademarks to make their use by competitors illegal. Because trademark protection applies only in individual countries where the owner registers the brand, unauthorized use of marks on counterfeit products is a huge headache for many companies.

A firm can claim protection for a brand even if it has not legally registered it. In the U.S., *common-law protection* exists if the firm has used the name and established it over a period of time (sort of like a common-law marriage). Although a registered trademark prevents others from using it on a similar product, it may not bar its use for a product in a completely different type of business. Consider the range of unrelated "Quaker" brands: Quaker Oats (cereals), Quaker Funds (mutual funds), Quaker State (motor oil), Quaker Bonnet (gift food baskets), and Quaker Safety Products Corporation (firemen's clothing). A court applied this principle when Apple Corp., the Beatles' music company, sued Apple Computers in 2006 over its use of the Apple logo. The plaintiff wanted to win an injunction to prevent Apple Computer from using the Apple logo in connection with its iPod and iTunes products; it argued that the application to music-related products came too close to the Beatles' musical products. The judge didn't agree; he ruled that Apple Computer clearly used the logo to refer to the download service, not to the music itself.[20]

Why Brands Matter

A brand is *a lot* more than just the product it represents—the best brands build an emotional connection with their customers. Think about the most popular diapers—they're branded Pampers and Luvs, not some functionally descriptive name like Absorbency Master or Dry Bottom. The point is that Pampers and Luvs evoke the joys of parenting, not the utility of the diaper.

Marketers spend huge amounts of money on new product development, advertising, and promotion to develop strong brands. When they succeed, this investment creates **brand equity**. This term describes a brand's value over and above the value of the generic version of the product. For example, how much extra will you pay for a shirt with the

trademark
The legal term for a brand name, brand mark, or trade character; trademarks legally registered by a government obtain protection for exclusive use in that country.

brand equity
The value of a brand to an organization.

American Eagle Outfitters logo on it than for the same shirt with no logo or, worse, the logo of an "inferior" brand? The difference reflects the eagle's brand equity in your mind.

Brand equity means that a brand enjoys customer loyalty because people believe it is superior to the competition. For a firm, brand equity provides a competitive advantage because it gives the brand the power to capture and hold on to a larger share of the market and to sell at prices with higher profit margins. For example, among pianos, the Steinway name has such powerful brand equity that its market share among concert pianists is 95 percent.[21]

Marketers identify different levels of loyalty (or lack thereof) by observing how customers feel about the product. At the lowest level, customers really have no loyalty to a brand, and they will change brands for any reason—often they will jump ship if they find something else at a lower price. At the other extreme, some brands command fierce devotion, and loyal users will go without rather than buy a competing brand.

Escalating levels of attachment to a brand begin when consumers become aware of a brand's existence. Then they might look at the brand in terms of what it literally does for them or how it performs relative to competitors. Next, they may think more deeply about the product and form beliefs and emotional reactions to it. The truly successful brands, however, are those that truly "bond" with their customers so that people feel they have a real relationship with the product. Here are some of the types of relationships a person might have with a product:

- *Self-concept attachment:* The product helps establish the user's identity. (For example, do you feel better in Ralph Lauren or Cherokee clothing?)
- *Nostalgic attachment:* The product serves as a link with a past self. (Does eating the inside of an Oreo cookie remind you of childhood?)[22]
- *Interdependence:* The product is a part of the user's daily routine. (Could you get through the day without a Starbucks coffee?)
- *Love:* The product elicits emotional bonds of warmth, passion, or other strong emotion. (Hershey's Kiss, anyone?)[23]

Ultimately, the way to build strong brands is to forge strong bonds with customers—bonds based on **brand meaning**. This concept encompasses the beliefs and associations that a consumer has about the brand. In many ways, the practice of brand management revolves around the management of meanings. Brand managers, advertising agencies, package designers, name consultants, logo developers, and public relations firms are just some of the collaborators in a global industry devoted to the task of *meaning management*.

Today, for many consumers brand meaning builds virally as people spread its story online. "Tell to sell," once a mantra of top Madison Avenue ad agencies, has made a comeback as marketers seek to engage consumers with compelling stories rather than peddle products in hit-and-run fashion with interruptive advertising like 30-second TV commercials—which Gen Y and younger largely block out anyway. The method of **brand storytelling** captures the notion that powerful ideas do self-propagate when the audience is connected by digital technology. It conveys the constant reinvention inherent in interactivity in that whether it's blogging, content creation through YouTube, or sharing a board on Pinterest, there will always be new and evolving perceptions and dialogues about a brand in real time.

Airbnb is a great example of a company that has used brand storytelling to connect with consumers and further establish its identity. The company underwent a rebranding effort that included the changing of its brand logo to what the company calls the Bélo: the universal symbol of belonging. The symbol looks partially like an upside down heart, partially like an uppercase "A," and includes an element that resembles the location pin symbol. For Airbnb the rebrand and accompanying branding campaign provided an opportunity to tell a story that fits with the brand's identity, one that is centered on the experience

brand meaning
The beliefs and associations that a consumer has about the brand.

brand storytelling
Compelling stories told by marketers about brands to engage consumers.

of being able to feel a sense of belonging wherever a person uses those services provided through Airbnb.[24] If we could name the key elements that make a brand successful, what would they be? Here is a list of 10 characteristics of the world's top brands:[25]

1. The brand excels at delivering the benefits customers truly desire.
2. The brand stays relevant.
3. The pricing strategy is based on consumers' perceptions of value.
4. The brand is properly positioned.
5. The brand is consistent.
6. The brand portfolio and hierarchy make sense.
7. The brand makes use of and coordinates a full repertoire of marketing activities to build equity.
8. The brand's managers understand what the brand means to consumers.
9. The brand is given proper support, and that support is sustained over the long run.
10. The company monitors sources of brand equity.

Products with strong brand equity provide exciting opportunities for marketers. A firm may leverage a brand's equity via **brand extensions**—new products it sells with the same brand name. Because of the existing brand equity, a firm is able to sell its brand extension at a higher price than if it had given it a new brand, and the brand extension will attract new customers immediately. Of course, if the brand extension does not live up to the quality or attractiveness of its namesake, there is a risk of **brand dilution**, in which the contrast between the brand extension's less positive characteristics and the more positive characteristics of the brand can lead to a shift in how consumers perceive the brand. Ultimately this result can impact brand equity as well as brand loyalty and sales. In the pursuit of greater sales and market share many luxury automakers such as Audi and BMW have been using their brand names to sell lower-end models with prices more accessible to a less affluent segment of consumers. Some marketers have voiced concerns over the impact this may have on the value of these brands, which in the past have been heavily associated with luxury and exclusivity.[26]

One other related approach is **sub-branding**, or creating a secondary brand within a main brand that can help differentiate a product line to a desired target group. Virgin is the king of sub-brands, having launched dozens over the history of the company. From Virgin Atlantic to Virgin America, Virgin Mobile, Virgin Megastore, Virgin Wines, Virgin Radio, and on and on—founder Sir Richard Branson has shown the power of thematic threading when the principal brand is robust.[27]

brand extensions
A new product sold with the same brand name as a strong existing brand.

brand dilution
A reduction in the value of a brand typically driven by the introduction of a brand extension that possesses attributes that adversely contrast with the current attributes consumers associate with the brand.

sub-branding
Creating a secondary brand within a main brand that can help differentiate a product line to a desired target group.

Branding Strategies

Because brands contribute to a marketing program's success, a major part of product planning is to develop and execute branding strategies. Marketers have to determine which branding strategy approach(es) to use. 📷 Figure 9.6 illustrates the options: individual or family brands, national or store brands, generic brands, licensing, and cobranding. This decision is critical, but it is not always an easy or obvious choice.

Individual Brands versus Family Brands

Part of developing a branding strategy is to decide whether to use a separate, unique brand for each product item—an *individual brand strategy*—or to market multiple items under the same brand name—a **family brand** or *umbrella brand* strategy. Individual brands may do a better job of communicating clearly and concisely what the consumer can expect from the product, whereas a well-known company like Hyatt Hotels may find that its high brand equity and reputation in one category (e.g., Hyatt Regency at the high end) can sometimes "rub off" on a brands in newer categories like Hyatt Place and Hyatt House.

family brand
A brand that a group of individual products or individual brands share.

Figure 9.6 📷 *Snapshot* | Branding Strategies

Marketers have several branding strategy options to choose from.

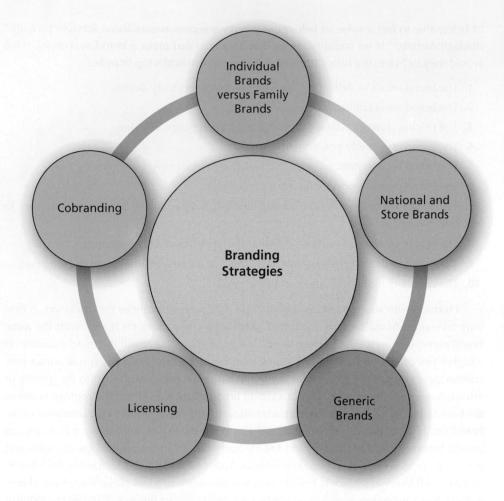

The decision whether to family brand often depends on characteristics of the product and whether the company's overall product strategy calls for introduction of a single, unique product or for the development of a group of similar products. For example, Microsoft serves as a strong umbrella brand for a host of diverse, individually branded products like Windows 10, Office 2016, Xbox One, and Bing. In contrast, Unilever and P&G prefer to brand each of their beauty care and household products separately (for most of the products, you'd never know who the manufacturer is unless you look at the small print on the back label).

But there's a potential dark side to having too many brands, particularly when they become undifferentiated in the eyes of the consumer as a result of poor positioning, or alternatively, when those brands begin to stray too far from a related parent brand, which results in a loss of synergy. For example, The Coca-Cola Company decided to implement its "One Brand" global strategy to address growing divisions between the various sub-brands that share the Coca-Cola name. Specifically, the strategy seeks to place Coca-Cola, Diet Coke, Coca-Cola Zero, and Coca-Cola Life more firmly under the Coca-Cola brand identity with each product's differences framed principally in terms of their product attributes as opposed to differing brand identities. To attempt to shift perceptions in this direction, Coke took a number of actions including having all of the products share a single tagline "Taste the Feeling," developing marketing campaigns that cover all of the different sub-brands, and in some areas, changing the packaging of each product to highlight the differences in the product while at the same time clearly showing that each one is part of the single iconic Coca-Cola brand. For Coke this reunification of the different product variants offers an opportunity to help a larger group of consumers to understand that the parent brand is more than just its flagship high-sugar product, and that there are different offerings available to

Coca-Cola drinkers depending on their specific product preferences and needs. The "One Brand" strategy was initially tested out on a trial basis before the company made the decision to move forward with it on a global basis.[28]

National and Store Brands

Retailers today often are in the driver's seat when it comes to deciding what brands to stock and push. In addition to choosing from producers' brands, called **national or manufacturer brands**, retailers decide whether to offer their own versions. **Private-label brands**, also called *store brands*, are the retail store or chain's exclusive trade name. Costco, for example, features a fine line of more than 300 products under its own private label Kirkland Signature. Representative categories include housewares, luggage, pet food and bedding, baby wipes, diapers, baby formula, apparel, wine, snacks, and more.[29] During the Great Recession that began in the late 2000s, store brands gained substantially in popularity for many value-conscious shoppers, and many consumers did not switch back to the parallel national brands as the economy rebounded because they are satisfied with the private labels.

Campbell's uses a family branding strategy to identify its Chunky line of soups.

Interestingly, if a retailer stocks a unique brand that consumers can't find in other stores, it's much harder for shoppers to compare "apples to apples" across stores and simply buy the brand where they find it sold for the lowest price. As such, private labels represent a major roadblock to price transparency online because consumers can't easily use the Internet to compare private label prices to national brand prices before purchase. Loblaws, Canada's largest supermarket chain, sells more than 4,000 food items under the "premium quality" President's Choice label, from cookies to beef, olive oil, curtains, and kitchen utensils. Sales of President's Choice items run from 30 to 40 percent of total store volumes. Under the private label, Loblaws can introduce new products at high quality but for lower prices than brand names. It can also keep entire categories profitable with its mix of pricing options. Competitors that sell only national brands can cut prices on those brands, but that hurts their overall profitability. Loblaws can reduce prices on national brands but still make money on its private-label products.[30]

national or manufacturer brands
Brands that the product manufacturer owns.

private-label brands
Brands that a certain retailer or distributor owns and sells.

Generic Brands

An alternative to either national or store branding is **generic branding**, which is basically no branding at all. Generic branded products are typically packaged in white with black lettering that names only the product itself (e.g., "Green Beans"). Generic branding is one strategy to meet customers' demand for the lowest prices on standard products such as dog food or paper towels. Generic brands first became popular during the inflationary period of the 1980s when consumers became especially price conscious. More recently, Walmart has aggressively disrupted the pharmacy business by offering some types of generic prescriptions, such as basic antibiotics, for $4.[31]

generic branding
A strategy in which products are not branded and are sold at the lowest price possible.

Licensing

Some firms choose to use a **licensing** strategy to brand their products. This means that one firm sells another firm the right to use a legally protected brand name and other associated elements for a specific purpose and for a specific period of time. Why should an organization sell its name? Licensing can provide instant recognition and consumer interest in a new product, and this strategy can quickly position a product for a certain target market as it trades on the high recognition of the licensed brand among consumers in that segment. For example, the popular mobile phone and tablet game Angry Birds was able to become a licensee for *Star Wars*, which enabled Rovio, the company responsible for the game, to

licensing
An agreement in which one firm sells another firm the right to use a brand name for a specific purpose and for a specific period of time.

Jelly Belly cobrands with several soft drink brands to offer new flavor options.

cobranding
An agreement between two brands to work together to market a new product.

ingredient branding
A type of branding in which branded materials become "component parts" of other branded products.

package
The covering or container for a product that provides product protection, facilitates product use and storage, and supplies important marketing communication.

create the popular Angry Birds Star Wars game. Angry Birds also has been able to license its popular brand and related characters to Hasbro to develop a line of Angry Birds' themed toys and physical games.[32]

A familiar form of licensing occurs when movie producers license their properties to manufacturers of a seemingly infinite number of products. Remember how each time a blockbuster Harry Potter movie hit the screens, a plethora of Potter products packed the stores? In addition to toys and games, there was Harry Potter candy, clothing, all manner of back-to-school items, home items, and even wands and cauldrons. In 2010, with considerable fanfare, Harry and the gang showed up in the form of a major attraction at Universal Orlando called "The Wizarding World of Harry Potter." The latest addition, called "Diagon Alley," opened for business in the summer of 2014. Since then other "Wizarding Worlds" have opened in Los Angeles and Osaka, Japan.[33]

Cobranding

Frito-Lay sells Tapatío flavored potato chips (with a hint of lime). Taco Bell sells Spicy Chicken Cool Ranch Doritos Locos Tacos, and General Mills sells Reese's Puffs cereal. Strange marriages? Not at all! Actually, these are examples of an innovative strategy called **cobranding**. Cobranding benefits both partners when combining the two brands provides more recognition power than either enjoys alone. For example, Sony markets its line of digital Cyber-shot cameras that use Zeiss lenses, which are world famous for their sharpness.[34] Sony is known for its consumer electronics. Combining the best in traditional camera optics with a household name in consumer electronics helps both brands.

A new and fast-growing variation on cobranding is **ingredient branding**, in which branded materials become "component parts" of other branded products.[35] This was the strategy behind the classic "Intel inside" campaign, which convinced millions of consumers to ask by name for a highly technical computer part (a processor) that they wouldn't otherwise recognize if they fell over it.[36] Today, consumers can buy Breyer's Ice Cream with chunks of Snickers bars, M&M's candies, Girl Scout Cookies Thin Mints, and several other decadent ingredients.

The practice of ingredient branding has two main benefits. First, it attracts customers to the host brand because the ingredient brand is familiar and has a strong brand reputation for quality. Second, the ingredient brand's firm can sell more of its product, not to mention the additional revenues it gets from the licensing arrangement.[37]

Packages and Labels: Branding's Little Helpers

How do you know if the soda you are drinking is "regular" or "caffeine free"? How do you keep your low-fat grated cheese fresh after you have used some of it? Why do you like that little blue box from Tiffany's so much? The answer to all these questions is effective packaging and labeling. So far, we've talked about how marketers create product identity with branding. In this section, we'll learn that packaging and labeling decisions also help to create product identity. We also talk about the strategic functions of packaging and some of the legal issues that relate to package labeling.

A **package** is the covering or container for a product, but it's also a way to create a competitive advantage. So the important functional value of a package is that it protects the product. For example, packaging for computers, TV sets, and stereos protects the units from damage during shipping and warehousing. Cereal, potato chips, or packs of grated cheese wouldn't be edible for long if packaging didn't provide protection from moisture, dust, odors, and insects. The multilayered, soft box for the chicken broth you see in 📷 Figure 9.7 prevents the ingredients inside from spoiling. In addition to protecting the product, effective packaging makes it easy for consumers to handle and store the product.

Metrics Moment

Recall from our previous discussion that brand equity represents the value of a product with a particular brand name compared to what the value of the product would be without that brand name (think Coca-Cola versus generic supermarket soda). Companies, market research firms, and creative agencies create metrics of brand equity because this is an important way to assess whether a branding strategy has been successful. For example, The Harris Poll EquiTrend® study is conducted on an annual basis to measure the brand equity of more than 1,400 brands in more than 148 categories. The company interviews over 38,000 consumers to determine how they feel about competing brands.[38] You can review the latest results at www.theharrispoll.com, then hover over "Solutions" and select "EQUITREND" from the resulting list.

If consumers have strong, positive feelings about a brand and are willing to pay extra to choose it over others, marketers are on Cloud Nine. Each of the following approaches to measuring brand equity has some good points and some bad points:

- *Customer mind-set metrics* focus on consumer awareness, attitudes, and loyalty toward a brand. However, these metrics are based on consumer surveys and don't usually provide a single objective measure that a marketer can use to assign a financial value to the brand.
- *Product-market outcome metrics* focus on the ability of a brand to charge a higher price than that of an unbranded equivalent. This

usually involves asking consumers how much more they would be willing to pay for a certain brand compared to others. These measures often rely on hypothetical judgments and can be complicated to use.

- *Financial market metrics* consider the purchase price of a brand if it is sold or acquired. They may also include subjective judgments about the future stock price of the brand.
- A team of marketing professors proposed a simpler measure that they claim reliably tracks the value of a brand over time. Their *revenue premium metric* compares the revenue a brand generates with the revenue generated by a similar private-label product (that doesn't have any brand identification). In this case, brand equity is just the difference in revenue (net price times volume) between a branded good and a corresponding private label.[39]

Apply the Metrics

1. Work with one or more other students to come up with a short list of five to seven of your collective favorite brands.
2. Consider the various aspects of branding you've read about in this chapter. What characteristics of each brand caused you to include it on your short list?

Figure 9.7 📷 *Snapshot* | Functions of Packaging

Great packaging provides a covering for a product, and it also creates a competitive advantage for the brand.

Pour spout: easy to use

Recognizable brand name and logo

Package material protects product from spoilage and is environmentally friendly

Product benefits

Recipes for alternative uses

Warnings

Nutritional information

Ingredients

Toll-free number

Directions for use

UPC code

Photo of actual product

Photo of product in use

Package shape easy to store in cabinet and refrigerator

QR codes are becoming commonplace on everything from cereal boxes to airline boarding passes because they hold more data and can be read by smartphones.

Universal Product Code (UPC)
A set of black bars or lines printed on the side or bottom of most items sold in grocery stores and other mass-merchandising outlets that correspond to a unique 10-digit number.

sustainable packaging
Packaging that involves one or more of the following: elements of the packaging that can be produced from previously used materials, elements of the packaging that use materials in their development that can be repurposed after use, the use of materials that require fewer resources to cultivate, and the use of materials and processes that are generally less harmful to the environment.

Review the different elements pointed out in Figure 9.7—collectively, they illustrate how packaging serves a number of different functions.

Over and above these utilitarian functions, however, a package communicates brand personality. Effective product packaging uses colors, words, shapes, designs, and pictures to provide brand and name identification for the product. In addition, packaging provides product facts, including flavor, fragrance, directions for use, suggestions for alternative uses (e.g., recipes), safety warnings, and ingredients. Packaging may also include warranty information and a toll-free telephone number for customer service.

A final communication element is the **Universal Product Code (UPC)**, which is the set of black bars or lines printed on the side or bottom of most items sold in grocery stores and other mass-merchandising outlets. The UPC is a national system of product identification. It assigns each product a unique 10-digit number. These numbers supply specific information about the type of item (grocery item, meat, produce, drugs, or a discount coupon), the manufacturer (a five-digit code), and the specific product (another five-digit code). At checkout counters, electronic scanners read the UPC bars and automatically transmit data to a computer in the cash register so that retailers can easily track sales and control inventory.

Design Effective Packaging

Should the package have a resealable zipper, feature an easy-to-pour spout, be compact for easy storage, be short and fat so it won't fall over, or be tall and skinny so it won't take up much shelf space? Effective package design involves a multitude of decisions.

Planners must consider the packaging of other brands in the same product category. For example, when Pringles potato chips were introduced, they were deliberately packaged in a cylindrical can instead of in bags like Lay's and others. This was largely out of necessity because Pringles doesn't have all the local trucks to deliver to stores that Frito-Lay does, and the cans keep the chips fresher much longer. However, quickly after product introduction, Pringles discovered that not all customers will accept a radical change in packaging, and retailers may be reluctant to adjust their shelf space to accommodate such packages. To partly answer the concern, Pringles now comes in a diverse array of products and package types and sizes, including Stix, Snack Stacks, Grab & Go, and, for the healthier eaters, Lightly Salted, Reduced Fat, Fat Free, and 100 Calorie.[40]

Packaging can speak to some of the intangible characteristics of a product's brand, such as its personality, heritage, and premium image. Jim Beam recently underwent a global packaging redesign to reflect a more premium and unified image for the products within its portfolio. Specific changes meant to help unify the products under the brand included the prominent display of the Jim Beam signature "rosette" logo. In addition, to keep the heritage of the brand in the minds of consumers the portraits on the side of the Jim Beam White bottle, which feature seven generations of Beam family distillers, were refreshed to improve the quality of the images. Specific Jim Beam products also had elements of the bottle updated to further communicate the premium nature of the different product offerings within the brand. This was the first ever global packaging redesign in the 220-plus-year history of the brand![41]

Firms that wish to act in a socially responsible manner must also consider the environmental, social, and economic impact of packaging. For instance, shiny gold or silver packaging transmits an image of quality and opulence, but certain metallic inks are not biodegradable. Some firms are developing innovative **sustainable packaging** that involves one or more of the following: elements of the packaging that can be produced from previously used materials, elements of the packaging that use materials in their development that can be repurposed after use, the use of materials that require fewer resources to cultivate, and the use of materials and processes that are generally less harmful to the environment. Of course, there is no guarantee that consumers will accept such packaging. They didn't take to plastic pouch refills for certain spray bottle products even though the pouches may take up less space in landfills than the bottles do. They didn't like pouring the refill into their old spray bottles. Still, customers have accepted smaller packages of concentrated products, such as laundry detergent, dishwashing liquid, and fabric softener.

What about the shape: Square? Round? Triangular? Hourglass? Toiletry manufacturer Mennen once had an aftershave and cologne line called Millionaire that it packaged in a gold pyramid-shaped box. How about an old-fashioned apothecary jar that consumers can reuse as an attractive storage container? What color should it be? White to communicate purity? Yellow because it reminds people of lemon freshness? Brown because the flavor is chocolate? Sometimes, we can trace these decisions back to personal preferences. The familiar Campbell's Soup label—immortalized as art by Andy Warhol—is red and white because a company executive many years ago liked the football uniforms at Cornell University!

Finally, there are many specific decisions brand managers must make to ensure that a product's packaging reflects well on its brand and appeals to the intended target market. What graphic information should the package show? Someone once quipped, "Never show the dog eating the dog food." Translation: Should there be a picture of the product on the package? Must green bean cans always show a picture of green beans? Should there be a picture that demonstrates the results of using the product, such as beautiful hair? Should there be a picture of the product in use, perhaps a box of crackers that shows them with delicious-looking toppings arranged on a silver tray? Should there be a recipe or coupon on the back? Of course, all these decisions rely on a marketer's understanding of consumers, ingenuity, and perhaps a little creative luck.

Store brands have unique packaging opportunities. Some store brands opt for **copycat packaging**, mimicking the look of the national branded product they want to knock off. Walgreens is a master of such copycat packaging—look on any shelf in its medicinal categories, and you will see a Walgreens brand proudly merchandised on the shelf right next to the leading national brand in that category, with the package design and colors so similar that you have to look carefully to discern what you are actually buying.[42]

A range of package sizes allows a company to expand its product line.

copycat packaging
Packaging designed to mimic the look of a similar or functionally identical national branded product often meant to lead the consumer to perceive the two products as comparable.

Labeling Regulations

The Federal Fair Packaging and Labeling Act of 1966 controls package communication and labeling in the U.S. This law aims to make labels more helpful to consumers by providing useful information. More recently, the requirements of the *Nutrition Labeling and Education Act of 1990* forced food marketers to make sweeping changes in how they label products. Since August 18, 1994, the U.S. Food and Drug Administration (FDA) requires most foods sold in the U.S. to have labels telling, among other things, how much fat, saturated fat, cholesterol, calories, carbohydrates, protein, and vitamins are in each serving of the product. These regulations force marketers to be more accurate when they describe the contents of their products. Juice makers, for example, must state how much of their product is real juice rather than sugar and water.

As of January 1, 2006, the FDA also requires that all food labels list the amount of trans fat in the food directly under the line for saturated fat content. The new labeling reflects scientific evidence showing that consumption of trans fat, saturated fat, and dietary cholesterol raises "bad" cholesterol levels, which increase the risk of coronary heart disease. The new information is the first significant change on the Nutrition Facts panel since it was established.[43]

Some store brands opt for copycat packaging, mimicking the look of the national branded product they want to knock off. Walgreens is a master of such copycat packaging—look on any shelf in its medicinal categories and you will see a Walgreens brand proudly merchandised on the shelf right next to the leading national brand in that category, with the package design and colors so similar that you have to look carefully to discern what you are actually buying.

9.4 Organize for Effective Product Management

OBJECTIVE

Describe how marketers structure organizations for new and existing product management.

(pp. 308–309)

Of course, firms don't create great products, brands, and packaging—people do. Like all elements of the marketing mix, product strategies are only as effective as their managers make them and carry them out. In this section, we talk about how firms organize both to manage existing products and to develop new products.

Manage Existing Products

In small firms, a single marketing manager usually handles the marketing function. This individual is responsible for new product planning, advertising, working with the company's few sales representatives, marketing research, and just about everything else. But in larger firms, there are a number of managers who are responsible for different brands, product categories, or markets. As illustrated in 📷 Figure 9.8, depending on the organization's needs and the market situation, product management may include brand managers, product category managers, and market managers. Let's take a look at how each operates.

Brand Managers

Sometimes, a firm sells several or even many different brands within a single product category. Take the laundry section in the supermarket, for example. In the detergent category, P&G brands are Bold, Gain, and Tide. In such cases, each brand may have its own **brand manager** who coordinates all marketing activities for a brand; these duties include positioning, identifying target markets, research, distribution, sales promotion, packaging, and evaluating the success of these decisions.

Although this job title and assignment (or something similar) is still common throughout industry, some big firms are changing the way they allocate responsibilities. For example, today P&G's brand managers function more like internal consultants to cross-functional teams located in the field that have responsibility for managing the complete business of key retail clients across all product lines. Brand managers still are responsible for positioning of brands and developing and nurturing brand equity, but they also work heavily with folks from sales, finance, logistics, and others to serve the needs of the major retailers that make up the majority of P&G's business.

By its very nature, the brand management system is not without potential problems. If they act independently and sometimes competitively against each other, brand managers may fight for increases in short-term sales for their own brand, potentially to the detriment of the overall product category for the firm. They may push too hard with coupons, cents-off packages, or other price incentives to a point at which customers will refuse to buy the product when it's not "on deal." Such behavior can hurt long-term profitability and damage brand equity.

Product Category Managers

Some larger firms have such diverse product offerings that they need more extensive coordination. Take IBM, for example. Originally known as a computer manufacturer, IBM now generates much of its revenue from a wide range of consulting and related client services across the spectrum of IT applications (and the company doesn't even sell personal computers anymore, having long ago spun off its ThinkPad business to the Chinese firm Lenovo). In cases such as IBM, organizing for product management may include

brand manager
An individual who is responsible for developing and implementing the marketing plan for a single brand.

Figure 9.8 📷 *Snapshot* | Types of Product Management

Product management can take several forms: brand managers, product category managers, and market managers, depending on the firm's needs and the market situation.

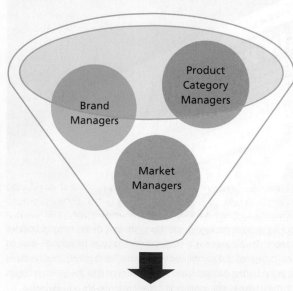

Three Types of Product Management

product category managers, who coordinate the mix of product lines within the more general product category and who consider the addition of new product lines based on client needs.

Market Managers

Some firms have developed a **market manager** structure in which different people focus on specific customer groups rather than on the products the company makes. This type of organization can be especially useful when firms offer a variety of products that serve the needs of a wide range of customers. For example, GE serves three broad markets: consumers, with products such as microwaves and light-bulbs; businesses, with products such as jet engines and imaging equipment for hospitals; and governments, with components used in production of naval vessels and military aircraft. Such firms serve their customers best when they focus separately on each of these very different markets.

Organize for New Product Development

You read in Chapter 8 about the steps in new product development and learned earlier in this chapter about the importance of the introduction phase of the PLC. Because launching new products is so important, the management of this process is a serious matter. In some instances, one person handles new product development, but within larger organizations, new product development almost always requires many people. Often especially creative people with entrepreneurial skills get this assignment.

The challenge in large companies is to enlist specialists in different areas to work together in **venture teams**, which focus exclusively on the new product development effort. Sometimes the venture team is located away from traditional company offices in a remote location called a "skunk works." This colorful term originated with the Skunk Works, an illicit distillery in the comic strip *Li'l Abner*. Because illicit distilleries were bootleg operations, typically located in an isolated area with minimal formal oversight, organizations adopted the colorful description "skunk works" to refer to a small and often isolated department or facility that functions with minimal supervision (not because of its odor).[44]

product category managers
Individuals who are responsible for developing and implementing the marketing plan for all the brands and products within a product category.

market manager
An individual who is responsible for developing and implementing the marketing plans for products sold to a particular customer group.

venture teams
Groups of people within an organization who work together to focus exclusively on the development of a new product.

MyLab Marketing™
Go to **mymktlab.com** to complete the problems marked with this icon ⭐ as well as additional Marketing Metrics questions only available in MyLab Marketing.

Objective Summary ➡ Key Terms ➡ Apply

CHAPTER 9
Study Map

9.1 Objective Summary (pp. 288–294)

Discuss the different product objectives and strategies a firm may choose.

Product planning is guided by the continual process of product management. Objectives for individual products may be related to introducing a new product, expanding the market of a regional product, or rejuvenating a mature product. For multiple products, firms may decide on a full- or a limited-line strategy. Often, companies decide to extend their product line with an upward, downward, or two-way stretch or with a filling-out strategy, or they may decide to contract a product line. Firms that have multiple product lines may choose a wide product mix with many different lines or a narrow one with few. Product quality objectives refer to the durability, reliability, degree of precision, ease of use and repair, or degree of aesthetic pleasure. One way that companies can improve quality is to use the Six Sigma method.

Key Terms

product management, p. 288

product line, p. 290

product line length, p. 291

stock-keeping unit (SKU), p. 291

cannibalization, p. 292

product mix, p. 292

product mix width, p. 292

product quality, p. 292

total quality management (TQM), p. 293

internal customers, p. 293

internal customer mind-set, p. 293

ISO 9000, p. 293

Six Sigma, p. 294

9.2 Objective Summary (pp. 295–298)

Understand how firms manage products throughout the product life cycle.

The product life cycle explains how products go through four stages from birth to death. During the introduction stage, marketers seek to get buyers to try the product and may use high prices to recover R&D costs. During the growth stage, characterized by rapidly increasing sales, marketers may introduce new product variations. In the maturity stage, sales peak and level off. Marketers respond by adding desirable new product features or market-development strategies. During the decline stage, firms must decide whether to phase a product out slowly, drop it immediately, or, if there is residual demand, keep the product.

Key Terms

product life cycle (PLC), p. 295

introduction stage, p. 295

growth stage, p. 297

maturity stage, p. 297

decline stage, p. 298

9.3 Objective Summary (pp. 298–307)

Explain how branding and packaging strategies contribute to product identity.

A brand is a name, term, symbol, or other unique element of a product used to identify a firm's product. A brand should be selected that has a positive connotation and that is recognizable and memorable. Brand names need to be easy to say, spell, read, and remember and should fit the target market, the product's benefits, the customer's culture, and legal requirements. To protect a brand legally, marketers obtain trademark protection. Brands are important because they help maintain customer loyalty and because brand equity or value means a firm is able to attract new customers. Firms may develop individual brand strategies or market multiple items with a family or umbrella brand

strategy. National or manufacturer brands are owned and sold by producers, whereas private-label or store brands carry the retail or chain store's trade name. Licensing means a firm sells another firm the right to use its brand name. In a cobranding strategy, two brands form a partnership to market a new product.

Packaging is the covering or container for a product and serves to protect a product and to allow for easy use and storage of the product. The colors, words, shapes, designs, pictures, and materials used in package design communicate a product's identity, benefits, and other important product information. Package designers must consider cost, product protection, and communication in creating a package that is functional, aesthetically pleasing, and not harmful to the environment. Product labeling in the U.S. is controlled by a number of federal laws aimed at making package labels more helpful to consumers.

Key Terms

brand, p. 298

trademark, p. 299

brand equity, p. 299

brand meaning, p. 300

brand storytelling, p. 300

brand extensions, p. 301

brand dilution, p. 301

sub-branding, p. 301

family brand, p. 301

national or manufacturer brands, p. 303

private-label brands, p. 303

generic branding, p. 303

licensing, p. 303

cobranding, p. 304

ingredient branding, p. 304

package, p. 304

Universal Product Code (UPC), p. 306

sustainable packaging, p. 306

copycat packaging, p. 307

9.4 Objective Summary (pp. 308–309)

Describe how marketers structure organizations for new and existing product management.

To successfully manage existing products, the marketing organization may include brand managers, product category managers, and market managers. Large firms, however, often give new product responsibilities to new product managers or to venture teams, groups of specialists from different areas who work together for a single new product.

Key Terms

brand manager, p. 308

product category managers, p. 309

market manager, p. 309

venture teams, p. 309

Chapter **Questions** and **Activities**

Concepts: Test Your Knowledge

9-1. What are some reasons a firm might determine it should expand a product line? What are some reasons for contracting a product line? Why do many firms have a product mix strategy?

9-2. Why is quality such an important product strategy objective? What are the dimensions of product quality? How has e-commerce affected the need for quality product objectives?

9-3. Explain the product life cycle concept. What are the stages of the product life cycle?

9-4. How are products managed during the different stages of the product life cycle?

9-5. What is a brand? What are the characteristics of a good brand name? How do firms protect their brands?

9-6. What is a brand extension? What is sub-branding?

9-7. What are individual and family brands? A national brand? A store brand?

9-8. What does it mean to license a brand? What is co-branding?

9-9. What are the functions of packaging? What are some important elements of effective package design?

9-10. What should marketers know about package labeling?

9-11. Describe some of the ways firms organize the marketing function to manage existing products. What are the ways firms organize for the development of new products?

Activities: Apply What You've Learned

9-12. *In Class, 10–25 Minutes for Teams* You have been asked to give a presentation on the product life cycle to a small group of students who are interning at your firm this summer. Describe each of the stages of the product life cycle—introduction, growth, maturity, and decline—and give examples of products in the various stages. Include examples of products that are in transition stages as well as examples of some product failures and some products that have been discontinued.

⭐ **9-13.** *For Further Research (Individual)* Select a company that has products under the same corporate brand name that includes products that represent a downward line stretch as well as products that represent an upward line stretch. Identify at least one product that fits within each category and identify what specific attributes separate each from the other.

9-14. *Creative Homework/Short Project* You have been recently promoted at P&G and have been tasked with identifying five cobranding opportunities. These cobranded products could be P&G products or a P&G product cobranded with another firm's brand. Describe each of the cobranding opportunities and define the advantages that would result from each.

9-15. *For Further Research (Individual)* The wine industry over the years has undergone a number of changes in the elements that make up the packaging of a bottle (or other type of individual package) of wine sold for consumption. Conduct research to identify some of the specific differences in the features of wine's packaging. Identify both the pros and cons of each packaging approach observed from a sustainability and marketing perspective (that is, consider different preferences and ideas held by different segments of the wine market affected by the related packaging features).

9-16. *In Class, 10–25 Minutes for Teams* Assume that you are working in the marketing department of a major manufacturer of athletic shoes. Your firm is introducing a new product, a line of disposable sports clothing. That's right—wear it once and toss it! You wonder if it would be better to market the line of clothing with a new brand name or use the family brand name that has already gained popularity with your existing products. Make a list of the advantages and disadvantages of each strategy. Develop your recommendation.

9-17. *In Class, 10–25 Minutes for Teams* As an entrepreneur, you know you want to open a new grocery store, but you aren't sure what kind of products you want to carry. Discuss the importance of national brands, store brands, and generic brands. Which brand or brands will your new store carry? Briefly explain your decision.

9-18. *For Further Research (Individual)* Find an example of a brand extension that you believe negatively impacted consumer perceptions of the brand. Explain why you believe this to be the case by citing aspects of the brand extension that you believe were most detrimental as well as specific evidence, if available.

9-19. *Creative Homework/Short Project* Assume that you have been recently hired by Kellogg, the cereal manufacturer. You have been asked to work on a plan for redesigning the packaging for Kellogg's cereals. In a role-playing situation, present the following report to your marketing superior:

   a. Discussion of the problems or complaints customers have with current packaging

   b. Several different package alternatives

   c. Your recommendations for changing packaging or for keeping the packaging the same

9-20. *For Further Research (Individual)* You are interested in the role that Six Sigma plays with regard to product quality. Using the Internet, research the concept of Six Sigma and find at least two case studies on companies that employ Six Sigma in their day-to-day activities. Summarize your findings in a short report.

Concepts: Apply Marketing Metrics

The chapter introduced you to the concept of brand equity, an important measurement of the value vested in a product's brand in and of itself. Different formulas for calculating brand equity exist. One well-publicized approach is that of Interbrand, which annually publishes its Best 100 Global Brands list. Go to the location on the Interbrand website where they provide these rankings for the present and past years (www.interbrand.com), then click on "Best Global Brands." Peruse the list of brands and select any five in which you have interest. For each, observe whether brand equity has been trending up or down over the past few years.

9-21. How does Interbrand explain the changes (or stability) in each?

9-22. Do you agree with Interbrand's assessment or do you have another opinion about why your brand's equity is what it is?

Choices: What Do You Think?

⭐ **9-23.** *Critical Thinking* Brand equity means that a brand enjoys customer loyalty, perceived quality, and brand-name awareness. To what brands are you personally loyal? What is it about the product that creates brand loyalty and, thus, brand equity?

9-24. *Critical Thinking* Are there specific products that you purchase where branding does not matter and has never mattered to you? What characteristics of the related products and your own individual preferences can help explain why this might be the case?

9-25. *Critical Thinking* When we hear the word "quality," we typically think of durability and/or performance, but product quality is a much broader term. Do you agree that consumers perceive quality across the aspects indicated by Figure 9.3 or do most consumers use a relatively simple approach to assessing quality?

Think of some products that provide quality based on the aspects indicated in this model and discuss how an array of quality aspects may influence how the product is marketed and positioned.

9-26. *Critical Thinking* Many times firms take advantage of their popular, well-known brands by developing brand extensions because they know that the brand equity of the original or parent brand will be transferred to the new product. If a new product is of poor quality, it can damage the reputation of the parent brand, whereas a new product that is of superior quality can enhance the parent brand's reputation. What are some examples of brand extensions that have damaged and that have enhanced the parent brand equity?

⭐ **9-27.** *Ethics* According to a U.K. study of 1,000 people, 91 percent felt that "the way a company behaves towards its customers and communities is influential when making a purchase."[45] Do you share the same belief? Have you ever looked up, for example, a company's environmental initiatives before making a purchase? How important is a brand's ethical behavior to you? Have you ever *not* purchased a brand because of the ethics of the company behind the brand?

9-28. *Critical Thinking* Sometimes marketers seem to stick with the same packaging ideas year after year regardless of whether they are the best possible design. Following is a list of products. For each one, discuss what (if any) problems you have with the package of the brand you use. Then think of ways the package could be improved. Why do you think marketers don't change the old packaging? What would be the results if they adopted your package ideas?
   a. Dry cereal
   b. Laundry detergent
   c. Frozen orange juice
   d. Gallon of milk
   e. Potato chips
   f. Loaf of bread

9-29. *Critical Thinking* In recent years, for packaged products the FDA has proposed that companies include the percentage daily value for added sugar on the nutrition label. The primary reasoning behind this proposal is that it would provide information on added sugars comparable to what consumers have been exposed to for nutrients such as saturated fat and sodium that the FDA advises should be limited in consumption.[46] Do you think that this update to include added sugar is necessary? Do you believe that this update will alter how people consume and make consumption decisions on products containing added sugars? Explain the reasoning behind your answers.

9-30. *Ethics* If a company knows that a snack or beverage is typically consumed in a single sitting (such as a bottle of soda or a bag of chips), is it ethical for that company to include on the product's nutrition label values based on the identification of multiple servings within the product (that is, the nutrition values displayed would represent a single serving of the product that is less than the whole product, making it necessary to multiply those values by the number of servings to identify the total nutritional value of the package)?

9-31. *Critical Thinking* Should a brand be viewed as socially responsible if the parent company of which the brand is a part engages in activities in direct contradiction to (and generally outweighing) the socially responsible actions engaged in by the brand itself?

9-32. *Critical Thinking* Brand elements and brand equity are distinct. Virtually all products will have a brand name, a logo, utilize certain colors, have a slogan, and so on, yet the degree of brand equity varies significantly.

Outline the key differences between brand elements and brand equity. What advantages do strong brands have over weak brands in the marketplace? In your opinion, what are some of the most effective ways to build a strong brand?

Miniproject: Learn by Doing

MP3 players such as the Apple iPod are now in the decline stage of their product lifecycle. Conduct some Internet-based research to find out the sales levels of iPods over the last 15 years or so. What you should find is a sales pattern that reflects the typical product lifecycle curve (keep in mind that there is always a seasonal bump for the Christmas period). Based upon this overall sales pattern for iPods, consider the questions below.

9-33. Given that entertainment technology often has a relatively short adoption period, why do you think it took some time for MP3s/iPods to progress through the introduction stage of the PLC? Thinking about your knowledge of Apple and the review of the introduction stage outlined in the textbook, what were some of the marketing actions that Apple had to implement in order to help the product become successful?

Why is the iPod currently in its decline stage? Is there a way to extend the life of the product, or should Apple look for other new product opportunities?

9-34. Given that the overall lifecycle of this product is relatively short (around 15–20 years), how does this impact a technology-driven company like Apple?

Marketing in **Action** Case Real Choices at Blue Diamond

Do you know how many different ways there are to enjoy an almond? According to agricultural cooperative Blue Diamond Growers, quite a few! After a price spike for almonds earlier in this decade, a market correction has occurred, prices have fallen, and demand has risen. Mark Jansen, Blue Diamond Growers President and CEO, says "I think almonds are more appropriately valued from a price standpoint, and I think we're in a place where we can get back to encouraging and growing fundamental consumer demand for almonds around the world." Much of that growth will likely be through product development.

The California Almond Grower's Exchange began in 1910, and today it represents the world's largest tree nut processing companies, serving more than 3,500 growers. The cooperative produces over 80 percent of the world's almond supply. The cooperative offers almonds in a range of forms and markets its products through the Blue Diamond Growers, which is dedicated to discovering and building customers by establishing new products, finding new uses, and creating new opportunities. Core brands include Blue Diamond roasted almonds, Almond Breeze almond milk, and Nut Thins nut and rice cracker snacks.

The original product, snack almonds, already comes in many tasty varieties but that doesn't stop Blue Diamond from seeking out new ways to grow the brand. The latest family of flavors is branded "Bold," with tastes described as "bold, brash and daring enough to stand out in any crowd." Example flavors include Sriracha, Jalapeno Smokehouse, Wasabi & Soy Sauce, and Habanero BBQ.

Because of growing consumer desire for lower fat and more nutritious alternatives, milk drinkers have been seeking alternatives to dairy. Almond Breeze Almondmilk is low in calories and saturated fat, and is a good source of calcium and vitamin E. These benefits are one of the reasons why USA Volleyball adopted the product as its Official almond milk for the 2016

Summer Olympic Games. Almond Breeze was available for the USA Volleyball team members, coaches, trainers, chefs, and nutritionists as a good alternative to dairy beverages.

Nut Thins are a crunchy cracker made with rice and nuts. The snacks are baked, not fried, and contain no genetically modified organisms (GMOs), gluten, artificial ingredients, or trans fats. They are promoted as ideal for snacking or as a tasty appetizer. Examples of flavors include Smokehouse, Pepper Jack Cheese, Cheddar Cheese, and Hint of Sea Salt.

A recent growth approach for Blue Diamond is a line of honey-flavored products. The new theme is applied across its Snack Almonds, Nut Thins, and Almond Breeze brands (examples: Honey Dijon Almonds, Honey Almond Milk). Al Greenlee, Director of Marketing at Blue Diamond Growers, asserts, "Honey is growing in popularity as a great natural alternative to sugar."

Clearly Blue Diamond is using products and branding successfully to spark new growth opportunities. The question is, how do they keep up the momentum?

You Make the Call

9-35. What is the decision facing Blue Diamond?

9-36. What factors are important in understanding this decision situation?

9-37. What are the alternatives?

9-38. What decision(s) do you recommend?

9-39. What are some ways to implement your recommendation?

Based on: Ann-Marie Jeffries, "Almond Industry 2016 Preview," *Growing Produce* (January 27, 2016), http://www.growingproduce.com/nuts/almond industry 2016-preview/ (accessed May 10, 2016); Mark Anderson. "Blue Diamond Goes Spicy with Sriracha-Flavored Almonds," *Sacramento Business Journal* (July 8, 2015), http://www.bizjournals.com/sacramento/news/2015/07/08/blue-diamond-goes-spicy-with-sriracha-flavored.html (accessed May 10, 2016); "Our Products," Blue Diamond Almonds, https://www.bluediamond.com/index.cfm?navid=3 (accessed May 10, 2016).

MyLab Marketing™

Go to **mymktlab.com** for the following Assisted-graded writing questions:

9-40. *Creative Homework/Short Project.* You may think of your college or university as an organization that offers a line of different educational products. Assume that you have been hired as a marketing consultant by your university to examine and make recommendations for extending its product line. Develop alternatives that the university might consider:
  a. Upward line stretch
  b. Downward line stretch
  c. Two-way stretch
  d. Filling-out strategy
  Describe how each extension might be accomplished. Evaluate each alternative.

9-41. *Creative Homework/Short Project.* Assume that you are the vice president of marketing for a firm that markets a large number of specialty food items (gourmet sauces, marinades, relishes, and so on). Your firm is interested in improving its marketing management structure. You are considering several alternatives: using a brand manager structure, having product category managers, or focusing on market managers. Outline the advantages and disadvantages of each type of organization. What is your recommendation?

Price: What Is the Value Proposition Worth?

Courtesy of Betsy Fleming, Converse College

Betsy Fleming
▼ A Decision Maker at Converse College

Betsy Fleming has served as president of Converse College in Spartanburg, South Carolina, since October 2005. She graduated magna cum laude from Harvard University with an AB in fine arts, received an MA in the history of design from the Royal College of Art in London, and earned a PhD in the history of art from Yale University. Her career began with administrative and curatorial positions at the Frick Collection and the Metropolitan Museum of Art in New York, the J. Paul Getty Trust in Los Angeles, the Yale University Art Gallery, and the Victoria and Albert Museum in London. She has taught at Yale and Parsons School of Design. Immediately before her arrival at Converse, Betsy was executive director of the Gibbes Museum of Art in Charleston, South Carolina. An Aspen Institute Liberty Fellow, she has served on the boards of the Women's College Coalition and the National Association of Independent Colleges and currently serves on the Board of Directors for the Federal Reserve Bank of Richmond, Charlotte Branch, and BlueCross BlueShield of South Carolina.

Betsy's Info

What I do when I'm not working?
For the body, biking, power walking, and yoga; for the spirit, indulging my love of the arts; and, for the mind, reading nonfiction, especially biographies.

First job out of school?
Selling expensive socks and gloves at Gorsuch, Ltd. in Vail, Colorado.

A job-related mistake I wish I hadn't made?
Publicly criticizing an important member of my senior leadership team during a team meeting.

Business book I'm reading now?
Mindset: The New Psychology of Success by Carol Dweck and *Lean In* by Sheryl Sandberg.

My heroes?
Teddy Roosevelt and Gloria Steinem.

My motto to live by?
Think and live out of the box.

What drives me?
Empowering and celebrating human creativity, expression and accomplishment.

My management style?
Collaborative with a priority on accountability.

My pet peeve?
Telling me, "But, we've always done it this way."

Here's my problem...

In 2013, the administration of Converse College, a private master's university located in South Carolina, realized that escalating tuition costs were creating serious problems for current and potential students. Higher-education costs are exploding, even while median U.S. household income has remained mostly flat for the past 10 years. Betsy and her staff decided to take a serious look at the college's pricing model. Their objective was threefold: (1) address the affordability concerns of private higher education within the marketplace, (2) recapture a greater portion of the middle-class market that was feeling priced out of the private college experience, and (3) develop a more sustainable and transparent operating model for the college. Betsy launched a strategic enrollment planning process that involved extensive research to guide data-driven decisions. The outcomes of this work would allow her to partner with the Board of Trustees and key stakeholders to cultivate buy-in and approval for a new pricing model. The working group identified possible solutions to the high-tuition dilemma.

Betsy considered her **Options** 1·2·3

1 **Option**

Reset tuition to a significantly lower price for traditional undergraduate students. The upward spiral of tuition prices within higher education is of national concern and being a leader in offering a different business model was an attractive opportunity to help the school stand out from the crowd. Because Converse projected that tuition would increase on average 3.5 percent each year, students would save quite a bit over several years because of the compounded savings that would result from a price drop. This option would enable Converse to promote a discounted tuition to encourage a larger number of qualified applicants to consider the school; many were unwilling to take a first look because they assumed that a small private school like Converse would be too expensive. However, this would be a risky move because some people who equate high tuition with prestige might assume that Converse's quality is lower than private schools with much higher tuition prices. A price reduction would also require Converse to reduce scholarships proportionately to the tuition decrease. This would create a healthier operating model for the school since scholarships would come from endowed funds alone rather than being supplemented by revenue from inflated tuition. But it could hamper the school's ability to recruit well-qualified students from families who still could not afford even reduced private school tuition (which was only marginally higher than in-state public universities).

2 **Option**

Freeze tuition for each incoming student from the time she matriculated until she graduated with an undergraduate degree. Families would be secure in the knowledge that they would not face annual increases in tuition that leave them challenged to afford college over a four-year period. This action would provide an immediate incentive and financial relief for classes entering Converse in the next year or two. On the other hand, a temporary freeze would provide only a short-term "Band-Aid" for a long-term problem. Converse incurs annual increases in operating costs, and it must generate additional revenue to offset that cost. Rather than having the entire student body share those increased costs through the form of an annual tuition increase, the next incoming class would shoulder the cost in the form of a much higher tuition increase. This would ultimately make tuition spiral upward at an even faster rate.

3 **Option**

Provide students with a Loan Repayment Program (LRP), which guarantees that any undergraduate student without employment after college would have her loans covered by an insurance policy. This guarantee would relieve the financial burden for graduates who could not find employment and provide some peace of mind for their families. It would demonstrate quite forcefully that the school had "skin in the game" in terms of preparing its students to be competitive in the workplace. However, Converse would pay an insurance premium for each student who enrolled, which would increase costs and ultimately result in tuition increases (thus perpetuating the upward spiral). And, paradoxically, this benefit contradicted the school's mission to help students find gainful employment; it would only reward graduates who were not successful at finding a job.

Now, put yourself in Betsy's shoes. Which option would you choose, and why?

You Choose

Which **Option** would you choose, and **why**?

☐ **Option 1**   ☐ **Option 2**   ☐ **Option 3**

See what **option** Betsy chose in **MyLab Marketing**™

MyLab Marketing™

⭐ **Improve Your Grade!**

Over 10 million students improved their results using the Pearson MyLabs.
Visit **mymktlab.com** for simulations, tutorials, and end-of-chapter problems.

Chapter 10

10.1

OBJECTIVE

Explain the importance of pricing and how marketers set objectives for their pricing strategies.

(pp. 316–320)

"Yes, but What Does It Cost?"

"If you have to ask how much it is, you can't afford it!" We've all heard that, but how often do you buy something without asking the price? If price weren't an issue, we'd all drive dream cars, take trips to exotic places, and live like royalty. In the real world, though, most of us need to at least consider a product's price before we buy it.

In the past two chapters, we've talked about creating and managing products. But to create value for customers, marketers must do more than just create a fantastic new (or existing) widget with all the bells and whistles consumers want. Equally (if not more) important is pricing the new offering so that consumers are willing to fork over their hard-earned cash to own the product. The question of what to charge for a product is a central part of the marketing plan.

In this chapter, we'll tackle the basic question—what is price? We'll look at pricing objectives and the roles that demand, costs, revenues, and the environment play in the pricing decision process. Then we'll explore specific pricing strategies and tactics. Finally, we'll look at the dynamic world of pricing on the Internet and at some psychological, legal, and ethical aspects of pricing.

price
The assignment of value, or the amount the consumer must exchange to receive the offering.

Bitcoin
The most popular and fastest-growing digital currency.

What Is Price?

As we said in Chapter 1, **price** is the assignment of value, or the amount the consumer must exchange to receive the offering or product. Price, of course, has many names. We pay college *tuition, rent* for our apartment, *interest* on our credit card balance, a lawyer's or a doctor's professional *fee*, an insurance *premium*, a taxi, airplane, or bus *fare*, and a *toll* to use a road or a bridge.

Payment may also be in the form of goods, services, favors, votes, or anything else that has *value* to the other party. Long before societies minted coins or printed paper money, people exchanged one good or service for another. This practice, called *bartering*, still occurs today. For example, someone who owns a home at a mountain ski resort may exchange a weekend stay for car repair or dental work. No money changes hands, but there still is an exchange of value (just ask the Internal Revenue Service).

The most recent addition to the value exchange is digital currency such as **Bitcoin**. Many believe that our future will be financed by digital currency. Bitcoin is the most popular but not the only digital currency today. The top three after Bitcoin are Ethereum, Ripple, and Litecoin. Digital currency is a bit hard to understand and quite controversial but is quickly establishing itself as an alternative to traditional Benjamins. You can buy this new digital currency on several *Bitcoin exchanges*, or individuals can purchase them from each other using mobile apps that store their Bitcoins in a "virtual wallet." Note: Don't plan on walking around with a shiny new Bitcoin in your pocket; they don't really exist in the sense that you can touch or see one!

Why are Bitcoins so controversial? The main reason is that unlike other "real" currencies, they are not controlled by a single entity like the U.S. Treasury, which puts Bitcoins beyond the grasp of governmental control. There are no "middlemen" (like banks) involved in the process that collects transaction fees (which is why many businesses like this option). However, it also means that transactions occur only from person to person, so there is no record of them, and this opens the potential for Bitcoins to show up in illegal transactions (such as funding terrorism or laundering drug money).

Digital currency systems such as Bitcoin may disrupt the way we think about money.

Jim West/Alamy Stock Photo

There are a number of distinct advantages to digital currency. For consumers, it eliminates the risk of credit card fraud that attracts criminals to steal personal customer information and credit card numbers. To pay for your purchase, you use your smartphone to take a picture of the QR code displayed by the cash register. You click "Confirm," and your app pays for your purchase with Bitcoins. There is also a societal benefit from the use of Bitcoin. Many lower-income consumers do not have bank accounts. Instead, they must often pay fees of 10 percent or higher each time they need to send a money order to a payee. With Bitcoin, such payments would cost only a fraction of that amount. Many believe that the advantages of Bitcoin or other digital currencies will contribute to increased quality of life for those living in the world's poorest countries.

Other nonmonetary costs often are important to marketers. What is the cost of wearing seat belts? What is it worth to people to camp out in a clean national park? It is also important to consider an *opportunity cost*, or the value of something we give up to obtain something else. For example, the cost to obtain a college degree includes more than tuition; it also includes the income that the student could have earned by working instead of going to classes (no, we're not trying to make you feel guilty). And what about a public service campaign designed to reduce alcohol-related accidents? The cost to the individual is either agreeing to abstain and be a designated driver or shelling out for taxi or Uber fare. The value is reducing the risk of having a serious or possibly fatal accident. Unfortunately, too many people feel the chance of having an accident is so slim that the cost of abstaining from drinking is too high.

As Figure 10.1 shows, the elements of price planning include six steps: developing pricing objectives, estimating demand, determining costs, evaluating the pricing environment, choosing a pricing strategy, and developing pricing tactics. In this chapter, we talk about how marketers go through these steps for successful price planning.

The first crucial step in price planning is to develop pricing objectives. These must support the broader objectives of the firm, such as maximizing shareholder value, as well as its overall marketing objectives, such as increasing market share. Figure 10.2 provides examples of different types of pricing objectives. Let's take a closer look at these.

Profit Objectives

As we discussed in Chapter 2, often a firm's overall objectives relate to a certain level of profit it hopes to realize. When pricing strategies are determined by profit objectives, the focus is on a target level of profit growth or a desired net profit margin. A profit objective is important to firms that believe profit is what motivates shareholders and bankers to invest in a company.

Because firms usually produce an entire product line or a product mix, profit objectives may focus on pricing for the firm's entire portfolio of products. In such cases, marketers develop pricing strategies that maximize the profits of the entire portfolio rather than focusing on the costs or profitability of each individual product. For example, it may be better to price one product especially high and lose sales on it if that decision causes customers to instead purchase a product that has a higher profit margin.

Although profits are an important consideration in the pricing of all goods and services, they are critical when the product is a *fad*. Just as the Hula Hoop and poodle skirts were popular fads in the 1950s, Mopeds and Pet Rocks in the 1970s, and Beanie Babies, Furby, and Rollerblades in the 1990s, today's fads include the mobile game Angry Birds, cupcake stores, the *Duck Dynasty* TV show, food trucks, gluten-free diets, twerking,

Figure 10.1 Process | Elements of Price Planning

Successful price planning includes a series of orderly steps beginning with setting pricing objectives.

Step 1: Set Pricing Objectives
- Profit
- Sales
- Market share
- Competitive effect
- Customer satisfaction
- Image enhancement

Step 2: Estimate Demand
- Shifts in demand
- Price elasticity of demand

Step 3: Determine Costs
- Variable costs
- Fixed costs
- Break-even analysis
- Markups and margins

Step 4: Examine the Pricing Environment
- The economy
- The competition
- Government regulation
- Consumer trends
- The international environment

Step 5: Choose a Pricing Strategy
- Based on cost
- Based on demand
- Based on the competition
- Based on customers' needs
- New-product pricing

Step 6: Develop Pricing Tactics
- For individual products
- For multiple products
- Distribution-based tactics
- Discounting for channel members

Figure 10.2 *Process* | Pricing Objectives

The first step in price planning is to develop pricing objectives that support the broader objectives of the firm.

Sales or Market Share
Develop bundle pricing offers in order to increase market share

Profit
Set prices to allow for an 8 percent profit margin on all goods sold.

Image Enhancement
Alter pricing policies to reflect the increased emphasis on the product's quality image.

Pricing Objectives

Competitive Effect
Alter pricing strategy during first quarter of the year to increase sales during competitor's introduction of a new product.

Customer Satisfaction
Alter price levels to match customer expectations.

and Pilates. Because fads such as these have a very short market life, the profit objective is essential to allow the firm to recover its investment in a short time. In such cases, the firm must harvest profits before customers lose interest and move on to the next cool idea.

Sales or Market Share Objectives

Often the objective of a pricing strategy is to maximize sales (either in dollars or in units) or to increase market share. Does setting a price intended to increase unit sales or market share simply mean pricing the product lower than the competition? Sometimes, yes. Providers of cable and satellite TV services such as Time Warner, Comcast, DIRECTV, and AT&T U-verse relentlessly offer consumers better deals that include more TV, wireless Internet, and telephone service. But lowering prices is not always necessary to increase market share. If a company's product has a competitive advantage, keeping the price at the same level as other firms may satisfy sales objectives. And such "price wars" can have a negative effect when consumers switch from one producer to another simply because the price changes.

Competitive Effect Objectives

Sometimes strategists design the pricing plan to dilute the competition's marketing efforts. In these cases, a firm may deliberately try to preempt or reduce the impact of a rival's pricing changes. That's what happened in Australia when Virgin Australia airlines began undercutting competitor Qantas's prices on domestic routes in 2013 to attract Qantas passengers. Qantas fought back

Virgin Australia uses an aggressive pricing strategy to compete with rival Qantas.

Metrics Moment

One criticism of marketing is that these operations lag behind other business areas in terms of measuring performance and how much they contribute to the success of the overall business. In fact, for most of marketing's history as a field, sales volume response to marketing expenditures was the most frequently cited metric, either in sales units or in dollar revenue. But, of course, many factors influence sales volume, so it is hard for marketing to claim a direct one-to-one relationship between marketing effectiveness and increases in sales.

Market share is the percentage of a market (defined in terms of either sales units or revenue) accounted for by a specific firm, product lines, or brands. Market share is quoted within the context of a particular set of competitors.[1] For example, the set of global auto manufacturers (which is only a few firms) might claim market share figures that add up to 100 percent of total U.S. sales. Market share is often a "bragging right" for a firm—sort of a "We're number one!" cheer. But some strategy gurus question whether a market share number is actually very useful as a marketing performance metric because there are numerous cases in which firms, product lines, or brands that do not have number one bragging rights in market share are consistently more profitable than their higher-share competitors. Why would this be? In this chapter, you will learn about cost concepts like *contribution margin* that tell the full story.

Here's an example. Everybody has heard of the brands Gillette and Schick in the U.S. razor and blade market. For years when Gillette was an independent firm (it has since been acquired by Procter & Gamble), the company boasted about a 60 percent share of the U.S. market versus Schick's share of less than 20 percent. Yet the Schick line consistently outperformed Gillette in bottom-line financial contribution—not just percentage profit but actual dollar profit! This was due largely to huge differences in costs, mainly the research-and-development and marketing expenses Gillette incurred in always trying to be the market innovator and grand advertiser (think Super Bowl ads). As a result, Gillette became a takeover target and the rest is history. Lesson: The old adage that "we'll make it up on volume" doesn't work when your variable costs per unit are ridiculously high versus the competition. (Don't worry, we'll explain variable costs with Learning Objective 2 in this chapter.)

Apply the Metrics

1. Pick any industry and identify the main competitors—this can be any type of product or service line of your choice as long as there are several easily identified competing brands (Hint: Publicly traded firms are easier to research then privately held firms.) Do a little research to find out how their market shares stack up.

2. Then, for the same firms, take a look at their most recent reported profits. Based on your findings, does a higher market share translate into a better profit picture?

---

to defend its 65 percent market share with plans to add capacity and reduce prices. Early in 2014, Qantas announced a $235 million loss and 5,000 jobs cut. By April 2014, Qantas reported its number of passengers down 1.5 percent.[2]

market share
The percentage of a market (defined in terms of either sales units or revenue) accounted for by a specific firm, product lines, or brands.

Customer Satisfaction Objectives

Many quality-focused firms believe that profits result from making customer satisfaction the primary objective. These firms believe that if they focus solely on short-term profits, they will lose sight of their objective to retain customers for the long term that we discussed in Chapter 1. Retail giant Walmart, long known as the "Every Day Low Price" leader, hopes to make its customers even more satisfied with its pricing. Following the lead of stores like Target and Best Buy that offer to meet the lower prices of their rivals, Walmart introduced Savings Catcher, a tool within its mobile app, that customers can use to ensure they're getting the lowest price on more than 80,000 food and household products when compared to the advertised prices of those of the competitors in the same geographic area. Customers need only scan the receipt with their phone or enter the receipt number on Walmart.com, and the Savings Catcher tool will automatically compare the prices on the receipt with the advertised prices at other local stores. Savings are returned to the customer in the form of an e-gift card that can be used for future Walmart purchases.[3]

Image Enhancement Objectives

Consumers often use price to make inferences about the quality of a product. In fact, marketers know that price is often an important means of communicating not only quality but also image to prospective customers. The image-enhancement function of pricing is particularly important with **prestige products** (or luxury products) that have a high price and appeal to status-conscious consumers. Most of us would agree that the high price tag

prestige products
Products that have a high price and that appeal to status-conscious consumers.

on a Rolex watch, a Louis Vuitton handbag, or a Rolls-Royce car, although representing the higher costs of producing the product, is vital to shaping an image of an extraordinary product that only the wealthy can afford (not counting the "real" Rolex you buy for $10 from that guy on the street).

10.2 Costs, Demand, Revenue, and the Pricing Environment

OBJECTIVE

Describe how marketers use costs, demand, revenue, and the pricing environment to make pricing decisions.

(pp. 320–332)

Once a marketer decides on its pricing objectives, it is time to begin the actual process of price setting. To set the right price, marketers must understand a variety of quantitative and qualitative factors that can mean success or failure for the pricing strategy. As shown in 🔀 Figure 10.3, these include an estimate of demand, knowledge of costs and revenue, and an understanding of the pricing environment.

Step 2: Estimate Demand

The second step in price planning is to estimate demand. *Demand* refers to customers' desire for a product: How much of a product are they willing to buy as the price of the product goes up or down? Obviously, marketers should know the answer to this question before they set prices. Therefore, one of the earliest steps marketers take in price planning is to estimate demand for their products.

Demand Curves

Economists use a graph of a *demand curve* to illustrate the effect of price on the quantity demanded of a product. The demand curve, which can be a curved or straight line, shows the quantity of a product that customers will buy in a market during a period of time at various prices if all other factors remain the same.

📷 Figure 10.4 shows demand curves for normal and prestige products. The vertical axis for the demand curve represents the different prices that a firm might charge for a product (P). The horizontal axis shows the number of units or quantity (Q) of the product demanded. The demand curve for most goods (that we show on the left side of Figure 10.4) slopes downward and to the right. As the price of the product goes up (P_1 to P_2), the number of units that customers are willing to buy goes down (Q_1 to Q_2). If prices decrease, customers will buy more. This is the *law of demand*. For example, if the price of bananas goes up, customers will probably buy fewer of them. And if the price gets really high, customers will eat their cereal without bananas.

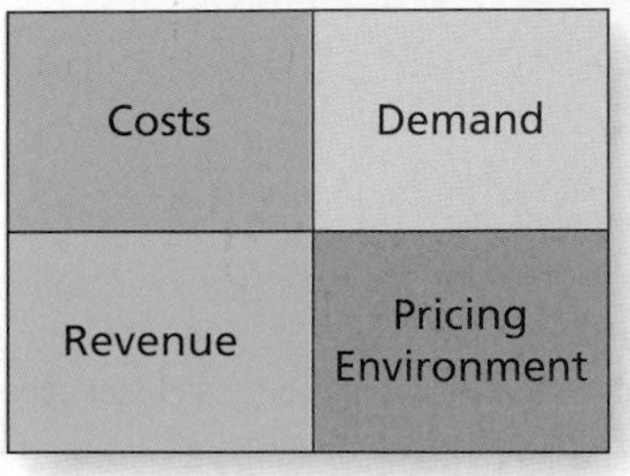

There are, however, exceptions to this typical price–demand relationship. In fact, there are situations in which (otherwise sane) people desire a product more as it *increases* in price. For prestige products such as luxury cars or jewelry, a price hike may actually result in an *increase* in the quantity consumers demand because they see the product as more valuable. In such cases, the demand curve slopes upward. The right-hand side of Figure 10.4 shows the "backward-bending" demand curve we associate with prestige products. If the price decreases, consumers perceive the product to be less desirable, and demand may decrease. You can see that if the price decreases from P_2 to P_3, the quantity demanded decreases from Q_2 to Q_1. On the other hand, if the price increases, consumers think the product is more desirable. This is what happens if the price begins at P_3 and then goes up to P_2; quantity increases from Q_1 to Q_2. Still, the higher-price/higher-demand relationship has its limits. If the firm increases the

Figure 10.3 🔀 *Process* | Factors in Price Setting

To set the right price, marketers must understand a variety of quantitative and qualitative factors.

Costs	Demand
Revenue	Pricing Environment

Figure 10.4 📷 *Snapshot* | Demand Curves for Normal and Prestige Products

There is an inverse relationship between price and demand for normal products. For prestige products, demand will increase—to a point—as price increases or will decrease as price decreases.

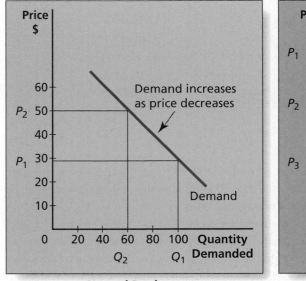

Normal Products

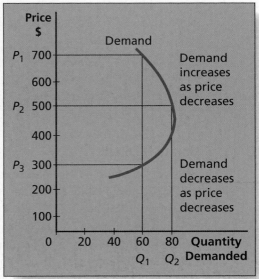

Prestige Products

price too much (say, from P_2 to P_1), making the product unaffordable for all but a few buyers, demand will begin to decrease. The direction the backward-bending curve takes shows this.

Shifts in Demand

The demand curves we've shown assume that all factors other than price stay the same. But what if they don't? What if the company improves the product? What happens when there is a glitzy new advertising campaign that turns a product into a "must-have" for a lot of people? What if stealthy *paparazzi* catch Brad Pitt using the product at home? Any of these things could cause an *upward shift* of the demand curve. An upward shift in the demand curve means that at any given price, demand is greater than before the shift occurs. And the demand shift would no doubt be steeper if Pitt's daughter Shiloh Nouvel Jolie-Pitt also showed up in the pic!

📷 Figure 10.5 shows the upward shift of the demand curve as it moves from D_1 to D_2. At D_1, before the shift occurs, customers will be willing to purchase the quantity Q_1 (or 80 units in Figure 10.5) at the given price, P (or $60 in Figure 10.5). For example, customers at a particular store may buy 80 barbecue grills at $60 a grill. But then the store runs a huge advertising campaign featuring Queen Latifah on her patio using the barbecue grill. The demand curve shifts from D_1 to D_2. (The store keeps the price at $60.) Take a look at how the quantity demanded has changed to Q_2. In our example, the store is now selling 200 barbecue grills at $60 per grill. From a marketing standpoint, this shift is the best of all worlds. Without lowering prices, the company can sell more of its product. As a result, total revenues go up, and so do profits, unless, of course, the new promotion costs as much as those potential additional profits.

Demand curves may also shift downward. For example, if a rumor spread at warp speed on Twitter that the gas grill was faulty and could cause dangerous fires, even with the price remaining at $60, the curve would shift downward, and the quantity demanded would drop so that the store could sell only 30 or 40 grills.

Figure 10.5 📷 *Snapshot* | Shift in the Demand Curve

Changes in the environment or in company efforts can cause a shift in the demand curve. A great advertising campaign, for example, can shift the demand curve upward.

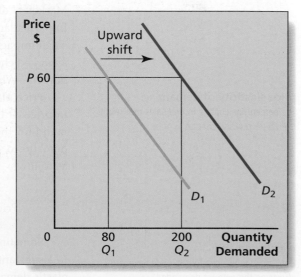

Table 10.1 | Estimating Demand for Pizza

Number of families in market	180,000
Average number of pizzas per family per year	6
Total annual market demand	1,080,000
Company's predicted share of the total market	3 percent
Estimated annual company demand	32,400 pizzas
Estimated monthly company demand	2,700 pizzas
Estimated weekly company demand	675 pizzas

Estimate Demand

It's extremely important for marketers to understand and accurately estimate demand. Plans for production of the product as well as marketing activities and budgets must all be based on reasonably accurate estimates of potential sales.

So how do marketers reasonably estimate potential sales? Marketers predict total demand first by identifying the number of buyers or potential buyers for their product and then multiplying that estimate times the average amount each member of the target market is likely to purchase. Table 10.1 shows how a small business, such as a start-up pizza restaurant, estimates demand in markets it expects to reach. For example, the pizza entrepreneur may use U.S. Census data to determine that there are 180,000 consumer households in his geographic market who normally buy pizza from various retail pizza outlets in the area and that each household would purchase an average of six pizzas a year. The total annual demand is 1,080,000 pizzas (hold the anchovies on at least one of those, please).

Once the marketer estimates total demand, the next step is to predict what the company's market share is likely to be. The company's estimated demand is then its share of the whole (estimated) pie. In our pizza example, the entrepreneur may feel that he can gain 3 percent of this market, or about 2,700 pizzas per month—not bad for a new start-up business. Of course, such projections need to take into consideration other factors that might affect demand, such as new competitors entering the market, the state of the economy, and changing consumer tastes, such as a sudden demand for low-carb takeout food.

Price Elasticity of Demand

Marketers also need to know how their customers are likely to react to a price change. In particular, it is critical to understand whether a change in price will have a large or a small impact on demand. How much can a firm increase or decrease its price until it sees a marked change in sales? If the price of a pizza goes up $1, will people switch to subs and burgers? What would happen if the pizza went up $2? Or even $5?

price elasticity of demand
The percentage change in unit sales that results from a percentage change in price.

Price elasticity of demand is a measure of the sensitivity of customers to changes in price: If the price changes by 10 percent, what will be the percentage change in demand for the product? The word *elasticity* indicates that changes in price usually cause demand to stretch or retract like a rubber band. We calculate price elasticity of demand as follows:

$$\text{Price elasticity of demand} = \frac{\text{Percentage change in quantity demanded}}{\text{Percentage change in price}}$$

elastic demand
Demand in which changes in price have large effects on the amount demanded.

Sometimes customers are sensitive to changes in prices and a change in price results in a substantial change in the quantity they demand. In such instances, we have a case of **elastic demand**. In other situations, a change in price has little or no effect on the quantity

Elastic demand

Price changes from $10 to $9.

$10 – 9 = $1

1/10 = 10% change in price

Demand changes from 2,700 per month to 3,100 per month

$$3,100$$
$$- 2,700$$

Increase   400 pizzas

Percentage increase   400/2,700 = .148 ~ 15% change in demand

$$\text{Price elasticity of demand} = \frac{\text{percentage change in quantity demanded}}{\text{percentage change in price}}$$

$$\text{Price elasticity of demand} = \frac{15\%}{10\%} = 1.5$$

Inelastic demand

Price changes from $10 to $9.

$10 – 9 = $1

1/10 = 10% change in price

Demand changes from 2,700 per month to 2,835 per month

$$2,835$$
$$- 2,700$$

Increase   135 pizzas

Percentage increase   135/2,700 = 0.05 ~ 5% change in demand

$$\text{Price elasticity of demand} = \frac{\text{percentage change in quantity demanded}}{\text{percentage change in price}}$$

$$\text{Price elasticity of demand} = \frac{5\%}{10\%} = 0.5$$

Figure 10.6 📷 *Snapshot* | Price Elasticity of Demand

Marketers know that elasticity of demand is an important pricing metric.

consumers are willing to buy. We describe this as **inelastic demand**. Let's use the formula in this example: Suppose the pizza maker finds (from experience or from marketing research) that lowering the price of his pizza 10 percent (from $10 per pizza to $9) will cause a 15 percent increase in demand. He would calculate the price elasticity of demand as 15 divided by 10. The price elasticity of demand would be 1.5. If the price elasticity of demand is greater than one, demand is elastic; that is, consumers respond to the price decrease by demanding more. Or, if the price increases, consumers will demand less. 📷 Figure 10.6 shows these calculations.

As 📷 Figure 10.7 illustrates, when demand is elastic, changes in price and in total revenues (total sales) work in opposite directions. If the price is increased, revenues decrease. If the price is decreased, total revenues increase. With elastic demand, the demand curve shown in Figure 10.7 is more horizontal. With an elasticity of demand of 1.5, a decrease in price will increase the pizza maker's total revenue.

If demand is price inelastic, can marketers keep raising prices so that revenues and profits will grow larger and larger? And what if demand is elastic? Does it mean that marketers can never raise prices? The answer to these questions is "no" (surprise!). Elasticity of demand for a product often differs for different price levels and with different percentages of change.

Other factors can affect price elasticity and sales. Consider the availability of *substitute* goods or services. If a product has a close substitute, its demand will be elastic; that is, a change in price will result in a change in demand as consumers move to buy the substitute product. For example, all but the most die-hard cola fans might consider Coke and Pepsi close substitutes. If the price of Pepsi goes up, many people will buy Coke instead.

inelastic demand
Demand in which changes in price have little or no effect on the amount demanded.

Figure 10.7 📷 *Snapshot*|
Price-Elastic and Price-Inelastic Demand

Price elasticity of demand represents how demand responds to changes in prices. If there is little change in demand, then demand is said to be price inelastic. If there is a large change in demand, demand is price elastic.

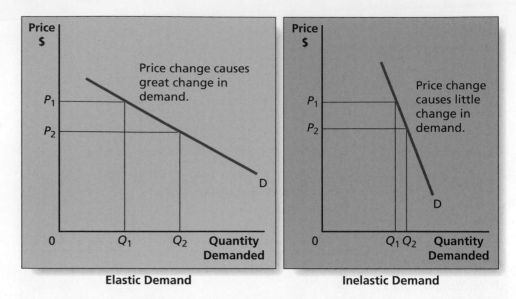

Elastic Demand   Inelastic Demand

Marketers of products with close substitutes are less likely to compete on price because they recognize that doing so could result in less profit as consumers switch from one brand to another.

Changes in prices of other products also affect the demand for an item, a phenomenon we label **cross elasticity of demand**. When products are substitutes for each other, an increase in the price of one will increase the demand for the other. For example, if the price of bananas goes up, consumers may instead buy more strawberries, blueberries, or apples. However, when products are *complements*—that is, when one product is essential to the use of a second—an increase in the price of one decreases the demand for the second. So if the price of gasoline goes up, consumers may drive less, carpool, or take public transportation, and thus demand for tires (as well as gasoline) will decrease.[4]

cross-elasticity of demand
When changes in the price of one product affect the demand for another item.

Step 3: Determine Costs

Estimating demand helps marketers to determine possible prices to charge for a product. It tells them how much of the product they think they'll be able to sell at different prices. Knowing this brings them to the third step in determining a product's price: making sure the price will cover costs. Before marketers can determine price, they must understand the relationship of cost, demand, and revenue for their product. In this next section, we'll talk about different types of costs that marketers must consider in pricing. Then we'll show how marketers use that information to make pricing decisions.

Variable and Fixed Costs

It's obvious that the cost of producing a product plays a big role when firms decide what to charge for it. If an item's selling price is lower than the cost to produce it, it doesn't take a rocket scientist to figure out that the firm will lose money. Before we look at how cost influences pricing decisions, we need to understand the different types of costs that firms incur.

First, a firm incurs **variable costs**—the per-unit costs of production that will fluctuate depending on how many units or individual products a firm produces. For example, if it takes 25 cents worth of nails—a variable cost—to build one bookcase, it will take 50 cents worth for two, 75 cents worth for three, and so on. Make cents? For the production of bookcases, variable costs would also include the cost of lumber and paint as well as the wages the firm would pay factory workers.

variable costs
The costs of production (raw and processed materials, parts, and labor) that are tied to and vary, depending on the number of units produced.

Figure 10.8 📷 *Snapshot* | Variable Costs at Different Levels of Production

Variable Costs to Produce 100 Bookcases		Variable Costs to Produce 200 Bookcases		Variable Costs to Produce 500 Bookcases	
Wood	$13.25	Wood	$13.25	Wood	$9.40
Nails	0.25	Nails	0.25	Nails	0.20
Paint	0.50	Paint	0.50	Paint	0.40
Labor (3 hours × $12.00 per hr)	$36.00	Labor (3 hours × $12.00 per hr)	$36.00	Labor (2½ hours × $12.00 per hr)	$30.00
Cost per unit	$50.00	Cost per unit	$50.00	Cost per unit	$40.00
Multiply by number of units	100	Multiply by number of units	200	Multiply by number of units	500
Cost for 100 units	$5,000	Cost for 200 units	$10,000	Cost for 500 units	$20,000

One bookcase = one unit.

📷 Figure 10.8 shows some examples of the average variable cost (the variable cost per unit) and the total variable costs at different levels of production (for producing 100, 200, and 500 bookcases). If the firm produces 100 bookcases, the average variable cost per unit is $50, and the total variable cost is $5,000 ($50 × 100). If it doubles production to 200 units, the total variable cost now is $10,000 ($50 × 200).

In reality, it's usually more complex to calculate variable costs than what we've shown here. As the number of bookcases the factory produces increases or decreases, average variable costs may change. For example, if the company buys just enough lumber for one bookcase, the lumberyard will charge top dollar. If it buys enough for 100 bookcases, the guys at the lumberyard will probably offer a better deal. And if it buys enough for thousands of bookcases, the company may cut variable costs even more. Even the cost of labor goes down with increased production because manufacturers are likely to invest in labor-saving equipment that allows workers to produce bookcases faster. Figure 10.8 shows this is the case. By purchasing wood, nails, and paint at a lower price (because of a volume discount) and by providing a means for workers to build bookcases more quickly, the company reduces the cost per unit to produce 500 bookcases to $40 each.

Variable costs don't always go down with higher levels of production. Using the bookcase example, at some point the demand for the labor, lumber, or nails required to produce the bookcases may exceed the supply: The bookcase manufacturer may have to pay employees higher overtime wages to keep up with production. The manufacturer may have to buy additional lumber from a distant supplier that will charge more to cover the costs of shipping. The cost per bookcase rises. You get the picture.

Fixed costs are costs that *do not* vary with the number of units produced—the costs that remain the same whether the firm produces 1,000 bookcases this month or only 10. Fixed costs include rent or the cost of owning and maintaining the factory, utilities to heat or cool the factory, and the costs of equipment, such as hammers, saws, and paint sprayers, used in the production of the product. Although the wages of factory workers to build the bookcases are part of a firm's variable costs, the salaries of a firm's executives, accountants, human resources specialists, marketing managers, and other personnel not involved in the production of the product are fixed costs. So too are other costs, such as advertising and other marketing activities, at least in the short term. All these costs are constant no matter how many units of the product the factory manufactures.

fixed costs
Costs of production that do not change with the number of units produced.

average fixed cost
The fixed cost per unit produced.

total costs
The total of the fixed costs and the variable costs for a set number of units produced.

break-even analysis
A method for determining the number of units that a firm must produce and sell at a given price to cover all its costs.

break-even point
The point at which the total revenue and total costs are equal and beyond which the company makes a profit; below that point, the firm will suffer a loss.

contribution per unit
The difference between the price the firm charges for a product and the variable costs.

Average fixed cost is the fixed cost per unit—the total fixed costs divided by the number of units (bookcases) produced and sold. Although total fixed costs remain the same no matter how many units are produced, the average fixed cost will decrease as the number of units produced increases. Say, for example, that a firm's total fixed costs of production are $300,000. If the firm produces one unit, it applies the total of $300,000 to the one unit. If it produces two units, it applies $150,000, or half of the fixed costs, to each unit. If it produces 10,000 units, the average fixed cost per unit is $30 and so on. As we produce more and more units, average fixed costs go down, and so does the price we must charge to cover fixed costs.

Of course, like variable costs, in the long term, total fixed costs may change. The firm may find that it can sell more of a product than it has manufacturing capacity to produce, so it builds a new factory, its executives' salaries go up, and more money goes to purchase manufacturing equipment.

Combining variable costs and fixed costs yields **total costs** for a given level of production. As a company produces more and more of a product, both average fixed costs and average variable costs may decrease. As output continues to increase, average variable costs may start to increase. These variable costs ultimately rise faster than average fixed costs decline, resulting in an increase to average total costs. As total costs fluctuate with differing levels of production, the price that producers have to charge to cover those costs changes accordingly. Therefore, marketers need to calculate the minimum price necessary to cover all costs—the *break-even price*.

Break-Even Analysis

Break-even analysis is a technique marketers use to examine the relationship between costs and price. This method lets them determine what sales volume the company must reach at a given price before it will completely cover its total costs and past which it will begin to turn a profit. Simply put, the **break-even point** is the point at which the company doesn't lose any money and doesn't make any profit. All costs are covered, but there isn't a penny extra. A break-even analysis allows marketers to identify how many units of a product they will have to sell at a given price to exceed the break-even point and be profitable.

📷 Figure 10.9 uses our bookcase example to demonstrate break-even analysis assuming the manufacturer charges $100 per unit. The vertical axis represents the amount of costs and revenue in dollars, and the horizontal axis shows the quantity of goods the manufacturer produces and sells. The break-even model assumes that there is a given total fixed cost and that variable costs per unit do not change with the quantity produced.

In this example, let's say that the total fixed costs (the costs for the factory, the equipment, the marketing and electricity) are $200,000 and that the average variable costs (for materials and labor) are constant. The figure shows the total costs (variable costs plus fixed costs) and total revenues if varying quantities are produced and sold. The point at which the total revenue and total costs lines intersect is the break-even point. If sales are above the break-even point, the company makes a profit. Below that point, the firm will suffer losses.

To determine the break-even point, the firm first needs to calculate the **contribution per unit**, or the difference between the price the firm charges for a product (the revenue per unit) and the variable costs. This figure is the amount the firm has after it pays for the wood, nails, paint, and labor to

Figure 10.9 📷 *Snapshot* | Break-Even Analysis Assuming a Price of $100

Using break-even analysis, marketers can determine what sales volume must be reached before the company makes a profit. This company needs to sell 4,000 bookcases at $100 each to break even.

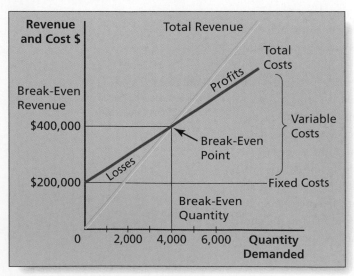

contribute to meeting the fixed costs of production and any profit. For our example, we will assume that the firm sells its bookcases for $100 each. Using the variable costs of $50 per unit that we had before, contribution per unit is $100 − $50 = $50. Using the fixed cost for the bookcase manufacturing of $200,000, we can now calculate the firm's break-even point in units of the product:

$$\text{Break-even point (in units)} = \frac{\text{Total fixed costs}}{\text{Contribution per unit to fixed costs}}$$

$$\text{Break-even point (in units)} = \frac{\$200,000}{\$50} = 4{,}000 \text{ units}$$

We see that the firm must sell 4,000 bookcases at $100 each to meet its fixed costs and to break even. We can also calculate the break-even point in dollars. This shows us that to break even, the company must sell $400,000 worth of bookcases:

$$\text{Break-even point (in dollars)} = \frac{\text{Total fixed costs}}{1 - \dfrac{\text{Variable cost per unit}}{\text{Price}}}$$

$$\text{Break-even point (in dollars)} = \frac{\$200,000}{1 - \dfrac{\$50}{\$100}} = \frac{\$200,000}{1 - 0.5} = \frac{\$200,000}{0.5} = \$400,000$$

After the firm's sales have met and passed the break-even point, it begins to make a profit. How much profit? If the firm sells 4,001 bookcases, it will make a profit of $50. If it sells 5,000 bookcases, we calculate the profit as follows:

$$\text{Profit} = \text{Quantity above break-even point} \times \text{Contribution per unit}$$
$$= 1{,}000 \times \$50$$
$$= \$50{,}000$$

Often a firm will set a *profit goal*, the dollar profit figure it wants to earn. Its managers may calculate the break-even point with a certain dollar profit goal in mind. In this case, it is not really a "break-even" point we are calculating because we're seeking profits. It's more of a "target amount." If our bookcase manufacturer thinks it is necessary to realize a profit of $50,000, his calculations look like this:

$$\text{Break-even point (in units) with target profit included} = \frac{\text{total fixed costs} + \text{target profit}}{\text{contribution per unit to fixed costs}}$$

$$\text{Break-even point (in units)} = \frac{\$200,000 + 50,000}{\$50} = 5{,}000 \text{ units}$$

Knowing the break-even point is equally important to small or large businesses. The owner of a restaurant that is already meeting its fixed costs and making a profit knows that if he can increase his sales, the contribution margin portion of all new sales will be profit. If an automaker can cut its costs by obtaining component parts for a lower price, the contribution margin and profits will increase with no increase in sales. This is the reason many U.S. firms have moved overseas where labor costs are lower or where governments have lower corporate tax rates.

Break-even analysis does not provide an easy answer for pricing decisions. Yes, it provides answers about how many units the firm must sell to break even and to make a profit, but without knowing whether demand will equal that quantity at that price, companies can make big mistakes.

markup
An amount added to the cost of a product to create the price at which a channel member will sell the product.

gross margin
The markup amount added to the cost of a product to cover the fixed costs of the retailer or wholesaler and leave an amount for a profit.

retailer margin
The margin added to the cost of a product by a retailer.

wholesaler margin
The amount added to the cost of a product by a wholesaler.

list price or manufacturer's suggested retail price (MSRP)
The price that the manufacturer sets as the appropriate price for the end consumer to pay.

Markups and Margins: Pricing through the Channel

So far, we've talked about costs simply from the perspective of a manufacturer selling directly to a consumer. But in reality, most products are not sold directly to consumers or business buyers. Instead, a manufacturer may sell a consumer good to a wholesaler, distributor, or jobber who in turn sells to a retailer who finally sells the product to the ultimate consumer. In organizational markets, the manufacturer may sell his or her product to a distributor who will then sell to the business customer. Each of these members of the channel of distribution buys a product for a certain amount and adds a **markup** amount to create the price at which they will sell a product. This markup amount is the **gross margin**, also referred to as the **retailer margin** or the **wholesaler margin**. The margin must be great enough to cover the fixed costs of the retailer or wholesaler and leave an amount for a profit. When a manufacturer sets a price, he or she must consider these margins. To understand pricing through the channel better, 📷 Figure 10.10 shows a simple example of channel pricing.

Many times, a manufacturer builds its pricing structure around list prices. A **list price**, which we also refer to as a **manufacturer's suggested retail price (MSRP)**, is the price that the manufacturer sets as the appropriate price for the end consumer to pay. In Figure 10.10 we have a consumer good with an MSRP of $20, the price that the retailers will charge a consumer. But, as we said, retailers need money to cover their fixed costs and their profits. Thus, the retailer may determine that he must have a certain percentage gross or retailer margin, say 30 percent. This means that the retailer must be able to buy the product for no more than $14.00. If the channel of distribution also includes a wholesaler, the wholesaler must be able to mark up the product to pay his fixed costs and profits. This means that the wholesaler must also have a certain percentage gross or wholesaler margin, say 20 percent.

Figure 10.10 📷 *Snapshot* | Markups through the Channel

Producers of products need to remember that organizations at each level of the channel must set the price of the product to cover their fixed costs and make a profit.

Retailer	
Manufacturer's suggested retail price (MSRP) or list price	$20.00
Retailer's required margin to cover fixed costs and make a profit	−30% = $ 6.00
	$14.00
Price to the retailer must be $14.00 or less	

Wholesaler	
Price the retailer pays for the product	$14.00
Wholesaler's required margin to cover fixed costs and make a profit	−20% = $ 2.80
	$11.20
Price the manufacturer charges the Wholesaler must be $11.20 or less.	

Manufacturer	
Manufacturer's revenue from sale of Item to the wholesaler	$11.20
Manufacturer's variable costs per unit	− $7.85
Manufacturer's contribution margin	$3.35

This means that the wholesaler must be able to buy the product for no more than $11.20 to cover his fixed costs and profits. Thus, the manufacturer will sell the product not for $20 but for $11.20. Of course, the manufacturer may sell the product to the wholesaler for less than that, but he cannot sell it for more and meet the margin requirements of the retailer and the wholesaler. If the manufacturer's variable costs for producing the product are $7.85, then his contribution to fixed costs is $3.35. This is the manufacturer's contribution margin and the amount that would be used to calculate the break-even point.

Many retail organizations or chains such as Walmart, Walgreens Drug Stores and Kroger Supermarkets have found that it makes good sense to handle the tasks of the wholesaler themselves through **vertical integration**. This means these retail chains have their own distribution centers and move products to stores in their own trucks, thus saving money while maintaining greater control over the availability and delivery of products to their stores. Hopefully, they are able to offer lower prices to their consumers. We'll talk more about these vertical marketing systems in Chapter 11.

Step 4: Examine the Pricing Environment

In addition to demand and costs, marketers look at factors in the firm's external environment when they set prices. The fourth step in developing pricing strategies is to examine and evaluate the external pricing environment. In this section we will discuss some important external influences on pricing strategies—the economic environment, competition, and consumer trends.

The Economy

Broad economic trends, like those we discussed in Chapter 2, tend to influence pricing strategies. The business cycle, inflation, economic growth, and consumer confidence in the economy all help to determine whether a firm should keep prices stable, reduce them, or even raise them. Of course, the upswings and downturns in a national economy do not affect all product categories or all regions equally. Marketers need to understand how economic trends will affect their particular business.

In general, during *recessions* like the Great Recession that began in late 2007, consumers grow more price sensitive. They switch brands to get a better price and patronize discount stores and warehouse outlets. They are less likely to take luxury vacations; instead, they're happy with a "staycation" where they entertain the family at home. Many consumers lose their jobs, and others are fearful of losing theirs. Even wealthy households, relatively unaffected by the recession, tend to cut back on their consumption. As a result, to keep businesses in operation during periods of recession, some firms find it necessary to cut prices to levels at which they cover their costs but don't make a profit. During the Great Recession, Starbucks' strategy to cope with the downturn was to keep a premium image while the chain retained price-sensitive customers who threatened to defect to lower-priced competitors, such as McDonald's. To do this, Starbucks raised the prices of its sugary coffees with several ingredients, such as frappuccinos and caramel macchiatos, by 10, 15, or even 30 cents. At the same time, the company reduced

It's common for services like insurance to rely on price as a competitive advantage.

vertical integration
the combining of manufacturing operations with channels of distribution under a single ownership to reduce costs and increase profits.

Consumers are very price-sensitive when economic conditions are bleak.

P&G responded to a difficult economic environment by lowering prices on products from Duracell batteries to Pampers diapers.

prices of more popular beverages, such as lattes and brewed coffee, from 5 to 15 cents.

P&G is the world's biggest producer of consumer goods, including many premium-priced brands, some at prices twice the category average. But during the recession, P&G found sales, market share, and profits declining as consumers switched to store brands and other cheaper options. P&G responded with a number of price-cutting and product enhancement strategies. For example, P&G began offering larger packs of Duracell batteries and more absorbent Pampers Baby Diapers without increasing prices.

There are also some economic trends that influence what consumers see as an acceptable or unacceptable price range for a product and thus allow firms to change prices. *Inflation* may give marketers causes to either increase or decrease prices. First, inflation gets customers accustomed to price increases, even when inflation goes away. This allows marketers to make real price increases, not just those that adjust for the inflation. Of course, during periods of inflation, consumers may cut back on purchases because they grow fearful of the future and worry about whether they will have enough money to meet basic needs. Then, as in periods of recession, inflation may cause marketers to lower prices and temporarily sacrifice profits to maintain sales levels.

The Competition

Marketers try to anticipate how the competition will respond to their pricing actions. It's not always a good idea to fight the competition with lower and lower prices. Pricing wars can change consumers' perceptions of what is a "fair" price, leaving them unwilling to buy at previous price levels.

As we discussed in Chapter 2, most industries belong to one of three industry structures—an oligopoly, monopolistic competition, or pure competition. The industry structure a firm belongs to will influence price decisions. In general, firms like Delta Airlines that do business in an oligopoly, in which the market has few sellers and many buyers, are more likely to adopt status quo pricing objectives in which the pricing of all competitors is similar. Such objectives are attractive to oligopolistic firms because avoiding price competition allows all players in the industry to remain profitable. Of course, this doesn't mean that firms in an oligopoly can just ignore pricing by the competition. When one airline raises or lowers the price for its flights, the other airlines follow.

In a business like the restaurant industry, which is characterized as monopolistic competition in which there are many sellers, each offering a slightly different product, it is possible for firms to differentiate products and to focus on nonprice competition. Then each firm prices its product on the basis of its cost without much concern for matching the exact price of competitors' products.

Organizations like wheat farmers that function in a market characterized as pure competition have little opportunity to raise or lower prices. Rather, supply and demand directly influence the price of wheat, soybeans, corn, or fresh peaches.

Government Regulation

Another important factor in the environment that influences how marketers develop pricing strategies is government regulation. Governments in the U.S. and some other countries develop two different types of regulations that affect pricing. First, regulations for employee health care, environmental protection, occupational safety, and highway safety, just to mention a few, cause the costs to produce many products to increase. Other regulations on specific industries, such as those imposed by the Food and Drug Administration on the production of food and pharmaceuticals, increase the costs of developing and producing those products.

In addition, some regulations directly address prices. Recently, Congress enacted the Credit Card Responsibility and Disclosure Act, which limits credit card rates and other fees.[5] In March 2010, a massive healthcare overhaul bill known as the Affordable Care Act was enacted. The legislation, which took effect in 2013–2014, offers all Americans access to health care, including those with preexisting conditions who in the past have often been denied coverage. We have yet to see the full effects (e.g., the predicted layoffs or drastic increases in insurance premiums), but so far, despite annual price increases, the plan seems to be working.[6]

Government regulations create some problems in the international environment. In countries including Egypt, the Philippines, Thailand, Bangladesh, and Zimbabwe to name a few, the government dictates prices for a range of products from bread to pharmaceuticals. Pricing regulations are enacted to maintain affordability of staple foods and goods, to prevent price gouging during shortages, and to slow inflation. When this kind of government control makes it impossible to produce their products and make a profit, a firm's only options are to use cheaper ingredients or not make their products available in that market.

Consumer Trends

Consumer trends also can strongly influence prices. Culture and demographics determine how consumers think and behave, so these factors have a large impact on all marketing decisions. One current consumer trend is saving time by *buying time*. More and more consumers are choosing to buy ready-made food, shop locally or online, enjoy "daycation" deals where hotels and spas offer access to a room or hotel amenities such as a pool for the day, and use digital timesaving devices such as robot vacuum cleaners. Consumers are also *eating greener* by cutting down on food waste, avoiding unhealthy food and overeating while eating local and seasonal food. **Shopping for control** is a response to the almost daily reports of terrorism and political unrest that have made the world a scary place for many consumers. This has led consumers to value products and services that provide some degree of predictability and control in an uncertain world, such as installing smart home technology or moving to gated communities.[7]

shopping for control
Consumers, facing a world with terrorism and political unrest, value products and services that provide some degree of control, such as installing smart home technology or moving to gated communities.

The International Environment

As we discussed in Chapter 2, the marketing environment often varies widely from country to country. This can have important consequences in developing pricing strategies. Can a company standardize prices for all global markets, or must it adjust to local conditions?

For some products, such as jet airplanes, companies like Boeing and Airbus standardize their prices. This is possible, first, because about the only customers for the wide-bodies and other popular jets are major airlines and governments of countries that buy for their military or for use by government officials. Second, companies that build planes have little or no leeway to cut their costs without sacrificing safety.

For other products, including most consumer goods, unique environmental factors in different countries mean that marketers must adapt their pricing strategies. As we noted in Chapter 2, the economic conditions in developing countries often mean that consumers simply cannot afford $3 or $4 or more for a bottle of shampoo or laundry detergent. As a result, marketers offer their brands at lower prices, often by providing them in one-use packages called sachets that we discussed in Chapter 2. In other cases, companies must save on costs by using less expensive ingredients in their brands to provide toothpaste or soap that is affordable.

Finally, channels of distribution often vary both in the types and sizes of available intermediaries and in the availability of an infrastructure to facilitate product distribution. Often these differences can mean that trade margins will be higher, as will the cost of getting the products to consumers.

10.3 Identify Strategies and Tactics to Price the Product

OBJECTIVE

Understand key pricing strategies and tactics.

(pp. 332–339)

An old Russian proverb says, "There are two kinds of fools in any market. One doesn't charge enough. The other charges too much."[8] In modern business, there seldom is any one-and-only, now-and-forever, best pricing strategy. Like playing a game of chess, making pricing moves and countermoves requires thinking two and three moves ahead. Figure 10.11 provides a summary of different pricing strategies and tactics. Price planning is influenced by psychological issues and strategies and by legal and ethical issues.

Step 5: Choose a Pricing Strategy

The next step in price planning is to choose a pricing strategy. Some strategies work for certain products, with certain customer groups, in certain competitive markets, whereas others do not. When is it best for the firm to undercut the competition and when to just meet the competition's prices? When is the best pricing strategy one that considers costs only, and when is it best to use one based on demand?

Pricing Strategies Based on Cost

Marketing planners often choose cost-based strategies because they are simple to calculate and are relatively risk free. They promise that the price will at least cover the costs the company incurs to produce and market the product.

Cost-based pricing methods have drawbacks, however. They do not consider factors such as the changing prices of inputs, the nature of the target market, demand, competition, the product life cycle, and the product's image. Moreover, although the calculations for setting the price may be simple and straightforward, estimating costs accurately may prove difficult.

Figure 10.11 Snapshot | Pricing Strategies and Tactics

Marketers develop successful pricing programs by choosing from a variety of pricing strategies and tactics.

Pricing strategies	Pricing tactics

• Based on cost
  Cost plus
• Based on demand
  Target costing
  Yield management
• Based on the competition
  Price leadership
• Based on customers' needs
  Value (EDLP) pricing
• New product pricing
  Skimming pricing
  Penetration pricing
  Trial pricing
	• Pricing for individual products
	  Two-part pricing
	  Payment pricing
	• Pricing for multiple products
	  Price bundling
	  Captive pricing
	• Distribution-based pricing
	• Discounting for channel members

Think about firms such as 3M, General Electric, and Nabisco, all of which produce many different products. How does a cost analysis allocate the costs for the plant, research and development, equipment, design engineers, maintenance, and marketing personnel among the different products so that the pricing plan accurately reflects the cost to produce any one product? For example, how do you allocate the salary of a marketing executive who oversees many different products? Should the cost be divided equally among all products? Should costs be based on the actual number of hours spent working on each product? Or should costs be assigned based on the revenues generated by each product? There is no one right answer. Even with these limitations, though, cost-based pricing strategies often are a marketer's best choice.

The most common cost-based approach to pricing a product is **cost-plus pricing**, in which the marketer totals all the costs for the product and then adds an amount (or marks up the cost of the item) to arrive at the selling price. Many marketers, especially retailers and wholesalers who often must set the price for tens of thousands of products, use cost-plus pricing because of its simplicity; users need only know or estimate the unit cost and add the markup.

You may wonder how a retailer or a wholesaler determines the markup percentage. In many cases the markup percentage is a matter of tradition or rules of thumb. Many retailers mark up clothing, gifts, and other items by keystone pricing or **"keystoning"** in which the retailer simply doubles the cost of the item (100 percent markup) to determine the price.[9] Restaurants typically triple the costs (200 percent markup) of the food that goes into a menu item and quadruple (300 percent markup) the cost of alcoholic beverages.[10]

To calculate cost-plus pricing, marketers usually calculate either a markup on cost or a markup on selling price. With both methods, you calculate the price by adding a predetermined percentage to the cost, but as the names of the methods imply, for one the calculation uses a percentage of the costs and for the other a percentage of the selling price. Which of the two methods is used seems often to be little more than a matter of the "the way our company has always done it." You'll find more information about cost-plus pricing and how to calculate markup on cost and markup on selling price in the Chapter 10 Supplement at the end of this chapter.

Pricing Strategies Based on Demand

Demand-based pricing means that the firm bases the selling price on an estimate of volume or quantity that it can sell in different markets at different prices. To use any of the pricing strategies based on demand, firms must determine how much product they can sell in each market and at what price. As we noted previously, marketers often use customer surveys, in which consumers indicate whether they would buy a certain product and how much of it they would buy at various prices. They may obtain more accurate estimates by conducting an experiment like the ones we described in Chapter 4. Two specific demand-based pricing strategies are target costing and yield management pricing. Let's take a quick look at each approach.

Today, firms find that a new product can be more successful if they match price with demand using a **target costing** process.[11] With target costing, firms first use marketing research to identify the quality and functionality needed to satisfy attractive market segments and what price they are willing to pay *before* they design the product. As Figure 10.12 shows, the next step is to determine what margins retailers and dealers require as well as the profit margin the producer firm requires. On the basis of this information, managers can calculate the target cost—the maximum it can cost the firm to manufacture the product. If the firm can meet customer quality and functionality requirements and control costs to meet the required price, it will manufacture the product. If not, it abandons the product.

Yield management pricing is another type of demand-based pricing strategy that hospitality businesses like airlines, hotels, and cruise lines use. These businesses charge

cost-plus pricing
A method of setting prices in which the seller totals all the costs for the product and then adds an amount to arrive at the selling price.

keystoning
retail pricing strategy in which the retailer doubles the cost of the item (100 percent markup) to determine the price.

demand-based pricing
A price-setting method based on estimates of demand at different prices.

target costing
A process in which firms identify the quality and functionality needed to satisfy customers and what price they are willing to pay before the product is designed; the product is manufactured only if the firm can control costs to meet the required price.

yield management pricing
A practice of charging different prices to different customers to manage capacity while maximizing revenues.

Figure 10.12 📷 *Snapshot* | Target Costing Using a Jeans Example

With target costing, a firm first determines the price at which customers would be willing to buy the product and then works backward to design the product in such a way that it can produce and sell the product at a profit.

Step 1: Determine the price customers are willing to pay for the jeans
$79.99

Step 2: Determine the markup required by the retailer
40% (.40)

Step 3: Calculate the maximum price the retailer will pay, the price customers are willing to pay minus the markup amount

Formula: Price to the retailer = Selling price × (1.00 − markup percentage)
Price to the retailer = $79.99 × (1.00 − .40)
= $79.99 × 0.60 = **$47.99**

Step 4: Determine the profit required by the firm
15% (.15)

Step 5: Calculate the target cost, the maximum cost of producing the jeans
Formula: Target cost = Price to the retailer × (1.00 − profit percentage)
Target cost = $47.99 × 0.85 = **$40.79**

---

different prices to different customers to manage capacity while they maximize revenues. Many service firms practice yield management pricing because they recognize that different customers have different sensitivities to price; some customers will pay top dollar for an airline ticket, whereas others will travel only if there is a discount fare. The goal of yield management pricing is to accurately predict the proportion of customers who fall into each category and allocate the percentages of the airline's or hotel's capacity accordingly so that no product goes unsold.

An airline, for example, may charge two prices for the same seat, say, a full fare of $899 and a discount fare of $299. (In reality, of course, the airlines charge a much greater number of different fares.) The airline uses information about past flights to predict how many seats it can fill at full fare and how many it can sell only at the discounted fare. The airline begins months ahead of the date of the flight with a basic allocation of seats—perhaps it will place 25 percent of the seats in the full-fare "bucket" and 75 percent in the discount-fare "bucket." As flight time gets closer, the airline might make a series of adjustments to the allocation of seats in the hope of selling every seat on the plane at the highest price possible. If the New York Mets need to book the flight, chances are the airline will be able to sell some of the discount seats at full fare, which in turn decreases the number available at the discounted price. If, as the flight date nears, the number of full-fare ticket sales falls below the forecast, the airline will move some of those seats over to the discount bucket. Then the suspense builds! The pricing game continues until the day of the flight as the airline attempts to fill every seat by the time the plane takes off. This is why you may find one price for a ticket on Travelocity.com or Expedia.com a month before the flight, a much higher price two weeks later, and a very low price the last few days before the flight. This also tells you why you often see the ticket agents at the gate frantically looking for "volunteers" who are willing to give up their seats because the airline sold more seats than actually fit in the plane.

Pricing Strategies Based on the Competition

Sometimes a firm's pricing strategy involves pricing its wares near, at, above, or below the competition's prices. In the "good old days," when U.S. automakers had the American market to themselves, pricing decisions were straightforward: Industry giant General Motors would announce its new car prices, and Ford, Chrysler, Packard, Studebaker, Hudson, and the others got in line or dropped out. A **price leadership**

price leadership
A pricing strategy in which one firm first sets its price and other firms in the industry follow with the same or similar prices.

strategy, which usually is the rule in an oligopolistic industry that a few firms dominate, may be in the best interest of all players because it minimizes price competition. Price leadership strategies are popular because they provide an acceptable and legal way for firms to agree on prices without ever coordinating these rates with each other.

Pricing Strategies Based on Customers' Needs

In 1960, Lee Iacocca, then the Ford Division general manager, noted forecasts that the Baby Boomer generation was coming of age, which meant that Ford would face an increasing number of young car buyers. There were also indications that these young car buyers would like a stylish sports car but couldn't afford the $4,000 to $7,000 price tag on the Ford Thunderbird or the GM Corvette. Under Iacocca's direction, Ford began developing a car that had the style and features young drivers desired but at a cost they could afford. This car, of course, was the iconic Ford Mustang. Priced at an amazingly low $2500, Ford sold more than 400,000 Mustangs in the first year and in two years made over $1 billion in profits from the car.[12]

Priceline uses hotels' excess capacity to its advantage as it provides rooms to guests at a discount.

Retailers typically practice one of two pricing strategies based on customer's needs: EDLP and high/low pricing. Firms that practice **value pricing** or **everyday low pricing (EDLP)** develop a pricing strategy that promises good quality and durable products at reasonable prices every day. Many successful retail chains around the world including Walmart, Kmart, Home Depot, Office Depot, Toys "R" Us, Target, and Tesco all adopt a deliberate policy of EDLP. Because of their size, these firms are able to demand billions of dollars in cost efficiencies from their suppliers and pass the savings on to customers.

value pricing or **everyday low pricing (EDLP)**
A pricing strategy in which a firm sets prices that provide ultimate value to customers.

The **high/low pricing** or **promo pricing** strategy means retailers have prices that are higher than EDLP chains, normally the MSRP or list price, but run frequent, often weekly, promotions that heavily discount some products. So what happens if retailers seek to switch from one strategy to the other? Sears, for example, has switched from high/low to EDLP and then back to high/low. JC Penney also tried to switch from a high/low strategy to EDLP and failed.

high/low pricing (also known as promo pricing)
A retail pricing strategy in which the retailer prices merchandise at list price but runs frequent, often weekly, promotions that heavily discount some products.

New Product Pricing

New products are vital to the growth and profits of a firm, but they also present unique pricing challenges. When a product is new to the market or when there is no established industry price norm, marketers may use a skimming price strategy, a penetration pricing strategy, or trial pricing.

A **skimming price** means that the firm charges a high, premium price for its new product with the intention of reducing it in the future in response to market pressures. If a product is highly desirable and offers unique benefits, demand is price inelastic during the introductory stage of the product life cycle, allowing a company to recover research and development (R&D) and promotion costs. When rival products enter the market, the firm lowers the price to remain competitive. Firms that focus on profit objectives when they develop their pricing strategies often set skimming prices for new products The Sony PlayStation 3 was originally sold at $599 in the U.S. market, but it was gradually reduced to less than $200.[13] For skimming pricing to be successful, there should be little chance that competitors can get into the market quickly. With highly complex, technical products, it will take time for competitors to put a rival product into production.

skimming price
A very high, premium price that a firm charges for its new, highly desirable product.

penetration pricing
A pricing strategy in which a firm introduces a new product at a very low price to encourage more customers to purchase it.

Penetration pricing is the opposite of skimming pricing. In this situation, the company prices a new product very low to sell more in a short time and gain market share early. Another reason marketers use penetration pricing is to discourage competitors from entering the market. The firm that first introduces a new product has an important advantage. Experience shows that a pioneering brand often is able to maintain dominant market share for long periods. Campbell's soup with the iconic red label is a brand that was first to market in 1895 and still dominates the industry today.[14]

trial pricing
Pricing a new product low for a limited period of time to lower the risk for a customer.

Trial pricing means that a new product carries a low price for a limited time to generate a high level of customer interest. Unlike penetration pricing, in which the company maintains the low price, in this case it increases the trial price after the introductory period. The idea is to win customer acceptance first and make profits later, as when a new health club offers an introductory membership to start pulling people in or a cable TV company offers a great low price for six months if you sign up for their TV, Internet, and phone bundle after which you will pay much more.

Price Segmentation

price segmentation
the practice of charging different prices to different market segments for the same product.

Most markets are made up of consumers who have widely different characteristics. As we discussed in Chapter 7, we refer to these as market segments. Just as the same product may not be best for all segments, the best price for a product differs among market segments. **Price segmentation** is the practice of charging different prices to different market segments for the same product. For example, some restaurants, segmenting by age, may offer senior citizens a 10 percent or larger discount on meals. Segmenting on quantity occurs when the price of one large pizza is $9.00 but you can get two for $15. Of course marketers must be careful when using customer characteristics as criteria for price differences to avoid some customers feeling discriminated against. The use of characteristics such as gender, race, religion, or ethnic group should generally be avoided.

peak load pricing
A pricing plan that sets prices higher during periods with higher demand.

When the demand for a product differs during predictable periods, sellers often develop a pricing plan that sets prices higher during periods with higher demand. In the same way, a seller may segment based on the time when the purchase is made. This **peak load pricing** received its name because it was originally used for pricing by electric utility companies. Movie theaters offer lower daytime ticket prices, restaurants offer "early bird" discounts, and the cost of resort hotel rooms is much higher during the summer for beach resorts and winter for resorts on the slopes.

surge pricing
A pricing plan that raises prices of a product as demand goes up and lowers it as demand slides.

Uber is a global online transportation company. Consumers can use the Uber app on their smartphones to request a trip, which is then routed to Uber drivers who use their own cars. Uber uses a **surge pricing** strategy; it raises the price of its product as demand goes up (as on a rainy Saturday night) and lowers it as demand declines.

Bottom of the Pyramid Pricing

bottom of the pyramid pricing
Innovative pricing that will appeal to consumers with the lowest incomes by brands that wish to get a foothold in bottom of the pyramid countries.

Marketers face a different challenge when they wish to get a foothold in countries with huge populations of people with the lowest incomes, the bottom of the pyramid countries. These marketers need to develop **bottom of the pyramid pricing**, prices that are low enough to appeal to the large numbers of these consumers. One approach (discussed in Chapter 2) is to sell nondurable products in smaller packages for just a few cents. A second option is for people, perhaps an entire village to share a product such as a cell phone, a computer, or a refrigerator.

Step 6: Develop Pricing Tactics

Once marketers have developed pricing strategies, the last step in price planning is to implement them. The methods companies use to set their strategies in motion are their *pricing tactics.*

Pricing for Individual Products

Pricing tactics, the way marketers present a product's price, can make a big difference in the success of the product:

- **Two-part pricing** requires two separate types of payments to purchase the product. For example, golf and tennis clubs charge yearly or monthly fees plus fees for each round of golf or tennis.

- **Payment pricing** makes the consumer think the price is "do-able" by breaking up the total price into smaller amounts payable over time. For example, at the online shopping channel QVC you can avoid the *sticker shock* (a negative reaction to the total retail price) of an iPad by paying for the product with low installment payments. For five easy payments of $159.99 (plus shipping and handling, of course), you can get a 16-gigabyte Apple iPad 2 with Bluetooth keyboard, case, and more. Just beware: The total cost of the iPad plus accessories totals $799.98—twice the price of the one you could have gotten at Best Buy for only $399![15]

Secondhand products often meet the price needs of frugal consumers. This ad for a used furniture store ran in Turkey.

- **Decoy pricing** is a strategy where a seller offers at least three similar products. Two of them have comparable but more expensive prices than the third, and one of these two is less attractive to buyers than the other. The result is that people will more often choose the more attractive of the two higher priced items. As an example, think about an electronics retailer who would like for his customers to buy a specific, higher-priced laptop with a higher margin that will mean more profits for him. With decoy pricing, he will offer three different laptops—we'll call them models A, B, and C. Model A is a stripped-down, no-name brand laptop, much lower priced than either model B or model C, and unlikely to attract many sales. One of the two higher priced items, say model B, has a larger hard drive, superior screen resolution and more RAM than model C. In this case, model C is the decoy. When consumers compare it to model B, they will naturally buy model B, just as the retailer wanted them to do.

Pricing for Multiple Products

A firm may sell several products that consumers typically buy at one time. As fast-food restaurants like Burger King know, a customer who buys a burger for lunch usually springs for a soft drink and fries as well. The purchase of a single-serve coffee brewer means you also need to purchase lots of K-cup coffee pods. The two most common tactics for pricing multiple products are price bundling and captive pricing.

Price bundling means selling two or more goods or services as a single package for one price—a price that is often less than the total price of the items if bought individually. Traditional cable TV providers like AT&T U-verse, Comcast, and Time Warner have gotten into the price bundling act as they entice their customers to sign on for a package of cable TV, high-speed Internet, and local or, in some cases, wireless phone service.

From a marketing standpoint, price bundling makes sense. If we price products separately, it's more likely that customers will buy some but not all the items. They might choose to put off some purchases until later, or they might buy from a competitor. Whatever revenue a seller loses from the reduced prices for the total package it often makes up for in increased total purchases.

Captive pricing is a pricing tactic a firm uses when it has two products that work only when used together. The firm sells one item at a very low price and then makes its profit

---

two-part pricing
Pricing that requires two separate types of payments to purchase the product.

payment pricing
A pricing tactic that breaks up the total price into smaller amounts payable over time.

decoy pricing
A pricing strategy where a seller offers at least three similar products; two have comparable but more expensive prices and one of these two is less attractive to buyers, thus causing more buyers to buy the higher priced more attractive item.

price bundling
Selling two or more goods or services as a single package for one price.

captive pricing
A pricing tactic for two items that must be used together; one item is priced very low, and the firm makes its profit on another, high-margin item essential to the operation of the first item.

The Art of Shaving, a division of Procter & Gamble, sells men's shaving products online, in department stores, and in its own free-standing stores. Customers often buy a "shaving kit" that consists of several of the company's products bundled together.

F.O.B. origin pricing (also known as F.O.B. factory pricing)
A pricing tactic in which the cost of transporting the product from the factory to the customer's location is the responsibility of the customer.

F.O.B. delivered pricing
A pricing tactic in which the cost of loading and transporting the product to the customer is included in the selling price and is paid by the manufacturer.

uniform delivered pricing
A pricing tactic in which a firm adds a standard shipping charge to the price for all customers regardless of location.

freight absorption pricing
A pricing tactic in which the seller absorbs the total cost of transportation.

on the second high-margin item. This tactic is commonly used to sell shaving products where the razor is relatively cheap but the blades are not. Similarly, companies such as HP and Canon offer consumers a desktop printer that also serves as a fax, copier, and scanner for under $100 to keep selling ink cartridges.

Distribution-Based Pricing

Distribution-based pricing is a pricing tactic that establishes how firms handle the cost of shipping products to customers near, far, and wide. Characteristics of the product, the customers, and the competition figure in the decision to charge all customers the same price or to vary according to shipping cost.

F.O.B. pricing is a tactic business-to-business (B2B) marketers use. F.O.B. stands for "free on board," which refers to who pays for the shipping. Also—and this is important—*title passes to the buyer* at the F.O.B. location. **F.O.B. factory pricing** or **F.O.B. origin pricing** means that the cost of transporting the product from the factory to the customer's location is the responsibility of the customer. **F.O.B. delivered pricing** means that the seller pays both the cost of loading and the cost of transporting to the customer, amounts it added into the selling price.

Delivery terms for pricing of products sold in international markets are similar:[16]

- *CIF* (cost, insurance, freight) is the term used for ocean shipments and means the seller quotes a price for the goods (including insurance), all transportation, and miscellaneous charges to the point of debarkation from the vessel.

- *CFR* (cost and freight) means the quoted price covers the goods and the cost of transportation to the named point of debarkation, but the buyer must pay the cost of insurance. The CFR term is also used for ocean shipments.

- *CIP* (carriage and insurance paid to) and *CPT* (carriage paid to) include the same provisions as CIF and CFR but are used for shipment by modes other than water.

When a firm uses **uniform delivered pricing**, it adds a preset shipping cost to the price, no matter what the distance from the manufacturer's plant—within reason. Uniform delivered pricing is most likely to be used when shipping charges are very low. For example, when you order a the latest Harry Potter book, you may pay the cost of the book plus $3.99 shipping and handling, no matter what the actual cost of the shipping to your particular location. Internet sales, catalog sales, home TV shopping, and other types of nonstore retail sales usually use uniform delivered pricing.

Freight absorption pricing means the seller takes on part or all of the cost of shipping. This policy works well for high-ticket items, for which the cost of shipping is a negligible part of the sales price and the profit margin. Marketers are most likely to use freight absorption pricing in highly competitive markets or when such pricing allows them to enter new markets. More recently, online marketers such as Amazon.com have found that offering free shipping makes a big difference to consumers and to their sales volume.

Discounting for Channel Members

So far, we've talked about pricing tactics used to sell to end customers. Now we'll talk about tactics firms use to price to members of their *distribution channels*:

- *Trade or functional discounts:* We discussed previously how manufacturers often set a list or suggested retail price for their product and then sell the product to members of the channel for less, allowing the channel members to cover their costs and make a profit.

Thus, the manufacturer's pricing structure will normally include **trade discounts** to channel intermediaries. These discounts are usually set percentage discounts off the suggested retail or list price for each channel level. In today's marketing environment dominated by large retail chains such as Walmart, Costco, and Target, the retailers dictate the amount of the trade discount, which because of their size have the most power in the channel. We'll talk more about channel power in Chapter 11.

- *Quantity discounts:* To encourage larger purchases from distribution channel partners or from large organizational customers, marketers may offer **quantity discounts**, or reduced prices for purchases of larger quantities. *Cumulative quantity discounts* are based on a total quantity bought within a specified time period, often a year, and encourage a buyer to stick with a single seller instead of moving from one supplier to another. Cumulative quantity discounts often take the form of *rebates*, in which case the firm sends the buyer a rebate check at the end of the discount period or, alternatively, gives the buyer credit against future orders. *Noncumulative quantity discounts* are based only on the quantity purchased with each individual order and encourage larger single orders but do little to tie the buyer and the seller together.

- *Cash discounts:* Many firms try to entice their customers to pay their bills quickly by offering **cash discounts**. For example, a firm selling to a retailer may state that the terms of the sale are "2 percent 10 (days), net 30 (days)," meaning that if the retailer or organizational customer pays the producer for the goods within 10 days, the amount due is cut by 2 percent. The total amount is due within 30 days, and after 30 days the payment is late.

- *Seasonal discounts:* **Seasonal discounts** are price reductions offered only during certain times of the year. For seasonal products such as snowblowers, lawn mowers, and water-skiing equipment, marketers use seasonal discounts to entice retailers and wholesalers to buy off-season and either store the product at their locations until the right time of the year or pass the discount along to consumers with off-season sales programs. Alternatively, they may offer discounts when products are in season to create a competitive advantage during periods of high demand.

trade discounts
Discounts off list price of products to members of the channel of distribution who perform various marketing functions.

quantity discounts
A pricing tactic of charging reduced prices for purchases of larger quantities of a product.

cash discounts
A discount offered to a customer to entice them to pay their bill quickly.

seasonal discounts
Price reductions offered only during certain times of the year.

10.4 Pricing and Electronic Commerce

OBJECTIVE
Understand the opportunities for Internet pricing strategies.
(pp. 339–341)

As we have seen, price planning is a complex process in any firm. But if you are operating in the "wired world," get ready for even more pricing options!

Because sellers are connected to buyers around the globe as never before through the Internet, corporate networks, and wireless setups, marketers can offer deals they tailor to a single person at a single moment. On the other hand, they're also a lot more vulnerable to smart consumers, who can easily check out competing prices with the click of a mouse.

Many experts suggest that technology is creating a consumer revolution that might change pricing forever—and perhaps create the most efficient market ever. The music industry provides the most obvious example: Music lovers from around the globe purchase and download tens of billions of songs from numerous Internet sites, including the iTunes Store, Google Play, and Amazon MP3.[17] More than 70 million people who live in the U.S. alone access music through their phones.[18] And as you know, some of those people pay little to nothing for their tunes.

The Internet also enables firms that sell to other businesses (B2B firms) to change their prices rapidly as they adapt to changing costs. For consumers who have lots of stuff in their attics that they need to put in someone else's attic, the Internet means an opportunity for sellers to find ready buyers through consumer-to-consumer (C2C) sites such as eBay and Etsy. And for B2C firms that sell to consumers, the Internet offers other opportunities. In this section, we'll discuss some of the more popular Internet pricing strategies.

Dynamic Pricing Strategies

dynamic pricing
A pricing strategy in which the price can easily be adjusted to meet changes in the marketplace.

One of the most important opportunities the Internet offers is **dynamic pricing**, in which the seller can quickly and easily adjust prices to meet changes in the marketplace. If a bricks-and-mortar retail store wants to change prices, employees/workers must place new price tags on items, create and display new store signage and media advertising, and input new prices into the store's computer system. For B2B marketers, employees/workers must print catalogs and price lists and distribute to salespeople and customers. These activities can be very costly to a firm, so they simply don't change their prices often.[19]

Internet Price Discrimination

Internet price discrimination
An Internet pricing strategy that charges different prices to different customers for the same product.

Of course, the Internet allows firms to do more than just adjust prices as a result of external factors such as changing costs or competitive activity. The promise of the Internet is that it allows consumers to quickly comparison shop for the lowest price, all the while sitting in their pajamas at home. Many firms, it seems, use the same technology to practice **Internet price discrimination**.

Internet price discrimination is an Internet pricing strategy that charges different prices to different customers for the same product.[20] A *Wall Street Journal* investigation found that a Swingline stapler on **Staples.com** was priced at $15.79 for one customer and $14.29 for another who lived just a few miles away based on their location and their distance from either an OfficeMax or an Office Depot store.[21]

Marketers know that they will maximize profits if they charge each customer the most that person is willing to pay. Although this is not practical, placing customers into groups based on where they live, how close they are to the retailer or a competitor, the cost of doing business in the area, or their Internet browsing history can greatly increase profits. Some sites even offer customers a discount if they use a mobile device. A shopper who uses a smartphone to find a hotel room on sites like Orbitz.com or CheapTickets.com may find rooms for as much as 50 percent less than they would otherwise pay.

Is internet price discrimination illegal? As we said in our discussion of price segmentation, as long as companies don't charge different prices based on a demographic characteristic such as gender or race, it is not. Sometimes, however, it's difficult to tell how the company makes these decisions. For example, a recent report found that *The Princeton Review*, which charges different prices for its SAT prep service to consumers who live in different zip codes, is almost twice as likely to offer a higher price to Asians who ask for an online quote compared to non-Asians. This doesn't necessarily mean the company is intentionally discriminating against Asians, but rather that these consumers are more likely to live in zip codes assigned to the higher rates. As the company responded, "The areas that experience higher prices will also have a disproportionately higher population of members of the financial services industry, people who tend to vote Democratic, journalists, and any other group that is more heavily concentrated in areas like New York City."[22]

Online Auctions

online auctions
E-commerce that allows shoppers to purchase products through online bidding.

Most consumers are familiar with eBay. But what about eCrater, Bonanzle, eBid, and CQout? These too are some of the many **online auctions** that allow shoppers to bid on everything from bobbleheads to health-and-fitness equipment to a Sammy Sosa home-run ball. Auctions are a powerful Internet pricing strategy. Perhaps the most popular auctions are the C2C auctions such as those on eBay. The eBay auction is an *open auction*, meaning that all the buyers know the highest price bid at any point in time. On many Internet auction sites, the seller can set a *reserve price*, a price below which the item will not be sold.

A *reverse auction* is a tool firms use to manage their costs in B2B buying. Although in a typical auction, buyers compete to purchase a product, in reverse auctions sellers compete for the right to provide a product at, the buyers hope, a low price.

Freemium Pricing Strategies

Perhaps the most exciting new pricing strategy is **freemium pricing** (a mix of "free" and "premium."). Freemium is a business strategy in which a product in its most basic version is provided free of charge, but the company charges money (the premium) for upgraded versions of the product with more features, greater functionality, or greater capacity.[23] The freemium pricing strategy has been most popular in digital offerings such as software media, games, or web services where the cost of one additional copy of the product is negligible. Companies that have followed the new pricing strategy include Dropbox, Inc., SurveyMonkey, Spotify, and Skype. The idea is that if you give your product away, you will build a customer base of consumers willing to pay for the added benefits. Whereas some products such as Skype have been highly successful, others have found that customers never upgrade to the premium version of the product. Pandora, the music streaming service, found that many consumers were unwilling to pay for their service and changed their business model to include a free service supported by paid advertising plus their Pandora One paid service without the ads.

freemium pricing
A business strategy in which a product in its most basic version is provided free of charge but the company charges money (the premium) for upgraded versions of the product with more features, greater functionality, or greater capacity.

Pricing Advantages for Online Shoppers

The Internet also creates unique pricing challenges for marketers as consumers and business customers gain more control over the buying process. Access to sophisticated "shopbots" and search engines means that consumers are no longer at the mercy of firms that dictate a price they must accept. The result is that customers have become more price sensitive. Many computer-savvy Internet shoppers find that shopbots provide them with the best price on all kinds of products. As one illustration, a comparison study found that the price of an Otter Box Defender Series iPhone case ranged from a high of $59.90 at OtterBox.com to a low of $44.20 at Amazon.com. Similarly, the price of a Michael Kors Signature Tote is $165.50 at Amazon.com but $198.00 online from Nordstrom (no, we're not working on commission).

Detailed information about what products actually cost manufacturers, available from sites such as Consumerreports.org, can give consumers more negotiating power when shopping for new cars and other big-ticket items. Finally, e-commerce potentially can lower consumers' costs because of the gasoline, time, and aggravation they save when they avoid a trip to the mall.

10.5 Psychological, Legal, and Ethical Aspects of Pricing

OBJECTIVE
Describe the psychological, legal, and ethical aspects of pricing.

(pp. 341–347)

So far, we've discussed how marketers use demand, costs, and an understanding of the pricing environment to plan effective pricing strategies and tactics. There are, however, other aspects of pricing that marketers must understand and deal with to maximize the effectiveness of their pricing plans. In this section, we discuss a number of psychological, legal, and ethical factors related to pricing that are important for marketers. Figure 10.13 provides a quick look at these aspects of pricing.

Figure 10.13 📷 *Snapshot* |
Psychological, Legal, and Ethical
Aspects of Pricing

Price planning is influenced by
psychological issues and strategies and
by legal and ethical issues.

Psychological Issues in Pricing	Psychological Pricing Strategies
• Buyer' Expectations • Internal Reference Prices • Price-Quality inferences	• Odd-Even Pricing • Price Lining • Prestige Pricing
Legal and Ethical Issues in B2C Pricing	Legal and Ethical Issues in B2B Pricing
• Bait-and-Switch • Loss-Leader pricing	• Price Discrimination • Price-Fixing • Predatory Pricing

Psychological Issues in Setting Prices

Much of what we've said about pricing depends on economists' notion of a customer who evaluates price in a logical, rational manner. For example, we express the concept of demand by a smooth curve, which assumes that if a firm lowers a product's price from $10 to $9.50 and then from $9.50 to $9 and so on, then customers will simply buy more and more. In the real world, though, it doesn't always work that way; consumers aren't nearly as rational as that! Let's look at some psychological factors that keep economists up at night.

Buyers' Pricing Expectations

Often consumers base their perceptions of price on what they perceive to be the customary or *fair price*. For example, for many years a candy bar or a pack of gum was priced at five cents (yes, five). Consumers would have perceived any other price as too high or low. It was a nickel candy bar—period. So when inflation kicked in and costs went up, some candy makers tried to shrink the size of the bar instead of changing the price. Eventually, inflation prevailed, consumers' salaries rose, and that candy bar goes for as much as 30 times one nickel today—a price that consumers would have found unacceptable a few decades ago.

When the price of a product is above or even sometimes when it's below what consumers expect, they are less willing to purchase the product. If the price is above their expectations, they may think it is a rip-off. If it is below expectations, consumers may think quality is below par. By understanding the pricing expectations of their customers, marketers are better able to develop viable pricing strategies. These expectations can differ across cultures and countries. For example, in one study researchers in southern California found that Chinese supermarkets charge significantly lower prices (only half as much for meat and seafood) than mainstream American supermarkets in the same areas.[24]

Internal Reference Prices

internal reference price
A set price or a price range in consumers' minds that they refer to in evaluating a product's price.

Sometimes consumers' perceptions of the price of a product depend on their **internal reference price**. That is, based on past experience, consumers have a set price or a price range in mind that they refer to when they evaluate a product's cost. The reference price may be the last price paid, or it may be the average of all the prices they know of for similar products. No matter what the brand, the normal price for a loaf of sandwich bread is about $2.00. In some stores it may be $1.89, and in others it is $2.89, but the average is $2.00. If consumers find a comparable loaf of bread priced much higher than this—say, $3.99—they will feel it is overpriced and grab a competing brand. If they find bread priced significantly lower—say, at $.89 or $.99 a loaf—they may shy away from the purchase as they wonder "what's wrong" with the bread (no, we don't think that's why they call it Wonder Bread).

In some cases, marketers try to influence consumers' expectations of what a product should cost when they use reference pricing strategies. For example, manufacturers may compare their price to competitors' prices when they advertise. Similarly, a retailer may display a product next to a higher-priced version of the same or a different brand. The consumer must choose between the two products with different prices.

Two results are likely: On the one hand, if the prices (and other characteristics) of the two products are fairly close, the consumer will probably feel the product quality is similar. This is an *assimilation effect*. The customer might think, "The price is about the same, they must be alike. I'll be smart and save a few dollars." And so the customer chooses the lower-price item because the low price makes it look attractive next to the higher-priced alternative. This is why store brands of deodorant, vitamins, pain relievers, and shampoo sit beside national brands, often accompanied by a shelf talker pointing out how much shoppers can save if they purchase the store brands. On the other hand, if the prices of the two products are too far apart, a *contrast effect* in which the customer equates the gap with a big difference in quality may result. The consumer may think, "Gee, this lower-priced one is probably not as good as the higher-priced one. I'll splurge on the more expensive one." Using this strategy, an appliance store may place an advertised $300 refrigerator next to a $699 model to convince a customer that the bottom-of-the-line model just won't do.

Price–Quality Inferences

Imagine that you go to a shoe store to check out running shoes. You notice one pair that costs $89.99. On another table you see a second pair that looks almost identical to the first pair—but its price is only $24.95. Which pair do you want? Which pair do you think is the better quality? Many of us will pay the higher price because we believe the bargain-basement shoes aren't worth the risk at any price.

Consumers make *price–quality inferences* about a product when they use price as a cue or an indicator of quality. (An inference means we believe something to be true without any direct evidence.) If consumers are unable to judge the quality of a product through examination or prior experience, they usually assume that the higher-priced product is the higher-quality product.

In fact, new research on how the brain works even suggests that the price we pay can subtly influence how much pleasure we get from the product. Brain scans show that—contrary to conventional wisdom—consumers who buy something at a discount experience *less* satisfaction than people who pay full price for the very same thing. For example, in one recent study, volunteers who drank wine that they were told cost $90 a bottle actually registered more brain activity in pleasure centers than did those who drank the very same wine but who were told it only cost $10 a bottle. Researchers call this the *price-placebo effect*. This is similar to the placebo effect in medicine where people who think they are getting the real thing but who are actually taking sugar pills still experience the effects of the real drug.[25]

Psychological Pricing Strategies

Setting a price is part science, part art. Marketers must understand psychological responses to prices when they decide what to charge for their products or services.

Odd–Even Pricing

In the U.S. market, we usually see prices in dollars and cents—$1.99, $5.98, $23.67, or even $599.95. We see prices in even dollar amounts—$2, $10, or $600—far less often. The reason? Marketers assume that there is a psychological response to odd prices that differs from the response to even prices. Habit might also play a role here. Whatever the reason, research on the difference in perceptions of odd versus even prices indeed supports the argument that prices ending in 99 rather than 00 lead to increased sales.[26]

But there are some instances in which even prices are the norm or perhaps a necessity. Theater and concert tickets, admission to sporting events, and lottery tickets tend to be priced in even amounts. Professionals normally quote their fees in even dollars. Would you want to visit a doctor or dentist who charged $39.99 for a visit, or would you be concerned that the quality of medical care was less than satisfactory? Many luxury items, such as jewelry, golf course fees, and resort accommodations, use even dollar prices to set them apart.

Restaurants (and the menu engineers who work with them) have discovered that how prices for menu items are presented has a major influence on what customers order—and how much they pay. When prices are given with dollar signs or even the word dollar, customers spend less. Thus, a simple 9 is better on a menu than $9. For high-end restaurants, the formats that end in 9, such as $9.99, indicate value but not quality.[27]

Price Lining

price lining
The practice of setting a limited number of different specific prices, called *price points*, for items in a product line.

Marketers often apply their understanding of the psychological aspects of pricing in a practice they call **price lining**, whereby items in a product line sell at different prices, or *price points*. If you want to buy a new digital camera, you will find that most of the leading manufacturers have one "stripped-down" model for $100 or less. A better-quality but still moderately priced model likely will be around $200, whereas a professional-quality camera with multiple lenses might set you back $1,000 or more. Price lining provides the different ranges necessary to satisfy each segment of the market.

Why is price lining a smart idea? From the marketer's standpoint, it's a way to maximize profits. In theory, a firm would charge each individual customer the highest price that customer is willing to pay. If the maximum one particular person is willing to pay for a digital camera is $150, then that will be the price. If another person is willing to pay $300, that will be his price. But charging each consumer a different price is really not possible. Having a limited number of prices that generally fall at the top of the different price ranges that customers find acceptable is a more workable alternative.

Prestige or Premium Pricing

prestige pricing or premium pricing
A pricing strategy used by luxury goods marketers in which they keep the price artificially high to maintain a favorable image of the product.

Finally, although a "rational" consumer should be more likely to buy a product or service as the price goes down, in the real world this assumption sometimes gets turned on its head. Remember that previously in the chapter we talked about situations where we want to meet an image-enhancement objective to appeal to status-conscious consumers. For this reason, sometimes luxury goods marketers use **prestige pricing**, also referred to as **premium pricing**, in which they keep the price of the product artificially high to maintain a favorable image of the product based on price only. Prestige pricing relies on the price-quality inference that we talked about before. Contrary to the "rational" assumption that we are more likely to purchase a product or service as the price goes down, in these cases, believe it or not, people tend to buy more as the price goes up!

Legal and Ethical Considerations in B2C Pricing

The free enterprise system is founded on the idea that the marketplace will regulate itself. Prices will rise or fall according to demand. Firms and individuals will supply goods and services at fair prices if there is an adequate profit incentive. Unfortunately, the business world includes the greedy and the unscrupulous.

Deceptive Pricing Practices: Bait and Switch

Unscrupulous businesses may advertise or promote prices in a deceptive way. The Federal Trade Commission (FTC), state lawmakers, and private bodies such as the Better Business Bureau have developed pricing rules and guidelines to meet the challenge. They say retailers (or other suppliers) must not claim that their prices are lower than a competitor's unless that claim is true. A going-out-of-business sale should be the last sale before going out of business. A fire sale should be held only when there really was a fire.

Another deceptive pricing practice is the **bait-and-switch** tactic, whereby a retailer will advertise an item at a very low price—the *bait*—to lure customers into the store. An example might be a budget model TV that has been stripped of all but the most basic features. But it is almost impossible to buy the advertised item—salespeople like to say (privately) that the item is "nailed to the floor." The salespeople do everything possible to get the unsuspecting customers to buy a different, more expensive, item—the *switch*. They might tell the customer "confidentially" that "the advertised item is really poor quality, lacking important features, and full of problems." It's complicated to enforce laws against bait-and-switch tactics because these practices are similar to the legal sales technique of "trading up." Simply encouraging consumers to purchase a higher-priced item is acceptable, but it is illegal to advertise a lower-priced item when it's not a legitimate, bona-fide offer that is available if the customer demands it. The FTC may determine if an ad is a bait-and-switch scheme or a legitimate offer by checking to see if a firm refuses to show, demonstrate, or sell the advertised product; disparages it; or penalizes salespeople who do sell it.

> **bait-and-switch**
> An illegal marketing practice in which an advertised price special is used as bait to get customers into the store with the intention of switching them to a higher-priced item.

Loss-Leader Pricing and Unfair Sales Acts

Not every advertised bargain is a bait and switch. Some retailers advertise items at very low prices or even below cost and are glad to sell them at that price because they know that once in the store, customers may buy other items at regular prices. Marketers call this **loss-leader pricing**; they do it to build store traffic and sales volume. For example, some office-supply stores and mass merchandisers recognize that "back-to-school" shopping means more than pencils and erasers and protractors.[28] These retailers use loss-leader pricing—eight pencils for a penny, 24 Crayola crayons for a quarter, or a watercolor set for 50 cents—to entice mothers to fork out $60 for a new Spiderman backpack. In the same way, you can buy a frozen turkey a week or so before Thanksgiving for less than half of what it is at other times of the year.

> **loss-leader pricing**
> The pricing policy of setting prices very low or even below cost to attract customers into a store.

Some states frown on loss-leader practices, so they have passed legislation called **unfair sales acts** (also called *unfair trade practices acts*). These laws or regulations prohibit wholesalers and retailers from selling products below cost. These laws aim to protect small wholesalers and retailers from larger competitors because the "big fish" have the financial resources that allow them to offer loss leaders or products at very low prices—they know that the smaller firms can't match these bargain prices.

> **unfair sales acts**
> State laws that prohibit suppliers from selling products below cost to protect small businesses from larger competitors.

Misleading Merchandising

Sometimes, the merchandising activities in the retail store are deceptive or at least suspicious. Consumers assume that items in an end-aisle display are being sold at a discounted price. When retailers display regularly priced merchandise in these displays, they may be accused of taking advantage of consumers.

Consumers also assume that the larger bottle or box of something is a better deal. Not always true! Although government regulations now require that grocers and other retailers of food post the price per ounce, pound, and such, on store shelves, few consumers seem to look at these labels.

Legal Issues in B2B Pricing

Of course, illegal pricing practices are not limited to B2C pricing situations. Some of the more significant illegal B2B pricing activities include price discrimination, price fixing, and predatory pricing.

Illegal B2B Price Discrimination

The *Robinson–Patman Act* includes regulations against price discrimination in interstate commerce. Price discrimination regulations prevent firms from selling the same product to different retailers and wholesalers at different prices if such practices lessen competition. In addition to regulating the price companies charge, the Robinson–Patman Act specifically prohibits offering such "extras" as discounts, rebates, premiums, coupons, guarantees, and free delivery to some but not all customers.

There are exceptions, however:

- The Robinson–Patman Act does not apply products sold to consumers—only those sold to resellers.
- A discount to a large channel customer is legal if it is based on the quantity of the order and the resulting efficiencies, such as transportation savings.
- The act allows price differences if there are physical differences in the product, such as different features. A name-brand appliance may be available through a large national retail chain at a lower price than an almost identical item a higher-priced retailer sells because only the chain sells that specific model.

Price-Fixing

price-fixing
The collaboration of two or more firms in setting prices, usually to keep prices high.

Price-fixing occurs when two or more companies conspire to keep prices at a certain level. *Horizontal price-fixing* occurs when competitors making the same product jointly determine what price they each will charge. Of course, parallel pricing among firms in industries in which there are few sellers is not in and of itself considered price-fixing. There must be an exchange of pricing information between sellers to indicate illegal price-fixing actions. The Sherman Antitrust Act of 1890 specifically makes this practice, referred to as *collusion*, illegal. In 2013, a U.S. district court found Apple guilty of price-fixing resulting from secret agreements it made with the publishers Macmillan, Penguin, Hachette, HarperCollins, and Simon & Schuster to raise the price of e-books to combat Amazon's strategy of discounting titles to sales of its Kindle reader. When the publishers joined forces to raise e-book prices, Amazon had no choice but to follow suit. As a result, consumers paid millions of dollars more for e-books regardless of where they purchased them.[29]

Vertical price fixing occurs when manufacturers or wholesalers attempt to force retailers to charge a certain price for their product. When vertical price-fixing occurs, the retailer that wants to carry the product must charge the "suggested" retail price. The *Consumer Goods Pricing Act* of 1976 limited this practice, leaving retail stores free to set whatever price they choose without interference by the manufacturer or wholesaler. Today, retailers don't need to adhere to "suggested" prices.

Predatory Pricing

predatory pricing
An illegal pricing strategy in which a company sets a very low price for the purpose of driving competitors out of business.

Predatory pricing means that a company sets a very low price for the purpose of driving competitors out of business. Later, when they have a monopoly, they turn around and increase prices. The Sherman Act and the Robinson–Patman Act prohibit predatory pricing. For example, in 1999 the Justice Department accused American Airlines of predatory pricing at its Dallas–Fort Worth hub.[30] In the mid-1990s, three small rivals started flying into the airport. American responded by lowering the prices of its flights on four routes. The Justice Department claimed that the airline planned to scare the three carriers away and monopolize the routes. Although American was exonerated in court, the case did send a message to airlines that they must be careful when they set prices.

Ripped from the Headlines

Ethical/Sustainable Decisions in the Real World

Are you one of the millions of proud owners of a Snuggie? The Snuggie is a fleece blanket with sleeves that, like many other products, was hawked on TV. First sold in 2008, more than 30 million Snuggies had been sold by March 2015. That's the same time that the Allstar Marketing Group LLC that sold the Snuggies agreed to pay an $8 million fine to the Federal Trade Commission (FTC) and the state of New York for providing inadequate information in their advertising. The results of the advertising were that buyers believed they were buying items at the price advertised on television, but ended up with hidden fees and extra merchandise they didn't mean to buy.

The FTC said that Allstar (which also sells the "perfect" brownie pan) attracted customers with "buy one, get one free" offers. The ads, however, did not tell consumers that there were additional fees and handling charges that equaled almost as much as the free Snuggie. According to the FTC, marketers must clearly disclose all costs, including processing and handling fees.

Of course Allstar's Snuggie is not alone in providing inadequate information to consumers. To attract customers, sellers sometimes offer prices that seem too low to believe but may not be as low as they seem to be, or worse, just plain dishonest. These price advertisements use such phrases as "save up to 50 percent" or "as low as 19.99." The ad that offers "three books for $0.01 each" is unclear that the buyer is also agreeing to buy three more books at the regular price during the year. Similarly, credit cards may offer one month free, but do not make it clear that the amount of the first payment will be added to the balance owed or that a single late payment may double the rate of interest.

Although these sales pitches do not meet the FTC's definition of deceptive advertising, the result is that consumers are misled into making a purchase they may not have made if they had full disclosure. Companies like Allstar would argue that it is the consumer's fault if he or she doesn't pay close attention to all the information provided, even if it is in fine print. Perhaps the moral of the story is, "If it seems too good to be true, it probably is."

ETHICS CHECK:

Do you believe that the FTC should create additional regulations on advertising that would create greater requirements for full disclosure in advertising?

☐ YES ☐ NO

MyLab Marketing™

Go to **mymktlab.com** to complete the problems marked with this icon ✪ as well as additional Marketing Metrics questions only available in MyLab Marketing.

Objective Summary ➡ Key Terms ➡ Apply

CHAPTER 10
Study Map

10.1 Objective Summary (pp. 316–320)

Explain the importance of pricing and how marketers set objectives for their pricing strategies.

Pricing is important to firms because it creates profits and influences customers to purchase or not. The newest addition to the exchange process is Bitcoin. Prices may be monetary or nonmonetary, as when consumers or businesses exchange one product for another. Effective pricing objectives are designed to support corporate and marketing objectives and are flexible. Pricing objectives often focus on a desired level of profit growth or profit margin, on sales (to maximize sales or to increase market share), on competing effectively, on increasing customer satisfaction, or on communicating a certain image.

Key Terms

price, p. 316

Bitcoin, p. 316

market share, p. 319

prestige products, p. 319

10.2 Objective Summary (pp. 320–332)

Describe how marketers use costs, demand, revenue, and the pricing environment to make pricing decisions.

In developing prices, marketers must estimate demand and determine costs. Marketers often use break-even analysis to help in deciding on the price for a product. Break-even analysis uses fixed and variable costs to identify how many units must be sold at a certain price to begin making a profit. Marketers must also consider the requirements for adequate trade margins for retailers, wholesalers, and other members of the channel of distribution. Like other elements of the marketing mix, pricing is influenced by a variety of external environmental factors. This includes economic trends such as inflation and recession and the firm's competitive environment—that is, whether the firm does business in an oligopoly, a monopoly, or a more competitive environment. Government regulations can also affect prices by increasing the cost of production or through actual regulations of a firm's pricing strategies. Consumer trends that influence how consumers think and behave may also influence pricing. Although marketers of some products may develop standardized pricing strategies for global markets, unique environmental factors in different countries mean marketers must localize pricing strategies.

Key Terms

price elasticity of demand, p. 322

elastic demand, p. 322

inelastic demand, p. 323

cross-elasticity of demand, p. 324

variable costs, p. 324

fixed costs, p. 325

average fixed cost, p. 326

total costs, p. 326

break-even analysis, p. 326

break-even point, p. 326

contribution per unit, p. 326

markup, p. 328

gross margin, p. 328

retailer margin, p. 328

wholesaler margin, p. 328

list price or manufacturer's suggested retail price (MSRP), p. 328

vertical integration, p. 329

shopping for control, p. 331

10.3 Objective Summary (pp. 332–339)

Understand key pricing strategies and tactics.

Although easy to calculate and "safe," frequently used cost-based strategies do not consider demand, the competition, the stage in the product life cycle, plant capacity, or product image. The most common cost-based strategy is cost-plus pricing.

Pricing strategies based on demand, such as target costing and yield management pricing, can require that marketers estimate demand at different prices in order to be certain they can sell what they produce. Strategies based on the competition may represent industry wisdom but can be tricky to apply. A price leadership strategy is often used in an oligopoly.

Firms that focus on customer needs may consider everyday low price or value pricing strategies. An alternative consumer pleasing strategy is a high/low pricing strategy. New products may be priced using a high skimming price to recover research, development, and promotional costs or a penetration price to encourage more customers and discourage competitors from entering the market. Trial pricing means setting a low price for a limited time.

Other pricing strategies include pricing segmentation, peak load pricing, surge pricing, bottom of the pyramid pricing, and decoy pricing.

To implement pricing strategies with individual products, marketers may use two-part pricing or payment pricing tactics. For multiple products, marketers may use price bundling, wherein two or more products are sold and priced as a single package. Captive pricing is often chosen when two items must be used together; one item is sold at a very low price and the other at a high, profitable price.

Distribution-based pricing tactics, including F.O.B., basing-point, and uniform delivered pricing, address differences in how far products must be shipped. Similar pricing tactics are used for products sold internationally.

Pricing for members of the channel may include trade or functional discounts, cumulative or noncumulative quantity discounts to encourage larger purchases, cash discounts to encourage fast payment, and seasonal discounts to spread purchases throughout the year or to increase off-season or in-season sales.

Key Terms

cost-plus pricing, p. 333

keystoning, p. 333

demand-based pricing, p. 333

target costing, p. 333

yield management pricing, p. 333

price leadership, p. 334

value pricing or everyday low pricing (EDLP), p. 335

high/low pricing or promo pricing, p. 335

skimming price, p. 335

penetration pricing, p. 336

trial pricing, p. 336

price segmentation, p. 336

peak load pricing, p. 336

surge pricing, p. 336

bottom of the pyramid pricing, p. 336

two-part pricing, p. 337

payment pricing, p. 337

decoy pricing, p. 337

price bundling, p. 337

captive pricing, p. 337

F.O.B. origin pricing (also known as F.O.B. factory pricing), p. 338

F.O.B. delivered pricing, p. 338

uniform delivered pricing, p. 338

freight absorption pricing, p. 338

trade discounts, p. 339

quantity discounts, p. 339

cash discounts, p. 339

seasonal discounts, p. 339

10.4 Objective Summary (pp. 339–341)

Understand the opportunities for Internet pricing strategies.

E-commerce may offer firms an opportunity to initiate dynamic pricing—meaning prices can be changed frequently with little or no cost. Auctions offer opportunities for customers to bid on items in C2C, B2C, and B2B e-commerce. The Internet also allows firms to practice freemium pricing, in which basic versions of digital products are given to customers for no charge. The Internet allows buyers to compare products and prices, gives consumers more control over the price they pay for items, and has made customers more price sensitive.

Key Terms

dynamic pricing, p. 340

Internet price discrimination, p. 340

online auctions, p. 340

freemium pricing, p. 341

10.5 Objective Summary (pp. 341–347)

Describe the psychological, legal, and ethical aspects of pricing.

Consumers may express emotional or psychological responses to prices. Customers may use an idea of a customary or fair price as an internal reference price in evaluating products. Sometimes marketers use reference pricing strategies by displaying products with different prices next to each other. A price–quality inference means that consumers use price as a cue for quality. Customers respond to odd prices differently than to even-dollar prices. Marketers may practice price lining strategies in which they set a limited number of different price ranges for a product line. With luxury products, marketers may use a prestige or premium pricing strategy, assuming that people will buy more if the price is higher.

Most marketers try to avoid unethical or illegal pricing practices. One deceptive pricing practice is the illegal bait-and-switch tactic. Many states have unfair sales acts, which are laws against loss leader pricing that make it illegal to sell products below cost. Federal regulations prohibit predatory pricing, price discrimination, and horizontal or vertical price-fixing.

Key Terms

internal reference price, p. 342

price lining, p. 344

prestige pricing or premium pricing, p. 344

bait-and-switch, p. 345

loss-leader pricing, p. 345

unfair sales acts, p. 345

price-fixing, p. 346

predatory pricing, p. 346

Chapter Questions and Activities

> **MyLab Marketing™**
>
> Go to **mymktlab.com** to watch this chapter's Rising Star video(s) for career advice and to respond to questions.

Concepts: Test Your Knowledge

10-1. What is price, and why is it important to a firm? What is digital currency, such as Bitcoin?

10-2. Describe and give examples of some of the following types of pricing objectives: profit, market share, competitive effect, customer satisfaction, and image enhancement.

10-3. Explain how the demand curves for normal products and for prestige products differ. What are demand shifts and why are they important to marketers? How do firms go about estimating demand? How can marketers estimate the elasticity of demand?

10-4. Explain variable costs, fixed costs, average variable costs, average fixed costs, and average total costs.

10-5. What is break-even analysis?

10-6. What are trade margins? How do they relate to the pricing for a producer of goods?

10-7. Give an example of how the competitive environment influences prices. What about government regulation and consumer trends? What are some ways the global environment can influence a firm's pricing strategies?

10-8. Explain and give an example of cost-plus pricing, target costing, and yield management pricing.

10-9. For new products, when is skimming pricing more appropriate, and when is penetration pricing the best strategy? When would trial pricing be an effective pricing strategy?

10-10. How do marketers customize pricing with pricing segmentation, peak load pricing, and surge pricing? How can marketers price to meet the need of bottom of the pyramid consumers?

10-11. Explain decoy pricing. Is decoy pricing ethical?

10-12. Explain two-part pricing, payment pricing, price bundling, captive pricing, and distribution-based pricing tactics.

10-13. Why do marketers use trade or functional discounts, quantity discounts, cash discounts, and seasonal discounts in pricing to members of the channel?

10-14. What is dynamic pricing? What is discriminatory pricing? What is the difference between the two?

10-15. Explain these psychological aspects of pricing: price–quality inferences, odd–even pricing, internal reference price, price lining, and prestige pricing.

10-16. Explain how unethical marketers might use bait-and-switch tactics, price-fixing, and predatory pricing.

Activities: Apply What You've Learned

⭐ 10-17. *Creative Homework/Short Project* Assume that you are an entrepreneur who runs a bakery that sells gluten-free breads and cakes. You believe that the current economic conditions merit an increase in the price of your baked goods. You are concerned, however, that increasing the price might not be profitable because you are unsure of the price elasticity of demand for your products. Develop a plan for the measurement of price elasticity of demand for your products. What findings would lead you to increase the price? What findings would cause you to rethink the decision to increase prices? Develop a presentation for your class outlining (1) the concept of elasticity of demand, (2) why raising prices without understanding the elasticity would be a bad move, (3) your recommendations for measurement, and (4) the potential impact on profits for elastic and inelastic demand.

10-18. *In Class, 10–25 Minutes for Teams* For each of the following products, determine at least three different prices that might be charged. Then survey each of the individuals within your group to find out how much of each product they would buy at each price point for each of the products. For each product, calculate the price elasticity of demand to determine whether the demand is elastic or inelastic.
   a. Cheese pizzas per month
   b. Movie tickets per month
   c. Concert tickets per year

10-19. *Creative Homework/Short Project* Assume that you have been hired as the assistant manager of a local store that sells fresh fruits and vegetables. As you look over the store, you notice that there are two different displays of tomatoes. In one display, the tomatoes are priced at $2.39 per pound, and in the other, the tomatoes are priced at $1.69 per pound. The tomatoes look very much alike. You notice that many people are buying the $2.39 tomatoes. Write a report explaining what is happening and give your recommendations for the store's pricing strategy.

10-20. *For Further Research (Individual)* Assume you are the owner of a local Mexican restaurant. You are seeking ways to increase your business. You believe that bundling items on the menu will increase the average ticket per customer. A suggested bundle offer would include the items below:

Item	Menu price
Chips, Salsa, and Guacamole	$4.00
Chicken Burrito with rice and beans	$10.50
Flan	$3.00
Non-alcoholic beverage	$2.50

You are considering three different prices that you might charge for the bundle: $14.00, $16.00, and $18.50. Design and conduct research to determine which price will maximize profits.

10-21. *For Further Research (Individual)* In this chapter, we talked about how airlines use yield management pricing to ensure that every seat is filled on every flight, thus maximizing profits. Go to the websites of at least two different airlines. Check the prices of a flight for each airline approximately three weeks from "now." Then check the prices for the same flights in less than a week, in one week and in two weeks. Write a report on your findings and what they tell you about airline pricing.

10-22. *For Further Research (Groups)* Select one of the product categories below. Identify two different firms that offer consumers a line of product offerings in the category. For example, Dell, HP, and Apple each market a line of laptop computers, whereas Hoover, Dyson, and Bissell offer lines of vacuum cleaners. Using the Internet or by visiting a retailer who sells your selected product, research the product lines and pricing of the two firms. Based on your research, develop a presentation on the price lining strategies of the two firms. Your presentation should discuss (1) the specific price points of the product offerings of each firm and how the price lining strategy maximizes revenue, (2) your ideas for why the specific price points were selected, (3) how the price lining strategies of the two firms are alike and how they are different, and (4) possible reasons for differences in the strategies.
   a. Laptop computers
   b. Vacuum cleaners
   c. Smart TVs
   d. Smartphones

Concepts: Apply Marketing Metrics

Contribution analysis and break-even analysis are popular and often used marketing metrics. These analyses are essential to determine if a firm's marketing opportunity will mean a financial loss or profit. As explained in the chapter, *contribution* is the difference between the selling price per unit and the variable cost per unit. Break-even analysis that includes contribution tells marketers how much must be sold to break even or to earn a desired amount of profit.

Touch of Beirut Brands is a Los Angeles–based specialty manufacturer of Lebanese specialty foods and ingredients. In the past, the firm has marketed primarily through restaurant distributors to small mom-and-pop Lebanese cuisine restaurants around the U.S. But they've developed a marketing plan to sell a combination hummus and pita slices packaged product that is ready to eat—sort of like the famous boxed Oscar Meyer Lunchables. They've branded the new product "Happy Hummus." Outlets will be Whole Foods and other new-age supermarkets.

The company plans to use social media to gain buzz around the new product but will also be spending money on advertising and sales promotion through coupons to consumers and price incentives to distributors and retailers. Whole Foods would like to be able to sell the boxes at retail for $5. Because the retailer typically requires a 30 percent markup, Touch of Beirut's price to the supermarkets will be $3.50 per box. The unit variable costs for the product including packaging will be $1.25.

The company estimates its advertising and promotion expenses for the first year will be $2,500,000.

⭐ **10-23.** What is the contribution per unit for Happy Hummus?

⭐ **10-24.** What is the break-even volume for the first year that will cover the planned advertising and promotion (1) in units and (2) in dollars?

⭐ **10-25.** How many units of Happy Hummus must Touch of Beirut sell to earn a profit of $1,000,000?

⭐ **10-26.** Does this seem like a good business venture to you? Why or why not?

Choices: What Do You Think?

⭐ **10-27.** *Critical Thinking* Governments sometimes provide price subsidies to specific industries; that is, they reduce a domestic firm's costs so that it can sell products on the international market at a lower price. What reasons do governments (and politicians) use for these government subsidies? What are the benefits and disadvantages to domestic industries in the long run? To international customers? Who would benefit and who would lose if all price subsidies were eliminated? Do you feel that the U.S. government should or should not use price subsidies for some U.S. industries? Why do you feel that way?

10-28. *Ethics* Several online stores now sell products to consumers at different prices based on the user's information, such as geographic location—which determines your proximity to competitors and your area's average income. Although this practice, known as Internet price discrimination, is not illegal, some would say it is unethical. Do you believe this practice is unethical? Should this practice be illegal? If you think the practice should be legal, should retailers be required to put a disclaimer on their site? Explain your reasoning.

⭐ **10-29.** *Critical Thinking* In many oligopolistic industries, firms follow a price leadership strategy, in which an accepted industry leader sets, raises, or lowers prices and the other firms follow. In what ways is this policy good and bad for the industry? In what ways is this good or bad for consumers? What is the difference between price leadership and price fixing? Should governments allow industries to use price leadership strategies? If not, how can they prevent it?

10-30. *Ethics* Many successful retailers use a loss leader pricing strategy, in which they advertise an item at a price below their cost and sell the item at that price to get customers into their store. They feel that these customers will continue to shop with their company and that they will make a profit in the long run. Do you consider this an unethical practice? Who benefits and who is hurt by such practices? Do you think the practice should be made illegal, as some states have done? How is this different from bait-and-switch pricing?

10-31. *Critical Thinking* Cost-plus pricing used to be the most common approach to setting prices in the marketplace. It has the advantages of being simple and ensuring that a profit margin is achieved on every unit sold. However, as highlighted in the chapter, there are alternative approaches to setting prices.

Do you think that cost-plus pricing is still applicable in today's world, or are there more suitable approaches to setting prices? For what type of products or industries do you think cost-plus pricing can still be used effectively?

10-32. *Critical Thinking* Penetration pricing is one approach to pricing for a new product launch. It is a helpful tactic to gain initial trials, build market share, discourage competitors, and pursue economies of scale. However, the initial price may set an expectation of value among consumers and essentially position the brand as a low-quality offering. This may result in some consumer resistance to purchasing the new product in the future if prices increase.

In light of this trade-off between benefits and potential risks, to what extent do you think penetration pricing is a suitable approach to helping a new product become successful in the marketplace? Would it be more appropriate to have some form of sales promotion or other incentive to encourage initial sales instead of some form of discounting? Do you think that a low price, even for an introductory period, would result in a negative perception of the brand?

10-33. *Critical Thinking* Many firms wish to market their products to consumers in bottom-of-the-pyramid countries. Being successful now will create consumer familiarity with the brand, establishing a presence in the countries for the future, when their economies improve. In addition to the ways we discussed in the chapter, what are some innovative strategies that could be successful for firms wishing to sell the following products?
1. Disposable diapers
2. Body wash
3. Toothpaste

Miniproject: Learn by Doing

Price segmentation, also referred to as price discrimination, is the practice of charging different prices for the same product to different people based upon age, usage, loyalty, time (day or season), and so on. For example, movie cinemas will generally price differently for children, students, and even retirees. They often have reduced prices for certain days of the week or for morning sessions, and some cinemas will provide discount tickets for regular moviegoers via some form of loyalty program. This means that different people will see the same movie in the same facilities, but pay a different price to attend.

Your initial task for this mini project is to research a number of different cinema outlets in order to determine their pricing approach, primarily on a segmentation and time/day approach. Determine whether the practice of price segmentation is relatively consistent across different cinema chains and whether the practice extends to smaller or independent cinemas. You should include four or five competitors in your initial research and then address the questions below.

10-34. Compare the pricing approach adopted by different competitors. Is there general consistency in the approach to price segmentation, or is there a variety of approaches being implemented? Are there cinema chains or independent cinemas that have primarily adopted a price-based approach to competing in the market, or do they tend to emphasize their facilities, locations, service, choice of movies, flexible times, and other service attributes?

10-35. Discuss price segmentation in cinemas with different people among your family and friends (that is, a cross-section of ages and demographics). To what extent is price a factor in their decision to visit a particular cinema? Are the consumers who benefit from price segmentation more likely to visit a cinema because of the reduced price? Is there any resentment from consumers who do not benefit from price segmentation (that is, they are required to pay the full price)?

Marketing in **Action** Case Real Choices at Disney

What happens when you are no longer "the Happiest Place on Earth"? The Walt Disney Company doesn't want to find out and is "reimagining" its pricing strategy. Responding to the ever-increasing demand for theme park tickets, especially at peak times, Disney has implemented "demand-based pricing" at both Walt Disney World in Florida and Disneyland in California.

Airlines and hotels have used demand-based pricing for years by charging higher prices during summer vacation season and around holidays when demand for flights and hotel accommodations is highest. Similarly, demand-based pricing has been in use by Disney competitor, Universal Studios, and other theme park operators in the United States. The idea is to redistribute customer demand by lowering prices during times with less demand to encourage more sales and increase prices at times when demand is higher to encourage customers to switch some of their visits to lower-priced times.

Visitors to Disneyland were previously charged a single-day ticket price of $99.00. Under demand-based pricing, there are three prices. "Value" tickets for Mondays through Thursdays during weeks when children are in school are only $95, a reduction of $4.00. "Regular" tickets for most weekends and summer months are $105. "Peak" tickets for visitors during December, spring break weeks, and July weekends are highest at $119. For Orlando's Disney World, the pricing is similar but more complex as a result of having four different parks at the site. The new demand-based pricing is only for single-day tickets and does not affect the price of annual passes or multiday tickets, which most families buy when they travel to Disney.

The unknown is how consumers will respond to this new pricing strategy long term. Will they see it as a more equitable system in which you pay more if you want to visit Disney at the "best" times to travel and pay less if you can vacation at "off" times. Of course, consumers may perceive the new strategy as a pricing gimmick to gouge consumers during heavy travel times to increase Disney profits.

Certainly, demand-pricing tactics airlines employ are not thought of kindly and have contributed to negative consumer attitudes toward the airlines. Although Disney stresses that it is using the new demand-based pricing to more efficiently manage its customer experience, it should be obvious that this policy can also lead to greater profits. Even more important, how will consumers think of Disney and its theme parks long term? Will Disney still be the happiest place in the world?

You Make the Call

10-36. What is the decision facing Disney?
10-37. What factors are important in understanding this decision situation?
10-38. What are the alternatives?
10-39. What decision(s) do you recommend?
10-40. What are some ways to implement your recommendation?

Based on: Brooks Barnes, "Disney Introduces Demand-Based Pricing at Theme Parks," *The New York Times* (February 27, 2016), http://www.nytimes.com/2016/02/28/business/disney-introduces-demand-based-pricing-at-theme-parks.html?_r=0 (accessed April 26, 2016); Hugo Martin, "Disneyland 'Demand Pricing' Will Cost You $5 Less on Slow Days and $20 More When It's Busy," *The Los Angeles Times* (February 27, 2016), http://www.latimes.com/business/la-fi-disney-adopts-demand-pricing-20160226-story.html (accessed April 26, 2016); Ben Fritz, "Disney Parks Consider Off-Peak Prices," *Wall Street Journal* (October 4, 2015), http://www.wsj.com/articles/disney-parks-consider-higher-prices-during-busy-times-1443960001 (accessed April 26, 2016).

MyLab Marketing™

Go to **mymktlab.com** for the following Assisted-graded writing questions:

10-41. This chapter states, "Often consumers base their perception of price on what they believe to be the customary or fair price." Explain the meaning of this statement and provide an example.

10-42. Some firms have profit as a pricing objective, whereas others set prices for customer satisfaction. What are the major differences between these two? Which is better?

Marketing Math

To develop marketing strategies to meet the goals of an organization effectively and efficiently, it is essential that marketers understand and use a variety of financial analyses. This supplement provides some of these basic financial analyses, including a review of the income statement and balance sheet, as well as some basic performance ratios. In addition, this supplement includes an explanation of some of the specific calculations that marketers use routinely to set prices for their goods and services.

Income Statement and Balance Sheet

The two most important documents used to analyze the financial situation of a company are the income statement and the balance sheet. The *income statement* (which is sometimes referred to as the *profit and loss statement* or the *P&L*) provides a summary of the revenues and expenses of a firm—that is, the amount of income a company received from sales or other sources, the amount of money it spent, and the resulting income or loss that the company experienced.

The major elements of the income statement are as follows:

- **Gross sales** are the total of all income the firm receives from the sales of goods and services.

- **Net sales revenue** is the gross sales minus the amount for returns and promotional or other allowances given to customers.

- **Cost of goods sold** (sometimes called the *cost of sales*) is the cost of inventory or goods that the firm has sold.

- **Gross margin** (also called *gross profit*) is the amount of sales revenue that is in excess of the cost of goods sold.

- **Operating expenses** are expenses other than the cost of goods sold that are necessary for conducting business. These may include salaries, rent, depreciation on buildings and equipment, insurance, utilities, supplies, and property taxes.

- **Operating income** (sometimes called *income from operations*) is the gross margin minus the operating expenses. Sometimes accountants prepare an *operating statement*, which is similar to the income statement except that the final calculation is the operating income—that is, other revenues or expenses and taxes are not included.

- **Other revenue and expenses** are income or expenses other than those required for conducting the business. These may include items such as interest income and expenses and any gain or loss experienced from the sale of property or plant assets.

- **Taxes** are the amount of income tax the firm owes calculated as a percentage of income.

- **Net income** (sometimes called *net earnings* or *net profit*) is the excess of total revenue over total expenses.

Table 10S.1 shows the income statement for an imaginary company, DLL Incorporated. DLL is a typical merchandising firm. Note that the income statement is for a specific year and includes income and expenses inclusively from January 1 through December 31.

| **Table 10S.1** | **DLL Income Statement for the Year Ended December 31, 2016** |

Gross sales		$253,950
Less: sales returns and allowances	$ 3,000	
Sales discounts	2,100	5,100
Net sales revenue		$248,850
Cost of goods sold		
Inventory, January 1, 2016		60,750
Purchases	135,550	
Less: purchase returns and allowances	1,500	
Purchase discounts	750	
Net purchases	133,300	
Plus: freight-in	2,450	135,750
Goods available for sale		196,500
Less: inventory, December 31, 2016		60,300
Cost of goods sold		136,200
Gross margin		112,650
Operating expenses		
Salaries and commissions		15,300
Rent		12,600
Insurance		1,500
Depreciation		900
Supplies		825
Total operating expenses		31,125
Operating income		81,525
Other revenue and (expenses)		
Interest revenue		1,500
Interest expense		(2,250)	(750)
Income before tax		80,775
Taxes (40%)		32,310
Net income		$ 48,465

The following comments explain the meaning of some of the important entries included in this statement.

- DLL Inc. has total or gross sales during the year of $253,950. This figure was adjusted, however, by deducting the $3,000 worth of goods returned and special allowances given to customers and by $2,100 in special discounts. Thus, the actual or net sales generated by sales is $248,850.
- The cost of goods sold is calculated by adding the inventory of goods on January 1 to the amount purchased during the year and then subtracting the inventory of goods on December 31. In this case, DLL had $60,750 worth of inventory on hand on January 1. During the year, the firm made purchases in the amount of $135,550. This amount, however, was reduced by purchase returns and allowances of $1,500 and by purchase discounts of $750, so the net purchases are only $133,300.

There is also an amount on the statement labeled "Freight-In." This is the amount spent by the firm in shipping charges to get goods to its facility from suppliers. Any expenses for freight from DLL to its customers (Freight-Out) would be an operating expense. In this case, the Freight-In expense of $2,450 is added to net purchase costs. Then these costs of current purchases are added to the beginning inventory to show that during the year the firm had a total of $196,500 in goods available for sale. Finally, the inventory of goods held on December 31 is subtracted from the goods available for sale, to reveal the total cost of goods sold of $136,200.

We mentioned that DLL Inc. is a merchandising firm—a retailer of some type. If DLL were instead a manufacturer, calculation of the cost of goods sold would be a bit more complicated and would probably include separate figures for items such as inventory of finished goods, the "work-in-process" inventory, the raw materials inventory, and the cost of goods delivered to customers during the year. Continuing down the previous income statement we have the following:

- The cost of goods sold is subtracted from the net sales revenue to get a gross margin of $112,650.
- Operating expenses for DLL include the salaries and commissions paid to its employees, rent on facilities or equipment, insurance, depreciation of capital items, and the cost of operating supplies. DLL has a total of $31,125 in operating expenses, which is deducted from the gross margin. Thus, DLL has an operating income of $81,525.
- DLL had both other income and expenses in the form of interest revenues of $1,500 and interest expenses of $2,250, making a total other expense of $750, which was subtracted from the operating income, leaving an income before taxes of $80,775.
- Finally, the income before taxes is reduced by 40 percent ($32,310) for taxes, leaving a net income of $48,465. The 40 percent is an average amount for federal and state corporate income taxes incurred by most firms.

The *balance sheet* lists the assets, liabilities, and stockholders' equity of the firm. Whereas the income statement represents what happened during an entire year, the balance sheet is like a snapshot; it shows the firm's financial situation at one point in time. For this reason, the balance sheet is sometimes called the *statement of financial position*.

Table 10S.2 shows DLL Inc.'s balance sheet for December 31. Assets include any economic resource that is expected to benefit the firm in the short or long term. *Current assets* are items that are normally expected to be turned into cash or used up during the next 12 months or during the firm's normal operating cycle. Current assets for DLL include cash, securities, accounts receivable (money owed to the firm and not yet paid), inventory on hand, prepaid insurance, and supplies: a total of $84,525. *Long-term assets* include all assets that are not current assets. For DLL, these are furniture and fixtures (less an amount for depreciation) and land, or $45,300. The *total assets* for DLL are $129,825.

A firm's *liabilities* are its economic obligations, or debts that are payable to individuals or organizations outside the firm. *Current liabilities* are debts due to be paid in the coming year or during the firm's normal operating cycle. For DLL, the current liabilities—the accounts payable, unearned sales revenue, wages payable, and interest payable—total $72,450. *Long-term liabilities* (in the case of DLL, a note in the amount of $18,900) are all liabilities that are not due to be paid during the coming cycle. *Stockholders' equity* is the value of the stock and the corporation's capital or retained earnings. DLL has $15,000 in common stock and $23,475 in retained earnings for a total stockholders' equity of $38,475. Total liabilities always equal total assets—in this case $129,825.

Table 10S.2 | DLL Inc. Balance Sheet: December 31, 2016

Assets			
Current assets			
Cash		$ 4,275	
Marketable securities		12,000	
Accounts receivable		6,900	
Inventory		60,300	
Prepaid insurance		300	
Supplies		150	
Total current assets			84,525
Long-term assets—property, plant and equipment			
Furniture and fixtures	$42,300		
Less: accumulated depreciation	4,500	37,800	
Land		7,500	
Total long-term assets			45,300
Total assets			$129,825
Liabilities			
Current liabilities			
Accounts payable	$70,500		
Unearned sales revenue	1,050		
Wages payable	600		
Interest payable	300		
Total current liabilities		72,450	
Long-term liabilities			
Note payable		18,900	
Total liabilities			91,350
Stockholders' equity			
Common stock		15,000	
Retained earnings		23,475	
Total stockholders' equity			38,475
Total liabilities and stockholders' equity			$129,825

Important Financial Performance Ratios

How do managers and financial analysts compare the performance of a firm from one year to the next? How do investors compare the performance of one firm with that of another? As the book notes, managers often rely on various metrics to measure performance.

Often, a number of different financial ratios provide important information for such comparisons. Such *ratios* are percentage figures comparing various income statement items to net sales. Ratios provide a better way to compare performance than simple dollar sales or cost figures for two reasons. They enable analysts to compare the performance of large and small firms, and they provide a fair way to compare performance over time without having to take inflation and other changes into account. In this section, we will

Table 10S.3 | Hypothetical Operating Ratios for DLL Inc.

Gross margin ratio	=	$\dfrac{\text{Gross margin}}{\text{Net sales}}$	=	$\dfrac{\$112,650}{\$248,850}$	= 45.3%
Net Income ratio	=	$\dfrac{\text{Net income}}{\text{Net sales}}$	=	$\dfrac{\$48,465}{248,850}$	= 19.5%
Operating expense ratio	=	$\dfrac{\text{Total operating expenses}}{\text{Net sales}}$	=	$\dfrac{\$31,125}{248,850}$	= 12.5%
Returns and allowances ratio	=	$\dfrac{\text{Return and allowances}}{\text{Net sales}}$	=	$\dfrac{\$3,000}{248,850}$	= 1.2%

explain the basic operating ratios. Other measures of performance that marketers frequently use and that are also explained here are the inventory turnover rate and return on investment (ROI).

Operating Ratios

Measures of performance calculated directly from the information in a firm's income statement (sometimes called an *operating statement*) are called the *operating ratios*. Each ratio compares some income statement item to net sales. The most useful of these are the *gross margin ratio*, the *net income ratio*, the *operating expense ratio*, and the *returns and allowances ratio*. These ratios vary widely by industry but tend to be important indicators of how a firm is doing within its industry. The ratios for DLL Inc. are shown in Table 10S.3.

- **Gross margin ratio** shows what percentage of sales revenues is available for operating and other expenses and for profit. With DLL, this means that 45 percent, or nearly half, of every sales dollar is available for operating costs and for profits.
- **Net income ratio** (sometimes called the *net profit ratio*) shows what percentage of sales revenues is income or profit. For DLL, the net income ratio is 19.5 percent. This means that the firm's profit before taxes is about 20 cents of every dollar.
- **Operating expense ratio** is the percentage of sales needed for operating expenses. DLL has an operating expense ratio of 12.5 percent. Tracking operating expense ratios from one year to the next or comparing them with an industry average gives a firm important information about the efficiency of its operations.
- **Returns and allowances ratio** shows what percentage of all sales is being returned, probably by unhappy customers. DLL's returns and allowances ratio shows that only a little over 1 percent of sales is being returned.

Inventory Turnover Rate

The *inventory turnover rate*, also referred to as the *stockturn rate*, is the number of times inventory or stock is turned over (sold and replaced) during a specified time period, usually a year. Inventory turnover rates are usually calculated on the basis of inventory costs, sometimes on the basis of inventory selling prices, and sometimes by number of units.

In our example, for DLL Inc. we know that for the year the cost of goods sold was $136,200. Information on the balance sheet enables us to find the average inventory. By adding the value of the beginning inventory to the ending inventory and dividing by 2, we can compute an average inventory. In the case of DLL, this would be as follows:

$$= \frac{\$60{,}750 + \$60{,}300}{2} = \$60{,}525$$

Thus,

$$\frac{\text{Inventory turnover rate}}{\text{(in cost of goods sold)}} = \frac{\text{Costs of goods sold}}{\text{Average inventory at cost}} = \frac{\$136{,}200}{\$60{,}525} = 2.25 \text{ times}$$

Return on Investment

Firms often develop business objectives in terms of *return on investment (ROI)*, and ROI is often used to determine how effective (and efficient) the firm's management has been. First, however, we need to define exactly what a firm means by investment. In most cases, firms define investment as the total assets of the firm. To calculate the ROI, we need the net income found in the income statement and the total assets (or investment) found in the firm's balance sheet.

Return on investment is calculated as follows:

$$\text{ROI} = \frac{\text{Net income}}{\text{Total investment}}$$

For DLL Inc., if the total assets are $129,825 then the ROI is as follows:

$$\frac{\$48{,}465}{\$129{,}825} = 37.3\%$$

Sometimes, return on investment is calculated by using an expanded formula:

$$\text{ROI} = \frac{\text{Net profit}}{\text{Sales}} \times \frac{\text{Sales}}{\text{Investment}}$$

$$= \frac{\$48{,}465}{\$248{,}850} \times \frac{\$248{,}850}{\$129{,}825} = 37.3\%$$

This formula makes it easy to show how ROI can be increased and what might reduce ROI. For example, there are different ways to increase ROI. First, if the management focuses on cutting costs and increasing efficiency, profits may be increased while sales remain the same:

$$\text{ROI} = \frac{\text{Net profit}}{\text{Sales}} \times \frac{\text{Sales}}{\text{Investment}}$$

$$= \frac{\$53{,}277}{\$248{,}850} \times \frac{\$248{,}850}{\$129{,}825} = 41.0\%$$

But ROI can be increased just as much without improving performance simply by reducing the investment—by maintaining less inventory:

$$\text{ROI} = \frac{\text{Net profit}}{\text{Sales}} \times \frac{\text{Sales}}{\text{Investment}}$$

$$= \frac{\$48{,}465}{\$248{,}850} \times \frac{\$248{,}850}{\$114{,}825} = 42.2\%$$

Sometimes, however, differences among the total assets of firms may be related to the age of the firm or the type of industry, which makes ROI a poor indicator of performance. For this reason, some firms have replaced the traditional ROI measures with *return on assets managed* (ROAM), *return on net assets* (RONA), or *return on stockholders' equity* (ROE).

Price Elasticity

Price elasticity, discussed in Chapter 10, is a measure of the sensitivity of customers to changes in price. Price elasticity is calculated by comparing the percentage change in quantity to the percentage change in price:

$$\text{Price elasticity of demand} = \frac{\text{Percentage change in quantity}}{\text{Percentage change in price}}$$

$$E = \frac{(Q_2 - Q_1)Q_1}{(R_2 - R_1)R_1}$$

where Q = quantity and P = price.

For example, suppose a manufacturer of jeans increased its price for a pair of jeans from \$30.00 to \$35.00. But instead of 40,000 pairs being sold, sales declined to only 38,000 pairs. The price elasticity would be calculated as follows:

$$E = \frac{(38{,}000 - 40{,}000)/40{,}000}{(\$35.00 - 30.00)/\$30.00} = \frac{-0.05}{0.167} = 0.30$$

Note that elasticity is usually expressed as a positive number even though the calculations create a negative value.

In this case, a relatively small change in demand (5 percent) resulted from a fairly large change in price (16.7 percent), indicating that demand is inelastic. At 0.30, the elasticity is less than 1.

On the other hand, what if the same change in price resulted in a reduction in demand to 30,000 pairs of jeans? Then the elasticity would be as follows:

$$E = \frac{(30{,}000 - 40{,}000)/40{,}000}{(\$35.00 - 30.00)/\$30.00} = \frac{-0.25}{0.167} = 1.50$$

In this case, because the 16.7 percent change in price resulted in an even larger change in demand (25 percent), demand is elastic. The elasticity of 1.50 is greater than 1.

Note: Elasticity may also be calculated by dividing the change in quantity by the average of Q_1 and Q_2 and dividing the change in price by the average of the two prices. However, we have chosen to include the formula that uses the initial quantity and price rather than the average.

Cost-Plus Pricing

As noted in Chapter 10, the most common cost-based approach to pricing a product is *cost-plus pricing*, in which a marketer figures all costs for the product and then adds an amount to cover profit and, in some cases, any costs of doing business that are not assigned to specific products. The most frequently used type of cost-plus pricing is *straight markup pricing*. The price is calculated by adding a predetermined percentage to the cost. Most retailers and wholesalers use markup pricing exclusively because of its simplicity; users need only estimate the unit cost and add the markup.

The first step requires that the unit cost be easy to estimate accurately and that production rates are fairly consistent. As Table 10S.4 shows, we will assume that a jeans manufacturer has fixed costs (the cost of the factory, advertising, managers' salaries, etc.) of $2,000,000. The variable cost, per pair of jeans (the cost of fabric, zipper, thread, and labor) is $20.00. With the current plant, the firm can produce a total of 400,000 pairs of jeans, so the fixed cost per pair is $5.00. Combining the fixed and variable costs per pair means that the jeans are produced at a total cost of $25.00 per pair and the total cost of producing 400,000 pairs of jeans is $10,000,000.

The second step is to calculate the markup. There are two methods for calculating the markup percentage: markup on cost and markup on selling price. For *markup on cost pricing*, just as the name implies, a percentage of the cost is added to the cost to determine the firm's

Table 10S.4	Markup Pricing Using Jeans as an Example

Step 1: Determine Costs

1.a: Determine total fixed costs

Management and other nonproduction-related salaries	$ 750,000
Rental of factory	600,000
Insurance	50,000
Depreciation on equipment	100,000
Advertising	500,000
Total fixed costs	**$2,000,000**

1.b: Determine fixed costs per unit

Number of units produced = 400,000

Fixed cost per unit ($2,000,000/400,000)	**$5.00**

1.c: Determine variable costs per unit

Cost of materials (fabric, zipper, thread, etc.)	$ 7.00
Cost of production labor	10.00
Cost of utilities and supplies used in production process	3.00
Variable cost per unit	**$20.00**

1.d: Determine total cost per unit

$20.00 + $5.00 = $25.00

Total cost per unit	**$25.00**

Total cost for producing 400,000 units = $10,000,000

Step 2: Determine markup and price

Manufacturer's markup on cost (assuming 20% markup)

Formula: Price = total cost + (total cost × markup percentage)

Manufacturer's Price to the Retailer	**$30.00**

= $25.00 + ($25.00 × 0.20) = $25.00 + 5.00 =

Retailer's markup on selling price (assuming 40% markup)

Formula: $\text{Price} = \dfrac{\text{Total cost}}{(1.00 - \text{Markup percentage})}$

Retailer's Price to the Consumer = $\dfrac{\$30.00}{(1.00 \times 40)} = \dfrac{\$30.00}{0.60} =$	**$50.00**

Retailer's alternative markup on cost (assuming 40% markup)

Formula: Price = total cost + (total cost × markup percentage)

Retailer's Price to the Consumer

$30.00 + ($30.00 × 0.40) = $30.00 + $12.00 =	**$42.00**

selling price. As you can see, we have included both methods in our example shown in Table 10S.4.

Markup on Cost

For markup on cost, the calculation is as follows:

$$\text{Price} = \text{Total cost} + (\text{Total cost} \times \text{Markup percentage})$$

But how does the manufacturer or reseller know which markup percentage to use? One way is to base the markup on the total income needed for profits, for shareholder dividends, and for investment in the business. In our jeans example, the total cost of producing the 400,000 pairs of jeans is $10,000,000. If the manufacturer wants a profit of $2,000,000, what markup percentage would it use? The $2,000,000 is 20 percent of the $10 million total cost, so 20 percent. To find the price, the calculations would be as follows:

$$\text{Price} = \$25.00 + (\$25.00 \times 0.20) = \$25.0 + \$5.00 = \$30.00$$

Note that in the calculations, the markup percentage is expressed as a decimal; that is, $20\% = 0.20, 25\% = 0.25, 30\% = 0.30$, and so on.

Markup on Selling Price

Some resellers, that is, retailers and wholesalers, set their prices using a markup on selling price. The markup percentage here is the seller's gross margin, the difference between the cost to the wholesaler or retailer and the price needed to cover overhead items, such as salaries, rent, utility bills, advertising, and profit. For example, if the wholesaler or retailer knows that it needs a margin of 40 percent to cover its overhead and reach its target profits, that margin becomes the markup on the manufacturer's selling price. Markup on selling price is particularly useful when firms negotiate prices with different buyers because it allows them to set prices with their required margins in mind.

Now let's say a retailer buys the jeans from the supplier (wholesaler or manufacturer) for $30.00 per pair. If the retailer requires a margin of 40 percent, it would calculate the price as a 40 percent markup on selling price. The calculation would be as follows:

$$\text{Price} = \frac{\text{Total cost}}{1.00 - \text{Markup percentage}}$$

$$\text{Price} = \frac{\$30.00}{(1.00 - 0.40)} = \frac{\$30.00}{0.60} = \$50.00$$

Therefore, the price of the jeans with the markup on selling price is $50.00.

Just to compare the difference in the final prices of the two markup methods, Table 10S.4 also shows what would happen if the retailer uses a markup on cost method. Using the same product cost and price with a 40 percent markup on cost would yield $42.00, a much lower price. The markup on selling price gives you the percentage of the selling price that the markup is. The markup on cost gives you the percentage of the cost that the markup is. In the markup on selling price the markup amount is $20.00, which is 40 percent of the selling price of $50.00. In the markup on cost, the markup is $12.00, which is 40 percent of the cost of $30.00.

Supplement Problems Test Your Marketing Math

10S-1. Assume that you are in charge of pricing for a firm that produces pickles. You have fixed costs of $2,000,000. Variable costs are $0.75 per jar of pickles. You are selling your product to retailers for $0.89. You sell the pickles in cases of 24 jars per case.

a. How many jars of pickles must you sell to break even?

b. How much must you sell in dollars to break even?

c. How many jars of pickles must you sell to break even plus make a profit of $300,000?

d. Assume a retailer buys your product for $0.89. His business requires that he prices products with a 35 percent markup on cost. Calculate his selling price.

e. Assume you have an MSRP of $1.39 for the pickles. If a retailer has a required 35 percent retailer margin on all products he sells, what is the most he is willing to pay the producer for the pickles?

f. A clothing retailer knows that to break even and make a profit he needs to have a minimum retailer margin (also referred to as a contribution margin or gross margin) of at least 60 percent. If he is to sell a pair of shorts for the manufacturer's suggested retail price of $49.99, what is the most he can pay the manufacturer for the shorts and maintain his margin?

g. A salesperson is developing a quote for a quantity of disposable hospital gowns. His cost for each case of gowns is $85.00. His firm requires that he have a 20 percent margin so he is using a markup on selling price calculation to price the gowns. What will his quote be per case of gowns if he uses a 20 percent markup on selling price?

10S-2. Executives of Studio Recordings Inc. produced the latest compact disc by the Starshine Sisters Band, titled *Sunshine/Moonshine*. The following cost information pertains to the CD.

a. CD package	$1.25/CD
b. Songwriters' royalties	$0.35/CD
c. Recording artists' royalties	$1.00/CD
d. Advertising and promotion	$275,000
e. Studio Recording Inc.'s overhead	$250,000
f. Selling price to the CD distributor	$9.00

Calculate the following:

1. Contribution per CD unit

2. Break-even volume in CD units and dollars

3. Net profit if 1 million CDs are sold

4. Necessary CD unit volume to achieve a $200,000 profit

Deliver the Goods: Determine the Distribution Strategy

Courtesy of Michael J. Ford, BDP International

Michael Ford

▼ **A Decision Maker at BDP International**

Michael Ford is a career professional in international transportation, specializing in import/export documentation and regulatory compliance. He is responsible for BDP International's Regulatory Compliance unit. Michael's activities include developing and administering the company's consulting arm in value-added product offerings such as Regulatory Compliance, Supply Chain Security, Duty Drawback, Customer Education and Logistics Process Analysis/Management, and all topical governmental issues connected with the handling and administration of export and import cargo. Michael's leadership in communication and system logic on governmental rules and regulations is central to BDP's ability to understand and resolve complex regulatory issues quickly, decisively and with minimal impact on customers.

Michael has been associated with BDP for more than 36 years. Before his current role he headed the company's regional ocean export service division as Vice President. For the past 20 years, he has worked with and served as an advocate for some of the world's leading companies, interacting with the U.S. Customs Service and the Department of Commerce/Census Bureau, in the development, piloting and automation of import and export programs. Among his other affiliations, Ford is the Co-chair for Trade on the Export Committee in the development of the new Customs ACE system and has served with Customs as a member of the Commercial Operations Advisory Council (COAC), Chair of the Mid-Atlantic District Export Council, and chairs the Partner sector with the American Chemistry Council, Responsible Care Committee. He also teaches an MBA International Logistics course at Saint Joseph's University in Philadelphia. He received a B.A. in Business Administration from Temple University in 1979.

Michael's Info

What I do when I'm not working:
Spending time with family and playing basketball

Business book I'm reading now:
Leading Change by John Kotter

My motto to live by:
Work hard and keep things simple

What drives me:
The opportunity to learn and then share my new knowledge

My management style:
Trust the people who work for you and allow them to make their decisions

Don't do this when interviewing with me:
Ask me questions about me

Here's my problem...

BDP International, Inc. is the world's premiere international logistics company, specializing in customized logistics solutions powered by exceptional people, industry-leading execution processes, and proprietary technology. BDP is non-asset based; this means it does not own the planes, vessels, and trucks it uses to move clients' goods around the world. This structure gives BDP a lot of flexibility because it can pick and choose the right transportation company to meet the needs of a specific client.

BDP was founded in 1966 in a one-room office of the Philadelphia Customs House with the goal to redefine the business of freight forwarding. The Company's founder, Richard Bolte, Sr., identified the opportunity to reinvent the complex documentation process of international sales and purchase orders to yield long-term and meaningful savings for his customers.

Since its inception, BDP has focused on finding solutions to complex logistics problems and creating significant value for customers rather than simply moving freight. BDP remains family owned. The continuity of family ownership, during BDP's transformation from start-up into a global enterprise, has fostered and institutionalized a unique service culture that has remained a hallmark of BDP's unparalleled industry reputation. BDP is one of the only U.S. headquartered, privately owned, freight forwarders with global scale.

PepsiCo is one of BDP's many large corporate clients; we work with their organization to move their products around the world. PepsiCo is the parent company of 22 brands that range from Pepsi beverages to Quaker Oats and Frito-Lay. In January 2015, the World Economic Forum (WEF) was holding an important meeting in Davos, Switzerland. Economic decision makers from around the world would be attending, and many of them were involved in leading discussions about many of the current world issues that impact large companies like PepsiCo as well as consumers and the environment. This prominent world stage was the perfect setting for the company's Quaker Foods brand to host a "café" at the conference and use the opportunity to provide attendees with samples of its new "breakfast bars." Quaker's PR/marketing team was eager to showcase this new product line because the company was introducing the bars to the consumer market and this event would provide a global stage for their debut. Two weeks before the start of the conference, Quaker asked us to help them get a total of 102 boxes full of these bars to the venue in Davos.

This request wasn't as easy as it sounds. The problem is that the breakfast bars are made in the U.S., and the manufacturing site is not approved by the European Union (EU). The EU imposes very strict controls on the ingredients it allows for import. Switzerland is a member country of the EU, so it follows EU regulations. BDP had a short window to move the goods from the U.S. and persuade Swiss Customs to clear the shipment in time for the conference. If the Quaker products didn't show up in time, the bare shelves at the café would make the client look bad—and this failure in turn would be a major black eye for BDP.

We had to scramble to understand all of the possible regulatory issues that might gum up the works. The biggest sticking point was that the EU requires all food products to carry a label that lists all of their ingredients, and this label has to be printed in Italian, German, or French; Swiss Customs would not grant a special exemption for English for the conference. If BDP had to unpack each box and relabel more than 4000 Quaker bars in one of the permitted languages, the additional resources required would make it unrealistic to move the order.

Michael considered his **Options** 1·2·3

1 Option
Convince Swiss Customs to allow us to put a new label on the outside of each of the 102 boxes rather than on each of the 4020 individual bars in the shipment. This compromise would allow the products to enter the country. However, the cost to label each box as well as the time required to do so raised the possibility that we couldn't move the goods in time to make the start of the conference. If we had to add another label in a different language this solution would also cover up the normal package and hide other product information.

2 Option
Identify a different Quaker Foods product that is manufactured in Europe and convince the client to substitute this for the breakfast bars. The client would be able to provide a local product for the conference attendees. On the other hand, Quaker wanted to impress the participants who would come from around the world with its innovativeness, and its new breakfast bars would do that.

3 Option
Provide the list of required ingredients in the requested language as our contact at Swiss Customs proposed. This option would eliminate the cost of labeling every bar or box as well as the additional labor costs and time required to move the boxes on schedule. However, the suggested solution was verbal only; as a result of the bureaucratic process involved we would have to approach Customs when the physical products actually arrived to be cleared and remind the person working at the time about this suggestion. The odds are this would not be the same person who made the suggestion, so we would have to take our chances. Inspectors who are confronted with more than 100 boxes to clear sometimes rely on their own judgment about how to handle the shipment. And, we would still have to move the boxes from the manufacturing site in the midwestern U.S. to Switzerland in less than a week. The client would have to pay for all the associated costs and they might not be too happy about that.

Now put yourself in Michael's shoes. Which option would you choose, and why?

You Choose

Which **option** would you choose, and **why**?

☐ Option 1   ☐ Option 2   ☐ Option 3

See what **option** Michael chose in **MyLab Marketing™**

MyLab Marketing™

⭐ **Improve Your Grade!**

Over 10 million students improved their results using the Pearson MyLabs.
Visit **mymktlab.com** for simulations, tutorials, and end-of-chapter problems.

11.1 Types of Distribution Channels and Wholesale Intermediaries

OBJECTIVE

Explain what a distribution channel is, identify types of wholesaling intermediaries, and describe the different types of distribution channels.

(pp. 366–377)

So you've done all the work to understand your target market. You've created your product, and you've priced it, too. Your Facebook page is attracting legions of brand fans. But sorry, you're still not done with the marketing mix—now you need to get what you make out into the marketplace (i.e., distribute it). The delivery of goods to customers involves **physical distribution**, which refers to the activities that move finished goods from manufacturers to final customers. As introduced in Chapter 1, a *channel of distribution* is the series of firms or individuals that facilitates the movement of a product from the producer to the final customer. In many cases, these channels include an organized network of producers (or manufacturers), wholesalers, and retailers that develop relationships and work together to make products conveniently available to eager buyers. And, as Michael Ford's decision at BDP International illustrates, the delivery of goods across national borders requires an in-depth understanding of laws and regulations specific to a particular nation or international governing body.

Distribution channels come in different shapes and sizes. The bakery around the corner where you buy your cinnamon rolls is a member of a channel, as is the baked-goods section at the local supermarket, the Starbucks that sells biscotti to go with your double-mocha cappuccino, and the bakery outlet store that sells day-old rolls at a discount.

A channel of distribution consists of, at a minimum, a producer—the individual or firm that manufactures or produces a good or service—and a customer. This is a **direct channel**, and when you buy a loaf of bread at a mom-and-pop bakery, you're buying through a direct channel. Firms that sell their own products directly to customers through websites, catalogs, toll-free numbers, or factory outlet stores also use direct channels.

But life (and marketing) usually isn't that simple: Channels often are *indirect* because they include one or more **channel intermediaries**—firms or individuals such as wholesalers, agents, brokers, and retailers who in some way help move the product to the consumer or business user. For example, a bakery may choose to sell its cinnamon buns to a wholesaler that will in turn sell boxes of buns to supermarkets and restaurants that in turn sell them to consumers. Another older term for intermediaries is *middlemen*.

physical distribution
The activities that move finished goods from manufacturers to final customers, including order processing, warehousing, materials handling, transportation, and inventory control.

direct channel
A channel of distribution in which a manufacturer of a product or creator of a service distributes directly to the end customer.

channel intermediaries
Firms or individuals such as wholesalers, agents, brokers, or retailers who help move a product from the producer to the consumer or business user. An older term for intermediaries is *middlemen*.

Functions of Distribution Channels

Channels that include one or more organizations or intermediaries often can accomplish certain distribution functions more effectively and efficiently than can a single organization. As we saw in Chapter 2, this is especially true in international distribution channels, where differences among countries' customs, beliefs, and infrastructures can make global marketing a nightmare. Even small companies can succeed in complex global markets when they rely on distributors such as BDP that know local customs and laws.

Overall, channels provide the place, time, and possession utility we described in Chapter 1. They make desired products available when, where, and in the sizes and quantities that customers desire. Suppose, for example, you want to buy that perfect bouquet of flowers for a special someone. You *could* grow them yourself or even "liberate" them from a cemetery if you were *really* desperate (very classy!). Fortunately, you can probably accomplish this task with just a simple phone call or a few mouse clicks, and "like magic" a local florist delivers a bouquet to your honey's door.

Distribution channels provide a number of logistics or physical distribution functions that increase the efficiency of the flow of goods from producer to customer (more on this later in the chapter). How would we buy groceries without our modern system of supermarkets? We'd have to get our milk from a dairy, our bread from a bakery, our tomatoes and corn from a local farmer, and our flour from a flour mill. And forget about specialty items such as Coca-Cola or Little Debbie snack cakes. The companies that make these items would have to handle literally millions of transactions to sell to every individual who craves a junk-food fix.

Distribution channels create *efficiencies* because they reduce the number of transactions necessary for goods to flow from many different manufacturers to large numbers of customers. This occurs in two ways. The first is **breaking bulk**. Wholesalers and retailers purchase large quantities (usually cases) of goods from manufacturers but sell only one or a few at a time to many different customers. Second, channel intermediaries reduce the number of transactions when they **create assortments**; they provide a variety of products in one location, so that customers can conveniently buy many different items from one seller at one time.

Figure 11.1 provides a simple example of how distribution channels work. This simplified illustration includes five producers and five customers. If each producer sold its product to each individual customer, 25 different transactions would have to occur—not exactly an efficient way to distribute products. But with a single intermediary who buys from all 5 manufacturers and sells to all 5 customers, we quickly cut the number of transactions to 10. If there were 10 manufacturers and 10 customers, an intermediary would reduce the number of transactions from 100 to just 20. Do the math: Channels are efficient.

The **transportation and storage** of goods is another type of physical distribution function. That is, retailers and other channel members move the goods from the production point to other locations where they can hold them until consumers want them. Channel intermediaries also perform a number of **facilitating functions** that make the purchase process easier for customers and manufacturers. For example, intermediaries often provide customer services, such as offering credit to buyers.

Many of us like to shop at brick-and-mortar department stores because if we are not happy with the product, we can take it back to the store, where cheerful customer service personnel are happy to give us a refund (at least in theory). But the same facilitating

breaking bulk
Dividing larger quantities of goods into smaller lots in order to meet the needs of buyers.

create assortments
To provide a variety of products in one location to meet the needs of buyers.

transportation and storage
Occurs when retailers and other channel members move the goods from the production point to other locations where they can hold them until consumers want them.

facilitating functions
Functions of channel intermediaries that make the purchase process easier for customers and manufacturers.

Figure 11.1 *Process* | Reduce Transactions via Intermediaries

One of the functions of distribution channels is to provide an assortment of products. Because the customers can buy a number of different products at the same location, this reduces the total costs of obtaining a product.

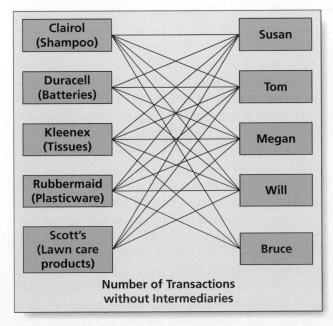

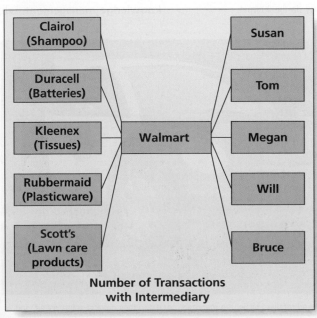

risk-taking functions
The chance retailers take on the loss of a product when they buy a product from a manufacturer because the product sits on the shelf because no customers want it.

communication and transaction functions
Happens when channel members develop and execute both promotional and other types of communication among members of the channel.

disintermediation (of the channel of distribution)
The elimination of some layers of the channel of distribution to cut costs and improve the efficiency of the channel.

knowledge management
A comprehensive approach to collecting, organizing, storing, and retrieving a firm's information assets.

intranet
An internal corporate communication network that uses Internet technology to link company departments, employees, and databases.

online distribution piracy
The theft and unauthorized repurposing of intellectual property via the Internet.

function happens online with Zappos, Lands' End, and a host of other customer-friendly retailers. These same customer services are even more important in business-to-business (B2B) markets where customers purchase larger quantities of higher-priced products. And channel members perform **risk-taking functions**. For example, if a retailer buys a product from a manufacturer and it just sits on the shelf because no customers want it, he or she is stuck with the item and must take a loss. But hey, that's what outlet malls are for, right? Perishable items present an even greater risk of spoilage and loss, hence potentially a high risk. Blueberries in the U.S. are in season for only a very short period of time. Retailers want to stock up to meet the annual high demand; on the other hand, a carton of semisoft blueberries on the shelf a few weeks past prime is beyond unappealing.

Finally, intermediaries perform **communication and transaction functions** by which channel members develop and execute both promotional and other types of communication among members of the channel. Wholesalers buy products to make them available for retailers, and they sell products to other channel members. Retailers handle transactions with final consumers. Channel members can provide two-way communication for manufacturers. They may supply the sales force, advertising, and other types of marketing communication necessary to inform consumers and persuade them that a product will meet their needs. And the channel members can be invaluable sources of information on consumer complaints, changing tastes, and new competitors in the market.

The Evolution of Distribution Functions

In the future, channel intermediaries that physically handle the product may become obsolete. Already companies are eliminating many traditional intermediaries because they find that they don't add enough value in the distribution channel—a process we call **disintermediation (of the channel of distribution)**. Literally, disintermediation means removal of intermediaries! For marketers, disintermediation reduces costs in many ways: fewer employees, no need to buy or lease expensive retail property in high-traffic locations, and no need to furnish a store with fancy fixtures and decor. You can also see this process at work when you pump your own gas, withdraw cash from an ATM, or book a roundtrip flight and a hotel stay with a website such as Kayak.

As with many other aspects of marketing, the Internet is radically changing how companies coordinate among members of a supply chain to make it more effective in ways that end consumers never see. These firms develop better ways to implement **knowledge management**, which refers to a comprehensive approach that collects, organizes, stores, and retrieves a firm's information assets. Those assets include databases and company documents as well as the practical knowledge of employees whose past experience may be relevant to solve a new problem. In the world of B2B, this process probably occurs via an **intranet**, which, as you read in Chapter 6, is an internal corporate communication network that uses Internet technology to link company departments, employees, and databases. But it can also facilitate sharing of knowledge among channel partners because it is a secure and password-protected platform. This more strategic management of information results in a win-win situation for all the partners.

But as with most things cyber, the Internet as a distribution channel brings pain with pleasure. One of the more vexing problems with Internet distribution is the potential for **online distribution piracy**, which is the theft and unauthorized repurposing of intellectual

Some wholesalers and retailers assist the manufacturer when they provide setup, repair, and maintenance service for products they handle. Best Buy's Geek Squad is a perfect example.

B Christopher/Alamy Stock Photo

property via the Internet. Bringing things close to home, the college textbook industry has high potential for online piracy. It's not uncommon for U.S.-produced textbooks to make their way to unscrupulous individuals outside the home country who translate the core content into the native language and post it online for distribution. This practice completely devalues the knowledge contained therein and results in zero return to the knowledge creators (namely, your humble textbook authors!). Many students don't realize that the only people who profit from used or pirated books are the middlemen who have obtained them (sometimes illegally). Used books do sell for less, but because the publisher does not see any revenue from these sales, it is forced to raise prices to return a profit. This results in a vicious circle as new books become more and more expensive, which motivates more students to buy them illegitimately, and so the madness continues.

Let's look at a similar distribution issue in a product category that's probably more familiar to you. Unauthorized downloads of music continue to pose a major challenge to the "recording" industry—to the point where the whole nature of the industry has turned topsy-turvy in search of a new business model that works. Many in the music business are rethinking exactly what—and where—is the value-added for what they do. To the majority of modern consumers of music, the value of a physical CD has diminished—to the point where many listeners are unwilling to pay anything at all for the artist's work. And more and more musical artists opt to defect from traditional record labels and introduce their tunes online, where they can control at least some of the channel of distribution. As you may know, a few years ago the band Radiohead even tried a "name your own price" strategy when it released its studio album *In Rainbows* on its website.

In addition to music, TV shows and movies also tend to be obvious targets for piracy online. For a company such as Netflix that legally partners with content providers to make their content available online for a fee, distribution piracy is a serious issue for both parties. Interestingly, Netflix actually adjusts its prices lower in markets outside the U.S. that have higher rates of piracy to attract a larger number of consumers to the legitimate offerings through the company website. In addition, Netflix believes that making legal access to content an easier and more convenient experience can lead to decreases in piracy. The company cites evidence of a 50 percent decline in BitTorrent traffic (a web-based communications protocol used both for the legal and illegal download of online content) after the introduction of Netflix in Canada.[1]

So far, we've learned what a distribution channel is and talked about some of the functions it performs. Now let's find out about specific types of channel intermediaries and channel structures.

Wholesaling Intermediaries

How can you get your hands on a new Drake T-shirt or hoodie? You could pick one up at your local music store, at a trendy clothing store like Hot Topic, or maybe at its online store. You might join hordes of others and buy an "official Drake concert T-shirt" from vendors during a show. Alternatively, you might get a "deal" on a bootlegged, unauthorized version of the same shirt that a shady guy who stands *outside* the concert venue sells from a battered suitcase. Perhaps you shop online at www.drakeofficial.com. Each of these distribution alternatives traces a different path from producer to consumer. Let's look at the different types of wholesaling intermediaries and at different channel structures. Note that we will hold off focusing on retailers, which are usually the last link in the chain, until Chapter 12. Retailers are a big deal and deserve a chapter of their own. 📷 Figure 11.2 portrays key intermediary types, and Table 11.1 summarizes the important characteristics of each.

Figure 11.2 📷 *Snapshot* | Key Types of Intermediaries

Intermediaries can be independent or manufacturer owned.

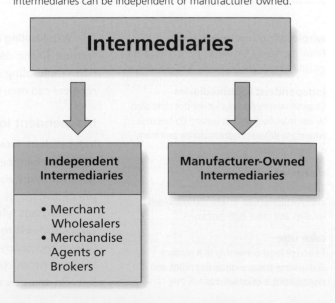

Table 11.1 | Types of Intermediaries

Intermediary Type	Description	Advantages
Independent intermediaries	Do business with many different manufacturers and many different customers	Used by most small to medium-size firms
• **Merchant wholesalers**	Buy (take title to) goods from producers and sell to organizational customers; either full or limited function	Allow small manufacturers to serve customers throughout the world with competitive costs
• Cash-and-carry wholesalers	Provide products for small-business customers who purchase at wholesaler's location	Distribute low-cost merchandise for small retailers and other business customers
• Truck jobbers	Deliver perishable food and tobacco items to retailers	Ensure that perishable items are delivered and sold efficiently
• Drop shippers	Take orders from and bill retailers for products drop shipped from manufacturer	Facilitate transactions for bulky products
• Mail-order wholesalers	Sell through catalogs, telephone, or mail order	Provide reasonably priced sales options to small organizational customers
• Rack jobbers	Provide retailers with display units, check inventories, and replace merchandise for the retailers	Provide merchandising services to retailers
• **Merchandise agents and brokers**	Provide services in exchange for commissions	Maintain legal ownership of product by the seller
• Manufacturers' agents	Use independent salespeople; carry several lines of noncompeting products	Supply sales function for small and new firms
• Selling agents, including export/import agents	Handle entire output of one or more products	Handle all marketing functions for small manufacturers
• Commission merchants	Receive commission on sales price of product	Provide efficiency primarily in agricultural products market
• Merchandise brokers, including export/import brokers	Identify likely buyers and bring buyers and sellers together	Enhance efficiency in markets where there are many small buyers and sellers
Manufacturer-owned intermediaries	Limit operations to one manufacturer	Create efficiencies for large firms
• **Sales branches**	Maintain some inventory in different geographic areas (similar to wholesalers)	Provide service to customers in different geographic areas
• **Sales offices**	Carry no inventory; availability in different geographic areas	Reduce selling costs and provide better customer service
• **Manufacturers' showrooms**	Display products attractively for customers to visit	Facilitate examination of merchandise by customers at a central location

wholesaling intermediaries
Firms that handle the flow of products from the manufacturer to the retailer or business user.

independent intermediaries
Channel intermediaries that are not controlled by any manufacturer but instead do business with many different manufacturers and many different customers.

merchant wholesalers
Intermediaries that buy goods from manufacturers (take title to them) and sell to retailers and other B2B customers.

take title
To accept legal ownership of a product and assume the accompanying rights and responsibilities of ownership.

Wholesaling intermediaries are firms that handle the flow of products from the manufacturer to the retailer or business user. There are many different types of consumer and B2B wholesaling intermediaries. Some of these are independent, but manufacturers and retailers can own them, too.

Independent Intermediaries

Independent intermediaries do business with many different manufacturers and many different customers. Because no manufacturer owns or controls them, they make it possible for many manufacturers to serve customers throughout the world while they keep prices low.

Merchant wholesalers are independent intermediaries that buy goods from manufacturers and sell to retailers and other B2B customers. Because merchant wholesalers **take title** to the goods (i.e., they legally own them), they assume certain risks and can suffer losses if products are damaged, become outdated or obsolete, are stolen, or just don't sell. On the other hand, because they own the products, they are free to develop their own marketing strategies, including setting the prices they charge their customers. Wait, it gets better: There are several different kinds of merchant wholesalers:

- **Full-service merchant wholesalers** provide a wide range of services for their customers, including delivery, credit, product-use assistance, repairs, advertising, and other promotional support—even market research. Full-service merchant wholesalers often have their own sales force to call on businesses and organizational customers. Some general merchandise wholesalers carry a large variety of different items, whereas specialty wholesalers carry an extensive assortment of a single product line. For example, a candy wholesaler carries only candy and gum products but stocks enough different varieties to give your dentist nightmares for a year.

- In contrast, **limited-service merchant wholesalers** provide fewer services for their customers. Like full-service wholesalers, limited-service wholesalers *take title* to merchandise but are less likely to provide services such as delivery, credit, or marketing assistance to retailers. Specific types of limited-service wholesalers include the following:

  - *Cash-and-carry wholesalers* provide low-cost merchandise for retailers and industrial customers that are too small for other wholesalers' sales representatives to call on. Customers pay cash for products and provide their own delivery. Some popular cash-and-carry product categories include groceries, office supplies, and building materials.

  - *Truck jobbers* carry their products to small business customer locations for their inspection and selection. Truck jobbers often supply perishable items such as fruit and vegetables to small grocery stores. For example, a bakery truck jobber calls on supermarkets, checks the stock of bread on the shelves, removes outdated items, and suggests how much bread the store needs to reorder.

  - *Drop shippers* are limited-function wholesalers that take title to the merchandise but never actually take possession of it. Drop shippers take orders from and bill retailers and industrial buyers, but the merchandise is shipped directly from the manufacturer. Because they take title to the merchandise, they assume the same risks as other merchant wholesalers. Drop shippers are important to both the producers and the customers of bulky products, such as coal, oil, or lumber.

  - *Mail-order wholesalers* sell products to small retailers and other industrial customers, often located in remote areas, through catalogs rather than a sales force. They usually carry products in inventory and require payment in cash or by credit card before shipment. Mail-order wholesalers supply products such as cosmetics, hardware, and sporting goods.

  - *Rack jobbers* supply retailers with specialty items, such as health and beauty products and magazines. Rack jobbers get their name because they own and maintain the product display racks in grocery stores, drugstores, and variety stores. These wholesalers visit retail customers on a regular basis to maintain levels of stock and refill their racks with merchandise. Think about how quickly magazines turn over on the rack; without an expert who pulls old titles and inserts new ones, retailers would have great difficulty ensuring that you can buy the current issue of *People* magazine on the first day it hits the streets.

Merchandise agents or brokers are a second major type of independent intermediary. Agents and brokers provide services in exchange for commissions. They may or may not take possession of the product, but they *never* take title; that is, they do not accept legal

Free shipping provides a competitive advantage for a large retailer.

full-service merchant wholesalers
Wholesalers that provide a wide range of services for their customers, including delivery, credit, product-use assistance, repairs, advertising, and other promotional support.

limited-service merchant wholesalers
Wholesalers that provide fewer services for their customers.

merchandise agents or brokers
Channel intermediaries that provide services in exchange for commissions but never take title to the product.

ownership of the product. Agents normally represent buyers or sellers on an ongoing basis, whereas clients employ brokers for a short period of time:

- *Manufacturers' agents*, or *manufacturers' reps*, are independent salespeople who carry several lines of noncompeting products. They have contractual arrangements with manufacturers that outline territories, selling prices, and other specific aspects of the relationship but provide little if any supervision. Manufacturers normally compensate agents with commissions based on a percentage of what they sell. Manufacturers' agents often develop strong customer relationships and provide an important sales function for small and new companies.

- *Selling agents*, including *export/import agents*, market a whole product line or one manufacturer's total output. They often work like an independent marketing department because they perform the same functions as full-service merchant wholesalers but do not take title to products. Unlike manufacturers' agents, selling agents have unlimited territories and control the pricing, promotion, and distribution of their products. We find selling agents in industries such as furniture, clothing, and textiles.

- *Commission merchants* are sales agents who receive goods, primarily agricultural products such as grain or livestock, on *consignment*—that is, they take possession of products without taking title. Although sellers may state a minimum price they are willing to take for their products, commission merchants are free to sell the product for the highest price they can get. Commission merchants receive a commission on the sales price of the product.

- *Merchandise brokers*, including export/import brokers, are intermediaries that facilitate transactions in markets such as real estate, food, and used equipment, in which there are lots of small buyers and sellers. Brokers identify likely buyers and sellers and bring the two together in return for a fee they receive when the transaction is completed.

Manufacturer-Owned Intermediaries

Sometimes manufacturers set up their own channel intermediaries. In this way, they can operate separate business units that perform all the functions of independent intermediaries while still maintaining complete control over the channel:

- *Sales branches* are manufacturer-owned facilities that, like independent wholesalers, carry inventory and provide sales and service to customers in a specific geographic area. We find sales branches in industries such as petroleum products, industrial machinery and equipment, and motor vehicles.

- *Sales offices* are manufacturer-owned facilities that, like agents, do not carry inventory but provide selling functions for the manufacturer in a specific geographic area. Because they allow members of the sales force to locate close to customers, they reduce selling costs and provide better customer service.

- *Manufacturers' showrooms* are manufacturer-owned or leased facilities in which products are permanently displayed for customers to visit. Merchandise marts are often multiple buildings in which one or more industries hold trade shows and many manufacturers have permanent showrooms. Retailers can visit either during a show or all year long to see the manufacturer's merchandise and make B2B purchases.

Types of Distribution Channels

Firms face many choices when they structure distribution channels. Should they sell directly to consumers and business users? Would they benefit if they included wholesalers, retailers, or both in the channel? Would it make sense to sell directly to some customers but use retailers to sell to others? Of course, there is no single best channel for all products. The marketing manager must select a channel structure that creates a competitive advantage for the firm and its products based on the size and needs of the target market. Let's consider some of the factors these managers need to think about.

When they develop distribution (place) strategies, marketers first consider different **channel levels**. This refers to the number of distinct categories of intermediaries that make up a channel of distribution. Many factors have an impact on this decision. What channel members are available? How large is the market? How frequently do consumers purchase the product? What services do consumers require? 📷 Figure 11.3 summarizes the different structures a distribution channel can take. The producer and the customer are always members, so the shortest channel possible has two levels. Using a retailer adds a third level, a wholesaler adds a fourth level, and so on. Different channel structures exist for both consumer and B2B markets.

And what about services? You will learn in Chapter 12 that services are intangible, so there is no need to worry about storage, transportation, and the other functions of physical distribution. In most cases, the service travels directly from the producer to the customer. However, an intermediary we call an *agent* can enhance the distribution of some services when he helps the parties complete the transaction. Examples of these agents include insurance agents, stockbrokers, and travel agents (no, not everyone books their travel online).

Consumer Channels

As we noted previously, the simplest channel is a direct channel. Why do some producers sell directly to customers? One reason is that a direct channel may allow the producer to serve its customers better and at a lower price than is possible if it included a retailer. A baker who uses a direct channel makes sure that customers enjoy fresher bread than if the tasty loaves are sold through a local supermarket. Furthermore, if the baker sells the bread through a supermarket, the price will be higher because of the supermarket's costs of doing business and its need to make its own profit on the bread. In fact, sometimes this is the *only* way to sell the product because using channel intermediaries may boost the price above what consumers are willing to pay.

Another reason to use a direct channel is *control*. When the producer handles distribution, it maintains control of pricing, service, and delivery—all elements of the transaction. Because distributors and dealers carry many products, it can be difficult to get their sales forces to focus on selling one product. In a direct channel, a producer works directly with customers, so it gains insights into trends, customer needs and complaints, and the effectiveness of its marketing strategies.

Even for a consumer packaged goods giant such as P&G that is able to maintain a strong presence within the storefronts of the largest physical and digital retailers, the allure of a direct channel is appealing, as evidenced by the company's launch of the "P&G Shop." This move was heavily driven by the desire to be where consumers shopped and to have the opportunity to listen to and engage with them online in a different way. P&G certainly does not have plans to cut ties with its retailers, but the creation of a direct-to-consumer channel offers the company some interesting opportunities to further engage with consumers and bolster sales.[2]

Why do producers choose to use indirect channels to reach consumers? A reason in many cases is that customers are familiar with certain retailers or other intermediaries; it's where they always go to look for what they need. Getting customers to change their normal buying behavior— for example, convincing consumers to buy their laundry detergent or frozen pizza from a catalog or over the Internet instead of from the corner supermarket— can be difficult.

In addition, intermediaries help producers in all the ways we described previously. By creating utility and transaction efficiencies, channel members make producers' lives easier and enhance their ability to reach customers. The *producer–retailer–consumer channel* in Figure 11.3 is the shortest indirect channel. Samsung uses this channel when it sells TVs

channel levels
The number of distinct categories of intermediaries that make up a channel of distribution.

In order to maintain creative control, recording artist Aimee Mann licenses her own music rather than working with a major record label.

Daria Khazel/PacificCoastNews/Newscom

Figure 11.3 📷 *Snapshot* | Different Types of Channels of Distribution

Channels differ in the number of channel members that participate.

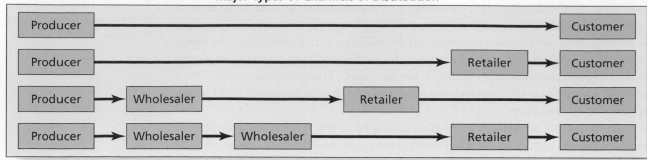

Major Types of Channels of Distribution

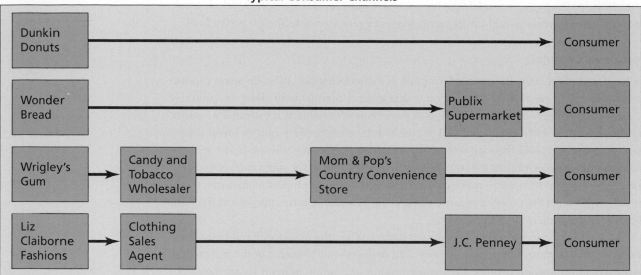

Typical Consumer Channels

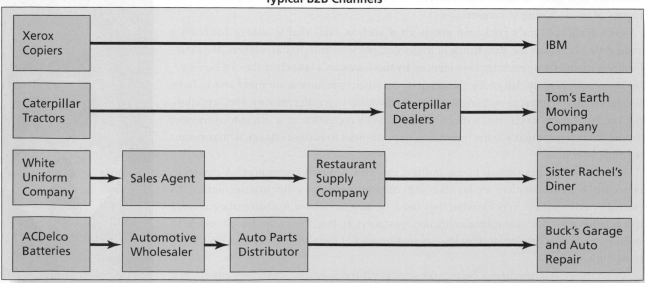

Typical B2B Channels

through large retailers such as Best Buy (either their brick-and-mortar stores or their online store). Because the retailers buy in large volume, they can obtain inventory at a low price and then pass these savings on to shoppers (this is what gives them a competitive advantage over smaller, more specialized stores that don't order so many items). The size of these retail giants also means they can provide the physical distribution functions that wholesalers handle for smaller retail outlets, such as transportation and storage.

The *producer–wholesaler–retailer–consumer channel* is a common distribution channel in consumer marketing. An example would be a single ice cream factory that supplies, say, four or five regional wholesalers. These wholesalers then sell to 400 or more retailers, such as grocery stores. The retailers, in turn, each sell the ice cream to thousands of customers. In this channel, the regional wholesalers combine many manufacturers' products to supply grocery stores. Because the grocery stores do business with many wholesalers, this arrangement results in a broad selection of products.

B2B Channels

B2B distribution channels, as the name suggests, facilitate the flow of goods from a producer to an organizational or business customer. Generally, B2B channels parallel consumer channels in that they may be direct or indirect. For example, the simplest indirect channel in industrial markets occurs when the single intermediary—a merchant wholesaler we refer to as an *industrial distributor* rather than a retailer—buys products from a manufacturer and sells them to business customers.

Direct channels are more common in B2B markets versus consumer markets. As we saw in Chapter 6, this is because B2B marketing often means that a firm sells high-dollar, high-profit items (a single piece of industrial equipment may cost hundreds of thousands of dollars) to a market made up of only a few customers. In such markets, it makes sense financially for a company to develop its own sales force and sell directly to customers—in this case, the investment in an in-house sales force pays off.

Dual and Hybrid Distribution Systems

Figure 11.3 illustrates how simple distribution channels work. But, once again, we are reminded that life (or marketing) is rarely that simple: Producers, dealers, wholesalers, retailers, and customers alike may actually participate in more than one type of channel, as illustrated earlier by P&G adding its own online store. Similarly, the online giant Amazon is opening more than 300 brick-and-mortar stores in the U.S. Even though it has helped to put many independent bookstores out of business, the company plans to stock its stores with books that Amazon users have rated highly as part of its strategy to dominate the book category.[3] We call these **dual or multiple distribution systems**.

dual or multiple distribution systems
A system where producers, dealers, wholesalers, retailers, and customers participate in more than one type of channel.

The pharmaceutical industry provides a good example of multiple-channel usage. Pharmaceutical companies distribute their products in at least three types of channels:

1. They sell to hospitals, clinics, and other organizational customers directly. These customers buy in quantity, and they purchase a wide variety of products. Because hospitals and clinics dispense pills one at a time rather than in bottles of 50, these outlets require different product packaging than when the manufacturer sells medications to other types of customers.

2. They rely on an indirect consumer channel when they sell to large drugstore chains, like Walgreens, that distribute the medicines to their stores across the country. Alternatively, some of us would rather purchase our prescriptions in a more personal manner from the local independent drugstore where we can still get an ice cream soda while we wait. In this version of the indirect consumer channel, the manufacturer sells to drug wholesalers that, in turn, supply these independents.

Internet intermediaries like eBay provide new distribution channel options so consumers can buy new or used items from other consumers in addition to producers.

hybrid marketing system
A marketing system that uses a number of different channels and communication methods to serve a target market.

3. Finally, the companies sell directly to third-party payers such as HMOs, PPOs, and insurance companies. After healthcare reform in the U.S. fully kicks in, who knows what the channel configuration might be!

Instead of serving a target market with a single channel, some companies combine channels—direct sales, distributors, retail sales, and direct mail—to create a **hybrid marketing system**.[4] Believe it or not, the whole world of business actually has not gone paperless (we know it's hard to accept)! Hence, companies actually do still buy copying machines (sounds so 1999)—and in large quantities. At one time, you could buy a Xerox copier only directly through a Xerox salesperson. Today, unless you are a very large business customer, you likely will purchase a Xerox machine from a local Xerox authorized dealer or possibly through the Xerox "Online Store." Xerox turned to an enhanced dealer network for distribution because such hybrid marketing systems offer companies certain competitive advantages, including increased coverage of the market, lower marketing costs, and a greater potential for customization of service for local markets.

Distribution Channels and the Marketing Mix

How do decisions regarding place relate to the other *three Ps*? For one, place decisions affect pricing. Marketers that distribute products through low-priced retailers such as Walmart, T.J. Maxx, and Marshalls will have different pricing objectives and strategies than will those that sell to specialty stores like Tiffany or high-end department stores like Nordstrom. And, of course, the nature of the product itself influences the retailers and intermediaries that are used for distribution. Manufacturers select mass merchandisers to sell mid–price-range products while they distribute top-of-the-line products such as expensive jewelry through high-end department and specialty stores.

Distribution decisions can sometimes give a product a distinct position in its market. For example, Ultradent Products, Inc. sells its teeth whitening product Opalescence® exclusively through licensed dental professionals. Many other companies' teeth whitening products are typically sold through traditional retail channels, making them much more easily available. However, Ultradent's approach allows the company to position Opalescence® as a higher-end product endorsed by professional experts. They rely on the dentist and staff to pitch the benefits of the product in a way that carries far more credibility with a patient than an ad by a retailer or manufacturer.[5]

In addition, the distribution channel *itself*—a cool new way you get the product—may help to position a product in a unique way vis-à-vis the competition. That is, the way you obtain a product can be one of the attributes that makes it appealing. A great example is the hot trend of **subscription boxes**, a new business model that generates more than $5 billion in revenue per year. Many people love to get surprises in the mail (as long as they're not bills or a jury summons). Today numerous upstart companies supply these surprises by sending out a box each month filled with items you never knew you wanted but you just have to have. Birchbox is one of the pioneers in this area, sending different boxes to women and men each month with samples of trendy new cosmetics, personal care products, and even socks and underwear. Many other competitors have entered the market to offer beauty boxes such as Ipsy, Boxycharm, Vegan Cuts Beauty Box (guess what kind of beauty products are in there)—even Walmart offers a beauty box. The subscription model includes

subscription boxes
A new business model for distribution that supplies surprises by sending out a box each month filled with items you never knew you wanted but you just have to have.

other distribution channels as well including gourmet food (Taste Club, Graze, BoCandy), fitness and weight loss products (Bulu Box, Jacked Pack), razors and blades (Dollar Shaving Club), rental clothing for plus-size women (Gwynnie Bee), and phone cases (Phone Case of the Month). Subscription Addiction, one of the many websites devoted to this new business model, lists more than 900 subscription plans.[6] What are you waiting for? Run, don't walk, to your mailbox!

Ethics in the Distribution Channel

Companies' decisions about how to make their products available to consumers through distribution channels can create ethical dilemmas. For example, because their size gives them great bargaining power when they negotiate with manufacturers, many large retail chains force manufacturers to pay a **slotting allowance**—a fee in exchange for agreeing to place a manufacturer's products on a retailer's valuable shelf space. Although the retailers claim that such fees pay the cost of adding products to their inventory, many manufacturers feel that slotting fees are more akin to highway robbery. Certainly, the practice prevents many smaller manufacturers that cannot afford the slotting allowances from getting their products into the hands of consumers.

It may seem odd to you that in some cases products end up being sold through one or more channels that the manufacturer did not authorize. This practice is known as **product diversion**, and it can be a big problem for manufacturers due to loss of control that results once the product is in the hands of unauthorized distributors and retailers. An additional concern for many manufacturers is that their products, once diverted, will end up being sold at a price or in a form that damages both the brand and the firm's relationship with its authorized distributors. Such practices are common for beauty products that are sold exclusively through salons and other hair care professionals. Redken is one such company that notes that once its products have been diverted there is a risk that the product being offered has been tampered with.[7]

So who perpetrates product diversion? Most often, a **diverter** turns out to be one or more of the manufacturer's own regular customers that purposefully overbuys product when it is offered at special promotional prices, holds it in inventory until the promotion is over, and then sells the product within the channel. Also, retailers or distributors may be tempted to simply divert incidental excess inventory of a product that they do not expect be able to sell through legitimate means.

Another ethical issue involves the sheer size of a particular channel intermediary—be it manufacturer, wholesaler, retailer, or other intermediary. Walmart, the poster child for giant retailers, has been vilified for years as contributing to the demise of scores of independent competitors (i.e., mom-and-pop stores). In more recent years, the company has begun a very visible program to help its smaller rivals. The program offers financial grants to hardware stores, dress shops, and bakeries near its new urban stores; training on how to survive with a Walmart in town; and even free advertising in Walmart stores. Although certainly beneficial to the small fry, Walmart also hopes to benefit from the program in urban settings like Los Angeles and New York, where its plan to build new stores in inner-city neighborhoods has met with mixed reactions from local communities.[8]

Overall, it is important for all channel intermediaries to behave and treat each other in a professional, ethical manner—and to do no harm to consumers (financially or otherwise) through their channel activities. Every intermediary in the channel wants to make money, but behavior by one to maximize its financial success at the expense of others' success is a doomed approach, as ultimately cooperation in the channel will break down. Instead, it behooves intermediaries to work cooperatively in the channel to distribute products to consumers in an efficient manner—making the channel a success for everybody participating in it (including consumers)! Win-win!

slotting allowance
A fee paid in exchange for agreeing to place a manufacturer's products on a retailer's valuable shelf space.

product diversion
The distribution of a product through one or more channels not authorized for use by the manufacturer of the product.

diverter
An entity that facilitates the distribution of a product through one or more channels not authorized for use by the manufacturer of the product.

11.2 Develop a Channel Strategy

OBJECTIVE
List and explain the steps to plan a distribution channel strategy.
(pp. 378–384)

Do customers want products in large or small quantities? Do they insist on buying them locally, or will they purchase from a distant supplier? How long are they willing to wait to get the product? Inquiring marketers want to know!

Channel of distribution planning works best when marketers follow the steps in [icon] Figure 11.4. In this section, we first look at how manufacturers decide on distribution objectives and then examine what influences distribution decisions. Finally, we talk about how firms select different distribution strategies and tactics.

Firms that operate within a channel of distribution—manufacturers, wholesalers, and retailers—do **distribution planning**, which is a process of developing distribution objectives, evaluating internal and external environmental influences on distribution, and choosing a distribution strategy. In this section, our perspective focuses primarily on distribution planning by producers/manufacturers rather than intermediaries because manufacturers, more often than intermediaries, take a leadership role to create a successful distribution channel. (There are notable exceptions, such as with a retailer like Walmart, which clearly is the biggest fish in any channel in which it operates.)

distribution planning
The process of developing distribution objectives, evaluating internal and external environmental influences on distribution, and choosing a distribution strategy.

Step 1: Develop Distribution Objectives

The first step in a distribution plan is to develop objectives that support the organization's overall marketing goals. How can distribution work with the other elements of the marketing mix to increase profits? To increase market share? To increase sales volume? In general, the overall objective of any distribution plan is to make a firm's product available when, where, and in the quantities customers want at the minimum cost. More specific distribution objectives, however, depend on the characteristics of the product and the market.

For example, if the product is bulky, a primary distribution objective may be to minimize shipping costs. If the product is fragile, a goal may be to develop a channel that minimizes handling. In introducing a new product to a mass market, a channel objective may be to provide maximum product exposure (like BDP's work with its client Quaker) or to make the product available close to where customers live and work. Sometimes marketers make their product available where similar products are sold so that consumers can compare prices.

Figure 11.4 [icon] *Process* | Steps in Distribution Planning

Distribution planning begins with setting channel objectives and evaluating the environment and results in developing channel strategies and tactics.

Step 1: Develop distribution objectives

↓

Step 2: Evaluate internal and external environmental influences

↓

Step 3: Choose a distribution strategy
- Number of channel levels
- Conventional, vertical, or horizontal marketing system
- Intensive, exclusive, or selective distribution

↓

Step 4: Develop Distribution Tactics
- Select channel partners
- Manage the channel
- Develop logistics strategies
  - Order processing
  - Warehousing
  - Materials handling
  - Transportation
  - Inventory control

Step 2: Evaluate Internal and External Environmental Influences

After they set their distribution objectives, marketers must consider their internal and external environments to develop the best channel structure. Should the channel be long or short? Is intensive, selective, or exclusive distribution best? Short, often direct channels may be better suited for B2B marketers for whom customers are geographically concentrated and require high levels of technical know-how and service. Companies frequently sell expensive or complex products directly to final customers. Short channels with selective distribution also make more sense with perishable products because getting the product to the final user quickly is a priority. However, longer channels with more intensive distribution are generally best for inexpensive, standardized consumer goods that need to be distributed broadly and that require little technical expertise.

The organization must also examine issues such as its own ability to handle distribution functions, what channel intermediaries are available, the ability of customers to access these intermediaries, and how the competition distributes its products. Should a firm use the same retailers as its competitors? It depends. Sometimes, to ensure customers' undivided attention, a firm sells its products in outlets that don't carry the competitors' products. In other cases, a firm uses the same intermediaries as its competitors because customers expect to find the product there. For example, you will find Harley-Davidson bikes only in selected Harley "boutiques" and Piaggio's Vespa scooters only at Vespa dealers (no sales through Walmart for those two!), but you can expect to find Coca-Cola, Colgate toothpaste, and a Snickers bar in every possible outlet that sells these types of items (remember our discussion in Chapter 8 about the nature of convenience products).

Harley-Davidson tries to keep customers focused only on its brand of motorcycles by selling products in exclusive boutiques. No Yamahas or Indians in here.

Finally, when they study competitors' distribution strategies, marketers learn from their successes and failures. If the biggest complaint of competitors' customers is delivery speed, developing a system that allows same-day delivery can make the competition pale in comparison.

Step 3: Choose a Distribution Strategy

Planning a distribution strategy means making several decisions. First, of course, distribution planning includes decisions about the number of levels in the distribution channel. We already discussed these options in the previous section on consumer and B2B channels, illustrated by Figure 11.3. Beyond the number of levels, distribution strategies also involve two additional decisions about channel relationships: (1) whether a conventional system or a highly integrated system will work best and (2) the proper **distribution intensity**, meaning the number of intermediaries at each level of the channel. The next sections provide insight into making these two distribution strategy decisions.

distribution intensity
The number of intermediaries at each level of the channel.

Decision 1: Conventional, Vertical, or Horizontal Marketing System?

Participants in any distribution channel form an interrelated system. In general, these marketing systems take one of three forms: conventional, vertical, or horizontal.

1. A **conventional marketing system** is a multilevel distribution channel in which members work independently of one another. Their relationships are limited to simply buying and selling from one another. Each firm seeks to benefit, with little concern for other channel members. Even though channel members work independently, most conventional channels are highly successful. For one thing, all members of the channel work toward the same goals—to build demand, reduce costs, and improve customer satisfaction. And each channel member knows that it's in everyone's best interest to treat other channel members fairly.

2. A **vertical marketing system (VMS)** is a channel in which there is formal cooperation among channel members at two or more different levels: manufacturing, wholesaling, and retailing. Firms develop VMSs as a way to meet customer needs better by reducing costs incurred in channel activities. Often, a VMS can provide a level of cooperation and efficiency not possible with a conventional channel, maximizing the effectiveness of the channel while also maximizing efficiency and keeping costs low. Members share information and provide services to other members; they recognize that such coordination makes everyone more successful when they want to reach a desired

conventional marketing system
A multiple-level distribution channel in which channel members work independently of one another.

vertical marketing system (VMS)
A channel of distribution in which there is formal cooperation among members at the manufacturing, wholesaling, and retailing levels.

target market. There are three types of vertical marketing systems: administered, corporate, and contractual:

administered VMS
A vertical marketing system in which channel members remain independent but voluntarily work together because of the power of a single channel member.

corporate VMS
A vertical marketing system in which a single firm owns manufacturing, wholesaling, and retailing operations.

contractual VMS
A vertical marketing system in which cooperation is enforced by contracts (legal agreements) that spell out each member's rights and responsibilities and how they will cooperate.

a. In an **administered VMS**, channel members remain independent but voluntarily work together because of the power of a single channel member. Strong brands are able to manage an administered VMS because resellers are eager to work with the manufacturer so they will be allowed to carry the product.

b. In a **corporate VMS**, a single firm owns manufacturing, wholesaling, and retailing operations. Thus, the firm has complete control over all channel operations. Retail giant Macy's, for example, owns a nationwide network of distribution centers and retail stores.

c. In a **contractual VMS**, cooperation is enforced by contracts (legal agreements) that spell out each member's rights and responsibilities and how they will cooperate. This arrangement means that the channel members can have more impact as a group than they could alone. In a wholesaler-sponsored VMS, wholesalers get retailers to work together under their leadership in a voluntary chain. Retail members of the chain use a common name, cooperate in advertising and other promotion, and even develop their own private-label products. Examples of wholesaler-sponsored chains are Independent Grocers' Alliance (IGA) food stores and Ace Hardware stores.

retailer cooperative
A group of retailers that establishes a wholesaling operation to help them compete more effectively with the large chains.

In other cases, retailers themselves organize a cooperative marketing channel system. A **retailer cooperative** is a group of retailers that establishes a wholesaling operation to help them compete more effectively with the large chains. Each retailer owns shares in the wholesaler operation and is obligated to purchase a certain percentage of its inventory from the cooperative operation. Associated Grocers and True Value hardware stores are examples of retailer cooperatives.

franchise organizations
A contractual vertical marketing system that includes a *franchiser* (a manufacturer or a service provider) who allows an entrepreneur (the *franchisee*) to use the franchise name and marketing plan for a fee.

Franchise organizations are a third type of contractual VMS. Franchise organizations include a *franchiser* (a manufacturer or a service provider) who allows an entrepreneur (the *franchisee*) to use the franchise name and marketing plan for a fee. In these organizations, contractual arrangements explicitly define and strictly enforce channel cooperation. In most franchise agreements, the franchiser provides a variety of services for the franchisee, such as helping to train employees, giving access to lower prices for needed materials, and selecting a good location. In return, the franchiser receives a percentage of revenue from the franchisee. Usually, the franchisees are obligated to follow the franchiser's business format very closely to maintain the franchise.

From the manufacturer's perspective, franchising a business is a way to develop widespread product distribution with minimal financial risk while at the same time maintaining control over product quality. From the entrepreneur's perspective, franchises are a helpful way to get a start in business.

horizontal marketing system
An arrangement within a channel of distribution in which two or more firms at the same channel level work together for a common purpose.

3. In a **horizontal marketing system**, two or more firms at the same channel level agree to work together to get their product to the customer. Sometimes, unrelated businesses forge these agreements. Most airlines today are members of a horizontal alliance that allows them to cooperate when they provide passenger air service. For example, American Airlines is a member of the oneworld alliance, which also includes Air Berlin, British Airways, Cathay Pacific, Finnair, Iberia, Japan Airlines, LAN, Malaysia Airlines, Qantas, Qatar Airways, Royal Jordanian, S7 Airlines, SriLankan Airlines, and TAM Airlines. These alliances increase passenger volume for all

RosalreneBetancourt 7/Alamy Stock Photo

Wetzel's Pretzels is a successful franchise operation.

airlines because travel agents who book passengers on one of the airline's flights will be more likely to book a connecting flight on the other airline. To increase customer benefits, they also share frequent-flyer programs and airport clubs.[9]

Decision 2: Intensive, Exclusive, or Selective Distribution?

How many wholesalers and retailers should carry the product within a given market? This may seem like an easy decision: distribute the product through as many intermediaries as possible. But guess again. If the product goes to too many outlets, there may be inefficiency and duplication of efforts. For example, if there are too many Honda dealerships in town, there will be a lot of unsold Hondas sitting on dealer lots, and no single dealer will be successful. But if there are not enough wholesalers or retailers to carry a product, the manufacturer will fail to maximize total sales of its products (and its profits). If customers have to drive hundreds of miles to find a Honda dealer, they may instead opt for a Toyota just because of convenience, Thus, a distribution objective may be to either increase or decrease the level of distribution in the market.

The three basic choices are intensive, exclusive, and selective distribution. Table 11.2 summarizes five decision factors—company, customers, channels, constraints, and competition—and how they help marketers determine the best fit between distribution system and marketing goals. Read on, and you will find that these categories connect with the concept of convenience products, shopping products, and specialty products you learned about in Chapter 8.

Intensive distribution aims to maximize market coverage by selling a product through all wholesalers or retailers that will stock and sell the product. Marketers use intensive distribution for *convenience products*, such as chewing gum, soft drinks, milk, and bread, that consumers quickly consume and must replace frequently. Intensive distribution is necessary for these products because availability is more important than any other consideration in customers' purchase decisions.

intensive distribution
Selling a product through all suitable wholesalers or retailers that are willing to stock and sell the product.

In contrast to intensive distribution, **exclusive distribution** means to limit distribution to a single outlet in a particular region. Marketers often sell pianos, cars, executive training programs, TV programs, and many other *specialty products* with high price tags through exclusive distribution arrangements. They typically use these strategies with products that are high priced and have considerable service requirements and when a limited number of buyers exist in any single geographic area. Exclusive distribution enables wholesalers and retailers to better recoup the costs associated with longselling processes for each customer and, in some cases, extensive after-sale service.

exclusive distribution
Selling a product only through a single outlet in a particular region.

Table 11.2 | Characteristics That Favor Intensive versus Exclusive Distribution

Decision Factor	Intensive Distribution	Exclusive Distribution
Company	Oriented toward mass markets	Oriented toward specialized markets
Customers	High customer density	Low customer density
	Price and convenience are priorities	Service and cooperation are priorities
Channels	Overlapping market coverage	Nonoverlapping market coverage
Constraints	Cost of serving individual customers is low	Cost of serving individual customers is high
Competition	Based on a strong market presence, often through advertising and promotion	Based on individualized attention to customers, often through relationship marketing

For luxury products, employing an exclusive distribution strategy can support the associations the marketer wants consumers to have with the product (such as exclusivity, quality, or mystique) and ensure that the product is offered by retailers who are well-suited and matched to the task. For example, the ultra-high-end watch maker Patek Phillippe only sells its products through a small group of authorized retailers and in many cases each retailer only receives one unit of a new model each year. Authorized dealers are heavily vetted and ultimately are selected based on their fit and ability to sell and service the watches, which can range from 10,000 Euros to more than 1 million Euros in price. The company does not sell its watches online and does not expect its retailers to do so either.[10]

That said, if you search for a Patek Philippe watch online you will undoubtedly find some e-commerce sites selling the company's products they were able to acquire through the **gray market**. Gray markets often emerge around high-end luxury goods sold through exclusive distribution. Related to the concept of product diversion introduced previously in the chapter, the gray market represents those channels of distribution that are not formally defined and authorized by the manufacturer for sale of the product. Exchanges that occur in the gray market are not technically illegal (unlike the concept of an illegal "black market") hence the use of the intermediate color gray makes sense. But the original manufacturer of the product does not view gray markets as appropriate or beneficial.

Of course, not every situation neatly fits a category in Table 11.2. (you didn't *really* think it would be that simple, did you?) For example, consider professional sports. Customers might not shop for games in the same way they shop for pianos. They might go to a game on impulse, and they don't require much individualized service. Nevertheless, professional sports use exclusive distribution. A team's cost of serving customers is high because of those million-dollar player salaries and multi-million-dollar stadiums.

The alert reader (and/or sports fan) may note that there are some exceptions to the exclusive distribution of sports teams. New York has two football teams and two baseball teams, Chicago fields two baseball teams, and so on. We call market coverage that is less than intensive distribution but more than exclusive distribution **selective distribution** (yes, this type falls between the two). This model fits when demand is so large that exclusive distribution is inadequate but selling costs, service requirements, or other factors make intensive distribution a poor fit. Although a White Sox baseball fan may not believe that the Cubs franchise is necessary (and vice versa), Major League Baseball and even some baseball fans think the Chicago market is large enough to support both teams.

Selective distribution strategies are suitable for most *shopping products*, such as household appliances and electronic equipment, for which consumers are willing to spend time visiting different retail outlets to compare alternatives. For producers, selective distribution means freedom to choose only those wholesalers and retailers that have a good credit rating, provide good market coverage, serve customers well, and cooperate effectively. Wholesalers and retailers like selective distribution because it results in higher profits than are possible with intensive distribution, in which sellers often have to compete on price.

gray market
A distribution channel in which a product's sale to a customer may be technically legal, but is at a minimum considered inappropriate by the manufacturer of the related product. Gray markets often emerge around high-end luxury goods sold through exclusive distribution.

selective distribution
Distribution using fewer outlets than intensive distribution but more than exclusive distribution.

The Chicago baseball market is large enough to support a selective distribution model as evidenced by its two Major League Baseball teams—the Cubs and the White Sox.

Step 4: Develop Distribution Tactics

As with planning for the other marketing Ps, the final step in distribution planning is to develop the tactics for distribution necessary to implement the distribution strategy. These decisions are usually about the type of distribution system to use, such as a direct or an indirect channel or a conventional or an integrated channel. Distribution tactics relate to two aspects of the implementation of these strategies: (1) how to select individual channel members and (2) how to manage the channel. We provide insights into making each of these two decisions.

First, it is essential to understand that these two decisions are important because they often have a *direct impact on customer satisfaction*; nobody wants to have to wait for something they've bought! For many small businesses, partnering with Amazon to take advantage of its great distribution prowess is highly attractive. For a competitive fee, fulfillment by Amazon offers third parties the ability to outsource the storage and shipping of products to them. A company such as Tech Armor, which has rapidly gone from a mobile phone and tablet accessories startup to sales in the millions of units, relies on Amazon as a channel member to distribute its products efficiently and at a competitive price. Consumers who are signed up for Amazon Prime and thus get access to free two-day shipping provide an added bonus for companies that sell their products through Amazon. Because of Amazon's size, companies such as Tech Armor can feel more confident that as they scale out their business Amazon will be able to stay ahead of their need for increased distribution. And in times of peak demand, a real advantage of outsourcing distribution versus an internal approach is that Amazon can easily flex to handle the spikes in demand. This flexibility saves a firm like Tech Armor a lot of stress.[11]

Decision 1: Select Channel Partners

When firms agree to work together in a channel relationship, they become partners in what is normally a long-term commitment. Like a marriage, it is important to both manufacturers and intermediaries to select channel partners wisely, or they'll regret the match-up later (and a divorce can be really expensive!). In evaluating intermediaries, manufacturers try to answer questions such as the following: Will the channel member contribute substantially to our profitability? Does the channel member have the ability to provide the services customers want? What impact will a potential intermediary have on channel control?

For example, what small to midsize firm wouldn't jump at the chance to have retail giant Walmart distribute its products? With Walmart as a channel partner, a small firm could double, triple, or quadruple its business. But believe it or not, some firms that recognize that size means power in the channel actually decide against selling to Walmart because they are not willing to relinquish control of their marketing decision making. There is also a downside to choosing one retailer and selling only through that one retailer. If that retailer stops carrying the product, for example, the company will lose its one and only customer (perhaps after relinquishing other smaller customers), and it will be back to square one.

Another consideration in selecting channel members is competitors' channel partners. Because people spend time comparing different brands when purchasing a shopping product, firms need to make sure they display their products near similar competitors' products. If most competitors distribute their electric drills through mass merchandisers, a manufacturer has to make sure its brand is there also.

A firm's dedication to social responsibility may also be an important determining factor in the selection of channel partners. Many firms run extensive programs to recruit minority-owned channel members. Starbucks's famous organizational commitment to good corporate citizenship translates in one way into its "supplier diversity program" that works to help minority-owned business thrive.[12]

Decision 2: Manage the Channel

Once a manufacturer develops a channel strategy and aligns channel members, the day-to-day job of managing the channel begins. The **channel leader or channel captain** is the dominant

channel leader or **channel captain**
The dominant firm that controls the channel.

channel power
The ability of one channel member to influence, control, and lead the entire channel based on one or more sources of power.

firm that controls the channel. A firm becomes the channel captain because it has more **channel power** relative to other channel members. Channel power is the ability of one channel member to influence, control, and lead the entire channel based on one or more sources of power. This power comes from different potential sources, among which are the following:

- A firm has *economic power* if it has the ability to control resources.
- A firm such as a franchiser has *legitimate power* if it has legal authority to call the shots.
- A producer firm has *reward* or *coercive power* if it engages in exclusive distribution and has the ability to give profitable products and to take them away from the channel intermediaries.

As we mentioned, historically producers have held the role of channel captain. P&G, for example, developed customer-oriented marketing programs, tracked market trends, and advised retailers on the mix of products most likely to build sales. As large retail chains have evolved, giant retailers such as Best Buy, Home Depot, Target, Walmart, and Walgreens began to assume a leadership role because of the sheer size of their operations. Today, it is much more common for the big retailers to dictate their needs to producers instead of producers controlling what products they offer to retailers.

As an example, Amazon tried to use its channel power to "persuade" publisher Hachette to meet Amazon's terms regarding e-book pricing by subjecting its books to artificial purchase delays and by limiting the visibility of some Hachette titles in search results. During the time of the dispute some popular Hachette titles no longer were available for preorder. Ultimately, Amazon and Hachette reached a settlement in which the publisher was still able to set its own prices, but evidence suggests the publisher made some concessions as well behind closed doors.[13]

channel cooperation
Occurs when producers, wholesalers, and retailers depend on one another for success.

Because producers, wholesalers, and retailers depend on one another for success, **channel cooperation** helps everyone. Channel cooperation is stimulated when the channel leader takes actions that make its partners more successful. Examples of this, such as high intermediary profit margins, training programs, cooperative advertising, and expert marketing advice, are invisible to end customers but are motivating factors in the eyes of wholesalers and retailers.

channel conflict
Incompatible goals, poor communication, and disagreement over roles, responsibilities, and functions among firms at different levels of the same distribution channel that may threaten a manufacturer's distribution strategy.

Of course, relations among members in a channel are not always full of sweetness and light. Because each firm has its own objectives, **channel conflict** may threaten a manufacturer's distribution strategy. Such conflict most often occurs between firms at different levels of the same distribution channel. Incompatible goals, poor communication, and disagreement over roles, responsibilities, and functions cause conflict. For example, a producer is likely to feel the firm would enjoy greater success and profitability if intermediaries carry only its brands, but many intermediaries believe they will do better if they carry a variety of brands.

In this section, we've been concerned with the distribution channels firms use to get their products to customers. In the next section, we'll look at the area of logistics—physically moving products through the supply chain—and end by introducing the concept of the supply chain.

11.3 Logistics and the Supply Chain

OBJECTIVE
Discuss the concepts of logistics and supply chain.

(pp. 384–392)

Some marketing textbooks tend to depict the practice of marketing as 90 percent planning and 10 percent implementation. Not so! In the "real world" (and in our book), many managers argue that this ratio should be reversed. Marketing success is very much the art of getting the timing right and delivering on promises—*implementation*.

That's why marketers place so much emphasis on efficient **logistics**: the process of designing, managing, and improving the movement of products through the supply chain. Logistics includes purchasing, manufacturing, storage, and transport. From a company's viewpoint, logistics takes place both *inbound* to the firm (raw materials, parts, components, and supplies) and *outbound* from the firm (work in process and finished goods).

Logistics is also a relevant consideration regarding product returns, recycling and material reuse, and waste disposal—**reverse logistics**.[14] As we saw in previous chapters, that's becoming even more important as firms start to more seriously consider *sustainability* as a competitive advantage and put more effort into maximizing the efficiency of recycling to save money and the environment at the same time. So you can see that logistics is an important issue across all elements of the supply chain. Let's examine this process more closely.

The Lowdown on Logistics

Have you ever heard the saying, "An army travels on its stomach"? *Logistics* was originally a term the military used to describe everything necessary to deliver troops and equipment to the right place, at the right time, and in the right condition. In business, logistics is similar in that its objective is to deliver exactly what the customer wants—at the right time, in the right place, and at the right price. As 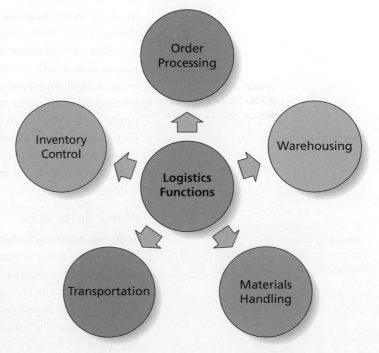 Figure 11.5 shows, logistics activities include order processing, warehousing, materials handling, transportation, and inventory control. This process impacts how marketers physically get products where they need to be, when they need to be there, and at the lowest possible cost.

When a firm does logistics planning, however, the focus also should be on the customer. In the old days when managers thought of logistics as physical distribution only, the objective was to deliver the product at the lowest cost. Today, forward-thinking firms consider the needs of the customer first. The customer's goals become the logistics provider's priorities. And this means that when they make most logistics decisions, firms must decide on the best trade-off between low costs and high customer service. The appropriate goal is not just to deliver what the market needs at the lowest cost but rather to provide the product at the lowest cost possible *as long as the firm meets delivery requirements*. Although it would be nice to transport all goods quickly by air (even by drone, as Amazon wants to do), that is certainly not practical. But sometimes air transport is necessary to meet the needs of the customer, no matter the cost.

When they develop logistics strategies, marketers must make decisions related to each of the five functions of logistics depicted in Figure 11.5. For each decision, managers need to consider how to minimize costs while maintaining the service customers want. Let's look closely at each of the five logistics functions.

Order Processing

Order processing includes the series of activities that occurs between the time an order comes into the organization and the time a product goes out the door. After a firm receives an order, it typically sends it electronically to an office for record keeping and then on to the warehouse to fill it. When the order reaches the warehouse, personnel there check to see if the item

logistics
The process of designing, managing, and improving the movement of products through the supply chain. Logistics includes purchasing, manufacturing, storage, and transport.

reverse logistics
Includes product returns, recycling and material reuse, and waste disposal.

order processing
The series of activities that occurs between the time an order comes into the organization and the time a product goes out the door.

Figure 11.5 *Process* | The Five Functions of Logistics

When developing logistics strategies, marketers must make decisions related to order processing, warehousing, materials handling, transportation, and inventory control.

enterprise resource planning (ERP) systems
A software system that integrates information from across the entire company, including finance, order fulfillment, manufacturing, and transportation, and then facilitates sharing of the data throughout the firm.

is in stock. If it is not, they put the order on back-order status. That information goes to the office and then to the customer. If the item is available, the company locates it in the warehouse, packages it for shipment, and schedules it for pickup by either in-house or external shippers.

Fortunately, many firms automate this process with **enterprise resource planning (ERP) systems**. An ERP system is a software solution that integrates information from across the entire company, including finance, order fulfillment, manufacturing, and transportation. Data need to be entered into the system only once, and then the organization automatically shares this information and links it to other related data. For example, an ERP system ties information on product inventories to sales information so that a sales representative can immediately tell a customer whether the product is in stock.

Warehousing

warehousing
Storing goods in anticipation of sale or transfer to another member of the channel of distribution.

Whether we deal with fresh-cut flowers, canned goods, or computer chips, at some point goods (unlike services) must be stored. Storing goods allows marketers to match supply with demand. For example, gardening supplies are especially big sellers during spring and summer, but the factories that manufacture them operate 12 months of the year. **Warehousing**—storing goods in anticipation of sale or transfer to another member of the channel of distribution—enables marketers to provide *time utility* to consumers by holding on to products until consumers need them.

Part of developing effective logistics means making decisions about how many warehouses are needed and where and what type of warehouse each should be. A firm determines the location of its warehouse(s) by the location of customers and access to major highways, airports, or rail transportation. The number of warehouses often depends on the level of service that customers require. If customers generally demand fast delivery (today or tomorrow at the latest), then it may be necessary to store products in a number of different locations from which the company can quickly ship the goods to the customer.

For example, over the years Amazon has invested billions of dollars in high-tech fulfillment centers across the U.S. and abroad to keep up with customer demand and ensure that products get to consumers as quickly as possible. Amazon has even rolled out same-day, one-hour, and Sunday delivery options depending on a consumer's location (if you live in a major metropolitan area in the U.S. chances are good that these premium services will become available to you soon if you don't have them already).[15]

distribution center
A warehouse that stores goods for short periods of time and that provides other functions, such as breaking bulk.

Firms use private and public warehouses to store goods. Those that use private warehouses have a high initial investment, but they also lose less of their inventory as a result of damage. Public warehouses are an alternative that allows firms to pay for a portion of warehouse space rather than having to own an entire storage facility. Most countries offer public warehouses in all large cities and many smaller cities to support domestic and international trade. A **distribution center** is a warehouse that stores goods for short periods of time and that provides other functions, such as breaking bulk. Most large retailers have their own distribution centers so that their stores do not need to keep a lot of inventory in the back room.

Materials Handling

materials handling
The moving of products into, within, and out of warehouses.

Materials handling is the moving of products into, within, and out of warehouses. When goods come into the warehouse, they must be physically identified, checked for damage, sorted, and labeled. Next, they are taken to a location for storage. Finally, they are recovered from the storage area for packaging and shipment. All in all, the goods may be handled over a dozen separate times. Procedures that limit the number of times a product must be handled decrease the likelihood of damage and reduce the cost of materials handling.

Transportation

Logistics decisions take into consideration options for **transportation**, the mode by which products move among channel members. Again, making transportation decisions entails a compromise between minimizing cost and providing the service customers want. As Table 11.3 shows, modes of transportation, including railroads, water transportation, trucks, airways, pipelines, and the Internet, differ in the following ways:

- *Dependability:* The ability of the carrier to deliver goods safely and on time
- *Cost:* The total transportation costs to move a product from one location to another, including any charges for loading, unloading, and in-transit storage
- *Speed of delivery:* The total time to move a product from one location to another, including loading and unloading
- *Accessibility:* The number of different locations the carrier serves
- *Capability:* The ability of the carrier to handle a variety of different products, such as large or small, fragile, or bulky
- *Traceability:* The ability of the carrier to locate goods in shipment

Each mode of transportation has strengths and weaknesses that make it a good choice for different transportation needs. Table 11.3 summarizes the pros and cons of each mode:

- *Railroads:* Railroads are best to carry heavy or bulky items, such as coal and other mining products, over long distances. Railroads are about average in their cost and provide moderate speed of delivery. Although rail transportation provides dependable, low-cost service to many locations, trains cannot carry goods to every community.

Amazon is experimenting with an Amazon Prime Air drone delivery service that may someday add a whole new dimension to transportation options for logistics companies.

transportation
The mode by which products move among channel members.

Table 11.3 | A Comparison of Transportation Modes

Transportation Mode	Dependability	Cost	Speed of Delivery	Accessibility	Capability	Traceability	Most Suitable Products
Railroads	Average	Average	Moderate	High	High	Low	Heavy or bulky goods, such as automobiles, grain, and steel
Water	Low	Low	Slow	Low	Moderate	Low	Bulky, nonperishable goods, such as automobiles
Trucks	High	High for long distances; low for short distances	Fast	High	High	High	A wide variety of products, including those that need refrigeration
Air	High	High	Very fast	Low	Moderate	High	High-value items, such as electronic goods and fresh flowers
Pipeline	High	Low	Slow	Low	Low	Moderate	Petroleum products and other chemicals
Internet	High	Low	Very fast	Potentially very high	Low	High	Services such as banking, information, and entertainment

- *Water:* Ships and barges carry large, bulky goods and are very important in international trade. Water transportation is relatively low in cost but can be slow.

- *Trucks:* Trucks or motor carriers are the most important transportation mode for consumer goods, especially for shorter hauls. Motor carrier transport allows flexibility because trucks can travel to locations missed by boats, trains, and planes. Trucks also carry a wide variety of products, including perishable items. Although costs are fairly high for longer-distance shipping, trucks are economical for shorter deliveries. Because trucks provide door-to-door service, product handling is minimal, and this reduces the chance of product damage.

- *Air:* Air transportation is the fastest and also the most expensive transportation mode. It is ideal to move high-value items such as important mail, fresh-cut flowers, and live lobsters. Passenger airlines, air-freight carriers, and express delivery firms, such as FedEx, provide air transportation. Ships remain the major mover of international cargo, but air transportation networks are becoming more important as international markets continue to develop. Drones are an interesting option for transporting items over short distances by air. Some companies, such as Amazon and Walmart, have publically announced a keen interest in using drone technology to enhance their logistics operations in the future. The goal of Amazon Prime Air service (now being tested) is to safely get packages to customers in 30 minutes or less using a fleet of these small unmanned aerial vehicles.[16] Ahead of the curve, tech company Matternet since 2011 has been using its self-guiding drones on a test basis to deliver medical supplies, specimens, and mail in countries where regulations allow such field tests (Haiti and Switzerland, for example).[17]

- *Pipeline:* Pipelines carry petroleum products such as oil and natural gas and a few other chemicals. Pipelines flow primarily from oil or gas fields to refineries. They are very low in cost, require little energy, and are not subject to disruption by weather.

- *The Internet:* As we discussed previously in this chapter, marketers of services such as banking, news, and entertainment take advantage of distribution opportunities the Internet provides.

Inventory Control

inventory control
Activities to ensure that goods are always available to meet customers' demands.

radio frequency identification (RFID)
Product tags with tiny chips containing information about the item's content, origin, and destination.

Another component of logistics is **inventory control**, which means developing and implementing a process to ensure that the firm always has sufficient quantities of goods available to meet customers' demands—no more and no less. This explains why firms work so hard to track merchandise in order to know where their products are and where they are needed in case a low-inventory situation appears imminent.

Some companies are even phasing in a sophisticated technology (similar to the EZ Pass system many drivers use to speed through tollbooths) known as **radio frequency identification (RFID)**. As we saw in Chapter 2, RFID lets firms tag clothes, pharmaceuticals, or virtually any kind of product with tiny chips that contain information about the item's content, origin, and destination. This technology has the potential to revolutionize inventory control and help marketers ensure that their products are on the shelves when people want to buy them. Great for manufacturers and retailers, right? But some consumer groups are creating a backlash against RFID, which they refer to as "spy chips." Through blogs, boycotts, and other anticompany initiatives, these groups proclaim that RFID is a personification of the privacy violations George Orwell predicted in his classic book *1984*.[18] One blogger, for example, convinced that Gillette is using "spy chips" in the packaging of its razors to spy on and take pictures of customers, decided to start his own "Boycott Gillette" website. The site warns consumers which Gillette products not to buy and lets them know how to contact Gillette as well as their lawmakers to fight against the use of RFID tags.[19]

Firms store goods (i.e., they create an *inventory*) for many reasons. For manufacturers, sometimes the pace of production may not match seasonal demand and as a result a firm might engage in a practice known as **level loading**. This is a manufacturing approach intended to balance the inventory holding capabilities and production capacity constraints of a manufacturer for a particular product through the implementation of a consistent production schedule, employed both during and beyond periods of peak demand. For example, it may be more economical to produce snow skis year-round and pay to store them for the colder months than to produce them only during the winter season. This is a result of capacity issues related to the number of snow skis that a manufacturer can produce in a given span of time on existing production lines and with its available work force.

Similarly, for channel members that purchase goods from manufacturers or other channel intermediaries, it may be economical to order a product in quantities that don't exactly parallel demand. For example, delivery costs make it prohibitive for a retail gas station to place daily orders for just the amount of gas that people will use that day. Instead, stations usually order truckloads of gasoline, holding their inventory in underground tanks. **Stock-outs**, which are zero-inventory situations resulting in lost sales and customer dissatisfaction, may be very negative. Ever go to the store based on an ad in the newspaper, only to find the store doesn't have the product on hand?

Inventory control has a major impact on the overall costs of a firm's logistics initiatives. If supplies of products are too low to meet fluctuations in customer demand, a firm may have to make expensive emergency deliveries or else lose customers to competitors. If inventories are above demand, unnecessary storage expenses and the possibility of damage or deterioration occur. To balance these two opposing needs, manufacturers turn to **just in time (JIT)** inventory techniques with their suppliers. JIT sets up delivery of goods just as they are needed on the production floor. This minimizes the cost of holding inventory while ensuring the inventory will be there when customers need it.

A supplier's ability to make on-time deliveries is the critical factor in the selection process for firms that adopt this kind of system. JIT systems reduce stock to very low levels (or even zero) and time deliveries very carefully to maintain just the right amount of inventory. The advantage of JIT systems is the reduced cost of warehousing. For both manufacturers and resellers that use JIT systems, the choice of supplier may come down to one whose location is nearest. To win a large customer, a supplier may even have to be willing to set up production facilities close to the customer to guarantee JIT delivery.[20]

Place: Pulling It All Together through the Supply Chain

A **supply chain** includes all the activities necessary to turn raw materials into a good or service and put it into the hands of the consumer or business customer. Sam's Club and its sister company, Walmart, are iconic when it comes to global supply chain effectiveness. To both reduce overall excess inventory and more effectively meet the needs of consumers who increasingly shop both in the company's physical locations and on its website, Walmart has put a strategy in place that enables greater agility within the company's supply chain. Specifically, the retail giant has reduced its total inventory, increased the variety of products sold, and shifted more of its inventory from its physical stores to its distribution centers. With an increasing number of consumers shopping online, this significant operational change allows Walmart to serve those customers more nimbly. The company can avoid the big increase in overall inventory costs it would incur if it had to maintain separate approaches to inventory management for online versus in-store shoppers.

level loading
A manufacturing approach intended to balance the inventory holding capabilities and production capacity constraints of a manufacturer for a particular product through the implementation of a consistent production schedule, employed both during and beyond periods of peak demand.

stock-outs
Zero-inventory situations resulting in lost sales and customer dissatisfaction.

just in time (JIT)
Inventory management and purchasing processes that manufacturers and resellers use to reduce inventory to very low levels and ensure that deliveries from suppliers arrive only when needed.

supply chain
All the activities necessary to turn raw materials into a good or service and put it in the hands of the consumer or business customer.

Metrics Moment

One of the most used measures of inventory control is **inventory turnover or inventory turns**, which is the number of times a firm's inventory completely cycles through during a defined time frame (usually in one year). Marketers can measure inventory turnover by using the value of the inventory at cost or at retail, or this metric can even be expressed in units. Just make sure that you're using the same unit of measure in both the numerator and the denominator. [22] One of the most common formulas is the following:

$$\text{Inventory turnover} \times \text{Annual cost of sales} \div \frac{\text{Average inventory}}{\text{level for the period}}$$

However, the formula requires waiting until the end of the year (or end of the business's fiscal year). An alternative is using the following "snapshot" number, which takes a rolling approach so that turns can be calculated at any time by looking at cost of sales for the immediately prior 12 months and the current inventory at the end of that period:

$$\text{Inventory turnover} \times \text{Rolling 12-month cost of sales} \div \text{Current inventory}$$

Benchmarks for inventory turnover vary greatly by industry and product line. High-volume/low-margin settings like supermarkets may have 12 or more inventory turns per year overall, but some staple goods that are bought at every trip (e.g., milk and bread) may have significantly higher turnover rates. All else equal, a firm can up its profitability substantially by targeting increases in inventory turnover—selling through Product X 15 times a year instead of 12 naturally improves the bottom line. However, if price reductions or promotional expense increases are needed to up the turns, management will have to carefully calculate whether increased volume really adds to profits (this is where marketers can get into trouble with the old saying, "We're losing money but we'll make it up in volume!").

Apply the Metrics

1. Spider's Auto Parts Store ended its fiscal year last month with a cost of sales of $3,600,000 and an average inventory of $450,000. What is Spider's inventory turnover for that fiscal year?
2. Spider's would like to boost its turns to 10 during the next fiscal year. What suggestions do you have that will help them accomplish this objective?

inventory turnover or inventory turns

The number of times a firm's inventory completely cycles through during a defined time frame.

In addition, distribution centers are much more efficient at getting products to stores when an expected increase in demand is observed at one location versus implementing an inventory transfer between stores. Yet another added benefit of this change is that it frees up in-store employees to focus more on other value-added activities (such as assisting customers) because less time will be required to manage inventory in the stock room. All of that said a reduction of inventory in each store potentially means that some customers will not be able to get a specific product exactly when they wanted it due to increased stock-outs.[21]

Walmart clearly understands the potential for supply chain practices to enhance organizational performance and profits, and scores of other firms across most every industry with physical products benchmark against them for best practices. The truth is that distribution may be the "final frontier" for marketing success. To understand why, consider these facts about the other three Ps of marketing. After years of hype, many consumers no longer believe that "new and improved" products really *are* new and improved. Nearly everyone, even upscale manufacturers and retailers, tries to gain market share through aggressive pricing strategies. Advertising and many other forms of promotion are so commonplace today that they have lost some of their impact. Even hot new social media strategies can't sell overpriced or poorly made products, at least not for long. Marketers have come to understand that *place* (the "distribution P") may be the only one of the *four Ps* to offer an opportunity for really long-term competitive advantage—especially because many consumers now expect "instant gratification" by getting just what they want instantaneously when the urge strikes.

That's why savvy marketers are always on the lookout for novel ways to distribute their products. A large part of the marketer's ability to deliver a value proposition rests on the ability to understand and develop effective supply chain strategies. Often, of course, firms may decide to bring in outside companies to accomplish these activities—this is *outsourcing*, which as we learned about in Chapter 6 occurs when firms obtain outside vendors to provide goods or services that might otherwise be supplied in-house. In the case of supply chain functions, outsource firms are most likely organizations with whom the company has developed some form of partnership or cooperative business arrangement.

Supply chain management is the coordination of flows among the firms in a supply chain to maximize total profitability. These "flows" include not only the physical movement of goods but also the sharing of information about the goods—that is, supply chain partners must synchronize their activities with one another. For example, they need to communicate information about which goods they want to purchase (the procurement function), about which marketing campaigns they plan to execute (so that the supply chain partners can ensure there will be enough product to supply the increased demand that results from the promotion), and about logistics (such as sending advance shipping notices to alert their partners that products are on their way). Through these information flows, a company can effectively manage all the links in its supply chain, from sourcing to retailing.

In his famous book *The World Is Flat: A Brief History of the Twenty-First Century*, author Thomas Friedman addresses a number of high-impact trends in global supply chain management.[23] One such development is the trend whereby companies we traditionally know for other things remake themselves as specialists who take over the coordination of clients' supply chains for them. UPS is a great example of this trend. UPS, which used to be "just" a package delivery service, today is much more because it also specializes in **insourcing**. This process occurs when companies contract with a specialist who services their supply chains. Unlike the *outsourcing process* where a company delegates nonessential tasks to subcontractors, insourcing means that the client company brings in an external company to run its essential operations. Although we tend to associate UPS with those little brown trucks that zip around town delivering boxes, the company actually positions itself in the B2B space as a broad-based supply chain consultancy!

supply chain management
The management of flows among firms in the supply chain to maximize total profitability.

insourcing
A practice in which a company contracts with a specialist firm to handle all or part of its supply chain operations.

Ripped from the Headlines

Ethical/Sustainable Decisions in the Real World

Supply chains commonly span multiple continents and involve numerous organizations that add value at various stages of the chain. For restaurants (and also other retailers), this can mean managing a very complex configuration of upstream supplier companies, each of which plays a important part. Because the restaurant is the final link in the chain before the end consumer, it often falls to this business to ensure that its customers trust the companies that supply it.

The Chipotle chain has been at the forefront of responsible food sourcing and handling for years, and for that reason the company became a favorite of many consumers who value its philosophy. Thus, the chain's highly publicized series of foodborne illness outbreaks (*Escherichia coli*) that began in 2015 hit especially hard. The problem shook both consumer trust and shareholder confidence in the highly regarded restaurant chain. The company responded with a number of changes designed to prevent future outbreaks, including a new key safety measure targeted at its upstream suppliers. Specifically, Chipotle began requiring all suppliers, before shipping ingredients to its stores, to use "DNA-based tests" on a small batch of each actual shipment to confirm there are no *E. coli* issues.

In reality, whether or not the issues could be traced to one or more suppliers, it's natural that Chipotle's consumers and investors would wonder

what the company could have, or should have, done differently to ensure that the contaminated ingredients were detected before reaching consumers, both in the stores and within the full supply chain. Some experts have also suggested that part of Chipotle's supply chain challenge is unique to the company's practice of sourcing a significant portion of its ingredients from small farms, as opposed to sourcing ingredients primarily from large producers and distributors that could be much more easily monitored and controlled by Chipotle. That is, increasing the number of suppliers naturally increases the complexity within a supply chain so it's harder to detect problems in individual shipments.[24] Ironically, Chipotle's attempts to be a good corporate citizen by supporting small, local businesses may have unwittingly contributed to the contamination problem.

In February 2016 the U.S. Centers for Disease Control and Prevention declared that the *E. coli* outbreak at Chipotle appeared to be over.[25] Going forward there is no doubt that Chipotle will be increasingly vigilant on all fronts in its efforts to avoid a repeat of this fiasco.

ETHICS CHECK:

If a restaurant knows that an upstream supplier has had problems in the past related to the improper production or handling of ingredients (even if it did not necessarily affect this particular restaurant chain), should the restaurant continue to work with that supplier?

☐ YES ☐ NO

Finally, in case you're wondering about the difference between a supply chain and a channel of distribution, the major distinguishing feature is the number of members and their functions. A supply chain is broader, consisting of those firms that supply the raw materials, component parts, and supplies necessary for a firm to produce a good or service *plus* the firms that facilitate the movement of that product to the ultimate users of the product. This last part—the firms that get the product to the ultimate users—is the channel of distribution.

MyLab Marketing™

Go to **mymktlab.com** to complete the problems marked with this icon ⭐ as well as additional Marketing Metrics questions only available in MyLab Marketing.

Objective Summary ➥ Key Terms ➥ Apply

CHAPTER 11
Study Map

11.1 Objective Summary (pp. 366–377)

Explain what a distribution channel is, identify types of wholesaling intermediaries, and describe the different types of distribution channels.

A channel of distribution is a series of firms or individuals that facilitates the movement of a product from the producer to the final customer. Channels provide place, time, and possession utility for customers and reduce the number of transactions necessary for goods to flow from many manufacturers to large numbers of customers by breaking bulk and creating assortments. Channel members make the purchasing process easier by providing important customer services.

Wholesaling intermediaries are firms that handle the flow of products from the manufacturer to the retailer or business user. Merchant wholesalers are independent intermediaries that take title to a product and include both full-service merchant wholesalers and limited-service merchant wholesalers. Merchandise agents and brokers are independent intermediaries that do not take title to products. Manufacturer-owned channel members include sales branches, sales offices, and manufacturers' showrooms.

Distribution channels vary in length from the simplest two-level channel to longer channels with three or more channel levels. Distribution channels include direct distribution, in which the producer sells directly to consumers, and to indirect channels, which may include a retailer, wholesaler, or other intermediary. B2B distribution channels facilitate the flow of goods from a producer to an organizational or business customer. Producers, dealers, wholesalers, retailers, and customers may participate in more than one type of channel, called a dual or multiple distribution system. Finally, some companies combine channels—direct sales, distributors, retail sales, and direct mail—to create a hybrid marketing system.

Key Terms

physical distribution, p. 366

direct channel, p. 366

channel intermediaries, p. 366

breaking bulk, p. 367

create assortments, p. 367

transportation and storage, p. 367

facilitating functions, p. 367

risk-taking functions, p. 368

communication and transaction functions, p. 368

disintermediation (of the channel of distribution), p. 368

knowledge management, p. 368

intranet, p. 368

online distribution piracy, p. 368

wholesaling intermediaries, p. 370

independent intermediaries, p. 370

merchant wholesalers, p. 370

take title, p. 370

full-service merchant wholesalers, p. 371

limited-service merchant wholesalers, p. 371

merchandise agents or brokers, p. 371

channel levels, p. 373

dual or multiple distribution systems, p. 375

hybrid marketing system, p. 376

subscription boxes, p. 376

slotting allowance, p. 377

product diversion, p. 377
diverter, p. 377

channel cooperation, p. 384
channel conflict, p. 384

11.2 Objective Summary (pp. 378–384)

List and explain the steps to plan a distribution channel strategy.

Firms that operate within a channel of distribution—manufacturers, wholesalers, and retailers—do distribution planning, which is a process of developing distribution objectives, evaluating internal and external environmental influences on distribution, and choosing a distribution strategy. Marketers begin channel planning by developing distribution channel objectives and considering important internal and external environmental factors. The next step is to decide on a distribution strategy, which involves determining the type of distribution channel that is best. Finally, distribution tactics include the selection of individual channel members and management of the channel.

Key Terms

distribution planning, p. 378
distribution intensity, p. 379
conventional marketing system, p. 379
vertical marketing system (VMS), p. 379
administered VMS, p. 380
corporate VMS, p. 380
contractual VMS, p. 380
retailer cooperative, p. 380
franchise organizations, p. 380
horizontal marketing system, p. 380
intensive distribution, p. 381
exclusive distribution, p. 381
gray market, p. 382
selective distribution, p. 382
channel leader or channel captain, p. 383
channel power, p. 384

11.3 Objective Summary (pp. 384–392)

Discuss the concepts of logistics and supply chain.

Logistics is the process of designing, managing, and improving supply chains, including all the activities that are required to move products through the supply chain. Logistics contributes to the overall supply chain through activities including order processing, warehousing, materials handling, transportation, and inventory control.

A supply chain includes all the activities necessary to turn raw materials into a good or service and put it into the hands of the consumer or business customer. Supply chain management is the coordination of flows among the firms in a supply chain to maximize total profitability.

Key Terms

logistics, p. 385
reverse logistics, p. 385
order processing, p. 385
enterprise resource planning (ERP) systems, p. 386
warehousing, p. 386
distribution center, p. 386
materials handling, p. 386
transportation, p. 387
inventory control, p. 388
radio frequency identification (RFID), p. 388
level loading, p. 389
stock-outs, p. 389
just in time (JIT), p. 389
supply chain, p. 389
inventory turnover or inventory turns, p. 390
supply chain management, p. 391
insourcing, p. 391

Chapter Questions and Activities

MyLab Marketing™

Go to **mymktlab.com** to watch this chapter's Rising Star video(s) for career advice and to respond to questions.

Concepts: Test Your Knowledge

11-1. What is a channel of distribution? What are channel intermediaries?
11-2. Explain the functions of distribution channels.
11-3. List and explain the types of independent and manufacturer-owned wholesaling intermediaries.
11-4. What factors are important in determining whether a manufacturer should choose a direct or indirect channel? Why do some firms use hybrid marketing systems?

11-5. What are conventional, vertical, and horizontal marketing systems?
11-6. Explain intensive, exclusive, and selective forms of distribution.
11-7. Explain the steps in distribution planning.
11-8. What is logistics? Explain the functions of logistics. What is reverse logistics?
11-9. What are the advantages and disadvantages of shipping by rail? By air? By ship? By truck?
11-10. What is inventory control, and why is it important?
11-11. What is a supply chain, and how is it different from a channel of distribution?

Activities: Apply What You've Learned

⭐ **11-12.** *Creative Homework/Short Project* Assume that you are the director of marketing for a firm that manufactures cleaning chemicals used in industries. You have traditionally sold these products through manufacturer's reps. You are considering adding a direct Internet channel to your distribution strategy, but you aren't sure whether this will create channel conflict. Make a list of the pros and cons of this move. What do you think is the best decision?

11-13. *For Further Research (Individual)* Find an example of disintermediation that has been employed by a particular firm. Research the specific impact of the disintermediation on the organization's operations and its customers' experience with the firm. Evaluate both the pros and the cons of the related example of disintermediation.

11-14. *Creative Homework/Short Project* Your friend's small business makes hand-crafted papers that she sells directly to her customers online. Fortunately, her business is growing quickly, and she is considering selling her unique product to other businesses. From your marketing class, you know that different channel structures exist for both consumer and B2B markets. Summarize the differences between these two channel structures. What advice can you give her?

11-15. *In Class, 10–25 Minutes for Teams* As the one-person marketing department for a candy manufacturer (your firm makes high-quality, hand-dipped chocolates using only natural ingredients), you are considering making changes in your distribution strategy. Your products have previously been sold through a network of food brokers that call on specialty food and gift stores. But you think that perhaps it would be good for your firm to develop a corporate vertical marketing system (i.e., vertical integration). In such a plan, a number of company-owned retail outlets would be opened across the country. The president of your company has asked that you present your ideas to the company executives. In a role-playing situation with one of your classmates, present your ideas to your boss, including the advantages and disadvantages of the new plan compared to the current distribution method.

11-16. *For Further Research (Individual)* Do a little research and find an example of a firm that attempted to sell a product or set of products online and failed.
- **a.** What do you believe are the key factors that led to the failure?
- **b.** What could the firm have done differently to increase the chances for success?

11-17. *In Class, 15–20 Minutes for Teams* An efficient logistics system can enable companies to ensure that their products are delivered to the right wholesalers and retailers at the right time, ensuring better supply to the end consumer. Logistics can also provide a competitive advantage, as firms can create a lower underlying cost structure, which can deliver either an increased profit margin or lower prices to consumers.

Think about different supermarket chains that you have visited. Are there some chains that usually have all their products in stock and other chains (or smaller stores) that frequently experience stock-out situations? In addition, think about the different pricing practices of the supermarkets. Are there any supermarkets that sell brands that are similar to others but at a much lower price? If so, how do you think they're able to do this? Do you think that their logistics system plays an important role?

Now let's consider the potential impact frequent stock-out situations would have on potential consumer behavior. Think about this consumer behavior change from the viewpoint of both the retailer and any brands that are regularly stocked out.

11-18. *In Class, 10–25 Minutes for Teams* Assume that you have recently been hired by a firm that manufactures furniture. You feel that marketing should have an input into supplier selection for the firm's products, but the purchasing department says that should not be a concern for marketing. You need to explain to the department head the importance of the value chain perspective. In a role-playing exercise, explain to the purchasing agent the value chain concept, why it is of concern to marketing, and why the two of you should work together.

11-19. *For Further Research (Individual)* It is increasingly important for companies to find ways to make their supply chains more sustainable. Find examples of how a company has implemented a sustainable practice within each of the following components of the supply chain: raw materials sourcing, distribution, warehousing, and retailing. For each component a separate company can be selected for use as your example.

⭐ **11-20.** *Creative Homework/Short Project* Your friend is studying for an upcoming marketing test but doesn't quite understand logistics. Write up a summary of the various logistics functions and devise a short multiple-choice quiz that will help him test his comprehension of the subject.

Concepts: Apply Marketing Metrics

Companies track a wide range of metrics within the supply chain area. Some of the most common ones are the following:

- On-time delivery
- Accuracy of forecasted inventory needs
- Returns processing cost as a percentage of product revenue
- Customer order actual cycle time
- Perfect order measurement

Let's take a look at the last measure in more detail. The perfect order measurement calculates the error-free rate of each stage of fulfilling a purchase order.[26] This measure helps managers track the multiple steps involved in getting a product from a manufacturer to a customer so that opportunities for process improvement can be pinpointed. For example, a company can calculate its error-free rate at each stage and then combine these rates to create an overall metric of order quality. Suppose the company identifies the following error rates:

- Order entry accuracy: 99.95 percent correct (can be thought of as 0.5 errors per 1,000 order lines)
- Warehouse pick accuracy: 99.2 percent (8 errors per 1,000 items picked by warehouse staff)
- Delivered on time: 96 percent (40 errors per 1,000 deliveries)

- Shipped without damage: 99 percent (10 damaged items per 1,000 deliveries)
- Invoiced correctly: 99.8 percent (2 errors per 1,000 invoices)

To calculate the perfect order measurement, all the company has to do is combine these individual rates into an overall metric by multiplying them together.

11-21. Calculate the perfect order measurement for the above purchase order process. Interpret your result.

11-22. Do you think the firm should be satisfied with this level of performance? Why or why not? What particular areas need attention, if any?

11-23. Is a zero error rate realistic? How close should a firm be expected to come to zero errors? How do you suggest motivating employees toward reducing these errors?

11-24. Given this particular example, what are some things the manufacturer might work on to bring the overall perfect order measurement higher? What would be the advantages to the firm of investing in making this already good number even better for customers?

Choices: What Do You Think?

11-25. *Critical Thinking* Many entrepreneurs choose to start a franchise business rather than "go it alone." Do you think franchises offer the typical businessperson good opportunities? What are some positive and negative aspects of purchasing a franchise?

11-26. *Critical Thinking* Would you purchase a durable product (such as a watch) online at a significantly lower price than the MSRP (Manufacturer Suggested Retail Price) if you knew that the retailer was not officially authorized by the product's manufacturer to sell it? Putting ethical concerns aside for a moment, what risks would most concern you about making such a purchase and what steps could the related retailer take to lessen those risks?

11-27. *Critical Thinking* As colleges and universities are looking for better ways to satisfy their customers, an area of increasing interest is the distribution of their product (which of course is a student's education). Describe the characteristics of your school's channel(s) of distribution. What types of innovative distribution might make sense for your school to try?

11-28. *Critical Thinking* Can a company's reverse logistics system have a significant influence on how a consumer views the organization and its brand? Are there specific types of products for which a company's reverse logistics system could play a more important role in contributing to a customer's view of the organization? For those companies what characteristics would you expect their reverse logistics systems to have in order to create high added value for a customer?

11-29. *Critical Thinking* One of the goals of modern-day logistics systems is to ensure a more suitable level of product supply through the chain that is matched to end-consumer demand. This requires a degree of flexibility in terms of production, warehousing, and transportation. However, along with greater supply flexibility, there is greater risk of increased costs (as the scale of production becomes less efficient).

Therefore, do you think that logistics should primarily focus on the needs and requirements of end consumers, or do you think that the prime goal of logistics is to distribute the product as cheaply and efficiently as possible? (In other words, do consumers primarily seek out low prices or convenience and reliability?) Do you think that there a way for a logistics company to balance both of these goals, or are they mutually exclusive?

11-30. *Critical Thinking* "To cut out the middleman" is a common phrase, usually referring to dropping wholesalers in an effort to increase profit margins for all other players in the channel and pass on reduced prices to the end consumer. Evaluate this statement. Think about the role that wholesalers play in the overall logistics and distribution system for the end consumer.

What impact would the removal of a wholesaler from a channel have on its efficiency and its overall cost structure? In particular, consider how both manufacturers and retailers would be affected by this approach. Are there any industries or product categories that are more highly reliant upon wholesalers than others?

11-31. *Critical Thinking* The supply chain concept looks at both the inputs of a firm and the firms that facilitate the movement of the product from the manufacturer to the consumer. Do you think *marketers* should be concerned with the total supply chain concept? Why or why not?

11-32. *Ethics* To bring cost-effective products to your door, retailers like Walmart use suppliers, some of which may contract work out to other suppliers and so on. And while the initial suppliers that Walmart contracts with may be socially responsible, not all suppliers are. What should retailers do to protect themselves from working with unethical companies or selling products made by such companies? How far down the supply chain should retailers be responsible for the business practices of their vendors?

Miniproject: Learn by Doing

Research a large supermarket chain by looking at their corporate site (as a guide, look for investor information for any chains that are publicly listed on the stock market). You should find information about their strategy and, in particular, their interest in logistics and supplier relationships, which is a common strategic approach across major supermarkets throughout the world.

11-33. Look for information on the supermarket's approach to logistics. You should look for their references to supplier relationships, their investment in any technology, and any other infrastructure that is relevant to sales and production data.

First, make a summary of the things they are doing in terms of logistics and supplier relationships and then consider how important their overall logistics and supplier practices appear to be in their overall strategy. Finally, how do they highlight the ways their investments in these areas will benefit end consumers?

Marketing in **Action** Case   Real Choices at Target

When can offering too many choices become too much to handle? Target has gone through a period of bad press as a result of an unacceptable level of stock-outs that upset customers and decreased sales. The discount retailer believes that it can solve the problem by reducing the number of brands and varieties of product options on the shelves. Brian Cornell, CEO, believes that the increased efficiency will allow for more focus on priority categories "like wellness, stylish home goods, apparel, and baby products."

Target's distribution process became more complicated with the expansion of its grocery business to include perishables like meat, fresh produce, and dairy products. Then, the situation became even more complex when it began allowing online customers to receive orders directly from its warehouses or pick up their online orders in stores. Because of the mess, Target has committed to redesigning its supply chain to make it more streamlined.

Target has a rich history of success. In 1902, George Dayton founded a company in Minneapolis, Minnesota, called Dayton Dry Goods Company. Over the years the company went through various retail format changes and in 1962, the first Target store opened in Roseville, Minnesota. It called itself the "new idea in discount stores" differentiated by merging key department store features with the lower prices of a discounter. Target became "a store you can be proud to shop in, a store you can have confidence in, a store that is fun to shop and exciting to visit." The retailer is the third largest U.S. store chain, operating over 1,800 retail locations throughout the United States.

Despite this lofty history, more recently growth at its established stores has been hindered by unacceptable stock levels because of their overly complicated supply chain. Target is spending more than $5 billion (yes, BILLION), to upgrade its distribution network and technology infrastructure to reduce stock shortages and facilitate the capability for online growth. In addition, the retailer is shrinking the number of different products it keeps in stock and reducing the number of sizes across those products. These changes will result in less overall inventory and improved handling efficiency. Amy Koo, an analyst with Kantar Retail, says, "In theory, everything can move faster, and they will have less stuff in the system."

Target's supply chain transformation includes other changes as well. Store shelves are being physically restructured to hold more product, pushing inventory out of backrooms and onto the sales floor. Suppliers are being required to adjust case sizes (how many individual items are inside a shipped carton) to increase inventory turnover and decrease the number of times a store employee has to handle the merchandise. In addition, Target wants suppliers to give a single-day arrival date for shipments to Target's warehouses, eliminating the prior practice of a "grace period" that allows shipments to arrive a few days after the promised date without penalties. These and other changes will help Target achieve its goal of better inventory management.

John Mulligan, chief operating officer, thinks that including suppliers in planning and executing the transformation is a key to success. Stock-outs not only hurt Target, the lost sales also mean that everyone in the supply chain suffers. How well the company uses this reinvigorated supply chain to deliver its value proposition to customers will be critical to its future competitive success.

You Make the Call

11-34. What is the decision facing Target?

11-35. What factors are important in understanding this decision situation?

11-36. What are the alternatives?

11-37. What decision(s) do you recommend?

11-38. What are some ways to implement your recommendation?

Based on: Phil Wahba, "This Is How Target Is Solving Its Out-of-Stock Problems," *Fortune* (March 2, 2016), http://fortune.com/2016/03/02/target-inventory/ (accessed May 6, 2016); "Target through the Years," *Target*, https://corporate.target.com/about/history/Target-through-the-years (accessed May 6, 2016); Nandita Bose and Nathan Layne, "Target Gets Tough with Vendors to Speed Up Supply Chain," Reuters (May 4, 2016), http://www.reuters.com/article/us-target-suppliers-exclusive-idUSKCN0XV096 (accessed May 6, 2016); Nandita Bose, "Target Gets Tough with Vendors to Speed Up Supply Chain," *Reuters* (March 2, 2016), http://www.reuters.com/article/us-target-outlook-idUSKCN0W42Q3 (accessed May 6, 2016).

MyLab Marketing™

Go to **mymktlab.com** for the following Assisted-graded writing questions:

11-39. *Creative Homework/Short Project.* Your new boss thinks that intermediaries cost the company too much money, but you know he is looking only at the bottom line. He has asked you to investigate the issue. In a short memo to your boss, describe the efficiencies that intermediaries create and identify the tangible and intangible benefits that these intermediaries provide.

11-40. *Creative Homework/Short Project.* Assume that your firm recently gave you a new marketing assignment. You are to head up development of a distribution plan for a new product line—a series of do-it-yourself instruction videos for home gardeners. These videos would show consumers how to plant trees, shrubbery, and bulbs; how to care for their plants; how to prune; and so on. You know that as you develop a distribution plan, it is essential that you understand and consider a number of internal and external environmental factors. Make a list of the information you will need before you can begin to write the distribution plan. How will you adapt your plan based on each of these factors?

Deliver the Customer Experience: Goods and Services via Bricks and Clicks

Courtesy of Stan Clark, Eskimo Joe's

Stan Clark

▼ A Decision Maker at Eskimo Joe's

Stan Clark is a native of Tulsa, Oklahoma. He graduated from Oklahoma State University (OSU) in May 1975 with a bachelor of science degree in business administration. For more than a decade, Stan's entrepreneurial success story has captivated audiences all over Oklahoma and across the country. Among other honors he was a Regional Finalist for *Inc.* magazine's Entrepreneur of the Year.

Stan's Info

First job out of school?
Eskimo Joe's. I graduated from OSU in May 1975 and opened Joe's about two weeks later. To do that, I turned down an assistantship to go into the OSU MBA program.

A job-related mistake I wish I hadn't made?
Killing the annual Joe's Anniversary Party in 1993. It attracted tens of thousands of people but was getting unwieldy.

My hero?
My dad, who inspired me to be an entrepreneur, and my mom, who gave me a positive outlook on life.

Business book I'm reading now?
Hug Your Customers by Jack Mitchell and *Discovering the Soul of Service* by Len Berry.

Career high?
During his 1990 commencement address at Lewis Field at OSU, President George H. W. Bush mentioned Eskimo Joe's in his speech. In 2006, George W. Bush did the same thing.

My motto to live by?
Live passionately and make a difference.

Here's my problem...

Real **People**, Real **Choices**

Stan Clark, the colorful entrepreneur behind the toothy grin of the Eskimo Joe caricature, and his dog Buffy faced a big problem. In 1975, Stan opened Eskimo Joe's bar in Stillwater, Oklahoma—the home of Oklahoma State University (OSU). By the mid-1980s, the watering hole had become a huge favorite among OSU students. Situated right across from the OSU campus, Joe's carved out a niche as the place to go for beer, music, pool, and foosball in this college town. Trading on the popularity of the bar as well as its quirky logo, Stan had also begun to sell some logo apparel over the counter. Before long, students, friends, parents, alums, and other visitors simply couldn't get enough of the T-shirts sporting the wide smiles by the boy and his faithful dog. For Stan, life was good and also lots of fun.

So what could possibly go wrong? Try the fact that Oklahoma had just passed a statewide "liquor by the drink" law. Prior to this, Oklahoma had a patchwork quilt of post–Prohibition era liquor laws, including "club card" requirements at bars and bring-your-own-bottle rules. Liquor by the drink opened up normal serving of beer, wine, and spirits at any establishment with a proper state liquor license; however, part of the new law was an increase in the legal drinking age from 18 to 21. Oops—a beer bar in a college town when you have to be 21 to drink? Not exactly an attractive business proposition. But, in the eight years since Eskimo Joe's opening, Stan had come to understand that the place represented a whole lot more to people than just pitchers of cold Bud on hot summer nights. There was a certain mystique and a strong sense of community around the brand that made it more than just a place to drink. Brisk sales of T-shirts and other clothing over the counter were evidence that people saw something else in the retailer—something that made them want to wear these items again and again. The affection and interest reached almost cult-like proportions and were not limited to Stillwater or even to Oklahoma. Stan had hit on something big, but what could he do? Big Brother in the State of Oklahoma was about to regulate him right out of his core business.

Stan had to take a couple of steps back, take a new look at his business, and think about what he might do to ensure that his retail enterprise would survive the new law. The situation could be life or death for Eskimo Joe's.

Stan considered his **Options** 1·2·3

1 Option

Convert the beer bar into a full-service restaurant that focuses on selling great food. This option assumes that the equity of the Eskimo Joe's brand would transfer into a brand-new market and product space. To accomplish this transformation, Stan would have to extensively remodel the facility. He would have to figure out who the new target market is and what type of menu fare would be most appealing to that customer. This was a risky proposition because restaurants open and close all the time. On the other hand, if Stan could morph the location into a restaurant that also happens to serve alcohol (which, under the new liquor law, would be legal—and potentially quite profitable), he would hopefully be able to continue to build the fledgling logo apparel business around the new restaurant theme, à la the Hard Rock Café.

2 Option

Continue operating as a beer bar at the core and work to offset declining beer sales with an increase in apparel sales. From 1975 to 1984, Joe's was "Stillwater's Jumpin' Little Juke Joint." It was by far one of the highest-volume beer bars in the region, and it had built its entire reputation on this image. As the number-one competitor in this market space, Stan had every reason to believe that the weaker competitors would be forced out of business by the law change, leaving their share of the market to him. Stan could continue to operate the bar in much the way it had always been operated, and if he liked, he could use it as a cash cow to generate revenues and then invest the money elsewhere for growth. The upside of this plan would be that any attempt to rebrand Eskimo Joe's as something other than what it had always been would be risky. However, the downside was the unknown of what it would mean to a retailer over the long run to lose its primary customer base of 18- to 20-year-olds in a town brimming with college students.

3 Option

Close Eskimo Joe's bar and refocus resources on building the growing apparel business. The cult-like status of the Eskimo Joe's brand and image may have begun at the physical location of the bar in Stillwater, but the way to replicate and perpetuate it on a national or international scale is by marketing the now-hip logo. Stan could build a small retail clothing boutique in Stillwater but turn primarily to direct marketing through catalogs focused on his target primary age and demographic groups. A key benefit of this approach is avoiding any unexpected problems with the bar that might occur in the liquor law transition, especially the negative publicity that would result if Joe's got caught selling beer to underage drinkers. The Eskimo Joe spirit would be maintained through the direct marketing and also through accompanying word of mouth. On the downside, to Joe's loyal fans, closing Stillwater's "Jumpin' Little Juke Joint" would be like Harley-Davidson ceasing to make motorcycles: Who wants the logo apparel when there's no product or place that still sports it? However, this option was tempting in that it would redirect Stan's resources to the high-growth (and high-profit-margin) apparel retailing sector.

Now put yourself in Stan's shoes. Which option would you choose, and why?

You Choose

Which **Option** would you choose, and **why**?

☐ Option 1   ☐ Option 2   ☐ Option 3

See what **option** Stan chose in **MyLab Marketing™**

MyLab Marketing™

⭐ **Improve Your Grade!**

Over 10 million students improved their results using the Pearson MyLabs. Visit **mymktlab.com** for simulations, tutorials, and end-of-chapter problems.

| Chapter 12 |

12.1

OBJECTIVE
Define retailing, understand how retailing evolves, and consider some ethical issues in retailing.

(pp. 400–407)

retailing
The final stop in the distribution channel in which organizations sell goods and services to consumers for their personal use.

Retailing, Twenty-First-Century Style

Shop 'til you drop! For many people, obtaining the product is only half the fun. Others, of course, would rather walk over hot coals than spend time in a store. Marketers like Stan need to find ways to deliver goods and services that please both types of consumers. **Retailing** is the final stop on the distribution path—the process by which organizations sell goods and services to consumers for their personal use.

As we said in Chapter 11, planning for distribution of product offerings includes decisions about where to make the product available. Thus, when marketers of consumer goods and services plan their distribution strategy, they talk about the retailers they will include in their channel of distribution. This means they need to understand retailing and the ever-changing retailer landscape.

Of course, retailers also develop their own marketing plans. Although the sample marketing plan we provided for your use in Appendix A relates to a manufacturer, we find essentially the same elements in retailers' marketing plans. Like producers, they must decide which consumer groups they can best serve, what product assortment and services they will provide for their customers, what pricing policies they will adopt, how they will promote their retail operations, and where they will locate their stores. This chapter will explore the many different types of retailers as we keep one question in mind: How does a retailer—whether store or nonstore (selling via TV, mobile phone, vending machine, or the Internet)—successfully make its goods or services available to the consumer?

So, this chapter has plenty "in store" for us. Let's start with an overview of where retailing has been and where it's going.

Retailing: A Mixed (Shopping) Bag

Retailing is big business. In 2015, U.S. retail sales totaled $4.87 trillion, 7 percent of which came from e-commerce.[1]

Over 1 million retail businesses employ nearly 16 million workers—more than 1 of every 10 U.S. workers.[2] Although we tend to associate huge stores such as Walmart and Sears with retailing activity, in reality most retailers are small businesses like Eskimo Joe's. Certain retailers, such as Home Depot and Costco, are both wholesalers and retailers because they provide goods and services to both businesses and end consumers.

As we said in Chapter 11, retailers are members of a channels of distribution. As such, they provide time, place, and ownership utility to customers. Some retailers save people time or money when they provide an assortment of merchandise under one roof. Others search the world for the most exotic delicacies; they allow shoppers access to goods they would otherwise never see. Still others, such as Starbucks, Apple, or REI, provide us with interesting environments in which to spend our leisure time and, they hope, our money. Service retailers such as banks, hospitals, and hair stylists satisfy our needs and wants for intangible products.

Globally, retailing has different faces in different parts of the world. In some European countries, don't even think about squeezing a tomato to see if it's too soft or picking up a cantaloupe to see if it smells ripe. Such mistakes will quickly gain you a reprimand from the store clerk, who will choose your oranges and bananas for you. In developing countries like those in Asia, Africa, and South America, retailing often includes many small butcher shops where you won't find hygienically sealed packages of steaks and lamb chops. Instead, sides of beef and lamb proudly hang in store windows so everyone will be assured that the meat comes from healthy animals. Other vendors sit cross-legged on the sidewalk where they sell lettuce, tomatoes, and cucumbers while men and boys offer passersby watermelons, neatly stacked on a donkey cart. Women cook small breakfast items and sell them in the front of their homes for workers and schoolchildren who pass by in the mornings. Neat store shelves stacked with bottles of shampoo may be replaced, as we said in Chapter 10, by hanging displays that hold one-use size sachets of shampoo and fabric softener, the only size that a woman can afford to buy and then only for special occasions. Street vendors may sell cigarettes one at a time. The local pharmacist may also give customers injections and recommends antibiotics and other medicines for patients who come in with a complaint and who can't afford to see a doctor. Don't feel like cooking tonight? There's no drive-through window for pickup; but even better—there's delivery from McDonald's, Hardees, KFC, Pizza Hut, Fuddruckers, Chili's, and a host of local restaurants via motor scooters that dangerously dash in and out of traffic is just a few minutes away. You can even order your Big Mac or a spicy vegetable dragon roll for delivery online through sites such as Egypt's Otlob.com or Mumbai's Foodkamood.com.

McDonald's is experimenting with delivery service in Vienna and other cities.

The Evolution of Retailing

Retailing has taken many forms over time, including the peddler who hawked his wares from a horse-drawn cart, a majestic urban department store, an intimate boutique, and a huge "hyperstore" that sells everything from potato chips to snow tires. But now the cart you see inside at your giant local mall that sells new-age jewelry or monogrammed golf balls to passersby has replaced the horse-drawn cart and you've traded the local hypermarket for your computer, tablet, or smartphone. As the economic, social, and cultural pictures change, different types of retailers emerge, and they often squeeze out older, outmoded types. How can marketers know what the dominant types of retailing will be tomorrow or 10 years from now?

One of the oldest and simplest explanations for these changes is the **wheel-of-retailing hypothesis**. 📷 Figure 12.1 shows that new types of retailers begin at the entry phase with low-end strategies as they offer goods at lower prices than their competitors.[3] After they gain a foothold, they gradually trade up as they improve facilities and upgrade merchandise. Finally, retailers move on to a high-end strategy with even higher prices, better

wheel-of-retailing hypothesis
A theory that explains how retail firms change, becoming more upscale as they go through their life cycle.

Vulnerability Phase

High prices
Luxurious facilities
Excellent services and amenities

Entry Phase

Low margin
Low prices
Limited or no services
Low-end facilities

Trading-up Phase

Moderate prices
Better facilities
Some services
Increased quality merchandise

Figure 12.1 📷 *Snapshot* | The Wheel of Retailing

The Wheel of Retailing explains how retailers change over time.

facilities, and amenities such as parking, gift wrapping, and maybe even spa treatments. *Upscaling* results in greater investment and operating costs, so the store must raise its prices to remain profitable. This makes it vulnerable to still newer entrants that can afford to charge lower prices. And so the wheel turns.

That's the story behind Pier 1 Imports. Pier 1 started as a single store in San Mateo, California, that sold low-priced beanbags, love beads, and incense to post–World War II baby boomers. Today, it sells quality home furnishings and decorative accessories to the same customers, who are now among the more affluent of the American population.[4]

The wheel of retailing helps us explain the development of some but not all forms of retailing. For example, some retailers never trade up; they simply continue to occupy a niche as discounters. Others, such as upscale specialty stores, start out at the high end and then move "downscale" as when Gap Stores opened Old Navy,

The Evolution Continues: What's "In Store" for the Future?

As our world continues to change rapidly, retailers scramble to keep up. A few of the factors that motivate innovative merchants to reinvent the way they do business are the economic environment, changing demographics and consumer preferences, technology, and globalization.

The Changing Economy

Recently, changes in the economic environment have been especially important both to consumers and to retailers. The economic downturn that began in 2007 meant that consumers worldwide were less willing to spend their discretionary income. Instead, they chose to lower their level of debt and to save. Retail sales, including the all-important Christmas sales, fell in nearly all retail segments.[5] Sales for most upscale retailers were especially vulnerable, whereas stores such as TJ Maxx, Marshalls, Dollar General, and online retailer Amazon.com that offer consumers low prices or discounted merchandise thrived. A number of retailers filed for bankruptcy, including Sharper Image, Circuit City, CompUSA, and Waldenbooks.[6]

During the economic downturn, some stores changed their merchandise assortment to meet consumers' desires for lower- or value-priced products. Sales of private-label brands continued to grow and in 2013 reached an all-time high in sales of $108 billion, which included 19 percent of supermarket sales.[7] Walmart and other mass merchandisers responded to this trend by allocating more shelf space to their own private-label brands and less to national brands. (Walmart later found that this strategy angered many consumers and hurt overall sales, and the chain quickly returned many items to its shelves.[8]) Although the recession is formally over, consumer spending has not grown as expected and retailer sales, even Christmas sales, remain fairly level.

Even private-label wines have become more popular. Many retailers have found that offering private label products during a downturn in the economy is good business. Trader Joe's exclusively carries Charles Shaw (aka "Two Buck Chuck"), Whole Foods uniquely offers Three Wishes, and Total Wine & More sells its very own Pacific Peak—and all sell for the low price of about $3 a bottle. Costco, which sells more than $1 billion of wine a year and is the largest retailer of fine wine in the U.S., buys wine from all over the world and sells it under its own Kirkland label. Can your palate detect the difference between private labels and the pricier brands if you remove the labels first?[9]

Randy Duchaine/Alamy Stock Photo

Retailers adapted to a weak economy by offering low-price wines.

Changing Demographics and Consumers Preferences

As we noted in Chapter 7, keeping up with changes in population characteristics including demographics and product preferences is at the heart of many marketing efforts. Here are some of the ways changing consumer demographics and preferences are altering the face of retailing.

Like other marketers, retailers need to stay on top of cultural trends that affect demand for the merchandise they sell, such as fur-free, vegan, or sustainable products.

- Retailers can no longer afford to stand by and assume that their customer base is the same as it has always been. Costco, for example, built its success on selling to upscale baby-boomers who own their own homes. As that demographic is replaced by Generation X and Generation Y consumers who prefer to shop online on Amazon.com, stores like Costco may have to reinvent themselves.[10]

- As more time-challenged consumers (especially women) are involved in the workforce, they demand greater convenience. In response retailers adjust their operating hours and services to meet the needs of working consumers who have less time to shop. Other retailers, including banks, dry cleaners and pharmacies, add drive-up windows to meet the needs of both working consumers and older consumers. A phone app called "ShowInRoom" reproduces your room on your phone and lets you "virtually" rearrange furniture without breaking a sweat. And walk-in medical clinics located at retailer, pharmacy, or grocery stores not only provide convenience but also save both patients and insurers money on routine care.[11]

- A change in consumer preferences has led retailer to develop creative **experiential merchandising**. Instead of shopping being a passive activity where a sales associate suggests what they should purchase, consumers want to convert shopping into a more interactive activity. Build-A-Bear provides such an experience with unique merchandise, store design, and customer activities. After all, it's not a store; it's a "Workshop." At Build-A-Bear, you don't just buy a toy with predetermined accessories, you get the excitement of "building" your very own bear. Once the customer (a child or the friend of a child) has selected the perfect color bear, he or she can select one or more outfits from a wide variety of well-made clothes (underwear and shoes included). Would your furry friend look best in a college or pro sports uniform? A career outfit? What about a Wonder Woman or Sleeping Beauty play costume? Better try on several! Probably need to buy more than one or come back another day. Build-A-Bear will also plan a child's birthday party complete with a party leader, games and activities, a Heart Ceremony for the Birthday child, and a party hat for each guest and their furry friends.[12]

experiential merchandising
Tactic whose intent is to convert shopping from a passive activity into a more interactive one, by better engaging the customer.

- Another trend is the appearance of the **destination retailer**, which is a store that consumers view as distinctive enough to go out of their way to shop there. Destination retailers come with different faces: an upscale strategy for status-conscious consumers, a convenience strategy for customers wanting easier shopping, and a unique way of doing business for bored consumers. Verizon has become a destination retailer with its 10,000 square foot retail space in Bloomington, Minnesota. Not your typical store, it's an interactive playground in the Mall of America that tends to blur the lines between online experiences and traditional brick-and-mortar retail. As more and more consumers spend more time with their smartphones and tablets, retailers' physical environments must compete with the online virtual world. Verizon's Destination Store demonstrates how mobile technologies can enhance every-day living using digital signage and video walls. The store's Lifestyle Zones include 1. Get Fit, 2. Amplify It (with an Amplify It Music Mixer and a Wall of Sound with 299 speakers), 3) Have Fun (a virtual golf course), 4) Home and On the Go (with smart home accessories guests can try out), 5) Anywhere Business (with business-friendly smart accessories), and 6) Customize It (with a digital photo booth).[13]

destination retailer
Firm that consumers view as distinctive enough to become loyal to it. Consumers go out of their way to shop there.

- Although members of every ethnic group can usually find local retailers that cater to their specific needs, larger companies must tailor their strategies to the cultural makeup of specific areas. For example, in Texas, California, and Florida, where there are large numbers of customers who speak only Spanish, many retailers make sure that there are sales associates who "habla Español."

Technology

- The same technology that has brought us the tablet and the smartphone now fuels consumers' craving for wearable technology—headsets, smart watches, fitness devices, and healthcare monitoring devices, just to name a few. Retailers will need to create a shopping experience that will be enhanced by these devices.

omnichannel (omni-channel) marketing
A retail strategy that provides a seamless shopping experience, whether the customer is shopping online from a desktop or mobile device, by telephone or in a brick-and-mortar store.

- **Omnichannel** (also spelled **omni-channel) marketing** is a strategy that provides a seamless shopping experience, whether the customer is shopping online from a desktop or mobile device, by telephone, or in a brick-and-mortar store. For example, new tech enables the sales associate in the store to access the customer's preferences, previous purchases, returns, frequency of shopping and all the other data that is currently only available when the shopper engages in a web chat with a customer service representative. As the shopper moves from a desktop to a tablet to a mobile phone, his or her search history and online shopping "basket" will remain intact and if they choose they can then pick up their purchase in the store of their choice the same day as they order it online.[14]

point-of-sale (POS) systems
Retail computer systems that collect sales data and are hooked directly into the store's inventory-control system.

perpetual inventory unit control system
Retail computer system that keeps a running total on sales, returns, transfers to other stores, and so on.

automatic reordering system
Retail reordering system that is automatically activated when inventories reach a certain level.

- Technology is revolutionizing retailing in ways that are not even visible to shoppers, such as advanced electronic **point-of-sale (POS) systems**. These devices contain computer brains that collect sales data and connect directly to the store's inventory-control system. Stores may use POS systems to create **perpetual inventory unit control systems** that keep a running total on sales, returns, transfers to other stores, and so on. This technology allows stores to develop computerized **automatic reordering systems** that are activated when inventories decline to a certain level.[15]

beacon marketing
A retail marketing strategy in which beacon devices are placed strategically throughout a store and emit a Bluetooth signal to communicate with shoppers' smartphones as they browse the aisles of the store.

- The hottest retail tech innovation right now is called a **beacon marketing**. As we noted in Chapter 8, these devices are placed strategically throughout a store and they use a Bluetooth signal to communicate with shoppers' smartphones as they browse the aisles. A beacon can share a coupon with your phone or reward you with points or discounts for specific merchandise just as you "coincidentally" stand next to the item. Macy's, Target, and American Apparel are among the large retailers that are starting to deploy beacon to keep in touch with what shoppers do in real-time. But wait, it gets scarier: Some retailers including Uniqlo, Lord & Taylor, and Saks are trying a version of beacons that get embedded inside store mannequins. These supposedly lifeless bodies can talk to you on your phone as you pass by a store window, and even send you photos of the outfits they're wearing.[16]

digital wallets
The use of Bluetooth technology that connects with customer smartphones and allows customers to pay for items without cash or even swiping a credit card.

- The store of the future will use RFID tags (and other technology) to assist the shopper in ways we haven't even thought of. For example, an RFID tag on a bottle of wine can tip off a nearby plasma screen that will project an ad for Barilla pasta and provide a neat recipe for fettuccine with bell peppers and shrimp. Some restaurants already use technology to let diners order their food tableside directly from a screen complete with photos of the dishes they offer. The *e-menus* help customers because they can see what every item on the menu will look like and, it is hoped, avoid a surprise when the waiter arrives.[17] This innovation also increases sales at the restaurant—who can avoid that mouth-watering picture of the eight-layer chocolate cake with peppermint stick ice cream on top?

- So-called **digital wallets**, discussed in Chapter 8, allow you to pay for items without cash or even swiping a credit card are making it even easier to burn through your paycheck. Already many of us routinely pay even for small items with apps like

Google Wallet, PayPal, Square, LevelUp, and Venmo. Now, Google is testing a hands-free payment system that uses voice-activation software in Silicon Valley branches of McDonald's and Papa John's. You just say, "I'll pay with Google" to a cashier and a Bluetooth sensor will activate the app in your phone and send you a bill.[18]

- Of course, technology is important to service industries also. Banking, for example, has become much simpler for both consumers and business customers. For many years, electronic banking offered ATMs and websites where consumers can check their bank balance or transfer funds. Today, most banks also offer automatic bill-pay services that allow consumers to pay their bills online, and the bank will write the check and mail it. Also, many banks now let you make deposits at the ATM or with your smartphone.

Retailing is alive and well at Taiwan's airport.

Globalization

As we learned in Chapter 1, many consumers and marketers have adopted a triple-bottom line orientation. This means that marketing organizations, including retailers, are concerned about their *social bottom line,* that is, their contribution to communities in which the company operates. The idea of social bottom line is especially relevant when it comes to operations in developing countries. Sometimes you will see the following phrase on a product label: "fair trade good," "fair trade certified," or something similar. These phrases on a product label assure that fair prices were paid to exporters as well as compliance with higher social and environmental and social standards.

Retailtainment to Satisfy Experiential Shoppers

For many customers, shopping is not just about making a purchase. Instead, they shop because it satisfies their experiential needs, that is, their desire for fun. These **experiential shoppers** regard shopping as entertainment. When the retail experience includes surprise, excitement, and a unique experience, experiential shoppers are more likely to make impulsive purchase decisions.[19]

With the tremendous growth on online retailing, brick-and-mortar retailers have to do more than just sell stuff.[20] **Retailtainment** is all about marketing strategies that enhance the shopping experience. Retailers from Disney to Bass Pro Shops create excitement, encourage impulse purchases (that are made spur-of-the-moment), and an emotional connection with the brand through retailtainment. For example, Thirsty Bear, a London pub, installed iPads at tables so customers could set up electronic bar tabs (and check their Facebook pages). Lark Lagerfeld, a London clothing retailer, installed iPads in dressing rooms that allow customers to send "selfies" to friends to get their opinions of the purchase. The new H&M store in New York City offers smart dressing rooms with iPads so customers can buy items while they still are in the dressing room and then leave, wearing their purchase. The store also boasts a DJ booth and a catwalk performance that is projected on external LED screens for passersby to see.[21] Cabela's refers to itself as the "world's foremost outfitter

experiential shoppers
Shoppers who shop because it satisfies their experiential needs, that is, their desire for fun.

retailtainment
The use of retail strategies that enhance the shopping experience and create excitement, impulse purchases, and an emotional connection with the brand.

Planet Hollywood is a retail chain with outposts in London and Paris.

RosaIreneBetancourt 1/Alamy Stock Photo

Andre Jenny Stock Connection Worldwide/Newscom

Ripped from the Headlines

Ethical/Sustainable Decisions in the Real World

Most clothing consumers in the U.S. and other developed countries buy is made in developing countries where workers are paid only pennies an hour. Often workers must work overtime without extra pay and they may even be physically punished for minor infractions by their employers. They arrive at work every day wondering if they will get fired. In many of these countries, the minimum wage is less than a living wage, that is, enough money to meet a family's basic needs of food and shelter.

One attempt to change this is the Fair Trade movement that promotes greater equity in international trading partnerships, encourages sustainable development, and secures the rights of marginalized producers and workers in developing countries. Members of the movement advocate the payment of higher prices to exporters from these countries, as well as improved social and environmental standards. Fair trade supporters believe that buying products from producers and workers in developing countries is a better way of promoting sustainable development than traditional charity and aid.

Fair Trade USA appears to be having some success. During the past few years, the number of firms certified by the group Fair Trade USA to label their products Fair Trade has grown. Patagonia, Williams-Sonoma, Inc.'s West Elm unit, and Bed Bath and Beyond Inc. are a few of the retailers now selling Fair Trade–Certified apparel or home furnishings. Under the Canopy's Fair Trade Certified line of bedding sold by Bed Bath & Beyond for the back-to-school season sold out immediately.

Alta Gracia is an example of a Fair Trade producer. The company sells collegiate branded apparel made in the Dominican Republic through campus book stores in the U.S. The organization's employees in the Dominican Republic are paid a living wage. This means they make three times the nation's minimum wage of $150 a month. That's enough to buy their own home and provide for their families. In addition, the Alta Gracia workers receive health insurance, a pension, vacation days, and maternity leave.[22]

> **ETHICS CHECK:** ↖
>
> Should all retailers seek out and buy Fair Trade goods?
>
> ☐ YES ☐ NO

---

for hunting, fishing, camping, and outdoor gear" and devotes up to 45 percent of its store space to retailtainment featuring taxidermy displays and a shooting gallery.[23]

Ethical Problems in Retailing

shrinkage
Losses experienced by retailers as a result of shoplifting, employee theft, and damage to merchandise.

Retailers must deal with ethical problems that involve both their customers and their employees. Losses resulting from **shrinkage** are a growing problem. *Shrinkage* is the term retailers use to describe stock losses due to shoplifting, employee theft, and damage to merchandise and a variety of errors. Shrinkage costs retailers $44 billion, or 1.38 percent, of all retail sales.[24] Guess who winds up paying for these "five-finger discounts?"

Shoplifting

organized retail crime (ORC)
Retail shoplifting by organized gangs of thieves that get away with thousands of dollars in goods in a single day.

Shoplifting has grown in recent years to giant proportions. In the U.S., shoplifting accounts for 38 percent of the total $44 billion in shrinkage. These thefts in turn drive consumer prices up and hurt the economy and sometimes even cause smaller retailers to go out of business. Increasingly, shoplifting is an organized criminal activity. **Organized retail crime (ORC)** is no different from other organized crime with organized gangs of thieves that use store floor plans and foil-lined bags to evade security sensors and get away with thousands of dollars in goods in a single day.[25] Many believe the Internet has increased ORC. Instead of selling their stolen watches or tee shirts on street corners, criminals can now join those who sell their legitimate items on online auction sites such as eBay and Etsy.

Of course, some shoplifting is more amateurish, and some shoplifters are just not that clever. One woman in California was caught stashing expensive items in her purse each time employees turned their backs. But after three trips into the store to steal, her luck ran out when she wrote down her real name and address while signing up for a raffle contest the store was hosting.[26] It's a safe bet to say she wasn't the sharpest tool in the shed.

Employee Theft

A second major source of shrinkage in retail stores is employee theft of both merchandise and cash. In the U.S., it accounted for 34.5 percent in 2014, less than shoplifting for the first time.[27] On a case-by-case basis, dishonest employees steal nearly five times the amount shoplifters do.[28] Employees not only have access to products but also are familiar with the store's security measures. "Sweethearting" is an employee practice in which a cashier consciously undercharges, gives a cash refund, or allows a friend to walk away without paying for items.[29] Sometimes a dishonest employee simply carries merchandise out the backdoor to a friend's waiting car.

Retail Borrowing

A third source of shrinkage is an unethical consumer practice the industry calls **retail borrowing**. Merchants over recent decades have developed liberal policies of accepting returns from customers because the product performs unsatisfactorily or even if the customer simply changes her mind. Retail borrowing refers to the return of nondefective merchandise for a refund after it has fulfilled the purpose for which it was purchased.[30] Popular objects for retail borrowing include a dress for a high school prom, a new suit for a job interview, and or a large-screen TV for a big football game. For the consumer, the practice provides short-term use of a product for a specific occasion at no cost. For the retailer, the practice results in lower total sales and in damaged merchandise, unsuitable for resale.

retail borrowing
The consumer practice of purchasing a product with the intent to return the nondefective merchandise for a refund after it has fulfilled the purpose for which it was purchased.

Ethical Treatment of Customers

The other side of the retail ethics issue is how retailers and their employees treat customers. Although it may be illegal if a store doesn't provide equal access to consumers of different ethnic groups, behavior that discourages customers who appear economically disadvantaged or socially unacceptable from shopping at a store is not. One study, for example, showed that restaurant servers based their level of service on the customer's perceived ability to pay and leave a good tip.[31]

In other **customer profiling** situations, where the level of customer service is tailored based on a customer's perceived ability to pay, some customers were followed around the store by associates and made so uncomfortable that they left before making a purchase, or the customer was ignored altogether to the point he or she left the store disgusted and angry.[32] As a classic scene in the movie *Pretty Woman* starring Julia Roberts depicted, stores that try to maintain an image of elite sophistication may not be real helpful to customers who don't look like they belong there.

customer profiling
The act of tailoring the level of customer service based on a customer's perceived ability to pay.

Many critics argue that retailers have an obligation not to sell products to customers if the products can be harmful. For example, for many years some teens and young adults abused potentially harmful over-the-counter medicines. While government regulations removed many of these drug products from store shelves in recent years, retailers still have to carefully police their distribution. The same is true for products such as alcohol and cigarettes, which by law are limited for sale to adult customers.

12.2 Types of Brick-and-Mortar Retailers

OBJECTIVE
Understand how we classify traditional retailers.

(pp. 407–413)

The field of retailing covers a lot of ground—from mammoth department stores to **service retailers** like Massage Envy, websites like Amazon.com, and restaurants like Eskimo Joe's. Retail marketers need to understand the possible ways they might offer their products in the market, and they also need a way to benchmark their performance relative to other, similar retailers.

service retailer
Organization that offers consumers services rather than merchandise. Examples include banks, hospitals, health spas, doctors, legal clinics, entertainment firms, and universities.

Classify Retailers by What They Sell

To keep this discussion of retailers from being confusing, we need to discuss two different ways we talk about services. First, there are retailers whose main products are services— your dry cleaner who cleans your clothes, the coiffure where you get your hair cut, and the garage that repairs your car. We also use the word *service* to refer to the extras we receive when we buy goods (i.e., the delivery and set-up of your new washer, instructions on how to set your new home security system and, at the supermarket, bagging your groceries and helping you put them in your car).

In classifying retailers by what they sell, we will first distinguish between retailers who primarily sell goods and those who primarily sell services. For a goods-oriented retailer, one of the most important strategic decisions is *what* to sell—its **merchandise mix**. Service retailers similarly decide what services they will offer consumers. Massage Envy, for example, as their name says, specializes in massages. Canyon Ranch Health Resort in Arizona offers exercise, nutrition instruction, a selection of indoor and outdoor pools complete with underwater treadmills, manicures, pedicures, beauty treatments, and even massages. Later in this chapter, we'll talk more about retailers whose main business is to provide consumers with quality services and other intangibles that meet their needs.

If a store's merchandise mix is too limited, it may not have enough potential customers, whereas if it is too broad, the retailer runs the risk of being a "jack of all trades, master of none." Because what the retailer sells is central to its identity, one way we describe retailers is in terms of their merchandise mix.

Although as we learned in Chapter 9 that a manufacturer's product line consists of product offerings that satisfy a single need, in retailing a *product line* is a set of related products a retailer offers, such as kitchen appliances or leather goods. The *Census of Retail Trade* that the U.S. Bureau of the Census conducts classifies all retailers by North American Industry Classification System (NAICS) codes (the same system we described in Chapter 6 that classifies industrial firms). A retailer that wants to identify direct competition simply looks for other firms with the same NAICS classification codes.

However, a word of caution: As marketers experiment with different retail merchandise mixes, it's getting harder to make these direct comparisons. For example, even though marketers like to distinguish between food and nonfood retailers, in reality these lines are blurring. **Combination stores** offer consumers food and general merchandise in the same store. **Supercenters**, such as Walmart Supercenters and SuperTargets, are larger stores that combine an economy supermarket with other lower-priced merchandise. Other retailers like CVS, RiteAid, and Walgreens drugstores, carry limited amounts of food.

We can also classify retailers by their **merchandise assortment**, or selection of products they sell. Merchandise assortment has two dimensions: breadth and depth. **Merchandise breadth**, or variety, is the number of different product lines available. A *narrow assortment*, such as we encounter in convenience stores, means that shoppers will find only a limited selection of product lines, such as candy, cigarettes, and soft drinks. A *broad assortment*, such as a warehouse store like Costco or Sam's Club offers, means there is a wide range of items from pizzas to barbecue grills.

Merchandise depth is the variety of choices available within each specific product line. A *shallow assortment* means that the selection within a product category is limited, so a factory outlet store may sell only white and blue men's dress shirts (all made by the same manufacturer, of course) and only in standard sizes. In contrast, a men's specialty store may feature a *deep assortment* of dress shirts (but not much else) in varying shades and in hard-to-find sizes. 📷 Figure 12.2 illustrates these assortment differences for one product: science fiction books.

Classify Retailers by Level of Service

In addition to classifying goods retailers by the merchandise they sell, we also characterize them by the amount extra help and assistance, that is, the services they offer customers who buy their merchandise. Firms recognize that there is a trade-off between service and low prices, so they tailor their strategies to the level of service they offer. Customers who demand higher levels of service must be willing to pay for that service, and those who want lower prices must be willing to give up services.

---

merchandise mix
The total set of all products offered for sale by a retailer, including all product lines sold to all consumer groups.

combination stores
Retailers that offer consumers food and general merchandise in the same store.

supercenters
Large combination stores that combine economy supermarkets with other lower-priced merchandise.

merchandise assortment
The range of products a store sells.

merchandise breadth
The number of different product lines available.

merchandise depth
The variety of choices available for each specific product line.

Figure 12.2 📷 *Snapshot* | Classification of Book Retailers by Merchandise Selection

Marketers often classify retail stores on the breadth and depth of their merchandise assortment. In this figure, we use the two dimensions to classify types of bookstores that carry science fiction books.

| | **Breadth** | |
	Narrow	Broad
Shallow	Airport Bookstore: A few *Lord of the Rings* books	Sam's Club: A few *Lord of the Rings* books and a limited assortment of *Lord of the Rings* T-shirts and toys
Deep	www.legendaryheroes.com: Internet retailer selling only merchandise for *Lord of the Rings*, *The Highlander*, *Zena: Warrior Princess*, *Legendary Swords*, *Conan*, and *Hercules*	www.Amazon.com: Literally millions of current and out-of-print books plus a long list of other product lines including electronics, toys, apparel, musical instruments, jewelry, motorcycles, and ATVs

(*Depth* labels the vertical axis on the left.)

Retailers like Sam's Club that promise cut-rate prices often are self-service operations. When customers shop at *self-service retailers*, they make their product selection without any assistance, they often must bring their own bags or containers to carry their purchases, and they may even handle the checkout process with self-service scanners. A new supermarket in Sweden called Näraffär Viken pushes the envelope to the extreme: It has no employees at all. Shoppers use a smartphone app to open the doors, scan barcodes, and pay for items. Note: The store operates on an honor system; but just in case, it's also monitored by CCTV.[33]

Contrast that experience to visiting a *full-service retailer*. Department stores like Bloomingdale's and specialty stores like Victoria's Secret provide supporting services such as gift wrapping, and they offer trained sales associates who can help us select that perfect gift. Nordstrom's, an upscale department store, is recognized for its exceptional service. The sales associates, known as "Nordies," have even been known to procure a desired item from another retailer for the shopper if it's not available at a good price in the Nordstrom inventory.

Other specialized services are available based on the merchandise the store offers. For example, many full-service clothing retailers will provide alteration services. Retailers like Macy's, Bed Bath & Beyond, Best Buy, and even Amazon.com that carry china, silver, housewares, appliances, electronics, or other items that brides (and grooms) might also offer special bridal consultants or bridal gift registries.

Limited-service retailers fall in between self-service and full-service retailers. Stores like Walmart, Target, Old Navy, and Kohl's offer credit and merchandise return but little else. Customers select merchandise without much assistance, preferring to pay a bit less rather than have more assistance from sales associates.

Major Types of Retailers

Now that we've seen how retailers differ in the breadth and depth of their assortments, let's review some of the major forms these retailers take. Table 12.1 provides a list of these types and their characteristics.

Convenience Stores

Convenience stores carry a limited number of frequently purchased items, including basic food products, newspapers, and sundries. They cater to consumers willing to pay a premium for the ease of buying staple items close to home. In other words,

convenience stores
Neighborhood retailers that carry a limited number of frequently purchased items and cater to consumers willing to pay a premium for the ease of buying close to home.

Table 12.1 | Different Retailers Offer Varying Product Assortments, Levels of Service, Store Sizes, and Prices

Type	Merchandise	Level of service	Size	Prices	Examples
Convenience stores	Limited number of choices in narrow number of product lines; frequently purchased and emergency items	Self-service	Small	Low-priced items sold at higher than average prices	7-Eleven
Supermarkets	Large selection of food items and limited selection of general merchandise	Limited service	Medium	Moderate	Publix, Kroger
Box stores	Limited selection of food items; many store brands	Self-service Bag your own purchases	Medium	Low	ALDI
Specialty stores	Large selection of items in one or a few product lines	Full service	Small and medium	Moderate to high	Yankee Candle Co., Things Remembered
Category killers	Large selection of items in one or a few product lines	Full service	Large	Moderate	Toys "R" Us, Home Depot, Best Buy
Leased departments	Limited selection of items in a single product line	Usually full service	Small	Moderate to high	Picture Me portrait studios in Walmart stores
Variety stores	Small selection of items in limited product lines; low-priced items; may have a single price point	Self-service	Small	Low	Dollar General, Dollar Tree
General merchandise discount stores	Large selection of items in a broad assortment of product lines	Limited service	Large	Moderate to low	Walmart, Kmart
Off-price retailers	Moderate selection of limited product lines; buy surplus merchandise	Limited service	Moderate	Moderate to low	T.J. Maxx, Marshall's
Warehouse clubs	Moderate selection of limited product lines; many items in larger than normal sizes	Self-service	Large	Moderate to low	Costco, Sam's Club, BJ's
Factory outlet stores	Limited selection from a single manufacturer	Limited service	Small	Moderate to low	Gap Outlet, Liz Claiborne Outlet, Coach Outlet
Department stores	Large selection or many product lines	Full service	Large	Moderate to high	Macy's, Bloomingdale's, Nordstrom
Hypermarkets	Large selection of items in food and a broad assortment of general merchandise product lines	Self-service	Very large	Moderate to low	Carrefour
Pop-up stores	Often a single line or brand; frequently used for seasonal products	Self-service	Very small	Low to moderate	Halloween costume pop-ups

convenience stores meet the needs of those who are pressed for time, who buy items in smaller quantities, or who shop at irregular hours. But these stores are starting to change, especially in urban areas, where many time-pressed shoppers prefer to visit these outlets even for specialty items. Store chains such as 7-Eleven and Wawa now offer customers a coffee bar, fresh sandwiches, and pastries. A great example of the wheel of retailing at work!

Think convenience stores are just for convenience and a late-night gallon of milk? Maverik Country Stores, Inc. doesn't think so. The 250-store chain transformed itself from an Old West country store to match its slogan, "Adventure's First Stop." Customers from soccer moms to mountain bikers think it's a fun place. The Adventure First Stop stores feature cascading waterfalls of fountain drinks, a winding river of coffee, and snowy mountains made of frozen yogurt. Unique names are also a part of the fun. Destination areas of the stores include Bodacious Bean coffee stations, Fountain Falls beverage dispensers, Big Moon restrooms (no comment), Big Bear Bakery, and Room with a Brew walk-in beer coolers. The stores even wrap their fuel pumps and tanker delivery trucks in murals of sports images, such as jet skis and snowmobiles.[34]

Supermarkets

Supermarkets are food stores that carry a wide selection of edible and nonedible products. Although the large supermarket is a fixture in the U.S., it has not caught on to the same extent in other parts of the world. In many European countries where small, compact towns dominate, for example, consumers walk or bike to small stores near their homes. They tend to have smaller food orders per trip and to shop more frequently, partly because many lack the freezer space to store a huge inventory of products at home. Wide variety is less important than quality and local ambiance to Europeans, but their shopping habits are starting to change as huge hypermarkets become popular around the globe.

supermarkets
Food stores that carry a wide selection of edibles and related products.

Box Stores

Box stores are food stores that have a limited selection of items, few brands per item, and few refrigerated items. Generally, they are open fewer hours than supermarkets, are smaller, and carry fewer items than warehouse clubs. Items are displayed in open boxes (hence the name), and customers bag their own purchases. ALDI stores, for example, carry only about 1,400 regularly stocked items, while a typical supermarket may carry up to 50,000 items.[35] (About 95 percent of ALDI items are store brands with a few national brands that are special-buy purchases and are available for limited periods.)

box stores
Food stores that have a limited selection of items, few brands per item, and few refrigerated items.

Specialty Stores

Specialty stores have narrow and deep inventories. They do not sell a lot of product lines, but they offer a good selection of brands within the lines they do sell. For many women with less-than-perfect figures, shopping at a store that sells only swimsuits means there will be an adequate selection so they can find a suit that really fits. The same is true for larger, taller men who can't find suits that fit in regular department stores but who have lots of choices in stores that cater to big-and-tall guys. Specialty stores can tailor their assortment to the specific needs of a targeted consumer, and they often offer a high level of knowledgeable service.

specialty stores
Retailers that carry only a few product lines but offer good selection within the lines that they sell.

A category killer is a very large specialty store that carries a vast selection of products in its category. Some examples of category killers are Home Depot, Toys "R" Us, Best Buy, and Staples.

category killer
A very large specialty store that carries a vast selection of products in its category.

leased departments
Departments within a larger retail store that an outside firm rents.

variety stores
Stores that carry a variety of inexpensive items.

general merchandise discount stores
Retailers that offer a broad assortment of items at low prices with minimal service.

off-price retailers
Retailers that buy excess merchandise from well-known manufacturers and pass the savings on to customers.

warehouse clubs
Discount retailers that charge a modest membership fee to consumers who buy a broad assortment of food and nonfood items in bulk and in a warehouse environment.

factory outlet store
A discount retailer, owned by a manufacturer, that sells off defective merchandise and excess inventory.

Discount department stores like Kohl's are a go-to source for fashion today.

Category Killers

The **category killer** is one type of specialty store that has become especially important in retailing today. A category killer is a very large specialty store that carries a vast selection of products in its category. Some examples of category killers are Home Depot, Toys "R" Us, Best Buy, and Staples.

Leased Departments

Leased departments are departments within a larger retail store that an outside firm rents. This arrangement allows larger stores to offer a broader variety of products than they would otherwise carry. Some examples of leased departments are in-store banks, photographic studios, pet departments, fine jewelry departments, and watch and shoe repair departments.

Variety Stores

Variety stores originated as the five-and-dime or dime stores that began in the late 1800s. In these early variety stores, such as the iconic Woolworth's, all items were sold for a nickel or a dime. Today's variety stores carry a variety of inexpensive items from kitchen gadgets to toys to candy and candles. It's tough to buy something for a dime today, but many variety stores still stick to a single price point, and some offer products that don't cost more than a dollar. Some examples of today's variety stores include Dollar General Stores, Family Dollar stores, and Dollar Tree.

Discount Stores

General merchandise discount stores, such as Target, Kmart, and Walmart, offer a broad assortment of items at low prices and with minimal service and are the dominant outlet for many products. Discounters are tearing up the retail landscape because they appeal to price-conscious shoppers who want easy access to a lot of merchandise. These stores increasingly carry designer-name clothing at bargain prices as companies like Liz Claiborne create new lines just for discount stores.[36] The glow may have faded on some general merchandise stores. Early in 2016, Walmart announced that it would close 269 stores, 154 of them in the U.S. as a result of increased competition from online retailers like Amazon.[37]

Some discount stores, such as T.J. Maxx, Tuesday Morning, Marshalls, Home Goods, and A.J. Wright, are **off-price retailers**. These stores obtain surplus merchandise from manufacturers and offer brand-name, fashion-oriented goods at low prices.

Warehouse clubs, such as Costco and BJ's, are a newer version of the discount store. These establishments do not offer any of the amenities of a full-service store. Customers buy many of the products in larger-than-normal packages and quantities—nothing like laying in a three-year supply of paper towels or five-pound boxes of pretzels, even if you have to build an extra room in your house to store all this stuff! These clubs often charge a membership fee to consumers and small businesses. A recent survey showed that the typical warehouse shopper shops about once a month, is intrigued by bulk buying, hates long lines, and is drawn to the club retailer because of specific product areas such as fresh groceries.[38] And, consistent with the wheel of retailing, even these stores "trade up" in terms of what they sell today; shoppers can purchase fine jewelry and other luxury items at many warehouse clubs.

The **factory outlet store** is still another type of discount retailer. A manufacturer owns these stores. Some factory outlets enable the manufacturer to sell off defective merchandise or excess inventory, while others carry items not available at full-price retail outlets and are designed to provide an additional distribution channel for the manufacturer. Although the assortment found in a Gap, Adidas, or J. Crew outlet store is not wide because a store carries products only one manufacturer makes, we find most factory outlet stores in *outlet malls*, where a large number of factory outlet stores cluster together in the same location.

Department Stores

Department stores sell a broad range of items and offer a deep selection organized into different sections of the store. Grand department stores dominated urban centers in the early part of the twentieth century. In their heyday, these stores sold airplanes and auctioned fine art. Lord & Taylor even offered its customers a mechanical horse to ensure the perfect fit of riding habits.

In many countries, department stores continue to thrive, and they remain consumers' primary place to shop. In Japan, department stores are always crowded with shoppers who buy everything from a takeaway sushi dinner to a string of fine pearls. In Spain, a single department store chain, El Corte Inglés, dominates retailing. Its stores include store-size departments for electronics, books, music, and gourmet foods, and each has a vast supermarket covering one or two floors of the store.

In the U.S., however, department stores have struggled in recent years. On the one hand, specialty stores lure department store shoppers away with deeper, more cutting-edge fashion selections and better service. On the other hand, department stores have also been squeezed by discount stores, catalogs, and online stores that offer the same items at lower prices because they don't have the expense of rent, elaborate store displays and fixtures, or high salaries for salespeople. This decline of middle-of-the-market retailing as a result of the popularity of both low-end discount/variety stores and upscale specialty retailing is called **bifurcated retailing**.[39] To remain major players in the minds and pocketbooks of consumers, department stores are spinning off lower-priced store formats such as Neiman-Marcus' Last Call and Macy's Backstage divisions.[40]

Hypermarkets

Hypermarkets combine the characteristics of warehouse stores and supermarkets. A European invention, these are huge establishments several times larger than other stores. A supermarket might be 40,000 to 50,000 square feet, whereas a hypermarket takes up 200,000 to 300,000 square feet, or four football fields. They offer one-stop shopping and feature restaurants, beauty salons, and children's play areas. The French company Carrefour has more than 10,000 stores in 33 countries around the globe including about 1500 hypermarkets; each carries 20,000 to 80,000 food and non-food items.[41] More recently, Carrefour is expanding to developing countries and now has 236 hypermarkets in China, where a burgeoning population and a lack of large retailers provide hyperopportunities.

Pop-Up Stores

Pop-up stores are retail experiences that "pop up" one day and then disappear after a period of one day to a few months. In addition to being a low-cost way to start a business, pop-up stores provide a number of advantages, including building consumer interest, creating buzz, and test marketing products and locations. Seasonal pop-up stores are frequently opened to sell Halloween costumes, Christmas gifts and decorations, and fireworks. In addition, traditional retailers, such as Target, Kate Spade, Gucci, and Louis Vuitton, have experimented with pop-ups.

department stores
Retailers that sell a broad range of items and offer a good selection within each product line.

bifurcated retailing
With the decline of middle-of-the-market retailing, both mass merchandising and niche retailing dominate the retail market.

hypermarkets
Retailers with the characteristics of both warehouse stores and supermarkets; hypermarkets are several times larger than other stores and offer virtually everything from grocery items to electronics.

pop-up stores
Retail stores, such as Halloween costume stores, that "pop up" one day and then disappear after a period of one day to a few months.

12.3 E-Commerce and Other Types of Nonstore Retailers

OBJECTIVE

Describe business-to-consumer (B2C) e-commerce and the other common forms of nonstore retailing.

(pp. 414–419)

Stores like The Limited succeed because they put cool merchandise in the hands of young shoppers who can't get it elsewhere. But competition for shoppers' dollars comes from sources other than traditional stores that range from bulky catalogs to dynamic websites. Debbie in Dubuque can easily log on to Forever21.com at 3:00 A.M. and order the latest belly-baring fashions without leaving home.

As the founder of the Neiman Marcus department store once noted, "If customers don't want to get off their butts and go to your stores, you've got to go to them."[42] Indeed, many products have been available in places other than stores for a long time. The Avon Lady, the Fuller Brush man, and Tupperware parties are all part of the rich history and present reality of retailing. These along with the fast growing world of e-commerce are part of **nonstore retailing**.

Of course, it's really hard to separate e-commerce from conventional retailers. Most, from upscale specialty stores such as Tiffany's to discounter Walmart to warehouse club Costco, have found it critical that they offer nonstore websites for customers who want to buy their merchandise online. For other companies, such as Internet retailer Amazon.com, nonstore retailing is their entire business. In Chapter 14, we will discuss what direct marketing retailers do through the mail, telephone, and TV. In this section, we'll look at other types of nonstore retailing, shown in Figure 12.3: B2C e-commerce, direct selling, and automatic vending.

nonstore retailing
Any method used to complete an exchange with a product end user that does not require a customer visit to a store.

B2C E-Commerce

B2C e-commerce
Online exchanges between companies and individual consumers.

M-commerce
Promotional and other e-commerce activities transmitted over mobile phones and other mobile devices, such as smartphones and personal digital assistants.

B2C e-commerce is online exchange between companies and individual consumers. According to Forrester Research, e-commerce sales are expected to reach $373 billion in 2016 and are projected to account for $523 billion by 2020.[43] Consumers are increasingly using their smartphones to make **M-commerce** purchases. Mobile phones will generate 15 percent of ecommerce sales by 2020, and tablets will generate 33 percent of ecommerce sales.[44]

Forrester Research estimates that by 2017, 60 percent of all U.S. retail sales will involve the web in some way—that means either a direct purchase of a product online or doing online research before making a product purchase in a traditional store (a web-influenced purchase).[45] Forrester also estimates that offline web-influenced sales will increase to $1.8 trillion by 2017.[46]

A number of factors prevent online sales from growing even more. Most consumers prefer stores where they can touch and feel items and avoid issues with returns and shipping costs. Also, many consumers don't like to buy online because they want the product immediately. To address some of these issues, many retailers, such as Best Buy, have merged their online and in-store sales functions. Consumers can select an item and pay for it online, then pick it up at their local store within hours; no wandering over the store to find the item or waiting in line to pay and no concerns about stock-outs.

Benefits of B2C E-Commerce

For both consumers and marketers, B2C e-commerce provides a host of benefits and some limitations. Table 12.2 lists some of these.

From the consumer's perspective, electronic marketing increases convenience because it breaks down many of the barriers time and location create. You can shop 24/7 without leaving home. Consumers

Figure 12.3 Snapshot | Types of Nonstore Retailing

Traditional retailers must compete with a variety of nonstore retailers from automatic vending to dynamic websites.

Direct Selling
- Door to door
- Parties and networks
- Multilevel networks and activities

Automatic Vending

B2C E-Commerce

in even the smallest of communities can purchase funky shoes or a hot swimsuit from Bloomingdales.com just like big-city dwellers. The website Ideeli.com offers its customers the chance to buy heavily discounted luxury items in a kind of online "blue-light special" on your cell phone. At the red-hot WarbyParker.com, you can upload your photo and virtually try on different sunglasses before you buy. The company will even send you several pairs if you're undecided; you just return the ones you don't want. In less developed countries, the Internet lets consumers purchase products that may not be available at all in local markets. Thus, the Internet can improve the quality of life without the necessity of developing costly infrastructure, such as opening retail stores in remote locations.

Although most online consumers engage in goal-directed behavior and want to satisfy their shopping goal as quickly as possible, between 20 and 30 percent shop online because they enjoy the "thrill of the hunt" as much as or more than the actual acquisition of the item. The desire to be entertained motivates these online experiential shoppers, and they linger at sites longer. Consequently, marketers who wish to attract these customers must design websites that offer surprise, uniqueness, and excitement. Today, marketers provide **virtual experiential marketing** when they add online enhancements including colors, graphics, layout and design, interactive videos, contests, games, and giveaways.[47] Because more than half of all retail customers say that friends influence their purchases, some online retailers have developed groups of "brand friends" who will share the news from the retailer.[48]

Marketers realize equally important benefits from e-commerce. Because an organization can reach such a large number of consumers via e-commerce, it is possible to develop very specialized businesses that could not be profitable if limited by geographic constraints. The Internet provides an excellent opportunity to bring merchants with excess merchandise and bargain-hunting consumers together.[49] When retailers become concerned that, due to economic downturns or

Brick-and-mortar bookstores, like this chain in Lithuania, struggle to provide unique experiences to buyers who are otherwise tempted to shop online.

virtual experiential marketing
An online marketing strategy that uses enhancements, including colors, graphics, layout and design, interactive videos, contests, games, and giveaways, to engage experiential shoppers online.

Table 12.2 | Benefits and Limitations of E-Commerce

Benefits	Limitations
For the Consumer	**For the Consumer**
Shop 24 hours a day	Lack of security
Less traveling	Fraud
Can receive relevant information in seconds from any location	Can't touch items
More product choices	Exact colors may not reproduce on computer monitors
More products available to less developed countries	Expensive to order and then return
Greater price information	Potential breakdown of human relationships
Lower prices, so less affluent can purchase	
Participate in virtual auctions	
Fast delivery	
Electronic communities	
For the Marketer	**For the Marketer**
The world is your marketplace	Lack of security
Decreases costs of doing business	Must maintain site to reap benefits
Very specialized businesses can succeed	Fierce price competition due to total transparency for branded products
Real-time pricing	Conflicts with conventional retailers
	Legal issues not resolved

other factors, consumers may not buy enough, they may use online liquidators, such as Overstock.com and Bluefly.com, that offer consumers great bargains on apparel and accessories, items that retailers refer to as "distressed inventory." At the same time, the Internet provides consumers with price transparency making it harder for online retailers to compete at prices that are higher than those of their competitors.

Even high-fashion designers whose retail outlets we associate with Rodeo Drive in Los Angeles, Fifth Avenue in New York, and the Magnificent Mile in Chicago are setting up shop on the Internet to sell $3,000 skirts and $5,000 suits. In 2014, $30 billion in luxury apparel and footwear were bought online.[50] According to Forrester Research, it makes sense to sell luxury online because 8 of 10 affluent customers use the Internet to research and purchase luxury goods.[51] The luxury fashion site Net-a-Porter.com sells designer clothing and accessories from Givenchy, Jimmy Choo, Victoria Beckman, and other top designers.[52] Bottega Veneta bolero jackets sell for $5,600, and Oscar de la Renta lace and tulle gowns sell for $9,290.

As we discussed in Chapter 11, one of the biggest advantages of e-commerce is that it's easy to get price information. Want to buy a new Hellboy action figure, a mountain bike, an MP3 player, or just about anything else you can think of? Instead of plodding from store to store to compare prices, many web surfers use search engines or "shopbots," (discussed in Chapter 6) such as Ask.com, that compile and compare prices from multiple vendors. With readily available pricing information, shoppers can browse brands, features, reviews, and information on where to buy that particular product.

E-commerce also allows businesses to reduce costs. Compared to traditional brick-and-mortar retailers, e-tailers' costs are minimal—no expensive mall sites to maintain and no sales associates to pay. And, for some products, such as computer software and digitized music, e-commerce provides fast, almost instantaneous delivery. Newer entertainment downloads have gone a step further with sites such as Amazon.com, Netflix.com, and iTunes that offer online shoppers the opportunity to purchase or rent movies. Just download a flick to your new high-definition LED smart TV and pop some corn. You're set for the evening.

Limitations of B2C E-Commerce

But all is not perfect in the virtual world. E-commerce does have its limitations. One drawback compared to shopping in a store is that customers must wait a few days to receive most products, which are often sent via private delivery services, so shoppers can't achieve instant gratification by walking out of a store clutching their latest "finds." The electronics chain Best Buy thinks it can address this issue with a new form of hybrid retailing we discussed previously; a customer can order a big-screen TV on the company's website and then drive to a brick-and-mortar store to pick it up the same day.

Of course, some e-commerce sites still suffer from poor design that frustrates consumers and leads to **shopping cart abandonment** where customers leave the site with unpurchased items in their cart. An average of 68 percent of all online shopping customers leave items in their carts costing e-marketers dearly.[53] Customers are less likely to return to sites that are difficult to navigate or that don't provide easy access to customer service personnel, such as the online chats that better sites provide. Customers are often frustrated with sites where their shopping baskets "disappear" as soon as they leave the site. Retailers need to take these navigational problems seriously. When consumers have problems shopping on a site, they are less likely to return to shop another day.

Security is a concern to both consumers and marketers. We regularly hear news of yet another retail chain's data system being hacked and information from millions of consumers' credit cards stolen. Although in the U.S., an individual's financial liability in most theft cases is limited because credit card companies usually absorb most or all of the loss, the damage to one's credit rating can last for years.

Consumers also are concerned about Internet fraud. Although most of us feel competent to judge a local brick-and-mortar business by its physical presence, by how long it's been around, and from the reports of friends and neighbors who shop there, we have little

shopping cart abandonment
Occurs when e-commerce customers leave an e-commerce site with unpurchased items in their cart.

or no information on the millions of Internet sites offering their products for sale—even though sites like eBay.com and the Better Business Bureau try to address these concerns by posting extensive information about the reliability of individual vendors.

As with catalogs, even though most online companies have liberal return policies, some companies do not pay return shipping costs and the consumer may get stuck with these charges for items that don't fit or simply aren't the right color.

Developing countries with primarily cash economies pose yet another obstacle to the global success of B2C e-commerce. In these countries, few people use credit cards, so they can't easily pay for items they purchase over the Internet. Furthermore, banks are far less likely to offer consumers protection against fraudulent use of their cards, so a hacked card number can literally wipe you out. For consumers in these countries, there are a growing number of alternatives for safely paying for online purchases. PayPal is a global leader in online payments. Founded in 1998 and acquired by eBay in 2002, PayPal has more than 184 million active customer accounts and services customers in 202 countries where customers can get paid in more than 100 currencies. In 2015, PayPal processed 4.9 billion payments around the world.[54] Twitpay is a service that permits consumers to send payments using the social network site Twitter. Twitpay's RT2Giv service offers consumers the opportunity to easily make payments to nonprofits. For example, the nonprofit group Malaria No More joined with Twitter to raise money for its Help Us End Malaria campaign—donations were used to buy mosquito nets for African children and their families.[55]

As major marketers beef up their presence on the web, they worry that inventory they sell online will *cannibalize* their store sales (we discussed the strategic problem of cannibalization in Chapter 9). This is a big problem for companies like bookseller Barnes & Noble, which has to be careful as it steers customers toward its website and away from its chain of stores bursting with inventory. Barnes & Noble has to deal with competitors such as Amazon (with 300 million worldwide customers and annual sales of not only books but myriad products from apparel to cell phones of more than $107 billion in 2015), which sells its books and music exclusively over its 13 global websites and so doesn't have to worry about this problem.[56] Of course, today, books, including textbooks like the awesome one you're reading now, have gone digital and can be purchased and downloaded online. Tablet e-book readers, such as Amazon's Kindle and Apple's iPad, make e-books even more attractive.

B2C's Effect on the Future of Retailing

Does the growth of B2C e-commerce mean the death of brick-and-mortar stores as we know them? Don't plan any funerals for your local stores prematurely. Although some argue that virtual distribution channels will completely replace traditional ones because of their cost advantages, this is unlikely. For example, although a bank saves 80 percent of its costs when customers do business online from their home computers, Wells Fargo found that it could not force its customers to use PC-based banking services. And for many products, people need "touch-and-feel" information before they buy. For now, clicks will have to coexist with bricks.

However, this doesn't mean that physical retailers can rest easy. Stores as we know them will continue to evolve to lure shoppers away from their computer screens. In the future, the trend will be *destination retail*; that is, consumers will visit retailers not so much to buy a product as for the entertainment they receive from the total experience. As we saw in our discussion

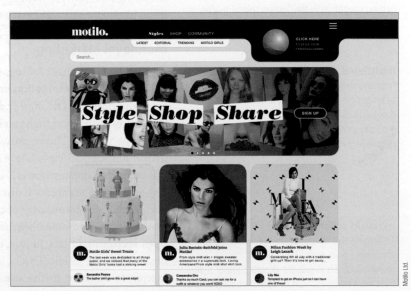

The online shopping site Motilo tries to make clothes shopping more fun as it offers user-generated suggestions, prizes, and other engaging activities.

Motilo Ltd.

of retailtainment, many retailers already offer ways to make the shopping in brick-and-mortar stores an experience rather than just a place to pick up stuff. Bass Pro Shops Mega Outdoor Stores are a store, museum, and art gallery all built into one. Hand-painted murals, 15,000-gallon saltwater aquariums, wildlife exhibits, a full-service restaurant, and a gift and nature center beckon customers to linger. In fact, the average Bass Pro Shop customer spends two and a half hours in the store after driving an average distance of 50-plus miles to get there.[57] This is definitely not your grandfather's bait-and-tackle store!

Direct Selling

direct selling
An interactive sales process in which a salesperson presents a product to one individual or a small group, takes orders, and delivers the merchandise.

Direct selling occurs when a salesperson presents a product to one individual or a small group, takes orders, and delivers the merchandise. The Direct Selling Association reported that in 2014, 18.2 million people were engaged in direct selling in the U.S., and these activities generated over $34 billion in sales.[58] Of this, 71.5 percent of revenues came from face-to-face sales and 22.4 percent from party plan or group sales. The major product categories for direct sales include home/family care products (such as cleaning products), wellness products (such as weight loss products), personal care products (such as cosmetics), clothing and accessories, and services. Major players in this huge industry include Amway, Mary Kay, Avon, Rodale & Fields, Advocare, Scentsy, and Tupperware.

Door-to-Door Sales

Door-to-door selling is still popular in some countries, such as China. But it's declining in the U.S., where two-income households are the norm, because fewer people are home during the day and those who *are* home are reluctant to open their doors to strangers. Door-to-door selling is illegal in communities that have **Green River Ordinances**; they prohibit door-to-door selling unless prior permission is given by the household.

Green River Ordinances
Community regulations that prohibit door-to-door selling unless prior permission is given by the household.

Parties and Networks

At *home shopping parties*, also called *in-home selling*, a company representative known as a consultant, distributor, or adviser makes a sales presentation to a group of people who have gathered in the home of a friend.[59] One reason that these parties are so effective is that people who attend may get caught up in the "group spirit" and buy things they would not normally purchase if they were alone—even Botox injections to get rid of those nasty wrinkles. We call this sales technique a **party plan system**. Perhaps the most famous home shopping parties were the Tupperware parties popular in the 1950s. Today, though, you're more likely to go to a Thirty-One or Scentsy party.

party plan system
A sales technique that relies heavily on people getting caught up in the "group spirit," buying things they would not normally buy if they were alone.

Multilevel Marketing

Another form of direct selling, which the Amway Company epitomizes, is **multilevel marketing or network marketing**. In this system, a *master distributor* recruits other people to become distributors. The master distributor sells the company's products to the people he or she entices to join and then receives commissions on all the merchandise sold by the people he or she recruits. Today, Amway has over 3 million independent business owners who distribute personal care, home care, and nutrition and commercial products in more than 100 countries and territories.[60] Amway and other similar network marketers use revival-like techniques to motivate distributors to sell products and find new recruits.[61]

multilevel or network marketing
A system in which a master distributor recruits other people to become distributors, sells the company's product to the recruits, and receives a commission on all the merchandise sold by the people recruited.

Despite the popularity of this technique, some network systems are illegal. They are really **pyramid schemes**: illegal scams that promise consumers or investors large profits from recruiting others to join the program rather than from any real investment or sale of goods to the public. Often, large numbers of people at the bottom of the pyramid pay money to advance to the top and to profit from others who might join. At recruiting meetings, pyramid promoters create a frenzied, enthusiastic atmosphere complete with promises of easy money. Promoters also use high-pressure tactics to get people to sign up,

pyramid schemes
An illegal sales technique that promises consumers or investors large profits from recruiting others to join the program rather than from any real investment or sale of goods to the public.

suggesting that if they don't sign on now, the opportunity won't come around again. Some pyramid schemes are disguised as multilevel marketing—that is, people entering the pyramid do not pay fees to advance, but they are forced to buy large, costly quantities of non-returnable merchandise.[62] That's one of the crucial differences between pyramid schemes and legitimate network marketers.

Automatic Vending

Coin-operated vending machines are a tried-and-true way to sell convenience goods, especially snacks and drinks. These machines are appealing because they require minimal space and personnel to maintain and operate. Some of the most interesting innovations are state-of-the-art vending machines that dispense everything from baguettes (which are good any time of day) to ballet flats (which you'll want after a late night out dancing).[63] Chinese customers can purchase live crabs from vending machines, and in Japan customers can buy draft beers. In the U.S., vending machines that use touch screens and accept credit card or mobile payments dispense pricey items like Beats by Dr. Dre headphones and Ray-Ban sunglasses.[64]

In general, however, vending machines are best suited to the sales of inexpensive merchandise, food, and beverages. Most consumers are reluctant to buy pricey items from a machine. New vending machines may spur more interest, however, as technological developments loom on the horizon, including video kiosk machines that let people see the product in use, have the ability to accept credit card or mobile payments, and have inventory systems that signal the operator when malfunctions or stock-outs occur.

12.4 Retailing What Isn't There: Services and Other Intangibles

OBJECTIVE
Understand the marketing of services and other intangibles.
(pp. 419–427)

As we said at the beginning of this chapter, retailing is about selling goods and services to consumers for their personal use. Thus, to understand retailing, we must also understand *services* and how marketers provide consumers with quality services (and other intangibles) that meet their needs.

Marketing What Isn't There

What do a Rihanna concert, a college education, a Cubs baseball game, and a visit to Walt Disney World have in common? Easy answer—each is a product that combines experiences with physical goods to create an event that the buyer consumes. You can't have a concert without musical instruments (or maybe a pink wig, in Rihanna's case), a college education without textbooks (Thursday night parties don't count), a Cubbies game without a hot dog, or a Disney experience without the mouse ears. But these tangibles are secondary to the primary product, which is some act that, in these cases, produces enjoyment, knowledge, or excitement.

In this section, we'll consider some of the challenges and opportunities that face marketers whose primary offerings are **intangibles**: services and other experience-based products that we can't touch. The marketer whose job is to build and sell a better football, automobile, or smartphone—all tangibles—deals with issues that are somewhat different from the job of the marketer who wants to sell tickets to a basketball game, limousine service to the airport, or allegiance to a hot new rock band. Services are one type of intangible that also happens to be the fastest-growing sector in our economy. As we'll see, all services are intangible, but not all intangibles are services.

intangibles
Experience-based products.

services
Intangible products that are exchanged directly between the producer and the customer.

Services are acts, efforts, or performances exchanged from producer to user without ownership rights. In 2014, service industry jobs accounted for four out of every five jobs in the U.S.[65] and almost 78 percent of the gross domestic product.[66] If you pursue a marketing career, it's highly likely that you will work somewhere in the services sector of the economy. Got your interest?

The service industry includes many consumer-oriented services, ranging from dry cleaning to body piercing. It also encompasses a vast number of services directed toward organizations. Some of the more common *business services* include vehicle leasing, information technology services, insurance, security, legal advice, food services, cleaning, and maintenance. In addition, businesses also purchase some of the same services as consumers, such as electricity, mobile phone service, and natural gas.

Characteristics of Services

Services come in many forms, from those done *to* you, such as a massage or a teeth cleaning, to those done to *something you own*, such as having your computer tuned or getting a new paint job on your classic 1965 Mustang. Regardless of whether they affect our bodies or our possessions, all services share four characteristics, which 📷 Figure 12.4 summarizes: intangibility, perishability, inseparability, and variability. The discussion that follows shows how marketers can address the unique issues related to these characteristics of services that don't pop up when they deal with tangible goods.

Intangibility

intangibility
The characteristic of a service that means customers can't see, touch, or smell good service.

Marketing of services might be called "marketing the product that isn't there." The essence is that unlike a bottle of Izzo soda or a Samsung 60" 4K Ultra HD TV—both of which have physical, tangible properties—services do not assume a tangible form. **Intangibility** means customers can't see, touch, or smell good service. This makes it much more difficult for consumers to evaluate many services. Although it may be easy to evaluate your new haircut, it is far less easy to determine whether the dental hygienist did a great job when she cleaned your teeth.

perishability
The characteristic of a service that makes it impossible to store for later sale or consumption.

Because they're buying something that isn't there, customers look for reassuring signs before they purchase; so marketers must ensure that these signs are readily available. That's why they try to overcome the problem of intangibility by providing *physical cues* to reassure the buyer. These cues for a service provider (such as a bank) might be the "look" of the facility; its furnishings, logo, stationery, business cards, or appearance of its employees; or well-designed advertising and websites.

capacity management
The process by which organizations adjust their offerings in an attempt to match demand.

Perishability

Perishability refers to the characteristic of a service that makes it impossible to store for later sale or consumption; it's a case of use it or lose it. When rooms go unoccupied at a ski resort, there is no way to make up for the lost opportunity to rent them for the weekend. As we discussed in Chapter 10, they may use yield management pricing or another marketing strategy to encourage demand for the service during slack times. Carnival Cruise Lines, after a series of service fiascos including what was dubbed the "Poop Cruise" (where stranded customers had no working toilets for five days), began offering heavily discounted tickets in an effort to lure customers back to its empty ships. Cabins could be purchased for as little as $50 a day—assuming you were willing to chance it, of course.[67]

Capacity management is the process by which organizations adjust their services in an attempt to match supply with demand. This strategy may mean adjusting the product, or it may mean adjusting the price. In the summer, for example, the Winter Park ski resort in Colorado combats its perishability problem when it opens its lifts to mountain bikers who tear down the

Figure 12.4 📷 *Snapshot* | Characteristics of Services

Services have four unique characteristics versus products.

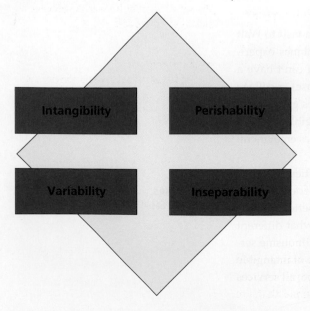

Intangibility

Perishability

Variability

Inseparability

sunny slopes. Capacity management is the reason behind Disney's new pricing structure described in the Marketing in Action case at the end of Chapter 10.

Variability

A National Football League quarterback may be red hot one Sunday and ice cold the next, and the same is true for most services. **Variability** means that over time, even the same service that the same individual performs for the same customer changes—even if only in minor ways. It's rare when you get exactly the same cut from a hairstylist each time you visit him or her. Even your physician might let a rough day get in the way of his or her usual charming bedside manner with patients.

It's difficult to standardize services because service providers and customers vary. Think about your experiences in your college classes. A school can standardize its offerings to some degree—course catalogs, course content, and classrooms are fairly controllable. Professors, however, vary in their training, life experiences, and personalities, so there is little hope of being able to make teaching uniform (not that we'd want to do this anyway). And because students with different backgrounds and interests vary in their needs, the lecture that you find fascinating might put your friend to sleep (trust us on this). The same is true for customers of organizational services. Differences in the quality of individual security guards or cleaning personnel mean variability in how organizations deliver these services.

The truth is, if you really stop and think about it, we don't necessarily *want* standardization when we purchase a service. Most of us desire a hairstyle that fits our face and personality and a personal trainer who will address our unique physical training needs. Businesses like McDonald's, Wendy's, and Burger King want their ad agencies to create unique advertising campaigns to set them apart from each other.

Inseparability

In services, **inseparability** means that it is impossible to divide the production of a service from the consumption of that service. Think of the concept of inseparability this way: A firm can manufacture goods at one point in time, distribute them, and then sell them later (likely at a different location than the original manufacturing facility). In contrast, by its nature, a service can take place only at the time the actual service provider performs an act on either the customer or the customer's possession.

Still, it's difficult if not impossible to detach the expertise, skill, and personality of a provider or the quality of a firm's employees, facilities, and equipment from the service offering itself. The central role that employees play in making or breaking a service underscores the importance of the **service encounter**, or the interaction between the customer and the service provider.[68] The most expertly cooked meal is just plain mush if a surly or incompetent waiter brings it to the table.

To minimize the potentially negative effects of bad service encounters and to save on labor costs, some service businesses turn to **disintermediation**, which means removing the "middleman" and thus eliminating the need for customers to interact with people at all. Examples include self-checkouts at the supermarket or home improvement store, self-service gas pumps, and bank ATMs. Even salad and dessert bars reduce reliance on a restaurant server.

As we said previously, the Internet provides many opportunities for disintermediation, especially in the financial services area. Banking customers can access their accounts, transfer funds from one account to another, apply for a loan and pay their bills with the click of a mouse.

The Service Encounter

Earlier, we said that a service encounter occurs when the customer comes into contact with the organization—which usually means he or she interacts with one or more employees who represent that organization. The *service encounter* has several dimensions that are

variability
The characteristic of a service that means that even the same service performed by the same individual for the same customer can vary.

inseparability
The characteristic of a service that means that it is impossible to separate the production of a service from the consumption of that service.

service encounter
The actual interaction between the customer and the service provider.

disintermediation
The elimination of some layers of the channel of distribution to cut costs and improve the efficiency of the channel.

important to marketers.[69] First, there is the *social contact dimension*—one person interacting with another person. The *physical dimension* is also important—customers often pay close attention to the environment where they receive the service.

Despite all the attention (and money) firms pay to create an attractive facility and deliver a quality product, this contact is "the moment of truth"—the employee often determines whether the customer will come away with a positive or a negative impression of the service. Our interactions with service providers can range from the most superficial, such as when we buy a movie ticket, to telling a psychiatrist (or bartender) our most intimate secrets. In each case, though, the quality of the service encounter exerts a big impact on how we feel about the service we receive. In other words, *the quality of a service is only as good as its worst employee.*

However, the customer also plays a part in the type of experience that results from a service encounter. When you visit a doctor, the quality of the health care you receive depends not only on the physician's competence. It's also influenced by your ability to accurately and clearly communicate the symptoms you experience and how well you follow the regimen he or she prescribes to treat you. In the same way, the business customer must provide accurate information to his or her accounting firm.

Physical Elements of the Service Encounter: Servicescapes and Other Tangibles

As we noted previously, because services are intangible, marketers have to be mindful of the *physical evidence* that goes along with them. An important part of this physical evidence is the **servicescape**: the environment in which the service is delivered and where the firm and the customer interact. Servicescapes include facility exteriors—elements such as a building's architecture, the signage, parking, and even the landscaping. They also include interior elements, such as the design of the office or store, equipment, colors, air quality, temperature, and smells. For hotels, restaurants, banks, airlines, and even schools, the servicescape is quite elaborate. For other services, such as an express mail drop-off, a dry cleaner, or an ATM, the servicescape can be very simple.

Marketers know that carefully designed servicescapes can have a positive influence on customers' purchase decisions, their evaluations of service quality, and their ultimate satisfaction with the service. Thus, for a service such as a pro basketball game, much planning goes into designing not only the actual court but also the exterior design and entrances of the stadium, landscaping, seating, restrooms, concession stands, and ticketing area. Similarly, marketers pay close attention to the design of other tangibles that facilitate the performance of the service or provide communications. For the basketball fan, these include the signs that direct people to the stadium, the game tickets, the programs, the team's uniforms, and the hundreds of employees who help to deliver the service.

How We Provide Quality Service

If a service experience isn't positive, it can quickly turn into a *disservice* with nasty consequences. Quality service ensures that customers are satisfied with what they have paid for. However, satisfaction is relative because the service recipient compares the current experience to some prior set of expectations. That's what makes delivering quality service tricky. What may seem like excellent service to one customer may be mediocre to another person who has been "spoiled" by earlier encounters with an exceptional service provider. So, marketers must identify customer expectations and then work hard to exceed them.

In air travel, lots of "little things" that used to be considered a normal part of the service are now treated by most airlines as extras. Many fliers believe the airlines are "nickel and diming" them for extra bag weight, blankets and pillows, small snacks and drinks, and prime seat locations. Soon they'll be charging us to use the restroom in flight! Southwest,

servicescape
The actual physical facility where the service is performed, delivered, and consumed.

though, has continued to offer all these perks as part of the basic service. Thus, by essentially doing nothing different from what they've always done, Southwest now stands out from the crowd and exceeds customer expectations. No surprise that year after year Southwest continues to be ranked among the top three in customer satisfaction among low-priced carriers by J.D. Power and Associates.[70]

Strategic Issues When We Deliver Service Quality

We've seen that delivering quality is the goal of every successful service organization. What can the firm do to maximize the likelihood that a customer will choose its service and become a loyal customer? Because services differ from goods in so many ways, decision makers struggle to market something that isn't there. But, just as in goods marketing, the first step is to develop effective marketing strategies. Table 12.3 illustrates how three different types of service organizations might devise effective marketing strategies.

Of course, no one (not even your marketing professor) is perfect, and mistakes happen. Some failures, such as when your dry cleaner places glaring red spots on your new white sweater, are easy to see at the time the firm performs the service. Others, such as when the dry cleaner shrinks your sweater, are less obvious, and you recognize them only at a later time when you're running late and get a "smaller than expected surprise." But no matter when or how you discover the failure, the important thing is that the firm takes fast action to resolve the problem. A timely and appropriate response means that the problem won't occur again (it is hoped) and that the customer's complaint will be satisfactorily

Table 12.3	Marketing Strategies for Service Organizations		
	Dry Cleaner	**City Opera Company**	**A State University**
Marketing objective	Increase total revenues by 20 percent within one year by increasing business of existing customers and obtaining new customers	Increase to 1,000 the number of season memberships to opera productions within two years	Increase applications to undergraduate and graduate programs by 10 percent for the coming academic year
Target markets	Young and middle-aged professionals living within a five-mile radius of the business	Clients who attend single performances but do not purchase season memberships	Primary market: prospective undergraduate and graduate students who are residents of the state
		Other local residents who enjoy opera but do not normally attend local opera performances	Secondary market: prospective undergraduate and graduate students living in other states and in foreign countries
Benefits offered	Excellent and safe cleaning of clothes in 24 hours or less	Experiencing professional-quality opera performances while helping ensure the future of the local opera company	High-quality education in a student-centered campus environment
Strategy	Provide an incentive offer to existing customers, such as one suit cleaned for free after 10 suits cleaned at regular price	Correspond with former membership holders and patrons of single performances encouraging them to purchase new season memberships	Increase number of recruiting visits to local high schools; arrange a special day of events for high school counselors to visit campus
	Use newspaper and direct mail advertising to communicate a limited-time discount offer to all customers	Arrange for opera company personnel and performers to be guests for local TV and radio talk shows	Communicate with alumni encouraging them to recommend the university to prospective students they know

Metrics Moment

We can easily measure service quality. The **SERVQUAL** scale is one popular instrument to measure customers' perceptions of service quality. SERVQUAL identifies five dimensions, or components, of service quality:

- *Tangibles:* The physical evidence of service quality, such as the physical facilities and equipment, professional appearance of personnel, and the look and functionality of the website
- *Reliability:* The ability to provide dependably and accurately what was promised to the customer
- *Responsiveness:* The willingness to help customers and provide prompt service
- *Assurance:* The knowledge and courtesy of employees and the ability to convey trust and confidence
- *Empathy:* The degree to which the service provider genuinely cares about customers and takes the customer perspective into account when delivering service.[71]

The SERVQUAL scale is reliable and valid (concepts discussed in Chapter 4), and service businesses usually administer the scale in a survey format through a written, online, or phone questionnaire to customers.

Firms often track their own SERVQUAL scores over time to understand how their service quality is, it is hoped, improving. They also can use it to collect data on customers' service quality perceptions of key competitors and then compare those scores to their own to see where to improve.

Gap analysis (no, nothing to do with a Gap clothing store) is a related measurement approach that gauges the difference between a customer's expectation of service quality and what actually occurs. By identifying specific places in the service system where there is a wide gap between what customers expect and what they receive, services marketers can get a handle on what needs improvement.

Apply the Metrics

1. Think back on a service encounter you've had in the past few days. This could be either in person or by phone.
2. Rate the quality of the service on each of the five SERVQUAL dimensions (consider if each aspect was low, medium, or high) and then give an overall rating for the service encounter. Explain why you gave the ratings that you did.

SERVQUAL

A multiple-item scale used to measure service quality across dimensions of tangibles, reliability, responsiveness, assurance, and empathy.

gap analysis

A marketing research method that measures the difference between a customer's expectation of a service quality and what actually occurred.

resolved. The key is speed; research shows that customers whose complaints are resolved quickly are far more likely to buy from the same company again than from those that take longer to resolve complaints.[72]

To make sure that they keep service failures to a minimum and that, when they do blow it, they can recover quickly, managers should first understand the service and the potential points at which failures are most likely to occur so they can plan how to recover ahead of time. That's why it's so important to identify critical incidents. In addition, employees should be trained to listen for complaints and be empowered to take appropriate actions immediately. Many hoteliers allow front-desk employees the discretion to spend up to a certain amount per service failure to compensate guests for certain inconveniences.

Marketing People, Places, and Ideas

By now, you understand that services are intangibles that marketers work hard to sell. But as we said previously, services are not the only intangibles that organizations need to market. Intangibles such as people, places, and ideas often need to be "sold" by someone and "bought" by someone else. Let's consider how marketing is relevant to each of these.

Marketing People

As we saw in Chapter 1, people are products, too. If you don't believe that, you've never been on a job interview or spent a Saturday night in a singles bar! Many of us find it distasteful to equate people with products. In reality, though, a sizable number of people hire personal image consultants to devise a marketing strategy for them, and others undergo plastic surgery, physical conditioning, or cosmetic makeovers to improve their "market position" or "sell" themselves to potential employers, friends, or lovers.[73] Let's briefly touch on a few prominent categories of *people marketing*.

Sophisticated consultants create and market politicians when they "package" candidates (clients) who then compete for "market share" as measured by votes. We trace

Table 12.4 | Strategies to Sell a Celebrity

Marketing Approach	Implementation
Pure selling approach	Agent presents a client to the following: Record companies Movie studios TV production companies Talk show hosts Advertising agencies Talent scouts
Product improvement approach	Client is modified: New name New image Voice lessons Dancing lessons Plastic surgery New backup band New music genre
Market fulfillment approach	Agent looks for market opening: Identify unmet need Develop a new product (band or singer) to the specifications of consumer wants

this perspective all the way back to the 1952 and 1956 presidential campaigns of Dwight Eisenhower. Advertising executive Rosser Reeves (one of the original "Mad Men" who shaped the industry) repackaged the bland but amiable U. S. Army general as he invented jingles and slogans such as "I like Ike" and contrived man-on-the-street interviews to improve the candidate's market position.[74] For better or worse, Reeves's strategies revolutionized the political landscape as people realized they could harness the tactics they use to sell soap to sell candidates for public office. Today, the basic idea remains the same, even though the techniques are more sophisticated.

From actors and musicians to athletes and supermodels, the famous and near-famous jockey for market position in popular culture. Agents carefully package celebrities as they connive to get their clients exposure on TV, starring roles in movies, recording contracts, or product endorsements.[75] Like other products, celebrities even rename themselves to craft a "brand identity." They use the same strategies marketers use to ensure that their products make an impression on consumers, including memorability (Flo Rida), suitability (fashion designer Oscar Renta reverted to his old family name of de la Renta because it sounded more elegant), and distinctiveness (Alicia Beth Moore became Pink).

In addition to these branding efforts, there are other strategies marketers use to "sell" a celebrity, as Table 12.4 shows. These include the following:

1. The *pure selling approach:* An agent presents a client's qualifications to potential "buyers" until he or she finds one who is willing to act as an intermediary.

2. The *product improvement approach:* An agent works with the client to modify certain characteristics that will increase his or her market value.

3. The *market fulfillment approach:* An agent scans the market to identify unmet needs. After identifying a need, the agent then finds a person or a group that meets a set of minimum qualifications and develops a new "product."

place marketing
Marketing activities that seek to attract new businesses, residents, or visitors to a town, state, country, or some other site.

idea marketing
Marketing activities that seek to gain market share for a concept, philosophy, belief, or issue by using elements of the marketing mix to create or change a target market's attitude or behavior.

Marketing Places

Place marketing strategies regard a city, state, country, or other locale as a brand. Marketers use the marketing mix to create a suitable identity so that consumers choose this brand over competing destinations when they plan their travel. Because of the huge amount of money tourism generates, the competition to attract visitors is fierce. There are about 1,600 visitors' bureaus in the U.S. alone that try to brand their locations. In addition, almost every town or city has an economic development office charged with luring new businesses or residents. Marketers invite would-be tourists to come and visit "Pure Michigan." In the commercials, which feature the calm, soothing voice of actor Tim Allen, the state of Michigan shows off its off-the-beaten path outdoor beauty as well as its big-city adventures. And these popular ads pay off; they brought in $1.2 billion in revenue in 2013. In addition to the current U.S. campaign, "Pure Michigan" commercials are set to air soon in Canada, Germany, and China, reaching ever more consumers and bringing in ever more revenue.[76] Then, there's the more unfortunate campaign in 2016 to brand the State of Rhode Island. Intense social media criticism forced the state's chief marketing officer to resign after she spent more than $500,000 to develop the slogan: "Cooler & Warmer." Let's just say Rhode Island's residents were cooler rather than warmer to the idea. Of course, it didn't help that some of the footage planned for use in the accompanying tourism ad campaign actually came from Iceland.[77]

Marketing Ideas

You can see people. You can stand in a city. So how do you market something you can't see, smell, or feel? **Idea marketing** refers to strategies that seek to gain market share for a concept, philosophy, belief, or issue. Even religious organizations market ideas about faith and desirable behavior when they adopt secular marketing techniques to attract young people. Some evangelists offer slickly produced services complete with live bands and professional dancers that draw huge audiences.[78]

But make no mistake about it; the marketing of ideas can be even more difficult than marketing goods and services. Consumers often do not perceive that the *value* they receive when they recycle garbage or designate a driver or even when they conserve to reduce global warming is worth the *cost*—the extra effort necessary to realize these goals. Governments and other organizations use marketing strategies, often with only limited success, to sell ideas that will save the lives of millions of unwilling consumers or that will save our planet.

The Future of Services

As we look into the future, we recognize that service industries will continue to play a key role in the growth of both the U.S. and the global economy. 📷 Figure 12.5 provides several trends for us to consider that will provide both opportunities and challenges for the marketers of services down the road (that means you). In the future, we can expect services we can't even imagine yet. Of course, they will also provide many new and exciting job opportunities for future marketers. These trends include the following:

- *Changing demographics:* As the population ages, service industries that meet the needs of older consumers will see dramatic growth. Companies that offer recreational opportunities, health care, and living assistance for seniors will be in demand.
- *Globalization:* The globalization of business will increase the need for logistics and distribution services to move goods around the world (discussed in Chapter 11) and for accounting and legal services that facilitate these global exchanges. In addition, global deregulation will affect the delivery of services by banks, brokerages, insurance, and

Figure 12.5 [📷] *Snapshot* | Factors That Shape the Future of Services

Changing demographics, globalization, technological advances, and proliferation of information all impact services.

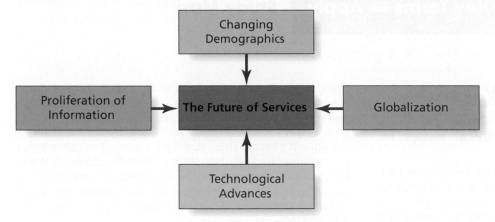

other financial service industries because globalization means greater competition. For example, many "medical tourists" now journey to countries like Thailand and India to obtain common surgical procedures that may cost less than half what they would in the U.S. Meanwhile, hospitals back home often look more like luxury spas as they offer amenities such as adjoining quarters for family members, choice of different ethnic cuisines, and in-room Internet access. In the hotel industry, demand for luxury properties is growing around the world. Hyatt Worldwide is aggressively expanding its Waldorf-Astoria and Conrad brands in China, with at least 16 luxury properties either open or scheduled to open by 2020.[79]

- *Technological advances:* Changing technology provides opportunities for growth and innovation in global service industries, such as telecommunications, health care, banking, and Internet services. And we can also expect technological advances to provide opportunities for services that we haven't even thought of yet but that will dramatically change and improve the lives of consumers.

- *Proliferation of information:* In many ways, we have become an information society. The availability of, flow of, and access to information are critical to the success of organizations. These changes will provide greater opportunities for database services, artificial intelligence systems, communications systems, and other services that facilitate the storage and transfer of knowledge.

MyLab Marketing™

Go to **mymktlab.com** to complete the problems marked with this icon ✪ as well as additional Marketing Metrics questions only available in MyLab Marketing.

Objective Summary ➡ **Key Terms** ➡ **Apply**

12.1 Objective Summary (pp. 400–407)

Define retailing, understand how retailing evolves, and consider some ethical issues in retailing.

Retailing is the process by which goods and services are sold to consumers for their personal use. The wheel-of-retailing hypothesis suggests that new retailers compete on price and over time become more upscale, leaving room for other new, low-price entrants. Four factors that motivate retailers to evolve are changing economic conditions, demographics, technology, and globalization. Changing demographics has led to the growth of M-commerce, experiential merchandising, and destination retailing while technology has brought beacon marketing, digital wallets, and omnichannel marketing to retailing. One of the ethical issues retailers face is shrinkage as a result of shoplifting, employee theft, and retail borrowing. Retailers and their employees must also be cognizant of the ethical treatment of customers.

Key Terms

retailing, p. 400

wheel-of-retailing hypothesis, p. 401

experiential merchandising, p. 403

destination retailer, p. 403

omnichannel (omni-channel) marketing, p. 404

point-of-sale (POS) systems, p. 404

perpetual inventory unit control system, p. 404

automatic reordering system, p. 404

beacon marketing, p. 404

digital wallets, p. 405

experiential shoppers, p. 405

retailtainment, p. 405

shrinkage, p. 406

organized retail crime (ORC), p. 406

retail borrowing, p. 407

customer profiling, p. 407

12.2 Objective Summary (pp. 407–413)

Understand how we classify traditional retailers.

Retailers are classified by NAICS codes based on product lines sold; however, new retail models, such as combination stores, offer consumers more than one product line. Merchandise assortment is described in terms of breadth and depth, which refer to the number of product lines sold and the amount of variety available for each. Retailers may also be classified by the level of service offered (self-service, full-service, and limited-service retailers) and by the merchandise assortment offered. Thus, stores are classified as convenience stores, supermarkets, box stores, specialty stores, category killers, leased departments, variety stores, general merchandise discount stores, off-price retailers, warehouse clubs, factory outlet stores, department stores, hypermarkets, and pop-up stores.

Key Terms

service retailers, p. 407

merchandise mix, p. 408

combination stores, p. 408

supercenters, p. 408

merchandise assortment, p. 408

merchandise breadth, p. 408

merchandise depth, p. 408

convenience stores, p. 409

supermarkets, p. 411

box stores, p. 411

specialty stores, p. 411

category killer, p. 412

leased departments, p. 412

variety stores, p. 412

general merchandise discount stores, p. 412

off-price retailers, p. 412

warehouse clubs, p. 412

factory outlet store, p. 412

department stores, p. 413

bifurcated retailing, p. 413

hypermarkets, p. 413

pop-up stores, p. 413

12.3 Objective Summary (pp. 414–419)

Describe business-to-consumer (B2C) e-commerce and the other common forms of nonstore retailing.

The three more common types of nonstore retailing are B2C e-commerce, direct selling, and automatic vending machines. B2C e-commerce, online exchanges between companies and consumers, is growing rapidly. For consumers, B2C benefits include greater convenience, greater product variety, and increased price information. For marketers, B2C offers a world market, decreased costs of doing business, opportunities for specialized businesses, and real-time pricing. The downside of B2C e-commerce for consumers includes having to wait to receive products, security issues, and the inability to touch and feel products. For Internet-only marketers, success on the Internet may be difficult to achieve, whereas cannibalization may be a problem with traditional retailers' online operations.

In direct selling, a salesperson presents a product to one individual or a small group, takes orders, and delivers the merchandise. Direct selling includes door-to-door sales, party or network sales, and multilevel marketing (network marketing). State-of-the-art self-service vending machines can dispense products from live crabs to draft beers.

Key Terms

nonstore retailing, p. 414

B2C e-commerce, p. 414

M-commerce, p. 414

virtual experiential marketing, p. 415

shopping cart abandonment, p. 416

direct selling, p. 418

Green River Ordinances, p. 418

party plan system, p. 418

multilevel or network marketing, p. 418

pyramid schemes, p. 418

12.4 Objective Summary (pp. 419–427)

Understand the marketing of services and other intangibles.

Services are products that are intangible and that are exchanged directly from producer to customer without ownership rights. Generally, services are acts that accomplish some goal and may be directed either toward people or toward an object. Important service characteristics include the following:

(1) intangibility, (2) perishability, (3) variability, and (4) inseparability from the producer.

Marketers know that both the social elements of the service encounter (i.e., the employee and the customer) and the physical evidence, including the servicescape, are important to a positive service experience. To measure service quality, marketers use the SERVQUAL scale, which measures five dimensions of service quality: tangibles, reliability, responsiveness, assurance, and empathy. Gap analysis, a related measurement, gauges the difference between a customer's expectation of service quality and what actually occurs.

Managers follow the steps for marketing planning when marketing other intangibles as well. People, especially politicians and celebrities, are often packaged and promoted. Place marketing aims to create or change the market position of a particular locale, whether a city, state, country, resort, or institution. Idea marketing (gaining market share for a concept, philosophy, belief, or issue) seeks to create or change a target market's attitude or behavior. The future of services will be determined by changing demographics, globalization, technological advances, and the proliferation of information.

Key Terms

intangibles, p. 419

services, p. 420

intangibility, p. 420

perishability, p. 420

capacity management, p. 420

variability, p. 421

inseparability, p. 421

service encounter, p. 421

disintermediation, p. 421

servicescape, p. 422

SERVQUAL, p. 424

gap analysis, p. 424

place marketing, p. 426

idea marketing, p. 426

Chapter **Questions** and **Activities**

MyLab Marketing™

Go to **mymktlab.com** to watch this chapter's Rising Star video(s) for career advice and to respond to questions.

Concepts: Test Your Knowledge

12-1. Define retailing. What is the role of retailing in today's world?

12-2. How does the wheel-of-retailing theory explain the evolution of retailing? How do the economic environment, demographics, technology, and globalization affect the future of retailing?

12-3. Describe experiential merchandising, destination retailing and omnichannel marketing.

12-4. What is beacon marketing? What are digital wallets?

12-5. Explain retail store shrinkage and the ways shrinkage normally occurs. What is "sweehearting"? What is retail borrowing? What are some of the ethical issues in retailers' treatment of consumers?

12-6. How do marketers classify retail stores? Explain merchandise breadth and depth.

12-7. Describe the differences in merchandise assortments for convenience stores, supermarkets, box stores, specialty stores, category killers, leased departments, variety stores, general merchandise discount stores, off-price retailers, warehouse clubs, factory outlet stores, department stores, hypermarkets, and pop-up stores.

12-8. Explain the different types of direct selling. What is the difference between multilevel marketing and a pyramid scheme?

12-9. What is B2C e-commerce? What are some benefits of B2C e-commerce for consumers and for marketers? What are the limitations of B2C e-commerce?

12-10. What are some possible effects of B2C e-commerce on traditional retailing?

12-11. What are intangibles? How do basic marketing concepts apply to the marketing of intangibles?

12-12. What is a service? What are the important characteristics of services that make them different from goods?

12-13. What dimensions do consumers and business customers use to evaluate service quality? How should marketers respond to failures in service quality?

12-14. What do we mean by marketing people? Marketing places? Marketing ideas?

Activities: Apply What You've Learned

★12-15. *Creative Homework/Short Project* Assume you are an entrepreneur who is seeking funding to start up your new retail business specializing in handcrafted fair-trade artisan goods from developing and least developed countries. Customers would be able to acquire a unique product and at the same time receive a good feeling knowing that a portion of the price paid for the product would go toward the people who produced the product earning a living wage. How might you merchandise the product to provide an experience for your customers?

12-16. *Creative Homework/Short Project* Assume that you are the director of marketing for a national chain of convenience stores. Your firm has about 200 stores located in 43 states. The stores are fairly traditional both in design and in the merchandise they carry. Because you want to be proactive in your marketing planning, you are concerned that your firm may need to consider making significant changes because of the current economic, demographic, technological, and global trends in the marketplace. You think it is important to discuss these things with the other executives at your firm. Develop a presentation that includes the following:

a. A discussion of the economic changes that might impact your stores

b. A discussion of the demographic changes that will impact your stores

c. A discussion of the technological changes that will impact your stores

d. A discussion of how global changes may provide problems and opportunities for your organization

e. Your recommendations for how your firm might meet the challenges faced in each of these areas

12-17. *In Class, 10–25 Minutes for Teams* Retailers are faced with the problem of shrinkage and what to do about it. Shrinkage comes, of course, from shoplifting and employee theft. Subtler, however, is shrinkage that involves customers, such as "sweethearting" and "retail borrowing." Many consumers feel that such practices are okay. Conduct a short survey of

students in your group to study these two sources of shrinkage. You might want to include questions about the following:

a. If and how frequently students engage in such practices

b. The attitudes of students as to whether such practices are unethical and why or why not

c. What harm comes from such practices

d. What respondents think retailers should do to prevent such shrinkage

Develop a short report on your findings and present it to your class.

★12-18. *Creative Homework/Short Project* You just started working for a firm that makes and sells baseball caps. Currently, the firm sells its products only in specialty stores, like Lids. You think you can improve sales by branching out to other types of retailers. Prepare a presentation that identifies the additional types of retailers your firm could sell to and what the advantages of selling to those types of retailers would be. Also, how would you change your retail strategy for these different retailers?

12-19. *For Further Research (Individual):* One problem that traditional retailers face when they open online stores is cannibalization. Select a traditional retailer where you and your fellow students might normally shop that also sells products online. You might, for example, select Best Buy, Banana Republic, Gap, Walmart, or Target. Visit the retailer's online store and make notes on the site's product offering, pricing, customer service policies, and so on. (If the store you have chosen offers many different product lines, you might wish to limit your research to one or two different product lines.) Then visit the store and compare what is offered there with the online offerings. Develop a report that summarizes your findings and discusses the potential for cannibalization and its implications for the retailer. Also, discuss any changes in either the online or store strategies that you would recommend.

12-20. *Creative Homework/Short Project* Because of increased competition in its community, you have been hired as a marketing consultant by a local day spa. You know that the spa's quality is judged by both the service provide and the goods (food). The characteristics of services (intangibility, perishability, variability, and inseparability) create unique marketing challenges, however, these challenges can be met with creative marketing strategies. Outline the challenges for marketing the spa created by each of the four characteristics of services. List your ideas for what might be done to meet each of these challenges.

12-21. *In Class, 10–25 Minutes for Teams* You are currently a customer for a college education, an expensive service product. You know that a service organization can create a competitive advantage by focusing on how the service is delivered after it has been purchased—making sure the service is efficiently and comfortably delivered to the customer. Develop a list of recommendations for your school for improving the delivery of its service. Consider both classroom and non-classroom aspects of the educational product.

12-22. *In Class, 15–20 Minutes for Teams* One way that retailers are still a relevant and attractive alternative to Internet-based shopping is when they become destination retailers.

Explain what a destination retailer means and provide some examples that you aware of.

If you opened a shoe store, what are some of the design and in-store facilities you could offer to ensure that you become a destination retailer? Do you think that this would provide a sufficient competitive advantage over online shoe retailers?

12-23. *In Class, 15–20 Minutes for Teams* A key challenge with the marketing of services is that they are intangible. Service firms that have retail outlets design their servicescape appropriately to help communicate their overall service quality and attract potential customers (which falls under the marketing mix element of physical evidence).

Think about the different types of restaurants that you have visited. How have they used the various elements of their servicescape to highlight their offering and service quality and attract new customers? How important do you think the servicescape is for a service provider such as a restaurant?

Choices: What Do You Think?

12-24. *Critical Thinking* Most retail store shrinkage can be attributed to shoplifting, employee theft, and retail borrowing. What are some ways that retail store managers can limit or stop shrinkage? What are some problems inherent in security practices? Should retailers create stricter merchandise return policies?

⭐**12-25.** *Ethics* Studies have shown—and court rulings have confirmed—that "customer profiling" does take place in U.S. retail stores, whether or not intentional. Have you ever been the victim of profiling? Have you ever seen a customer treated in such a way that you would assume he or she was a victim of profiling? What were the circumstances? Did you make a complaint? Why or why not? As the store manager of an employee who is accused of profiling, what actions would you take for both the customer and the employee?

⭐**12-26.** *Critical Thinking* Experts predict the future of B2C e-commerce to be very rosy indeed, with exponential increases in Internet sales of some product categories within the next few years. What effect do you think the growth of e-retailing will have on traditional retailing? Do you think we will have a future of empty malls and stores? In what ways will this be good for consumers, and in what ways will it not be so good?

12-27. *Critical Thinking* Most U.S. consumers have purchased a product online at one time or another. What products have you ever purchased online? How did you pay for these products? Do you consider a site's security methods at the time of purchase? Why or why not? Should retailers be required to post information about how they're keeping your information secure? How should retailers be held accountable if the personal information they keep on you is hacked?

12-28. *Critical Thinking* Disintermediation is becoming more commonplace in the service industry, often eliminating a customer's interaction with, for example, bank tellers or supermarket clerks. How does this lack of interaction affect the customer's experience? How does this lack of interaction affect a firm's ability to provide superior customer service?

12-29. *Critical Thinking* Sometimes service quality may not meet customers' expectations. What problems have you experienced with quality in the delivery of the following services?
   a. A haircut
   b. A dental visit
   c. Computer repairs
   d. Your college education
What do you think is the reason for the poor quality? How would you improve the quality of service?

12-30. *Critical Thinking* There has been a lot of criticism about the way politicians have been marketed in recent years. What are some of the ways marketing has helped our political process? What are some ways the marketing of politicians might have an adverse effect on our government?

12-31. *Ethics* Many not-for-profit and religious organizations have found that they can be more successful by marketing their ideas. What are some ways that these organizations market themselves that are similar to and different from the marketing by for-profit businesses? Is it *ethical* for churches and religious organizations to spend money on marketing? Why or why not?

12-32. *Critical Thinking* Many developed countries, including the U.S., have in recent decades become primarily service economies; that is, there is relatively little manufacturing of goods, and most people in the economy are employed by service industries. Why do you think this has occurred? In what ways is this trend a good and/or a bad thing for a country? Do you think this trend will continue?

Concepts: Apply Marketing Metrics

Inventory management is an important aspect of retail strategy. For example, it is important to know *when* it is time to reorder and *how much* to order at a time, a metric called *reorder point*.

As consumers buy a product day after day, the inventory level declines. The question for retailers is how low they should allow the inventory level to decline before they place an order; that is, when is the optimal time to reorder? If you order too late, you take a chance of losing sales because you are out of stock. If you order too soon, consumer tastes may change, and you will be stuck with excess and unsellable merchandise. And generally, retailers do not want more inventory on hand than is necessary to avoid stock-outs because inventory ties up cash.

Hence, the decision of when to order and how much to order is critical to a retailer's bottom line. The simplest formula to determine the reorder point is the following:

$$\text{Reorder point} \times \text{Usage rate} + \text{Lead time}$$

Usage rate is basically how quickly the inventory sells, and lead time is the length of time from reorder to delivery. Retailers tend to keep a little extra stock on hand—"safety stock"—just in case their historical data on usage rate and lead time might vary from any one particular reorder experience. Adding in safety stock, the formula becomes the following:

$$\text{Reorder point} \times (\text{Usage rate} \times \text{Lead time}) + \text{Safety stock}$$

Sam's 24-Hour Gas 'n' Sip sells 97 large sodas a day. It takes five days to place an order and receive a new shipment of large cups. But to be prepared for the possibility of extra sales or a late shipment, they need to have a safety stock equal to three days of sales.

⭐**12-33.** What is the reorder point for large cups for Sam's gas station?

Miniproject: Learn by Doing

Miniproject 1

Select a good that you, as a consumer, would like to purchase in the next week or so. Shop for this product both online and at a physical retailer.

12-34. As you shop, record the details of both shopping experiences, including the following:
  a. Type of retailer
  b. Clerks available to assist you
  c. Website or physical facilities
  d. Product variety
  e. Product availability
  f. Product price
  g. Store hours
  h. Ease of transaction
  i. Ease of return

12-35. Explain why you would be more likely to purchase this product online or at a physical retailer in the future.

Miniproject 2

The wheel-of-retailing theory (refer to Figure 12.1) suggests that retailers change their overall strategy over time as they become more established. Your task for this mini project is to conduct Internet-based research into three well-established retail chains. Review their history, which is often provided in an "About Us" page on their website, to determine where and when they were originally established and what their retail strategy (that is, merchandise, service levels, servicescape, pricing) was at that time. You may also be able to find additional information from older newspaper and magazine articles and even older advertisements for the retailer on the Internet.

12-36. To what extent have these retailers' strategies evolved over time? To what extent are their in-store offerings, range of merchandise, pricing, service levels, etc. different to when they first started their retail chain? To what extent is their development over time consistent with the wheel-of-retailing model provided in the chapter?

12-37. Given your responses above, how helpful is the wheel-of-retailing model in describing the evolution of retailers over time? That is, did the three retail firms that you reviewed generally follow the model? Do you think that this model is more applicable to certain types of retailers? How helpful would this model be in helping guide the future direction of a retailer?

Marketing in **Action** Case   Real Choices at Alibaba

When you're already big it can be hard to get bigger. That's why Alibaba is working hard to continue to expand its e-tailing empire.

In 1999, Jack Ma, inspired by a trip to the U.S. where he first encountered the Internet, led a group of 17 friends to form Alibaba.com. Initially, the website was a business-to-business portal to bring together Chinese exporters, manufacturers, and entrepreneurs with overseas buyers. Today, the Alibaba Group, often called the Chinese Amazon, is a leading online and mobile marketplace in retail and wholesale trade, cloud computing, and other services. As of 2016, the group's retail businesses had more than 423 million active users, 12.7 million annual orders in its marketplace, and 86.2 percent of the Chinese mobile shopping market.

According to research by McKinsey Digital, only 19 percent of rural China is using online buying services. Due to the constraints of lower incomes, dispersed populations, and poor logistics, rural traditional retail options are limited, have higher prices, and inferior product quality. These limitations make for tremendous prospects for expansion of online sales. To take advantage of this opportunity, Alibaba's e-commerce business, Taobao, has opened service centers in many rural villages. There, residents can search for deals on products like mobile phones, toothpaste, apparel, and more using company-provided computers. To implement this strategy, Alibaba has committed to investing over USD$1.5 billion on logistics, hardware, and training in more than 100,000 villages.

Michael Evans, President of Alibaba, says "Globalization is a critical strategy for the growth of Alibaba Group today and well into the future." E-commerce accounts for less than 1 percent of retail sales in Southeast Asia, compared with 6 percent in Europe and 8 percent in China and the U.S., according to data from consulting firm A.T. Kearney. Credit Suisse, a multinational financial services company, found that as a share of total retail sales, e-commerce may soon be larger in emerging markets than in developed countries. They assert that nearly 1 billion online shoppers will emerge in these markets in the next few years.

The company recently acquired a controlling stake in Singapore e-commerce firm, the Lazada Group, which operates e-commerce portals in other Asian countries including Indonesia, Malaysia, the Philippines, Singapore, Thailand, and Vietnam. The portals are online shopping and selling destinations that offer mobile and web access, multiple payment methods, customer care, and free returns. Alibaba will be able to contribute its extensive infrastructure and advanced logistics abilities to Lazada. The shared tools and knowledge are important because parts of Southeast Asia do not have the necessary distribution networks and information technology management.

Of course, there are still challenges for the Alibaba Group. The company's home market of China is struggling with slowing development as the overall economy faces some challenges. Expansion means dealing with Southeast Asia's weak infrastructure and slower Internet speeds. Alibaba also faces growing competition. Western competitors such as Amazon.com and eBay.com are less of a threat that homegrown competitors. These include Tencent, primarily an entertainment and social media company, that is getting into e-commerce; JD.com, more like Amazon.com involving direct sales, holding inventory, and managing logistics and shipping; and Baidu, China's dominant Internet-search engine, that is very similar to Google in both services and products.

You Make the Call

12-38. What is the decision facing Alibaba?

12-39. What factors are important in understanding this decision situation?

12-40. What are the alternatives?

12-41. What decision(s) do you recommend?

12-42. What are some ways to implement your recommendation?

Based on: Dexter Roberts and Lulu Yilun Chen, "China's Hunt for Growth in the Countryside," *Bloomberg Businessweek* (August 27, 2015), http://www.bloomberg.com/news/articles/2015-08-27/china-s-hunt-for-growth-in-the-countryside (accessed May 1, 2016); "History and Milestones," *Alibaba Group*, http://www.alibabagroup.com/en/about/history (accessed May 1, 2016); Alyssa Abkowitz and Newley Purnell, "Alibaba to Invest $1 Billion in E-Commerce Startup Lazada," *Wall Street Journal* (April 13, 2016), http://www.wsj.com/articles/alibaba-to-invest-1-billion-in-e-commerce-startup-lazada-1460445117 (accessed May 1, 2016); Prableen Bajpai, CFA (ICDAI), "Alibaba's Top Competitors," Investopedia http://www.investopedia.com/articles/investing/110714/alibabas-top-competitors.asp (accessed May 17, 2016).

MyLab Marketing™

Go to **mymktlab.com** for the following assisted-graded writing questions:

12-43. Today, traditional brick-and-mortar retailers are faced with competition from B2C e-commerce. What are some of the benefits and limitations of B2C e-commerce?

12-44. In this chapter, we learned that the characteristics of services are intangibility, perishability, variability, and inseparability. Explain each of these characteristics and how they create challenges for marketing services.

Promotion I: Advertising and Sales Promotion

Courtesy of Sara Bamossy, Pitch

Sara Bamossy

▼ **A Decision Maker at the Pitch Agency**

Sara Bamossy is Chief Strategy Officer of Pitch, a full-service advertising agency in Los Angeles. She brings a broad range of brand and retail experience on global clients including Toyota, P&G, Burger King, Netflix, Waldorf Astoria, and Nestlé. Sara's specialty is a deep understanding of a wide range of consumer groups and she has been consulted by publications such as *Advertising Age* and *Forbes* for her expertise on Millennials and Boomers. Sara's strategic thinking has inspired campaigns that have earned numerous industry awards including the Effies and Cannes Lions. She graduated summa cum laude from UCLA with a BA in Marketing and Communications. She also completed the distinguished EPWL program at Stanford's Graduate School of Business. Sara's personal metric for a well-lived life is a passport full of stamps. She loves travel, as well as coming home again to approach everything with fresh eyes and new ideas.

Sara's Info

What I do when I'm not working:
Yoga, Netflix, reading on the beach

First job out of school:
In high school I worked at the Gallup Poll doing market research surveys … and the rest is history.

Career high:
As someone who loves my job it's hard to pick! I still remember the first time I was sent to Japan to test drive prototype cars as a young strategist leading a vehicle launch…. it was a pinch-myself-to-make-sure-this-is-real career moment.

A job-related mistake I wish I hadn't made:
Leaving a specific role that wasn't right for me sooner; I knew in my heart and in my mind it wasn't right after three months and I muscled on for too long.

Business book I'm reading now:
Yes Please by Amy Poehler.

My hero:
It would be amazing to be reincarnated as a superhuman combination of JK Rowling, Gwen Stefani, and Tina Fey.

My motto to live by:
If you don't have a clear goal in life, you are destined to work for someone who does.

What drives me:
The thrill of solving a complicated problem.

My management style:
Chameleon Coach. I prefer strengths-based management style that best fits each individual's needs.

Don't do this when interviewing with me:
Tell me that you view the role as just a short-term stop on your career path.

My pet peeve:
Wasting time (see also: being unprepared, making excuses, finger pointing)

Here's my problem...

Real People, Real Choices

After a series of enormously successful business decisions across promotions, operations, and menu innovation, Burger King was posting U.S. sales gains when competitors were failing or stagnant. By mid-2015 Burger King was outperforming McDonald's and Wendy's by significant margins in sales. However, the brand was lagging its main competitors in imagery. In the third quarter we turned our attention to refining our advertising strategy and optimizing communications.

Mass communications for quick-serve restaurants (QSRs) must drive traffic quickly, often to promote specific menu items with immediate and ambitious sales gains. We needed to find a way to develop and implement long-range brand planning within the business reality of this fast-moving industry. My role was to create a strategy that would enable Burger King to tell a consistent brand story with the flexibility to support a wide range of new and core menu items across all day parts. BK has always been known and loved for "Have it Your Way," flame-grilling, and the Whopper. As the brand evolved, The King was introduced to bring a younger audience and later he was retired in favor of a broader reaching "Taste is King" campaign. The question became, what's next for BK marketing?

As CSO (Chief Strategy Officer) of Pitch, I partnered with Burger King North America on an action plan to get us to the ultimate strategy, with inputs from data mining, consumer research, and competitive analysis. Along the way we reached a key decision point for the Burger King brand: Should we bring back The King or find a new road? Should Burger King's new long-range strategy take advantage of latent equity in a past icon?

Sara considered her Options 1·2

1
Option

Leave The King in the past where he belongs. The QSR landscape, the economy, and consumer attitudes toward fast food had all evolved since Burger King stopped using The King in 2011. The rise of fast casual dining options (like Chipotle), health macro trends (clean eating, organic), and fast meal behavior changes (i.e., Starbucks and meal replacement bars) all impacted the fast-food industry. Also, even at the height of his popularity, The King was a bit tricky as a company spokesman. When depictions were not carefully crafted, he became "creepy" and relevant to a narrow audience of Millennial men. His edgy persona differentiated him among this group, because as a brand icon he was a part of pop culture and a departure from the typical overly wholesome "mascots" many companies use. Clearly, during the time of his reign The King was a well-recognized advertising icon, but he was not an automatic traffic driver. Some people thought he had nothing to do with where they're going to eat lunch today.

On the other hand, it is difficult to create a brand new icon from scratch. If a QSR brand doesn't have highly identifiable brand markers (think Ronald McDonald or Wendy), customers can easily misattribute its mass communications to similar products—so you wind up advertising for the competition. The King was like a giant sponge that sucked up *earned media coverage* (exposure as a result of natural publicity rather than paid advertising) and kept Burger King in the pop-culture spotlight. That kind of exposure is hard to replicate.

2
Option

Bring back The King as an instantly recognizable icon. The King still had high awareness even after several years away from the spotlight. Using The King boosts brand attribution, especially for promotions. As an icon, he has the potential to drive PR and buzz when he authentically and organically fits into pop-culture moments. Using a brand icon is one of the fastest ways to optimize media impact because he brings an instant branding kick.

On the other hand, brand spokespeople (even imagined ones) need to be very carefully crafted and follow strictly adhered-to guidelines or they can become gimmicks. By the end of his reign in 2011, the use of The King in messaging was no longer directly tied to business and brand needs. A perception existed that The King had become overexposed by the time he retired. To take full advantage of The King's earned media potential, the brand must be willing to make and act on decisions *very quickly* to take full advantage of a constantly churning Internet news cycle. That would mean resuscitating a new and improved King who would be able to rule over a kingdom that's shaped by unpredictable social media trends rather than the predictable television campaigns of days past.

Now put yourself in Sara's shoes.

You Choose

Which **Option** would you choose, and **why**?

☐ **Option 1**   ☐ **Option 2**

See what **option** Sara chose in **MyLab Marketing™**

MyLab Marketing™

⭐ **Improve Your Grade!**

Over 10 million students improved their results using the Pearson MyLabs.
Visit **mymktlab.com** for simulations, tutorials, and end-of-chapter problems.

13.1 Communication Models in a Digital World That Is "Always On"

OBJECTIVE

Understand the communication process and the traditional promotion mix.

(pp. 436–442)

Test your advertising memory:*

1. Which fast-food chain encourages you to "Live Más"?
2. What product advertises that you can "Go Commando?"
3. What hair product brand says "Because you're worth it"?
4. What pet food "Tastes so good, cats ask for it by name?"
5. Which credit card says, "There are some things money can't buy. For everything else, there's …"

Did you get them all right? You owe your knowledge about these and a thousand other trivia questions to the efforts of people who specialize in marketing communication. Of course today, these slogans are "old school" as marketers have followed consumers onto Facebook and Twitter and into virtual worlds to talk with their customers.

So far, we've talked about creating, managing, pricing, and delivering products. But it's not enough just to produce great products—successful marketing plans must also provide effective marketing communication strategies. As we said in Chapter 1, *promotion* is the coordination of marketing communication efforts to influence attitudes or behavior. This function is the last of the famous *four Ps* of the marketing mix, and it plays a vital role—whether the goal is to sell hamburgers, insurance, ringtones, or healthy diets. Of course, virtually *everything* an organization says and does is a form of marketing communication. The ads it creates, the packages it designs, the uniforms its employees wear, and what other consumers say about their experiences with the brand contribute to the thoughts and feelings people have of the company and its products. Today, what both the company and others say in the digital world plays an increasingly important role in the marketing communication process. Just what do we mean by communication? Today, messages assume many forms: quirky TV commercials, innovative websites, viral videos, blogs, Internet advertising, mobile apps, social media sites, sophisticated magazine ads, funky T-shirts, blimps blinking messages over football stadiums—even do-it-yourself, customer-made advertising on the Super Bowl broadcast. Some marketing communications push specific products (like the Apple iPad) or actions (like donating blood), whereas others try to create or reinforce an image that represents the entire organization (like General Electric or the Catholic Church).

Marketing communication in general performs one or more of four roles:

1. It *informs* consumers about new goods and services.
2. It *reminds* consumers to continue using certain brands.
3. It *persuades* consumers to choose one brand over others.
4. It *builds* relationships with customers.

Today, marketing experts believe a successful promotion strategy should coordinate diverse forms of marketing communication to deliver a consistent message. **Integrated marketing communication (IMC)** is the process that marketers use "to plan, develop, execute, and evaluate coordinated, measurable, persuasive brand communication programs over time to targeted audiences."[1] The IMC approach argues that consumers come in contact with a company or a brand in many different ways before,

integrated marketing communication (IMC)

A strategic business process that marketers use to plan, develop, execute, and evaluate coordinated, measurable, persuasive brand communication programs over time to targeted audiences.

* Answers: (1) Taco Bell, (2) Cottonelle toilet paper, (3) L'Oréal hair products, (4) Meow Mix cat food, (5) MasterCard.

after, and during a purchase. Consumers see these points of contact—a TV commercial, a company website, a coupon, an opportunity to win a sweepstakes, or a display in a store—as a whole, as a single company that speaks to them in different places and different ways.

To achieve their marketing communication goals, marketers must selectively use some or all of these to deliver a consistent message to their customers in a **multichannel promotion strategy** where they combine traditional marketing communication activities (advertising, sales promotion, public relations, and direct marketing) with social media and other online buzz-building activities. That's a lot different from most traditional marketing communication programs of the past that made little effort to coordinate the varying messages consumers received. When a TV advertising campaign runs independently of a sweepstakes, which in turn has no relation to a NASCAR racing sponsorship, consumers often get conflicting messages that leave them confused and unsure of the brand's identity. We'll talk more about multichannel strategies later in this chapter.

To better understand marketing communications today, let's look at the three different models of marketing communication, as shown in 📷 Figure 13.1. The first, the traditional communication model, is a "one-to-many" view in which a single marketer develops and sends messages to many, perhaps even millions of, consumers at once. The one-to-many approach involves traditional forms of marketing communication, such as *advertising*, including traditional mass media (TV, radio, magazines, and newspapers); *out-of-home*, such as billboards; and Internet advertising, such as banners and pop-ups. This model also

multichannel promotion strategy
A marketing communication strategy where they combine traditional advertising, sales promotion, and public relations activities with online buzz-building activities.

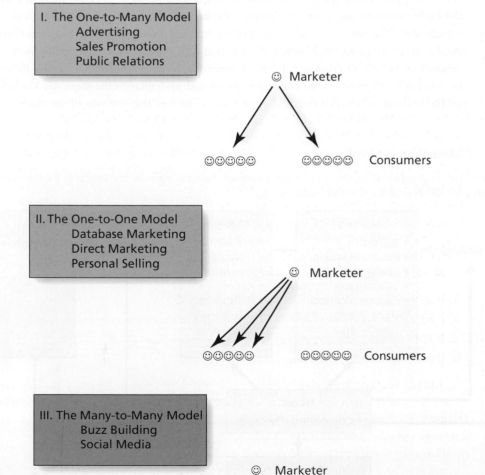

Figure 13.1 📷 *Snapshot* |
Three Models of Marketing Communication

Marketers today make use of the traditional one-to-many communication model and the updated many-to-many communication model as well as talking one to one with consumers and business customers.

benefits from *consumer sales promotions*, such as coupons, samples, rebates, or contests, and press releases and special events that *public relations* professionals organize.

We also need to expand our traditional communication model to include the *one-to-one model*, where marketers speak to consumers and business customers individually. The one-to-one forms of marketing communication include *personal selling, trade sales promotion activities* used to support personal selling, and a variety of *database marketing* activities that include direct marketing.

In today's "always on" world that we discussed in Chapter 1, the importance of the *updated* "many-to-many" model of marketing communication increases exponentially. This newer perspective recognizes the huge impact of social media and its use in **word-of-mouth communication**, where consumers look to each other for information and recommendations. Many of us are more likely to choose a new restaurant based on users' reviews we read on Yelp than because we saw a cool commercial for the place on TV.

In the updated model, marketers add new tools to their communications toolbox, including *buzz-building* activities that use *viral* and *evangelical marketing techniques* as well as new social media platforms, such as *brand communities, product review sites*, and *social networking sites* where consumers talk to lots of other consumers. The odds are you're using many of these platforms already. In this chapter and the following one, we'll examine each of these three different ways to communicate with our customers.

word-of-mouth communication
When consumers provide information about products to other consumers.

The Communication Model

communication model
The process whereby meaning is transferred from a source to a receiver.

Of course, promotion strategies can succeed only if we are able to get customers to understand what we're trying to say. The **communication model** in Figure 13.2 is a good way to understand the basics of how any kind of message works—from you telling your friends about your great spring break in Key West to that little green gecko telling millions of consumers to buy GEICO insurance. In this perspective, a *source* transmits a *message* through some *medium* to a *receiver* who (we hope) listens and understands the message. Marketers need to understand the function and importance of each of the elements of the model.

Figure 13.2 *Process* | Communication Model

The communication model explains how organizations create and transmit messages from the marketer (the source) to the consumer (the receiver) who (we hope) understands what the marketer intends to say.

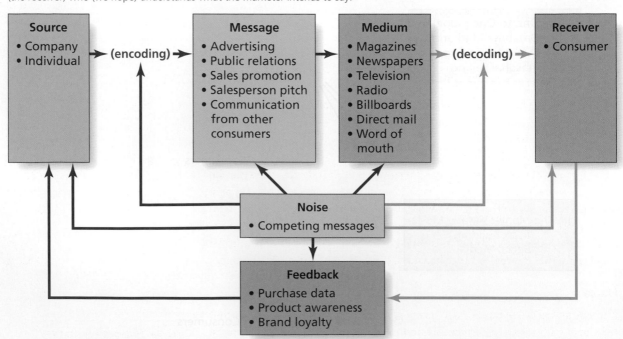

The Source Encodes

Let's start to explore this basic model from a good place: the beginning. First, there is a person or organization—the **source**—that has an idea it wants to communicate to a receiver, such as potential customers. To do this, the source must translate the idea into a physically perceivable form (like a TV commercial) that conveys the desired meaning. This **encoding** process means the source may translate the idea into different forms to convey the desired meaning. We may just use words, music, a celebrity (Ashton Kutcher for Nikon cameras or Sofia Vergara for Cover Girl Cosmetics[2]), an unknown actor, an actual customer or even that animated gecko to speak to consumers.

The Message

The **message** is the actual content of that physically perceivable form of communication that goes from the source to a receiver. The message may be in the form of advertising, public relations, sales promotion, a salesperson's pitch, a direct marketing infomercial, a Facebook post, a video on YouTube, or a customer's comment on a blog. It includes (hopefully) the information necessary to persuade, inform, remind, or build a relationship. The marketer must select the ad elements carefully so that the message connects with end consumers or business customers in its target market.

The Medium

No matter how the source encodes the message, it must then transmit that message via a **medium**, a communication vehicle that reaches members of a target audience. For marketers, this vehicle can be TV, radio, social media sites such as Facebook or Twitter, a magazine, a company website, an Internet blog, a billboard, or even a coffee mug that displays a product logo. Marketers face two major challenges when they select a medium: first, that the target market will be exposed to the medium, and second, that the characteristics of the product are not in conflict with the medium.

The Receiver Decodes

If a tree falls in the forest and no one hears it, did it make a sound? Zen mysteries aside, communication cannot occur unless a **receiver** is there to get the message. The receiver is any individual or organization that intercepts and interprets the message. **Decoding** is the process whereby a receiver assigns meaning to a message; that is, he or she translates the message he or she sees or hears back into an idea that makes sense to him or her.

Marketers hope that the target consumer will decode the message the way they intended, but effective communication occurs only when the source and the receiver have had similar experiences and thus share a mutual frame of reference. Too often, sources and receivers aren't on the same page, a mismatch that is especially likely to happen when the source and the receiver don't share the same cultural background, experiences, values, or language.

Noise

The communication model also acknowledges that **noise**—anything that interferes with effective communication—can block messages. As the many

Campbell's uses the familiar symbolism of a gold star to encode a desired meaning.

source
An organization or individual that sends a message.

A simple and straightforward message.

encoding
The process of translating an idea into a form of communication that will convey meaning.

message
The communication in physical form that goes from a sender to a receiver.

medium
A communication vehicle through which a message is transmitted to a target audience.

receiver
The organization or individual that intercepts and interprets the message.

decoding
The process by which a receiver assigns meaning to the message.

noise
Anything that interferes with effective communication.

feedback
Receivers' reactions to the message.

promotion mix
The communication elements that the marketer controls.

mass communication
Relates to TV, radio, magazines, and newspapers.

Surrender, tough messes. Conquer them with our thick wipes.

For effective decoding to occur, the source and the receiver must share a mutual frame of reference. In this ad the receiver needs to understand the meaning of a "white flag" in order for the message to make sense.

arrows between noise and the other elements of the communication model in Figure 13.2 indicate, this interference can occur at any stage of communication.

Feedback

To complete the communication loop, the source gets **feedback** from receivers. Of course, the best feedback for marketing communication is for consumers to purchase the product. Other types of feedback occur with a phone call or an e-mail to the manufacturer. More often, though, marketers must actively seek their customers' feedback through marketing research.

The Traditional Promotion Mix

As we said previously, promotion, or marketing communication, is one of the famous four Ps. Marketers use the term **promotion mix** to refer to the communication elements that the marketer controls. The elements of the traditional promotion mix include the following:

- Advertising
- Sales promotion
- Public relations
- Personal selling
- Direct marketing

Promotion works best when the marketer skillfully combines all of the elements of the promotion mix to deliver a single consistent message about a brand. Table 13.1 presents some of the pros and cons of each element of the traditional promotion mix.

In addition, the promotion mix must work in harmony with the overall *marketing mix* to combine elements of promotion with place, price, and product to position the firm's offering in people's minds. For example, marketers must design ads for luxury products such as Rolex watches or Jaguar automobiles to communicate that same luxury character of the product, and the ads should appear in places that reinforce that upscale image. A chic commercial that appears during the commercial breaks of an episode of *Swamp People* or *Duck Dynasty* just won't cut it.

Marketers have a lot more control over some kinds of marketing communication messages than they do over others. As 📷 Figure 13.3 shows, *mass-media advertising* and *sales promotion* are at one end of the continuum, where the marketer has total control over the message he or she delivers. At the other end is *word-of-mouth (WOM) communication*, where everyday people rather than the company run the show. WOM includes the social media that consumers use today to keep in touch with friends and potentially millions of other consumers. Sandwiched between the ends we find *personal selling* and *direct marketing*, where marketers have some but not total control over the message they deliver, and *public relations*, where marketers have even less control.

Mass Communication: The One-to-Many Model

Some elements of the promotion mix include messages intended to reach many prospective customers at the same time. Whether a company offers customers a coupon for 50 cents off or airs a TV commercial to millions, it promotes itself to a mass audience. These are the elements of the promotion mix that use traditional **mass communication**, that is, TV radio, magazines, and newspapers:

Table 13.1 | A Comparison of Elements of the Traditional Promotion Mix

Promotion Element	Pros	Cons
Advertising	• The marketer has control over what the message will say, when it will appear, and who is likely to see it.	• Because of the high cost to produce and distribute, it may not be an efficient means of communicating with some target audiences. • Some ads may have low credibility or be ignored by the audience.
Sales promotion	• Provides incentives to retailers to support one's products. • Builds excitement for retailers and consumers. • Encourages immediate purchase and trial of new products. • Price-oriented promotions cater to price-sensitive consumers.	• Short-term emphasis on immediate sales rather than a focus on building brand loyalty. • The number of competing promotions may make it hard to break through the promotion clutter. • If marketers use too many price-related sales promotion activities, consumers' perception of a fair price for the brand may be lowered.
Public relations	• Relatively low cost. • High credibility.	• Lack of control over the message that is eventually transmitted and no guarantee that the message will ever reach the target. • It is difficult to measure the effectiveness of public relations efforts.
Personal selling	• Direct contact with the customer gives the salesperson the opportunity to be flexible and modify the sales message to coincide with the customer's needs. • The salesperson can get immediate feedback from the customer.	• High cost per contact with customer. • Difficult to ensure consistency of message when it is delivered by many different company representatives. • The credibility of salespeople often depends on the quality of their company's image, which has been created by other promotion strategies.
Direct marketing	• Targets specific groups of potential customers with different offers. • Marketers can easily measure the results. • Provides extensive product information and multiple offers within a single appeal. • Provides a way for a company to collect feedback about the effectiveness of its messages in an internal database.	• Consumers may have a negative opinion of some types of direct marketing. • Costs more per contact than mass appeals.

Figure 13.3 📷 *Snapshot* | Control Continuum

The messages that consumers receive about companies and products differ in terms of how much the marketer can control the content.

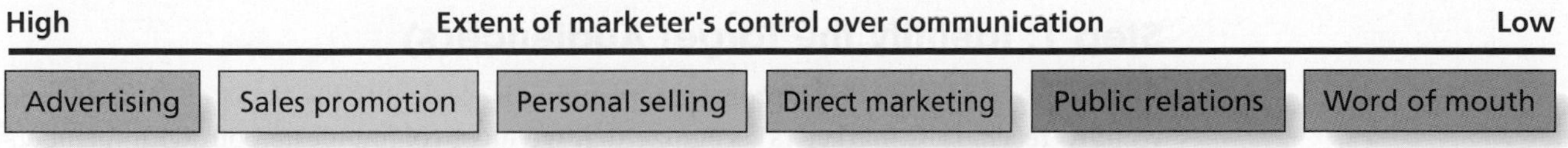

High	Extent of marketer's control over communication				Low
Advertising	Sales promotion	Personal selling	Direct marketing	Public relations	Word of mouth

- *Advertising:* Advertising is, for many, the most familiar and visible element of the promotion mix. Advertising reaches large numbers of consumers at one time and can convey rich and dynamic images that establish and reinforce a distinctive brand identity. Advertising also is useful to communicate factual information about the product or to remind consumers to buy their favorite brand. In recent years, Internet advertising has grown exponentially and it has become an important part of the one-to-many model as our small screens fill with promotional messages. We'll talk more about Internet advertising and social media in Chapter 14.

- *Sales promotion: Consumer sales promotion* includes programs such as contests, coupons, or other incentives that marketers design to build interest in or encourage purchase of a product during a specified period. Unlike other forms of promotion, sales promotion intends to stimulate immediate action (often in the form of a purchase) rather than to build long-term loyalty.

- *Public relations: Public relations* describes a variety of communication activities that seek to create and maintain a positive image of an organization and its products among various *publics*, including customers, government officials, and shareholders. Public relations programs also include efforts to present negative company news in the most positive way so that this information will have less damaging consequences.

Personal Communication: The One-to-One Model

Sometimes, marketers want to communicate with consumers on a personal, one-to-one level. The most immediate way for a marketer to make contact with customers is simply to tell them how wonderful the product is. This is part of the *personal selling* element of the promotion mix we mentioned previously. It is the direct interaction between a company representative and a customer that can occur in person, by phone, or even over an interactive computer link.

Marketers also use direct mail, telemarketing, and other *direct marketing* activities to create personal appeals. Like personal selling, direct marketing provides direct communication with a consumer or business customer.

13.2 Overview of Promotion Planning

OBJECTIVE
Describe the steps in traditional and multichannel promotion planning.
(pp. 442–448)

Now that we've talked about communication and some of the tools marketers can use to deliver messages to their customers, we need to see how to make it all happen. How do we go about the complex task of developing a promotion plan—one that delivers just the right message to a number of different target audiences when and where they want it in the most effective and cost-efficient way?

Just as with any other strategic decision-making process, the development of this plan includes several steps, as ⬈ Figure 13.4 shows. First, we'll go over the steps in promotion planning, and then we'll take a look at how marketers today develop multichannel promotion strategies.

Step 1: Identify the Target Audience(s)

An important part of overall promotion planning is to identify the target audience(s) you want to reach. IMC marketers recognize that we must communicate both with members of our target market and with a variety of stakeholders who influence that target market. After all, we learn about a new product not just from the company that produces it, but also from the news media, from our friends and family, and even from the producers of competitive products. Of course, the intended customer is the most important target audience and the one that marketers focus on the most.

Step 2: Establish the Communication Objectives

As we said, marketers develop communication programs for different target audiences. The whole point of communicating with customers and prospective customers, the most important target audiences, is to let them know in a timely and affordable way that the

Figure 13.4 *Process* | Steps to Develop the Promotion Plan

Development of successful promotion plans involves organizing the complex process into a series of several orderly steps.

Step 1: Identify the Target Audiences

Step 2: Establish the Communication Objectives

Step 3: Determine and Allocate the Marketing Communication Budget
- Determine the Total Promotion Budget
- Decide on a Push or a Pull Strategy
- Allocate the Budget to a Specific Promotion Mix

Step 4: Design the Promotion Mix

Step 5: Evaluate the Effectiveness of the Communication Program

organization has a product to meet their needs. It's bad enough when a product comes along that people don't want or need. An even bigger marketing sin is to have a product that they *do* want, but you fail to let them know about it. Of course, seldom can we deliver a single message to a consumer that magically transforms him or her into a loyal customer. In most cases, it takes a series of messages that moves the consumer through several stages.

We view this process as an uphill climb, such as the one 📷 Figure 13.5 depicts. The marketer "pushes" the consumer through a series of steps, or a **hierarchy of effects**, from initial awareness of a product to brand loyalty. At almost any point in time, different members of the target market may have reached each of the stages in the hierarchy. Marketers develop different communication objectives to "push" people to the next level.

To understand how this process works, imagine how a firm would have to adjust its communication objectives as it tries to establish a presence in the market for Hunk, a new men's cologne. Let's say that the primary target market for the cologne is single men ages 18 to 24 who care about their appearance and who are into health, fitness, working out, and looking ripped. The company would want to focus more on some promotion methods (such as advertising) and less on others (such as personal selling). Next, we'll discuss some communication objectives the company might develop for its Hunk promotion.

hierarchy of effects

A series of steps prospective customers move through, from initial awareness of a product to brand loyalty.

Create Awareness

The first step in the hierarchy of effects is to make members of the target market aware that there's a new brand of cologne on the market. The promotion objective might be to create an 80 percent awareness of Hunk cologne among 18- to 24-year-old men in the first two months.

Note how this objective is worded: Objectives are best when they are quantitative (80 percent), when they specify the target consumer or business group (18- to 24-year-old men), and when they specify the time frame during which the plan is expected to reach the objective (in the first two months). To accomplish this, the fragrance's marketers might place simple, repetitive advertisements that push the brand name in magazines, on TV, and on the radio.

Figure 13.5 📷 *Snapshot* | The Hierarchy of Effects

Communication objectives move consumers through the hierarchy of effects.

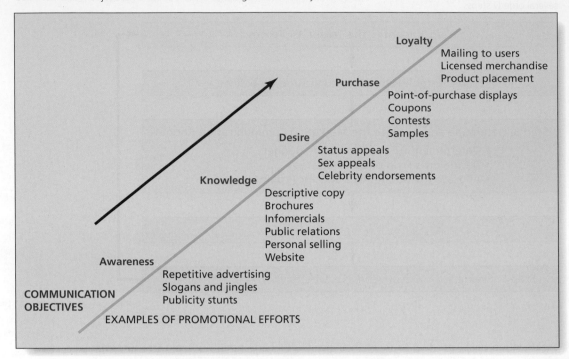

Inform the Market

For those consumers who have heard the name "Hunk" but don't really know anything about it, the challenge is to provide knowledge about the benefits the new product has to offer—to *position* it relative to other colognes (see Chapter 7). The objective at this point might be to communicate the connection between Hunk and muscle building so that 60 percent of the target market develops some interest in the product in the first six months of the communication program. To accomplish this, promotion would focus on advertising and other communications that emphasize the muscle-building connection.

Create Desire

The next step in the hierarchy is *desire*. The task of marketing communications is to create favorable feelings toward the product and to convince at least some members of this group that they would rather splash on some Hunk instead of other colognes. The specific objective might be to create positive attitudes toward Hunk cologne among 50 percent of the target market and brand preference among 30 percent of the target market. Communication at this stage might consist of splashy advertising spreads in magazines, perhaps with an endorsement by a well-known celebrity.

Encourage Purchase and Trial

As the expression goes, "How do ya know 'til ya try it?" The company needs to get some of the men who have become interested in the cologne to try it. The specific objective now might be to encourage trial of Hunk among 25 percent of 18- to 24-year-old men. A promotion plan might encourage trial by mailing samples of Hunk to members of the target market, inserting "scratch-and-sniff" samples in bodybuilding magazines, placing elaborate displays in stores that dispense money-saving coupons, or even sponsoring a contest in which the winner gets to have WWE wrestler Roman Reigns as his personal trainer for a day.

Build Loyalty

Loyalty, the final step in the hierarchy of effects, means customers decide to stay with Hunk after they've gone through the first bottle. The objective might be to develop and maintain regular usage of Hunk cologne among 10 percent of men from 18 to 24 years old. Promotion efforts must maintain ongoing communication with current users to reinforce the bond they feel with the product.

Step 3: Determine and Allocate the Marketing Communication Budget

Although setting a budget for marketing communication might seem easy—you just calculate how much you need to accomplish your objectives—in reality it's not that simple. Figure 13.6, we shows the three distinct decisions required to develop the budget.

Budget Decision 1: Determine the Total Marketing Communication Budget

To determine the total amount to spend on marketing communication, most firms rely on one of two types of budgeting techniques: top down and bottom up. With **top-down budgeting techniques**, managers establish the overall amount that the organization will allocate to promotion activities.

The most common top-down technique is the **percentage-of-sales method**, in which the marketing communication budget is based on last year's sales or on estimates for the present year's sales. The advantage of this method is that it ties spending on promotion to sales and profits. Unfortunately, this method can imply that sales cause promotion spending rather than viewing sales as the *outcome* of marketing communication efforts.

The **competitive-parity method** is a fancy way of saying "keep up with the Joneses." In other words, match whatever competitors spend. Another approach is to begin at the beginning: identify promotion objectives and allocate enough money to accomplish them. That is what **bottom-up budgeting techniques** attempt. This bottom-up logic is at the heart

top-down budgeting techniques
Allocation of the promotion budget based on management's determination of the total amount to be devoted to marketing communication.

percentage-of-sales method
A method for promotion budgeting that is based on a certain percentage of either last year's sales or estimates of the present year's sales.

competitive-parity method
A promotion budgeting method in which an organization matches whatever competitors are spending.

bottom-up budgeting techniques
Allocation of the promotion budget based on identifying promotion goals and allocating enough money to accomplish them.

Figure 13.6 *Process* | Steps in Developing the Marketing Communication Budget

Budgeting decisions allow marketers to systematically plan IMC spending.

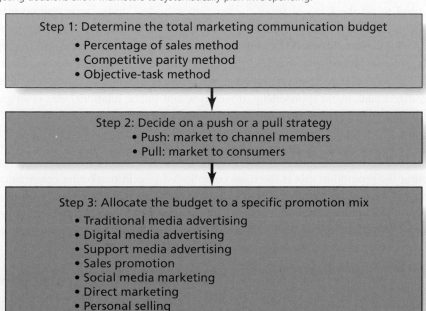

Step 1: Determine the total marketing communication budget
- Percentage of sales method
- Competitive parity method
- Objective-task method

Step 2: Decide on a push or a pull strategy
- Push: market to channel members
- Pull: market to consumers

Step 3: Allocate the budget to a specific promotion mix
- Traditional media advertising
- Digital media advertising
- Support media advertising
- Sales promotion
- Social media marketing
- Direct marketing
- Personal selling
- Public relations

objective-task method
A promotion budgeting method in which an organization first defines the specific communication goals it hopes to achieve and then tries to calculate what kind of promotion efforts it will take to meet these goals.

push strategy
The company tries to move its products through the channel by convincing channel members to offer them.

pull strategy
The company tries to move its products through the channel by building desire for the products among consumers, thus convincing retailers to respond to this demand by stocking these items.

of the **objective-task method**. When it uses this approach, the firm first defines the specific communication goals it hopes to achieve, such as increasing by 20 percent the number of consumers who are aware of the brand. It then tries to figure out how much advertising, sales promotion, buzz marketing, and so on, it will take to meet that goal. Although this is the most rational approach, it is hard to implement because it obliges managers to specify their objectives and attach dollar amounts to them. This method requires careful analysis— and a bit of lucky "guesstimating."

Budget Decision 2: Decide on a Push or a Pull Strategy

The second important decision in marketing communication budgeting is whether the company will use a push or a pull strategy. A **push strategy** means that the company wants to move its products by convincing channel members to offer them and entice their customers to select these items; it pushes them through the channel. This approach assumes that if consumers see the product on store shelves, they will be motivated to make a trial purchase. In this case, marketers spend the promotion budget on personal selling, trade advertising, and trade sales promotion activities that will "push" the product from producer through the channel of distribution to consumers.

In contrast, a company that relies on a **pull strategy** is counting on consumers to demand its products. This popularity will then convince retailers to respond by stocking these items. In this case, communication budgets are used primarily for media advertising and consumer sales promotion to stimulate interest among end consumers who will "pull" the product onto store shelves and then into their shopping carts.

Budget Decision 3: Allocate the Budget to a Specific Promotion Mix

The final step in planning the communication budget is to allocate the total budget among the elements in the promotion mix. In today's dynamic media environment, there are few clear guidelines to divide up the promotion pie—though we are witnessing a steady shift away from traditional advertising media and toward so-called "new media" like Facebook and Google. In some cases, managers may simply have a preference for advertising versus sales promotion or other elements of the promotion mix. Also, consumers vary widely in the likelihood that they will respond to various communication elements. College students for example are especially likely to spend most of their time on the Internet (but you knew that).

Although traditional media advertising (TV, newspaper, radio, magazine, and outdoor) used to get the lion's share of the promotion budget, today spending on Internet advertising is almost a third of total advertising spending. Overall U.S. advertising spending in 2015, for example, was $182.7 billion, an increase over 2014 spending of 3.6 percent. Of that, Internet advertising was $59.7 billion or almost as much as total broadcast and cable TV at $66.6 billion. Spending on other marketing services (sales promotion, telemarketing, direct mail, event sponsorship, directories, and public relations) was even greater than advertising at $224.4 billion, 30 percent of which went for sales promotion.[3]

Step 4: Design the Promotion Mix

Designing the promotion mix is the most complicated step in marketing communication planning. It includes determining the specific communication tools to use, what message to communicate, and the communication channel(s) that will be used to send the message.

In the "old days" before the Internet, this was a simple process of primarily deciding on advertising and sales promotion programs. Today the decisions are much more complicated. Do we continue to use traditional mass media advertising? How will we include digital communications? Buzz marketing? Sales promotion? And even more important, how will we make sure these are all integrated to provide our customers with a seamless, consistent experience? Not only are the questions complicated, but also they are different for each product and for each target audience,

Step 5: Evaluate the Effectiveness of the Communication Program

As marketers are faced with the need for greater accountability and they often have to document the ROMI (discussed in Chapter 3) of their marketing communications and other marketing activities, evaluating the effectiveness of the communication program is more important than ever. It would be nice if a marketing manager could simply report, "The $3 million campaign for our revolutionary glow-in-the-dark surfboards brought in $15 million in new sales!" It's not so easy. There are many random factors in the marketing environment that are out of the control of the marketer and that can impact sales: a rival's manufacturing problem, a coincidental photograph of a movie star toting one of the boards, or perhaps a surge of renewed interest in surfing sparked by a cult movie hit like *Blue Crush*.

As we discussed in Chapter 4, marketers use a variety of different methods to monitor and evaluate the company's communication efforts. The catch is that it's easier to determine the effectiveness of some forms of communication than others. As a rule, various types of sales promotion are the easiest to evaluate because they occur over a fixed, usually short period, making it easier to link to sales volume. Traditional advertising, on the other hand, has lagged or delayed effects so that an ad people see this month might influence a car purchase next month or even a year from now. Typically, researchers measure brand awareness, recall of product benefits communicated through advertising, and even the image of the brand before and after an advertising campaign. They use similar measures to assess the effectiveness of salespeople and of public relations activities.

Multichannel Promotion Strategies

As we said previously in this chapter, marketers today recognize that the traditional one-to-many communication model in which they spent millions of dollars broadcasting ads to a mass audience is less and less effective. At the same time, it isn't yet clear how effective the new many-to-many model is—or what marketing metrics we should use to measure how well these new media work.

Thus, many marketers opt for multichannel promotion strategies where they combine traditional advertising, sales promotion, public relations, and direct marketing activities with social media activities. The choice to employ multichannel marketing yields important benefits. First, these strategies boost the effectiveness of either online or offline strategies used alone. And multichannel strategies allow marketers to repeat their messages across various channels, strengthening brand awareness and providing more opportunities to convert customers.

Perhaps the best way to really understand how marketers develop multichannel strategies is to look at how some actually do it. When Jaguar launched its all-new F-type sports car, the luxury carmaker left nothing to chance when it came to its multichannel strategy. The global "Your Turn" campaign spanned TV, cinema (a short film), print, digital, mobile, experiential, and social activations. For example, in addition to TV, print, and digital ads, Jaguar partnered with USA Network's series *Covert Affairs* to feature the car, teamed up with *Playboy* to announce the Playmate of the Year, and sponsored an episode of ESPN SportsCenter. Jaguar also created a #MyTurnToJag social media contest where consumers could enter for a chance to win a drive in a Jaguar in New York, Los Angeles, Miami, or Chicago that was then shown across various social media venues.[4]

In the remainder of this chapter and the next, we will look at the various marketing communication activities that marketers may include in the multichannel promotion strategy we discussed already in this chapter. In this chapter, we look at media that support the one-to-many communication model. We begin with traditional advertising that consumers access through traditional media. Then we discuss some of the fine details of one-to-many digital media activities followed by consumer and business-to-business sales promotion— all in this chapter. In Chapter 14 we continue, as we turn to new many-to-many marketing communication techniques that include social media marketing; direct marketing; personal selling; and public relations.

You know from your own daily experience that you interact with brands in many different ways. Maybe you see a TV commercial, check out a T-shirt with a brand logo, look at a billboard on the highway, read a Facebook post' where someone in your network rants or raves about a product … and that's all before lunch! Today successful marketers know they must use multichannel marketing communication campaigns that provide information and also enhance the customer experience. The multichannel campaign may include traditional media, social media, mobile applications, e-mail, websites, direct mail, call centers, and the salesforce, maximizing the strengths of each. And it's not just about the information. Multichannel campaigns need to provide a customer experience that will engage the customer and add something of value (in addition to the product) to the customer's life.

13.3 Advertising

OBJECTIVE

Tell what advertising is, describe the major types of advertising, discuss some of the major criticisms of advertising, and describe the process of developing an advertising campaign and how marketers evaluate advertising.

(pp. 448–468)

advertising
Nonpersonal communication from an identified sponsor using the mass media.

A long-running Virginia Slims cigarettes advertising campaign proclaimed, "You've come a long way, baby!" We can say the same about advertising itself. Advertising has been with us a long time. In ancient Greece and Rome, ad messages appeared on walls, were etched on stone tablets, or were shouted by criers, interspersed among announcements of successful military battles, lost slaves, or government proclamations. As the technology that's available to connect us with companies and other consumers continues to evolve, we see that advertising evolves as well. And the differences between advertising and other types of marketing communications have blurred as advertising agencies find new ways to take advantage of all the exciting communications options that are available to them today.

We traditionally define **advertising** as nonpersonal communication from an identified sponsor using the mass media. Advertising is so much a part of marketing that many people think that advertising *is* marketing (but remember that product, price, and distribution strategies are crucial as well). And, as we saw previously, there are many ways to get a message out to a target audience in addition to advertising. But make no mistake; traditional advertising is still important, especially because the Internet gives marketers yet another important medium to use when they want to talk to large numbers of customers at once. In 2015, total U.S.ad spending for *Advertising Age's* top 200 advertisers was a record $142.5 billion. Of all product categories, automotive advertising tops the list with spending on measured advertising (magazines, newspapers, radio, TV, and Internet), of $13.8 billion.[5]

One thing is sure: as the media landscape continues to change, so will advertising. Sales of Internet-ready smart TVs are booming, as is the number of households with digital video recorders (DVRs) that let viewers skip through the commercials. Watching TV through your mobile devices also is on the rise because many cable and satellite providers now let you use apps to stream your favorite TV episodes. It's so popular that there's even a name for it: **TV Everywhere.** TV Everywhere, which is also known as **authenticated streaming**, is a term that describes using your Internet-enabled device, like a tablet or smartphone, to stream content from your cable or satellite provider.[6] This new way to consume media is growing rapidly; digital video viewing increased from 7 percent in the third quarter of 2013 to 39 percent in the same quarter of 2015.[7]

TV everywhere (also known as authenticated streaming)
The use of an Internet-enabled device, like a tablet or smartphone, to stream content from a cable or satellite provider.

So, with almost everyone spending so much time looking at small screens instead of TVs, billboards, and newspapers, is traditional advertising dead? Don't write any obituaries yet. Mass media communication remains the best way to reach a large audience. For that reason, producers of FMCGs (fast-moving consumer goods that we discussed in Chapter 8) such as P&G and Unilever will continue to rely on these traditional channels of communication to reach their customers even as they add newer digital communications.

Types of Advertising

Because they spend so much on advertising, marketers must decide which type of ad will work best to get their money's worth given their organizational and marketing goals. As 📷 Figure 13.7 shows, the advertisements an organization runs can take many forms, so let's review the most common kinds.

Product Advertising

When people think about advertising, they are likely to recall the heartwarming stories from Hallmark's ads, Nike's encouragement to "Just do it," or the funny squawks from the AFLAC duck. These are examples of **product advertising**, where the message focuses on a specific good or service.

Institutional Advertising

Rather than a focus on a specific brand, **institutional advertising** promotes the activities, personality, or point of view of an organization or company. The three forms of institutional advertising include the following:

- **Corporate advertising** promotes the company as a whole instead of the firm's individual products. Privately held, family-owned SC Johnson, for example, maker of familiar household brands including Windex, Ziploc, and Pledge, launched a corporate branding campaign that included digital, PR, social media, shopper marketing, and TV advertising. In addition, the company offered 3,000 free plane tickets to help reunite families for Thanksgiving. The aim of the campaign was to be the most trusted company in the industry, for consumers to know the products are SC Johnson products and that it's a family company. The tagline was "Making life better for the next generation in ways only a family company can."[8]
- **Advocacy advertising** seeks to influence public opinion on a specific issue in the interest of the public or a specific group. AT&T's "Close to Home," ad is part of the multiyear "It Can Wait" campaign meant to show consumers that they too can cause fatalities when they use their phones for e-mail, social media, and other activities while they drive. "Close to Home" shows a mother driving with her child in the back seat who quickly checks a social-media post on her phone leading to devastating consequences; it is difficult to watch. Data from the Departments of Transportation in Texas, Kentucky, and other states have suggested there is a relationship between the "It Can Wait" campaign and a reduction in crashes.[9]

Figure 13.7 📷 *Snapshot* | Types of Advertising

Advertisements that an organization runs can take many different forms.

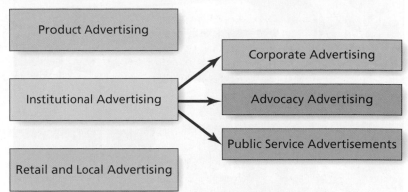

Product Advertising

Institutional Advertising → Corporate Advertising / Advocacy Advertising / Public Service Advertisements

Retail and Local Advertising

product advertising
Advertising messages that focus on a specific good or service.

institutional advertising
Advertising messages that promote the activities, personality, or point of view of an organization or company.

corporate advertising
Advertising that promotes the company as a whole instead of a firm's individual products.

advocacy advertising
A type of public service advertising where an organization seeks to influence public opinion on an issue because it has some stake in the outcome.

Non-profit organizations often use vivid imagery to communicate the seriousness of their causes.

The GEICO Gecko is the popular star of one of the company's several advertising campaigns.

- **Public service advertisements (PSAs)** are messages in the public interest, run by the media at no charge, that seek to change attitudes and behavior toward a social issue. Advertising agencies often offer their services on a pro bono (for free, not the U2 singer) basis. The most frequent topics for PSAs are health and safety issues.

Retail and Local Advertising

Both major retailers and small, local businesses advertise to encourage customers to shop at a specific store or use a local service. Local advertising informs us about store hours, location, and products that are available or on sale. While historically, newspapers have been the medium of choice for retail and local advertising, today, these ads may take the form of pop-up ads online or text messages on your mobile device.

Who Creates Advertising?

An **advertising campaign** is a coordinated, comprehensive plan that carries out promotion objectives and results in a series of creatively similar advertisements placed in various media over a period of time. GEICO, for example, has sponsored multiple advertising campaigns over the past few years, often with several running simultaneously. Five of its more recognized campaigns are (1) the GEICO gecko campaign; (2) the caveman campaign that even spawned a short-lived TV sitcom ("so easy a caveman can do it"); (3) the "money you could be saving" campaigns with the googly-eyed dollar bills; (4) the "Rhetorical Questions" campaign that included ads featuring Charlie Daniels (Does Charlie Daniels play a mean fiddle?), Elmer Fudd, and the Waltons; and (5) the Maxwell the pig campaign. Although all of these campaigns promote the same company and its products and all use the same tagline, "Fifteen minutes could save you 15 percent or more on car insurance," each is creatively distinct. Each includes multiple ads (there have been at least 22 caveman TV commercials), but each obviously is part of its own unique, coordinated advertising campaign.

Although some firms create their own advertising in-house, in most cases firms hire *outside advertising agencies* to develop an advertising campaign:

- A **limited-service agency** provides one or more specialized services, such as media buying or creative development.

- A **full-service agency** supplies most or all of the services a campaign requires, including research, creation of ad copy and art, media selection, and production of the final messages.

An advertising campaign has many elements; agencies provide the services of many different people to pull it all together:

- *Account management:* The **account executive**, or account manager, is the "soul" of the operation. This person supervises the day-to-day activities on the account and is the primary liaison between the agency and the client. The account executive has to ensure that the client is happy while verifying that people within the agency execute the desired strategy. The **account planner** combines research and account strategy to act as the voice of the consumer in creating effective advertising. It is the job of the account planner to use market data, qualitative research, and product knowledge to become intimately familiar with the consumer and to translate what customers are looking for to the creative teams who create the ads.

public service advertisements (PSAs)
Advertising run by the media for not-for-profit organizations or to champion a particular cause without charge.

retail and local advertising
Advertising that informs consumers about store hours, location, and products that are available or on sale.

advertising campaign
A coordinated, comprehensive plan that carries out promotion objectives and results in a series of advertisements placed in media over a period of time.

limited-service agency
An agency that provides one or more specialized services, such as media buying or creative development.

full-service agency
An agency that provides most or all of the services needed to mount a campaign, including research, creation of ad copy and art, media selection, and production of the final messages.

account executive
A member of the account management department who supervises the day-to-day activities of the account and is the primary liaison between the agency and the client.

account planner
A member of the account management department who combines research and account strategy to act as the voice of the consumer in creating effective advertising.

RosaIreneBetancourt 4/Alamy Stock Photo

- *Creative services: Creatives* are the "heart" of the communication effort. The **creative services** department includes the people who actually dream up and produce the ads. They include the agency's creative director, art director, copywriters, and photographers. Creatives are the artists who breathe life into marketing objectives and craft messages that, it is hoped, will interest consumers.

- *Research and marketing services:* In **research and marketing services**, *researchers* are the "brains" of the campaign. They collect and analyze information that will help account executives develop a sensible strategy. They assist creatives in getting consumer reactions to different versions of ads or by providing copywriters with details on the target group.

- *Media planning:* The **media planner** is the "legs" of the campaign. He or she helps to determine which communication vehicles are the most effective and recommends the most efficient means to deliver the ad by deciding where, when, and how often it will appear.

Today, more and more agencies practice IMC, in which advertising is only one element of a total communication plan. Client teams composed of people from account services, creative services, media planning, digital and social media marketing, research, public relations, sales promotion, and direct marketing may work together to develop a plan that best meets the communication needs of each client.

Land Rover uses attention-getting imagery to promote the adventurous side of the car.

User-Generated Advertising Content

One of the most recent and important promotional innovations is to let your customers create your advertising for you. User-generated content (UGC) or consumer-generated media that we discussed in Chapter 1, includes the millions of online consumer comments, opinions, advice, consumer-to-consumer discussions, reviews, photos, images, videos, podcasts and webcasts, and product-related stories available to other consumers through digital technology.

Some marketers encourage consumers to contribute their own **do-it-yourself (DIY) ads**. For advertisers, DIY advertising offers several benefits. First, consumer-generated spots cost only one-quarter to one-third as much as professional TV and Internet ads—about $60,000 compared to the $350,000 or more to produce a traditional 30-second spot. This can be especially important for smaller businesses and emerging brands. Equally important, even to large companies with deep pockets, is the feedback on how consumers see the brand and the chance to gather more creative ideas to tell the brand's story.[10]

Marketers need to monitor (and sometimes encourage) UGC for two reasons. First, consumers are more likely to trust messages from fellow consumers than from companies. Second, social media is proliferating everywhere; a person who searches online for a company or product name is certain to access any number of blogs, forums, homegrown commercials, or online complaint sites that the product manufacturer had nothing to do with.

As introduced in Chapter 1, consumers also generate content for firms through a process called *crowdsourcing*. Put simply, this is a way to harness "crowds" to "source" solutions to business problems. Marketers use this technique to come up with new product ideas, brand names, and product redesigns, but in many cases they look to their customers to create advertising messages for them. One of the most successful applications of crowdsourcing is the Doritos "Crash the Super Bowl" contest, which has run for more than a decade. When the idea was first suggested, the company's managers thought it was too risky to invest $2 million in a consumer-generated ad. Ten years later, the Doritos ads have earned top-five rankings on the *USA Today* Ad Meter every

creative services
The agency people (creative director, copywriters, and art director) who dream up and produce the ads.

research and marketing services
The advertising agency department that collects and analyzes information that will help account executives develop a sensible strategy and assist creatives in getting consumer reactions to different versions of ads.

media planners
Agency personnel who determine which communication vehicles are the most effective and efficient to deliver the ad.

do-it-yourself (DIY) ads
Product ads that are created by consumers.

year in which they have aired, including four No. 1 rankings—and that's in competition with Coke and Pepsi and Budweiser. As one ad executive said, "It just shows that great creative can come from anywhere."[11]

Ethical Issues in Advertising

Advertising, more than any other aspect of marketing, has been sharply criticized as unethical for decades. Much of this criticism may be based less on actual unethical advertising and more on the high visibility of advertising and the negative attitudes of consumers who find ads an intrusion into their lives. The objections to advertising are similar to those some people have to marketing in general, as we discussed in Chapter 2. Here are the main ones:

- *Advertising is manipulative.* Advertising causes people to behave like robots and do things against their will—to make purchases they would not otherwise make were it not for the ads. However, consumers are not robots. Because they are consciously aware of appeals made in advertising, they are free to choose whether to respond to an ad or not. Of course, consumers can and often do make bad decisions that advertising may influence, but that is not the same as manipulation.

- *Advertising is deceptive and untruthful.* According to the Federal Trade Commission, (FTC), deceptive advertising means that an ad falsely represents the product and that consumers believe the false information and act on it. Indeed, there is a small amount of false or deceptive advertising, but as a whole advertisers try to present their brands in the best possible light while being truthful.

corrective advertising
Advertising that clarifies or qualifies previous deceptive advertising claims.

To protect consumers from being misled, the FTC has specific rules regarding unfair or deceptive advertising. If the FTC finds that an ad is deceptive, it can fine the offending company and the ad agency. In addition, the FTC has the power to require firms to run **corrective advertising**—messages that clarify or qualify previous claims.[12] In 2016, the FTC announced a $2 million settlement with Lumos Labs, whose commercials for Lumosity "brain training" games were deemed deceptive. The FTC said Lumosity "preyed on consumers' fears about age-related cognitive decline suggesting their game would stave off memory loss, dementia, and even Alzheimer's disease."[13]

puffery
Claims made in advertising of product superiority that cannot be proven true or untrue.

Other ads, although not illegal, may create a biased impression of products when they use **puffery**—claims of superiority that neither sponsors nor critics of the ads can prove are true or untrue. For example, Tropicana claims it has the "world's best fruit and vegetable juice," Pizza Hut claims that it has "America's best pizza," and Simply Lemonade says it's okay for other people to say it's "the best lemonade ever."

greenwashing
A practice in which companies promote their products as environmentally friendly when in truth the brand provides little ecological benefit.

Many consumers today are concerned about **greenwashing**, a practice in which companies promote their products as environmentally friendly when in truth the brand provides little ecological benefit. The carmaker Mazda received a significant amount of backlash after it released its commercial for the Mazda CX-5 compact SUV with fuel-efficient SkyActiv technology. The problem? The SUV is only slightly more environmentally friendly than similar vehicles, but because the commercial starred the popular tree-hugging Dr. Seuss character The Lorax, the ad made it seem as though the SUV was much more environmentally friendly than it really was.[14]

- *Advertising is offensive and in bad taste.* To respond to this criticism, we need to recognize that what is offensive or in bad taste to one person may not be to another. Whereas advertisers seek to go the distance using humor, sex appeals, or fear appeals to get audiences' attention, most shy away from presenting messages that offend the very audience they want to buy their products.

- *Advertising causes people to buy things they don't really need.* The truth of this criticism depends on how you define a "need." If we believe that all consumers need is the basic functional benefits of products—the transportation a car provides, the nutrition we get from food, and the clean hair we get from shampoo—then advertising may be guilty as charged. If, on the other hand, you think you need a car that projects a cool image, food that tastes fantastic, and a shampoo that makes your hair shine and smell ever so nice, then advertising is just a vehicle that communicates those more intangible benefits.

Develop the Advertising Campaign

The advertising campaign is about much more than creating a cool ad and hoping people notice it. The campaign should be intimately related to the organization's overall communication goals. That means that the firm (and its outside agency if it uses one) must have a good idea of whom it wants to reach, what it will take to appeal to this market, and where and when it should place its messages. Let's examine the steps required to do this, as Figure 13.8 shows.

Step 1: Understand the Target Audience

The best way to communicate with an audience is to understand as much as possible about them and what turns them on and off. An ad that uses the latest teen text slang (e.g., OMG, BFF, and GR8) may relate to teenagers but not to their parents, and this strategy may backfire if the ad copy reads like an "ancient" 40-year-old trying to sound like a 20-year-old.

Step 2: Establish Message and Budget Objectives

Advertising objectives should be consistent with the overall communication plan. That means that both the underlying message and the expenditures for delivering that message need to be consistent with what the marketer is trying to say about the product and the overall marketing communication budget. Thus, advertising objectives generally will include objectives for both the message and the budget.

1. Set Message Objectives: As we noted previously, because advertising is the most visible part of marketing, many people assume that marketing *is* advertising. In truth, advertising alone is quite limited in what it can achieve. What advertising *can* do is inform, persuade, and remind. Accordingly, some advertisements aim to make the customer knowledgeable about features of the product or how to use it. At other times, advertising seeks to persuade consumers to like a brand or to prefer one brand over the competition. But many ads simply aim to keep the name of the brand in front of the consumer; reminding consumers that this brand is the one to choose when they look for a soft drink or a laundry detergent.

2. Set Budget Objectives: Advertising is expensive. P&G, which leads all U.S. companies in advertising expenditures, spent $4.3 billion in 2015, whereas second-, third-, and fourth-place ad spenders AT&T, General Motors, and Comcast spent more than $3 billion each.[15]

An objective of many firms is to allocate a percentage of the overall communication budget to advertising, depending on how much and what type of advertising the company can afford. The major approaches and techniques to setting overall promotion budgets discussed previously in this chapter, such as the percentage-of-sales and objective-task methods, also set advertising budgets.

Figure 13.8 *Process* | Steps to Develop an Advertising Campaign

Developing an advertising campaign includes a series of steps that will ensure that the advertising meets communication objectives.

Step 1: Understand the Target Audience

Step 2: Establish Message and Budget Objectives

Step 3: Create the Ads

Step 4: Pretest What the Ads Will Say

Step 5: Choose the Media Type(s) and Media Schedule

Step 6: Evaluate the Advertising

Step 3: Create the Ads

Using the terminology of the Communication Model, this is where the sender of a message encodes the idea into a physically perceivable form, the message. The creation of the advertising begins when an agency formulates a **creative strategy**, which gives the advertising creatives the direction and inspiration they need to begin the creative process. The strategy is summarized in a written document known as a **creative brief**, a rough blueprint that guides the creative process. A creative brief provides relevant information and insights about the marketing situation, the advertising objective, the competition, the advertising target, and most important, the message that the advertising must deliver.

It's one thing to know *what* a company wants to say about itself or its products and another to figure out *how* to say it. The role of the creative brief is to provide the spark that helps the ad agency come up with "the big idea," the visual or verbal concept that delivers the message in an attention-getting, memorable, and relevant manner. From this, the creatives develop the ads by combining already-known facts, words, pictures, and ideas in new and unexpected ways. Specifically, to come up with finished ads, they must consider four elements of the ads shown in 📷 Figure 13.9: the appeal, the format, the tonality, and the creative tactics and techniques.[16]

Advertising Appeals

creative strategy
The process that turns a concept into an advertisement.

creative brief
A guideline or blueprint for the marketing communication program that guides the creative process.

An **advertising appeal** is the central idea of the ad and the basis of the advertising messages. It is the approach used to influence the consumer. Generally, we think of appeals as informational versus emotional. Often, informational appeals are based on a **unique selling proposition (USP)** that gives consumers a clear, single-minded reason why the advertiser's product is better than other products at solving a problem. Because consumers often buy products based on social or psychological needs, advertisers also use emotional appeals that focus on an emotional or social benefit the consumer may receive from the product, such as safety, love, excitement, pleasure, respect, or approval. Of course, not all ads fit into these two appeal categories. Well-established brands like Coca-Cola and Pepsi often use **reminder advertising** just to keep their name in people's minds. Sometimes advertisers use **teaser ads or mystery ads** to generate curiosity and interest in a to-be-introduced product.

advertising appeal
The central idea or theme of an advertising message.

unique selling proposition (USP)
An advertising appeal that focuses on one clear reason why a particular product is superior.

Execution Format

Execution format describes the basic structure of the message. Some of the more common formats include the following:

reminder advertising
Advertising aimed at keeping the name of a brand in people's minds to be sure consumers purchase the product as necessary.

- *Comparison.* A **comparative advertisement** explicitly names one or more competitors. Comparative ads can be very effective, but there is a risk of turning off consumers who don't like the negative tone. This format is best for brands that have a smaller share of the market and for firms that can focus on a specific feature that makes them superior to a major brand.

teaser ad or mystery ad
Ads that generate curiosity and interest in a to-be-introduced product by drawing attention to an upcoming ad campaign without mentioning the product.

- *Demonstration.* A demonstration ad format shows a product "in action" to prove that it performs as claimed: "It slices, it dices!" Demonstration advertising is most useful when consumers are unable to identify important benefits except when they see the product in use.

execution format
The basic structure of the message, such as comparison, demonstration, testimonial, slice of life, and lifestyle.

- *Brand storytelling.* In Chapter 9 we introduced the concept of *brand storytelling*. From an advertising execution perspective, brand storytelling commercials are like 30-second movies with plots that involve the product in a more peripheral way. An example is the Subaru commercial that depicts a loving dad handing his six-year-old daughter the car keys and telling her to be careful. We eventually learn that she is a teenager but he still sees her as a little girl. The Subaru brand is not even revealed until we see the logo and slogan at the end.

comparative advertising
Advertising that compares one brand with a second named brand.

- *Testimonial.* A celebrity, an expert, or a "man in the street" states the product's effectiveness. The use of a *celebrity endorser* is a common but expensive strategy.

Figure 13.9 📷 *Snapshot* | Creative Elements of Advertising

Creating good ads includes making decisions about the four different ad elements.

Creative Element	Element Options	Description	Example
Appeals: the central idea of the ad	Informational/Rational	Satisfies customers' practical need for information; emphasize the features or benefits of the product. Example Unique Selling Proposition (USP)	Weathertec floor liners' ads show their factory and workers and advertise that they are made in the U.S.
	Emotional	Try to influence our emotions, "pull our heartstrings"	Ads that make us cry can be provided by non-profits who wish us to give for abused animals, sick and starving children, or helping wounded veterans. Even ads for greeting cards can touch our hearts.
	Reminder Advertising	Just to keep the name of the brand in people's minds so they will repurchase	Coke and Pepsi make sure their names are seen in ads on TV programs, in movies, in college and professional sports venues, inside retail stores—just about everywhere.
	Teaser/Mystery Ads	Generate curiosity and interest in a yet-to-be-introduced product.	Most used to attract consumers to be eager to see upcoming movies and TV shows.
Execution Formats: the basic structure of the message	Comparison	Explicitly names one or more competitors	Peanut butter ads frequently say one brand is better than another. "Jif tastes more like real peanuts."
	Demonstration	Shows the product in action or the results of using the results of using the product	A device used frequently for floor cleaning, car polishing, exercise equipment, and diet aids.
	Storytelling	A 30-second movie that involves the product in a more peripheral way	The 90-second Toyota Prius Hybrid ad for Superbowl 50 told the story of two bank robbers who outran police and got away in a Prius.
	Testimonial	A celebrity, expert, or "man on the street" states the products benefits	In a recent TV commercial, sports celebrities Kevin Nealon, Brian Vickers and Arnold Palmer talked about their experience with prescription drug Zyrelto for reducing the risk of blood clots.
	Slice of Life	A dramatized scene from everyday life showing that "real people" buy and use the product	Coca-Cola has aired slice-of-life commercials including one in which a father teaches his daughter to dance for her wedding.

	Lifestyle	Shows people who are attractive to the target market in a scene that demonstrates a certain lifestyle	As automobiles have become more like commodities with the same features, Subaru has found success through focusing on its cars meeting the desires of people who have or want a certain lifestyle.
Tonality: the mood or attitude the ad conveys	Straightforward	Simply present the information to the audience in a clear manner	
	Humor	People enjoy humorous ads so they break through the "clutter" however, humor is different for different people so others may find humorous ads offensive of stupid; humor may overpower other elements of the ad so consumers remember the ad in detail but can't remember what brand it was for	Mountain Dew's 50th Super Bowl ad received rave reviews for its puppymonkeybaby.
	Dramatic	A dramatization that presents a problem and a solution, often in a manner that is exciting and suspenseful	Pantene in Thailand aired a commercial showing a deaf and mute girl who learns to play the violin against all odds and wins top prize in a music competition.
	Romantic	Presenting a romantic situation, effective at getting attention and selling products people associate with dating and mating	Ads for luxury resorts, cruises, and Internet dating sites often use romance and may seem to promise romance if you purchase the product.
	Sex appeals	Appear like selling sex; effective at getting attention and at selling when there is a connection between sex and the product	Victoria's Secret advertises its lingerie worn by voluptuous models.
	Apprehension/Fear	Highlight the negative consequences of not using a product; can be social disapproval or physical harm	Used by marketers of deodorant, dandruff shampoo, auto insurance, and home security systems.
Creative Tactics and Technology	Animation and Art	Use art, illustration, or animation to attract attention and a unique "look" to the ad	Geico's Gekko is an animated character.
	Celebrities	When celebrities appear in ads, they attract attention and may influence people's favorable attitude toward a product	Movie actor, former champion body builder, and former California Governor Arnold Schwarzenegger stars in ads for game, Mobile Strike, "Command Center."
	Music, Jingles, and Slogans	Original words and/or music can make an ad memorable. Slogans link the brand to a memorable linguistic device	"Fifteen minutes can save you 15 percent or more on car insurance"

- *Slice of life.* A **slice of life** format presents a (dramatized) scene from everyday life. Slice-of-life advertising can be effective for everyday products such as peanut butter and headache remedies that consumers may feel good about if they see that "real" people buy and use them.

- *Lifestyle.* A **lifestyle** format shows a person or persons attractive to the target market in an appealing setting. The advertised product is "part of the scene," implying that the person who buys it will attain the lifestyle. For example, a commercial on MTV might depict a group of "cool" California skateboarders who take a break for a gulp of milk and say, "It does a body good."

- *Rich media.* Rich media advertising, which we discussed in Chapter 6, provides digital ads that have advanced features such as video, audio, games, or other elements that offer more ways for a consumer to interact and engage with the content and thus generate greater user response. For example, a simple website button ad for an international hotel chain includes the following interaction opportunities: links for different languages, "Roll over and learn more link," View exclusive offers link, 10 city/country locations links, each with multiple links for different properties in each city; links in each property site to access special discounts and links to book online, and links to sign up for special e-mail offers. There are also many large interior and exterior photos of each property. You can easily spend (or waste) an hour or more with this rich media ad.

Tonality

Tonality refers to the mood or attitude the message conveys. Some common tonalities include the following:

- *Straightforward.* Straightforward ads simply present the information to the audience in a clear manner.

- *Humor.* Consumers, in general, like humorous, witty, or outrageous ads, so these often provide an effective way to break through advertising clutter. But humor can be tricky because what is funny to one person may be offensive or stupid to another. In addition, humor can overpower the message. It's not unusual for a person to remember a hilarious ad but have no idea what product it advertised.

- *Dramatic.* A dramatization, like a play, presents a problem and a solution in a manner that is often exciting and suspenseful—a fairly difficult challenge in 30 or 60 seconds.

- *Romantic.* Ads that present a romantic situation can be especially effective at getting consumers' attention and at selling products that people associate with dating and mating. That's why fragrance ads often use a romantic format.

- *Sexy.* Some ads appear to sell sex rather than products. In an ad for the Fiat 500 Abarth, an Italian-speaking woman first angrily slaps a man for looking at her but then turns the tables and begins to seduce him. As the man leans in to kiss her, the camera pans in on the Fiat and "reality" sets in. Although sex appeal ads are known to get an audience's attention, they may or may not be effective in other ways. *Sex appeal* ads are more likely to be effective when there is a connection between the product and sex (or at least romance). For example, sex appeals will work well with a perfume but are less likely to be effective when you're trying to sell a lawn mower.

- *Apprehension/fear.* **Fear appeal ads** highlight the negative consequences of *not* using a product. Some fear appeal ads focus on physical harm,

slice of life advertising
A slice of life ad presents a (dramatized) scene from everyday life.

lifestyle advertising
Lifestyle ads show a person(s), attractive to the target market, in an appealing setting with the advertised product as "part of the scene," implying that the person who buys it will attain the lifestyle.

tonality
The mood or attitude the message conveys (straightforward, humor, dramatic, romantic, sexy, and apprehension/fear).

fear appeals
Advertisements that highlight the negative consequences of *not* using a product by either focusing on physical harm or social disapproval.

Humorous, witty or outrageous ads can be an effective way to break through advertising clutter.

whereas others try to create concern for social harm or disapproval. Mouthwash, deodorant, and dandruff shampoo makers and life insurance companies successfully use fear appeals. So do ads aimed at changing behaviors, such as messages discouraging drug use or smoking. In general, fear appeals can be successful if the audience perceives that the level of intensity in the fear appeal is appropriate for the product being advertised. For example, graphic photos of teens lying on the highway following an auto accident can be quite effective in public service advertisements designed to persuade teens not to text and drive, but they are likely to backfire if an insurance company tries to "scare" people into buying life insurance.

Creative Tactics and Techniques

In addition to ad formats and tonality, the creative process may also include a number of different creative tactics and techniques. Some of these are the following:

- *Animation and art.* Not all ads are executed with film or photography. Sometimes, a creative decision is made to use art, illustration, or animation to attract attention or to achieve the desired look for a print ad or TV commercial.
- *Celebrities.* Sometimes, celebrities appear in testimonials or for endorsements, such as Jessica Simpson's pitches for Weight Watchers.
- *Jingles.* **Jingles** are original words and music written specifically for advertising executions. Many of us remember classic ad jingles such as "I wish I were an Oscar Mayer Wiener" and "I am stuck on Bandaid and Bandaid's stuck on me." Today, jingles are used less frequently than in the past.
- *Slogans.* **Slogans** link the brand to a simple linguistic device that is memorable but without music. We usually have no trouble reciting successful slogans (sometimes years after the campaign has ended); think of such die-hards as "Finger lickin' good" (KFC), "Got milk?" (the California Milk Processor Board), "Just do it" (Nike), and "Even a caveman can do it" (Geiko insurance).

jingles
Original words and music written specifically for advertising executions.

slogans
Simple, memorable linguistic devices linked to a brand.

Step 4: Pretest What the Ads Will Say

Now that the creatives have performed their magic, how does the agency know if the campaign will work? Advertisers try to minimize mistakes by pretesting the ads, that is, getting reactions to ad messages before they actually place them. Much of this **pretesting** goes on in the early stages of campaign development. It centers on gathering basic information that will help planners to be sure they've accurately defined the product's market, consumers, and competitors. As we saw in Chapter 4, this information often comes from quantitative sources, such as surveys, and qualitative sources, such as focus groups.

pretesting
A research method that seeks to minimize mistakes by getting consumer reactions to ad messages before they appear in the media.

Step 5: Choose the Media Type(s) and Media Schedule

Media planning is a problem-solving process that gets a message to a target audience in the most effective way. In terms of the communication model, it's selecting the medium to deliver the message. Planning decisions include audience selection and where, when, and how frequent the exposure should be. Thus, the first task for a media planner is to find out when and where people in the target market are most likely to be exposed to the communication. Many college students read the campus newspaper in the morning (believe it or not, sometimes even during class!), so advertisers may choose to place ad messages aimed at college students there.

For the advertising campaign to be effective, the media planner must match the profile of the target market with specific media vehicles. For example, many Hispanic American consumers, even those who speak English, are avid users of Spanish-language media. To reach this segment, marketers might allocate a relatively large share of their advertising

media planning
The process of developing media objectives, strategies, and tactics for use in an advertising campaign.

budget to buying Spanish-language newspapers, magazines, TV, and Spanish web casts available on the Internet.

The choice of the right media mix is no simple matter, especially because new options, including videos and DVDs, video games, personal computers, streaming TV and movies via the Internet, social media, hundreds of new TV channels, and even satellite radio, now vie for our attention. In 1965, TV signals came into most consumers' living rooms through wires from the TV to a tall antenna on top of the house or via "rabbit ears" on top of the TV. Consider, however, that advertisers could reach 80 percent of 18- to 49-year-olds in the U.S. with only three 60-second TV spots placed on the three networks available: ABC, CBS, and NBC. That kind of efficiency is just a pipe dream in today's highly fragmented media marketplace. Later, we'll discuss the many choices marketers have in where to say it.

Step 6: Evaluate the Advertising

John Wanamaker, a famous Philadelphia retailer, once complained, "I am certain that half the money I spend on advertising is completely wasted. The trouble is, I don't know which half."[17] Now that we've seen how advertising is created and executed, let's step back and see how we decide if it's working.

There's no doubt that a lot of advertising is ineffective. With so many messages competing for the attention of frazzled customers, it's especially important for firms to evaluate their efforts to increase the impact of their messages. How can they do that?

Posttesting means conducting research on consumers' responses to advertising messages they have seen or heard (as opposed to *pretesting*, which, as we've seen, collects reactions to messages *before* they're actually placed in "the real world"). Ironically, many creative ads that are quirky or even bizarre make an advertising agency look good within the industry (and on the résumé of the creative director) but are ultimately unsuccessful because they don't communicate what the company needs to say about the product itself. Three ways to measure the impact of an advertisement are *unaided recall, aided recall,* and *attitudinal measures*:

1. **Unaided recall** tests by telephone survey or personal interview whether a person remembers seeing an ad during a specified period without giving the person the name of the brand.

2. An **aided recall** test uses the name of the brand and sometimes other clues to prompt answers. For example, a researcher might show a group of consumers a list of brands and ask them to choose which items they have seen advertised within the past week.

posttesting
Research conducted on consumers' responses to actual advertising messages they have seen or heard.

unaided recall
A research technique conducted by telephone survey or personal interview that asks whether a person remembers seeing an ad during a specified period without giving the person the name of the brand.

aided recall
A research technique that uses clues to prompt answers from people about advertisements they might have seen.

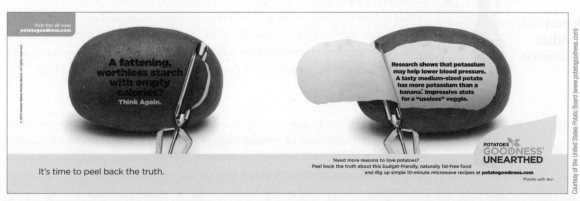

A communication objective may focus on educating consumers about a product like potatoes. The sponsor can measure the effectiveness of a campaign by assessing people's knowledge before and after the messages have run to determine if they had any impact.

attitudinal measures

A research technique that probes a consumer's beliefs or feelings about a product before and after being exposed to messages about it.

3. **Attitudinal measures** probe a bit more deeply by testing consumers' beliefs or feelings about a product before and after they are exposed to messages about it. If, for example, Pepsi's messages about "freshness-dating" make enough consumers believe that the freshness of soft drinks is important, marketers can consider the advertising campaign successful.

Where to Say It: Traditional Mass Media

What does a 50-inch plasma TV with Dolby Surround Sound have in common with an ink pen? Each is a media vehicle that permits an advertiser to communicate with a potential customer. In this section, we'll take a look at the major categories of traditional mass media, Internet advertising, and some less traditional indirect forms of advertising. Table 13.2 summarizes some of the pros and cons of each type.

Television

Because of TV's ability to reach so many people at once, it's often the medium of choice for regional and national companies. However, advertising on a TV network can be very expensive. The cost to air a 30-second ad on a popular prime-time network TV show one time normally ranges between $75,000 and $200,000, with higher costs for top-rated shows such as *The Big Bang Theory* ($348,300), *Modern Family* ($239,994), and *Sunday Night Football* ($603,000)[18] For the 50th Super Bowl in 2016, the cost of a single 30-second ad was between $4.6 and $5 million.[19]

Radio

Radio as an advertising medium dates back to 1922, when a New York City apartment manager went on the air to advertise properties for rent. One advantage of radio advertising is flexibility. Marketers can change commercials quickly, often on the spot by an announcer and a recording engineer.[20] Traditional radio advertising has declined in recent years as satellite radio, mostly by subscription only and without ads, has gained in popularity.

Newspapers

The newspaper is one of the oldest communication platforms. Retailers in particular relied on newspaper ads since before the turn of the twentieth century to inform readers about sales and deliveries of new merchandise. Although most newspapers are local, *USA Today*, the *Wall Street Journal*, and the *New York Times* have national circulations and provide readerships in the millions. Newspapers are an excellent medium for local advertising and for events (such as store sales) that require a quick response. Today, most newspapers also offer online versions of their papers to expand their exposure, but most of these do not include the ads we see in the paper versions. Some, such as the *New York Times*, offer online subscribers downloads of the actual newspaper, including all the ads, at a much lower cost than the paper version. The future of the newspaper industry is not clear because more people choose to get their news online.

Magazines

Today, in addition to general audience magazines such as *Reader's Digest*, there are literally thousands of special-interest magazines from *Decanter* to *Garden Railways*. New technology, such as *selective binding*, allows publishers to localize their editions so that they can include advertisements for local businesses in issues they mail to specific locations. For advertisers, magazines also offer the opportunity for multipage spreads as well as the ability to include special inserts so they can deliver samples of products such as perfumes and other "scratch-and-sniff" treats.

Print media like magazines can provide vivid messages and images to readers.

Table 13.2 | Pros and Cons of Media Vehicles

Vehicle	Pros	Cons
TV	• TV is extremely creative and flexible. • Network TV is the most cost-effective way to reach a mass audience. • Cable and satellite TV allow the advertiser to reach a selected group at relatively low cost. • A prestigious way to advertise. • Can demonstrate the product in use. • Can provide entertainment and generate excitement. • Messages have high impact because of the use of sight and sound.	• The message is quickly forgotten unless it is repeated often. • The audience is increasingly fragmented. • Although the relative cost of reaching the audience is low, prices are still high on an absolute basis—often too high for smaller companies. A 30-second spot on a prime-time TV sitcom costs well over $250,000. • Fewer people view network TV. • People switch from station to station and zap commercials. • Rising costs have led to more and shorter ads, causing more clutter.
Radio	• Good for selectively targeting an audience. • Is heard outside the home. • Can reach customers on a personal and intimate level. • Can use local personalities. • Relatively low cost, both for producing a spot and for running it repeatedly. • Because of short lead time, radio ads can be modified quickly to reflect changes in the marketplace. • Use of sound effects and music allows listeners to use their imagination to create a vivid scene.	• Listeners often don't pay full attention to what they hear. • Difficulty in buying radio time, especially for national advertisers. • Not appropriate for products that must be seen or demonstrated to be appreciated. • The small audiences of individual stations means ads must be placed with many different stations and must be repeated frequently.
Newspapers	• Wide exposure provides extensive market coverage. • Flexible format permits the use of color, different sizes, and targeted editions. • Provides the ability to use detailed copy. • Allows local retailers to tie in with national advertisers. • Readers are in the right mental frame to process advertisements about new products, sales, etc. • Timeliness, that is, short lead time between placing ad and running it.	• Most people don't spend much time reading the newspaper. • Readership is especially low among teens and young adults. • Short life span—people rarely look at a newspaper more than once. • Offers a cluttered ad environment. • The reproduction quality of images is relatively poor. • Not effective to reach specific audiences.
Magazines	• Audiences can be narrowly targeted by specialized magazines. • High credibility and interest level provide a good environment for ads. • Advertising has a long life and is often passed along to other readers. • Visual quality is excellent. • Can provide detailed product information with a sense of authority.	• With the exception of direct mail, it is the most expensive form of advertising. The cost of a full-page, four-color ad in a general-audience magazine typically exceeds $100,000. • Long deadlines reduce flexibility. • The advertiser must generally use several magazines to reach the majority of a target market. • Clutter.
Directories	• Customers actively seek exposure to advertisements. • Advertisers determine the quality of the ad placement because larger ads get preferential placement.	• Limited creative options. • May be a lack of color. • Ads are generally purchased for a full year and cannot be changed.

(continues)

Table 13.2 | Pros and Cons of Media Vehicles (*continued*)

Vehicle	Pros	Cons
Out-of-home media	• Most of the population can be reached at low cost. • Good for supplementing other media. • High frequency when signs are located in heavy traffic areas. • Effective for reaching virtually all segments of the population. • Geographic flexibility.	• Hard to communicate complex messages because of short exposure time. • Difficult to measure advertisement's audience. • Controversial and disliked in many communities. • Cannot pinpoint specific market segments.
Internet websites	• Can target specific audiences and individualize messages. • Web user registration and cookies allow marketers to track user preferences and website activity. • Is interactive—consumers can participate in the ad campaign; can create do-it-yourself ads. • An entertainment medium allowing consumers to play games, download music, etc. • Consumers are active participants in the communication process, controlling what information and the amount and rate of information they receive. • Websites can facilitate both marketing communication and transactions. • Consumers visit websites with the mind-set to obtain information. • Banners can achieve top-of-mind awareness, even without click-throughs.	• Limited to Internet users only. • Banners, pop-ups, unsolicited e-mail, etc., can be unwanted and annoying. • Declining click-through rates for banners—currently less than 0.03 percent. • If web pages take too long to load, consumers will abandon the site. • *Phishing* is e-mail sent by criminals to get consumers to go to phony websites that will seek to gain personal information, such as credit card numbers. • Because advertisers' costs are normally based on the number of click-throughs, competitors may engage in click fraud by clicking on a sponsored link. • Difficult to measure effectiveness.
Place-based media	• Effective for certain markets such a pharmaceutical companies to reach their target audience. • In retail locations, it can reach customers immediately before purchase; this provides a last opportunity to influence the purchase decision. • In locations such as airports, it receives a high level of attention because of lack of viewer options.	• Limited audience. • Difficult to measure effectiveness.
Branded entertainment	• Brand presented in a positive context. • Brand message presented in a covert fashion. • Less intrusive and thus less likely to be avoided. • Connection with a popular movie plot or TV program and with entertaining characters can help a brand's image. • Can build emotional connection with the audience. • Can create a memorable association that serves to enhance brand recall.	• Little control of how the brand is positioned—is in the hands of the director. • Difficult to measure effectiveness. • Costs of placement can be very high.
Advergaming	• Companies can customize their own games or incorporate brands into existing popular games. • Some game producers now actively pursue tie-ins with brands. • Millions of gamers play an average of 40 hours per game before they tire of it. • Millions of consumers have mobile phones "in their hands."	• Audience limited to gamers.
Mobile phones	• A large variety of different formats using different mobile phone apps.	• Consumers may be unwilling to receive messages through their phones.

Sources: Adapted from J. Thomas Russell and Ron Lane, *Kleppner's Advertising Procedure*, 15th ed. (Upper Saddle River, NJ: Prentice Hall, 2002); Terence A. Shimp, *Advertising, Promotion and Supplemental Aspects of Integrated Marketing Communications*, 8th ed. (Sydney: Thomson Southwestern, 2010); and William Wells, John Burnett, and Sandra Moriarty, *Advertising: Principles and Practice*, 6th ed. (Upper Saddle River, NJ: Prentice Hall, 2003).

Where to Say It: Branded Entertainment

Today more and more marketers rely on **branded entertainment**, also known as **product placement**, and **embedded marketing** to grab the attention of consumers who tune out traditional ad messages as fast as they see them. All of these terms refer to paid placement of brands within entertainment venues including movies, TV shows, videogames, novels, and even retail settings.

Is branded entertainment a solid strategy? The idea is that when consumers see a popular celebrity who uses a specific brand in their favorite movie or TV program, they might develop a more positive attitude toward that brand. Successful brand placements include the Harley-Davidson motorcycles characters rode in FX's popular *Sons of Anarchy* show and the opening of a Subway restaurant in NBC's *Community*. And from 2001 to 2013, AT&T's name came up every time viewers were asked to vote on their favorite *American Idol* contestants.[21]

Beyond movies and TV shows, what better way to promote to the video generation than through brand placements in video games? The industry calls this technique **advergaming**. If you are a video gamer, watch for placements of real-life brands such as the Audi R7S Sportback in *Forza Motorsport 5* or the Nissan Leaf electric car in *Gran Turismo*. Auto marketers aren't the only ones that place their products in video games, however. All told, the in-game advertising industry is worth about $2.8 billion annually. Nissan alone spent $500,000 on advergaming in 2013, about 25 percent of its overall advertising budget.[22]

We mentioned previously that increasingly the once-solid line between traditional advertising and other forms of promotion is rapidly blurring. Nowhere is this trend more evident than in the growth of a technique marketers call **native advertising**. This term refers to sponsored messages that mimic or resemble the normal content of the media vehicle where they appear. Basically, the ad looks like part of the program, as when an article about the Tesla electric car gets inserted in the middle of a magazine feature on new advances in green products.

Native advertising most commonly appears on the Internet, but it also pops up in other types of media such as print magazines or TV—in some cases the actors in a sitcom may also appear in a commercial so that you're not really sure if you're still watching the show or not.

Even though the label "sponsored content" usually appears somewhere in the message, consumers may not notice. Nationwide, for example, a regular sponsor of AMC's *Mad Men* series, aired a special commercial designed to resemble programming in which the chief marketing officer (CMO) of Nationwide discusses the company's advertising history. In the commercial, the CMO refers to a 1964 memo that resulted in the Nationwide slogan changing from "In service with the People" to "The man from Nationwide is on your side," later shortened to "Nationwide is on your side."[23]

Content marketing, which we mentioned in Chapter 7, also referred to as branded content, is another form of branded entertainment in which a marketer provides useful information through blogs, websites, and videos. This kind of promotion provides customers with information about the use of a product or a related subject that is valuable to them. For example, companies that sell avocados or pomegranates often create helpful videos to demonstrate the best way to use these items in a great guacamole or dessert.

Where to Say It: Support Media

Although marketers (and consumers) typically think of advertising as messages that pop up on television, magazines, and radio, in reality many of the ads we see today show up in other places as well such as public venues like restrooms, on coasters we get in restaurants and bars, or on signs that trail behind airplanes. These **support media** reach people who

branded entertainment (also known as product placements or embedded marketing) A form of advertising in which marketers integrate products into entertainment venues.

advergaming Brand placements in video games.

native advertising An execution strategy that mimics the content of the website where the message appears.

support media Media such as directories or out-of-home media that may be used to reach people who are not reached by mass-media advertising.

may not have been exposed to mass-media advertising, and these platforms also reinforce the messages traditional media delivers. Here we'll look at some of the more important support media advertisers use.

Directory Advertising

Directory advertising is the most "down-to-earth," information-focused advertising medium. In 1883, a printer in Wyoming ran out of white paper while printing part of a telephone book, so he substituted yellow paper instead. Today, the *Yellow Pages*, including the online *Yellow Pages*, posts revenues of more than $16 billion in the U.S. and more than $45 billion globally.[24] Often consumers look through directories just before they are ready to buy.

Out-of-Home Media

out-of-home media
Communication media that reach people in public places.

digital signage
Out-of-home media that use digital technology to change the message at will.

Out-of-home media include outdoor advertising (billboards and signs), transit advertising (signs placed inside or outside buses, taxis, trains, train stations, and airports), and other types of messages that reach people in public places. In recent years, outdoor advertising has pushed the technology envelope with **digital signage** that enables the source to change the message at will. Swedish carmaker Volvo placed interactive digital signs for its new V40 model at train and bus stops throughout the United Kingdom. The signed teased, "Do you want to know more about yourself?" and let passersby use the touch screen to customize their own V40.[25] Of course, many consumers dislike out-of-home media, especially outdoor advertising, because they feel it is unattractive.

Place-based Media

place-based media
Advertising media that transmit messages in public places, such as doctors' offices and airports, where certain types of people congregate.

Place-based media, like CNN's *Airport Channel*, transmit messages to "captive audiences" in public places, such as airport waiting areas. The channel, which appears at more than 2,000 gates and other viewing areas in 50 major U.S. airports, offers on-the-go news and entertainment.[26] Similar place-based video screens are now in thousands of shops, offices, and health clubs across the country, including stores like Best Buy, Foot Locker, and Target. The *Walmart Smart Network* reaches more than 7.9 million consumers each week, with monitors in high-traffic marketing zones, such as checkout aisles or electronics.[27]

Where to Say It: Digital Media

Here's where things get really confusing. We've talked about traditional advertising and about traditional media. But as we said previously, marketers are relying less and less on these traditional forms of marketing communication and moving more of their communications to digital media. Although we can name the traditional media pretty much on one hand, there are many different forms of communication on digital media.

digital media
Media that are digital rather than analog, including websites, mobile or cellular phones, and digital video, such as YouTube.

The term **digital media** refers to any media that are digital rather than old-school analog, the technology used for land-line telephones and non-digital watches. The more popular types of digital media advertisers use today include e-mail, their own websites, ads placed on other websites and blogs, social media sites such as Facebook, search engines such as Google, and digital video such as YouTube, available via a variety of devices. Marketers also send advertising text messages to consumers via mobile phones.

Digital media can be classified as owned, paid, and earned.[28]

owned media
Internet sites, such as websites, blogs, Facebook, and Twitter accounts, that are owned by an advertiser.

- Companies can control their **owned media**, including their own websites, blogs, Facebook pages, YouTube channels and Twitter accounts. The advantage of these owned media is that they are effective means for companies to build relationships with their customers while they maintain control of content.

- **Paid media**, the most similar model to traditional media, includes display ads, sponsorships, and paid key word searches. Consumers generally dislike paid ads, reducing their effectiveness.
- **Earned media** refers to word of mouth or buzz on social media. The positive of earned media is that it is the most credible to consumers, just like their friends and families have been most credible pretty much forever. The challenge is that marketers have little control over earned media; they can only listen and respond.

Website Advertising

Online advertising no longer is a novelty; companies now spend more than $121 billion a year to communicate via digital media.[29] That's because today Americans over the age of 18 spend more time on their mobile devices (just over five hours daily) than they do watching TV (about four and a half hours daily).[30]

Online advertising offers several advantages over other media platforms. First, the Internet provides new ways to finely target customers. Web user registrations and *cookies* allow sites to track user preferences and deliver ads based on previous Internet behavior. In addition, because the website can track how many times an ad is "clicked," advertisers can measure in real time how people respond to specific online messages.

Specific forms of Internet advertising include banners, buttons, pop-up ads, search engines and directories, and e-mail:

Banners, rectangular graphics at the top or bottom of web pages, were the first form of web advertising.

Buttons are small banner-type advertisements that a company can place anywhere on a page.

A **pop-up ad** is an advertisement that appears on the screen while a web page loads or after it has loaded. Many surfers find pop-ups a nuisance, so most Internet access software provides an option that blocks all pop-ups.

E-Mail Advertising

E-mail advertising that transmits messages to very large numbers of in-boxes simultaneously is one of the easiest ways to communicate with consumers; —it's basically the same price whether you send 10 messages or 10,000. One downside to this platform is the explosion of **spam**, defined as the practice of as sending unsolicited e-mail to five or more people not personally known to the sender. Many websites that offer e-mail give surfers the opportunity to allow or refuse e-mail. This **permission marketing** strategy gives the consumer the power to *opt in* or out. Marketers in the U.S. send about 258 billion e-mails to consumers every year, so they hope that a good portion of these will be opened and read rather than being sent straight to the recycle bin.[31]

Search Engines

Search engines are Internet programs that search for documents with specified key words. Increasingly, consumers use the Internet to search for information about products. Search engines, sites such as Google (www.google.com) and Bing (www.bing.com), help us locate useful information as they search millions of web pages for key words and return a list of sites that contain those key words.

Of course, the problem for marketers is that consumers seldom follow up on more than a page or two of results they get from these searches; we're all bombarded by way too much information these days to ever look at all of it. This has led marketers to develop sophisticated **search marketing** techniques. With search engine optimization (SEO), which we discussed in Chapter 5, marketers first find what key words consumers use most in

---

paid media
Internet media, such as display ads, sponsorships, and paid key word searches, that are paid for by an advertiser.

earned media
Word-of-mouth or buzz using social media where the advertiser has no control.

banners
Internet advertising in the form of rectangular graphics at the top or bottom of web pages.

buttons
Small banner-type advertisements that can be placed anywhere on a web page.

pop-up ad
An advertisement that appears on the screen while a web page loads or after it has loaded.

spam
The use of electronic media to send unsolicited messages in bulk.

permission marketing
E-mail advertising in which online consumers have the opportunity to accept or refuse the unsolicited e-mail.

search engines
Internet programs that search for documents with specified key words.

search marketing
Marketing strategies that involve the use of Internet search engines.

Ripped from the Headlines

Ethical/Sustainable Decisions in the Real World

The Internet is an open source revolution, where everyone can join in creating and sharing unlimited entertainment, news, information and commerce in ways we've never before imagined. It's almost like a fairy tale—too good to be real. And like any good fairy tales, there's a villain threatening the future of unfettered web usage. The villain's name is **ad fraud** and his sidekick is **ad blocking**.

Advertisers create digital ads to deliver to potential customers who are online reading articles in from publications such as the *New York Times*, searching websites for a new pair of shoes, visiting their Facebook page, or using a search engine. Here is where ad fraud comes in. Advertising on-line networks, the intermediaries between the advertiser and your phone or tablet, seek to make as much money as they can. Because they are paid per view or click-through, the more of these connections they can generate, the richer they become. Cybercriminals use *fraud bots*, automated browsers programmed to cause ads to load and then click on them in the background of the device where they will not make contact with real consumers and thus falsify the number of views or click-throughs the advertisers must pay for. One study that looked at this **mobile hijacking** found consumers had unknowingly downloaded "zombie apps" onto 12 million devices over a 10-day period, each of which can run up to 16,000 ads in the background of a phone without the owner ever

knowing it. Although it may only cost consumers some battery life, ad fraud is estimated to cost advertisers more than $8 billion a year. Some estimates are much higher—as much as $18 billion.

One solution is to use powerful ad-blocking software created to stop ad fraud by stripping ads from the website at the network level. But is this the way to go? Just like TV commercials are essential to pay for TV programming, online ads power the open Internet so that consumers can enjoy unlimited content for free. Certainly, individuals can block ads from their own devices, but that is their choice. Network ad blocking takes away consumers' ability to control what they see and don't see, the foundation of the World Wide Web. An argument against network ad blocking is that it creates censorship and destroys freedom of the press and will eventually mean that consumers pay more and more for less and less information. In other words, it would be the end of the open and free web as we know it.

Some experts argue that ad and content blocking is inevitable. As the amount on web content grows exponentially every year, consumers will eventually want to block ads and other content.

Finally, some feel that much of the ad fraud would be cut out if advertisers simply follow good basic business practices. Some basics include vetting channel partners, especially new ones, using address information, tax IDs and background checks.

ETHICS CHECK:

Is it ethical for ad networks to block ads intended for consumers' devices?

☐ YES ☐ NO

---

ad fraud
The use of automated browsers to falsify the number of views or click-throughs the advertisers must pay for.

ad blocking
The use of powerful ad-blocking software created to stop ad fraud by stripping ads from the website at the network level.

mobile hijacking
The use of automated browsers to falsify the number of views or click-throughs the advertisers must pay for.

search engine marketing (SEM)
Search marketing strategy in which marketers pay for ads or better positioning.

sponsored search ads
Paid ads that appear at the top or beside the Internet search engine results.

mobile advertising
A form of advertising that is communicated to the consumer via a handset.

text message advertising
Delivering ads to consumers as mobile phone text messages.

their searches. Then they edit their site's content or HTML to increase its relevance to those key words so that they can try to place their site high up in the millions of sites the search might generate. With **search engine marketing (SEM)**, the search engine company charges marketers to display **sponsored search ads** that appear at the top or beside the search results. Google, which has 67 percent of all U.S. web searches,[32] has total global revenues of more than $50 billion.[33] Who have you Googled today?

Mobile Advertising

The Mobile Marketing Association defines **mobile advertising** as "a form of advertising that is communicated to the consumer via a handset."[34] Mobile marketing offers advertisers a variety of ways to speak to customers (ideally with the customer's permission), including mobile websites, mobile applications or apps, **text message ads**, and mobile video and TV.

Newer phones with GPS features that pinpoint your location allow additional mobile advertising opportunities. This technology enables smartphone geo-targeting, discussed in Chapter 7, which is the ability to identify where customers are and deliver ads that are relevant to that location, increasing the relevancy of the message. Geo-targeting is also used with social media apps with location check-in features such as FourSquare, Gowalla, and Facebook Places that enable marketers to deliver promotional offers at the right time and place and can also be used to deliver coupons within a store at the point of sale. Restaurants and other retailers can use geo-targeting to contact consumers to let them know where the closest outlet is. Within stores, advertisers can send ads to your smartphone as soon as you stand in front of a product.[35] When a buyer or human resources manager searches for these services, AFLAC's name will surely be at the top of the list. Now there's a duck that's not out of water![36]

Most smartphone users prefer free apps; many refuse to pay for any. Therefore, developers of mobile apps must find some way to **monetize** their product. **In-app advertising** is often the best way to do this. The best strategy for in-app advertising is often to use advertising that not only creates revenue but also entertains and engages the user to the maximum possible extent.[37]

QR code advertising offers another way to engage consumers via their mobile phones. Marketers print QR codes in magazines and other forms of advertising, in stores, and even on "House for Sale" signs in yards. Smartphones are used as QR code scanners and convert the code to a usable form such as a URL for a website. For the consumer it is an easier and faster way to access a brand's website. For marketers, because consumers choose to access the website, the conversion rate (the chance that a sale will result from the contact) is much higher.

Video Sharing: Check It Out on YouTube

Video sharing describes the strategy of uploading video recordings or **vlogs** (pronounced "vee-logs") to Internet sites. Although YouTube is certainly the most popular video-sharing site, it is not the only one. After YouTube, the top seven video sharing sites include Vimeo, Vevo, Dailymotion, Veoh, Metacafe, Flickr, and Break.[38]

For marketers, YouTube and other video platforms provide vast opportunities to build relationships with consumers. Cuisinart and other appliance makers post videos to show consumers how to use their new products. Nike, in preparation for the World Cup kickoff, released a five-minute World Cup–themed short film featuring animated versions of some of the world's best football (or soccer, for you U.S. fans) players. Titled "Risk Everything," the video was watched by more than 18.6 million viewers in the first three months.[39] Universities and their students also have gotten into video sharing. Have students in your university created a "Happy" video and placed it on YouTube or Facebook?

When and How Often to Say It: Media Scheduling

After he or she chooses the advertising media, the planner then creates a **media schedule** that specifies the specific outlets the campaign will use as well as when and how often the message will appear. 📷 Figure 13.10 shows a hypothetical media schedule for the promotion of a new video game. Note that much of the advertising reaches its target audience in the months just before Christmas and that much of the expensive TV budget focuses on advertising during specials just prior to the holiday season.

monetize
The act of turning an asset into money. Websites and mobile apps monetize their content through advertisers.

in-app advertising
To monetize free mobile phone apps, developers use advertising to create revenue and to engage the consumer.

QR code advertising
QR (quick response) code advertising uses smartphone GPS technology to deliver ads and other information to consumers in stores and in other locations.

video sharing
Uploading video recordings on to Internet sites such as YouTube so that thousands or even millions of other Internet users can see them.

vlogs
Video recordings shared on the Internet.

media schedule
The plan that specifies the exact media to use and when to use it.

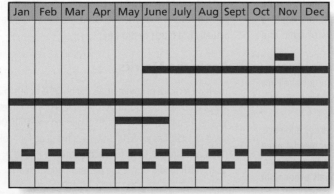

Figure 13.10 📷 *Snapshot* | Media Schedule for a Video Game

Media planning includes decisions on where, when, and how much advertising to do. A media schedule, such as this one for a video game, shows the plan visually.

reach
The percentage of the target market that will be exposed to the media vehicle.

frequency
The average number of times a person in the target group will be exposed to the message.

gross rating points (GRPs)
A measure used for comparing the effectiveness of different media vehicles: average reach × frequency.

cost per thousand (CPM)
A measure used to compare the relative cost-effectiveness of different media vehicles that have different exposure rates; the cost to deliver a message to 1,000 people or homes.

The media schedule outlines the planner's best estimate of which media (TV or magazines for example) will be most effective to attain the advertising objective(s) and which specific media vehicles (TV shows such as *Game of Thrones* or *The Big Bang Theory*) will be the most effective. The media planner considers qualitative factors, such as the match between the demographic and psychographic profile of a target audience and the types of people a media vehicle reaches, the advertising patterns of competitors, and the capability of a medium to adequately convey the desired information. The planner must also consider factors such as the compatibility of the product with editorial content. For example, viewers might not respond well to a serious commercial about preventing animal cruelty that tugs at one's heartstrings while they watch a "fun" show like *Keeping Up with the Kardashians*.

After deciding where and when to advertise, the planner must decide how often he or she wants to send the message. What time of day? And what overall pattern will the advertising follow?

A *continuous schedule* maintains a steady stream of advertising throughout the year. This is most appropriate for products that we buy on a regular basis, such as shampoo or bread. A *pulsing schedule* varies the amount of advertising throughout the year based on when the product is likely to be in demand. A suntan lotion might advertise year-round but more heavily during the summer months. *Flighting* is an extreme form of pulsing, in which advertising appears in short, intense bursts alternating with periods of little to no activity.

Metrics Moment

Media planners use a number of quantitative factors to develop the media schedule. **Reach** is the percentage of the target market that will be exposed to the media vehicle at least once during a given period of time, usually four weeks, expressed as a whole number. For example, if the target market includes 100 million adults age 18 and older and a specific TV program has an audience that includes 5 million adults in this age group, the program has a reach of 5. Developing a media plan with high reach is particularly important for widely used products when the message needs to get to as many consumers as possible. **Frequency** is simply the average number of times that an individual or a household will be exposed to the message. High levels of frequency are important for products that are complex or those that are targeted to relatively small markets for which multiple exposures to the message are necessary to make an impact.

Gross rating points (GRPs) are a measure of the quantity of media included in the media plan. Just as we talk about buying 15 gallons of gas or a pound of coffee, media planners talk about a media schedule that includes the purchase of 250 GRPs of radio and 700 GRPs of TV.

Marketers calculate GRPs by multiplying a media vehicle's rating by the number of planned ad insertions. If 30 percent of a target audience watches *The Big Bang Theory* and you place 12 ads on the show during a four-week period, you buy 360 GRPs of that show (30 × 12).

Although some media vehicles deliver more of your target audience, they may not be cost efficient. More people will see a commercial aired during the Super Bowl than during a 3:00 A.M. rerun of a Tarzan movie. But the advertiser could probably run late-night commercials every night

for a year for less than the cost of one 30-second Super Bowl spot. To compare the relative cost-effectiveness of different media and of spots run on different vehicles in the same medium, media planners use a measure they call **cost per thousand (CPM)**. This figure reflects the cost to deliver a message to 1,000 people.

Assume that the cost of each 30-second commercial on *The Big Bang Theory* is $400,000, but the number of target audience members the show reaches is 20 million, or 20,000 units of 1,000 (in CPM, everything is broken down into units of 1,000). Hence, the CPM of *The Big Bang Theory* is $400,000/20,000 = $20 CPM.

Compare this to the cost of advertising in *Fortune* magazine: A full-page four-color ad costs approximately $115,000, and the readership includes approximately 2 million members of our target audience, or 2,000 units of 1,000. Thus, the cost per thousand for *Fortune* is $115,000/2,000 = $57.50 CPM. As a result of this standardization to units of 1,000, you end up comparing "apples to apples," and the comparison reveals that *The Big Bang Theory*, which has a higher total cost, actually is a much better buy!

Apply the Metrics

You have a choice of commercials during *NCIS* or ads in *The Wall Street Journal* (*WSJ*). *NCIS* reaches 30 million members of the target audience, while *WSJ* reaches 15 million members. CBS is quoting you $500,000 per 30-second spot on *NCIS*; *WSJ* charges $200,000 for a full-page four-color ad.

1. Calculate the CPM for each option.
2. Which media buy is the better financial deal?

13.4 Sales Promotion

OBJECTIVE

Explain what sales promotion is and describe the different types of consumer and B2B sales promotion activities.

(pp. 469–474)

Sometimes when you walk through your student union on campus, you might get assaulted by a parade of people eager for you to enter a contest, taste a new candy bar, or take home a free T-shirt with a local bank's name on it. These are examples of **sales promotion**; programs that marketers design to build interest in or encourage purchase of a good or service during a specified period.[40]

How does sales promotion differ from advertising? Great question! Both are paid promotion activities from identifiable sponsors to change consumer behavior or attitudes. Often, a traditional advertising medium actually publicizes the sales promotion, as when Applebee's restaurant used TV advertising to tell military personnel and veterans about its free entrée offer for Veterans Day.[41]

But while marketers carefully craft advertising campaigns to create long-term positive feelings about a brand, company, or store, sales promotions are more useful if the firm has an *immediate* objective, such as bolstering sales for a brand quickly or encouraging consumers to try a new product. Indeed, the purpose of many types of sales promotion is to induce action by the consumer or business buyer.

Marketers today place an increasing amount of their total marketing communication budget into sales promotion. Several reasons account for this increase. First, due to the growth of very large grocery store chains and mass merchandisers such as Walmart, there has been a shift in power in the channels. These large chains can pressure manufacturers to provide deals and discounts. A second reason for the growth in sales promotion is declining consumer brand loyalty. This means that consumers are more likely to purchase products based on cost, value, or convenience. A special sales promotion offer is more likely to cause price-conscious customers to switch brands.

Marketers target sales promotion activities either to ultimate consumers or to members of the channel, such as retailers that sell their products. Thus, we divide sales promotion into two major categories: *consumer-oriented sales promotion* and *trade-oriented sales promotion*. We'll talk about the consumer type first, after which we'll discuss trade promotion. You'll see some examples of common consumer-oriented sales promotions in Table 13.3.

sales promotion
Programs designed to build interest in or encourage purchase of a product during a specified period.

Sales Promotion Directed toward Consumers

One of the reasons for an increase in sales promotion is because it works. For consumer sales promotion, the major reason for this is that most promotions temporarily change price/value relationships. A coupon for 50 cents off the price of a bottle of ketchup reduces the price, whereas a special "25 percent more" jar of peanuts increases the value. And if you get a free hairbrush when you buy a bottle of shampoo, this also increases the value. As shown in 📷 Figure 13.11, we generally classify consumer sales promotions as either price-based or attention-getting promotions.

Price-Based Consumer Sales Promotion

Many sales promotions target consumers where they live—their wallets. They emphasize *short-term price reductions* or *rebates* that encourage people to choose a brand—at least during the deal period. Price-based consumer promotions, however, have a downside similar to trade promotions that involve a price break. If a company uses them too frequently, this "trains" its customers to purchase the product at only the lower promotion price. Price-based consumer sales promotion includes the following:

- *Coupons.* Try to pick up any Sunday newspaper without spilling some coupons. These certificates, redeemable for money off a purchase, are the most common price

Table 13.3 | Consumer Sales Promotion Techniques: A Sampler

Technique	Description	Example
Coupons (newspaper, magazine, in the mail, on product packages, in-store, and on the Internet)	Certificates for money off on selected products, often with an expiration date, are used to encourage product trial.	Crest offers $5 off its WhiteStrips.
Price-off packs	Specially marked packages offer a product at a discounted price.	Tide laundry detergent is offered in a specially marked box for 50 cents off.
Rebates/refunds	Purchasers receive a cash reimbursement when they submit proofs of purchase.	Uniroyal offers a $40 mail-in rebate for purchasers of four new Tiger Paw tires.
Continuity/loyalty programs	Consumers are rewarded for repeat purchases through points that lead to reduced price or free merchandise.	Airlines offer frequent fliers free flights for accumulated points; a carwash offers consumers a half-price wash after purchasing 10 washes.
Special/bonus packs	Additional amount of the product is given away with purchase; it rewards users.	Maxell provides 10 free blank CDs with the purchase of a pack of 50.
Contests/sweepstakes	Offers consumers the chance to win cash or merchandise. Sweepstakes winners are determined strictly by chance. Contests require some competitive activity, such as a game of skill.	Publisher's Clearing House announces its zillionth sweepstakes.
Premiums: Free premiums include in-pack, on-pack, near pack, or in-the-mail premiums; consumers pay for self-liquidating premiums	A consumer gets a free gift or low-cost item when a product is bought; reinforces product image and rewards users.	A free makeup kit comes with the purchase of $20 worth of Clinique products.
Samples (delivered by direct mail, in newspapers and magazines door-to-door, on or in product packages, and in-store)	Delivering an actual or trial-size product to consumers to generate trial usage of a new product.	A free small bottle of Clairol Herbal Essences shampoo arrives in the mail.

promotion. Indeed, they are the most popular form of sales promotion overall. Companies distribute billions of them annually in newspapers and magazines, in the mail, in stores, by e-mail, and through the Internet. Even industries such as pharmaceuticals that never tried this approach before now use it in a big way. This industry offers coupons that customers can redeem for free initial supplies of drugs in hopes that patients will ask their physician for the specific brand instead of a competing brand or a more economical generic version.[42]

Figure 13.11 📷 *Snapshot* | Types of Consumer Sales Promotions

Consumer sales promotions are generally classified as price-based or attention-getting promotions.

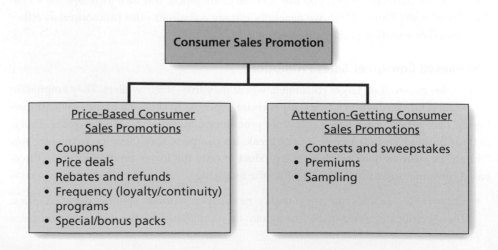

- *Price deals, refunds, and rebates.* In addition to coupons, manufacturers often offer a temporary price reduction to stimulate sales. This price deal may be printed on the package itself, or it may be a price-off flag or banner on the store shelf. Alternatively, companies may offer refunds or **rebates** that allow the consumer to recover part of the purchase price via mail-ins to the manufacturer.

- *Frequency (loyalty/continuity) programs.* **Frequency programs**, also called *loyalty* or *continuity programs*, offer a consumer a discount or a free product for multiple purchases over time. Mike Gunn, former vice president of marketing at American Airlines, is widely credited with developing this concept in the early 1980s when he coined the phrase "frequent flyer" miles. Of course, all the other airlines were quick to follow suit, as were a host of other firms, including retailers, auto rental companies, hotels, restaurants—you name it, and they have a customer loyalty program.

- *Special/bonus packs.* Another form of price promotion involves giving the shopper more products instead of lowering the price.[43] How nice to go to Walgreens and find the normal 16-ounce jar of Planters peanuts made larger to contain four ounces or 25 percent more free! A special pack also can be in the form of a unique package, such as a reusable decorator dispenser for hand soap.

rebates
Sales promotions that allow the customer to recover part of the product's cost from the manufacturer.

frequency programs
Consumer sales promotion programs that offer a discount or free product for multiple purchases over time; also referred to as *loyalty* or *continuity programs*.

Attention-Getting Consumer Sales Promotions

Attention-getting consumer promotions stimulate interest in a company's products. Some typical types of attention-getting promotions include the following:

- *Contests and sweepstakes.* According to their legal definitions, a contest is a test of skill, whereas a sweepstakes is based on chance.
  - To tap into a "younger, hotter" audience, Perrier, the number-one sparkling water in the world, hosted an immersive Secret Place sweepstakes, where contestants had to find clues to locate a secret bottle of Perrier that unlocked their ticket into the sweepstakes. The prize? An invite to one of five global megaparty destinations.[44]
  - In an effort to launch the new Axe Apollo brand of men's grooming products and do something that's epic, the Axe Apollo Big Game Sweepstakes was designed to send 22 everyday people up to 64 miles into space where they would be weightless for up to six minutes. All contestants had to do was plead their case about why they wanted to become astronauts. Popular vote would determine the top 100 finalists, and both the brand and the transport company would determine the winners.[45]

- *Premiums.* **Premiums** are items you get free when you buy a product. General Mills Cheerios brand cereal gave away millions of bilingual children's books inside Cheerios boxes during a 12-year period. In 2015, the company switched to offering free e-books that can be downloaded using a code provided in Cheerios boxes.[46]

premiums
Items offered free to people who have purchased a product.

- *Sampling.* How many starving college students at one time or another have managed to scrape together an entire meal by scooping up free food samples at their local grocery store? Some stores, like Publix and Sam's Club, actually promote Saturdays as sampling day in their advertising. **Product sampling** encourages people to try a product by distributing trial-size and sometimes regular-size versions in stores in public places such as student unions or through the mail. Companies like P&G, Unilever, S.C. Johnson, and GlaxoSmithKline are readily taking advantage of websites such as Freesamples.com and Startsampling.com that distribute the firms' samples and then follow up with consumer-satisfaction surveys.

product sampling
Distributing free trial-size versions of a product to consumers.

Trade Sales Promotion: Targeting the B2B Customer

As we said, sales promotions also target the B2B customer—located somewhere within the supply chain. Such entities are traditionally referred to as "the trade." Hence, **trade sales promotions** focus on members of the supply chain, which include distribution channel members that we discussed in Chapter 11.

Trade promotions take one of two forms: (1) those designed as discounts and deals and (2) those designed to increase company visibility. Let's take a look at both types of trade promotions in more detail. To help you follow along, [📷] Figure 13.12 portrays several of the most important types of trade sales promotion approaches, and Table 13.4 provides more details about each approach. You will note that some of the techniques, although targeted primarily to the trade, also appeal to consumers.

Discount Promotions

Discount promotions (deals) reduce the cost of the product to the distributor or retailer or help defray its advertising expenses. Firms design these promotions to encourage stores to stock the item and be sure it gets a lot of attention. Marketers offer these discounts for a limited period of time and should not be confused with discounts that are part of the pricing strategy and are offered long term.

One form of trade promotion is a short-term *price break*. A manufacturer can reduce a channel partner's costs with a sales promotion that discounts its products. For example, a manufacturer can offer a **merchandising allowance** to reimburse the retailer for in-store support of a product, such as when a store features an off-shelf display for a brand. Another way in which a manufacturer can reduce a channel partner's cost is with a **case allowance** that provides a discount to the retailer or wholesaler during a set period based on the sales volume of a product the retailer or wholesaler orders from the manufacturer.

However, allowances and deals have a downside. As with all sales promotion activities, the manufacturer expects these to be of limited duration, after which the distribution channel partner will again pay full price for the items. Unfortunately, some channel members engage in a practice the industry calls *forward buying*: They purchase large quantities of the product during a discount period, warehouse them, and don't buy them again until the manufacturer offers another discount. Some large retailers and wholesalers take this to an extreme when they engage in *diverting*. This describes an ethically questionable practice where the retailer buys the product at the discounted promotional price and warehouses it. Then, after the promotion has expired, the retailer sells the hoarded inventory to other retailers at a price that is lower than the manufacturer's nondiscounted price but high enough to turn a profit. Obviously, both forward buying and diverting go against the manufacturer's intent in offering the sales promotion.

Co-Op Advertising

Another type of trade allowance is **co-op advertising**. These programs offer to pay a portion, usually 50 percent, of the cost of any retailer advertising that features the manufacturer's product. Co-op advertising is a win-win situation for manufacturers because most local media vehicles offer lower rates to local businesses than to national advertisers. Both the retailer and the manufacturer pay for only part of the advertising, plus the manufacturer gets the lower rate. Normally, the amount available to a retailer for co-op advertising is limited to a percentage of the purchases the retailer makes during a year from the manufacturer.

trade sales promotions
Promotions that focus on members of the "trade," which include distribution channel members, such as retail salespeople or wholesale distributors, that a firm must work with in order to sell its products.

merchandising allowance
Reimburses the retailer for in-store support of the product.

case allowance
A discount to the retailer or wholesaler based on the volume of product ordered.

co-op advertising
A sales promotion where the manufacturer and the retailer share the cost.

Figure 13.12 [📷] *Snapshot* | Trade Sales Promotions

Trade sales promotions come in a variety of forms. Some are designed as discounts and deals for channel members, and some are designed to increase industry visibility.

Table 13.4 | Characteristics of Trade Sales Promotion Approaches

Technique	Primary Target	Description	Example
Allowances, discounts, and deals	Trade	Retailers or other organizational customers receive discounts for quantity purchases or for providing special merchandising assistance.	Retailers get a discount for using a special Thanksgiving display unit for Pepperidge Farm Stuffing Mix.
Co-op advertising	Trade and consumers	Manufacturers pay part of the cost of advertising by retailers who feature the manufacturer's product in their ads.	Toro pays half of the cost of Brad's Hardware Store newspaper advertising that features Toro lawn mowers.
Trade shows	Trade	Many manufacturers showcase their products to attendees.	The National Kitchen and Bath Association trade shows allow manufacturers to display their latest wares to owners of kitchen and bath remodeling stores.
Promotional products	Trade and consumers	A company builds awareness and reinforces its image by giving out "premiums" with its name on them.	Coors distributors provide bar owners with highly sought-after "Coors Light" neon signs. Caterpillar gives customers caps with the Caterpillar logo.
Point-of-purchase displays	Trade and consumers	In-store exhibits attract consumers' attention. Many point-of-purchase displays also serve a merchandising function.	The Behr's paint display in Home Depot stores allow consumers to select from more than 1,600 colors, including 160 Disney colors.
Incentive programs	Trade	A prize is offered to employees who meet a pre-specified sales goal or who are top performers during a given period.	Mary Kay cosmetics awards distinctive pink cars to its top-selling representatives.
Push money	Trade	A particular type of incentive program in which salespeople are given a bonus for selling a specific manufacturer's product.	A retail salesperson at a cosmetics counter gets $5 every time she sells a bottle of Glow perfume by JLo.

Sales Promotion to Increase Industry Visibility

Other types of trade sales promotions increase the visibility of a manufacturer's products to channel partners within the industry. Whether it is an elaborate exhibit at a trade show or a coffee mug with the firm's logo it gives away to channel partners, these aim to keep the company's name topmost when distributors and retailers decide which products to stock and push. These forms of sales promotion include the following:

- *Trade shows.* The thousands of industry **trade shows** in the U.S. and around the world each year are major vehicles for manufacturers and service providers to show off their product lines to wholesalers and retailers. Usually, large trade shows are held in big convention centers where many companies set up elaborate exhibits to show their products, give away samples, distribute product literature, and troll for new business contacts. Today, we also see more and more online trade shows that allow potential customers to preview a manufacturer's products remotely.

- *Promotional products.* We have all seen them: coffee mugs, visors, T-shirts, ball caps, key chains, and even more expensive items, such as golf bags, beach chairs, and luggage emblazoned with a company's logo. They are examples of **promotional products**. Unlike licensed merchandise we buy in stores, sponsors give away these goodies to build awareness for their organization or specific brands.

- *Point of purchase displays.* **Point of purchase (POP) materials** include signs, mobiles, banners, shelf ads, floor ads, lights, plastic reproductions of products, permanent

trade shows
Events at which many companies set up elaborate exhibits to show their products, give away samples, distribute product literature, and troll for new business contacts.

promotional products
Goodies such as coffee mugs, T-shirts, and magnets given away to build awareness for a sponsor. Some freebies are distributed directly to consumers and business customers; others are intended for channel partners, such as retailers and vendors.

point of purchase (POP) displays
In-store displays and signs.

and temporary merchandising displays, in-store TV, and shopping card advertisements. Marketers use POP displays because it keeps the name of the brand in front of the consumer, reinforces mass-media advertising, calls attention to other sales promotion offers, and stimulates impulse purchasing. Generally, manufacturers must give retailers a promotion allowance for use of POP materials. For retailers, the POP displays are useful if they encourage sales and increase revenues for the brand. Many are invaluable aids for shoppers. How would you like to buy paint for your bedroom without those wonderful paint displays with hundreds of color cards to take home and compare with the color of your favorite purple hippopotamus?

push money
A bonus paid by a manufacturer to a salesperson, customer, or distributor for selling its product.

- *Incentive programs.* In addition to motivating distributors and customers, some promotions light a fire under the firm's own sales force. These incentives, or **push money**, may come in the form of cash bonuses, trips, or other prizes. Mary Kay Corporation—the in-home party plan cosmetics seller—is famous for giving its more productive distributors pink cars to reward their efforts. Another cosmetics marketer that uses a retail store-selling model, Clinique, provides push money to department store cosmeticians to demonstrate and sell the full line of Clinique products. This type of incentive has the nickname *SPIF* for "sales promotion incentive funds."

MyLab Marketing™

Go to **mymktlab.com** to complete the problems marked with this icon ⭐ as well as additional Marketing Metrics questions only available in MyLab Marketing.

Objective Summary ➡ Key Terms ➡ Apply

CHAPTER 13
Study Map

13.1 Objective Summary (pp. 436–442)

Understand the communication process and the traditional promotion mix.

Firms use promotion and other forms of marketing communication to inform consumers about new products, remind them of familiar products, persuade them to choose one alternative over another, and build strong customer relationships. Recognizing that consumers come in contact with a brand in many different ways, firms today often practice integrated marketing communications (IMC) to reach consumers through a multichannel promotion strategy. Because marketers understand the impact of word-of-mouth communication, they are likely to supplement the traditional one-to-many communication model with a newer many-to-many model and also talk one to one with consumers.

The traditional communication model includes a message source that creates an idea, encodes the idea into a message, and transmits the message through some medium. The message is delivered to the receiver, who decodes the message and may provide feedback to the source. Anything that interferes with the communication is called "noise."

The promotion mix refers to the marketing communication elements that the marketer controls. Advertising, sales promotion, and public relations use the mass media to reach many consumers at a single time, whereas personal selling and direct marketing allow marketers to communicate with consumers one-on-one.

Key Terms

integrated marketing communication (IMC), p. 436

multichannel promotion strategy, p. 437

word-of-mouth communication, p. 438

communication model, p. 438

source, p. 439

encoding, p. 439

message, p. 439

medium, p. 439

receiver, p. 439

decoding, p. 439

noise, p. 439

feedback, p. 440

promotion mix, p. 440

mass communication, p. 440

13.2 Objective Summary (pp. 442–448)

Describe the steps in traditional and multichannel promotion planning.

Recognizing the importance of communicating with a variety of stakeholders who influence the target market, marketers begin the promotion planning process by identifying the target audience(s). Next, they establish communication objectives. Objectives often are to create awareness, inform the market, create desire, encourage purchase and trial, or build loyalty.

Marketers develop promotion budgets from rules of thumb such as the percentage-of-sales method, the competitive-parity method, and the objective-task method. They then decide on a push or a pull strategy and allocate monies from the total budget to various elements of the promotion mix.

Next, marketers design the promotion mix by deciding how they can use advertising, sales promotion, personal selling, and public relations most effectively to communicate with different target audiences. The final step in any advertising campaign is to evaluate its effectiveness. Marketers evaluate advertising through posttesting. Posttesting research may include aided or unaided recall tests that examine whether the message had an influence on the target market.

Marketers today often opt for multichannel promotion strategies where they combine traditional advertising, sales promotion, and public relations activities with social media and online buzz-building activities. Multichannel strategies boost the effectiveness of either online or offline strategies used alone and allow marketers to repeat their messages across various channels, thus strengthening brand awareness and providing more opportunities to convert customers.

Key Terms

hierarchy of effects, p. 443

top-down budgeting techniques, p. 445

percentage-of-sales method, p. 445

competitive-parity method, p. 445

bottom-up budgeting techniques, p. 445

objective-task method, p. 446

push strategy, p. 446

pull strategy, p. 446

13.3 Objective Summary (pp. 448–468)

Tell what advertising is, describe the major types of advertising, discuss some of the major criticisms of advertising, and describe the process of developing an advertising campaign and how marketers evaluate advertising.

Advertising is nonpersonal communication from an identified sponsor using mass media to persuade or influence an audience. Advertising informs and reminds consumers and creates consumer desire. Product advertising seeks to persuade consumers to choose a specific product or brand. Institutional advertising is used to develop an image for an organization or company (corporate advertising), to express opinions (advocacy advertising), or to support a cause (public service advertising). Retail and local advertising informs customers about where to shop. Most firms rely on the services of advertising agencies to create successful advertising campaigns. Full-service agencies include account management, creative services, research and marketing services, and media planning, whereas limited-service agencies provide only one or a few services.

User-generated content (UGC), also known as consumer-generated media (CGM), includes online consumer comments, opinions, advice, consumer-to-consumer discussions, reviews, photos, images, videos, podcasts and web casts, and product-related stories available to other consumers through digital technology. To take advantage of this phenomenon, some marketers encourage consumers to contribute their own do-it-yourself (DIY) ads. Crowdsourcing is a practice in which firms outsource marketing activities (such as selecting an ad) to a community of users, that is, a crowd.

Advertising has been criticized for being manipulative, for being deceitful and untruthful, for being offensive and in bad taste, for creating and perpetuating stereotypes, and for causing people to buy things they don't really need. Although some advertising may justify some of these criticisms, most advertisers seek to provide honest ads that don't offend the markets they seek to attract.

Development of an advertising campaign begins with understanding the target audiences and developing objectives for the message and the ad budget. To create the ads, the agency develops a creative strategy that is summarized in a creative brief. To come up with finished ads, they must decide on the appeal, the format, the tonality, and the creative tactics and techniques. Pretesting advertising before placing it in the media prevents costly mistakes.

Media planning gets a message to a target audience in the most effective way. The media planner must decide whether to place ads in traditional mass media or in digital media. Digital media are classified as owned media, paid or bought media, and earned media. Website advertising includes banners, buttons, and pop-up ads. Other types of digital media include e-mail advertising and search engine strategies. Mobile advertising includes text message advertising, in-app advertising, geotargeting, and QR code advertising. Video sharing allows marketers to upload videos to websites such as YouTube. Product placements, a type of branded entertainment, integrate products into movies, TV shows, video games, novels, and even retail settings. Advergaming, native advertising, and content marketing are additional types of branded content. Support media include directories, out-of-home media, and place-based media. A media schedule specifies the exact media the campaign will use and when and how often the message should appear.

The final step in any advertising campaign is to evaluate its effectiveness. Marketers evaluate advertising through posttesting. Posttesting research may include aided or unaided recall tests that examine whether the message had an influence on the target market.

Key Terms

advertising, p. 448

TV Everywhere (also known as **authenticated streaming**), p. 448

product advertising, p. 449

institutional advertising, p. 449

corporate advertising, p. 449

advocacy advertising, p. 449

public service advertisements (PSAs), p. 450

retail and local advertising, p. 450

advertising campaign, p. 450

limited-service agency, p. 450

full-service agency, p. 450

account executive, p. 450

account planner, p. 450

creative services, p. 451

research and marketing services, p. 451

media planner, p. 451

do-it-yourself (DIY) ads, p. 451

corrective advertising, p. 452

puffery, p. 452

greenwashing, p. 452

creative strategy, p. 454

creative brief, p. 454

advertising appeal, p. 454

unique selling proposition (USP), p. 454

reminder advertising, p. 454

teaser ads or mystery ads, p. 454

execution format, p. 454

comparative advertising, p. 454

slice of life advertising, p. 457

lifestyle advertising, p. 457

tonality, p. 457

fear appeals, p. 457

jingles, p. 458

slogans, p. 458

pretesting, p. 458

media planning, p. 458

posttesting, p. 459

unaided recall, p. 459

aided recall, p. 459

attitudinal measures, p. 460

branded entertainment (also known as **product placement or embedded marketing**), p. 463

advergaming, p. 463

native advertising, p. 463

support media, p. 463

out-of-home media, p. 464

digital signage, p. 464

place-based media, p. 464

digital media, p. 464

owned media, p. 464

paid media, p. 465

earned media, p. 465

banners, p. 465

buttons, p. 465

pop-up ad, p. 465

spam, p. 465

permission marketing, p. 465

search engines, p. 465

ad fraud, p. 466

ad blocking, p. 466

mobile hijacking, p. 466

search marketing, p. 465

search engine marketing (SEM), p. 466

sponsored search ads, p. 466

mobile advertising, p. 466

text message advertising, p. 466

monetize, p. 467

in-app advertising, p. 467

QR code advertising, p. 467

13.4 Objective Summary (pp. 469–474)

Explain what sales promotion is and describe the different types of consumer and B2B sales promotion activities.

Sales promotions are programs that marketers design to build interest in or encourage purchase of a good or service during a specified period. Marketers target sales promotion activities either to ultimate consumers or to members of the channel such as retailers that sell their products. Price-based consumer sales promotions include coupons, price deals, refunds, and rebates, frequency (loyalty/continuity) programs, and special/bonus packs. Attention-getting consumer sales promotions include contests and sweepstakes, premiums, and sampling.

Trade sales promotions come in a variety of forms. Some are designed as discounts and deals, including co-op advertising, for channel members, and some are designed to increase industry visibility. Approaches aimed at increasing industry visibility include trade shows, promotional products, point-of-purchase (POP) displays, incentive programs, and push money.

Key Terms

Chapter **Questions** and **Activities**

MyLab Marketing™

Go to **mymktlab.com** to watch this chapter's Rising Star video(s) for career advice and to respond to questions.

Concepts: Test Your Knowledge

13-1. What is promotion? What is integrated marketing communication? What are multichannel promotion strategies?

13-2. Describe the traditional communication model.

13-3. List the elements of the promotion mix and describe how they are used to deliver personal and mass appeals.

13-4. List and explain the steps in promotion planning.

13-5. Explain the hierarchy of effects and how it is used in communication objectives.

13-6. Describe the major ways in which firms develop marketing communication budgets.

13-7. Describe push versus pull strategies. What is advertising, and what types of advertising do marketers use most often? What is an advertising campaign?

13-8. Firms may seek the help of full-service or limited-service advertising agencies for their advertising. Describe each.

13-9. What is consumer-generated advertising, and what are its advantages? What is crowdsourcing, and how is it used in advertising?

13-10. What are some of the major criticisms of advertising? What is corrective advertising? What is puffery?

13-11. Describe the steps in developing an advertising campaign. What is a creative brief? What is meant by the appeal, execution format, tonality, and creative tactics used in an ad campaign?

13-12. What is media planning? What are the strengths and weaknesses of traditional media, that is, TV, radio, newspapers, and magazines?

13-13. What is digital media? What are owned, paid, and earned media? What are the different advertising activities or techniques included in website advertising, mobile advertising, and video sharing?

13-14. What are different types of branded content? How do marketers use branded entertainment and support media, such as directories, out-of-home media, and place-based media, to communicate with consumers?

13-15. How do marketers pretest their ads? How do they posttest ads?

13-16. What is media planning? How do media planners use reach, frequency, gross rating points, and cost per thousand in developing effective media schedules?

13-17. What is sales promotion? Explain some of the different types of consumer sales promotions marketers frequently use.

13-18. Explain some of the different types of trade sales promotions marketers frequently use.

Activities: Apply What You've Learned

★13-19. *Creative Homework/Short Project* You work in the marketing department at your local Red Cross blood center. Because donations are down, it's important that you reach out to the community for blood donor volunteers. Using the communication model, explain how you will create and transmit this message to the consumer. Then describe how you will determine whether consumers successfully received this message.

★13-20. *In Class, 15–20 Minutes for Teams* One of the components of the communications model (refer to Figure 13.2) suggests that the choice of the medium will influence the overall communication process and how the end consumer will decode the message. For this activity, assume that you want to communicate to your target market that your brand of canned soup, which now comes in a new exciting flavor, is ideal as a main meal during winter for families.

Assuming that you were going to use a billboard/outdoor ad as well as a radio ad, map out how you would design each of these marketing messages. You should keep in mind that radio commercials are typically around 30 seconds in length and that consumers only have one or two seconds to process a billboard ad.

13-21. *In Class, 15–20 Minutes for Teams* One of the steps in gauging the marketing communication budget is to determine whether the firm should adopt a push or pull strategy. Let's consider two products that are to be sold through a typical convenience store. The first is a well-known brand of chocolate and the second is an unknown brand of peanuts.

As you can see, both products fall into the snack food category for consumers and are typically bought on an impulse or convenience basis. When it comes to snacks, many consumers like variety and choice.

If you were a marketer responsible for promoting these products, to what extent would you focus on a push or pull strategy for each of them? How would your decision to pursue either a push or pull approach impact your choice of which promotional tools you would use?

13-22. *For Further Research (Individual)* More and more firms are engaged in multichannel promotion programs. You can learn about many of these by searching library or Internet sources. Some Internet sources that may be useful are the following:

Brandchannel.com
Adweek.com (*Adweek* magazine)
NYTimes.com (*New York Times*)
Adage.com (*Advertising Age* magazine)

Gather information on one or more multichannel promotion programs. Develop a report that describes the program(s) and makes suggestions for how it or they might be improved.

13-23. *Critical Thinking* Sales promotions are designed to generate short-term sales and, as a result, are often associated with some sort of discount or special offer. The end goal is to increase market share through increased volume of purchases and drawing business from consumers switching from competing brands.

However, is there a downside for the brand in using a sales promotion or launching them too frequently? Generally, strong brands like to achieve a price premium in the market to increase their long-term level of profitability. Therefore, if a brand frequently uses various price-based sales promotions, how would it impact the brand equity? Would it influence consumers to "rethink" the true value of the brand?

Are there any brands that you are aware of that may have damaged their brand equity through the overuse of aggressive sales promotions? Are there brands that you are aware of that never or rarely use price-based sales promotions?

13-24. *In Class, 10–25 Minutes for Teams* Assume that you are a member of the marketing department for a firm that produces several brands of snack foods. Your assignment is to develop recommendations for consumer and trade sales promotion activities for a new low-fat, low-calorie, high-protein snack food. Develop an outline of your recommendations for these sales promotions. In a role-playing situation, present and defend your recommendations to your boss.

13-25. *In Class, 10–25 Minutes for Teams* Timing is an important part of a sales promotion plan. Trade sales promotions must be properly timed to ensure channel members fully maximize the opportunity to sell your product. Assume that the introduction of the new snack food in question 13.24 is planned for April 1. Place the activities you recommended in question 13.25 onto a 12-month calendar of events. (Hint: The calendar needs to start *before* the product introduction.) In a role-playing situation, present your plan to your boss. Be sure to explain the reasons for your timing of each trade sales promotion element.

Concepts: Apply Marketing Metrics

13-26. You learned that media planners use a variety of metrics to help in making decisions on what TV show or which magazines to include in their media plans. Two of these are gross rating points (GRPs) and cost per thousand (CPM).

Assume you are developing a media plan for a new brand of gourmet frozen meals. Your target market includes females ages 25 to 64. The table that follows lists six possible media buys you are considering for the media plan, along with some relevant information about each (Note that the numbers are fictitious, created for example purposes only). The plan is based on a four-week period:

a. Calculate the GRPs for each media buy based on the information given.

b. Calculate the CPM for each media buy.

c. Based on the cost of each buy, the reach or rating of each buy, and any qualitative factors (e.g., decision criteria beyond the numbers) that you believe are important, select the top three media buys that you would recommend.

d. Explain why you would select these three.

Media Vehicle	Rating	Cost per Ad or Insertion	Number of Insertions	CPM	GRPs for This Number of Insertions
Dancing with the Stars	30	$500,000	4 (one per weekly episode)		
Big Bang Theory	20	$400,000	4 (one per weekly episode)		
CBS Evening News	12	$150,000	20 (one per weeknight news program)		
Time magazine	5	$40,000	4 (one per weekly publication)		
Better Homes and Gardens magazine	12	$30,000	1 (one per monthly publication)		
USA Today	4	$10,000	12 (three ads per week)		

Choices: What Do You Think?

13-27. *Critical Thinking* Marketers are spending less on mass-media advertising today than in previous times. Nevertheless, TV, radio, magazine, and newspaper advertising remains an important means of communicating with customers for many products and is preferred over spending on digital and mobile advertising. What products do you think most benefit from digital and mobile advertising? Why is this so? Do you feel traditional advertising will continue to decline in importance as a means for marketing communication, or will it rebound in the future?

13-28. *Ethics* The use of branded content is on the rise, especially in digital marketing. This includes content marketing, native advertising, product placements, branded entertainment, and advergaming. How do you think consumers respond to these tactics? Are you aware that these are forms of advertising? Is this deceptive? How do you suggest this approach could be improved to address potential ethical issues?

✪**13-29.** *Critical Thinking* Advertising and other forms of marketing communications have changed radically during the last decade or so as a result of digital technology. List some of these changes. What about each of these changes has benefitted consumers? Harmed consumers? Benefitted marketers? Harmed marketers? What changes would you recommend?

✪**13-30.** *Critical Thinking* Greenwashing is a practice in which companies promote their products as environmentally friendly when in truth the brand provides little ecological benefit. What are your thoughts on greenwashing? How much of a product should be environmentally friendly for it to be considered a truly green brand? Fifty percent? Eighty percent? Should the practice of greenwashing be regulated?

13-31. *Ethics* Firms are increasing their use of search engine marketing in which they pay search engines such as Google and Bing for priority position listings. Social media sites such as Twitter generate revenue by offering to sell "search words" to firms so that their posting appears on top. Are such practices ethical? Are consumers being deceived when a firm pays for priority positioning?

13-32. *Critical Thinking* Companies sometimes teach consumers a "bad lesson" with the overuse of sales promotions. As a result, consumers expect the product always to be "on deal" or have a rebate available. What are some examples of products for which this has occurred? How do you think companies can prevent this?

Miniproject: Learn by Doing

13.33. The hierarchy of effects model (refer to Figure 13.5) highlights the need for different communication goals that will utilize different forms of promotion and tools in order to advance the target market through various awareness, attitudinal, and behavior stages.

For this mini project, you need to design a long-term communications plan for a new business that is planning to provide educational international travel tours for older and retired people. Educational travel is becoming more common and is attracting new competitors to the marketplace. Therefore, you need to design a long-term communications plan showing how a firm could approach its promotional mix.

Work through the hierarchy of effects model and list some promotional tools that could be used at each stage of the model to achieve success for this new firm.

Marketing in **Action** Case   Real Choices at Domino's

Pizza is big business. Americans spend over $40 billion on pizza every year. With more than 59,000 U.S. stores that sell and deliver pizza, customers have lots of options from which to choose. Dominos wants more and more of them to make Domino's their only pizza delivery store.

In 1960, with a $500 down payment and $900 borrowed, Michigan-based brothers Tom and James Monaghan, purchased a small pizza store called DomiNick's. Soon after that, James sold his half of the business to Tom, who in 1965 renamed the company Domino's Pizza, Inc. For the next two decades, the company continued to grow and in 1983 opened its 1,000th Domino's store and its first international store in Winnipeg, Manitoba, Canada. In 2010 Domino's Pizza's celebrated its 50th anniversary and opened its 9,000th store worldwide. Today it has almost 12,000 stores including those in 80 international markets with global sales in 2014 of $89 billion. This success has led to the company to consistently being ranked in the Top 10 in *Entrepreneur* magazine's annual listing of great franchise opportunities.

Recently, growth of the retail pizza industry has slowed because of intensified competition from other types of restaurants and an increased level of consumer demand for healthier food choices. In this market, where there is little room for growth, Domino's must give current customer reasons to stay loyal and persuade potential customers to give them a try.

Domino's spends the majority of its $100 million-plus advertising budget on traditional television ads. The message of the recent "AnyWare" campaign is that you can use any device to place your Domino's order whether via text, tweet, TV, or smartwatch. The individual commercials highlight different celebrities showing how easy it is to order food using their favorite devices. Eva Longoria orders a pizza using her TV remote, Sarah Hyland, an actress on *Modern Family*, texts her order with a pizza emoji, and *The Avengers* actor Clark Gregg orders by tapping on his smartwatch.

Following the AnyWare campaign, Domino's latest advertising campaign is not even about pizza—it's about the specialty "delivery expert" car, the DXP. The DXPs are refashioned Chevrolet Sparks that come equipped with a working "warming oven" in the rear of the car. The cars can hold 80 pizzas per trip as well as a large number of drinks, side items, and other delivery products. According to Dominos, "the DXP comes equipped with a puddle light projecting the Domino's logo on the ground. The front fascia displays the Domino's logo, and the side panel displays the reflective graphic of the Domino's brand. Other details include hubcaps with the Domino's logo and the recognizable illuminated Domino's car topper."

The humorous DXP ads mimic auto advertising. In one, the little delivery car races across the desert, in another, a guy in a white lab coat talks about the features of the car and another promotes a $5.99 pizza deal with 0 percent APR for an unlimited time. The message that Dominos hopes consumers get is that everything Dominos offers—from emoji orders to a delivery vehicle—improves the pizza ordering process. Of course, there's no guarantee that the DXP ads can have a positive impact on sales, that they can convince consumers to make Domino's their first and maybe only option.

You Make the Call

13-34. What is the decision facing Domino's?

13-35. What factors are important in understanding this decision situation?

13-36. What are the alternatives?

13-37. What decision(s) do you recommend?

13-38. What are some ways to implement your recommendation?

Based on: Evan Schuman, "Domino's Again Uses Technology Illusion Brilliantly," *Computerworld* (February 29, 2016), http://www.computerworld.com/article/3038872/retail-it/dominos-again-uses-technology-illusion-brilliantly.html (accessed May 5, 2016); "About Us—Our History," *Domino's Pizza*, http://dominospizza.com.ng/index.php/about/our-history/ (accessed May 5, 2016); Jessica Wohl, "Celebs Click, Text, Tweet, and Tap to Order Domino's," *Advertising Age* (August 14, 2015), http://adage.com/article/cmo-strategy/celebs-click-text-tweet-tap-order-domino-s/299965/ (accessed May 5, 2016); Jessica Wohl, "This New Car Ad Isn't for a Car—It's for Pizza," *Advertising Age*, (February 22, 2016), http://adage.com/article/cmo-strategy/car-advertising-a-car-company-pizza/302752/ (accessed June 2, 2016).

MyLab Marketing™

Go to **mymktlab.com** for the following assisted-graded writing questions:

___

13-39. As an account executive for an advertising agency, you have been assigned to a new client, a company that has developed a new energy drink. As you begin development of the creative strategy, you are considering different types of ad execution formats and tonality:
   a. Comparative advertising
   b. A fear appeal
   c. A celebrity endorsement
   d. A slice-of-life ad
   e. Sex appeal
   f. Humor
   Outline the strengths and weaknesses of each of these appeals for advertising the new energy drink.

13-40. *Creative Homework/Short Project.* As a marketing consultant, you are frequently asked by clients to develop recommendations for marketing communication strategies. The traditional elements used include advertising, sales promotion, public relations, and personal selling. Which of these do you feel would be most effective for each of the following clients?
   a. A bookstore
   b. An all-inclusive resort hotel
   c. A university
   d. A company that produces organic snacks
   e. A sports equipment company

Promotion II: Social Media Marketing, Direct/Database Marketing, Personal Selling, and Public Relations

Courtesy of Rohan Deuskar, Stylitics

Rohan Deuskar

▼ **A Decision Maker** at Stylitics, Inc.

Rohan Deuskar was born and raised in India and came to the U.S. at the age of 18 to attend Northwestern University. After college, Rohan joined Vibes Media, a mobile marketing start-up that was pioneering the use of text messaging in interactive marketing campaigns.

At Vibes, Rohan worked in a variety of sales and account roles before starting the company's Innovation Team and helping to grow the company from six people to 80 and 15-fold revenues. He helped create some of the first marketing campaigns in the U.S. to use mobile. His work has won the Chicago Innovation Award, the Mobile Marketing Award, and many other awards as well as a U.S. patent.

Rohan left Vibes after five years to get an MBA in entrepreneurship from the Wharton School, where he became president of the entrepreneurship and rowing clubs. While at Wharton, he started Stylitics, a company designed to unlock the data in people's closets to power personalization and analytics through a "digital closet" platform. Since 2011, under Rohan's leadership, Stylitics has grown to a team of 16 people, raised more than $4 million in funding, and counts a number of the world's leading fashion brands and retailers as clients. The company has been featured extensively in the *New York Times*, the *Wall Street Journal, Vogue, Women's Wear Daily*, and others. Rohan is a frequent speaker on the intersection of fashion, tech, and data at events like New York Fashion Week and DataBeat.

Rohan's Info

What I do when I'm not working?
Play guitar, read a lot, explore New York City.

First job out of school?
A tiny mobile marketing start-up called Vibes Media. I got the job after I overheard the founder discussing the idea at a coffee shop and went up to him as he was leaving!

Career high?
Picking up the *Wall Street Journal* in a New York deli and seeing a three-page profile of my year-old company, just 10 months after moving to New York City. A bit surreal.

A job-related mistake I wish I hadn't made?
Most of my mistakes have been about being too optimistic and hiring the wrong people despite warning signs.

Business book I'm reading now?
Ben Franklin's autobiography. Not a business book but the profile of an inspiring and unique man in his own words. Lots to learn.

My hero?
One of them is Ben Franklin. He not only was a creative genius but also was able

to bring people together to achieve great things toward the common good.

My motto to live by?
Put in more than you take out. That applies to a job, a relationship, or the world in general.

What drives me?
The opportunity to create something that is good and useful in the world.

My management style?
(1) Listen. (2) Be kind.

My pet peeve?
Apathy. I can't stand the phrase "Whatever."

Here's my problem...

Stylitics was born from the confluence of my personal need as a consumer and a major need in the fashion industry. The spark was my frustration that, although like most people I was spending a decent amount of money and time on buying clothes and deciding what to wear, my closet was still one of the most inefficient parts of my life. I'd wear only 20 percent of my stuff, I'd forget what I owned, and I'd buy duplicates of clothes I already owned. It struck me that the closet was one of those central experiences in people's lives that is still completely analog and tied to one or two physical locations. I realized that if you had a digital version of your closet—essentially all your clothing data in one place online—then you could unlock an amazing set of new capabilities. Imagine putting together packing lists on the go, tracking stats like cost per wear of each item, or getting online outfit advice from your friend or a digital stylist. And not only would consumers be better off, but, with the user's permission, brands and retailers could see what people are wearing and buying in real time for the first time. That means better and more personal recommendations, more targeted offers, and better insights.

That's exactly what we've built. Today, we're the largest digital closet platform in the world and, for a while, the number one free fashion app in the App Store. Our apps are on iOS, Android, and the web and used by a large number of people around the world. Our trend reports are used by some of the world's top brands and retailers to help them serve their customers better. And we're just getting started! Anyone interested in finding out more (and being more organized!) should visit Stylitics.com.

In the fall of 2012, the team at Stylitics was discussing how to grow our social media presence. We'd had a year of strong user growth on our digital closet platform, driven by word of mouth and some good press. But my cofounder Zach Davis and I felt that it was time to do more to grow our brand using social media, primarily Twitter, Facebook, Instagram, and Pinterest. We had accounts on all these platforms, but they weren't really contributing very much to our goals of new user sign-ups and brand engagement. We'd seen the success that larger companies had via these channels through sophisticated campaigns. If we wanted to continue to drive user growth, we needed to step up our social media game.

As we began to discuss our options, we observed a few things. First, although we all used social media as individuals, we didn't have any experience in using social media to grow a brand. Second, while we were active on the @Stylitics Twitter and Facebook accounts, we were posting without a clear purpose or strategy. And third, and most important, we were missing a unique voice. A lot of our posts were reposts or retweets of fashion-related articles; something any company could do. Zach and I felt strongly that unless we had something to offer that was unique to our products or our vision, we should not simply add to the social media noise.

Another issue was reach. As a small company, we didn't have the budget for expensive paid social media campaigns. Even if we created an engaging and unique campaign, we still had to figure out how to make sure it would spread far enough to make an impact. Large companies hire social media agencies and invest in search engine optimization (SEO) and ads to spread the word. Our total budget was $5,000 at most—less than most large companies spend in a week. It was all very well to talk about content "going viral," but that is extremely rare, and even when it happens, it typically requires hitting a critical mass of people through paid promotion before achieving virality.

As leaders, my cofounder Zach Davis and I had to decide what our social media strategy would be. Our marketing team needed direction. Also, we knew that potential users, customers, reporters, and investors often judge young companies based on their follower counts and social media sophistication. It was not something we could ignore for much longer.

Rohan considered his **Options** 1·2·3

1 Option
Spend more money. We could increase our budget to pay a social media agency to create a campaign or pay for advertising on social platforms. We could also hire writers to create original content. This would be a safe choice, and it would require much less time and effort on our part. We could focus on other things and leave it to the experts. Of course, the funds to achieve this goal would have to come at the cost of something else. There was also no guarantee of good results, and we didn't know if consumer engagement would disappear after we exhausted our budget.

2 Option
Create our own campaign. We could try to come up internally with a concept for a social media campaign that would be unique and compelling. This would involve identifying external partners who would promote our content to their own followers in exchange for some kind of benefit to them. A "homegrown" strategy would be cheaper, and Stylitics would retain more control over the initiative. Engaging partners would mean extending our reach without spending money. However, an internal approach would take a lot of creativity as well as substantial effort to convince others to participate. It could easily take up a lot of time, use up our whole budget, and still flop badly.

3 Option
Continue as before. We could also choose to continue as we had been. We could accept that until we had the resources to upgrade our social media efforts, we weren't going to be able to do much. Hopefully, as we continued to build a community of avid Stylitics users, they would spread the word organically to their social networks. We could repurpose our social media budget elsewhere and focus on other priorities. A "stay-the-course" approach would allow us to focus on the areas where we have more control. Start-ups are always strapped for time and cash; this would save us both. On the other hand, Stylitics would continue to have a generic social media presence like so many other companies.

Now put yourself in Rohan's shoes. Which option would you choose, and why?

You Choose

Which **Option** would you choose, and **why**?

☐ **Option 1**   ☐ **Option 2**   ☐ **Option 3**

See what **option** Rohan chose in **MyLab Marketing™**

14.1 Social Media Marketing

OBJECTIVE

Understand how marketers communicate using an updated communication model that incorporates new social media and buzz marketing activities.

(pp. 484–489)

In Chapter 13, we saw how advertising and sales promotion follow the one-to-many marketing communication model. In this chapter, we first look at social media marketing that provides many-to-many marketing communication and then at two types of one-to-one communication: direct marketing and personal selling. Finally, we will learn about public relations. Public relations is the final element of the promotion mix and it includes a variety of communication activities,

It seems as if most of us are "on" 24/7 these days, whether we're checking our e-mail while on vacation, walking all over campus playing Pokémon Go on our smartphone, tweeting about the fabulous new restaurant we discovered, or just checking Facebook on our iPad while in class. Authors Charlene Li and Josh Bernoff refer to the changing communication landscape as the **groundswell**: "a social trend in which people use technology to get the things they need from each other, rather than from traditional institutions like corporations."[1] In other words, today's consumers increasingly get their information and news via their social interaction with friends and family and even their entertainment from one another.

Millions of people around the globe surf the web, talk with their friends, watch TV, and purchase products from traditional marketers, from Internet-only marketers, and from each other on their computers, smartphones, or tablets. For example, at last report, Facebook had 1.55 billion monthly active users; Facebook founder and CEO Mark Zuckerberg had more than 73 million followers.[2] All these users have the potential to connect with each other and to share feedback—whether it's about how hard that statistics test was this morning or where they bought a great new swimsuit for summer and how much they paid for it.

The new many-to-many communication model is altering the face of marketing. Marketers no longer are the only ones who talk about their products; millions of consumers also have the ability and the desire to spread the good (or bad) news about the goods and services they buy.

At the same time, traditional advertising has diminished as a way to talk to customers as consumers, especially younger ones, spend more and more time online and less time watching TV (and forget about reading newspapers!).[3] Magazine readership in 2015 reached 1.7 billion for a 7.1 percent increase over the previous year.[4] Mobile readership, in contrast, increased 429 million or a 53 percent increase.[5] U.S. advertiser spending on digital has now overtaken TV ad spending. Forrester Research projects that by 2019, U.S. advertisers will spend $85.8 billion on TV, or 30 percent of overall ad spending, while digital advertising will be $103 billion or 36 percent. Although some of the spending on digital will come from funds previously spent on TV, most will come from new money.[6] And, for those who still watch TV on a TV set rather than on their phones or other streaming devices, the average home now has 189 channels to choose from.[7] The abundance of choices makes the job of reaching a mass market even more complex and costly.

Retailers also find that their online business is growing, but that the Internet customer is harder to please and less loyal. This is not surprising because people have

groundswell

A social trend in which people use technology to get the things they need from each other rather than from traditional institutions like corporations.

Creative ads continue to draw our attention, but today the competition for "eyeballs" is even fiercer as traditional advertising competes with online messages and video content.

Turns Birdie into man's best friend.

easy access to competing prices and to the reviews of products and sellers from other online shoppers. The growth of Internet consumer-to-consumer (C2C) shopping sites such as eBay, Etsy, and Craigslist means more and more consumers buy from each other rather than (gulp) pay retail prices. To better understand this new communication model and its consequences, we need to first look at how marketers encourage and enable consumers to talk about their products in "buzz-building" activities. Then we'll look at some of the specific new media trending in the marketing communication landscape.

Game sites like Candystand are "sticky" (this one is built around candy, after all) so many advertisers find these media outlets an attractive place to advertise.

Social Media

Social media is an important part of the *updated communication model*. This term refers to Internet-based platforms that allow users to create their own content and share it with others who access these sites. It's hard to grasp just how much these new formats will transform the way we interact with marketers; they "democratize" messages because they give individual consumers a seat at the table where organizations shape brand meanings and promote themselves in the marketplace. This makes it much easier for companies to tap into their brand evangelists to help them spread the word. The flip side is that the bad stuff also gets out much quicker and reaches people a lot faster: In one survey, 20 percent of respondents said they had used social media to share a negative experience with a brand or service.[8]

There's no doubt that social media is the place to be in marketing communications now. In 2016, social media advertising spending was $10.9 billion, an increase of $7 billion from the previous year.[9] American Express leverages social media to connect with its card members. For example, American Express used Twitter hashtags that let members load special merchant offers onto their cards, and they tweeted special hashtags so that members could make purchases from companies like Sony and Amazon.[10] American Express also boosted their social media engagement by posting historical brand images to Facebook, Twitter, and Google. The result on Facebook alone was an astounding 127 percent increase in Facebook likes and a 100 percent increase in shares of Facebook posts.[11]

Social media include social networking sites such as Facebook, blogs, and microblogs such as Twitter, picture- and video-sharing sites such as Pinterest and YouTube, product review sites such as Yelp, wikis, and other collaborative projects such as Wikipedia, and virtual worlds such as Second Life. Let's take a brief tour of some of the most important social media platforms for marketers.

social media
Internet-based platforms that allow users to create their own content and share it with others who access these sites.

Social Networks

Social networks are sites that connect people with other people. Successful networking sites ask users to develop profiles of themselves so that those with similar backgrounds, interests, hobbies, religious beliefs, racial identities, or political views can "meet" online. Social networks such as Facebook and LinkedIn are some of the most popular sites on the Internet with millions of users from around the globe. Once a user has created a profile, it's easy to connect with old and new friends.

So what's in all this social networking for marketers? First, by monitoring social networks, marketers learn what consumers are thinking and what they are saying to each other about their brand and about the competition. Such information can be invaluable to improve advertising messages or even to correct defects in products.

By participating in the conversations, marketers can reach influential people such as journalists and consumers who are opinion leaders. But even more important is the opportunity social networks provide to create a **brand community**, a group of social network

social networks
Online platforms that allow a user to represent himself or herself via a profile on a website and provide and receive links to other members of the network to share input about common interests.

brand community
A group of social network users who share an attachment to a product or brand, interact with each other and share information about the brand.

users who share an attachment to a product or brand. Members of the brand community interact with each other, sharing information about the brand or just expressing their affection for it. As a result, the relationships between the consumers and the brand grow even stronger.

Sometimes, brand communities develop spontaneously among consumers, while at other times, the brand's marketers purposely create them—or at least nurture them along. Harley-Davidson, for example, set about to create a "brotherhood" of riders and met them on their own terms. To do this, the company's marketers set up outreach events and staffed them with employees. This tactic allowed the employees to get up close and personal with Harley riders so they could better understand how their customers actually relate to the bikes. In the process, some employees got interested in the bikes and became riders, and some riders wound up working for Harley.[12] Today, this extremely active community of enthusiasts, known as Harley Owners Group (HOGs), displays fierce loyalty to the brand; they wouldn't imagine riding anything but a Harley.

Now that we've discussed brand communities, let's examine a couple of the most popular social media sites.

Facebook

Facebook is the most popular of all social networking sites with, as we said previously, more than 1.55 billion monthly active users as we write this book—and no doubt tons of new ones even as you're reading it.[13] Users of Facebook first develop a profile that remains private unless they choose to connect with a "friend." Although this social media site was originally created to allow college students to keep in touch with their friends (in those days, you had to have ".edu" in your e-mail address to join), it is no longer just for students. Today, there are many significant user segments, including baby-boomer women and even grandparents who use the platform to locate long-lost friends (and keep tabs on their grandchildren).[14]

Although Facebook remains the most popular social media site for college students today, many 18- to 24-year-olds are moving away from it (maybe because of the "creep factor" as their parents increasingly sign on). Instead, they spend more time on other sites, including Instagram, Twitter, Tumblr, Snapchat, and Vine.[15] Another change is how college students access social media sites. Many prefer to use their mobile phones to access social media sites, receive and send e-mail, and otherwise interact on social media.

Twitter

Twitter
A free microblogging service that lets users post short text messages with a maximum of 140 characters.

Twitter is a free microblogging service that lets users post short text messages with a maximum of 140 characters. People who subscribe to an individual's Twitter feed are called "followers." Users can follow anyone they like, unlike Facebook, where you have to be recognized and accepted as a "friend." Attesting to its popularity, Twitter now has 320 million registered users who "tweet" 500 million posts a day.[16] Recently Twitter has altered its 140-character limit so followers now have a greater opportunity for expression by adding photos, videos, hashtags, Vines, and more. In 2016, Twitter announced plans for even more changes to the 140-character limit.[17]

Because of this ongoing activity, it is especially important for marketers to monitor Twitter to understand what consumers say about their products. Unlike some other social media that work only on closed networks, Twitter is a *broadcast medium*. This means that marketers can send messages to hundreds of thousands of people at a time, and they can encourage users to rally around a cause (or brand) when they include the now familiar # (hashtag). Today, it seems that everyone from political figures to music and movie celebrities uses Twitter. In fact, Twitter seems to be creating news, as newscasters request feedback from TV viewers or ask them to vote on what they like and dislike. As part of its show *Morning Express with Robin Meade*, HLN (part of CNN), has featured a salute to troops every hour where viewers can tweet a video to @ireport.com for their chosen serviceman.

Virtual Worlds

Virtual worlds are online, highly engaging digital environments where **avatars**—graphic representations of users—live and interact with other avatars in real time. The blockbuster movie *Avatar* exposed many people to this basic idea as it told the story of a wounded soldier who takes on a new (10 feet tall and blue) identity in the world of Pandora.

In virtual worlds, residents can hang out at virtual clubs, shop for clothing and bling for their avatars, buy furniture to deck out virtual homes, and yes, even go to college in virtual universities. Some people find it hard to believe, but it's common for people to spend real money to buy digital products that don't exist in the real world. Indeed, the **virtual goods** market is booming; consumers across the globe spend more than $11 billion per year to buy items they use only in virtual worlds![18]

The Sims is one of the largest and best-known virtual worlds, although in reality there are several hundred of these environments up and running. These platforms are a booming marketplace for budding fashion designers, musicians, and businesspeople who sell their goods and services. A few have even become real-world millionaires by selling virtual goods to users who want to buy bling for their avatars. A sampling of virtual worlds includes the following:

- Disney's *Club Penguin*, geared toward a younger audience, offers more than 20 games for visitors to play and earn coins, which they can then use to deck out their penguins. Players can also adopt and care for Pet Puffles in this virtual world.

- *Smeet*, a virtual world for adults, lets visitors play, flirt, and chat in a three-dimensional (3D) interface. Users start by building their own 3D home, but they can meet new people in public hangouts or attend live events.

- *Habbo Hotel* is a virtual world where kids inhabit a room (a "habbo") and decorate it with furniture they purchase with Habbo credits.

- *FooPets*, especially popular with 12- to 14-year-old girls, allows users to "adopt" digitally animated pets, then care for them, and feed them. If the pets are not properly cared for, they will be taken to a virtual shelter.[19]

Most virtual goods, whether sold in virtual worlds or through other social media sites, have microprices—from less than $1 to $3. So what's in it for real-world marketers? Some firms enter the market for virtual goods to keep in touch with consumers, improve the brand's image, and develop loyal customers. And even micropriced items, such as digital clothing for avatars, start to add up when you sell many thousands of them.

Product Review Sites

Product review sites are social media sites that enable people to post stories about their experiences with goods and services. Marketers hope that product review sites create a connection between the consumer and the brand. Product review sites give users both positive and negative information about companies:

- *TripAdvisor* provides unbiased hotel reviews complete with photos and advice. The site gives consumers an opportunity to rate and comment on a hotel that they recently stayed in or to use other consumers' comments to select a hotel for an upcoming trip. Consumers can also rate local attractions.

- *Yelp* is a product review site that provides reviews of local businesses, such as places to eat, shop, drink, or play. Consumers can access *Yelp* through either the Internet or a mobile phone. Businesses can create pages to post photos and send messages to their customers.

virtual worlds
Online, highly engaging digital environments where avatars live and interact with other avatars in real time.

avatars
Graphic representations of users of virtual worlds.

virtual goods
Digital products consumers buy for use in online contexts.

product review sites
Social media sites that enable people to post stories about their experiences with goods and services.

Virtual worlds are a new and exciting frontier for marketers to communicate with millions of users around the world.

Courtesy of Allaray Roo

The Pokémon Go craze revived a popular videogame from many years ago—but, more importantly, it was a breakthrough for augmented reality applications as people around the world scrambled to find cartoon characters in all kinds of real-world settings.

location-based social networks
Networks that integrate sophisticated GPS technology that enables users to alert friends of their exact whereabouts via their mobile phones.

augmented reality (AR)
A view of a physical, real world that is enhanced or altered by computer-generated sounds, videos, graphics, or GPS data.

• *Angie's List* and *Home Advisor* are sites for consumers who are "tired of lousy service." Angie's List members, who cannot remain anonymous, rate service companies in more than 700 categories, and a certified data collection process ensures that companies don't report on themselves or their competitors.[20]

Mobile Apps and Location-Based Social Networks

Location-based social networks, as we mentioned in Chapter 13, integrate sophisticated GPS technology (like the navigation system you may have in your car) that enables users to alert friends of their exact whereabouts via their mobile phones.

In July 2016, the **augmented reality (AR)** mobile app game "Pokémon Go" (which also relies on GPS technology in smart phones) took the world by storm, attracting more than 10 million daily users in less than a week.[21] Augmented reality is a view of a physical, real world that is enhanced or altered by computer-generated sounds, videos, graphics, or GPS data. In the case of Pokémon Go, players chase cartoon Pokémon characters at "pokestops" and "gyms" plotted on a customized version of Google Maps. Players' smartphone GPS alerts them when a Pokémon creature appears on their phone. Players are thus encouraged to "level-up" (move to a higher level) by Pokémon. The popularity of Pokémon Go creates an opportunity for advertisers to reach consumers highly engaged with the.[22] Any organization, company, or store can pay to put a pokestop or gym in their location.

Foursquare, a social network that uses GPS, was one of the most popular location-based networks with more than 50 million users, but in May 2014, the *Foursquare* folks announced they were splitting the app in two: *Foursquare* for discovering new places and *Swarm* for checking in at places you visit. Like *Foursquare*, the new *Swarm* app has the popular "Mayor" feature, but instead of competing against everyone who uses *Swarm* for the most check-ins, you compete only against your friends. The new app also offers stickers so you can let others know how you're feeling; to unlock more stickers, just check in at more places.

Businesses can ride this wave by offering discounts or free services to people who check in to their locations. For example, Boloco, a burrito chain in Boston, used a feature from the *LevelUp* app, which offered customers $5 off of a food and drink purchase of $10. To "level up," customers returned to the restaurant for $10 off a $25 purchase and then $14 off a $45 purchase. Boloco saw 26 percent of its customers return for the Level 3 reward.[23]

It's obvious to almost anyone who has a pulse today that the future of marketing communication lies in that magic little device you practically sleep with—your smartphone. Combine web-browsing capability with built-in cameras, and the race is on to bring the world to your belt or purse. Apple lit up this market when it introduced the iPhone, and now everyone is scrambling to "monetize" the mobile market through sales of ringtones, on-demand video, online coupons, and "apps" that entertain or educate. A few to watch include the following:[24]

• *ShopSavvy* finds the lowest prices online and at nearby brick-and-mortar retailers. Users can like products to get price alerts or follow their favorites stores to get alerts about when items go on sale.
• *Hot5 Fitness* is a fitness app that offers hundreds of five-minute video workouts that you can add on to the end of your current fitness routine or mix together to create a

longer workout. The high-quality videos feature custom music synced to the workout for maximum intensity.

- *Fastmall* provides interactive maps of malls, highlights the quickest route to stores, and even helps shoppers remember where they parked their cars. Even better: Shake your phone, and it shows you the nearest restroom location.

- *Flipboard* lets you pull content from social networks like *Facebook and Twitter*, as well as news content from the *New York Times* or *People* magazine, and organize it into a visual, magazine-like format.

The Internet of Things

We would be remiss if we ended our discussion of social media without mentioning the Internet of Things that we introduced in Chapter 5. This term refers to the network of physical things, vehicles, devices, buildings in which designers have embedded sensors, electronics, and network connectivity. With this technology, "things" can collect data and communicate it to each other—the many to many of things.

Many analysts believe the Internet of Things will dominate marketing's future as more and more devices get "smart." Already providers of Internet services are offering to "connect" your home with your phone to turn off your TV, lock your doors, adjust your heat and on and on. Leave your keys to your new Tesla at the resort hotel where you stayed on your holiday? No problem! Tesla will text message you to ask if you want your car unlocked and started remotely.[25] Just as the Internet has created a revolution in marketing communication, the Internet of Things will change our lives again.

14.2 Direct Marketing

OBJECTIVE
Understand the elements of direct marketing.
(pp. 489–492)

Are you one of those people who loves to get lots of catalogs in the mail or pore over online catalogs for hours and then order just exactly what you want without leaving home? Maybe you're the one who ordered the Donatella Arpaia Multifunctional Pizza Oven from the Home Shopping Network for two easy payments of only $29.98 or responded to an infomercial on TV for the DashCam Pro or the Pedi Paws pet nail trimmer. All these are examples of direct marketing, the fastest-growing type of marketing communication.

Direct marketing, a form of one-to-one marketing communication, refers to "any direct communication to a consumer or business recipient that is designed to generate a response in the form of an order, a request for further information, or a visit to a store or other place of business for purchase of a product."[26] Spending on direct marketing continues to increase. Direct and digital ad spending in 2015 was $153.2 billion, up 8 percent from the previous year. Direct mail spending alone increased 2.9 percent to $46.8 billion.[27]

direct marketing
Any direct communication to a consumer or business recipient designed to generate a response in the form of an order, a request for further information, or a visit to a store or other place of business for purchase of a product.

Why do so many marketers love direct marketing? One reason is simple but powerful: You know almost immediately whether your pitch worked. Unlike traditional advertising, every message can link directly to a response (hence the term *direct marketing*). For this reason, organizations that want to see evidence of a promotion's ROI ("show me the money!") can get very specific feedback about what worked and what didn't.

Let's look at the four most popular types of direct marketing as portrayed in Figure 14.1: mail order (including catalogs and direct mail), telemarketing, direct-response advertising, and m-commerce. We'll start with the oldest—buying through the mail—which is still incredibly popular!

Figure 14.1 📷 *Snapshot* | Key Forms of Direct Marketing

Key forms of direct marketing are mail order (including catalogs and direct mail), telemarketing, direct-response advertising, and m-commerce.

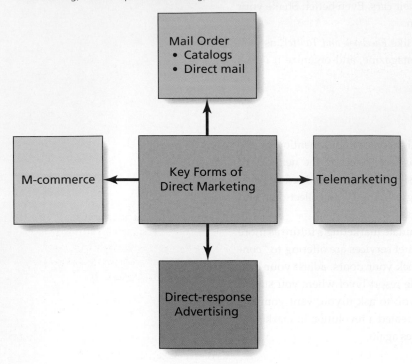

Mail Order

In 1872, Aaron Montgomery Ward and two partners put up $1,600 to mail a one-page flyer that listed their merchandise with prices, hoping to sell to farmers through the mail.[28] The mail-order industry was born, and today consumers can buy just about anything through the mail. Mail order comes in two forms: catalogs and direct mail.

A **catalog** is a collection of products offered for sale in book form, usually consisting of product descriptions accompanied by photos of the items. The early catalogs Montgomery Ward and other innovators such as Sears and JC Penney pioneered targeting people in remote areas who lacked access to stores.

Today, despite the growth in online shopping, the catalog is still alive and appears to be making a comeback. After years of decline, U.S. retailers mailed 11.9 billion catalogs in 2013, an increase of 1 percent. For many brands the catalog drives both online and in-store sales. According to the Direct Marketing Association, approximately 90 million Americans, 60 percent of whom are women, make purchases from catalogs. Customers who receive catalogs spend an average of $850 annually on catalog purchases. Of course, many catalogs are available and viewed online, often on mobile devices.

Why do retailers think catalogs are still so important? The answer is because they drive sales. In 2000, Lands' End reduced the number of catalogs it distributed. The result was a $100 million decrease in sales.

Retailer Neiman Marcus is famous for its *Christmas Book*, which always includes a number of one-of-a-kind "Fantasy Gifts." In the 2015 catalog, the gifts included Guitars designed by ZZ Top's guitarist Billy Gibbons for $30,000 and a Neiman Marcus Mustang for $95,000. The top gift for 2015 was a 12-day dream trip to India for two people including travel by private planes and vintage autos, dinners hosted by real royals and a dance lesson on a private Bollywood movie set, all for a mere $400,000.[29]

Direct Mail

Unlike a catalog retailer that offers a variety of merchandise through the mail, **direct mail** is a brochure or pamphlet that offers a specific good or service at one point in time. A direct mail offer has an advantage over a catalog because the sender can personalize it. Charities, political groups, and other not-for-profit organizations also use a lot of direct mail.

Just as with e-mail spamming, Americans are overwhelmed with direct-mail offers—"junk mail"—that may end up in the trash. Of course, many consumers not only open but also respond with cold cash to their direct mail. Research from the Direct Marketing Association found that four-fifths (79 percent) of consumers act on direct mail immediately compared to only 45 percent who say they deal with e-mail right away.[30] The direct-mail industry constantly works on ways to monitor what companies send through the mail and it allows consumers to "opt out" of at least some mailing lists.

Telemarketing

Telemarketing is direct marketing an organization conducts over the telephone (but why do they always have to call during dinner?). It might surprise you to learn that telemarketing actually is more profitable for business markets than for consumer markets.

catalog
A collection of products offered for sale in book form, usually consisting of product descriptions accompanied by photos of the items.

direct mail
A brochure or pamphlet that offers a specific good or service at one point in time.

telemarketing
The use of the telephone to sell directly to consumers and business customers.

When business-to-business (B2B) marketers use the telephone to keep in contact with smaller customers, it costs far less than a face-to-face sales call yet still lets these clients know they are important to the company.

The Federal Trade Commission (FTC) established the National Do Not Call Registry to allow consumers to limit the number of telemarketing calls they receive. The idea is that telemarketing firms check the registry at least every 31 days and clean their phone lists accordingly. Consumers responded very positively to the regulation, and more than 220 million have posted their home numbers and mobile numbers on the registry.[31] Some direct marketers initially challenged this action; they argued that it would put legitimate companies out of business while unethical companies would not abide by the regulation and continue to harass consumers. However, the National Do Not Call Registry, along with similar operations at the state level, now is an accepted part of doing business through direct marketing. The FTC maintains a list of violators on its website.[32]

Direct-Response Advertising

Direct-response advertising allows the consumer to respond to a message by immediately contacting the provider to ask questions or order the product. Although for many companies the Internet has become the medium of choice for direct marketing, this technique is still alive and well in magazines, in newspapers, and on TV.

As early as 1950, the Television Department Stores channel brought the retailing environment into the TV viewer's living room when it offered a limited number of products the viewer could buy when he or she called the advertised company. TV sales picked up in the 1970s when two companies, Ronco Incorporated and K-Tel International, began to peddle products such as the Kitchen Magician, Pocket Fisherman, Mince-O-Matic, and Miracle Broom on TV sets around the world.[33] And who can forget the late Billy Mays's enthusiastic hawking of Oxy Clean, Jupiter Jack, and nearly 20 other products on TV? Make a simple phone call, and one of these wonders could be yours ("but wait, there's more …").

Direct-response TV (DRTV) includes short commercials of less than two minutes, 30-minute or longer infomercials, and the shows that home shopping networks such as QVC and HSN broadcast. Top-selling DRTV product categories include exercise equipment, self-improvement products, diet and health products, kitchen appliances, and music. Of course, even home shopping networks have gone online, so you if you miss the show, you can still order the product.

The primitive sales pitches of the old days have largely given way to the slick **infomercials** we all know and love (?) today. These half-hour or hour-long commercials resemble a talk show, often with heavy product demonstration and spirited audience participation, but of course they really are sales pitches. Although some infomercials still carry a low-class, sleazy stereotype, in fact over the years, numerous heavyweights from Apple Computer to Volkswagen have used this format.

M-Commerce

One final type of direct marketing is m-commerce. The "m" stands for "mobile," but it could also stand for "massive"—because that's how big the market will be for this platform. **M-commerce** refers to the promotional and other e-commerce activities transmitted over mobile phones and other mobile devices, such as smartphones and tablets with phone capabilities. With more than 7 billion mobile phones in use worldwide—more and more of them Internet enabled—it makes sense that

direct-response advertising
A direct marketing approach that allows the consumer to respond to a message by immediately contacting the provider to ask questions or order the product.

direct-response TV (DRTV)
Advertising on TV that seeks a direct response, including short commercials of less than two minutes, 30-minute or longer infomercials, and home shopping networks.

infomercials
Half-hour or hour-long commercials that resemble a talk show but actually are sales pitches.

m-commerce
Promotional and other e-commerce activities transmitted over mobile phones and other mobile devices, such as smartphones and personal digital assistants.

Infomercials are a commonly used form of direct-response TV.

marketers would want to reach out and touch this large audience, which is just over 85 percent of the world's population. That means there are more mobile phones throughout the world than working toilets![34]

M-commerce through text messages (such as an ad for a concert or a new restaurant) is known as *short-messaging system* (SMS) marketing. In terms of unwanted "junk mail," m-commerce has the same potential dark side as other forms of direct marketing, such as snail mail and e-mail. And the rise of the all-in-one smartphone on which the user engages in 24/7 social networking has created an up-and-coming industry of social networking activity tracking and analytics, such as Google Analytics and similar programs that we discussed in Chapter 5.

14.3 Personal Selling: Adding the Personal Touch to the Promotion Mix

OBJECTIVE

Understand the important role of personal selling, the different types of sales jobs and the steps in the creative selling process.

(pp. 492–501)

Now we turn our attention to one of the most visible—and most expensive—forms of marketing communication: personal selling. Like direct marketing, personal selling is an example of one-to-one marketing communications.

personal selling

Marketing communication by which a company representative interacts directly with a customer or prospective customer to communicate about a good or service.

Personal selling occurs when a company representative interacts directly with a customer or prospective customer to communicate about a good or service. This form of promotion is a far more intimate way to talk to customers. Another advantage of personal selling is that salespeople are the firm's eyes and ears in the marketplace. They learn which competitors talk to customers, what they offer, and what new rival goods and services are on the way—all valuable competitive intelligence.

Many organizations rely heavily on personal selling because at times the "personal touch" carries more weight than mass-media material. For a B2B market situation, the personal touch translates into developing crucial relationships with clients. Also, many industrial goods and services are too complex or expensive to market effectively in impersonal ways (such as through mass advertising). An axiom in marketing is: The more complex, technical, and intangible the product, the more heavily firms tend to rely on personal selling to promote it.

Personal selling has special importance for students (that's *you*) because many graduates with a marketing background will enter professional sales jobs. The U.S. Bureau of Labor Statistics estimates job growth of about 7 percent for sales representatives in manufacturing and wholesaling between 2014 and 2024. For technical and scientific products, the growth projection is also 7 percent. Overall, sales job growth ranks high among all occupations surveyed.[35] Jobs in selling and sales management often provide high upward mobility if you are successful because firms value employees who understand customers and who can communicate well with them. The old business adage "nothing happens until something is sold" translates into many firms placing quite a bit of emphasis on personal selling in their promotion mixes. And the sales role is even more crucial during tricky economic times, when companies look to their salespeople to drum up new business and to maintain the business they already have.

Sold on selling? All right, then let's take a close look at how personal selling works and how professional salespeople develop long-term relationships with customers.

The Role of Personal Selling in the Marketing Mix

When a woman calls the 800 number for the MGM Grand Hotel in Las Vegas to book a room for a little vacation trip and comes away with not only a room but also show tickets,

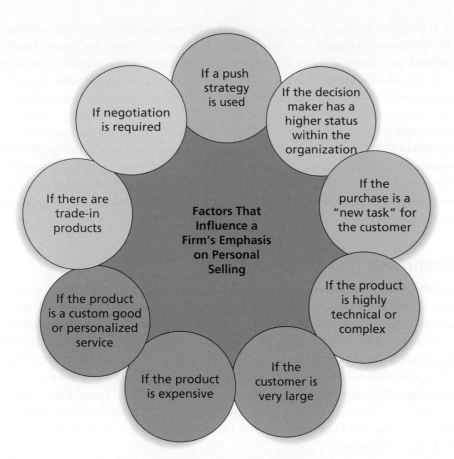

Figure 14.2 ⬚ *Snapshot* | Factors That Influence a Firm's Emphasis on Personal Selling

A variety of factors influence whether personal selling is a more or less important element in an organization's overall promotion mix.

a massage booking at the hotel spa, and a reservation for dinner at Emeril's, she deals with a salesperson. When she sits in on a presentation at work by a website consultant who proposes a new content management system for her firm's website, she deals with a salesperson. When she tries on five pairs of stiletto heels in a shoe store, she deals with a salesperson. And when that same woman agrees over lunch at a swanky restaurant to invest some of her savings with a financial manager's recommended mutual fund, she also deals with a salesperson.

For many firms, some element of personal selling is essential to land a commitment to purchase or a contract, so this type of marketing communication is a key to the success of their overall marketing plan. To put the use of personal selling into perspective, ⬚ Figure 14.2 illustrates some of the factors that make it a more or less important element in an organization's promotion.

In general, a personal selling emphasis is more important when a firm engages in a *push strategy*, in which the goal is to "push" the product through the channel of distribution so that it is available to consumers. As a vice president at Hallmark Cards once observed, "We're not selling *to* the retailer, we're selling *through* the retailer. We look at the retailer as a pipeline to the hands of consumers."[36]

Personal selling also is likely to be crucial in B2B contexts where the firm must interact directly with a client's management to clinch a big deal—and often when intense negotiations about price and other factors will occur before the customer signs on the dotted line. In consumer contexts, inexperienced customers may need the hands-on assistance that a professional salesperson provides. Firms that sell goods and services that consumers buy infrequently—houses, cars, computers, lawn mowers, and even college educations—often rely heavily on personal selling. (*Hint:* Your school didn't pick just any student at random to conduct campus tours and help those clueless freshmen.) Likewise, firms whose goods or services are complex or very expensive often need a salesperson to explain, justify, and sell them—in both business and consumer markets.

If personal selling is so useful, why don't firms just scrap their advertising and sales promotion budgets and hire more salespeople? There are some drawbacks that limit the role personal selling plays in the marketing communication mix. First, when the dollar amount of individual purchases is low, it doesn't make sense to use personal selling—the average cost per contact with each customer is more than $300, much higher than other forms of promotion. The per-contact cost of a national TV commercial is minuscule by comparison. A 30-second prime-time commercial may run $300,000 to $500,000 (or as we said in Chapter 13, more than $4 million for a 30-second commercial aired during the Super Bowl), but with millions of viewers, the cost per contact may be only $25 or $35 per 1,000 viewers. For low-priced consumer packaged goods such as Doritos or beer, personal selling to end users simply doesn't make good financial sense.

Technology and Personal Selling

Personal selling is supposed to be, well, "personal." By definition, a company uses personal selling for marketing communications in situations when one person (the salesperson) interacts directly with another person (the customer or prospective customer) to communicate about a good or service. All sorts of technologies can enhance the personal selling process, and clearly today the smartphone is the communication hub of the relationship between salesperson and client. However, as anyone making sales calls knows, technology itself cannot and should not *replace* personal selling. Today, a key role of personal selling is to manage customer *relationships*—and remember that relationships occur between people, not between computers (as much as you love your *Facebook* friends or checking in on *Swarm*).

However, there's no doubt that a bevy of technological advancements makes it easier for salespeople to do their jobs more effectively. One such technological advance is *customer relationship management (CRM) software*. For years now, *account management software* such as ACT and GoldMine has helped salespeople manage their client and prospect base. These programs are inexpensive, easy to navigate, and allow salespeople to track all aspects of customer interaction. As we saw with our discussion of Oracle in Chapter 3, currently many firms turn to *cloud computing* CRM applications, which are more customizable and integrative than ACT or OnContact yet are less expensive than major companywide CRM installations. A market leader in such products is SalesForce.com, which is particularly user friendly for salespeople. A key benefit of cloud computing versions of CRM systems is that firms "rent" them for a flat fee per month (at SalesForce.com, monthly prices are as low as $20 per user), so they avoid major capital outlays.[37]

partner relationship management (PRM)
Similar to a CRM, the PRM system allows both selling and buying firms to share some of their information.

Recently, some sales organizations have turned to a new-generation system called **partner relationship management (PRM)**, which links information between selling and buying firms. PRM differs from CRM in that both supplier and buyer firms share at least some of their databases and systems to maximize the usefulness of the data for decision-making purposes. Firms that share information are more likely to work together toward win-win solutions.

Beyond CRM and PRM, numerous other technology applications enhance personal selling, including teleconferencing, videoconferencing, and improved corporate

Telemarketing, sometimes called teleselling, involves person-to-person communication that takes place on the phone.

websites that offer frequently asked questions (FAQs) pages to answer customers' queries. Many firms also use intranets and blogs to facilitate access to internal and external communication.

Voice-over Internet protocol (VoIP)—systems that rely on a data network to carry voice calls—get a lot of use in day-to-day correspondence between salespeople and customers. With VoIP, the salesperson on the road can just plug into a fast Internet connection and then start to make and receive calls just as if in the office. Unlike mobile phones, there are no bad reception areas, and unlike hotel phones, there are no hidden charges.

One popular VoIP product is Skype. Thanks to Skype, built-in laptop and tablet web cams, instant messaging, and the like, customers of all types are becoming more comfortable with the concept of doing business with a salesperson who is not actually in the same room. As such, a good portion of the future of face- to-face sales calls may occur on your own computer screen. Since its purchase by Microsoft in 2011, Skype has introduced Skype for Business, which offers the Skype technology for meetings of up to 250 people for a monthly fee.

New technology such as VoIP has made a major change in the attractiveness of sales jobs. In the past, salespeople were expected to travel and be away from home as much as four nights a week, entertaining customers with a big expense account. This type of job was hard on families because it left little time for the employee to hang out at home. Today, firms and their salespeople use computer networks, e-mail, and video conferencing. These technological advances and changing cultural values that require a balance in life mean that an increasing number of salespeople **telecommute** from a **virtual office**. Telecommuting is a win-win opportunity. Companies spend less on office space and travel and salespeople are able to balance their time between work and home and can respond to family responsibilities.[38]

Consider the following hypothetical transaction related to buying a set of solar panels for your roof—a complex and expensive purchase. The sales consultant calls at an appointed time. You open her e-mail message, click a link to start the presentation, and a picture of your roof appears, courtesy of satellite imaging. Colorful charts show past electricity bills and the savings from a solar-panel system. A series of spreadsheets examine the financing options available—and these are dynamic documents, not static images, so the salesperson can tinker with the figures right before your eyes. Would more panels be justified? A few keystrokes later, new charts displayed the costs and savings. Could they be shifted to another part of the roof? With a mouse, she moves some black panels from the east side to the west side. How about more cash up front? She scrolls to the spreadsheets, highlights three payment options, and computes the numbers over the next 15 years. In less than an hour, the exchange is over.

Perhaps for a few days or a week, you mull over the choices and study the fine print in the contract, but the sale was essentially closed by the time you hung up the phone. You decided to make a major, complex purchase, worth thousands of dollars, without ever meeting anyone in the flesh and without holding any product in your hands. And unlike many purchases, you had no *buyer's remorse* despite the fact it was done online—or maybe *because* it was online.[39]

For years now, all of us have been shopping online, taking in the bargains and wide selection, usually for relatively straightforward goods and services and without any human contact unless a problem arises with the ordering technology itself. The brave new world of virtual selling adds another dimension and is yet another example of how the Internet transforms business and remakes job descriptions. These more sophisticated virtual selling capabilities won't replace all face-to-face salesperson–client encounters any more than e-commerce replaced brick-and-mortar retailers. But smart sales organizations can find the right blend of technology and personal touch, tailored to their particular clientele and product offerings, which make the most of building strong customer relationships.

voice-over Internet protocol (VoIP)
Communication systems that use data networks to carry voice calls.

telecommute
Working with fellow employees from a distant location using Internet communication technology such as VoIP.

virtual office
The use of Internet technology to work and participate from a distant physical office.

Figure 14.3 📷 *Snapshot* | Types of Sales Jobs

A wide range of different types of sales jobs are available, each of which has different job requirements and responsibilities.

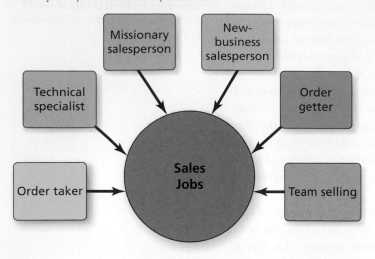

order taker

A salesperson whose primary function is to facilitate transactions that the customer initiates.

technical specialist

A sales support person with a high level of technical expertise who assists in product demonstrations.

missionary salesperson

A salesperson who promotes the firm and tries to stimulate demand for a product but does not actually complete a sale.

new-business salesperson

The person responsible for finding new customers and calling on them to present the company's products.

order getter

A salesperson who works to develop long-term relationships with particular customers or to generate new sales.

team selling

The sales function when handled by a team that may consist of a salesperson, a technical specialist, and others.

key account

Very large customer organizations with the potential for providing significant sales revenue.

cross-functional team

A form on selling team where the team includes individuals from various areas of the firm.

multilevel selling

A form of team selling in which the team consists of company personnel from various managerial levels, each calling on their counterpart in the customer organization.

Types of Sales Jobs

Maybe you aspire to work in sales someday, or perhaps you've already held a sales job at some point. If you see sales in your future, there are several different types of sales jobs from which you can choose, each with its own unique characteristics. Let's look more closely at some of the different types of sales positions. 📷 Figure 14.3 summarizes the most important types.

As you might imagine, sales jobs vary considerably. The person who answers the phone at Zappos to take your order for a new pair of UGG boots (if anybody orders them by phone anymore instead of online) is primarily an **order taker**—a salesperson who processes transactions the customer initiates. Many retail salespeople are order takers, but often wholesalers, dealers, and distributors also employ salespeople to assist their business customers. Because little creative selling is involved taking, this type of sales job typically is the lowest-paid sales position.

In contrast, a **technical specialist** contributes considerable expertise in the form of product demonstrations, recommendations for complex equipment, and setup of machinery. The technical specialist provides *sales support* rather than actually closing the sale. He or she promotes the firm and tries to stimulate demand for a product to make it easier for colleagues to actually seal the deal.

Then there is the **missionary salesperson**, whose job is to stimulate clients to buy. Like technical specialists, missionary salespeople promote the firm and encourage demand for its goods and services but don't actually take orders.[40] Pfizer (one of the world's largest pharmaceutical companies) salespeople do missionary sales work when they call on physicians to influence them to prescribe the latest-and-greatest Pfizer medications instead of competing drugs. However, no sale actually gets made until doctors or their patients get the prescriptions to pharmacies, which then place orders for the drug through their wholesalers or directly from the maker of the drug.

The **new-business salesperson** is responsible for finding new customers and calls on them to present the company's products. As you might imagine, gaining the business of a new customer usually means that the customer stops doing business with one of the firm's competitors (and they won't give up without a fight). New-business selling requires a high degree of creativity and professionalism, so this type of salesperson is usually very well paid.

Once a new-business salesperson establishes a relationship with a client, he or she often continues to service that client as the primary contact as long as the client continues to buy from the company. In that long-term-relationship-building role, this type of salesperson is an **order getter**. Order getters are usually the people most directly responsible for a particular client's business; they may also hold the title of "account manager."[41]

More and more, firms find that the selling function works best via **team selling**. A selling team may consist of a salesperson, a technical specialist, someone from engineering and design, and other players who work together to develop products and programs that satisfy the customer's needs. With multiple individuals participating in a selling team, all working with a single account, team selling becomes very expensive. Thus, team selling is usually limited to large customers or **key accounts** where potential business justifies the extra human resource commitment.

When the company includes people from a range of areas, it often calls this group a **cross-functional team**. **Multilevel selling** is a form of team selling in which the selling team consists of company personnel from various managerial levels, each calling on their counterpart in the customer organization.[42]

Another popular sales model is *direct selling*. Direct sellers bypass channel intermediaries and sell directly from manufacturer to consumer through personal, one-to-one contact. Typically, independent sales representatives sell in person in a customer's home or place of business. Tupperware, Thirty-One, Scentsy, Avon, Mary Kay, and the Pampered Chef are some well-known examples. Many direct-selling firms use a *party plan* approach where salespeople demonstrate products in front of groups of friends and neighbors. Direct selling is on a big upswing. In 2015, more than 20 million people were involved in direct selling, more than two-thirds of whom were aged 35 and over. Direct retail sales in 2015 were more than $35 billion, up 4.8 percent from the previous year.[43]

Two Approaches to Personal Selling

Personal selling is one of the oldest forms of marketing communication. Unfortunately, over the years, smooth-talking pitchmen who will say anything to make a sale have tarnished its image. Pulitzer Prize–winning playwright Arthur Miller's famous character Willie Loman in *Death of a Salesman*—a must-read for generations of middle and high school students—didn't help. Loman (as in "low man" on the totem pole—get it?) is a pathetic, burned-out peddler who leaves home for the road on Monday morning and returns late Friday evening selling "on a smile and a shoeshine." His personal life is in shambles with two dysfunctional sons and a disaffected wife who hardly knows him. Great public relations for selling as a career, right?

Fortunately, personal selling today is nothing like Miller's harsh portrayal. Selling has moved from a transactional, hard-sell approach to an approach based on relationships with customers. Let's see how.

Transactional Selling: Putting on the Hard Sell

Loman practiced a high-pressure, hard-sell approach. We've all been exposed to the pushy electronics salesperson who puts down the competition when telling shoppers that if they buy elsewhere, they will be stuck with an inferior home theater system that will fall apart in six months. Or how about the crafty used car salesman who plays the good-cop/bad-cop game, gives you an awesome price, but then sadly informs you that the boss, the sales manager, won't go for such a sweet deal. These hard-sell tactics reflect **transactional selling**, an approach that focuses on making an immediate sale with little concern for developing a long-term relationship with the customer.

transactional selling
A form of personal selling that focuses on making an immediate sale with little or no attempt to develop a relationship with the customer.

As customers, the hard sell makes us feel manipulated and resentful, and it diminishes our satisfaction and loyalty. It's a shortsighted approach to selling. As we said previously in the book, constantly finding new customers is much more expensive than getting repeat business from the customers you already have. And the behaviors transactional selling promotes (i.e., doing anything to get the order) contribute to the negative image many of us have of salespeople as obnoxious and untrustworthy. Such salespeople engage in these behaviors because they don't care if they ever have the chance to sell to you again. This is really bad business!

Relationship Selling: Building Long-Term Customers

Relationship selling is the process by which a salesperson secures, develops, and maintains long-term relationships with profitable customers.[44] Today's professional salesperson is more likely to practice relationship selling than transactional selling. This means that the salesperson tries to develop a mutually satisfying, win-win relationship with the customer. Securing a customer relationship means converting an interested prospect into someone who is convinced that the good or service holds value for him or her. Developing a customer relationship means ensuring that you and the customer work together to find more ways to add value to the transaction. Maintaining a customer relationship means building

relationship selling
A form of personal selling that involves securing, developing, and maintaining long-term relationships with profitable customers.

Figure 14.4 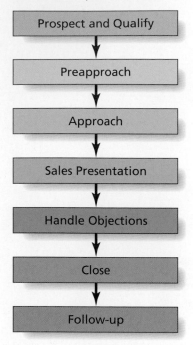 *Process* | Steps in the Creative Selling Process

In the creative selling process, salespeople follow a series of steps to build relationships with customers.

creative selling process
The process of seeking out potential customers, analyzing needs, determining how product attributes might provide benefits for the customer, and then communicating that information.

prospecting
A part of the selling process that includes identifying and developing a list of potential or prospective customers.

preapproach
A part of the selling process that includes developing information about prospective customers and planning the sales interview.

customer satisfaction and loyalty—thus, you can count on the customer to provide future business and stick with you for the long haul. And if doing business with the customer isn't profitable to you, unless you're a charitable organization, you would probably like to see that customer go somewhere else.

The Creative Selling Process

Many people find selling to be a great profession, partly because something different is always going on. Every customer, every sales call, and every salesperson is unique. Some salespeople are successful primarily because they know so much about what they sell. Others are successful because they've built strong relationships with customers so that they're able to add value to both the customer and their own firm—a win-win approach to selling. Successful salespeople understand and engage in a series of activities to make the sales encounter mutually beneficial.

A salesperson's chances of success increase when following a systematic series of steps we call the **creative selling process**. These steps require the salesperson to seek out potential customers, analyze their needs, determine how product attributes provide benefits, and then decide how best to communicate this to prospects. As Figure 14.4 shows, there are seven steps in the process. Let's take a look at each.

Step 1: Prospect and Qualify

Prospecting is the process by which a salesperson identifies and develops a list of *prospects* or *sales leads* (potential customers). Leads come from existing customer lists, telephone directories, commercially available databases, and of course, the diligent use of web search engines like Google. The local library may own directories of businesses (including those state and federal agencies publish) and directories of association memberships. Of course, many of these directories are now online, which makes the search easier than ever. Sometimes companies generate sales leads through their advertising or sales promotion when they encourage customers to request more information. As we discussed in Chapter 13, trade shows also are an important source of sales leads.

Another way to generate leads is through *cold calling*, in which the salesperson simply contacts prospects "cold," without prior introduction or arrangement. It always helps to know the prospect, so salespeople might rely instead on *referrals*. Current clients who are satisfied with their purchase often recommend a salesperson to others—yet another reason to maintain good customer relationships.

However, the mere fact that someone is willing to talk to a salesperson doesn't guarantee a sale. After they identify potential customers, salespeople need to *qualify* these prospects to determine how likely they are to become customers. To do this, they ask questions such as the following:

- Are the prospects likely to be interested in what I'm selling?
- Are they likely to switch their allegiance from another supplier or product?
- Is the potential sales volume large enough to make a relationship profitable?
- Can they afford the purchase?
- If they must borrow money to buy the product, what is their credit history?

Step 2: Preapproach

In the **preapproach** stage, you compile background information about prospective customers and plan the sales interview. Firms don't make important purchases lightly, and it's often difficult even to get an appointment to see a prospect. It's foolish for a salesperson to blindly call on a qualified prospect and risk losing the sale because of a lack of preparation. Salespeople try to learn as much as possible about qualified prospects early on. They may probe a prospect's prior purchase history or current needs or, in some cases, may even try to learn about their personal interests. Does the customer like for a salesperson to spend time informally talking about golf or football, or does he or she prefer a salesperson who gets to the point quickly and leaves? And, of course, it's always good to know which football team the customer roots for.

Salespeople can draw information about a prospect from a variety of sources. In the case of larger companies, they can find financial data, names of top executives, and other information about a business from outlets such as *Standard & Poor's 500 Directory* or Dun & Bradstreet's *Million Dollar Directory*. They can also find a great deal of information for the preapproach on customers' websites. And the inside scoop on a prospect often comes from informal sources, such as noncompeting salespeople who have dealt with the prospect before.

Of course, if the salesperson's firm has a CRM system, he or she can use it to see whether the database includes information about the prospect. Say, for example, a salesperson at Mike's Bikes plans to call on a buyer at Greg's Vacation Rentals to see about selling some new bikes for guests to use at Greg's various resort properties. If Mike's has had a CRM system in place for some time, any contacts with customers and potential customers (prospects) are recorded in the database. The salesperson can simply run an inquiry about Greg's Vacation Rentals, and with luck, the CRM database will deliver information on the company, prior purchases from Mike's, when and why customers stopped buying from the company, and perhaps even the preferences of the particular buyer.

Step 3: Approach

After the salesperson lays the groundwork with the preapproach, it's time to **approach**, or contact, the prospect. During these important first minutes, several key events occur. The salesperson tries to learn even more about the prospect's needs, create a good impression, and build rapport. If the salesperson found prospect Emily Groves through a referral, he or she will probably say so to Emily up front: "Stephanie Wall with Prentice Industries suggested I call on you."

During the approach, the customer decides whether the salesperson has something to offer that is of potential value. The old saying "You never get a second chance to make a good first impression" rings true here. A professional appearance tells the prospect that the salesperson means business and is competent to handle the sale. Of course, what is appropriate depends on industry norms. Today, you may be out of place calling on some customers in a suit and tie. Even so, "casual Friday" rarely cuts it in the sales world.

Step 4: Sales Presentation

Many sales calls involve a formal **sales presentation**, which lays out the benefits of the product and its advantages over the competition. When possible and appropriate, salespeople should incorporate a great multimedia presentation shown on their tablet or laptop integrated into their sales presentations to jazz things up. A picture is worth a thousand words and a video showing how each weld in the grocery carts is triple welded—well, you know.

The focus of the sales presentation should always be on ways the salesperson, the goods and services, and the company can add value to the customer (and in a B2B setting, to the customer's company). It is important for the salesperson to present this value proposition clearly and to invite the customer's involvement in the conversation. Let the customer ask questions, give feedback,

approach
The first step of the actual sales presentation in which the salesperson tries to learn more about the customer's needs, create a good impression, and build rapport.

sales presentation
The part of the selling process in which the salesperson directly communicates the value proposition to the customer and invites two-way communication.

A good salesperson is well groomed and wears appropriate business dress. She doesn't chew gum, use poor grammar or inappropriate language, mispronounce the customer's name, or seem uninterested in the call. Visible tattoos, body piercings, and the like are controversial in professional selling.

and discuss his or her needs. Canned approaches to sales presentations are a poor choice for salespeople who want to build long-term relationships. In fact, sales managers rate *listening* skills, not talking skills, as the single most important attribute they look for when they hire relationship salespeople.[45] In a sales call, it's a good idea to put the *80/20 rule* to work—that is, spend 80 percent of your time listening to the client and assessing his or her needs and only 20 percent talking (Note: This rule of thumb is a spin-off of the 80/20 rule for market segmentation we discussed in Chapter 7).

Step 5: Handle Objections

It's rare when a prospect accepts everything the salesperson offers without question. The effective salesperson anticipates *objections*—reasons why the prospect is reluctant to make a commitment—and prepared to respond with additional information or persuasive arguments. Actually, the salesperson should welcome objections because they show that the prospect is at least interested enough to consider the offer and seriously weigh its pros and cons. Handling the objection successfully can move a prospect to the decision stage. For example, the salesperson might say, "Ms. Wall, you've said before that you don't have room to carry our new line of trail bikes, although you mentioned that you may be losing some sales by carrying only one brand with very few different models. If we could come up with an estimate of how much business you're losing, I'll bet you'd consider making room for our line, wouldn't you?"

Step 6: Close the Sale

close
The stage of the selling process in which the salesperson actually asks the customer to buy the product.

The win-win nature of relationship selling should take some of the pressure off salespeople to make "the dreaded close." But there still comes a point in the sales call at which one or the other party has to move toward gaining commitment to the objectives of the call—presumably a purchase. This is the decision stage, or **close**. Directly asking the customer for his or her business doesn't need to be painful or awkward: If the salesperson has done a great job in the previous five steps of the creative selling process, closing the sale should be a natural progression of the dialogue between the buyer and seller.

There are a variety of approaches salespeople use to close the sale:

- A *last objection close* asks customers if they are ready to purchase, providing the salesperson can address any concerns they have about the product: "Are you ready to order if we can prove our delivery time frames meet your expectations?"

- An *assumptive* or *minor points close* mean the salesperson acts as if the purchase is inevitable with only a small detail or two to be settled: "What quantity would you like to order?"

- A *standing-room-only* or *buy-now close* injects some urgency when the salesperson suggests the customer might miss an opportunity if he or she hesitates: "This price is good through Saturday only, so to save 20 percent we should book the order now." When making such closes, salespeople must be sure the basis they state for buying now is truthful, or they'll lose a valuable relationship for the price of a one-time sale!

Step 7: Follow-Up

follow-up
Activities after the sale that provide important services to customers.

Understanding that the process doesn't end after the salesperson earns the client's business is basic to a relationship selling perspective that emphasizes the importance of long-term satisfaction. The **follow-up** after the sale includes arranging for delivery, payment, and purchase terms. It also means the salesperson makes sure the customer received delivery and is satisfied. Follow-up also allows the salesperson to *bridge* to the next purchase. Once a relationship develops, the selling process is only beginning. Even as one cycle of purchasing draws to a close, a good salesperson already lays the foundation for the next one.

Metrics Moment

Now you know quite a bit about selling, but how does a firm know whether a salesperson is effective? Obviously, the short answer is that he or she produces high sales volume and meets or exceeds sales goals. But just increasing total dollar or unit sales volume is not always an adequate indicator of salesperson success. The problem is that, everything else being equal, salespeople who are compensated strictly on sales volume may simply sell whatever products are easiest to sell to pile up total sales. And what's wrong with this, you might ask? It is that the easiest products to sell may not be the products with the highest *profit* margins, and they also may not be the products the firm believes are important to build to ensure future success in the market.

Because of these problems with using raw sales volume as the sole indicator of salesperson success, some firms turn to a variety of other metrics, including input and output measures. **Input measures** are "effort" measures—things that go into selling, such as the number and type of sales calls, expense account management, and a variety of nonselling activities, such as customer follow-up work and client service. **Output measures**, or the results of the salesperson's efforts, include sales volume but also include things like the number of orders, size of orders, number of

new accounts, level of repeat business, customer satisfaction, and quantity of particular key products sold. Profitability of the sale to the company is also an output measure, although many salespeople resist being judged on their profit contribution because they claim (not entirely incorrectly) that they cannot control many of the costs that impact product profits.

Ultimately, the best approach to measure salesperson success is to use a variety of metrics that are consistent with the goals of the particular firm, to ensure the salesperson thoroughly understands the goals and related metrics being used, and then to link salesperson rewards to the achievement of those goals.

Apply the Metrics

1. Assume that you are a professional salesperson and consider the various input and output metrics of salesperson effectiveness described.
2. Which of the metrics would you prefer to be evaluated against? Why do you prefer these?
3. Which of the metrics would you least like being evaluated against? Why?

14.4

OBJECTIVE

Explain the role of public relations and the steps in developing a public relations campaign.

(pp. 501–510)

Public Relations

Public relations (PR) is the communication function that seeks to build good relationships with an organization's *publics*; these include consumers, stockholders, legislators, and other stakeholders in the organization. Today marketers use PR activities to influence the attitudes and perceptions of various groups not only toward companies and brands but also toward politicians, celebrities, and not-for-profit organizations.

One basic rule of good PR is, *Do something good, and then talk about it*. A company's efforts to get in the limelight—and stay there—can range from humanitarian acts to sponsoring band tours. For example, after Baylor University's star center Isaiah Austin, expected to be a first-round National Basketball Association (NBA) draft pick, announced that he had been diagnosed with Marfan syndrome and would never play professional basketball, Commissioner Silver invited Austin to the draft and surprised everyone by announcing that the NBA was picking Isaiah Austin for "Team NBA."[46] The next day, Austin and his family were interviewed on CNN, and the story was covered on sports Internet sites and in newspapers around the world.

The big advantage of this kind of communication is that when PR messages are placed successfully, they are more credible than if the same information appeared in a paid advertisement. As one marketing executive observed, "There's a big difference between hearing about a product from a pitchman and from your trusted local anchorman."[47]

PR strategies are crucial to an organization's ability to establish and maintain a favorable image. *Proactive*

input measures
Efforts that go into selling, such as the number and type of sales calls, expense account management, and a variety of nonselling activities, such as customer follow-up work and client service.

output measures
The results of the salesperson's efforts.

public relations (PR)
Communication function that seeks to build good relationships with an organization's publics, including consumers, stockholders, and legislators.

The Isaiah Austin story was a PR success for the NBA.

Jason Szenes/epa european pressphoto agency b.v./Alamy Stock Photo

publicity
Unpaid communication about an organization that appears in the mass media.

crisis management
The process of managing a company's reputation when some negative event threatens the organization's image.

PR activities stem from the company's marketing objectives. For example, marketers create and manage **publicity**, unpaid communication about an organization that gets media exposure. It's interesting to note that this aspect of PR is blending into other promotional strategies as social media continue to mushroom. Essentially, buzz marketing is also one form of PR because it tries to motivate consumers to talk up a brand or service to one another (ideally for free).

As many of the other functions of PR blend into buzz-marketing activities, perhaps the most important function it still "owns" is **crisis management**. This refers to the process of managing a company's reputation when some negative and often unplanned event threatens the organization's image. Think about the newly hired CEO at GM, for example, who had to apologize to the public about GM's faulty ignition switches that resulted in 31 crashes and the deaths of 13 people while still trying to instill confidence in the GM brand.[48] Or what about the team at Malaysia Airlines who had to respond to the mysterious disappearance of Flight MH370, which had more than 200 passengers and crew on board?

The goal in such situations is to manage the flow of information to address concerns so that consumers don't panic and distributors don't abandon the product. Although some organizations don't seem to learn this lesson, typically the best strategy is to be honest about the problem and to quickly take responsibility for correcting it. Carnival Cruise Lines learned this lesson all too well when a fire in the engine room on its ship *Triumph* caused 3,100 passengers and crew to be stranded at sea for five days without air conditioning or working toilets. Thanks to social media, word of the conditions on the "Poop Cruise" quickly spread. Then Carnival's crisis team jumped into action, launching a Facebook page and using Twitter to send out updates and mobilizing more than 200 Carnival employees to assist disembarking passengers when the ship finally docked. Carnival also gave a full refund to passengers, reimbursement for most of their onboard expenses, a flight home, $500 cash, and a credit toward a future cruise in an effort to make up for the unplanned disaster.[49]

PR professionals know that when a firm handles a crisis well, it can minimize damage and help the company make things right. Thus, a vitally important role of PR is to prepare a *crisis management plan*. This is a document that details what an organization will do *if* a crisis occurs—who will be the spokesperson for the organization, how the organization will deal with the press, and what sort of messages it will deliver to the press and the public.

Plan a PR Campaign

public relations campaign
A coordinated effort to communicate with one or more of the firm's publics.

A **public relations campaign** is a coordinated effort to communicate with one or more of the firm's publics. This is a three-step process that develops, executes, and evaluates PR objectives. Let's review each step, and then we'll examine some of the more frequently used objectives and tactics shown in 📷 Figure 14.5.

Like an advertising campaign, the organization must first *develop* clear objectives for the PR program that define the message it wants people to hear. For example, the International Apple Institute, a trade group devoted to increasing the consumption of apples, had to decide if a campaign should focus on getting consumers to cook more with apples, drink more apple juice, or simply buy more fresh fruit. Because fresh apples brought a substantially higher price per pound to growers than apples used for applesauce or apple juice, the group decided to push the fresh fruit angle. It used the theme "An apple a day ..." (sound familiar?) as it mounted a focused campaign to encourage people to eat more apples by placing articles in consumer media extolling the fruit's health benefits.

Marketing communication experts know that PR strategies are best used in concert with advertising, sales promotion, and personal selling to send a consistent message to

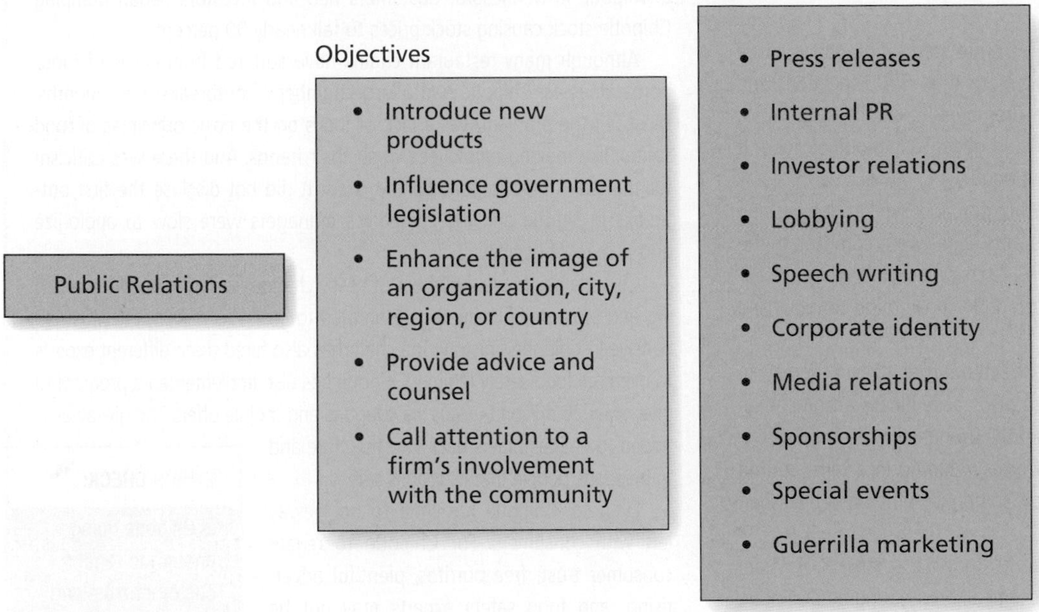

Figure 14.5 📷 *Snapshot* | Objectives and Tactics of Public Relations

Successful PR campaigns include clearly defined objectives and the use of the right PR activities.

Public Relations

Objectives

- Introduce new products
- Influence government legislation
- Enhance the image of an organization, city, region, or country
- Provide advice and counsel
- Call attention to a firm's involvement with the community

Activities

- Press releases
- Internal PR
- Investor relations
- Lobbying
- Speech writing
- Corporate identity
- Media relations
- Sponsorships
- Special events
- Guerrilla marketing

customers and other stakeholders. As part of the total marketing communication plan, they often rely on PR to accomplish the following objectives:

- *Introduce new products to retailers and consumers.* As we discussed in Chapter 2, Amazon CEO Jeff Bezos created great excitement when he announced the company's work on Prime Air, a new delivery system that would deliver packages to customers in 30 minutes or less using drones. Of course, the excitement calmed down when a few months later the Federal Aviation Administration ruled that Amazon and other firms could not use drones to deliver packages.[50] Fortunately for Amazon, that ruling has since been reversed.

- *Influence government legislation.* Airplane maker Boeing spent more than a decade in public relations activities to persuade regulators that jetliners with two engines are as safe as those with three or four engines even for nonstop international flights, some as long as 16 hours.[51]

- *Enhance the image of an organization.* The Ladies Professional Golf Association used a variety of public relations and other promotion activities—from product endorsements to player blogs to sexy calendars—in its "These Girls Rock" campaign. The program to change the image of ladies' golf to a hip sport seems to be working, as both tournament attendance and TV audiences have increased.[52]

- *Provide advice and counsel.* Because of their expertise and understanding of the effects of communication on public opinion, PR professionals also provide *advice and counsel* for top management. When a firm needs to shut down a plant or to build a new one, to discontinue a product or add to the product line, to fire a vice president, or to give an award to an employee who spends hundreds of hours a year doing volunteer work in his community, it needs the advice of its PR staff. What is the best way to handle the situation? How should the announcement be made? Who should be told first? What is to be said, and how?

- *Enhance the image of a city, region, or country.* The city of Brooklyn Park, a suburb of Minneapolis, Minnesota, hired a PR firm to revamp its image. Once known as high-crime area, the city also suffered from "suburban blah." Brooklyn Park hopes its

Ripped from the Headlines

Ethical/Sustainable Decisions in the Real World

Begun on borrowed money in 1993 as a burrito stand, Chipotle is a true success story. At its peak, Chipotle had more than 2000 locations and a market value of $23 billion. Chipotle promotes its emphasis on fresh, locally sourced ingredients and has rejected genetically modified food. It follows the notion of doing well by doing good.

In November 2015, 19 people in Washington and 3 in Oregon became sick from eating at local Chipotle restaurants. Eight were admitted to the hospital. No one died, but there were links to six different Chipotle restaurants in the Seattle and Portland areas. Chipotle chose to be cautious and closed 43 restaurants in those markets.

The cause was *Escherichia coli*, a bacteria that lives naturally in people's intestines, but some strains can also cause illness accompanied by vomiting and diarrhea, and even death. This usually occurs when a person ingests tiny amounts of feces from swimming in a lake, petting an animal, or eating food prepared by someone who hasn't washed their hands.

In December, things got worse when 80 students, at least 8 of whom were on the school's basketball team, became ill after eating at a Chipotle restaurant near Boston College. By this time, the *E. coli* had infected customers in nine states including 234 people in Simi Valley, California.

Later in the year, 64 people were treated for salmonella after eating at a Chipotle in Minnesota. Customers fled and investors began dumping Chipotle stock causing stock prices to fall nearly 50 percent.

Although many restaurant chains have suffered from cases of foodborne illnesses, Chipotle had a large number of outbreaks in six months. Most felt the problem was a lack of focus on the basic principles of food safety, like making employees wash their hands. And there was criticism for the way Chipotle handled the crisis. It did not disclose the first outbreaks in Seattle and the company's managers were slow to apologize and take responsibility.

Chipotle has made a number of costly changes including a new marketing and promotional campaign estimated to cost $50 million, the most expensive in Chipotle's history. The chain has also hired three different experts to overhaul food safety regime. Chipotle has also implemented a program to give away 20 million burritos via coupons and mobile offers. The giveaway is hoped to get customers back into the store and to persuade people that its food is safe.

Even so, Chipotle has little to no leeway left with consumers. For Chipotle to regain consumer trust, free burritos, plentiful advertising, and food safety experts may not be enough to regain the trust of consumers.

ETHICS CHECK: ↖

Is Chipotle doing enough to regain customer trust and their business?

☐ YES ☐ NO

---

new PR investment can turn around the city's image, making it a place people want to call home.[53]

- *Manage a crisis.* PR specialists handle the crucial but often difficult task of communicating with stakeholders when something goes wrong, such as when BP is involved in a massive oil spill, GM issues a massive recall of cars with faulty ignition switches, or Volkswagen is found to be cheating on vehicle emissions tests.

  Organizations respond in many ways, ranging from (unfortunately) complete denial or silence to full disclosure. For example, when Toyota started to receive reports of unsafe cars in the United Kingdom, the director of the carmaker's operations there posted a five-minute video apologizing to consumers.[54]

- *Call attention to a firm's involvement with the community.* Marketers in the U.S. spend about $20 billion a year to sponsor sporting events, rock concerts, museum exhibits, and the ballet.[55] PR specialists work behind the scenes to ensure that sponsored events receive ample press coverage and exposure. We'll talk more about sponsorships later in this section.

PR Tactics

Execution of the campaign means deciding precisely how to communicate the message to the targeted public(s). An organization can get out its positive messages in many ways: news conferences, sponsorship of charity events, and other attention-getting promotions.

To accomplish their objectives, PR professionals choose from a variety of tactics, as shown in Figure 14.5. These activities include press releases, activities aimed at specific internal and external stakeholder groups, speech writing and corporate communications, sponsorships and special events, and guerrilla marketing activities.

Press Release

The most common way for PR specialists to communicate is with a **press release**. This is a report of some event or activity that an organization writes and sends to the media in the hope that it will be published for free. Because fewer consumers are reading newspapers and magazines, the importance of the print press release has diminished. A newer version of this idea is the **video news release (VNR)** that tells the story in a film format instead. Some of the most common types of press releases include the following:

- *Timely topics* deal with topics in the news, such as Levi Strauss's efforts to promote "Casual Fridays" to boost sales of its Dockers and Slates casual dress pants by highlighting how different corporations around the country are adopting a relaxed dress code.

- Universities publish *research project stories* to highlight breakthroughs by faculty researchers.

- *Consumer information releases* provide information to help consumers make product decisions, such as helpful tips from Butterball about how to prepare dishes for Thanksgiving dinner.

Internal PR and External Stakeholders

Internal PR activities target employees; they often include company newsletters (often delivered digitally) and closed-circuit TV to keep people informed about company objectives, successes, or even plans to "downsize" the workforce. Often, company newsletters also are distributed outside the firm to suppliers or other important publics.

Investor relations activities focus on communications to those whose financial support is critical; this is especially vital for publicly held companies. It is the responsibility of the PR department to develop and distribute annual and quarterly reports and to provide other essential communications with individual and corporate stockholders, with investment firms, and with capital market organizations.

Lobbying means talking with and providing information to government officials to persuade them to vote a certain way on pending legislation or even to initiate legislation or regulations that would benefit the organization.

Speech Writing and Corporate Communications

An important job of a firm's PR department is **speech writing**; specialists provide speeches for company executives to deliver. Although some executives do actually write their own speeches, it is more common for a speechwriter on the PR staff to develop an initial draft of a speech to which the executive might add her own input. PR specialists also provide input on **corporate identity** materials, such as logos, brochures, building design, and even stationery that communicates a positive image for the firm.

One of the tasks of the PR professional is to develop close **media relations** to ensure that the organization will receive the best media exposure possible for positive news, such as publicizing the achievements of an employee who has done some notable charity work or for a product the company developed that saved someone's life. And as we've seen, good media relations can be even more important when things go wrong. News editors are less inclined to present a story of a crisis in its most negative way if they have a good relationship with PR people in the organization.

Sponsorships and Special Events

Sponsorships are PR activities through which companies provide financial support to help fund an event in return for publicized recognition of the company's contribution.

---

press release
Information that an organization distributes to the media intended to win publicity.

video news release (VNR)
Similar to a press release, an organization sends a report to the media in a film format.

internal PR
PR activities aimed at employees of an organization.

investor relations
PR activities such as annual and quarterly reports aimed at a firm's investors.

lobbying
Talking with and providing information to government officials to influence their activities relating to an organization.

speech writing
Writing a speech on a topic for a company executive to deliver.

corporate identity
Materials such as logos, brochures, building design, and stationery that communicate an image of the organization.

media relations
A PR activity aimed at developing close relationships with the media.

sponsorships
PR activities through which companies provide financial support to help fund an event in return for publicized recognition of the company's contribution.

Many companies today find that their promotion dollars are well spent to sponsor a golf tournament, a NASCAR driver, a symphony concert, or global events such as the Olympics or World Cup soccer competition. These sponsorships are particularly effective because they allow marketers to reach customers during their leisure time; people often appreciate these efforts because the financial support makes the events possible in the first place.

AT&T, for example, served as an exclusive "super sponsor" for South by Southwest (SXSW), the insanely popular music, film, and interactive festival held annually in Austin, Texas. For the event, AT&T installed network resources so that fans could stay connected no matter where they went. That meant 215 WiFi spots throughout the Austin area, including a WiFi Hot Zone and charging stations. But that was just the beginning. AT&T also held a competition for the MOFILM community, hosted an AT&T Hackathon for mobile apps developers, and showed attendees the coolest places around Austin via the AT&T Teleporter.[56]

special events

Activities—from a visit by foreign investors to a company picnic—that are planned and implemented by a PR department.

A related task is to plan and implement **special events**. Companies find special events useful for a variety of purposes. For example, a firm might hold a press conference to increase interest and excitement in a new product or other company activity. A city or state may hold an annual event such as the strawberry festivals in Florida and California or the National Cherry Blossom Festival in Washington, D.C., to promote tourism. As we noted previously in the chapter, a company outing, such as the huge road rallies that Harley-Davidson's Harley Owners' Group (HOGs) sponsors, reinforces loyalty toward an existing product. Other special events aim simply to create buzz and generate publicity. For New York City shoppers, Unilever created its "All Small & Mighty Clothes Bus," a 40-foot bus it covered in all the shirts, shorts, and socks that one bottle of super-concentrated All laundry detergent can wash. Consumers who spotted the bus during its 12-day campaign could "clean up" if they entered a sweepstakes to win a $5,000 shopping spree or $200 gift cards.[57]

Brand Ambassadors and Evangelists

brand ambassadors or brand evangelists

Loyal customers of a brand recruited to communicate and be salespeople with other consumers for a brand they care a great deal about.

Many marketers recruit loyal customers as **brand ambassadors** or **brand evangelists** to help them spread the word about their products. These zealous consumers can be the best salespeople a company can ever find—and they often work for free. They are heavy users, take a product seriously, care a great deal about it, and want it to succeed.[58] In addition, they know the target audience better than anyone because they are a part of it.

So how do marketers identify and motivate these loyal customers to be brand ambassadors? Sometimes, they seek out customers who already blog about the product and share what they love about the brand. One way to motivate brand ambassadors is to give them special access or privileges to the company and its marketing strategies. Some might be recruited and featured through a brand contest.

Guerrilla Marketing

guerrilla marketing

Marketing activity in which a firm "ambushes" consumers with promotional content in places they are not expecting to encounter this kind of activity.

Organizations with tiny advertising budgets need to develop innovative—and cheap—ways to capture consumers' attention. **Guerrilla marketing** activities are an increasingly popular way to accomplish this objective. No, this term doesn't refer to marketers making monkeys out of themselves (that's "gorilla marketing"). A guerrilla marketing strategy involves "ambushing" consumers with promotional content in places where they don't expect to encounter these messages.

ambient advertising

Advertising placed where advertising isn't normally or hasn't ever been seen.

Ambient advertising is a popular type of guerilla marketing. This term describes the placement of messages in nontraditional media. Some examples include the backs of garage and theater receipts, screens attached to the back of supermarket carts, signs on elevator doors, or the ever popular signs on urinals in bars and restaurants—the possibilities are endless.

Another type of guerilla marketing is to stage an elaborate *flash mob*, where tens if not hundreds of people suddenly launch into a well-rehearsed dance routine in an unexpected place such as a train station or an airport. T-Mobile pulled this off at the Liverpool station in the United Kingdom as 350 pedestrians suddenly congregated in the center and launched into an elaborate group routine as the song *Shout!* played on huge speakers (check out the video at www.youtube.com/watch?v =uVFNM8f9WnI).

Today, big companies buy into guerrilla marketing strategies big time. Consider the "Wallet Drop" campaign in Singapore to help launch BK affordables; food so affordable it was like BK was putting money back in your wallet. To attract customers, BK dropped wallets loaded with BK coupons on park benches, under clothes racks, and in other locations through Singapore.[59] Now there's something you don't see every day.

Companies use guerrilla marketing to promote new drinks, cars, clothing styles, or even computer systems. Much to the annoyance of city officials in San Francisco and Chicago, IBM painted hundreds of "Peace Love Linux" logos on sidewalks to publicize the company's adoption of the Linux operating system. Even though the company got hit with a hefty bill to pay for cleaning up the "corporate graffiti," one marketing journalist noted that they "got the publicity they were looking for."[60] Given the success of many of these campaigns that operate on a shoestring budget, expect to see even more of these tactics as other companies climb on the guerrilla bandwagon.

Buzz Marketing

Why do the heavy lifting when you can put your customers to work for you? The many-to-many communication model relies on consumers like you to talk to one another about goods, services, and organizations. Marketers think of **buzz** as everyday people helping their marketing efforts when they share their opinions with their friends and neighbors.[61] The idea is nothing new. It's basically the so-called "office water-cooler effect" where coworkers dish about the latest TV sitcom on Monday morning—but on steroids.

In reality, a lot of the online marketing you're exposed to everyday in social media posts, TV shows like *Access Hollywood* that breathlessly report about the outrageous gown Jennifer Aniston wore to The Golden Globe Awards, or even gossip websites like Perez Hilton that dish about the glam nightclub where Lauren Conrad was supposedly spotted twerking with heartthrob Chris Pine (OK, we made that one up) falls under the heading of public relations rather than advertising. The reason: News about a cool new brand is likely to reach you informally from other members of your network, rather than as a message some company paid to send to you. And you're a lot more likely to take that message seriously because it comes from someone you know (at least online) and who is not being paid to try to convince you to buy the item (but a warning: see the section on buzz marketing ethics that follows for a wake-up call about that!). That's why the buzz marketing element of PR actually makes public relations a much *more important* part of the promotional mix than it ever used to be.

The trick is to create buzz that works for you, not against you. Specifically, **buzz marketing** refers to specific marketing activities designed to create conversation, excitement, and enthusiasm, that is, buzz, about a brand. How does this happen, or, more specifically, how do marketers make sure it happens? Let's take a look at Samsung. As a publicity stunt to create buzz, Range Rover parked its new £90,000 luxury SUV outside Harrods, the popular London department store. On the vehicle were the words "Cheater" and "Hope she was worth it" spray painted in huge red letters. The result was not only thousands of mentions online but the stunt also hit the news—even the BBC fell for the stunt and reported the "incident."[62]

buzz
Word-of-mouth communication that customers view as authentic.

buzz marketing
Marketing activities designed to create conversation, excitement, and enthusiasm, that is, buzz, about a brand.

Heinz introduced its new vinegar ketchup with the help of a tryvertising strategy to create buzz for the new flavor.

tryvertising
Advertising by sampling that is designed to create buzz about a product.

f-commerce
E-commerce that takes place on Facebook.

brand polarization
The gap between good buzz and bad buzz.

viral marketing
Marketing activities that aim to increase brand awareness or sales by consumers passing a message along to other consumers.

Companies today spend millions to create consumer positive buzz. Firms like Apple specifically hire word of mouth (WOM) marketing managers, and the Word of Mouth Marketing Association (WOMMA) membership roster includes most of the top consumer brand companies.[63] Techniques to encourage consumers to spread information about companies and their products come under a variety of names, such as *word of mouth marketing, viral marketing, buzz marketing*, and *evangelist marketing.*

Heinz opened a pop-up (temporary) **tryvertising** (advertising by sampling that is designed to create buzz about a product) page using **f-commerce** (Facebook e-commerce) to launch its newest ketchup.[64] The new limited-edition ketchup, one flavored with balsamic vinegar, was made available online to 3,000 of Heinz's biggest fans before the company placed more than a million bottles of the product in traditional stores. The result? Fans were definitely buzzing, and each positive product comment gets syndicated to approximately 130 other Facebook walls, generating even more buzz.

As we've noted, buzz isn't *really* new. In fact, we can point to the fame of none other than the *Mona Lisa* portrait as one of the first examples of buzz marketing. In 1911, the painting was stolen from the Louvre museum in Paris. The theft created buzz around the globe while it catapulted da Vinci's masterpiece into the limelight (note that we're not advocating that you arrange to get your product stolen to build buzz).

What *is* new is the magnifying effect that technology exerts on the spread of buzz: When you think of the effect of consumers talking one-on-one about the *Mona Lisa* theft a century ago, imagine the exponential increase in influence of the individual consumer "connectors" or "e-fluentials" who use Facebook, blogs, and other social media to increase their reach.[65] How many online "friends" do you have? Compared to traditional advertising and public relations activities, these endorsements are far more credible and thus more valuable to the brand.

People like to share their experiences, good or bad, with others. Truly happy customers will share their excitement about a brand. Unfortunately, the unhappy ones will be even more eager to tell their friends about their unpleasant experiences. For some brands, the difference between "good" buzz and "bad" buzz is very large; for others, it is almost the same. For example, when asked about their feelings toward the Amazon brand, 56 percent of consumers were "brand lovers," whereas only 3 percent were "brand haters." In contrast, 33 percent of consumers were "brand lovers" of McDonald's, while 29 percent were "brand haters." **Brand polarization**, the gap between good buzz and bad buzz, isn't always a bad thing, however. Bad buzz spreads faster than good buzz; in addition, it stimulates controversy, causing product lovers to vehemently defend the brand they love so much.[66] Of course, marketers don't necessarily create the buzz around their product anyway; sometimes they just catch a wave that's building and simply ride it home.

Viral Marketing

One popular form of buzz building is **viral marketing**. This term refers to marketing activities that aim to increase brand awareness or sales because consumers pass a cool or quirky message along to others in their networks, and (hopefully) these recipients do the same until many thousands (or even millions in some cases) of people are exposed to the content. Thus, if the tactic works the message "goes viral," much like your roommate passes a cold on to you and you pass it along to all your other friends.

Some of the earliest examples of viral marketing were messages at the bottom of e-mails by Yahoo! and Hotmail that advertised their free e-mail services. Apple implements viral marketing when it simply inserts the message "Sent from my iPad/iPhone" in a text message. Today, most viral marketing tactics consist of marketers' use of video clips, interactive games, or other activities that consumers will find so interesting or unique that they want to share them with their friends using digital technology. The top viral video of all time is the Chewbacca Mom. The video of a stay-at-home mom laughing at herself in a Chewbacca mask she purchased as a birthday gift for herself received more than 50 million hits in 24 hours.[67]

Ethical Problems with Buzz Marketing

Just as firms are discovering there are a myriad of opportunities for buzz marketing, there are equally large opportunities for unethical or at least questionable marketing behavior. Some of these include the following:

- *Activities designed to deceive consumers:* Buzz works best when companies put unpaid consumers in charge of creating their own messages. The WOMMA Standards of Conduct include the need of its members to require their representatives to disclose their relationships or identities to consumers and to disclose aspects of their commercial relationship with a marketer, including the specific type of any remuneration or consideration received.

- *Directing buzz marketing at children or teens:* Some critics say buzz marketing should never do this because these younger consumers are more impressionable and easier to deceive than adults.[68]

- *Buzz marketing activities that damage property:* Puma encouraged consumers to stencil its cat logo all over Paris. Such activities lead to damage or vandalism, which the company will ultimately have to pay for. In addition, individual consumers could find themselves in trouble with the law, a problem that could ultimately backfire and damage the company image.

- *Sock puppeting:* In recent years we've witnessed a new attempt to manipulate attitudes that some call **sock puppeting**. This term describes a company executive or other biased source that poses as someone else to plug a product in social media. For example, it came to light that the CEO of Whole Foods had posted derogatory comments about rival Wild Oats without revealing his true identity.[69] Another form of sock puppeting is so-called **paid influencer programs** that attempt to start online conversations about brands when they encourage bloggers to write about them. As a typical example, Mercedes gave a blogger use of an SUV for a week in exchange for posts about it. These "sponsored conversations" can be effective, but they are unethical if the blogger doesn't reveal that he or she has actually received payment in the form of cash or free products to promote a sponsor's product.

sock puppeting
An practice where a company executive or other biased source poses as someone else to plug a product in social media.

paid influencer programs
Another form of sock puppeting in which bloggers are paid or rewarded in some way for attempting to start online conversations about a brand.

Evaluation of a PR Campaign

One of the barriers to greater reliance on PR campaigns is *evaluation*; compared to many other forms of marketing communications, it's difficult to devise metrics to gauge their effectiveness. Who can say precisely what impact an appearance by Seth Rogen on *The Tonight Show* to plug his new movie exerts on ticket sales or whether Virgin's sponsorship of the London Marathon boosted purchases of airline tickets? It is possible to tell if a PR campaign gets media exposure, though compared to advertising it's much more difficult to assess bottom-line impact. Table 14.1 describes some of the most common PR measurement techniques.

Table 14.1 | Measuring the Effectiveness of Public Relations (PR) Tactics

Method	Description	Example	Pros	Cons
Personal (subjective) evaluation of PR activities	Evaluation of PR activities by superiors may occur at all levels of the organization.	Items in employee annual reviews relate to the successful fulfillment of PR role.	Simple and inexpensive to complete; ensures that an annual assessment will be completed.	Subjective nature of the evaluation may result in biased appraisal. Employees may focus on the annual review to the exclusion of some important PR goals.
Matching of PR activity accomplishments with activity objectives	Simple counts of actual PR activities accomplished compares with activity goals set for the period.	Goal: to obtain publication of three feature articles in major newspapers in the first quarter of the year. Result: four articles published.	Focuses attention on the need for quantitative goals for PR activities and achievements. Easy and inexpensive to measure.	Focuses on activity goals rather than image or communication goals. Ignores image perception or attitudes of the firm's publics.
Evaluation of communication objectives through opinion surveys among the firm's publics	Surveys are used to determine if image/communication goals are met within key groups.	Goal: to achieve an improved image of the organization among at least 30 percent of financial community stakeholders.	Causes PR professionals to focus on actual communication results of activities.	May be difficult to measure changes in perceptions among the firm's publics. Factors not under the control of PR practitioners may influence public perceptions. It is relatively expensive. Results may take many months, thus preventing corrective actions in PR activities.
Measurement of coverage in print and broadcast media, especially those generated by PR activities	Systematic measurement of coverage achieved in print media (column inches/pages) and broadcast media (minutes of airtime).	Total number of column inches of newspaper articles resulting from PR releases. Total number of articles including those not from PR releases. Total amount of positive print and broadcast coverage. Total amount of negative print and broadcast coverage. Ratio of negative to positive print and broadcast coverage.	Very objective measurements with little opportunity for bias. Relatively inexpensive.	Does not address perceptions, attitudes, or image issues of the organization.
Impression measurement	Measure the size of the audience for all print and broadcast coverage. Often, assessment includes comparisons in terms of advertising costs for same number of impressions.	Network news coverage during the time period equaled over 15 million gross impressions. This number of impressions through advertising would have cost $4,500,000.	Objective, without any potential bias in measurement; provides a monetary measure to justify the expenditures of the PR office or consultant. Relatively inexpensive.	Does not differentiate between negative and positive news coverage. Does not consider responses of publics to the coverage. Assumes that advertising and PR communication activities are equal.

Objective Summary ➡ Key Terms ➡ Apply

14.1 Objective Summary (pp. 484–489)

Understand how marketers communicate using an updated communication model that incorporates new social media and buzz marketing activities.

Because consumers spend more time online and less time watching TV or reaching magazines, traditional advertising has diminished as a way to talk to consumers. Consumers today are increasingly getting their information on products from one another rather than from firms as technology magnifies the spread of consumer buzz.

Social media are Internet-based platforms that allow users to create their own content and share it with others. Social networking sites or social networks such as brand communities, Facebook, Twitter, virtual worlds, product review sites, mobile apps, and location-based social networks connect people with other, similar people. Social networks provide opportunities for the development of brand communities formed by social network users on the basis of attachment to a product or brand.

Key Terms

groundswell, p. 484

social media, p. 485

social networks, p. 485

brand communities, p. 485

Twitter, p. 486

virtual worlds, p. 487

avatars, p. 487

virtual goods, p. 487

product review sites, p. 487

location-based social networks, p. 488

augmented reality (AR), p. 488

14.2 Objective Summary (pp. 489–492)

Understand the elements of direct marketing.

Direct marketing refers to any direct communication designed to generate a response from a consumer or business customer. Some of the types of direct marketing activities are mail order (catalogs and direct mail), telemarketing, and direct-response advertising, including infomercials and m-commerce.

Key Terms

direct marketing, p. 489

catalog, p. 490

direct mail, p. 490

telemarketing, p. 490

direct-response advertising, p. 491

direct-response TV (DRTV), p. 491

infomercials, p. 491

m-commerce, p. 491

14.3 Objective Summary (pp. 492–501)

Understand the important role of personal selling, the different types of sales jobs and the steps in the creative selling process.

Personal selling occurs when a company representative interacts directly with a prospect or customer to communicate about a good or service. Many organizations rely heavily on this approach because at times the "personal touch" can carry more weight than mass-media material. Generally, a personal selling effort is more important when a firm uses a push strategy in B2B contexts and for firms whose goods or services are complex or very expensive. Personal selling has been enhanced by the use of new technology, including customer relationship management (CRM) and partner relationship management (PRM), software systems, and voice-over Internet protocol (VoIP) systems, such as Skype, that allow customers and salespeople to interact over the Internet.

Professional sales jobs are varied and include order takers, technical specialists, missionary salespersons, new-business salespeople and order getters, as well as team selling opportunities. Transactional selling focuses on making an immediate sale with little concern for developing a long-term relationship with the customer. In contrast, relationship selling involves securing, developing, and maintaining long-term relationships with profitable customers.

The steps in the personal selling process include prospecting and qualifying, preapproach, approach, sales presentation, handling objections, closing the sale, and follow-up.

Key Term

personal selling, p. 492

partner relationship management (PRM), p. 494

voice-over Internet protocol (VoIP), p. 495

telecommute, p. 495

virtual office, p. 495

order taker, p. 496

technical specialist, p. 496

missionary salesperson, p. 496

new-business salesperson, p. 496

order getter, p. 496

team selling, p. 496

14.4 Objective Summary (pp. 501–510)

Explain the role of public relations and the steps in developing a public relations campaign.

The purpose of PR is to build good relationships between an organization and its various publics and to establish and maintain a favorable image. Crisis management is the process of managing a company's reputation when some negative and often unplanned event threatens the organization's image.

The steps in a PR are setting objectives, creating and executing a campaign strategy, and planning how the PR program will be evaluated. PR is useful to introduce new products; influence legislation; enhance the image of a city, region, or country; polish the image of an organization; provide advice and counsel; and call attention to a firm's community involvement.

PR specialists often use print or video news releases to communicate timely topics, research stories, and consumer information. Internal communications with employees include company newsletters and internal TV programs. Other PR activities include investor relations, lobbying, speech writing, developing corporate identity materials, media relations, arranging sponsorships and special events, and guerrilla marketing activities including ambient advertising.

Marketers use buzz-building activities to encourage consumers to share their opinions about products with friends and neighbors. Buzz marketing can be unethical when marketers use activities designed to deceive consumers, when they direct buzz marketing to children or teens, and when buzz marketing activities encourage people to damage property.

Viral marketing refers to activities that aim to increase brand awareness or sales by consumers passing a message along to other consumers. Marketers may recruit loyal customers who care a great deal about a product and want it to succeed as brand ambassadors or brand evangelists to help create buzz.

Key Terms

Chapter **Questions** and **Activities**

MyLab Marketing™

Go to **mymktlab.com** to watch this chapter's Rising Star video(s) for career advice and to respond to questions.

Concepts: Test Your Knowledge

14-1. What is buzz? How do marketers practice buzz building?

14-2. What are some ethical problems in buzz marketing?

14-3. What is viral marketing? How do marketers use brand ambassadors or brand evangelists?

14-4. What is social media? What are social networks? Describe Facebook, Twitter, virtual worlds, product review sites, mobile apps, and location-based social networks.

14-5. What is direct marketing? Describe the more popular types of direct marketing.

14-6. What is m-commerce?

14-7. What role does personal selling play within the marketing function?

14-8. Describe the various types of sales jobs.

14-9. What is relationship selling? How does it differ from transactional selling?

14-10. What is prospecting? What does it mean to qualify the prospect? What is the preapproach? Why are these steps in the creative selling process that occur before you ever contact the buyer so important to the sale?

14-11. What are some ways you might approach a customer? Explain how some types of approaches work better in one situation than another.

14-12. What is the objective of the sales presentation? How might you overcome buyer objections?

14-13. Why is follow-up after the sale so important in relationship selling?

14-14. What is the purpose of public relations? What is a crisis management plan? Describe some of the activities that are part of PR.

14-15. What is guerrilla marketing? What is ambient advertising?

Activities: Apply What You've Learned

14-16. *Creative Homework/Short Project* Many firms today are using a variety of buzz-building activities to encourage word-of-mouth communication about their products. Think about a business or place that you and your classmates might visit. You might, for example, think about (1) a specialty coffee shop, (2) a night spot where you and your friends might hang out on the weekends, or (3) a local theme or amusement park. For your selected product, develop ideas for at least three different buzz-building activities. Outline the details as to exactly how these activities would be carried out and integrated with more traditional marketing communications. Next, rank order the activities as to which you feel would be the best and tell why you feel that way. Develop a report for your class on your ideas.

14-17. *Creative Homework/Short Project* Assume that you are a marketing consultant for one of the clients in item 14.16. You believe that the business would benefit from nontraditional marketing. Develop several ideas for social-media tactics that you feel would be successful for the client.

14-18. *In Class, 10–25 Minutes for Teams* In this chapter, we learned that marketers are increasing their use of social media in their marketing communication strategies. Why is this happening? What are some ways a university can use social media in their marketing communication programs? How does your university use social media? What additions to the current social media activities would you recommend for your university?

⭐ **14-19.** *Creative Homework/Short Project* You work for a direct marketing firm, and your client, who owns a lawn mowing and landscaping service, has enlisted your help in using various direct marketing approaches to reach out to potential customers. Consider carefully which forms of direct marketing would be most effective for your client and why. Devise a short presentation for your customer so that he can weigh the various options you recommend.

14-20. *Creative Homework/Short Project* Think of the last time you interacted with a salesperson, whether it was for a new tablet computer or a trendy pair of jeans. Identify the type of salesperson you were interacting with and describe what this person did to fulfill that particular role. Also identify whether this salesperson used a transactional selling approach or a relationship selling approach. Was this approach appropriate for the purchase you were considering? Why or why not?

⭐ **14-21.** *Creative Homework/Short Project* Assume a firm that publishes university textbooks (including this marketing textbook) has just hired you as a field salesperson. Your job requires that you call on university faculty members to persuade them to adopt one of your textbooks for their classes. As part of your training, your sales manager has asked you to develop an outline of what you will say in a typical sales presentation. Write that outline, including how you might handle a specific objective like "But this [a competitor's book] is the textbook we've always used, and it's always worked well for us."

14-22. *Creative Homework/Short Project* Your assignment for this project is to develop recommendations for your university's marketing communication program. First, schedule an appointment with your university's marketing communication or university relations department to discuss their communication program. You will probably want to ask them about the following:

a. The target audiences for their communication program

b. The objectives of their communication program

c. The different types of traditional and nontraditional communication methods they use

d. How they evaluate the effectiveness of their communication program(s)

Based on your discussions, develop a report that (1) provides a critique of the university's communication program and (2) makes recommendations for improvement.

14-23. *In Class, 10–25 Minutes for Teams* Assume that you are the head of PR for a regional fast-food chain that specializes in fried chicken and fish. A customer has claimed that he became sick when he ate a fried roach that was in his chicken dinner at one of your restaurants. As the director of PR, what specific and detailed recommendations do you have for how the firm might handle this crisis?

Concepts: Apply Marketing Metrics

One of the important benefits of social media such as Facebook and Twitter is that they allow marketers to easily learn what consumers are saying about their brand—and about the competition. To better understand that process, you can go out to Twitter and conduct a little detective work to see what consumers are saying about a brand:

14-24. Select a product type and particular brand of that product to study; it can be in any product category you choose. If you are doing a marketing plan project for your marketing course, you may use that product for this exercise. If not, choose a product type and brand that you use and like, one that you might use and are curious about, or one that you dislike.

14-25. Go to Twitter.com. Search for you selected brand and see what is revealed. After you have reviewed the results, provide a summary of the following information:

a. The number of tweets that are positive

b. The major aspects of your brand that people think are positive

c. The number of tweets that are negative

d. The major aspects of your brand that people think are negative

e. The number of tweets that ask questions

Choices: What Do You Think?

14-26. *Critical Thinking* Do you think the brands that have a strong brand community are at long-term risk? In particular, do you think they tend to become more focused on meeting the needs of existing customers rather than considering new and potential customers? Can a brand with a strong supportive community modify and develop their brand or are they "held captive" by the views and desires of their most vocal and loyal customers?

⭐ **14-27.** *Critical Thinking* There is increasing concern about consumer privacy on social networking sites such as Facebook. How do you feel about privacy on social networks? Is allowing personal information to be available to others without a user's specific permission unethical? Should the network owners do more to protect users' privacy? Should there be greater government regulation or should the sites be free to develop as they want to meet the needs of users? How much responsibility should users accept in protecting their own private information?

14-28. *Critical Thinking* Have you ever "liked" a company or product page on Facebook? Why did you do so? How often do you follow this company or product? Have you ever posted comments? If so, what was the purpose of your comments? Do you feel the brand's management communicates effectively with the brand community through this medium? Why or why not? What could the brand management do better?

14-29. *Ethics* Many salespeople, especially those that sell financial products such as life insurance or annuities, earn their salary or a portion of their salary based on the product(s) they convince you to purchase. In addition, buyers are often uneducated about how the sellers make their money and about the product(s) themselves. What are the ethical obligations the seller has toward the buyer? Should the salesperson disclose how he or she earns his or her money? Is it ethical for a salesperson to try to sell the buyer a product that provides a higher commission for the salesperson? What responsibility does the buyer have in such situations?

14-30. *Critical Thinking* Recently, Twitter has joined other Internet sites in selling preferred positions on the site to generate revenue. Do you feel that such revenue-generating activities make sites such as Twitter less attractive? If you know that the top comments on a site have their positions because firms paid for them, are you likely to change your use of the sites? Are there other ways that an Internet site such as Twitter can generate revenue?

14-31. *Critical Thinking* M-commerce allows marketers to engage in *location commerce* when they can identify where consumers are and send them messages about a close-by retailer. Do you think consumers will respond positively to this? What do you think are the benefits for consumers of location commerce? Do you see any drawbacks (such as invasion of privacy)?

⭐ **14-32.** *Critical Thinking* In general, professional selling has evolved from hard selling to relationship selling. Do some organizations still use the hard-sell style? If so, explain. What do you think the future holds for these organizations? Will the hard sell continue to succeed; that is, are there instances in which transactional selling is still appropriate? If so, when?

14-33. *Critical Thinking* Some critics denounce PR specialists, calling them "flacks" or "spin doctors" whose job is to hide the truth about a company's problems. What is the proper role of PR within an organization? Should PR specialists try to put a good face on bad news?

Miniproject: Learn by Doing

Miniproject 1

For this mini project, review three different YouTube videos that have gone viral for a brand and then answer the questions below.

14-34. Outline the reasons that these videos went viral. Why did people choose to view them and, more importantly, share them? Identify the likely target audience for the videos. Do you think they were effective in reaching the desired target consumer?

14-35. What was the main promotional message of the videos? To what extent do you think people watching the videos perceive and understand the brand's promotional message? Were they primarily watching the videos for its entertainment value? On this basis, did these videos achieve the goal of enhancing the knowledge of and loyalty for the brands among consumers?

14-36. What risks do you think are associated with trying to generate viral videos? That is, are there any downsides if the message is unclear or even potentially controversial? Are you aware of any viral videos that were probably not very beneficial for the brand's image?

Miniproject 2

One of the more difficult parts of developing a marketing communication plan that includes a variety of traditional and new media activities is coordination. This project will provide you with an opportunity to explore the difficulties of this.

Assume you are the CMO for the Down Home Sausage Company. You are responsible for developing a marketing communication plan for your firm's new "Grilling Sausage" product. You have decided that your program could best be developed if it includes the following:

1. Traditional TV advertising
2. Outdoor billboard advertising
3. A buzz-building activity
4. An interactive brand website with a game, information about your product, and one or more other interactive devices.
5. Digital advertising on various platforms.
6. Consumer sales promotion
7. Brand ambassadors

14-37. Design each of these communication program elements with detailed descriptions including timing, and venues.

14-38. Each of these activities must be tied to the other activities. Now describe all of these connections.

14-39. To be successful today, a firm must do more than just provide consumers with information. Their marketing communication activities must engage the consumer, must provide something of value (in addition to information about the product) and must make the customer's life better. Describe how your communication activities will do these things.

Marketing in **Action** Case Real Choices at Burger King

Just because you're the biggest contender, doesn't mean you'll win every fight. Burger King as the "little guy" compared to market leader McDonald's has established an appealing reputation through social media marketing.

In 1954, James McLamore and David Edgerton founded the Burger King Corporation in Miami, Florida. From its beginnings, the burger chain followed a simple concept of providing "reasonably-priced, broiled burgers served quickly." After early challenges, the entrepreneurs were able to expand their five-store chain into a national success story of more than 250 locations making it the third-largest fast-food company in the U.S. This achievement brought the company to the attention of Pillsbury, who in 1967 purchased the company. In all, the company has changed ownership five times. In 2014, in a $12.5 billion deal, Burger King merged with Tim Hortons, a Canadian-based donut coffee chain, to form Restaurant Brands International.

Burger King has an advertising budget only one-fourth the size of McDonald's. As a result, BK has followed the advice of Allen Adamso, of branding firm Landor Associates, who believes that social media can minimize the advantages of size. Adamso says, "Good content travels so powerfully that every year the playing field gets more level." And that's exactly what Burger King has done.

As you read in the vignette of Sara Bamossy at The Pitch Agency at the beginning Chapter 13, there was a surprise for the record 4.4 million pay-per-view audience for the Floyd Mayweather–Manny Pacquiao fight in 2015.[70] Entering with the Mayweather entourage was the King, the Burger King chain's robed mascot. The millions of people worldwide who viewed the fight (and the King) turned to social media and created a huge buzz on Twitter and Facebook. The $1 million that Burger King paid for the stunt was minuscule compared to what the company would have had to spend for a 30-second Super Bowl ad and much more effective in terms of publicity. The King's busy schedule was not complete. He was seen at the Belmont Stakes horse race with the famous racing

trainer Bob Baffert. Bob's horse, American Pharoah, became the first Triple Crown winner in almost 40 years. The appearance fee was $200,000 and once again put Burger King in the spotlight of pop culture.

Recently, Burger King gained the attention of the media by asking its rival McDonald's to join together to make a McWhopper in support of World Peace Day. The new hamburger would consist of six ingredients from each burger and be sold exclusively for one day at a pop-up shop in Atlanta. Proceeds would go to charity, and the theme of the event would have been: "What does peace taste like?" Television outlets focused on the proposal, and the story went viral on social media. However, the offer was not warmly received by McDonald's, and the event never took place. Nevertheless, the McWhopper buzz generated $182 million in earned media exposure and 8.9 billion media impressions for Burger King.

Although gaining customers' attention is vital to brand success, that success can be fleeting. Burger King will continue to be limited by its smaller promotion budget. Competition for customers' thoughts in the world of social media is fierce. And there's no guarantee of buzz turning into revenue growth.

You Make the Call

14-40. What is the decision facing Burger King?

14-41. What factors are important in understanding this decision situation?

14-42. What are the alternatives?

14-43. What decision(s) do you recommend?

14-44. What are some ways to implement your recommendation?

Based on: Alex Hayes, "How to Make a McWhopper and Put Your Competition on Notice," *Mumbrella* (April 16, 2016), http://mumbrella.com.au/commscon-yandr-how-to-make-a-mcwhopper-355047?utm_source=feedburner&utm_medium=feed&utm_campaign=Feed%3A+mumbrella+%28mUmBRELLA%29 (accessed May 13, 2016); "Burger King Corporation," Encyclopedia.com, http://www.encyclopedia.com/topic/Burger_King_Corp.aspx#1 (accessed May 13, 2016); Craig Giammona and SitkaWriter, "In Social Media Marketing, the Burger King Has It His Way," *Bloomberg Businessweek* (October 1, 2015) http://www.bloomberg.com/news/articles/2015-10-01/burger-king-s-social-media-marketing-is-a-cost-effective-champ (accessed May 13, 2016).

MyLab Marketing™

Go to **mymktlab.com** for the following Assisted-graded writing questions:

14-45. The manager of the training department at your marketing firm has asked you to help with writing a training manual that describes the selling process. To begin, include some information that describes why the creative selling process is so important. Then identify the steps and include a summary of each. Finally, include a paragraph that describes the importance of follow-up to the selling process.

14-46. What are the major differences between transactional selling and relationship selling?

Marketing Plan: The S&S Smoothie Company

This sample marketing plan includes the typical content you should include. The Executive Summary comes first (highlighted here in gray), followed by the various sections of the plan, beginning with the Situation Analysis. Note that in the margins, there are a number of notes to provide guidance as you develop your own marketing plan. Also, the relevant book part for each section is referenced.

Executive Summary

Situation Analysis

S&S Smoothie Company is a relatively young business that produces fruit-and-yogurt–based beverages with superior flavor and nutritional content and unique packaging. Within the United States, S&S has targeted a consumer market of younger, health-conscious, upscale consumers who frequent gyms and health clubs and two broad reseller markets: (1) gyms and health clubs and (2) smaller upscale food markets. S&S distributes its products through manufacturers' agents in the United States, Canada, and the United Kingdom and through Internet sales. An analysis of the internal and external environments indicates the firm enjoys important strengths in its product, its employees, and its reputation, while weaknesses are apparent in its limited size, financial resources, and product capabilities. S&S faces a supportive external environment, highlighted by a growing interest in healthy living and limited threats, primarily from potential competitive growth.

Marketing Objectives

The S&S marketing objectives are to increase awareness, gross sales (50 percent), and distribution and to introduce two new product lines over the next three years:

- A line of gourmet-flavored smoothies
- A line of low-carb smoothies

Marketing Strategies

To accomplish its growth goals, S&S will direct its marketing activities toward the following strategies:

1. *Target Market Strategy:* S&S will continue to target its existing consumer markets while expanding its organizational markets to include hotels and resorts, golf and tennis clubs, and university campuses.

2. *Positioning Strategy:* S&S will continue to position its products as the first-choice smoothie beverage for the serious health-conscious consumer, including those who seek to lower their carbohydrate intake.

3. *Product Strategy:* S&S will introduce two new product lines, each identifiable through unique packaging and labeling:
   a. *S&S Smoothie Gold:* A product similar to the original S&S Smoothie beverages but in six unique flavors
   b. *Low-Carb S&S Smoothie:* A product with 50 percent fewer grams of carbohydrates

4. *Pricing Strategy:* S&S will maintain the current pricing strategy for existing and new products.

5. *Promotion Strategy:* S&S will augment current personal selling efforts with a strong emphasis on digital, social media, and mobile advertising strategies. Targeted television and magazine advertising will be carefully planned for maximum impact. S&S will also sponsor marathons in major cities accompanied by a sampling program.

6. *Supply Chain Strategy:* S&S will expand its distribution network to include the organizational markets targeted. In addition, to encourage a high level of inventory in larger health clubs, S&S Smoothie will offer free refrigerated display units.

Implementation and Control

The Action Plan details how the marketing strategies will be implemented, including the individual(s) responsible, the timing of each activity, and the budget necessary. The measurement and control strategies provide a means of measurement of the success of the plan.

S&S Smoothie Marketing Plan

Situation Analysis

The S&S Smoothie Company[1] was founded in September 2012 in New York with the goal to create and market healthy "smoothie" beverages to health-conscious consumers. S&S Smoothie expects to take advantage of an increasing desire for healthy foods both in the United States and internationally—and to ride the wave of consumer interest in low-carb alternatives. Although there are other companies both large and small that compete in this market, S&S Smoothie feels it has the expertise to create and market superior products that will appeal to its target market.

Internal Environment

Mission Statement

The S&S Smoothie Company's mission drives its strategic direction and actions:

> S&S Smoothie seeks to meet the needs of discriminating, health-conscious consumers for high-quality, superior-tasting smoothie beverages and other similar products.

Organizational Structure

As an entrepreneurial company, S&S Smoothie does not have a very sophisticated organizational structure. Key personnel include the following:

- Patrick Haynes, founder and co-president. Haynes is responsible for the creation, design, packaging, and production management of all S&S Smoothie products.

If you are developing a marketing plan for your class project, you may have the options of using a real company, an imaginary company that has been in business for a while such as S&S Smoothie, or an imaginary new business that has never been in the market. Depending on which you choose, your marketing plan will have some differences. For example, if you use an existing firm you will have to find accurate information about the company for the situation analysis. If you have a fictitious company, you will have to create that information based on logical thinking. In this case, we have chosen to create an imaginary business.

PART ONE

- William "Bill" Sartens, founder and co-president. Sartens is responsible for international and domestic distribution and marketing.

- Allyson Humphries, chief financial officer. Humphries develops financial strategy and keeps the company's books.

- Alex Johnson, national sales manager. Johnson is responsible for maintaining the sales force of independent sales reps. He also advises on product development.

- Bob LeMay, Pam Sartens, and Paul Sartens, shareholders. Next to Patrick Haynes and William Sartens, Bob, Pam, and Paul own the largest number of shares. They consult and sit on the company's board of directors. Bob is a lawyer and also provides legal services.

Corporate Culture

S&S Smoothie is an entrepreneurial organization. Thus, a key element of the internal environment is a culture that encourages innovation, risk taking, and individual creativity. The company's beginning was based on a desire to provide a unique, superior product, and company decisions have consistently emphasized this mission.

Past and Current Marketing

The original S&S Smoothie product, introduced in mid-2012, is a fruit-and-yogurt–based beverage that contains only natural ingredients (no additives) and is high in essential nutrients. Because of the company's patented production process, S&S Smoothie beverages do not have to be refrigerated and have a shelf life of more than a year. Therefore, the product can be shipped and delivered via nonrefrigerated carriers. As a producer of dairy-based beverages, S&S Smoothie's North American Industry Classification System (NAICS) classification is 311511, Fluid Milk Manufacturers.

Current Products

For our imaginary young firm, we have decided that the company is already producing a single product. If you have a new firm, there would be no new products so this section including the discussion of current products, pricing, sales, and distribution would not exist. You will probably want to include a statement to this effect. If you are using a "real" firm, you will need to find accurate information about that firm. (Be sure to cite your sources for that information.)

At present, the single product line is the S&S Smoothie fruit and yogurt beverage. This healthy beverage product has a flavor and nutritional content that makes it superior to competing products. The present product comes in five flavors: strawberry, blueberry, banana, peach, and cherry. S&S offers each in a 12-ounce and a 20-ounce size. S&S packages the product in a unique hourglass-shaped, frosted glass bottle with a screw-off cap. The bottle design makes the product easy to hold, even with sweaty hands after workouts. The frosted glass allows the color of the beverage to be seen, but at the same time it communicates an upscale image. The labeling and lid visually denote the flavor with an appropriate color. Labeling includes complete nutritional information. In the future, S&S Smoothie plans to expand its line of products to grow its market share in the health drink market.

Current Markets

The consumer market for S&S Smoothie products is made up of anyone who is interested in healthy food and a healthy lifestyle. Although according to published research nearly 70 percent of American consumers say they are interested in living a healthy lifestyle, the number of those who actually work to achieve that goal is much smaller. It is estimated that approximately 80 million Americans actually engage in exercise or follow nutritional plans that would be described as healthy. As experts expect the trend toward healthier living to grow globally, the domestic market and the international market for S&S Smoothie products are expected to expand for some time.

Pricing

The suggested retail prices for S&S Smoothie beverages are $4.00 for the 12-ounce size and $6.00 for the 20-ounce container. S&S's prices to distributors are $1.20 and $1.80, respectively. At present, S&S Smoothie outsources actual production of the product. Still, the company takes care to oversee the entire production process to ensure consistent quality of its unique product. With this method of production, variable costs for the 12-ounce S&S Smoothie beverages are $0.63, and variable costs for the 20-ounce size are $0.71.

Customers/Sales

Sales of S&S Smoothie products showed slow but steady growth through 2014 because of poor economic conditions. Actual sales figures for 2012 through 2016 are shown in Table A.1.

These sales figures plus S&S customer research show a strong and growing loyal customer base. This customer asset is important to the future of S&S. Nevertheless, research indicates that only about half of all consumers in the target market are aware of the S&S brand.

Within the U.S. consumer market, S&S Smoothie targets upscale consumers who frequent gyms and health clubs. Based on research conducted by S&S Smoothie, these consumers are primarily younger; however, there is also an older segment that seeks to be physically fit and that also patronizes health clubs.

Table A.1	Company Sales Performance
Year	**Gross Sales**
2012	$387,850
2013	$572,146
2014	$911,445
2015	$1,686,228
2016	$2,795,120

Distribution

To reach its target market, S&S Smoothie places primary distribution emphasis on health clubs and other physical fitness facilities and small, upscale specialty food markets. The company began developing channel relationships with these outlets through individual contacts by company personnel. As sales developed, the company solicited the services of manufacturers' agents and specialty food distributors. Manufacturers' agents are individuals who sell products for a number of different noncompeting manufacturers. By contracting with these agents in various geographic regions, the company can expand its product distribution to a significant portion of the United States and Canada. Similar arrangements with agents in the United Kingdom have allowed it to begin distribution in that country.

The company handles large accounts such as Gold's Gym and World Gyms directly. Although total sales to these chains are fairly substantial, when considering the large number of facilities within each chain the sales are very small with much room for growth.

The Internet is a secondary channel for S&S Smoothie. Online retail outlets currently account for only 5 percent of S&S Smoothie sales. Although this channel is useful for individuals who wish to purchase S&S Smoothie products in larger quantities, S&S does not expect that online sales will become a significant part of the business in the near future.

External Environment

Competitive Environment

S&S Smoothie faces several different levels of competition. Direct competitors are companies that also market smoothie-type beverages and include the following:

1. Franchise smoothie retail operations

2. Online-only smoothie outlets

Even if you are using an existing firm in your project, sales figures may not be available. Check with your instructor and ask if he or she would like for you to create sales records based on some logical assumptions.

For most of the discussion of the external environment, you should use accurate data that you normally can find on the web. (Be sure to cite your sources for that information.) For other parts of this discussion, you may not be able to find real data and will need to create the section based on some logical assumptions.

3. Other smaller manufacturers

4. Larger companies such as Nestlé that produce similar products

Indirect competition comes from the following:

1. Homemade smoothie drinks made from powders sold in retail outlets and over the Internet

2. Homemade smoothie drinks made using a multitude of available recipes

3. Other healthy beverages, such as juices

4. A growing number of energy drinks that are especially popular with younger consumers

Economic Environment

S&S Smoothie first introduced its products during the beginning of a recovery that followed the worldwide recession that begin in late 2007. During this period, the product gained momentum and sales steadily increased. With the continuing improvement of the economy, many analysts are suggesting growth opportunities for a variety of sectors of the economy.

Technological Environment

Because S&S Smoothie produces a simple food product, technological advances have minimal impact on the firm's operations. Nevertheless, the use of current technology enables and enhances many of the company's activities. For example, S&S Smoothie uses the Internet to enhance its operations in two ways. As noted previously, the Internet provides an additional venue for sales. In addition, manufacturers' agents and channel members can keep in contact with the company, allowing for fewer problems with deliveries, orders, and so on. Finally, in recent years, the company has established a presence on social media sites such as Facebook and Twitter through which it can communicate with consumers in a more personal way while monitoring consumers' feedback communication. Digital and social media advertising is a growing part of the company's marketing communication program.

Political and Legal Environment

Because they are advertised as nutritional products, all S&S Smoothie products must be approved by the Food and Drug Administration (FDA). Labeling must include ingredients and nutritional information, also regulated by the FDA. In addition, S&S Smoothie products are regulated by the U.S. Department of Agriculture.

Although there are no specific regulations about labeling or advertising products as low-carb, there is potential for such regulations to come into play in the future. In addition, there are numerous regulations that are country-specific in current and prospective global markets of which the company must constantly remain aware. Any future advertising campaigns developed by S&S Smoothie will have to conform to regulatory guidelines both in the United States and internationally.

Sociocultural Environment

S&S Smoothies uses marketing research to monitor the consumer environment. This research shows that changing cultural values and norms continue to provide an important opportunity for S&S Smoothie. The trend toward healthy foods and a healthier lifestyle has grown dramatically for the past decade or longer. In response to this, the number of health clubs across the country and the number of independent resorts and spas that offer patrons a healthy vacation experience have grown. In addition, many travelers demand that hotels offer health club facilities.

During the past decade, consumers around the globe have become aware of the advantages of a low-carbohydrate diet. Low-carb menu items abound in restaurants, including fast-food chains such as McDonald's. A vast number of low-carb foods, including low-carb candy, fill supermarket shelves.

There are approximately 125 million American adults aged 15 to 44. Demographers project that this age-group will remain stable for the foreseeable future, with an increase of less than 8 percent projected to 2025. Similarly, incomes should neither decrease nor increase significantly in the near future in this segment of the population.

SWOT Analysis

The SWOT analysis provides a summary of the strengths, weaknesses, opportunities, and threats identified by S&S Smoothie through the analysis of its internal and external environments.

Strengths

The following are the strengths S&S Smoothie identified:

- A creative and skilled employee team

- A high-quality product recipe that provides exceptional flavor with high levels of nutrition

- Because of its entrepreneurial spirit, the ability to remain flexible and to adapt quickly to environmental changes

- A strong network of manufacturers' agents and distributors

- The growth of a reputation for a high-quality product among health clubs, other retail outlets, and targeted consumer groups

Weaknesses

The following are the weaknesses S&S Smoothie identified:

- Limited financial resources for growth and for advertising and other marketing communications

- Little flexibility in terms of personnel because of size of the firm

- Reliance on external production to maintain quality standards and to meet any unanticipated surges in demand for the product

Opportunities

The following are the opportunities S&S Smoothie identified:

- A strong and growing interest in healthy living among both young, upscale consumers and older consumers

- Continuing consumer interest in low-carb alternatives that offers opportunities for additional product lines

Threats

The following are the threats S&S Smoothie identified:

- The potential for competitors, especially those with large financial resources who can invest more in promotion, to develop products that consumers may find equal or superior to the S&S Smoothie products

- Fizzling of the low-carb craze if other forms of dieting gain in popularity

- Increase in popularity of energy drinks like Rockstar, etc.

Many but not all experts recommend that the SWOT analysis should be a summary of the material covered in the discussions of the various internal and external environments. Strengths and weaknesses come from the facts presented in the discussion of the internal environment, whereas opportunities and threats are based on discussions about the external environments. Be sure you check with your instructor on his or her perspective on the SWOT analysis.

Remember that you will need to measure the success of your marketing strategies against your objectives. Therefore, your objectives should be quantitative, realistic, and measurable.

PART TWO

Because the S&S Smoothie Company has an existing product that was discussed in the Internal Environment Section, we were able to say we were continuing some of those same strategies in our Marketing Strategies sections. If you have determined that your marketing plan is for a new business without any marketing history, you will have to provide complete details on the target market, product, price, promotion and distribution.

Marketing Objectives

The following are the marketing objectives set by S&S Smoothie:

- To increase the awareness of S&S Smoothie products by at least 10 percent among the target market during the next year.

- To increase gross sales by 50 percent over the next two years

- To introduce two new product lines: a line of low-carb smoothies and a line of gourmet-flavored smoothies

- To increase distribution of S&S Smoothie products to include hotels and resorts, golf and tennis clubs, and university campuses both in the United States and globally during the next two years.

Marketing Strategies

Target Markets

S&S Smoothie has identified a number of consumer and organizational markets for its products.

Consumer Markets

S&S Smoothies will continue to target its existing consumer markets. Company research shows that the primary consumer target market for S&S Smoothie beverages can be described as follows:

Demographics

- Male and female teens and young adults

- Ages: 15–39

- Household income: $50,000 and higher

- Education of head of household: College degree or higher

- Primarily located in midsize to large urban areas or college towns

Psychographics

- Health-conscious; interested in living a healthy lifestyle

- Spend much time and money taking care of their bodies

- Enjoy holidays that include physical activities

- Live very busy lives and need to use time wisely to enjoy all they want to do

- Enjoy spending time with friends

Media Habits

- Individuals in the target market use the Internet as their primary source of news and entertainment. When they watch television, it is usually on a computer or more often on a tablet or smartphone. Many simply avoid the news altogether and only get secondhand news through Facebook or other social media.

- When they do watch television programming, these consumers prefer watching edgier shows such as *The Walking Dead*, *Breaking Bad*, *The Big Bang Theory*, and *Game of Thrones*.

- They are likely to have satellite radio installed in their automobiles.

- They are heavy users of social media, spending between two and three hours a day on sites including Facebook, Twitter, LinkedIn, and Foursquare.

- They frequently read magazines such as *Men's Health, BusinessWeek, Sports Illustrated,* and *The New Yorker.*

Organizational Markets

In the past, S&S Smoothie has targeted two categories of reseller markets: (1) health clubs and gyms, and (2) small, upscale specialty food markets. To increase distribution and sales of its products, S&S Smoothie will target the following in the future:

1. Hotels and resorts in the United States and in selected international markets

2. Golf and tennis clubs

3. College and university campuses

Upscale young professionals frequently visit hotels and resorts, and they demand that even business travel should include quality accommodations and first-rate health club facilities. The membership of golf and tennis clubs, although including many older consumers, also is an excellent means of providing products conveniently for the targeted groups. College and university students, probably more than any other consumer group, are interested in health and in their bodies. In fact, many universities have built large, fairly elaborate health and recreational facilities as a means of attracting students. Thus, providing S&S Smoothie beverages on college campuses is an excellent means of meeting the health beverage needs of this group.

Positioning the Product

S&S Smoothie seeks to position its products as the first-choice smoothie beverage for the serious health-conscious consumer, including those who are seeking to lower their carbohydrate intake. The justification for this positioning is as follows: Many smoothie beverages are available. The S&S Smoothie formula provides superior flavor and nutrition in a shelf-stable form. S&S Smoothie has developed its product, packaging, pricing, and promotion to communicate a superior, prestige image. This positioning is thus supported by all its marketing strategies.

Product Strategies

To increase its leverage in the market and to meet its sales objectives, S&S Smoothie needs additional products. Two new product lines are planned:

PART THREE

1. *S&S Smoothie Gold:* This product will be similar to the original S&S Smoothie beverage but will come in six unique flavors:

   a. Piña colada

   b. Chocolate banana

   c. Apricot nectarine madness

   d. Pineapple berry crush

   e. Tropical tofu cherry

   f. Peaches and dreams

The nutritional content, critical to the success of the new products, will be similar to that of the original S&S Smoothie beverages. Nutritional apnformation is shown in Table A.2.

The packaging for the new S&S Smoothie product will also be similar to that used for the original product, utilizing the unique, easy-to-hold, hourglass-shaped, frosted glass

Table A.2 | Nutritional Information: S&S Smoothie Beverage

	S&S Smoothie Gold		Low-Carb S&S Smoothie	
	Amount per Serving	% Daily Value	Amount per Serving	% Daily Value
Calories	140		130	
Calories from fat	6		7	
Total fat	<0.5	1%	<0.5	1%
Saturated fat	<0.5	2%	<0.5	2%
Cholesterol	6 mg	2%	6 mg	2%
Sodium	70 mg	3%	70 mg	3%
Potassium	100 mg	3%	100 mg	3%
Total carbs	20 g	8%	10 g	4%
Dietary fiber	5 g	20%	5 g	20%
Protein	25 g	50%	25 g	50%
Vitamin A		50%		50%
Vitamin C		50%		50%
Calcium		20%		20%
Iron		30%		30%
Vitamin D		40%		40%
Vitamin E		50%		50%
Thiamin		50%		50%
Riboflavin		50%		50%
Niacin		50%		50%
Vitamin B^6		50%		50%
Vitamin B^{12}		50%		50%
Biotin		50%		50%
Pantothenic acid		50%		50%
Phosphorus		10%		10%
Iodine		50%		50%
Chromium		50%		50%
Zinc		50%		50%
Folic acid		50%		50%

Serving Size: 12 ounces
For 20-ounce sizes, multiply the amounts by 1.67.

bottle and providing the new beverage with the same upscale image. To set the product apart from the original-flavor Smoothie beverages in store refrigerator cases, labels will include the name of the beverage and the logo in gold lettering. The bottle cap will also be gold.

2. *Low-Carb S&S Smoothie:* As shown in Table A.2, the Low-Carb S&S Smoothie beverage will have approximately 50 percent fewer grams of carbohydrates than the original Smoothie beverage or the S&S Smoothie Gold. Low-Carb S&S Smoothie will come in the following four flavors:

   a. Strawberry

   b. Blueberry

   c. Banana

   d. Peach

Packaging for the Low-Carb S&S Smoothie will be similar to other S&S Smoothie beverages but will include the term "Low-Carb" in large type. The label will state that the beverage has 50 percent fewer carbs than regular smoothies. The bottle cap will be black.

Pricing Strategies

The current pricing strategy will be maintained for existing and new products. This pricing is appropriate for communicating a high-quality product image for all S&S Smoothie products. The company feels that creating different pricing for the new beverages would be confusing and create negative attitudes among consumers. Thus, there is no justification for increasing the price of the new products.

Pricing through the channel including margins is shown in Table A.3.

S&S Smoothie will continue to outsource actual production of the new offerings as it does with its existing product. As noted previously, with this method of production, variable costs for the 12-ounce S&S Smoothie beverages are $0.63 and variable costs for the 20-ounce size are $0.71. Anticipated annual fixed costs for S&S Smoothie office space, management salaries, and expenses related to sales, advertising and other marketing communications are as follows:

Salaries and employee benefits	$525,000
Office rental, equipment, and supplies	$124,600
Expenses related to sales (travel, etc.)	$132,000
Advertising and other marketing communications	$450,000
Total fixed costs	$1,231,600

Sales of the two sizes of all S&S products are expected to be approximately equal; that is, half of sales will be for the 12-ounce size and half will be for the 20-ounce size. Thus, there will be an average contribution margin of $0.83 per bottle. Based on this, to achieve breakeven in units, S&S Smoothie must sell the following:

$$\frac{\$1,231,600}{.83} = 1,483,856 \text{ bottles}$$

Again, assuming equal sales of the two sizes of products, the break-even point in dollars is $2,225,784.

Promotion Strategies

In the past, S&S Smoothie has used mainly personal selling to promote its products to the trade channel. To support this effort, signage has been provided for the resellers to promote the product at the point of purchase. Posters and stand-alone table cards show appealing photographs of the product in the different flavors and communicate the brand name and

Even if you are using an existing firm in your project, fixed and variable costs may not be available. Check with your instructor and ask if he or she would like for you to estimate these figures based on some logical assumptions.

PART THREE

PART FOUR

Table A.3 | Pricing of S&S Smoothie Beverages

	12 Ounces	20 Ounces
Suggested retail price	$4.00	$6.00
Retailer margin	50%/$2.00	50%/$3.00
Price to retail outlets (health clubs, etc.)	$2.00	$3.00
Distributor/sales agent margin	40%/$0.80	40%/$1.20
Price to distributor/discount to sales agent	$1.20	$1.80
Variable costs	$0.63	$0.71
S&S contribution margin	$0.57	$1.09

the healthy benefits of the product. Similar signage will be developed for use by resellers who choose to stock the S&S Smoothie Gold and the Low-Carb Smoothies.

Selling has previously been handled by a team of more than 75 manufacturers' agents who sell to resellers. In addition, in some geographic areas, an independent distributor does the selling. To support this personal selling approach, S&S Smoothie plans for additional promotional activities to introduce its new products and meet its other marketing objectives. These include the following:

1. *Television advertising:* The major objectives of television advertising are to increase awareness and knowledge of S&S Smoothies' superior product quality and to introduce the two new lines of Smoothies. Television advertising will be limited to programming related to healthy athletes such as the Olympics, major tennis matches, and golf tournaments. Ads will project health and happiness among young people who live a healthy lifestyle.

2. *Magazine and newspaper advertising:* Because consumers in the target market are not avid magazine readers, magazine advertising will be limited and will supplement other promotion activities. During the next year, S&S Smoothie will experiment with limited magazine advertising in such titles as *Men's Health*. The company will also investigate the potential of advertising in university newspapers.

3. *Sponsorships:* S&S Smoothie will attempt to sponsor several marathons in major cities. The advantage of sponsorships is that they provide visibility for the product while at the same time showing that the company supports activities of interest to the target market.

4. *Digital, social media, and mobile marketing:* S&S Smoothie will increase its use of digital and social media marketing to leverage its popularity among members of the target market. The objectives of these activities will be (1) to engage consumers with the company and the product, (2) to provide a benefit (i.e., something of value to the consumers delivered through the communication), (3) to better understand and, when possible, respond to the positive and negative comments about the S&S products by monitoring consumer postings on social media sites, and (4) to enhance the awareness and knowledge of the S&S products through the company website, YouTube videos and entries on related blogs.

   The key to successful digital and social media marketing is to provide more than just information. As noted, the challenge is to provide content that engages the consumer and that provides a benefit. For example, S&S could offer through its website and YouTube videos content such as how to make healthy dishes or meals, new exercise techniques, evaluation of different exercise equipment, stories about amateur athletes, their victories, their techniques, and so on. Inviting consumers to add to this information with their own videos would be one of many ways to encourage consumer engagement. The specifics of these activities should be developed as soon as possible. One of S&S's greatest assets is its loyal customer base, so a priority will be to turn avid users into ambassadors for the brand who will help to promote positive word of mouth on social media platforms.

5. *Sampling:* Sampling of S&S Smoothie beverages at select venues will provide an opportunity for prospective customers to become aware of the product and to taste the great flavors. Sampling will include only the two new products being introduced. Venues for sampling will include the following:

   a. Marathons

   b. Weightlifting competitions

   c. Gymnastics meets

   d. Student unions located on select college campuses

Supply Chain Strategies

As noted previously, S&S Smoothie distributes its beverages primarily through health clubs and gyms, and small, upscale specialty food stores. S&S Smoothie plans to expand its target reseller market to include the following:

1. Hotels and resorts in the United States and in targeted international markets

2. Golf and tennis clubs

3. College campuses

To increase leverage in larger health clubs, S&S Smoothie will offer free refrigerated display units that feature a prominent product logo. This will encourage the facility to maintain a high level of inventory of S&S Smoothie beverages.

Implementation

The action plan details the activities necessary to implement all marketing strategies. In addition, the action plan includes the timing for each item, the individual(s) responsible, and the budgetary requirements. Table A.4 shows an example of one objective (to increase distribution venues) and the action items S&S Smoothie will use to accomplish it.[2]

PART FOUR

PART ONE

Table A.4 | Action Items to Accomplish Marketing Objective Regarding Supply Chain

Objective: Increase Distribution Venues

Action Items	Beginning Date	Ending Date	Responsible Party	Cost	Remarks
1. Identify key hotels and resorts, golf clubs, and tennis clubs where S&S Smoothies might be sold	July 1	September 1	Bill Sartens (consulting firm will be engaged to assist in this effort)	$25,000	Key to this strategy is to selectively choose resellers so that maximum results are obtained from sales activities. Because health club use is greater during the months of January to May, efforts will be timed to have product in stock no later than January 15.
2. Identify 25 key universities where S&S Smoothies might be sold	July 1	August 1	Bill Sartens	0	Information about colleges and universities and their health club facilities should be available on the university web pages.
3. Make initial contact with larger hotel and resort chains	September 1	November 1	Bill Sartens	Travel: $10,000	
4. Make initial contact with larger individual (non-chain) facilities	September 1	November 1	Bill Sartens	Travel: $5,000	
5. Make initial contact with universities	August 15	September 15	Manufacturers' agents	0	Agents will be assigned to the 25 universities and required to make an initial contact and report back to Bill Sartens on promising prospects.
6. Follow up initial contacts with all potential resellers and obtain contracts for coming six months	September 15	Ongoing	Bill Sartens, manufacturers' agents	$10,000	$10,000 is budgeted for this item, although actual expenditures will be on an as-needed basis, as follow-up travel cannot be preplanned.

PART ONE

Measurement and Control Strategies

A variety of activities will ensure effective measurement of the success of the marketing plan and allow the firm to make adjustments as necessary. These include targeted market research and trend analysis. It is also important to maintain the stats on consumer access of digital media and social media marketing.

Research

Firms need to regularly engage in marketing research activities to understand brand awareness and brand attitudes among their target markets. S&S Smoothie will therefore continue its program of focus group research and descriptive studies of its target consumer and reseller markets.

Trend Analysis

S&S Smoothie will do a monthly trend analysis to examine sales by reseller type, geographic area, chain, agent, and distributor. These analyses will allow S&S Smoothie to take corrective action when necessary.

Your Future in a Marketing Career

Do you just hate it when someone asks, "What are you going to do when you graduate?" Perhaps you avoid the question by saying, "Get a job—I hope."

Many college students like you have an idea of the type of career they might like but don't have a clue as to how to get there. Still others just don't even have any idea about what job they would enjoy—they just want to get one. In this appendix, we will be talking about how you can use marketing strategies to not only choose a job but also assist you in actually landing the job you want.

It's all about thinking of yourself as a product—a unique brand—and how to best market that brand. In fact, *you* are a product. That may sound weird, but companies like LinkedIn couldn't exist if you were not a product with value. As we have said, *value* refers to the benefits a customer receives from buying a good or service.

You have "market value" as a person—you have qualities that set you apart from others and abilities other people want and need. After you finish this course, you'll have even more value because you'll know about the field of marketing and how this field relates to you both as a future businessperson *and* as a consumer. In addition to learning about how marketing influences each of us, you'll have a better understanding of what it means to be "Brand You"—and, it is hoped, some ideas about what you can do to increase your value to employers and maybe even to society.

Although it may seem strange to think about the marketing of people, in reality we often talk about ourselves and others in marketing terms. It is common for us to speak of "positioning" ourselves for job interviews or to tell our friends not to "sell themselves short." Some people who are cruising for potential mates even refer to themselves as "being on the market." In addition, many consumers hire personal image consultants to devise a "marketing strategy" for them, and others undergo plastic surgery or makeovers to improve their "product images." The desire to package and promote ourselves is the reason for personal goods and services markets ranging from cosmetics and exercise equipment to résumé specialists and dating agencies.[1]

So the principles of marketing apply to people, just as they apply to coffee, convertibles, and computer processors. Sure, there are differences in how we go about marketing each of these, but the general idea remains the same: Marketing is a fundamental part of our lives both as consumers and as players in the business world. Perhaps a good place to start a discussion of careers is to look at the *who* and *where* of Marketing.

The *Who* and *Where* of Marketing

Marketers come from many different backgrounds. Although many have earned marketing degrees, others have backgrounds in areas such as engineering or agriculture. Retailers and fashion marketers may have training in merchandising or design. Advertising copywriters often have degrees in English or in psychology. E-marketers who do business over the Internet may have studied computer science.

Marketers work in a variety of locations. They work in consumer goods companies such as Quaker Foods and in retail organizations like Eskimo Joe's. You'll see them in companies that provide services to consumers such as Weight Watchers, International, and those that sell their services to other companies like BDP that offers regulatory compliance and logistics solutions to companies like Quaker Foods through their consulting services. You'll see them at philanthropic organizations such as the Red Cross or Product (RED) and at cutting-edge advertising and social media agencies like The Pitch Agency and Twitter.

And, although you may assume that the typical marketing job is in a large, consumer-oriented company like Disney, marketers work in other types of organizations too. There are many exciting marketing careers in companies that sell to other businesses. In small organizations, one person (perhaps the owner) may handle all the marketing responsibilities. In large organizations, marketers work on different aspects of the marketing strategy. No matter where they work, all marketers are real people who make choices that affect themselves, their companies, and very often thousands or even millions of consumers.

Marketing's Role in the Firm: Cross-Functional Relationships

What role do marketers play in a firm? The importance organizations assign to marketing activities varies a lot. Top management in some firms is very marketing oriented (especially when the chief executive officer comes from the marketing ranks), whereas in other companies marketing is an afterthought. However, analysts estimate that at least one-third of CEOs come from a marketing background—so stick with us!

Sometimes a company uses the term *marketing* when what it really means is sales or advertising. In some organizations, particularly small, not-for-profit ones, there may be no one in the company specifically designated as "the marketing person." In contrast, some firms realize that marketing applies to all aspects of the firm's activities. As a result, there has been a trend toward integrating marketing with other business functions (such as management and accounting) instead of making it a separate function.

No matter what size the firm, a marketer's decisions affect—and are affected by—the firm's other operations. Marketing managers must work with financial and accounting officers to figure out whether products are profitable, to set marketing budgets, and to determine prices. They must work with people in manufacturing to be sure that products are produced on time and in the right quantities. Marketers also must work with research-and-development specialists to create products that meet customers' needs.

Where Do You Fit In? Careers in Marketing

Marketing is an incredibly exciting, diverse discipline that brims with opportunities. There are many paths to a marketing career. To see an excellent overview of marketing-related jobs, including up-to-date starting salaries, we strongly recommend you visit the

Occupational Outlook Handbook website maintained by the Bureau of Labor Statistics, U.S. Department of Labor. Just look under Management and then Advertising, Promotions, and Marketing Managers, or go directly to this link: http://www.bls.gov/ooh/management /advertising-promotions-and-marketing-managers.htm#tab-8.[2] Next we'll talk about how you can use your knowledge of marketing to find a successful career whether in marketing or some other field.

Create Your Personal Marketing Plan

Because we think the best way to start a career includes much of what we know from marketing, we'll talk about developing your career as the process as creating and marketing your own personal brand. It's not about what kind of job you want after graduation, it's about what career you want and what you want to be doing 5, 10, or 15 years from now.

In Chapter 3 of this text, we talked about the steps in developing a marketing plan. And, you can find a sample marketing plan in Appendix A. We'll use those same steps in your plan to develop a great career.

Step 1: Define Your Mission

As we discussed in Chapter 3, a first step for an organization—or for you—is to define your mission—a statement of your overall purpose and what you hope to achieve. Just like a firm's mission statement guides the plans of all the functional areas of the firm, from human resources to marketing, your mission statement will guide you in your career search. It will provide the foundation of goal-directed behavior now and in the future.

As a beginning to developing a personal mission statement, you will probably want to think about what you enjoy doing the most in your life. This is important because you'll be most successful if you enjoy your career—if you like going to work every day. Some examples of what you might include in this list are the following:

- Helping people

- Developing and executing creative ideas

- Working with other people—or alone

- Working with quantitative concepts—or with words

Based on this, you can develop a concise statement of what you want in your career.

Example: "To work in a creative, value-focused environment with the goal of providing unique and useful products that help make lives better."

Step 2: Perform a Situation Analysis

The next important step in any planning process is to have a clear, honest, and accurate understanding of where you are—your situation analysis. The situation analysis includes an understanding of the internal environment, an examination of the external environment in which you will look for a job and work, and a SWOT analysis.

The Internal Environment

What are your skills, talents, values, strengths, weaknesses? Are you good at writing or at persuading others to accept your ideas? Do you motivate other people? Are you good at developing strategies to achieve goals, generating innovative ideas, or initiating change? Are you a detail person? Do you persevere until you find the solution to a problem? Are you dependable? Can you accept criticism? Do you like or dislike being in charge? Do you like working alone or do you prefer to be a part of a team and work with other people? Do you hate wearing a suit and dream of a career where you can wear jeans, a T-shirt and flip-flops? Are there some things that you really hate doing such as learning new things? Have you created a large debt in loans to pay for your college so that salary is critically important to you in a job? Are you tied to a specific location by family or unwillingness to relocate? Do you have any physical limitations? What are your plans and dreams for a family? It's important that you carefully and critically examine yourself before you begin a career exploration.

The External Environment

There are many factors in the external environment, factors that you have no control over and that you need to recognize and understand. These include factors that exist now, that you can expect to change in the future, and that will affect you and others who are entering the workforce. Some of these might be the following:

- Changing technology

- A changing competitive environment

- The state of the national and global economy

- Changing cultural values, tastes, and trends

- The movement of work to other locations both in and outside your home country

- Computers and smart machines replacing people in jobs

- Changing population demographics

- Changing environmental and other government regulations

- The increasing importance of digital communication and social media for consumers and for businesses

Your Personal SWOT Analysis

A SWOT analysis is kind of a summary of the examination of your internal and external environments. It focuses on what you have learned about yourself and identified as strengths that you can offer an employer and weaknesses that you need to address or make sure they will not create a road to disaster in your career.

Strengths:

- You probably have personal characteristics that set you apart from others. You may be detail-oriented, tech savvy, persistent, creative, good with quantitative analysis, or getting along with others.

- You also have gained knowledge and skills that will make you a "better hire." Through an internship or other work experience you may have gained valuable skills such as developing and implementing plans, organizing events, public speaking, handling conflict, conducting research, or writing reports.

Weaknesses:

- We all have weaknesses, but what are yours? You may be easily defeated if things don't go well. Some people find it very difficult to accept the ideas of others if they are different from their own. Your weakness may be difficulty in expressing your ideas to others. You will be better off in your marketing strategy if you admit your weaknesses at the beginning and develop ways to overcome them.

Opportunities: What is happening in the external environment that provides good opportunities where your strengths are needed and your weaknesses are not a "deal breaker"?

- As the population ages, more job opportunities will open up.

- New opportunities in growing industries such as Internet communications, services for the aging population, and the demand for improved education including new delivery methods

Threats: What factors that you can't control may have a negative impact on your career success?

- Predictions for the economic environment in the short term and in the long term may provide threats to career success. Of course, they may also provide opportunities.

- With the growing importance of digital and social media marketing, employers may become less interested in employees with only traditional marketing skills.

- As marketing communication changes, new skills will be needed that you may not have.

- The increasing number of college graduates means a highly competitive hiring environment in which only the best will succeed.

Step 3: Develop Your Marketing/Career Objectives

Objectives, whether for an organization or for you as an individual seeking a career need to be specific, quantitative, measurable, attainable, and realistic. You can find out more about this in Chapter 3.

Depending on where you are in your education and career search, some examples may be the following:

- To obtain two internships in marketing areas of organizations before graduation

- To obtain an entry-level marketing position with a firm that has at least $50 million in sales within the first three years after graduation

- To earn a salary of at least $30,000 within the first year after graduation

Step 4: Develop Marketing Strategies

Once you have identified your career objectives, it's time to develop your plans to reach those objectives. Just as marketers know that their success in selling a new brand of toothpaste depends on developing target marketing, product, pricing, promotion, and distribution strategies, you need to develop great strategies for career success.

Step 4A: Develop Target Marketing Strategies

Firms large and small must conduct research to determine the best target market for their new laundry detergent or jeans. You need to conduct research to identify your ideal job. Your research will seek to discover (1) if a potential employer is somewhere you would like to work and (2) if the employer has a job in which you can be successful.

Organizational Culture

One important aspect of a job and a career that you should consider is the organizational culture. Many young people today feel that their personal happiness is just as if not more important than the money they make. Companies like Zappos are creating a paradigm shift in terms of the work environment. At Zappos, the company's goal is to "wow" the customer, not just satisfy them. All employees, including the top people, have the same size desk and space, which they are encouraged to decorate any way they choose. There are no private offices but lots of small conference rooms are available to everyone for meetings. Healthy snacks are available for everyone for free, and less healthy snacks are in vending machines for a price. And if you ever see a coat and tie in the building, it will be a guest who is wearing this outfit. Jeans and flip-flops are more the norm. Does this kind of work atmosphere appeal to you?

Of course, there are other, often more important aspects of an organization's culture. Your research should include such things as the following:

- The management philosophy

- The history of the company

- The size of the organization

- The ethical values of the firm

- The opportunities for upward mobility within the firm

- Does the firm believe in risk taking or are they more conservative?

One of the best ways to find out about a company is the web. Company websites, social media, blogs, and other sites will provide you with useful information about organizations.

Finding Potential Jobs

As we said previously, your research should also look at identifying employers who are looking for someone with your knowledge and skills. Again, the three most important activities for finding the right job are research, research, and research. Go beyond just searching what is available today. Investigate what trends are changing the job scene. What careers are expected to be important in the future? What industries are growing? How is technology expected to influence the job market?

You will, of course, need to identify specific jobs A few sources that might be useful for you are listed in Table B.1.

Positioning Yourself

As you recall, the third step in target marketing is positioning yourself. Positioning is placing yourself in the customer's (the hiring firm's) mind in relation to the competition (other candidates for the job). If you will be applying for several different types of jobs, you may need to develop slightly different positioning for different jobs by focusing on specific skills or experiences. There are some characteristics that are universally important that you should use in positioning yourself for a job. These include the following:

- Written and oral communication skills

- Dependability

- Honesty and integrity

- Teamwork

- A strong work ethic

- Initiative

- Flexibility

- Problem solving

- Computer skills

Table B.1 | Sources of Career and Job Information

What Information Is Available?	Sources
News, trends, and general information on industries.	www.hoovers.com www.bls.gov/oco www.online.onetcenter.org
Advice on career planning.	Your campus career center http://career-advice.monster.com www.salary.com
Professional trade organizations in the area which you are interested. These often include internship and full-time job listings.	www.associationjobboards.com
Individual industry publications that often include job listings.	Advertising: www.adage.com www.aaf.org Accounting and finance: www.afponline.org Marketing: www.marketingjobs.com Marketing research: www.mra-net.org Sales and marketing: www.smei.org
Local business journals provide news on local businesses and local job listings.	For business journal websites in your community, www.bizjournals.com
Lists of top businesses can provide lists of businesses that might be target companies.	Publications such as www.businessweek.com www.wsj.com For marketing related firms, www.marketingpower.com
Professional social networks allow you to create a network of people to make contacts.	www.linkedin.com

Step 4B: Develop Product Strategies

Just as we discussed in Chapter 8, developing a product concept means thinking in terms of the product layers, that is, the core, the actual, and the augmented product:

- *The core product:* The core product includes benefits the firm will receive if they hire you. In your job search, you should be prepared to offer arguments and evidence that through your education and experience (such as an internship) you have gained the skills and knowledge that will provide the benefits they look for. Remember, the firm wants someone who will be an asset in helping them achieve their goals. These may be related to higher sales, increased customer satisfaction, lower costs, or something else. If they don't see you as providing that benefit, they will look for someone else. That's where that list of strengths comes in.

- *The actual product:* The actual product is all about your perceivable "features." These include not only your skills related to the specific positions, such as knowledge of research methods or experience in developing branding strategies, but also those personal characteristics listed previously.

- *The augmented product:* The augmented product for a job includes those benefits you will provide for the employer that are not requirements of the job. Are you willing to travel? Will you work overtime? Do you have some additional skills not required of the job but which you feel will be useful to the firm?

Step 4C: Develop Pricing Strategies: What Salary Should You Ask For?

When you think about price you will expect for your work, you need to consider not only the salary but also the benefits and perks the employer is offering. In many jobs, there is a base salary plus other monetary compensation in terms of a commission, bonus, or stock options. Employee benefits normally include a variety of insurance plans (medical, dental, etc.), sick leave, vacation time, day care, tuition reimbursement, and retirement plans. Perks offered by employers might be on-site cafeterias offering meals at low prices, health/workout facilities, free coffee and healthy snacks, flexible working hours, on-site day care facilities, or on-site basic medical care.

Sooner or later, you will have to answer the question of what salary you will need. To answer this question, some advance preparation is necessary. You may want to begin thinking about the minimum you will need to pay your basic expenses. How much more than this would you like to earn to have some discretionary income? Based on that, you can ask for a salary range a little above that to give yourself some negotiating room. For example, if your minimum to pay your expenses is $30,000 but you would like at least $33,000, then you might ask for $35,000 to $40,000 to get what you want after salary negotiations. And don't forget in your calculations to consider what you need for transportation, taxes, insurance, Social Security, deductions for retirement plans and other costs of being employed.

Most experts say that you should not bring up the subject of compensation (salary and benefits) but rather wait until the employer brings it up. If asked what you need, you may be wise not to give a specific amount unless it is demanded. A good answer might be "I'm sure you have a competitive compensation plan."

Step 4D: Develop Promotional Strategies: Your Personal Marketing Communication Plan

Of course, you want to develop a great integrated marketing communication plan to let potential employers know about you. Two very important opportunities for communication include online and person to person networking and advertising.

Networking

Word of mouth is probably the most influential source of information for employers. Many employers would prefer not to even post a job. You might think of networking as a sort of personal selling. Just like a salesperson practices customer relationship management by regularly contacting prospective customers, you need to keep in touch with contacts and try to be helpful to them.

- Family and friends: Your networking should begin with your family and friends. You should also be sure to obtain contact information to maintain relationships with your college peers and professors. If there is a business professional as a guest speaker in your class or for a school club, make a point to meet him or her and get his or her card before he or she leaves. Follow up with a thank-you note to ensure that the speaker remembers you.

- LinkedIn: Just having and updating your LinkedIn doesn't count as making LinkedIn work for you in your job search.[2] The best strategy is to continuously work on increasing the size of your LinkedIn network. If you have a hundred folks in your network and every member of your network has a hundred or so members in each of their networks, you are connected to literally thousands of individuals who may work for a firm that has your perfect job. If not, then one of these thousands surely knows someone who works there, or has a relative or friend who works there. It's always a good idea to get someone on LinkedIn to provide an introduction for you.

You also need to make sure your LinkedIn account communicates the best about "Brand You." Your name, your headline and a photo is all someone will see when your LinkedIn profile comes up. This means your headline is critical to communicating your brand. Consider how you can create a headline that says you are the perfect solution to a firm's hiring problem or at least tells a story that makes you as real as possible and a great prospect for a hiring manager. You may want to enhance your LinkedIn account by including a video of you making a presentation or your very best PowerPoint presentation slides.

- Career fairs: Career fairs can be great places to meet a number of different potential employers. Be sure to "dress for success" and bring copies of your cover letter and your résumé. Always ask for a business card so that you can follow up with the career fair contact with a note.

- Company websites: Company websites based on a list of companies you have developed as discussed previously.

- Online job boards and recruiting websites: Some general job boards and recruiting sites include www.collegegrad.com, www.careerbuilder.com, www.black-collegian.com, www.hotjobs.yahoo.com, www.monster.com, and your own campus career website. Some industry-specific boards include www.marketingjobs.com, www.marketingsherpa .com, and www.thebossgroup.com .

Advertising: Your Résumé and Cover Letter

The résumé and the cover letter are the most important elements of marketing communication for any job applicant. They're your advertising. It's important that both communicate that you have the knowledge and skills the employer is looking for. And it isn't enough just to say you know how to write a press release or create a marketing plan; you need to indicate that you have actually written the release or plan, perhaps in a class or for an internship. In this way, you can set yourself apart from your competitors, that is, the other job applicants. Most important, both your résumé and your cover letter must be well-written if you want to "sell" yourself to the employer. A cover letter *is not* a social media post! Abbreviations, slang or emoticons won't cut it. A single misspelled word or incorrect grammar can mean the end to your dream for a great job.

Résumé

Writing a résumé for the first time can be overwhelming. Fortunately, most universities have career services personnel who will help you in the task. Of course, they will probably ask that you put together a first draft, and then they will help you fine-tune it. Some suggestions for that first draft follow.

1. Get organized before you begin writing. Make notes on your jobs, internships, honors, extracurricular activities, leadership experiences, community service, class projects, and course work. But don't just create a list; you also need to describe exactly what you did, what you learned, what skills you gained, and so on, with each experience. And be sure to keep a record of any names and addresses of people whom you came in contact with in these activities. Accuracy is important in these notes. One thing you must never do is to *lie or exaggerate* on your résumé.

2. Tailor to the job. Your individual experiences, skills, etc., may be more or less important for different jobs. Because you should tailor your résumé for different jobs, you should think about which are more important for the job at hand.

3. Section headings. Heading are important for any document and especially so for a résumé. The normal headings for a résumé for a college student seeking a first career position are "Education," "Honors and Scholarships," and "Work Experience."

Other headings may be "Leadership Experience," "Athletic Achievements," "Professional Associations," "Extracurricular Experience," "International Language Skills," "Software Skills," and "Community Service." If you have had important internship or employment experience, you will probably want to list three to five accomplishments for each.

4. The "look" of the résumé. Looks are important in a resume. In general, your résumé should not exceed one page, should be in a single font, and should have lots of white space so that it is easy to read.

5. Be sure there are no typos, misspellings, or grammatical errors and print on white or neutral-colored paper.

Cover Letter

A good cover letter is as important or even more important than a good résumé. If the cover letter has typos or other errors, the employer will likely never even read the résumé. The logic is that if you can't write a good letter, they simply don't want you.

You may choose to format your cover letter with a series of paragraphs, or you may choose to use an introductory sentence or two followed by bullets. That decision is based on what and how much you want to say. The letter should do the following:

- Include your name, address, and the date

- Include an inside address

- Be addressed to an individual person by name

- Include a personal salutation: "Dear Mr.... ."

- Have an introductory paragraph that talks about the position you are seeking, how you learned about it, and why you are interested in the position.

- Discuss your experience and skills that make you a good candidate for the job in the body of the letter

- Make sure that each paragraph or bullet covers a single subject—when you start a new subject, you should start a new paragraph or bullet.

- Include a final paragraph that provides a strategy for an interview; that is, you will call or ask the employer to call you to set up an interview.

Delivering your advertising by direct mail: To let prospective employers know about you, send them a letter—a real paper and envelope letter (not e-mail)—and your résumé. Be sure you send the letter and resume to the right person or people at a company. A well-written letter on paper, delivered in an envelope, can make you stand out from the crowd. We can't say it too many times—be sure that you don't have any spelling, grammatical, or punctuation errors in your letter or your résumé.

Step 4E: Develop Supply Chain Strategies: Delivering Value with a Successful Interview

No matter how great your cover letter and résumé are, your delivery in the interview process is critical to landing the job. Planning is critical for ensuring great success in both telephone and personal interviews.

To make your interview successful, do the following:

- Be sure you know as much as possible about the job and the company. Don't be concerned that the employer will disapprove of this; employers recognize that the best candidates do their research.

- Prepare for interview questions. By this, we mean developing a list of questions you expect the interviewer to ask you and your answers. For example, in many interviews, you will be asked, "Tell us about yourself." You also need to develop a list of questions that you can ask the interviewer when requested.

- Prepare your key selling points. These are the things you would like to make sure you say to one or more of the questions. You want to focus on the benefits you can provide for the employer, but you have to do this in response to questions.

- Dress for success. Dressing professionally is probably the best advice for any interview, even if you have found in your research that employees of the organization dress casually. In general, this means a professional dress or suit in a conservative color for women and a suit in a conservative color for men. For both, it's best to wear conservative shoes and not to have any tattoos or piercings visible. You can probably find more information on how to dress for an interview from your school's career services advisers or online.

- Follow up the interview with a thank-you note within 24 hours. A handwritten note is often best, but today many businesspeople prefer the convenience of an e-mail thank-you. Also, e-mail will arrive immediately, whereas snail mail will take a few days. Time may be critical if the hiring decision is to be made quickly.

What to Bring to the Interview

One of the best things you can bring to an interview is a portfolio of your work. This may include class projects and items that showcase your work in an internship or a job or a volunteer project. You will probably want to include these in a portfolio enclosed in plastic sleeves.

You should also bring extra copies of your cover letter and résumé. Although you have already sent the interviewer a copy of these, they may be lost at the bottom of a pile on the desk. Having an extra copy available can save the interviewer from embarrassment and greatly enhance the interview process.

Accepting the Offer

Experts suggest that you never accept an offer immediately. It is expected that you will take a day or so to think about the offer before you accept it. This gives you time to consider the salary and benefits offered, ask any questions that you may have, and determine if you want to negotiate anything.

After you have verbally accepted the offer, you should ask for an offer letter that includes the terms of the offer. If it includes all the elements of your verbal offer and negotiations, you can sign the offer letter, make a copy for yourself, and return the original. Then enjoy your career!

▶ Notes

CHAPTER 1

1. American Marketing Association, "About AMA," www.ama.org/AboutAMA/Pages/Definition-of-Marketing.aspx (accessed April 4, 2014).

2. American Marketing Association, "About AMA," www.ama.org/AboutAMA/Pages/Definition-of-Marketing.aspx (accessed April 4, 2014).

3. Thomas Hobbs, "Over 20% of FTSE 100 CEOs Now Come from a Marketing Background," *Marketing Week*, October 23, 2015, https://www.marketingweek.com/2015/10/23/over-20-of-ftse-100-ceos-now-come-from-a-marketing-background/" (accessed March 19, 2016).

4. "USA, GDP Services," World Bank Cross Country Data, https://www.quandl.com/data/WORLDBANK/USA_NV_SRV_TETC_ZS-United-States-Services-etc-value-added-of-GDP (accessed March 23, 2016).

5. Lee D. Dahringer, "Marketing Services Internationally: Barriers and Management Strategies," *Journal of Service Marketing* 5 (1991): 5–17.

6. Stuart Elliott, "Introducing Kentucky, the Brand," *The New York Times*, June 9, 2004, www.nyt.com.

7. Julie Jargon, "McDonald's All-Day Breakfast Is Luring In Consumers, Study Finds," *The Wall Street Journal*, December 8, 2015, http://www.wsj.com/articles/mcdonalds-all-day-breakfast-is-luring-in-customers-study-finds-1449609778?cb=logged0.9060535116359343 (accessed March 3, 2016).

8. Julie Weeddec, "For Uber, Airbnb and Other Companies, Customer Ratings Go Both Ways," *The New York Times*, December 1, 2014, http://www.nytimes.com/2014/12/02/business/for-uber-airbnb-and-other-companies-customer-ratings-go-both-ways.html (accessed March 23, 2016). Uber.com

9. Target Corporation, "2012 Corporate Responsibility Report," https://corporate.target.com/_media/TargetCorp/csr/pdf/2012-corporate-responsibility-report.pdf (accessed April 5, 2014).

10. Mark Strassman, "A Dying Breed: The American Shopping Mall," March 23, 2014, www.cbsnews.com/news/a-dying-breed-the-american-shopping-mall (accessed April 6, 2014).

11. Paula D. Englis, Basil G. Englis, Michael R. Solomon, and Aard Groen, "Strategic Sustainability and Triple Bottom Line Performance in Textiles: Implications of the Eco-Label for the EU and Beyond," Business as an Agent of World Benefit Conference, United Nations and the Academy of Management, Cleveland, OH, 2006.

12. Compare M. K. Khoo, S. G. Lee, and S. W. Lye, "A Design Methodology for the Strategic Assessment of a Product's Eco-Efficiency," *International Journal of Production Research* 39 (2001): 245–74; C. Chen, "Design for the Environment: A Quality-Based Model for Green Product Development," *Management Science* 47, no. 2 (2001): 250–64; McDonough Braungart Design, *Chemistry's Design Paradigm*, www.mbdc.com/c2c_home.htm (accessed April 15, 2006); Elizabeth Corcoran, "Thinking Green," *Scientific American* 267, no. 6 (1992): 44–46; Amitai Etzioni, "The Good Society: Goals beyond Money," *The Futurist* (2001): 68–69; and M. H. Olson, "Charting a Course for Sustainability," *Environment* 38, no. 4 (1996): 10–23. See also U.S. Environmental Protection Agency, "What Is Sustainability," www.epa.gov (accessed April 7, 2014).

13. Lew Blaustein, "How Adidas Is Pioneering Open-Source Sustainability for Sports," *Green Biz* July 24, 2015, https://www.greenbiz.com/article/how-adidas-pioneering-open-source-sustainability-sports (accessed March 25, 2016).

14. Jeff Lowe, *The Marketing Dashboard: Measuring Marketing Effectiveness*, February 2003, www.brandchannel.com/images/papers/dashboard.pdf; G. A. Wyner, "Scorecards and More: The Value Is in How You Use Them," *Marketing Research*, Summer, 6–7; C. F. Lunbdy and C. Rasinowich, "The Missing Link: Cause and Effect Linkages Make Marketing Scorecards More Valuable," *Marketing Research*, Winter 2003, 14–19.

15. Marketing Accountability Standards Board, "Finance and Marketing Bond at MillerCoors," March 10, 2016, https://themasb.org/finance-and-marketing-bond-at-millercoors/ (accessed March 27, 2016).

16. Jeff Beer, "25 Predictions for What Marketing Will Look Like in 2020," *Fastcocreate*, March 4, 2015, http://www.fastcocreate.com/3043109/sector-forecasting/25-predictions-for-what-marketing-will-look-like-in-2020; Daniel Newman, "10 Top Trends Driving the Future of Marketing," *Forbes*, CMO Network, April 14, 2015, http://www.forbes.com/sites/danielnewman/2015/04/14/10-top-trends-driving-the-future-of-marketing/#1f71d350662c (accessed March 25, 2016).

17. Jessica Oaks, "4 Big Companies Using Big Data Successfully" *Smart Data Collective*, July 14, 2015, http://www.smartdatacollective.com/jessoaks11/330428/4-big-companies-using-big-data-successfully (Accessed March 21, 2016).

18. Claire Groden, "Here's How Many Americans Sleep with Their Smartphones," *Fortune* (June 29, 2015), http://fortune.com/2015/06/29/sleep-banks-smartphones/ (accessed March 28, 2016).

19. Liat Hughes Joshi, "Perils of Screen Addiction," *The Vancouver Sun*, January 25, 2016, http://www.vancouversun.com/life/perils+screen+addiction/11675328/story.html (accessed March 21, 2016).

20. Jess Oaks, "Big-Companies-Using-Big-Data-Successfully," http://www.smartdatacollective.com.

21. Jeep, "Frequently Asked Questions," http://jeepjamboreeusa.com/faq (accessed April 6, 2014).

22. Roberto A. Ferdman, "How Coca-Cola Has Tricked Everyone into Drinking So Much of It," *The Washington Post*, October 5, 2015, https://www.washingtonpost.com/news/wonk/wp/2015/10/05/how-coca-cola-gets-its-way/ (accessed March 20, 2016).

23. Michael E. Porter, *Competitive Advantage: Creating and Sustaining Superior Performance* (New York: Free Press, 1985).

24. Siddharth Cavale, "Coke Revenue Misses Estimates as Soda Sales Slow," February 18, 2014, www.reuters.com/article/2014/02/18/us-cocacola-results-idUSBREA1H0WH20140218 (accessed April 7, 2014). Neil Hughes, "Apple's Domestic Mac Sales Surge 28.5% as Overall PC Market Shrinks 7.5%," January 9, 2014, http://appleinsider.com/articles/14/01/09/apples-domestic-mac-sales-surge-285-as-overall-pc-market-shrinks-75 (accessed April 7, 2014). Southwest Airlines, "2014 Media Kit," www.southwest.com/assets/pdfs/customer_service/swcom_media_kit.pdf (accessed April 7, 2014). Andrew Rhomberg, "Is Amazon Invincible?" July 23, 2013, www.digitalbookworld/2013/is-amazon-invincible (accessed April 7, 2014). Annalyn Censky, "Dunkin' Donuts to Double U.S. Locations," January 4, 2012, http://money.cnn.com/2012/01/04/news/companies/dunkin_donuts_locations (accessed April 7, 2014).

25. Karlene Lukovitz, "Ghirardelli Streams User Content in Times Square," March 9, 2010, www.mediapost.com/publications/index.cfm?fa=Articles.showArticle&art_aid=123852 (accessed June 8, 2010).

26. CNN, "About CNN iReport," http://ireport.cnn.com/about.jspa (accessed April 6, 2014).

27. James Yang, "Here's an Idea: Let Everyone Have Ideas," *New York Times*, March 30, 2006.

28. Frito-Lay North America, "PepsiCo's Doritos Brand Reveals the Five Consumer-Created Commercials Competing for $1 Million Grand Prize," January 2, 2014, www.fritolay.com/about-us/press-release-20140102.html (accessed April 6, 2014).

29. Kenneth E. Clow and Donald E. Baack, *Integrated Advertising, Promotion, and Marketing Communications*, 7th ed. (Upper Saddle River, NJ: Pearson, 2016).

30. Jess Fee, "The Beginners Guide to the Cloud," *Mashable*, August 26, 2013, http://mashable.com/2013/08/26/what-is-the-cloud/#djXLUOtpvkq7 (accessed March 22, 2016).

31. Some material adapted from a presentation by Matt Leavey, Prentice Hall Business Publishing, July 18, 2007.

32. This section adapted from Michael R. Solomon, Consumer Behavior: Buying, Having, and Being, 8th ed. (Upper Saddle River, NJ: Prentice Hall, 2008).

33. Jeff Surowiecki, The Wisdom of Crowds (New York: Anchor, 2005); Jeff Howe, "The Rise of Crowdsourcing," June 2006, www.wired.com/wired/archive/14.06/crowds.html (accessed October 3, 2007).

34. Jolie Lee, "Lego to Release 'Ghostbusters' Set Tied to Anniversary," February 27, 2014, www.usatoday.com/story/news/nation-now/2014/02/17/lego-ghostbusters-ecto-1/5551069 (accessed April 6, 2014).

35. Jack Ewing, "VW Says Emissions Cheating Was Not a One-Time Error," *New York Times*, December 10, 2015, http://www.nytimes.com/2015/12/11/business/international/vw-emissions-scandal.html (accessed March 20, 2016).

36. Larry Edwards, "The Decision Was Easy," Advertising Age, August 26, 1987, 106. For research and discussion related to public policy issues, see Paul N. Bloom and Stephen A. Greyser, "The Maturing of Consumerism," Harvard Business Review, November/December 1981, 130–39; George S. Day, "Assessing the Effect of Information Disclosure Requirements," Journal of Marketing, April 1976, 42–52; Dennis E. Garrett, "The Effectiveness of Marketing Policy Boycotts: Environmental Opposition to Marketing," Journal of Marketing 51 (January 1987): 44–53; Michael Houston and Michael Rothschild, "Policy-Related Experiments on Information Provision: A Normative Model and Explication," Journal of Marketing Research 17 (November 1980): 432–49; Jacob Jacoby, Wayne D. Hoyer, and David A. Sheluga, Misperception of Televised Communications (New York: American Association of Advertising Agencies, 1980); Gene R. Laczniak and Patrick E. Murphy, Marketing Ethics: Guidelines for Managers (Lexington, MA: Lexington Books, 1985): 117–23; Lynn Phillips and Bobby Calder, "Evaluating Consumer Protection Laws: Promising Methods," Journal of Consumer Affairs 14 (Summer 1980): 9–36; Donald P. Robin and Eric Reidenbach, "Social Responsibility, Ethics, and Marketing Strategy: Closing the Gap between Concept and Application," Journal of Marketing 51 (January 1987): 44–58; Howard Schutz and Marianne Casey, "Consumer Perceptions of Advertising as Misleading," Journal of Consumer Affairs 15 (Winter 1981): 340–57; and Darlene Brannigan Smith and Paul N. Bloom, "Is Consumerism Dead or Alive? Some New Evidence," in Advances in Consumer Research, ed. Thomas C. Kinnear (Provo, UT: Association for Consumer Research, 1984): 569–73.

37. Parts of this section are adapted from Michael R. Solomon, *Consumer Behavior: Buying, Having, and Being*, 7th ed. (Upper Saddle River, NJ: Prentice Hall, 2007).

38. Thomas C. O'Guinn and Ronald J. Faber, "Compulsive Buying: A Phenomenological Explanation," *Journal of Consumer Research* 16 (September 1989): 154.

39. Associated Press, "Center Tries to Treat Web Addicts," September 5, 2009, www.nytimes.com/2009/09/06/us/06internet.html (accessed June 8, 2010); Samantha Manas, "Addicted to Chapstick: The World of Chapstick Addicts Revealed," July 5, 2006, www.associatedcontent.com/article/41148/addicted_to_chapstick.html (accessed May 13, 2008).

40. "Advertisers Face Up to the New Morality: Making the Pitch," July 8, 1997.

41. http://green.yahoo.com/pledge (accessed August 30, 2010).

42. www.carbonfootprint.com/carbonfootprint.html (accessed August 30, 2010).

CHAPTER 2

1. Marcella Kelly and Jim McGowen, *BUSN 5* (Mason, OH: South-Western Cengage Learning, 2013).

2. Myron Levin and Stuart Silverstein, "Asbestos Found in Imported Crayons and Toy Fingerprint Kits," Fairwarning, July 8, 2015, http://www.fairwarning.org/2015/07/asbestos-in-toys/ (accessed April 3, 2016); Emily Stewart, "China Has a History of Selling Dangerous Products to U.S. Consumers," The Street, March 3, 2015, http://www.thestreet.com/story/13063992/1/china-has-a-history-of-selling-dangerous-products-to-us-consumers.html (accessed April 4, 2016).

3. European Commission, "Clothing and Toys Top List of Dangerous Consumer Items in EU," March 26, 2014, http://ec.europa.eu/news/environment/140326_en.htm (accessed April 15, 2014).

4. http://www.starbucks.com/business/international-stores.

5. http://www.starbucks.com/business/international-stores.

6. World Trade Organization, "Annual Report 2014," https://www.wto.org/english/res_e/booksp_e/anrep_e/anrep15_e.pdf (accessed April 1, 2016).

7. Katie Thomas, "Facing Black Market, Pfizer Is Looking Online to Sell Viagra," *The New York Times*, May 6, 2013, http://nytimes.com/2013/05/07/business/pfizer-begins-selling-viagra-online.htm (accessed April 14, 2014).

8. The World Bank Group, "Glossary," http://www.worldbank.org/depweb/english/beyond/global/glossary.html (accessed April 4, 2016).

9. Todaro and Smith, "Economic Development Glossary," *Economic Development*, 8th ed. (New York: Addison Wesley, 2003), http://www.compilerpress.ca/ElementalEconomics/270%20Developmental/Todano%20&%20Smith%20Glossary%208th%20Ed.htm (accessed April 4, 2016; Food and Agricultural Organization of the United Nations, "Document 10: Glossary of Economic and Institutional Terminology," http://www.fao.org/docrep/006/y5137e/y5137e0f.htm, accessed April 4, 2016.

10. Amy Qin, "U.S.-China Adventure Film Already Creating Buzz," *The New York Times*, July 2, 2015, http://sinosphere.blogs.nytimes.com/2015/07/02/sino-zhang/ (accessed April 3, 2016.

11. Investopedia, "What are examples of products and companies that rely on protective tariffs to survive?" http://www.investopedia.com/ask/answers/051315/what-are-examples-products-and-companies-rely-protective-tariffs-survive.asp (accessed April 5, 2016).

12. Mike McPhate, "Zica Car Will Be Renamed, Tata Motors of India Says," *The New York Times* (February 2, 2016), http://www.nytimes.com/2016/02/03/business/tata-renaming-zica-car.html?_r=0, accessed April 6, 2016.

13. United Nations, "World Economic Situation and Prospects 2015: Global Economic Outlook (Chapter 1)," December 18, 2013, https://www.wto.org/english/res_e/booksp_e/anrep_e/anrep15_e.pdf (accessed April 1, 2016).

14. C. K. Prahalad, *The Fortune at the Bottom of the Pyramid* (Upper Saddle River, NJ: Wharton School Publishing, 2010), xiv.

15. Mark Koba, "BRICS: CNBC Explains," CNBC, August 11, 2011, http://www.cnbc.com/id/44006382 (accessed April 4, 2016); Ian Talley, "'BRICS' New World Order Is Now on Hold, *The Wall Street Journal*, January 19, 2016, http://www.wsj.com/articles/brics-new-world-order-is-now-on-hold-1453240108 (accessed April 4, 2916).

16. Alison Smale and Michael D. Shear, "Russia Is Ousted from Group of 8 by U.S. and Allies," *The New York Times*, March 24, 2014, www.nytimes.com/2014/03/25/world/europe/obama-russia-crimea.html (accessed April 15, 2014).

17. G8 Information Center, "What Is the G8?" http://www.g7.utoronto.ca/what_is_g8.html (accessed February 12, 2010).

18. Donald Armbrecht, "What Do Different Nationalities Spend Their Money On?" *World Economic Forum* (January 2016), https://www.weforum.org/agenda/2016/01/what-do-different-nationalities-spend-their-money-on/?utm

_content=buffer9f3f3&utm_medium=social&utm_source
=twitter.com&utm_campaign=buffer, (accessed April 6, 2016).

19. CBS News, "Amazon Unveils Futuristic Plan: Delivery by drone," December 01, 2013, http://www.cbsnews.com/news/amazon -unveils-futuristic-plan-delivery-by-drone/ (accessed April 4, 2016.

20. Federal Aviation Administration, Press Release, "DOT and FAA Finalize Rules for Small Unmanned Aircraft Systems," June 21, 2016, https://www.faa.gov/news/press_releases/news_story .cfm?newsId=20515 (accessed August 5, 2016).

21. www.hhs.gov/healthcare/rights/index.html (accessed April 22, 2014).

22. Masha Gessen, "What the Russians Crave: Cheese," *The New York Times*, July 5, 2015, http://www.nytimes.com/2015/07/05 /opinion/sunday/what-the-russians-crave-cheese.html (accessed April 4, 2016).

23. Stephan Nielsen, "Brazil Local Content Rules Hurting Major Wind Suppliers," www.renewableenergy.com, October 7, 2013, www.renewableenergy.com/rea/news/article/2013/10/brazil -local-content-rules-hurting-major-wind-manufacturers (accessed April 16, 2014).

24. Max Nielsen, "How Nike Solved Its Sweatshop Problem," May 9, 2013, www.businessinsider.com/hwo-nike-solved-its-sweatshop -problem (accessed April 16, 2014).

25. Choe Sang-Hun, "In South Korea, Spam Is The Stuff Gifts Are Made of," *The New York Times* (January 26, 2014), http://www .nytimes.com/2014/01/27/world/asia/in-south-korea-spam-is -the-stuff-gifts-are-made-of.html (accessed April 6, 2016).

26. Joe Cochran, "Tupperware's Sweet Spot Shifts to Indonesia," *The New York Times* (February 28, 2015), http://www.nytimes .com/2015/03/01/world/asia/tupperwares-sweet-spot-shifts -to-indonesia.html?hp&action=click&pgtype=Homepage&modu le=second-column-region&region=top-news&WT.nav=top-news, (accessed April 6, 2016).

27. Richard W. Pollay, "Measuring the Cultural Values Manifest in Advertising," *Current Issues and Research in Advertising* 6 (1983): 71–92.

28. Laurie Burkitt, "Mattel Gives Barbie a Makeover for China," *The Wall Street Journal*, November 7, 2013, http://www.wsj .com/articles/SB10001424052702304672404579183324082672770 (accessed April 5, 2016); Helen H. Wang, "Can Mattel Make A Comeback In China?" *Forbes*, November 17, 2013, http://www .forbes.com/sites/helenwang/2013/11/17/can-mattel-make-a -comeback-in-china/#3bee4a585b84 (accessed April 5, 2016); Helen H. Wang, "Why Barbie Stumbled in China and How She Could Re-invent Herself," *Forbes*, October 24, 2012, http://www.forbes .com/sites/helenwang/2012/10/24/why-barbie-stumbled-in -china-and-how-she-could-re-invent-herself/#14203be300b1 (accessed April 5, 2016).

29. Daniel Goleman, "The Group and the Self: New Focus on a Cultural Rift," *The New York Times*, December 25, 1990, http://www .nytimes.com/1990/12/25/science/the-group-and-the-self-new -focus-on-a-cultural-rift.html, (accessed December 4, 2014). 37; Harry C. Triandis, "The Self and Social Behavior in Differing Cultural Contexts," *Psychological Review* 96 (July 1989): 506; Harry C. Triandis et al., "Individualism and Collectivism: Cross-Cultural Perspectives on Self-Ingroup Relationships," *Journal of Personality and Social Psychology* 54 (February 1988): 323.

30. Getta Anand, "A Yoga Master, the King of 'Baba Cool,' Stretches Out an Empire," *The New York Times*, April 1, 2016, http://www .nytimes.com/2016/04/02/world/asia/a-yoga-master-the-king -of-baba-cool-stretches-out-an-empire.html?smprod=nytcore -iphone&smid=nytcore-iphone-share&_r=0 (accessed April 6, 2016).

31. "Oh, Crap: Audi Mucks Up E-Tron Name in French," *AutoBlog* (September 13, 2010), http://www.autoblog.com/2010/09/13 /oh-crap-audi-mucks-up-e-tron-name-in-french/ (accessed April 6, 2016).

32. Shaun Rein, "Shanghai Disney Must Deliver 'Big' Experience," CNBC, April 11, 2011, www.cnbc.com/id/42528017 (accessed April 21, 2014).

33. https://www.shanghaidisneyresort.com/en/destinations /theme-park/.

34. Matt Viser, "Dunkin' Donuts Jumps on Asia's Coffee Craze," *Boston Globe*, March 30, 2014, www.bostonglobe.com/news /world/2014/03/29/from-massachusetts-seoul-dunkin -donuts-finds-new-markets-coffee-craze-sweeps-asia/ aykwWhGnFNjG85ahVxJIFL/story.html (accessed April 14, 2014).

35. Brooks Barnes, "Thomas the Tank Engine's Expanding World," The New York Times (March 25, 2016), http://www.nytimes .com/2016/03/26/business/media/thomas-the-tank-engines -expanding-world.html?_r=0, accessed April 6, 2016.

36. International Energy Agency, "Access to Electricity," World Energy Outlook, 2009, www.iea.org/weo/electricity.asp (accessed February 16, 2010).

37. Deciwatt, "The Challenge," http://deciwatt.org/the-challenge (accessed April 10, 2014).

38. Ben Schiller, "A $5 Light for the Developing World with an Ingenious Fuel: Gravity," December 14, 2012, www .fastcoexist.com/1681067/a-5-light-for-the-developing-world -with-an-ingenious-fuel-gravity#1 (accessed April 10, 2014).

39. Jack Neff, "Lipton Uses Oscars (and Muppets) to Launch Global Campaign for Unified Brand," February 26, 2014, http:// adage.com/article/media/lipton-launcing-global-campaign -oscars/291873 (accessed April 17, 2014).

40. Amy Harder and Mike Spector, "EPA Accuses Volkswagen of Dodging Emissions Rules," *The Wall Street Journal,* September 22, 2015, http://www.wsj.com/articles/epa-accuses-volkswagen-of -dodging-emissions-rules-1442595129 (accessed March 25, 2016); Reuters, "Volkswagen admits rigging of 8 mln cars in EU— Handelsblatt," October 5, 2015, http://www.reuters.com/article /volkswagen-emissions-eu-idUSL8N12548G20151005 (accessed March 25, 2016); Jeannie Naujeck, "Dodging a Disaster With Volkswagen?" *Memphis Daily News*, March 26, 2016, https://www .memphisdailynews.com/news/2016/mar/26/dodging-a-disaster -with-volkswagen/ (accessed April 7, 2016).

41. AT&T, "AT&T's Code of Business Conduct," www.att.com /Common/about_us/downloads/att_code_of_business _conduct.pdf (accessed April 16, 2014).

42. Duff Wilson, "Cigarette Giants in Global Fight on Tighter Rules," *The New Work Times*, November 13, 2010, www.nytimes .com/2010/11/14/business/global/14smoke.html?_r=1 (accessed April 16, 2014).

43. "Foreign Corrupt Practices Act of 1977 (as Amended)," www.usdoj .gov/usao/eousa/foia_reading_room/usam/title9/47mcrm.htm (accessed May 15, 2008).

44. Joan Voight, "Green Is the New Black: Nike among Marketers Pushing Sustainability," *Adweek*, October 23, 2013, www.adweek .com/news/advertising-branding/green-new-black-levi-s-nike -among-marketers-pushing-sustainability-153318 (accessed March 10, 2014).

45. www.commondreams.org/headline/2012/05/08 (accessed April 23, 2014).

46. Center for Sustainability at Aquinas College, www .centerforsustainability.org/resources.php?root=176&category=89 (accessed April 4, 2016); Jeanelle Schwartz, Beth Beloff, and Susan Beaver, "Use Sustainability Metrics to Guide Decision-Making," July 2002, http://people.clarkson.edu/~wwilcox/Design/sustain .pdf (accessed April 4, 2016).

CHAPTER 3

1. Twitter, "About," https://about.twitter.com/company (accessed March 18, 2016).

2. Samsung Electronics, "Vision 2020," http://www.samsung.com /us/aboutsamsung/corporateprofile/visionmission.html (accessed March 18, 2016).

3. Anthony D'Allesandro, "Star Wars: The Force Awakens' Reaches Unprecedented Height At Domestic B.O. With $900M, $2B Worldwide," February 5, 2016, http://deadline.com/2016/02/star

-wars-the-force-awakens-box-office-900m-1201696190/ (accessed March 18, 2016).

4. Sandra Pedicini, "Disney parks to break ground on Star Wars lands next month" *Orlando Sentinel*, March 3, 2016, http://www.orlandosentinel.com/travel/attractions/the-daily-disney/os-disney-star-wars-lands-break-ground-april-20160303-story.html (accessed March, 18,2016).

5. Michael Cieply and Brooks Barnes, "Disney Sells Miramax for $660 Million," *The New York Times*, July 30, 2010, www.nytimes.com/2010/07/31/business/media/31miramax.html?_r=0 (accessed April 22, 2014).

6. Thomas Heath, "Disney Backs Out of National Harbor, in Blow to Prince George's," *Washington Post*, November 25, 2011, www.washingtonpost.com/business/economy/in-a-blow-to-prince-georges-disney-backs-out-of-national-harbor/2011/11/25/gIQAM2OKxN_story.html (accessed April 22, 2014).

7. Mohid Ahmed, "Amazon's Alexa Set to Take Over US Households and the World," February 8, 2016, http://www.bidnessetc.com/62980-amazons-alexa-set-to-take-over-us-households-and-the-world/ (accessed March, 18, 2016).

8. Mary Wisniewski, "Why Banks Have an Ear to Amazon Echo," March 11, 2016, http://www.americanbanker.com/news/bank-technology/why-banks-have-an-ear-to-amazons-echo-1079871-1.html (accessed March 18, 2016).

9. Nancy Trejos, "Starwood: 1st Company to Run Cuban Hotels in Decades," *USA Today*, March 21, 2016, http://www.usatoday.com/story/travel/roadwarriorvoices/2016/03/19/starwood-become-first-us-hotel-company-run-cuba-hotels-decades/82040434/ (accessed March 22, 2016).

10. Brian Sozzi, "The 6 Most Interesting New Menu Items McDonald's is Testing in 2016," February 27, 2016, http://www.thestreet.com/story/13473716/1/the-6-most-interesting-new-menu-items-mcdonald-s-is-testing-in-2016.html (accessed March 22, 2016).

11. Prudence Ho, "Coke Acquires Chines Maker of Multigrain Drinks," *The Wall Street Journal*, April 17, 2015, http://www.wsj.com/articles/coke-acquires-chinese-maker-of-multigrain-drinks-1429273291 (accessed March 18, 2016).

12. Megan Clark, "Struggling Soda Companies Diversify, Following Tobacco's Lead," October 23, 2014, http://www.ibtimes.com/struggling-soda-companies-diversify-following-tobaccos-lead-1709264 (accessed March 18, 2016).

13. Rick Mullin, "Tufts Study Finds Big Rise in Cost of Drug Development," November, 20, 2014, http://cen.acs.org/articles/92/web/2014/11/Tufts-Study-Finds-Big-Rise.html (accessed March 18, 2016).

14. Paul R. La Monica, "Martin Shkreli Quits as Turing CEO," CNN.com, (December 18, 2015, http://money.cnn.com/2015/12/18/investing/martin-shkreli-arrest-turing-kalobios/ (accessed March 31, 2016).

15. Andrew Pollack, "Drug Goes from $13.50 a Tablet to $750, Overnight" *The New York Times*, September 20, 2015, http://www.nytimes.com/2015/09/21/business/a-huge-overnight-increase-in-a-drugs-price-raises-protests.html?_r=0 (accessed March 18, 2016).

16. Alaska Airlines Increases Overhead Storage Nearly 50 Percent with First 737 Featuring New Boeing Space Bins," *PR Newswire*, October 09, 2015, http://www.prnewswire.com/news-releases/alaska-airlines-increases-overhead-storage-nearly-50-percent-with-first-737-featuring-new-boeing-space-bins-300157186.html (accessed March 22, 2016).

17. Ibid.

18. Delta, "Delta Comfort+™," http://www.delta.com/content/www/en_US/traveling-with-us/onboard-experience/delta-comfort-plus.html#board (accessed March 23,2016)/

19. Ben Mutzabaugh, "Is Emirates Targeting U.S. Airlines with Jennifer Aniston Ad," *USA Today*, October 5, 2015, http://www.usatoday.com/story/todayinthesky/2015/10/05/is-emirates-targeting-us-airlines-with-new-jennifer-aniston-ad/73381332/ (accessed March 23, 2016).

20. "#TimeForVacay: Expedia Rolls Out Big Midwinter Sale and Leap Day Savings," *PR Newswire*, February 18, 2016, http://www.prnewswire.com/news-releases/timeforvacay-expedia-rolls-out-big-midwinter-sale-and-leap-day-savings-300221974.html (accessed March 23, 2016).

21. Gordon A. Wyner, "Beyond ROI: Make Sure the Analytics Address Strategic Issues," *Marketing Management* 15 (May/June 2006): 8–9.

22. Guy R. Powell, *Return on Marketing Investment* (Albuquerque, NM: RPI Press, 2002), 4–6.

23. Ibid.

24. Tim Ambler, "Don't Cave in to Cave Dwellers," *Marketing Management*, September/October 2006, 25–29.

25. International Data Corporation, "PC Market Finishes 2015 As Expected, Hopefully Setting the Stage for a More Stable Future, According to IDC," January 12, 2016, http://www.idc.com/getdoc.jsp?containerId=prUS40909316 (accessed March 19, 2016).

CHAPTER 4

1. Reuters, "U.S. TV Networks Embrace 'Binge-Watching,' Taking Cue from Netflix," March 11, 2016, http://www.newsmax.com/Finance/Companies/television-tv-binge-view-networks/2016/03/11/id/718640/ (accessed March 25, 2016).

2. Marketing Evaluations Inc., "The Q Scores Company," http://www.qscores.com (accessed April 4, 2016).

3. Emmet McDermott, "Who Is America's Most Disliked Celebrity? An Explainer," *Hollywood Reporter*, August 13, 2015, http://www.hollywoodreporter.com/news/disliked-celebrity-bill-cosby-ariana-814857 (accessed March 25, 2016).

4. Heather Clancy, "MasterCard Uses a Command Center to Track Its Marketing Spend," *Fortune*, January 29, 2016, http://fortune.com/2016/01/29/mastercard-data-analytics/?iid=sr-link10 (accessed March 25, 2016).

5. Quoted in Dale Buss, "Unapologetically, Volvo Aims Its New Campaign at True Believers," April 15, 2013, *Forbes*,www.forbes.com/sites/dalebuss/2013/04/15/unapologetically-volvo-aims-its-new-ads-at-true-believers (accessed April 4, 2015).

6. Experian, "Simmons National Consumer Study," www.experian.com/simmons-research/consumer-study.html (accessed April 6, 2016).

7. Michael R. Solomon, *Conquering Consumerspace: Marketing Strategies for a Branded World* (New York: AMACOM Books, 2003).

8. ResearchLive, "'Incredible Things Happen When You Have the Right Insight,' Says Reckitt Benckiser," March 16, 2016, https://www.research-live.com/article/news/incredible-things-happen-when-you-have-the-right-insight-says-reckitt-benckiser/id/5004402 (accessed March 25, 2015).

9. Greg Trotter, "MillerCoors Works to Keep Leninkeugel, Blue Moon Rising," *Chicago Tribune*, March 22, 2016, http://www.chicagotribune.com/business/ct-blue-moon-leinenkugel-craft-beer-0323-biz-20160322-story.html (accessed March 25, 2016).

10. Tom De Ruyck, "Inspirational Online Dialogues," October 14, 2013, rwcommect.esomar.org/inspirational-online-dialogues (accessed August 12, 2016).

11. http://www.decisionanalyst.com/services/onlinecommunities.dai (accessed April 9, 2016).

12. Karl Greenberg, "Volvo Uses Twitter Chat for Digital Focus Group," May 29, 2013, www.mediapost.com/publications/article/201309/volvo-uses-twitter-chat-for-digital-focus-group.html?edition=60600 (accessed August 12, 2016).

13. John Kell, "Coke Spent More on Health Research Than Previously Reported," *Fortune*, March 25, 2016, http://fortune.com/2016/03/25/coke-health-research-spending/ (accessed March 25. 2016).

14. Mike Estrel, "Coca-Cola Has Spent Millions on Health Research, Fitness Programs," September 22, 2015, *The Wall Street*

Journal, http://www.wsj.com/articles/coca-cola-spent-nearly -120-million-on-research-health-programs-since-2010-1442919600 (accessed March 25, 2016).

15. Paul Marsden, "Consumer Advisory Panels," http:// digitalintelligencetoday.com/downloads/Marsden_CAB.pdf (accessed April 2, 2016).

16. Matt Richtel, "The Parable of the Beer and Diapers," August 15, 2006, www.theregister.co.uk/2006/08/15/beer_diapers (accessed April 8, 2016).

17. John Carney, "Hemlines Are Plunging, Is Economy Next?" *CNBC*, February 16, 2012, www.cnbc.com/id/46414411 (accessed April 4, 2016).

18. Kristen Schweizer, "Marketer's Next Trick: Reading Byers' Minds," *Bloomberg*, July 2, 2015, http://www.bloomberg.com /news/articles/2015-07-02/advertisers-use-neuroscience-to -craft-consumer-messages (accessed March 26, 2016).

19. Direct Marketing Association, "Where Marketers Can Obtain State Do-Not-Call Lists," http://www.the-dma.org/government /donotcalllists.shtml (accessed April 2, 2016).

20. John D. Stoll and Anne Steele, "The Evolution of Auto Show 'Booth Babes,'" *Wall Street Journal* (January 14, 2015), http:// www.wsj.com/articles/the-evolution-of-auto-show-booth -babes-1421257095?KEYWORDS=auto+show+model&cb=logg ed0.45785790963341455 (accessed April 5, 2016).

21. The Praxi Group, Inc., "Research Overview: Telephone versus On-line Research—Advantages and Pitfalls," Fall 2007, http://www .praxigroup.net/TPG%20Phone%20Versus%20Online%20WP.pdf (accessed April 1, 2016).

22. Basil G. Englis and Michael R. Solomon, "Life/Style OnLine ©: A Web-Based Methodology for Visually-Oriented Consumer Research," *Journal of Interactive Marketing* 14, no. 1 (2000): 2–14; Basil G. Englis, Michael R. Solomon, and Paula D. Harveston, "Web-Based, Visually Oriented Consumer Research Tools," in *Online Consumer Psychology: Understanding and Influencing Consumer Behavior in the Virtual World*, ed. Curt Haugtvedt, Karen Machleit, and Richard Yalch (Hillsdale, NJ: Lawrence Erlbaum Associates, 2005): 511–527.

23. Nielsen, "Online Measurement," http://www.nielsen.com/us /en/nielsen-solutions/nielsen-measurement/nielsen-online -measurement.html (accessed March 26, 2016).

24. Nielsen Social, http://www.nielsensocial.com/product /nielsen-twitter-tv-ratings/ (accessed March 26, 2016).

25. Nielsen, http://www.nielsen.com/us/en/solutions/capabilities /audio.html (accessed March 26, 2016).

26. Corey Deitz, "What Is the Portable People Meter and How Does It Work?" http://radio.about.com/od/forprofessionals/a/What -Is-Arbitrons-Portable-People-Meter-And-How-Does-It-Work .htm (accessed March 26, 2016).

27. Tobii Pro, http://www.tobiipro.com/fields-of-use/marketing -consumer-research/advertising/ (accessed March 26, 2016).

28. Ray Nelson, "How to Use Social Media for Marketing Research," March 19, 2013, http://socialmediatoday.com/raywilliamnelson /1313496/marketing-research-how-use-social-media-market -research (accessed April 5, 2016).

29. Amazon Mechanical Turk, https://www.mturk.com/mturk /help?helpPage=overview, (accessed March 26, 2016).

30. Douglas Macmillan and Elizabeth Dwoskin, "Smile! Marketing Firms Are Mining Your Selfies," *The Wall Street Journal* (October 9, 2014), http://www.wsj.com/articles/smile-marketing-firms-are -mining-your-selfies-1412882222?KEYWORDS=selfies (accessed April 5, 2016).

31. Alexis Madrigal, "How Netflix Reverse Engineered Holly-wood," *The Atlantic*, January 2, 2014, http://www.theatlantic .com/technology/archive/2014/01/how-netflix-reverse -engineered-hollywood/282679 (accessed April 5, 2016).

32. Jack Neff, "Chasing the Cheaters That Undermine Online Research," *Advertising Age*, March 31, 2008, 12.

33. Matt Quinn, "How to Reduce Your Website's Bounce Rate," *Inc.*, January 31, 2011, http://www.inc.com/guides/2011/01/how-to -reduce-your-website-bounce-rate.html (accessed April 8, 2016); Paul W. Farris, Neil T. Bendle, Phillip E. Pfeifer, and David J. Reib-stein, *Marketing Metrics: The Definitive Guide to Measuring Marketing Performance* (Upper Saddle River, NJ: Pearson Education, 2010).

34. Bruce L. Stern and Ray Ashmun, "Methodological Disclosure: The Foundation for Effective Use of Survey Research," *Journal of Applied Business Research* 7 (1991): 77–82.

35. Malcom Gladwell, *Blink* (New York: Hachette Book Group, 2007), 159.

36. Michael E. Ross, "It Seemed Like a Good Idea at the Time," MSNBC, April 22, 2005, www.msnbc.msn.com/id/7209828 (accessed April 7, 2016).

37. Gary Levin, "New Adventures in Children's Research," *Advertising Age*, August 9, 1993, 17.

38. Diane Bowers and Michael Brereton, "The 2015 AMA Gold Top 50 Report," https://www.ama.org/publications/MarketingNews /Pages/the-2015-ama-gold-top-50-report.aspx (accessed March 26, 2015).

39. Paul W. Farris, Neil T. Bendle, Phillip E. Pheifer, and David J. Reibstein, *Marketing Metrics: 50+ Metrics Every Executive Should Master* (Upper Saddle River, NJ: Wharton School Publishing, 2006), 292.

CHAPTER 5

1. Sarah K. White, "As CMOs Start to Outspend CIOs, Collaboration Remains Key," *CIO*, August 25, 2015, http://www.cio.com /article/2975828/cio-role/as-cmos-start-to-outspend-cios -collaboration-remains-key.html (accessed May 30, 2016).

2. "A Crash Course in Customer Relationship Management," *Harvard Management Update*, March 2000 (Harvard Business School reprint U003B); Nahshon Wingard, "CRM Definition—Customer-Centered Philosophy," October 26, 2009, http:// ezinearticles.com/?CRM-Definition—Customer-Centered -Philosophy&id=933109 (accessed May 7, 2016).

3. Don Peppers and Martha Rogers, *The One-to-One Future* (New York: Doubleday, 1996).

4. Don Peppers, Martha Rogers, and Bob Dorf, "Is Your Company Ready for One-to-One Marketing?" *Harvard Business Review*, January–February 1999, 151–60.

5. Quoted in Cara B. DiPasquale, "Navigate the Maze," Special Report on 1:1 Marketing, *Advertising Age*, October 29, 2001, S1: 2.

6. Oracle Marketing Cloud, "JD Williams Increases Customer Email Conversion 92% with Personalisation," https://www.oracle.com /marketingcloud/customers/success-stories/jd-williams .html (accessed May 7, 2016); https://www.oracle.com /marketingcloud/content/documents/casestudies/jd-williams -customer-success-oracle.pdf (accessed May 7, 2016).

7. Leonard L. Berry, *On Great Service: A Framework for Action* (New York: Free Press, 1995); Paul T. Ringenbach, *USAA: A Tradition of Service* (San Antonio, TX: Donning, 1997).

8. Gartner, "Gartner Says Customer Relationship Management Software Market Grew 13.3 percent," May 19, 2015, http://www .gartner.com/newsroom/id/3056118 (accessed May 7, 2016).

9. Gartner, "Gartner Says Modernization and Digital Transformation Projects are Behind Growth in Enterprise Application Software Market," August 27, 2015, http://www.gartner.com/newsroom /id/3119717 (accessed May 7, 2016).

10. JP Mangalindan, "Amazon's Recommendation Secret," July 30, 2012, http://fortune.com/2012/07/30/amazons-recommendation -secret/ (accessed May 8, 2016).

11. Jeff Oxford, "6 Things Online Retailers Can Learn from Amazon," September 24, 2013, http://www.forbes.com/sites /groupthink/2013/09/24/6-things-online-retailers-can-learn -from-amazon/#7159afcc53b8 (accessed May 8, 2016).

12. Salesforce, "Tommy Bahama," http://www.salesforce.com /customers/stories/tommy-bahama.jsp (accessed May 8, 2016); Alicia Fioletta, "Tommy Bahama Collects Real-Time Feedback with Medallia," July 11, 2014, http://www.retailtouchpoints

.com/features/retail-success-stories/tommy-bahama-collects -real-time-feedback-with-medallia (accessed May 8, 2016).

13. "My Magic Plus," http://mousehints.com/my-magic-plus (accessed May 8, 2016).

14. Elie Ofek, "Customer Lifetime Value (CLV) vs. Customer Lifetime Return on Investment (CLROI)," October 2014, *Harvard Business School Technical Note*: 515–49.

15. SAS, "Big Data, Bigger Marketing," www.sas.com/en_us/insights /big-data/big-data-marketing.html (accessed April 9, 2016).

16. David Carr, "Giving Viewers What They Want," February 24, 2013, http://www.nytimes.com/2013/02/25/business/media /for-house-of-cards-using-big-data-to-guarantee-its-popularity .html?_r=0 (accessed May 9, 2016).

17. Friedemann Mattern and Christian Floerkemeier, "From the Internet of Computers to the Internet of Things," *Informatik-Spektrum* 33 (2010): 107–21.

18. Teradata Customer Success and Engagement Team, "Volvo Cars: Fueling Innovation with Data, Analytics and the Internet of Things So that Every Volvo is 'Designed around You,'" December 18, 2015, http://blogs.teradata.com/customers /volvo-cars-fueling-innovation-with-data-analytics-and-the -internet-of-things-so-that-every-volvo-is-designed-around -you/ (accessed May 9, 2016).

19. Luke Fretwell, "'Open Data Now' Author Joel Gurin on How Businesses and Government Are Building the Data Economy," April 17, 2014, http://govfresh.com/2014/04/open-government -data-open-business-interview (accessed May 14, 2016).

20. Jim Edwards, "Yes, Your Credit Card Company Is Selling Your Purchase Data to Online Advertisers," April 16, 2013, www .businessinsider.com/credit-cards-sell-purchase-data-to -advertisers-2013-4 (accessed May 9, 2016).

21. Todd Traub, "Wal-Mart Used Technology to Become Supply Chain Leader," July 2, 2012, www.arkansasbusiness.com/article /85508/wal-mart-used-technology-to-become-supply-chain -leader?page=all (accessed May 9, 2016).

22. IBM, "IBM Closes Deal to Acquire the Weather Company's Product and Technology Businesses," January 29, 2016, http://www-03 .ibm.com/press/us/en/pressrelease/48884.wss (accessed May 9, 2016); Leonard Kile, "IBM Merges Weather and Business Forecasts," January 2016, http://www.destinationcrm.com/Articles/Columns -Departments/Insight/IBM-Merges-Weather-and-Business -Forecasts-108306.aspx (accessed May 9, 2016).

23. Constance L. Hays, "What Wal-Mart Knows About Customers' Habits," *New York Times* (November 4, 2004), http://www.nytimes .com/2004/11/14/business/yourmoney/what-walmart-knows -about-customers-habits.html?_r=0 (accessed May 30, 2016).

24. Christophe Giraud-Carrier, "Success Stories in Data/Text Mining," http://dml.cs.byu.edu/~cgc/docs/mldm_tools/Reading /DMSuccessStories.html#_ftn1 (accessed May 10, 2016).

25. Dana Mattioli, "On Orbitz, Mac Users Steered to Pricier Hotels," August 23, 2016, http://www.wsj.com/articles/SB100014240527 02304458604577488822667325882 (accessed May 10, 2016).

26. Pan-Ning Tan, Michael Steinbach, and Vipin Kumar, *Introduction to Data Mining* (New York: Addison-Wesley, 2005).

27. Emil Protalinski, "Facebook Passes 1.55B Monthly Active Users and 1.01B Daily Active Users," November 4, 2015, http://venturebeat .com/2015/11/04/facebook-passes-1-55b-monthly-active-users -and-1-01-billion-daily-active-users/ (accessed May 9, 2016).

28. Chris Baraniuk, "The Bad Things that Happen when Algorithms Run Online Shops," August 20, 2015, http://www.bbc .com/future/story/20150820-the-bad-things-that-happen -when-algorithms-run-online-shops (accessed May 12, 2016).

29. Michael Nunez, "Former Facebook Workers: We Routinely Suppressed Conservative News," May 9, 2016, http://gizmodo .com/former-facebook-workers-we-routinely-suppressed-conser -1775461006 (accessed May 12, 2016).

30. Farhad Manjoo, "Facebook's Bias Is Built-in, and Bears Watching," *The New York Times*, May 11, 2016, http://www.nytimes .com/2016/05/12/technology/facebooks-bias-is-built-in-and

-bears-watching.html?_r=0&module=ArrowsNav&contentCollec tion=Technology&action=keypress&region=FixedLeft&pgtype=a rticle (accessed May 12, 2016).

31. Joe F. Hair Jr., "Knowledge Creation in Marketing: The Role of Predictive Analytics," *European Business Review* 19 (2007): 303–15.

32. Goutam Chakraborty and Murali Krishna Pagolu, "Analysis of Unstructured Data: Applications of Text Analytics and Sentiment Mining," *SAS Paper* 1288 (2014): 1–14.

33. Todd Spangler, "Viacom to Track Emotional Responses to Social Ads, Content," January 25, 2016, http://variety.com/2016 /digital/news/viacom-canvs-emotional-social-media -ads-1201687790/ (accessed May 13, 2016).

34. Josh Leibowitz, Kelly Ungermena, and Maher Masri, "Know Your Customers Wherever They Are," October 16, 2012, http://blogs.hbr .org/2012/10/know-your-customers-wherever-t (accessed May 13, 2016).

35. Tan et al., *Introduction to Data Mining*.

36. Werner Reinartz, and V. Kumar, "The Mismanagement of Customer Loyalty," *Harvard Business Review* 80 (7): 86–97.

37. Robert Nelson, "Sprint May Cancel Your Service If You Call Customer Service Too Often," July 6, 2007, www.gadgetell.com/tech /comment/sprint-may-cancel-your-service-if-you-call-customer -service-to-often (accessed May 13, 2016); Samar Srivasta, "Sprint Drops Clients over Excessive Inquiries," July 7, 2007, http://online .wsj.com/public/article_print/SB118376389957059668-IpRTFYV QbLGbXKvlbPELi83M_8A_20080710.html (accessed February 7, 2010).

38. IBM, "What Is a Data Scientist?" www-01.ibm.com/software /data/infosphere/data-scientist (accessed May 13, 2016).

39. Glassdoor, https://www.glassdoor.com/Salaries/data-scientist -salary-SRCH_KO0,14.htm (accessed May 13, 2016).

40. Thomas H. Davenport and D. J. Patil, "Data Scientist: The Sexiest Job of the 21st Century," October 2012, http://hbr.org/2012/10 /data-scientist-the-sexiest-job-of-the-21st-century/ar/1 (accessed May 13, 2016).

41. Wikipedia, "Analytics," https://en.wikipedia.org/wiki/Analytics (accessed May 13, 2016).

42. SAS, "Marketing Analytics: What It Is and Why It Matters," www .sas.com/en_us/insights/marketing/marketing-analytics.html (accessed May 13, 2016).

43. Pew Internet Research Project, "Internet Use over Time," www .pewinternet.org/data-trend/internet-use/internet-use-over -time (accessed May 14, 2016); Pew Internet Research Project, "Social Media Use over Time," www.pewinternet.org/data-trend /social-media/social-media-use-all-users (accessed June 1, 2014).

44. Gartner, "Gartner Survey Reveals that Digital Marketing Is Now Mainstream," November 19, 2015, http://www.gartner.com /newsroom/id/3170017 (accessed May 14, 2016).

45. Nathan Ingrahan, "Imgur's New Analytics Tools Let Users and Advertisers See How Their Images Go Viral," January 28, 2014, http://www.theverge.com/2014/1/28/5351618/imgurs-new -analytics-tool-lets-users-and-advertisers-see-how-images-go -viral (accessed May 14, 2016).

46. Jeff Standridge, "Can You Really Measure Direct Mail Success?" March 12, 2015, http://www.acxiom.com/can-really-measure -direct-mail-success/ (accessed May 15, 2016).

47. Greg Bensinger, "Amazon Wants to Ship Your Package before You Buy It," January 14, 2014, http://blogs.wsj.com/digits/2014/01/17 /amazon-wants-to-ship-your-package-before-you-buy-it (accessed May 13, 2016).

48. Hair, "Knowledge Creation in Marketing."

49. Samuel Greengard, "Predictive Analytics Helps Vodafone Ring Up Sales," June 3, 2014, www.baselinemag.com/analytics-big -data/predictive-analytics-helps-vodafone-ring-up-sales.html (accessed June 5, 2014).

50. IBM, "XO Communications: Insights into Customer Behavior Help Prevent Customer Churn," https://www.ibm.com/smarterplanet /global/files/us__en_us__leadership__xo_communications.pdf (accessed May 14, 2016).

51. Paul W. Farris, Neil T. Bendle, Phillip E. Pfeifer, and David J. Reibstein, *Marketing Metrics: 50+ Metrics Every Executive Should Master* (Philadelphia: Wharton School Publishing, 2006), 291.

52. Google, "Conversion Overview," https://support.google.com/analytics/answer/1006230?hl=en (accessed June 7, 2014).

53. Farris et al., *Marketing Metrics*, 294–95.

54. Farris et al., *Marketing Metrics*, 49–50.

55. Brad Reed, "Sprint Just Made a Huge Move to Steal You Away from AT&T and Verizon," http://bgr.com/2014/12/02/sprint-vs-att-vs-verizon/ (accessed May 15, 2015).

56. RJ Metrics, "What Is Churn Rate," http://churn-rate.com/ (accessed May 15, 2016).

57. Wes Nichols, "Secrets of Successful Analytics Adoption," *Forbes*, July 22, 2013, www.forbes.com/sites/forbesinsights/2013/07/22/secrets-of-successful-marketing-analytics-adoption (accessed May 16, 2016).

CHAPTER 6

1. Geoff Williams, "The Heavy Price of Losing Weight," *U.S. News & World Report* January 2, 2013, http://money.usnews.com/money/personal-finance/articles/2013/01/02/the-heavy-price-of-losing-weight (accessed December 24, 2015).

2. James R. Bettman, "The Decision Maker Who Came In from the Cold," Presidential Address, in *Advances in Consumer Research*, vol. 20, ed. Leigh McAllister and Michael Rothschild (Provo, UT: Association for Consumer Research, 1990); John W. Payne, James R. Bettman, and Eric J. Johnson, "Behavioral Decision Research: A Constructive Processing Perspective," *Annual Review of Psychology* 4 (1992): 87–131; for an overview of recent developments in individual choice models, see Robert J. Meyer and Barbara E. Kahn, "Probabilistic Models of Consumer Choice Behavior," in *Handbook of Consumer Behavior*, ed. Thomas S. Robertson and Harold H. Kassarjian (Englewood Cliffs, NJ: Prentice Hall, 1991), 85–123.

3. Gary L. Clark, Peter F. Kaminski, and David R. Rink, "Consumer Complaints: Advice on How Companies Should Respond Based on an Empirical Study," *Journal of Services Marketing* 6 (Winter 1992): 41–50.

4. Catherine Valenti, "No Oscar? How About a Gift Bag?" March 24, http://abcnews.go.com/Business/story?id=86683&page=1 (accessed April 26, 2014).

5. Michael Lev, "No Hidden Meaning Here: Survey Sees Subliminal Ads," *New York Times*, May 3, 1991, D7.

6. "ABC Rejects KFC Commercial, Citing Subliminal Advertising," *Wall Street Journal Interactive Edition*, March 2, 2006.

7. Quoted in Natasha Singer, "YOU FOR SALE: Your Online Attention, Bought in an Instant," New York Times (November 17, 2012), http://www.nytimes.com/2012/11/18/technology/your-online-attention-bought-in-an-instant-by-advertisers.html?pagewanted=1 (accessed April 7, 2016).

8. http://www.chevrolet.com/spark-fuel-efficient-car.html

9. Nicholas Bakalar, "If It Says McDonald's, Then It Must Be Good," *New York Times* (August 14, 2007), www.NewYorkTimes.com (accessed August 14, 2007).

10. Abraham H. Maslow, *Motivation and Personality*, 2nd ed. (New York: Harper & Row, 1970).

11. Robert A. Baron and Donn Byrne, *Social Psychology: Understanding Human Interaction*, 5th ed. (Boston: Allyn & Bacon, 1987).

12. Rae Ann Fera, "The Rise of Sadvertising: Why Brands are Determined to Make You Cry," *Fast Company* (May 4, 2014), http://www.fastcocreate.com/3029767/the-rise-of-sadvertising-why-brands-are-determined-to-make-you-cry?partner=newsletter, (accessed April 13, 2016).

13. Ryan Nakashima, "Disney to Create Lab to Test Ads for ABC, ESPN," *USA Today*, May 12, 2008, www.usatoday.com/tech/products/2008-05-12-1465558386_x.htm (accessed February 24, 2010).

14. David Moye, "Millennials Are Surprisingly Chill with Funeral Selfies," *The Huffington Post*, September 28, 2015, http://www.huffingtonpost.com/entry/selfie-survey-20-percent-funerals_us_5605bddee4b0af3706dc592c (accessed April 13, 2016).

15. Sheila Shayon, "Target Launches First Plus-Size Collection Following Blogger Boycott," *Brandchannel* (January 21, 2015), http://brandchannel.com/2015/01/21/target-launches-first-plus-size-collection-following-blogger-boycott/?utm_campaign=150121-Target-Plus-Size&utm_source=newsletter&utm_medium=email (accessed April 13, 2016).

16. Alex Williams, "High Times Wants to Be the Playboy of Pot," *The New York Times*, April 2, 2016, http://www.nytimes.com/2016/04/03/style/high-times-wants-to-be-the-playboy-of-pot.html?ref=media (accessed April 13, 2016).

17. Alfred S. Boote, "Psychographics: Mind over Matter," *American Demographics*, April 1980, 26–29; William D. Wells, "Psychographics: A Critical Review," *Journal of Marketing Research* 12 (May 1975): 196–213.

18. Shiv, "Sensory Marketing: Using the Senses for Brand Building," March 3, 2014, http://marketingfaq.net/branding/sensory-marketing-and-branding (accessed April 29, 2014).

19. Aroma Marketing, "Research/Case Studies," www.sensorymax.com/aroma-marketing/research-case-studies-aroma.html (accessed April 29, 2014).

20. Roxie Hammill and Mike Hendricks, "Scent Received, With a Tap of a Smartphone," *The New York Times* (July 8, 2015), http://www.nytimes.com/2015/07/09/technology/personaltech/scent-received-with-a-tap-of-a-smartphone.html?ref=business&_r=1 (accessed April 13, 2016).

21. Ibid.

22. Jack Grant, "Shoppers Make More Purchase Decisions In-Store," June 2012, http://www.cpgmatters.com/In-StoreMarketing0612.html (accessed April 27, 2014).

23. Sally Delta, "Farmville Funeral Home Offering Drive-Thru Viewing," June 24, 2013, www.wset.com/story/22673593/farmville-funeral-home-offering-drive-thru-viewings (accessed July 14, 2014).

24. Betsy Morris, "More Consumers Prefer Online Shopping," June 3, 2013 http://online.wsj.com/news/articles/SB10001424127887324063304578523112193480212 (accessed April 27, 2014).

25. Glenn Llopis, "Don't Sell to Me! Hispanics Buy Brands That Empower Their Cultural Relevancy," May 14, 2012, www.forbes.com/sites/glennllopis/2012/05/14/dont-sell-to-me-hispanics-buy-brands-that-empower-their-cultural-relevancy (accessed April 29, 2014).

26. Richard W. Pollay, "Measuring the Cultural Values Manifest in Advertising," Current Issues and Research in Advertising 6, no. 1 (1983): 71–92.

27. Michelle Saettler, "General Mills, Clorox Target Hispanic Mobile Shoppers via Bilingual Promotions App," 14, 201, www.mobilemarketer.com/cms/news/strategy/17575.html (accessed April 29, 2014).

28. Bruce Horovitz, "Axe Showerpool Promo Raises Eyebrows," *USA Today* (September 17, 2012), http://usatoday30.usatoday.com/money/business/story/2012/09/17/axe-showerpool-promo-raises-eyebrows/57797640/1 (accessed March 1, 2013).

29. Emily Burg, "Whole Foods Is Consumers' Favorite Green Brand," *Marketing Daily*, www.mediapost.com (accessed May 10, 2007).

30. Stuart U. Rich and Subhash C. Jain, "Social Class and Life Cycle as Predictors of Behavior," Journal of Marketing Research 5 (February 1968): 41–49.

31. Nathan Kogan and Michael A. Wallach, "Risky Shift Phenomenon in Small Decision-Making Groups: A Test of the Information Exchange Hypothesis," Journal of Experimental Social Psychology 3 (January 1967): 75–84; Arch G. Woodside and M. Wayne DeLozier, "Effects of Word-of-Mouth Advertising on Consumer Risk Taking," Journal of Advertising (Fall 1976): 12–19.

32. Brooks Barnes, "For Lucasfilm, the Way of Its Force Lies in Its 'Star Wars' Fans," *The New York Times* (April 17, 2015), http://www.nytimes.com/2015/04/18/business/media/for-lucasfilm-the-way-of-its-force-lies-in-its-star-wars-fans.html?smid=nytcore

-iphone-share&smprod=nytcore-iphone&assetType=nyt_now &_r=0&mtrref=www.nytimes.com (accessed April 13, 2016).

33. Everett M. Rogers, Diffusion of Innovations, 3rd ed. (New York: Free Press, 1983).

34. Kathleen Debevec and Easwar Iyer, "Sex Roles and Consumer Perceptions of Promotions, Products, and Self: What Do We Know and Where Should We Be Headed," in Advances in Consumer Research, vol. 13, ed. Richard J. Lutz (Provo, UT: Association for Consumer Research, 1986), 210–14; Lynn J. Jaffe and Paul D. Berger, "Impact on Purchase Intent of Sex-Role Identity and Product Positioning," Psychology and Marketing, Fall 1988, 259–71.

35. Mike Pomranz, "Italian Woman Facing Up to 6 Years in Jail for Not Cooking Enough," Foodandwine.com February 8, 2016, http://www.foodandwine.com/fwx/food/italian-woman-facing -6-years-jail-not-cooking-enough (accessed April 13, 2016).

36. Reuters, "Mattel's Quarterly Sales Grow as Barbie Doll Choices Expand," February 1, 2016, The New York Times, http://www .nytimes.com/2016/02/02/business/mattels-quarterly-sales -grow-as-barbie-doll-choices-expand.html?rref=collection%2Ftim estopic%2FBarbie%20%28Doll%29&action=click&contentCollect ion=timestopics&region=stream&module=stream_unit&version =latest&contentPlacement=4&pgtype=collection (accessed April 11, 2016).

37. Melissa Dahl, "Six-Pack Stress: Men Worry More about Their Appearance Than Their Jobs," February 28, 2014, www.today .com/health/six-pack-stress-men-worry-more-about-their -appearance-their-2D12117283 (accessed April 27, 2014).

38. Matthew Boyle, "Yes, Real Men Drink Beer and Use Skin Moisturizer," October 23, 2013, www.businessweek.com /articles/2013-10-03/men-now-spend-more-on-toiletries-than -on-shaving-products (accessed April 27, 2014).

39. Catharine Skipp and Arian Campo-Flores, "Looks: A Manly Comeback," August 20, 2007, http://services.newsweek.com /search.aspx?offset50&pageSize510&sortField5pubdatetime&so rtDirection5descending&mode5summary&q5Looks%2C1a1manl y1comeback (accessed August 17, 2007).

40. www.boeing.com/commercial/prices (accessed March 10, 2010).

41. Walmart, "Where in the World Is Walmart?" http://corporate .walmart.com/our-story/our-business/locations (accessed April 26, 2014).

42. U.S. Census Bureau, The 2012 Statistical Abstract of the United States (Washington, DC: U.S. Census Bureau, 2012); U.S. Census Bureau, "The 2012 Statistical Abstract," www.census.gov/compendia /statab (accessed April 29, 2014).

43. U.S. Census Bureau, "North America Industry Classification System (NAICS)," www.census.gov/eos/www/naics (accessed February 23, 2010).

44. F. Robert Dwyer and John F. Tanner, Business Marketing: Connecting Strategy, Relationships, and Learning (Boston: McGraw-Hill, 2008); Edward F. Fern and James R. Brown, "The Industrial/Consumer Marketing Dichotomy: A Case of Insufficient Justification," Journal of Marketing, Spring 1984, 68–77.

45. Porsche, "All Boxter Models," www.porsche.com/usa/models /boxster (accessed February 22, 2010).

46. Aflac, "Aflac for Business," www.aflac.com/business/default .aspx (accessed February 23, 2010).

47. Michael Riley, Ben Elgin, Dune Lawrence, and Carol Matlack, "Missed Alarms and 40 Million Stolen Credit Card Numbers: How Target Blew It," Bloomberg Businessweek, March 13, 2014, www.businessweek.com/articles/2014-03-13/target-missed -alarms-in-epic-hack-of-credit-card-data (accessed April 26, 2014).

48. Tom Pick, "83 Exceptional Social Media and Marketing Statistics for 2014," April 20, 2014, www.business2community.com /social-media/83-exceptional-social-media-marketing-statistics -2014-0846364#!FfTg2 (accessed March 19, 2014).

49. Ryan Nakashima, "Disney to Create Lab to Test Ads for ABC, ESPN," USA Today, May 12, 2008, www.usatoday.com/tech /products/2008-05-12-1465558386_x.htm (accessed February 24, 2010); Sylvia Jensen, "How Do B2B Companies Use Social Media?"

www.scu.edu/ethics/practicing/decision (accessed March 21, 2014); J. J. McCorvey, "How to Use Social Media for B2B Marketing," Inc., July 29, 2010, www.inc.com/guides/2010/07/how -to-use-social-media-for-b2b-marketing.html (accessed March 15, 2014); Allen Narcisse, "Planning Your B2B Marketing Approach to Social Media: 3 Key Angles," http://contentmarketinginstitute .com/2014/01/planning-b2b-marketing-approach-social-media (accessed March 21, 2014).

CHAPTER 7

1. www.foxnews.com/leisure/2014/05/20/burger-king-ditches -have-it-your-way-slogan (accessed April 1, 2016).

2. Brooks Barnes, "But It Doesn't Look Like a Marriott: Marriott International Aims to Draw a Younger Crowd," The New York Times (January 4, 2014), http://www.nytimes.com/2014/01/05 /business/marriott-international-aims-to-draw-a-younger -crowd.html?ref=business (accessed April 18, 2016).

3. http://www.sneakerwatch.com/article/020496/the-65-most -expensive-sneakers-at-flight-club-right-now (April 10, 2016).

4. Anne Gammon and Kristen Harmeling, "Children Have Refined Pester Power and Make Savvy Shoppers," June 11, 2015, https:// today.yougov.com/news/2015/06/11/children-make-savvy -shoppers-have-refined-pester-p/ (accessed April 1, 2016).

5. Drew Harwell, "Netflix is Coming for Your Kids," Washington Post, March 28, 2016, https://www.washingtonpost.com/news /the-switch/wp/2016/03/28/netflix-is-coming-for-your-kids/ (accessed April 1, 2016).

6. Ruth Bernstein, "Move Over Millennials—Here Comes Gen Z," Advertising Age, January 21, 2015, http://adage.com/article /cmo-strategy/move-millennials-gen-z/296577/ (accessed April 20, 2015); Laurence Benhamou, "Everything You Need to Know About Generation Z," Business Insider, February 12, 2015, http:// www.businessinsider.com/afp-generation-z-born-in-the-digital -age-2015-2#ixzz3XsRYBXX6 (accessed April 20, 2015); https:// www.youtube.com/user/evantherock (accessed April 20, 2015).

7. Adapted from Michael R. Solomon, Consumer Behavior; Buying, Having, and Being, 12th ed. (Hoboken, NJ: Pearson Education, 2016).

8. Kit Barmann, "Purchasing Power of Teens," May 12, 2014, http:// www.fona.com/resource-center/blog/purchasing-power-teens (accessed April 1, 2016).

9. Amy Barrett, "To Reach the Unreachable Teen," BusinessWeek, September 18, 2000, 78–80.

10. Max Chafkin and Sarah Frier, "How Snapchat Build a Business Confusing Olds," March 3, 2016, http://www.bloomberg.com /features/2016-how-snapchat-built-a-business/ (accessed April 1, 2016).

11. Jacqueline Doherty, "On the Rise," April 29, 2013, http://online .barrons.com/news/articles/SB5000142405274870388940457844 0972842742076 (accessed April 10, 2016).

12. Eileen Patten and Richard Fry, "How Millennials Today Compare with Their Grandparents 50 Years Ago," March 19, 2015, http:// www.pewresearch.org/fact-tank/2015/03/19/how-millennials -compare-with-their-grandparents/#!1 (accessed April 1, 2016).

13. Douglas Coupland, Generation X: Tales for an Accelerated Culture (New York: St. Martin's Press, 1991).

14. Marshall Lager, "The Slackers' X-cellent Adventure," November 2008, www.destinationcrm.com/Articles/Editorial/Magazine -Features/The-Slackerse28099-X-cellent-Adventure-51406.aspx (accessed April 10, 2016).

15. John H. Fleming, "Baby Boomers Are Opening Their Wallets," January 30, 2015, http://www.gallup.com/businessjournal/181367 /baby-boomers-opening-wallets.aspx (accessed April 1, 2016).

16. U.S. Census Bureau, "Millennials Outnumber Baby Boomers and Are Far More Diverse, Census Bureau Reports," June 25, 2015, https://www.census.gov/newsroom/press-releases/2015/cb15 -113.html (accessed April 1, 2016).

17. Ibid.

18. Jeffrey Zaslow, "Get Back to Where You Once Belonged," *The Wall Street Journal*, January 20, 2010, http://online.wsj.com/article/SB10001424052748704561004575012964067490650.html (accessed April 10, 2016).

19. "Dirty Dancing Remake Ordered Starring Abigail Breslin," *Entertainment Weekly* (December 8, 2015), http://www.ew.com/article/2015/12/08/dirty-dancing-abc (accessed April 18, 2016).

20. Associated Press, "California Brewer Uses Slogan 'Queen Of Beers' But Budweiser 'King of Beers' Isn't Having It," http://sanfrancisco.cbslocal.com/2015/08/22/california-she-beverage-brewery-uses-slogan-queen-of-beer-but-king-of-beer-budweiser-isnt-having-it/ (accessed April 1, 2016).

21. Ray A. Smith, "Men are Shopping Like Women," *The Wall Street Journal*, February 16, 2016, http://www.wsj.com/articles/men-are-shopping-like-women-1455657516 (accessed April 1, 2016).

22. Wendy Wang, "Record Share of Wives Are More Educated Than Their Husbands," February 12, 2014, www.pewresearch.org/fact-tank/2014/02/12/record-share-of-wives-are-more-educated-than-their-husbands (accessed April 10, 2016).

23. Sonya Rhodes, "The Upside of 'Marrying Down,'" *The Wall Street Journal*, April 18, 2014, http://online.wsj.com/news/articles/SB10001424052702303663604579503800504978432 (accessed April 10, 2016).

24. Daniel Bachman and Akrur Barua, "Single-Person Households: Another Look at the Changing American Family," November 12, 2015, http://dupress.com/articles/single-person-households-and-changing-american-family/ (accessed April 1, 2016).

25. NPD Group, "Growing Single-Person Households Have Increasing Influence on Snacking Behavior," August, 11, 2015, https://www.npd.com/wps/portal/npd/us/news/press-releases/2015/growing-single-person-households-have-increasing-influence-on-snacking-behavior/ (accessed April 1, 2015).

26. John Stanton, "A Closer Look at the Single Household," July 18, 2013, www.foodprocessing.com/articles/2013/market-view-single-household (accessed April 10, 2016).

27. "Glass Baby Bottles in Demand," June 1, 2008, www.brandpackaging.com/CDA/Articles/Trends_Next_Now/BNP_GUID_9-5-2006_A_10000000000000352222 (accessed April 10, 2016).

28. Anne Fleming, "2013—The Year of the Woman Car Buyer: Capture This Powerful & Ever-Growing Segment," January 22, 2013, www.autoremarketing.com/trends/2013-%E2%80%93-year-woman-car-buyer-capture-powerful-ever-growing-segment (accessed April 10, 2016).

29. Jack Neff, "Survey Finds the Rich Returning to Familiar Spending Habits," September 15, 2009, http://adage.com/article/news/marketing-rich-returning-familiar-spending-habits/139009/ (accessed April 10, 2016).

30. Christopher Rauwald and Mark Clothier, "Luxury Car Makers Bet on Lower-Priced Rides," January 16, 2014, http://www.bloomberg.com/news/articles/2014-01-16/luxury-car-makers-bet-on-lower-priced-rides (accessed April 10, 2016); Tom Randall, "How Tesla's Model 3 Could Conquer Low-End Luxury," March 22, 2016, http://www.bloomberg.com/news/features/2016-03-22/how-tesla-model-3-can-complete-its-take-over-of-the-u-s-luxury-market (accessed April 18, 2016); Ben Thompson, "Can Elon Musk Meet Demand for the Tesla Model 3?" *The Christian Science Monitor*, April 4, 2016, http://www.csmonitor.com/Business/2016/0404/Can-Elon-Musk-meet-demand-for-the-Tesla-Model-3-video (accessed April 18, 2016).

31. U.S. Census Bureau, http://quickfacts.census.gov/qfd/states/00000.html (accessed March 16, 2013).

32. Elizabeth A. Harris and Tanzina Vega, "Race in Toyland: A Nonwhite Doll Crosses Over," *New York Times*, July 26, 2014, http://www.nytimes.com/2014/07/27/business/a-disney-doctor-speaks-of-identity-to-little-girls.html?_r=0, accessed February 23, 2015.

33. Nielsen, "Meet the Fastest-Growing Multicultural Segment in the U.S.: Asian-Americans," June 11, 2015, http://www.nielsen.com/us/en/insights/news/2015/meet-the-fastest-growing-multicultural-segment-in-the-us-asian-americans.html (accessed April 1, 2016).

34. Yuriy Boykiv, "How BuzzFeed Is Winning with Asian-Americans," August 5, 2015, http://adage.com/article/digitalnext/buzzfeed-winning-asian-americans/299823/ (accessed April 1, 2015).

35. U.S. Census Bureau, "United States Census 2000," www.census.gov/main/www/cen2000.html (accessed March 22, 2006); "Latinas Are a Driving Force behind Hispanic Purchasing Power in the U.S.," August 1, 2013, www.nielsen.com/us/en/newswire/2013/latinas-are-a-driving-force-behind-hispanic-purchasing-power-in-.html (accessed May 28, 2014); Elinor Kinnier, "Five Trends Emerging among U.S. Hispanics: The New General Market," April, 2008, www.amg-inc.com/AMG/news/4-08-5trends-hispanicmkt.html (accessed February 25, 2010).

36. Nielsen, "A Fresh View of Hispanic Consumers," April 15, 2014, http://www.nielsen.com/us/en/insights/news/2014/a-fresh-view-of-hispanic-consumers.html (accessed April 1, 2016).

37. Lucette B. Comer and J. A. F. Nicholls, "Communication between Hispanic Salespeople and Their Customers: A First Look," *Journal of Personal Selling and Sales Management* 20 (Summer 2000): 121–27; Elena del Valle, "Relationship Building and Brand Loyalty," January 21, 2009, www.hispanicmpr.com/2009/01/21/relationship-building-and-brand-loyalty (accessed April 10, 2016).

38. Nielsen, "Measuring the Bicultural Hispanic Consumer beyond Just Language and Demographic Data," September 03, 2015, http://sites.nielsen.com/newscenter/measuring-the-bicultural-hispanic-consumer-beyond-just-language-and-demographic-data/ (accessed April 2, 2016).

39. Michael Freedman, Mythili Vutukuru, Nick Feamster, and Hari Balakrishnan, "Geographic Locality of IP Prefixes," Internet Measurement Conference, 2005.

40. Alex Samuely, "Campari Unscrews Real-Time Data for Lyft Offer Targeting Bar-Goers," June 29, 2015, http://www.mobilemarketer.com/cms/news/strategy/20764.html (accessed April 2, 2016).

41. Robert D. Hof, "Marketing in the Moments, to Reach Customers Online," *The New York Times*, January 17, 2016, http://www.nytimes.com/2016/01/18/business/media/marketing-in-the-moments-to-reach-customers-online.html?_r=0 (accessed April 2, 2016).

42. See Lewis Alpert and Ronald Gatty, "Product Positioning by Behavioral Life Styles," *Journal of Marketing* 33 (April 1969): 65–69; Emanuel H. Demby, "Psychographics Revisited: The Birth of a Technique," *Marketing News*, January 2, 1989, 21; and William D. Wells, "Backward Segmentation," in *Insights into Consumer Behavior*, ed. Johan Arndt (Boston: Allyn & Bacon, 1968), 85–100.

43. Lisa Jennings, "Starbucks Takes a Hit for My Starbucks Rewards Changes," March 4, 2016, http://nrn.com/starbucks-coffee/starbucks-takes-hit-my-starbucks-rewards-changes (accessed April 2, 2016).

44. "Choose Where and When Ads Appear," https://support.google.com/adwords/topic/3119119?hl=en&ref_topic=3119071 (accessed April 10, 2016).

45. Polly Mosendz, "Why Hamburger Helper's Rap-Mixtape Marketing Stunt Worked," April 2016, http://www.bloomberg.com/news/articles/2016-04-01/why-hamburger-helper-s-rap-mixtape-marketing-stunt-worked (accessed April 2, 2016).

46. GreatCall, https://www.greatcall.com/phones-devices (accessed April 2, 2016); Dyna, http://dynallc.com/dynas-work/great-call-jitterbug/ (accessed April 2, 2016).

47. Aaron M. Kessler, "A 3-D Printed Car, Ready for the Road," *The New York Times* (January 15, 2015), http://www.nytimes.com/2015/01/16/business/a-3-d-printed-car-ready-for-the-road.html?smid=nytcore-iphone-share&smprod=nytcore-iphone&_r=0 (accessed April 19, 2016).

48. Chip Bayers, "The Promise of One to One (a Love Story)," *Wired*, May 1998, 130.

49. http://www.levis.com.au/curve-id (accessed April 18, 2016).

50. Better Business Bureau, "Children's Food and Beverage Advertising Initiative," https://www.bbb.org/council/the-national

-partner-program/national-advertising-review-services/childrens -food-and-beverage-advertising-initiative/ (accessed April 2, 2016).

51. Alexandra Sifferlin, "Kids See More Candy Ads on TV Now Than in the Past," *Time*, September 10, 2015, http://time.com/4029230 /kids-candy-advertisements/ (accessed April 2, 2016).

52. Ben Popken, "Major Candy Companies Will Stop Advertising to Kids," March 17, 2016, http://www.nbcnews.com/business /consumer/major-candy-companies-will-stop-advertising-kids -n540736 (accessed April 2, 2016).

53. Andrea K. Walker, "Under Armour in Public Eye," July 24, 2008, www.commercialalert.org/issues/culture/product-placement /under-armour-in-public-eye (accessed March 1, 2010).

54. Jonathan Chew, "This is How Much Stephen Curry Is Worth to Under Armour," March 4, 2016, http://fortune.com/2016/03/04 /stephen-curry-under-armour/ (accessed April 3, 2016).

55. Arundhati Parmar, "Where Are They Now? Revived, Repositioned Products Gain New Life," *Marketing News*, April 14, 2003, 1(3).

56. Jay Moye, "Meet the Three Guys behind the Movement to Bring Back Surge," September 18, 2014, http://www.coca-colacompany .com/stories/meet-the-three-guys-behind-the-movement-to -bring-back-surge/%23TCCC (accessed April 3, 2016).

57. Kevin Hunt, "The Doughboy Is 50!" November 5, 2015, http:// www.blog.generalmills.com/2015/11/the-doughboy-is-50/ (accessed April 4, 2016).

58. For an example of how consumers associate food brands with a range of female body shapes, see Martin R. Lautman, "End-Benefit Segmentation and Prototypical Bonding," *Journal of Advertising Research*, June/July 1991, 9–18.

CHAPTER 8

1. Woodstream Corp., www.victorpest.com (accessed April 11, 2016).

2. Leah Yamson, "Apple Music FAQ: The Ins and Outs of Apple's New Streaming Music Service," *Macworld*, September 27, 2015, http://www.macworld.com/article/2934744/software-music /apple-music-faq-the-ins-and-outs-of-apples-new-streaming -music-service.html (accessed April 8, 2016).

3. Gerrick D. Kennedy, "Drake Issues Two New Singles as Apple Exclusives, Reunites Jay Z and Kanye West," *Los Angeles Times*, April 5, 2016, http://www.latimes.com/entertainment/music/posts /la-et-ms-drake-apple-singles-20160405-story.html (accessed April 8, 2016).

4. Apple, "Apple Support Communities," https://discussions .apple.com/community/ipad (accessed April 8, 2016).

5. Olga Kharif, "Shoppers' 'Mobile Blinders' Force Checkout-Aisle Changes," March 21, 2013, www.bloomberg.com/news/2013-03 -21/shoppers-mobile-blinders-force-checkout-aisle-changes.html (accessed April 11, 2016).

6. Jack Loechner, "Digital Coupons Becoming Core Promotional Element," February 17, 2016, http://www.mediapost.com /publications/article/269005/digital-coupons-becoming-core -promotional-element.html (accessed April 8, 2016).

7. Ariel Adams, "10 Things Every Rolex Owner Should Know," *Business Insider*, January 30, 2015, http://www.businessinsider .com/10-things-every-rolex-owner-should-know-2015-1 (accessed April 8, 2016).

8. www.wikipedia.com.

9. Michael D. Mumford, "Where Have We Been, Where Are We Going? Taking Stock in Creativity Research." *Creativity Research Journal* 15 (2003): 107–20.

10. Darren Dahl, "Meet the Travel App That Helps You Talk Like a Local," *Forbes*, February 5, 2014, www.forbes.com/sites/united /2014/02/05/meet-the-travel-app-that-helps-you-talk-like-a -local (accessed April 11, 2016).

11. Jon Chase, "The 12 Best Apps for International Travelers," August 12, 2014, http://www.cntraveler.com/galleries/2014-08-12/the -12-best-apps-for-international-travelers (accessed April 8, 2016).

12. Apple Inc., "iPod + iTunes Timeline," https://www.apple.com /pr/products/ipodhistory (accessed April 11, 2016); http:// www.everymac.com/systems/apple/ipod/ipod-faq/how -many-songs-does-ipod-hold-capacity.html (accessed April 11, 2016).

13. http://www.statista.com/statistics/276307/global-apple-ipod -sales-since-fiscal-year-2006/ (accessed April 28, 2016); Jason Cipriani, "The Real Reason Apple Decided to Release a New iPod Touch," *Fortune*, July 15, 2015, http://fortune.com/2015/07/15 /apple-ipod-touch/ (accessed April 8, 2016); Vindu Goel, "IPhone Sales Drop, and Apple's 13-Year Surge Ebbs," *The New York Times*, April 26, 2016, http://www.nytimes.com/2016/04/27/technology /apple-q2-earnings-iphone.html?_r=0, accessed April 28, 2016.

14. Tim Ambler, *Marketing and the Bottom Line*, 2nd ed. (Edinburgh Gate: FT Press, 2004), 172.

15. Jens Hansegard, "Lego's Plan to Find the Next Big Hit: Crowdsource It," *The Wall Street Journal*, February 25, 2015, http://blogs .wsj.com/digits/2015/02/25/legos-plan-to-find-the-next-big -hit-crowdsource-it/ (accessed April 8, 2016); Lego Ideas, "How it Works," https://ideas.lego.com/howitworks (accessed April 8, 2016).

16. Anita Li, "Smartphone-Controlled Toilet Features Remote Lid, Speakers, App," *Mashable*, December 15, 2012, http://mashable .com/2012/12/15/smartphone-controlled-toilet/?utm_source =feedburner&utm_medium=email&utm_campaign=Feed%3 A+Mashable+%28Mashable%29#hhvMklnHAZqp (accessed April 29, 2016).

17. Green Vehicle Guide, "Vehicle Emissions," http://www .greenvehicleguide.gov.au/pages/Information/VehicleEmissions (accessed April 8, 2016)

18. Russell Hotten, "Volkswagen: The Scandal Explained," BBC, December 10, 2015, http://www.bbc.com/news/business-34324772 (accessed April 8, 2016).

19. Alex Davies, "The Real Winner in the VW Diesel Car Scandal? Hybrid Cars," *Wired*, September 24, 2015, http://www.wired .com/2015/09/volkswagen-diesel-cheating-scandal-is-good-for -hybrid-cars/ (accessed April 8, 2016).

20. goTenna, "How It Works," http://www.gotenna.com/pages/ how-it-works (accessed April 9, 2016).

21. Simon Pitman, "Pfizer Sues P&G over Mouthwash Ad Claims," March 6, 2006, http://www.cosmeticsdesign.com/Market-Trends /Pfizer-sues-P-G-over-mouthwash-ad-claims (accessed April 11, 2016).

22. Chance Barnett, "Top 10 Crowdfunding Sites for Fundraising," *Forbes*, May 8, 2013, www.forbes.com/sites/chancebarnett/2013 /05/08/top-10-crowdfunding-sites-for-fundraising (accessed April 11, 2016).

23. Brad Stone, "Analysts Ask If the iPad Can Live Up to Its Hype," *The New York Times*, March 28, 2010, www.nytimes.com/2010/03/29 /technology/29apple.html (accessed April 11. 2016).

24. Malcolm Gladwell, *The Tipping Point* (Newport Beach, CA: Back Bay Books, 2002).

25. Ewan Spence, "Samsung's Sneaky Viral Strategy to Sell the Galaxy S7," *Forbes*, http://www.forbes.com/sites/ewanspence/2016/02 /18/samsung-galaxy-s7-unboxing-video-review/#3460a03f3dd8 (accessed April 8, 2016).

26. Samsung, "Seven Days of Unboxing," http://www.samsung .com/se/sevendaysofunboxing/?CID=AFL-hq-mul-0813 -11000170 (accessed April 8, 2016).

27. Michelle Castillo, "Lil Wayne Help Samsung Reach Viral Success," CNBC, March 23, 2016, http://www.cnbc.com/2016/03/23 /lil-wayne-helps-samsung-reach-viral-success.html (accessed April 8, 2016).

28. Taylor Bloom, "Multiple Players at the Masters Are Using Clubs Designed by Boeing," April 9, 2016, http://www.sporttechie .com/2016/04/09/multiple-players-at-the-masters-are-using -clubs-designed-by-boeing/ (accessed April 9, 2016).

29. Tamagotchi Friends, "Tamagotchi Friends™ Debuts!" February 18, 2014, http://us.tamagotchifriends.com/2014/02/18/tamagotchi -friends-debuts/ (accessed April 11, 2016).

30. "Mtn Dew® Kickstart™ Launches Two New Flavors With Coconut Water And Introduces 'It All Starts With A Kick' Campaign," *PRNewswire*, January 21, 2015, http://www.prnewswire.com/news-releases/mtn-dew-kickstart-launches-two-new-flavors-with-coconut-water-and-introduces-it-all-starts-with-a-kick-campaign-300023487.html (accessed April 9, 2016).

31. Everett Rogers, *Diffusion of Innovations* (New York: Free Press, 1983), 247–51.

32. Techopedia, "Bleeding Edge," https://www.techopedia.com/definition/23222/bleeding-edge (accessed April 11, 2016).

33. Sources used in this section: "Wi-Fi's Big Brother," *Economist*, March 13, 2004, 65; William J. Gurley, "Why Wi-Fi Is the Next Big Thing," *Fortune*, March 5, 2001, 184; Joshua Quittner, "Cordless Capers," *Time*, May 1, 2000, 85; Scott Van Camp, "Intel Switches Centrino's Gears," *Brandweek*, April 26, 2004, 16; Benny Evangelista, "SBC Park a Hot Spot for Fans Lugging Laptops," *San Francisco Chronicle*, April 26, 2004, A1; Todd Wallack, "Santa Clara Ready for Wireless," *San Francisco Chronicle*, April 19, 2004, D1; Glenn Fleishman, "Three Essays on Muni-Fi You Should Read," http://wifinetnews.com.

34. Christine Chen and Tim Carvell, "Hall of Shame," *Fortune*, November 22, 1999, 140.

35. "Top 10 Failed Products," www.smashinglists.com/top-10-failed-products/2 (accessed April 11, 2016).

36. Market Watch, "12 Worst American Product Flops," April 10, 2015, http://www.marketwatch.com/story/12-worst-american-product-flops-2015-04-10 (accessed April 9, 2016).

37. Rogers, *Diffusion of Innovations*, chap. 6.

38. Patrick Sarkissian, "Why Metrics Are Killing Creativity in Advertising," March 10, 2010, http://adage.com/article/guest-columnists/viewpoint-metrics-killing-creativity-advertising/142600 (accessed April 11, 2016).

CHAPTER 9

1. David Kiley, "The MINI Bulks Up," NBC News, January 27, 2006, http://www.nbcnews.com/id/10992248/ns/business-us_business/t/mini-bulks/ (accessed April 15, 2016).

2. Trader Joe's, "Timeline," http://www.traderjoes.com/our-story/timeline (accessed April 15, 2016).

3. Frito-Lay, "Lay's Classic Potato Chips," http://www.fritolay.com/snacks/product-page/lays (accessed April 15, 2016).

4. Tiffany Burlingame, "Lay's Southern Biscuits And Gravy Flavored Chips Is 2015 'Do Us A Flavor' Contest Winner," October 22, 2015, http://www.fritolay.com/blog/blog-post/snack-chat/2015/10/22/lays-southern-biscuits-and-gravy-flavored-chips-is-2015-do-us-a-flavor-contest-winner.htm (accessed April 15, 2016).

5. Campbell's Soups, https://www.campbells.com/campbell-soup/ (accessed July 15, 2016).

6. Rolls-Royce Motor Cars, www.rolls-roycemotorcars.com (accessed April 15, 2016).

7. Trefis Team, "Estee Lauder Increasing Focus on Its Fragrance Business with Another High End Brand Acquisition," *Forbes*, February 29, 2016, http://www.forbes.com/sites/greatspeculations/2016/02/29/estee-lauder-increasing-focus-on-its-fragrance-business-with-another-high-end-brand-acquisition/#54f68e4d5cad (accessed April 15, 2016).

8. Bernie Woodall, "Kia Tries to Burnish Image with $66,000 Luxury K900 Car," *Chicago Tribune*, May 16, 2014, http://articles.chicagotribune.com/2014-05-16/marketplace/sns-rt-us-kia-motors-k900-20140515_1_luxury-brand-bernie-woodall-k900 (accessed April 15, 2016).

9. Jay Ramey, "2015 Kia K900 Luxury Sedan Gets $5,000 Price Cut," January 28, 2015, http://autoweek.com/article/car-news/2015-kia-k900-luxury-sedan-gets-5000-price-cut (accessed April 15, 2016).

10. Jack Neff, "P&G Makes It Official with Beauty Divestiture to Coty," July 9, 2015, http://adage.com/article/adroll/p-g-makes-official-beauty-divestiture-coty/299408/ (accessed April 15, 2015).

11. Jennifer Kaplan, "Constellation to Buy Ballast Point Brewing for $1 Billion," *Bloomberg*, November 16, 2015, http://www.bloomberg.com/news/articles/2015-11-16/constellation-to-acquire-ballast-point-brewery-for-1-billion (accessed April 15, 2016).

12. David Gelles, "Social Responsibility That Rubs Right Off," October 17, 2015, *The New York Times*, http://www.nytimes.com/2015/10/18/business/energy-environment/social-responsibility-that-rubs-right-off.html (accessed April 16, 2016).

13. Karina Basso, "Huggies Maker Sued in Natural Label Class Action Lawsuit," August 11, 2015, http://topclassactions.com/lawsuit-settlements/lawsuit-news/94041-huggies-maker-sued-in-natural-label-class-action-lawsuit/ (accessed April 15, 2016).

14. Geoffrey Colvin, "The Ultimate Manager," *Fortune*, November 22, 1999, 185–87.

15. www.iso.org/iso/home/standards.htm (accessed April 15, 2016).

16. Al Ries and Laura Ries, *The Origin of Brands* (New York: Collins, 2005).

17. Matt Swider, "PS$ Vs Xbox One: Which Console Is Better," *TechRadar*, December 4, 2015, http://www.techradar.com/news/gaming/consoles/ps4-vs-xbox-720-which-is-better-1127315/4 (accessed April 16, 2016); Charles Poladian, "PS4 Launch Cost Vs. PS4: Oh How the Prices Have Dropped," *International Business Times*, November 12, 2013, http://www.ibtimes.com/ps4-launch-cost-vs-ps3-oh-how-prices-have-dropped-1466806 (accessed April 16, 2016); Jacob Siegal, "All the Reasons Why the PS4 Is Consistently Crushing the Xbox One," *BGR*, July 10, 2014, http://bgr.com/2014/07/10/why-is-the-ps4-outselling-the-xbox-one/ (accessed April 16, 2016).

18. Laurie Burkitt and Ken Bruno, "New, Improved … and Failed," NBC News, March 24, 2010, http://www.nbcnews.com/id/36005036/ns/business-forbescom#.VxIWo6QrKM8 (accessed April 16, 2016).

19. Steve Dent, "iPhone 6s Breaks Apple Sales Record with 13 Million Sold," September 28, 2015, http://www.engadget.com/2015/09/28/apple-iphone-6s-sales-record/ (accessed April 16, 2016).

20. "'Apple' Wins Logo Lawsuit against Beatles," May 8, 2006, www.macnn.com/articles/06/05/08/apple.wins.logo.lawsuit (accessed April 16, 2016).

21. "The Most Famous Name in Music," *Music Trades* 118, no. 12 (September 2003).

22. Suzanne Vranica, "McDonald's Vintage T-Shirts Sizzle," *Post-Gazette*, April 27, 2006, www.post-gazette.com/pg/06117/685629-28.stm (accessed April 16, 2016).

23. Susan Fournier, "Consumers and Their Brands: Developing Relationship Theory in Consumer Research," *Journal of Consumer Research* 24 (March 1998): 343–73.

24. Austin Carr, "Airbnb Unveils a Major Rebranding Effort that Paves the Way for Sharing More than Homes," *Fast Company*, July 16, 2014, http://www.fastcompany.com/3033130/most-innovative-companies/airbnb-unveils-a-major-rebranding-effort-that-paves-the-way-for-sh (accessed April 16, 2016).

25. Kevin Lane Keller, "The Brand Report Card," *Harvard Business Review*, January–February 2000 (Harvard Business School reprint R00104).

26. Jeremy Sinek, "As Luxury Makers Offer Cheaper Cars, Does It Help or Devalue the Brand?" *The Globe and Mail*, April 12, 2016, http://www.theglobeandmail.com/globe-drive/news/industry-news/as-luxury-makers-offer-cheaper-cars-does-it-help-or-devalue-the-brand/article29539479/ (accessed April 16, 2016).

27. www.brandingstrategyinsider.com/2010/08/exploring-the-value-of-sub-brands.html#.U5Ul5H7D9Mw (accessed April 16, 2016).

28. Duane D. Stanford "Coca-Cola Makes over Look of Cans to Shake Calorie Stigma," *Bloomberg*, March 5, 2015, http://www.bloomberg.com/news/articles/2015-03-05/coca-cola-ripping-up-old-can-look-in-europe-to-shake-calorie-hex (accessed July 16, 2016); Thomas Hobbs, "Coca-Cola Takes 'One Brand' Marketing Strategy Global with 'Taste the Feeling' Campaign," *Marketing Week*, January 19, 2016, https://www.marketingweek.com/2016/01/19/coca-cola

-takes-one-brand-marketing-strategy-global-as-it-unveils-new -tagline/ (accessed April 16, 2016); Jay Moye, "'One Brand' Strategy, New Global Campaign Unite Coca-Cola Trademark," January 19, 2016, http://www.coca-colacompany.com/tastethefeeling/ (accessed April 16, 2016).

29. www.costco.com/insider-guide-ks-products.html (accessed April 16, 2016).

30. "Psst! Wanna See Loblaws' New Products?" *Private Label Buyer* 10, no. 1 (January 2003); Len Lewis, "Turf War!," *Grocery Headquarters* 13, no. 6 (November 2002).

31. www.walmart.com/cp/1078664?povid=cat5431-env198764 -moduleB120712-lLinkFC44DollarPrescriptions (accessed April 16, 2016).

32. "Hasbro and Rovio Enter into Expanded Angry Birds Licensing Agreement," June 17, 2013, http://www.rovio.com/hasbro -and-rovio-enter-expanded-angry-birds-licensing-agreement (accessed April 16, 2016).

33. Tony Lisanti, "Warner Bros. and the Magic World of Harry Potter," June 1, 2009, http://www.licensemag.com/license-global /warner-bros-and-magic-world-harry-potter (accessed April 16, 2016); Morgan Korn, "Universal Makes Big Bet on Harry Potter Again," June 23, 2014, http://finance.yahoo.com/blogs/daily -ticker/universal-s-diagon-alley-opens-july-8-131552766.html (accessed April 16, 2016); Leo Sun, "Theme Park Sales Again," April 1, 2016, http://www.fool.com/investing/general/2016/04 /01/harry-potter-may-boost-comcast-corps-theme-park-sa.aspx (accessed April 16, 2016).

34. Zeiss, "Sony and Zeiss: What Photographers Should Know about the Partnership," July 29, 2015, http://lenspire.zeiss.com/en /sony-and-zeiss-what-photographers-should-know-about-the -partnership/ (accessed April 16, 2016).

35. D. C. Denison, "The Boston Globe Business Intelligence Column," *Boston Globe*, May 26, 2002.

36. "Putting Zoom into Your Life," *Time International*, March 8, 2004, 54.

37. Stephanie Thompson, "Brand Buddies," *Brandweek*, February 23, 1998, 26–30; Jean Halliday, "L.L. Bean, Subaru Pair for Co-Branding," *Advertising Age*, February 21, 2000, 21.

38. The Harris Poll, "Enduring Brands Top 2015 Harris Poll EquiTrend® List," March 24, 2015, http://www.theharrispoll.com/business /Enduring-Brands-Top-2015-Harris-Poll-EquiTrend-List.html (accessed April 15, 2016).

39. Kusum L. Ailawadi, Donald R. Lehmann, and Scott A. Neslin, "Revenue Premium as an Outcome Measure of Brand Equity," *Journal of Marketing* 67 (October 2003): 1–17.

40. www.pringles.com/en_US/home.html (accessed April 16, 2016).

41. Packaging World, "Jim Beam Family DNA Informs Bourbon Bottle Redesign," April 16, 2016, http://www.packworld.com/package -design/redesign/jim-beam-family-dna-informs-bourbon-bottle -redesign (accessed April 16, 2016).

42. Aaron Baar, "Accidental Purchases: Blame Package Design, *Marketing Daily/MediaPost News*, October 29, 2010 http://www.mediapost.com/publications/article/116283 /accidental-purchases-blame-package-design.html (accessed April 16, 2016).

43. "Labels to Include Trans Fat," *San Fernando Valley Business Journal*, January 19, 2004, 15.

44. Professor Jakki Mohr, University of Montana, personal communication (April 2004).

45. Russell Parsons, "Consumers Rate a Brand's Ethics before Buying, Study Finds," July 29, 2011, http://www.marketingweek.com /2011/07/29/consumers-rate-a-brands-ethics-before-buying-study -finds/ (accessed April 16, 2016).

46. FDA, "FDA Revises Propose Nutrition Facts Label Rule to Include a Daily Value for Added Sugars," July 24, 2015, http://www.fda .gov/NewsEvents/Newsroom/PressAnnouncements/ucm455837 .htm (accessed April 17, 2016).

CHAPTER 10

1. Paul W. Farris, Neil T. Bendle, Phillip E. Pfeifer, and David J. Reibstein, Marketing Metrics: The Definitive Guide to Measuring Marketing Performance (Upper Saddle River, NJ: Pearson Education, 2010).

2. Max Mason, "Virgin Battle Testing Qantas' Domestic Strategy," May 21, 2014, www.smh.com.au/business/aviation/virgin-battle-testing -qantas-domestic-strategy-20140521-38nh9.html#ixzz32Urapa3N (accessed May 22, 2014).

3. Associated Press, "Walmart's New Tool Gives You Competitors' Prices," March 21, 2014, www.dailyfinance.com/2014/03/21 /walmart-new-tool-provides-competitors-prices (accessed May 22, 2014).

4. "This Day in History," www.history.com/this-day-in-history /seventeen-states-put-gasoline-rationing-into-effect (accessed May 23, 2014).

5. Jennifer Waters, "It's a New Day for Credit Cards," *The Wall Street Journal*, February 21, 2010, http://online.wsj.com/article /SB126670472534749217.html?KEYWORDS5credit1card1rate1reg ulations (accessed March 3, 2010).

6. "Key Features of the Affordable Care Act by Year," www.hhs .gov/healthcare/facts/timeline/timeline-text.html (accessed May 10, 2014); Rick Ungar, "The Real Numbers on 'The Obamacare Effect' Are In—Now Let the Crow Eating Begin," *Forbes*, March 10, 2014, www.forbes.com/sites/rickungar/2014/03/10 /the-real-numbers-on-the-obamacare-effect-are-in-now-let-the -crow-eating-begin (accessed May 20, 2014).

7. Daphne Kasriel-Alexander, *Top 10 Global Consumer Trends for 2016*, White paper, 2016, Euromonitor International.

8. Steward Washburn, "Pricing Basics: Establishing Strategy and Determining Costs in the Pricing Decision," *Business Marketing*, July 1985, reprinted in Valerie Kijewski, Bob Donath, and David T. Wilson, eds., *The Best Readings from Business Marketing Magazine* (Boston: PWS-Kent, 1993), 257–69.

9. Robert L. Steiner, "The Inverse Association Between the Margins of Manufacturers and Retailers," *Review of Industrial Organization* 8 (1993): 717–40, As cited in Robert M. Schindler, *Pricing Strategies: A Marketing Approach* (Thousand Oaks, CA: SAGE Publications, Inc., 2012), 23.

10. Charles L. Ilvento, *Profit Planning and Decision Making in the Hospitality Industry* (Dubuque, IA: Kendall/Hunt Publishing Company, 1996), 154. As cited in Robert M. Schindler, *Pricing Strategies: A Marketing Approach* (Thousand Oaks, CA: SAGE Publications, Inc., 2012), 23.

11. Robin Cooper and W. Bruce Chew, "Control Tomorrow's Costs through Today's Design," *Harvard Business Review*, January–February 1996, 88–97.

12. David Adodaher, Iacocca (New York: Macmillan Publishing Co., 1982), 126, as cited in Robert M. Schindler, *Pricing Strategies: A Marketing Approach* (Thousand Oaks, CA: SAGE Publications, Inc., 2012), 37.

13. http://www.tutor2u.net/blog/index.php/business-studies /comments/qa-explain-price-skimming (accessed May 12, 2014).

14. Campbell's, "About Us," www.campbellsoupcompany.com /about-campbell (accessed May 8, 2014).

15. Laura Northrup, "QVC Bundles Some Accessories with iPad 2, Doubles the Price," March 22, 2012, http://consumerist .com/2012/03/22/qvc-bundles-some-accessories-with-ipad -2-doubles-the-price (accessed May 8, 2014).

16. Export 911, "International Commercial Terms," www.export911 .com/e911/export/comTerm.htm (accessed May 27, 2008).

17. Megan Gibson, "Happy 10th Birthday, iTunes!" April 28, 2013, http://entertainment.time.com/2013/04/28/happy-10th-birthday -itunes (accessed May 8, 2014).

18. "Music Goes Mobile as More Smartphone Users Stream Songs," August 13, 2013, www.emarketer.com/Article/Music-Goes-Mobile -More-Smartphone-Users-Stream-Songs/1010126 (accessed May 10, 2014).

19. Adam Tanner, "Different Customers, Different Prices, Thanks to Big Data," *Forbes*, March 26, 2014, www.forbes.com/sites/adamtanner/2014/03/26/different-customers-different-prices-thanks-to-big-data (accessed May 23, 2014).

20. "Definition of 'Price Discrimination,'" www.investopedia.com/terms/p/price_discrimination.asp (accessed May 23, 2014).

21. Jennifer Valentino-DeVries, Jeremy Singer-Vine, and Ashkan Soltani, "Websites Vary Prices, Deals Based on Users' Information," *The Wall Street Journal*, December 24, 2012, http://online.wsj.com/news/articles/SB10001424127887323777204578189391813881534 (accessed May 1, 2014).

22. Quoted in Julia Angwin, Surya Mattu, and Jeff Larson, "The Tiger Mom Tax: Asians Are Nearly Twice as Likely to Get a Higher Price from Princeton Review," *Pro Publica*, September 1, 2015, https://www.propublica.org/article/asians-nearly-twice-as-likely-to-get-higher-price-from-princeton-review (accessed April 20, 2016).

23. "What Is Freemium?" www.freemium.org/what-is-freemium-2 (accessed May 22, 2014).

24. David Ackerman and Gerald Tellis, "Can Culture Affect Prices? A Cross-Cultural Study of Shopping and Retail Prices," *Journal of Retailing* 77 (2001): 57–82.

25. Shankar Vedantam, "Eliot Spitzer and the Price-Placebo Effect," *Washington Post*, March 17, 2008, www.washingtonpost.com/wp-dyn/content/article/2008/03/16/AR2008031602168.html (accessed May 27, 2008).

26. William J. Boyes, Allen K. Lynch, and William Stewart, "Why Odd Pricing?" *Journal of Applied Social Psychology* 37, no. 5 (May 2007): 1130–40; Robert M. Schindler and Thomas M. Kibarian, "Increased Consumer Sales Response through Use of 99-Ending Prices," *Journal of Retailing* 72 (1996): 187–99.

27. Sarah Kershaw, "Using Menu Psychology to Entice Diners," *The New York Times*, December 22, 2009, www.nytimes.com/2009/12/23/dining/23menus.html?scp51&sq5Using%20Menu%20Psychology%20to%20Entice%20Diners&st5cse (accessed March 3, 2010).

28. Stephanie Rosenbloom, "Back-to-School Discounts Are Deeper, More Creative," *The New York Times*, August 14, 2008, www.nytimes.com/2008/08/15/business/15retail.html?scp51&sq5Back-to-School%20Discounts%20Are%20Deeper,%20More%20Creative&st5cse (accessed March 4, 2010).

29. Sam Gustin, "Apple Found Guilty in E-Book Price Fixing Conspiracy Trial," *Time*, July 10, 2013, http://business.time.com/2013/07/10/apple-found-guilty-in-e-book-price-fixing-conspiracy-trial (accessed May 8, 2014).

30. Adam Bryant, "Aisle Seat Bully?" *Newsweek*, May 24, 1999, 56.

CHAPTER 11

1. Rob Price, "Netflix Has an Ingenious, Piracy-Combating Way to Set Its International Pricing," *Business Insider*, April 17, 2015, http://www.businessinsider.com/netflix-piracy-international-pricing-streaming-earnings-2015-4?r=UK&IR=T (accessed April 24, 2016); Tori Floyd, "Netflix Says Service's Presence in Canada has Helped Drop Piracy by 50 Percent," September 19, 2013, https://ca.news.yahoo.com/blogs/right-click/netflix-says-presence-canada-helped-drop-piracy-50-133215784.html (accessed April 24, 2016).

2. Procter & Gamble, "The eStore Featuring P&G Brands Launches Today to U.S. Consumers," May 20, 2010, http://news.pg.com/press-release/pg-corporate-announcements/estore-featuring-pg-brands-launches-today-us-consumers (accessed April 24, 2016); The CMO Survey, "The Lure of Disintermediation," December 6, 2011, https://cmosurvey.org/blog/the-lure-of-disintermediation/#more-2506 (accessed April 24, 2016).

3. Pavithra Mohan, "Report: Amazon to Open Hundreds of Brick-And-Mortar Bookstores," *Fast Company*, February 2, 2016, http://www.fastcompany.com/3056266/fast-feed/amazon-to-open-hundreds-of-brick-and-mortar-bookstores?utm_source=mailchimp&utm_medium=email&utm_campaign=fast-company-daily-newsletter&position=1&partner=newsletter&campaign_date=02032016 (accessed May 2, 2016).

4. Rowland T. Moriarty and Ursula Moran, "Managing Hybrid Marketing Systems," *Harvard Business Review*, November– December 1990, 2–11.

5. Ultradent Products Inc., "The Opalescence® Story," https://www.ultradent.com/en-us/Dental-Products-Supplies/Tooth-Whitening/Pages/Opalescence-Story.aspx?s_cid=1396 (accessed April 24, 2016).

6. http://www.mysubscriptionaddiction.com/2016/01/subscription-boxes-you-can-try-for-10.html (accessed May 2, 2016); Elizabeth Segran, "From Socks to Sex Toys: Inside America's Subscription-Box Obsession," *Fast Company*, April 6, 2015, http://www.fastcompany.com/3044527/most-creative-people/from-socks-to-sex-toys-inside-americas-subscription-box-obsession (accessed May 2, 2016).

7. Redken, "Anti-Diversion Policy," http://www.redken.com/anti-diversion (accessed April 25, 2016).

8. www.washingtonpost.com/blogs/capital-business/post/wal-mart-invites-local-business-to-join-it-on-georgia-avenue/2013/04/30/bc9a60fe-b1ae-11e2-9a98-4be1688d7d84_blog.html (accessed April 25, 2016).

9. Oneworld, "Member Airlines," www.oneworld.com/member-airlines/overview (accessed April 25, 2016).

10. Sophie Doran, "In Conversation with Thierry Stern, President, Patek Philippe," April 22, 2014, http://luxurysociety.com/articles/2014/04/in-conversation-with-thierry-stern-president-patek-philippe (accessed April 25, 2016); PatekPhilippe, "Authorized Retailers," http://www.patek.com/en/retail-network/authorized-retailers (accessed April 25, 2016).

11. Jordan England-Nelson, "Small Businesses Tap Amazon's Shipping Prowess to Sell More, Earn More," *Daily Breeze*, http://www.dailybreeze.com/business/20140815/small-businesses-tap-amazons-shipping-prowess-to-sell-more-earn-more (accessed April 25, 2016).

12. Starbucks, "Supplier Diversity Program," http://www.starbucks.com/responsibility/sourcing/suppliers (accessed April 25, 2016).

13. David Streitfeld, "Amazon and Hachette Resolve Dispute," *The New York Times*, November 13, 2014, http://www.nytimes.com/2014/11/14/technology/amazon-hachette-ebook-dispute.html (accessed April 25, 2016).

14. Toby B. Gooley, "The Who, What, and Where of Reverse Logistics," *Logistics Management* 42 (February 2003): 38–44; James R. Stock, *Development and Implementation of Reverse Logistics Programs* (Oak Brook, IL: Council of Logistics Management, 1998), 20.

15. Danielle Kucera, "Amazon Ramps Up $13.9 Billion Warehouse Building Spree," *Bloomberg*, August 21, 2013, http://www.bloomberg.com/news/articles/2013-08-20/amazon-ramps-up-13-9-billion-warehouse-building-spree; http://www.bloomberg.com/news/articles/2013-08-20/amazon-ramps-up-13-9-billion-warehouse-building-spree (accessed April 25, 2016); Lisa Easdiccio, "How Amazon Delivers Packages in Less than an Hour," *Time*, December 22, 2015, http://time.com/4159144/amazon-prime-warehouse-new-york-city-deliveries-christmas/ (accessed April 25, 2016).

16. Amazon Prime Air, http://www.amazon.com/b?node=8037720011 (accessed May 2, 2016).

17. John Biggs, "Matternet to Test the First Real Drone Delivery System in Switzerland," *Tech Crunch*, April 23, 2015, http://techcrunch.com/2015/04/23/matternet-to-test-the-first-real-drone-delivery-system-in-switzerland/ (accessed April 25, 2016).

18. "Spychipped Levi's Brand Jeans Hit the U.S.," April 27, 2006, www.spychips.com/press-releases/levis-secret-testing.html (accessed April 25, 2016); Katherine Albrecht and Liz McIntyre, *Spychips: How Major Corporations and Government Plan to Track Your Every Purchase and Watch Your Every Move* (New York: Plume, 2006).

19. "Boycott Gillette," www.boycottgillette.com/index.html (accessed April 25, 2016).

20. Faye W. Gilbert, Joyce A. Young, and Charles R. O'Neal, "Buyer-Seller Relationships in Just-in-Time Purchasing Environments," *Journal of Organizational Research* 29 (February 1994): 111–20.

21. Loretta Chao, "Wal-Mart Reins Back Inventory in a Revamped Supply Chain," *The Wall Street Journal*, August 18, 2015, http://www.wsj.com/articles/wal-mart-reins-back-inventory-in-a-revamped-supply-chain-1439933834 (accessed April 26, 2016).

22. www.supplychainmetric.com/inventoryturns.htm (accessed April 25, 2016).

23. Thomas L. Friedman, *The World Is Flat 3.0: A Brief History of the Twenty-First Century* (New York: Picador, 2007).

24. Emma Court, "What Chipotle's Farm-to-Fork Approach Looks Like Post-Food Safety Scandals," *Market Watch*, February 8, 2016, http://www.marketwatch.com/story/can-chipotles-farm-to-fork-approach-be-sustained-2016-01-07 (accessed April 26, 2016).

25. Sarah Whitten, "CDC Declares Chipotle-Linked E. coli outbreak Over," CNBC, February 1, 2016, http://www.cnbc.com/2016/02/01/cdc-declares-chipotle-linked-e-coli-outbreak-over.html (accessed April 27, 2016).

26. "Perfect Order Measure," www.supplychainmetric.com/perfect.htm (accessed April 25, 2016).

CHAPTER 12

1. Dan Berthiaume, "Retail Sales to Reach $4.9 Trillion in 2015," *Chain Store Age*, February 19, 2015, http://www.chainstoreage.com/article/retail-sales-reach-49-trillion-2015 (accessed July 15, 2016).

2. Bureau of Labor Statistics, U.S. Department of Labor, "The Employment Situation—June 2016," http://www.bls.gov/news.release/pdf/empsit.pdf (accessed July 15, 2016).

3. Stanley C. Hollander, "The Wheel of Retailing," *Journal of Retailing*, July 1960, 41.

4. "Pier 1 Imports History," http://www.pier1.com/public-relations/pr_history,default,pg.html (accessed May 5, 2016).

5. Stephanie Rosenbloom and Jack Healy, "Retailers Post Weak Earnings and July Sales," *The New York Times*, August 13, 2009, www.nytimes.com/2009/08/14/business/14shop.html?scp52&sq5christmas%20sales%20percentage%20of%20annual&st5cse (accessed March 15, 2010).

6. Bruce Lambert, "Once Robust, Retail Scene on the Island Is Smarting," *The New York Times*, May 7, 2009, www.nytimes.com/2009/05/10/nyregion/long-island/10roosevltli.html?scp55&sq5retail%20bankruptcies&st5cse (accessed March 15, 2010).

7. Christopher Durham, "Private Brand Sales Outpace National Brands—PLMA's 2013 Private Label Yearbook," June 28, 2013, http://mypbrand.com/2013/06/28/private-brands-sales-outpace-national-brands-plmas-2013-private-label-yearbook (accessed May 10, 2014).

8. Jack Neff, "Walmart Reversal Marks Victory for Brands," *Ad Age*, March 22, 2010, http://adage.com/article?article_id5142904 (accessed September 30, 2010).

9. John Ewoldt, "Total Wine & More Superstore May Steer You to Its Private Labels," *Star Tribune*, November 4, 2013, www.startribune.com/blogs/230540151.html (accessed May 15, 2014); Kim Peterson, "12 Things About Costco You Ought to Know," CBS News Money Watch, July 16, 2014, http://www.cbsnews.com/media/12-things-about-costco-that-may-surprise-you/13/ (accessed April 23, 2016).

10. Peterson, "12 Things About Costco you Ought to Know."

11. www.trendhunter.com/trends/augmented-pixels-showinroom (accessed May 18, 2014); Thomas M. Anderson, "Checkups on the Run," *Kiplinger Personal Finance*, May 2006, 96.

12. "Build-a-Bear Workshop, Build a Party" http://www.buildabear.com/party/ (accessed April 29, 2016).

13. Robin Nicol, "Verizon Destination Store Opens at Mall of America®, New Retail Experience Helps Customers Discover the Latest in Wireless Technology," Verizon.com, November 19, 2013, (accessed April 24, 2016).

14. "Omnichannel Retailing: The New Normal," National Retailing Federation, https://nrf.com/resources/retail-library/omnichannel-retailing-the-new-normal (accessed April 25, 2016); http://www.slideshare.net/SonataSoftware/omni-channel-retail-the-new-normal.

15. Barry Berman and Joel R. Evans, *Retail Management: A Strategic Approach*, 11th ed. (Upper Saddle River, NJ: Pearson Education, 2010).

16. Rachel Abrams, "Psst! It's Me, the Mannequin. This Would Look Great on You."*The New York Times*, December 18, 2014, http://www.nytimes.com/2014/12/19/business/psst-its-me-the-mannequin-this-would-look-great-on-you.html?smid=nytcore-iphone-share&smprod=nytcore-iphone&_r=1 (accessed April 26, 2016).

17. Rebecca Harrison, "Restaurants Try E-Menus," Reuters, February 25, 2008, http://uk.reuters.com/article/internetNews/idUKL204599320080226.

18. "Google Is Testing Hands-Free Payments," *Canvas8*, March 4, 2016, http://www.canvas8.com/signals/2016/03/04/google-hands-free.html (accessed April 26, 2016).

19. Nancy D. Albers-Miller, "Utilitarian and Experiential Buyers, http://facultyweb.berry.edu/nmiller/classinfo/601/Module%203/util_and_exp.htmn (accessed May 22, 2014).

20. "Retailtainment: The Future of Shopping?" May 25, 2014, www.independent.co.uk/news/business/analysis-and-features/retailtainment-the-future-of-shopping-2303942.html (accessed May 25, 2014).

21. "Thirsty for Innovation," March 28, 2014, http://saatchixlondon.wordpress.com/2014/04/10/on-the-move-with-ikea (accessed May 25, 2014); "Karl Lagerfeld Puts Social Shopping at the Heart of Its New Store," March 20, 2014, http://saatchixlondon.wordpress.com/2014/04/10/on-the-move-with-ikea (accessed May 25, 2014); "H&M's Innovative Store," January 15, 2014, http://saatchixlondon.wordpress.com/2014/04/10/on-the-move-with-ikea (accessed May 25, 2014).

22. http://www.altagraciaapparel.com/news_entry.php?blog_id=11363; "Company Background," Company Background http://www.altagraciaapparel.com/about.html (accessed April 24, 2016).

23. Sean Deale, "Retailtainment: 10 Great Ideas to Increase Store-Based Retail Traffic," *In Store Trends*, December 21, 2011, www.instoretrends.com/index.php/2011/12/21/retailtainment-10-great-ideas-to-increase-store-based-retail-traffic/#sthash.8u7fjeF9.dpuf (accessed May 25, 2014).

24. Kathy Grannis Allen, "Retailers Estimate Shoplifting, Incidents of Fraud Cost $44 Billion in 2014," National Retail Federation, June 23, 2015, https://nrf.com/media/press-releases/retailers-estimate-shoplifting-incidents-of-fraud-cost-44-billion-2014 (accessed May 11, 2016).

25. Joel Griffin, "Study: Retailers' Shrink Reduction Efforts Pay Off," *Security Infowatch*, June 30, 2015, http://www.securityinfowatch.com/article/12088376/retailers-shrink-reduction-efforts-pay-off-2015-national-retail-security-survey-finds (accessed May 11, 2016).

26. Allen, "Retailers Estimate Shoplifting, Incidents of Fraud Cost $44 Billion in 2014."

27. Ibid.

28. Ibid.

29. Kelly Gates and Dan Alaimo, "Solving Shrink," *Supermarket News*, October 22, 2007, 43.

30. Francis Piron and Murray Young, "Retail Borrowing: Insights and Implications on Returning Used Merchandise," *International Journal of Retail & Distribution Management* 28, no. 1 (2000): 27–36.

31. Barbara Farfan, "Customer Service Research Reveals Profiling and Discrimination as Common Employee Practices—How Nordstrom, Costco, Trader Joe's Replace Customer Profiling with Service," March 31, 2013, http://retailindustry.about.com/b/2013/03/31/customer-service-research-reveals-profiling-and-discrimination

-as-common-employee-practices-how-nordstrom-costco-trader -joes-replace-customer-profiling-with-service.htm (accessed May 17, 2014).

32. Brandon A. Perry, "Civil Rights Commission Probes Complaints about Retail Discrimination," *Indianapolis Recorder*, May 16, 2013, www.indianapolisrecorder.com/news/article_87bcda4e-be36 -11e2-909e-0019bb2963f4.html (accessed May 17, 2014).

33. "Näraffär Viken Is a Staffless Supermarket," *Canvas8*, March 2016, http://www.canvas8.com/signals/2016/03/16/automated -supermarket.html (accessed April 26, 2016).

34. Linda Lisanti, "Adventure's Next Stop," *Convenience Store News*, March 3, 2008, 28–34; Michael Browne, "Maverik's Big Adventure," *Convenience Store News*, November 15, 2005, 50–54.

35. "About ALDI," www.aldifoods.com/us/html/company/about _aldi_ENU_HTML.htm?WT.z_src5main (accessed March 28, 2010).

36. Mark Albright, "Kohl's Debut with Fresh New Look," *St. Petersburg Times*, September 28, 2006, 1D.

37. Tribune Wire Reports, "Wal-Mart to Close 269 Stores, 154 of Them in the U.S.," *Chicago Tribune*, January 16, 2016, http:// www.chicagotribune.com/business/ct-walmart-closing-stores -20160115-story.html (accessed April 24, 2016).

38. "Proof of Club Popularity in the 64-Ounce Pudding," *DSN Retailing Today*, December 19, 2005, 64.

39. Barry Berman and Joel R. Evans, *Retail Management: A Strategic Approach*, 12th ed. (Upper Saddle River, NJ: Pearson Education 2013).

40. Ashley Lutz, "Macy's Just Announced the End of Department Stores as We Know Them," *Business Insider*, January 19, 2016, http://www.businessinsider.com/macys-testing-discount-outlets -in-stores-2016-1 (accessed April 26, 2016).

41. http://www.carrefour.com/sites/default/files/2015_Overview .pdf.

42. Quoted in Stratford Sherman, "Will the Information Superhighway Be the Death of Retailing?" *Fortune*, April 18, 1994, 110.

43. Forrester Research, "Forrester Forecasts US Online Retail To Top $500B By 2020," April 28, 2016, https://www.forrester.com/Forr ester+Forecasts+US+Online+Retail+To+Top+500B+By+2020/-/E -PRE9146 (accessed July 15, 2016).

44. Chantal Tode, "Mcommerce Sales to Reach $142B in 2016: Forrester," *Luxury Daily*, October 9, 2015, https://www.luxurydaily.com /mcommerce-sales-to-reach-142b-in-2016-forrester/ (accessed July 15, 2016).

45. Amy Dusto, "60% of U.S. Retail Sales Will Involve the Web by 2017," *Internet Retailer*, October 30, 2013, www.internetretailer .com/2013/10/30/60-us-retail-sales-will-involve-web-2017 (accessed May 15, 2014).

46. Ibid.

47. Jashen Chen and Russell K. H. Ching, "Virtual Experiential Marketing on Online Customer Intentions and Loyalty," *Proceedings of the 41st Hawaii International Conference on System Sciences*, 2008, http://citeseerx.ist.psu.edu/viewdoc/download?doi=10. 1.1.133.4967&rep=rep1&type=pdf (accessed May 23, 2014); Randall Stone, "Retailtainment to the Rescue," January 14, 2008, www.lippincott.com/en/insights/retailtainment-to-the-rescue (accessed May 22, 2014).

48. The Network Experiential, "Creating a Storm: Two Retail Trends That Demonstrate the Real Value of Experiential Marketing," February 2, 2014, www.thenetwork-experiential.com/blogview .asp?ID={27BA6D5C-85F0-428C-833C-37D7067AB651} (accessed May 22, 2014).

49. Bob Tedeschi, "A Quicker Resort This Year to Deep Discounting," *The New York Times*, December 17, 2007, www.nytimes.com /2007/12/17/technology/17ecom.html?scp541&sq5forrester1res earch&st5nyt (accessed May 1, 2008).

50. Tode, "Mcommerce Sales to Reach $142B in 2016: Forrester."

51. Lauren Indvik, "Luxury Brands Still Tread Lightly with Social Media," *Forbes*, October 19, 2010, www.forbes.com/2010/10/19 /burberry-christian-louboutin-technology-social-media.html (accessed May 20, 2014).

52. http://www.net-a-porter.com (accessed May 19, 2014).

53. ECP Team, "Reducing Shopping Cart Abandonment by Giving the Customer What They Want," *Ecommizer*, June 24, 2016, http:// www.ecommercepartners.net/blog/reducing-shopping-cart -abandonment.html (accessed July 7, 2016).

54. "About PayPal," https://www.paypal.com/us/webapps/mpp /about (accessed July 7, 2016).

55. Amy Sample Ward, "Social Philanthropy: Raising Money on You-Tube and Twitter," March 12, 2012, www.thenonprofittimes.com /news-articles/social-philanthropy-raising-money-on-youtube -and-twitter (accessed May 15, 2014).

56. Amazon.com, "Amazon.com Announces Fourth Quarter Sales up 22% to $35.7 Billion," Press Release, January 28, 2016, http://phx.corporate-ir.net/phoenix.zhtml?c=176060&p=irol -newsArticle&ID=2133284 (accessed July 15, 2016).

57. Bass Pro Shops, "Bass Pro Shops Announces New Features of Mega Outdoor Store in Tampa/Hillsborough County, Fla." April 4, 2014, www.basspro.com/webapp/wcs/stores/servlet/CFPage?storeId =10151&catalogId=10051&langId=-1&appID=34&template=news _display.cfm&newsID=559 (accessed May 17, 2014).

58. Direct Selling Association, "Direct Selling in 2014: An Overview," http://www.dsa.org/docs/default-source/research /research2014factsheet.pdf?sfvrsn=0 (accessed April 24 2016).

59. Direct Selling Association, "Ready, Set, Shop!" www.dsa.org /about/dsaoprahinsert.pdf (accessed May 16, 2014).

60. Amway, "Business Opportunity," www.amway.com/about-amway /business-opportunity (accessed May 15, 2014).

61. "Amway Corporation Company Profile," http://biz.yahoo.com/ ic/103/103441.html (accessed May 15, 2014).

62. Direct Selling Association, "The Difference between Legitimate Direct Selling Companies and Illegal Pyramid Schemes," www .dsa.org/ethics/legitimatecompanies.pdf (accessed May 19, 2014).

63. Kathleen Davis, "9 Things You Never Thought You Would Buy from a Vending Machine," *Entrepreneur*, July 30, 2013, www .entrepreneur.com/slideshow/227452 (accessed May 15, 2014); Ariel Knutson, "24 Vending Machines You Won't Believe Exist," *Buzz Feed*, www.buzzfeed.com/arielknutson/vending-machines -you-wont-believe-exist (accessed May 15, 2014).

64. Jill Becker, "Vending Machines for All Your Needs," CNN, August 16, 2012, www.cnn.com/2012/08/16/travel/odd-vending-machines (accessed May 15, 2014).

65. Bureau of Labor Statistics, "Employment Projections: Employment by Major Industry Sector," December 8, 2015, http://www .bls.gov/emp/ep_table_201.htm (accessed May 11, 2016).

66. Central Intelligence Agency, "The World Factbook," https://www .cia.gov/library/publications/the-world-factbook/geos/us.html (accessed May 11, 2016).

67. Brad Tuttle, "Travelers Still Avoiding Carnival After 'Poop Cruise,'" May 28, 2013, *Time*, http://business.time.com /2013/05/28/travelers-still-avoiding-carnival-after-poop-cruise (accessed May 26, 2014).

68. John A. Czepiel, Michael R. Solomon, and Carol F. Surprenant, eds., *The Service Encounter: Managing Employee/Customer Interaction in Service Businesses* (Lexington, MA: D. C. Heath, 1985).

69. Cengiz Haksever, Barry Render, Roberta S. Russell, and Robert G. Murdick, *Service Management and Operations* (Englewood Cliffs, NJ: Prentice Hall, 2000), 25–26.

70. http://businesscenter.jdpower.com/news/pressrelease.aspx ?ID52010092 (accessed June 20, 2010).

71. A. Parasuraman, Leonard L. Barry, and Valarie A. Zeithaml, "SERVQUAL: A Multiple-Item Scale for Measuring Consumer Perceptions of Service Quality," *Journal of Retailing* 64, no. 1 (1988): 12–40; A. Parasuraman, Leonard L. Barry, and Valarie A. Zeithaml, "Refinement and Reassessment of the SERVQUAL Scale," *Journal of Retailing* 67, no. 4 (1991): 420–50.

72. Cynthia Webster, "Influences upon Consumer Expectations of Services," *Journal of Services Marketing* 5 (Winter 1991): 5–17.

73. Michael R. Solomon, "The Wardrobe Consultant: Exploring the Role of a New Retailing Partner," *Journal of Retailing* 63 (Summer 1987): 110–28.

74. Irving J. Rein, Philip Kotler, and Martin R. Stoller, *High Visibility* (New York: Dodd, Mead, 1987).

75. Michael R. Solomon, "Celebritization and Commodification in the Interpersonal Marketplace," unpublished manuscript, Rutgers University, 1991.

76. Matt Rousch, "State Says Pure Michigan Campaign Drove $1.2 Billion Visitor Spending," March 11, 2014, http://detroit.cbslocal.com/2014/03/11/state-says-pure-michigan-campaign-drove-1-2-billion-visitor-spending (accessed May 16, 2014).

77. Ted Nesi and Perry Russom, "RI Chief Marketing Officer Resigns After 'Cooler & Warmer' Debacle," WPRI.com (April 1, 2016), http://wpri.com/2016/04/01/ri-chief-marketing-officer-resigns-after-cooler-warmer-debacle/ (accessed April 26, 2016).

78. Gustav Niebuhr, "Where Religion Gets a Big Dose of Shopping-Mall Culture," *New York Times*, April 16, 1995, 1(2).

79. George Chen, "Hilton to Open More Waldorf, Conrad Hotels in China, Add 40,000 Jobs," June 12, 2013, www.scmp.com/business/companies/article/1258695/hilton-open-more-waldorf-conrad-hotels-china-add-40000-jobs (accessed May 16, 2014).

CHAPTER 13

1. Don E. Schultz and Heidi Schultz, *IMC. The Next Generation. Five Steps for Delivering Value and Measuring Returns Using Marketing Communication* (New York: McGraw-Hill, 2003), 20–21.

2. Barbara Lippert, "Windows Debut: Almost 7th Heaven," October 26, 2009, www.adweek.com/aw/content_display/creative/critique/e3i7a4f853fe57e4c0b5bf8e3a501635ead (accessed May 12, 2009).

3. *Advertising Age Marketing Fact Book,* 2016 ed., Crain Publications, December 21, 2015.

4. Tricia Carr, "Jaguar Sharpens F-Type Push to Reach Men Ages 25–54," May 15, 2013, www.luxurydaily.com/jaguar-sharpens-f-type-push-to-25-54-year-old-males (accessed June 12, 2014).

5. *Advertising Age Marketing Fact Book,* 2016 ed., Crain Publications, December 21, 2015.

6. Molly Wood, "TV Apps Are Soaring in Popularity, Report Says," June 4, 2014, http://bits.blogs.nytimes.com/2014/06/04/report-tv-apps-are-soaring-in-popularity/?_php=true&_type=blogs&_r=0 (accessed June 10, 2014).

7. "Tablet Video Viewing Slightly Decreases as a Share of the Total," *eMarketer,* December 28, 2015, http://www.emarketer.com/Article/Smartphones-Continue-Drive-Mobile-Video-Consumption/1013389?ecid=NL1001#sthash.BX13V4ag.dpuf (accessed May 12, 2016).

8. Jack Neff, "SCJohnson Brand Effort Aims to Edge Out Public Rivals," *Advertising Age,* October 19, 2015, http://adage.com/article/contact-us/scjohnson-launches-brand-effort-edge-rivals-trust/300958/ (accessed May 11, 2016).

9. Ann-Christine Diaz, "Best of 2015 #8 TV/Film: A Mom's Social Media Post Shatters Lives in AT&T's Gut-Wrenching Ad," Creativity online, Advertising Age, July 20, 2015, http://creativity-online.com/work/att-it-can-wait-close-to-home/42768 (accessed May 11, 2016); Ann-Christine Diaz, "The Story Behind AT&T's Disturbing Phone-Safety Ad," July 27, 2015, *Advertising Age,* http://adage.com/article/behind-the-work/story-disturbing-mobile-phone-safety-ad/299678/ (accessed May 11, 2016).

10. Karen E. Klein, "Should Your Customers Make Your Ads?" January 3, 2008, www.businessweek.com/stories/2008-01-02/should-your-customers-make-your-ads-businessweek-business-news-stock-market-and-financial-advice (accessed August 24, 2014).

11. E. J. Schultz, "How 'Crash the Super Bowl' Changed Advertising," *Advertising Age,* January 4, 2016, http://adage.com/article/special-report-super-bowl/crash-super-bowl-changed-advertising/301966/ (accessed April 28, 2016).

12. Natasha Singer, "A Birth Control Pill That Promised Too Much," *The New York Times,* February 11, 2009, B1.

13. "FTC Calls B.S. on Lumosity's Deceptive 'Brain Training' Advertising," *Advertising Age,* January 5, 2016, www.adage.com/article/news/ftc-calls-b-s-lumosity-brain-training-company-pay-2m/302006/ (accessed April 28, 2016).

14. Ed Gillespie, "Greenwash and Hamming It Up—Mazda Makes a Mess of CX-5 Advert," February 27, 2012, www.theguardian.com/environment/blog/2012/feb/27/mazda-advert-dr-seuss-lorax (accessed June 16, 2014).

15. Bradley Johnson, "100 Leading National Advertisers," *Advertising Age,* June 27, 2016, 10–26.

16. Peter Cornish, personal communication, March 2010.

17. This remark has also been credited to a British businessman named Lord Leverhulme; see Charles Goodrum and Helen Dalrymple, *Advertising in America: The First 200 Years* (New York: Harry N. Abrams, 1990).

18. *Advertising Age Marketing Fact Book,* 2016 ed., Crain Publications, December 21, 2015.

19. Ad Age Staff, "Super Bowl 50 Complete Ad Chart: Who Bought Commercials in the Big Game," *Advertising Age,* February 7, 2016, http://adage.com/article/special-report-super-bowl/super-bowl-50-ad-chart-buying-big-game-commercials/301183/ (accessed May 11, 2016).

20. Phil Hall, "Make Listeners Your Customers," *Nation's Business,* June 1994, 53R.

21. Michael Sebastian and Nat Ives, "Top 10 Product Placements of the Last 10 Years," *Ad Age,* May 13, 2014, http://adage.com/article/media/top-10-product-placements-10-years/293140 (accessed June 27, 2014).

22. Christiaan Hetzner and Harro Ten Wolde, "Putting Cars in Video Games Is Now a $2.8 Billion Industry," *Huffington Post,* August 22, 2013, www.huffingtonpost.com/2013/08/22/car-in-video-games_n_3793607.html (accessed June 10, 2014).

23. Stuart Elliott, "Nationwide Insurance Teams with 'Mad Men,'" *The New York Times,* April 4, 2013, www.nytimes.com/2013/04/05/business/media/nationwide-insurance-teams-up-with-mad-men.html?_r=0 (accessed June 27, 2014).

24. "Interactive Advertising Revenues to Reach $147B Globally, $62.4B in US," www.marketingchartscom/direct/interactive-advertising-revenues-to-reach-147b-globally-624b-in-us-3567 (accessed April 21, 2008).

25. "Volvo Uses a Campaign of Interactive Digital Signage for the Launch of Its New Model V40," *Digital AV Magazine,* www.digitalavmagazine.com/en/2012/09/07/volvo-recurre-a-una-campana-de-digital-signage-interactivo-para-el-lanzamiento-de-su-nuevo-modelo-v40 (accessed June 30, 2014).

26. "CNN Airport Network Adds New Entertainment and Sports Programming to Lineup," CNN, June 18, 2013, http://cnnpressroom.blogs.cnn.com/2013/06/18/cnn-airport-network-adds-new-entertainment-and-sports-programming-to-lineup (accessed June 16, 2014).

27. Walmart, "Building a Relationship with Shoppers," www.walmartsmartnetwork.info/howWePartner.htm (accessed June 16, 2014).

28. Sean Corcoran, "Defining Earned, Owned and Paid Media," December 16, 2009, http://blogs.forrrester.com/interactive_marketing/2009/12/defining-earned-owned-and-paid-media.html (accessed April 27, 2010).

29. Ingrid Lunden, "Internet Ad Spent to Reach $121 in 2014, 23% of $547B Total Ad Spend, Ad Tech Boosts Display," *Tech Crunch,* April 7, 2014, http://techcrunch.com/2014/04/07/internet-ad-spend-to-reach-121b-in-2014-23-of-537b-total-ad-spend-ad-tech-gives-display-a-boost-over-search (accessed June 9, 2014).

30. "Digital Set to Surpass TV in Time Spent with US Media," *eMarketer,* August 1, 2013, www.emarketer.com/Article/Digital-Set-Surpass-TV-Time-Spent-with-US-Media/1010096 (accessed June 11, 2014).

31. Mobile Marketing Association, "Mobile Marketing Industry Glossary," http://mmaglobal.com/uploads/glossary.pdf (accessed April 27, 2010).

32. Ashley Zeckman, "Google Search Engine Market Share Nears 68%," May 20, 2014, http://searchenginewatch.com/article/2345837/Google-Search-Engine-Market-Share-Nears-68 (accessed June 9, 2014).

33. Tim Peterson, "Google Finally Crosses $50 Billion Annual Revenue Mark," *Ad Week*, January 22, 2013, www.adweek.com/news/technology/google-finally-crosses-50-billion-annual-revenue-mark-146710 (accessed June 9, 2014);

34. Kyle Christensen, "Still Running Marketing Campaigns? Chances Are, You're Running Out of Time," www.responsys.com/blogs/nsm/cross-channel-marketing/marketing-orchestration-still-running-marketing-campaigns-chances-youre-running-time (accessed June 10, 2014).

35. Joshua Brustein, "If Your Phone Knows What Aisle You're in, Will It Have Deals on Groceries?" *Bloomberg Businessweek*, January 26, 2014, www.businessweek.com/articles/2014-01-06/apples-ibeacon-helps-marketer-beam-ads-to-grocery-shoppers-phones (accessed June 16, 2014).

36. Aflac, "Aflac for Business," www.aflac.com/business/default.aspx (accessed February 23, 2010).

37. Priya Viswanathan, "Methods to Achieve Success with In-App Advertising, About.com, updated December 2, 2015, http://mobiledevices.about.com/od/additionalresources/tp/Methods-To-Achieve-Success-With-In-App-Advertising.htm (accessed May 11, 2016).

38. Selin, "Top 7 Free Video Sharing Sites," March 7, 2013, www.freemake.com/blog/top-7-free-video-sharing-sites (accessed June 27, 2014).

39. Mark J. Miller, "Nike Risks Everything on Soccer Promotions as World Cup Kickoff Nears," June 9, 2014, www.brandchannel.com/home/post/2014/06/09/140609-Nike-World-Cup-Risk-Everything.aspx?utm_campaign=140609nikeriskeverything&utm_source=newsletter&utm_medium=email (accessed June 30, 2014).

40. "Virgin Atlantic Rolls Out Space Miles," http://promomagazine.com/incentives/virgin_atlantic_miles_011106/index.html (accessed June 12, 2006).

41. Alex Palmer, "Applebee's, Chilie's, Outback Conduct Veterans Day Promotions," November 11, 2010, www.dmnews.com/applebees-chilis-outback-conduct-veterans-day-promotions/article/190659 (accessed June 12, 2014).

42. Michael Fielding, "C'est Délicieux," Marketing News, September 15, 2010, 10.

43. "Lengthy Research Leads Disney to Global 'Dreams' Theme," http://promomagazine.com/research/disney_research_061206/index.html (accessed June 12, 2006).

44. Sheila Shayon, "Perrier, at 150, Lures Younger, Hotter Audience to Its 'Secret Place,'" April 5, 2013, www.brandchannel.com/home/post/2013/04/05/Perrier-Secret-Place-040513.aspx (accessed June 27, 2014).

45. Dale Buss, "Super Bowl Ad Watch: With Space Trips, Axe Strives for 'Something That's Epic,'" January 23, 2013, www.brandchannel.com/home/post/2013/01/23/SuperBowl-ApolloUpdate.aspx (accessed June 27, 2014).

46. General Mills, "Cheerios Serves Spoonfuls of Stores for the 11th Year to Get Books into Children's Hands," April 25, 2013, www.generalmills.com/ChannelG/NewsReleases/Library/2013/April/spoonfuls.aspx (accessed June 9, 2014).

CHAPTER 14

1. Charlene Li and Josh Bernoff, *Groundswell: Winning in a World Transformed by Social Technologies* (Boston: Harvard Business School Publishing, 2008), 9.

2. "Facebook Posted Quarterly Results That Topped Analysts' Expectations," CNBC, November 4, 2015, https://www.facebook.com/search/top/?q=number%20of%20facebook%20users (accessed July 22 2016).

3. Brian Stelter, "Nielsen Reports a Decline in Television Viewing," http://mediadecoder.blogs.nytimes.com/2012/05/03/nielsen-reports-a-decline-in-television-viewing/?_php=true&_type=blogs&_r=0 (accessed June 18, 2014).

4. "Magazine Media Increased Total Audience by More than 110 Million Across Platforms in 2015," *MPA—The Association of Magazine Media*, http://www.magazine.org/magazine-media-360%C2%B0/mm360-press-releases/magazine-media-increased-total-audience-more-110-million (accessed May 11, 2016).

5. "Magazine Media 360 Brand Audience Report," *MPA—The Association of Magazine Media*, December 2015, http://www.magazine.org/sites/default/files/December%20360%C2%B0%20BAR%20Month%20%26%20YTD_0.pdf (accessed May 11, 2016).

6. Tim Peterson, "Digital to Overtake TV Ad Spending in Two Years, Says Forrester," *Advertising Age*, November 4, 2014, http://adage.com/article/media/digital-overtake-tv-ad-spending-years-forrester/295694/ (accessed May 15, 2016).

7. Andrew Burger, "Nielsen: Despite Hundreds of Choices, Average Number of TV Channels Watched Is 17," May 9, 2014, www.telecompetitor.com/nielsen-average-number-of-tv-channelswatched-is-17 (accessed June 18, 2014).

8. Erik Sass, "20% of Social Network Users Have Shared Negative Brand Experiences," April 29, 2010, www.mediapost.com/publications/?fa5Articles.showArticle&art_aid5127224 (accessed April 30, 2010).

9. George Slefo, "Digital Ad Spending Surges to Record High as Mobile and Social Grow More Than 50%," *Advertising Age*, April 21, 2016, http://adage.com/article/digital/iab-digital-advertising-generated-60-billion-2016/303650/ (accessed May 20 2016).

10. Chanelle Bessette, "Social Media Superstars 2014," *Fortune*, January 16, 2014, http://fortune.com/2014/01/16/social-media-superstars-2014-fortunes-best-companies-to-work-for (accessed June 18,2014).

11. Christopher Heine, "AmEx's Social Data Shows That Nostalgia Is Just Swell," *Adweek*, October 11, 2013, www.adweek.com/news/technology/amexs-social-data-shows-nostalgia-just-swell-153053 (accessed June 18, 2014).

12. Susan Fournier and Lara Lee, "Getting Brand Communities Right," April 2009, http://hbr.org/2009/04/getting-brandcommunities-right/ar/1 (accessed June 18, 2014).

13. "Leading Social Networks Worldwide as of April 2016, Ranked by Number of Active Users (in Millions)," Statistica, http://www.statista.com/statistics/272014/global-social-networks-ranked-by-number-of-users/ (accessed May 20, 2016).

14. Myra Frazier, "The Networked Boomer Woman: Hear Us Roar," December 18, 2009, www.brandchannel.com/features_effect.asp?pf_id5496 (accessed April 4, 2010).

15. John McDermott, "Facebook Losing Its Edge among College-Aged Adults," January 21, 2014, http://digiday.com/platforms/social-platforms-college-kids-now-prefer (accessed June 18, 2014).

16. "Leading Social Networks Worldwide as of April 2016, Ranked by Number of Active Users (in Millions)," Statistica, http://www.statista.com/statistics/272014/global-social-networks-ranked-by-number-of-users/ (accessed May 20, 2016); Twitter, "About," https://about.twitter.com/company (accessed June 18, 2014).

17. Todd Sherman, "Coming Soon: Express Even More in 140 Characters," *Tweet*, May 24, 2016, https://blog.twitter.com/express-even-more-in-140-characters (accessed July 22, 2016).

18. Lim Yung-Hui, "1.6% of Facebook Users Spent Over $1 Billion on Virtual Goods," *Forbes*, August 2, 2012, www.forbes.com/sites/limyunghui/2012/08/02/1-6-of-facebook-users-spent-over-1-billion-on-virtual-goods (accessed June 18, 2014).

19. Sheila Shayon, "Kwedit Promise: You Can Keep That Virtual Puppy, for a Price," February 8, 2010, www.brandchannel.com/home/post/2010/02/08/Kwedit-Promise-You-Can-Keep-That-Virtual-Puppy-For-A-Price.aspx (accessed March 5, 2010).

20. Angie's List, "How It Works," www.angieslist.com/how-itworks.htm (accessed June 19, 2014).

21. Robert Hof, "You Knew This Was Coming: Ads Are Headed to Pokémon Go," *Forbes*, http://www.forbes.com/sites/roberthof

/2016/07/13/you-knew-this-was-coming-ads-are-headed-to-pokemon-go/#50d306104d6f (accessed July 23, 2016).

22. Maureen Morison, "Sponsored Locations Are Coming to Pokémon Go on a Cost-Per-Visit Basis, Retailers Will Have the Biggest Opportunity to Advertise," *Advertising Age,* July 14, 2016, http://adage.com/article/digital/pokemon-s-ad-model-a-cost-visit-basis/304952/ (accessed July 23 2016); Christopher Heine, "Pokémon Go Is Inspiring Small Retailers. So Has Augmented Reality Gone Mainstream?" *Adweek*, July 12, 2016, http://www.adweek.com/news/technology/pok-mon-go-inspiring-small-retailers-so-has-augmented-reality-gone-mainstream-172478 (accessed July 23, 2016).

23. Todd Wasserman, "5 Creative Location-Based Campaigns for Small Businesses to Learn From," Mashable, http://mashable.com/2011/06/21/small-business-foursquare-scvngr (accessed June 19, 2014).

24. Natalie Zmuda, "An App for That, Too: How Mobile Is Changing Shopping," *Ad Age*, March 1, 2010, http://adage.com/print?article_id5142318 (accessed March 14, 2010); Jenna Wortham, "Telling Friends Where You Are (or Not)," *The New York Times*, March 14, 2010, www.nytimes.com/2010/03/15/technology/15locate.html (accessed April 30, 2010).

25. Malcolm Maiden, "The Internet of Things: It's Arrived and It's Eyeing Your Job," May 21, 2016, Business Day, *The Sydney Morning Herald*, http://www.smh.com.au/business/innovation/the-internet-of-things-its-finally-arrived-and-its-eyeing-your-job-20160520-gozz1f.html (accessed May 21, 2016).

26. Direct Marketing Association, www.the-dma.org/index.php (accessed May 2, 2010).

27. Ginger Conlon, "2016 Will Be a Growth Year in Marketing Spending," *Direct Marketing News*, February 1, 2016, http://www.dmnews.com/marketing-strategy/2016-will-be-a-growth-year-in-marketing-spending/article/469545/ (accessed July 23. 2016).

28. Leslie Kaufman with Claudia H. Deutsch, "Montgomery Ward to Close Its Doors," *The New York Times*, December 29, 2000, www.nytimes.com/2000/12/29/business/montgomery-ward-to-close-itsdoors.html (accessed August 29, 2014).

29. Phil Wahba, "Neiman Marcus' Outlandish Christmas Gifts: Keanu Motorbikes, $400,000 Trip to India," *Fortune*, October 7, 2015, http://fortune.com/2015/10/07/neiman-marcus-christmas/ (accessed May 25, 2016).

30. Ishbel Macleod, "Infographic: Consumers More Likely to Deal with Direct Mail Immediately Compared to Email," *The Drum*, October 23, 2013, www.thedrum.com/news/2013/10/23/infographicconsumers-more-likely-deal-direct-mail-immediately-comparedemail (accessed June 18, 2014).

31. Alan Farnham, "Fighting Telemarketers: When Do-Not-Call List Fails, These Strategies Work," ABC News, January 21, 2014, http://abcnews.go.com/Business/best-ways-turn-tables-telemarketers/story?id=21534413 (accessed June 19, 2014).

32. Federal Trade Commission, "National Do Not Call Registry," www.ftc.gov/donotcall (accessed May 8, 2010).

33. Alison J. Clarke, "'As Seen on TV': Socialization of the Tele-Visual-Consumer," paper presented at the Fifth Interdisciplinary Conferenceon Research in Consumption, University of Lund, Sweden, August 1995.

34. Yue Wang, "More People Have Cell Phones Than Toilets, U.N. Study Shows," March 25, 2013, http://newsfeed.time.com/2013/03/25/more-people-have-cell-phones-than-toilets-un-study-shows (accessed June 19, 2014).

35. Bureau of Labor Statistics, *Occupational Outlook Handbook*, December 17, 2015, http://www.bls.gov/ooh/home.htm (accessed May19, 2016).

36. Quoted in Jaclyn Fierman, "The Death and Rebirth of the Salesman," *Fortune*, July 25, 1994, 88.

37. Salesforce.com, www.salesforce.com (accessed May 1, 2010).

38. Mark W. Johnston and Greg W. Marshall, *Sales Force Management, Leadership, Innovation, Technology*, 12th ed. (New York: Routledge, Taylor & Francis, 2016).

39. Adapted from Mitchell Schnurman, "The Game-Changing Reality of Virtual Sales Pitches," *Star-Telegram*, April 9, 2010, www.star-telegram.com/2010/04/09/2103717_p2/the-game-changing-reality-ofvirtual.html (accessed May 1, 2010).

40. Dan C. Weilbaker, "The Identification of Selling Abilities Needed for Missionary Type Sales," *Journal of Personal Selling & Sales Management* 10 (Summer 1990): 45–58.

41. Derek A. Newton, *Sales Force Performance and Turnover* (Cambridge, MA: Marketing Science Institute, 1973), 3.

42. Johnston and Marshall, *Sales Force Management, Leadership, Innovation, Technology*.

43. Direct Selling Association, "Industry Fact Sheets," http://www.dsa.org/benefits/research/factsheets (accessed July 23, 2016).

44. Mark W. Johnston and Greg W. Marshall, *Relationship Selling*, 3rd ed. (Boston: McGraw-Hill, 2010).

45. Greg W. Marshall, Daniel J. Goebel, and William C. Moncrief, "Hiring for Success at the Buyer-Seller Interface," *Journal of Business Research* 56 (April 2003): 247–255.

46. Darren Heitner, "How Isiah Austin Became NBA's Most Valuable Draft Pick," *Forbes*, June 27, 2014, www.forbes.com/sites/darrenheitner/2014/06/27/how-isaiah-austin-became-nbas-most-valuabledraft-pick (accessed June 30, 2014).

47. Kate Fitzgerald, "Homemade Bikini Contest Hits Bars, Beach for10th Year," *Advertising Age*, April 13, 1998, 18.

48. Jim Jelter, "General Motors CEO Mary Barra's BP Moment," March12, 2014, http://blogs.marketwatch.com/thetell/2014/03/12/general-motors-ceo-mary-barras-bp-moment (accessed June 19, 2014).

49. Rich Thomaselli, "PR Response Has Been Swift and Active, But Test Will Come When Ship Finally Docks," *Ad Age*, February 14, 2013, http://adage.com/article/news/carnival-cruises-pr-responsetriumph-crisis/239819 (accessed June 20, 2014).

50. Mark Prigg, "Amazon's Drone Dreams Come Crashing Down, U.S. Regulators Ban Package Delivery Services Using 'Model Aircraft,'" *Daily Mail*, June 24, 2014, www.dailymail.co.uk/sciencetech/article-2668411/Amazons-drone-dreams-come-crashing-USregulators-ban-package-delivery-services-using-model-aircraft.html#ixzz35rMKW4VF (accessed June 30, 2014).

51. Andy Pasztor, "FAA Ruling on Long-Haul Routes Would Boost Boeing's Designs," *The Wall Street Journal*, June 5, 2006, A3.

52. Amy Chozick, "Star Power: The LPGA Is Counting on a New Marketing Push to Take Women's Golf to the Next Level," *The Wall Street Journal*, June 12, 2006, R6.

53. Shannon Prather, "Identity Crisis: Brooklyn Park Hires PR Firm to Improve Its Reputation," *Star Tribune*, April 8, 2014, www.startribune.com/local/north/254292091.html#FLeReIJRQyImAWVq.97 (accessed June 24, 2014).

54. Carol Driver, "Five-Minute YouTube Apology from Toyota Boss as First Lawsuit Filed over Faulty Pedal Recall," *Daily Mail*, February 5, 2010, http://www.dailymail.co.uk/news/article-1248588/Fiveminute-YouTube-apology-Toyota-boss-lawsuit-filed-faulty-pedalrecall.html (accessed March 15, 2010).

55. IEG Sponsorship Report, "Sponsorship Spending Growth Slows in North America as Marketers Eye New Media and Marketing Options," January 7, 2014, www.sponsorship.com/iegsr/2014/01/07/Sponsorship-Spending-Growth-Slows-In-North-America.aspx (accessed June 24, 2014).

56. AT&T, "AT&T Is An Exclusive 'Super Sponsor' of SXSW," March 2013, www.att.com/gen/press-room?pid=22489 (accessed June 24, 2014).

57. Quoted in Michelle Kessler, "IBM Graffiti Ads Gain Notoriety," *USA Today*, April 26, 2001, 3B.

58. Tamar Weinbert, *The New Community Rules: Marketing on the Social Web* (Sebastopol, CA: O'Reilly Media, 2009).

59. Campaign Asisa, "Case Study: Burger King's Wallet Drop Stunt Creates Online Buzz in Singapore, July 22, 2010, www.campaignasia.com/agencyportfolio/CaseStudyCampaign/220642,case-studyburger-kings-wallet-drop-guerilla-stunt-creates-online-buzz-insingapore.aspx#.U6jGlKhKvDk (accessed June 23, 2014).

60. Michelle Kessler, "IBM Graffiti Ads Gain Notoriety," February 6, 2002, http://usatoday30.usatoday.com/tech/news/2001-04-25-ibm-linux-graffiti.htm (accessed August 29, 2014).

61. Lois Geller, "Wow—What a Buzz," *Target Marketing*, June 2005, 21.

62. Natasha Salmon, "Revealed: Watch the TRUTH behind Viral 'Cheater' Spray Painted Range Rover Left Outside Harrods," Mirror.com (*Daily Mirror*), May 15, 2016 http://www.mirror.co.uk/news/uk-news/revealed-watch-truth-behind-viral-7972090 (accessed May 16, 2016.)

63. Matthew Creamer, "In Era of Consumer Control, Marketers Crave the Potency of Word-of-mouth," *Advertising Age*, November 28, 2005, 32.

64. Paul Marsden, "F-Commerce: Heinz Innovates with New 'Tryvertising' F-Store," March 8, 2011, http://digitalintelligencetoday.com/f-commerce-heinz-innovate-with-new-tryvertising-f-storescreenshots (accessed June 23, 2014).

65. Todd Wasserman, "Blogs Cause Word-of-Mouth Business to Spread Quickly," *Brandweek*, October 3, 2005, 9.

66. Pano Mourdoukoutas, "Good Buzz, Bad Buzz Brand Management: A Social Media Strategy That Pays Off," *Forbes*, November 7, 2013, www.forbes.com/sites/panosmourdoukoutas/2013/11/07/goodbuzz-bad-buzz-brand-management-a-social-media-strategythat-pays-off (accessed June 18, 2014).

67. Ryan Parker, "Chewbacca Mask-Wearing Mom Hits 50 Million Facebook Views in 24 Hours, *The Hollywood Reporter*, May 20, 2016, http://www.hollywoodreporter.com/heat-vision/chewbacca-mask-wearing-mom-hits-896120 (accessed July 22, 2016).

68. Todd Wasserman, "Word Games," *Brandweek*, April 24, 2006, 24.

69. Stephanie Strom, "Nonprofit Punishes a 2nd Founder for Ruse," *The New York Times*, January 15, 2008, www.nyt.com/2008/01/15/us/15givewell.html?ex=1201064400&en=97effb249 (accessed January 15, 2008); Ross D. Petty and J. Craig Andrews, "Covert Marketing Unmasked: A Legal and Regulatory Guide for Practices That Mask Marketing Messages," *Journal of Public Policy & Marketing* (Spring 2008): 7–18; James B. Stewart, "Whole Foods CEO Threatens Merger, Fuels Arbitrage," *Smart Money* (July 18, 2007), www.smartmoney.com/investing/stocks/whole-foods-ceo-threatens-merger-fuels-arbitrage-21550/?hpadref=1 (accessed June 4, 2009); Brian Morrissey, "'Influencer Programs' Likely to Spread," *Adweek* (March 2, 2009), http://www.adweek.com/news/advertising-branding/influencer-programs-likely-spread-98542 (accessed March 2, 2009); Katie Hafner, "Seeing Corporate Fingerprints in Wikipedia Edits," *The New York Times*, August 19, 2007, www.nyt.com/2007/08/19/technology/19wikipedia.html?_r=1&oref=slogin (accessed August 19, 2007); Brian Bergstein, "New Tool Mines: Wikipedia Trustworthiness Software Analyzes Reputations of the Contributors Responsible for Entries," MSNBC, September 5, 2007, www.msnbc.msn.com/id/20604175 (accessed September 5, 2007); http://wikiscanner.virgil.gr (accessed June 4, 2009).

70. You can read more about the Burger King campaign in the "Real People, Real Choices" vignette at the beginning of Chapter 13.

APPENDIX A

1. S&S Smoothie Company is a fictitious company created to illustrate a sample marketing plan.

2. Note that the action plan for the final marketing plan should include objectives, action items, timing information, and budget information necessary to accomplish all marketing objectives. We have included only one objective in this sample marketing plan.

APPENDIX B

1. John W. Schouten, "Selves in Transition: Symbolic Consumption in Personal Rites of Passage and Identity Reconstruction," *Journal of Consumer Research*, March 17, 1991, 412–25; Michael R. Solomon, "The Wardrobe Consultant: Exploring the Role of a New Retailing Partner," *Journal of Retailing* 63 (1987): 110–28; Michael R. Solomon and Susan P. Douglas, "Diversity in Product Symbolism: The Case of Female Executive Clothing," *Psychology & Marketing* 4 (1987): 189–212; Joseph Z. Wisenblit, "Person Positioning: Empirical Evidence and a New Paradigm," *Journal of Professional Services Marketing* 4, no. 2 (1989): 51–82.

2. Bureau of Labor Statistics, U.S. Department of Labor, *Occupational Outlook Handbook, 2016–17 Edition*, Advertising, Promotions, and Marketing Managers, on the Internet at http://www.bls.gov/ooh/management/advertising-promotions-and-marketing-managers.htm (visited August 18, 2016).

3. Liz Ryan, "Ten Ways To Use LinkedIn In Your Job Search," *Forbes*, May 19, 2014, http://www.forbes.com/sites/lizryan/2014/05/19/ten-ways-to-use-linkedin-in-your-job-search/3/#7e505b19b4dc (accessed June 5, 2016).

▶ Glossary

80/20 Rule A marketing rule of thumb that 20 percent of purchasers account for 80 percent of a product's sales.

A

A/B test A method used for testing the effectiveness of altering one characteristic of a marketing asset (e.g., a web page, a banner advertisement, or an e-mail). The test is conducted by randomly exposing some users to the original version and other users to an altered version. The behavior of users within each group is recorded and the results are used to determine if the altered version performs better on some measure of interest (e.g., click-through rates).

accountability A process of determining just how much value an organization's marketing activities create and their impact on the bottom line.

account executive A member of the account management department who supervises the day-to-day activities of the account and is the primary liaison between the agency and the client.

account planner A member of the account management department who combines research and account strategy to act as the voice of the consumer in creating effective advertising.

action plans Individual support plans included in a marketing plan that provide the guidance for implementation and control of the various marketing strategies within the plan. Action plans are sometimes referred to as "marketing programs."

activities, interests, and opinions (AIOs) Measures of consumer activities, interests, and opinions used to place consumers into dimensions.

activity metrics Metrics focused on measuring and tracking specific activities taken within a firm that are part of different marketing processes.

actual product The physical good or the delivered service that supplies the desired benefit.

ad blocking The use of powerful ad-blocking software created to stop ad fraud by stripping ads from the website at the network level.

ad fraud The use of automated browsers to falsify the number of views or click-throughs the advertisers must pay for.

administered VMS A vertical marketing system in which channel members remain independent but voluntarily work together because of the power of a single channel member.

adoption pyramid Reflects how a person goes from being unaware of an innovation through stages from the bottom up of awareness, interest, evaluation, trial, adoption, and confirmation.

advergaming Brand placements in video games.

advertising appeal The central idea or theme of an advertising message.

advertising campaign A coordinated, comprehensive plan that carries out promotion objectives and results in a series of advertisements placed in media over a period of time.

advertising Nonpersonal communication from an identified sponsor using the mass media.

advocacy advertising A type of public service advertising where an organization seeks to influence public opinion on an issue because it has some stake in the outcome.

affect The feeling component of attitudes; refers to the overall emotional response a person has to a product.

aided recall A research technique that uses clues to prompt answers from people about advertisements they might have seen.

ambient advertising Advertising placed where advertising isn't normally or hasn't ever been seen.

anticonsumption The deliberate defacement of products.

approach The first step of the actual sales presentation in which the salesperson tries to learn more about the customer's needs, create a good impression, and build rapport.

Arab Spring a series of anti-government protests and uprisings in a number of Arab countries facilitated by new social media tools available to people in the region.

attention The extent to which a person devotes mental processing to a particular stimulus.

attitude A learned predisposition to respond favorably or unfavorably to stimuli on the basis of relatively enduring evaluations of people, objects, and issues.

attitudinal measures A research technique that probes a consumer's beliefs or feelings about a product before and after being exposed to messages about it.

attributes Include features, functions, benefits, and uses of a product. Marketers view products as a bundle of attributes that includes the packaging, brand name, benefits, and supporting features in addition to a physical good.

augmented product The actual product plus other supporting features such as a warranty, credit, delivery, installation, and repair service after the sale.

augmented reality (AR) A view of a physical, real world that is enhanced or altered by computer-generated sounds, videos, graphics, or GPS data.

automatic reordering system Retail reordering system that is automatically activated when inventories reach a certain level.

avatars Graphic representations of users of virtual worlds.

average fixed cost The fixed cost per unit produced.

B

B2C e-commerce Online exchanges between companies and individual consumers.

baby boomers The segment of people born between 1946 and 1964.

back-translation The process of translating material to a foreign language and then back to the original language.

backward invention Product strategy in which a firm develops a less advanced product to serve the needs of people living in countries without electricity or other elements of a developed infrastructure.

badge A milestone or reward earned for progressing through a video game.

bait-and-switch An illegal marketing practice in which an advertised price special is used as bait to get customers into the store with the intention of switching them to a higher-priced item.

balance of payments a statement of how much trade a country has going out compared to how much it has coming in. If a country is buying more than it is selling, it will have a negative balance of payments.

banners Internet advertising in the form of rectangular graphics at the top or bottom of web pages.

BCG growth–market share matrix A portfolio analysis model developed by the Boston Consulting Group that assesses the potential of successful products to generate cash that a firm can then use to invest in new products.

beacon marketing A retail marketing strategy in which beacon devices are placed strategically throughout a store and emit a Bluetooth signal to communicate with shoppers' smartphones as they browse the aisles of the store.

behavior The doing component of attitudes; involves a consumer's intention to do something, such as the intention to purchase or use a certain product.

behavioral learning theories Theories of learning that focus on how consumer behavior is changed by external events or stimuli.

behavioral segmentation A technique that divides consumers into segments on the basis of how they act toward, feel about, or use a good or service.

benefit The outcome sought by a customer that motivates buying behavior that satisfies a need or want.

beta test Limited release of a product, especially an innovative technology, to allow usage and feedback from a small number of customers who are willing to test the product under normal, everyday conditions of use.

bifurcated retailing With the decline of middle-of-the-market retailing, both mass merchandising and niche retailing dominate the retail market.

Big Data A popular term to describe the exponential growth of data—both structured and unstructured—in massive amounts that are hard or impossible to process using traditional database techniques.

Bitcoin The most popular and fastest-growing digital currency.

bleeding edge technology An innovative technology that is not yet ready for release to the market as a whole, potentially because of issues related to reliability and stability, but is in a suitable state to be offered for beta testing to evaluate consumer perceptions of its performance and identify any potential issues in its usage.

bottom of the pyramid (BOP) The collective name for the group of consumers throughout the world who live on less than $2 a day.

bottom of the pyramid pricing Innovative pricing that will appeal to consumers with the lowest incomes by brands that wish to get a foothold in bottom of the pyramid countries.

bottom-up budgeting techniques Allocation of the promotion budget based on identifying promotion goals and allocating enough money to accomplish them.

bounce rate A marketing metric for analyzing website traffic. It represents the percentage of visitors who enter the site (typically at the home page) and "bounce" (leave the site) rather than continuing to view additional pages on the site.

box stores Food stores that have a limited selection of items, few brands per item, and few refrigerated items.

brand ambassadors or brand evangelists Loyal customers of a brand recruited to communicate and be salespeople with other consumers for a brand they care a great deal about.

brand anthropomorphism The assignment of human characteristics and qualities to a brand.

brand community A group of social network users who share an attachment to a product or brand, interact with each other and share information about the brand.

brand competition When firms offering similar goods or services compete on the basis of their brand's reputation or perceived benefits.

brand dilution A reduction in the value of a brand typically driven by the introduction of a brand extension that possesses attributes that adversely contrast with the current attributes consumers associate with the brand.

brand equity The value of a brand to an organization.

brand extensions A new product sold with the same brand name as a strong existing brand.

brand loyalty A pattern of repeat product purchases, accompanied by an underlying positive attitude toward the brand, based on the belief that the brand makes products superior to those of its competition.

brand manager An individual who is responsible for developing and implementing the marketing plan for a single brand.

brand meaning The beliefs and associations that a consumer has about the brand.

brand personality A distinctive image that captures a good's or service's character and benefits.

brand polarization The gap between good buzz and bad buzz.

brand storytelling Compelling stories told by marketers about brands to engage consumers.

brand A name, a term, a symbol, or any other unique element of a product that identifies one firm's product(s) and sets it apart from the competition.

branded content Marketing communication developed by a brand to provide educational or entertainment value rather than to sell the brand in order to develop a relationship with consumers; may indicate the brand is the sponsor.

branded entertainment (also known as product placements or embedded marketing) A form of advertising in which marketers integrate products into entertainment venues.

brandfests Events that companies host to thank customers for their loyalty.

break-even analysis A method for determining the number of units that a firm must produce and sell at a given price to cover all its costs.

break-even point The point at which the total revenue and total costs are equal and beyond which the company makes a profit; below that point, the firm will suffer a loss.

breaking bulk Dividing larger quantities of goods into smaller lots in order to meet the needs of buyers.

bribery When someone voluntarily offers payment to get an illegal advantage.

BRICS countries Also referred to as the BRICS, Brazil, Russia, India, China, and South Africa are the fastest growing of the developing countries. With more than 3 billion people, they represent over 42% of the world's population and about 20% of the gross world product.

business analysis The step in the product development process in which marketers assess a product's commercial viability.

business cycle The overall patterns of change in the economy—including periods of prosperity, recession, depression, and recovery—that affect consumer and business purchasing power.

business ethics Basic values that guide a firm's behavior.

business plan A plan that includes the decisions that guide the entire organization.

business planning An ongoing process of making decisions that guides the firm both in the short term and in the long term.

business portfolio The group of different products or brands owned by an organization and characterized by different income-generating and growth capabilities.

business-to-business (B2B) e-commerce Online exchanges between two or more businesses or organizations.

business-to-business (B2B) markets The group of customers that include manufacturers, wholesalers, retailers, and other organizations.

business-to-business marketing The marketing of goods and services from one organization to another.

buttons Small banner-type advertisements that can be placed anywhere on a web page.

buyclass One of three classifications of business buying situations that characterizes the degree of time and effort required to make a decision.

buying center The group of people in an organization who participate in a purchasing decision.

buying power A concept in segmentation that can help marketers to determine how to better match different products and versions of products to different consumer groups based on an understanding of what discretionary and nondiscretionary allocations of funds they are able to make.

buzz marketing Marketing activities designed to create conversation, excitement, and enthusiasm, that is, buzz, about a brand.

buzz Word-of-mouth communication that customers view as authentic.

C

cannibalization The loss of sales of an existing brand when a new item in a product line or product family is introduced.

capacity management The process by which organizations adjust their offerings in an attempt to match demand.

captive pricing A pricing tactic for two items that must be used together; one item is priced very low, and the firm makes its profit on another, high-margin item essential to the operation of the first item.

case allowance A discount to the retailer or wholesaler based on the volume of product ordered.

case study A comprehensive examination of a particular firm or organization.

cash cows SBUs with a dominant market share in a low-growth-potential market.

cash discounts A discount offered to a customer to entice them to pay their bill quickly.

catalog A collection of products offered for sale in book form, usually consisting of product descriptions accompanied by photos of the items.

category killer A very large specialty store that carries a vast selection of products in its category.

causal research A technique that attempts to understand cause-and-effect relationships.

channel conflict Incompatible goals, poor communication, and disagreement over roles, responsibilities, and functions among firms at different levels of the same distribution channel that may threaten a manufacturer's distribution strategy.

channel cooperation Occurs when producers, wholesalers, and retailers depend on one another for success.

channel intermediaries Firms or individuals such as wholesalers, agents, brokers, or retailers who help move a product from the producer to the consumer or business user. An older term for intermediaries is *middlemen*.

channel leader or channel captain The dominant firm that controls the channel.

channel levels The number of distinct categories of intermediaries that make up a channel of distribution.

channel of distribution The series of firms or individuals that facilitates the movement of a product from the producer to the final customer.

channel partner model A relationship between channel partners in which a two-way exchange of information between purchasing organizations and their respective vendors is facilitated through shared or integrated IT systems.

channel power The ability of one channel member to influence, control, and lead the entire channel based on one or more sources of power.

churn rate The percentage of a company's customers (for a given span of time) who by the end of that time span can no longer be considered customers of the company (e.g. because they have cancelled their contract for a service or they have stopped shopping at the related retail location).

classical conditioning The learning that occurs when a stimulus eliciting a response is paired with another stimulus that initially does not elicit a response on its own but will cause a similar response over time because of its association with the first stimulus.

click-through A metric that indicates the percentage of website users who have decided to click on an advertisement to visit the website or web page associated with it.

close The stage of the selling process in which the salesperson actually asks the customer to buy the product.

Cloud A network of servers that provide an almost infinite amount of storage space.

co-op advertising A sales promotion where the manufacturer and the retailer share the cost.

cobranding An agreement between two brands to work together to market a new product.

code of ethics Written standards of behavior to which everyone in the organization must subscribe.

cognition The knowing component of attitudes; refers to the beliefs or knowledge a person has about a product and its important characteristics.

cognitive dissonance The anxiety or regret a consumer may feel after choosing from among several similar attractive choices.

cognitive learning theory Theory of learning that stresses the importance of internal mental processes and that views people as problem solvers who actively use information from the world around them to master their environment.

collaborative consumption A term used to refer to the activities practiced by rentrepreneurs.

collectivist cultures Cultures in which people subordinate their personal goals to those of a stable community.

combination stores Retailers that offer consumers food and general merchandise in the same store.

commercial success Indicates that a product concept is feasible from the standpoint of whether the firm developing the products believes there is or will be sufficient consumer demand to warrant its development and entry into the market.

commercialization The final step in the product development process in which a new product is launched into the market.

common good approach Ethical philosophy that advocates the decision that contributes to the good of all in the community.

communication and transaction functions Happens when channel members develop and execute both promotional and other types of communication among members of the channel.

communication model The process whereby meaning is transferred from a source to a receiver.

comparative advertising Advertising that compares one brand with a second named brand.

comparison shopping agents or shopbots Web applications that help online shoppers find what they are looking for at the lowest price and provide customer reviews and ratings of products and sellers.

compatibility The extent to which a new product is consistent with existing cultural values, customs, and practices.

compensatory decision rules The methods for making decisions that allow information about attributes of competing products to be averaged in some way.

competitive advantage A firm's edge over its competitors that allows it to have higher sales, higher profits, more customers and enjoy greater success year after year.

competitive intelligence (CI) The process of gathering and analyzing publicly available information about rivals.

competitive-parity method A promotion budgeting method in which an organization matches whatever competitors are spending.

complexity The degree to which consumers find a new product or its use difficult to understand.

component parts Manufactured goods or subassemblies of finished items that organizations need to complete their own products.

concentrated targeting strategy Focusing a firm's efforts on offering one or more products to a single segment.

conscientious consumerism A continuation of the consumerism movement in which consumers are much more mindful of environmental issues in their daily purchases and marketers support consumerism issues in their advertising.

consideration set The alternative brands a consumer seriously considers in making a decision.

consumer addiction A physiological or psychological dependency on goods or services including alcoholism, drug addiction, cigarettes, shopping, and use of the Internet.

consumer ethnocentrism Consumers' feeling that products from their own country are superior or that it is wrong to buy products produced in another country.

consumer goods The goods individual consumers purchase for personal or family use.

consumer packaged good (CPG) or fast-moving consumer good (FMCG) A low-cost good that is consumed quickly and replaced frequently.

consumer satisfaction/dissatisfaction The overall feelings or attitude a person has about a product after purchasing it.

consumerism A social movement that attempts to protect consumers from harmful business practices.

content marketing The strategy of establishing thought leadership in the form of bylines, blogs, commenting opportunities, videos, sharable social images, and infographics.

continuous innovation A modification of an existing product that sets one brand apart from its competitors.

contractual VMS A vertical marketing system in which cooperation is enforced by contracts (legal agreements) that spell out each member's rights and responsibilities and how they will cooperate.

contribution per unit The difference between the price the firm charges for a product and the variable costs.

control A process that entails measuring actual performance, comparing this performance to the established marketing objectives, and then making adjustments to the strategies or objectives on the basis of this analysis.

convenience product A consumer good or service that is usually low priced, widely available, and purchased frequently with a minimum of comparison and effort.

convenience sample A nonprobability sample composed of individuals who just happen to be available when and where the data are being collected.

convenience stores Neighborhood retailers that carry a limited number of frequently purchased items and cater to consumers willing to pay a premium for the ease of buying close to home.

conventional marketing system A multiple-level distribution channel in which channel members work independently of one another.

convergence The coming together of two or more technologies to create a new system with greater benefits than its separate parts.

conversion Signifies an event that occurs on a web page that indicates the meeting of a predefined goal associated with the consumer's interaction with that page.

cookies Text files inserted by a website sponsor into a web surfer's hard drive that allows the site to track the surfer's moves.

copycat packaging Packaging designed to mimic the look of a similar or functionally identical national branded product often meant to lead the consumer to perceive the two products as comparable.

core product All the benefits the product will provide for consumers or business customers.

corporate VMS A vertical marketing system in which a single firm owns manufacturing, wholesaling, and retailing operations.

corporate advertising Advertising that promotes the company as a whole instead of a firm's individual products.

corporate citizenship Also referred to a corporate social responsibility, refers to a firm's responsibility to the community in which they operate and to society in general.

corporate identity Materials such as logos, brochures, building design, and stationery that communicate an image of the organization.

corrective advertising Advertising that clarifies or qualifies previous deceptive advertising claims.

cost per thousand (CPM) A measure used to compare the relative cost-effectiveness of different media vehicles that have different exposure rates; the cost to deliver a message to 1,000 people or homes.

cost-per-click An online ad purchase in which the cost of the advertisement is charged only each time an individual clicks on the advertisement and is directed to the web page that the marketer placed within the advertisement.

cost-per-impression An online ad purchase in which the cost of the advertisement is charged each time the advertisement shows up on a page that the user views.

cost-per-order The cost of gaining an order in terms of the marketing investment made to turn a website visitor into a customer who has chosen to make a transaction.

cost-plus pricing A method of setting prices in which the seller totals all the costs for the product and then adds an amount to arrive at the selling price.

countertrade A type of trade in which goods are paid for with other items instead of with cash.

create assortments To provide a variety of products in one location to meet the needs of buyers.

creative brief A guideline or blueprint for the marketing communication program that guides the creative process.

creative selling process The process of seeking out potential customers, analyzing needs, determining how product attributes might provide benefits for the customer, and then communicating that information.

creative services The agency people (creative director, copywriters, and art director) who dream up and produce the ads.

creative strategy The process that turns a concept into an advertisement.

creativity A phenomenon whereby something new and valuable is created.

crisis management The process of managing a company's reputation when some negative event threatens the organization's image.

cross-elasticity of demand When changes in the price of one product affect the demand for another item.

cross-functional team A form on selling team where the team includes individuals from various areas of the firm.

cross-sectional design A type of descriptive technique that involves the systematic collection of quantitative information.

crowdfunding Online platforms that allow thousands of individuals to each contribute small amounts of money to fund a new product from a startup company.

crowdsourcing A practice where firms outsource marketing activities (such as selecting an ad) to a community of users.

cultural diversity A management practice that actively seeks to include people of different sexes, races, ethnic groups, and religions in an organization's employees, customers, suppliers, and distribution channel partners.

cultural values A society's deeply held beliefs about right and wrong ways to live.

culture The values, beliefs, customs, and tastes a group of people values.

consumer The ultimate user of a good or service.

consumer behavior The process involved when individuals or groups select, purchase, use, and dispose of goods, services, ideas, or experiences to satisfy their needs and desires.

customer relationship management (CRM) A systematic tracking of consumers' preferences and behaviors over time to tailor the value proposition as closely as possible to each individual's unique wants and needs.

custom research Research conducted for a single firm to provide specific information its managers need.

customer equity The financial value of a customer throughout the lifetime of the relationship.

customer insights The collection, deployment, and interpretation of information that allows a business to acquire, develop, and retain their customers.

customer orientation A business approach that prioritizes the satisfaction of customers' needs and wants.

customer profiling The act of tailoring the level of customer service based on a customer's perceived ability to pay.

customer reference program A formalized process by which customers formally share success stories and actively recommend products to other potential clients, usually facilitated through an online community.

customized marketing strategy An approach that tailors specific products and the messages about them to individual customers.

D

data Raw, unorganized facts that need to be processed.

data brokers Companies that collect information on consumers, use it to create detailed profiles of individuals, and sell or share the information with others.

data mining Sophisticated analysis techniques to take advantage of the massive amount of transaction information now available.

data scientist An individual who searches through multiple, disparate data sources to discover hidden insights that will provide a competitive advantage.

data warehouse A system to store and process the data that result from data mining.

database An organized collection (often electronic) of data that can be searched and queried to provide information about contacts, products, customers, inventory, and more.

decline stage The final stage in the product life cycle, during which sales decrease as customer needs change.

decoding The process by which a receiver assigns meaning to the message.

decoy pricing A pricing strategy where a seller offers at least three similar products; two have comparable but more expensive prices and one of these two is less attractive to buyers, thus causing more buyers to buy the higher priced more attractive item.

demand-based pricing A price-setting method based on estimates of demand at different prices.

demand Customers' desires for products coupled with the resources needed to obtain them.

demographics Statistics that measure observable aspects of a population, including size, age, gender, ethnic group, income, education, occupation, and family structure.

department stores Retailers that sell a broad range of items and offer a good selection within each product line.

derived demand Demand for business or organizational products caused by demand for consumer goods or services.

descriptive research A tool that probes more systematically into the problem and bases its conclusions on large numbers of observations.

destination retailer Firm that consumers view as distinctive enough to become loyal to it. Consumers go out of their way to shop there.

determinant attributes The features most important to differentiate and compare among the product choices.

developed countries A country that boasts sophisticated marketing systems, strong private enterprise, and bountiful market potential for many goods and services.

developing countries Countries in which the economy is shifting its emphasis from agriculture to industry.

differential benefit Properties of products that set them apart from competitors' products by providing unique customer benefits.

differentiated targeting strategy Developing one or more products for each of several distinct customer groups and making sure these offerings are kept separate in the marketplace.

diffusion The process by which the use of a product spreads throughout a population.

digital marketing channels The paths of distribution through which a company's digital marketing communications can be delivered to reach their respective audiences.

digital media Media that are digital rather than analog, including websites, mobile or cellular phones, and digital video, such as YouTube.

digital natives Individuals who spend a big chunk of their time online, so they expect brands to engage them in two-way digital conversations.

digital signage Out-of-home media that use digital technology to change the message at will.

digital wallets The use of Bluetooth technology that connects with customer smartphones and allows customers to pay for items without cash or even swiping a credit card.

direct channel A channel of distribution in which a manufacturer of a product or creator of a service distributes directly to the end customer.

direct mail A brochure or pamphlet that offers a specific good or service at one point in time.

direct marketing Any direct communication to a consumer or business recipient designed to generate a response in the form of an order, a request for further information, or a visit to a store or other place of business for purchase of a product.

direct selling An interactive sales process in which a salesperson presents a product to one individual or a small group, takes orders, and delivers the merchandise.

direct-response TV (DRTV) Advertising on TV that seeks a direct response, including short commercials of less than two minutes, 30-minute or longer infomercials, and home shopping networks.

direct-response advertising A direct marketing approach that allows the consumer to respond to a message by immediately contacting the provider to ask questions or order the product.

discontinuous innovation A totally new product that creates major changes in the way we live.

discretionary income The portion of income people have left over after paying for necessities such as housing, utilities, food, and clothing.

disintermediation (of the channel of distribution) The elimination of some layers of the channel of distribution to cut costs and improve the efficiency of the channel.

distinctive competency A superior capability of a firm in comparison to its direct competitors.

distribution center A warehouse that stores goods for short periods of time and that provides other functions, such as breaking bulk.

distribution intensity The number of intermediaries at each level of the channel.

distribution planning The process of developing distribution objectives, evaluating internal and external environmental influences on distribution, and choosing a distribution strategy.

diversification strategies Growth strategies that emphasize both new products and new markets.

diverter An entity that facilitates the distribution of a product through one or more channels not authorized for use by the manufacturer of the product.

do-it-yourself (DIY) ads Product ads that are created by consumers.

dogs SBUs with a small share of a slow-growth market. They are businesses that offer specialized products in limited markets that are not likely to grow quickly.

drones Unmanned aerial vehicles or flying robots controlled remotely using GPS technology.

dual or multiple distribution systems A system where producers, dealers, wholesalers, retailers, and customers participate in more than one type of channel.

dumping A company tries to get a toehold in a foreign market by pricing its products lower than it offers them at home.

durable goods Consumer products that provide benefits over a long period of time, such as cars, furniture, and appliances.

dynamic pricing A pricing strategy in which the price can easily be adjusted to meet changes in the marketplace.

dynamically continuous innovation A change in an existing product that requires a moderate amount of learning or behavior change.

E

e-commerce The buying or selling of goods and services electronically, usually over the Internet.

early adopters Those who adopt an innovation early in the diffusion process but after the innovators.

early majority Those whose adoption of a new product signals a general acceptance of the innovation.

earned media Word-of-mouth or buzz using social media where the advertiser has no control.

economic communities Groups of countries that band together to promote trade among themselves and to make it easier for member nations to compete elsewhere.

economic infrastructure The quality of a country's distribution, financial, and communications systems.

elastic demand Demand in which changes in price have large effects on the amount demanded.

embargo A quota completely prohibiting specified goods from entering or leaving a country.

emergency products Products we purchase when we're in dire need.

emotion analysis A sophisticated process for identifying and categorizing the emotions a follower possesses in relation to a product or brand by assessing the content of that communication.

encoding The process of translating an idea into a form of communication that will convey meaning.

encryption The process of scrambling a message so that only another individual (or computer) with the right "key" can unscramble it.

enterprise resource planning (ERP) systems A software system that integrates information from across the entire company, including finance, order fulfillment, manufacturing, and transportation, and then facilitates sharing of the data throughout the firm.

equipment Expensive goods that an organization uses in its daily operations that last for a long time.

ethical relativism Suggests that what is ethical in one culture is not necessarily the same as in another culture.

ethnography An approach to research based on observations of people in their own homes or communities.

evaluative criteria The dimensions consumers use to compare competing product alternatives.

evoked set All of the alternative brands a consumer is aware of when making a decision.

exchange The process by which some transfer of value occurs between a buyer and a seller.

exclusive distribution Selling a product only through a single outlet in a particular region.

execution format The basic structure of the message, such as comparison, demonstration, testimonial, slice of life, and lifestyle.

experiential merchandising Tactic whose intent is to convert shopping from a passive activity into a more interactive one, by better engaging the customer.

experiential shoppers Shoppers who shop because it satisfies their experiential needs, that is, their desire for fun.

experiments A technique that tests predicted relationships among variables in a controlled environment.

exploratory research A technique that marketers use to generate insights for future, more rigorous studies.

export merchants Intermediaries a firm uses to represent it in other countries.

exposure The extent to which a stimulus is capable of being registered by a person's sensory receptors.

expropriation When a domestic government seizes a foreign company's assets without any reimbursement.

external environment The uncontrollable elements outside an organization that may affect its performance either positively or negatively.

external validity The extent to which the results of a research study can be generalized to the population its sample was intended to represent, providing a higher level of confidence that the findings can be applied outside of the setting where the research was conducted.

extortion   When someone in authority extracts payment under duress.

extranet   A private, corporate computer network that links company departments, employees, and databases to suppliers, customers, and others outside the organization.

eye tracking technology   A type of mechanical observation technology that uses sensors and sophisticated software to track the position and movement of an individual's eyes to gain context-specific insights into how individuals interact with and respond to different visual elements and stimuli.

F

F.O.B. delivered pricing   A pricing tactic in which the cost of loading and transporting the product to the customer is included in the selling price and is paid by the manufacturer.

F.O.B. origin pricing (also known as F.O.B. factory pricing)   A pricing tactic in which the cost of transporting the product from the factory to the customer's location is the responsibility of the customer.

f-commerce   E-commerce that takes place on Facebook.

facilitating functions   Functions of channel intermediaries that make the purchase process easier for customers and manufacturers.

factory outlet store   A discount retailer, owned by a manufacturer, that sells off defective merchandise and excess inventory.

fair trade suppliers   Companies that pledge to pay a fair price to producers in developing countries, to ensure that the workers who produce the goods receive a fair wage, and to ensure that these manufacturers rely where possible on environmentally sustainable production practices.

fairness or justice approach   Ethical philosophy that advocates the decision that treats all human beings equally.

family branding   A brand that a group of individual products or individual brands share.

family life cycle   A means of characterizing consumers within a family structure on the basis of different stages through which people pass as they grow older.

fear appeals   Advertisements that highlight the negative consequences of *not* using a product by either focusing on physical harm or social disapproval.

feedback   Receivers' reactions to the message.

firewall   A combination of hardware and software that ensures that only authorized individuals gain entry into a computer system.

fixed costs   Costs of production that do not change with the number of units produced.

focus group   A product-oriented discussion among a small group of consumers led by a trained moderator.

folksonomy   A classification system that relies on users rather than preestablished systems to sort contents.

follow-up   Activities after the sale that provide important services to customers.

foreign exchange rate (forex rate)   the price of a nation's currency in terms of another currency.

Four Ps   Product, price, promotion, and place.

franchise organizations   A contractual vertical marketing system that includes a *franchiser* (a manufacturer or a service provider) who allows an entrepreneur (the *franchisee*) to use the franchise name and marketing plan for a fee.

franchising   A form of licensing involving the right to adapt an entire system of doing business.

free trade zones   Designated areas where foreign companies can warehouse goods without paying taxes or customs duties until they move the goods into the marketplace.

freemium pricing   A business strategy in which a product in its most basic version is provided free of charge but the company charges money (the premium) for upgraded versions of the product with more features, greater functionality, or greater capacity.

freight absorption pricing   A pricing tactic in which the seller absorbs the total cost of transportation.

frequency programs   Consumer sales promotion programs that offer a discount or free product for multiple purchases over time; also referred to as *loyalty* or *continuity programs*.

frequency   The average number of times a person in the target group will be exposed to the message.

full-service agency   An agency that provides most or all of the services needed to mount a campaign, including research, creation of ad copy and art, media selection, and production of the final messages.

full-service merchant wholesalers   Wholesalers that provide a wide range of services for their customers, including delivery, credit, product-use assistance, repairs, advertising, and other promotional support.

functional planning   A decision process that concentrates on developing detailed plans for strategies and tactics for the short term, supporting an organization's long-term strategic plan.

G

gamer segment   A consumer segment that combines a psychographic/lifestyle component with a heavy dose of generational marketing.

gamification   A strategy in which marketers apply game design techniques, often by awarding of points, badges, or levels, to non-game experiences to drive consumer behavior.

gap analysis   A marketing research method that measures the difference between a customer's expectation of a service quality and what actually occurred.

gender roles   Society's expectations regarding the appropriate attitudes, behaviors, and appearance for men and women.

General Agreement on Tariffs and Trade (GATT)   International treaty to reduce import tax levels and trade restrictions.

general merchandise discount stores   Retailers that offer a broad assortment of items at low prices with minimal service.

Generation X   The group of consumers born between 1965 and 1978.

Generation Y (millennials)   The group of consumers born between 1979 and 1994.

Generation Z   The group of consumers born after 1994.

generational marketing   Marketing to members of a generation, who tend to share the same outlook, values, and priorities.

generic branding   A strategy in which products are not branded and are sold at the lowest price possible.

geodemography   A segmentation technique that combines geography with demographics.

geographic information system (GIS)   A system that combines a geographic map with digitally stored data about the consumers in a particular geographic area.

geographic segmentation   An approach in which marketers tailor their offerings to specific geographic areas because people's preferences often vary depending on where they live.

geotargeting   Determining the geographic location of a website visitor and delivering different content to that visitor based on his or her location.

global warming   a warming of the planet that will have disastrous effects on the planet.

good   A tangible product that we can see, touch, smell, hear, or taste.

government markets   The federal, state, county, and local governments that buy goods and services to carry out public objectives and to support their operations.

gray market   A distribution channel in which a product's sale to a customer may be technically legal, but is at a minimum considered inappropriate by the manufacturer of the related product. Grey markets often emerge around high-end luxury goods sold through exclusive distribution.

gray market goods   Items manufactured outside a country and then imported without the consent of the trademark holder.

green customers   Those consumers who are most likely to actively look for and buy products that are eco-friendly.

green marketing   A marketing strategy that supports environmental stewardship, thus creating a differential benefit in the minds of consumers.

greenwashing   A practice in which companies promote their products as environmentally friendly when in truth the brand provides little ecological benefit.

gross domestic product (GDP)   The total dollar value of goods and services produced by a nation within its borders in a year.

gross margin   The markup amount added to the cost of a product to cover the fixed costs of the retailer or wholesaler and leave an amount for a profit.

gross rating points (GRPs)   A measure used for comparing the effectiveness of different media vehicles: average reach × frequency.

Greenhouse Effect   The turning of our atmosphere into a kind of greenhouse as a result of the addition of carbon dioxide and other greenhouse gasses.

Green River Ordinances   Community regulations that prohibit door-to-door selling unless prior permission is given by the household.

groundswell   A social trend in which people use technology to get the things they need from each other rather than from traditional institutions like corporations.

Group of 7 (G7)   An informal forum of the seven most economically developed countries that meets annually to discuss major economic and political issues facing the international community. Formerly the G8, Russia was excluded from the group as a result of its invasion of Crimea in 2014.

growth hackers   Experts who work on apps and sites to better hook consumers and keep them coming back and staying longer.

growth stage   The second stage in the product life cycle, during which consumers accept the product and sales rapidly increase.

guerrilla marketing   Marketing activity in which a firm "ambushes" consumers with promotional content in places they are not expecting to encounter this kind of activity.

H

haul videos   Videos consumers post on YouTube that detail the latest stuff they bought.

heuristics   A mental rule of thumb that leads to a speedy decision by simplifying the process.

hierarchy of effects   A series of steps prospective customers move through, from initial awareness of a product to brand loyalty.

hierarchy of needs   An approach that categorizes motives according to five levels of importance, the more basic needs being on the bottom of the hierarchy and the higher needs at the top.

high/low pricing   A retail pricing strategy in which the retailer prices merchandise at list price but runs frequent, often weekly, promotions that heavily discount some products.

horizontal marketing system   An arrangement within a channel of distribution in which two or more firms at the same channel level work together for a common purpose.

hybrid marketing system   A marketing system that uses a number of different channels and communication methods to serve a target market.

hypermarkets   Retailers with the characteristics of both warehouse stores and supermarkets; hypermarkets are several times larger than other stores and offer virtually everything from grocery items to electronics.

I

idea generation (ideation)   A phase of product development in which marketers use a variety of sources to come up with great new product ideas that provide customer benefits and that are compatible with the company mission.

idea marketing   Marketing activities that seek to gain market share for a concept, philosophy, belief, or issue by using elements of the marketing mix to create or change a target market's attitude or behavior.

import quotas   Limitations set by a government on the amount of a product allowed to enter a country.

impulse products   A product people often buy on the spur of the moment.

impulse purchase   A purchase made without any planning or search effort.

in-app advertising   To monetize free mobile phone apps, developers use advertising to create revenue and to engage the consumer.

independent intermediaries   Channel intermediaries that are not controlled by any manufacturer but instead do business with many different manufacturers and many different customers.

individualist cultures   Cultures in which people tend to attach more importance to personal goals than to those of the larger community.

industrial goods   Goods that individuals or organizations buy for further processing or for their own use when they do business.

inelastic demand   Demand in which changes in price have little or no effect on the amount demanded.

infomercials   Half-hour or hour-long commercials that resemble a talk show but actually are sales pitches.

information overload   A state in which the marketer is buried in so much data that it becomes nearly paralyzing to decide which of the data provide useful information and which do not.

information search   The process whereby a consumer searches for appropriate information to make a reasonable decision.

information   Interpreted data.

ingredient branding   A type of branding in which branded materials become "component parts" of other branded products.

innovation   A product that consumers perceive to be new and different from existing products.

innovators   The first segment (roughly 2.5 percent) of a population to adopt a new product.

input measures   Efforts that go into selling, such as the number and type of sales calls, expense account management, and a variety of nonselling activities, such as customer follow-up work and client service.

inseparability   The characteristic of a service that means that it is impossible to separate the production of a service from the consumption of that service.

insourcing   A practice in which a company contracts with a specialist firm to handle all or part of its supply chain operations.

institutional advertising   Advertising messages that promote the activities, personality, or point of view of an organization or company.

intangibility   The characteristic of a service that means customers can't see, touch, or smell good service.

intangibles Experience-based products.

intensive distribution Selling a product through all suitable wholesalers or retailers that are willing to stock and sell the product.

integrated marketing communication (IMC) A strategic business process that marketers use to plan, develop, execute, and evaluate coordinated, measurable, persuasive brand communication programs over time to targeted audiences.

internal PR PR activities aimed at employees of an organization.

internal customer mind-set An organizational culture in which all organization members treat each other as valued customers.

internal customers Coworkers that interact who harbor the attitude and belief that all activities ultimately impact external customers.

internal environment The controllable elements inside an organization, including its people, its facilities, and how it does things that influence the operations of the organization.

internal reference price A set price or a price range in consumers' minds that they refer to in evaluating a product's price.

internal validity The extent to which the results of a research study accurately measure what the study intended to measure by ensuring proper research design, including efforts to ensure that any potentially confounding factors were not included or introduced at any point during the execution of the research study.

Internet of Things Describes a system in which everyday objects are connected to the Internet and in turn are able to communicate information throughout an interconnected system.

Internet price discrimination An Internet pricing strategy that charges different prices to different customers for the same product.

International Monetary Fund (IMF) An international organization that seeks to ensure the stability of the international monetary exchange by controlling fluctuations in exchange rates.

interpretation The process of assigning meaning to a stimulus based on prior associations a person has with it and assumptions he or she makes about it.

intranet An internal corporate communication network that uses Internet technology to link company departments, employees, and databases.

introduction stage The first stage of the product life cycle, in which slow growth follows the introduction of a new product in the marketplace.

inventory control Activities to ensure that goods are always available to meet customers' demands.

inventory turnover or inventory turns The number of times a firm's inventory completely cycles through during a defined time frame.

investor relations PR activities such as annual and quarterly reports aimed at a firm's investors.

involvement The relative importance of perceived consequences of the purchase to a consumer.

ISO 9000 Criteria developed by the International Organization for Standardization to regulate product quality in Europe.

J

jingles Original words and music written specifically for advertising executions.

joint demand Demand for two or more goods that are used together to create a product.

joint venture A strategic alliance in which a new entity owned by two or more firms allows the partners to pool their resources for common goals.

just in time (JIT) Inventory management and purchasing processes that manufacturers and resellers use to reduce inventory to very low levels and ensure that deliveries from suppliers arrive only when needed.

K

key account Very large customer organizations with the potential for providing significant sales revenue.

keystoning retail pricing strategy in which the retailer doubles the cost of the item (100 percent markup) to determine the price.

knockoff A new product that copies, with slight modification, the design of an original product.

knowledge management A comprehensive approach to collecting, organizing, storing, and retrieving a firm's information assets.

L

laggards The last consumers to adopt an innovation.

lagging indicators Performance indicators that provide insight into the performance of an action plan based on outcomes realized.

landing page A single page on a website that is built for a particular direct marketing opportunity.

late majority The adopters who are willing to try new products when there is little or no risk associated with the purchase, when the purchase becomes an economic necessity, or when there is social pressure to purchase.

leading indicators Performance indicators that provide insight into the performance of *current efforts* in a way that allows a marketer to adjust relevant marketing activities (hopefully) resulting in performance improvements against the current action plan.

learning A relatively permanent change in behavior caused by acquired information or experience.

leased departments Departments within a larger retail store that an outside firm rents.

least developed country (LDC) A country at the lowest stage of economic development.

level loading A manufacturing approach intended to balance the inventory holding capabilities and production capacity constraints of a manufacturer for a particular product through the implementation of a consistent production schedule, employed both during and beyond periods of peak demand.

level of economic development The broader economic picture of a country.

licensing agreement An agreement in which one firm gives another firm the right to produce and market its product in a specific country or region in return for royalties.

licensing An agreement in which one firm sells another firm the right to use a brand name for a specific purpose and for a specific period of time.

lifestyle advertising Lifestyle ads show a person(s), attractive to the target market, in an appealing setting with the advertised product as "part of the scene," implying that the person who buys it will attain the lifestyle.

lifestyle The pattern of living that determines how people choose to spend their time, money, and energy and that reflects their values, tastes, and preferences.

lifetime value of a customer The potential profit a single customer's purchase of a firm's products generates over the customer's lifetime.

limited-service agency An agency that provides one or more specialized services, such as media buying or creative development.

limited-service merchant wholesalers Wholesalers that provide fewer services for their customers.

list price or manufacturer's suggested retail price (MSRP) The price that the manufacturer sets as the appropriate price for the end consumer to pay.

lobbying Talking with and providing information to government officials to influence their activities relating to an organization.

local content rules A form of protectionism stipulating that a certain proportion of a product must consist of components supplied by industries in the host country or economic community.

location-based social networks Networks that integrate sophisticated GPS technology that enables users to alert friends of their exact whereabouts via their mobile phones.

locavorism The trend for shoppers to actively look for products that come from farms within 50 to 100 miles of where they live.

logistics The process of designing, managing, and improving the movement of products through the supply chain. Logistics includes purchasing, manufacturing, storage, and transport.

long tail A new approach to segmentation based on the idea that companies can make money by selling small amounts of items that only a few people want, provided they sell enough different items.

longitudinal design A technique that tracks the responses of the same sample of respondents over time.

loss-leader pricing The pricing policy of setting prices very low or even below cost to attract customers into a store.

M

m-commerce Promotional and other e-commerce activities transmitted over mobile phones and other mobile devices, such as smartphones and personal digital assistants.

maintenance, repair, and operating (MRO) products Goods that a business customer consumes in a relatively short time.

mall intercept A study in which researchers recruit shoppers in malls or other public areas.

malware Software designed specifically to damage or disrupt computer systems.

mar-tech Short for "marketing technology," this term is commonly used to denote the fusion of marketing and technology. A particular focus is placed on the application of marketing through digital technologies.

margin on sales The difference between the price at which a product is sold and the cost of the product.

market development strategies Growth strategies that introduce existing products to new markets.

market fragmentation The creation of many consumer groups due to a diversity of distinct needs and wants in modern society.

market intelligence system A method by which marketers get information about what's going on in the world that is relevant to their business.

market manager An individual who is responsible for developing and implementing the marketing plans for products sold to a particular customer group.

market penetration strategies Growth strategies designed to increase sales of existing products to current customers, nonusers, and users of competitive brands in served markets.

market planning The functional planning marketers do. Market planning typically includes both a broad three- to five-year marketing plan to support the firm's strategic plan and a detailed annual plan for the coming year.

market research ethics Taking an ethical and aboveboard approach to conducting market research that does no harm to the participant in the process of conducting the research.

market research online community (MROC) A privately assembled group of people, usually by a market research firm or department, utilized to gain insight into customer sentiments and tendencies.

market research The process of collecting, analyzing, and interpreting data about customers, competitors, and the business environment in order to improve marketing effectiveness.

market segment A distinct group of customers within a larger market who are similar to one another in some way and whose needs differ from other customers in the larger market.

market share The percentage of a market (defined in terms of either sales units or revenue) accounted for by a specific firm, product lines, or brands.

market test or test market Testing the complete marketing plan in a small geographic area that is similar to the larger market the firm hopes to enter.

market All the customers and potential customers who share a common need that can be satisfied by a specific product, who have the resources to exchange for it, who are willing to make the exchange, and who have the authority to make the exchange.

marketing analytics A group of technologies and processes that enable marketers to collect, measure, analyze, and assess the effectiveness of marketing efforts.

marketing automation A group of systems and technologies that can be used to establish a set of rules for handling different marketing related processes in an automated fashion.

marketing concept A management orientation that focuses on identifying and satisfying consumer needs to ensure the organization's long-term profitability.

marketing decision support system (MDSS) The data, analysis software, and interactive software that allow managers to conduct analyses and find the information they need.

marketing information system (MIS) A process that first determines what information marketing managers need and then gathers, sorts, analyzes, stores, and distributes relevant and timely marketing information to system users.

marketing metrics Specific measures that help marketers watch the performance of their marketing campaigns, initiatives, and channels and, when appropriate, serve as a control mechanism.

marketing mix A combination of the product itself, the price of the product, the promotional activities that introduce it, and the place where it is made available, that together create a desired response among a set of predefined consumers.

marketing plan A document that describes the marketing environment, outlines the marketing objectives and strategy, and identifies how the company will implement and control the strategies embedded in the plan.

marketing scorecards Feedback vehicles that report (often in quantified terms) how the company or brand is actually doing in achieving various goals.

marketing Marketing is the activity, set of institutions, and processes for creating, communicating, delivering, and exchanging offerings that have value for customers, clients, partners, and society at large.

marketplace Any location or medium used to conduct an exchange.

markup An amount added to the cost of a product to create the price at which a channel member will sell the product.

mass class The hundreds of millions of global consumers who now enjoy a level of purchasing power that's sufficient to let them afford high-quality products—except for big-ticket items like college educations, housing, or luxury cars.

mass communication Relates to TV, radio, magazines, and newspapers.

mass customization An approach that modifies a basic good or service to meet the needs of an individual.

mass market All possible customers in a market, regardless of the differences in their specific needs and wants.

materials handling   The moving of products into, within, and out of warehouses.

maturity stage   The third and longest stage in the product life cycle, during which sales peak and profit margins narrow.

mechanical observation   A method of primary data collection that relies on machines to capture human behavior in a form that allows for future analysis and interpretation.

media blitz   A massive advertising campaign that occurs over a relatively short time frame.

media planners   Agency personnel who determine which communication vehicles are the most effective and efficient to deliver the ad.

media planning   The process of developing media objectives, strategies, and tactics for use in an advertising campaign.

media relations   A PR activity aimed at developing close relationships with the media.

media schedule   The plan that specifies the exact media to use and when to use it.

medium   A communication vehicle through which a message is transmitted to a target audience.

merchandise agents or brokers   Channel intermediaries that provide services in exchange for commissions but never take title to the product.

merchandise assortment   The range of products a store sells.

merchandise breadth   The number of different product lines available.

merchandise depth   The variety of choices available for each specific product line.

merchandise mix   The total set of all products offered for sale by a retailer, including all product lines sold to all consumer groups.

merchandising allowance   Reimburses the retailer for in-store support of the product.

merchant wholesalers   Intermediaries that buy goods from manufacturers (take title to them) and sell to retailers and other B2B customers.

message   The communication in physical form that goes from a sender to a receiver.

metrics   Measurements or "scorecards" that marketers use to identify the effectiveness of different strategies or tactics.

metrosexual   A straight, urban male who is keenly interested in fashion, home design, gourmet cooking, and personal care.

microcultures   Groups of consumers who identify with a specific activity or art form.

micromarketing   The ability to identify and target very small geographic segments that sometimes amount to individuals.

mission statement   A formal statement in an organization's strategic plan that describes the overall purpose of the organization and what it intends to achieve in terms of its customers, products, and resources.

missionary salesperson   A salesperson who promotes the firm and tries to stimulate demand for a product but does not actually complete a sale.

mobile advertising   A form of advertising that is communicated to the consumer via a handset.

mobile hijacking   The use of automated browsers to falsify the number of views or click-throughs the advertisers must pay for.

mobile marketing   Interacting with consumers via mobile devices (i.e., phones, tablets, and wearable screens such as smart watches).

modified rebuy   A buying situation classification used by business buyers to categorize a previously made purchase that involves some change and that requires limited decision making.

monetize   The act of turning an asset into money. Websites and mobile apps monetize their content through advertisers.

monopolistic competition   A market structure in which many firms, each having slightly different products, offer unique consumer benefits.

monopoly   A market situation in which one firm, the only supplier of a particular product, is able to control the price, quality, and supply of that product.

motivation   An internal state that drives us to satisfy needs by activating goal-oriented behavior.

multichannel promotion strategy   A marketing communication strategy where they combine traditional advertising, sales promotion, and public relations activities with online buzz-building activities.

multilevel or network marketing   A system in which a master distributor recruits other people to become distributors, sells the company's product to the recruits, and receives a commission on all the merchandise sold by the people recruited.

multilevel selling   A form of team selling in which the team consists of company personnel from various managerial levels, each calling on their counterpart in the customer organization.

multiple sourcing   The business practice of buying a particular product from several different suppliers.

multitasking   Moving back and forth between various activities such as e-mails TV, instant messages, and so on.

N

national or manufacturer brands   Brands that the product manufacturer owns.

nationalization   When a domestic government reimburses a foreign company (often not for the full value) for its assets after taking it over.

native advertising   An execution strategy that mimics the content of the website where the message appears.

need   The recognition of any difference between a consumer's actual state and some ideal or desired state.

neuromarketing   A type of brain research that uses technologies such as functional magnetic resonance imaging (fMRI) to measure brain activity to better understand why consumers make the decisions they do.

new product development (NPD)   The phases by which firms develop new products, including idea generation, product concept development and screening, marketing strategy development, business analysis, technical development, test marketing, and commercialization.

new-business salesperson   The person responsible for finding new customers and calling on them to present the company's products.

new-task buy   A new business-to-business purchase that is complex or risky and that requires extensive decision making.

noise   Anything that interferes with effective communication.

nondurable goods   Consumer products that provide benefits for a short time because they are consumed (such as food) or are no longer useful (such as newspapers).

nonprobability sample   A sample in which personal judgment is used to select respondents.

nonstore retailing   Any method used to complete an exchange with a product end user that does not require a customer visit to a store.

North American Industry Classification System (NAICS)   The numerical coding system that the United States, Canada, and Mexico use to classify firms into detailed categories according to their business activities.

not-for-profit organizations (also known as nongovernmental organizations [NGOs])   Organizations with charitable, educational, community, and other public service goals that buy goods and services to support their functions and to attract and serve their members.

O

objective-task method A promotion budgeting method in which an organization first defines the specific communication goals it hopes to achieve and then tries to calculate what kind of promotion efforts it will take to meet these goals.

observability How visible a new product and its benefits are to others who might adopt it.

observational learning Learning that occurs when people watch the actions of others and note what happens to them as a result.

off-price retailers Retailers that buy excess merchandise from well-known manufacturers and pass the savings on to customers.

offshoring A process by which companies contract with companies or individuals in remote places like China or India to perform work they used to do at home.

oligopoly A market structure in which a relatively small number of sellers, each holding a substantial share of the market, compete in a market with many buyers.

omnichannel (omni-channel) marketing A retail strategy that provides a seamless shopping experience, whether the customer is shopping online from a desktop or mobile device, by telephone or in a brick-and-mortar store.

one-to-one marketing Facilitated by CRM, one-to-one marketing allows for customization of some aspect of the goods or services that are offered to each customer.

online auctions E-commerce that allows shoppers to purchase products through online bidding.

online distribution piracy The theft and unauthorized repurposing of intellectual property via the Internet.

operant conditioning Learning that occurs as the result of rewards or punishments.

operational planning A decision process that focuses on developing detailed plans for day-to-day activities that carry out an organization's functional plans.

operational plans Plans that focus on the day-to-day execution of the marketing plan. Operational plans include detailed directions for the specific activities to be carried out, who will be responsible for them, and time lines to accomplish the tasks.

opinion leader A person who is frequently able to influence others' attitudes or behaviors by virtue of his or her active interest and expertise in one or more product categories.

order getter A salesperson who works to develop long-term relationships with particular customers or to generate new sales.

order processing The series of activities that occurs between the time an order comes into the organization and the time a product goes out the door.

order taker A salesperson whose primary function is to facilitate transactions that the customer initiates.

organizational demographics Organization-specific dimensions that can be used to describe, classify, and organize different organizations for the purpose of segmenting business-to-business markets.

organizational markets Another name for business-to-business markets.

organized retail crime (ORC) Retail shoplifting by organized gangs of thieves that get away with thousands of dollars in goods in a single day.

out-of-home media Communication media that reach people in public places.

outcome metrics Metrics focused on measuring and tracking specific events identified as key business outcomes that result from marketing processes.

output measures The results of the salesperson's efforts.

outsourcing The business buying process of obtaining outside vendors to provide goods or services that otherwise might be supplied in house.

owned media Internet sites, such as websites, blogs, Facebook, and Twitter accounts, that are owned by an advertiser.

P

package The covering or container for a product that provides product protection, facilitates product use and storage, and supplies important marketing communication.

paid influencer programs Another form of sock puppeting in which bloggers are paid or rewarded in some way for attempting to start online conversations about a brand.

paid media Internet media, such as display ads, sponsorships, and paid key word searches, that are paid for by an advertiser.

partner relationship management (PRM) Similar to a CRM, the PRM system allows both selling and buying firms to share some of their information.

party plan system A sales technique that relies heavily on people getting caught up in the "group spirit," buying things they would not normally buy if they were alone.

patent A legal mechanism to prevent competitors from producing or selling an invention, aimed at reducing or eliminating competition in a market for a period of time.

payment pricing A pricing tactic that breaks up the total price into smaller amounts payable over time.

peak load pricing A pricing plan that sets prices higher during periods with higher demand.

penetration pricing A pricing strategy in which a firm introduces a new product at a very low price to encourage more customers to purchase it.

perceived risk The belief that choice of a product has potentially negative consequences, whether financial, physical, or social.

percentage-of-sales method A method for promotion budgeting that is based on a certain percentage of either last year's sales or estimates of the present year's sales.

perception The process by which people select, organize, and interpret information from the outside world.

perceptual map A technique to visually describe where brands are "located" in consumers' minds relative to competing brands.

perfect competition A market structure in which many small sellers, all of whom offer similar products, are unable to have an impact on the quality, price, or supply of a product.

perishability The characteristic of a service that makes it impossible to store for later sale or consumption.

permission marketing E-mail advertising in which online consumers have the opportunity to accept or refuse the unsolicited e-mail.

perpetual inventory unit control system Retail computer system that keeps a running total on sales, returns, transfers to other stores, and so on.

personal selling Marketing communication by which a company representative interacts directly with a customer or prospective customer to communicate about a good or service.

personality The set of unique psychological characteristics that consistently influences the way a person responds to situations in the environment.

physical distribution The activities that move finished goods from manufacturers to final customers, including order processing, warehousing, materials handling, transportation, and inventory control.

place marketing Marketing activities that seek to attract new businesses, residents, or visitors to a town, state, country, or some other site.

place-based media Advertising media that transmit messages in public places, such as doctors' offices and airports, where certain types of people congregate.

place The availability of the product to the customer at the desired time and location.

point-of-purchase (POP) displays In-store displays and signs.

point-of-sale (POS) systems Retail computer systems that collect sales data and are hooked directly into the store's inventory-control system.

pop-up ad An advertisement that appears on the screen while a web page loads or after it has loaded.

pop-up stores Retail stores, such as Halloween costume stores, that "pop up" one day and then disappear after a period of one day to a few months.

portfolio analysis A management tool for evaluating a firm's business mix and assessing the potential of an organization's strategic business units.

positioning statement An expression of a product's positioning that is internally developed and maintained in order to support the development of marketing communication that articulates the specific value offered by a product.

positioning Developing a marketing strategy to influence how a particular market segment perceives a good or service in comparison to the competition.

posttesting Research conducted on consumers' responses to actual advertising messages they have seen or heard.

preapproach A part of the selling process that includes developing information about prospective customers and planning the sales interview.

predatory pricing An illegal pricing strategy in which a company sets a very low price for the purpose of driving competitors out of business.

predictive analytics Uses large quantities of data within variables that have identified relationships to more accurately predict specific future outcomes.

predictive technology Analysis techniques that use shopping patterns of large numbers of people to determine which products are likely to be purchased if others are.

premiums Items offered free to people who have purchased a product.

press release Information that an organization distributes to the media intended to win publicity.

prestige pricing or premium pricing A pricing strategy used by luxury goods marketers in which they keep the price artificially high to maintain a favorable image of the product.

prestige products Products that have a high price and that appeal to status-conscious consumers.

pretesting A research method that seeks to minimize mistakes by getting consumer reactions to ad messages before they appear in the media.

price The assignment of value, or the amount the consumer must exchange to receive the offering.

price bundling Selling two or more goods or services as a single package for one price.

price elasticity of demand The percentage change in unit sales that results from a percentage change in price.

price fixing The collaboration of two or more firms in setting prices, usually to keep prices high.

price leadership A pricing strategy in which one firm first sets its price and other firms in the industry follow with the same or similar prices.

price lining The practice of setting a limited number of different specific prices, called *price points*, for items in a product line.

price segmentation the practice of charging different prices to different market segments for the same product.

primary data Data from research conducted to help make a specific decision.

private-label brands Brands that a certain retailer or distributor owns and sells.

probability sample A sample in which each member of the population has some known chance of being included.

problem recognition The process that occurs whenever the consumer sees a significant difference between his or her current state of affairs and some desired or ideal state; this recognition initiates the decision-making process.

processed materials Products created when firms transform raw materials from their original state.

producers The individuals or organizations that purchase products for use in the production of other goods and services.

product adaptation strategy Product strategy in which a firm offers a similar but modified product in foreign markets.

product adoption The process by which a consumer or business customer begins to buy and use a new good, service, or idea.

product advertising Advertising messages that focus on a specific good or service.

product category managers Individuals who are responsible for developing and implementing the marketing plan for all the brands and products within a product category.

product competition When firms offering different products compete to satisfy the same consumer needs and wants.

product concept development and screening The second step of product development in which marketers test product ideas for technical and commercial success.

product development strategies Growth strategies that focus on selling new products in existing markets.

product diversion The distribution of a product through one or more channels not authorized for use by the manufacturer of the product.

product invention strategy Product strategy in which a firm develops a new product for foreign markets.

product life cycle (PLC) A concept that explains how products go through four distinct stages from birth to death: introduction, growth, maturity, and decline.

product line length Determined by the number of separate items within the same category.

product line A firm's total product offering designed to satisfy a single need or desire of target customers.

product management The systematic and usually team-based approach to coordinating all aspects of a product's strategy development and execution.

product mix width The number of different product lines the firm produces.

product mix The total set of all products a firm offers for sale.

product quality The overall ability of the product to satisfy customer expectations.

product review sites Social media sites that enable people to post stories about their experiences with products and services.

product sampling Distributing free trial-size versions of a product to consumers.

product specifications A written description of the quality, size, weight, and other details required of a product purchase.

product A tangible good, service, idea, or some combination of these that satisfies consumer or business customer needs through the exchange process; a bundle of attributes including features, functions, benefits, and uses.

production orientation   A management philosophy that emphasizes the most efficient ways to produce and distribute products.

promo pricing   A different name for high/low pricing.

promotion mix   The communication elements that the marketer controls.

promotion   The coordination of a marketer's communication efforts to influence attitudes or behavior.

promotional products   Goodies such as coffee mugs, T-shirts, and magnets given away to build awareness for a sponsor. Some freebies are distributed directly to consumers and business customers; others are intended for channel partners, such as retailers and vendors.

prospecting   A part of the selling process that includes identifying and developing a list of potential or prospective customers.

protectionism   A policy adopted by a government to give domestic companies an advantage.

prototypes   Test versions of a proposed product.

psychographics   The use of psychological, sociological, and anthropological factors to construct market segments.

public relations (PR)   Communication function that seeks to build good relationships with an organization's publics, including consumers, stockholders, and legislators.

public relations campaign   A coordinated effort to communicate with one or more of the firm's publics.

public service advertisements (PSAs)   Advertising run by the media for not-for-profit organizations or to champion a particular cause without charge.

publicity   Unpaid communication about an organization that appears in the mass media.

puffery   Claims made in advertising of product superiority that cannot be proven true or untrue.

pull strategy   The company tries to move its products through the channel by building desire for the products among consumers, thus convincing retailers to respond to this demand by stocking these items.

push money   A bonus paid by a manufacturer to a salesperson, customer, or distributor for selling its product.

push strategy   The company tries to move its products through the channel by convincing channel members to offer them.

pyramid schemes   An illegal sales technique that promises consumers or investors large profits from recruiting others to join the program rather than from any real investment or sale of goods to the public.

Q

QR code advertising   QR (quick response) code advertising uses smartphone GPS technology to deliver ads and other information to consumers in stores and in other locations.

quantity discounts   A pricing tactic of charging reduced prices for purchases of larger quantities of a product.

question marks   SBUs with low market shares in fast-growth markets.

R

radio frequency identification (RFID)   Product tags with tiny chips containing information about the item's content, origin, and destination.

raw materials   Products of the fishing, lumber, agricultural, and mining industries that organizational customers purchase to use in their finished products.

reach   The percentage of the target market that will be exposed to the media vehicle.

rebates   Sales promotions that allow the customer to recover part of the product's cost from the manufacturer.

receiver   The organization or individual that intercepts and interprets the message.

reciprocity   A trading partnership in which two firms agree to buy from one another.

reference group   An actual or imaginary individual or group that has a significant effect on an individual's evaluations, aspirations, or behavior.

relationship selling   A form of personal selling that involves securing, developing, and maintaining long-term relationships with profitable customers.

relative advantage   The degree to which a consumer perceives that a new product provides superior benefits.

reliability   The extent to which research measurement techniques are free of errors.

reminder advertising   Advertising aimed at keeping the name of a brand in people's minds to be sure consumers purchase the product as necessary.

rentrepreneurs   Enterprising consumers who make money by renting out their possessions when they aren't using them.

repositioning   Redoing a product's position to respond to marketplace changes.

representativeness   The extent to which consumers in a study are similar to a larger group in which the organization has an interest.

research and development (R&D)   A well-defined and systematic approach to how innovation is done within the firm.

research and marketing services   The advertising agency department that collects and analyzes information that will help account executives develop a sensible strategy and assist creatives in getting consumer reactions to different versions of ads.

research design   A plan that specifies what information marketers will collect and what type of study they will do.

resellers   The individuals or organizations that buy finished goods for the purpose of reselling, renting, or leasing to others to make a profit and to maintain their business operations.

retail and local advertising   Advertising that informs consumers about store hours, location, and products that are available or on sale.

retail borrowing   The consumer practice of purchasing a product with the intent to return the nondefective merchandise for a refund after it has fulfilled the purpose for which it was purchased.

retailer cooperative   A group of retailers that establishes a wholesaling operation to help them compete more effectively with the large chains.

retailing   The final stop in the distribution channel in which organizations sell goods and services to consumers for their personal use.

retailer margin   The margin added to the cost of a product by a retailer.

retailtainment   The use of retail strategies that enhance the shopping experience and create excitement, impulse purchases, and an emotional connection with the brand.

retro brands   A once-popular brand that has been revived to experience a popularity comeback, often by riding a wave of nostalgia.

return on investment (ROI)   The direct financial impact of a firm's expenditure of a resource, such as time or money.

return on marketing investment (ROMI)   Quantifying just how an investment in marketing has an impact on the firm's success, financially and otherwise.

reverse engineering   The process of physically deconstructing a competitor's product to determine how it's put together.

reverse logistics   Includes product returns, recycling and material reuse, and waste disposal.

reverse marketing   A business practice in which a buyer firm attempts to identify suppliers who will produce products according to the buyer firm's specifications.

rich media   A digital advertising term for an ad that includes advanced features like video and audio that encourage viewers to interact and engage with the content.

rights approach   Ethical philosophy that advocates the decision that does the best job of protecting the moral rights of all.

risk-taking functions   The chance retailers take on the loss of a product when they buy a product from a manufacturer because the product sits on the shelf because no customers want it.

S

sachet   Affordable one-use packages of cleaning products, fabric softeners, shampoo, etc., for sale to consumers in least developed and developing countries.

sadvertising   Advertising designed to arouse more negative emotions to get our attention and create a bond with their products.

sales presentation   The part of the selling process in which the salesperson directly communicates the value proposition to the customer and invites two-way communication.

sales promotion   Programs designed to build interest in or encourage purchase of a product during a specified period.

sampling   The process of selecting respondents for a study.

scanner data   Data derived from items that are scanned at the cash register when you check out with your loyalty card.

screen addicts   Consumers who spend so much time on smartphones, tablets, and computers that it interferes with more normal activities and productivity.

search engine marketing (SEM)   Search marketing strategy in which marketers pay for ads or better positioning.

search engine optimization (SEO)   A systematic process to ensure that your firm comes up at or near the top of lists of typical search phrases related to your business.

search engines   Internet programs that search for documents with specified key words.

search marketing   Marketing strategies that involve the use of Internet search engines.

seasonal discounts   Price reductions offered only during certain times of the year.

secondary data   Data that have been collected for some purpose other than the problem at hand.

segment profile   A description of the "typical" customer in a segment.

segmentation variables   Dimensions that divide the total market into fairly homogeneous groups, each with different needs and preferences.

segmentation   The process of dividing a larger market into smaller pieces based on one or more meaningfully shared characteristics.

selective distribution   Distribution using fewer outlets than intensive distribution but more than exclusive distribution.

self-concept   An individual's self-image that is composed of a mixture of beliefs, observations, and feelings about personal attributes.

selling orientation   A managerial view of marketing as a sales function, or a way to move products out of warehouses to reduce inventory.

sensory branding   The use of distinct sensory experiences not only to appeal to customers but also to enhance their brand.

sensory marketing   Marketing techniques that link distinct sensory experiences such as a unique fragrance with a product or service.

sentiment analysis   The process of identifying a follower's attitude (e.g., "positive," "negative," or "neutral") toward a product or brand by assessing the context or emotion of his or her comments.

service encounter   The actual interaction between the customer and the service provider.

service retailer   Organization that offers consumers services rather than merchandise. Examples include banks, hospitals, health spas, doctors, legal clinics, entertainment firms, and universities.

services   Intangible products that are exchanged directly between the producer and the customer.

servicescape   The actual physical facility where the service is performed, delivered, and consumed.

SERVQUAL   A multiple-item scale used to measure service quality across dimensions of tangibles, reliability, responsiveness, assurance, and empathy.

share of customer   The percentage of an individual customer's purchase of a product that is a single brand.

shopping cart abandonment   Occurs when e-commerce customers leave an e-commerce site with unpurchased items in their cart.

shopping for control   Consumers, facing a world with terrorism and political unrest, value products and services that provide some degree of control, such as installing smart home technology or moving to gated communities.

shopping products   Goods or services for which consumers spend considerable time and effort gathering information and comparing alternatives before making a purchase.

shrinkage   Losses experienced by retailers as a result of shoplifting, employee theft, and damage to merchandise.

simulated market test   Application of special computer software to imitate the introduction of a product into the marketplace allowing the company to see the likely impact of price cuts and new packaging—or even to determine where in the store it should try to place the product.

single sourcing   The business practice of buying a particular product from only one supplier.

situation analysis   An assessment of a firm's internal and external environments.

Six Sigma   A process whereby firms work to limit product defects to 3.4 per million or fewer.

skimming price   A very high, premium price that a firm charges for its new, highly desirable product.

slice-of-life advertising   A slice-of-life ad presents a (dramatized) scene from everyday life.

slogans   Simple, memorable linguistic devices linked to a brand.

slotting allowance   A fee paid in exchange for agreeing to place a manufacturer's products on a retailer's valuable shelf space.

social class   The overall rank or social standing of groups of people within a society according to the value assigned to factors such as family background, education, occupation, and income.

social media   Internet-based platforms that allow users to create their own content and share it with others who access these sites.

social networking platforms   Online platforms that allow a user to represent himself or herself via a profile on a website and provide and receive links to other members of the network to share input about common interests.

social networks   Online platforms that allow a user to represent himself or herself via a profile on a website and provide and receive links to other members of the network to share input about common interests.

social norms   Specific rules dictating what is right or wrong, acceptable or unacceptable.

societal marketing concept A management philosophy that marketers must satisfy customers' needs in ways that also benefit society and deliver profit to the firm.

sock puppeting An practice where a company executive or other biased source poses as someone else to plug a product in social media.

source An organization or individual that sends a message.

spam The use of electronic media to send unsolicited messages in bulk.

special events Activities—from a visit by foreign investors to a company picnic—that are planned and implemented by a PR department.

specialized services Services that are essential to the operation of an organization but are not part of the production of a product.

specialty products Goods or services that have unique characteristics and are important to the buyer and for which he or she will devote significant effort to acquire.

specialty stores Retailers that carry only a few product lines but offer good selection within the lines that they sell.

speech writing Writing a speech on a topic for a company executive to deliver.

sponsored search ads Paid ads that appear at the top or beside the Internet search engine results.

sponsorships PR activities through which companies provide financial support to help fund an event in return for publicized recognition of the company's contribution.

stakeholders Buyers, sellers, or investors in a company; community residents; and even citizens of the nations where goods and services are made or sold; in other words, any person or organization that has a "stake" in the outcome.

standard of living An indicator of the average quality and quantity of goods and services consumed in a country.

staple products Basic or necessary items that are available almost everywhere.

stars SBUs with products that have a dominant market share in high-growth markets.

status symbols Visible markers that provide a way for people to flaunt their membership in higher social classes (or at least to make others believe they are members).

stock-keeping unit (SKU) A unique identifier for each distinct product.

stock-outs Zero-inventory situations resulting in lost sales and customer dissatisfaction.

straight extension strategy Product strategy in which a firm offers the same product in both domestic and foreign markets.

straight rebuy A buying situation in which business buyers make routine purchases that require minimal decision making.

strategic alliance Relationship developed between a firm seeking a deeper commitment to a foreign market and a domestic firm in the target country.

strategic business units (SBUs) Individual units within the firm that operate like separate businesses, with each having its own mission, business objectives, resources, managers, and competitors.

strategic planning A managerial decision process that matches an organization's resources and capabilities to its market opportunities for long-term growth.

structured data Data that (1) are typically numeric or categorical; (2) can be organized and formatted in a way that is easy for computers to read, organize, and understand; and (3) can be inserted into a database in a seamless fashion.

sub-branding Creating a secondary brand within a main brand that can help differentiate a product line to a desired target group.

subculture A group within a society whose members share a distinctive set of beliefs, characteristics, or common experiences.

subliminal advertising Supposedly hidden messages in marketers' communications.

subscription boxes A new business model for distribution that supplies surprises by sending out a box each month filled with items you never knew you wanted but you just have to have.

supercenters Large combination stores that combine economy supermarkets with other lower-priced merchandise.

supermarkets Food stores that carry a wide selection of edibles and related products.

supply chain management The management of flows among firms in the supply chain to maximize total profitability.

supply chain All the activities necessary to turn raw materials into a good or service and put it in the hands of the consumer or business customer.

support media Media such as directories or out-of-home media that may be used to reach people who are not reached by mass-media advertising.

surge pricing A pricing plan that raises prices of a product as demand goes up and lowers it as demand slides.

sustainability metrics Tools that measure the benefits an organization achieves through the implementation of sustainability.

sustainability A product design focus that seeks to create products that meet present consumer needs without compromising the ability of future generations to meet their needs.

sustainable packaging Packaging that involves one or more of the following: elements of the packaging that can be produced from previously used materials, elements of the packaging that use materials in their development that can be repurposed after use, the use of materials that require fewer resources to cultivate, and the use of materials and processes that are generally less harmful to the environment.

SWOT analysis An analysis of an organization's strengths and weaknesses and the opportunities and threats in its external environment.

syndicated research Research by firms that collect data on a regular basis and sell the reports to multiple firms.

T

take title To accept legal ownership of a product and assume the accompanying rights and responsibilities of ownership.

target costing A process in which firms identify the quality and functionality needed to satisfy customers and what price they are willing to pay before the product is designed; the product is manufactured only if the firm can control costs to meet the required price.

target market The market segments on which an organization focuses its marketing plan and toward which it directs its marketing efforts.

target marketing strategy Dividing the total market into different segments on the basis of customer characteristics, selecting one or more segments, and developing products to meet the needs of those specific segments.

targeting A strategy in which marketers evaluate the attractiveness of each potential segment and decide in which of these groups they will invest resources to try to turn them into customers.

tariffs Taxes on imported goods.

team selling The sales function when handled by a team that may consist of a salesperson, a technical specialist, and others.

teaser ad or mystery ad Ads that generate curiosity and interest in a to-be-introduced product by drawing attention to an upcoming ad campaign without mentioning the product.

technical development   The step in the product development process in which company engineers refine and perfect a new product.

technical specialist   A sales support person with a high level of technical expertise who assists in product demonstrations.

technical success   Indicates that a product concept is feasible purely from the standpoint of whether or not it is possible to physically develop it, regardless of whether it is perceived to be commercially viable.

telecommute   Working with fellow employees from a distant location using Internet communication technology such as VoIP.

telemarketing   The use of the telephone to sell directly to consumers and business customers.

text message advertising   Delivering ads to consumers as mobile phone text messages.

time poverty   Consumers' belief that they are more pressed for time than ever before.

tipping point   In the context of product diffusion, the point when a product's sales spike from a slow climb to an unprecedented new level.

tonality   The mood or attitude the message conveys (straightforward, humor, dramatic, romantic, sexy, and apprehension/fear).

top-down budgeting techniques   Allocation of the promotion budget based on management's determination of the total amount to be devoted to marketing communication.

total costs   The total of the fixed costs and the variable costs for a set number of units produced.

total quality management (TQM)   A management philosophy that focuses on satisfying customers through empowering employees to be an active part of continuous quality improvement.

touchpoint   Any point of direct interface between customers and a company (online, by phone, or in person).

trade discounts   Discounts off list price of products to members of the channel of distribution who perform various marketing functions.

trade sales promotions   Promotions that focus on members of the "trade," which include distribution channel members, such as retail salespeople or wholesale distributors, that a firm must work with in order to sell its products.

trade shows   Events at which many companies set up elaborate exhibits to show their products, give away samples, distribute product literature, and troll for new business contacts.

trademark   The legal term for a brand name, brand mark, or trade character; trademarks legally registered by a government obtain protection for exclusive use in that country.

transactional selling   A form of personal selling that focuses on making an immediate sale with little or no attempt to develop a relationship with the customer.

transportation and storage   Occurs when retailers and other channel members move the goods from the production point to other locations where they can hold them until consumers want them.

transportation   The mode by which products move among channel members.

trial pricing   Pricing a new product low for a limited period of time to lower the risk for a customer.

trialability   The ease of sampling a new product and its benefits.

triple-bottom-line orientation   A business orientation that looks at financial profits, the community in which the organization operates, and creating sustainable business practices.

tryvertising   Advertising by sampling that is designed to create buzz about a product.

TV everywhere (also known as authenticated streaming)   The use of an Internet-enabled device, like a tablet or smartphone, to stream content from a cable or satellite provider.

Twitter   A free microblogging service that lets users post short text messages with a maximum of 140 characters.

two-part pricing   Pricing that requires two separate types of payments to purchase the product.

U

U.S. Generalized System of Preferences (GSP)   A program to promote economic growth in developing countries by allowing duty-free entry of goods into the U.S.

unaided recall   A research technique conducted by telephone survey or personal interview that asks whether a person remembers seeing an ad during a specified period without giving the person the name of the brand.

undifferentiated targeting strategy   Appealing to a broad spectrum of people.

unfair sales acts   State laws that prohibit suppliers from selling products below cost to protect small businesses from larger competitors.

uniform delivered pricing   A pricing tactic in which a firm adds a standard shipping charge to the price for all customers regardless of location.

unique selling proposition (USP)   An advertising appeal that focuses on one clear reason why a particular product is superior.

Universal Product Code (UPC)   A set of black bars or lines printed on the side or bottom of most items sold in grocery stores and other mass-merchandising outlets that correspond to a unique 10-digit number.

unmanned aerial vehicles (UAVs)   Another name for drones.

unobtrusive measures   Measuring traces of physical evidence that remain after some action has been taken.

unsought products   Goods or services for which a consumer has little awareness or interest until the product or a need for the product is brought to his or her attention.

unstructured data   Nonnumeric information that is typically formatted in a way that is meant for human eyes and not easily understood by computers.

usage occasions   An indicator used in behavioral market segmentation based on when consumers use a product most.

usage rate   A measurement that reflects the quantity purchased or frequency of use among consumers of a particular product or service.

user-generated content (also referred to as consumer-generated content)   Marketing content and activities created by consumers and users of a brand such as advertisements, online reviews, blogs, social media, input to new product development or serving as wholesalers or retailers. online reviews, blogs, and social media.

utilitarian approach   Ethical philosophy that advocates a decision that provides the most good or the least harm.

utility   The usefulness or benefit that consumers receive from a product.

V

validity   The extent to which research actually measures what it was intended to measure.

VALS™   A psychographic segmentation system that divides U.S. adults into eight groups according to what drives them psychologically as well as by their economic resources.

value chain   A series of activities involved in designing, producing, marketing, delivering, and supporting any product. Each link in the chain has the potential to either add or remove value from the product the customer eventually buys.

value co-creation The process by which benefits-based value is created through collaborative participation by customers and other stakeholders in the new product development process.

value pricing or everyday low pricing (EDLP) A pricing strategy in which a firm sets prices that provide ultimate value to customers.

value proposition A marketplace offering that fairly and accurately sums up the value that will be realized if the good or service is purchased.

variability The characteristic of a service that means that even the same service performed by the same individual for the same customer can vary.

variable costs The costs of production (raw and processed materials, parts, and labor) that are tied to and vary, depending on the number of units produced.

variety stores Stores that carry a variety of inexpensive items.

venture teams Groups of people within an organization who work together to focus exclusively on the development of a new product.

vertical integration the combining of manufacturing operations with channels of distribution under a single ownership to reduce costs and increase profits.

vertical marketing system (VMS) A channel of distribution in which there is formal cooperation among members at the manufacturing, wholesaling, and retailing levels.

video news release (VNR) Similar to a press release, an organization sends a report to the media in a film format.

video sharing Uploading video recordings on to Internet sites such as YouTube so that thousands or even millions of other Internet users can see them.

viral marketing Marketing activities that aim to increase brand awareness or sales by consumers passing a message along to other consumers.

virtual experiential marketing An online marketing strategy that uses enhancements, including colors, graphics, layout and design, interactive videos, contests, games, and giveaways, to engage experiential shoppers online.

virtual goods Digital products consumers buy for use in online contexts.

virtual office The use of Internet technology to work and participate from a distant physical office.

virtual worlds Online, highly engaging digital environments where avatars live and interact with other avatars in real time.

virtue approach Ethical philosophy that advocates the decision that is in agreement with certain ideal values.

vlogs Video recordings shared on the Internet.

voice-over Internet protocol (VoIP) Communication systems that use data networks to carry voice calls.

W

want The desire to satisfy needs in specific ways that are culturally and socially influenced.

warehouse clubs Discount retailers that charge a modest membership fee to consumers who buy a broad assortment of food and nonfood items in bulk and in a warehouse environment.

warehousing Storing goods in anticipation of sale or transfer to another member of the channel of distribution.

web scraping The process of using computer software to extract large amounts of data from websites.

Web 1.0 The beginning phase of the Internet that offered static content provided by the owner of the site.

Web 2.0 The second generation of the World Wide Web that incorporated social networking and user interactivity via two-way communication.

Web 3.0 The current generation of the web that offers consumers real-time instant communications through live chats and instant messaging and marketers the ability to track customers' online behavior.

Web 4.0 The web gives consumers access to thousands of apps and makes the ability to use their smartphones and tablets to access brands anywhere and anytime a necessity.

wheel-of-retailing hypothesis A theory that explains how retail firms change, becoming more upscale as they go through their life cycle.

wholesaler margin The amount added to the cost of a product by a wholesaler.

wholesaling intermediaries Firms that handle the flow of products from the manufacturer to the retailer or business user.

wisdom of crowds Under the right circumstances, groups are smarter than the smartest people in them, meaning that large numbers of consumers can predict successful products.

World Bank An international lending institution that seeks to reduce poverty and improve the lives of people by improving economies and promoting sustainable development.

word-of-mouth communication When consumers provide information about products to other consumers.

World Trade Organization (WTO) An organization that replaced GATT; the WTO sets trade rules for its member nations and mediates disputes between nations.

world trade The flow of goods and services among different countries— the value of all the exports and imports of the world's nations.

Y

yield management pricing A practice of charging different prices to different customers to manage capacity while maximizing revenues.

▶ Name Index

▶ Subject Index

583